A

MANUAL

OF

THE NÍLAGIRI DISTRICT

IN THE

MADRAS PRESIDENCY

A

MANUAL

OF

THE NÍLAGIRI DISTRICT

IN THE

MADRAS PRESIDENCY.

BY H. B. GRIGG, B.A., OXON

GYAN

Published by

Gyan Publishing House
5, Ansari Road
Daryaganj, New Delhi-110002
Phone: 011-47034999, 9811692060
E-mail: books@gyanbooks.com

Distribution Network
gyanbooks.com
India, USA, Canada, UK, Australia

ISBN: 978-93-6208-067-7 (PB)
First Published, 1880

2nd Impression 2024

Printed at: Gyan Press, Delhi.

A MANUAL OF THE NÍLAGIRI DISTRICT IN THE MADRAS PRESIDENCY

Author: H. B. GRIGG

A

MANUAL

OF

THE NÍLAGIRI DISTRICT

IN THE

MADRAS PRESIDENCY.

COMPILED AND EDITED

BY H. B. GRIGG, B.A., OXON,

MADRAS CIVIL SERVICE. LATE ASSISTANT COMMISSIONER, NÍLAGIRIS.

MADRAS:

PRINTED BY E. KEYS, AT THE GOVERNMENT PRESS.

1880.

CONTENTS.

CHAPTER I.

GENERAL DESCRIPTION.

Geographical position.—Configuration and aspect.—Hill Ranges and Peaks.—Streams and Waterfalls.—Valleys.—Scenery.—Changes in features and aspect ... ... Pages 1—10

CHAPTER II.

GENERAL DESCRIPTION—(*Continued*).

Length and Breadth.—Boundaries.—Area.—Divisions.—Stations.—Ghâts and Hill Passes.—Roads.—Bungalows.—Chuttrums ... ... Pages 11—24

CHAPTER III.

POPULATION.

Early notices.—Captain Ward's Report.—Major Ouchterlony's.—Quinquennial return.—Census of 1871.—Distribution.—Houses.—Proportion of Sexes.—Increase in number of Hill Tribes.—Incorrectness of Returns.—Population of Villages.—Of Nâds.—Religion.—Castes.—Occupations.—Education.—General remarks ... ... Pages 25—34

CHAPTER IV.

PART I.—CLIMATE, METEOROLOGY, AND HEALTH.

First notices of the climate.—Reports on the medical topography.—Climates.—Thermometrical and barometrical observations.—Doddabetta Observatory.—Wellington Observatory.—Meteorological tables.—Temperature compared.—Winds.—Table of winds.—Hurricanes.—Effect of wind on barometer.—Rainfall.—Average fall.—Extremes.—Rain-gauge stations.—Hygrometrical observations.—Vital statistics.—Comparative tables.—Vaccination.—Results.—Special reports, Ootacamand—Wellington ... ... Pages 35—45

PART II.—THE PHYSICAL AND MEDICAL CLIMATE AND TOPOGRAPHY OF OOTACAMAND AND THE SURROUNDING PLATEAU OF THE NÍLAGIRIS, TOGETHER WITH REMARKS ON PERSONAL HYGIENE, FOR THE USE OF VISITORS, INVALIDS, &c.

(*By* Surgeon-Major WHITTON, M.B., B.A., *Civil Surgeon, Ootacamand.*)

Physical topography.—Elevation.—Climate.—Health.—Rainfall.—Temperature.—Hygienic rules.—Diseases peculiar to residents and new-comers.—Lawrence Asylums.—Climates of Coonoor and Kótagiri ... ... Pages 46—63

PART III.—WELLINGTON.

(*Extracts from a Report furnished by Surgeon-Major* W. H. CORBETT, *Army Medical Department, in Medical charge of Convalescent Depôt, to the Surgeon-General, British Medical Service.*)

Description of the Hills.—Approach from the plains.—Topography.—Geology.—Botany, table productions and vegetation.—Seasons.—Meteorology.—Ozone.—Climate, and its influence on health.—Places to be visited.—Period for visiting the Hills.—Precautions to be taken.—Those who benefit.—Those who do not benefit.—Barracks.—Cantonment.—Sanitary condition.—The bazaar.—Water-supply.—Commissariat supplies.—Amusements.—Duties of the troops.—Mortality and sickness ... ... Pages 64—82

CHAPTER V.

GEOLOGY AND MINERALOGY.

Early papers.—Geological Survey.—General description.—Action of water—fresh—marine.—Rock formation.—Granite absent.—Gneissose rocks—foliations.—Minerals—iron—hornblendic gneiss.—Other varieties.—Landslips.—Intruded rocks.—Dislocations.—Three systems of faults.—Disturbances.—Upheaval of the gháts.—Quartz veins.—Withering of rocks.—Laterite.—Kaolin.—Clays.—Escarpments.—Kaity valley.—Kúndas.—Alluvial.—Economic geology.—Limestone.—Mr. King's note.—Gold.—South-East Wainád ... Pages 83—97

CHAPTER VI.

FLORA.

(*By* Lieutenant-Colonel R. H. BEDDOME, M.S.C., *Conservator of Forests, Madras Presidency.*)

General remarks.—Botanical divisions of the Hills.—Deciduous forests on slopes—characteristic trees—valuable timbers.—Moist evergreen forests on slopes—characteristic trees—timbers.—Woods of the plateau—characteristic trees—timbers—ferns and mosses.—Grass-land of the plateau—characteristic trees and plants (beautiful plants) of the Hills.—List of flowering plants—Dicotyledones—Monocotyledones—Gramineæ.—List of Ferns and Mosses—Cryptogams—Jungermanniaceæ—Bryaceæ.—Lichenales.—Fungales.—Books of reference.—Introduced plants ... ... Pages 98—132

CHAPTER VII.

THE USEFUL PLANTS OF THE NÍLAGIRIS.

(*By* Surgeon-Major BIDIE, M.B., *Government Museum, Madras.*)

Introductory remarks.—SUBSTANCES USED AS FOOD, &c.—pulses—cereals—roots and tubers—fruits and seeds—greens—substances used in the preparation of drinks—intoxicating substances—spices and condiments.—SUBSTANCES USED IN MANUFACTURES—oils and seeds—dyes and tanning substances—fibres.—DRUGS ... ... Pages 133—149

CHAPTER VIII.

ZOOLOGY.

PART I.—MAMMALS, BIRDS AND FISHES.

(*By* Surgeon-Major G. BIDIE, M.B., *Supt. of the Central Museum, Madras.*)

General.—Mammals.—Birds.—Fishes.—Introduction of Fish from low country and from England ... ... Pages 150—170

PART II.—LIZARDS, SNAKES AND FROGS.

(*By* Lieutenant-Colonel R. H. BEDDOME, M.S.C., *Conservator of Forests, Madras Presidency.*)

Lazards, Snakes and Frogs ... ... Pages 171—176

PART III.—LAND AND FRESH-WATER SHELLS.

(*By* Lieutenant-Colonel R. H. BEDDOME, M.S.C., *Conservator of Forests, Madras Presidency.*)

Inoperculated shells.—Operculated shells.—Remarks.—Fresh-water shells. Pages 177—179

CHAPTER IX.

ETHNOLOGY.

INTRODUCTION.

The tribes.—General view of their history.—Sources of information.—Local distribution ... ... Pages 180—182

PART I.—THE TÓDAS.

Origin.—Derivation of name.—Physical characteristics.—Dress.—Census.—Divisions.—Mode of life.—Dwellings.—The mand—Situation.—Family and inheritance.—Pastimes.—Music and song.—Salutation.—Religion.—Priests.—Temples.—Rites and ceremonies.—Birth.—Marriage.—Funerals, green and dry.—Traditions.—Language ... ... Pages 183—202

PART II.—THE KÓTAS.

Length of residence.—Derivation of name.—Language.—Physical characteristics. Dress.—Census.—Divisions.—Mode of life.—Habits.—Habitations.—Religion.—Rites.—Birth.—Marriage.—Death.—Traditions ... Pages 203—207

PART III.—KÚRUMBAS.

Origin.—Physical characteristics.—Dress.—Census.—Divisions.—Mode of life.—Dwellings.—Livelihood.—Religion.—Rites.—Birth.—Marriage.—Death.—Traditions ... ... Pages 208—213

PART IV.—IRULAS.

Origin.—Language.—Physical characteristics.—Dress.—Census and Divisions.—Mode of life.—Dwellings.—Religion.—Rites and ceremonies.—Traditions ... ... Pages 214—217

PART V.—THE BADAGAS.

Origin.—Physical characteristics.—Dress.—Castes.—Wódeas.—Kongas.—Adhikáris.—Kanakas.—Chittre.—Bellis.—Háruvas.—Minor Castes.—Mode of life.—Music and song.—Character.—Dwellings.—Religion.—Temples.—Rites and ceremonies.—Traditions.—Language ... ... Pages 218—228

CHAPTER X.

ANTIQUITIES.

Varieties of monuments, by whom described.—CAVES.—CAIRNS, position, contents, size, probable age.—BARROWS, size, contents, compared with European tumuli.—KISTVAENS, size, contents.—STONE CIRCLES.—AZARAMS.—CROMLECHS OR DOLMENS, groups, contents, origin.—RUINED VILLAGES.—FORTS ... ... Pages 229—247

CHAPTER XI.

EARLY HISTORY.

Sketch of the history of peninsular India.—Early race movements.—Early religions of the peninsula.—Relation of early hill-tribes to race movements.—Divisions of South India.—Kongu or Chera.—Chólas.—Kadamba dynasty.—Hoysala Bellála.—Vijayanagar.—Mysore.—Fall of Seringapatam.—Malayálam.—Early Portuguese Missionaries ... ... Pages 248—275

CHAPTER XII.

RECENT HISTORY.

Marquis of Wellesley's policy.—Dr. Buchanan's mission.—Colonel Colin Mackenzie's survey.—Mr. Keys' visit.—Mr. John Sullivan's exploration.—Attention of Governor-General drawn to the Hills.—M. Leschenault's remarks.—Infanticide.—Ootacamand.—Captain Ward's survey.—Mr. Sullivan opens out roads.—Ootacamand laid out.—Sir Thomas Munro's visit.—Mr. S. R. Lushington's scheme.—Ootacamand constituted a sanitarium.—Military Commandant appointed.—Official complications.—Convalescent Depôt established.—Mr. Sullivan's departure.—Portion of Nílagiris transferred to Malabar.—Mr. Sullivan protests.—Rapid extension of Ootacamand.—Bishop Daniel Wilson.—Court of Directors ask for report.—Committee of inquiry appointed.—Government orders on report.—Mr. Lushington's departure.—Sir Frederick Adam succeeds.—Medical Report.—Abolition of Convalescent Depôt.—Administration defective.—Massacre of Kúrumbas.—Special legislation proposed, but negatived by Imperial Government.—Destruction of woods.—Draft Act.—Ootacamand constituted a Military bazaar.—Lord Elphinstone at Kaity.—Mr. Sullivan urges the re-annexation of that part of the plateau transferred to Malabar.—Government declines to make the transfer.—Commandant appointed Joint Magistrate and District Munsif.—Marquis of Tweeddale, Governor.—Re-transfer of the second portion of the Hills to Coimbatore.—Coffee-planting begun.—Plans submitted for barracks at Wellington.—Coonoor Church built.—Small Cause Court Judge at Ootacamand.—Proposals to appoint Civil and Sessions Court rejected.—Assistant Judge transferred from Combaconum to Ootacamand.—Kúndas and Nídumalé annexed.—First Commissioner, Mr. Breeks.—Ouchterlony Valley added to the district.—Industries.—Prospects of District ... ... Pages 276—310

CHAPTER XIII.

REVENUE HISTORY.

INTRODUCTION.

Subject divided.—Revenue system of North Coimbatore prevails.—Major McLeod's settlement ... ... Pages 311—313

PART I.—(*a.*) CULTIVATING TRIBES: the Badagas, Kótas, Irulas, Kúrumbas.

First settlement of the Nílagiris.—Mr. Sullivan proposes a survey.—Revenue.—Rates of assessment.—Changes proposed, 1862.—The shifting system.—" Ain " grass and " Grazing " puttas.—Revenue Board's proposals.—Decision of Government.—Revision of assessment.—Rates settled by Government—approved by Secretary of State.—Settlement introduced—extends to plateau only.—State of revenue accounts.—Settlement of Kúndas.—Lands for cultivation to be obtained under Waste Land Rules only.—Effects of the measure.—Kótas and other aboriginal cultivators.—Mode of assessing lands ... Pages 314—327

(*b.*) THE GRAZIERS: the Tódas.

Claim of Tódas to lordship over plateau—nature of claim—its extent—conditions operating against it.—Restrictions on purchases of land from Tódas.—Claims of the Tódas partially admitted.—Occupation of lands by Europeans attracts attention of Court of Directors.—Change in policy of Madras Government.—Grants made without mention of Tódas' claims.—Settlers continue to purchase from the Tódas.—Sir Frederick Adam's action.—Mr. Sullivan's views—endorsed by Government—approved by Court of Directors.—Difficulties in carrying policy into effect.—Matters still unsettled in 1839, and Court of Directors interfere.—Mr. Conolly's views.—Mr. C. M. Lushington strongly opposes policy of Government.—Marquis of Tweeddale refers questions to the Court of Directors.—After further report from the Collector of Malabar the Court's despatch, 1843, settles questions finally and orders payment of compensation for Ootacamand to Tódas.—Manual of Land Rules to be prepared—provisions of the manual relating to the Tódas—rescinded by the Waste Land Rules.—Present revenue system ... ... Pages 327—343

PART II.—EUROPEAN AND OTHER IMMIGRANTS.

Absence of restrictions on acquisition of land by Europeans.—Policy of Lord Amherst's Government.—Rules promulgated.—Orders of Madras Government regarding acquisition of lands on the Hills.—Mr. Lushington encourages settlements of Anglo-Indians.—Rates on lands in the Mélnád prohibitive—Mr. Sullivan proposes changes—determination of Government—subsequent modifications.—Radical changes in the policy of Government in 1842.—Rules in the Dehra Doon despatch.—Manual of Land Rules to be prepared.—Right of settlers to use of water.—Résumé of the Manual.—Modification in 1858.—Redemption of land-tax sanctioned.—Causes of variety of tenure on the Hills.—Discussion on land policy of Government of India after the Mutiny—Lord Stanley's despatches — Lord Canning's Resolution — action of the Madras Government — discussions in Parliament.—Waste Lands Bill.—Nílagiri Land Rules sanctioned.—Debate in the House of Commons.—Changes in the Rules and their causes.—Auction system called in question.—Appointment of a Committee of Inquiry and results.—Table of Sales of Waste Lands.—Absence of Tope Rules.—Firewood allotments ... ... Pages 344—360

PART III.—REVENUE SURVEY.

First survey.—Major Ouchterlony's survey.—Surveyors appointed on introduction of Waste Land Rules.—Special Assistant Collector placed in charge.—Work transferred to Superintendent, Revenue Survey.—Settlement limits.—Rules for conduct of operations.—Survey operations after creation of Nílagiri Commission.—Work performed ... ... Pages 361—364

CHAPTER XIV.

REVENUE ADMINISTRATION.

Revenue powers of the Commissioner and his Assistant.—Deputy Tahsildars.—Revenue Inspectors.—Maniyagar and Karnams.—Hukamnáma.—South-East Wainád.—Local Funds.—Pound Fund ... ... Pages 365—369

CHAPTER XV.

HEADS OF REVENUE AND EXPENDITURE.

(*a.*) Imperial.

Land Revenue.—Excise on Spirits and Malt Liquors.—Stamps.—Forests.—Miscellaneous ... ... Pages 370—371

(*b.*) Provincial.

Jails.—Registration.—Police.—Medical.—Printing.—Miscellaneous Charges. Page 372

(*c.*) Local.

Local Funds.—Act IV of 1871—Pound Fund—Village Service Fund—Endowment Fund—Municipal Funds ... ... Page 372

CHAPTER XVI.

CRIMINAL AND CIVIL JUSTICE AND REGISTRATION.

Constitution by Act I of 1868.—Sessions Judge and Magistrates—jurisdiction.—Benches of Magistrates—statement of operations.—Civil Courts—statement of operations.—Village Munsifs—appeals to the High Court.—Cost of Law and Justice.—Registration—operations ... ... Pages 373—377

CHAPTER XVII.

MUNICIPALITIES AND STATIONS.

The four Settlements.—Description of *Ootacamand*—area and population—limits of the Municipality—elevation—Municipal Commission—receipts and expenditure—sanitation—market—public buildings—the gardens—hotels—rents—early sketch.—*Coonoor*—description—area—municipal limits—elevation—Municipal Commission—receipts and expenditure—public buildings—population—hotels and rents.—*Wellington*—description, &c.—*Kótagiri*—description ... ... Pages 378—390

CHAPTER XVIII.

NOTES ON THE PUBLIC WORKS OF THE NÍLAGIRI DISTRICT.

(*By* Major J. L. L. Morant, R.E., *District Engineer.*)

Sums expended.—Establishment.—Roads.—Railway scheme.—Military buildings.—Lawrence Asylums.—Building materials.—Wages and cost of materials.—Nílagiris and Coimbatore compared.—Cost of the various edifices. Pp. 391—399

CHAPTER XIX.

PRISONS.

(*By* Lieut.-Colonel CLEMENTSON, M.S.C., *Superintendent of Prisons, Ootacamand, and Joint Magistrate, Nílagiris.*)

EUROPEAN PRISON—buildings—prisoners—discipline—industries—diet—dress—health—instruction—cost — establishment. — DISTRICT JAIL—situation—buildings—industries—diet—health.—SUBSIDIARY JAILS ... ... Pages 400—406

CHAPTER XX.

POSTAL DEPARTMENT.

Number of Post Offices.—History of Ootacamand Post Office.—Old postal rates.—Hill Post Offices brought under inspection.—Present establishment.—Number of letters received and despatched.—Revenue.—Coonoor and Kótagiri.—Wellington.—South-East Wainád.—Old postal route of the Hills.—Tonga.—Rates for passengers.—Post hours at Ootacamand and other offices. Pages 407—409

CHAPTER XXI.

TELEGRAPH DEPARTMENT.

(*Supplied by the Superintendent, Malabar Coast Division.*)

Position.—The Indian system.—Strength of lines.—Number of Telegraph Offices.—Staff.—Cost of construction ... ... Page 410

CHAPTER XXII.

POLICE DEPARTMENT.

The village system.—Crime.—Reforms necessary.—New constabulary.—Present organization.—Stations on the Nílagiris—in Wainád section.—Proportion of Police to population, &c., &c.—Appendices ... ... Pages 411—413

CHAPTER XXIII.

MEDICAL.

Establishments.—Cost.—Ootacamand—St. Bartholomew's Hospital.—Coonoor—Hospital.—Wellington.—Kótagiri.—South-East Wainád ... Pages 414—416

CHAPTER XXIV.

ECCLESIASTICAL.

Establishment—its cost.—Churches in Ootacamand, St. Stephen's, St. Thomas'.—Coonoor, All Saints'.—Kótagiri.—Wellington.—Roman Catholic Churches—Convent.—C. M. S. Tamil Mission.—The Basel Mission ... Pages 417—422

CHAPTER XXV.

EDUCATIONAL.

History of education among the hill-tribes.—Badaga schools—Scheme of Union Schools.—Schools for Anglo-Indians.—The Breeks' Memorial School.—Convent Schools.—Tamil Mission School.—Hobart Girls' School.—Private Schools.—Educational needs.—Coonoor.—Lawrence Asylums—history—amalgamation with the Military Male Orphan Asylum—revenue—instruction—medical—domain ... ... Pages 423—437

CHAPTER XXVI.

FORESTS.

WOODS ON THE PLATEAU—early efforts to preserve shólas—first conservancy establishment—Dr. Cleghorn's suggestions—Conservancy Rules sanctioned in 1860—additional establishment—transfer of forests and plantations to the Commissioner under Jungle Conservancy—Special Forest Officer—retransfer to Forest Department—operations under Jungle Conservancy—Forest Commission—present system of firewood sales, &c. PLANTATIONS ON PLATEAU—early private enterprise—Government plantation at Jackatalla—planting at Ootacamand—other plantations—particulars—Ootacamand plantations—Wellington plantations—Conservator's remarks—yield of *eucalyptus*—financial statement—system of working. FORESTS AND PLANTATIONS BELOW THE GHATS—Múdúmalé forest—plantations—receipts and expenditure—Benné forest—plantations—Segúr—forest—sandalwood plantation—receipts and expenditure—management—finances of the range—minor products—timber trees ... Pages 438—454

CHAPTER XXVII.

AGRICULTURE.

INTRODUCTION.

Mr. Sullivan's enterprise.—Mr. S. R. Lushington's farm at Kaity.—The Committee's report.—Major Ouchterlony's proposal.—Silk-worm culture.—Grant to Mr. John McIvor.—Private effort.—Lord Napier's Minute.—Major Ouchterlony's statement of produce ... ... Pages 455—463

MONOGRAPH ON AGRICULTURE.

(*By* Major-General MORGAN, *formerly Deputy Conservator of Forests, Nilagiris.*)

(*a.*) SOILS.

Black soil.—Brown soil.—Yellow and red soils ... ... Page 464

(*b.*) NATIVE AGRICULTURE.

Corps—korali—raggi—barley—wheat—sámé—naomi—mustard—keré—poppy—onions—garlic—peas—potatoes.—Yield per acre.—Average price of staple food-grains.—Manuring.—Ploughing.—Sowing.—Weeding.—Area under each crop.—Cost of cultivation.—Implements.—Cattle.—Rotation of crops.—Terracing and fencing.—Reaping, thrashing, storing.—Price of cattle.—Land for pasturage.—Fodder.—Cows.—Modes of bringing produce to market.—Markets.—Results of agriculture ... . Pages 465—470 (c.) ENGLISH FARMING.

Tracts and soils best suited.—Expenses.—Seasons for cultivating.—Field crops.—Degeneration of seed.—Draining, terracing, and ploughing.—Cultivation.—Manuring — lime — potash. — Horticulture. — Garden crops.— Fruit trees.—Market prices.— Live-stock — cattle — sheep — pigs — horses — poultry.—Diseases.—Treatment—murrain—foot-and-mouth disease.—General remarks. Pages 471—481

CHAPTER XXVIII.

COFFEE CULTIVATION.

INTRODUCTION.

Introduction of the coffee plant into South India.—Abbé Dubois.—Coffee on the Baba Booden Hills—in the Wainád—on the Nilagiris.—Major Ouchterlony's note.—The Ouchterlony Valley.—Area of coffee land under cultivation in the district.—Statistics of coffee exports.—Estimation of cost of cultivation and profits.—Books on coffee cultivation ... ... Pages 482—487

MONOGRAPH ON THE CULTIVATION OF COFFEE.

(*By* A. H. STEEDMAN, Esq., *Balcarres Estate, Wainád.*)

Selection of land—elevation—opening out land—nurseries—shade—felling—burning—road tracing—lining—pitting—planting—weeding—draining—handling and pruning.—Manuring—composts—poudrette—fish-manure—bones—blood and slaughter-house refuse—guano—superphosphate of lime.—Irrigation.—Buildings—bungalow—cooly lines—pulper-house and store—barbacues and drying tables—cattle sheds.—Machinery—sprouting—pulper.—Crops—picking and curing.—Enemies of the coffee plant—bug—the borer—the coffee rat—leaf rot—leaf disease—its remedies ... ... Pages 487—509

CHAPTER XXIX.

TEA.

INTRODUCTION.

Plant introduced, 1835.—Mr. Mann's efforts, 1854.—Dr. Cleghorn's reports.—Government policy.—Mr. Rae opens an estate near Ootacamand.—Government introduces tea-makers and forms a nursery at Doddabetta.—Agricultural Exhibition and its results as regards tea.—Area under tea.—Exports and imports. Pages 510—514

MONOGRAPH ON THE CULTIVATION OF TEA ON THE NÍLAGIRIS.

(*By* E. J. C. BRACE, Esq., *of Kótagiri.*)

Suitability of climate and soils of the district for growth of tea.—Varieties of the plant—the China—the indigenous—the hybrid.—Selection of seed.—Selection of land—aspect and soil—lay of land—clearing—shelter—terracing—lining—pitting—planting.—Nurseries—propagation by cuttings—cultivation and pruning—yield.—Manuring—manures and their application.—Weeding.—Fodder crops.—Manufacture—difference between black and green teas.—Manufacture of black tea—withering—rolling—second rolling—rolling by machinery—colouring—drying appliances—drying off—storing—tasting teas.—Manufacture of green tea—sifting—packing ... ... Pages 515—547

CHAPTER XXX.

CHINCHONA CULTURE.

Botanical Order—species—native countries—distribution—discovery of medicinal qualities—by whom described.—Threatened failure of American supplies of bark.—Suggestions for introduction of chinchona into the East Indies—attempts to introduce made by the French and Dutch—the Indian Government recommends the sending of a Collector to South America—the Court of Directors select Mr. Markham for the duty—his search—Mr. Spruce's search for *Red barks*—Mr. Pritchett's search for Grey barks—Mr. Cross procures *Crown bark* seeds—Pitayo barks.—Selection of sites on the Nilagiris and formation of plantations—area of plantations—financial results.—Policy of Government in regard to the plantation scheme.—The manufacture of alkaloids in the country.—Mr. Broughton appointed quinologist—his researches—Amorphous quinine.—Alkaloid manufactory.—Analysis of barks.—Chief species and varieties of chinchona in India—Cultivation.—Manure.—Harvesting the bark.—Drying the bark.—Packing.—Publications on chinchona ... Pages 548—570

CHAPTER XXXI.

HORTICULTURE.

Origin of the Ootacamand Gardens.—Mr. McIvor appointed Superintendent.—Site.—Defective management.—Dr. Wight's report.—Receipts and expenditure to 1852.—Gardens placed under Government.—Mr. Markham's description of the Gardens.—Medicinal plants.—Mr. Jamieson appointed.—Gardens placed under the Commissioner.—Agri-Horticultural Society.—Recent improvements.—Superintendent's reports.—Receipts and expenditure of each garden.
Pages 571—576

CHAPTER XXXII.

WEIGHTS AND MEASURES.

Land measure.—Capacity measures.—Measure used for house sites.—Long measure.—Weights.—Precious metals and coins ... ... Pages 577—578

APPENDIX.

No.		Page
1.—	Statement showing the Number of Villages and Hamlets in the District of Nilagiris as they stood in Fasli 1285	ii
2.—	Statement of Population arranged with reference to Caste, according to the Census of 1871	iii
2-A.—	Statement showing the Male Population arranged with reference to Occupation, according to the Census of 1871	iv
2-B.—	Statement showing the Number of Houses, Population, and Cattle in each Taluk	*ib.*
3.—	Statement of Rent Roll for Fasli 1281	v

No.		PAGE
4.—	Statement showing the Rainfall for a Series of Ten Years in the District ...	vi
5.—	Statement showing Rainfall in certain places in the District of Nílagiris from Fasli Year 1870-71 to 1876-77 ...	vii
6.—	Statement showing the Prices of Grain for a Series of Ten Years in the District of Nílagiris per Garce of 3,200 Madras Measures ...	x
7.—	Statement showing the Particulars of Cultivation, &c., for a Series of Ten Years ...	xi
7-A.—	Statement showing the Area under the principal Crops cultivated in Fasli 1285 ...	xii
8.—	Statement showing the Collections under the several Heads of Revenue in the District of Nílagiris for a Series of Ten Years...	*ib.*
9.—	Statement showing the Number and Value of Suits disposed of in the Civil and Revenue Courts for a Series of Ten Years ...	xiii
10.—	Statement showing the Receipts and Expenditure of Local Funds under Act IV of 1871, for the Five Years ending 1875-76 ...	xiv
11.—	Statement showing Receipts and Expenditure for Special Local Funds for the Five Years ending 1875-76 ...	xvi
12.—	Statement showing the Progress of Education for a Series of Ten Years ...	xvii
13.—	Deaths registered in the Rural Circle and Towns of the District of Nílagiris during each Month from the Year 1870 to 1877 ...	xxii
14.—	Deaths registered among Europeans and Eurasians from different causes in the District of Nílagiris ...	xxvii
15-A.—	Wellington—Statement of Rainfall at the Observatory, 1873-1876 ...	xxviii
15-B.—	Wellington—Statement of Readings of Barometer at the Observatory, 1873-1876 ...	xxix
15-C.—	Wellington—Statement of Ozone Readings at the Observatory, 1873-1876 ...	xxx
15-D.—	Wellington—Statement of Readings of Thermometer at the Observatory, 1873-1876 ...	xxxi
16.—	Expenditure on Public Works in the Nílagiri District during the 17 Years from 1860-61 to 1876-77, a rupee being taken at two shillings ...	xxxiii
16-A.—	Detailed particulars of the Wellington Barracks in the Nílagiri District ...	xxxiv
16-B.—	Detailed particulars of the Ootacamund Lawrence Asylums, Nílagiri District ...	xxxvi
16-C.—	Rates of Wages and Cost of Materials in the Nílagiri District during the past quarter of a Century arranged in Triads, a rupee being taken at two shillings ...	xl
16-D.—	Comparative Statement of the Rates for Labor, Carriage, and Work in Coimbatore and the Nílagiri Hills in the Year 1877 ...	xli
16-E.—	Nature and Cost of Construction of various Edifices in the Nílagiri District ...	xliv
17.—	A Topographical Description of the Neelaghery Mountains ...	xlviii
18.—	Copy of a letter dated 30th January 1819, to the Editor of the Government Gazette, published in the "Madras Courier" of the 23rd February 1819 ...	lii
19.—	From Lieutenant EVANS MACPHERSON, Superintendent, Neelgherry Road, to JOHN SULLIVAN, Esq., dated Neelgherry, 12th June 1820 ...	lv
20.—	Geographical and Statistical Memoir of a Survey of the Neelgherry Mountains in the Province of Coimbatore made in 1821 under the superintendence of Captain B. S. Ward, Deputy Surveyor-General ...	x

No. PAGE

21-A.—Statement showing the Strength and Cost of the Police Force of the Nílagiri District, excluding South-East Wainád Division, for the Year 1878 lxxxvi

21-B.—Statement showing the Strength and Cost of the Police Force of the South-East Wainád Division in Nílagiri District for the Year 1878 lxxxvii

22.—Statement of Grave Crimes occurred in the Years 1870-71 and 1875-76 in the District of Nílagiris lxxxviii

23.—Comparative Statement showing the Result of Police Operations in regard to each Great Class of Crime usually dealt with by the Police in the Nílagiri District during the Year 1875-76 ... lxxxix

24.—Comparative Statement showing the Result of Police Operations in regard to each Great Class of Crime usually dealt with by the Police in the Nílagiri District during the Year 1870-71 ... xcii

25.—Detail List showing Strength, &c., of the Police Force of the Nílagiri District, 1878 xcv

26.—Detail List showing Strength, &c., of the Police Force of the South-East Wainád Division in Nílagiri District, 1878 xcvi

27.—Rules for the sale of Waste Lands on the Neilgherry Hills, passed by the Hon'ble the Governor in Council on the 6th March 1863, and numbered 478A xcvii

28.—Rules of the Ootacamand Lawrence Asylum cvii

INDEX cxvii

MANUAL

OF THE

NÍLAGIRI DISTRICT.

CHAPTER I.

GENERAL DESCRIPTION.

Geographical position.—Configuration and aspect.—Hill Ranges and Peaks.—Streams and Waterfalls.—Valleys.—Scenery.—Changes in features and aspect.

CHAP. I.

GENERAL DESCRIPTION.

Geographical position.

THE Nílagiri[1] District,—as it existed prior to the annexation, on the 31st March 1877, of the tracts known as the Nambalakód, Cheramkód, and Munnanád Amshoms,[2] hitherto appertaining to the Wainád[3] Taluq of the Malabar District,—lies between Latitude 11° 8′ and 11° 37′ north, and Longitude 76° 27′ and 77° 4′ east. Within these limits, rise the Nílagiri Hills, a vast mountain block, comprising two more or less distinct hill ranges, usually known as the Nílagiris Proper and the Kúndas.[4]

Configuration and aspect.

This mountain mass, which may be described as an irregular rectangular triangle, its shortest side, or base, being the western, its longest the south-eastern, and its apex the hill known as Rangasámi's Peak, to the extreme east, is a gigantic headland marking the point of union of the Eastern and Western Gháts, or Sáhyádri Hills. These ranges constitute the eastern and western boundaries of the great triangular table-land of the Dekhan, which rests to the north upon the Vindya Mountains. As the Eastern approach the Western Gháts, they gradually lose,

[1] Derived from *Nílam* (Sans.) blue, and *giri* (Sans.) a hill—so called from the blue appearance the hills present to people living in the subjacent districts.

[2] Amshom (*Mal.*), a share, a territorial division.

[3] Lit. the open or champaign country. *Bailu* (Karn.), a field having water suitable for growing rice, a plain. *Nádu* (Karn.), a division of a district.

[4] So called from a village of that name. It signifies small, or little hill, from *Kinnud* (Tóda), *Sinna* (Karn.), *Chinna* (Tam.), small.—F. METZ. *Kundru* (Tam.), *Konda* (Tel.), means literally a small hill.—DR. CALDWELL.

CHAP. I. — GENERAL DESCRIPTION.

in great part, their rough and irregular conformation, until they merge in the undulating uplands of South-West Mysore and the Wainád. The ridge of the Eastern Ghâts is divided from the Nílagiris at their north-east extremity opposite the Gajalhatti[1] Pass by the Moyár River.

The Western Ghâts, meanwhile, after almost touching the coast line in North Malabar, trend to the south-east, becoming more precipitous and broken in character as they proceed, until at last they culminate at two lofty points, known as Nílagiri[2] and Múkartébetta[3] Peaks, the latter the Teneriffe of Southern India. Thence they divide into two branches running north and south, called respectively the Nídumalé or Himagála,[4] and the Kúnda ranges. In conformation and physical aspect, they differ greatly. The Nídumalé[5] range assumes a more and more undulating character as it slopes away towards the north, until it reaches the confines of the plateau overlooking the Mysore country. There the fall to the table-land below is precipitous, though the physical aspect of precipice and gorge is still somewhat rounded. The western slopes of this range, towards the Wainád country, are generally gradual. The Kúndas, on the other hand, form a lofty ridge or crest, the western side of which is wild, rugged, and precipitous in the extreme. In many parts their lofty crags rise almost perpendicularly to the height of several thousand feet from the Nellambúr[6] country beneath. To the distant gaze from the

[1] Probably from *gajam* (Tam.), an elephant, and *hatti* (Karn.), a herdsman's hamlet.

[2] Sometimes called Ellémalé, the boundary hill, from *ellei*, boundary, frontier, and *malei*, a hill.

[3] The spelling above adopted is in accordance with Badaga pronunciation. The word seems to be a compound of *múk*, nose, *ar* or *aru*, cut, and the suffix *té*, signifying the feminine gender.—*aruthal*, "she who was cut," has been changed into *arté*. Mr. Stokes of Kaity inclines to this derivation, which is the basis of the Badaga tradition. This tradition, on the authority of a Badaga catechist, he gives as follows:—A woman came to this spot, where her nose was cut off by some one. Disgraced, she turned herself into a mountain, and thus acquired the honors of a goddess, and formed the three streams which flow at her feet in different directions, afterwards uniting into one river. The first stream year by year washes down an elephant and says to her sister streams, "I have brought an elephant from the hills"; the second washes down a buffalo, and proclaims the fact to her sisters likewise; the third brings down a man and repeats the same tale. Another derivation connects the word with *maha*, great, and *kúr* (Drav.), a sharp point. The popular pronunciation militates against this suggestion. In Badaga ballads, "From Múkarté to Molemava" (a fabulous tree on the eastern extremity of the Hills) is the phrase equivalent to our "From Land's End to John o'Groat's."

[4] See Blandford's Geological Memoir.

[5] Lit. the long hill or mountain. *Nídu* (Tam.) long, extended; and *malei* (Tam.), a hill or mountain.

[6] A zemindári in Malabar celebrated for its teak forests and plantations. Name derived probably from *nella* (Mal.), paddy, unhusked rice.

west they appear like the battlemented wall of some gigantic fortress. Dense, but intensely green, tropical forest, interspersed with bamboo palm and fern-tree, clothes the ravines and even the precipitous buttress-like spurs, to the very crest of gháts, the eastern face of which is covered only with wiry brownish green grass, in which appear here and there dwarfed rhododendron and other subalpine shrubs. From the extreme south-west angle of the district the range runs in a southerly direction, rapidly decreasing in height, until it reaches the open country, known as the Coimbatore Gap, to the south of which rise the A'némalé[1] Hills. This gap, in breadth about twenty miles, forms the great historic pass between the Carnatic and Malabar, formerly commanded by the Palghát Fort.

To return to the Kúndas: the ghát line pursues first an easterly direction as far as the Mélkúnda promontory, which is divided from the Nílagiris proper by the Kúnda river. Thence it pursues a north-easterly direction, gradually becoming less serrated, rugged and abrupt in character, though still broken by ravine and gorge, precipice and promontory. This character it maintains along its northern limit, though the table-land from which the Nílagiris spring, gradually rises from below one thousand feet on their eastern, to above three thousand feet on their northern side.

Apart from the Kúnda and Nídumalé ranges, the surface of the Nílagiris is divided into an upper and lower plateau. The lower forming an irregular shelf, rests upon the north-eastern and southern slopes of the Doddabetta,[2] or great central range and its offshoots, including the north-east angle of the plateau, sometimes, though without sufficient reason, called the Kótagiri range. The higher plateau, known amongst the aborigines as the "Mél,"[3] or upland, nád, comprises the tract lying between the western slopes of Doddabetta and the Nídumalé and Kúnda ranges. The average elevation of this higher plateau above the lower may be roughly stated at from 1,000 to 1,500 feet.

Hill Ranges and Peaks.

The great ranges already mentioned cross the Hill plateau from south to north with an inclination towards the east, but they appear to be traversed, at the ghát line already described, by ridges running from east to west. These traversing lines appear to have been thrown up at a later geological period, as explained in another chapter.

Hills—central.

The Doddabetta range proper, seen from the east, might be termed a great cradle mountain, with Doddabetta as its southern,

---

[1] Or Elephant Hills. *A'né* (elephant).

[2] Lit. the great hill; from *dodda* (Karn.), great, and *betta* (Karn.), a hill.

[3] *Mél* (Karn.), above or west, and *nádu*.

CHAP. I.

GENERAL DESCRIPTION.

and Snowdon its northern eminence, for the distance between these two points is little over two miles. Doddabetta stands in Lat. 11° 24′ 5″ 40, Long. 76° 46′ 44″ 39. Its height is 8,760 feet above sea level, as ascertained by the Great Trigonometrical Survey, 8,642 feet as calculated in 1871 by Colonel Saxton, Deputy Superintendent of Topographical Survey. It is remarkable, even among the mammiform hills so common on the Nílagiris, for the flattened curve of its summit. The hollows of its slopes are clothed with thick woods; and rhododendron trees, though somewhat stunted, are found even within a few yards of the top, which is covered with thick coarse grass and flowering sub-alpine shrubs and herbs. Snowdon, formerly known as Dévashólabetta[1] on the other hand, is almost a perfect cone, the line of its northern slope, a fall of some 1,500 feet, being remarkably even, though steep. Its height is 8298·9 feet, or by the Great Trigonometrical Survey, 8,380 feet.

—to the West. Standing on the Doddabetta range, and looking westward, the first important eminences which meet the eye are the hills of Kalkúdiúr[2] (8002·4 feet) and Kuttakádu[3] (7933·4 feet). A few miles to the north lies the Paikaré[4] Hill (7511·7 feet). Some ten miles behind Kalkúdiúr rises Múkarté Peak (8380·3 feet, or 8,403 feet, G. T. S.), and a little to the north-west, the Nílagiri Peak and Dévar-betta, the heights of which, I believe, have not been correctly ascertained, nor, owing to its precipitous character, has any traveller as yet reached the summit of the former, though the ascent has been attempted.[5] The ascent of Múkarté is by a zigzag path cut on its eastern face. Its western is an almost unbroken wall-like precipice, several thousand feet in depth. A little to the south-east of Múkarté is Pichulbetta (8,348 feet), the northern extremity of the Kúndas. Between these two peaks the Paikaré river takes its rise. Some four or five miles to the north of Múkarté stands Velingiri (8,246 feet). About the same distance to the south is seen the Káléri (8,622 feet), and the Kúdikádu[6] hills (8,491—8,502 feet G.T.S.) at the head of the Avalanché Valley; and about two miles further south, the cone known as Dérbetta (8,303—8,353 feet, G.T.S.) This hill is

---

[1] *Déva*, God, and *shóla* (Karn.), a wood.

[2] Lit. the village of the stone circle or temple. From *Kal* (Tam.), stone, *kudi* (Karn.), a circle, a hut, a temple (see Caldwell, p. 503), and *úr*, a village.

[3] Derived probably from *Kuddan* (Tam.), a hollow, and *kádu*, a forest, or a jungle tract.

[4] Called after the river Paikaré, which seems to be derived from *payam* (Tam.), water, or river; and *karei* (Tam.), a bank or boundary. It may be rendered the boundary or frontier river. The name is significant.

[5] This ascent, I have learnt since writing the above, has been accomplished by Mr. Fraser, Sub-Assistant, Revenue Survey.

[6] *i.e.*, the temple tract.

CHAP. I.

GENERAL DESCRIPTION.

known to sportsmen as bear-hill. The highest hill to the west is probably Nádgáni; the Sisapára Peak is however the most interesting feature in the western region. On the eastern slope of these hills rise the chief tributaries of the Kúnda river; on the western and southern, the chief feeders of the Bhavání and the Nellambúr rivers. The Kúnda peaks, owing to their exposure to the full violence of the south-west monsoon and the poorness of the soil, are but sparingly covered with vegetation. Such trees and shrubs as exist within the hollows shew, by their gnarled and rugged appearance, how severe the struggle for life has been.

—to the South and East.

On the southern side of the hills the principal eminences are Mélkúnda (6,923 feet) overlooking the Bhavání Valley, Dévashóla (7,416 feet), half way between it and Doddabetta, and still nearer to Ootacamand, Chinna Doddabetta, which rises behind the Lawrence Asylum to the height of 7,848 feet. To the south and south-east of Ootacamand the principal hills needing mention are Kátéri and Kólakambé (5,600 feet), Húlikal[1] Drúg (about 6,000 feet), and on the opposite side of the gorge the Coonoor Peak (6,893 feet). Two or three miles north of Coonoor[2] stands Kúndamúgi, round the eastern face of which the road to Kótagiri passes; and on the approach to Kótagiri, a short distance to the north, is seen Dimhatti Hill, or Úrbetta (6,903—6,915 feet, G. T. S.), at the foot of which the old Sanitarium stood. Some ten or twelve miles to the north of Kótagiri is the Kódanád Hill (6,740 feet), and, at a still greater distance, to the east is Rangasámi's Peak (5,937 feet), a very conspicuous hill of a conical shape, dedicated to the god Rangasámi. To the north-west of Kótagiri, at almost an equal distance from it and Ootacamand, is Kúkalbetta (7,160 feet). Nearly due north of Ootacamand, overhanging the Moyár Valley, is the quaint shaped hill known as Chinna Coonoor, and about a mile to the west the Segúr, or Kónabetta Peak (6,777 feet). Further away to the west at the head of the Segúr Pass stands Muttinád-betta, and beyond it Ibex hill, a bluff-like eminence, the last hill needing special mention.

—to the North.

Streams.

Only three rivers of any importance have their source in the Nílagiris—the Moyár, the Chinna or Súr-Bhavání, and the Beypúr river, but the streams which help to form these rivers are very numerous. The Moyár rises at Múkarté and flows in a north-easterly direction, under the appellation of the Paikaré. This river is remarkable among hill streams for its long reaches or pools

---

[1] *Húli* (Karn.), a tiger, *kal* (Karn.), a rock or stone.

[2] *Kún* (Tam.), crookedness, a humped-back; and *úr*, village. The meaning may also more properly be "The village on the little hill" or "The little village." See note on derivation of Kúnda.

CHAP. I. GENERAL DESCRIPTION.

divided from each other by rocky rapids formed by shelving bands of rock on which lie loose boulders. In these pools are now to be found, though rare, trout and other fish, the ova of which were imported from England by the late Mr. W. G. McIvor, Superintendent of the Cinchona Plantations. On reaching the edge of the plateau it turns to the west, and passing through the Government Cinchona Plantations, falls in a succession of cascades to the table-land beneath. Thence it wends its way to the east, through a gorge known as the Mysore ditch, having the appearance of a long deep moat, as seen from the crest of the gháts, which forms the boundary between the table-land lying at the foot of the Nílagiris and Mysore, and entering the Coimbatore country, mingles its waters with those of the Bhaváni, at Dévanaikenkóta, below Rangasámi's Peak. The Bhaváni, taking its rise in the spot already mentioned, flows along the southern base of the Hills, receiving in its course the waters of the Kúnda and Coonoor rivers. The former drains the south-western slopes of Doddabetta and the south-eastern slopes of the Kúnda range, the latter rising on Doddabetta drains the whole southern face of the plateau, its principal feeder being the Kátéri.[1] The Beypúr river is formed mainly by two streams—the Pándi and the Nellambúr,—which have their origin on the hill ranges to the north and south of Múkarté.

Waterfalls.

The Waterfalls[2] are numerous and picturesque, though not of any great depth or volume. The highest is that of Kólakambé, north of the hill of that name, having an unbroken fall of about 400 feet. Second to this is St. Catherine's Fall (250 feet) in a stream south of Kótagiri. Then follows the lower Fall of Paikaré (200 feet) and after it the upper (180 feet.) Of nearly the same height as this latter is the Kalhatti Fall (170 feet) on the Segúr Pass. The Kátéri Fall in the river of the same name, six miles from Ootacamand,[3] is 180 feet in depth.

Lakes.

There are no natural lakes in the plateau, but art has attempted to supply in the neighbourhood of Ootacamand the defects of nature. In the neighbourhood of this station there are some artificial lakes or reservoirs, formed by banking up the stream at a narrow part of the valley. The most important is that known as the Ootacamand lake, a marked feature in the station, and one which

---

[1] *Kádu* (Tam.), a forest tract, *éri* (Tam.), a river.

[2] I am indebted to Captain Freeth, of the Revenue Survey, for these measurements.

[3] The derivation of this name is doubtful, but the most probable is *whotai* (dwarf bamboo), *kai* (Tam.), fruit, or green food, and mand. Dwarf bamboo abounds in some of the shólas near the ancient mand by the Public Gardens, still known as Whatakai-mand, and this spelling of the name appears in the earliest reports. The fresh shoots are eaten. Another derivation is *udakam* (Tam.), water.

adds greatly to its beauty. Its form is serpentine or sinuous, the bends being caused by the projecting spurs of the hills on either side. Its length is about two miles and a half, its breadth from three to four hundred yards. A road follows the windings of its banks throughout and forms the principal drive of the station, its length being nearly eight miles.

Valleys.

Owing to their peculiar conformation, there are few, if any, true valleys among the Nílagiris. The base of one hill rises so close to that of another, that the space between them more often resembles a narrow ravine or hollow, than a true valley. A level space is still more rare. The principal localities to which the term has been applied, and which possess at least some of the requisite characteristics, are the Nanjanád, the Kúnda, the Paikaré, the Kaity, the Arvenkád, and the Orange Valleys.

The Nanjanád valley on the upper plateau, lying south-west of Ootacamand, takes its name from a village on its western slope. Its head is a ravine formed by two spurs of Doddabetta, and known as Lovedale. It gradually opens out, and stretches for some miles in the direction of the Avalanché[1] valley. It is watered by a tributary of the Paikaré and consists, mainly, of undulating stretches of grazing land.

The valley of the Kúnda river, which in its descent to the low country, forms a deep gorge, is, in its upper stretch, very similar in character to the Nanjanád, though its slopes are more steep. There is some cultivated land in this valley, and some tea estates are being opened out in it.

The Paikaré river gives its name to the valley which follows the line of the lower slopes of the Nídumalé range. Its most remarkable features are the broad reaches, referred to above, of the river which are found here and there in the wider openings, and are supposed to be the beds of ancient lakes. This and the Kúnda valley are favorite grazing grounds of the Tódas.

The Kaity valley, which forms the upper basin of the Kátéri river, lies to the south of the Doddabetta range, and is enclosed to the north and west by that branch of the same range which runs out towards Dévashóla. It is of considerable extent, and contains numerous thriving Badaga villages, the greater portion being under cultivation. The soil is so well suited for the growth of the staple Hill crops, that even the steepest hill-sides are utilised by the ryots. In the lower portion of the valley stands the German Mission House, surrounded by a plantation of exotic

[1] So called from the post-house formerly located here. From *aval* (Karn.), first, *anché* (Karn.), stage or post. The name has nothing to do with the apocryphal avalanche or landslip said by Mr. Blandford to have occurred in the neighbourhood.—BLANDFORD'S *Geological Memoir*.

CHAP. I.

GENERAL DESCRIPTION.

trees. It was formerly the residence of Lord Elphinstone when Governor of Madras.

Separated from the Kaity valley by a spur, on which is built the Rest-house on the Ootacamand and Coonoor road, is Arvenkád, a valley of a similar configuration and character. The drainage of this valley flows into the Coonoor river. The old road to Ootacamand runs up the hollow of this valley; the present one is formed by a cutting along its northern side, a spur of Doddabetta.

The Orange Valley is so called from the wild oranges and limes with which it abounds. It starts from the north-east angle of Doddabetta, and skirting the Kótagiri table-land, breaks through the edge of the plateau, and descends to the low country at a spot exactly opposite the Gajalhatti Pass. It is a deep indentation, not above 4,500 feet above the sea level, and being shut in by lofty hills, the temperature is very high. Owing to this feature and to the richness of the soil, the vegetation in this valley is more nearly tropical than in any other locality above the gháts.

Scenery.

I know of no description which brings out the peculiar features of the Nílagiri scenery so truthfully or effectively as the following.[1] After remarking upon the configuration of the hills, their aspect from the plains, and the different appearance which the forest of the slopes assumes as the table-land is approached from below, the writer continues :—

" The interior of the plateau consists chiefly of grassy undulating hills, divided by narrow valleys, which invariably contain a stream or a swamp. In the hollows of the hill-sides nestle small beautiful woods, locally known as shólas. It is seldom that so much variety of beauty is found in so small a compass. From the bleak heights of the Kúndas, with their storm-beaten, moss-hung woods and rank, coarse grass, to the springy turf and many colored shólas of Ootacamand, and the tropical vegetation of the western slopes, every five or ten miles brings the traveller to a new climate and new scenery. Even on the summit of the plateau the rainfall varies with each different aspect, and ranging from about 30 inches to 150 or more, produces a corresponding range of vegetation. It is, however, the views over the edges of the table-land that are most singular and striking, from the extreme abruptness of the descent. Let a visitor take a short ride in almost any direction from almost any part of the plateau, and passing along shady English-looking lanes, sheltered by thickets of blackberry and wild rose; across bare breezy downs, sometimes dotted with twisted crimson flowering rhododendron trees, and intersected by swampy valleys, where buffaloes wade and wallow, through dense woods carpeted with rare beautiful ferns and gorgeous

[1] BREEKS' *Nílagiris.*

CHAP. I.

GENERAL DESCRIPTION.

in spring-tints, beside which the coloring of an English autumn is faint and dull, by native villages, with their patches of cultivation and their magnificent single trees, he will find himself on some ridge or promontory, looking straight down from 4,000 to 6,000 feet, on a scene that changes like the figures in a kaleidoscope. In the morning a sea of clouds lies at his feet, and gradually rises round him. In the afternoon this has cleared away, and reveals, perhaps, a vast crimson plain, veined by dark lines of wood, dotted with isolated hummocks like giant ant-hills, and terminating in faint blue lines of mountains, the furthest of which seems to hang half-way up the sky; perhaps on a tumbled mass of hills and valleys, a perfect dissolving view, for the eye has hardly traced the outline of some rocky ridge, glowing red in the sun-light, before a blue cloud-shadow blots it out, and a fresh series of crests and ravines starts into sight beyond. Broken peaks, hung with wood, frame the picture, and on all sides lies tropical sun-light, intensified by the keen thin mountain air."

Changes in features and aspect.

Great changes, however, are rapidly taking place in the aspect of the plateau and the slopes, due to three causes, the wide extension of cultivation by the hill tribes of cereal and other crops, the increase in the area under tea and coffee, and, lastly, the numerous plantations of Australian and exotic trees, especially in the neighbourhood of the large stations. Thus it has happened that much of the indigenous forest has been felled, and many grand shólas, which existed twenty years ago, have wholly disappeared. To the lover of the scenery peculiar to the Hills, this may seem an irreparable loss, but many will find a more than counter-balancing gain in the variety afforded by the rich green of the tea and coffee bushes, the larch-like forests of gums (*Eucalypti*) and the pyramidal shapes of the Australian blackwood (*Acacia melanoxylon*). These make a pleasing contrast with the almost universally rounded forms of the primeval forest, only here and there relieved by the white stems, spreading branches, and flattened tops of a few of the indigenous trees. Long, however, before Europeans reached the Hills, the process of the destruction of the woodlands had been going on in the tracts occupied by the Badagas, on the slopes of the Doddabetta range, the western alone excepted. There can be little question that these tracts, which are now given up almost wholly to the plough or hoe, were once covered with dense jungle, except the more stony ridges and heights. This is evidenced by the numerous shóla trees, single or in groups of two or three, standing generally near a rock or stream, which have owed their escape from the general destruction to the superstitious fears of the people, who regard them as the homes of the unseen genii of the place. The frequent occurrence of the suffix *kád*, jungle or forest, in names of localities, where now hardly a tree is to be found, is

CHAP. I.

GENERAL DESCRIPTION.

an additional proof of this assertion, as is also the character of much of the soil, which is well suited to carry heavy timber.

There has been some speculation as to whether the grassy downs and hollows lying to the west of Doddabetta were ever covered with forest, which has been cleared away for cultivation or pasture. This, however, is very improbable, as the character of the soil, with its thick subjacent layer of cold gravelly clay, has doubtless been hostile to the growth of large vegetation, but at the same time it is probable that some of the protected valleys, which have long been relinquished to the herds of the Tódas, were at some earlier era cultivated. This hypothesis rests mainly on the facts that some of the shólas do not bear the marks of great antiquity,[1] whilst the lands of the valleys are often smooth and even, as if the surface had once been levelled by the plough.[2] It is, however, to be remembered that the present park-like appearance of the higher plateau, with its downs and woodlands, is also, in a great measure, due to the annual recurrence of fires which sweep over the hills, burning the grass and outlying scrub and even the smaller shólas, and checking the larger woods in their persistent efforts to extend their domain further along the sides of the valleys.

Such is a brief description of the principal natural features of the district. The following chapter deals with subjects of a more artificial or administrative nature.

---

[1] The age of some shóla trees is said to be not less than 800 years.

[2] Some inquirers have thought that they can trace in mounds on the plateau remains of ruined villages.

CHAPTER II.

GENERAL DESCRIPTION—(*Continued*).

Length and Breadth.—Boundaries.—Area.—Divisions.—Stations.—Gháts and Hill Passes.—Roads.—Bungalows.—Chuttrums.

CHAP. II. — GENERAL DESCRIPTION. — Length and breadth.

THE length of the district from east to west, *i.e.*, from a point near Rangasámi's Peak to the Pándi river in Wainád, is 40 miles. Its breadth from north to south, *i.e.*, from the Moyár river to the Coimbatore frontier, near Mélkúnda, is 29 miles. The plateau, between its extreme north-east and south-west points, is in length approximately 42 miles. Its breadth, in the centre, from north to south, is 15 miles; but its average breadth is only about 10 miles.

Boundaries.

The district is bounded on the south-east, east, and north-east by the Coimbatore District, namely, from the south-eastern extremity of the Kúnda range, near Mélkúnda Hill, to the Mysore frontier and the Moyár river, in Lat. 11° 35′, Long. 76° 52′; on the north by the Mysore territory and the Moyár river; on the west and south by the Malabar District, the line running from the Mysore frontier near Tippukádú on the Moyár, along that river to a point below Neduwattam,[1] and thence along a line known as "Richardson's line" to a hill called Aratapára. It then follows the course of a stream running into the Pándi, and that river itself, until it falls over the Western Gháts, near Karkúr, thence up the Yellamalé Spur to the Nílagiri Peak, and along the western and southern crests of the Kúnda range to the Coimbatore frontier.

Area.

The total[2] area, exclusive of the Ouchterlony Valley, has been hitherto shown in official reports as 749 square miles, or 479,360

[1] From *nídu* (long) and *vattam*, a circle, a tank, a valley; probably the latter meaning applies here; the word is also applied to a circle of hamlets or small district.—WILSON'S *Glossary*. The ordinary spelling is retained to avoid confusion.

[2] The areas of the three amshoms of South-East Wainád transferred to the Nílagiris, are estimated as follows:—

	SQ. MS.
Nambalakód	140
Cheramkód	37
Munnanád	62
	239

Thus the total area of the district, as now constituted, is 988 square miles.

By the transfer of these three amshoms the tri-junction point of Malabar, Mysore, and Nílagiris is shifted from the junction of the Kakkanholla and Mysore streams to a point about Lat. 11° 40′ North, and Long. 76° 30′ East, at the junction of the Dodholla and Marégathé streams, thence the boundary runs southwards

CHAP. II. — GENERAL DESCRIPTION.

acres. From more recent calculations made by the Deputy Superintendent of the Revenue Survey, Lieutenant-Colonel Cloete, this figure appears to be excessive. Colonel Cloete estimates the area, exclusive of the Ouchterlony Valley, approximately at 695 square miles, or 444,800 acres. The following statement shows this estimate in detail:—

		SQ. MILES.	
Correct Areas Surveyed.			
Ootacamand Settlement	... ...	30·31	
Coonoor "	... ...	11·97	
Kotagiri "	... ...	11·42	
Mékanád (Plateau)	... ...	58·88	
" (Slopes)	... ...	33·71	
		——	146·29
Approximated Areas.			
Tódanád[1] (Plateau)	... ...	163·	
" (Slopes)	... ...	135·	
Péranganád (Plateau)	... ...	90·	
" (Slopes)	... ...	40·	
Kúndas ...	... ...	120·	
Ouchterlony Valley	... ...	30·	
		——	578·
		Total ...	724·29

The area of the plateau is estimated approximately at 478·87 square miles. Of this extent more than a fourth part is under occupation, probably about 79,360 acres, or 124 square miles. By the revenue accounts the ayacut[2] area of the district, excluding the Ouchterlony Valley, is 480 square miles, of which about 114 square miles are termed assessed, or culturable.

The swamps occupy about one-sixtieth part, or 8·87 miles, the woods and plantations one-tenth, or 45 square miles. Thus there remain 303 square miles of waste, rather less than 200,000 acres, which is chiefly utilised for grazing cattle by the hill tribes.

In 1847, by Major Ouchterlony's survey,[3] the area of the plateau, excluding the Kúndas and slopes, is returned as 268,494 acres, 420 square miles, of which 23,772 acres, or 37 square miles, were

up the latter stream to Gúlúr Hill, then west and south round Benné Teak Forest, crossing two paths from Múdúmalé to the Battery (Sultan's) and Gúndalpet road, and crossing the main road from Gúdalúr to the Battery at the 17th mile stake from Gúdalúr; the boundary then follows a crooked line, generally westerly through paddy flats to the tri-junction of the Ganapathi, Cheramkód, and Mupeinád amshoms on the banks of the Choladi river, then south, down the course of that river, and eastward along a line generally a little below the crest of the gháts up to Nílagiri Peak.

[1] The areas of the three náds do not include the areas of the Settlements.

[2] Lands belonging to a village and entered in the village register of lands.

[3] See Report, Madras Journal L. S., December 1848.

under cultivation, and 244,772 acres, 382·45 square miles, waste. Thus in 30 years the occupied area of the plateau has trebled itself. This result is mainly due to the extension of cultivation by the Badaga villagers. Major Ouchterlony estimated that about 31,500 acres of land were subject to Badaga cultivation, but that only about 17,000 acres were actually cultivated annually.

CHAP. II. — GENERAL DESCRIPTION.

The following statistics, relating to each nád, or revenue division, will be interesting. In regard to Mékanád only, however, are the statistics reliable, for of this nád only has the survey been completed. As to the other náds the statistics are derived from the revenue accounts, which are admittedly more or less inaccurate.

Divisions.

The district is divided into four compartments or náds, viz., Péranganád, Mékanád, Kúndanád, and Tódanád. These náds originally were exclusive of the Ouchterlony Valley, the portion lying between the foot of the Segúr Pass and the Moyár, and the lands attached to Irula villages on the eastern slopes. For convenience, however, these lower tracts are included in the superjacent náds.

Péranganád.

Péranganád[1] derives its names from the god Rangasámi worshipped by the Badagas, whose temple is located on the peak of that name within the arrondissement. It forms the eastern division, and is separated from Tódanád, on the west by the Múdukkádu stream, and Orange Valley, and the north-east spur of the Doddabetta range. On the west and south it is divided from the Mékanád by the southern spur of the same range, and the Kátéri river. It contains the settlements of Coonoor and Kótagiri and the Military Depôt of Wellington.

Distribution of Occupied Area.

	ACRES.
Lands held under Patta by the Hill Tribes ...	15,831·57
Lands held by Europeans and Natives under the Waste Land Rules	2,439·81
Inám Lands	461·43
Lands held by Europeans and Natives under other tenures than the Waste Land Rules	4,073·65
Múlachapoi Kambé and Velléru Kambé.	
Lands held under Patta by Hill Tribes ...	734·43
Lands held by Europeans and Natives under Waste Land Rules	285·50
Inám Lands	126·57
Lands held by Europeans and Natives under other tenures than the Waste Land Rules ...	16·50
Total ...	23,969·46

[1] The initial syllable is probably a contraction of *periya* (Tamil), great an honorific prefix. Comp. Pérangalúr in Púdúkóta, and Pérambúr, Madras.

CHAP. II. — GENERAL DESCRIPTION. — Mékanád.

The Mékanád,[1] which properly signifies the Western Nád (west), is divided from Péranganád by the boundaries already mentioned, from Tódanád on the north-west by a spur of the Doddabetta range, and the eastern branch of the Biguli or Kúnda river, which flows through the Lovedale and the Nanjanád Valleys to the main stream. The Biguli river also separates it from the Kúndanád on the south-west.

The total area, including the slopes, is 92·59 square miles, or 59,247·86 acres, 37,685 acres being above the gháts. The land above the gháts is distributed as follows according to the survey register:—

	ACRES.
Pattas	22,833·17
Under Waste Land Rules	2,793·67
Freehold	15·39
Under Tope Rules	151·67
Squatters	6·45
Government River Tracts	427·30
Do. Roads	223·84
Do. Streams	290·44
Do. Swamp	162·55
Do. Building Sites	0·21
Village Sites	132·44
Unappropriated Waste	10,647·98
	37,685·11

or 58·88 square miles.

Land on the Slopes.

	ACRES.
Approximate area of Patta Lands	500·00
Unappropriated Waste	21,062·75
	21,562·75

The Revenue accounts give the following figures:—

Patta Lands held by Hill Tribes	20,161·19
Do. Europeans and Natives under the Waste Land Rules ...	2,722·73
Inám Lands	367·81
Europeans and Natives on other Tenures ...	3,311·74
Total ...	26,563·47

Kúndanád.

The Kúndanád lies to the west and south of the Kúnda river, its northern boundary, separating it from the Tódanád, being the

[1] Der. *mérku* (Tamil), west. It is really the south-eastern division of the plateau, but is west of Péranganád, originally the most important Sub-division. The name indicates the course of the early immigrants.

western branch of this stream, and another stream known as the Arakádholla[1] which constitutes the principal source of the Nellambúr river.

Distribution of Occupied Area according to the Revenue Accounts.

Lands held under Patta by Hill Tribes ...	1,608·37
Lands held by Europeans and Natives under Waste Land Rules	504·41
Lands held by Europeans and Natives on other Tenures	7·10
Total ...	2,119·88

Tódanád.

The Tódanád occupies the whole of the plateau north-west of the other three náds, the table-land at the foot of the northern slopes. The Ouchterlony Valley may now be regarded as appertaining to this nád. It is divided by the hill tribes into two divisions, or náds, known as the Mélnád and Kílnád,[2] the latter occupying the country lying east and north of the Doddabetta range, and north of the Málemand Hill line, as far as Kalhatti and Shólúr. The Mélnád has already been described. The town of Ootacamand lies within the Mélnád, though the southern portion of the settlement, including the Lawrence Asylums, appertains to Mékanád.

Distribution of Area according to the Revenue Accounts.

	Lands held under Patta by Hill tribes ...	17,652·14
	Lands held by Europeans and Natives under the Waste Land Rules	4,506·17
	Inám Lands	651·86
	Lands held by Europeans and Natives under other tenures than the Waste Land Rules...	936·95
Segúr.	Lands held under Patta by Hill tribes and low-country natives	2,242·63
Segúr.	Lands held by Europeans and Natives under Waste Land Rules	74·50
Segúr.	Inám Lands	43·00
Segúr.	Lands held by Europeans and Natives under other tenures than Waste Land Rules	1,034·45
Ouchterlony Valley.	Area under cultivation in full bearing (coffee)	3,951·10
	Total ...	31,092·80

[1] *Holla* (Badaga), *hole* (Karn.), a stream or river.

[2] For meaning of Mélnád, see note *ante*, Kílnád; der. *kíl*, below.

CHAP. II. — GENERAL DESCRIPTION. — Stations.

The stations are Ootacamand, Coonoor, Wellington, and Kótagiri. Full particulars regarding them will be found in a later chapter. I would, however, here remark that the station of Kótagiri, strictly speaking, is not a civil station, as for magisterial, revenue, civil, and police purposes it is an appendage of Coonoor.

Gháts and Hill Passes.

The Passes to the Hills, of which six deserve notice from their importance, have generally followed, though far from closely, the tracks which were in existence long before Europeans visited the Hills. Of the six Passes, two, viz., Coonoor and Kótagiri, are on the east or south-east angle of the plateau, and terminate at Mettapollium in the Coimbatore District, a small town situate to the south of the Bhavání river, and the present terminus of that section of the Madras Railway which branches off at Pothanúr in the direction of the Nílagiris. It is 942 feet above the sea. At the north-west and south-west angles of the plateau are the Gúdalúr and the Sisapára or Kúnda Gháts, the former communicating with Wainád and the northern portion of Malabar, the latter the direct route to Calicut. On the north, communicating with Mysore and Bangalore, is the Segúr Pass. On the south, the now almost deserted passage known as the Mélúr Pass.

Of the lines above mentioned the Coonoor (new), the Gúdalúr (new), the Kótagiri (new), and the Segúr gháts are open to wheel-traffic. I proceed to give a more detailed account of each.

—Kótagiri Pass.

There are two lines of road, known as the Old and New Gháts. The Old Ghát was the first road cut by Government for the ascent to the Hills. It was completed in 1822—a Corps of Pioneers having carried out the work. Originally it started from Srimúgai, a village on the Bhavání, two or three miles to the north of Mettapollium. Its destination was the early sanitarium at Dimhatti, above Kótagiri. The distance from Srimúgai to Dimhatti is reported to be sixteen miles; from thence to Ootacamand by the nearest track eleven; in all twenty-seven miles. This line was originally much used by persons proceeding to the Hills from the southern and eastern districts of the Presidency, but was finally deserted by through-passengers after the completion of the Coonoor Pass. Subsequent to the opening of this line the point of departure was changed from Srimúgai to the Bhavání bridge near Mettapollium. The lower portion of the ascent was up a spur of the Hills, which stretches out a considerable distance into the plain towards Mettapollium, and then up the south side of the gorge of the Érkád river. The ascent was generally easy, until within the last few miles of Kótagiri. The New Ghát,—which was aligned and constructed by Major Morant, R.E., District Engineer, the work having been begun in

1872 and completed in 1875,—also follows this spur and valley. Its total length is 20 miles. It has a uniform gradient of one in seventeen feet, excepting the two miles at the foot, which are nearly level. It is bridged, and in no part less than nine feet, and generally fifteen feet wide. This road is little used except by passengers and traffic connected with estates in the neighbourhood of Kótagiri. There was also an ascent from Dévanaikenkóta to Dimhatti by Ténád and Kíl-Kótagiri below Rangasámi's Peak, and Nídunkúlum. The distance is 20 miles. CHAP. II. GENERAL DESCRIPTION.

—Coonoor Pass.

Some years after the construction of the Kótagiri ghát, this line was projected. It was completed in the year 1833. Starting from Mettapollium it runs due west to the village of Kalár along the level, a distance of nearly six miles, crossing in its course two streams—the Bhavání and Kalár. From Kalár the ascent begins. The road follows the northern side of the gorges of the Kátéri and Coonoor rivers, the distance from the foot to the Coonoor bridge at the head of the Pass being nearly nine miles. This ghát, the original alignment of which is very faulty, was constructed by the Corps of Pioneers under Lieutenant LeHardy. The average gradient is about 1 in 12, but towards the top the gradient is as steep as 1 in 5, and in some places it is reversed. The new ghát, which was completed in 1871, was traced and constructed chiefly by Lieutenant, now Colonel, Law. It begins the ascent at Kalár, and is 16 miles long. Its gradient is 1 in 18½ feet. It has 32 timber bridges, of spans varying from 12 to 70 feet. Its width is about 18 feet. It follows the northern side of the gorge for about 13 miles, crossing and recrossing the old ghát at no less than nine points. It then passes to the western side of the gorge of the Coonoor river, and meets the old pass at the bridge at the head of the ghát. Its great defect is its numerous zigzags, of which there are no less than twelve.

The views in the ascent are very striking, the road winding through deep ravines and under lofty crags, whilst far below rushes the Coonoor river, forming beautiful cascades in its downward course. On the opposite side stands the Húlikal Drúg—a grand bluff, wonderfully diversified with scarp and crag, relieved with bright green foliage in each cleft or hollow, whilst its base is covered with rich tropical forest, gradually passing into stretches of waving bamboo. Much primeval forest, above the elevation of three or four thousand feet, has been destroyed, and its place supplied by coffee plantations, among which are seen here and there the houses, sheds and huts belonging to the estates.

CHAP. II.

GENERAL DESCRIPTION.

—Segúr Pass.

The head of this pass is distant from Ootacamand four miles and three-quarters, the road being fairly level. The descent is about seven miles in length, though the distance from the crest to the old bungalow at Segúr is eight miles and one-quarter. About half way down is the village of Kalhatti, with its picturesque waterfall not far below. From the foot of the ghát to Tippukádu on the Moyár on the Mysore frontier the distance is ten miles and a half. This road is generally undulating, but in some parts the gradients are as steep as 1 in 12. The Moyár is crossed by a wooden bridge constructed in 1841. Near this point the road into Wainád branches off. The town of Mysore by this route is sixty-nine miles from Ootacamand. The road for twenty-five miles passes through much dense jungle, in which large game abounds. The gradient of this ghát, though severe, never exceeds 1 foot in 10, the average being 1 in 12. It is bridged with timber structures throughout. It is partly metalled. It was constructed in 1838, and took the place of the old path by Bellikal[1] further to the east. At one time it was the favorite approach to the Hills by the visitors from the northern parts of the Presidency and Madras.[2] It is still much used for the carriage of teak and other timber to the Hills.

—Gúdalúr Pass.

This pass is so named from the village of Gúdalúr, not far from its base. The old trace was exceedingly rough and steep, the descent being only four miles in length. The new ghát, which follows mainly the northern face of a spur of the Hills, was completed in the year 1868. It was traced by Captain, now Colonel, Farewell, M.S.C., but the construction was left to Mr. T. Browning. From the crest at Neduwattam, near the Government Cinchona Plantations, to its base the distance is eight miles, and from thence to Gúdalúr three miles. The gradient is very easy, being in no case more than 1 in 19. It has eight zigzags. The traffic on this ghát is at present light. From Gúdalúr a road runs to the north-east, and connects this line with the Segúr line near Tippukádu, a distance of eleven miles.

—Mélúr or Súndaputté Pass.

This pass was constructed next in order to the Kótagiri Ghát, about the year 1828. It was at one time much used by passengers from the Southern and Western districts. From the village of Súndaputté, at its foot westwards up the Bhavání Valley, runs the very ancient track to Manárghát and Calicut, crossing the ridge near the gorge known as the Silent Valley, which lies between two spurs of the Kúnda range. Eastwards a path runs down the left bank of the Bhavání to Mettapollium, thence to

---

[1] *i.e.*, white rock: der. *belli* (Kar.), white, *kal* (Tam.), rock.

[2] Lord Macaulay journeyed to the Hills by this route. See his Life.

CHAP. II. GENERAL DESCRIPTION.

Coimbatore. There was also another path more direct to Coimbatore from Súndaputté. The pass reaches the summit of the ghát below the hill called Súndabetta, not far from the village of Mélúr. It is little used now except by the hill people; but at one time there was a good deal of passenger traffic by it, the road across the plateau to Ootacamand being good. It was also once much used by tobacco-smugglers. The abandonment of this line was probably chiefly due to the rapid growth in public favor of Coonoor, both as a resort for invalids and as a good field for coffee cultivation. There was also another ghát to the west of this, known as the Tallapoya Pass. Leaving the lowland at a point on the Bhaváni some distance above Súndaputté, it reaches the plateau near Mélkúnda. It appears to have been used solely by the hill people.

—Sisapára or Kúnda Pass.

This pass, which was begun in 1832 and completed in 1838, the pioneers being employed for the work, was once used as the tappal[1] line between Ootacamand and the West Coast. It was, however, finally abandoned, owing to the severity of the climate of the Kúndas. It was traced by Lieutenant LeHardy, the tracer of the Coonoor Ghát. The pass begins at Shólakal in Nellambúr at the base of the Hills, ascends through a wooded ravine for a distance of eleven miles and a half to the crest of the Kúndas at Sisapára (6,742 feet above the sea). From this point to Ootacamand the distance is thirty-one miles and a half; from Shólakal to Wúndúr ten miles, and from thence to Arriakód, on the Beypúr river, fourteen miles and a half. The gradient in parts is very steep. The view from the head of the pass, with the tower-like Sisapára rock on the right, is perhaps the grandest on the Hills. There was formerly a bungalow at this spot, but it was burnt down some years ago, and has not been rebuilt.

Plateau Roads.

Ootacamand is the centre of the road system of the district. From it branch roads to the several gháts already described, but of these the roads to the Coonoor and Segúr Passes only are metalled and suitable for heavy traffic at all seasons of the year. The road to Gúdalúr is only metalled in parts, though bridged throughout. The road to Sisapára was formerly traversable by carts as far as the Avalanché, but is no longer so. The road to Kótagiri crosses Doddabetta and follows a spur of this range until it reaches the main road leading from Kótagiri to Coonoor. In its present state wheeled vehicles cannot traverse it, and carriages have to make a circuit by Wellington. Besides the roads mentioned there is a driving road from Ootacamand to Dévashóla on the south, whence an extension, more or less complete, to Kátéri on

---

[1] *i.e.*, Post.

CHAP. II. — GENERAL DESCRIPTION.

the east, and Témalé[1] Estate on the south. Another road, though not complete, leads in the direction of the country to the south and east of the Avalanché.

Half way between Coonoor and Ootacamand a road strikes off to Kátéri on the south, whence branch three lines,—the first traverses the Kólakambé coffee district, a second runs along the southern escarpment of the Drúg range, the third leads down the Kátéri Valley to the Coonoor Ghát. These roads are all suitable for wheeled traffic, but are not bridged throughout. Moreover, the Drúg road, though sanctioned, has not yet been completed. A road connecting Mélkúnda with Kátéri is also projected. Coonoor and Wellington are connected with Kótagiri by a good road bridged throughout. There is an extension to the Kódanád district to the north. The road to Gúdalúr crosses the Paikaré river by a good bridge with masonry piers. It was constructed in the year 1857. At the summit of the range, two or three miles from Paikaré a road branches away to the north, communicating with coffee and cinchona estates on the slopes to the east of the Paikaré Falls.

The following table gives the trunk and subordinate lines of district roads, with mileage—these lines are marked in the plane map attached. Over and above these roads the whole plateau is traversed in every direction by a network of paths connecting village with village, or these with the main road lines. Except in a few precipitous localities they may be used as bridle-paths :—

Roads—Trunk and District.

Group	Description of Road.	Miles.	Furlongs.	Total.
New Roads.	From *Ootacamand* to Coonoor	12	...	
	„ Coonoor to Burliár	12	...	
	„ Burliár to Kalár	4	...	
	„ Kalár to *Mettapollium*	6	...	34 miles.
	From Coonoor to Lamb's Rock	3	...	
	„ Lamb's Rock to the Dolphin's Nose	3	...	
Old Roads.	From *Ootacamand* to Coonoor	10	2	
	„ Coonoor to Burliár	6	5	
	„ Burliár to Kalár	2	6½	
	„ Kalár to *Mettapollium*	4	6½	24 ms. 4 fs.
New Roads.	From *Ootacamand* to Wellington	10	...	
	„ Wellington to Kótagiri	10	...	
	„ (1.) Kótagiri to *Mettapollium*	20	...	40 miles.
	„ (2.) Kótagiri to *Kódanád*	8	...	28 „
Old Roads.	From *Ootacamand* to Kótagiri	14	6	
	„ (1.) Kótagiri to *Mettapollium* ...	11	6	26 ms. 4 fs.
	„ (2.) Kótagiri to *Kódanád*	8	..	22 ms. 6 fs.

[1] *i.e.*, God's hill. *Té* or *tévan* (Tam.) God, and *malei*, a hill. By some the name is pronounced Taimalé, *i.e.*, the hill of the mother goddess—Dúrga or Bhavání—from *tai* (Tam.), mother.

Description of Road.	Miles.	Furlongs.	Total.
From *Ootacamand* to Kalhatti	9	...	
„ Kalhatti to Segúr	4	...	
„ Segúr to *Tippukádu*	10	4	
			23 ms. 4 fs.
From Tippukádu to *Mysore*	...	...	45 ms. 4 fs.
„ Ootacamand to Bellikal	6	...	59 miles.
New Roads. From *Ootacamand* to Paikaré	12	...	
New Roads. „ Paikaré to Neduwattam	9	...	
New Roads. „ Neduwattam to *Gúdalúr*	11	...	
			32 miles.
Old Roads. From *Ootacamand* to Paikaré	10	6	
Old Roads. „ Paikaré to Neduwattam	7	2	
Old Roads. „ Neduwattam to *Gúdalúr*	4	...	
			22 miles.
From Gúdalúr to Calicut by Karkúr	...	...	69 miles.
„ Gúdalúr to Cannanore	...	...	126 ms. 2 fs.
From *Ootacamand* to Krúrmand	10	...	
„ Krúrmand to *Múkarté*	6	...	
			16 miles.
From Ootacamand to Paikaré Falls by Paikaré road.	14	...	
New Road Ootacamand to Avalanché	16	...	
Old Roads. From *Ootacamand* to Avalanché	13	4	
Old Roads. „ Avalanché to Banghi Tappal	9	...	
Old Roads. „ Banghi Tappal to Sisapára	8	7	
Old Roads. „ Sisapára to *Shólakal*	10	4	
			41 ms. 7 fs.
From Ootacamand to Calicut	...	...	103 ms. 3 fs.
„ *Ootacamand* to McIvor's Bund	12	...	
„ McIvor's Bund to *Mélkúnda*	9	...	
			21 miles.
From *Ootacamand* to Dévashóla	9	4	
„ Dévashóla to Témalé	6	4	
„ Dévashóla to Mélúr	3	...	
„ Dévashóla to *Kátéri*	9	...	
From Ootacamand to Kátéri (old road)	7	...	
„ Ootacamand to Ellanhalli Chuttrum	6	...	
„ Ellanhalli to Kátéri	5	...	
„ Kátéri to Kólakambé	6	...	
„ Kátéri to Húlikal (Pillúr)	7	...	
„ Kátéri to Coonoor	4	...	
„ Coonoor to Húlikal (Pillúr)	5	...	

NOTE.—The final stations of the several lines of road are shown in italics, and the total distances between each in the last column.

Travellers' Bungalows.—There are seven bungalows in the district besides the Segúr, which has been abandoned. Of these, the Avalanché, the Neduwattam, the Paikaré and Kalhatti belong to the Local Fund Board; the Pérmand and Púrthé are Government property, whilst Krúrmand is private. These bungalows are all situated at spots well suited for the enjoyment of the sport and scenery of the Hills. Travellers' bungalows.

A wooden structure with zinc roof. It consists of a dining-hall, with front and back verandahs, four bed and two bath rooms, and stable accommodation for about six horses. The bungalow is about fifteen miles from Ootacamand. Half of the way is impracticable for vehicles. It is in charge of a peon paid by Government, —Avalanché.

CHAP. II. — GENERAL DESCRIPTION.

who serves either as cook or maity. No provisions of any kind are procurable at this place. A moderate quantity of crockery and cutlery form part of the furniture. The rooms are furnished, but there is no bedding.

—Neduwattam. This is a fairly large building, consisting of a dining-hall 24 × 15, with verandahs in the front and in the sides, two bed-rooms, each $18\frac{3}{4}$ × 15, two dressing-rooms, and two bath-rooms, each $8\frac{3}{4}$ × $5\frac{3}{4}$, and stabling for four horses. The bungalow is twenty-two miles from Ootacamand by the new road and seventeen by the old. The former is a carriage road throughout. The Local Fund Board maintain a paid servant and a sweeper. The maity holds a liquor license, and will provide provisions if timely notice is given by excursionists.

—Paikaré. This bungalow contains a dining-room, two bed, two dressing, and two bath-rooms, and supplies stabling for four horses. The bungalow is leased by a contractor, who pays the Local Fund Board ten rupees a month for the privilege. The bungalow is twelve miles by the new road and ten by the old from Ootacamand.

—Kalhatti. The bungalow here commands a fine view of the waterfall. It consists of two spacious rooms with dressing and bath rooms attached. A couple of horses may find stabling. The bungalow is eight miles from Ootacamand, six of which are a fine carriage road. A peon is in charge of the building. He can cook.

—Pérmand. This bungalow has not yet been taken over by the Local Fund Board. It is under the Commissioner, and the peon of the Avalanché Bungalow is in charge. The usual fees are demanded. The building consists of a dining-room, a bed-room, each 20 × 16, with a bath-room attached, 10 × 5. There are stables for four horses.

—Púrthé, near McIvor's Bund. This building was erected by the late Mr. McIvor at the site of his bund across the Púrthé or Kúnda stream when carrying out the silting process in 1868-69. On the abandonment of the bund the Local Fund Board did not take charge of the building, but it is available for travellers. The bungalow is small.

—Krúrmand. This bungalow, which stands on the bank of the Paikaré river, was built by subscription by Mr. C. B. Thomas in January 1862. It has a thatched roof, and the following accommodation : a dining-room, two bed and two bath rooms, and stabling for four horses. It is ten miles from Ootacamand, for seven of which there is a cart road. There is crockery for six people. There is a servant in charge who can cook. It is the halting place for visitors to Múkarté Peak.

In accordance with the Local Fund Board's rules, travellers occupying the abovenamed bungalows have to pay the following charges :—

	RS.	A.	P.
For a single person, per day	1	0	0
Do. do. for part of a day ...	0	8	0
For a family, per day	2	0	0
Do. for part of a day	1	0	0
For a horse-stable—charges, per day ...	0	4	0

Chuttrums.

Chuttrums or Native Rest Houses.—There are sixteen chuttrums in the district; of these twelve are under the Local Fund Board, three under the Municipalities, and one is still retained by Government. There are also one or two private chuttrums, the best of which is on the new Coonoor Ghát, about four miles from the top of the Pass, built by a trader, Nanjappa Row.

—Ellanhalli.

This chuttrum is situated near the fifth milestone on the road from Ootacamand to Coonoor. It is a large building, 50′×25′, and can accommodate about fifty travellers. It is much used, especially by travellers posting relays. The space is undivided, except on the left, which is divided off and forms a room.

—Craigmore.

This is a small building immediately behind the toll-gate at Craigmore. It measures 15′ × 12′.

—Arvenkád.

This is a small building on the old road from Coonoor to Ootacamand, about four miles from the former station.

—Kótagiri.

The building is 54′ × 24′. It has a reserve space for those who bring goods for sale to the market, of 90′ × 60′, including the ground occupied by the chuttrum. The interior is not divided into compartments, and may accommodate about sixty people.

—Nanjanád.

This chuttrum is about seven miles from Ootacamand, on the road to the Avalanché Bungalow. It is 39′ long by 37′ wide, and is in three compartments, each 10½′ × 24′, with a verandah in front. It can accommodate about thirty people.

—Paikaré.

This is a building 53′ × 25′. It contains two small rooms. The main room can accommodate about thirty-three travellers. It is ten miles from Ootacamand by the old and twelve miles by the new road.

—Neduwattam.

This chuttrum is of the same size as the one at Paikaré. It is twenty-two miles from Ootacamand by the new road and seventeen by the old.

—Ouchterlony's.

This chuttrum was built by the late Mr. Ouchterlony. It consists of a room 20′ × 12′, and may be able to accommodate about ten people at a time. The cooly class use this chuttrum. It is five miles from Ootacamand on the old road.

—Burliár.

This chuttrum is about eleven miles down the ghát by the new and six miles by the old road. It is 45′ × 26′, and is divided into two compartments, 18′ × 16′.

CHAP. II. — GENERAL DESCRIPTION. — New chuttrum.

This chuttrum is situated midway between Paikaré and Neduwattam. It is 28′ × 18′. The main room is 28′ × 10′, and can accommodate about twenty travellers. It was erected in 1869, partly by aid afforded by planters. The servant in charge of the Neduwattam Chuttrum looks after this chuttrum also.

—Segúr.

The chuttrum is 40′ × 12′, and is situated not far from the river. It is eleven miles and a half from Ootacamand by the Segúr Ghát. It accommodates about twenty people. There are two compartments, 18′ × 9′ each, and there is also a small bungalow at the head of the Pass.

—Ootacamand Agraharam.

The outer measurements of the building are 58′ × 37½′. It consists of seven small enclosed compartments and two halls or covered enclosures. It is the only caste chuttrum in the district. It was originally built by one Subaon, who in 1856 made it over to Government on condition that they would maintain an establishment, keep the building in repair, and restrict its use to Brahmans. The establishment and contingencies cost Government Rupees 120 per annum.

—Ootacamand.

This chuttrum is under the Municipal Commissioners of Ootacamand. It is 66′ × 75′, and can comfortably accommodate twenty or twenty-five travellers. People coming up to the weekly market use it.

—Coonoor (Market).

There are two chuttrums at Coonoor, both under the Municipality. The Market Chuttrum is the larger. It consists of two rooms 18′ × 16′, a small room 16′ × 7′, and a long verandah 51′ × 7½′. The accessories are a cook-room, a stable and a latrine. Respectable natives sometimes take shelter in this chuttrum; about twelve people can be accommodated.

—Coonoor (Cooly).

This structure adjoins the bridge. It is 47′ × 15′, without partitions; about thirty coolies find comfortable accommodation, but the number usually occupying the building is much larger. It was erected in 1871 by one Narrainsámi, who was an extensive landholder. His family are in possession of property extending from Kalhatti almost to the head of the Pass.

—Kalhatti.

The chuttrum is 47′ × 26′, and is capable of accommodating about fifty people. It is divided into six compartments—three each 11′ × 11′, one 17′ × 6½′, one 14′ × 6½′, and another 11′ × 6½′.

The Government chuttrums in the district are, with the exception noted, in charge of the Local Fund Board. They were made over to this body in 1871 on the introduction of the Local Fund Act. A fee of Rs. 2-8-0 is paid to the servants in charge of each building, and an assignment of two acres of land is also allowed, but utilized only at the following chuttrums, viz., Neduwattam, Paikaré, Burliár, Kótagiri, and Ellanhalli.

CHAPTER III.

POPULATION.

Early notices.—Captain Ward's Report.—Major Ouchterlony's.—Quinquennial.—Census of 1871.—Distribution.—Houses.—Proportion of Sexes.—Increase in number of Hill Tribes.—Incorrectness of Returns.—Population of Villages.—Of Náds.—Religion.—Castes.—Occupations.—Education.—General remarks.

CHAP. III. — POPULATION. — Early Notices.

The earliest notice of the population of the Nílagiri Hills will be found in Keys' and Macmahon's Survey Report, dated the 12th June 1812[1]. "The population," they observe, "male and female in the three náds[2] amounts to 2,516 individuals, of which number 1,647 are Badagas, 292 Lingbund or Shevaacharas, 268 Thorayers, 179 Thothavurs and 130 Cothurs." They mention also the number of villages as "41 principal and 119 subordinate." These figures were probably obtained from the Taluq Office at Dévanaikenkóta, to which taluq the Nílagiris then appertained.

Captain Ward's Census.

In 1821 Captain B. S. Ward[3] appears to have made a more detailed census. The results are as follows :—

[1] Printed in the Appendices.

[2] Péranganád, Mékanád and Tódanád.

[3] Printed in the Appendices.

A Statistical Table of the three Náds on the Nílagiris.

Number.	Names of the Náds.	No. of Villages.			No. of Munds.	No. of Peons.	Husbandmen.												Herdsmen.		Artificers		Cussuvers.		Number of Ploughs.
							Lingavunts.		Budagers.		Torayens.		Kycolens.		Mulu-Curumbers.		Baders.		Thodawars.		Cothurs.				
		Principal.	Subordinate.	Total.			Male.	Female.	Male.	Female.	Male.	Female.	Male.	Female.	Male.	Female.	Male.	Female.	Male.	Female.	Male.	Female.	Male.	Female.	
1	Péranganád ...	32	25	57	3	62	59	62	621	532	80	70	...	...	17	10	...	...	13	7	69	57	...	...	166
2	Mékanád ...	7	37	44	2	34	12	11	446	411	27	21	...	...	...	...	...	...	7	5	22	22	...	...	81
3	Tódanád ...	12	47	59	39	55	23	15	696	647	10	9	12	9	...	...	3	2	120	70	81	66	5	4	161
	Total ...	51	109	160	44	151	94	88	1763	1590	117	100	12	9	17	10	3	2	140	82	172	145	5	4	408
	Total of Male and Female ...						182		3,353		217		21		27		5		222		317		9		

Male ...	2,323
Female ...	2,030
Grand Total ...	4,353

CHAP. III. POPULATION.

Captain Ouchterlony's Report.

Twenty-six years later or in December 1847 Captain Ouchterlony[1] found the population to stand thus :—

No. of Villages or Mands	Houses.	Names of Tribes.	Adult. Male.	Adult. Female.	Children. Male.	Children. Female.	Total.
85	209	Tódas	86	70	87	94	337
227	2,092	Burghers	2,017	1,997	1,269	1,316	6,599
6	81	Kothers	93	92	64	58	307
22	150	Irulas	148	151	77	85	461
340	2,532	Grand Total ...	2,344	2,310	1,497	1,553	7,704
...	...	Hindoos	...	...	...	...	3,045
...	...	Mussulmans	...	...	...	...	901
...	...	Pariahs	...	...	...	...	4,941
...	...	East Indians	...	...	...	...	154
...	...	Europeans	...	...	...	...	342
		Total Population of the Nílagiris ...					17,087

Hill Tribes—numbers in 1856.

In the year 1856, the number of the hill tribes, exclusive of Irulas, was as follows; but I have not been able to ascertain the figures of the Hindu, European, Eurasian and Mussulman population at this date.

—	Male.	Female.	Total.
Badagas	6,574	6,778	13,352
Tódas	185	131	316
Kótas	238	246	484
Kúrumbas	72	79	151
Total ...	7,069	7,234	14,333

—In 1866-67. Quinquennial Report.

In the year 1866-67, the total population had risen to 38,142 souls, but this figure was too low owing to the omission, probably, of the Tamil and European population; as five years later, according to the census of 1871, the numbers were 49,501, or 66·0 per square mile. Since this date the Ouchterlony Valley, hitherto appertaining to South-East Wainád, and still more recently the greater part of the remaining portion of that section of the Wainád Taluq, have been added to the district, containing in 1871 a total population of 37,347 souls, or 156·26 to the square mile. Thus the total population, allowing for the natural increase and immigration since the year 1871, may be roughly estimated at little short of 100,000 souls, or about 100 persons to the square mile.

Distribution of Population.

Within the limits of the district as it stood in 1871, the population is distributed as follows. These statistics are drawn mainly from Dr. Cornish's Census Report. For the portions since annexed, I am unable to give information in detail.

[1] Then employed on the Topographical Survey of the Plateau.

Divisions.	Houses.			Population.											
				Children.		Adults.		Total.							
	Inhabited.	Uninhabited.	Total.	Boys under 12 years of age.	Girls under 10 years of age.	Males.	Females.	Males.	Females.	Hindus.	Mahomedans.	Christians.	Buddhists & Jains.	Others.	Total.
Nílagiris	10,893	...	10,893	6,482	5,621	12,168	9,703	18,650	15,324	32,907	272	783	...	12	33,974
Ootacamand Municipality	2,062	...	2,062	1,648	1,458	3,617	3,259	5,265	4,717	6,391	1,199	2,362	...	30	9,982
Coonoor Municipality ...	536	...	536	447	390	1,211	1,010	1,658	1,400	2,236	233	588	...	1	3,058
Wellington Cantonment....	360	...	360	279	216	766	480	1,045	696	690	203	847	...	1	1,741
Lawrence Asylum ...	70	...	70	176	49	281	123	457	172	120	21	488	...	...	629
Lovedale Jail[1]	1	...	1	...	...	117	...	117	...	107	8	2	...	...	117
Total ...	13,922	...	13,922	9,032	7,734	18,160	14,575	27,192	22,309	42,451	1,936	5,070	...	44	49,501

[1] In 1871 prisoners were still employed in the Lawrence Asylum works, Lovedale.

CHAP. III. — POPULATION. — Houses. Proportion of Sexes.

This population was dwelling in 13,922 houses, of which all save 1,914 were thatched. The average number of inmates was low, viz., 3·6: and excluding the cantonments it was 3·1 only. The excess in the proportion of males over females is noteworthy. This is mainly due to the fact that native traders, servants, coolies, and other temporary residents on the Hills are not, to any great extent, accompanied by their women. Among the hill tribes the proportion, except in the case of the Tódas and Kúrumbas, is fairly satisfactory, as appears from the following table :—

—	1871-72.		Total.
	Males.	Females.	
Badagas	9,775	9,701	19,476
Tódas	405	288	693
Kótas	534	578	1,112
Kúrumbas	330	283	613
Irulas	746	724	1,470
Total ...	11,790	11,574	23,364

Increase in number of Hill Tribes.

Incorrectness of early returns.

After making every allowance for the incorrectness of the earlier statistics, the increase in the number of some of the hill tribes is very satisfactory. There is no evidence in support of the assertion that the Tódas are gradually dying out. In the case of the other wild tribes and the Kótas, the defectiveness of these early figures is manifest, but as regards the Badagas, the returns are probably not so incorrect. The average annual percentage of increase, however, in the periods noted below, after including the Badagas, shows the great inaccuracy of the early returns :—

—	1812.	1821.	1847.	1856.	1866.	1871.
Badagas	2,207	3,778	6,569	13,352	17,778	19,476
Tódas	179	222 [1]	337	316	704	693
Kótas	130	317	307	484	802	1,112
Kúrumbas	...	27	...	151	505	613
Irulas	...	...	461	...	102	1,470 [2]

Period.	Percentage of Increase annually.
1812—21 ...	7·9
1821—47 ...	2·7
1847—56 ...	11·4
1856—66 ...	3·3
1866—71 ...	1·9

[1] The census of 1825-26 gave 326 Tódas.

[2] The villages at the foot of the ghâts have been included. See following tatement.

CHAP. III.
POPULATION.

The low figures for the period ending 1847, as compared with the preceding and succeeding percentages are, I conclude, in a measure due to Ouchterlony's numbers being rigorously restricted to the plateau, whilst Ward's in 1821, and the returns in 1856, seem to include the lower slopes also. If the Badaga population of 1812 is compared with that returned in 1847, the annual average increase was 5·6 per cent. only. More reliance may be placed on the census of 1825, the results of which were as follows. The small number of girls, however, is suspicious, though, to some extent, early marriages may account for it.

Men	1,668
Women	1,696
Boys	1,151
Girls	632
Total ...	5,147
Villages	35
Houses	1,651

Village Population.

The distribution of these tribes among the several villages[1] is as follows:—

Number.	Divisions.	Kótas.	Badagas.	Tódas.	Kúrumbas.	Irulas.	Total.
1	Arakád	...	...	...	41	160	201
2	Aranád	...	...	...	...	105	105
3	Búdinattam	...	...	...	164	250	414
4	Kokád	...	...	...	...	30	30
5	Mékanád	243	4,707	33	60	5	5,048
6	Malachippa	...	...	...	23	52	75
7	Péranganád	331	7,713	105	208	6	8,363
8	Sembanaré	...	...	...	2	45	47
9	Sembanattam ...	...	...	...	1	72	73
10	Segúr	...	...	...	...	24	24
11	Tódanád	420	6,260	517	6	334	7,537
12	Ariyúr	...	...	...	36	...	36
13	Kúndas	118	776	...	15	...	909
14	Kúniapáni	...	...	...	...	139	139
15	Siral Kambé	...	4	...	...	99	103
16	Vagapáni	...	...	...	2	50	52
17	Velléru Kambé ...	...	...	...	55	98	153
18	Ootacamand Municipality	...	15	38	...	1	54
19	Coonoor Municipality.	...	1	...	...	...	1
	Total ...	1,112	19,476	693	613	1,470	23,364

[1] A village on the Nílagiris often embraces a number of hamlets, some of which may be as extensive as the parent village. The Péranganád and Mékanád villages are co-terminous with the sub-divisions of these names.

CHAP. III. — POPULATION.

If these villages be assigned to their proper náds, the result stands thus:—

Mékanád	5,048
Tódanád (including Segúr Villages) ...	8,102
Péranganád	9,305
Kúndanád	908
Total ...	23,364

Religion.

The people are classed thus under religions, the hill tribes being included under Hindus:—

Hindus	42,451
Mahamedans	1,936
Christians	5,070
Others	44

Among the Hindus Sivaism prevails, 37,264 being Sivaites, 3,504 only Vishnaites. There are 1,467 Lingaites, a sect of Sivaites. The Badagas are mostly Sivaites. The Mussulmans, who have more than doubled their number in the 25 years preceding 1871, are chiefly Soonees, 1,589 out of the 1,936 belonging to this sect, or 81·0 per cent. They are distributed among the following nationalities and tribes:—

Labbés[1]	273
Arabs	4
Sheiks	853
Syuds	156
Pattans	178
Moguls	8
Other Mahamedans	464
Total ...	1,936

Of this total number 787 only are females.

The Christians are classified thus:—

	Roman Catholics.	Protestants.	Total.
Europeans	209	1,130	1,339
Eurasians	128	668	796
Natives	2,437	498	2,935
Total ...	2,774	2,296	5,070

It is not to be forgotten that these numbers include the Wellington Depôt and the Lawrence Asylum. Among the

[1] These Labbés are half-breds sprung from Arab fathers and native mothers.

CHAP. III.
POPULATION.

Europeans and Eurasians, the Protestants have a large majority, but no less than 83·0 per cent. of the Native Christians are Roman Catholics.[1]

Castes.

The castes are arranged as follows:—

Castes.	Males.	Females.	Total.	Percentage of Females to 100 Males.	Percentage to the Hindu Population.
Brahmans (Priests)	107	89	196	83·2	·4
Kshatriyas (Warriors)	31	19	50	61·3	·1
Chetties (Traders)	362	110	472	30·4	1·0
Vellálas (Cultivators)	2,851	1,779	4,630	62·4	10·2
Idaiyas (Shepherds)	421	350	771	83·1	1·7
Kammalas (Artisans)	270	220	490	81·5	1·1
Kannakkas (Writers)	65	49	114	75·4	·3
Kaikkalas (Weavers)	148	84	232	56·8	·5
Vannias (Laborers)	708	526	1,234	74·3	2·9
Kusavas (Potters)	20	3	23	15·0	·05
Satani (Mixed Castes)	1,077	882	1,959	81·9	4·3
Sembadavas (Fishermen) ...	36	24	60	66·7	·1
Shánás (Toddy-drawers) ...	16	...	16	...	·04
Ambattas (Barbers)	51	57	108	111·8	·2
Vunnás (Washermen)	107	87	194	81·3	·4
Others	12,695	11,914	24,609	93·9	54·2
Pareiyas	5,705	4,523	10,228	79·3	22·5
Total ...	24,670	20,716	45,386	83·9	100·0

The Hill tribes are classed under "Others," the impression being that they acknowledge no divisions other than tribal. This, however, is not the case, so far as the Badagas are concerned, for among them the following principal caste divisions are found:—

Badagas.

1. Wúdeáru and Kongáru.[2]
2. Haruváru.
3. Adhikáris { Lingadhikáris. / Meat-adhikáris.
4. Kanukáru.
5. Badakáru.
6. Thoriáru.

The male portion of the population pursue the following occupations, 40 per cent. being devoted to agriculture:—

[1] The census being taken in November, gives a low average for the European Christian population.

[2] Mr. Metz divides the Wúdeáru and Kongaváru into two distinct classes. See Chapter on "Ethnology."

CHAP. III.

POPULATION.

Occupations.

Major headings.	Minor headings.	Number employed.	Total.	Percentage to the Male Population.
Professional ...	Government	78		·3
	Military	578		2·8
	Learned Professions ...	56		·2
	Minor do.	482		1·8
			1,186	
Domestic	Personal Service	964		3·5
			964	
Commercial ...	Traders	824		3·0
	Conveyors	608		2·2
			1,422	
Agricultural ...	Cultivators	6,963		25·6
			6,963	

Those employed in Government service are mostly Europeans, Vellálas and Pareiyas. The learned professions occupy 35 Europeans and Eurasians, 10 Pareiyas and 6 Mahamedans. As might be supposed, the personal servants are chiefly Pareiyas. Of the traders nearly 30 per cent. are Mussalmans, the rest Chetties, Vellálas and Pareiyas. The conveyors are chiefly Vellálas and Pareiyas. The cultivators are mainly Hill-men, Vellálas, Vannias and Pareiyas. To these classes also mainly belong the laborers.

Education.

The state of education on the Hills is very backward, especially among the hill-men. The following table exhibits the condition of the population in this respect :—

—	Gross Population.	Number able to Read and Write.	Proportions.
Hindus	42,451	1,555	3·7
Mahamedans	1,936	298	15·4
Europeans and Eurasians	2,135	1,500	70·3
Native Christians	2,935	631	21·5
Others	44	6	13·6
Total ...	49,501	3,990	8·1

General remarks.

The foregoing statistics represent the numbers and conditions of the population, permanent and temporary, found on the Hills at the close of 1871. There can, however, be little doubt that as already stated, it has considerably increased since then, especially as regards the immigrant populations, Canarese and Tamil; this increase being due to the extension of coffee, tea, and cinchona

CHAP. III.

POPULATION.

cultivation, and also to the numerous public works which have been undertaken during the last five years, especially in Ootacamand and Wellington; meanwhile, however, until the year 1877 no epidemic disease has to any considerable extent prevailed among these people. The same causes have also tended to improve the condition of the hill-people. In the early notices the miserable condition of the Badaga villagers is more than once referred to. The women are spoken of as lean and emaciated, the children as having protuberant stomachs, thin and fleshless legs, —the true signs of short and hard fare. The appearance their women and children now present forms a striking contrast to this description. Dr. Cornish, the Sanitary Commissioner, remarks: "I have no doubt the native population is increasing, and that the position of the Badaga has materially improved. I notice especially the facts that they are now tiling their houses, that their women and children earn money on the tea and coffee estates, and that they buy rági and grain from the low country, and get a better market for their straw and cattle. They wear jewels of gold and silver, saved from their earnings. Of course 1877 was a bad year for them, but, as a rule, according to my observation of them, they have borne the famine pressure better than the low-country people."

CHAPTER IV.

CLIMATE, METEOROLOGY, AND HEALTH.

First notices of the climate.—Reports on the medical topography.—Climates. —Thermometrical and barometrical observations.—Doddabetta Observatory. —Wellington Observatory.—Meteorological tables.—Temperature compared. —Winds.—Table of winds.—Hurricanes.—Effect of wind on barometer.—Rainfall.—Average fall.—Extremes.—Rain-gauge stations.—Hygrometrical observations.—Vital statistics.—Comparative tables.—Vaccination.—Results.—Special reports, Ootacamand.—Wellington.

PART I.

CHAP. IV, PART I. — CLIMATE, &c. — First notices of climate.

THE climate of these hills has been the subject of frequent discussion from their first occupation by Europeans in 1819 up to recent years. The discovery of a spot within the tropics possessing a climate with many of the advantages and but few of the disadvantages of the climates of those countries, within the temperate zones, with which Anglo-Indians of the day were familiar, excited the keenest interest.[1]

"When you look over the register of the thermometer which I now send you," writes a prophetic friend of the writer, whose letter is published in the *Madras Gazette*, 17th June 1820, and who had been three months on the plateau, "the wonderful equality of the temperature in the shade throughout the month must strike you as remarkable, the difference between the highest and lowest degrees at 6 in the morning being only 7½, at 8 o'clock 5, at noon 7, and the same at 8 o'clock at night. This cool and equal temperature ought to prove highly beneficial to invalids suffering from the diseases or debility produced by a long residence in a hot climate. We have here none of those hot close nights which allow no rest to the sick; it is always agreeable to sleep under a blanket; and one awakes in the morning revived and refreshed. You are aware that I came up here much debilitated from the effects of a severe fever. I speak, therefore, from

[1] See letters in the *Madras Courier*, 23rd February 1819, printed in the Appendix.
Letters in the *Madras Gazette*, 19th April and 17th June 1820, 14th March 1821, 15th June 1822, 20th August and 22nd October 1825; also a series of letters during 1825 and 1826 by "Philanthropos" in the Bengal *Hárkaru*, republished in the *Madras Courier*.

CHAP. IV, PART I. — CLIMATE, &c.

experience; a week's residence here produced the greatest possible change in my health and feelings, and I have no doubt that the day will come when this will be esteemed the Montpellier of India, and that people will resort to it from all quarters."

In another portion of his letter this correspondent remarks: "I don't remember to have seen the glass lower than 56 degrees at the coldest season, and in the coldest portion of the Isle of France. If my memory is correct, it usually rose to 75 or 76 degrees during the day. This was during the months of May, June, July, August, and part of September; during the remainder of the year the weather is very much better. If this statement is correct, the temperature of the air on the Nilagerry Mountains in the hot season is about equal to the temperature of the Isle of France in the cold. I have no means of knowing what the temperature at the Cape is, but it is not much cooler, I imagine, than the climate of the Isle of France, as the mountainous parts of the island are much higher than any habitable lands at the Cape. The mean temperature for the month of March (when the hot season is over) is stated in a periodical publication to be 72 degrees. I remember to have seen the glass at the Government House at the Cape rise to above 100 degrees on Christmas-day, the hottest season of the year." * * * "Particulars of the climate of New South Wales are given in Wentworth's recent account of that colony, but I think he states the thermometer to rise as high as 85 degrees or 90 in the shade. In the summer months of March, April, and May on the Nilagerries it got as high as 79. * * * These facts are abundantly sufficient to prove the very extraordinary coolness of the Nilagerry Mountains throughout the year."

Reports on the medical topography.

When this letter was written only fifteen or twenty travellers had visited the Hills, but the number of visitors rose rapidly, and still more rapidly did the climate rise in popular estimation for coolness and salubrity. But some of the doctors were diffident. The main point at issue was whether or not the Hills would supply suitable sanitaria firstly for the invalids of the Honorable Company's European troops, and, secondly, as a residence for Civil and Military officers not invalids. Report after report was called for. Finally a complete digest of all information collected on the medical topography and climate of the Hills was submitted to Government by the Medical Board on the 13th March 1828, together with an excellent paper on the meteorology, contributed by Surgeon Dalmahoy, then stationed at Kótagiri.

Later, in 1832, a full report was submitted to the Court of Directors respecting "the extent and permanence of the benefit derived by European soldiers and public officers" from a resort to these Hills. The officer from whom the Medical Board derived most of the information furnished with their letter, 24th December 1832, was Dr. Baikie, and the general results of his intelligent and indefatigable labors will be found in the chapter of his book devoted to the climate of the Nílagiris.

They concurred in the opinion that there were "no grounds for anticipating from such an establishment[1] any results of much importance, in a financial or political point of view, if indeed its maintenance should not be attended with positive loss," and, further, that, while the medical reports generally represent the climate in the most favorable point of view, "they tend to show that it is not well adapted for the cure of those chronic diseases attributable to a tropical climate which chiefly lead to inefficiency, and consequently to discharge from the service or transfer to the invalid or pension establishments."

The Board, however, passed over in silence Dr. Baikie's scheme, to which reference is made in a later chapter, for the location of fresh recruits and European regiments on the Hills—a scheme which has already been partially carried into effect by the establishment of the depôt at Wellington, and which bids fair to attain, as time goes on, a more complete development.

In addition to Dr. Baikie's book, already referred to, published in 1833, and the report on the meteorology of the hills by Mr. Dalmahoy, the most important papers on the subject of the climate and meteorology subsequently given to the public were—a report by Dr. Birch (*Madras Journal of Literature and Science*, 1838, No. 20), a paper on the medical topography of the Hills, published by Government, with similar reports on the Ceded Districts and Coorg in 1844; a paper in the selections of Government papers on "Our Marine and Hill Sanitaria" published in 1860. In Major Ouchterlony's Survey Report (1847) will also be found many valuable observations on the subject and some important tables. The latter chiefly apply to Kótagiri. A pamphlet was published by Mr. Pachman in 1850, and another in 1870 by Dr. Mackay. Both of these contain valuable information.

The climate, or rather climates, of the Nílagiri Hills—for that of each hill and valley seems to vary according to its exposure to the monsoons, its elevation, or other local causes[2]—may be generally described as for the greater part of the year dry, bracing, and exhilarating, and more equable than those of Europe; the maximum range of the thermometer being only

---

[1] Invalid Depôt.

[2] This is curiously illustrated by the fact that whilst 31·45 inches of rain fell at Coonoor in October and November 1875, only 16·71 inches fell at Wellington in the same months, though only two miles distant.

CHAP. IV, PART I. — CLIMATE, &c.

from 8 to 9 degrees at Ootacamand, and from 12 to 15 degrees at Wellington throughout the year, in the middle of the day, as against 28 degrees in London.

Thermometrical and barometrical observations.

As already stated a vast amount of diligent inquiry has been bestowed on the meteorology of the plateau. The scientific value, however, of such observations is by no means commensurate with the labor bestowed thereon, as they were not conducted on system, or carried on with identical or relatively-adjusted instruments. To supply this defect in accordance with the expressed wish of the Honorable Court of Directors, the Madras Government, during the reign of the Marquis of Tweeddale, allotted funds for the establishment of an Observatory.

Doddabetta Observatory.

The summit of Doddabetta[1] was chosen as farthest removed from disturbing local conditions affecting the air currents and temperature, &c., and in 1846 a plain brick-building was erected there. Instruments were provided from England for the new institution, which was placed under the general control of Mr. T. G. Taylor, the H. C. Astronomer, Madras, with an Assistant or Writer, and a Lascar on the spot. Observations were begun in 1847 and continued till May 1859. The observations, however, were published till 1855, but I have seen those for the first three years only. A discussion on the results will be found in a paper by Colonel Sykes, F.R.S., in the Philosophical Transactions of the Royal Society, Part II, 1850. This experiment eventually proved a failure from various causes. The thermometric observations are not to be relied on, but those of the atmospheric pressure and rainfall, though not accurate, are, Mr. Pogson informs me, less open to suspicion.

Wellington Observatory.

Some years after the closing of the Doddabetta Observatory, another was established at Wellington under G.O., 27th August 1866, and is in the charge of the Cantonment Surgeon.

Meteorological tables.

The following comparative tables exhibit the thermometrical and barometrical conditions of Ootacamand, Wellington, and Kótagiri :—

[1] About 50 miles from the sea on the west and 240 on the east.

CHAP. IV, PART I. CLIMATE, &c.

Thermometrical Observations.

Months.	Ootacamand—Mean Temperature from Sun-rise to Sun-set, 1832.	Kótagiri—Mean Temperature from Sun-rise to Sun-set, 1832.	Wellington—Mean Temperature calculated on the Years 1873-74-75.
January	54·33	59·16	58·00
February	56·33	60·83	59·00
March	60·00	61·33	63·46
April	61·66	62·66	64·46
May[1]	61·66	62·83	65·40
June	58·66	64·00	64·50
July	57·00	65·00	64·33
August	57·00	65·33	64·50
September	56·66	64·00	63·76
October	56·33	62·50	62·76
November	55·00	60·66	59·30
December	53·33	59·33	57·50
Mean Average ...	57·33	62·305	62·36

Barometrical Observations.

Months.	Mean Height of Barometer, Ootacamand, 1831-32.	Mean Height of Barometer, Kótagiri, 1847-48.	Mean Height of Barometer, Wellington, 1873-74.
March	23·175	24·113	24·230
April	23·085	24·126	24·208
May	22·983	...	24·203
June	22·910	24·459	24·192
July	22·861	24·027	24·179
August	22·820	22·834	24·178
September	22·785	23·894	24·214
October	23·056	24·112	24·185
November	23·070	24·138	24·188
December	23·174	24·890	24·252
January	23·375	24·152	24·276
February	23·364	24·337	24·257
Mean Average ...	23·055	24·098	24·213

Temperature, &c. compared.

The mean temperature of the hill stations stands thus as compared with that of Great Britain and the Presidency capitals.

London	50·0
Ootacamand ...	57·0
Wellington	62·0
Kótagiri	62·0
Coonoor	64·0
Calcutta	78·0
Bombay	81·0
Madras	85·0

[1] The temperature of this month in Ootacamand was first registered in 1822: mean 62, maximum 72, minimum 52, range 20.

CHAP. IV, PART I. — CLIMATE, &c.

The following comparative statement of temperature, rainfall, and elevation of several of the more important hill sanitaria in India may be found useful :—

Names of Hills or Hill Stations.		Mean Temperature in												Ascertained Heights.	Average Fall of Rain per Annum in Inches.
		January.	February.	March.	April.	May.	June.	July.	August.	September.	October.	November.	December.		
Bengal Presidency.	Darjeeling	40	41	51	55	61	62	63	64	63	55	50	44	8,008	12¾
	Simla	40	44	53	61	66	80	75	78	70	67	52	46	8,000	70
	Muree	...	...	...	...	...	69	68	66	62	62	...	...	6,786	...
	Kussowlie	42	47	58	64	77	73	70	70	72	66	...	...	6,400	70
	Nainee Tal	42	46	56	61	69	69	67	69	65	61	50	47	6,200	82½
Madras Presidency.	Ootacamand ...	54	56	60	61	61	57	63	63	63	56	54	53	7,361	60
	Kótagiri	59	60	61	63	63	64	65	65	64	62	60	59	6,100	55
	Wellington	59	61	67	68	68	64	70	70	70	63	61	60	5,840	50
	Coonoor	60	62	68	68	68	65	70	70	70	65	62	62	5,761	50
	Pulnis	51	53	60	61	Is about 69°								7,000	...
	Shevaroys	65	65	68	71	71	68	68	68	67	66	66	65	5,260	40
	Ramandroog	70	76	80	80	75	73	71	70	70	71	71	67	3,400	46
Bombay Presidency.	Mahableshwur ...	63	65	72	74	72	67	63	64	64	66	64	63	4,700	239¾
	Poorendhur	67	73	77	78	73	70	67	65	67	71	69	64	4,200	72¼
	Matheran		Temperature throughout the year about 10° under that of Bombay.											2,500	...
	Mount Aboo	61	61	69	77	77	77	69	69	69	69	69	71	4,015	78¼

Vide page 21, Mountain and Marine Sanitaria, 1862.

CHAP. IV, PART I. — CLIMATE, &c. — Winds.

The Nílagiris, from their geographical position, come within the full influence of the south-west monsoon as far as the western and upland tracts are concerned. The other portions are greatly protected by the Doddabetta range and its spurs, which form the dividing wind and water line between the south-west and north-east monsoons. On the other hand those portions which are sheltered from the south-west receive the full burst of the north-east monsoon. The former sets in at Ootacamand about the middle of June, the latter towards the end of October.

During the south-west monsoon the wind usually blows from the west and north-west, gradually trending more and more towards the north and east until October. From the end of this month until the beginning of April the winds blow fairly constantly from the east, working round to the west, as the sun travels towards the north. The direction of winds, however, on the plateau is far less constant than might be expected considering the great comparative height and almost insular position of the Nílagiri Mountain range. This variability, apart from local disturbing causes, such as hill, gorge, and valley present, is due probably to the fact that it is rather a headland than an island from which the Western and Eastern Ghâts recede in a northerly and easterly direction respectively.

The air currents meeting these ranges receive an impulse, turning them southwards. This seems to account for the remarkable phenomenon that for the greater portion of the year the winds blow, more or less, constantly and directly from the north.

The following table illustrates this:—

Table of Winds.

Winds at Doddabetta.

—	North-west.	North-east.	South-west.	South-east.
1847.	Days.	Days.	Days.	Days.
February	5	6	...	17
March	4	25	...	2
April	7	18	3	2
May	3	18	8	2
June	4	...	26	...
July	18	...	13	...
August	27	3	...	1
September	21	4	5	...
October	9	10	...	12
November	5	15	7	3
December	6	17	...	8
1848.				
January	2	13	...	16
Year ...	111	129	62	63
Total ...	240		125	

CHAP. IV, PART I. — CLIMATE, &c.

Col. Sykes' remarks.

Colonel Sykes remarks :—

"The winds of the south-west monsoon, however, terminate in July instead of October. This is the more remarkable, as Doddabetta lies between Madras, where these winds are the prevailing winds of May, June, July, August, and September, and Bombay, where the same winds prevail in the same months. It is probable, therefore, that Doddabetta is situated just above the upper surface of the stratum of wind and aqueous vapour which supplies the south-west monsoon to Western India, and therefore has comparatively a small supply of rain from this source. But it is not situated (although on the Western Coast) above the stratum of wind and aqueous vapour which supplies the Coromandel Coast during the north-east monsoon, as it has the same prevailing winds between the north and east points in the same months as at Madras from October to February, when the north-east ceases at Madras, but continues at Doddabetta until late in May. The *prevalence* of winds from points between north and west in the months of July, August, and September is peculiar to Doddabetta : neither Mahableshwur, at 4,500 feet, nor Madras, Bombay, nor Calcutta, has similar indications. However, as this so-denominated north-west wind very frequently blows from only one or two points to the northward of west, the wind may belong to the monsoon of the Western India, local physical circumstances having given it a slant."

Hurricanes.

Hurricanes are of rare occurrence, and the storms, accompanied with great electric disturbance which usher in the monsoons, generally take their course along the crests of the range.

Effect of wind on barometer.

The slight effect of the pressure of the wind on the barometer on the plateau is noteworthy. Colonel Sykes observes :—

Col. Sykes' remarks.

"It is usually understood that very high winds materially depress the barometer, but the records at Doddabetta do not support this view. On the 17th and 18th of April 1847 the wind blew with a mean pressure of 21 lbs. and 14 lbs. respectively upon the square foot ; but the barometers only fell from 21·955 on the 16th to 21·917 on the 17th, and rose to 21·984 on the 18th ; and there was a maximum pressure from the wind on the 17th at one time of 35 lbs. 26th of May, maximum wind 28·5 lbs., barometer not affected more than 0·010 inch ; 12th of June 30 lbs. ; 26th June 32 lbs. ; 10th of September 35 lbs. ; and 14th of October 22 lbs. ; but these pressures of the wind had little or no effect upon the barometer."[1]

Rainfall.

The register of the rainfall from the several stations of the Hills was recorded but irregularly, and mainly by private individuals until within the last few years. The most trustworthy returns kept until quite recently are probably those taken by Drs. Baikie and Ross and Major Ouchterlony.

---

[1] *Phil. Transactions, Royal Society*. Part II, 1850.

CHAP. IV, PART I. — CLIMATE, &c.

The following facts will be of interest :—

Average Rainfall, Ootacamand.

	INCHES.
1829 to 1836 inclusive	47·78
1851 to 1860 do.	52·38
1869 to 1875 do.	46·00

Average fall. Extremes.

The highest rainfall that I have found on record is 63·18 in 1858-59, the lowest 33·84 in 1832. However, 35·50 inches only fell in 1869-70, and 34·65—35·76 inches in 1875-76 and 1876-77 respectively.[1]

Rain-gauge stations.

The localities where the rain gauges are now kept are Ootacamand, Wellington, Coonoor, Mélkúnda, Kaity, Kódanád, and Neduwattam. The average fall at each of these points for each month of the year for the quinquennium ending 1874-75 will be found in Appendix No. 5 compared with the fall in 1875-76 and 1876-77, the years ending 31st July. If the rainfall in the western Kúndas were included, the average would be considerably raised.

The following table exhibits the results :—

Average Rainfall.

Stations.	Period. 1870-71—1874-75.	Period. 1875-76—1876-77.
Ootacamand	48·10	35·20
Coonoor	68·12	58·25
Wellington	51·47	40·09
Mélkúnda	56·28	40·08
Kaity	50·95	39·12
Kódanád	61·69	41·69
Neduwattam	113·61	101·51
Average ...	64·31	50·85

Hygrometrical observations.

With regard to the hygrometric state of the air on the Hills, Dr. Baikie observes :—

Dr. Baikie's remarks.

"The air during the months of January, February, and March is intensely dry, the points of saturation (or temperature to which the air must be reduced to deposit any part of its moisture) being occasionally as low as 13 degrees, the temperature of the air being 60 degrees. In

[1] Mr. Broughton has recorded some observations as to the amount of organic matter in the rainfall during the north-east and south-west monsoons which are especially important from a health point of view. He found marked differences of organic impurity in rain falling during the south-west monsoon from that in storms from the land side. The south-west rains were nearly absolutely free of organic matter, while rain from the north-east or north-west was charged with organic impurity. The rain washes the air and brings down impurities, and the difference in the healthiness of south-west and north-east wind seasons is in part accounted for by the purity of the air in one case and its contamination by terrestrial exhalations in the other.

CHAP. IV, PART I. — CLIMATE, &c.

April it begins to fluctuate, and in May the quantity of moisture increases very perceptibly, being accompanied by rapid changes of the electrical condition of the atmosphere, indicated by thunder-storms and heavy showers, but of short duration. During June, July, and August it is nearly charged with moisture; in September it is again fluctuating; in October and November moist; and in December it begins to reassume its dry state."

"The following table," he adds, "presents the actual state of the weather in Ootacamand for 366 days, from 1st March 1831 to 29th February 1832, which, from all I can learn, may be considered an average season":—

Number of days of heavy rain	19
Do. occasional showers with fair intervals...	81
Do. cloudy	28
Do. clear and fine	238
	366

Vital statistics.

A separate register of the births and deaths was begun in 1869. In the Appendix Table No. 13 appear the results since the year 1870-71. The statistics for the rural tracts are, as the figures themselves seem to indicate, of comparatively little value. Those of the Municipal towns are more trustworthy, especially as regards deaths, but even here the registration of the deaths of children is probably very defectively carried out.

Comparative table.

The following comparative statement of deaths of all ages will be of use:—

—	Infants.		Adolescents.		Adults.		Old People.		Total.		Total.
	Males.	Females.	Males.	Females.	Males.	Females.	Males.	Females.	Males.	Females.	
1874	85	57	127	118	232	138	94	66	538	379	917
1875	88	68	139	110	234	156	83	48	544	382	926
1876	92	75	146	146	342	246	118	109	698	576	1,274[1]

In Appendix No. 14 information will be found of the deaths among Europeans and Eurasians in 1874-75.

Vaccination.

Vaccination has been unusually successful in the Hills, as the statistics of deaths from small-pox will show. In the year 1869 the deaths are reported as 109; in the seven subsequent years they amounted to only 76, of which 33 were in 1873—an annual average of 10·85.

The following table exhibits the operations of the Vaccinators for the five years ending 1875-76. The establishment consists

[1] Exclusive of 13 born dead.

of four Vaccinators, two working under the Local Fund Board in the rural villages, and one in each of the Municipalities, all being under the general supervision of the Medical Officers of Ootacamand and Coonoor :— CHAP. IV, PART I. CLIMATE, &c.

Years.	Total No. vaccinated.	Successful.	Unsuccessful.	Unknown.
1871-72	1,198	1,060	62	76
1872-73	1,468	1,346	44	78
1873-74	2,378	2,376	58	144
1874-75	1,899	1,755	61	83
1875-76	1,746	1,609	67	70
Total ...	8,889	8,146	292	451

In the foregoing paragraphs I have endeavoured to exhibit briefly the principal facts in connection with the meteorology and health of the district. Considering, however, the vast importance of these subjects in relation to hill sanitaria, I append two papers, furnishing detailed information regarding Ootacamand and Wellington, contributed by the Medical Officers of those stations, Surgeons-Major Whitton and Corbett respectively. From these papers I have omitted certain portions supplying information which is furnished elsewhere, or which seemed otherwise unsuited for a work of this description. Concluding remarks.

PART II.

THE PHYSICAL AND MEDICAL CLIMATE AND TOPOGRAPHY OF OOTACAMAND AND THE SURROUNDING PLATEAU OF THE NÍLAGIRIS, TOGETHER WITH REMARKS ON PERSONAL HYGIENE, FOR THE USE OF VISITORS, INVALIDS, &c.

(*By* Surgeon-Major WHITTON, M.B., B.A., *Civil Surgeon, Ootacamand.*)

Physical topography.—Elevation.—Climate.—Health.—Rainfall.—Temperature.—Hygienic rules.—Diseases peculiar to residents and new-comers.—Lawrence Asylums.—Climates of Coonoor and Kótagiri.

CHAP. IV, PART II. — PHYSICAL AND MEDICAL CLIMATE, &c. — Causes of physical climate of Ootacamand.

AMONGST the combined circumstances which influence and produce the climate peculiar to the Nílagiri plateau may be mentioned—

1. Local elevation.
2. Geographical position.
3. The geological structure of the soil, its vegetation, and configuration.

Effects of local elevation.

As air receives its warmth from the earth, its temperature must diminish as the elevation increases; moreover, warm air, as it ascends, expands, its capacity for heat becoming greater; much of its heat therefore becomes latent, and sensible heat, as shown by the thermometer, is diminished. Another effect of elevation is the increase of the power of the sun's rays, a result which is, however, here greatly modified by strong winds, clouds and mist, or by the abundant moisture exhaled from the vegetation which covers the surface of the soil.

Effects of geographical position.

The Nílagiris, being situated but a short distance, some fifty miles, from the Indian Ocean, are exposed to the full force of the south-west monsoon, more especially the higher and western portions of the range. The great height of the Nílagiri also brings it in a marked degree under the influence of the north-east monsoon, especially towards the north and east. These monsoons, especially the south-west, exercise a most beneficial influence on the climate; for instance, during the months of June, July, and August, the sun is vertical, and would prove injurious in its effects on animal and vegetable life were it not that the clouds and mist, which are the usual concomitant

---

NOTE.—General description has been omitted, as it repeats matter already given; also other matter which seemed unsuitable to a paper for a manual.—ED.

of the monsoon during these months, moderate the power of its rays, and reduce the radiation from the ground. The strong gales which accompany the monsoons thoroughly ventilate the surface and remove effluvia, whilst the condensation of their aqueous vapour induces the frequent heavy showers, by which means everything which floats in the atmosphere and is not essential to its constitution is carried to the earth. The south-west monsoon, being a pure sea-breeze, is remarkably healthy and refreshing. The north-east monsoon, on the contrary, after it has parted with its moisture, becomes cold and dry, and consequently less wholesome. Moreover it brings with it air which has lain stagnant on the plains of India during some previous months.

Effects produced by the geological nature of the superficial strata and vegetation.

The geological nature of the soil and its vegetation also exert a marked influence on the configuration and climate of these Hills. Were the granitic[1] basement rocks of the Nílagiris unprotected from the denuding effects of meteorological forces, they would doubtless have assumed the rugged physical characters and contour which are found to be identical in mountain masses of a similar kind in other parts of the globe; but, owing to the protection afforded by local peculiarities of vegetation and surface soil, they rather resemble, in their rounded forms and elevated table-land, with abrupt declivities, the general appearance of mountains composed of calcareous rocks.

Valleys.

The valleys between the Hills are usually damp and marshy, and in these situations, owing to an accumulation of soil washed down from the hills above, particularly when forests have aided in retaining and enriching the soil, very fertile spots are to be found. Many forests in these situations have been felled for cultivation. This may in part account for the comparative absence of forest in the cultivable parts of the plateau in the present day. Peat swamps, so useful for the supply of fuel, are often found at the lower part of these valleys.

Springs, &c.

Springs are to be found in almost every hill-side. Occasionally the water from these springs contains iron in minute quantities. Many of these springs are perennial, whilst others cease to flow towards the end of the dry season. Being fed by the rain which has percolated through the primitive rocks, of which the hills are composed, they are, as is usual with waters derived from a similar source, of the most wholesome quality. At Ootacamand a great number of small rivulets, derived from springs on the Doddabetta range, converge, forming a stream which passes through the lowest part of the valley.

[1] See chapter on Geology. There is no granite on the Hills. The rocks referred to are gneissose.—ED.

CHAP. IV, PART II. — PHYSICAL AND MEDICAL CLIMATE, &c.

Station of Ootacamand.

The principal station, Ootacamand, is about 7,400 feet above the level of the sea. It is situated in the centre of the Nílagiri range, and from its elevation it is the coldest of the stations. It is located in an extensive valley, which permits of the free course of the winds, and which is sufficiently inclined to allow of good natural drainage from every part of it. It is enclosed on all sides but the west by a lofty range of hills. In the west centre of the station an artificial lake has been formed. Its western position and its unsheltered western aspect expose it more than either Coonoor or Kótagiri to the force of the south-west monsoon, which is broken only by the Kúndas, situated about 15 miles off.

Sanitary condition of the station.

The sanitary condition of Ootacamand is defective. It has now been occupied for fifty-five years, during the last twenty-five years of which successive Medical Officers have not failed to point out dangers from the neglect of sanitation. For several years past the Municipal Commission, established in 1868, has been doing much towards checking the evils resulting from previous neglect, but the funds at their disposal have not been sufficient to carry out sanitary works of any magnitude, such as a drainage system, or adequate water-supply. It says much for the natural salubrity of the station that it has so long remained comparatively free from serious endemic disease, but the experience of the famine year shows that a similar immunity cannot be calculated upon for the future. For years past the occurrence of occasional cases of typhoid fever of local origin point to the likelihood of further serious results from neglect of sanitary laws.

Water-supply of Ootacamand.

The chief water-supplies of Ootacamand are brought by open channels from tolerably pure sources situated at a considerable distance from the centre of the station, but it is obvious that water conveyed through a town by this means must be liable to pollution in a variety of ways. It should therefore be invariably boiled and filtered before use, but it would be better if water for drinking purposes were procured from some of the numerous springs. The water of the lake at Ootacamand is not likely to be used for domestic purposes by Europeans, but it is well to repeat that, being the receptacle for all the natural and artificial drainage of the station of Ootacamand, including the native bazaar, its water must be polluted in no ordinary degree.

Climate.

The climate of Ootacamand for the greater portion of the year is decidedly salubrious. The air is pure and bracing, and has a sensible effect in exhilarating the spirits and increasing the disposition to exercise. Inconvenience is seldom experienced under great or unusual exertion, and languor or lassitude are never felt as in the sultry plains of India.

CHAP. IV, PART II. — PHYSICAL AND MEDICAL CLIMATE, &c.

The prevailing winds are those of the north-east and south-west monsoons. The following table, showing the direction of the wind, has been compiled from the meteorological observations made in the years 1848, 1849, and 1850 :—

Prevailing winds and rainfall as recorded in the summit of Doddabetta.

Months.	1848.		1849.		1850.		Mean of the three Months.	Average fall of Rain for three years.	Direction of the Wind.
	* Wind.	Rain.	* Wind.	Rain.	* Wind.	Rain.	Wind	Rain.	
January ...	79	0·00	86	1·77	67	1·66	76	1·47	E. by N.
February...	79	0·00	56	0·00	116	2·62	84	0·87	E. by N.
March ...	79	0·55	88	2·15	79	0·69	82	1·13	E. by N.
April ...	68	4·09	56	7·72	65	5·52	63	5·77	E. N. E.
May ...	30	6·40	55	6·05	40	6·48	42	6·33	N. E.
June ...	281	5·66	270	8·45	281	6·70	278	6·70	W. by N.
July ...	292	13·06	303	10·59	281	11·44	292	11·69	W. N. W.
August ...	304	8·63	312	9·51	256	19·31	291	12·48	W. N. W.
September.	337	14·05	299	12·26	330	9·42	322	11·91	N.W. by N.
October ...	340	4·36	4	15·37	143	13·84	48	11·19	N. N. E.
November.	40	8·48	79	6·50	67	10·06	62	8·34	N. E. by E.
December.	59	2·59	81	1·87	114	4·91	85	3·12	E.
Total ...	...	65·53	...	82·24	...	92·65	...	80·14	

* Mean of hourly observations for the month.

The figures under wind, representing the direction of the wind, are reckoned from north towards the east on to 360 degrees, which again represents the north.

Remarks on the above tables.

From a perusal of the above table, it will be apparent that, notwithstanding the elevation of Doddabetta, it is still situated within the stratum of wind and aqueous moisture brought by both monsoons; but the comparatively small quantity of rain which it receives annually would, however, seem to show that it is not situated far below the upper surface of the current of aqueous moisture. A peculiarity in the direction of the wind, not observed in other parts of India during the prevalence of the south-west monsoon, may be seen in the above table. Instead of being from the south-west it is almost invariably from points between the west and north. This very curious phenomenon is doubtless due to some local physical circumstance, in all probability the Kúnda hills, which impart a slant to the wind.[1]

Rainfall at Ootacamand.

The rainfall received upon the plateau is considerably less than at Doddabetta.

[1] See remarks in Part I.—ED.

CHAP. IV, PART II.

PHYSICAL AND MEDICAL CLIMATE, &c.

	—	Ootacamand. Average Rain-fall for five Years.	Ootacamand. Total.	Coonoor. Average Rain-fall for five Years.	Coonoor. Total.	Average Number of Days on which Rain fell for five Years. Ootacamand.		Coonoor.	
North-east Monsoon.	October ...	8·06		10·83		17·6		17·0	
	November.	5·52		16·76		11·0		16·0	
	December.	1·16		5·37		3·4		6·4	
	January...	0·01		0·52		0·2		1·4	
	February.	0·73		4·28		1·8		2·8	
	March ...	1·02	16·50	1·23	38·99	2·8	36·80	2·2	45·8
Interme-diate.	April ...	2·65		4·44		86·0		8·0	
	May ...	6·71	9·36	6·22	10·66	13·0	21·6	9·4	17·4
South-west Monsoon.	June ...	5·73		3·34		15·6		9·6	
	July ...	5·22		3·07		18·0		11·2	
	August ...	4·04		3·30		15·0		10·4	
	September.	5·55	20·54	5·92	15·63	14·4	63·0	12·8	44·0
Annual Mean ...		...	46·40	...	65·28	...	121·4	...	107·2

The above table has been prepared from the daily records of the rainfall for five years from July 1871 to July 1876 inclusive.

The mean annual rainfall at Ootacamand for the last five years has been 46·40, and the average number of days on which rain fell during each of these years was 121·4.

Dr. Baikie gives 47·78 inches as annual mean rainfall at Ootacamand for seven years from the 1st June 1829 to the 31st May 1836, or only 1·38 inches more than the mean annual fall recorded during the past five years. This shows that the seasons, after an interval of forty years, have altered but little in regard to the amount of rainfall.

Temperature at Ootacamand.

According to the thermometric observations made by Dr. Baikie, the mean maximum temperature for the years 1831, 1832, and 1833 was 67·16, and the mean minimum for the same period was 48·05, giving a mean temperature of 57·60. According to Mr. Ross, whose observations refer to the years 1853, 1854, 1855, and 1856, the mean maximum is 61·87 and the mean minimum is 47·36, the mean temperature being 54·61. If the mean between these results be taken as 56·10, we shall probably have the correct mean temperature. There are some later observations, but they bear unmistakable traces of error arising from the unsuitable position in which the thermometers were placed.

In the absence of later trustworthy observations, the following extracts from remarks by Professor Oldham on the observations recorded by Dr. Baikie and Mr. Ross will be of interest as proving the equability and temperate nature of the climate:—

"The range of the temperature of the air during the hottest hours of the day, or at its maximum, throughout the whole year, appears to be not quite nine degrees; at the coldest hours of the night, or at the minimum, only 9·15 degrees; that is, the hottest hours of the day, whether in summer or in the depth of winter, do not vary more than nine degrees. The extreme variation from the hottest *day* temperature to the coldest *night* temperature during the whole year (average of seven years) was only 21·25. The extreme average range between day and night temperature was about the same as the extreme annual range, or 21·15. The mean daily range for the whole year (from seven years' observations) was 16·17 degrees."

Temperate nature of the climate proved by its botanical productions.

In further illustration of the temperate nature of the climate, it may be mentioned that English vegetables (potatoes, beans, cabbage, cauliflower, beet, carrots, turnips, cellery, and lettuce,) grow almost as well as in England; that English garden flowers are here produced in profusion almost all the year round; and that the indigenous botanical productions resemble chiefly those of a temperate climate. A late writer on medical topography states with justice that "the character of a climate is much more faithfully indicated by such a natural test as its influence on vegetable products than by any instrumental or artificial means whatever."

North-east monsoon.

The north-east monsoon usually begins about the middle of October. In the early part of October the direction of the wind is variable from the north and north-west, but, as the monsoon sets in, the wind blows from the north-east. It is ushered in with about three weeks of rain, after which the atmosphere clears up and the cold weather sets in. This usually lasts from the beginning of December until the end of February.

Cold season.

During the cold season the sky is remarkably clear, and the force of the sun is very great. The nights are, on the contrary, cold and frosty. Sometimes in the morning the valleys and hollows of hills, owing to radiation and evaporation, are covered with hoar-frost. This deposition, however, does not indicate a similar general decrease of temperature, for, although the thermometer falls to 20° F. or even lower when placed in contact with the ground in valleys and sheltered but open situations, it seldom ranges lower than 38° or 40° F. when exposed to the breeze at an elevation of a few feet from the ground. Owing to the frost and the exceeding dryness of the air at this season of the year, all the more delicate plants, garden vegetables, and the grasses wither, leaving a mass of decayed vegetable matter on the surface of the ground.

From the beginning of the year and until the end of April, north-easterly winds prevail. These prove most trying to the invalid. From April until June the winds are variable, some-

CHAP. IV, PART II. — PHYSICAL AND MEDICAL CLIMATE, &c.

times shifting to the north, south, or east. Their mean direction, however, is from a point about north-east.

Hot season. The months of April and May are the hottest in the year. The thermometer in the higher station of Ootacamand, however, seldom ranges about 70° F. in the shade, although, when exposed to the direct rays of the sun, it will sometimes rise to 120° or even more. From the time that the heavy rains set in in the early part of June, there is a marked improvement in the public health.

South-west monsoon. In the early part of June the wind sets in steadily from the west, or west by north, and, soon becoming intensified, is accompanied with electrical disturbances and heavy showers.

For some days before the setting in of this monsoon heavy banks of clouds are to be observed in the direction of the Kúndas, and on these is expended its first violence.

During the south-west monsoon, which usually prevails until the early part of October, much rain falls, and the air is generally saturated with moisture. The hills become quickly covered with luxuriant grasses and the forest trees put forth their fresh leaves. During the months of August and September breaks, as they are called, occur. The mists clear off, and the sun shines forth for several days successively. The scenery, usually beautiful, is now surpassingly so, the undulating ground of the whole plateau being clothed with verdure of peculiar richness. This season is usually considered to be the most salubrious period of the year, and Europeans who have resided for any length of time upon the Hills, and judge of the climate by experience, invariably prefer the rainy season to any other.

Effects of climate on the prevalence of disease. The effects of the climate on the prevalence of diseases during different seasons of the year are more or less remarkable. During the early months, from December until April, affections of the respiratory organs, including catarrhs and whooping-cough, are very prevalent. Neuralgia and affections of the throat are also very common. During the months of March, April, and May diarrhœa, derangements of the hepatic functions, and sometimes fevers of an intermittent character are met with. These latter months may be considered the most unhealthy part of the year. The occasional showers which fall during these months, owing to their washing off surface impurities and replenishing the springs, are often looked forward to with anxiety as harbingers of an improved state of the public health. It may be remarked that at this season visitors with their followers arrive in great numbers, and some of the apparent unhealthiness is due to sickness induced by a sudden transition from the plains.

Hygienic rules for the guidance of visitors. Most illnesses which the medical man is called upon to treat at Ootacamand are due to individual imprudence. How important then is it that the visitor in quest of health or relaxation should be possessed of such a knowledge of hygiene, or preventive medicine, as will enable him to preserve intact that measure of health with which he may be endowed. If this be true with regard to the healthy and the strong, of how much more importance is it that the invalid should not only be acquainted with rules for his guidance, but be prepared to act up to them? The following notes on preventive medicine as applicable to visitors to this sanitarium may therefore prove useful to those who may be unacquainted with the peculiarities of this hill climate.

The ascent to Ootacamand being usually made in from five to ten hours, according to the mode of conveyance, the visitor finds himself suddenly transported from a climate with a temperature of 85° F. or more to one whose mean temperature reaches only 56° F. To be unprepared to meet this sudden change is merely to invite disease or such a derangement of the principal functions as will incapacitate the traveller from deriving benefit or pleasure from his visit. Warm clothing should therefore be used as soon as a change of temperature is sensibly felt, and in the case of young children their flannel under-clothing had better be put on before the journey up the ghát is commenced. In case any portion of the journey up the gháts be made during the day-time, it will be necessary to guard against the action of the sun's rays, which are here, owing to the stillness of the atmosphere, often very powerful. As several tempting streams pass the ghát road, the possibility of fever resulting from their use should generally be known. It is better therefore to come provided with a few bottles of sodawater or cold tea. Those who are in a weakly state, but whose destination is Ootacamand, should halt a few hours for rest and refreshment at Coonoor.

On arrival at Ootacamand it will be well to see that bedding is suitable and sufficient and that the sheets are well aired. It is necessary to point out this latter as an occasional cause of illness, for, from the difficulty experienced in drying linen, &c. during wet weather, clothes are often found to be quite damp on being brought from the wash. The windows of the sleeping apartments should be always kept closed at nights. Some people keep them open, thinking that, as they have done so even in England, they can do so here with impunity, but the cases are different, for here, in addition to cold and damp, we have occasionally malaria. Unoccupied houses are often damp and close; fires lighted for a day or two previous to occupancy will help to remove these defects.

Precautions in damp weather.

The cold moist state of the atmosphere during the monsoons does not appear to be prejudicial to the European residents or invalids when sufficient attention is paid to the judicious adaptation of clothing to the state of the weather. In consequence of the

CHAP. IV, PART II. — PHYSICAL AND MEDICAL CLIMATE, &c.

damp, well-made boots and woollen stockings should be worn: by this means many an attack of diarrhœa or other illness may be warded off. Wet clothing should always be changed on a return home; with this precaution, exposure in the rain seldom does any harm. It will be well for visitors at this season of the year to come provided with light, well-ventilated, water-proof clothing for use as occasion may require.

First transitory effects of climate.

Owing to the exhilarating effect of the climate, the visitor on first arrival usually feels inclined to exert himself far beyond his strength, and the appetite, generally keen for the time being, is indulged. Invalids particularly should be cautious in these respects. Visitors on first arrival are apt to be affected with oppression of the breathing, sleeplessness, headache, and coldness of the extremities arising from the highly-rarified state of the atmosphere. These symptoms generally pass off after a short residence.

Dangers of undue exposure.

It should also be remembered that the low temperature on these hills is due to elevation, and not latitude. That the almost vertical sun's rays, shining with great fierceness through a rarified atmosphere, are at certain seasons of the year as powerful as when experienced on the plains, and that the alternations of temperature, and particularly the rapid fall which follows sun-set, are fruitful sources of derangement of the principal functions. From a consideration of the above peculiarities of climate, the importance of wearing suitable clothing, protection to the head from the sun's rays, and of avoiding undue exposure to cold will be apparent. In the case of young children, especially those lately arrived, unsuitable clothing and exposure to the sun are frequent sources of disease. Woollen under-clothing should always be worn by such. With care and attention to these details, children usually do remarkably well.

Amongst adults lately arrived, exposure to cold causes temporary congestion of the internal organs, more particularly of the liver, due to sudden chill and cessation of the action of the skin. Hence it follows that this climate must be prejudicial in all cases of visceral disease, and those predisposed to weakness of this nature should be provided with a flannel belt to be worn round the loins and stomach. A comfortable over-coat or warm wrappers should always be worn after sun-set, particularly if from any cause perspiration may have been induced.

Early rising undesirable.

The habit of early rising so necessary in the plains is not desirable here; between seven and eight o'clock is sufficiently early, and delicate persons and children should not venture out until the sun has warmed the atmosphere and dissipated mist.

Bathing.

As to bathing in cold water, strong healthy people may generally do so from the first with advantage, but it is desirable that others should have the chill taken off it. With young children and elderly people a warm or tepid bath will suit better. Reaction should always take place after a cold bath; should it not take place, it may generally be regarded as a sign that cold bathing is unsuitable and should be discontinued. This term reaction merely implies that the blood which has been driven from the surface has returned as shown by a glow of superficial warmth which is experienced, and the redness imparted to the previously pale surface. If, after immersion in warm water, and whilst standing in the bath, a few vessels of cold water be poured over the surface of the body, a feeling of reaction will be experienced shortly after even by persons of delicate constitution. This is an excellent mode of bathing for all who shrink from, or who feel doubtful of, salutary reaction from the use of cold water. The following rules as to bathing should be observed:—Never to bathe in cold water within two hours after a meal, or when exhausted from fatigue or any other cause, or when the body is cooling after perspiration.

Use of stimulants.

Those accustomed to the use of stimulants on the plains may generally continue to use them but in diminished quantities. They are seldom necessary for health in this climate, except for some invalids, and many people give them up altogether with advantage. Light sound claret with water or sodawater will be found a suitable beverage for most people.

Remarks on diet, exercise, &c.

Stimulating food and hot-seasoned dishes had better be eschewed by the invalid. They are unnecessary, and often injurious. Early dinners are recommended. Unripe peaches, mushrooms, and improperly-fed pork, sometimes brought about for sale, are unsafe articles of consumption. Visitors from the plains often crave for a vegetable diet on first arrival, and the abundance of delicious vegetables here produced enables them to gratify their taste in this respect. They should be well cooked and eaten with moderation.

On the selection of a house.

The houses in these hill stations are usually placed upon the summits of minor spurs or ridges, but some are located on sites excavated on the sides of some of the larger undulations, and are consequently backed by a steep cutting. When possible, a preference should always be given to the former and for the following obvious reasons: being placed relatively at a higher elevation to the soil, they are drier, the air is purer, and the drainage is more perfect; whilst, being more fully exposed to the morning and afternoon sun, they are generally speaking warmer. Houses situated near the lower part of the valleys in sheltered situations are, owing to the greater radiation, colder, and, being exposed to dew and fog, are comparatively damp during the rainy seasons. Sleeping rooms are usually badly ventilated, but a little fire wire-gauze, or finely-perforated zinc placed in the upper

CHAP. IV, PART II.

PHYSICAL AND MEDICAL CLIMATE, &c.

part of the window, obviates this defect. There is a great difference in houses variously situated with respect to their water-supply for drinking purposes, for whilst some are bountifully supplied with streams from the Doddabetta range, or from local springs of good quality, others, and more particularly those situated to the western side of Ootacamand, have during the dry season to procure water sufficiently pure for drinking purposes from a distance. It may be remarked that in the case of children, who it is desirable should enjoy as much fresh air as possible, a few clumps of shady trees near the dwelling will prove an advantage, as it will enable them to enjoy the open air when otherwise, from the heat of the sun, they would be confined to the house. Some of the houses at Ootacamand have open verandahs similar to those on the plains. These are in themselves cold and draughty, and by sheltering the walls from the sun make them at some seasons damper than they would otherwise be. Children are liable to be laid up from colds, or accidental exposure to the sun, from being allowed to play in such unsuitable places.

Sanitary condition of compounds.

All residents on the hills should look carefully after the state of their compounds, for, if neglected, noxious matters accumulate which, if not periodically removed, become a source of disease. A small sum paid to the Municipality will ensure the removal of all offensive matter within the limits of the compound weekly or oftener if required.

Danger attending a visit to the jungle surrounding the base of the Nílagiris.

The danger of visiting the belts of jungle which surround and clothe the base of the Nílagiris to a height of from 2,000 to 3,500 feet, was exemplified in the early months of the year 1876. A party of 35 Constables proceeded to arrest certain criminals who had taken refuge there. On their return, after remaining for about two months in this unhealthy locality, all without exception suffered from malarious fever, so much so that two died shortly after their return to Ootacamand, seventeen had to proceed on sick leave, and of the remainder several, after a lapse of several months, occasionally complain of the return of the fever and other attendant ills. This account speaks for itself, and should deter sportsmen and others from running a similar risk.

Although some of the above remarks hardly apply to visitors in general, yet to the invalid, for whom in particular they are framed, they will doubtless prove of advantage, for he of all others should be placed under conditions most favorable to health. After a residence of some months the visitor becomes acclimatized, and can then venture to do many things which could not be attempted with impunity by one not so acclimatized.

Diseases which are of rare occurrence on the Hills.

There are no diseases peculiar to the Hills. Diarrhœa and dysentery, said to be endemic in some of the Himalayan sanitaria, are not met with in this form on these hills. Variola is comparatively rare amongst natives, probably owing to careful vaccination of late years, and is seldom met with in the European. Cholera[1] originating on the Hills is practically unknown, at least in the higher portion of the plateau. Hardly a year passes however, but some cases are imported from the low country. Occasionally it is communicated to one, two, or more persons, and then speedily dies out. Although so far removed above the so-called fever range, yet there is a strong probability that malaria is, at certain seasons of the year, carried by the dry cold winds from the belt of jungle which surrounds the base of these hills, and cases of intermittent fever are occasionally observed amongst Europeans residing on the plateau who have never been absent for a day.

Recently abundant evidence has been furnished of its occasional existence in a severe form amongst the native population by the excessive mortality which occurred in the months of April, May, and June 1876 from this disease. This exceptional state of the public health was probably due partly to the above cause and partly to a season of excessive drought, and the liberation of the deleterious material from the soil by solar desiccation.

The milder cases of uncomplicated intermittent fever, contracted either here or on the plains, usually do well on these hills, for although a return of paroxysms may be induced by the rapid alternations of temperature, yet they appear gradually to lose their intensity in succeeding attacks.

Rheumatism originating on the Hills is also, strange to say, a rather rare disease with Europeans, but frequent with Natives.

Diseases commonly met with in Europeans, and the effects of climate on same.

Diarrhœa is common enough amongst the newly-arrived, but in these cases it is seldom intractable, and is usually due to errors of diet or exposure to cold. Amongst children it is one of the most troublesome diseases to which they are liable, and when it occurs during dentition it is more than usually serious.

Whooping-cough and measles are sometimes very prevalent in the early months of the year: croup is also occasionally met with. In European children, who of course are carefully looked after, these diseases generally run a mild course, but in the case of Native children they not unfrequently prove fatal. In all of the above cases cold and particularly the cold dry winds of the early months of the year have to be carefully guarded against, but otherwise the climate does not act prejudicially in any of them.

Asthmatic cases seldom do well even in the milder climate of Coonoor. The same may be said of consumptive cases. The former seldom originate here, and the cases observed have been those sent from the plains for change.

---

[1] An outbreak occurred in 1877, resulting in many deaths. Though originally imported, its prevalence was probably due to bad drinking-water and defective drainage, and to the fact that the town had not been cleansed by the usual monsoon rains in 1876.—ED.

CHAP. IV, PART II. — PHYSICAL AND MEDICAL CLIMATE, &c.

Chicken-pox is a common disease with both European and Native children, but it is always a mild disease.

Febricula in children is frequently met with; its usual cause is undue exposure to the sun.

The class of diseases peculiar to females almost invariably improves in this climate, and cases of dyspepsia and derangement of the bowels generally do well. Uncomplicated cases of dysentery originating here are seldom severe, and rapidly yield to treatment. Diseases of a local nature, such as ulcers, fractures, and wounds, usually heal rapidly, and cutaneous diseases also, under appropriate treatment, make good recoveries. Simple debility in young people almost always yields rapidly to the effects of the climate and nourishing food. Parturition is probably unattended with any special risk due to the climate or altitude. Convalescence from it is usually rapid, and nursing is unaccompanied with the debility often experienced on the plains. Miscarriage is frequent in the early months, but it is more generally due to over-exertion on ascending hills, &c., than to any peculiarity of the climate.

Neuralgia when it accompanies anæmia or debility, or when it remains as a relic of former malarial agency, gradually becomes milder in its visitations, much depending on the general state of the health, appropriate medical treatment, and a residence for some time is required before an improvement can be expected.

Delicate strumous children do very well upon the Hills, but a change to the Madras coast in the cold weather is very desirable when it can be accomplished. Young children moreover should not be brought to the Hills whilst they are cutting their first teeth.

Anæmia and chlorosis, although distinct diseases, may here be classed together, for both derive marked benefit from change of air, moderate exercise, cheerful scenery, and nutritious diet; such cases, with judicious medical treatment, do remarkably well.

The more severe tropical diseases are seldom seen here. The climate being known to be unsuitable, such cases requiring a change are sent to Europe.

Persons suffering from heart disease invariably complain of an aggravation of their symptoms on ascending the Hills. The same may be said of persons suffering from diseases of the brain.

Serious diseases met with in Natives of the plains.

Natives of the plains are liable, on first arrival, to diseases, the result of climatic vicissitudes and insufficiency or unsuitability of food, but, after they become acclimatized by a short residence, they enjoy good health as a rule. Older natives frequently succumb to disease from deficient vital energy and from an inability to resist the depressing effects of cold. Among the more serious diseases to which they are liable on first arrival are dysentery, diarrhœa, rheumatism, fevers, and bronchitis. This

CHAP. IV, PART II. PHYSICAL AND MEDICAL CLIMATE, &c.

latter sometimes terminates in pneumonia or inflammation of the lungs. Europeans do not suffer from these diseases to the same extent as the Natives, and doubtless these diseases are for the most part induced by exposure to cold with unsuitable clothing, impure drinking water, and bad food. Visitors should therefore be careful that their servants are suitably clothed and housed, and it is of equal importance that they should not be allowed to sleep upon the ground, a common practice with many of them. The sickness and mortality which affects the class of Natives who visit the Hills to obtain employment on the various coffee estates is very great. During the cold season many of these travellers perish from cold and starvation, whilst others suffering from fever or diarrhœa through neglect and exposure fall victims to more serious diseases.

Cases of illness which derive most benefit from a change to the Hill climate.

On the Nílagiri table-land we have a climate essentially temperate, and one which experience tells us is capable of conferring the greatest benefit in suitable cases. The cool refreshing breezes, together with the lovely mountain scenery, and relaxation from work, combine to effect an improvement in the health of those who have been exposed for any length of time to the enervating influences of the plains. For the following classes the climate will be found unquestionably most suitable and invigorating. Young people of weakly constitution, who have broken down through overwork in a tropical climate, or who, from having come out to India before their constitution may be said to have been properly formed, and in consequence have been reduced to a state of general debility after their arrival in the country. Older persons who, by reason of a prolonged residence on the plains without any change, or who, after suffering from some slight illness, have been troubled with dyspepsia, nervous debility, mental depression, or loss of appetite, and who in consequence feel an inability to perform their accustomed duties. These are the cases which derive the most permanent benefit from a residence on the hills. It is presumed that in the above cases there is a freedom from all structural disease. Convalescene from many of the more trivial diseases to which Europeans are subject on the plains is generally hastened by a residence on these hills, attention being paid to the selection of a station for such cases in due accordance with the age and state of the patient and the season of the year.

Unsuitable cases.

The climate of the Nílagiris has been found by experience to be quite unsuitable in the following cases: those who have long suffered on the plains from remittent or repeated attacks of intermittent fevers, chronic diarrhœa, dysentery, hepatitis, and syphilitic affections, as also cases of organic disease generally.

True value of the climate.

Although the climate of the Nílagiris has nothing in it to recommend it to the invalid suffering from the more serious

CHAP. IV, PART II. — PHYSICAL AND MEDICAL CLIMATE, &c.

tropical diseases, yet, in addition to the cases for which its climate has by experience been proved to be suitable, it will be found that the European can retain his health and vigour, as evidenced by the robust constitutions of those who have been, for the greater portion of their lives, resident upon the hills. It is usual to look upon these mountain ranges as sanitaria where health may be regained, but their true value will be found to consist in their possessing a climate in which Europeans can maintain their health and vigour, or a periodical resort to which will enable them, on their return to the plains, to resist the debilitating influences of surrounding adverse conditions.

Influence of the climate on the health of the children at the Lawrence Asylum.

The following tables represent the sickness and mortality for the past five years of the children of the Lawrence Asylum near Ootacamand. It is believed that few, if any, of the great schools of England can compare to advantage with these in so far as the comparative absence of serious diseases or the low rate of mortality are concerned. There are two branches of this Asylum. One is intended for the reception of sons, and the other for the daughters, of European and Eurasian soldiers serving in India. Their ages vary from about eight years on admission to sixteen on discharge.

MALE BRANCH, OOTACAMAND LAWRENCE ASYLUM, LOVEDALE.

Statement showing the Number of Admissions and Deaths, &c., of the Diseases that came under Treatment during the past five Years.

Years	1871-72.		1872-73.		1873-74.		1874-75.		1875-76.		Yearly Average Admissions of five Years.
Diseases.	Admitted.	Died.	Admitted.	Died.	Admitted.	Died.	Admitted.	Died.	Admitted.	Died.	
Measles	...	...	87	...	...	...	...	...	...	...	
Chicken-pox	22	...	...	...	11	...	12	...	8	...	
Febricula	13	..	9	...	5	...	1	...	3	...	
Ague	3	...	1	...	1	...	..	...	...	...	
Sun-stroke	...	...	1	1	...	...	..	...	...	...	
Remittent fever ...	2	...	...	...	...	...	...	...	..	...	
Typhoid fever... ...	...	...	...	...	...	...	...	...	2	1	
Rheumatism	3	...	...	...	3	...	...	...	5	...	
Conjunctivitis ...	5	...	11	...	7	...	5	...	11	...	
Bronchitis	...	...	...	...	...	...	2	...	1	...	
Pneumonia	...	...	...	...	...	...	2	...	...	...	
Dysentery	4	...	5	...	9	...	12	...	5	...	
Other diseases ...	47	...	33	...	36	..	40	...	11	...	
Total ...	99	...	147	1	72	...	74	...	46	1	87
Average daily number of sick	2·31		4·03		2·10		3·43		2·05		2·78
Percentage of daily sick to average annual strength ..	0·78		1·13		0·64		0·23		0·14		·58
Strength	295		336		319		325		326		320

FEMALE BRANCH, OOTACAMAND LAWRENCE ASYLUM, LOVEDALE.

CHAP. IV, PART II.

PHYSICAL AND MEDICAL CLIMATE, &c.

Statement showing the Number of Admissions and Deaths, &c., of the Diseases that came under Treatment during the past five Years.

Years	1871-72.		1872-73.		1873-74.		1874-75.		1875-76.		Yearly Average of five Years.
Diseases.	Admitted.	Died.	Admitted.	Died.	Admitted.	Died.	Admitted.	Died.	Admitted.	Died.	
Measles	...	...	20	..	1	...	...	...	...	...	
Chicken-pox ...	10	...	1	...	3	...	...	...	...	...	
Febricula	5	...	4	...	...	...	3	...	4	...	
Febris remittent ...	...	...	...	...	...	...	...	...	1	...	
Ague	...	...	2	...	...	...	...	...	1	...	
Parotitis	2	...	...	...	18	...	...	...	...	...	
Conjunctivitis ...	1	...	...	...	2	...	1	...	...	...	
Tonsilitis	...	...	...	...	...	...	...	...	1	...	
Dyspepsia	2	...	...	...	...	...	...	...	1	...	
Dysentery	1	...	...	...	...	...	3	...	4	...	
Bronchitis	...	...	1	...	2	...	1	...	...	...	
Pneumonia	...	...	...	...	...	...	1	1	1	...	
Other diseases ...	2	...	2	...	2	...	5	...	3	...	
Total ...	23	...	30	...	28	...	14	1	16	...	·22
Average daily number of sick	·72		·92		·81		·32		·80		·71
Percentage of daily sick to average annual strength ...	1·14		1·44		1·40		0·21		0·27		·89
Strength	63		64		60		60		60		61

The annual average strength for the past five years has been 320 in the Male branch, and 61 in the Female branch. In the Male branch the average number of admissions into hospital for each of the five years was 87, and the average number of daily sick was only 2·78, and the percentage of daily sick to average annual strength was 0·58. In the Female branch the average number of admissions into hospital for each year was 22; the average number of daily sick was 0·71, and the percentage of daily sick to average annual strength was 0·89. There were in all but three deaths during the five years, and the two cases of typhoid fever were both imported from a distance. The European population of Ootacamand is so fluctuating that the effects of a continuous residence in these hills are difficult to tabulate; however, in the foregoing returns there is satisfactory statistical evidence of the healthy nature of the climate.

Erroneous views on the subject of the climate.

It has already been remarked that the climate is faithfully indicated by its influence on vegetable products, and its healthy influence on the European constitution has also been noticed. These are probably the soundest tests of the suitability or

CHAP. IV, PART II. PHYSICAL AND MEDICAL CLIMATE, &c.

otherwise of a climate, for, as Sir J. R. Martin, when speaking of climate, justly observes, "For this much is certain, that the framers of elaborate tables of the winds and of the degrees of the thermometer have as yet done little to inform our minds or guide our inquiry." It is erroneous to suppose that the climate of the Nílagiris is possessed of any specific qualities by means of which it directly cures disease, for neither of these will produce much benefit unless aided by dietetic and hygienic rules, directed with due regard to the constitution, the general state of each individual case, and the season of the year. It is therefore necessary to be cautious about expecting too much from a mere change of climate, as this confidence leads to neglect of other circumstances which are at least equally essential to recovery. It is better to look upon this climate as a medium through which a cure may be wrought than as the direct instrument by which the change is to be effected.

Varieties of climate possessed by the Nílagiri sanitaria.

The Nílagiris enjoy a very great advantage over other Hill sanitaria in India, as an invalid has the means afforded him of selecting out of three stations the climate most suitable to his state of health. The other stations besides Ootacamand are those of Coonoor and Kótagiri, but these, owing to differences in altitude, locality, aspect, and surrounding physical features, have well-marked differences in the respective climates, and although this report has special reference to the climate, &c., of Ootacamand, yet a passing glance at the salient differences between its climate and that of the other stations may not be out of place.

Brief sketch of the climate of Coonoor.

Coonoor is situated in the south-eastern crest of the mountains, and is distant about 12 miles by the new road from Ootacamand in a south-easterly direction. Its elevation is 5,886 feet above the level of the sea, or about 1,530 feet less than that of Ootacamand. Its mean annual range of temperature is about eight degrees higher than the latter station. It is sheltered from the south-west monsoon by the lofty Doddabetta range, and during this season its climate is particularly mild and genial, for, as the sun is frequently obscured by hazy mists and the rain is only occasional, it is possible to enjoy daily open air exercise. From the exposed situation of this station on the crest of the hills, unprotected as it is by any barrier on its north-east side, it receives the whole force of this monsoon, the weather during the short period it prevails being most inclement. Towards the end of November or beginning of December this monsoon has generally expended itself, and by Christmas-time the climate is delightful. This is the cold season, and it lasts until towards the close of February; but at this season the cold north-east winds experienced here are not nearly so trying as at Ootacamand. Owing to radiation, ice is occasionally found in sheltered spots as at Ootacamand, but in a smaller quantity. On proceeding from the more bracing climate of Ootacamand to Coonoor, the change is often accompanied with a feeling of languor and oppression, doubtless owing to the increase in temperature and the more sultry and relaxing nature of its climate.

Kótagiri.

The station of Kótagiri is situated on the north-eastern crest of the plateau and overlooks the plains; it is about 17 miles east of Ootacamand, and about 12 miles from Coonoor by road. From its position it must be even more fully exposed to the north-east monsoon than Coonoor, and, owing to its greater distance from the Doddabetta range, it cannot be so well protected from the south-west monsoon as the latter station. Its elevation being about 500 feet above that of Coonoor, and being more exposed than either of the other stations during the north-east monsoon, it follows that its climate is a medium between those of Ootacamand and Coonoor. Notwithstanding the advantages offered by its climate, it is seldom resorted to in the present day, probably from want of house accommodation.

Selection of a station for an invalid.

As a general rule, medical advice should be sought by the invalid as to which station will be the most suitable in each individual case, and it is not possible to do more here than lay down general remarks on the climate, &c., for guidance, as every case must be considered with due regard to age, the general health, temperament, previous history, and the season of the year in which the proposed visit is to be made. It may, however, be stated that elderly people as well as young children, the delicate, and those who have suffered from a prolonged residence on the plains will derive more benefit by a residence, in the first instance, at the milder stations of Coonoor or Kótagiri than by at once proceeding to Ootacamand.

PART III.

WELLINGTON.

(*Extracts from a report furnished by Surgeon-Major* W. H. CORBETT, *Army Medical Department, in Medical charge of Convalescent Depôt, to the Surgeon-General, British Medical Service.*) [1]

Description of the Hills.—Approach from the plains.—Topography.—Geology.—Botany, table productions and vegetation.—Seasons.—Meteorology.—Ozone.—Climate, and its influence on health.—Places to be visited.—Period for visiting the Hills.—Precautions to be taken.—Those who benefit.—Those who do not benefit.—Barracks.—Cantonment.—Sanitary condition.—The bazaar.—Water-supply.—Commissariat supplies.—Amusements.—Duties of the troops.—Mortality and sickness.

CHAP. IV, PART III. — WELLINGTON. MEDICAL REPORT ON CLIMATE, &c. — Position of Wellington.

THE station of Wellington, which is the Convalescent Depôt for the British troops in the Madras Presidency, is in the Péranganád Division of the Nílagiri District, and lies in latitude 11° 5′ north, and longitude 77° 5″ east, with an area of 446 acres, or nearly two square miles, and a native population of 1,567. It is 6,100 feet above the level of the sea, situated on a spur running to the south-east from the Doddabetta or middle range of mountains, is well sheltered, only partially exposed to the monsoons, and well adapted from situation for a sanitarium. It is bounded on the north by the Doddabetta mountain, which is 8,760 feet above sea-level, and is sheltered by it partially from the south-west monsoon; on the south by Coonoor, two miles distant, from which it is separated by a deep ravine; on the east by Kótagiri, 13 miles distant; and on the west by a spur of the Doddabetta range stretching towards Kátéri.

Approach from the plains.

These hills are easily and speedily accessible from the three presidencies. A line of rail runs to Mettapollium within six miles of the foot of the Hills, to the south-east. Here there is a good hotel for travellers and a rest-house with the following accommodation: 3 rooms—one holding 6 men, or 3 families, a middle room holding 10 men, or 5 families, and an end room holding 6 men, or 3 families; and 3 European soldiers' tents, in which, for the short time they may be occupied, the Rest-house Superintendent has authority to place 42 men. Troops halt here during the day. The married portion and baggage-guard leave in the evening and come up the long ghát, a distance of 24 miles, with a gradual ascent, not exceeding 1 foot in 18 or 20. This party should always be provided with torches, as it is difficult to prevent their being the greater portion of the night on the road. The remaining portion leave at midnight and come up

[1] Portions of this paper have been omitted which contained information furnished elsewhere or were otherwise unsuited to a paper of this description.

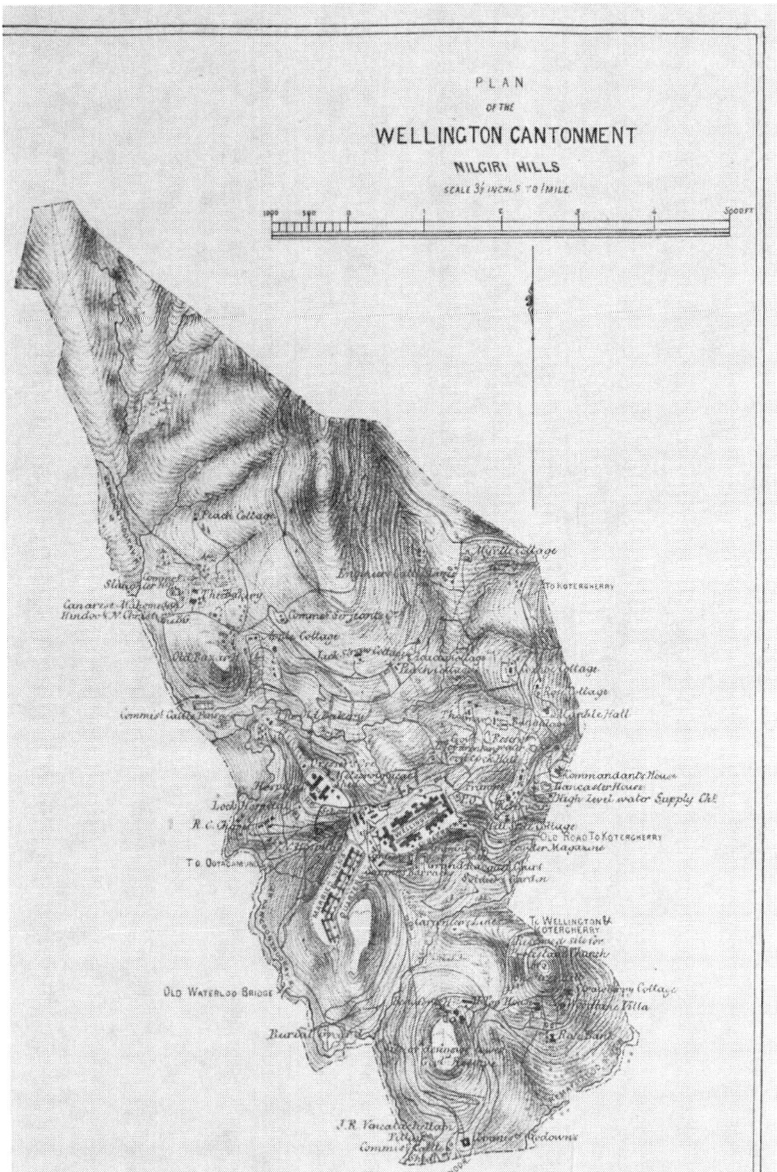
PLAN
OF THE
WELLINGTON CANTONMENT
NILGIRI HILLS
SCALE 3½ INCHES TO 1 MILE
Peach Cottage
Myrtle Cottage
TO KOTERGHERRY
The Bakery
Old Bazaar
Gamble Hall
Kommandant's House
Lancaster House
High Level water Supply Chl.
R. C. Church
OLD ROAD TO KOTERGHERRY
TO OOTACAMUND
Soldiers Garden
TO WELLINGTON & KOTERGHERRY
OLD WATERLOO BRIDGE
Strawberry Cottage
Burial Ground
J. R. Vencatachellam
NEW ROAD FROM COONOOR
Survey Office
Madras
August 1877
Major R.E.
Acting Supt. Madras Survey

the short ghát, a distance of nine miles. They are conveyed by transit to Kalár, from which place those able are expected to march. This arrangement I do not altogether think for the best, as the men arrive at Kalár, which is in the midst of a low swampy jungle with bad water and filled with malarious exhalations, at the most trying time to the constitution, from sun-set to sun-rise.

The road up the ghát runs from east to west. On the first portion of the ascent the bamboo grows in abundance, sheltering the road. On going higher, one observes the indigenous forest trees, among which are conspicuous the teak, of an inferior quality, the blackwood, which is useful for furniture, and takes a handsome polish, the sál, wild jack, and vengay. Vengay is a superior timber considered by some equal to teak, and from it the bridges throughout the ghát are made. Lastly, the red and white cedars, the woods of which are suitable for building or making furniture. These trees are conspicuous for their great girth. About two-thirds up the ghát it is a pleasing relief to meet a resting-place, known as the "Toll-bar." Here coffee is provided for troops coming up. It is well shaded, and a perennial spring of clear water flows close by. The ascent from Mettapollium to Coonoor is about 4,500 feet.

Topography.

The barracks are in a slight hollow bounded by high mountains and extensive ravines. They were built in 1852 and 1853. The station was then called Jackatalla after a neighbouring Badaga village, which name the ravine to the north still retains. The site was chosen by the Marquis of Tweeddale in 1847. Much of the country surrounding the station is undulating, but broken by ravines and rugged hills. To the west of the barracks is a ravine which extends towards the south and through which there is a bridle-path to the Wellington bazaar; to the north and west are the married quarters, and, almost due north, the hospital. The natural drainage of the plateau is good. There are numbers of private residences, conspicuous among which is the house of the Commandant, about 200 feet above the barracks to the eastward. On all sides mountain streams and brooks flow and empty themselves into ravines to the north-west and south.

There are no gheels, marshes, lakes, or rivers of any extent in the vicinity of Wellington. The principal stream flows along the south-west of the cantonment below the married quarters. It drains the eastern side of Doddabetta range, and is joined near the Wellington bazaar by a stream of fair size flowing from the north. These together form the Kancunthuré river, and pass down under the Coonoor bridge, where also another considerable stream which rises in the south and east of the cantonment after passing through the race-course joins it. It is also joined by other streams, which pour down in every direction, along the Coonoor ghát,

CHAP. IV, PART III.

until it reaches the Kátéri river. The combined stream passes Kalár, and empties itself into the Bhaváni.

WELLINGTON. MEDICAL REPORT ON CLIMATE, &c.

Geology.

The soil in and about Wellington is of a rich red ferruginous clay or marl, resting on a granitic[1] base, with sienite in many places, and here and there felspar, mica, and veins of quartz. Flint and amethyst appear to be embedded in the granite, sienite, or gneiss, in the form of crystallized silica.

Botany, table productions and vegetation.

The station is planted throughout with numerous ornamental trees which afford shelter and add to its beauty. Within the last four years there has been an average of 2,000 young trees planted out in various parts of the station. Some of them have failed from climate and exposure, but a large proportion continue to thrive. These consist of rapidly-growing exotic trees, such as the Australian blue gum, or *Eucalyptus globulus.*

The intersecting valleys, sides of the hills, and plateaus possess a rich soil, the result of sub-tropical forest growth, producing luxuriant vegetation, where almost all the European vegetables thrive. As many as three or four crops of potatoes have been raised during one year. The ground to the west of the barracks is utilized as a soldiers' garden. The men to whom it is allotted pay a monthly subscription for which they are supplied with garden tools, and periodically with seeds, the produce being entirely their own property. There is an agreement with the Commissariat to take their produce, which is served with the rations. Here onions, cabbage, cauliflower, beans, tomatoes, peas, lettuce, beet-root, knol-khol, carrots, sweet potatoes, &c. grow well. The work affords amusement and profit to the owners. Fruits of all kinds grow luxuriantly at Wellington, particularly oranges, peaches, the wild gooseberry, red and white raspberry, Brazil cherry, limes, and citrons, pears and apples coming from the more sheltered neighbourhood of Kótagiri.

Places to be visited.

Coonoor, two miles to the south, is a pretty little station, about 6,000 feet above the level of the sea, encircled by hills, irregular in shape and elevation, and sheltered from the south-west monsoon. Being nearer the edge of the Hills, it is more subject to fogs; the variations of temperature are often sudden and great. The climate is less bracing and more suitable for cases of chest, bowel, and liver derangements than Wellington. There are several excellent hotels. There are small shops, kept by natives, in Coonoor; but, as a rule, European articles of good quality that are required should be obtained from Ootacamand. Near Coonoor visitors should see the spots known as "Lady Canning's Seat," "Dolphin's Nose," "Lamb's Rock," "Húlikal," "Tódamand," and the "Drúg," from which latter views of the

[1] The old view.—ED.

Ánémalé and Kúnda mountains, Mettapollium, Coimbatore and the plains, Kótagiri, Doddabetta, Wellington, and the Lawrence Asylum can be obtained.

Kótagiri lies to the east and north of Wellington, about 13 miles distant, with a population of 31 Europeans and 600 Natives. There is a good road winding through the mountains. It is in a sheltered plateau, protected from the south-west monsoon, at an elevation of about 6,200 feet. It has not received proper trial as a sanitarium, but I cannot help thinking that the climate is such as to deserve its receiving greater attention than it has done heretofore. Many years ago there was an experiment of the kind tried by establishing a small sanitarium at Dimhatti near the Orange Valley to the north, but I am informed that the place is now in ruins, and I have not records to show whether it was satisfactory or otherwise. The soil in the vicinity is good for vegetables and fruit, and tea is grown on the slopes of excellent quality, particularly in the plantation known as Catsfield. There are no hotels or public bungalows. The principal house is surrounded by beautiful grounds with a small lake. It belongs to Mr. Gordon Forbes, and is called "Kóta Hall." There is a small church, but no resident clergyman. Also a well-conducted dispensary, and a small bazaar.

Doddabetta may be visited from Wellington, either by skirting the mountains to the eastward, following those bearing to the north and west, or by passing through the Jackatalla valley and old race-course up the mountain side. From the top, as it is the highest elevation in Southern India, on a clear day views may be had of Ootacamand, to the west, lying at its base; the Kúndas to the west and south, and the Ánémalés to the south, Kótagiri to the eastward, Coonoor and the hills overlooking Coimbatore to the south and east, and Mysore to the north.

Seasons.

January, February, and March are intensely dry and cold at nights, the atmosphere throughout the day being clear and free from clouds, but the sun's rays are very powerful and require to be guarded against. This is the season at which sun-strokes occur on the Hills. There are great variations of the temperature between day and night; ice forms in the ravines, and hoar-frost and heavy dews are of ordinary occurrence. As a general rule a heavy shower may be expected about the end of January, or before the 10th of February.

During February and March there is still a hard dry east wind blowing, but, if it is a good year, heavy rain may be expected about the 25th of March with thunder, which clears the air. Should there not be rain at the end of March and beginning of April, the air becomes heavy and hot, with frequent thunder-storms from the south, but damp and cold by night, rendering, under these circumstances, the season sickly.

CHAP. IV, PART III. — WELLINGTON. MEDICAL REPORT ON CLIMATE, &c.

In April, May, and June, thunder-storms continue. The south-east winds draw round to the south and eventually to the south-west. May is the hottest month, a steamy heat with high temperature, averaging 81 degrees in the shade. In June there are heavy winds from the south-west, from which point the monsoon is looked for, which, as a rule, breaks about the 20th. In July, August, and September the south-west monsoon prevails, and the season is usually delightful, the rain never being so continuous as to prevent a certain amount of out-door exercise, although it is heavier and more tropical here than at Ootacamand. August is wet, but the atmosphere is still and hot. During September it becomes muggy, the monsoon ending about the 20th. Then there is a break, as a rule, until the 20th of October.

In October, November, and December the weather is splendid, though cold, and occasionally damp and wet, but very wholesome. The north-east monsoon begins about the middle of October, and is ushered in with heavy thunder-storms. During November there is very heavy rain with thunder-storms and fogs.

In December the rain begins to fail. There are usually two or three days' break at a time. The weather is cold, and frost begins to form ; hoar-frost is constant. During this monsoon heavy floods are common on the eastern slopes. In November 1865 they were so severe that the water was three feet over the Coonoor bridge, setting in without warning and doing immense damage in about four hours. Similar floods occurred in December 1875 in the race-course valley. From the 16th December the rain gradually draws off, and is not usually expected to return till about the 12th March.

Meteorology.

The atmosphere at Wellington from its rarified condition, due to elevation, will only support a column of mercury 24 inches high, that at the sea being 30. This shows it to be about 6,100 feet above that level. Consequently persons visiting the Hills are relieved of an atmospheric pressure of the difference between 15 lbs. per square inch, which is that at the level of the sea, and that of 12¼ lbs., which is the pressure at Wellington. The changes, which are observed in climate or in weather, may be traced in general to preponderance or deficiency of the vapour of water in the air. The steadiness of the barometers in these latitudes is a very remarkable phenomenon. Except during hurricanes there seems to be an absolute freedom from irregular variations. The annual atmospheric tide is due to the varying position of the locality with reference to the sun, the atmosphere being lighter (as will be seen by reference to the meteorological tables), from expansion at the summer solstice than at the winter one.

The average mean reading for the winter months will be found in excess of those for the centre of the year. The sun's rays are as powerful here as at the level of the sea, but the heat that composes it is modified by free radiation.

The mean annual range and the mean daily range of temperature are small, the warmest month being May with the mean temperature of 66·4, and the coldest month December with the mean temperature of 57·5. The mean annual height of the barometer uncorrected is 24·246, and the mean daily variation of the radiation thermometer is 25·2. The respective readings of the sun's maximum in vacuo between this and the level of the sea shows that the diminished heat of the earth and atmosphere of elevated regions is not due to any less quantity of solar influence received, but to the latter being radiated away into space, almost as fast as it is received, and, if it were not for the difference in the amount of obscuration of the sun between Madras and Wellington, the reading of the thermometer showing the sun's maximum in vacuo would be exactly the same. Between the maximum thermometer fully exposed at Wellington and that at Madras there is a difference of 21° Fahrenheit, which is the amount of heat lost by radiation, between this and the level of the sea, and here, as is usual near the equator, the annual and daily range of the barometer is not very great. In May 1872 the barometer fell to 24·018, but this was contemporaneous with the cyclone which devastated the Madras roads; also, on the 6th May 1874, during a cyclone at Madras, the barometer at Wellington fell to 24·052. Rain, which is one of the most important elements in determining climate, amounts annually, on an average, to 46·75 inches. Here it has small influence on the barometer, and the popular idea that the fall of the barometer indicates rain is a fallacy. It represents irregular currents of air forming wind. This is notorious in the tropics, where the wind is mostly ranged into uniform trades or monsoons, and rain is almost unnoticed by the barometer. A very simple rule for ascertaining heights of mountains and mean temperatures of such places may be noticed here. If we are able to obtain the pressure of the barometer, which is easily done by a pocket aneroid, and knowing that for every 1,000 feet of ascent the barometer falls very nealy one inch, we find that the pressure of the barometer at Wellington is 24 inches, whilst the reading at the level of the sea is always calculated at 30, which shows a less pressure of six inches, making its elevation 6,000 feet, which is very nearly correct. In the same way, if we admit that the mean temperature at the sea is to be calculated at 83° Fahrenheit, and for every 300 feet of ascent the thermometer falls a degree, we may calculate the mean temperature, if we know the height of a locality. Thus Wellington is looked on as 6,000 feet above the sea. Divide 300 into 6,000, and you will get 20 as the result. Deduct this 20° from the temperature at the level of the sea, viz., 83 degrees, and

CHAP. IV, PART III. it gives a result of 63 degrees, which is nearly correct, that of Wellington being 62°·6.

WELLINGTON. MEDICAL REPORT ON CLIMATE, &c.

Ozone.

Ozone is an electric condition of the air which is present at all times, but particularly during thunder-storms. The name is derived from the peculiar smell emitted when it is produced artificially by an electric machine. It is oxygen in an allotropic state, a bin-oxide of hydrogen, and is generated by the discharge of electricity into the air. A reference to the ozone tables for the months of October and June, when there is an electric condition present, prior to the bursting of the monsoons, shows that the atmosphere is filled with it. This is shown by the depth of color on the ozone papers. The mode by which oxygen passes into ozone is inexplicable. All we know is that it is produced when electricity is discharged into the air. It tends to cleanse and purify the atmosphere, but is in itself so powerful that animals expire when placed in pure ozone.

Climate, and its influence on health.

The climate at Wellington, although only 11 degrees from the equator, is most salubrious, temperate, and invigorating. The thermometer seldom rises in the shade above 75 degrees, and the days throughout the cold months are clear and bracing. The mornings are always refreshing, and, if the character and time of the setting in of the south-west monsoon is regular, the months of the middle part of the year are pleasant and healthy.

The objections to the Hills are that the valleys intersecting them contain jungle, where malarious fever may be contracted. These are to be particularly avoided, especially at night or in the evening after sun-set. This is in consequence of the variations of temperature being greater than in the higher situations.

The sun's rays, however, are powerful throughout the year, and one is never safe in being exposed to them without having the head properly protected. The health of the inhabitants greatly depends upon the regular periods of the monsoons, as by them the ravines, hill-sides, and gullies are washed of the decaying vegetation, and in consequence the atmosphere is rendered pure and free from malaria; whereas, if the monsoons are not regular or sufficient, this vegetation decomposes, the atmosphere becomes tainted and malarious. Fevers are endemic. For, although we are taught that an elevation of 4,500 feet is beyond malarial influence, experience shows that not only are attacks of fever frequent, but that they originate on these hills, and, as there is a good deal of marshy ground in the ravines about Wellington, owing to springs issuing from their sides and jungle growing on their slopes, malaria is generated especially in wet weather, producing relapses in persons whose constitutions are affected. It is most difficult to eradicate this malaria from the system.

Attacks of febricula from chill and exposure to the sun with high temperature, shiverings, with severe headache, suffused eyes, dilated pupils, and derangement of the stomach, especially in the younger soldiers, are common; but the climate, no doubt, is particularly adapted for newly-arrived troops from England, when preventive, rather than curative, results are looked for, and in it the European can maintain his health and vigour. Still it will always be necessary, especially with reference to the younger soldiers, that they should not expose themselves to the sun or venture into the valleys, and that they should be well provided with flannel shirts with sleeves, and avoid becoming overheated.

Period for visiting the Hills.

At present the troops begin to arrive from about the middle of March, which is very advantageous considering that they are out of the plains before the hot weather becomes very severe, and I think they should not be despatched from the plains later than the 15th March if it can be avoided. The pleasantest time to arrive would be April, May, or June.

Those who benefit.

The climate is particularly suitable to those who are suffering from ordinary depression or debility resulting from the heat of the plains, or who are failing either from long residence in the excessive temperature of India, and who have fallen into a condition of exhaustion without organic disease. It is particularly beneficial to young soldiers who have had their tone of constitution lowered by attacks of simple fever, or who have lost flesh and strength by climate. These persons rapidly regain strength; the blood resumes its red globules, the cheeks and lips become rosy, and the appetite and vigour are restored. Those suffering from wounds, injuries, suppurating bubos, abscesses, or from scrofula or malarious fever do well up here. Mild bowel derangements and even dysentery, when not complicated with disease of the liver (if precautions against chills are observed), improve, and even rheumatism and ulcers without syphilitic taint and chronic bronchitis, which frequently attacks old soldiers in the plains with diffuse expectoration, are benefited. Old soldiers without organic disease, who are showing symptoms of breaking down, thrive, improve their general health, are able to bear more fatigue, and regain strength up here, as is shown by settlers, pensioners, and others, who are holding positions under Government on these hills, or are independent.

Those who do not benefit.

The climate, although exhilarating, is peculiar, and from the rarified condition of the atmosphere, which at this elevation exerts a pressure of 2¾ lbs. to the square inch less than at the level of the sea, the system feels naturally the want of support, the blood-vessels dilate, and consequently this climate is totally unsuitable for valvular disease of the heart, or developed disease of the lungs; and even persons in fair health, from this peculiar condition of atmosphere, suffer from palpitation caused by the increased action of the heart, which becomes embarrassed in

CHAP. IV, PART III. — WELLINGTON. MEDICAL REPORT ON CLIMATE, &c.

endeavouring to propel the blood through the relaxed or dilated blood-vessels. This accounts for the number of people who complain of oppression and difficulty of breathing with increased action of the heart, amounting in some to cardialgia on first arrival from the plains. It is an unpleasant condition, which passes off as the system accommodates itself to the elevation. From the same cause persons on first arrival at the Hills suffer from sleeplessness and giddiness, with marked dilatation of the pupils, due to an insufficiency of blood being propelled to the brain by the embarrassed heart. This symptom is distressing and is not benefited, as a rule, by narcotics, but bromide of potassium with quassia is useful by its sedative and tonic action. For the same reason lung diseases, particularly phthisis, do badly throughout their whole course on the Hills. For a similar cause hæmorrhages are not of unfrequent occurrence, and the medical man has to guard against this, particularly in women after confinement. Cases of neuralgia during the easterly winds do badly, relapses are frequent; in fact it has been known to have originated by a residence here, and a change to the plains seems to be the only cure.

It may be stated then that the climate of the Hills is decidedly injurious to cases of organic disease of the abdominal and thoracic viscera, secondary syphilitic disease, and cases of dysentery complicated with liver, also diarrhœa of a chronic nature. It is particularly prejudicial to cardiac, cerebral, and lung affections, and to diseases of the liver and kidneys. This can be easily understood when one considers that action of the skin and lungs, which are the great contemporaneous channels of relief to these organs in the plains, is in the one instance, the skin, totally checked, and in the other, the lungs, called upon by elevation to do much more than double work. This is shown by persons going up hill suffering from dyspnœa, which results from the system demanding more oxygen.

Any violent exercise is prejudicial, as it is thought liable to produce disease of the circulatory system, and for this reason gymnastic exercises are discouraged, and shot drill is not allowed. Elderly persons are liable to irregularity of the bowels, due to torpid action of the liver, and diarrhœa is common on first arrival, unless great precautions are observed to avoid internal congestions, this being nature's mode of relief, considering that there is no transpiration through the skin; and women from the same cause, on first arrival, are liable to have their menstrual functions interrupted. Children cannot be too carefully looked after, and especially is it necessary to protect them from cold winds by warm clothing. Teething is a most trying ordeal, children at that period being more liable to acute abdominal and thoracic attacks. They should be clothed in flannel and all

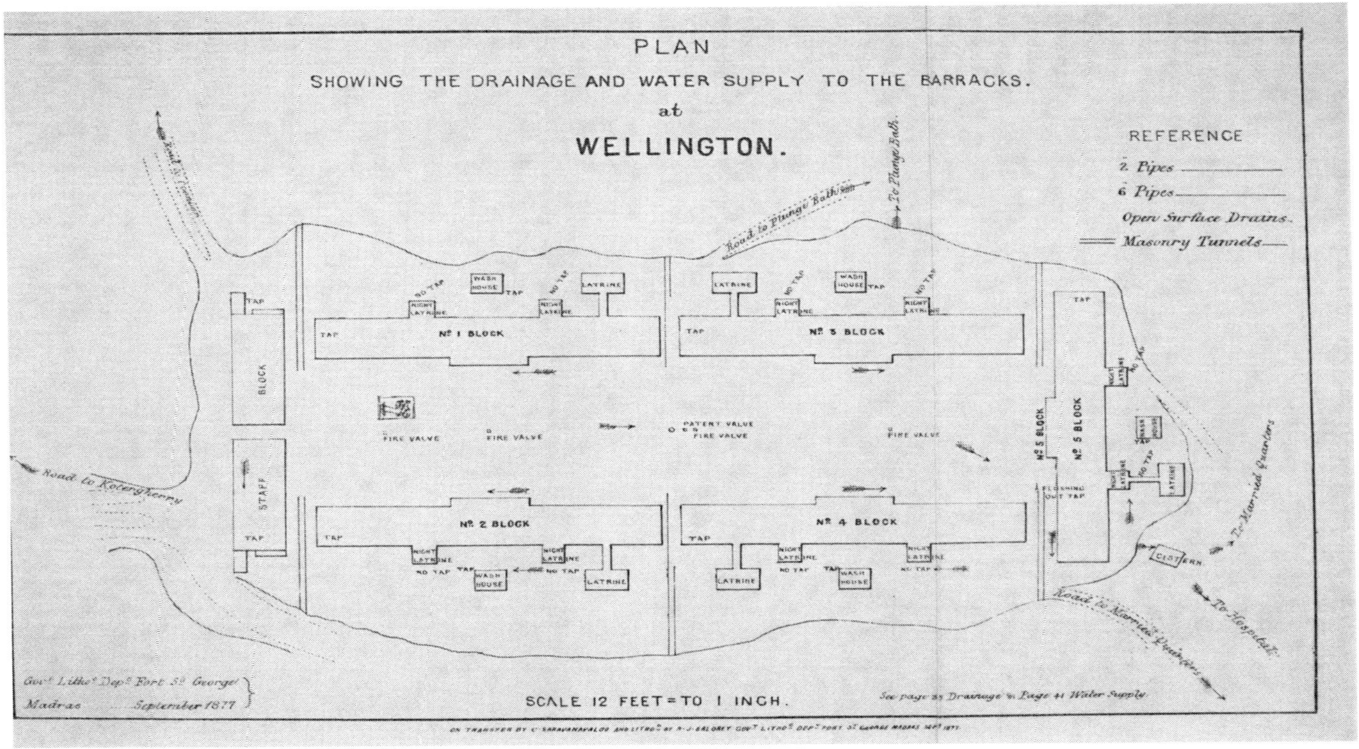
PLAN
SHOWING THE DRAINAGE AND WATER SUPPLY TO THE BARRACKS.
at
WELLINGTON.
REFERENCE
2 Pipes
6 Pipes
Open Surface Drains.
Masonry Tunnels
Road to Plunge Bath
To Plunge Bath
Road to Koterghery
To Married Quarters
Road to Married Quarters
To Hospital.
No. 1 BLOCK
No. 2 BLOCK
No. 3 BLOCK
No. 4 BLOCK
No. 5 BLOCK
BLOCK
STAFF
TAP
NO TAP
NIGHT LATRINE
LATRINE
WASH HOUSE
FIRE VALVE
PATENT VALVE
FLUSHING OUT TAP
CISTERN
SCALE 12 FEET = TO 1 INCH.
See page 35 Drainage & Page 41 Water Supply.
Govt. Litho. Dept. Fort St. George
Madras September 1877

CHAP. IV, PART III.

WELLINGTON. MEDICAL REPORT ON CLIMATE, &c.

changes of temperature avoided. Convulsions are common; whooping-cough and mumps are frequent; measles and ophthalmia have been epidemic; scarlet fever known, and small-pox also has been prevalent.

The greatest care is necessary, however, to avoid attacks of bowel-complaint, to which children, particularly at this depôt, are liable either from teething, chill, irregularity of diet, exposure to the sun, or imperfect clothing, and to avoid which latter a flannel roller should be always worn. Those above four or five years of age thrive well; their physical condition and mental development under most circumstances improve. The chances of sickness among children will now, no doubt, be much decreased by the late general order directing officers commanding regiments to observe particularly that women and children sent to Wellington for change should be provided with clothing suitable for the climate.

Barracks.

The barracks consist of six blocks of double-storied masonry buildings enclosing a parallelogram. They are all alike, except the one to the east, which is occupied by Staff Sergeants, Staff Office, and Court-martial room upstairs; Sergeants' mess, the coffee shop (at present utilised as a Roman Catholic Chapel), guard-room with lock-up room for prisoners off it, Quartermaster's store, Barrack store, and Carpenter's workshop on the lower story.

The square is entered by an arch in the centre of this barrack, which faces east and west. The remaining barracks are divided into open verandahs on each story, inside verandahs which are used for dining in, and long sleeping rooms which accommodate 35 men each, with rooms for two non-commissioned officers at either end, and the cook-houses are in the lower story of each building. The ventilation is good, although the flooring of the lower story is only 18 inches from the ground; but a free current of air passes under it through holes above the ground on either side, underneath the verandah. It is in consequence dry, and sickness cannot be attributed to dampness. There are fire-places at either end, and several small holes near the floor and ceiling, with open arches leading into the back verandahs connected with doors, which afford ample ventilation. The upper stories are lofty with pent roof, very freely ventilated by swinging windows; they afford the same acoommodation as the lower story, viz., 35 in the large rooms and four non-commissioned officers' rooms. One of these large rooms in the upper story is used for a Church of England, and, as it is one of the best situated, ventilated, and airy barracks, the misappropriation should, if possible, be prevented. The question that arises is, where can the church be put? A site has been selected for it on the rising ground to

10

CHAP. IV, PART III. — WELLINGTON. MEDICAL REPORT ON CLIMATE, &c.

the west of the married quarters, and with a garrison of the strength of the depôt, and a Resident Chaplain, it is to be hoped that Government will in time be able to erect a proper place of worship. The adjoining room in this upper barrack is used for a recreation and reading room, coffee shop, and theatre. The out-houses are situated on the flanks to the west, north, and south, and are covered buildings, well constructed and suitable for the purposes they are required for. The cook-houses, as stated before, are situated at the end and on the lower story of the building. They are provided with a range, and the cooking, which is conducted by the soldiers under a master-cook, is well carried out: variety is obtained, and the food supplied is liked by the men.

The married quarters are to the north and west of the plateau on which the soldiers' barracks are built. They are placed on a plateau formed by the hillside being scarped out, and consist of four ranges of double-storied buildings containing accommodation for 107 persons, allowing each family a front and back room. They are well raised, fairly ventilated, and well suited to the purpose, the only objection being the fire-place in the front room, which is required to be used for cooking purposes, and which occasionally smokes. The out-houses which are situated at the back, reached by covered ways, are very good and suitable.

The drainage of the barracks throughout is conducted by open masonry channels, which communicate with deeper trapped drains, and empty themselves on the slopes. These require to be frequently flushed, but answer well. The married quarters are drained by open masonry drains, which have not answered well, as the slope is hardly sufficient, but this state of things has lately been improved by keeping a stream of water constantly flowing into them, and by their being carefully and frequently swept by hand.

The hospital is to the north about 70 feet lower than the barracks on the summit of a hill, which renders it dry, and permits it to be drained easily and effectually. It consists of two single-storied masonry buildings, enclosing a parallelogram, with the west end composed of out-houses, and store rooms, and the east end free, or rather having the Meteorological Observatory shed facing to the north. The accommodation is (commencing with the building to the west and south) the Hospital Sergeant's quarters, two special wards, surgery and store rooms for medicines, two large wards, one known as the "non-commissioned officers' ward," which is capable of accommodating 12, and the one adjoining it of accommodating 15 men, with an enclosed verandah running the full length and facing to the square. At the west end is a small special ward for isolating serious cases. Facing outwards are open verandahs, which are used for smoking. The other

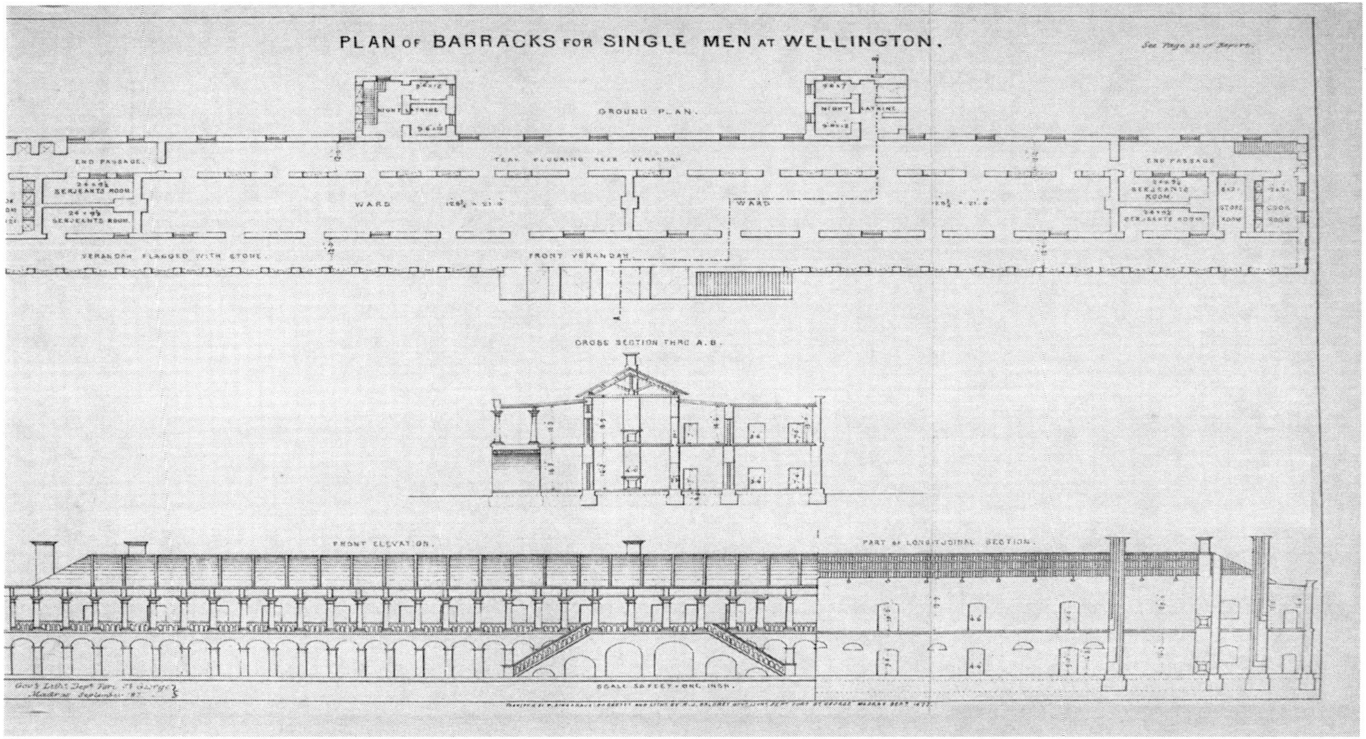
PLAN OF BARRACKS FOR SINGLE MEN AT WELLINGTON.
GROUND PLAN.
END PASSAGE.
TEAK FLOORING REAR VERANDAH
SERJEANTS ROOM.
WARD
STORE ROOM
COOK ROOM
NIGHT LATRINE
VERANDAH FLAGGED WITH STONE.
FRONT VERANDAH
CROSS SECTION THRO A.B.
FRONT ELEVATION.
PART OF LONGITUDINAL SECTION.
SCALE 50 FEET = ONE INCH.

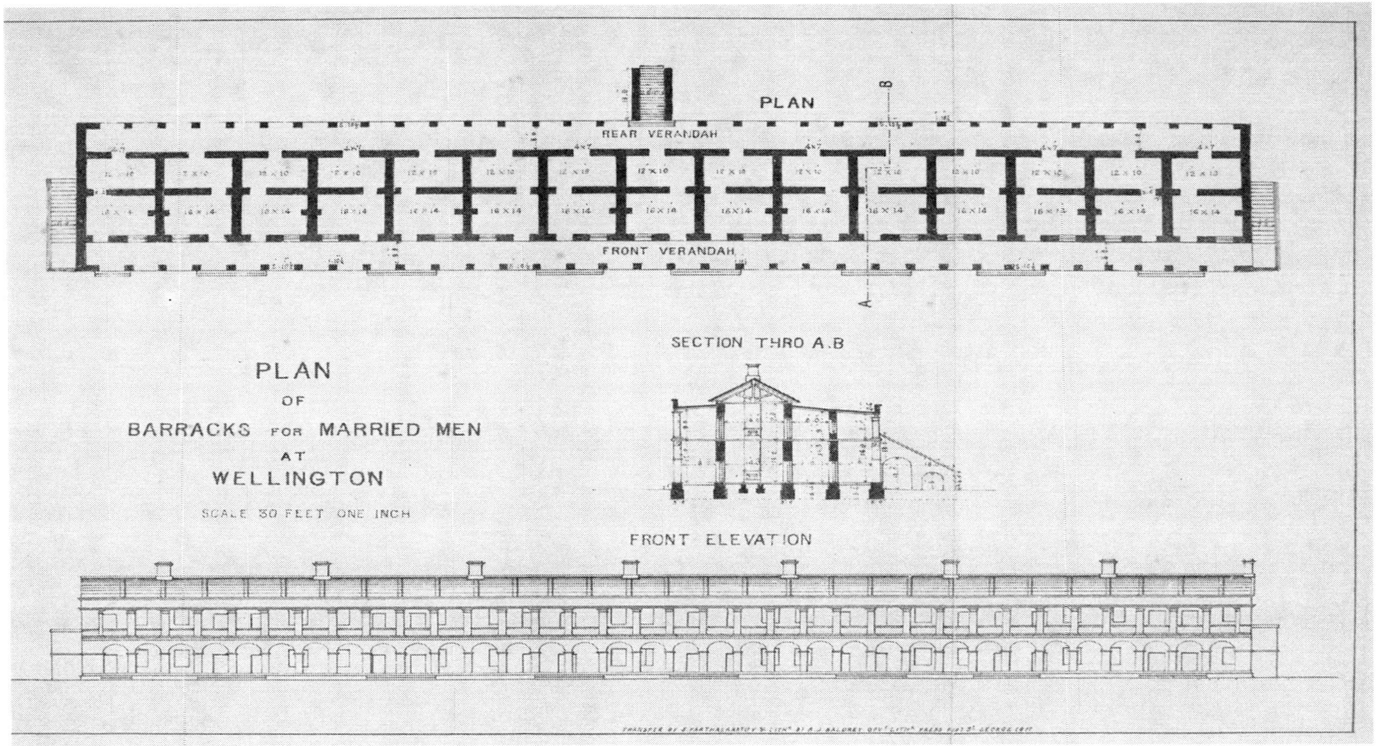
PLAN
REAR VERANDAH
FRONT VERANDAH
A
B
SECTION THRO A.B
PLAN
OF
BARRACKS FOR MARRIED MEN
AT
WELLINGTON
SCALE 30 FEET ONE INCH
FRONT ELEVATION

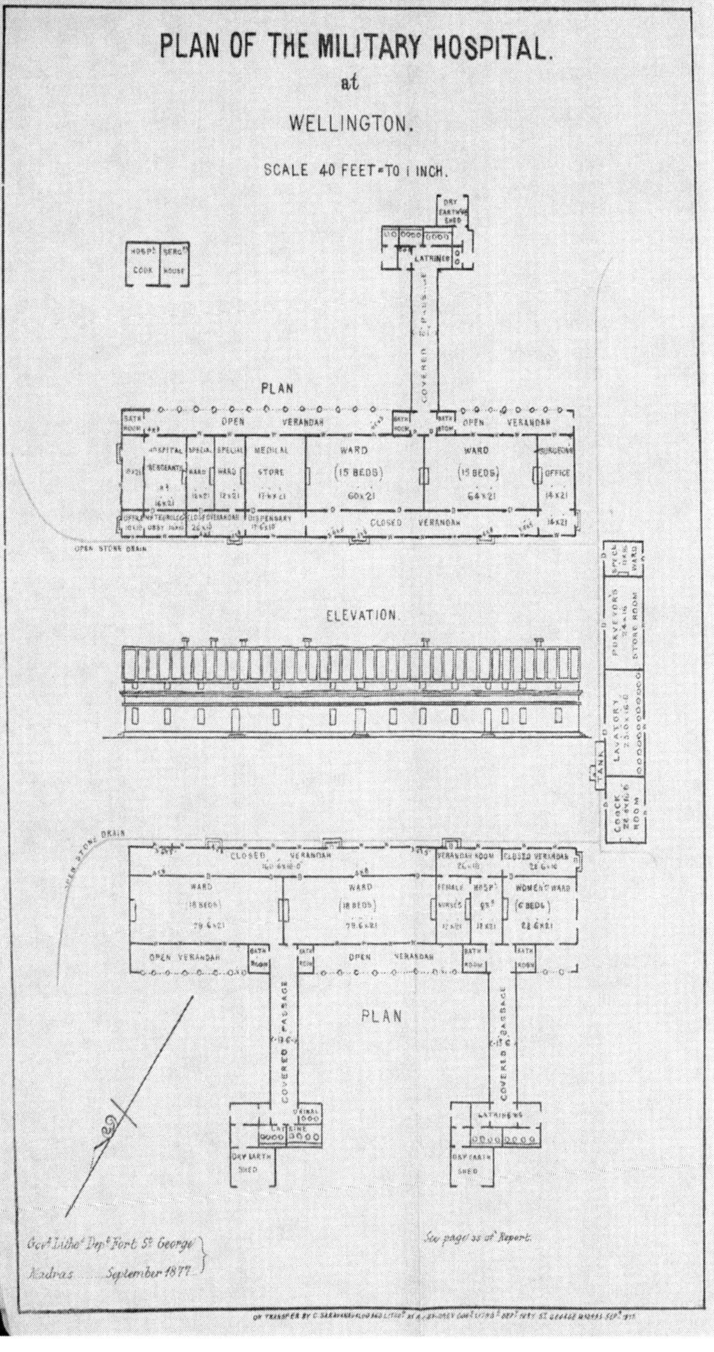
PLAN OF THE MILITARY HOSPITAL.
at
WELLINGTON.
SCALE 40 FEET = TO 1 INCH.
HOSPL COOK
SERGTS HOUSE
DRY EARTH SHED
LATRINES
COVERED PASSAGE
PLAN
OPEN VERANDAH
BATH ROOM
HOSPITAL SERGEANTS
SPECIAL WARD 12x21
SPECIAL WARD 12x21
MEDICAL STORE 17.6x21
WARD (15 BEDS) 60x21
WARD (15 BEDS) 64x21
SURGEONS OFFICE 14x21
DISPENSARY
CLOSED VERANDAH
OPEN STONE DRAIN
ELEVATION.
SPECL WARD
PURVEYORS STORE ROOM 24x16
LAVATORY 25.0x16.0
TANK
COOK ROOM
CLOSED VERANDAH
VERANDAH ROOM
WARD (18 BEDS) 79.6x21
WARD (18 BEDS) 79.6x21
FEMALE NURSES 12x21
HOSPL SERT
WOMEN'S WARD (6 BEDS) 22.6x21
OPEN VERANDAH
PLAN
COVERED PASSAGE
URINAL
LATRINE
LATRINES
DRY EARTH SHED
Govt Litho Dept Fort St George
Madras ...... September 1877
See page 55 of Report.

building facing to the north has also two large wards, each capable of accommodating 18 patients, with a verandah running its full length, facing the square, and an open verandah at the back used for smoking. At the west end are the Matron's quarters, and a small room known as the female hospital, which is divided, one section forming a ward for women during confinement. The latrines, which are on the flanks, reached by covered and closed passages, are suitable, well attended to, and conducted strictly on the dry-earth principle. The drainage is by open masonry channels conveying the waste wash and rain water down the slopes. The wash-house is suitable, and is provided with basins and taps, and a plentiful supply of water. Cooking is on a range and is performed by native cooks under the superintendence of a European orderly. It answers admirably, the men having various and savory dishes, and curries when allowed, soups, puddings, jellies, &c.

The hospital accommodation for women and children is insufficient, there being only room in the ward, known as the female hospital, for six beds, whereas seven and eight women and as many as 18 children have required hospital treatment at one time during the past season, 1876. The small room adjoining the female hospital is capable of accommodating one woman, but as many as three have been obliged to be placed in it. There are no small wards for the treatment of special cases. One woman, suffering from enteric fever, and a child suffering from the same, have been obliged to be placed in a small room at the end of the godown. This shows how great is the necessity for a new female hospital, and now, as it is believed the number of men at this depôt will be increased by the occupation of the new barrack, the whole of the men's hospital will be required for their own use. It will thus be necessary to vacate the present Matron's quarters and female hospital, and to provide others elsewhere. I have proposed that the present lock hospital, which is a well-raised, well-ventilated building with boarded floor, and will accommodate about 14 patients, should be converted for the purpose by verandahs being thrown out front and back, and a Matron's quarters with Medical Officer's room for out-patients being added, without any very great outlay of money, especially as Government are impressed with the necessity of erecting a new lock hospital in a less objectionable position than the present, and have sanctioned 13,000 rupees for this purpose.

Cantonment.

The cantonment extends on the west from the Commissariat store and godown, on the north to the Commissariat cattle-shed, near the Jackatalla valley, on the east to the Kótagiri road and Commandant's hill, and south to the race-course. The centre is at a point known as the fountain where ten roads meet,

CHAP. IV, PART III. — WELLINGTON. MEDICAL REPORT ON CLIMATE, &c.

that from Kótagiri, Coonoor, Barracks, and the Commissariat being most conspicuous. There are several houses of residents, who are nearly all connected with the depôt. The houses are scattered prettily on the sides, slopes, and summits of the smaller and sheltered hills.

Sanitary condition.

The cantonment is carefully supervised by a Committee, of which the Commandant is President, the Cantonment Magistrate Secretary, and the Senior Medical Officer Sanitary Officer. The roads, compounds, hill-sides, and valleys are kept free of overgrowing or decaying underwood, hedges are clipped, grass for grazing purposes preserved, drains kept clean, water-courses kept from defilement, and the lower branches of trees lopped, thus permitting a free current of air. For these duties the Conservancy Committee is responsible.

The bazaar.

The Wellington Bazaar is prettily situated on the slope of a hill extending to a valley leading from the west and south of the barracks. It is well cared for, clean, and from its position well drained throughout. It has masonry channels, which convey drinking water obtained from a mountain stream to the north and west, thus artificially turned to supply this bazaar. The number of houses has decreased within the last two years. No thatch is allowed, whilst ruinous houses have been removed, and regularity with regard to position and ventilation insisted upon. The natives are principally Pareiyas and Kanarese laborers with a few dealers in grain and produce from the low country. The Magistrate's Court is situated here, where criminal cases are tried and civil suits are heard. During the year 1875, of the former there were 880 cases, and of the latter 91. There is a Police station also. During 1875 there was an expensive latrine built here, which is worked on the dry-earth system, and adds greatly to the cleanliness, and thereby the health of the village. Its deposits are converted into poudrette, which meets with ready sale to the coffee planters.

There was a good deal of sickness in the bazaar during the season of 1876, but this was general throughout the district, and is attributed to the scarcity of rain. The inhabitants suffered from febrile and bowel disorders.

The natives of this station including camp followers, private servants, the establishments of the Commissariat and Magistrate, and the Sappers, which are composed of a detachment of 35 men, 3 Naigues, 2 Havildars, and 1 Native officer, are totally without any immediate supply of medicines or medical attendance, and are obliged to apply to the Coonoor Dispensary—a distance of two miles—for treatment.

In 1875 there were 141 persons living in the Wellington Bazaar who applied to the Coonoor Dispensary for treatment

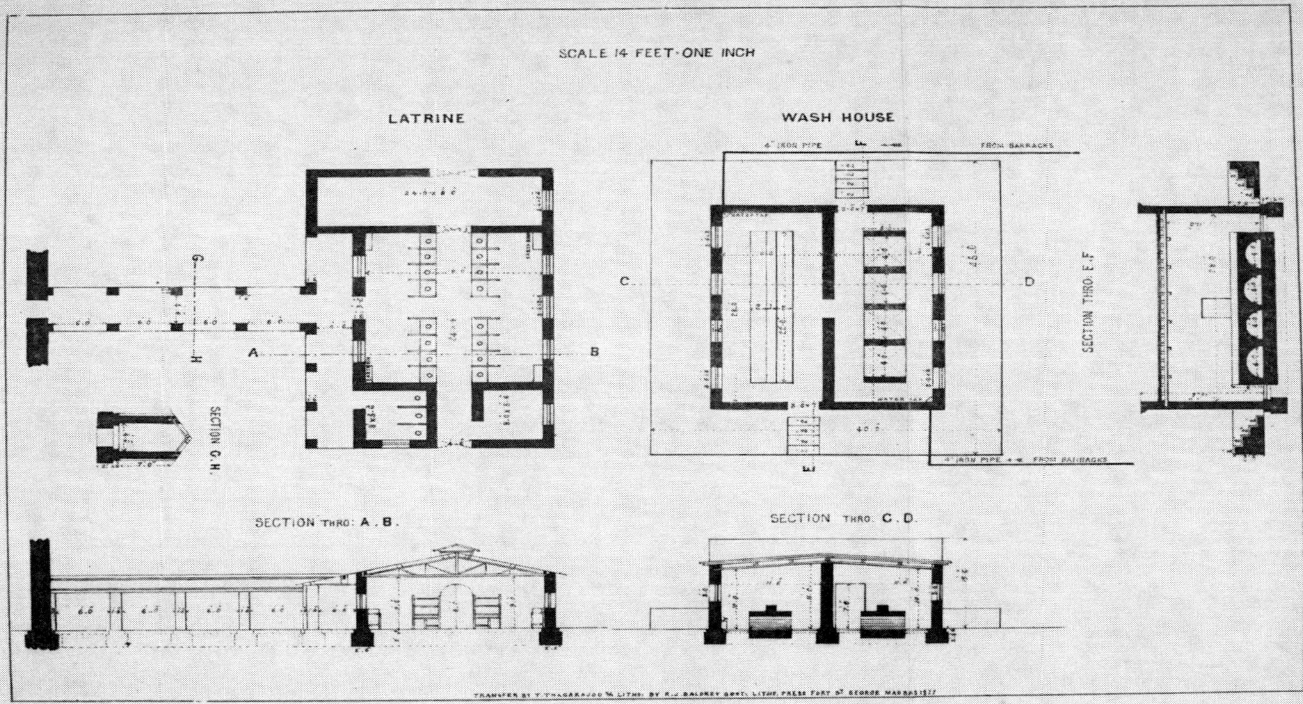
SCALE 14 FEET-ONE INCH
LATRINE
WASH HOUSE
4" IRON PIPE
FROM BARRACKS
SECTION THRO: E.F
SECTION G.H.
SECTION THRO: A.B.
SECTION THRO. C.D.
TRANSFER BY T. THAGARAJOO 1/4 LITHO: BY R.J. BALDREY GOVT. LITHO. PRESS FORT ST GEORGE MADRAS 1877

compared with 39 in 1874. From January to May ague, rheumatism, dysentery, diarrhœa, and bronchitis prevailed. It will be observed that the numbers applying for treatment are greatly on the increase (in 1876), and the Medical Officer of Coonoor has represented the totally insufficient accommodation there available. It has been recommended through the Cantonment Committee to Government that a Civil Dispensary or detached hospital should be built at Wellington.

Water-supply.

There is abundance of excellent water at and about Wellington. For ablution purposes, connected with the barracks, there is a large masonry reservoir on the hill, about 80 feet above the barracks on the eastern slope. The water is brought by artificial channels from the neighbourhood of Doddabetta, and is conveyed by hydrostatic pressure through iron pipes to the ablution rooms and Staff Sergeants' quarters, cook-houses, and married soldiers' out-houses, and finally to the wash-house at the hospital. This water is not fit for drinking, but for that purpose water is obtained, of abundant quantity and excellent quality, from two springs which arise beneath the rocks about 300 yards from the barracks to the east and north. Here the springs are enclosed with a masonry wall and protected by a small shady forest of trees. The sun's rays can never reach it, and the water is consequently cool and refreshing. It is collected at this spot in a cask with cover and lock and key, arranged so that the overflow is constantly passing into a channel conveying it to a reservoir, within about 30 feet of the barracks, from which it is conveyed by water-carriers to the filters and cook-houses. This arrangement has its objections: roots of trees get into the masonry channel; the water is contaminated, and repairs are expensive: whereas, if there was an iron pipe from the spring to the reservoir, this would be avoided. Again, the reservoir is not what it should be. At present there is merely a trough, and the flow of 380 gallons per hour passes off as waste.

Commissariat supplies.

The rations of the troops consist of beef five times a week and mutton twice; this is supplied by contract, the animals being brought from the plains of Coimbatore a short time before being required, as it has been found that keeping stock on the Hills does not answer. The animals suffer from bowel-complaint and rapidly fall off in flesh. The vegetables consist of potatoes and onions as a regular issue and the addition of other vegetables in season at the time. The bread is made at Coonoor and is of good quality. Beer and porter are supplied by the Commissariat for the troops, home-brewed, and of good quality. Locally-brewed beer is not used, as in the North-West Provinces. Excellent beer is brewed at Kussowlie and Muree, and is drunk generally by

CHAP. IV, PART III. — WELLINGTON. MEDICAL REPORT ON CLIMATE, &c.

troops serving in that part of India. It is a light refreshing beverage, possesses tonic properties from chiretta or other bitters that is added to improve its quality, and its use proves a great saving to Government. Spirits are not allowed under any circumstances, except in cases of sickness, to be issued to the convalescents at this depôt, and yet, on reference to the returns, it will be seen what a large number of cases of intemperance are treated, showing that it is obtained clandestinely to an enormous extent.

Amusements. The race-course, which is the great centre of attraction in the month of May, is situated in a valley to the south-east. It is well sheltered, planted with short grass, is kept in first-rate order, and, except for one or two sharp turns, is considered a favorite course by sportsmen. There is an excellent cricket ground on the course with a good pavilion, where tiffin is provided. Matches usually occur weekly, in which persons join from Ootacamand, Coonoor, and Kótagiri. Here foot-ball also might be played. Badminton and Lawn Tennis, and Archery are among the sports. At the barracks they have reading rooms, where many newspapers—Indian and English—are taken in. Games, such as drafts, chess, bagatelle, and cards are played and theatricals performed. Out-of-doors there are a fives' and racket courts and a skittle alley.

There is a good coffee-shop connected with the depôt, looked after by an officer, where men may obtain refreshments at a moderate rate.

Duties of the troops. The duties of the troops, which are light and conducive to health, consist of short parades, route-marches, inspections, and fatigue duties, the latter consisting in carrying the rations, working the fire-engines, looking after their barrack-rooms, superintending the filters and out-houses. Except for the latrines, no native servants are allowed.

The guards consist of the main guard furnishing four sentries under the command of a Sergeant—one over the magazine, one over the prisoners, and two over the cash-chests; and, when there are cell-prisoners, a Corporal's guard furnishing one sentry is detailed, and when there are court-martial prisoners in hospital a guard of the same strength is required at the hospital guard-room, as under ordinary circumstances no hospital guard has been considered necessary.

Serge and woollen cloth clothing is worn by the troops throughout the year, and at night the sentries, especially during the cold weather, wear their great coats. The parades do not take place very early in the day; that of church and inspections, as a rule, at 11 o'clock.

CHAP. IV, PART III.

WELLINGTON. MEDICAL REPORT ON CLIMATE, &c.

The accompanying table is intended to convey at a glance the sickness and mortality at the depôt for the past four years, showing the disposal, *i.e.*, men that have benefited and have returned to the plains and those who have not benefited, who have either been sent to the depôt at Poonamallee, retained at this depôt for another year, or invalided.

In 1873 the average strength of the depôt was 450·91 men, 66 women, and 138 children. Out of this number 107 men were treated for fever, of which 56 were ague; 33 were treated for lung affections, 32 for heart disease, and 240 for other complaints, including debility, accidents, and milder classes of disease. There were 401 men benefited; 28 were sent to Poonamallee; 40 invalided to England; 10 deaths occurred—2 from fever (one of which was enteric), 3 from lung affections (2 of which were phthisis and 1 pneumonia), 2 from aneurism, 1 from dysentery, and 2 from abscess of the liver. If we analyse these deaths, we will see that the two cases of phthisis ought never to have been sent to the Hills, that the case of dysentery could not have been expected to benefit, that the two aneurisms were decidedly unsuitable cases, and also the abscess of the liver, as all organic affections of this organ are objected to, if it could have been diagnosed. The result is only three cases of death due to the climate, whilst in the case of enteric fever it is doubtful whether it may not have been contracted elsewhere.

There were no deaths among the women in 1873, and the principal sicknesses from which they suffered were bowel-complaints, hepatitis, and debility.

Among the children there were 6 deaths, 1 from measles, 2 from debility, 1 from bronchitis, and 2 from diarrhœa, the latter showing the great necessity for warm clothing.

In 1874 the average strength of the depôt was 477·42 men, 85·52 women, and 189·71 children. There were 543 admissions to hospital among the men, of which 71 were fever, 49 lung diseases, 18 derangements of the liver, 19 intemperance, 85 bowels, and 176 from other complaints. 470 benefited and returned to the plains, 12 were sent to Poonamallee, 51 invalided home, and 7 died from the following causes:—1 calcareous degeneration of the aorta, 1 medullary cancer, 1 red softening of the brain, 1 meningitis, 2 pneumonia, and 1 enteric fever. To analyse these deaths, all, except the fever and pneumonia, might have occurred anywhere, and therefore cannot be attributed to any peculiarity of the Wellington climate.

Of the women there were 67 admissions and 4 deaths—1 from small-pox, 1 from consumption, 1 from angina pectoris, and 1 from abortion.

CHAP. IV, PART III. — WELLINGTON. MEDICAL REPORT ON CLIMATE, &c.

Of the children there were 77 admissions and 7 deaths—1 from measles, 1 from constitutional syphilis, 1 from cancer of the mouth, 1 from bronchitis, 1 from teething, and 1 from debility.

In 1875 the average strength of the depôt was 512·41 men, 95·50 women, 233·10 children. There were 478 men admitted to hospital, of whom 75 were cases of fever, 51 bowel disorders, 26 liver derangements, 88 venereal, and 73 other complaints; 430 benefited, 58 were invalided, 8 sent to Poonamallee, and 6 died. Of these three were from diseases of the circulatory system, all being aneurisms of the aorta, and three of abscess of the liver. These cases were not suitable to the climate of the Hills.

Of the women there were 95 admitted and 4 deaths, 1 from ague, 1 from pneumonia, 1 from retention of the placenta, and 1 from debility.

Of the children there were 101 admissions, and the great mortality of 20. Of these, 1 died of cancer of the mouth, 1 of tabes mesenterica, 1 of scrofula, 2 of tubercular meningitis, 2 of puerpera, 2 of convulsions, 2 of hydrocephalus, 1 of bronchitis, 3 teething, 1 dysentery, 1 tonsillitis, and 3 debility.

The year 1876 was a sickly one, due, it is supposed, to there not having been a proper fall of rain from the south-west monsoon, and there were, up to the end of September, as many as 632 admissions to hospital among the men.

CHAP. IV, PART III.

WELLINGTON. MEDICAL REPORT ON CLIMATE, &c.

Sickness and mortality.

Sickness and Mortality at Wellington during 1873, 1874, 1875, *and* 1876,* *showing the Numbers sent to the Depôt and how disposed of.*

Years		1873.						
Average Strength ...		450·91						
Diseases.	Remained from previous Year.	Number sent up.	Number admitted.	Number benefited.	Number sent to Poonamallee for change.	Number invalided Home.	Number died.	Number remained for another Season.
Fevers	18	75	107	64	...	6	2	20
Lungs	...	1	33	...	3	1	3	...
Bowels	...	5	90	2	4	1	1	...
Heart	...	...	32	...	7	1	2	...
Liver	...	1	53	...	9	3	2	..
Brain	...	3	36	...	2	5	...	...
Venereal	...	1	62	...	1	2	...	...
Intemperance ...	...	...	1	...	...	...	...	...
Accidents ...	...	...	23	...	...	...	...	...
Other complaints.	64	428	240	335	2	21	...	97
Total ...	82	514	677	401	28	40	10	117

Years	1874.						
Average Strength	477·42						
Diseases.	Number sent up.	Number admitted.	Number benefited.	Number sent to Poonamallee for change.	Number invalided Home.	Number died.	Number remained for another Season.
Fevers	68	71	66	...	2	1	18
Lungs	...	49	...	4	1	3	...
Bowels	21	85	20	5	1	...	...
Heart	...	7	...	2	2	1	...
Liver	...	18	...	...	...	...	...
Brain	10	21	6	...	7	2	...
Venereal	6	55	6	...	2	...	...
Intemperance	...	19	...	...	...	...	...
Accidents	8	42	1	...	4	..	...
Other complaints.	423	176	371	1	32	...	95
Total	536	543	470	12	51	7	113

Years	1875.						
Average Strength	512·41						
Diseases.	Number sent up.	Number admitted.	Number benefited.	Number sent to Poonamallee for change.	Number invalided Home.	Number died.	Number remained for another Season.
Fevers	31	75	31	...	...	...	6
Lungs	...	21	...	2	3	...	...
Bowels	22	51	21	3	5	...	...
Heart	2	6	...	...	2	3	...
Liver	...	26	...	...	...	3	...
Brain	4	11	4	...	2	...	...
Venereal	5	88	...	1	6	...	...
Intemperance	...	9	...	...	...	...	...
Accidents	1	18	...	...	1	...	...
Other complaints.	379	73	374	2	39	...	50
Total	444	478	430	8	58	6	56

Years	1876.						
Average Strength	403·12						
Diseases.	Number sent up.	Number admitted.	Number benefited.	Number sent to Poonamallee for change.	No. invalided Home.	Number died.	Number remained for another Season.
Fevers	584	191	...	...	...	3	...
Lungs	...	51	...	5	...	1	...
Bowels	...	107	...	4	...	5	...
Heart	...	20	...	3	...	...	...
Liver	...	29	...	2	...	1	...
Brain	...	6	...	...	...	1	...
Venereal	...	43	...	...	...	...	...
Intemperance	..	34	..	...	...	...	...
Accidents	...	34	...	...	...	...	...
Other complaints.	...	117	...	...	...	2†	...
Total	584	632	...	14	...	13	...

* The figures of 1876 are for the first nine months only.

† Fracture of the skull.

CHAP. IV, PART III.

WELLINGTON. MEDICAL REPORT ON CLIMATE, &c.

Sickness and Mortality at Wellington among Women and Children during the past four Years.

Women.

Years	1873.			1874.			1875.			1876.*		
Diseases.	Number sent up.	Number admitted.	Number died.	Number sent up.	Number admitted.	Number died.	Number sent up.	Number admitted.	Number died.	Number sent up.	Number admitted.	Number died.
Fevers		1	...		8	...		8	1		21	...
Lungs		4	...		10	1		4	1		1	...
Bowels		21	...		4	...		8	...		13	1
Heart	66	...	...	85·52	3	1	95·50	...	...	78·12	...	...
Liver		4	...		...	...		2	...		2	...
Child-birth ...		20	...		23	...		34	...		17	...
Uterine diseases...		4	...		1	1		3	1		4	...
Other complaints.		12	...		18	1		36	1		20	...
Total ...	66	66	...	85	67	4	95	95	4	78	78	1

Children.

Years	1873.			1874.			1875.			1876.*		
Diseases.	Number sent up.	Number admitted.	Number died.	Number sent up.	Number admitted.	Number died.	Number sent up.	Number admitted.	Number died.	Number sent up.	Number admitted.	Number died.
Fevers	...	9	1	...	23	1	...	18	...	...	32	...
Lungs	...	8	1	...	24	2	...	25	1	...	7	1
Bowels	...	17	2	...	14	...	...	19	4	...	39	9
Heart	...	...	...	...	...	...	...	...	...	...	...	...
Liver	...	...	...	...	...	...	...	...	...	...	...	...
Uterine diseases ...	...	...	...	...	1	...	...	...	...	...	...	...
Other complaints ...	...	20	2	...	15	4	...	49	15	...	42	7
Total ...	138	54	6	189	77	7	233	111	20	189	120	17

* The figures of 1876 are for the first nine months only.

CHAPTER V.

GEOLOGY AND MINERALOGY.

Early papers.—Geological Survey.—General description.—Action of water—fresh—marine.—Rock formation.—Granite absent.—Gneissose rocks—foliations.—Minerals—iron—hornblendic gneiss.—Other varieties—Landslips.—Intruded rocks.—Dislocations.—Three systems of faults.—Disturbances.—Upheaval of the ghâts.—Quartz veins.—Withering of rocks.—Laterite.—Kaolin.—Clays.—Escarpments.—Kaity valley.—Kúndas.—Alluvial.—Economic geology.—Limestone.—Mr. King's note.—Gold.—South-East Wainád.

CHAP. V.

GEOLOGY AND MINERALOGY.

Early papers.

SEVERAL papers on the geological and mineralogical structure of these hills have, from time to time during the last forty years, been laid before the public. The earliest of these was a "Geological Sketch of the Nilgiris," contributed to the Journal of the Asiatic Society of Bengal in 1835 by Dr. P. M. deBenza, the Surgeon to the Governor of Madras at the time. This paper, which is spoken of by Mr. Blandford as "very excellent," will be found in an improved form in Volume III of the Journal of the Madras Literary and Scientific Society. "The Report on the Medical Topography of the Neilgherry Hills," printed by order of Government in 1844, contains some valuable remarks on the geology of the hills. During this and the following year a series of letters on their topography, geology, and ethnology was contributed to the *Madras Spectator* by Captain Congreve and Dr. Burrell. Later, Captain Congreve, in the year 1861 (Vol. V, No. XVI, December) furnished another paper on the geology of the district to the Madras Literary and Scientific Society, in which his opinions and observations are given in a more systematic form than in the earlier brochures. In Major Ouchterlony's Survey Memoir (1847) there will also be found some information on the subject, as also in two papers contributed to the Journal of the Asiatic Society, Bengal, New Series, No. LXXXVI, about the year 1856.

CHAP. V. GEOLOGY AND MINERALOGY.

Geological Survey.

In the year 1857, in accordance with measures, proposed by the Government of India and approved by the Honorable Court of Directors, for the investigation of the geological structure and mineral character of the country comprised within the Presidency of Madras, Mr. Henry F. Blandford, of the Geological Survey of India, was deputed to carry out a systematic survey of the Presidency. Mr. Blandford began operations on the Nílagiris and the table-land of Mysore in the month of June of that year. The results of his inquiries, as respects the Nílagiris, which form the basis of the following monograph, will be found in the Memoirs of the Geological Survey, Vol. I, Part II, published in 1858. Mr. Blandford was accompanied by three assistants, Messrs. Oldham, King, and Geoghegan.

General description.

Of the Nílagiris Mr. Blandford observes that they, like most of the hill-tracts of the peninsula, *e.g.*, the Shevaroys, Pulnís, and Ánémalés, rise abruptly from the lower country round them, and are bounded on all sides by short precipitous spurs, the remains of a great former escarpment, which, in the course of long ages, has been broken up by the unceasing action of the numerous streams pouring down from their surface.

Action of water—fresh.

After describing the drainage system already explained in Chapter I, Mr. Blandford goes on to point out that the gorges which break into the lateral faces of the hills are the result of the attrital action of the water flowing down from the plateau. In his own words :

"They have, therefore, the precipitous sides, and are separated by the steep ridges which always result from extensive fresh water denudation in a mountainous country. The surface of the Neelgherries, on the other hand, is undulating in the extreme, and the streams which carry off its drainage meander with a comparatively gentle fall through rounded grassy hills, but rarely forming anything like a large rocky bluff; while the valleys never present the slightest approach to the character of a gorge, except in some of the deeper valleys of the Kundas, where * * * the rainfall is far greater than on the surface of Neelgherries proper, and the denudation produced thereby consequently greater. It might be inferred, therefore, even from a casual glance at the Neelgherries, that the hills on the plateau owe their form to marine action, it being a well established fact that rounded hills and an undulating country are invariably the result of such action. But on the Neelgherries we have a further proof that the sea has formerly washed over what is now the highest portion of the table-land, in the existence of a series of escarpments, imperfect indeed in many cases and much cut up by the subsequent action of surface water, but still distinctly recognisable to the practised eye, and sometimes traceable for a distance of many miles continuously.

Sea.

The most conspicuous of these superficial escarpments crosses the hills in a south-west direction from the rise of the Pykara near Makurty Peak, and forms the boundary of that elevated portion of the plateau to which the name of the Kundas has been given."

Rock formation.

The rocks which constitute the Nílagiris belong almost wholly to the schistose or foliated class, which are included by some geologists among metamorphic rocks. But for reasons given, Mr. Blandford regards this appellation as of but doubtful propriety, preferring to restrict himself to the term gneissose rocks, "gneiss being the most known and most typical of the series." The other rocks are chiefly alluvial deposits, small basaltic dykes, and some quartz veins. Nowhere above the ghåts has any trace of granite or of rocks belonging to that class been found, though in the district below the ghåts numerous small granite veins are observable.

Granite absent.

Gneissose rocks.

The rocks occurring in the district and neighbouring tracts are very varied in mineral character, and might easily be regarded as of Plutonic origin. But though at times their foliated structure is very indistinct, yet they invariably pass into a more markedly typical gneissose form. They never "form igneous veins or present any appearance of intrusion." Their foliated character is much more marked in the plains than in mountainous tracts.

Direction of foliations.

The direction of this foliation, which is fairly constant, approximately coincides with that of the "southern escarpment of the Neelgherries, the Bhowani River, the Eastern Ghåts, and many of the principal ridges on the surface of the plateau, especially those to the south of Ootacamund. Its prevailing strike is between N.E., S.W. and E.N.E. and W.S.W." A few variations occur, notably at Snowdon, but these are very local. The foliation is most distinct at Kótagiri, but it is rarely strongly marked, and never approaches to a schistose character. The foliation becomes more strongly marked as you descend the ghåts, especially the Coonoor ghåt, near Mettapollium. "A coarse hornblende schist, composed of thick alternating laminæ of quartz and hornblende, is seen protruding from the ground in large slabs resembling the old tombstones in a country churchyard." The foliation becomes more compact as you advance into the great Coimbatore plain.

Minerals.

The principal minerals generally found in varying proportions in these foliated rocks are garnet, felspar, quartz and hornblende. Mica occurs but rarely, and is stated by Mr. Blandford to be an exceptional mineral in South India. Besides the above minerals, "magnetic iron, hæmatite, specular iron and graphite, and, as the result of decomposition, the various earthy forms of the hydratid peroxide of iron, such as ochre and laterite and kaolin," are of local occurrence. Of these the oxide of iron is the most abundant.

CHAP. V. — GEOLOGY AND MINERALOGY. — Iron.

They occur " in short irregular bands or masses in the gneiss, such bands generally running in the direction of the foliation. Hæmatite and specular iron are far more common on the surface than magnetic iron, but from their manner, structure and mode of occurrence, they are probably magnetic iron peroxidized by atmospheric agency." Masses of ore occur above the village of Karrashóla, a mile and a half to the west of Kótagiri, and on a spur of the Doddabetta range above the Washermen's—Dhobies'—village at Ootacamand. Similar deposits also occur three miles to the east of Jackatalla or Wellington. Here the hæmatite is " interfoliated with the gneiss in broad strings of pure mineral."

Hornblendic gneiss.

In the north-western portion of the Nílagiris the gneiss contains a very large proportion of hornblende, with which is intermixed quartz and some garnets. This rock is described as " a hard, tough, black rock breaking with an even fracture." It contains but few traces of foliation in fresh fractures, but on weathered surfaces it is otherwise. A similar hornblendic gneissose formation constitutes the north-east or lofty section of the Kúndas, though here it is stated to be much decomposed, producing " a thick covering of ferruginous clay and lateritic gravel." It is these varieties of gneiss which, Mr. Blandford observes, had misled previous geological observers, who have described them as " syenite, greenstone, and kindred igneous rocks." " Such formations will be seen on the Segore Ghât, where the rock weathers into smooth rounded blocks " without any appearance of foliation.

Mistakes regarding these rocks.

Quartz felspathic gneiss.

Near Sisapára on the Kúndas appears another variety of gneissose rock, the component minerals of which are felspar and quartz. This variety was described by Dr. Benza as pegmatite, or graphic granite ; but from the fact that it gradually passes into the neighbouring gneiss, whilst the threads of quartz are " all arranged in the normal direction of foliation," Mr. Blandford does not hesitate to pronounce it a gneissose rock. A similar rock occurs in the valley north-west of Snowdon, and also a more extensive spread north of Mélúr, " forming a belt about three miles in width passing from the foot of the Kundas to the Kaity valley." This rock contains also garnets in abundance.

Quartzo-hornblendic gneiss.

Mr. Blandford observes that the most common kind of gneiss in the central portions of the plateau is " a finely grained rock composed of quartz, garnet and hornblende, with variable proportions of felspar." Its foliation is indistinct; it is very decomposible, except on the large precipitous faces, and in decomposition forms a large mass of ferruginous clay, embedded in which are large spheroidal boulders. In large exposed faces

CHAP. V. — GEOLOGY AND MINERALOGY. — Landslips.

the rock shows a tendency to split off in enormous slabs slightly curved to the form of the hill side." The probable cause of these splits is the heat of the sun, which makes the surface layers expand rapidly and then separate from the cooler rock beneath. After heavy rain the decomposing mass, being saturated with water, frequently breaks off from the main rock and rushes down, scattering the embedded boulders over the valley below. The mark of such landslips may be observed along the Doddabetta slopes forming the north-east side of the Kaity valley.

Banded structure of gneiss.

Mr. Blandford draws attention to the banded structure of the gneiss, which contains much hornblende, about Paikaré and Múkarté. The bands protrude from the hill-side and always run

FIG 1 — HARD BANDS IN GNEISS, NEAR NEDDIWUTTUM.

in the direction of the foliation. Traces of this banded structure also appear in the hills around Ootacamand, but it is rarely possible to trace them to any distance, as they " either become lenticular or break up and die away in the mass." He then refers to a remarkable limestone formation in Coimbatore[1] exhibiting the banded structure of these rocks more clearly. The limestone and the gneiss run in alternate bands. " The regularity and continuity of this rock for a distance of six miles and probably even more render it difficult " he writes, " to believe that it can be other than a really metamorphosed band of sedimentary

[1] See Notice, *Madras Journal of Literature and Science*, Vol. III, No. V, New Series.

CHAP. V. — GEOLOGY AND MINERALOGY.

rocks, and afford the strongest evidence of such an origin that has yet been obtained in this part of India."

FIG: III.—THIN ALTERNATIONS OF LIMESTONE AND GNEISS, WEATHERED,—NEAR COIMBATOOR.

Intruded rocks.

As already mentioned no granite is found on the hills, and the other rocks which were regarded by Dr. Benza as of igneous origin are now shown to be foliated. A few small dykes, however, of rocks which are undoubtedly trap occur. One will be observed north of the Paikaré road near Ootacamand and another on the northern slope of Snowdon, "about 200 yards from the summit, and again to the north-west in the bed of a small water-course on the western side of the valley, and in both cases consists of several small parallel dykes, varying from two to ten inches in width, and consisting of a tough compact basaltic rock." These dykes run north-west, or nearly at right angles to the foliation of the gneiss. Trap dykes also appear at the south-west extremity of the district near Sisapára. Mr. Blandford's paper contains a minute description of these dykes by his assistant, Mr. King. As regards the age of the trap dykes no evidence, Mr. Blandford observes, is forthcoming, consequently "it is impossible to say whether or not they are connected with the great outbreak of the Deckan." Similar dykes, however, occur in Mysore.

Dislocations.

Mr. Blandford's remarks on these subjects seem to me too valuable to be curtailed. After observing that ample evidence of the dislocations which have occurred is forthcoming in the physical features of the surface, and to some extent in the presence of mineral veins, he proceeds :—

Three systems of faults.

"There are three principal systems of faulting, two of them probably synchronous and at right angles to each other, being those which coincide with the lines of the Eastern and Western Ghâts respectively, and a third, probably subsequent to the above, and contemporaneous with the final upheaval of the Neelgherry plateau.

"The first of the systems of dislocation, viz., that to which the formation of the Eastern Ghâts is due, has an east-north-east direction, varying occasionally to north-east, and therefore about coincident with the general strike of the foliation. To this system belong the great faults, with a down-throw to south-east which have produced the Eastern Ghâts and the south-eastern escarpment of the Neel-gherries, and those with a north-western down-throw, which have given rise to the great Kunda escarpment and that at Neddiwuttum, both of which face towards the north-west. To the smaller dislocations of this system may be attributed the valley of Pykara at the foot of the Himagala range and the great south-eastern escarpment of the Dodabetta range, both on the plateau of the hills and having a down-throw to the south-east. First system. Eastern Ghâts and other line of escarpment.

"The second system is nearly at right angles to the preceding, and has a west-north-west direction, varying to north-west where it meets the former system in the Neelgherries. Second system.

"It comprises the Western Ghâts and the smaller Neelgherry escarpment of the Kunda range, or that which, facing to the north-east, commences at the Pykara River, and passing thence behind Avalanche, terminates near the village of Keel Kunda, overlooking the valley of the Bhowani River. These two escarpments, although in precisely the same line, face in different directions, and it is therefore probable that the disturbance which gave rise to the latter was of subsequent date to that which produced the former, but took place along the old line of dislocation, the upheaval being on the opposite side. Another line of fracture belonging to this system is that which crosses the hills from St. Katharine's Falls to the Elk Fall in the neighborhood of Kotergherry, on the north-eastern portion of the hills, and it is to this that the gorges below these two falls are originally due. There does not appear to have been any great amount of disturbance along this line, so far as can be judged from the present aspect of the country, but the evidences are sufficiently clear to warrant the belief that such a fracture exists." Western Ghâts and Kúnda escarpment. Faults near Kótagiri.

"The third great system of faults is that to which the northern boundary of the Neelgherries, the short southern escarpment of the Kunda range, the extreme terminal escarpment of the hill-country of Palghât, and probably some smaller dislocations in the hilly country intervening between the Neelgherries and Palghât belong. The first of these might, at first sight, seem to ramify from the line of disturbance of the Eastern Ghâts, which at their junction has very nearly the same direction; but the existence of parallel lines of faulting elsewhere, all of which are connected with the upheaval of the Neelgherries as a group, and the incompatibility of such a series as synchronous with either of the two systems above enumerated, induce the belief that it belongs to a separate and subsequent system of dislocations. Third system. Why regarded as a distinct system.

"According to the above, the following is the series of successive disturbances which have mainly given rise to the present physical aspect of the country. Succession of disturbances as deduced from the preceding.

CHAP. V. — GEOLOGY AND MINERALOGY. — Upheaval of the ghâts.

"The first great disturbance which took place was the upheaval of the ghâts and the intervening plateau of Mysore, the two main lines of dislocation meeting and possibly terminating in the Neelgherries. The great fault, or system of faults, along which the Neelgherry or Avalanche escarpment of the Kundas was afterwards upraised, probably gave rise to the terminal portion of the Western Ghâts, the down-throw at the period being towards the south. Many smaller dislocations, more or less parallel to the two main lines, would be produced during such an upheaval, and in some of these the isolated hill mass of the Neelgherries may have been subsequently upraised to a far greater elevation.

Formation of Nílagiris.

"The second great disturbance which produced the Neelgherries may have followed the former, either after a certain interval, or as the closing act of a long period of elevation, the upheaving force being more concentrated. The area upheaved was bounded partly by a pre-existing line of fracture and partly by a newly-formed series having an eastern and western direction. During the same period, minor disturbances broke up the country for some miles to the south, and also produced some of those escarpments which have been described as occurring on the Neelgherries, and which were subsequently much modified in form by marine action. It is not improbable that the Neelgherries have been upheaved *en masse* to some extent since the surface of the plateau received its present form and since that portion of the country has been raised above the sea, for the mural escarpments which bound the Neelgherries are far more precipitous than we could imagine them to have been had they been subjected to marine action during a long gradual process of upheaval from the sea.

—subsequent in part to the general upheaval of the country.

—epoch of upheavals not ascertainable.

"Of the geological periods during which the disturbances just enumerated took place we can learn nothing in this part of the country, there being no sedimentary rocks that can furnish any clue to this important problem.

"The Carnatic, and the country through which the Godavery flows, are the districts most likely to afford the much desired information as to the epochs of the disturbance in the Indian peninsula.

Quartz veins cannot be classed with any system.

"In describing the great lines of fracture in the rocks of the Neelgherries, no notice has been taken of the small quartz veins occurring in various parts of the hills, inasmuch as these minor disturbances can scarcely be referred to any distinct system. They are in most cases of no great length or width, and of no economic value. The vein stone in all of them is a pure white quartz, occasionally containing a few crystals of pyrites of tolerable size, and which appear to have the form of the pentagonal dodecahedron. In the vein which is seen cropping out on the hill side where the Avalanche road crosses a stream about seven miles from Ootacamund, there is a small quantity of brown hæmatite (limonite) filling the cavities in the quartz. This is sometimes seen forming irregular pseudomorphs of the pyrites, and it is evident that it has resulted from the decomposi-

—Of no economic value.

—Pyrites.

tion of that mineral. Captain Ouchterlony mentions having found a speck of copper pyrites in a loose block derived from one of these quartz veins, but no trace of that mineral has been found by the surveyors after careful and repeated examination of the vein stones. It is possible the iron pyrites or mundic above described may have been mistaken for the more valuable cupriferous mineral."

—Brown hæmatite how found.

—No copper pyrites.

Weathering of rocks.

With regard to the decomposition of the rocks already adverted to, Mr. Blandford observes that without a careful chemical analysis of the various descriptions of gneiss present on the hills, it is difficult to account for "the unequal and irregular decomposition which obtains in many cases in rocks of apparently identical mineral composition." Generally it seems that the rocks containing little or no felspar are little liable to decomposition; the same is also the case with rocks destitute of hornblende, though containing much felspar. The existence of hard gneiss bands, *e.g.*, at Múkarté, is due to the fact that some portions of the rock contain more quartz than others.

Laterite.

The laterite which exists in the hills, where no regular laterite beds are found, appears to be result of the decomposition of hornblendic gneiss. "The iron" observes Mr. Blandford, "originally contained in the hornblende becomes thoroughly peroxidized and hydrated, and by a species of crystallization forms a mammillated coating of impure limonite (brown hæmatite) exactly resembling the characteristic surface of laterite." A good instance of this occurs near the Paikaré River on the road to Múkarté.

Kaolin; Ochreous clays.

This mineral is found in several places on the hills. It may be seen on the Lake road at Ootacamand, near Fairlawns, and on the road between Paikaré and Neduwattam. It is stated to contain too much iron to be of much economic value. The hill kaolin is formed by felspathic gneiss decomposed *in situ*. Ordinarily it is formed from decomposed granite. Several kinds of ferruginous clays occur, of varying tints, some of which might possibly be used as pigments. Twenty-eight different varieties of clay were shown at the Agricultural Exhibition at Ootacamand in October 1869. Twenty cups manufactured from them at the Madras School of Arts were also shown, also a flower vase made of the pure white kaolin. The quality is stated to have been very fine.

Evidences of marine action.

The physical aspect of the Nílagiris has, as already pointed out, been greatly affected by the action of the rainfall, the erosion of the rocks being in proportion to the severity of the rainfall. It is in the Kúndas, for this reason, that we meet with steeper and more precipitous hills and deeper and more gorge-like valleys than in other portions of the range which are not open to the full burst of the south-west monsoon. It is, therefore, on the portions of the hills where this fresh-water influence has prevailed least, that we

CHAP. V. — GEOLOGY AND MINERALOGY.

find the most evident marks of former marine action. This is especially apparent in the escarpments of the Doddabetta range and spurs.

Mr. Blandford observes—

"The general outline of Dodabetta, as seen from a distance, is much rounded; it appears as a prominent mass of hills bounded on the greater part of its circumference by a tolerably distinct escarpment.

FIG: V.— VIEW OF THE DODABETTA AND KAITEE ESCARPMENT.

Escarpment —of Kaity Valley.

This escarpment is especially visible on its south-eastern side which overlooks Kaitee valley, and again to the north and north-west of Jackatalla, where the projecting terminations of several spurs present a striking resemblance to the rocky headlands of parts of the south coast of England. The ground between these prominent spurs has been much hollowed out by the streams pouring down from Dodabetta, and it is, therefore, only by viewing the general contour of these hills from some little distance that their cliff-like character becomes apparent. Passing from Jackatalla towards Kotergherry, the escarpment may still be traced, although much obliterated by the subsequent formation of valleys. About half-way between Jackatalla and Kotergherry it turns to the west, and seen from any point on the northern part of the hills it presents a bold rocky face terminating in Daversolabetta, a lofty conical peak a few miles north-east of Ootacamund. At this point the escarpment cannot be very distinctly made out, but to the west of Daversolabetta the upper part of the escarpment appears to turn round to the south and join that overlooking Ootacamund, while the lower part, which is extremely well marked, although of comparatively less elevation than that of Dodabetta and at a somewhat lower level, passes below Marlimund and Seven-Cairn hill, crossing the Seegoor road, and forming the termination of the pass of that name, and finally merges into the great boundary escarpment of the hills. To return to our starting point, the escarpment above Kaitee valley may be traced for some distance to the south-west, and finally dies away, or rather appears to be broken up into smaller escarpments, which, in the course of time, have become nearly obliterated by the erosion of the hill streams." CHAP. V.

GEOLOGY AND MINERALOGY.

The same features are, though less distinctly, observable on the eastern side of the Kúndas and in the range of hills extending from Múkarté to Paikaré, sometimes called the Himagála range. —of the Kúndas.

The following sketch is a view of Múkarté with the Paikaré river at its foot. Tukalhallibetta, the terminating point of the Kúndas on the north, is concealed by clouds. The Himagála range begins with Múkarté.

FIG VI—VIEW OF MAKURTY PEAK WITH PART OF THE HIMACALA RANGE AND THE VALLEY OF THE PYKARA

Mr. Blandford further remarks—

"There are several small insular outliers, such as that to the north-west of Mailur, the Hoolicaldroog and the adjoining hills, the hills to the east of Coonoor, and the two prominent hills * * * to the west of Ootacamund, all of which are bounded partly at least by escarpments more or less distinctly marked Subsequent fresh water denudation has much modified, where it has not destroyed, most of the pre-existing features of the hills, in some cases rendering the escarpments still deeper and more marked, in others cutting through them and making them up into rounded spurs, so that it is only by observing their *general* outline from some distance that an idea can be formed of original appearance."

Alluvial deposits.

In many of the valleys of the hills are found large deposits of alluvium, sometimes spreading into plains or flats of considerable extent. These deposits of the neighbouring mountains appear to have accumulated in the large serpentine lakes, many of which are believed to have existed at some early period of the geological history of the hills, and which were formed by dams or bunds of rock thrown up across the valleys, by which means the egress of the water was checked. Through these natural bunds of rock streams will often now be seen gradually wearing a path downwards to the bottom of the original valley. Of these

CHAP. V.
GEOLOGY AND MINERALOGY.

lakes Mr. Blandford says: "It is evident that any obstacle closing a valley excavated by running water must be of subsequent date to the formation of the valley, and, therefore, if the Neelgherry valleys now occupied by alluvium be really of fresh water origin, as seems most probable, there must have been subsequent to their formation some changes in the levels of the country, which, by stopping the drainage, converted the pre-existing valleys into lakes." Again: " The form of the valleys which they (the alluvial flats) occupy precludes the idea that the former were excavated by any other agent than the hill-streams, and such being the case, it is, as already stated, only by subsequent disturbance that they could be converted into lakes."

FIG. VII.—ALLUVIAL PLAIN ON A FEEDER OF THE PYKARA RIVER NEAR TUKULHULLYBETTA.

Economic geology. Limestone.

The rocks of the hills yield but few substances of any economic value. Limestone, which, as already stated, exists in the subjacent plain of Coimbatore, has not been found on the hills either in the crystalline or gravel form. Some of the gneissose rocks are fairly adapted for building purposes, but the localities where such varieties occur are generally inaccessible. In most cases the stone is either very loosely foliated or extremely bad and deficient in joints. Where the structure is loose the stone seems to have a great tendency to decompose. This is doubtless a great objection to the use of such stone for road metal, but in case of building the evil might probably be greatly neutralised by placing the blocks so that the cross section of the foliation only shall be exposed. The gneiss of the Kúndas in the neighbourhood of Sisapára, from its finely jointed character, is stated to promise well for quarrying purposes; but the distance precludes its use. The iron ore of the plateau would probably yield well, but the dearness of fuel militates against the financial success of any scheme for smelting it. Much quartz occurs, but though very white and free from iron, it is pronounced " not sufficiently pellucid to be of any value for optical purposes." Attention has already been called to the probable economic value of some highly-colored iron ores and clays for pigments or pottery. Garnets, as already stated, abound in some of the gneiss, and in the Madras Museum there is a small piece of pot-stone, the *lapis ollaris* of the ancients, said to have been found on the range. Peat occurs in many of the valleys, and for years past has been cut and used as fuel.

Such is an imperfect summary of the results of the geological survey. I am indebted to the kindness of Mr. King, of the Geological Survey, for the additional interesting note which has special reference to the Ouchterlony Valley and to the gold prospects of the Nílagiri range.

Additional note on the rocks of the Nílagiris and adjacent country.

Since Mr. H. F. Blandford's Memoir on the Nílagiri hills was written, the only further exploration of the country adjacent to the plateau proper was that made in 1874 during the survey of Wainád, at which time the Ouchterlony Valley was cursorily visited to note any extension of the Déwála gold-reefs.

Rocks of the valley.

The rocks of the Ouchterlony Valley belong, as might be expected, to the same series as the rest of the Nílagiris, though they are mainly of that particular variety of *quartzo-hornblendic gneiss*, constituting two or more of the several belts[1] or bands of the gneiss family of which this range of mountains is made up. Here, as on the upland, the foliation has a north-east—south-west strike, this being also the lie or direction of the belt across the valley, while the general dip is very high (50°–70°) to the south-east.

Folding and even reduplication of the strata is often visible, thus presenting local variations in both dip and strike; but the general lie is as given above.

The great band strikes right across the valley from the Moyár on the north by Neduwattam to the plains of Malabar below the Kúndas and is about six miles in width, and is bounded on the north-west side by a further belt of *felspathic* and *chloritic* gneisses in the country west of Gúdalúr and towards Nádgáni and Déwála. The general term *quartzo-hornblendic gneiss* is

[1] The same or nearly the same variety of gneiss forms what may be called the Doddabetta and Elk Hill belt on the Nílagiri plateau.

CHAP. V.
GEOLOGY AND MINERALOGY.

applied to the whole of the band, but variations in the prevalency of one mineral over the other are very frequent. On the Gúdalúr side, or in the lower part of the valley, the rock is more *quartzose,* at times *garnetiferous*, and is of a light grey color; while the more hornblendic varieties, or as they are sometimes called *syenitoid gneisses*, are higher up, and range through the Neduwattam country and among the more elevated coffee plantations. Towards the south-west there are frequent traces of veins of white *quartz* traversing the *gneiss* in a direction nearly at right angles to the foliation, or about north-north-west, south-south-east, with a dip to the eastward; and these are evidently southerly prolongations of some of the numerous gold-bearing reefs of South-East Wainád.

Gold—Wainád.

There is, however, no knowledge of gold having been obtained from any of the valley veins, though it appeared evident from the debris of quartz lying about the surface at one or two places near the outcrop of the veins, together with the broken character of the ground, that search for gold, if not actual workings, must have been carried on at some former period. The quartz-reefs are also not so strong as around Dévála, being from about two to four feet in width, and this narrowing or nipping out from the generally greater width of the lodes traversing the softer gneisses of Dévála resembles what has happened to the same reefs still further west, where they traverse the hard quartzose gneisses of the Marapannaddi ridge. As the veins are crossed from the Nádgáni or south-west end of the valley towards Gúdalúr they become less and less distinct, when also they gradually assume a granular structure and are largely interspersed with *mica,* until at Gúdalúr itself they become quite granitic in their constitution. This change in the character of the contents of the lodes is, as in Wainád, marked by an absence of gold, at least in any appreciable quantity; and this granitic and barren quality exists for some miles to the eastward into the Mysore country.

Nílagiris.

Since the late resuscitation of the gold industry in Wainád, attention has been directed to the possible auriferousness of the few quartz veins on the Nílagiri plateau, but as yet no definite exploration has been made among these. At the time of the geological survey in 1857 no trace of gold was found, nor did there appear to be any tradition of its existence. The veins were also so insignificant in number and size that anything like prolonged search was not considered advisable. Still, during the examination of Wainád, the appearance of many old sites of working-places and diggings for gold soon recalled to mind the existence of irregular patches of dug-up earth and quartz debris along the banks of the Lovedale streams, and again in a smaller valley to the south of and behind Bishop's Down which at this time could not be accounted for, and these were doubtless also sites of old gold-workings. Subsequent information seems to confirm this idea, as Colonel Beresford obtained, in 1874, traces of gold from fragments of quartz picked up in the neighborhood of these localities. This is, however, all that can at present be safely said as to the possibility of gold on these hills; while, at the same time, the general absence of any of the *chloritic* varieties of gneiss on the Nílagiris is, if we are guided by the character of other auriferous regions, a feature which ought to inspire great caution in the expectation of gold in any quantity in the Nílagiris quartz lodes.

South-East Wainád.

Though the Wainád, and more especially the south-east division, has been partially examined by the Geological Survey Department, no complete memoir has as yet appeared. From the "Preliminary Note on the Gold-field, South-East Wainád,"[1] by Mr. King, much information on the geological structure of this tract will be found, together with a map exhibiting the same. The paper also gives a brief narrative of the ancient gold mining history of Wainád and Nellambúr, fuller details of which were published by Government in 1874 in a pamphlet entitled "Correspondence regarding Gold Mines in Wainád." Further information on the subject, especially in relation to lands having gold, whether public or private, and the State's right to the metal will be found in the orders of Government, 2nd April 1875, No. 512, and 23rd January 1877, No. 319. The Government have not yet disposed of the questions raised. I must content myself with referring the readers to the above papers, as this paper has already reached to too great a length, and the questions relate more properly to the recently annexed portion of the district, of which I am not expected to treat in detail.

[1] Records of the Geological Survey of India, Vol. VIII, Part 2, 1875.

CHAPTER VI.

FLORA.

(*By* Lieutenant-Colonel R. H. Beddome, M.S.C., *Conservator of Forests, Madras Presidency.*)

General remarks.—Botanical divisions of the Hills.—Deciduous forests on slopes—characteristic trees—valuable timbers.—Moist evergreen forests on slopes—characteristic trees—timbers.—Woods of the plateau—characteristic trees—timbers—ferns and mosses.—Grass-land of the plateau—characteristic trees and plants (beautiful plants) of the Hills.—List of flowering plants—Dicotyledones—Monocotyledones—Gramineæ.—List of Ferns and Mosses—Cryptogams—Jungermanniaceæ—Bryaceæ.—Lichenales.—Fungales.—Books of reference.—Introduced plants.

CHAP. VI. — FLORA. — General remarks.

The Nílagiri Mountains, rising to upwards of 8,000 feet, and having a rainfall of less than 40 inches on some of the driest parts of the eastern side, and 300 inches on the moistest parts of the western slopes, possess, as might be expected, a very varied and interesting flora, exceedingly numerous in genera and species. With the exception of the dense evergreen moist forests on the western slopes, the whole area has been well explored by botanists, and it is probable that there are no plants now botanically unknown on the plateau and the deciduous forests of the slopes; but this cannot be said of the heavy moist forests of the western slopes. They are of immense extent, very difficult to get at, and very feverish at the lower elevations; and as there are no habitations, inhabitants, or supplies of any sort, the visits of botanists, who have often been attracted to them, have been generally of a flying nature. The trees in these tracts attain an immense size, 200 or 250 feet in height, and it is of course no easy matter to obtain their flowers; and there can be no doubt that there are still a good many undescribed species awaiting the botanist. Some flower in the cold season, some in the hot season, and some in the rains, some few are in flower all the year round; but it is believed that the majority flower between February and the middle of May, which is the most unhealthy time of the year. The shrubs, creepers and herbaceous plants in these tracts are pretty well known, but a careful search at any season of the year would undoubtedly be rewarded by some novelties.

Hills divided into four tracts.

Botanically we may divide these hills into four tracts, each having its own flora, very few species of which encroach upon the other tracts.

CHAP. VI.

FLORA.

Deciduous forests on slopes.

1st *Tract.—The deciduous Forests of the Slopes.*—These are of much the same character as the dry forests of the lesser hills and plains of the Presidency. The trees are all more or less deciduous in the dry months of January, February, and March, but the forests are never entirely bare, like the woods and forests in Europe in the winter. Many trees, such as the *Erythrinas, Butea frondosa*, the three *Dalbergias, Schleichera trijuga, Stereospermum xylocarpum, Odina Wodier, Terminalia Belerica*, and others burst into flower in February, and leaf themselves rapidly afterwards, before many other trees have finished shedding their leaves; but still these tracts have a very forlorn appearance at this season, and fire often sweeps through them greatly to the disgust of the Foresters. In these tracts a very great proportion of the tropical trees of this Presidency are to be met with, and about the lowest portions, very many of the tropical shrubs and weeds, which do not belong at all to our alpine flora, such as the weeds amongst *Capparids*, the small *Milkworts* (*Polygalas*), the herbs and shrubs of *Malvaceæ*, the *Grewias* and herbs of *Tiliaceæ, Zizyphus* (several species), *Vitis* (several species), *Cardiospermum*, leguminous weeds and herbs, most of the *Cucurbitaceæ*, many of the *Compositæ, Convolvulaceæ, Scrophulariaceæ, Amarantaceæ, Commelynaceæ*, and a large proportion of the sedges and grasses.

—characteristic trees.

The trees most characteristic of these tracts are as follows:—

Dillenia pentagyna.
Cochlospermum gossypium.
Kydia calycina.
Bombax Malabaricum.
Sterculia fœtida, urens, villosa, and colorata.
Eriolœna Hookeriana and quinquelocularis.
Boswellia serrata.
Garuga pinnata.
Cedrela Toona.
Chloroxylon Swietenia.
Elæodendron glaucum.
Schleichera trijuga.
Buchanania latifolia.
Mundulea suberosa.
Butea frondosa.
Dalbergia latifolia and paniculata.
Pterocarpus marsupium.
Hardwickia binata.
Xylia dolabriformis.
Acacia—many species.
Albizzia odoratissima and amara.
Terminalia tomentosa, paniculata, Belerica, and chebula.
Anogeissus latifolius.
Careya arborea.
Lagerstrœmia microcarpa and Regina.
Adina cordifolia.
Stephegyne parvifolia.
Stereospermum xylocarpum.
Tectona grandis.
Gmelina arborea.
Phyllanthus emblica.
Sponia Wightii.
Bambusa arundinacea } Bamboos.
Dendrocalamus strictus }

—valuable timbers.

These tracts yield many of the most valuable timbers of the Presidency, of which the following may be said to be the most important:—

Cedrela Toona (White Cedar).
Chloroxylon Swietenia (the Satinwood).
Schleichera trijuga (Puva).
Dalbergia latifolia (the Blackwood or Rosewood).
Pterocarpus marsupium (Vengay).
Hardwickia binata (Achâ).
Xylia dolabriformis (Irul).
Albizzia odoratissima (Karangilli).
Terminalia tomentosa (Matti).
Lagerstrœmia microcarpa (Venteak).
Tectona grandis (Teak).
Gmelina arborea.
Phyllanthus emblica (Nelli).
Santalam album (Sandalwood).

CHAP. VI.

FLORA.

Moist evergreen forests of the slopes.

2nd Tract.—The Moist Evergreen Forests of the Slopes.—These are grandest on the western slopes, and between 3,000 and 4,000 feet elevation, where the trees often attain 200 and 250 feet in height. They are all evergreen, and their great variety of foliage and colour renders them exceedingly beautiful, some of the young leaves coming out pure white, others a bright crimson, others all possible tints of brown, yellow, red, and green. These tracts are exceedingly moist from the first showers in March till the end of December, and during that season abound with leeches. The trees are often covered with epiphytic orchids, ferns, mosses, balsams, and *cyrtandraceæ,* and there is a glorious profusion of rattans, tree-ferns, climbing ferns, and fine creepers. But what may be said to be most characteristic of these forests is the genus *Strobilanthes* (*Acanthaceæ*), large shrubs, which form the principal underwood, and of which 29 species are found on these hills. Some of these flower every year, others however only after a growth of six or seven years, when they die down and renew themselves from seed. They almost all have showy flowers, and many are very beautiful. The two palms, *Caryota urens* and *Arenga Wightii,* are very conspicuous in these tracts, also several specimens of rattan (*Calamus*), and three very fine reed bamboos, *Beesha Rheedii, Oxytenanthera Thwaitesii* (Munro), and *Teinostachyum Wightii* (a very handsome broad-leaved species, described by Munro as a bambusa from specimens only in leaf). Ferns are in great profusion, including several tree-ferns, amongst which the *Alsophila crinita* (not yet introduced into English hot-houses) unmatched in any country, is very beautiful. *Sonerilas* and balsams are also in profusion. *Guttiferæ, Rubiaceæ,* and *Euphorbiaceæ* are the orders perhaps most copiously represented (next to *Acanthaceæ*), the first by trees, the two last by shrubs and trees.

Above 4,000 feet these forests begin to decrease in size, and towards the plateau they gradually pass into what will be treated of as the *Shólas* or woods.

—characteristic trees.

The following is a list of the trees most characteristic of these forests:—

Polyalthia coffeoides.
Garcinia Cambogia and Morella.
Calophyllum tomentosum.
Mesua speciosa and Coromandelina.
Pæciloneuron Indicum.
Dipterocarpus turbinatus.
Hopea parviflora and Malabarica.
Vateria Indica.
Cullenia excelsa.
Leptonychia moaccuroides.
Chickrassia tabularis.
Canarium strictum.
Aglaia Roxburghiana.
Beddomea Indica and simplicifolia.
Gomphandra axillaris and polymorpha.
Euonymus Indicus and angulatus.
Lophopetalum Wightianum.
Harpulia cupanoides.
Acrocarpus fraxinifolius.
Humboldtia Brunonis and Vahliana.
Saprosma fragrans, Wightii, and glomerata.
Bassia elliptica.
Pajanelia Rheedii.
Myristica laurifolia and corticosa.
Alseodaphne semicarpifolia.

Actinodaphne salicina.
Cryptocarya Wightiana.
Actephila excelsa.
Sarcoclinium longifolium.
Agrostistachys Indica.
Baccaurea sapida.
Ostodes Zeylanica.
Cephalocroton Indicum.
Bischoffia Javanica.
Hemicyclia venusta.
Artocarpus hirsuta.
Gironniera reticulata.
Laportea crenulata.

The timbers, as a rule, are not of such good quality as those in the deciduous forests, but there are valuable timbers, of which the following are the chief:— —timbers.

Calophyllum tomentosum (Poon spar).
Mesua, 2 species (Iron wood).
Hopea parviflora.
,, Malabarica.
Chickrassia tabularis (Chittagong wood).
Acrocarpus fraxinifolius (Red Cedar or Shingle Tree).
Diospyros ebenum (Ebony).
Artocarpus hirsuta (Angelli or Aynee).
Gironniera reticulata (Kho mongoe).

These moist forests never reach quite down to the plains anywhere round the Nílagiris, though they do so in parts of South Canara, Coorg, and Travancore. They always give way at 1,000 or more feet from the base to deciduous forests or tracts composed of nothing but reed bamboos (*Teinostachyum Wightii*).

3rd Tract.—The Shólas or Woods of the Plateau.—These are very similar in character to the moist evergreen forests of the slopes, but from being at a higher elevation the trees are of different genera and species, and their growth is much smaller, 70 feet being much beyond the average height. The shólas or woods of the plateau.

They are all evergreen, and the tints from the new growth at certain seasons very beautiful. *Myrtaceæ*, *Lauraceæ*, and *Styraceæ* are the orders most represented by trees, and the undergrowth is chiefly composed of *Rubiaceous* shrubs and *Strobilanthes* (*Acanthaceæ*).

The following are the principal trees growing in these shólas:— —characteristic trees.

Michelia Nilagirica.
Hydnocarpus alpinus.
Gordonia obtusa.
Elæocarpus oblongus, tuberculatus and ferrugineus.
Melicope Indica.
Heynea trijuga.
Gomphandra axillaris.
Apodytes Benthamiana.
Ilex Wightiana and denticulata.
Euonymus crenulatus.
Microtropis ramiflora and densiflora.
Turpinia pomifera.
Meliosma Arnottiana and pungens.
Photinia Notoniana and Lindleyana.
Eugenia—many species.
Pentapanax Leschenaultii.
Polyscias acuminata.
Heptapleurum racemosum.
,, rostratum.
,, venulosum.
,, obovatum.
Viburnum punctatum, erubescens, hebanthum, and coriaceum.
Vaccineum Leschenaultii, and Nilagiriense.
Sapota elengioides.
Symplocos—many species.
Lasiosiphon eriocephalum.
Machilus macrantha.
Phœbe Wightii.
Cinnamomum Zeylanicum, *var.* Wightii.
Tetranthera Wightiana.
Litsœa Zeylanica.
Glochidion—several species.

The timbers are of much less value than in either of the other tracts. The following are those chiefly in use:— —timbers.

Hydnocarpus alpinus.
Gordonia obtusa.
Ternströmia Japonica.
Elæocarpus oblongus.
Ilex Wightiana.
Eugenia—several species.
Euonymus crenulatus.

CHAP. VI. — FLORA. — —ferns and mosses.

Ferns and mosses abound. Amongst the former *Alsophila latebrosa,* a tree fern, is abundant. Orchids are very poorly represented. There is one species of reed bamboo (*Arundinaria Wightiana*) and some shrubby balsams and begonias, and the following herbaceous plants may be enumerated as characteristic :—

Desmodium strangulatum.
Crotalaria barbata.
Fragaria Indica and elatior.
Sonerila speciosa.
Hydrocotyle Javanica.
Sanicula Europæa.
Senecio corymbosus.
Chrysogonum heterophylla.
Halenia Perottetii.
Pogostemon rotundatus.
,, speciosus.
Gerardinia Leschenaultii.
Elatostema diversifolia.
,, sessile.
Pilea Wightii.
Chamabainia cuspidata.

The grass-land of the plateau.

4th Tract.—The Grass-land of the Plateau.—This tract is covered with many short, coarse species of grass which are quite burnt up with the frost and sun in December and January. After the first showers in March the growth is very rapid, and numerous herbaceous plants spring up. The following are the most characteristic :—

Anemone rivalis.
Ranunculus reniformis.
,, diffusus.
,, Wallichianus.
Viola serpens.
Impatiens Beddomii.
,, Chinensis.
,, inconspicua.
,, tomentosa.
Crotalaria Formosa.
Indigofera pedicellata.
Flemingia procumbens.
Potentilla Kleiniana.
,, Leschenaultii.
,, supina.
Drosera Burmaniana.
,, Indica.
,, lunata.
Sonerila grandiflora.
Pimpinella Leschenaultii.
Heracleum ringens.
Anaphalis—several species.
Gnaphalium hypoleucum.
,, marcescens.
Senecio—several species.
Gentiana pedicellata.
Ophelia corymbosa.
,, minor.
Micromeria biflora.
Prunella vulgaris.
Pedicularis Perottetii.
,, Zeylanica.
Satyrium Nepalense.
,, Wightianum.
Habenaria—many species.
Lilium Nílagiriense.
Pteris aquilina.
Gleichenia dichotoma.

—characteristic trees and plants.

Trees are only here and there loosely scattered about these tracts. These consist chiefly of *Rhododendron arboreum, Salix tetrasperma, Celtis serotina, Pittosporum,* two species, *Dodonæa viscosa, Wendlandia Nottoniana.* The following are the most characteristic shrubs :—

Berberis Nepalensis.
,, aristata.
Hypericum Mysorense.
,, Hookerianum.
Eurya Japonica.
Indigofera pulchella.
Desmodium rufescens.
Atylosia Candollei.
Sophora glauca.
Cassia Timoriensis.
,, tomentosa.
Rubus lasiocarpus.
,, flavus.
,, rugosus.
Rosa Leschenaultiana.
Cotoneaster buxifolia.
Rhodomyrtus tomentosa.
Osbeckia Gardneriana.
Osbeckia Wightiana.
Hedyotis Lawsoniæ.
,, stylosa.
,, articularis.
,, fruticosa.
,, pruinosa.
Lobelia excelsa.
Gualtheria fragrantissima.
Ligustrum Perottetii.
,, robustum.
Jasminum revolutum.
Clerodendron serratum.
Leucas—several species.
Elœagnus latifolia.
Strobilanthes sessilis.
,, sessiloides.
,, Kunthianus.

CHAP. VI.

FLORA.

The latter plant is often gregarious and covers several acres in extent, and when out in flower is one sheet of blue, and some people say that it is from this that the Nílagiris, or Blue Hills, derive their name.

—beautiful plants.

The following may be enumerated as the most beautiful plants found in these hills :—

Fagræa Coromandelina (Slopes).
Rhododendron arboreum (Plateau).
Ceropegia Decaisneana (Sisapára Ghát).
,, elegans (Coonoor).
Exacum Perottetii (,,).
Œgenetia pedunculata (Northern Slopes).
Impatiens acaulis (Sisapára Ghát).
,, rivalis.
,, Denisonii (Sisapára Ghát).
,, Munronii (,, ,,).
,, Jerdonii (,, ,,).
,, maculata (Paikaré).
,, latifolia } (Kótagiri and
,, fruticosa } Coonóor).
Vigna Wightii (Northern Slopes).
Bauhinia Phœnicea (Sisapára Ghát).
Osbeckia Gardneriana (Plateau).
,, Wightiana (,,).
Sonerila grandiflora (Avalanché).
,, speciosa (Ootacamand).
,, elegans (Sisapára Ghát).
,, versicolor (,, ,,).
,, axillaris (,, ,,).
Passiflora Leschenaultii (Coonoor).
Pavetta siphonantha (Sisapára Ghát).
Saprosma fragrans (,, ,,).
Hamiltonia suaveolens (Kalhatti Ghát).
Vaccineum Leschenaultii (Plateau).
,, Nílagiriense (,,).
Lysimachia Japonica (,,).
Symplocos pulchra (Sisapára Ghát).
Jasminum revolutum (Plateau).
Alstonia venenata (Coonoor Ghát).
Beaumontia Jerdoniana (Northern Slopes).
Hoya pauciflora (Sisapára Ghát).
Boucerosia diffusa } (Foot of Hills,
,, umbellata } Southern).
Porana racemosa (Western Slopes).
Rivea tiliæfolia } (Foot of Hills and
Ipomea campanulata } Western Slopes).
Argyreia splendens (Western Slopes).
,, speciosa (,, ,,).
Ipomea vitifolia (Southern Slopes).
Solanum ferox (Northern Slopes).
,, Wightii (Coonoor).
Torenia Asiatica (Sisapára Ghát).
Pedicularis Perottetii (Sisapára).
Æschynanthus Zeylanica (Sisapára Ghát).
Klugia Notoniana (Coonoor Ghát).
Pajanelia Rheedii (Western Slopes).
Thunbergia Hawteyniana (Kótagiri).
,, Mysorensis } (Western
,, Wightii } Slopes).
Strobilanthes gossypinus (Sisapára).
,, luridus (Neduwattam).
,, tristis (Sisapára Ghát).
,, sexennis (Ootacamand).
,, pulcherrimus (,,).
,, paniculatus (Western Slopes).
,, violaceus (Sisapára).
Barleria involucrata (Coonoor Ghát).
Hedychium coronarium (Western Slopes).
Alpinia Rheedii (,, ,,).
Musa ornata (,, ,,).
Gloriosa superba (Southern Slopes).
Lilium Nílagiriense (,, ,,).

All the above are well worthy of introduction into gardens and hot-houses. The orchids are very poor compared to those of the Himalayas and Burmah, but the following are well worthy of cultivation :—

Dendrobium aqueum (Western Slopes).
Cælogyne—all the species (Plateau).
Arundina bambusifolia (Western Slopes).
Ipsia Malabarica (,, ,,).
Cyrtoptera flava (,, ,,).
,, fusea (,, ,,).
Vanda spathulata (Northern Slopes).
,, Roxburghi(,, ,,)
Ærides crispum (Western Slopes).
,, Lindleyana (Kátéri and Coonoor).
Calanthe masuca (Plateau in Shólas).
Platanthera Susannæ (Western Slopes).

One hundred and seventy-eight species of ferns have been detected on these hills, and probably others only known from other districts will yet be discovered on the western slopes.

Two of these ferns, *Lastrœa scabrosa* and *ferruginea* are, it is believed, not found elsewhere.

CHAP. VI. — FLORA. — List of flowering plants.—Dicotyledones.

The following is a complete list of all the flowering plants, ferns, and mosses found on these hills :—

DICOTYLEDONES.

RANUNCULACEÆ.

Clematis smilacifolia, *Wall.*
„ Gouriana, *Roxb.*
„ Wightiana, *Wall.*
Naravelia Zeylanica, *D.C.*
Anemone rivularis, *Ham.*
Thalictrum Javanicum, *Bl.*
Ranunculus reniformis, *Wall.*
„ diffusus, *D.C.*
„ Wallichianus, *Ut.*

DILLENIACEÆ.

Dillenia Indica, *L.*
„ bracteata, *W.*
Dillenia pentagyna, *Roxb.*

MAGNOLIACEÆ.

Michelia champaca, *L.*
„ Nílagirica, *Zenk.*
Kadsura Wightiana, *Ait.*

ANONACEÆ.

Uvaria Zeylanica, *L.*
Artabotrys Zeylanicus, *H. f. et T.*
Unona pannosa, *Dalz.*
Polyalthia coffeoides, *Benth. et Hk. f.*
„ fragrans, *Benth. et H. f.*
„ cerasoides, *Benth. et H. f.*
„ korinti, *Benth. et H. f.*
„ suberosa, *Benth. et H. f.*
Phœanthus Malabaricus, *Bedd.*
Miliusa Indica, *Lesch.*
„ Nílagirica, *Bedd.*
Goniothalamus Wainádensis, *Bedd.*
Saccopetalum tomentosum, *H. f. et T.*
Alphonsea lutea, *H. f. et T.*
„ Madraspatana, *Bedd.*
Orophea Thomsoni, *Bedd.*
Bocagea Dalzellii, *H. f. et T.*

MENISPERMACEÆ.

Tinospora Malabarica, *Miers.*
„ cordifolia, *Miers.*
Anamirta cocculus, *W. et A.*
Tiliacora racemosa, *Colebr.*
Cocculus villosus, *D.C.*
Stephania rotunda, *Lour.*
„ hernandifolia, *Walp.*
Cissampelos Pareira, *Linn.*
Cyclea peltata, *H. f. et T.*

BERBERIDEÆ.

Berberis Nepalensis, *Spr.*
Berberis aristata *D.C.*

PAPAVERACEÆ.

Argemone Mexicana, *L.*

FUMARIACEÆ.

Fumaria parviflora, *Loun.*

CRUCIFERÆ.

Nasturtium officinale, *Br.*
„ Indicum, *D.C.*
Cardamine Africana, *L.*
„ subumbellata, *Hook.*
Cardamine hirsuta, *L.*
Capsella Bursa-pastoris, *Mönch.*
Lepidium sativum, *L.*

CAPPARIDEÆ.

Cleome monophylla, *L.*
„ viscosa, *L.*
Gynandropsis pentaphylla, *D.C.*
Niebuhria liearis, *D.C.*
Cratæva religiosa, *Forst.*
Cadaba Indica, *Lamk.*
Capparis grandiflora, *Wall.*
Capparis Zeylanica, *Linn.*
„ divaricata, *Lamk.*
„ aphylla, *Rottb.*
„ Roxburghii, *D.C.*
„ grandis, *L. f.*
„ horrida, *L. f.*
„ tenera, *Daly.*

VIOLACEÆ.

Viola Patrinii, *D.C.*
,, serpens, *Wall.*
Ionidium suffruticosum, *Guig.*

BIXINEÆ.

Cochlospermum gossypium, *D.C.*
Scolopia crenata, *Clos.*
Flacourtia montana, *Grah.*
Flacourtia sepiaria, *Roxb.*
Hydnocarpus Wightiana, *Bl.*
,, alpina, *Wight.*

PITTOSPOREÆ.

Pittosporum tetraspermum, *Ut.*
,, Nílagiriense, *W. et A.*
Pittosporum floribundum, *W. et A.*

POLYGALEÆ.

Polygala arillata, *Hom.*
,, Javana, *D.C.*
,, leptalea, *D.C.*
,, persicariæfolia, *D.C.*
,, erioptera, *D.C.*
,, elongata, *Kleni.*
Polygala Chinensis, *L.*
,, Sibirica, *L.*
,, telephioides, *Willd.*
Salomonia oblongifolia, *D.C.*
Xanthophyllum flavescens, *Roxb.*

CARYOPHYLLEÆ.

Silene gallica, *L.*
Cerastium Indicum, *W. et A.*
,, vulgatum, *L.*
Stellaria paniculata, *Edg.*
Stellaria uliginosa, *L.*
Arenaria Nílagiriensis, *W. et A.*
Spergula arvensis, *L.*
Drymaria cordata, *Willd.*

PORTULACACEÆ.

Portulaca oleracea, *L.*
,, Wightiana, *Wall.*
Talinum cuneifolium, *Willd.*

ELATINEÆ.

Elatine Americana, *Arnt.*
Bergia ammannioides, *Roxb.*
Bergia verticellata, *Willd.*

HYPERICINEÆ.

Hypericum Mysorense, *Heyne.*
,, Hookerianum, *W. et A.*
,, humifusum, *L.*
Hypericum Nepaulense, *Choisy.*
,, Japonicum, *Thunb.*

GUTTIFERÆ.

Garcinia Cambogia, *Desrouss.*
,, Morella, *Desrouss.*
,, ovalifolius, *Hook f.*
Calophyllum tomentosum, *W.*
,, Wightianum, *Wall.*
Calophyllum Walkeri, *Wight.*
Mesua speciosa, *Choisy.*
,, Coromandelina, *Wight.*
Pœciloneuron Indicum, *Bedd.*

TERNSTRÖMIACEÆ.

Ternströmia Japonica, *Thunb.*
Eurya Japonica, *Thunb.*
Gordonia obtusa, *Wall.*

DIPTEROCARPEÆ.

Dipterocarpus turbinatus, *Gært.*
Ancistrocladus Heyneanus, *Wall.*
Vatica Roxburghiana, *B.C.*
Shorea Talura, *Roxb.*
Hopea parviflora, *Bedd.*
,, Wightiana, *Wall.*
,, Malabarica, *Bedd.*
Vateria Indica, *L.*

MALVACEÆ.

Malva verticellata, *L.*
Sida humilis, *Willd.*
,, Mysorensis, *W. et A.*
,, spinosa, *L.*
,, carpinifolia, *L.*
,, rhombifolia, *L.*
,, cordifolia, *L.*
Abutilon Asiaticum, *G. Don.*
,, Indicum, *G. Don.*
,, graveolens, *W. et A.*
,, crispun, *G. Don.*
,, Nílagiriense, *Munro.*
Urena lobata, *L.*
,, sinuata, *L.*
,, repanda, *Roxb.*
Pavonia glechomifolia, *A. Rich.*
Pavonia odorata, *Willd.*
Decaschistia trilobata, *Wight.*
,, crotonifolia, *W. et A.*
Hibiscus solandra, *L'Her.*
,, canescens, *Heyne.*
,, lunariifolius, *Willd.*
,, panduræformis, *Burn.*
,, vitifolius, *L.*
,, cannabinus, *L.*
,, angulosus, *Most.*
Thespesia Lampas, *Dalz. and Gibs.*
Kydia calycina, *Roxb.*
Bombax Malabaricum, *D.C.*
Eriodendron anfraetuosum, *D.C.*
Cullenia excelsa, *Wight.*

STERCULIACEÆ.

Sterculia fœtida, *L.*
,, urens, *Roxb.*
,, villosa, *Roxb.*
,, guttata, *Roxb.*
,, colorata, *Roxb.*
Helicteres isora, *L.*
Pterospermum Heyneanum, *Wall.*
,, glabrescens, *W. et A.*
Eriolæna Hookeriana, *W. et A.*
,, quinquelocularis, *Wight.*
Melhania incana, *Heyne.*
,, cannabina *Wight.*
Melochia corchorifolia, *L.*
Waltheria Indica, *L.*
Leptonychia moacuroides, *Bedd.*

TILIACEÆ.

Grewia columnaris, *Sw.*
,, emarginata, *W. et A.*
,, populifolia, *Vahl.*
,, salvifolia, *Heyne.*
,, orbiculata, *Rottl.*
,, tiliæfolia, *Vahl.*
,, pilosa, *Lam.*
,, villosa, *Willd.*
,, multiflora, *Juss.*
,, lævigata, *Vahl.*
Grewia abutilifolia, *Juss.*
Triumfetta pilosa, *Roth.*
,, rhomboidea, *Jacq.*
,, rotundifolia, *Lam.*
Corchorus olitorius, *L.*
,, trilocularis, *L.*
Elæocarpus oblongus, *Gærtn.*
,, tuberculatus, *Roxb.*
,, ferrugineus, *Wight.*
,, Munronii, *Wight.*

LINEÆ.

Linum Mysorense, *Heyne.*
Hugonia mystax, *L.*
Erythroxylon monogynum, *Roxb.*

MALPIGHIACEÆ.

Hiptage madablota, *Gærtn.*

GERANIACEÆ.

Geranium Nepalense, *Sweet.*
Oxalis corniculata, *L.*
Biophytum polyphyllum, *Munro.*
Impatiens, Beddomii, *Hook f.*
,, modesta, *Wight.*
,, orchioides, *Bedd.*
,, acaulis, *Arn.*
,, rivalis, *Wight.*
,, Denisonii, *Bedd.*
,, Chinensis, *L.*
,, Gardneriana, *Wight.*
,, setosa, *H. f. et T.*
,, Kleinii, *W. et A.*
,, inconspicua, *Benth.*
Impatiens tenella, *Heyne.*
,, oppositifolia, *L.*
,, tormentosa, *Heyne.*
,, latifolia, *L.*
,, Leschenaultii, *Wall.*
,, lucida, *Heyne.*
,, Goughii, *Wight.*
,, balsamina, *L.*
,, Munronii, *Wight.*
,, dasysperma, *Wight.*
,, fruticosa, *D. C.*
,, Jerdoniæ, *Wight.*
,, campanulata, *Wight.*
,, maculata, *Wight.*

RUTACEÆ.

Evodia Roxburghiana, *Benth.*
Melicope Indica, *Wight.*
Zanthoxylon ovalifolium, *Wight.*
,, tetraspermum, *W. et A.*
,, Rhetsa, *D.C.*
Toddalia aculeata, *Pres.*
Acronychia laurifolia, *Bl.*
Glycosmis pentaphylla, *Corr.*
Murraya exotica, *L.*
Clausena Willdenovii.
Limonia acidissima, *L.*
,, alata, *W. et A.*
Luvunga eleutherandra, *Daly.*
Paramignya monophylla, *Wight.*
Atalantia monophylla, *Corr.*
,, racemosa, *W. et A.*
,, Ceylanica, *Wight.*
Citrus aurantium, *L.*
Feronia elephantum, *Corr.*
Ægle marmelos, *Corr.*

SIMARUBEÆ.

Ailanthus excelsa, *Roxb.*

OCHNACEÆ.

Ochna squarrosa, *L.*
Gomphia angustifolia, *Vahl.*

BURSERACEÆ.

Boswellia serrata, *Roxb.*
Garuga pinnata, *Roxb.*
Balsamodendron Berryi, *Arn.*
Protium caudatum, *W. et A.*
Canarium strictum, *Roxb.*

MELIACEÆ.

Naregamia alata, *W. et A.*
Munronia Wallichii, *Wight.*
Melia Azadirachta, *L.*
,, Azedarach, *L.*
Cipadessa fruticosa, *Bl.*
Dysoxylum Malabaricum, *Bedd.*
Aglaia Roxburghiana, *Miq.*
Lansium Ánémaléanum, *Bedd.*
Amoora Rohituka, *W. et A.*
Walsura piscidia, *Roxb.*
Heynea trijuga, *Roxb.*
Beddomea Indica, *Hook f.*
,, simplicifolia, *Bedd.*
Soymida febrifuga, *Juss.*
Chickrassia tabularis, *Juss.*
Cedrela Toona, *Roxb.*
Chloroxylon Swietenia, *D.C.*

CHAILLETIACEÆ.

Chailletia gelonioides, *Hook f.*

OLACINEÆ.

Olax Wightiana, *Wall.*
Cansjera Rheedii, *Gmel.*
Opilia amentacea, *Roxb.*
Gomphandra axillaris, *Wall.*
,, polymorpha, *Wight.*
Apodytes Benthamiana, *Wight.*
,, Beddomei, *Mast.*
Mappia fœtida, *Miers.*
Sarcostigma Kleinii, *W. et A.*

ILICINEÆ.

Ilex Malabarica, *Bedd.*
,, denticulata, *Wall.*
Ilex Gardneriana, *Wight.*
,, Wightiana, *Wall.*

CELASTRINEÆ.

Euonymus Indicus, *Heyne.*
,, crenulatus, *Wall.*
,, serratifolius, *Bedd.*
,, angulatus, *Wight.*
Glyptopetalum grandiflorum, *Bedd.*
Microtropis latifolia, *Wight.*
,, ramiflora, *Wight.*
,, densiflora, *Wight.*
,, microcarpa, *Wight.*
,, ovalifolia, *Wight.*
Lophopetalum Wightianum, *Arnt.*
Pleurostylia Wightii, *W. et A.*
Celastrus paniculata, *Willd.*
Gymnosporia emarginata, *Roth.*
,, montana, *Roxb.*
Elæodendron glaucum, *Pers.*
Hippocratea obtusifolia, *Roxb.*
Salacia prionoides, *D.C.*
,, oblonga, *Wall.*

RHAMNEÆ.

Ventilago Madraspatana, *Gærtn.*
„ Bombaiensis, *Dalz.*
Zizyphus jujuba, *Lamk.*
„ glabrata, *Heyne.*
„ nummularia, *W. et A.*
„ œnoplia, *Mill.*
„ xylopyrus, *Willd.*
„ incurva, *Roxb.*
Zizyphus horrida, *Roth.*
„ rugosa, *Lamk.*
Rhamnus Wightii, *W. et A.*
Scutea Indica, *Brongn.*
Sageretia oppositifolia, *Brongn.*
Colubrina Asiatica, *Brongn.*
Gouania microcarpa, *D.C.*

AMPELIDEÆ.

Vitis quadrangularis, *Wall.*
„ repens, *W. et A.*
„ discolor, *Daly.*
„ adnata, *Wall.*
„ tomentosa, *Heyne.*
„ latifolia, *Roxb.*
„ Indica, *L.*
Vitis Rheedii, *W. et A.*
„ Himalayana, *Brand.*
„ auriculata, *Roxb.*
„ lanceolaria, *Roxb.*
„ pedata, *Vahl.*
Leea macrophylla, *Roxb.*
„ sambucina, *Willd.*

SAPINDACEÆ.

Cardiospermum halicacabum, *L.*
„ canescens, *Wall.*
Hemigyrosa deficiens, *Bedd.*
Erioglossum edule, *B.C.*
Allophyllus cobbe, *Bl.*
Schleichera trijuga, *Willd.*
Sapindus erectus, *Hiern.*
Nephelium Longana, *Camb.*
Harpulia cupanoides, *Roxb.*
Dodonæa viscosa, *Lam.*
Turpina pomifera, *Vent.*

SABEACEÆ.

Meliosma Arnottiana, *Wight.*
„ pungens, *Wall.*
Meliosma simplicifolia, *Roxb.*

ANACARDIACEÆ.

Rhus Mysorensis, *Heyne.*
Mangifera Indica, *L.*
Buchanania latifolia, *Roxb.*
Odina Wodier, *Roxb.*
Semecarpus anacardium, *L.*
Semecarpus Grahami, *Wight.*
Holigarna longifolia, *Roxb.*
Nothopegia Colebrookiana, *Bl.*
Spondias mangifera, *Pers.*

CONNARACEÆ.

Connarus monocarpus, *L.*

LEGUMINOSÆ.

Sub-Order Papilionaceæ.

Crotalaria rubiginosa, *Willd.*
„ *var.* Wightiana, *Grah.*
„ calycina, *Schr.*
„ barbata, *Grah.*
„ Mysorensis, *Roth.*
„ hirta, *Willd.*
„ speciosa, *Heyne.*
„ fulva, *Roth.*
„ longipes, *W. et A.*
„ obtecta, *Grah.*
„ candicans, *W. et A.*
„ Madurensis, *Wight.*
„ juncea, *L.*
„ Formosa, *Grah.*
„ Leschenaultii, *D.C.*
„ retusa, *L.*
„ verrucosa, *L.*
Crotalaria tecta, *Roth.*
„ sericea, *Retzy.*
„ semperflorens, *Vent.*
„ evolvuloides, *Wight.*
„ dubia, *Grah.*
„ acicularis, *Ham.*
„ humifusa, *Grah.*
„ albida, *Heyne.*
„ linifolia, *L.*
„ biflora, *L.*
„ nana, *Burm.*
„ Notonii, *W. et A.*
„ laburnifolia, *L.*
„ clavata, *W. et A.*
Psoralea corylifolia, *L.*
Indigofera cordifolia, *Heyne.*
„ enneaphylla, *L.*

Indigofera uniflora, *Heyne.*
,, pentaphylla, *L.*
,, viscosa, *Lam.*
,, tenuifolia, *Rottl.*
,, pedicellata, *W. et A.*
,, parvifolia, *Heyne.*
,, flaccida, *Kœn.*
,, pulchella, *Roxb.*
,, cœrulea, *Roxb.*
Tephrosia tinctoria, *Pers.*
,, incana, *Grah.*
,, diffusa, *W. et A.*
,, calophylla, *Bedd.*
Mundulea suberosa, *Benth.*
Milletea splendens, *W. et A.*
Smithia capitata, *Dalz.*
,, setulosa, *Dalz.*
,, gracilis, *Benth.*
,, blanda, *Wall.*
Geissaspis cristata, *W. et A.*
Zornia angustifolia, *Sw.*
Ougeinia dalbergioides, *Benth.*
Desmodium cephalotes, *Wall.*
,, triquetrum, *D.C.*
,, latifolium, *D.C.*
,, gyrans, *D.C.*
,, polycarpum, *D.C.*
,, rufescens, *D.C.* (ferrugineum, *Wall.*)
,, scalpe, *D.C.*
,, heterophyllum, *D.C.*
,, pulchellum, *D.C.*
,, congestum, *Wight.*
Desmodium Wightii, *Grah.*
Pseudarthria viscida, *W. et A.*
Alysicarpus monilifer, *D.C.*
,, nummularifolius, *D.C.*
,, styracifolius, *D.C.*
,, rugosus, *D.C.*
,, racemosus, *Benth.*
Abrus precatorius, *L.*
Clitoria ternatea, *L.*
Dumasia villosa, *D.C.*
Shuteria vestita, *W. et A.*
Teramnus labialis, *L.*
Erythrina Indica, *L.*
,, stricta, *Roxb.*
,, suberosa, *Roxb.*
Mucuna monospermum, *D.C.*
,, gigantea, *D.C.*
Butea frondosa, *Roxb.*
Spatholobus parviflorus, *Roxb.*
Galactia tenuiflora, *W. et A.*
Pueraria tuberosa, *D.C.*
Phaseolus Mungo, *L.*
,, trinervius, *Heyne.*
,, semierectus, *L.*
Vigna Wightii, *Benth.*
Dolichos falcatus, *Klein.*
Dunbaria Heynei, *W. et A.*
Atylosia Candollei, *W. et A.*
,, albicans, *Benth.*
,, rugosa, *W. et A.*
,, scarabœoides, *Benth.*
Cylista scariosa, *Ait.*
Rhynchosia minima, *D.C.*
,, sericea, *Span.*
,, filipes, *Benth.*
Flemingia Grahamiana, *W. et A.*
,, procumbens, *Wight.*
Dalbergia latifolia, *Roxb.*
,, paniculata, *Roxb.*
,, frondosa, *Roxb.*
Pterocarpus marsupium, *Roxb.*
Derris oblonga, *Benth.*
,, scandens, *W. et A.*
Pongamia glabra, *Vent.*
Calpurnia aurea, *Lam.*
Sophora heptaphylla, *L.*
,, glauca, *Lesch.*

Sub-Order Cæsalpinieæ.

Mezoneuron cucullatum, *W. et A.*
Cæsalpinia paniculata, *Roxb.*
,, mimosoides, *Lam.*
Pterolobium lacerans, *Br.*
Acrocarpus fraxinifolius, *Wight.*
Wagatea spicata, *Dalz.*
Poinciana elata, *L.*
Cassia fistula, *L.*
,, tomentosa, *L.*
,, Timoriensis, *D.C.*
,, montana, *Heyne.*
,, auriculata, *L.*
,, occidentalis, *L.*
Cassia pumila, *Lam.*
,, Wallichiana, *D.C.*
,, Kleinii, *W. et A.*
Bauhinia racemosa, *Lam.*
,, Malabarica, *Roxb.*
,, purpurea, *L.*
,, Vahlii, *W. et A.*
,, Benthamii, *Bedd.*
Humboldtia Brunonis, *Wall.*
,, Vahliana, *Wight.*
Tamarindus Indicus, *L.*
Hardwickia binata, *Roxb.*

Sub-Order Mimosæ.

Entada Pursætha, *D.C.*
Prosopis spicigera, *L.*
Dicrostachys cinerea, *D.C.*
Mimosa rubicaulis, *Lam.*
Xylia dolabriformis, *Benth.*
Acacia Arabica, *Willd.*
,, leucophlœa, *Willd.*
,, Catechu, *Willd.*
,, sundra, *Roxb.*
,, ferruginea, *Willd.*
Acacia pennata, *Willd.*
,, cæsia, *W. et A.*
,, Intsia, *Willd.*
Albizzia Lebbek, *Willd.*
,, odoratissima, *Willd.*
,, stipulata, *D.C.*
,, amara, *Willd.*
,, procera, *Willd.*
Pithecolobium bigeminum, *Willd.*
,, dulce, *Willd.*

ROSACEÆ.

Parinarium Indicum, *Bedd.*
Pygeum Ceylanicum, *Gærtn.*
Rubus lasiocarpus, *Sw.*
„ flavus, *Ham.*
„ rugosus, *Sw.*
Fragaria Indica, *Andr.*
„ elatior, *W. et A.*
Potentilla Kleiniana, *W. et A.*
Potentilla Leschenaultiana.
„ supina, *W. et A.*
Alchemilla vulgaris, *L.*
Rosa Leschenaultiana, *Red. et Thor.*
Cotoneaster buxifolia, *Wall.*
Photinea Notoniana, *Wall.*
„ Lindleyana, *W. et A.*

SAXIFRAGEÆ.

Parnassia Wightiana, *Wall.*

CRASSULACEÆ.

Bryophyllum calycinum, *Salisb.*
Kalanchoe laciniata, *D.C.*
Kalanchoe grandiflora, *Wall.*

DROSERACEÆ.

Drosera Burmanni, *Vahl.*
„ Indica, *L.*
Drosera lunata, *Ham.*

HALORAGEÆ.

Serpicula Indica, *Thw.*
Myriophyllum Indicum, *Willd.*

RHIZOPHOREÆ.

Carallia integerrima, *D.C.*

COMBRETACEÆ.

Terminalia tomentosa, *Roxb.*
„ paniculata, *Roxb.*
„ Arjuna, *Roxb.*
„ Bellerica, *Roxb.*
„ catappa, *Willd.*
Terminalia chebula, *Retz.*
Anogeissus latifolius, *Wall.*
Combretum Wightiana, *Wall.*
Quisqualis Malabarica, *Bedd.*
Gyrocarpus Jacquini, *Roxb.*

MYRTACEÆ.

Psidium guyava, *L.*
Rhodomyrtus tomentosa, *D.C.*
Eugenia jambolana, *L.*
„ calophyllifolia, *Wight.*
„ Arnottiana, *Wight.*
„ montana, *Wight.*
„ Malabarica, *Bedd.*
„ lanceolata, *Wight.*
Eugenia Wightii, *Bedd.*
„ Munronii, *Wight.*
„ hemisphærica, *Wight.*
„ bracteata, *Roxb.*
„ Mooniana, *Wight.*
Barringtonia racemosa, *Roxb.*
Careya arborea, *Roxb.*

MELASTOMACEÆ.

Osbeckia Leschenaultiana.
„ Gardneriana, *Wight.*
„ Wightiana, *Benth.*
„ aspera, *Bl.*
Melastoma Malabathricum, *L.*
Sonerila grandiflora, *Wight.*
„ speciosa, *Zenker.*
Sonerila elegans, *Wight.*
„ versicolor, *Wight.*
„ axillaris, *Wight.*
„ Rheedii, *Wall.*
Medinilla radicans, *Don.*
Memecylon umbellatum, *Burm.*

LYTHRARIEÆ.

Woodfordia tomentosa, *Salisb.*
Lagerstrœmia Reginæ, *Roxb.*
Lagerstrœmia microcarpa, *Wight.*
„ lanceolata, *Wall.*

ONOGRARIEÆ.

Jussiæa villosa, *Lam.*
Ludwigia prostrata, *Roxb.*
Circæa alpina, *Wight.*

SAMYDACEÆ.

Casearia tomentosa, *Roxb.*
,, esculenta, *Roxb.*
Casearia Wainádensis, *Bedd.*
Homalium Ceylanicum, *Gard.*

PASSIFLOREÆ.

Passiflora Leschenaultii.
Modecca Wightiana, *Vahl.*

CUCURBITACEÆ.

Trichosanthes palmata, *Roxb.*
,, sp.
Gymnopetalum Wightii, *Arnt.*
Luffa pentandra, *Roxb.*
Momordica dioica, *Roxb.*
Cucumis pubescens, *Willd.*
Citrullus colocynthis, *L.*
Cephalandra Indica, *W. et A.* (Coccinia).
Bryonia laciniosa, *L.*
Mukia scabella, *Arn.*
Zanonia Indica, *L.*

BEGONIACEÆ.

Begonia Malabarica, *Dry.*
,, dipetala, *Grah.*
,, subpeltata, *Wight.*
Begonia fallax, *D.C.*
,, minima, *Bedd.*

DATISCEÆ.

Tetrameles nudiflora, *R. Br.*

FICOIDEÆ.

Mollugo spergula, *L.*

UMBELLIFERÆ.

Hydrocotyle conferta, *Wight.*
,, Javanica, *Thunb.*
Sanicula Europæa, *var.* elata, *Ham.*
Bupleurum distichophyllum, *W. et A.*
,, mucronatum, *W. et A.*
,, falcatum, *L.*
,, plantaginifolium, *Wight.*
Pimpinella Candolleana, *W. et A.*
,, Leschenaultii, *D.C.*
Schultzia involucrata, *Miq.*
Heracleum Sprenglianum, *W. et A.*
,, Hookerianum, *W. et A.*
,, rigens, *W. et A.*
,, ligusticifolia, *W. et A.*

ARALIACEÆ.

Aralia Malabarica, *Bedd.*
Pentapanax Leschenaultii, *D.C.*
Polyscias acuminata, *Wight.*
Heptapleurum racemosum, *Wight.*
Heptapleurum rostratum, *Wight.*
,, obovatum, *Wight.*
,, venulosum, *W. et A.*
,, sp. nov.? (Sisapára Ghát.)

LORANTHACEÆ.

Loranthus loniceroides, *L.*
,, Nílagiriensis, *W. et A.*
,, intermedius, *Wight.*
,, recurvus, *Wall.*
,, Buddleoides, *Desr.*
,, memecylifolius, *W. et A.*
,, longiflorus, *Desr.*
Loranthus tomentosus, *Heyne.*
,, lageniferus, *Wight.*
Viscum moniliforme, *Bl.*
,, orbiculatum, *Wight.*
,, orientale, *Willd.*
,, capitellatum, *Sm.*

CORNACEÆ.

Alangium Lamarckii, *Thw.*
Mastixia arborea, *Wight.*

CHAP. VI.

FLORA.

CAPRIFOLIACEÆ.

Lonicera ligustrina, *Wall.*
,, Leschenaultii, *Wall.*
Viburnum punctatum, *Ham.*
Viburnum erubescens, *Wall.*
,, hebanthum, *W. et A.*
,, coriaceum, *Bl.*

RUBIACEÆ.

Anthocephalus Cadambus, *Roxb.*
Adina cordifolia, *Roxb.*
Stephegyne parvifolia, *Roxb.*
Hymenodictyon obovatum, *Wall.*
,, excelsum, *Roxb.*
Wendlandia Notoniana, *Wall.*
Dentella repens, *Forst.*
Argostemma *sp.* ?
Neurocalyx Hookerianus, *Wight.*
Hedyotis Lawsoniæ, *W. et A.*
,, stylosa, *Br.*
,, articularis, *Br.*
,, fruticosa, *L.*
,, pruinosa, *W. et A.*
,, verticellaris, *Wall.*
,, hirsutissima, *Bedd.*
,, auricularia, *L.*
,, glabella, *Br.*
Oldenlandia Heynei, *Br.*
,, aspera, *Heyne.*
Anotis Leschenaultiana, *W. et A.*
,, monosperma, *W. et A.*
,, affinis, *W. et A.*
,, Rheedii, *W. et A.*
,, Wightiana, *Wall.*
Ophiorhiza mungos, *L.*
,, sp.
Mussænda frondosa, *L.*
Webera Asiatica, *L.*
Randia dumetorum, *Law.*
,, fragrans, *Kœn.*
,, speciosa *Bedd.*
Gardenia lucida, *Roxb.*
,, gummifera, *L.*
,, latifolia, *Ait.*
Diplospora apiocarpa, *Dalz.*
Knoxia corymbosa, *Willd.*
Canthium didymum, *Gærtn.*
,, parviflorum, *Roxb.*
,, Rheedii, *D.C.*
,, Leschenaultii, *D.C.*
,, Nílagiriense, *D.C.*
Ixora parviflora, *Vahl.*
,, acuminata, *Roxb.*
,, nigricans, *Br.*
,, lanceolata, *Cohb.*
Pavetta Indica, *L.*
,, tomentosa, *Roxb.*
,, breviflora, *D.C.*
,, siphonantha, *Dalz.*
Coffea alpestis, *Wight.*
,, grumelioides, *Wight.*
Morinda umbellata, *L.*
Psychotria elongata, *Wight.*
,, congesta, *W. et A.*
,, bisulcata, *W. et A.*
Charasia curviflora, *Wall.*
Geophila reniformis, *Desc.*
Lasianthus venulosus, *W. et A.*
,, cyanocarpus, *Jack.*
,, ciliatus, *Wight.*
,, capitulatus, *Wight.*
Saprosma Wightii, *Gardn.*
,, fragrans, *Bedd.*
,, glomerata, *Gardn.*
Fergusonia tetracocca, *Thw.*
Hamiltonia suaveolens, *Roxb.*
Spermacoce articularis, *L.*
,, hispida, *L.*
Rubia cordifolia, *L.*
Galium asperifolium, *Wall.*
,, Requienianum, *W. et A.*

VALERIANEÆ.

Valeriana Brunoniana, *W. et A.*
,, Leschenaultii, *Dec.*
Valeriana Arnottiana, *Wight.*

DIPSACEÆ.

Dipsacus Leschenaultii.

COMPOSITEÆ.

Centratherum reticulatum, *Wight.*
Vernonia divergens, *Benth.*
,, Wightiana, *D.C.*
,, pectiniformis, *D.C.*
,, Candolleana, *W.*
,, elliptica, *D.C.*
,, cinerea, *Lesc.*
Elephantopus scaber, *L.*
Adenostemma viscosum, *Forst.*
Ageratum conyzoides, *L.*
Dicrocephala chrysanthemifolia, *D.C.*
,, latifolia, *D.C.*
Centipeda minuta, *Benth.*
Cyathocline lyrata, *Car.*
Grangea Madraspatana, *Poir.*
Myriactis Wightii, *D.C.*
Pulicaria Wightiana, *Benth.*
Erigeron acre, *L.*
Conyza absinthifolia, *D.C.*
Blumea hieracifolia, *D.C.*
Laggera alata, *D.C.*
,, pterodonta, *D.C.*
Pluchea tomentosa, *D.C.*
Sphæranthus hirtus, *Wills.*
Anaphalis Nílagiriana, *D.C.*
,, Notoniana, *D.C.*

Anaphalis Wightiana, *Wall.*
„ aristata, *D.C.*
„ elliptica, *D.C.*
„ marcescens, *W.*
Gnaphalium hypoleucum, *D.C.*
Helichrysum Buddleoides, *D.C.*
Vicoa Indica, *D.C.*
Carpesium Nepalense, *Lesc.*
Chrysogonum heterophyllum, *Arnt.*
Xanthium strumarium, *L.*
Siegesbeckia orientalis, *L.*
Eclipta alba, *Hassk.*
Wedelia biflora, *Benth.*
„ „ *var.* urticæfolia, *Roxb.*
Glossocardia Boswellea, *D.C.*
Bidens pilosa, *Linn.*
Artemisia parviflora, *Roxb.*
„ vulgaris, *L.*
Gynura nitida, *D.C.*
Emilia scabra, *D.C.*
„ sonchifolia, *D.C.*
Notonia grandiflora, *D.C.*
Senecio araneosus, *D.C.*
„ Walkeri, *Wight.*
„ tomentosus, *Wight.*
„ Wightii, *D.C.*
„ multifidus, *Willd.*
„ polycephalus, *D.C.*
„ Lessengianus, *Arn.*
„ pinnatifidus, *Benth.*
„ Nílagirianus, *D.C.*
„ lavandulæfolius, *D.C.*
„ campylodes, *D.C.*
„ intermedius, *Wight.*
„ Wightianus, *D.C.*
Cnicus argyracanthus, *D.C.*
Volutarella procumbens, *Wight.*
Picris hieracioides, *L.*
Lactuca glabra, *Wight.*
„ hastata, *D.C.*
Sonchus arvensis, *L.*
„ oleraceus, *L.*
Lactuca Heyneana, *D.C.*

CAMPANULACEÆ.

Wahlenbergia agrestris, *D.C.*
„ Indica, *D.C.*
Campanula fulgens, *Wall.*
„ Alphonsii, *Wall.*
Campanula ramulosa, *Wall.*
Lobelia excelsa, *Lesch.*
„ rosea, *Wall.*
„ trigona, *Roxb.*

ERICACEÆ.

Vaccinium Leschenaultii, *Wight.*
„ Nilagiriense, *Wight.*
„ rotundifolium, *Wight.*
Gualtheria fragrantissima, *Wall.*
Rhododendrum arboreum, *Sw.*

PRIMULACEÆ.

Lysimachia Japonica, *Triml.*
„ Leschenaultii, *Dub.*
Anagallis arvensis, *L.*

MYRSINEÆ.

Mœsa Indica, *D.C.*
Embelia ribes, *Burm.*
„ robusta, *Roxb.*
„ glandulifera, *Wight.*
„ Gardneriana, *Wight.*
Samara viridiflora, *D.C.*
Myrsine capitellata, *Wall.*
Ardisia pauciflora, *Heyne.*
„ humilis, *Vahl.*
Antistrophe serratifolia, *Bedd.*

SAPOTACEÆ.

Chrysophyllum Roxburghii, *G. Don.*
Sapota elengioides.
Mimusops Roxburghiana, *Wight.*
Bassia elliptica, *Dalz.*
„ Wightiana, *D.C.*

EBENACEÆ.

Diospyros embryopteris, *Pers.*
„ montana, *Roxb.*
„ cordifolia, *Roxb.*
„ ebenum, *Retz.*
„ sylvatica, *Roxb.*
„ melanoxylon, *Roxb.*
Diospyros ovalifolia, *Wight.*
„ Candolliana, *Wight.*
„ paniculata, *Dalz.*
„ ramiflora, *Roxb.*
„ pruriens, *Dalz.*
Maba buxifolia, *Pers.*

STYRACEÆ.

Symplocos pendula, *Wight.*
„ spicata, *Roxb.*
„ obtusa, *Wall.*
„ pulchra, *Wight.*
Symplocos Gardneriana, *Wight.*
„ microphylla, *Wight.*
„ foliosa, *Wight.*
„ nervosa, *D.C.*

CHAP. VI.

FLORA.

JASMINEÆ.

Jasminum erectiflorum, *D.C.*
,, revolutum, *Linn.*
,, rigidum, *J.*
,, sambac, *Ait.*
,, cordifolium, *Wall.*
,, brevilobum, *D.C.*
,, flexile, *Vahl.*
Chondrospermum laurifolium, *Wight.*
Olea glandulifera, *Wall.*
,, robusta, *Wall.*
,, polygama, *Wight.*
Ligustrum Perottetii, *D.C.*
,, robustum, *Roxb.*
Chionanthus intermedia, *Wight.*
,, Malabarica, *Wall.*
Schrebera Swietenioides, *Roxb.*

APOCYNACEÆ.

Ophioxylon densiflorum, *Wall.*
,, serpentinum, *Wills.*
Carissa carandas, *L.*
Tabernamontana dichotoma, *Roxb.*
Wrightea tinctoria, *Br.*
,, tomentosa, *R. Seb.*
,, Wallichii, *D.C.*
Alstonia scholaris, *Br.*
,, venenata, *Br.*
Holarrhena antidysenterica, *Wall.*
Anodendron paniculatum, *D. C.*
Chonemorpha macrophylla, *Don.*
Beaumontia Jerdoniana, *Wight.*
Chilocarpus Malabarica, *Rudd.*
Ichnocarpus frutescens, *Br.*
,, elegans, *Don.*
Plumiera acutifolia, *L.*

ASCLEPIADEÆ.

Hemidesmus Indicus, *Br.*
Brachylepis nervosa, *Wight.*
Vincetoxicum pauciflorum, *Decaisne.*
,, callialata, *Ham.*
Holostemma Rheedii, *Spr.*
Calotropis gigantea, *Br.*
Dæmia extensa, *Br.*
Tylophora molissima, *Wall.*
,, fasciculata, *Ham.*
,, Iphsia, *D.C.*
,, pauciflora, *W. et A.*
,, asthmatica, *W. et A.*
Marsdenia tenacissima, *W. et A.*
Gymnema sylvestre, *Br.*
,, hirsutum, *W. et A.*
Hoya pauciflora, *Wight.*
,, viridiflora, *Br.*
,, pendula, *W. et A.*
Bidaria elegans, *Decaisne.*
Ceropegia elegans, *Wall.*
,, pusilla, *W. et A.*
,, Decaisneana, *Wight.*
Caralluma attenuata, *Wight.*
Boucerosia diffusa, *Wight.*
,, umbellata, *W. et A.*

LOGANIACEÆ.

Mitreola oldenlandioides, *Wall.*
Fagræa Coromandelina, *Wight.*
,, obovata, *Wall.*
Strychnos nux vomica, *L.*
Strychnos cinnamonifolia, *Thun.*
Gardnera ovata, *Wall.*
Buddleia Asiatica, *Lour.*

GENTIANEÆ.

Exacum Perottetii, *G.*
,, bicolor, *Roxb.*
,, pedunculatum, *L.*
,, sessile, *L.*
Canscora diffusa, *Br.*
,, decussata, *Reom. et Sch.*
,, sessiliflora, *Reom. et Sch.*
Canscora perfoliata, *Lam.*
Gentiana pedicellata, *Wall.*
Slevogtia orientalis, *Griseb.*
Ophelia corymbosa, *Griseb.*
,, minor, *Griseb.*
Halenia Perottetii, *D.C.*

BORAGINEÆ.

Cordia myxa, *L.*
,, Wallichii, *Don.*
,, monoica, *Roxb.*
,, Rothii, *Reom. et Sch.*
Ehretia lævis, *Roxb.*
,, aspera, *Roxb.*
,, ovalifolia, *Wight.*
Rhabdia viminea, *Dalz.*
Tournefortia reticosa, *Wight.*
Heliotropium linifolium, *Lehm.*
Heliophytum Indicum, *D.C.*
Cynoglossum furcatum, *Wall.*
Trichodesma Indicum, *L.*

CONVOLVULACEÆ.

Erycibe paniculata, *Roxb.*
Convolvulus rufescens, *Choisy.*
Porana racemosa, *Roxb.*
Rivea tiliæfolia, *Choisy.*
,, Zeylanica, *Gærtn.*
,, bona-nox, *Choisy.*
,, cuneata, *Wight.*
Argyreia aggregata, *Choisy.*
,, splendens, *Sweet.*
,, speciosa, *Sweet.*
,, Leschenaultii, *Choisy.*
,, cymosa, *Sweet.*
Ipomœa paniculata, *Br.*
,, nil, *Choisy.*
,, speciosum, *Choisy.*
Ipomœa campanulata, *L.*
,, pes-tigridis, *L.*
,, turpethum, *Br.*
,, Wightii, *Choisy.*
,, sepiaria, *Konig.*
,, rugosa, *Choisy.*
,, vitifolia, *Sweet.*
,, pilosa, *Sweet.*
,, sessiliflora, *Roth.*
,, obscura, *L.*
,, chryseides, *Choisy.*
Evolvulus alsinoides, *L.*
Breweria Roxburghii, *Choisy.*
Cuscuta reflexa, *Roxb.*

SOLANACEÆ.

Solanum verbascifolium, *L.*
,, ferox, *L.*
,, giganteum, *Jacq.*
,, denticulatum, *Wall.*
,, Wightii, *Nees.*
Physalis Peruviana, *L.*
Withania somnifera, *Dun.*
Datura alba, *L.*
,, fastuosa, *L.*

SCROPHULARIACEÆ.

Verbascum virgatum, *D.C.*
Limnophila hirsuta, *Bl.*
,, hypericifolia, *Benth.*
Herpestis monnieria, *H.B.K.*
Dopatrium junceum, *Ham.*
Artanema sesamoides, *Benth.*
Torenia Asiatica, *L.*
Vandellia crustacea, *Benth.*
Ilysanthes hyssopioides, *Benth.*
Bonnaya veronicæfolia, *Spr.*
Buchnera hispida, *Ham.*
Striga hirsuta, *Benth.*
Sopubia delphinifolia, *Don.*
,, trifida, *Ham.*
Centranthera Brunoniana, *Wall.*
,, hispida, *Br.*
Pedicularis Perottetii, *Benth.*
,, Zeylanica, *Benth.*
Campbellia aurantiaca, *Wight.*
,, cytinoides, *Wight.*

LENTIBULARIEÆ.

Utricularia flexuosa, *Vahl.*
,, diantha, *Roen. et Sch.*
,, cœrulea, *L.*
,, ,, *var.* B. affinis, *Wight.*
Utricularia reticulata, *L.*
,, bifida.
B. Wallichiana, *Wight.*

OROBANCHACEÆ.

Ægenetia pedunculata.

GESNERIACEÆ.

Æschynanthus Zeylanica, *Gardn.*
Didymocarpus tomentosa, *Wight.*
Klugia Notoniana, *D.C.*
Jerdonia Indica, *Wight.*
Ethithema Zeylanica, *Gardn.*

BIGNONIACEÆ.

Oroxylum Indicum, *L.*
Dolichandrone crispum, *Wall.*
,, Rheedii, *Wall.*
,, arcuatum, *Wight.*
Stereospermum suaveolens, *Roxb.*
,, xylocarpum, *Roxb.*
Pajanelia Rheedii, *Wight.*

ACANTHACEÆ.

Thunbergia Hawtaynii, *Wall.*
,, Wightiana, *Anders.*
,, Mysorensis, *Wight.*
,, fragrans, *Roxb.*
Thunbergia fragrans, *var.* tomentosa, *Anders.*
Elytraria crenata, *Vahl.*
Nelsonia tomentosa, *Willd.*
Ebermaiera glauca, *Nees.*

CHAP. VI.
FLORA.

Adenosma balsamea, *Spr.*
Hygrophila serpyllum, *Anders.*
,, salicifolia, *Nees.*
Ruellia patula, *Jacq.*
Phaylopsis parviflora, *Willd.*
Hemigraphis dura, *Nees.*
,, elegans, *Nees.*
Stenosiphonium confertum, *Nees.*
,, Russellianum, *Nees.*
Strobilanthes consanguineus, *Anders.*
,, cuspidatus, *Anders.*
,, Kunthianus, *Anders.*
,, gossypinus, *Anders.*
,, Wightianus, *Nees.*
,, punctatus, *Wight.*
,, Bolampattianus, *Bedd.*
,, Nilagiriensis, *Bedd.*
,, asper, *Wight.*
,, Perrottetianus, *Nees.*
,, anceps, *Nees.*
,, sessiloides, *Wight.*
,, sessilis, *Nees.*
,, Zenkerianus, *Nees.*
,, foliosus, *Wight.*
,, barbatus, *Nees.*
,, ciliatus, *Nees.*
,, papillosus, *Anders.*
,, micranthus, *Wight.*
,, luridus, *Wight.*
,, lupulinus, *Nees.*
,, tristis, *Wight.*
,, caudatus, *Anders.*
,, pallidus, *Anders.*
,, sexennis, *Nees.*
,, rubicundus, *Anders.*
,, pulcherrimus, *Anders.*
,, paniculatus, *Anders.*
,, violaceus, *Bedd.*
Dœdalacanthus montanus, *Roxb.*
,, roseus, *Vahl.*
Barleria cuspidata, *Wall.*
,, prionitis, *L.*
,, cristata, *L.*
,, longifolia, *L.*
,, cœrulea, *Roxb.*
,, involucrata, *Nees.*
Crossandra infundibuliformis, *Nees.*
Lepidagathis trinervis, *Nees.*
,, hyalina, *Nees.*
,, fasciculata, *Nees.*
Blepharis boerhaaviæfolia, *Pers.*
Andrographis Neesiana, *Wight.*
,, lineata, *Nees.*
,, echioides, *Nees.*
,, lobelioides, *Wight.*
Haplanthus verticellaris, *Nees.*
Gymnostachyum canescens, *Nees.*
,, serrulatum, *Anders.*
Justicia montana, *Wall.*
,, betonica, *L.*
,, procumbens, *L.*
,, Waínádensis, *Wall.*
,, Wallichii, *Nees.*
Monothecium aristatum, *Nees.*
Rungia pectinata, *Nees.*
,, repens, *Nees.*
,, latior, *Nees.*
,, Sisaparensis, *Anders.*
Dicliptera bivalvis, *Juss.*
Peristrophe bicalyculata, *Nees.*
Rhinacanthus communis, *Nees.*
Eranthemum ecbolium, *L.*
Asystasia Mysorensis, *Roth.*
,, chelonoides, *Nees.*
,, Gangetica, *L.*
,, crispata, *Benth.*

VERBENACEÆ.

Stachytarpheta Indica, *Vahl.*
Lantana alba, *Mill.*
,, mixta, *L.* (introduced).
Premna purpurescens, *Thw.* ?
,, tomentosa, *Willd.*
,, herbacea, *Roxb.*
Tectona grandis, *L.*
Clerodendron serratum, *Spr.*
Clerodendron infortunatum, *L.*
Callicarpa lanata, *L.*
Gmelina Asiatica, *L.*
,, arborea, *Roxb.*
Vitex altissima, *Heyne.*
,, leucoxylon, *Linn. f.*
,, negundo, *L.*

LABIATÆ.

Ocimum canum, *L.*
,, gratissimum, *L.*
,, sanctum, *L.*
Plectranthus bullatus, *Benth.*
,, Nilagiricus, *Benth.*
,, nigrescens, *Benth.*
,, coetsa, *Don.*
,, coleoides, *Benth.*
Coleus barbatus, *Benth.*
,, Wightii, *Benth.*
,, Malabaricus, *Benth.*
Anisochilus dysophylloides, *Benth.*
,, purpureus, *Wight.*
,, albidus, *Wight.*
,, suffruticosus, *Wight.*
Pogostemon Heyneanus, *Benth.*
,, paludosus, *Benth.*
Pogostemon atropurpureus, *Benth.*
,, rotundatus, *Benth.*
,, speciosus, *Benth.*
,, hirsutus, *Wight.*
Colebrookia ternifolia, *Benth.*
Micromeria biflora, *Benth.*
Calamintha chinopodium, *Benth.*
Prunella vulgaris, *L.*
Scutellaria violacea, *Heyne.*
,, rivularis, *Wall.*
Anisomeles ovata, *Br.*
,, Malabarica, *Br.*
Leucas cephalotes, *Spr.*
,, urticæfolia, *Br.*
,, pubescens, *Br.*
,, procumbens, *Desf.*
,, marubioides, *Desf.*

Leucas Zeylanica, *Br.*
„ suffruticosa, *Benth.*
„ rosmarinifolia, *Benth.*
„ helianthemifolia, *Desf.*
„ ternifolia, *Desf.*
Leucas lanceæfolia, *Desf.*
„ lamiifolia, *Desf.*
Gomphostemma Heyneanum, *Wall.*
Teucrium tomentosum, *Heyne.*

PLANTAGINEÆ.

Plantago major, *L.*

PODOSTOMACEÆ.

Dicræa dichotoma, *Tul.*
„ Wightii, *Tul.*
Dicræa rigida, *Tul.*
Hydrobryum griseum, *Tul.*

PHYTOLACCACEÆ.

Gieseckia pharnaceoides, *L.*

CHENOPODIACEÆ.

Chenopodium ambrosioides, *L.*
Atriplex heterantha, *Wight.*

AMARANTACEÆ.

Celosia pulchella, *Moq.*
„ argentea, *Moq.*
Chamissoa nodiflora, *Mart.*
Amaranthus oleraceus, *Roxb.*
„ frumentaceus, *Ham.*
„ caudatus, *Moq.*
Banalia thyrsiflora, *Moq.*
Ærua floribunda, *Wight.*
Ærua Javanica, *Juss.*
„ lanata, *Juss.*
„ Monsonia, *Mart.*
Achyranthes aspera, *L.*
„ „ *var.* argentea, *Lam.*
„ bidentata, *Bl.*
Cyathula prostrata, *Bl.*
Alternanthera sessilis, *Br.*

PARONYCHIACEÆ.

Polycarpæa spicata, *Wight.*
Drymaria cordata, *Willd.*

POLYGONACEÆ.

Polygonum barbatum, *L.*
„ glabrum, *Willd.*
„ minus, *Huds.*
„ strigosum, *Br.*
„ Donii, *Meissn.*
Polygonum perforatum, *Meissn.*
„ Wallichii, *Meissn.*
„ Chinense, *L.*
Rumex Nepalensis, *Spr.*

NYCTAGINEÆ.

Boerhaavia diffusa, *L.*
Pisonia aculeata, *L.*

MYRISTICEÆ.

Myristica laurifolia, *H. f. et T.*
„ corticosa, *Lour.*
Myristica Farquhariana, *Wall.*

PROTEACEÆ.

Helicia Nílagirica, *Bedd.*

THYMELÆACEÆ.

Lasiosiphon eriocephalus, *Dese.*
Cansjera Rheedii, *Gmel.*

ELŒAGNACEÆ.

Elœagnus latifolia, *L.*

SANTALACEÆ.

Santalum album, *L.*
Osyris arborea, *L.*
Thesium Wightianum, *Wall.*

SALICACEÆ.

Salix tetrasperma, *Roxb.*

LAURACEÆ.

Machilus macrantha, *Nees.*
Phœbe Wightii, *D.C.*
Cinnamomum Zeylanicum, *Breyn.* (several varieties.)
Alseodaphne semicarpifolia, *Nees.* (5,000 feet.)
Apollonias Arnottii, *Nees.*
Cryptocarya Wightiana, *Thw.* (4,000 ft.)
Tetranthera ligustrina, *Nees.* (7,000 feet.)
" Wightiana, *Nees.* (7,000 ft.)
" sebifera, *Bl.* (7,000 feet.)
Actinodaphne salicina, *D.C.* (4,000 feet.)
Litsæa Zeylanica, *Nees.*
Cassytha filiformis, *L.*

HERNANDIACEÆ.

Sarcostigma Kleinii, *W. et A.*

EUPHORBIACEÆ.

Tribe Phyllantheæ.

Actephila excelsa, *Dalz.*
Phyllanthus emblica, *L.*
" polyphyllus, *Willd.*
" Indicus, *Dalz.*
" Miquelianus, *Müll.*
" Leschenaultii, *Müll.*
" fimbriatus, *Müll.*
" Wightianus, *Müll.*
Glochidion fagifolium, *Müll.*
" Nílagiriense, *Wight.*
" Perrottetianum, *Müll.*
" velutinum, *Wight.*
" Daltoni, *Müll.*
Melanthesopsis patens, *Roxb.*
Breynia rhamnoides, *Willd.*
Putranjiva Roxburghii, *Wall.*
Securinega obovata, *Willd.*
" leucopyrus, *Kœn. in Roxb.*
Baccaurea sapida, *Roxb.*
Bischoffia Javanica, *Bl.*
Hemicyclia elata, *Bedd.*
" sepiaria, *W. et A.*
" venusta, *Wight.*
Cyclostemon macrophyllus, *Bl.*
Aporosa Lindleyana, *Wight.*
Antidesma Ghæsembilla, *Gærtn.*
" lanceolatum, *Tul.*
Sauropus quadrangularis, *Müll.*
Agyneia bacciformis, *Müll.*

Tribe Briedelieæ.

Briedelia retusa, *L.*
" stipularis, *L.*
" montana, *Willd.*
Cleistanthus patulus, *Roxb.*
" stipularis, *Hook.*
Lebidieropsis orbicularis, *Roth.*

Tribe Crotoneæ.

Croton Malabaricum, *Bedd.*
Croton aromaticum, *L.*

Tribe Acalypheæ.

Agrostistachys Indica, *Dalz.*
Sarcoclinium longifolium, *Wight.*
Cephalocroton Indicum, *Bedd.*
" leucocephalum, *Baill.*
Symphyllia mallotiformis, *Müll.*
Trewia nudiflora, *L.*
Mallotus albus, *Roxb.*
" muricatus, *Wight.*
" Philippinensis, *Lam.*
Cleidion Javanicum, *Bl.*
Macaranga tomentosa, *Wight.*
" Indica, *Wight.*
Homonoya riparia, *Lour.*
" retusa, *Wight.*
Acalypha paniculata, *Miq.*
" alnifolia, *Willd.*
" brachystachya, *Horn.*
Acalypha Indica, *L.*
Tragia Miqueliana, *Müll.*
" involucrata, *Müll.*
Claoxylon mercurialis, *L.*

Tribe Hippomaneæ.

Trigonostemon Lawianus, *Nimmo.*
Givotia Rottleriformis, *Griff.*
Ostodes Zeylanica, *Thw.*
Codiœum umbellatum, *Willd.*
Gelonium lanceolatum, *Willd.*
Excœcaria insignis, *Royle.*
Excœcaria Cochinchinensis, *Lour.*
" oppositifolia, *Jack.*
Jatropha Wightiana, *Müll.*
Baliospermum montanum, *Müll.*
Sebastiania chamælea, *Müll.*

Tribe Euphorbieæ.

Euphorbia antiquorum, *L.*
,, trigona, *Roxb.*
,, tirucalli, *L.*
,, bracteolaris, *Boiss.*
Euphorbia pycnostegia, *Boiss.*
,, pilulifera, *L.*
,, sanguinea, *Hoch. et Stend.*
,, oreophila, *Miq.*

Genera allied to Euphorbiaceæ.

Daphniphyllum gláucescens, *Bl.*
Sarcococca saligna, *Don.*

CALLITRICHACEÆ.

Callitriche verna, *L.*

CERATOPHYLLACEÆ.

Ceratophyllum verticellatum, *Roxb.*

URTICACEÆ.

Tribe Celtideæ.

Ulmus integrifolia, *Roxb.*
Celtis serotina, *Planch.*
,, Wightii, *Planch.*
Sponia Wightii, *Planch.*
Gironniera reticulata, *Thw.*

Tribe Artocarpeæ.

Artocarpus hirsuta, *Lam.*
,, integrifolia, *Willd.*
,, Lakoocha, *Roxb.*
Plecospermum spinosum, *Roxb.*
Antiaris innoxia, *Bl.*
Streblus aspera, *Lour.*
Taxotrophis Roxburghii, *Bl.*
Dorstenia Indica, *Wight.*
Ficus religiosa, *L.*
Ficus Bengalensis, *L.*
,, tomentosa, *Roxb.*
,, Tsiela, *L.*
,, retusa, *L.*
,, nervosa, *Roth.*
,, asperrima, *Roxb.*
,, glomerata, *Willd.*
,, guttata, *Wight.*

Tribe Urticeæ.

Fleurya interrupta, *Gand.*
Laportea terminalis, *Wight.*
,, crenulata, *Gand.*
Gerardinia Leschenaultii, *Decaisne.*
,, Zeylanica, *Dec.*
Pilea trinervia, *Wight.*
,, Wightii, *Wedd.*
Lecanthus peduncularis, *Wall.*
Pellionia Heyneana, *Wedd.*
Elatostema sessile, *Forst.*, *var.* cuspidatum, *Wight.*
,, lineolatum, *Wight.*
,, diversifolium, *Weddell* (sarcallosum, *Wight*).
,, approximatum, *Weddell* (cuneatum, *Wight*).
Procris lævigata, *Bl.*
Bœhmeria Malabarica.
Bœhmeria platyphylla, *Don. et Ham.*, *var.* macrostachya, *Wight.*
Chamabrinia cuspidata, *Wight.*
Pouzolzia auriculata, *Wight.*
,, ,, *var.* Rheedii, *Wight.*
,, diffusa, *Wight.*
,, cymosa, *Wight.*
,, Indica, *Gand.*, *var.* tetraptera, *Wight.*
Nemorialis pentandra, *Roxb.*, *var.* ramosissima, *Wight.*
,, Nílagiriensis, *Weddell.*
,, hirta, *Bl.*
,, ,, *var.* Bennettiana, *Wight.*
,, ,, *var.* tomentosa, *Wight.*
,, ,, *var.* Gardneri, *Wight.*
Debregeasia longifolia, *Gand.*
Droguetia pauciflora, *Weddell.*

ARISTOLOCHIACEÆ.

Aristolochia Indica, *L.*
Bragantia Wallichii, *R. Br.*

CHAP. VI.

FLORA.

PIPERACEÆ.

Peperomia Dindigulensis, *Miq.*
,, Heyneana, *Miq.*
,, reflexa, *A. Dictr.*
Pothomorphe subpeltata, *Miq.*
Chavica sphærostachya, *Miq.*
Chavica Betle, *Miq.* (Cultivated at foot of hills).
Muldera galeata, *Miq.*
Piper attenuatum, *Ham.*
,, nigrum, *L.*
,, arborescens, *Miq.*

CHLORANTHACEÆ.

Chloranthus brachystachys, *Bl.*

BALANOPHOREÆ.

Balanophora Indica, *Wall.*

CYCADEÆ.

Cycas circinalis, *L.*

—Monocotyledons.

MONOCOTYLEDONS.

ORCHIDACEÆ.

Section Malaxeæ.

Sub-Section Liparidæ.

Liparis biloba, *Wight.*
,, Wightii, *Lindl.* (=elliptica, *Wight*).
Microstylis luteola, *Wight.*
,, Rheedii, *Lindl.* (=versicolor, *Wight*).
Oberonia denticulata, *Wight.*
,, Brunoniana, *Wight.*
,, Lindleyana, *Wight.*
,, verticellata, *Wight.*
,, Wightiana, *Lindl.*
,, Arnottiana, *Wight.*

Sub-Section Dendrobiæ.

Dendrobium Pierardi, *Roxb.*
,, nutans, *Lindl.* (Jerdonianum, *Wight*).
,, aqueum, *Lindl.* (album, *W.*)
,, aureum, *Lindl.*
,, barbatulum, *Lindl.*
,, microbulbon, *A. Rich.* (humile, *W.*)
,, Macræi, *Lindl.*
Bulbophyllum Nílagiriense, *Wight.*
,, fuscopurpureum, *Wight.*
,, tremulum, *Wight.*
Cirrhopetalum Nílagiriense, *Wight.* (Bulbophyllum Kaitiense, *Walps*).
Cirrhopetalum albidum, *W.* (B. acutiflorum, *A. Rich.*)
Eria braccata, *Lindl.* (= reticosa, *Wight*).
,, polystachya, *Wight.*
,, nana, *A. Rich.*
,, pubescens, *Wight.*
,, Dalzelli, *Hook.* (= Dend. filiforme, *Wight*).
,, pauciflora, *Wight.*
Aggeianthus marchantioides, *Wight.*

Section Epidendreæ.

Sub-Section Cœlogynidæ.

Cœlogyne breviscapa, *Lindl.* (= angustifolia, *W.*)
,, odoratissima, *Lindl.*
,, glandulosa, *Lindl.* (= nervosa, *W.*)
Cœlogyne nervosa, *Lindl.*
,, corrugata, *Lindl.*
Pholidota imbricata, *Lindl.*

Sub-Section Blétidæ.

Arundina bambusæfolia, *Lindl.*
Ipsea Malabarica, *Rchb.* (= Pachystoma, *Bl.*) (? = speciosa).
Ania latifolia, *Lindl.*

Section Vandeæ.

Sub-Section Sarcanthidæ.

Eulophia virens, *Br.*
,, macrostachys, *Lindl.*
,, ramentacea, *Lindl.*
Cyrtopera fusca, *Wight.*
,, flava, *Lindl.* (= Cullenii, *W.*)
Luisia tenuifolia, *B.* (= Cymbidium tenuifolia, *W.*)
,, trichorhiza, *Bl.*
Cottonia peduncularis, *Lindl.* (= C. macrostachys, *Wight*).
Vanda Roxburghii, *Br.*
,, spathulata, *Spr.*
Acampe Wightiana, *Lindl.* (Vanda, *Wight*).
Chiloschista usucoides, *Wight.*
Saccolabium præmorsum, *Lindl.*
,, ringens, *Lindl.* (= S. rubrum, *Wight*).
Saccolabium paniculatum, *Wight.*
,, roseum, *Lindl.* (= sarcanthus, *Wight*).
,, filiformis, *Lindl.*
,, calceolaria, *Lindl.* (= Vanda pulchella, *Wight*).
Sarcanthus peninsularis, *Dalz.* (= S. pauciflorus, *Wight*).
Tœniophyllum Jerdonianum, *Wight.*
Ærides Wightianum, *Lindl.*
,, crispum, *Lindl.* (Saccolabium speciosum, *W.*)
• ,, Lindleyanum, *Wight.*
,, cylindricum, *Lindl.*
Diplocentrum congestum, *Wight.*
,, recurvum, *Lindl.* (= longifolium, *Wight*).
Josephia lanceolata, *Wight.*

Sub-Section Cryptochilidæ.

Acanthophippium bicolor, *Lindl.*

Sub-Section Brassidæ.

Cymbidium aloifolium, *Sw.*
Cymbidium erectum, *Wight.*

Sub-Section Maxillaridæ.

Polystachya luteola, *Hook.* (= P. Wightii, *Walpers*).

Sub-Section Calanthidæ.

Calanthe Masuca, *Lindl.* (= emarginata, *Wight*).
,, Perottetii, *A. Rich.*
Calanthe veratrifolia, *R. Br.*
Geodorum dilatatum, *R. Br.*

Section Ophreæ.

Sub-Section Satyriadæ.

Satyrium Nepalense, *Don.* (= Perottetianum, *Wight*, albidiflorum, *Wight*).
Satyrium Wightianum, *Lindl.*

Sub-Section Gymnadenidæ.

Ate virens, *Lindl.*
Habenaria viridiflora, *Br.*
,, plantaginea, *Lindl.*
,, crinifera, *Lindl.*
,, Heyneana, *Lindl.*
,, rariflora, *A. Rich.*
,, longicalcarata, *A. Rich.*
,, montana, *A. Rich.*
,, cephalotis, *Lindl.*
,, platyphylla, *Spr.*
,, foliosa, *A. Rich.*
Habenaria fimbriata, *Wight.*
,, Richardiana, *Wight.*
,, decipiens, *Wight.*
Platanthera Susannæ, *Lindl.*
,, brachyphylla, *Lindl.*
,, iantha, *Wight.*
Peristylus plantagineus, *Lindl.*
,, spiralis, *Wight.*
,, Richardianus, *Wight.*
Cœloglossum secundum, *Lindl.*

Sub-Section Corycidæ.

Disperis Nilagiriensis, *Wight.*
Disperis tripetaloidea, *Lindl.*

CHAP. VI.

FLORA.

Section *Arethuseæ.*

Sub-Section Pogonidæ.

Pogonia biflora, *Wight.*

Sub-Section Gastrodidæ.

Epipogium nutans, *Lindl.* (= Podanthera pallida, *Wight*).

Sub-Section Vanillidæ.

Podochilus Malabaricus, *Wight.*

Section *Neotteæ.*

Sub-Section Spiranthidæ.

Spiranthus australis.

Sub-Section Physuridæ.

Zeuxine sulcata, *Lindl.* (= robusta and brevifolia, *Wight*).
Cheirostylis flabellata, *Wight.*
Goodyera procera, *Hook.*
Anæctochilus setaceus, *Bl.*
,, elatus, *Lindl.*
Cnemidia nervosa (= Govindovia, *Wight*).

ZINGIBERACEÆ.

Globba bulbifera, *Roxb.*
Zingiber Wightianum, *Thur.*
,, Zerumbet, *Sm.*
Curcuma aromatica, *Salisb.*
,, Nílagiriensis, *Wight.*
Kæmpferia rotunda, *Willd.*
Amomum, *Sp.*
Elettaria cannæcarpa, *Wight.*
,, cardamomum, *Maton.*
Hedychium flavescens, *Roscoe.*
,, coronarium, *Willd.*
,, cernuum, *Wight.*
Alpinia Rheedii, *Wight.*
Costus speciosus, *Sm.*

MARANTACEÆ.

Maranta virgata, *Wall.*
Phrynium capitatum, *Willd.*
Canna Indica, *L.*

MUSACEÆ.

Musa ornata, *Roxb.*

PONTEDERACEÆ.

Monochoria hastæfolia, *Presl.*
Monochoria vaginalis, *Presl.*

COMMELYNACEÆ.

Commelyna salicifolia, *Roxb.*
,, Bengalensis, *L.*
,, obliqua, *Don.*
,, hirsuta } (=Heterocarpus,
,, glaber } *Wight*).
Aneilema ensifolium, *Wight* (also secunda, *W.*)
,, nudiflorum, *Kunth.*
,, nanum, *Kth.*
,, latifolium, *Wight.*
,, montanum, *Wight.* (= Dictyospermum, *Wight*).
Aneilema ovalifolium, *Wight* (= Dictyospermum).
Pollia Indica, *Wight.* (= Aclisia.)
Ploscopa paniculata, *Hassk.* (=Dithyrocarpus, *Wight.*)
Cyanotis cristata, *Roem & Sch.*
,, axillaris, *Roem & Sch.*
,, pilosa, *Roem & Sch.*
,, fasciculata, *Roem & Sch.* (=rosea and sarmentosa, *Wight.*)
,, lanceolata, *Wight.*
,, longifolia, *Wight.*

HYPOXIDACEÆ.

Hypoxis trichocarpa, *Wight.*
Curculigo orchidioides, *Gærtn.* (= brevifolia, *Wight*).
Curculigo Malabarica, *Wight.*

AMARYLLIDACEÆ.

Crinum defixum, *Gawl.*
Pancratium verecundum, *Soland.*
Pancratium Malabaricum, *Kth.*

BURMANNIACEÆ.

Burmannia triflora, *Roxb.*

DIOSCOREACEÆ.

Dioscorea oppositifolia, *L.*
„ pentaphylla, *L.*
Dioscorea bulbifera, *L.*
„ tomentosa, *Kth.*

PANDANEÆ.

Pandanus odoratissimus, *L.*

PALMACEÆ.

Areca catechu, *L.* (cultivated at foot of hills).
Caryota urens, *L.*
Phœnix Sylvestris, *Roxb.*
Phœnix farinifera, *Roxb.*
Calamus Wightii, *Griff.*
„ rotang, *L.*
and two species not identified

PISTIACEÆ.

Pistia stratiotes, *L.*

ALISMACEÆ.

Alisma obtusifolia, *L.*

NAJADACEÆ.

Aponogeton crispus, *Thunb.*

AROIDEÆ.

Lagenandra ovata, *L.*
Arum divaricatum, *L.*
„ Roxburghii, *Sch.*
Arisæma curvatum, *Kunth.*
„ Leschenaultii, *Bl.*
tortuosum, *Sch.*
Amorphophallus campanulatus, *Bl.*
„ dubius, *Bl.*
Colocina antiquorum, *Sch.*
„ vivipara, *Roxb.*
Scindapsus pertusus, *Sch.*
Pothos scandens, *L.*

LILIACEÆ.

Asparagus rubricaulis, *Kth.*
„ floribunda, *Kth.*
Sanseviera Roxburghiana, *Sch.*
Dianella ensifolia, *Red.*
Disporum Leschenaultianum, *Don.*
Smilax maculata, *Roxb.*
„ ovalifolia, *Roxb.*
„ Zeylanica, *L.*
Chlorophytum parviflorum, *Dalz.*=(Phalangium, *Wight*).
Gloriosa superba, *L.*
Ophiopogon intermedius, *Don.*
Peliosanthes Nilagiriensis, *Wight.*
Ledebouria hyacinthina, *Roth.*
Barnardi Indica, *Wight.*
Lilium Nilagiriensis, *Wight.*

JUNCACEÆ.

Juncus monticola, *Steudel.*

RESTIACEÆ.

Eriocaulon Nilagiriense, *Steudel.*
„ robustum, *Steudel.*
Eriocaulon bracteosum, *Steudel.*
„ sexangulare, *L.*

CHAP. VI.

FLORA.

CYPERACEÆ.

Cyperus polystachyus, *Rottb.*
„ puncticulatus, *Vahl.*
„ alopecuroides, *Rottb.*
„ Nilagiricus, *Hochst.*
„ atroferrugineus, *Steudel.*
„ petræus, *Hochst.*
„ rotundus, *L.*
„ aristatus, *Rottb.*
„ dubius, *Rottb.*
„ distans, *L.*
„ kyllingioides, *Steudel.*
„ umbellatus, *Vahl.*
Kyllingia monocephala, *L.*
„ brevifolia, *Rottb.*
„ melanosperma, *Nees.*
„ triceps, *Rottb.*
Hypolytrum latifolium, *Rich.*
Fuirena ciliaris, *Roxb.*
„ umbellata, *Rottb.*
Abilgaardia monostachya, *Vahl.*
Fimbristylis polytrichoides, *Br.*
Fimbristylis schænoides, *Vahl.*
„ argentea, *Nees.*
„ quinquangularis, *Kunth.*
„ miliacea, *Vahl.*
„ uliginosa, *Hochst.*
„ capillacea, *Hochst.*
„ monticola, *Hochst.*
Isolepis gracilis, *Nees.*
„ barbata, *Br.*
Scirpus juncoides, *Roxb.*
Eleocharis capitata, *Br.*
Schleria tessellata, *Willd.*
„ lithosperma, *Willd.*
„ androgyna, *Nees.*
Carex mercarensis, *Hochst.*
„ macrophylla, *Hochst.*
„ Nilagirica, *Hochst.*
„ platycarpa, *Hochst.*
„ gemella, *Hochst.*
„ nubigena, *Don.*

GRAMINEÆ.

ORYZEÆ.

Oryza sativa, *L.*

PHALERIDEÆ.

Coix Lachryma, *L.*

PANICEÆ.

Paspalum Metzii, *Steudel.*
„ scrobiculatum, *L.*
Panicum Wallichianum, *W. & A.*
„ Nilagiracum, *Steudel.*
„ multibrachiatum, *Hochst.*
„ nodibarbatum, *Hochst.*
„ Metzii, *Hochst.*
„ brachyglume, *Hochst.*
„ Burmanni, *Retz.*
Panicum Crus galli, *L.*
„ glaucum, *L.*
„ Helopus, *Trin.*
„ Javanicum, *Poir.*
„ montanum, *Roxb.*
„ Indicum, *L.*
„ trigonum, *Retz.*
„ verticellatum, *L.*
Pennisetum Hohenackeri, *Hochst.*

TRISTEGINEÆ.

Arundinella setifera, *Steudel.*
„ purpurea, *Hochst.*
Garnotia, *sp.*

ROTTBOELLIEÆ.

Oropetium Thomœum, *Trin.*
Rottboellia exaltata, *L.*
Manisuris granularis, *Sw.*

ANDROPOGONEÆ.

Apluda aristata, *L.*
Crysopogon aciculatus, *Trin.*
Anthistiria ciliata, *Retz.*
„ heteroclita, *Roxb.*
Andropogon Halapensis, *Sibth.*
„ Schænanthus, *Roxb.*
„ Martini, *Roxb.*
„ pertusus, *Willd.*
„ Hohenackeri, *Hochst.*
„ oliganthus, *Hochst.*
Andropogon confertiflorus, *Steudel.*
„ polyneuros, *Steudel.*
„ petiolatus, *Daly.*
„ nodulibarbis, *Hochst.*
„ breviaristatus, *Steudel.*
Ischæmum nervosum, *Rottb.*
Heteropogon hirtus, *Pers.*
Imperata arundinacea, *Cyr.*
Saccharum spontaneum, *L.*
Perotis latifolia, *Ait.*

AGROSTIDEÆ.

Sporobolus diander, *Beauv.*
Triachryum Nílagiricum, *Steudel.*

STIPACEÆ.

Aristida hystrix, *L.*
Aristida depressa, *Roxb.*

ARUNDINEÆ.

Phragmites Roxburghii, *Kth.*

CHLORIDEÆ.

Cynodon dactylon, *Pers.*
„ gracilis, *Nees.*
Dactyloctenium Ægyptiacum, *Beauv.*
Chloris barbata, *Seid.*
„ digitata, *Steudel.*
Eleusine Indica, *Gœrt.*

FESTUCACEÆ.

Eragrostis bifaria, *Vahl.*
„ unioloides, *R. & S.*
„ nutans, *Steudel.*
„ paniculata, *Steudel.*
„ parviglumis, *Hochst.*
Eragrostis atropurpurea, *Hochst.*
Lophatherium gracile, *Broug.*
Elytrophorus articulatus, *Beauv.*
Cœlachne pulchella, *Br.*
Tripogon bromoides, *Roth.*

BAMBUSEÆ.

Arundinaria Wightiana, *Nees.*
Bambusa arundinacea, *Retz.*
„ orientalis, *Nees.*
Oxytenanthera Thwaitesii, *Munro.*
Teinostachyum Wightii, *Bedd.*
Dendrocalamus strictus, *Nees.*
Beesha Rheedii, *Munro.*

CRYPTOGAMS.

LYCOPODIACEÆ.

Lycopodium cernuum, *L.*
„ phlegmaria, *L.*
„ serratum, *Thunb.*
„ complanatum, *L.*
„ clavatum, *L.*
Psilotum triquetrum.
Selaginella caudata, *Desv.*
„ atroviridis, *Spring.*
„ concinna, *Spring.*
„ rupestris, *Spring.*

FILICES.

Gleichenia dichotomum, *Willd.*

Cyathea spinulosa, *Wall.*
Alsophila latebrosa, *Wall.*
Alsophila crinita, *Hk.*
„ glabra, *Hk.*

Hymenophyllum exsertum, *Wall.*
„ polyanthos, *Sw.*
„ Javanicum, *Spr.*
Trichomanes Nílagiriense, *Bedd.*
„ exiguum, *Bedd.*
Trichomanes parvulum, *Poir.*
„ proliferum, *Bl.*
„ filicula, *Boug.*
„ pyxidiferum, *L.*
„ rigidum, *Sev.*

Humata pedata, *Sm.*
Leucostegia immersa, *Wall.*
„ pulchra, *Dm.*
Davallia bullata, *Wall.*
Microlepia strigosa, *Sw.*
Microlepia proxima, *Bl.*
„ hirta, *Kaulf.*
„ platyphylla, *Dm.*
Stenoloma tenuifolia, *Sw.*

CHAP. VI.
FLORA.

Lindsaya cultrata, *Sw.*
Schizoloma lobatum, *Poir.*
Schizoloma ensifolium, *Sw.*
,, heterophyllum, *Dry.*

Adiantum lanceolatum, *Burm.*
,, caudatum, *L.*
,, capillus-veneris, *L.*
,, Æthiopicum, *L.*
,, hispidulum, *Sw.*
Cheilanthus Mysorensis, *Wall.*
,, farninosa, *Kaulf.*
,, ,, *var.* Dalhousiæ.
,, tenuifolia, *Sw.*
Pellœa concolor, *Langs & Fisch.*
,, boivini, *Hk.*
,, falcata, *Fee.*
Pteris longifolia, *L.*
,, cretica, *L.*
Pteris pellucida, *Presl.*
,, ensiformis, *Burm.*
,, quadriaurita, *Retz.*
,, ,, *var.* argentea.
,, ,, *var.* aspericaulis.
,, patens.
,, longipes, *G. Don.*
,, aquilina, *L.*
Campteria biaurita, *L.*
,, Anémalénsis, *Bedd.*
Ceratopteris thalictroides, *Brong.*
Lomaria Patersoni, *Spr.*
,, *var.* elongata, *Bl.*
Blechnum orientale, *L.*

Asplenium nidus, *L.*
,, *var.* phyllitidis, *Don.*
,, ensiforme, *Wall.*
,, Trichomanes, *L.*
,, normale, *Don.*
,, Wightianum, *Wall.*
,, lunulatum, *Sw.*
,, Zenkerianum, *Kze.*
,, auritum, *Sw.*
,, falcatum, *Lam.*
,, caudatum, *Forst.*
,, crinicaule, *Bance.*
,, macrophyllum, *Sw.*
,, formosum, *Bl.*
,, resectum, *Sm.*
,, heterocarpum, *Wall.*
,, planicaule, *Wall.*
,, furcatum, *Thunb.*
Asplenium nitidum, *Sm.*
,, fontanum, *Bernh.*
,, ,, *var.* exiguum, *Bedd.*
,, varians, *Hk. & Grev.*
,, tenuifolium, *Dom.*
Athyrium Hohenackerianum, *Kze.*
,, macrocarpum, *Bl.*
,, nigripes, *Bl.*
,, aspidioides, *Schl.*
,, umbrosum, *J. Sm.*
,, *var.* australe.
Diplazium sylvaticum, *Presl.*
,, lasiopteris, *Mett.*
,, polypoidioides, *Mett.*
,, asperum, *Bl.*
,, latifolium, *Don.*
Anisogonium esculentum, *Presl.*
Actiniopteris radiata, *Link.*

Polystichum auriculatum, *Sw.*
,, aculeatum, *Sw.*
,, ,, *var.* angulatum.
Cyrtomium falcatum, *var.* caryotideum, *Wall.*
Aspidium polymorphum, *Wall.*
,, decurrens, *Presl.*
,, cicutarium, *L.*
Lastræa aristata, *Sw.*
,, coniifolia, *Wall.*
,, hirtipes, *Hk.*
,, gracilescens, *Hk.*
,, calcarata, *Hk.*
,, ,, *var.* falciloba, *Hk.*
,, ochthodes, *Kze.*
,, tylodes, *Kze.*
,, thelypteris, *Desv.*
,, syrmatica, *Willd.*
,, Filix mas *var.* patentissima.
,, ,, *var.* elongata.
,, ,, *var.* cochleata.
Lastræa sparsa, *Don.*
,, crenata, *Forsk.*
,, dissecta, *Forst.*
,, ferruginea, *Bedd.*
,, scabriosa, *Kze.*
,, Boryana, *Willd.*
,, setigera, *Bl.*
Nephrodium otaria, *Presl.*
,, unitum, *R. Br.*
,, pteroides, *Retz.*
,, extensum, *Bl.*
,, cucullatum, *Bl.*
,, Amboinense, *Presl.*
,, arbuscula, *Desv.*
,, pennigerum, *Bl.*
,, molle, *Desv.*
,, truncatum, *Presl.*
Nephrolepis cordifolia, *L.*
,, exaltata, *Sch.*
Oleandra musæfolia, *Kze.*

Phegopteris distans, *Don.*
„ ornata, *Wall.*
„ punctata, *Thunb.*
Polypodium parasiticum, *Mett.*
„ subfalcatum, *Bl.*
Niphobolus adnascens, *Sw.*
„ fissus, *Bl.*
Pleopeltis linearis, *Thunb.*
Pleopeltis lanceolata, *L.*
„ membranacea, *Don.*
„ punctata, *L.*
„ trifida, *Don.*
„ nigrescens, *Bl.*
„ leiorhiza, *Wall.*
Drynaria quercifolia, *L.*

Gymnogramma totta, *Schl.*
„ leptophylla, *Desv.*
Selliguea lanceolata, *Hk.*
„ involuta, *Don.*
Meniscium triphyllum, *Sw.*
Antrophyum plantagineum, *Kaulf.*
Antrophyum reticulatum, *Kaulf.*
Vittaria elongata, *Sw.*
Tæniopsis lineata, *Sw.*
Drymoglossum piloselloides, *Presl.*
Hemionitis arifolia, *Burm.*

Elaphoglossum conforme, *Sw.*
„ laurifolium, *Thouars.*
„ viscosum, *Sw.*
„ stigmatolepis, *Fer.*
Stenochlæna palustre, *L.*
Polybotrya appendiculata, *Willd.*
Polybotrya appendiculata *var* asplenii-folia.
Gymnopteris lanceolata, *Hk.*
„ axillaris, *Cav.*
„ contaminans, *Wall.*
„ terminalis, *Wall.*

Osmunda regalis, *L.*

Anemia tomentosa, *Sw.*
„ „ *var.* Wightiana, *Gardn.*
Lygodium scandens, *Sw.*
„ pinnatifidum, *Sw.*

Angiopteris evecta, *Hoffm.*
Marattia fraxinea, *Sm.*

OPHIOGLOSSACEÆ.

Ophioglossum reticulatum, *L.*
„ nudicaule, *L.*
Helminthostachys Zeylanica, *Hk.*
Botrychium paucifolium, *Wall.*
„ Virginianum, *Sw.*
„ „ *var.* lanuginosum, *Wall.*

JUNGERMANNIACEÆ—(SCALE MOSSES).

—Scale Mosses.

Plagiochila dichotoma, *Nees.*
Lophocolea muricata, *Nees.*
Gottschea aligera, *Nees.*
„ glaucescens, *Nees.*
Madotheca Perrottetii, *Mont.*
„ Nílagiriensis, *Mont.*
„ ligulifera, *Taylor.*
„ acutifolia, *Lehm. & Ldbg.*
Lejennia minutissima, *Dumort.*
„ cucullata, *Nees.*
„ Nílagiriana, *Gottsche.*
Frullania glomerata, *L. & Ldbg.*
„ Wallichiana, *Mitten.*
„ acutiloba, *Mitten.*
„ moniliata, *Nees.*
Steetzia crispata, *Nees.*
Dumortiera hirsuta, *Nees.*
Marchantia nitida, *L.*
Fimbriaria leptophylla, *Mont.*
Riccia fluitans, *Linn.*
Sendtnera dicrana, *Tayl.*
Gymnomitrium lutescens, *Mitt.*

EQUISETACEÆ.

Equisetum debile, *Roxb.*
Equisetum, sp.

MARSILEACEÆ.

Marsilea quadrifolia, *L.*

CHAP. VI.

FLORA.

BRYACEÆ—(URN MOSSES).

TRIBE I.—DICRANACEÆ.

Pleuridium denticulatum, *Mitt.*	Campylopus Nílagiriensis, *Mitt.*
Leptotrichum phascoides, *Mitt.*	„ albescens, *C. Müller.*
„ plicatum, *C. Müller.*	„ densus, *Schl.*
„ Schmidii, *C. Müller.*	„ latinerve, *Mitt.*
Trematodon Schmidii, *C. Müller.*	„ flagelliferus, *C. Müller.*
„ paucifolius, *C. Müller.*	„ involutus, *C. Müller.*
„ sp.	„ caudatus, *C. Müller.*
Cynontodium amænum, *T. & Mitt.*	„ ericetorum, *Mitt.*
Pæcilophyllum tenerum, *Mitt.*	„ tricolor, *C. Müller.*
„ Taylori, *Mitt.*	„ erythrognaphalon, *G. Müller.*
„ nitens, *Mitt.*	„ Schmidii, *C. Müller.*
„ amœne-virens, *Mitt.*	„ nodiflorus, *C. Müller.*
Campylopus recurvus, *Mitt.*	„ nitidus *Mitt.*
„ Goughii, *Mitt.*	Didymodon stenocarpus, *Mitt.*

TRIBE II.—GRIMMIEÆ.

Grimmia ovata, *Web. and Mohr.*	Glyphomitrium (Brachysteleum) tortula, *C. Muller.*
„ Nílagiriensis, *C. Müller.*	

TRIBE III.—LEUCOBRYEÆ.

Octoblepharum albidum, *Hedw.*	Leucobryum Nílagiriensis.
Leucobryum Javense, *Mitt.*	„ Bowringii, *Mitt.*
„ Wightii, *Mitt.*	

TRIBE IV.—SYRRHOPODONTEÆ.

Calymperes sp.

TRIBE V.—TORTULEÆ.

Weissia (Gymnostoma) involuta, *Hook.*	Tortula augustata, *Mitt.*
Tortula orthodonta, *Müller.*	„ (Syntrichia) Schmidii, *C. Müller.*
„ stenophylla, *Mitt.*	Anœctangium Schmidii, *C. Müller.*

TRIBE VI.—ORTHOTRICHEÆ.

Zygodon acutifolius, *C. Müller.*	Macromitrium Schmidii, *C. Müller.*
„ cylindricarpus, *C. Müller.*	„ Muellerianum, *Mitt.*
„ tetragonostomus, *Braun.*	„ sulcatum, *Brid.*
Ulota Schmidii, *Mitt.*	„ uncinatum, *C. Müller.*
Orthotrichum n.; sp. (No. 458 *Herb. Bed.*)	„ fasciculare, *Mitt.*
Macromitrium Perrottetii, *C. Müller.*	„ Nílagiriensis, *C. Müller.*
„ squarrulosum, *C. Müller.*	Schlotheimia Grevilliana, *Mitt.*

TRIBE VII.—FUNARIEÆ.

Entosthodon Buseanus, *Mitt.*	Entosthodon submarginatus, *Müller.*
„ Perrottetii, *Mitt.*	Funaria connivens, *Müller.*
„ physcomitrioides, *Müller.*	„ hygrometrica, *Dill.*
„ diversinervis, *Müller.*	

TRIBE VIII.—SPLACHNEÆ.

Tayloria subglabrata, *Mitt.*

TRIBE IX.—BARTRAMIEÆ.

Bartramia (Philonotis) Roylei, *Mitt.*	Bartramia (Philonotis) macrocarpa, *Müller.*
„ „ pseudofontana, *Müller.*	„ „ subpellucida, *Mitt.*
„ „ falcata, *Mitt.*	„ (Breutelia) Indica, *Mitt.*
	„ „ dicranacea, *Müller.*

Tribe X.—Bryeæ.

Bryum giganteum, *Hook.*
,, Wightii, *Mitt.*
,, argenteum, *Linn.*
,, ramosum, *Hook.*
,, Schmidii, *C. Müller.*
,, Harveyanum, *C. Müller.*
,, flaccidisetum, *C. Müller.*
,, Montagneanum, *C. Müller.*
,, rugosum, *C. Müller.*
,, porphyrioneuron, *C. Müller.*
,, alpinum, *L.*
,, lamprostegum, *C. Müller.*
,, (Dicranobryum) Weissiæ, *Mitt.*
Bryum (Brachymenium) velutinum, *C. Müller.*
,, (,,) clavariæforme, *C. Müller.*
,, (,,) Nepalense, *Hook.*
,, leptostomoides, *C. Müller.*
,, apalodictyoides, *C. Müller.*
,, Zollingeri, *Duby.*
,, medianum, *Mitt.*
Mnium rostratum, *Schr.*
,, rhyncophorum, *Hook.*
Rhizogonium spiniforme, *Brach.*
Anomodon planatus ? *Mitt.*

Tribe XI.—Hypopterygieæ.

Hypopterygium tenellum, *C. Müller.*
Hypopterygium struthiopteris, *Brid.*

Tribe XII.—Rhacopileæ.

Rhacopilum Schmidii, *C. Müller.*

Tribe XIII.—Hookerieæ.

Lepidopilum Ootacamandianum, *Mont.*
Distichophyllum (Mniadelphus) Montagnei, *C. Müller.*
Distichophyllum (Mniadelphus) succulentum, *Mitt.*
Hookeria (Calliostella) flabellata, *Mitt.*

Tribe XIV.—Erpodieæ.

Aulacopilum tumidulum, *Thw. and Mitt.*
Erpodium n : sp.

Tribe XV.—Neckereæ.

Hedwigia Indica, *C. Müller.*
Cryphœa (Braunia) Indica, *Mitt.*
,, (Dendropogon) ferruginea, *Mitt.*
Phyllogonium elegans, *Hook. and Wils.*
Pterobryum involutum, *T. and Mitt.*
,, Ceylanicum, *Thw. and Mitt.*
,, tumidum, *Mitt.*
Cyrtopus frondosus, *Mitt.*
Meteorium fuscescens, *Mitt.*
,, blandum, *Mitt.*
,, squarrosum, *Mitt.*
,, floribundum, *D. and M.*
,, flexipes, *Mitt.*
,, Foulkesianum, *Mitt.*
,, reclinatum, *Mitt.*
,, hispidum, *Mitt.*
Meteorium auro-nitens, *Mitt.*
,, convolvens, *Mitt.*
,, punctulatum, *C. Müller.*
,, Schmidii, *C. Müller.*
,, filamentosum, *Mitt.*
,, cuspidiferum, *Mitt.*
Neckera Montagneana, *C. Müller.*
,, Goughiana, *Mitt.*
,, æqualifolia, *C. Müller.*
,, arcuans, *Mitt.*
,, Schmidii, *Mitt.*
,, parvula, *Mitt.*
Porotrichum ligulæfolium, *Mitt.*
,, sp.
,, fruticosum, *Mitt.*
Homalia Targioniana, *Mitt.*

Tribe XVI.—Sematophylleæ.

Tribe XVII.—Stereodonteæ.

Stereodon (Taxicaulis) albescens, *Mitt.*
,, ,, Ivoreanus, *Mitt.*
,, subhumilis, *C. Müller.*
,, leptorhynchoides, *Mitt.*
Stereodon (Symphyodon) Perrottetii, *Mitt.*
Entodon plicatus, *C. Müller.*
,, (Leptohymenium) juliformis, *Mitt.*

CHAP. VI.

FLORA.

TRIBE XVIII.—HYPNEÆ.

Fabronia secunda, *Mont.*
„ Goughii, *Mitt.*
„ Schmidii, *C. Müller.*
Hypnum discriminatum, *Mont.*
„ Wightii, *Mitt.*
„ Bonplandi, *Mitt.*
„ plumosum, *Mitt.*
„ lychnitis, *C. Müller.*
„ procumbens, *Mitt.*
„ humillimum, *Mitt.*
„ Buchanani, *Hook.*
Rhegmatodon orthostegius, *Mont.*
Trachypus crispatulus, *Mitt.*
Trachypus bicolor, *Schw.*
„ atratus, *Mitt.*
„ Buchanani, *C. Müller.*
„ plicæfolius, *C. Müller.*
„ brevirameus, *C. Müller.*
Thuidium cymbifolium, *Dozy and M.*
„ glaucinum, *Mitt.*
„ blepharophylla, *C. Müller.*
„ pristocalyx, *C. Müller.*
„ tamariscella, *C. Müller.*
Pleuropus Nílagiriensis, *Mitt.*
Leskea consanguinea, *Mont.*
„ prionophylla, *Mitt.*

TRIBE XIX.—SKITOPHYLLEÆ.

Fissidens anomalus, *Mont.*
„ Schmidii, *C. Müller.*
Fissidens serratus, *C. Müller.*
„ Ceylonensis, *Dozy and M.*

TRIBE XX.—POLYTRICHEÆ.

Pogonatum Neesii, *C. Müller.*
„ microstomum, *Br.*
„ aloides, *Brid.*
Pogonatum hexagonum, *Mitt.*
Polytrichum perichætiale, *Mont.*

TRIBE XXI.—BUXHAUMIEÆ.

Diphyscium sp.
Diphyscium sp.

LICHENALES.

—Lichens.

There are numerous lichens on these hills, but they have never been worked out.

FUNGALES.

—Fungi.

Fungi are numerous, but little is known about them.

Books of reference.

The above is a complete catalogue of the flowering plants, ferns, and mosses of the Nílagiris as at present known. The descriptions are nowhere to be found in a collected form, though "The Flora of British India" by Dr. Hooker (very slowly progressing) will in time supply this want. For the present, the student must consult Wight and Arnott's "Prodromus" and DeCandolle's "Prodromus" for most of the plants; for the orchids, Dr. Lindley's "Genera and Species Orchidaceæ" and his papers in the Linnæan Journal; for the grasses Kunth's "Enumeratio Plantarum" and Steudel's "Syn. Pl. Gram.;" and for the mosses the works of Müller and Mitten.

Very many of the flowering plants are figured in Dr. Wight's "Icones," and most of the trees and shrubs, or at least one or more of each genus, in Colonel Beddome's "Flora Sylvatica," and all the ferns in Colonel Beddome's "Ferns of Southern India" and "Ferns of British India," all of which works are to be found in the Ootacamand Library.

Introduced plants.

The list does not include introduced plants. The Australian *Eucalypti* and *Acacias* have given quite a new character to Ootacamand and Coonoor, in and about which they have been planted very largely. The Forest Department have planted several hundred acres of *Eucalyptus globulus*, the blue-gum of Tasmania, and there are also extensive plantations of *Acacia melanoxylon* and *dealbata.* They are all excellent firewood, and, in the event of a railway being made up the gháts, plantations of this sort will be very profitable, the growth being exceedingly rapid and the yield per acre very large (probably not less than 25 tons per annum from *Eucalyptus globulus* and 15 tons from *Acacia dealbata*).

Numerous species of *Eucalyptus* have been introduced from Australia, amongst which may be mentioned *E. sideroxylon* (the iron bark), *E. obliqua* (stringy bark), *E. fissilis* (mess-mate), *E. viminalis* (manna-gum), *E. amygdalina* (the gigantic box-gum), *E. rostrata* (the red-gum), *E. perfoliata*, besides many other Victorian species as doing well. Some West Australian *Eucalypti*, such as *E. marginata* (the jarrah or mahogany tree, the wood of which stands exposure to sea-water, and in Australia is much in use for jetties, ship-building, railway sleepers, &c.) and *E. calophylla*, have been introduced and will grow with care, but they do not stand the frost when young, and have to be carefully covered up in December, January, and February until they attain certain dimensions.

Very many of the Australian *Acacias*, besides those above mentioned, have been introduced and ornament our gardens and roads, &c. Amongst them are *Acacia homolophylla* (the myall or violet wood), *Acacia pycnantha, A. salicina, A. decurrens, A. cultriformis, A. dodonæifolia, A. elata, A. longifolia, A. saligna, A. pulchella, Albizzia lophantha,* besides many others.

Many other Australian trees and shrubs have also been introduced into gardens on the plateau, amongst which are many species of *Hakea, Grevillea* and *Banksia, Casuarina quadrivalvis* and *suberosa* (the she-oak and he-oak), *Pomaderris* (three species), *Myoporum insulare, Pittosporum* (two species), *Melaleuca* (several species), *Leptospermum* (several species), *Callistemon* (two species), *Beaufortia, Kunzea, Calothamnus, Angophora, Tristania,* &c. Many of the *Coniferæ* have also been introduced from the Himalayas, Japan, and other countries, the most successful of which are *Cupressus macrocarpa, Lawsoniana, torulosa, sempervirens* and *Cashmeriana. Araucarias Bidwillii* and *Cunninghami. Criptomeria Japonica. Frenela species, Pinus pinaster* and *longifolia.*

Some of the European pines, such as the Larch and Scotch Fir (*P. laricio* and *P. sylvestris*) and some of the Himalayan *Abies* have quite failed to grow.

Coffee now covers many acres of the slopes between 2,000 and 5,000 feet.

CHAP. VI.

FLORA.

Cinchona and tea are also very largely grown; the former from 3,000 feet upwards, the latter from 4,500 feet.

The mangosteen fruits well in the garden at Burliar, about 4,000 feet elevation on the south-eastern slopes, where also the nutmeg of commerce, the clove, the cocoa, and the vanilla grow luxuriantly.

Oranges, apples, peaches, and pears grow well at Coonoor and Kalhatti; pears succeed also in the colder and damper climate of Ootacamand, where walnuts thrive and fruit well. Strawberries and raspberries grow and fruit, but do not answer very well except with constant attention to the supply of liquid manure and water. Cherries and gooseberries will not fruit at all, probably from the want of a regular winter, which is also the reason that the oak grows so badly, and the elm, birch, and most other European deciduous trees make no growth whatever. Currants very rarely fruit. In the gardens of the plateau most of the flowers found in English gardens and green-houses are to be met with. The growth of fuschias, geraniums, and heliotropes is most luxuriant; they are often made into hedges.

CHAPTER VII.

THE USEFUL PLANTS OF THE NÍLAGIRIS.

(*By* Surgeon-Major BIDIE, M.B., *Government Museum, Madras.*)

Introductory remarks.—SUBSTANCES USED AS FOOD, &c.—Pulses—Cereals—Roots and tubers—Fruits and seeds—Greens—Substances used in the preparation of drinks—Intoxicating Substances—Spices and condiments.—SUBSTANCES USED IN MANUFACTURES—Oils and seeds—Dyes and tanning substances—Fibres.—DRUGS.

CHAP. VII. — USEFUL PLANTS. — Introductory remarks.

As a supplement to the monograph on the Flora in this Manual, I have been asked to furnish a memorandum on the useful plants of the Nílagiris. As Colonel Beddome has enumerated the various timber trees belonging to the range, it remains for me only to notice other plants, used as food or medicines, or in the arts. The list of these in a district presenting such varieties of climate and possessing such a rich flora is, it need hardly be said, rather an extensive one. It will be impossible therefore, within a reasonable compass, to do more than notice the more important products, and even these notices must be brief. The most scientific mode of arranging the articles would of course be according to the natural orders to which the plants belong, but as the great majority of those who may have occasion to consult the list will not be botanists, it has been deemed preferable to subordinate the botanical classification to a practical one, grouping the plants, in the first instance, according to their economical uses. Except in the case of some very important products, such as cinchona, tea and coffee, no notice will be taken of plants which have been introduced from other countries and are merely cultivated as curiosities in gardens, or to a very limited extent. The three primary classes under which the several substances will be arranged are therefore as follows :—

I. Substances used as food, &c.
II. Substances used in manufactures.
III. Drugs.

I.—SUBSTANCES USED AS FOOD, &c.

Substances used as food.

Of these I shall first notice pulses and cereals.

CHAP. VII.

USEFUL PLANTS.

—Pulses.

A. PULSES.

N.O. LEGUMINOSÆ.

The varieties of pulses cultivated on the plains are rather numerous, but very few of them are suited for the cold wet climate of the Hills. English peas and beans are reared in gardens and find a ready sale in the weekly markets.

—Cereals.

B. CEREALS.

N.O. GRAMINEÆ.

The chief grain crops of the Nílagiris are as follows:—

PANICUM. *Tam.* Korali,[1] probably a form of *P. italicum* changed by climate.

PANICUM MILIARE. *Eng.* Millet. *Tam.* Sámé.

PANICUM MILIACEUM. *Eng.* Little Millet. *Duk.* China. *Tam.* Varágu. *Kan.* Navoné.

ELEUSINE CORACANA. *Eng.* Raggi. *Duk.* Raggi. *Tam.* Kaywur. *Kan.* Raggi.

TRITICUM VULGARE. *Eng.* Wheat. *Duk.* Gehun. *Tam.* Godumai. *Kan.* Godhi.

HORDEUM. *Eng.* Barley. *Tam.* Barli-arisi.

These well known grains need no explanatory notices. Of the six kinds named, *Korali* and *Barley* are the two most commonly cultivated. In addition to the grains proper a species of *Amaranthus* is raised to a small extent, and its seeds form a nutritious article of food.

—Roots and tubers.

C. ROOTS AND TUBERS.

N.O. SOLANACEÆ.

SOLANUM TUBEROSUM, the potato, has long been cultivated on the Hills, but of late years the crops have been more or less a failure owing to *potato-disease*, and from constantly growing the tubers in the same ground, by which the soil gets exhausted.

N.O. DIOSCOREACEÆ.

DIOSCOREA PENTAPHYLLA, a twining jungle plant yielding a kind of yam.

N.O. AROIDEÆ.

AMORPHOPHALLUS CAMPANULATUS. *Eng.* Telinga-potato. *Tam.* Karunai. The root of this *arum* attains a size as large or even larger than that of a man's head, and is eaten like yams.

—Fruits and seeds.

D. FRUITS AND SEEDS.

N.O. MALVACEÆ.

HIBISCUS ESCULENTUS. *Eng.* Edible Hibiscus. *Duk.* Bhendi. *Tam.* Vendaik-kai. *Kan.* Bendé-kaí.

A mucilaginous fruit, eaten as a vegetable.

---

[1] The native synonyms will be given as far as known, and the following are the contractions employed in rendering them:—*Tam.* Tamil. *Kan.* Kanarese. *Duk.* Dukhni (the form of Hindustani used in Southern India).

N.O. STERCULIACEÆ.

STERCULIA FŒTIDA. *Eng.* Sterculia seeds. *Tam.* Pinari-kai.

The kernels of the seeds are eaten by natives.

N.O. TILIACEÆ.

ELÆOCARPUS OBLONGUS, a pretty tree, belonging to the genus which yields the tubercular seeds worn by Brahmins as beads. The hard tubercular shells of the seeds of this tree are broken, and the kernel eaten by natives like almonds.

N.O. RUTACEÆ.

LIMONIA ACIDISSIMA, a very acid species of lime.

CITRUS AURANTIUM. *Eng.* Orange. *Duk.* Nárangi. *Tam.* Kichchilip-pazham. *Kan.* Kittale-hannu.

Of the orange there are several varieties, and when carefully cultivated they yield excellent fruit.

FERONIA ELEPHANTUM. *Eng.* Wood-apple. *Duk.* Kavit. *Tam.* Vilampazham. *Kan.* Byalada-hannu.

The pulp of the fruit has a strong flavour and sweetish taste and is eaten.

ÆGLE MARMELOS. *Eng.* Bael fruit. *Duk.* Bel-phal. *Tam.* Vilvapazham. *Kan.* Bilapatri-hannu.

The fruit when ripe is sweetish and aromatic, and when green it is astringent and used in diarrhœa and dysentery.

N.O. ANACARDIACEÆ.

BUCHANANIA LATIFOLIA. *Eng.* Cuddapah almond. *Tam.* Kat-manga. Shara-purpu. *Kan.* Chara-puppu.

Kernel of the seed.

N.O. ROSACEÆ.

FRAGARIA INDICA, this, the wild strawberry, is small and insipid.

RUBUS LASIOCARPUS and RUBUS FLAVUS, known as blackberries and edible.

N.O. COMBRETACEÆ.

TERMINALIA CATAPPA. *Eng.* Country Almond. *Duk.* Jangli.badam. *Tam.* Nattu Vadam-kottai. *Kan.* Nat-badami.

Kernels of seeds.

N.O. RHAMNACEÆ.

ZIZYPHUS JUJUBA. *Eng.* Ber-fruit. *Duk.* Ber. *Tam.* Elandap-pazham. *Kan.* Yalachi-hannu.

Known as the jujube-fruit, and is wholesome and palatable.

N.O. MYRTACEÆ.

PSIDIUM PYRIFERUM and P. POMIFERUM, the Guava, grows on the lower slopes, but the fruit does not attain great perfection.

CHAP. VII.

USEFUL PLANTS.

RHODOMYRTUS TOMENTOSA, this handsome shrub yields the fruit known as the hill-gooseberry.

EUGENIA JAMBOLANA. *Eng.* Jambolam or Blue apple. *Duk.* Jamun. *Tam.* Nagap-pazham. *Kan.* Nerale-hannu.

A sweetish and astringent fruit.

N.O. CUCURBITACEÆ.

MOMORDICA DIOICA. *Tam.* Palupaghel.

The young fruit of this member of the Cucumber family as well as its roots are eaten.

N.O. SOLANACEÆ.

SOLANUM MELONGENA. *Eng.* Brinjal. *Tam.* Kathrikkai.

The fruit is a well known vegetable.

PHYSALIS PERUVIANA. Cape-gooseberry. An introduced plant, but now growing wild all over the Hills. The fruit makes very good jam or tart.

N.O. PALMACEÆ.

PHŒNIX FARINIFERA. *Eng.* Small or Wild Date. *Duk.* Sandole. *Tam.* Isham-pazham.

Fruit eaten.

N.O. MUSACEÆ.

MUSA PARADISIACA. *Eng.* Plantain. *Duk.* Mouz. *Tam.* Vazhaip-pazham. *Kan.* Bale-hannu.

I have not noticed the apple, peach, pear, walnut and other introduced fruits, as their culture is confined to a few gardens and still in a very primitive state.

Greens.

E. GREENS.

N.O. CRUCIFERÆ.

NASTURTIUM OFFICINALE and NASTURTIUM INDICUM. Both these species yield edible cresses.

N.O. PORTULACACEÆ.

PORTULACA OLERACEA, P. WIGHTIANA. Leaves eaten as greens.

N.O. RUTACEÆ.

MURRAYA (BERGERA) KONIGII. *Eng.* Curry-leaf. *Duk.* Karya-pak. *Tam.* Karu-veppilai. *Kan.* Kari-bevina.

The leaves are used for flavouring curries.

N.O. AMARANTHACEÆ.

AMARANTHUS OLERACEUS, A. FRUMENTACEUS and A. CAUDATUS. The leaves of the three species are used as pot-herbs.

ACHYRANTHES ASPERA is also eaten at times.

N.O. LAURACEÆ.

CINNAMOMUM ZEYLANICUM. *Eng.* Cinnamon. *Duk.* Dal-chini. *Tam.* Lavangap-pattai. *Kan.* Dala-chinni.

The leaves of the cinnamon tree are used as flavouring agents in food.

F. SUBSTANCES USED IN THE PREPARATION OF DRINKS.

N.O. CAMELLIACEÆ.

THEA (species). *Eng.* Tea. *Duk.* Cha. *Tam.* Te-ilai.

Substances used in the preparation of drinks.

The first effort to introduce the tea plant into Southern India was made by the Agri-Horticultural Society of Madras, which imported plants from China in 1857. It is only of late years, however, that much attention has been paid to its culture. At the present time there are numerous plantations on the range situated at elevations ranging from 5,000 to 7,000 feet above sea level. The plants cultivated are the China, the Assam, and a hybrid, the last-named being usually preferred as being more prolific of leaf. The produce of the Nílagiri tea estates commands fair prices in the English market, and is extensively sold at high rates both locally and in Madras and other large towns in Southern India. The field for the extension of tea culture on the Nílagiris is limited, and the industry is likely to receive a check by the resolution of Government to preserve intact the wooded ravines, locally known as *shólas*. In 1874-75 there were 87,372 lb. of tea shipped from Madras to Europe.

N.O. RUBIACEÆ.

COFFEA ARABICA. *Eng.* Coffee. *Duk.* Bun, Bund. *Tam.* Kapi-kottai. *Kan.* Kapi-bija.

Coffee was introduced into Southern India about two centuries ago by a Mahomedan pilgrim, Baba-buden. This man on his return from Mecca brought a few berries in his wallet, and taking up his abode amongst the wilds of the hills in western Mysore, which still bear his name, planted them near his hut. For many years the culture was in the hands of natives, and confined to small gardens. Upwards of 50 years ago it began to attract the attention of Europeans, and at the present day there is an almost continuous chain of estates, belonging to Englishmen, extending from the north of Mysore down to Cape Comorin. On the eastern slopes of the Nílagiris the coffee estates are numerous and large, and on the western side the Ouchterlony Valley presents a magnificent expanse of coffee culture, unequalled as to fertility in Southern India. The exports of coffee have not been on the increase of late years, but this may be partly due to the fact that its consumption is increasing amongst the native population, and that much of it is, therefore, used locally. The exports of coffee from Madras ports in 1875 amounted to lb. 33,738,922.

G. INTOXICATING SUBSTANCES, &c.

Intoxicating substances.

N.O. LEGUMINOSÆ.

ACACIA CATECHU. *Eng.* Catechu. *Duk.* Katthah. *Tam.* Kashu-katti. *Kan.* Kachu.

The Extract made into pellets is chewed with betel-leaf.

CHAP. VII.

USEFUL PLANTS.

N.O. SOLANACEÆ.

NICOTIANA RUSTICA. *Eng.* Tobacco. *Duk.* Tamaqu. *Tam.* Pugai-ilai. *Kan.* Hogesappu.

In former years a good deal of tobacco culture was carried on on the Hills, but of late it has greatly declined as it can be grown much cheaper on the plains.

N.O. URTICACEÆ.

CANNABIS SATIVA. *Eng.* Indian Hemp. *Duk.* Siddhi. *Tam.* Bangi-ilai. *Kan.* Bhangi.

The leaves and flowering tops are used as intoxicants. The use of hemp for this purpose in India was first noticed by a Portuguese writer in 1563. The hemp is smoked and also made up in various preparations.

N.O. PIPERACEÆ.

CHAVICA BETLE. *Eng.* Betel-leaf. *Duk.* Pan. *Tam.* Vettilai. *Kan.* Vile-dele.

Used as a masticatory by both sexes and all classes, in conjunction with lime and areca nut.

N.O. PALMACEÆ.

ARECA CATECHU. *Eng.* Betel-nut. *Duk.* Supari. *Tam.* Kottai-pakku. *Kan.* Adike.

Astringent and constantly chewed, natives believing that it preserves the teeth and strengthens the gums.

Spices and condiments.

H. SPICES AND CONDIMENTS.

N.O. MALVACEÆ.

ERIODENDRON ANFRACTUOSUM. *Duk.* Khatyan-ka-kalli. *Tam.* Maratti-moggu.

The ovaries of the flower or very young fruits are used as condiments.

N.O. SOLANACEÆ.

CAPSICUM ? Species of chillies are cultivated at low elevations.

N.O. PIPERACEÆ.

PIPER NIGRUM. *Eng.* Black Pepper. *Duk.* Kali-mirchi. *Tam.* Milagu. *Kan.* Menasu.

The dry berry is used as a condiment.

N.O. ZINGIBERACEÆ.

ZINGIBER OFFICINALE. *Eng.* Ginger. *Duk.* Adrak. *Tam.* Inji. *Kan.* Hasisunthi.

The dried root is sometimes used in cookery.

CURCUMA LONGA. *Eng.* Turmeric. *Duk.* Haldi. *Tam.* Manjal. *Kan.* Arishina.
A constant ingredient in curries.

ELETTARIA CARDAMOMUM. *Eng.* Cardamoms. *Duk.* Elachi. *Tam.* Ellakai. *Kan.* Yalakkai.
A well known condiment.

N.O. LILIACEÆ.

ALLIUM SATIVUM. *Eng.* Garlic. *Duk.* Lassan. *Tam.* Vellaip-pundu. *Kan.* Belluli.
A strong smelling condiment.

ALLIUM CEPA. *Eng.* Onions. *Duk.* Piyaz. *Tam.* Vengayam. *Kan.* Irulli.
A well known cultivated bulb.

N.O. GRAMINEÆ.

ANDROPOGON SCHŒNANTHUS. *Eng.* Lemon-grass. *Duk.* Hazar-masaleh. *Tam.* Karpura-pullu. *Kan.* Vasane-hullu.
Used as a flavouring agent.

II.—SUBSTANCES USED IN MANUFACTURES.

A. OILS AND OIL SEEDS.

Oils and seeds.

N.O. PAPAVERACEÆ.

ARGEMONE MEXICANA. *Eng.* Mexican Thistle. *Duk.* Pila-dhatura. *Tam.* Birama-dandu. *Kan.* Datturi.
Oil extracted from the seeds.

N.O. LOGANIACEÆ.

STRYCHNOS NUX-VOMICA. *Eng.* Nux-vomica. *Duk.* Kuchlah. *Tam.* Ettik-kottai. *Kan.* Mushti-bija.
An oil is got from the seeds and they are also used for the manufacture of strychnia.

N.O. EUPHORBIACEÆ.

RICINUS COMMUNIS. *Eng.* Castor-oil seeds. *Duk.* Yarandi. *Tam.* Amanakkan-kottai. *Kan.* Haralu.
The seeds yield castor-oil.

B. DYES AND TANNING SUBSTANCES.

Dyes and tanning substances.

N.O. BERBERIDEÆ.

BERBERIS ARISTATA. *Eng.* Indian Barberry bark.
The roots contain 17 per cent. of yellow coloring matter.

CHAP. VII.

USEFUL PLANTS.

N.O. MALVACEÆ.

HIBISCUS ROSA-SINENSIS. *Eng.* Shoe-flower. *Duk.* Jasut. *Tam.* Shappattup-pu. *Kan.* Dasvalada-huvu.

The flowers yield a bluish-purple hue.

N.O. RUTACEÆ.

TODDALIA ACULEATA. *Duk.* Jangli-kali-mirchi. *Tam.* Milakaranai.

Roots contain yellow coloring matter.

ÆGLE MARMELOS. *Eng.* Bael Fruit. *Duk.* Bel-phal. *Tam.* Vilva-pazham. *Kan.* Bilapatri-hannu.

Rind of fruit astringent and yields a yellow color.

N.O. MELIACEÆ.

MELIA AZEDARACH. *Eng.* Persian Lilac. *Duk.* Gouli-nim. *Tam.* Malai-vembu. *Kan.* Bettada-bevina.

Leaves contain a green coloring matter.

N.O. RHAMNACEÆ.

ZIZYPHUS JUJUBA. *Eng.* Ber fruit. *Duk.* Ber. *Tam.* Elandap-pazham. *Kan.* Yalachi-hannu.

Bark used by dyers with other compound dyes.

VENTILAGO MADRASPATANA. *Tam.* Pappili-chakka or Sural-pattai. *Kan.* Papli-chakka.

Root-bark a valuable dye and much used by native dyers.

N.O. ANACARDIACEÆ.

BUCHANANIA LATIFOLIA. *Eng.* Cuddapah Almond. *Tam.* Kat-manga; Shara-purpu. *Kan.* Chara-puppu.

Bark astringent, used by dyers and tanners.

SEMECARPUS ANACARDIUM. *Eng.* Marking-nut. *Duk.* Bhilavan. *Tam.* Sheran-kottai. *Kan.* Geru.

The resinous juice of the pericarp is used in conjunction with lime for marking cotton clothing.

N.O. LEGUMINOSÆ.

ACACIA ARABICA. *Eng.* Babool Tree. *Duk.* Kali-kikar. *Tam.* Karu-velam. *Kan.* Kare-jali.

Bark highly astringent, used by tanners and dyers.

ACACIA CATECHU. *Eng.* Catechu. *Duk.* Katthah. *Tam.* Kashu-katti. *Kan.* Kachu.

Gum used for tanning, &c.

BUTEA FRONDOSA. *Eng.* Butea or Bastard Teak. *Duk.* Palas-ka-jhar. *Tam.* Murukka-maram. *Kan.* Muttuga-gidda.

Flowers yield a yellow dye.

CASSIA AURICULATA. *Eng.* Tanner's Cassia. *Duk.* Tarvar. *Tam.* Avarai. *Kan.* Avara-gida.

Bark a most valuable and generally used tanning agent.

N.O. COMBRETACEÆ.

TERMINALIA CHEBULA. *Eng.* Chebulic Myrabolans. *Duk.* Halda. *Tam.* Kaduk-kai. *Kan.* Alale-kai.

Fruit the *Myrabolan* of commerce, used as a dye and tanning stuff.

TERMINALIA BELLERICA. *Eng.* Belleric Myrabolans. *Duk.* Balda. *Tam.* Tanrik-kai. *Kan.* Tari-kai.

Fruit used for dyeing yellow and black.

TERMINALIA TOMENTOSA. *Duk.* Jangli-karanj. *Tam.* Karuppu-maruta-maram.

Bark used for dyeing black.

N.O. RUBIACEÆ.

RUBIA CORDIFOLIA. *Eng.* Indian Madder. *Duk.* Manjit. *Tam.* Manjitti. *Kan.* Manjushta.

Roots yield a kind of madder.

N.O. URTICACEÆ.

ARTOCARPUS INTEGRIFOLIA. *Eng.* Indian Jack Tree. *Duk.* Phunus. *Tam.* Palah-marum.

Saw-dust of the wood yields a yellow dye.

N.O. EUPHORBIACEÆ.

PHYLLANTHUS EMBLICA. *Duk.* Anvulah. *Tam.* Nelli-kai. *Kan.* Nelli-kai.

Bark astringent, used in dyeing.

MALLOTUS PHILIPPINENSIS. *Eng.* Kamela. *Tam.* Kamela.

A powder from the outer surface of the fruit gives a yellow dye.

C. FIBRES.

Fibres.

N.O. MALVACEÆ.

HIBISCUS CANNABINUS. *Eng.* Dukhaui Hemp. *Duk.* Ambari. *Tam.* Palungu.

This plant yields a very excellent fibre. In addition to this one there are six other species of *Hibiscus* on the Hills, all of which contain fibre. In fact, as a rule, all the herbaceous plants of the Mallow family contain fibre.

N.O. LEGUMINOSÆ.

Several *Crotalarias* and *Bauhinias* contain fibre. A large, climbing species of *Bauhinia* yields the fibrous bark used on the Government Cinchona Estates for tying on the moss, used in the mossing system of harvesting the cinchona bark.

N.O. ASCLEPIADEÆ.

CALOTROPIS GIGANTEA. *Eng.* Mudar. *Duk.* Akra. *Tam.* Erukkam. *Kan.* Yakkeda.

Yields a strong and durable fibre, used by native fishermen for making fishing lines.

CHAP. VII. — USEFUL PLANTS.

MARSDENIA TENACISSIMA. The stems yield a very superior fibre. Some of it prepared some years ago by me was nearly as fine as silk and very glossy and strong.

N.O. URTICACEÆ.

GIRARDINIA LESCHENAULTII. Contains a fine silk-like fibre used by the Hill tribes for making thread. Can be advantageously cultivated and will yield two or more crops per annum.

ANTIARIS INNOXIA. The inner bark yields a mesh of strong fibrous matting, which is made into bags by some Hill tribes.

N.O. MUSACEÆ.

MUSA ORNATA. All the plantains contain a quantity of very superior fibre.

N.O. PALMACEÆ.

PHŒNIX FARINIFERA. *Eng.* Date Tree. *Duk.* Sandole-ka-jhar. *Tam.* Ishan-chedi.

Leaf stalks yield a strong fibre.

N.O. PANDANEÆ.

PANDANUS ODORATISSIMUS. *Eng.* Fragrant Screwpine. *Duk.* Kedgi. *Tam.* Tazham. *Kan.* Kyadage.

Yields a very strong and superior fibre.

N.O. LILIACEÆ.

SANSEVIERA ZEYLANICA. *Eng.* Bowstring Hemp. *Duk.* Murgali. *Tam.* Marul.

Yields large quantities of very strong fibre and might easily be cultivated.

Drugs.

III.—DRUGS.[1]

Owing to the large number of articles coming under this class, it will not be possible to do more than simply specify their action as medicines.

N.O. MENISPERMACEÆ.

ANAMIRTA COCCULUS. *Eng.* Cocculus Indicus seeds. *Duk.* Kakmari-ke-binj. *Tam.* Kakkai-kolli-virai. *Kan.* Kakamari-bija.

Poisonous internally; used generally as an ointment.

TINOSPORA CORDIFOLIA. *Duk.* Gul-bel. *Tam.* Shindil-kodi. *Kan.* Amruta-balli.

Tonic and diuretic.

---

[1] The Superintendent of the Botanical Gardens, Ootacamand, is now cultivating experimentally various exotic medicinal plants, such as Rhubarb, Jalap, Peppermint and Ipecacuan, and there is every prospect of his shortly being able to supply these in quantities sufficient to meet the large demands of the Medical Department.

N.O. BERBERIDEÆ.

BERBERIS ARISTATA. *Eng.* Indian Barberry bark.
Tonic and febrifuge.

N.O. PAPAVERACEÆ.

ARGEMONE MEXICANA. *Eng.* Mexican Thistle. *Duk.* Pila-dhatura. *Tam.* Birama-dandu. *Kan.* Datturi.
Fresh juice used for muscular pains. Oil of seeds employed in skin diseases.

N.O. CRUCIFERÆ.

SINAPIS JUNCEA. *Eng.* Country Mustard. *Duk.* Rayan. *Tam.* Kadugu. *Kan.* Sasave.

N.O. CAPPARIDEÆ.

GYNANDROPSIS PENTAPHYLLA. *Duk.* Hulhul-ka-jhar. *Tam.* Velai.
Juice of leaves used as a rubefacient.

N.O. GUTTIFERÆ.

GARCINIA MORELLA. } *Eng.* Gamboge. *Duk.* Ausarahe-revan. *Tam.*
GARCINIA CAMBOGIA. } Makki.
Yield gamboge, a drastic purgative and pigment.

N.O. DIPTEROCARPEÆ.

DIPTEROCARPUS TURBINATUS. *Eng.* Gurjun Balsam ; Wood-oil. *Duk.* Garjan-ka-tel.
Used in leprosy.
VATERIA INDICA. *Eng.* White Dammer. *Tam.* Vellai-kunrikam.
Yields white dammer, which is allied to copal.

N.O. MALVACEÆ.

BOMBAX MALABARICUM. *Eng.* Red-cotton Tree. *Duk.* Kanton-ka-semal. *Tam.* Mul-ilava-maram. *Kan.* Mullu-buraga-mara.
Gum astringent; fruit yields silk-cotton.
ERIODENDRON ANFRACTUOSUM. *Duk.* Khatyan-ka-jhar. *Tam.* Ilava-maram. *Kan.* Bura-mara.
Yields gum and silk-cotton.

N.O. STERCULIACEÆ.

STERCULIA FŒTIDA. *Eng.* Sterculia-seeds. *Tam.* Pinari-kai.
Seeds yield an oil ; bark aperient.

N.O. LINACEÆ.

ERYTHROXYLON MONOGYNUM. *Eng.* Red Cedar. *Duk.* Dewadar. *Tam.* Tevadarum.
Leaves were largely eaten by the poor during the recent famine. Wood fragrant.

N.O. RUTACEÆ.

To this family belong the orange, lime, citron, &c., which are too well known to require any notice here.

ÆGLE MARMELOS. *Eng.* Bael Fruit. *Duk.* Bel-phal. *Tam.* Vilva-pazham. *Kan.* Bilapatri-hannu.

Half-ripe fruit astringent and used in dysentery.

TODDALIA ACULEATA. *Duk.* Jangli-kali-mirchi. *Tam.* Milakaranai.

Root-bark bitter, stimulant and febrifuge.

FERONIA ELEPHANTUM. *Eng.* Wood-apple. *Duk.* Kavit. *Tam.* Vilam-pazham. *Kan.* Byalada-hannu.

Leaves have the smell of anise ; half-ripe fruit astringent.

N.O. BURSERACEÆ.

CANARIUM STRICTUM. *Eng.* Black Dammer. *Duk.* Kala-damar. *Tam.* Karuppu-damar.

Yields the beautiful black dammer of Southern India.

N.O. MELIACEÆ.

MELIA AZADIRACHTA. *Eng.* Nim ; Margosa. *Duk.* Nim. *Tam.* Veppam. *Kan.* Bevina-mara.

Bark tonic and febrifuge. Mr. Broughton got from the bark an amorphous resin ; the bitter principle seeds yield an oil used in skin diseases.

N.O. CELASTRINEÆ.

CELASTRUS PANICULATA. *Eng.* Staff-tree. *Tam.* Atiparich-cham.

An empyreumatic oil made from the seeds is known as *Oleum nigrum* and used in beriberi.

N.O. ANACARDIACEÆ.

SEMECARPUS ANACARDIUM. *Eng.* Marking-nut. *Duk.* Bhilavan. *Tam.* Sheran-kottai. *Kan.* Geru.

The acrid juice of the nut is caustic and vesicant. It is also used with lime for marking cotton cloth, like marking ink.

ODINA WODIER. *Eng.* Annaickarai wood. *Duk.* Besharam-ka-jhar. *Tam.* Odiya-maram.

Bark astringent, used in skin diseases.

N.O. LEGUMINOSÆ.

ACACIA ARABICA. *Eng.* Babool-tree. *Duk.* Kali-kikar. *Tam.* Karu-velam. *Kan.* Kare-jali.

Bark astringent and used for tanning. The gum is that known in India as gum-arabic.

ACACIA LEUCOPHLÆA. *Eng.* Panicled Acacia. *Duk.* Sharab-ki-kikar. *Tam.* Vel-velam. *Kan.* Bilijali-mara.

Bark astringent, used in distilling spirit.

ACACIA CATECHU. *Eng.* Catechu. *Duk.* Katthah. *Tam.* Kashu-katti. *Kan.* Kachu.

Yields a kind of catechu, the *Catechu nigrum* of materia medica.

CASSIA FISTULA. *Eng.* Purging Cassia. *Duk.* Amaltas. *Tam.* Konraik-kai. *Kan.* Kakke-kai.

The pulp of the fruit is laxative.

PTEROCARPUS MARSUPIUM. *Eng.* Indian Kino. *Duk.* Nat-ka-dammul-akhvain. *Tam.* Kandamiruga-mirattum.

Yields the gum kino of commerce.

BUTEA FRONDOSA. *Eng.* Butea Gum. *Duk.* Palas-ka-gond. *Tam.* Murukkan-pishin. *Kan.* Muttaga-gondu.

Yields a kind of gum like kino. The seeds are used as an anthelmintic.

ABRUS PRECATORIUS. *Eng.* Indian Liquorice. *Duk.* Gumchi. *Tam.* Gundu-mani. *Kan.* Gul-ganji.

Root said to be used as a substitute for liquorice. The red seeds with black tips are used as weights by native jewellers and druggists.

N.O. COMBRETACEÆ.

TERMINALIA BELLERICA. *Eng.* Belleric Myrabolans. *Duk.* Balda. *Tam.* Tanrik-kai. *Kan.* Tari-kai.

The fruit is the astringent *Belleric myrabolans* of commerce.

TERMINALIA CHEBULA. *Eng.* Chebulic Myrabolans. *Duk.* Halda. *Tam.* Kaduk-kai. *Kan.* Alale-kai.

The common *myrabolans*, largely exported.

TERMINALIA CATAPPA. *Eng.* Country Almond. *Duk.* Jangli-badam. *Tam.* Nattu-vadam-kottai. *Kan.* Nat-badami.

Bark astringent, fruit used as a substitute for almonds.

TERMINALIA TOMENTOSA. *Duk.* Jangli-karanj. *Tam.* Karuppu-maruta-marum.

Bark astringent, used in dyeing and tanning.

N.O. MYRTACEÆ.

PSIDIUM PYRIFERUM and P. POMIFERUM. *Eng.* Guava root. *Duk.* Jam-ka-chal. *Tam.* Goyya-ver. *Kan.* Shíbe-hannu.

Bark of stem and root astringent and used in diarrhœa.

EUGENIA JAMBOLANA. *Eng.* Jambolam or Blue Apple. *Duk.* Jamun. *Tam.* Nagap-pazham. *Kan.* Nerale-hannu.

Bark astringent.

N.O. CUCURBITACEÆ.

CITRULLUS COLOCYNTHIS. *Eng.* Colocynth. *Duk.* Indaravan. *Tam.* Pey-komatti. *Kan.* Hava-mekke-kai.

Yields a kind of colocynth, an active purgative.

TRICHOSANTHES PALMATA. *Duk.* Guda-pandu. *Tam.* Shavari-pazham. *Kan.* Avagude-hannu.

A handsome climbing plant. Fruit said to be purgative.

N.O. RUBIACEÆ.

CINCHONA OFFICINALIS. *Eng.* Crown bark. *Duk.* Barak. *Tam.* Shurap-pattai.

CINCHONA SUCCIRUBRA. *Eng.* Red bark. *Duk.* Barak. *Tam.* Shurap-pattai.

These valuable plants, natives of South America, were introduced in 1861, and are now quite naturalised. Other species besides those mentioned above are cultivated, but only to a small extent. The area of the Government cinchona estates is a little over 842 acres. Besides distinct species there are also various varieties and hybrids which have appeared on the estates, and some of which promise to become very valuable. The bark hitherto has been chiefly harvested by what is called the mossing process. Under this system three kinds of bark are sent to market, viz., [1] *unmossed-bark*, *mossed-bark*, and *renewed bark*. The alkaloid on which the commercial value of bark chiefly depends is *quinine*, but it also yields *cinchonidine*, *quinidine* and *cinchonine*, all of which are also very efficacious as febrifuges. The average amount of alkaloids in Nílagiri bark is from 5 to 6 per cent., but some varieties and hybrids have yielded as much as 12 per cent. The crown bark is rich in quinine, and red bark contains chiefly cinchonidine.

RANDIA DUMETORUM. *Eng.* Emetic nut. *Duk.* Med-phal. *Tam.* Marukkalan-kai.

Fruit emetic.

GARDENIA LUCIDA. *Duk.* Dikamali. *Tam.* Kumbai. *Kan.* Dikke-malli.

Yields a fragrant resin, considered antispasmodic.

N.O. VALERIANEÆ.

VALERIANA LESCHENAULTII, V. BRUNONIANA. Roots have a smell like that of the officinal valerian and might be used as a substitute.

N.O. COMPOSITÆ.

VERNONIA ANTHELMINTICA. *Eng.* Purple Flea-bane. *Duk.* Kali-ziri. *Tam.* Kattu-shiragam. *Kan.* Kadu-jirage.

Used by natives as a remedy for leprosy and snake-bite. Also employed to kill parasites in the hair and as an anthelmintic.

N.O. CAMPANULACEÆ.

LOBELIA EXCELSA. Leaves poisonous, but may probably become a substitute for the officinal *Lobelia*.

N.O. EBENACEÆ.

DIOSPYROS EMBRYOPTERIS. *Eng.* Gab-fruit. *Duk.* Tendu. *Tam.* Tumbilik-kai.

Fruit astringent, a remedy in diarrhœa.

---

[1] *Unmossed-bark* is simply natural bark.

Mossed-bark is natural bark which has for some time been covered with moss.

Renewed-bark is the bark which forms under in covering of moss after the natural bark has been stripped off.

DIOSPYROS MELANOXYLON. *Eng.* Ebony tree. *Tam.* Tumballi-maram. Flowers used as a perfume ; bark astringent.

N.O. APOCYNEÆ.

HOLARRHENA ANTIDYSENTERICA. *Duk.* Karva-indarjou. *Tam.* Kulap-palai-virai.

Bark formerly exported to Europe as a remedy for dysentery under the name of *Conesse-bark*, *Corte de pala*, *Tellicherry bark*.

N.O. ASCLEPIADEÆ.

HEMIDESMUS INDICUS. *Eng.* Indian Sarsaparilla. *Duk.* Nannari. *Tam.* Nannari. *Kan.* Sugandha-palada-gida.

Used in all Government hospitals as a substitute for sarsaparilla.

TYLOPHORA ASTHMATICA. *Eng.* Indian Ipecacuanha. *Duk.* Pit-kari. *Tam.* Nach-churuppan.

The powdered leaves used as a substitute for ipecacuan.

DÆMIA EXTENSA. *Duk.* Jutup. *Tam.* Velip-parutti ; Uttamani. *Kan.* Hala-koratige.

Leaves emetic and expectorant.

HOYA VIRIDIFLORA. Leaves expectorant and emetic.

N.O. LOGANIACEÆ.

STRYCHNOS NUX-VOMICA. *Eng.* Nux-vomica. *Duk.* Kuchlah. *Tam.* Ettik-kottai. *Kan.* Mushti-bija.

The seeds are the commercial source of strychnia.

N.O. GENTIANEÆ.

There are several species of *Exacum*, two of *Ophelia* and one *Gentiana*, all of which are more or less bitter and possess the tonic properties of the European gentian. The gentian is a little prostrate plant of great beauty, and very common in dry pasture about Ootacamand.

N.O. CONVOLVULACEÆ.

PHARBITIS NIL. *Eng.* Kaladana. *Duk.* Kali-zirki-ke-binj. *Tam.* Kodi-kakkatan-virai ; Jiriki-virai.

The seeds are used as a substitute for jalap, and their active principle is a resin, *Pharbitisin*, discovered by me in 1861.

IPOMÆA TURPETHUM. *Eng.* Indian Jalap. *Duk.* Tikra. *Tam.* Shivadai-ver.

The *Turbith-root* of old writers. Purgative.

N.O. BORAGINACEÆ.

CORDIA MYXA. *Eng.* Sepistan-plum. *Duk.* Bari-gondni. *Tam.* Periya-naruvili.

Yields the *larger sebestens* of older writers. Emollient and demulcent.

N.O. SCROPHULARIACEÆ.

HERPESTIS MONNIERA. *Tam.* Nir-brami.

Regarded as diuretic and laxative.

CHAP. VII.

USEFUL PLANTS.

N.O. VERBENACEÆ.

VITEX NEGUNDO. *Eng.* Five-leaved Chaste tree. *Duk.* Shambali. *Tam.* Vellai-nochchi. *Kan.* Lakki-gida.

Heated leaves applied to swellings. Internally said to be anodyne and diuretic.

CLERODENDRON SERRATUM. *Duk.* Gand-baha-rangi. *Tam.* Shirutek.

Used by natives in fevers and colds.

N.O. SOLANACEÆ.

DATURA ALBA. Indian or White-flowered Datura. *Duk.* Ujla-dhaturah. *Tam.* Umattai. *Kan.* Ummatte-gida.

Anodyne and antispasmodic, used in medical practice.

N.O. LABIATÆ.

OCIMUM SANCTUM. *Eng.* Holy Basil. *Duk.* Tulsi. *Tam.* Tulashi. *Kan.* Tulashi-gida.

One of the sacred plants, the *tulsie*, said to be expectorant and diaphoretic.

N.O. AMARANTHACEÆ.

ACHYRANTHES ASPERA. *Duk.* Aghara. *Tam.* Nay-urivi. *Kan.* Utrani-gida.

Astringent and diuretic.

N.O. LAURACEÆ.

CINNAMOMUM ZEYLANICUM. *Eng.* Cinnamon. *Duk.* Dal-chini. *Tam.* Lavangap-pattai. *Kan.* Dala-chinni.

The bark is the cinnamon of commerce.

N.O. SANTALACEÆ.

SANTALUM ALBUM. *Eng.* Sandal-wood. *Duk.* Sandal. *Tam.* Shandanak-kattai. *Kan.* Gandhada-chekke.

Powder of wood used as a local application, essential oil used as a perfume, &c.

N.O. EUPHORBIACEÆ.

MALLOTUS PHILIPPINENSIS. *Eng.* Kamela. *Tam.* Kamela-mavu.

Yields a red powder *kamela*, used as a dye and anthelmintic.

RICINUS COMMUNIS. *Eng.* Castor-oil seeds. *Duk.* Yarandi. *Tam.* Amanakkan-kottai. *Kan.* Haralu.

Castor-oil plant.

EUPHORBIA ANTIQUORUM. *Duk.* Tin-dhari-send. *Tam.* Shadurak-kalli.

EUPHORBIA TIRUCALLI. *Eng.* Milk-hedge or Indian Tree-spurge. *Duk.* Bar-ki-send. *Tam.* Kalli. *Kan.* Bonta-kalli.

Juice very acrid.

PHYLLANTHUS EMBLICA. *Duk.* Anvulah. *Tam.* Nelli-kai. *Kan.* Nelli-kai.

Fruit astringent and antiscorbutic. Used also as a condiment.

ACALYPHA INDICA. *Eng.* Indian Acalypha. *Duk.* Kuppi. *Tam.* Kuppai-mani.
Emetic.

N.O. PIPERACEÆ.

PIPER NIGRUM. *Eng.* Black Pepper. *Duk.* Kali-mirchi. *Tam.* Milagu. *Kan.* Menasu.
Black pepper plant.

N.O. ZINGIBERACEÆ.

ELETTARIA CARDAMOMUM. *Eng.* Cardamoms. *Duk.* Ilachi. *Tam.* Ela-kai. *Kan.* Yalakkai.
Yields cardamoms, a well known spice.

CURCUMA AROMATICA. *Eng.* Wild Turmeric. *Duk.* Anbe-haldi. *Tam.* Kasturi-manjal. *Kan.* Kasturi-arishina.
Tonic and carminative.

N.O. LILIACEÆ.

LEDEBOURIA HYACINTHOIDES. *Duk.* Chhoti-jangli-piyaz. *Tam.* Shiru-nari-vengayam.
Bulbs expectorant.

GLORIOSA SUPERBA. *Duk.* Nat-ka-bachhnag. *Tam.* Kalaippaik-kiz-hangu.
Roots used to adulterate the aconite root imported from Northern India.

N.O. CYPERACEÆ.

CYPERUS ROTUNDUS. *Duk.* Kore-ki-jar. *Tam.* Korai.
The common korai, a troublesome weed. Root aromatic and diaphoretic and stimulant.

N.O. GRAMINEÆ.

ANDROPOGON CITRATUM. *Eng.* Lemon-grass. *Duk.* Hazar-masaleh. *Tam.* Karpura-pullu. *Kan.* Vasane-hullu.
Yields lemon-grass oil.

CHAPTER VIII.

ZOOLOGY.

PART I.—MAMMALS, BIRDS AND FISHES.
PART II.—LIZARDS, SNAKES AND FROGS.
PART III.—LAND AND FRESH-WATER SHELLS.

PART I.

MAMMALS, BIRDS AND FISHES.

(*By* Surgeon-Major G. BIDIE, M.B., *Supt. of the Central Museum, Madras.*)

General.—Mammals.—Birds.—Fishes.—Introduction of Fish from low country and from England.

CHAP. VIII, PART I. — ZOOLOGY. — General.

THERE has never been any attempt to give a complete description of the fauna of the Nílagiris,[1] such as was drawn up by the late Dr. Wight on the flora of this region. Indeed, the only available information on the subject consists of scattered notices in various general works, such as those of Jerdon, and these have reference chiefly to mammals and birds. As regards the reptiles and fish of the Blue Mountains not much is known, but there is even less recorded regarding the molluscs and hardly anything at all with reference to the rich insect fauna. There is not, therefore, much to be learned from books regarding the zoology of the Nílagiris, but fortunately there are in the Madras Museum a fair collection of birds from the district and specimens of the more remarkable mammals, together with a few reptiles and fish. These and the incidental notices already referred to have therefore supplied material for the present memoir.

MAMMALS.[2]

Mammals. —Monkeys.

Monkeys.—The most common and best known of this family on the hills is the Nílagiri langur, *Presbytis jubatus* of Jerdon, which inhabits retired shólas on the upper parts of the slopes and never descends to low elevations. It is covered throughout with a black glossy fur, except on the head and nape which have long

[1] Many interesting notes on the habits of wild animals on the Hills will be found in "*Game, by Hawkeye.*" Ootacamand, 1876.—ED.

[2] For facility of reference, the nomenclature of Jerdon has been used in the notices and lists of mammals and birds.

reddish-brown hair. The beauty of this unfortunate animal's coat is likely to lead to its extermination, as on account of the high price given for good skins the shikarees are indefatigable in shooting it down at all seasons. When caught young it becomes quite docile in captivity.

—The Lion Monkey.

The Lion Monkey.—This animal (*Inuus silenus*) is much more rarely seen than the previous one, as it is shy and inhabits dense and remote forests on the Malabar side of the hills. It was long designated the "Wanderoo," and believed to be a native of Ceylon, but does not exist in that island, being confined to the Western Gháts of the Indian peninsula. It is sometimes tamed, but is a sorry pet in captivity, being morose and bad tempered. The hair on its body is black, and there is a tuft at the tip of its tail; but the most remarkable feature in its appearance is the reddish white ring of hair surrounding the face, which gives it a very antiquated and venerable expression.

—Bats.

Bats.—There is very little known regarding the Nílagiri members of this family, only two, viz., *Nycticejus Temminckii* and *Hipposideros murinus*, having reached the Museum. As seen on the Nílagiris the "Little Horse-shoe Bat" is, according to Jerdon, of a light rufous colour, and found at Kaity and Rallia.

—Hedge-hog.

Hedge-hog.—There are several specimens of the South Indian hedge-hog (*Erinaceus micropus*) in the Museum, and we lately got a live animal, but it refused to eat and soon died. It is found chiefly on the eastern and lower slopes of the hills, and is smaller than the English hedge-hog. Its head and ears are nude and of a dark colour, and the spines are ringed with brown and tipped with white.

—Black Bear.

Black Bear.—This animal (*Ursus labiatus*), although a good deal hunted by English sportsmen, is still not uncommon on the hills. Its long, black, shaggy covering of hair is too well known to need any description. Its distinguishing marks are the light-coloured muzzle and feet, and the curved white band on the chest. Its particular vanities in the way of food are ants and beetles, but it has a sweet tooth for honey, and, by way of dessert, sometimes resorts to the fruit of the little date-palm found on various parts of the hills. One of its favourite relaxations is to scratch the bark of trees with its powerful claws. This, the Natives say, is done with the object of whetting the claws, but it is more probable that, as in the case of cats, it is done out of pure exuberance of animal life and spirits, or perhaps it may be intended to dislodge ants or other insects concealed in the crevices of the bark.

—Martens.

Martens, &c.— Two members of this family are found on the hills, viz., the Indian marten (*Martes flavigula*) and the Hill-otter, a species of *Lutra* much smaller than *L. nair* or *L. vulgaris*. There

CHAP. VIII, PART I. ZOOLOGY.

is only one skin of the Hill-otter in the Museum, and as the animal was not full grown, it is impossible to determine its species. It is by no means uncommon, but very shy and therefore rarely seen. Its dispersion over the range seems to indicate that fish are more plentiful in hill-streams than is generally supposed.

—Cats.

Cats, &c.—Of the cat family four species are found on the hills, but all of these are more common on, and rather belong to the fauna of, the plains. Chief of these is the tiger, which has been found at all elevations, although, of course, more common in jungles on the lower slopes than on the higher plateau. At times the tiger takes up its abode in some thicket quite close to one of the principal stations, a temerity which generally leads to its destruction, as it is soon marked down and pursued by ardent sportsmen. The tiger not unfrequently tries to carry off the buffaloes of the hill-men, but is often defeated in these attacks as the animals close up for mutual defence, and attempt to gore or trample their assailant to death. The cattle-herd on these occasions is said to take shelter within the irregular ring formed by his charge when on the defence. The leopard (*Felis pardus*) is also not uncommon on the hills, and does not lose in the cooler climate any of the predatory habits for which it is remarkable on the plains of India. Indeed, it might rather be said that it is even bolder in its depredations on the hills than elsewhere. Some years ago there appeared, in one of the Madras papers, an account of a leopard having ascended a tree on the Nílagiris to escape from its tormentors when hotly pursued by dogs and men, in which retreat it was potted like a rook. The other members of the feline family found on the Nílagiris are the leopard-cat (*Felis Bengalensis*), and the common jungle-cat (*Felis chaus*).

—Tree-cats.

Tree-cats.—The common tree-cat exists on the eastern side of the hills, and skins of another *Paradoxurus*, of much larger size, were recently got from the Ánémallé range and Kótagiri. This latter is called by the natives *Tree-dog*, and is, I believe, the *P. Zeylanicus*, var. *fuscus*, of Kelaart. It is not noticed by Jerdon, and has not hitherto been regarded as a native of Southern India.

—Mungoos.

Mungoos.—Three species of this animal are found on the hills, viz., (*Herpestes vitticollis*) the stripe-necked mungoos, (*H. fuscus*) the Nílagiri brown mungoos, and (*H. Smithii*) the ruddy mungoos. The first of these is found throughout the Western Ghâts and elsewhere, but the *H. fuscus* would appear to be peculiar to the Nílagiris. It is almost unnecessary to refer to the use of the mungoos in the economy of nature as an enemy of snakes, poisonous and non-poisonous. At one time it was believed that the animal, when wounded by a snake, resorted to some special plant as an antidote to the poison of the reptile, but it is now known that the mungoos does not have recourse to any specific when bitten. The impunity with which it comes out of such conflicts is entirely owing to the little animal's boldness and cunning mode of attack, and if fairly bitten by a poisonous snake, such as the cobra, there can be no doubt that the results would be fatal. CHAP. VIII, PART I. ZOOLOGY.

The Wild Dog.—This animal, *Cuon rutilans*, with its beautiful rusty red coat, large erect ears, eyes staring into the far distance, and cruel face, is certainly one of the most distinguished-looking of the *feræ naturæ* of Southern India. Its cousins, the jackal and fox, have always a sneaking expression about them, as befits their habits; but the bold look of the dog shows that it is made of sterner material, and its habits do not belie its physiognomy. Wild dogs always hunt in packs, chiefly during the day, and while thus engaged, keep up a peculiar sort of bark. When once they have fixed on their destined victim, they follow it with unfaltering perseverance until the animal becomes exhausted, when they rush in and worry it to death. They prey on deer and smaller animals, and Sir Walter Elliot mentions that he has known tigers leave a jungle in which a pack of wild dogs had taken up its quarters. This they possibly did not from any fear of the dogs, but because the presence of the latter would diminish the number of game and supply of food. Natives have rather a dread of the wild dogs, and consider it very unsafe to attack them, more especially if they are engaged in feeding on some animal they may have killed. —Wild Dog.

Squirrels.—Seven species of squirrels are found on the hills. One of these, the Nílagiri striped squirrel, is peculiar to the hill ranges of Southern India and Ceylon, but a nearly allied, if not identical, species, the *Sciurus insignis* of Horsfield, is found in Java. The flying squirrel also frequents dense forests at low elevations on the western slopes of the hills. It is very difficult to procure, being, like the bats, nocturnal in its habits; but specimens can generally be obtained when forest is being felled for coffee plantations. —Squirrels.

Rats.—Several species of rats and four of mice are found on the Nílagiris. One of these, *Golunda Elliotti*, is also common in Ceylon, and is well known to planters both there and in Southern India as the *coffee rat*. It is so called because in certain seasons it invades coffee estates in large numbers, and proves very destructive by cutting the young branches and eating the flowers of the coffee plant. Planters believe that it usually subsists on the seeds of the bamboo, and that when supplies of these fail it resorts to the coffee plantations. However this may be, it is very destructive owing to the immense numbers in which it appears. Its —Rats.

CHAP. VIII, PART I. — ZOOLOGY. — The Porcupine.

flesh is much relished by various castes of natives, and is said to be very palatable.

The Porcupine.—The porcupine is very common at various elevations on the Nílagiris, and most destructive to garden crops. It is especially fond of potatoes, and various engines of destruction, including spring-guns and steel-traps, are employed to get rid of the enemy. A deep narrow ditch with perpendicular sides is sometimes dug around the potato fields to keep the porcupines off, as they cannot cross this, and when they fall into the ditch they are unable to get out and are caught. They burrow like rabbits, and are nocturnal in their habits. When found abroad and pursued they are easily run down, but very dangerous either to men or dogs not acquainted with their system of defence, as when hotly pressed they suddenly charge backwards with spines erect, when ten to one the unwary pursuer is taken by surprise and gets impaled on the spines. Their coat of armour enables them to set at defiance blows with a stick and even a charge of shot from a gun, unless it takes effect in the head.

—The Elephant.

Elephant.—The *elephant* is only found low down on the slopes of the hills, and owing to the clearing away of jungle for coffee planting and the indiscriminate destruction by shooting which was carried on for some years, is not so common as it formerly was. The Indian elephant differs both from the African and that of Ceylon. The chief points of difference between the three species will be found in the shape of the head, the size of the ears, the disposition of the streaks of enamel in the teeth, and the number of the ribs. In all three species the number of pairs of true ribs is six, but in *Elephas Indicus* the pairs of false ribs number thirteen, while in the *E. Sumatranus* of Ceylon they number fourteen and in *E. Africanus* fifteen. Very exaggerated ideas have been entertained as to the height of the elephant. Of 201 elephants which were some years ago in the possession of the Madras Commissariat, the height of the tallest was exactly nine feet eight inches, and that of the majority below eight feet. The fossil remains of an elephant found at Jabbalpur are said to have shown a height of fifteen feet, but it is doubtful if, at the present day, any Indian elephant ever much exceeds ten feet in height. The Commissariat elephant which measured nine feet eight inches was a male captured in Coimbatore, and 36 years of age. Of late years certain restrictions have, very properly, been instituted by Government for the protection of wild elephants, and considerable numbers been captured in keddahs in Coimbatore and Mysore. As a rule, the wild elephant is a very timid animal, and *Rogue* or destructive individuals comparatively rare. For a more extended account of this noble animal

I would refer my readers to Tennent's charming "Natural History of Ceylon," to which I have been indebted for some of the facts already given.

—Deer.

Deer.—Both the *Samber* and *Spotted Deer* frequent the Nílagiris, but are getting scarce and shy owing to the constant persecution to which they are subjected by men, who, being on the hills and with nothing else to do, go out to shoot. The *Rib-faced* or *Barking Deer* receives the latter name from its peculiar call, which somewhat resembles a bark. Its face is marked with two long converging furrows, and it has large canines in the upper jaw, with which it wounds dogs when brought to bay. It is not gregarious, but leads a lonely life in remote jungle and is rather timid. Its horns are small with one snag, and its general color a bright rufous bay. The mouse-deer is also found in dense forest on the lower slopes.

—The Nílagiri Wild Goat, Ibex.

The *Nílagiri Wild Goat*, the *Ibex* of sportsmen, is now becoming rather scarce on the hills, and so wary that it is nearly impossible to get near it. It is quite peculiar to Southern India, being found only on the Nílagiris and other portions of the Western Gháts south of that range. The male, when full grown, is of a dark brownish color, with a pale saddle and stiff mane. The horns are short, curved, keeled internally, and closely ringed externally. The Nílagiri wild goat frequents the ledges of precipices and other difficult rocky retreats. It is gregarious and extremely wary. On the slightest alarm the herd melt away as if by magic, disappearing amongst the rocks. The *Tehr* or wild goat of the Himalayas belongs to the same genus.

Both the ibex and other game animals, at one time plentiful on the hills, are being fast exterminated, there being no close season. Bucks in soft-horn and does with young are wantonly shot down; and if measures be not adopted to protect the animals during the breeding season, there will not, in a few years, be one left on any part of the range.

A Bill has recently been introduced into the Legislative Council to secure protection for both game and fish, indigenous or introduced, on the Nílagiris.

—Bison.

The *Gaur* or *Bison* of the sportsman frequents the dense moist jungles of the western slopes of the Nílagiris. It has a very wide geographical distribution, being found wherever there is sufficient cover all along the Western Gháts, in the Pulní Hills, and in the remote ranges of the Northern Circars. It also occurs in Central India, the Terai and in Burmah. It is a very timid animal, and when alarmed the whole herd dashes into the forest regardless of every obstacle. It is also very wary, but when wounded a bull bison will often charge with great ferocity.

CHAP. VIII, PART I. — ZOOLOGY.

The following is a list of the mammalia found on the Nílagiris, in which the names given are those adopted by Jerdon in his "Mammals," a book likely to be in the hands of all taking an interest in the matter, and to which they can easily refer for further information.

ORDER PRIMATES.

FAMILY SIMIADÆ.

Presbytis jubatus. *The Nílagiri Langur.*
Inuus silenus. *The Lion Monkey.*

SUB-ORDER CHEIROPTERA.

FAMILY VAMPYRIDÆ.

Hipposideros murinus. *The Little Horse-Shoe Bat.*

FAMILY VESPERTILIONIDÆ.

Nycticejus Temminckii. *The Common Yellow Bat.*

ORDER INSECTIVORA.

FAMILY SORECIDÆ.

Sorex niger. *The Nílagiri Wood-Shrew.*
„ Perroteti. *The Nílagiri Pigmy-Shrew.*

FAMILY ERINACEIDÆ.

Erinaceus micropus. *The South-Indian Hedge-hog.*

ORDER CARNIVORA.

TRIBE PLANTIGRADA.

FAMILY URSIDÆ.

Ursus labiatus. *The Indian Black Bear.*

TRIBE SEMI-PLANTIGRADA.

FAMILY MUSTELIDÆ.

Martes flavigula. *The Indian Marten.*
Lutra sp. ? *The Hill Otter.*

TRIBE DIGITIGRADA.

FAMILY FELIDÆ.

Felis tigris. *The Tiger.*
„ pardus. *The Pard.*
„ Bengalensis. *The Leopard-Cat.*
„ chaus. *The Common Jungle-Cat.*

FAMILY VIVERRIDÆ.

Paradoxurus musanga. *The Common Tree-Cat.*
Paradoxurus sp. ?
Herpestes Smithii. *The Ruddy Mungoos.*
„ fuscus. *The Nílagiri Brown Mungoos.*
„ vitticollis. *The Stripe-necked Mungoos.*

FAMILY CANIDÆ.

Cuon rutilans. *The Wild Dog.*

ORDER RODENTIA.

FAMILY SCIURIDÆ.

Sciurus Malabaricus. *The Malabar Squirrel.*
„ Elphinstonei. *The Bombay Red Squirrel.*
„ macrourus. *The Grizzled Hill Squirrel.*
„ palmarum. *The Common Striped Squirrel.*
„ tristriatus. *The Jungle Striped Squirrel.*
„ sublineatus. *The Nílagiri Striped Squirrel.*
Pteromys petaurista. *The Brown Flying Squirrel.*

FAMILY MURIDÆ.

Nesokia Indica. *The Indian Mole-Rat.*
Mus Nílagiricus. *The Nílagiri Tree-Mouse.*
„ crassipes. *The Large-footed Mouse.*
„ Darjeelingensis. *The Darjeeling Mouse.*
Platacanthomys lasiurus. *The Long-tailed Spiny Mouse.*
Golunda Elliotti. *The Bush or Coffee Rat.*

FAMILY HYSTRICIDÆ.

Hystrix leucura. *The Indian Porcupine.*

ORDER UNGULATA.

TRIBE PROBOSCIDEA.

FAMILY ELEPHANTIDÆ.

Elephas Indicus. *The Indian Elephant.*

TRIBE CHÆRODIA.

FAMILY SUIDÆ.

Sus Indicus. *The Indian Wild Boar.*

TRIBE RUMINANTIA.

FAMILY CERVIDÆ.

Rusa aristotelis. *The Samber Stag.*
Axis maculatus. *The Spotted Deer.*

CHAP. VIII, PART I. — ZOOLOGY.

Cervulus aureus.	*The Rib-faced or Barking-Deer.*
Memimna Indica.	*The Mouse-Deer.*

FAMILY BOVIDÆ.

Hemitragus hylocrius.	*The Nílagiri Wild Goat.*
Gavæus gaurus.	*The Gaur or Bison.*

BIRDS.

Birds.

The avi-fauna of the Nílagiris is fairly represented in the Madras Museum, one of the taxidermists having made collections there during two successive years, and a large number was collected by me in 1877. Comparatively few birds are seen on the slopes and ravines on the higher ranges of the hills, but they become more numerous, both as to individuals and species, at elevations of from two to four thousand feet, that is to say where cover and food are most abundant. During the more rainy months of the south-west monsoon the majority of birds migrate to the eastern side of the range, where there is less rain and more sunshine. One of the most interesting birds found on the hills is the migratory wood-cock, and it is curious to notice the punctuality with which it annually appears, notwithstanding the systematic manner in which the bird is persecuted and shot down. Indeed there can be no doubt that if the woodcock had been a permanent resident, it would long ere now have been exterminated or frightened away from its haunts, but, being a pilgrim and stranger, it comes back yearly, all unconscious of, or forgetting the risks it will run, and the deadly gaps that will be made in its ranks. A list will be found farther on of the chief birds known to frequent the Nílagiris, the nomenclature and classification being those of Jerdon. This list contains species, and the order which first requires notice is that of the *Raptores*, or birds of prey. The most remarkable of these, as to size, are the long-billed brown vulture, and scavenger vulture, which are not uncommon, and are said to breed on the hills. Of hawks there is a goodly number including the kestril, two falcons, two goshawks and two sparrow hawks. There is no true eagle, but one kite-eagle, one hawk-eagle, and a serpent-eagle occur.

—Birds of prey.

—Owls.

Owls.—This group of birds is well represented, no less than eight species of owls being found on the Nílagiris. Of these the most remarkable is the brown wood-owl, which is regarded by Natives, both in India and Ceylon, with superstitious dread. It is purely a nocturnal bird, and its dismal yell is no doubt the reason for its being regarded with such fear. Most owls are more or less disliked by natives except the little spotted owlet, and it even is no favorite. A resident in Coorg informed me that he once put an owl in a cage, on which his Coorg friends besought him to set it at liberty, otherwise some disaster would certainly befall his family. He tried to argue with them as to the absurdity of their fears, and resolved to keep the bird to show that nothing would go wrong in consequence of its presence. On this resolution becoming known the bearers who attended on his children also pleaded with him to send the owl away, and threatened to resign his service if it were retained, as they were afraid to live on the premises with it. Hearing of this a missionary in the station volunteered to take charge of the bird to show that such superstitions were groundless, and it was accordingly lodged in his verandah. Shortly after this the missionary had to visit an unhealthy part of the district, where he got an attack of jungle fever which very nearly cost him his life. When this occurred the Natives at once triumphantly ascribed the fever to the presence of the owl, and some of the missionary's native friends lost no time in setting it at liberty. The missionary ultimately recovered, and this result was confidently attributed to the timely liberation of the caged bird.

—Perching birds.

Perching birds.—This large group is well represented on the Nílagiris.

Of *Swallows and Swifts* there are at least eleven species, and one of the most remarkable of these is the edible nest swiftlet (*Collocalia nidifica*). It breeds at various places on the hills, one site being a cave above the road from Ootacamand to Coonoor, near the first toll-bar out of Ootacamand. The nests as found here consist of a frame-work of grey lichen, glued together by inspissated mucus. *Night-jars*, *Bee-eaters*, *King-fishers*, and the Indian *Roller* are also more or less common, and the frugivorous *Great Horn-bill* occurs on the eastern slopes. Various writers have noticed the peculiar loud noise made by the wings of this bird when flying, and Hodgson, as quoted by Jerdon, compares its cry to the braying of a jackass. The list of climbing birds belonging to the Nílagiris is rather a long one. Of the beautiful plumaged wood-peckers eight species are found on the hills, and there are seven *cuckoos*, of which the pied-crested species is perhaps the most common. *Sun-birds*, *Shrikes* and *Fly-catchers* are also represented, and of *Thrushes*, including *Short-wings* and *Babblers* there are at least eighteen species. Of game-birds there are *Peacock*, *Jungle-fowl*, *Spur-fowl* and *Bush-quail*, not to mention the *Wood-cock* and *Wood* or *Solitary Snipe*. The beautiful Nílagiri or *Imperial Pigeon* also deserves notice, as being one of the prettiest of its family and somewhat limited in its geographical range. A list is appended of the birds known to frequent the Nílagiris.

—Climbing-birds.

CHAP. VIII, PART I.

ZOOLOGY.

ORDER RAPTORES.

FAMILY VULTURIDÆ.

Gyps Indicus. *The Long-billed Brown Vulture.*
Neophron perenopterus. *The White Scavenger Vulture.*

FAMILY FALCONIDÆ.

Falco peregrinator. *The Shahin Falcon.*
Tinnunculus alaudarius. *The Kestril.*
Erythropus cenchris. *The Lesser Kestril.*
„ vespertinus. *The Red-legged Falcon.*
Astur palumbarius. *The Goshawk.*
„ (Lophospiza) trivirgatus. *The Crested Goshawk.*
Accipiter nisus. *The European Sparrow-Hawk.*
„ virgatus. *The Besra Sparrow-Hawk.*
Neopus Malaiensis. *The Black Eagle.*
Nisaetus Bonelli. *The Crestless Hawk-Eagle.*
Spilornis cheela. *The Crested Serpent-Eagle.*
Buteo vulgaris. *The Common Buzzard.*
Milvus govinda. *The Common Pariah Kite.*
Pernis cristata. *The Crested Honey-Buzzard.*

FAMILY STRIGIDÆ.

Strix Javanica. *The Indian Screech-Owl.*
„ candida. *The Grass-Owl.*
Syrnium indranee. *The Brown Wood-Owl.*
Urrua Bengalensis. *The Rock Horned-Owl.*
Ketupa Ceylonensis. *The Brown Fish-Owl.*
Ephialtes pennatus. *The Indian Scops-Owl.*
Athene radiata. *The Jungle Owlet.*
Ninox scutellatus. *The Brown Hawk-Owl.*

ORDER INSESSORES.

TRIBE FISSIROSTRES.

FAMILY HIRUNDINIDÆ.

Hirundo rustica. *The Common Swallow.*
„ domicola. *The Nílagiri House-Swallow.*
„ daurica. *The Red-rumped Swallow.*
Cotyle concolor. *The Dusky Crag-Martin.*
„ rupestris. *The Mountain Crag-Martin.*
Chelidon urbica. *The English House-Martin.*
Acanthylis gigantea. *The Brown-necked Spine-tail.*
Cypselus melba. *The Alpine Swift.*
„ affinis. *The Common Indian Swift.*
Collocalia nidifica. *The Indian Edible-nest Swiftlet.*
Dendrochelidon coronatus. *The Indian Crested Swift.*

FAMILY CAPRIMULGIDÆ.

Batrachostomus moniliger. *The Wainád Frog-mouth.*
Caprimulgus Kelaarti. *The Nilagiri Night-jar.*
„ Mahrattensis. *Sykes' Night-jar.*

FAMILY TROGONIDÆ.

Harpactes fasciatus. *The Malabar Trogon.*

FAMILY MEROPIDÆ.

Merops quinticolor. *The Chesnut-headed Bee-eater.*
Nyctiornis Athertoni. *The Blue-necked Bee-eater.*

FAMILY CORACIADÆ.

Coracias Indica. *The Indian Roller.*

FAMILY HALCYONIDÆ.

Halcyon fuscus. *The White-breasted Kingfisher.*
Alcedo Bengalensis. *The Common Indian Kingfisher.*

FAMILY BUCEROTIDÆ.

Homraius bicornis. *The Great Horn-bill.*
Hydrocissa coronata. *The Malabar Pied Horn-bill.*

TRIBE SCANSORES.

FAMILY PSITTACIDÆ.

Palæornis rosa. *The Rose-headed Parrakeet.*
„ columboides. *The Blue-winged Parrakeet.*
Loriculus vernalis. *The Indian Lorikeet.*

FAMILY PICIDÆ.

Hemicircus canente. *The Heart-spotted Woodpecker.*
Chrysocolaptes sultaneus. *The Golden-backed Woodpecker.*
„ goensis. *The Black-backed Woodpecker.*
Mulleripicus Hodgsoni. *The Great Black Woodpecker.*
Gecinus striolatus. *The Small Green Woodpecker.*
Chrysophlegma chlorophanes. *The Southern Yellow-naped Woodpecker.*
Micropternus gularis. *The Madras Rufous Woodpecker.*
Chrysonotus Shorei. *The Large Three-toed Woodpecker.*

FAMILY MEGALAIMIDÆ.

Megalaima caniceps. *The Common Green Barbet.*
„ viridis. *The Small Green Barbet.*
Xantholæma Indica. *The Crimson-breasted Barbet.*
„ Malabarica. *The Crimson-throated Barbet.*

FAMILY CUCULIDÆ.

Cuculus canorus. *The European Cuckoo.*
„ Sonneratii. *The Banded Bay Cuckoo.*
Hierococcyx sparverioides. *The Large Hawk-Cuckoo.*
Polyphasia nigra. *The Indian Plaintive Cuckoo.*
Chrysococcyx Hodgsoni. *The Emerald-Cuckoo.*
Coccystes melanoleucos. *The Pied-crested Cuckoo.*
„ Coromandus. *The Red-winged Crested Cuckoo.*
Eudynamis orientalis. *The Indian Koel.*
Zanclostomus viridirostris. *The Small Green-billed Malkoha.*

Centropus rufipennis.	*The Common Coucal.*
Taccocua Leschenaultii.	*The Southern Sirkeer.*

TRIBE TENUIROSTRES.

FAMILY NECTARINIDÆ.

Arachnothera pusilla.	*The Little Spider-hunter.*
Leptocoma Zeylonica.	*The Amethyst-rumped Honey-sucker.*
„ minima.	*The Tiny Honey-sucker.*
Arachnechthra Asiatica.	*The Purple Honey-sucker.*
Dicæum concolor.	*The Nílagiri Flower-pecker.*

FAMILY CERTHIADÆ.

Sitta castaneoventris.	*The Chesnut-bellied Nuthatch.*
Dendrophila frontalis.	*The Velvet-fronted Blue Nuthatch.*

FAMILY UPUPIDÆ.

Upupa epops.	*The European Hoopoe.*
„ nigripennis	*The Indian Hoopoe.*

TRIBE DENTIROSTRES.

FAMILY LANIADÆ.

Lanius erythronotus.	*The Rufous-backed Shrike.*
Tephrodornis sylvicola.	*The Malabar Wood-Shrike.*
Hemipus picatus.	*The Little Pied Shrike.*
Volvocivora Sykesii.	*The Black-headed Cuckoo-Shrike.*
Pericrocotus flammeus.	*The Orange Minivet.*
„ brevirostris.	*The Short-billed Minivet.*
„ erythropygius.	*The White-bellied Minivet.*
Dicrurus longicaudatus.	*The Long-tailed Drongo.*
„ cærulescens.	*The White-bellied Drongo.*
Chaptia ænea.	*The Bronzed Drongo.*
Edolius Malabaricus.	*The Malabar Racket-tailed Drongo.*

FAMILY MUSCICAPIDÆ.

Tchitrea paradisi.	*The Paradise Fly-catcher.*
Myiagra azurea.	*The Black-naped Blue Fly-catcher.*
Leucocerca pectoralis.	*The White-spotted Fan-tail.*
Cryptolopha cinereocapilla.	*The Grey-headed Fly-catcher.*
Ochromela nigrorufa.	*The Black and Orange Fly-catcher.*
Eumyias melanops.	*The Verditer Fly-catcher.*
„ albicaudata.	*The Nílagiri Blue Fly-catcher.*
Cyornis ruficauda.	*The Rufous-tailed Fly-catcher.*
„ pallipes.	*The White-bellied Blue Fly-catcher.*
Erythrosterna leucura.	*The White-tailed Robin Fly-catcher.*

FAMILY MERULIDÆ.

Callene rufiventris.	*The Rufous-bellied Short-wing.*
Myiophonus Horsfieldii.	*The Malabar Whistling Thrush.*
Petrocossyphus cyaneus.	*The Blue Rock-Thrush.*
Orocetes cinclorhynchus.	*The Blue-headed Chat-thrush.*
Turdus Wardii.	*Ward's Pied Blackbird.*

Oreocincla Nílagiriensis.	*The Nílagiri Thrush.*
Pyctorhis sinensis.	*The Yellow-eyed Babbler.*
Alcippe poiocephala.	*The Nílagiri Quaker-Thrush.*
,, atriceps.	*The Black-headed Wren-Babbler.*
Pomatorhinus Horsfieldii.	*The Southern Scimitar-Babbler.*
Garrulax Delesserti.	*The Wainád Laughing-Thrush.*
Trochalopteron cachinnans.	*The Nílagiri Laughing-Thrush.*
,, Jerdoni.	*The Banasore Laughing Thrush.*
Malacocircus Malabaricus.	*The Jungle Babbler.*
,, Malcolmi.	*The Large Grey Babbler.*
Layardia subrufa.	*The Rufous Babbler.*
Chætornis striatus.	*The Grass Babbler.*
Schænicola platyura.	*The Broad-tailed Reed-bird.*

FAMILY BRACHYPODIDÆ.

Hypsipetes Nílagiriensis.	*The Nílagiri Black Bulbul.*
,, ganeesa.	*The Ghát Black Bulbul.*
Criniger ictericus.	*The Yellow-browed Bulbul.*
Kelaartia penicillata.	*The Yellow-eared Bulbul.*
Rubigula gularis.	*The Ruby-throated Bulbul.*
Brachypodius poiocephalus.	*The Grey-headed Bulbul.*
Otocompsa jocosa.	*The Red-whiskered Bulbul.*
Pycnonotus hæmorhous.	*The Common Madras Bulbul.*
Phyllornis Jerdoni.	*The Common Green Bulbul.*
,, Malabaricus.	*The Malabar Green Bulbul.*
Iora Zeylonica.	*The Black-headed Green Bulbul.*
Irena puella.	*The Fairy Blue-bird.*
Oriolus kundoo.	*The Indian Oriole.*
,, Ceylonensis.	*The Southern Black-headed Oriole.*

FAMILY SYLVIADÆ.

Copsychus saularis.	*The Magpie-Robin.*
Kattacincla macroura.	*The Shama.*
Pratincola atrata.	*The Nílagiri Black Robin.*
,, Indica.	*The Indian Bush-Chat.*
Larvivora cyana.	*The Blue Wood-chat.*
Acrocephalus dumetorum.	*The Lesser Reed-Warbler.*
Orthotomus longicauda.	*The Indian Tailor-Bird.*
Prinia socialis.	*The Dark-ashy Wren-Warbler.*
,, Hodgsoni.	*The Malabar Wren-Warbler.*
Drymoipus sylvaticus.	*The Jungle Wren-Warbler.*
Phylloscopus lugubris.	*The Dull-green Tree-Warbler.*
Motacilla Madraspatana.	*The Pied Wagtail.*
Nemoricola Indica.	*The Black-breasted Wagtail.*
Pipastes agilis.	*The Indian Tree-Pipit.*
,, montanus.	*The Hill Tree-Pipit.*
Agrodroma cinnamomea.	*The Rufous Rock-Pipit.*

FAMILY AMPELIDÆ.

Zosterops palpebrosus.	*The White-eyed Tit.*
Parus cinereus.	*The Indian Grey Tit.*
Machlolophus Jerdoni.	*The Southern Yellow Tit.*

TRIBE CONIROSTRES.

FAMILY CORVIDÆ.

Corvus culminatus.	*The Indian Corby.*
Dendrocitta leucogastra.	*The Long-tailed Magpie.*
„ rufa.	*The Common Indian Magpie.*

FAMILY STURNIDÆ.

Acridotheres fuscus.	*The Hill Bank-Myna.*
„ tristis.	*The Common Myna.*
Temenuchus Blythii.	*The White-headed Myna.*
Pastor roseus.	*The Rose-colored Starling.*
Eulabes religiosa.	*The Southern Hill Myna.*

FAMILY FRINGILLIDÆ.

Estrelda amandava.	*The Red Wax-bill.*
Munia undulata.	*The Spotted Munia.*
„ striata.	*The White-backed Munia.*
Alauda gulgula.	*The Indian Sky-lark.*
„ Malabarica.	*The Crested Malabar Lark.*

ORDER GEMITORES.

FAMILY TRERONIDÆ.

Osmotreron Malabarica.	*The Grey-fronted Green Pigeon.*
„ flavo-gularis.	*The Yellow-fronted Green Pigeon.*
Carpophaga insignis.	*The Bronze-backed Imperial Pigeon.*

FAMILY COLUMBIDÆ.

Palumbus Elphinstonei.	*The Nílagiri Wood-Pigeon.*
Turtur Suratensis.	*The Spotted Dove.*

FAMILY GOURIDÆ.

Chalcophaps Indicus.	*The Bronze-winged Dove.*

ORDER RASORES.

FAMILY PHASIANIDÆ.

Pavo cristatus.	*The Common Peacock:*
Gallus Sonneratii.	*The Grey Jungle-Fowl.*
Galloperdix spadiceus.	*The Red Spur-Fowl.*

FAMILY TETRAONIDÆ.

Perdicula Cambayensis.	*The Jungle Bush-quail.*
„ erythrorhyncha.	*The Painted Bush-quail.*

TRIBE LONGIROSTRES.

FAMILY SCOLOPACIDÆ.

Scolopax rusticola.	*The Wood-cock.*
Gallinago nemoricola:	*The Wood Snipe.*

TRIBE MERGITORES.

FAMILY PODICIPIDÆ.

Podiceps Philippensis. *The Little Grebe.*

FISHES.

Fishes.

The streams on the higher parts of the range contain very few fish, compared with what would be found in similar waters in any part of Europe. Standing by the Paikaré river, for instance, during a fresh, it is with a feeling of regret that one contemplates the utter barrenness of a stream apparently so well suited in every way to nourish hosts of fish, and afford sport for the lovers of the "gentle art." In 1866 Dr. Day attempted to introduce trout into the Nílagiri waters, but from various causes the experiment failed.[1] A full account of these experiments will be found in Dr. Day's first report, printed in Government Proceedings, 28th June 1866, No. 650, and of his further experiments to introduce fish from the low country in his second report, printed with their Proceedings of 9th May 1867, No. 1,052. These reports contain valuable contributions to the natural history of the district. Subsequently the late Mr. W. G. McIvor deposited live *trout*, *tench*, (the common sort, and also the beautiful German variety), *rudd*, *carp*, *gold-fish* and *silver eels* in the Ootacamand lake and several streams on the higher parts of the range.[2] Of the *trout* some were said to have been subsequently caught in a stream near Neduwattum, and some in a pool in the Paikaré river above the Bungalow towards the close of the year 1875.[3] These were seen and pronounced by Mr. H. S. Thomas to be undoubtedly trout. Of the other species the *carp* and *tench* have multiplied in the lake and elsewhere. The rest do not seem to have survived. Dr. Day also introduced *Barbus Carnaticus* into the Ootacamand and Bellikal lakes.[4] Whether these are living in the former is not known, but those put into the latter are flourishing. Subsequently Mr. H. S. Thomas deposited *Labes calbases* and *L. nigrescens* in a pond on the Adderley estate. These lived long enough to show they would stand the change of climate, but afterwards got into the coffee-pulper and were killed. Finally in 1877 Mr. Knox and Mr. Wapshare introduced into the Paikaré river

—Dr. Day's efforts to introduce fish from the low country and Europe.

---

[1] An attempt had previously been made in 1863, by Mr. E. C. G. Thomas, which also failed.

[2] Lady Napier and Ettrick placed the first fish in the Ootacamand Lake in August 1869.

[3] A full account of the method adopted by Mr. McIvor will be found in the Proceedings of the Madras Government, 6th January 1868, No. 31; 5th August 1869, No. 2,262; and G.O., 23rd August 1873, No. 899.

[4] Good Máh-seer (large carp, *Barbus mosal*) fishing may be had in the large streams at the base of the Nílagiris, see MR. THOMAS' *Rod in India*, 1873.—ED.

CHAP. VIII, PART I. — ZOOLOGY. —

some *Barbus Carnaticus* caught in the Hope-river, Ouchterlony valley. The fate of these is not yet known.

According to Dr. Day the only indigenous species found at high elevations on the plateau is *Danio Nilagiriensis.* He also caught in the rapids of streams on the slopes of the range a small roach, *Nemacheilus Guntheri,* a little carp, *Puntius Grayi* (*Barbus arulius,* Gunth.) and *Barilius rugosus,* erroneously called a "trout." The following is a list of the fish found on the plateau and slopes of these hills so far as known :—

GOBIIDÆ.

Gobius neglectus. *Jerdon.*

NANDIDÆ.

Nandus marginatus. *Jerdon.*

OPHIOCEPHALIDÆ.

Ophiocephalus marulius.	*Buch. Ham.*
„ gachua.	*Buch. Ham.*
„ striatus.	*Lacép.*

RHYNCHOBDELLIDÆ.

Mastacemblus armatus. *Lacép.*

SILURIDÆ.

Macrones punctatus.	*Jerdon.*
„ Cavasius.	*Buch. Ham.*
Wallago attu.	*Bloch.*
„ Malabaricus	*C. et V.*
Glyptosternum lonah.	*Sykes.*

SCOMBRESOCIDÆ.

Belone cancila. *Buch. Ham.*

CYPRINIDÆ.

Discognathus lamta	*Buch. Ham.*
Labeo Kontius.	*Jerdon.*
„ Dussumieri.	*C. et V.*
Mola melettinus.	*C. et V.*
Barbus dubius.	*Day.*
„ Mysorensis.	*Jerdon.*
„ Carnaticus.	*Jerdon.*
„ tor.	*Buch. Ham.*
„ melanampyx.	*Day.*
„ lepidus.	*Day.*
„ arulius.	*Gunth.*
Nuria Malabarica.	*Day.*
„ Madraspatensis.	*Day.*

Rasbora Nílagiriensis.	*Buch. Ham.*
„ daniconius.	*Buch. Ham.*
Barilius cocsa.	*Buch. Ham.*
„ gatensis.	*C. et V.*
Danio Nílagiriensis.	*Day.*
„ aurolineatus.	*Day.*
Perilampus atpar.	*Buch. Ham.*
Chela argentea.	*Day.*
Homaloptera Brucei.	*Gray & Hardw.*
Nemacheilus semiarmatus.	*Day.*
„ sinuatus.	*Day.*
„ striatus.	*Day.*
„ Denisonii.	*Day.*
„ Guntheri.	*Day.*

NOTOPTERIDÆ.

Notopterus kapirat. *Bonn.*

MURÆNIDÆ.

Muræna maculata. *Buch. Ham.*

—Mr. McIvor's success.

The following interesting account of the means employed by Mr. McIvor for the transport of live fish from England to the Nílagiris is extracted from G.O. No. 2,262 of 5th August 1869.

"I collected the young Trout-fry in July 1867, and had them kept in an aquarium till the date of my departure for India, to accustom them to the artificial condition to which they would be subjected during the voyage. When first placed in the aquarium, a rapid flow of water was allowed to pass through it; after ten days this flow of water was gradually diminished; but as many of the fry died, the flow of water was again increased, and continued for about six weeks, when it was again diminished with more favorable results. On leaving England I selected eighteen of the most healthy Trout-fry to be conveyed to India. The other species of fish had not this preparatory process, and I believe this was a disadvantage. On the 3rd November 1867, I left Southampton by the P. and O. Steamer with eighteen lake Trout-fry, twenty-four Tench, twelve Carp, twelve Gudgeon, twelve Rudd, twelve Silver Eels, and three Goldfish (one male and two females). Of those I succeeded in bringing to the Neilgherries, fifteen Trout, ten Carp, twenty-four Tench, twelve Rudd, twelve Silver Eels, and three Goldfish. The Gudgeon were all lost by an accident in the Red Sea; two Trout were subsequently lost by leaping out of the tubs in which they were placed. One female Goldfish died; nine of the Eels escaped into the running stream, and have not since been seen; the remaining three Eels were placed in a large pond in the gardens; and the other species of fish in a house, or rather enclosure covered with wire-netting, specially prepared for their reception, by forming

CHAP. VIII, PART I. — ZOOLOGY.

four ponds with a stream of clear water running through them. Previous to my departure I had the fry of each species placed separately in tin boxes, 15 × 10 inches, fitted with a small tap so as to allow a flow of water to pass from one box into the other, as per sketch below, Fig. I. The boxes should be placed in a

Fig. I.

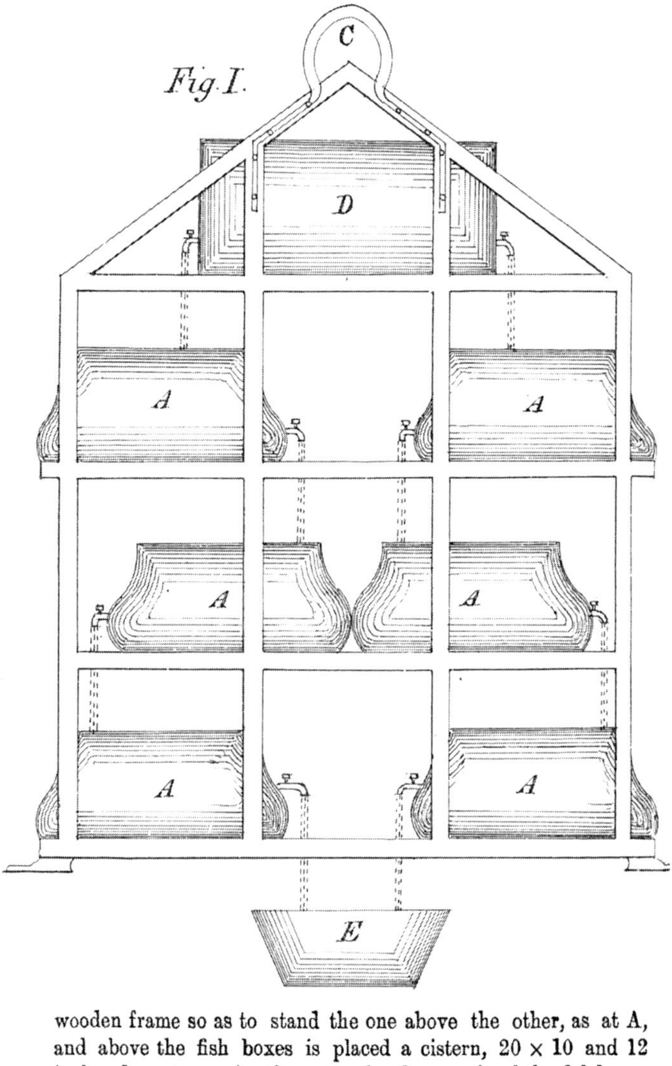

wooden frame so as to stand the one above the other, as at A, and above the fish boxes is placed a cistern, 20 × 10 and 12 inches deep, to receive the water for the supply of the fish boxes below. The wooden frame should be constructed so as either to be slung or stand on the deck. It is better, however, that it should be slung so as to swing to and fro with the motion of the ship. This can be effected by passing a rope through the iron loop C and suspending the frame in some convenient place exposed to a breeze. The same arrangement should be adopted when conveyed by land in a Railway carriage or otherwise. Fig. II is a longitudinal section of the fish box; A being a small flange for the lid to rest on; B the lid, made of perforated tin or zinc so as to allow the air to act on the water when the lid is shut. The lid should never be shut except in very stormy weather, and when there is a danger of the fish being thrown out of the boxes. In order to prevent all the water from being drawn off, the tap C should be placed about the centre of the box. Fig. III is a cross section; A the flange, B the lid, C the tap. The boxes are prepared for the reception of the fish, by placing about ½ an inch well-washed gravel at the bottom; they are then filled three parts full of water, and in this is placed a few aquatic plants to float in the water. These plants give off a small portion of oxygen and afford shelter to the fish. During the journey the water should be changed in the boxes and replaced in the cistern three times in twenty-four hours, or once every eight hours if possible. It is best to throw the fresh-water

Fig. II.

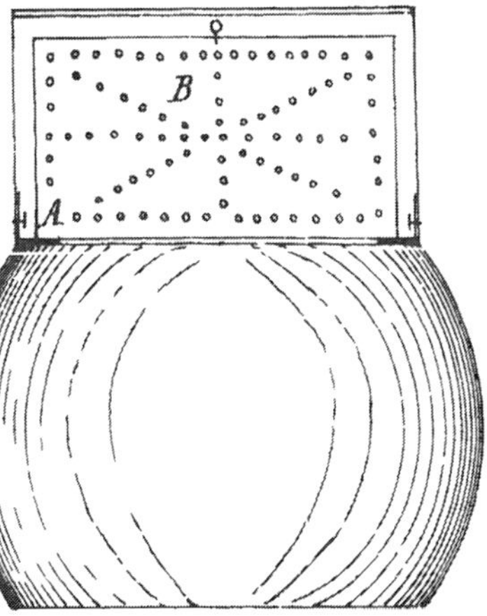

Fig. III.

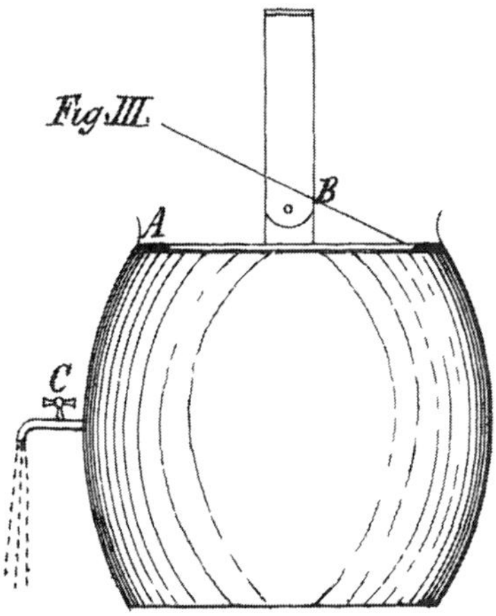

CHAP. VIII, PART I. ZOOLOGY.

into the boxes by means of a syringe, as in this way it catches the oxygen of the air in its descent. In addition to this the water prior to being used should be thoroughly aerated by forcing air through it by means of a bellows with a piece of elastic tubing (sufficient to reach the bottom of the water) attached to the end of the pipe. The smaller the fish-fry are, the safer they can be conveyed; but fish of considerable size could be conveyed with safety by increasing the size of the boxes in proportion, and thus placing at their disposal a greater quantity of water."

PART II.

LIZARDS, SNAKES AND FROGS.

REPTILIA.

(*By* Lieutenant-Colonel R. H. BEDDOME, M.S.C., *Conservator of Forests, Madras Presidency.*)

LIZARDS.

CHAP. VIII, PART II. ZOOLOGY. Lizards.

ORDER SAURIA.

VARANIDÆ.

Varanus dracœna, *L.* ... Southern slopes.
„ lunatus, *Gray.* ... Western slopes.

LACERTIDÆ.

Cabrita Leschenaultii, *D. et B.* ... About the foot and lower slopes on eastern and southern side.
„ Jerdoni, *Bedd.* ... Do.
Ophiops Jerdoni, *Blyth.* ... Do.

SCINCIDÆ.

Euprepes carinatus, *Schn.* ... Slopes everywhere.
„ macularius, *Blyth.* ... Do.
„ brevis, *Gunth.* ... Walaghát.
„ trilineatus, *Jerd.* ... Eastern slopes.
Hinulia Dussumieri, *D. et B.* ... Foot of Sisapára Ghát and western slopes.
Ristella Rurkii? *Gray.* ... Walaghát and western slopes.
„ n. sp. (an undescribed sp. with 2 large frontals). ... Foot of Sisapára Ghát.
Mocoa bilineata, *Gray.* ... Ootacamand, very common under stones.
Riopa albopunctata, *Gray.* ... All the slopes.
„ Hardwickii, *Gray.* ... Do.
„ punctata, *L.* ... Do.

GECKOTIDÆ.

Gecko Ánémaléam, *Gunth.* ... Slopes above Gajalhatti.
Hemidactylus trihedrus, *Dand.* ... Slopes, common.
„ maculatus, *D. et B.* ... Do. do.
„ Pieresii, *Kelaart.* ... Do. do.
„ Leschenaultii, *D. et B.* Do. do.

CHAP. VIII, PART II.

ZOOLOGY.

Gymnodactylus Kollegalensis, *Bedd.* Sisapára slopes near the foot, abundant.
„ Indicus, *Gray.* ... Ootacamand and Kúndas, very common under stones.
Goniodactylus planipes, *Bedd.* ... Foot of western slopes.
„ Wainádensis, *Bedd.* ... Walaghát, &c., and the Ouchterlony Valley.

AGAMIDÆ.

Draco Dussumieri, *D. et B.* ... Western slopes.
Sitana Pondiceriana, *Cuv.* ... Eastern slopes and foot.
Calotes nemoricola, *Jerd.* ... Coonoor slopes.
„ ophiomachus, *Merr.* ... All the slopes.
„ Elliotti, *Gunth.* ... Sisapára slopes.
„ versicolor, *Dand.* ... All the slopes, very common.
„ gigas, *Blyth.* ... Eastern slopes.
Salea Horsfieldii, *Gray.* ... Ootacamand and all the plateau, very common.
Charasia dorsalis, *Gray.* ... Abundant on rocks on all the gháts.

CHAMŒLIONIDÆ.

Chamœleo vulgaris, *L.* ... Southern slopes.

HARMLESS AND VENOMOUS SNAKES.

ORDER OPHIDIA.

Harmless snakes.

HARMLESS SNAKES.

TYPHLOPIDÆ.

Typhlops braminus, *Dand.* ... Common under stones on the slopes.
Onychocephalus acutus, *D. et B.* ... Rare about the foot on the western slopes.

UROPELTIDÆ.

Rhinophis sanguineus, *Bedd.* ... The Ouchterlony Valley.
Silybura Beddomei, *Gunth.* ... Walaghát.
„ Elliotii, *Gray.* ... Common on the slopes.
„ ocellata, *Bedd.* ... Common at Walaghát and in the Ouchterlony Valley.
„ Ceylanica, *D. et B.* ... Kalhatti, Walaghát, Shólúr and elsewhere.
„ brevis, *Gunth.* ... Walaghát.
Plectrurus Perottetii, *D. et B.* ... Ootacamand, very common.
„ Guntheri, *Bedd.* ... Walaghát.
Melanophidium Wainádense, *Bedd.* Ouchterlony Valley, very rare.

CALAMARIDÆ.

Geophis microcephalus, *Gunth.* ... Ootacamand, very common.

OLIGODONTIDÆ.

Oligodon subgriseus, *D. et B.* ... Eastern and southern slopes.
„ spilonotus, *Gunth.* ... Do.
„ Ellioti, *Gunth.* ... Do.
„ brevicauda, *Gunth.* ... Walaghát and the Ouchterlony Valley.
„ affinis, *Gunth.* ... Do.
Simotes venustus ... Ootacamand, not rare.

COLUBRIDÆ.

Ablabes olivaceus, *Bedd.* ... The Ouchterlony Valley, rare.
„ Humberti, *Jan.* ... Southern slopes.
Cyclophis Calamaria, *Gunth.* ... Slopes.
Coluber rubro-venter, *Bedd.*, n. sp.... Múdúmalé.
Cynophis Malabaricus, *Jerd.* ... Western slopes.
„ Helena. ... Eastern slopes, rare.
Ptyas mucosus, *L.* ... Slopes up to 4,000 feet, very common.
Zamenis fasciolatus, *Shaw.* ... Below Kótagiri, &c., rather rare.
Tropidonotus quincunciatus, *Schl.* ... Lower slopes.
„ Beddomei, *Gunth.* ... Múdúmalé and western slopes.
„ stolatus, *L.* ... Slopes, common.
„ monticola, *Jerd.* ... Western slopes and Múdúmalé.
„ plumbicolor, *Cantr.* ... Shólúr, Kalhatti, and all slopes, common.
Atretium schistosum, *Dand.* ... Múdúmalé, very common.

DENDROPHIDÆ.

Dendrophis pictus, *Gunth.* ... Slopes, common.
Chrysopelea ornata, *Shaw.* ... Do. do.

DRYIOPHIDÆ.

Tragops Perottettii, *D. et B.* ... Grass land of the plateau, very common.
Passerita mycterizans, *L.* ... Slopes, very common.
„ purpurascens, *Gunth.* ... Walaghát, rare.

DIPSADIDÆ.

Dipsas trigonata, *Boie.* ... Slopes, common.
„ Forsteni, *D. et B.* ... Do. rare.
„ nuchalis, *Gunth.* ... Western slopes, common.

CHAP. VIII, PART II. ZOOLOGY.

LYCODONTIDÆ.

Lycodon aulicus, *L.* ... Common up to 4,000 feet.
„ striatus, *Shaw.* ... Slopes, common.

PYTHONIDÆ.

Python molurus, *L.* ... All the slopes up to 4,000 feet, not common.

ERYCIDÆ.

Gongylophis conicus, *Schn.* ... Common under stones in dry forests up to 3,000 feet.
Eryx Johnii, *Russell.* ... Foot of Hills, east side.

Venomous snakes.

VENOMOUS SNAKES.

ELAPSIDÆ.

Naja tripudians, *Merr.* ... Common low down, rarely coming up to 5,000 feet.
Ophiophagus elops, *Gunth.* ... The Ouchterlony Valley and western slopes, rare.
Callophis nigrescens, *Gunth.* ... Slopes near Gajalhatti, rare.
„ Malabaricus, *Jerd.* ... Western slopes and up to Neduwattam, rare.
„ cerasinus, *Bedd.* ... Múdúmalé and western slopes.
„ trimaculatus, *Gunth.* ... This rare little snake, only hitherto known from the dry districts of Trichinopoly and Bellary, has just been discovered at the foot of the Sisapára Ghát.
Bungarus cœruleus, *Schn.* ... Eastern slopes.

VIPERIDÆ.

Daboia elegans, *Shaw.* ... Lower slopes, eastern side.
Echis carminata, *Schn.* ... Do. do.

CROTALIDÆ.

Trimeresurus Ánémaléensis, *Gunth.* ... Western slopes and northern slopes, common.
„ strigatus, *Gray.* ... Kúndas, very common.
Halys Elliotii, *Jerd.* ... Coonoor slopes, described briefly by Dr. Jerdon, but never detected since.
Hypnale nepa, *Lour.* ... Slopes, not uncommon.

Of the venomous snakes only two, viz., *Trimeresurus strigatus* and *Callophis Malabaricus* ascend to the plateau, and they appear to be confined to the western and northern sides of the Hills, never having been observed about Ootacamand or Coonoor, &c.

Trimeresurus A'némaléensis and *Hypnale nepa* are common in the moist forests and in coffee estates on the slopes. *Ophiophagus elops* (the hill cobra) and the four species of *Callophis* are very rare. *Naja tripudians* (the cobra), *Bungarus cœruleus* (the carpet snake), and *Daboia elegans* (the cobra monil or chain viper) are common only about the foot; the little *Echis* is very common in dry rocky ground, but not up to any elevation. It is very doubtful if the *Halys* is really a Nílagiri snake.

The above 45 innocuous and 13 venomous snakes are all that have as yet been detected in this district, but it is more than probable that other Uropelts, which occur in Wainád, and probably further new species will be found on the western slopes, and other Ánémalé snakes, such as *Simotes Russellii* and *Lycodon A'némaléensis*, probably occur there.

FROGS.

Frogs.

ORDER BATRACHIA.

RANIDÆ.

Rana Kuhlii, *Schl.*	... Walaghát.
„ pygmœa, *Gunth.*	... Do.
„ hexadactyla, *Les.*	... Eastern slopes.
„ cyanophlyctis, *Schn.*	... Do.
„ tigrina, *Dand.*	... Do.
„ gracilis, *Wiegm.*	... Plateau, the common frog in all swamps.
„ n. sp. (*var.* verrucosa, *Gunth.*)	... Western slopes.
Pyxicephalus breviceps, *Schn.*	... Slopes.

CYSTIGNATHIDÆ?

Crinia (or allied genus) n. sp.	... Walaghát. A minute frog with free toes, no parotids, maxillary teeth, and sacral vertebræ sometimes dilated.

PHRYNISCIDÆ.

Melanobatrachus Indicus, *Bedd.*	... This little frog, only lately discovered on the Ánémalés and Madura Hills, has just been found at Walaghát.

RHINODERMATIDÆ.

Cacopus systoma, *Schn.*	... Slopes.
Diplopelma ornatum, *D. et B.*	... Walaghát, &c.
„ Carnatica, *Jerd.*	... Eastern slopes.

CHAP. VIII, PART II. ZOOLOGY.

BUFONIDÆ.

Bufo melanostictus, *Schn.* ... Common everywhere.
„ Beddomei, *Gunth.* ... Western slopes.
„ hololius, *Gunth.* ... Do.

POLYPEDATIDÆ.

Polypedates maculatus, *Gunth.* ... Lower slopes.
„ pleurostictus, *Gunth.* ... Ootacamand and all the plateau.
„ brachytarsus, *Gunth.* ... Walaghát.
Hylorana temporalis, *Gunth.* ... Plateau and slopes.
„ curtipes, *Jerd.* ... Walaghát and the Ouchterlony Valley.
Ixalus variabilis, *Gunth.* ... Plateau and slopes.
„ opisthorhodus, *Gunth.* ... Western side, plateau, and slopes.
„ saxicola, *Jerd.* ... Western slopes, on rocks, beds of rivers.
„ tinniens, *Jerd.* ... The tinkling frog of Ootacamand.
„ diplostictus, *Gunth.* ... Walaghát.
Rhacophorus Malabaricus, *And.* ... Western slopes.

HYLŒDACTYLIDÆ.

Callula triangularis, *Gunth.* ... Paikaré.
„ olivacea, *Gunth.* ... Walaghát.
„ obscura, *Gunth.* ... Plateau, western side and slopes.
„ picta, *D. et B.* ... Slopes near Gajalhatti.

BATRACHIA APODA.

Epicrium glutinosum, *D. et B.* ... Western slopes.
Cecilia oxyura, *D. et B.* ... Do.

PART III.

LAND AND FRESH-WATER SHELLS.

(*By* Lieutenant-Colonel R. H. BEDDOME, M.S.C., *Conservator of Forests, Madras Presidency.*)

Inoperculated shells.—Operculated shells.—Remarks.—Fresh-water shells.

INOPERCULATED LAND SHELLS.

CHAP. VIII, PART III.

ZOOLOGY.

Inoperculated land shells.

Vitrina auriformis, *Bl.*
„ sp.
„ sp.
Helix ampulla, *Bens.*
„ apicata, *Bl.*
„ aspirans, *Bl.*
„ Barrackporensis, *Pf.*
„ bistrialis, *Beck.*
„ cacuminifera, *Bens.*
„ castra, *Bens.*
„ conulus, *Bl.*
„ crinigera, *Bens.*
„ cysis, *Bens.*
„ euomphalos, *Bl.*
„ fallaciosa, *Fer.*
„ fastigiata, *Hutt.*
„ febrilis, *Bl.*
„ Huttoni, *Pf.*
„ Indica, *Pf.*
„ injussa, *Bl.*
„ Kúndaensis, *Bl.*
„ lychnia, *Bl.*
„ Madraspatana, *Gray.*
„ mucosa, *Bl.*
„ Nílagirica, *Pf.*
„ retifera, *Pf.*
„ Shiplayi, *Pf.*
„ Sisapárica, *Bl.*
„ solata, *Bn.*
„ tertiana, *Bl.*
„ thyræus, *Bn.*
„ todarum, *Bl.*
„ Tranquebarica, *Bl.*
Streptaxis Perotteti, *Petil.*
„ Watsoni, *Bl.*

CHAP. VIII, PART III. ZOOLOGY.

Pupa (Ennea) bicolor, *Hutt.*
Bulimus mavortius, *Reeve.*
„ Nílagiricus, *Pfr.*
„ physalis, *Bn.*
„ prætermissus, *Bls.*
„ punctatus, *Ant.*
„ trutta, *Bl.*
Achatina Ceylanica, *Bn.*
„ oreas, *Bn.*
„ Perotteti, *Pf.*
„ Shiplayi, *Pf.*
„ hebes, *Bl.*
„ paupercula, *Bls.*
„ Jerdoni, *Bn.*
„ Bensoniana, *Pf.*
„ corrosula, *Pf.*
„ Botellus, *Bn.*
„ facula, *Bn.*

OPERCULATED LAND SHELLS.

Operculated land shells.

Diplommatina (Nicida) Nílagirica, *Bl.*
„ „ nitidula, *Bl.*
Jerdonia trochlea, *Bn.*
Craspidotropis cuspidatus, *Bl.*
Cyathopoma Coonoorense, *Bl.*
„ Dekhanense, *Bl.*
„ filacinctum, *Bl.*
„ Malabaricum, *Bl.*
„ malleatum, *Bl.*
„ Waináдense, *Bl.*
Opisthostoma Nílagiricum, *Bl.*
Alycæus expatriatus, *Bl.*
Pterocyclos bilabiatus, *Sow.*
„ rupestris, *Bns.*
Cyclophorus annulatus, *Tros.*
„ cælocomus, *Bn.*
„ deplanatus.
„ Indicus, *Desh.*
„ involvulus, *Mull.*
„ Jerdoni, *Bn.*
„ Nílagiricus, *Bn.*
„ ravidus, *Bn.*
„ Shiplayi, *Pf.*

Remarks.

The grand *Helix ampulla* is only found in the moist forest on the western slopes 3,000-4,000 feet elevation, where the rare and fine *Cyclophorus Nílagiricus* also occurs. Both these shells are very rare in collections, and of considerable value. *Diplommatina,*

Jerdonia, Craspidotropis, Opisthostoma, Cyclophorus, Shiplayi, and some of the *Cyathopomas, Streptaxis,* many small *Helices* and some of the *Achatinas* abound in the shólas or woods of the plateau. *Helix Madraspatana* abounds on the grass land of the plateau, sometimes in association with *Helix Nílagirica* and *Bulimus Nílagiricus.* The two species of *Pterocyclos* are found at or near the foot of the hills, and most of the *Cyclophori* in the woods on the slopes (Sisapára, Coonoor, and Kalhatti ghâts).

FRESH-WATER SHELLS.

Fresh-water shells.

There are very few fresh-water shells. *Neritina Perrottetii* occurs in some rivers on the plateau, and *Paludina Bengalensis, Planorbis exustus,* and *Ampullaria globosa* occur in tanks.

CHAPTER IX.

ETHNOLOGY.

PART I.—THE TO'DAS. | PART IV.—THE IRULAS.
PART II.—THE KO'TAS. | PART V.—THE BADAGAS.
PART III.—THE KU'RUMBAS.

INTRODUCTION.

The tribes.—General view of their history.—Sources of information.—Local distribution.

CHAP. IX. — ETHNOLOGY. — The tribes.

THE Nílagiris are inhabited by five native tribes, four of which may be regarded as primitive or aboriginal, viz., the Tódas, the Kótas, Kúrumbas and the Irulas, and the fifth as belonging to the Aryanized Hindu races now in ascendancy throughout Peninsula India.

General view of their history.

These tribes deserve, and have received the careful attention of ethnologists, and their language that of philologists. They are, in a measure, representatives of races which once overspread large portions of South India, some of which appear to have attained to a certain degree of civilization, and even to extended rule. In the Tódas we may perhaps see the remnants of tribes who occupied the river tracts of the Dekhan, and who tended their sacred herds of buffaloes long before their bovine rivals monopolised the veneration of the people;—in the Kótas, perhaps, the representatives of the early artisans of the south, who wrought metal and wood for the aborigines in the ages before the handicrafts became the monopoly of the present castes, who wear the thread of the twice-born and boldly dispute with the Brahmans their supremacy in the social scale;—again, in the Kúrumbas we may see the kinsmen of the primitive shepherds and goatherds of the southern uplands, who, unlike the more pliable Ideiyas, were too independent to ally themselves with the immigrant races from the north:—whilst in the Irulas we find the descendants of the hunting tribes of the south, who have attained to some civilization and power, as, for example, in the case of the Bédas and Náyaks. Lastly the Badagas, or *people of the north*, have a historic position, in that they bear witness to the fact that portions of the Nílagiris must have been long under the authority of Carnatic chiefs.

CHAP. IX.

ETHNOLOGY.

But although the primitive tribes are thus representatives, in a degree, of tribes whose power and influence was once widespread, yet they can be so only in a degree, for the constituent clans of each of those tribes, though known now under some general appellation, and possessing some generic qualities in common, were probably separated from one another in manifold ways. Through untold ages prior to the dawn of history, South India was probably occupied, like Central Africa of to-day, by numerous clans and tribes, springing up and then vanishing with a rapidity which is hardly conceivable in more civilized communities, where war, famine, and pestilence have lost some of their primal destructive force. Some of these clans would naturally, under favoring circumstances, have progressed, whilst others, under unaltered conditions, would have necessarily remained in their primitive state. But all would be known alike to strangers by one generic name, taken probably from some accident of their appearance or mode of life. This probably was the case with the Kúrumbas and Irulas, the *dwarfs* and *blacks* of the past. Clans belonging to each of these great divisions or tribes became civilized, partially at least, attained dominion, and exercised the arts of government and of politic life; but others never emerged from a state of barbarism and savagery. Among these were probably the forefathers of the Nílagiri Kúrumbas and Irulas. In fact the former are even now behind their kinsmen of the neighbouring plains, and obtain a livelihood by the pursuit of game, instead of by the care of sheep. Similarly, elsewhere, remnants of other large tribes, such as the Maravas and the Kallas, are scattered over the country, though some of their kindred have secured territory and power. But making allowance for these facts, still the isolated sections or remnants of tribes once powerful possess a greater interest than remnants which we know must have been greatly affected, both in language and manners, by contact with immigrant races, in that their very isolation has tended to preserve unchanged their dialect and race idiosyncracies. Thus in these dwellers in the wilderness, whether we regard them as descendants of, or merely as akin to the powerful tribes of their name of yore, we may find true indications of what their ancestors were before they succumbed to conquering invaders, and lost all their original brightness, by being driven back to seek subsistence under conditions of the savage life from which they had for a time emerged.

Sources of information.

In a work of this description, however, speculative inquiries are out of place, and therefore in the following monographs I have endeavoured simply to produce faithfully the recorded observations and views of the several competent writers on the subject.

By far the most trustworthy and exhaustive treatise thereon is the Report on the Primitive Tribes and Monuments of the

CHAP. IX. ETHNOLOGY.

Nílagiris, drawn up by the late Mr. Breeks, under the orders of the Madras Government, in pursuance of the general instructions of the Government of India, and to it I am mainly indebted, but have also made constant reference to the works of Messrs. Metz, Marshall, Harkness, Baikie, Ouchterlony, Jervis, Caldwell, Congreve, Shortt and Pope, and to several reports furnished to the Madras Government at different times.

Local distribution.

As regards the local distribution of the tribes, it may be roughly stated that the Irulas and Kúrumbas are scattered about the slopes, that the Badagas occupy the whole middle plateau, excepting, only, tracts in the north-eastern angle of Péranganád called Kódanád, as well as a small extent of pasture land in the vicinity of four mands[1] near Coonoor and Húlikal, which belong to the Tódas, and the lands attached to the six large villages of the Kótas, of which two are in Péranganád, two in Tódanád, one in Mékanád, and one in the Kúndas.

[1] Tóda Villages.

PART I.

The Tódas.

Origin.—Derivation of Name.—Physical characteristics.—Dress.—Census.—Divisions.—Mode of life.—Dwellings.—The mand—Situation.—Family and inheritance.—Pastimes.—Music and Song.—Salutation.—Religion—Priests.—Temples.—Rites and ceremonies.—Birth.—Marriage.—Funerals, green and dry.—Traditions.—Language.

CHAP. IX, PART I. — Ethnology. — Origin.

It has become the custom to consider this people as lords of the soil, not only on account of their self-assertion and independent bearing, but also on account of their practice of levying *gúdú*, or tribute in kind, from the other tribes. The Government have, in a measure, countenanced this claim of lordship over the lands of the plateau by paying to them quit-rent for certain lands within the towns of Ootacamand and Coonoor.[1]

The Tódas have probably inhabited the Nílagiris for many centuries, their occupation being anterior to that of any other of the tribes now dwelling thereon; but there are not sufficient reasons for considering them to be the earliest inhabitants of the hills.

Some remains of villages in no way resembling Tóda mands, as well as the cairns and barrows, are possibly the work of a race or races who preceded them, but of whom the Tódas can give no account. If Dr. Caldwell's theory is correct, that the Tódas are a Dravidian race of Scythian origin, they would seem to have left the plains after the Aryan invasions, but before the tenets of the Brahmans had taken any hold upon the minds of the people, and before there had been any extensive mixture of races.

But the date of their coming and their previous history are alike uncertain. Some think that they migrated to the Hills[2] about 800 years ago from the Kanarese country, and those who hold this theory, of the grounds of which I am ignorant, look upon them as a people who have degenerated from isolation, their religion containing only here and there some fossil remains of a former faith, and their language having dwindled to a mere skeleton. Colonel Marshall's researches have led him, on the contrary, to look on them as a primitive race still in its infancy. The Tódas themselves say that they came from the jungle tract of inferior hills situated between the Kanarese and Tamil Districts, in the direction of the Hásanúr Pass in the Eastern Gháts, north-east of the

[1] The history of the action of Government in regard to the land rights of the Tódas will be found in the chapter on the Revenue History of the District.

[2] Dr. Pope's *Tuda Grammar*; Mr. Metz's *Tribes inhabiting the Nilgherries.*

CHAP. IX. PART I. — ETHNOLOGY.

Nílagiris. In making this assertion, they are probably repeating parrot-like the Badaga tradition regarding the latter's advent to the hills, as is their wont, not being gifted with sufficient imagination to evolve a mythic history of their own. Another theory is that they came from the West Coast. The similarity of some of their customs to those of the Malayálams and the position of their mands, which are mostly in the western uplands of the plateau, whilst some are even in the Wainád, seem to lend colour to the view that their country lay to the west of the Nílagiris.

On the other hand, Dr. Caldwell remarks :—

"It has not been noticed by writers on the Nilgherries, but it is nevertheless a fact that, notwithstanding the long residence of the Tudas in a cold, cloudy mountain region, the color of their skin is considerably darker than that of the more modern hill race, the Badagas, a race of people who immigrated from the Canarese country not many centuries ago, and is many shades darker than that of the majority[1] of the natives of the Malabar Coast. The darkness of the complexion of the Tudas tends to prove that they came originally from the eastern or sun-burnt side of the range of Ghâts; and that, long before they took up their abode in the hills, they had formed a constituent portion of the low country population."

The mode of wearing the hair also seems to point the same way. The luxuriant crop or mop of hair, which is their pride, differs but little from the rough, shaggy and unkempt hair of many of the Pareiya and wandering castes of the Carnatic and Dekhan, except that it is oiled and combed. This pride in "these redundant locks, robustious to no purpose" is shared in an eminent degree by the women, whose desire to curl their hair, which has little natural wave in it, may be a point deserving the attention of the ethnologist, for this fashion is perhaps but an imitation of the *mode* of some superior race with whom their ancestors were familiar. The hazel or brown eye common to the Tóda, Kúrumba and Kóta, is also met with in the wild castes of the eastern plains.[2]

Nor does this view altogether militate against the notion that they *approached* the hills from the western side through the old Carnatic country. A race of drovers of semi-amphibious buffaloes is more likely to have gradually pushed forward its herds through the rich moist flats of Wainád to the grassy downs of the Nílagiris, than through the dry plains of Coimbatore and Salem. The fine species of buffalo which they possess may perhaps be found more nearly allied to the race of buffaloes known in Mysore as the Chokatti buffalo, which comes from the

---

[1] One tribe, the Puleiyas, in Malabar are very black.

[2] See FERGUSSON'S *Tree and Serpent Worship*, page 224; also DR. CALDWELL, Appendix, *Gram. Drav. Lang.*, page 566.

tracts along the Kistna river, than to the common and meaner animal of the plains.[1]

Derivation of the name Tóda.

Dr. Pope derives the name from the Tamil word *Tóru-van*, a herdsman. Mr. Metz and Dr. Caldwell doubt the correctness of this derivation, the *d* in Tóda being the dental, not the lingual *d*, and not related to the Tamil *r* or *l*. They consider the correct derivation still unknown.

Physical characteristics.

The Tódas surpass all the other tribes in physique and dignity of bearing, but they are not so tall as the Badagas. Still they may be spoken of as tall, the height of the men averaging 5 feet 3·30 inches, that of the women 5 feet 0·25 inches. Their features may best be described as European, with Roman noses and bright hazel eyes, good teeth and an abundance of rather coarse but glossy black hair, which is worn in a crop by the men and in long thick ringlets by the women. The expression of their countenances is open, fearless, and agreeable, and their smile invariably pleasant although rather vacant. Those who are interested in the lost tribes have been attracted by the peculiar noses of the Tódas. Their faces have sometimes a general resemblance to the Jewish type, but nothing in their customs or traditions connects them with the Jews. There is, however, a pastoral simplicity about them, when seen with their herds or in their homes, which agrees with our preconceived ideas of the primitive Hebrews. But it is rather beside the other races of the Nílagiris, than as compared with the natives of the plains, that the Tódas appear to great advantage.[2] Though admitting that they are a hardy, fine-looking race, as might be expected from their simple mode of life and the bracing mountain air they breathe, Dr. Caldwell remarks :—

"It is also certain that many of the statements that are commonly made, both in conversation and in books, respecting their physical characteristics are mere romance. As regards size and strength of body they will not bear comparison with the natives of the North-West Provinces, or even with the Telugu farmers and palanquin-bearers. The supporters of the Celtic Indo-European origin of the Tudas, are wont to rest the chief weight of their theory on the Roman noses of their *protégés*, but aquiline noses are not unfrequently met with amongst the people of the plains, though they have not had the good fortune to attract so much of the notice of tourists; and, after all, the nose which is most commonly seen on the Tuda face is not an aquiline, but simply a large nose. Even if it were universal, it would reveal nothing respecting the origin of the Tuda, for physiology makes little account of noses, but much of heads and the shape

[1] Dr. Shortt thinks all the breeds identical.

[2] The good food which the Badaga is now able to secure is improving his physique.

CHAP. IX, PART I. — ETHNOLOGY.

of the head, and the head of the Tuda does not differ in any material point from that of the low-country Dravidian." [1]

Though it cannot be denied that their facial peculiarities are not so marked as they at first appear, and that a good deal is due to their long beards and way of cutting their hair and to the absence of the turban, there is still something in the fearless manners and independent bearing of the Tódas, which makes them very attractive. They thoroughly enjoy a joke and never scruple to laugh heartily at anything which amuses them, showing no servile fear of Europeans, but rather treating them as equals if not inferiors. This fearlessness may in part arise from the superstitious awe with which other tribes regard them, which has enabled them to hold their own without the aid of arms or numbers. The Badaga regards the Tóda of the hills as a grand counterpoise in the art of necromancy to the malicious Kúrumba of the slopes.

Dress, &c.

The dress of the Tóda is simple in the extreme, but not ungraceful. It consists of a coarse species of cloth woven at Coimbatore, and white when new, having one or two bars of colour, generally red, woven into it at each end. By the men it is worn wound round the body, so as to form a kilt or petticoat, leaving the legs nearly bare ; then it is brought under the right arm and the end is thrown over the left shoulder. In general effect it is not unlike a Roman toga. The men also wear the lingúti or waistcloth called by them *kúvú* or *kónu*.

The female dress consists of the same kind of cloth, but it is merely thrown over the shoulders and held together in front, and is not worn so gracefully as by the men. Women also wear heavy brass armlets, generally two on one arm, called *Túwagi*.[2] They have necklaces of twisted hair or black thread with silver clasps, and here and there a bead or a bunch of cowrie shells, and sometimes a silver chain. They wear silver bracelets of rather a pretty pattern, and silver rings on their fingers and thumbs, also iron bracelets of peculiar design, one like a snake. Sometimes a silver chain is worn round the waist, to which is attached a small silver box opening with a screw, and used for carrying small coins.

Their ideas of cleanliness are extremely limited ; but, like most Natives, they clean their teeth. Their hair-dressing is by far the most elaborate feature of their toilette : according to Mr. Metz, who was well acquainted with their habits, the curling of their ringlets on long sticks occupies a considerable time every evening.

---

[1] *Grammar of Dravidian Languages*, Appendix, page 557.

[2] Weight about 5 lb.

CHAP. IX, PART I. ETHNOLOGY.

Census.

The following is a list of the Tóda population in the Nílagiri District according to the final census of 15th November 1871. Particulars will be found in Chapter II.

Villages.	Number of Persons.			Mands occupied.	Mands unoccupied.
	Male.	Female.	Total.		
Tódanád	319	212	531	30	38
Péranganád ...	53	49	104	5	3
Mékanád	2	2	4	1	...
Kúndas	...	...	...	...	2
Total ...	376	263	639	36	43

The number of mands has decreased since 1847.[1] There were then in

Tódanád	74
Mékanád	3
Péranganád	8

Divisions.

The Tódas are divided by Mr. Breeks into two classes, who cannot intermarry: 1, *Déválydl*[2]; 2, *Tarserzhál*. The first consists of the Peiki clan, corresponding in some respects to the Brahmans; the second, of the four remaining clans, called respectively Pehkans, Kuttans, Kennans and Tódis. Mr. Breeks states that the Peikis do not intermarry with the other clans, but Mr. Metz asserts that none of the clans intermarry.

Mode of life.

The Tódas are essentially a pastoral people, and, in a measure, nomadic, that is to say, the inhabitants of each mand or village possess one or two other mands, and[3] move from one to the other as they may find it convenient or necessary to do so, either to secure pasture for their herds or shelter from the monsoons, which are more felt in some localities than in others.

They never make any attempt to cultivate their lands. The *gúdú*, which they levy in kind from the Badagas and Kótas, supplies them with grain, and beyond this they depend entirely upon their large herds of buffaloes for support. Mr. Breeks humorously remarks:—

"Labor of any kind they hardly attempt; indeed, so entirely incomprehensible is the notion to them, that when, on one occasion, an unlucky mistake about the ownership of some buffaloes committed

[1] Ouchterlony's Report.

[2] Déválydl signifies "A man of God's house" from *Déválayam*, a temple, and *ál*, a person. Tarserzhál seems to signify servant, from *Tásan*, a servant or slave, a man of the fourth caste. Mr. Metz does not mention these names; possibly they are modern descendants of the high and low caste sections of the Tóda tribe. This caste distinction in an isolated and unbrahmanized race is suggestive.

[3] They also leave a mand for a time when one of their number dies.

CHAP. IX, PART I. — ETHNOLOGY.

an old Tóda to jail, it was found impossible to induce him to work with the convicts, and the authorities, unwilling to resort to hard measures, were compelled to save appearances by making him an overseer."

Besides their simple household duties, the women do a coarse kind of embroidery in blue and white thread obtained from the low country. They use Nílagiri nettle-thread for sewing their cloths and English needles.

Of late years some few Tódas, impelled by the example of the Badagas, whose industry is gradually making them rich, have applied for employment on plantations, but neither they nor their employers appear to have been much pleased with the experiment.

Dwellings.

The houses of the Tódas are well described by Dr. Shortt[1] as

"A peculiar kind of oval pent-shaped construction, usually 10 feet broad. The entrance or doorway into this building measures 32 inches in height and 18 in width, and is not provided with any door or gate; but the entrance is closed by means of a solid slab or plank of wood from 4 to 6 inches thick and of sufficient dimension to entirely block up the entrance. This sliding door is inside the hut, and so arranged and fixed on two stout stakes buried in the earth and standing to the height of 2½ to 3 feet as to be easily moved to and fro. There are no openings or outlets of any kind either for the escape of smoke or for the free ingress and egress of atmospheric air. The doorway itself is of such small dimensions, that to effect an entrance one has to go down on all fours, and even then much wriggling is necessary before an entrance can be effected. The houses are neat in appearance and are built of bamboo closely laid together, fastened with rattan and covered with thatch, which renders them water-tight. Each building has an end wall before and behind, composed of solid blocks of wood, which slopes down to the ground. The front wall or planking contains the entrance or doorway. The inside of a hut is from 8 to 15 feet square and is sufficiently high in the middle to admit of a tall man moving about with comfort. On one side there is a raised platform or pial formed of clay, about two feet high and covered with sambar[2] or buffalo skins, or sometimes with a mat. This platform is used as a sleeping-place. On the opposite side is a fire-place and a slight elevation on which the cooking utensils are placed. In this part of the building faggots of firewood are seen piled up from floor to roof, and secured in their places by loops of rattan. Here also the rice-pounder and pestle are fixed. The mortar is formed by a hole dug in the ground 7 to 9 inches deep and rendered hard by constant use. The other household goods consist of three or four brass dishes or plates, several bamboo measures, and sometimes a hatchet." * * * *

[1] *Tribes of the Neilgherries.*—SHORTT.

[2] Indian Elk.

CHAP. IX, PART I. ETHNOLOGY.

"Each hut or dwelling is surrounded by an enclosure[1] or wall formed of loose stones piled up from 2 to 3 feet high and includes a space or yard measuring 13 by 10 feet."

The mand.

A cluster of five or six of these houses, with a cattle kraal, forms a mand[2] or village, from *mané*, (Kan.) a house (Tam. *manei.*) One hut is always used as a dairy,[3] and one or two give shelter to the calves. The rest are simply dwelling-houses. Though the Tódas can hardly be said to possess any love for the beautiful, the picturesqueness of their mands, and the beauty of the sites which they choose for them, have probably helped to heighten their attractions as a people, and to add to the mystery which surrounds them.

Situation of mands.

One or two of these villages are perched on the extreme edge of the plateau, commanding glorious views of the plains and of the rich woods from which the mountains rise. Others nestle on the edge of a shóla, or are at least backed by some beautiful single trees. The presence of their buffaloes, seldom driven far away when pasture can be found near at hand, ensures a patch of short green velvet sward, sloping down to the stream which supplies the mand with water, or terminating in a marsh where their favourite animals wallow.

One remarkable feature in the Nílagiri shólas lends an additional, though perhaps a fictitious charm, to these villages, for it gives them, from a little distance, the one characteristic in which they are often wanting on a nearer view—a look of neatness and order. There is occasionally a strange resemblance in these shólas to carefully planted shrubberies, and some glades about Ootacamand might almost belong to the grounds of a well kept country place. The trees in the depth of the wood are often not high and of no great size, but their branches are gnarled and moss-grown, and nature has selected and placed them, as if with a view to variety of growth, foliage and colour. Shrubs, wreathed with jasmines and dog-roses, fringe the edges of these copses; and ferns and flowering plants, among which are the violet and a variety of the forget-me-not, make a border where they meet the sward. Periodical fires and the grazing of the buffaloes help to keep this line distinct; and if the trees are torn or cut for firewood,

---

[1] A cluster of huts always is, but not, as a rule, each hut.

[2] The Europeans who first ascended the hills probably confounded the word *mott* or *mortt*, which they used instead of *mand* with the latter. The former is the name used for the Irula villages on the slopes, with which the officers of the Coimbatore District were familiar; the words however may be of identical derivation. Mott or mortt is derived from *maram*, a tree, a word common to all Dravidian dialects. Dr. Pope derives mand from *mande*, a herd (Kanarese).

[3] *Páltchi. Pál*, milk + tchi? *tchi* = *erthchi*, it is. This suffix seems to be the third person of *er*, to be, and probably is equal to—milk is here, *i.e.*, the place where milk is kept.

CHAP. IX, PART I. — ETHNOLOGY.

nature restores the injury done to her with a lavish hand, and throws a mantle of rich green drapery over the wound. The woods are, however, too valuable as a shelter from rain and cold to be ruthlessly injured by the Tódas. They show great judgment in the selection of sites for their mands, shifting from one to another as the seasons change, and showing an intimate acquaintance with all the changeful moods of the Nílagiri climate. One peculiarity, the result of a great altitude within the Torrid Zone, has hardly been sufficiently dwelt on in a former chapter, although it sometimes has a prejudicial effect on the health of both Natives and Europeans,—I allude to the strange combat between summer and winter, between the chill frosty air of night and the burning tropical sun of mid-day,—all the fiercer for the transparent medium through which it shines,—which characterizes a winter in the hills. Its effect on vegetation, especially on flowers and fruit, is very marked, and some gardens and even portions of the shólas look as if Oberon and Titania had been quarrelling there, so well does her lament apply to them.

> " The seasons alter: hoary-headed frosts
> Fall in the fresh lap of the crimson rose;
> And on old Hyems' thin and icy crown,
> An odorous chaplet of sweet summer buds
> Is, as in mockery, set. The spring, the summer,
> The childing autumn, angry winter, change
> Their wonted liveries; and the 'maz'd world,
> By their increase, now knows not which is which.
> And this same progeny of evil comes
> From our debate, from our dissension:
> We are their parents and original."

Midsummer Night's Dream, Act II. Sc. I.

Family relations and inheritance.

To return to prose. It is said that the inhabitants of a mand are generally related to one another, and that, although each household has its head, the whole together forms but one family. The practice of polyandry, however, which still exists, tends to make their relationships most confusing; but, strange to tell, it does not appear to interfere with the domestic affections. This is probably in part due to the form of polyandry being that of several brothers or near kinsmen having one wife, a less gross institution than that existing among other polyandrists in South India. Polyandry is on the decline, and those men who can afford it have each their own wife. Often an elder brother indulges in this extravagance, whilst the younger are satisfied by a marital co-partnery. Female infanticide, which undoubtedly existed as a practice among them, but which has now entirely ceased, rendered polyandry a necessary institution. The position of the children in relation to the several husbands does not appear to be defined. Colonel Marshall asserts that each husband has an equal claim to parental right in the children born to them by the wife, and Mr. Metz that they claim the children on the principle of seniority, thus, the first child is given to the eldest brother, the second to the next, and so on. The differences are probably due to the varying customs of the several clans. I am not aware that these questions have ever been sifted in a court of justice. Women do not inherit, but the property is equally divided among the sons, the youngest taking the house, and with it accepting the duty of maintaining the females of the deceased. It is probable, however, that the father's wishes may to some extent determine the distribution of the estate. Inheritance goes in the male line,[1] not in the female as amongst the polyandrists of the West Coast.

Pastimes.

The Tódas have several games, which they play with much energy and apparent enjoyment. They are expert at a game called *Iláta,* which is played with a cylindrical piece of wood pointed at both ends and a bat. In fact Iláta is a variety of tipcat.

Another game is called *Narthpimi* and is thus described by Mr. Breeks :

"Close to some munds a stone table may be observed, consisting of two slabs stuck edgeways into the ground and another laid across them, leaving an opening just large enough for a man to drag himself through on his stomach. Two stones are fixed as starting posts, one at about thirty, the other about sixty yards from the table. A man stands by each of these, and the nearer of the two runs to the table and tries to wriggle under it, before the other, starting at the same time from the farther stone, can catch him. The rapidity with which they squeeze through the opening must be the result of long practice in crawling in and out of their house-doors."

A third game, called *Káriálapimi,* has some resemblance to *Puss in the Corner.*

Music and song.

They have only one musical instrument, a kind of flute, called *Búguri.* It is simply a hollow bamboo with holes at intervals, and is by no means sweet in tone. The singing of the Tódas is remarkable for an entire absence of tune. They lean their heads upon their hands, shut their teeth, and make a droning nasal sound which can hardly be dignified even with the name of a chant, and often approaches more nearly to a snore. As far as I know, they have no words for these songs, though one is known as the wedding song (*snori*). The Tóda word is graphic.

---

[1] It is remarkable, however, that in regard to the sacred buffaloes, the descent is through the females.—MARSHALL.

CHAP. IX, PART I. — ETHNOLOGY.

Mode of salutation.

Their mode of saluting one another is peculiar to themselves. A woman when she meets a man, lifts his feet,[1] first one and then the other, to her head as she crouches before him. In the case of an old woman, the ceremony is reversed, and she places her foot on the head of the man..

Badagas are called *máv*, or fathers-in-law, by the Tódas in token of respect. A Badaga greets a Tóda by laying his hand on the head of the latter.

Tenure of land.

The Tódas hold the lands on which their mands are built and the surrounding grazing lands on grazing puttas or leases. They pay two annas an acre. Further particulars will be found in the Revenue chapter.

Religion and religious beliefs.

Of the religion of the Tódas, as of their origin, very little remains to be said when the bare facts of the case, as far as they can be ascertained in one instance, and as far as they exist in the others, are divested of the hypothetic and romantic dress with which their chroniclers have adorned them. Their religion is either wholly rudimental, owing its few forms and ceremonies to recent contact with Hindus and others, or it is only the skeleton of an ancient but more developed cult.

Following the Tóda through the peaceful but monotonous course of his life, from the quaint ceremonies which herald his birth to his death-bed, surrounded by relatives who *mourn*, as orientals only can, we find no trace of any guiding or restraining power—apparently no sense of religious obligations or supernatural fears. He is too strong and fearless, or perhaps too dull and unimaginative, for superstitious horrors. His simple life presents few problems of good and evil, right and wrong. Hence he has little conscience or sense of wrong doing. It is startling, then, to find that after death he has a heaven[2] for the good and a hell for the bad, where, as they charitably aver, Badaga sinners at least must expiate their offences, and that the grim ceremonial of his funeral contains some words of prayer for the forgiveness of sins.

It is significant that such words as God, sin, ghost (Dév, Pápum, and Bhút) are almost pure Sanscrit, whilst the words

---

[1] This salutation is called *A'dabuddiken*, " I seize the foot."

[2] *Amnor*, heaven.—DR. POPE. Mr. Rice (Gazetteer of Mysore and Coorg) thinks this is a confusion, and that *Amnor* is a corruption of Marriamma or Amunnadáru, the mother or village goddess. Mr. Breeks, however, gives *Ammunád*, heaven; Colonel Marshall says, " The Toda has *Papum* for sin, but I more than doubt if he has any word for hell."

" All Todas go to *Amnor*."—MARSHALL.

Mr. Breeks remarks : " The Todas, as we have said, believe in a heaven and a hell, the latter being a swamp full of leeches" called Pufferingen, from *Pufa*, a leech, and *en*, a place. May not Amnúr or *Ammunád*, after all, be simply the village or country of the goddess Marriamma ?

which relate to ideas, which they have clearly borrowed from the Badagas, are Kanarese.

It has been supposed that the Tódas believe in the transmigration of the soul, but this is not very clear. They have, as has been said above, a distinct idea of a life after death, to be spent in a country, sometimes called "the other district."[1] As their buffaloes are their chief food in this world, they considerately kill a sufficient number at each funeral to supply the dead with milk in the next. The spirits of men and buffaloes are supposed to take a leap together into Hades from Múkarté Peak.

The Tóda has no idea then of an all-pervading Power, still less of a benevolent personal God; neither can he be said to act with any hopes of reward or fear of punishment of a supernatural kind. He has a half childish awe of any thing unusual or beyond his comprehension, and very soon exalts such things into objects of reverence, Dév or Swámi, though in the same category he includes occasionally the bones of his ancestors, a buffalo, a bell (Konku), an axe, an old knife, or the Pálál himself.

The absence of religious rites, except the annual[2] sacrifices of a buffalo-calf, and the extreme vagueness of what little can be illicited from them on the subject of religion, seems to have led to a report that they were not idolaters,[3] and the Jesuits of the west coast made several trips to the Hills in hopes of finding a colony of orthodox Christians, or at least of Manicheans[4] who had, though long estranged, preserved some features of their former faith. But in this they were disappointed. The exceedingly primitive worship of the Tódas is confined to one material object, the sacred buffalo-bell, which is hung round the neck of the best buffalo of the sacred herd, and is looked upon by them as the representative of Hiriadéva[5] or the chief god.

Besides this deity they have quite a pantheon of presiding gods, one in fact for each mand, and a hunting god called Bétakan,[6] whose temple is at Nambalakód in Wainád. He is the son of Dirkish, the son of En, the first Tóda, and is now, they say, attended by Brahmans. But to these gods they do not pray, and in what their religious worship consists it would be hard to say. It has few features of fetishism, no expiatory sacrifices,

---

[1] See METZ. The word alluded to by this gentleman is probably *Paradesam*, neighbouring country; *Paradise*.

[2] See RICE, *Mysore and Coorg*, on similar customs in Mysore, page 365, Vol. I.

[3] There is no Tóda word for idol. See DR. POPE's *Tuda Grammar*.

[4] There can be no doubt that, like the Manicheans, the Tódas reverence or even worship light, such as the sun, moon, or a lighted lamp. See Colonel MARSHALL.

[5] Hiriya = lord.

[6] *i.e.*, the hunter.—BREEKS.

CHAP. IX, PART I. ETHNOLOGY.

and there are but few traces of the joyous nature worship of Vedic times, still less any connection between its vague ideas of deity and its notions of right and wrong. "Some old men," Mr. Breeks writes, "of devout turn of mind, make salaam to the rising sun (Birsch) and at some seasons to the moon (Tiggul) and fast at eclipses, and occasionally they may prostrate themselves at the door of the *Páltchi*,[1] but no one except the *pujari* attempts any thing beyond this. "May all be well," "May the buffaloes be well" is the only form of prayer." * * * "They do not appeal to their mund god by name, nor do they seem to expect that he will show them any especial favor; in fact the names of their gods, like some of their funeral ceremonies, seem more like fossil remains of an extinct religion than parts of a living creed." It is also a curious fact that the Tóda does not pray by deputy. His priest, so far from offering up prayers for the people, regards himself as a god who needs not to pray.

Priests.

In spite of this apparent apathy, one division of the Tódas, the Peikis, is devoted to the priesthood, or rather resembles a tribe of Levites. There are five kinds of priests. The highest are the *Páláls*,[2] a mixture of herdsmen and priests. They live in isolated holy mands or groves called *Tiriéri*. No female may approach the mand, and no man may converse with the *Pálál* except from a distance, much less touch him. His own father must bow down before him. He is attended by a herdsman called the *Kávalál*[3] or watchman, who is also an ascetic, but by no means so holy as the Pálál, being merely his servant. He may converse with the Pálál, but may not touch him.

"Great sanctity attaches to the person of the Pálál in the eyes of his Toda brethren, and he exerts a powerful influence over their minds. They believe that God dwells in him, and makes known His will through him to those who come to him for counsel."[4]

Both *Pálál* and *Kávalál* are generally married men, and only lead a celibate life during their term of office. The preparation which a *Pálál* must undergo is by no means light. The aspirant is expected to retire to the jungles and there to live for eight days without any clothing to protect him from the severity of the weather and with hardly any food. Each day he strips some bark off the Túde tree (*Meliosma simplicifolia* or *Millingtonia*); and three times every day he performs the following ceremony[5]:—

---

[1] Sacred Dairy or Temple.

[2] *Pál* = milk, *ál* = a person, Man—appellative affix.

[3] *Kával* = watch, guard, and *ál* = person.

[4] Mr. Metz.

[5] Marshall.

"Squeezing some of the juice of the bark into a leaf-cup containing water from the stream or spring, he raises the cupful with the right hand to his forehead in token of respect; then lowering it to his mouth and drinking off the contents, passes the empty leaf round over his head and left shoulder, then depositing it behind his right side. This formula is repeated three times, using a fresh leaf each time. Next he takes the remainder of the bark and rubs his naked body all over with it, washing himself immediately with fresh water."

After thirty days of this exposure in the wilds, he is allowed to enter upon his duties, and from henceforth he inhabits a small hut in the lonely *Tiriéri-mand.*[1]

He renounces women and lives a life of rigid asceticism. The office of Pálál is seldom, if ever, held for life. There are instances of its being held for fourteen years, but the ordinary period is from two to three years.

The dress of a Pálál consists of a scanty black cloth. These are woven by the Badagas of Jackanéri.

Priests of the second order are called *Varzhál.*[2] They go through the same ceremonies as the *Pálál*, but hold office for a shorter period and are employed as milkmen. They wear only the *lingúti.*

The next two orders seem to be identical with the *Varzhál*, but their designation depends upon the mands to which they belong. They are called, respectively, *Kokváli* and *Kúrpúli.* The last, *Pálkápals*, *i.e.*, milk watchers, are a lower order. They are not obliged to lead a celibate life and may wear the *putkúli.*

It is said that the *Páláls* make up for their austerities by paying occasional visits to Badaga villages. They are held in great reverence for their sanctity and for their supposed acquaintance with the black arts by the timid Badagas, who readily supply them with such luxuries as they have to give. The *Pálál* appropriates all the milk of the sacred herd. It is considered too holy to be sold as milk, but what remains when the *Pálál* and *Kávalál* have had their shares is made into ghee, and in that state sold to the laity and the Badagas.

Temples.

There are two kinds of temples; one,[3] called *Bóa* or *Bóath*, is a conical roofed building surrounded by a wall. There are four in the hills:—

[4] 1, called *Manbóa* at Muttinád mand about four miles from Ootacamand on the left of the Segúr road.

---

[1] *i.e.*, the sacred buffalo mand, *tiri*, honorific prefix holy; *éri*—from *ér*, buffalo.
[2] From *Varusha*, year + *ál*—Kan.
[3] For a minute description of a Bóa interior and exterior see MARSHALL.
[4] BREEKS.

CHAP. IX, PART I. — ETHNOLOGY.

2, *Kinezh*, at the Tiriéri mand, near Shólúr.
3, called *Tarzkáva*, at the Tiriéri mand on the Kúndas.
4, called *Mutterzhva*, near Brikapatti.

There was formerly a fifth called *Katedva* near Múkarté, but it is now in ruins.

The second kind of temple is called a *Páltchi*. It resembles an ordinary house, but is larger. There are two varieties, one is merely a dairy house, such as every mand possesses, the other is something more, and its importance appears to depend upon the relics it contains. These are called *Kúrpús*[1] and the *Páltchi* in which they are kept is looked upon as a shrine. Mands where they are found are called *Etad*, or great mands, in contradistinction to *Buri*, or common mands.

The *Bóa* temples do not seem properly to belong to the Tódas, but to some earlier race. They are not attended by priests of the highest, but of the second grade. The particulars regarding them, however, are more appropriate to the following chapter.

Rites and ceremonies. —Birth.

Soon after a child is born a young buffalo-calf is brought. The father takes three bamboo measures and pours water from the third measure into the other two, holding them close to the hind quarters of the calf on its right side. The meaning of this singular rite is not clear, but it probably has reference to the future supply of milk for the infant's sustenance. The following custom is also noteworthy, but also inexplicable. The Tóda throws no light on the subject. He, like most other Hindus, is content to say and know that "it is mámúl" or custom.

The father and mother of a new-born child take each a leaf in their hands; water is poured over the leaf held by the father, and from it to the one in the mother's hand; she drinks and puts a drop into the child's mouth three times. After this mother and child are removed to a separate hut and remain there until the next new moon. No ceremony is used when girls are named, but boys are taken by the father to the door of the *Páltchi*. The father prostrates himself, and a name is then given to the infant, generally a few months old, by its maternal grandfather.

—Marriage.

Early betrothals are common among the Tódas and an interchange of buffaloes ratifies the agreement. Later, when the marriage is consummated, another exchange of buffaloes takes place. There is no ceremony, except that the woman bows down before her husband who places his foot upon her head. She then performs some simple household duty, such as drawing water and cooking food, and is thus installed. In the case of two or more brothers marrying one wife, the ceremony is performed by the eldest only.

[1] MARSHALL.

In the seventh month of a woman's first pregnancy an apparently meaningless rite is gone through, which is curious, because in it the bow and arrows, now fallen into disuse, play a part, as they also do at funerals.

It is thus described by Mr. Breeks:

"The woman's father visits the husband's hut. The husband asks 'Shall I tie the *tali*?'[1] The father consents. The husband then asks, 'Shall I give a bow?' The father answers, 'yes.' The husband makes a bow of the Hubbé shrub (*Sophora glauca*), the bark serving for a string. He takes this into a shola in the afternoon, and gives it to his wife, who, sitting down before a jungle tree, in the stem of which a convenient hole can be found to place a small earthenware lamp, asks the name of the bow, holds it a little while, and then places it at the foot of the tree. Each mand has a different name for the bow."

The husband and wife remain all night in the shóla.

—Funerals.

The ceremonies with which the Tóda surrounds his dead are strange and weird, with touches here and there full of pathos and beauty. But, again, we are haunted by the thought that the ritual is in places more suggestive to us than it can be to him, and that memory or imagination infuse a meaning for us into forms which to him are "mámúl" and nothing more.

When a Tóda is thought to be "sick unto death" he is dressed in all the ornaments and jewellery of his house, and his friends' last office is to give him milk to drink.[2] After death he is wrapped in a new mantle, into the pockets of which a supply of grain, sugar, &c., is put for his use on the road to *Amnúr*. No coin to fee the ferryman of the infernal river is placed in the mouth of the dying man as is done in the case of moribund Badagas. The omission seems simply to indicate the isolated position of the Tóda for many generations. They provide in kind for what a Badaga provides in coin. There are two funeral ceremonies, one, which includes the burning of the body and takes place as soon as possible after death. This is called the green[3] funeral. The other is celebrated some months later and may include all the members of the tribe who have died during the year. It is called the dry[4] funeral.

—Green funeral.

As soon as death occurs, the dead man is brought out of his house and laid upon a bier made of branches. On this he is

---

[1] Or necklace, answering to our wedding ring.

[2] The Phrenologist among the Tódas.

[3] *Háse Kédú*. From *Hásé* Drav. perhaps *pasu* (?) green, soft, tender. *Kédú*, (Tamil, Kanarese), destruction, death.—MARSHALL.

[4] Bara-Kédú—*Bara* or *Var*, Tamil; Kanarese and Telugu, *bar*, dry, parched, sterile.—MARSHALL.

Mr. Breeks gives *Kordzai Kédu*, green funeral; *Marvendli Kédu*, dry funeral.

CHAP. IX, PART I. — ETHNOLOGY.

carried by his nearest relatives, surrounded by a crowd of mourning friends to the nearest *Kédu* or burial mand, or, as it is often called, *Methgúdi* or burning-place.

A small herd of buffaloes is driven along with the *cortége* and all the friends of the deceased and the neighboring villagers assemble to do honor to the dead. Arrived at the *Methgúdi* a funeral pile is constructed on which the corpse is placed. Each buffalo has a little bell hung round its neck, and they are then driven close to the pile with the words "*Avan ọd atu*," "Go with him." Then the mourners, male and female, down to the youngest baby, take three handfuls of earth, throw them towards the buffaloes; then they throw earth three times upon the body, saying "*Purzh-ul-gama, Purzh-ul-gama, Purzh-ul-gama*," "Let him go into the soil." The recumbent corpse is now lifted up in the arms of his relatives, and each cow in succession is dragged by two men up to her master, whose arm is raised and made to touch the animal's horns. After this the pyre is lighted by fire made by the friction of two sticks. The body is lifted up and swung three times from side to side, then laid on the burning wood *face downwards*. As the flames devour the body the people cry "Shall we kill buffaloes for you?" "You are going to Amnúr;" "may it be well with you;" "may all thy sins go." One or two buffaloes are now killed, and as each creature falls dead from a blow from the butt end of an axe the people crowd round it, sobbing and lamenting and kissing its face. After this they sit round the bier in pairs with their faces together and their foreheads touching, weeping bitterly and wailing in true oriental fashion.

After the corpse is consumed, they collect the bones and the skull[1] to be kept in the house of the deceased until the dry funeral is celebrated. Any jewels or coins that may have been on the body are sought for,[2] but the ashes are "left to the winds." The friends then salute the place and leave it.

They never mention the dead by name. No prayer or religious ceremony seems to accompany a burning, nor are the priests necessarily in attendance.

—Dry funeral.

The dry funeral is a less solemn, although a more elaborate, ceremony. Probably the mere fact of its now being postponed until two or three funerals can be celebrated together has tended to make it more or less of a commemoration festival. The reasons for thus making one festival serve for all the dead of one tribe seem to

[1] *Norrzh, Nirru* (Dra.), ashes.—POPE.

[2] BREEKS. Colonel Marshall says they are buried with only valueless articles, such as knives, metal rings, &c.

have been chiefly economic, but Government[1] have also stepped in to restrain the reckless slaughtering of buffaloes which was customary on these occasions, on the ground of the cruelties practised, and this action may have helped to the same result. None were gainers by the death of the poor animals except the Kótas, who attend on these occasions as musicians and claim the carcases of all the buffaloes. When the Tódas are asked why they give them all to the Kótas, the stereotyped reply is " It is *mámúl shástra.*" " When the buffaloes are alive they are ours, when they are dead they are the Kótas'."

The ceremonies are spread over three days. On the first the Tódas assemble in large numbers at a *Kédmanei* or funeral-house.

" Each clan has its own and different ones for men and women. They are like ordinary Toda huts, but are sometimes decorated at the time of the funeral with silver coins."

Kóta musicians are in attendance as well as Badagas and other natives, and sometimes shopkeepers from Ootacamand selling biscuits and sweetmeats. The scene is busy and animated, singing and dancing go on; to pass the time panchayets[2] are held, and occasionally a Tóda becomes possessed of his god and makes a variety by doing a little prophesying in a wild and ecstatic manner, but like such "mediums" from the Pythian down to those of modern times, his communications are not of a very exalted nature, nor do they convey information which would be otherwise unattainable, but generally consist of denunciations of the present and praises " of the good old times."

Nothing further is done on the first day except the driving in of the buffaloes intended to be sacrificed. When they are safely enclosed in the kraal—two or three for each of the dead commemorated—the young men throw off their *pútkúlis* and rush among them, hanging on to the animals by the neck and horns, whilst a bell is tied round the neck of each. At this point the women begin to lament, but though the tears flow down their cheeks they are soon dried, and the rest of the day is spent in feasting.

The ceremonies of the second day are the most important. In the first place the *Kéd* is brought out, wrapped in a new *pútkúli* and placed within the stone wall which encloses the *Kédmanei*. Twenty or thirty men stand round it shouting the apparently irrelevant sentence " *Hah, Hoh, ér kár ultama,*" " May the buffaloes and calves be well," after which each lays his hand on the remains, bowing until his forehead touches the cloth in which they are wrapped. The *Kéd* is then carried to where a hole has

---

[1] Permission has to be obtained from the Commissioner before slaughtering the animals.

[2] Juries of five men to settle disputes.

CHAP. IX, PART I. — ETHNOLOGY.

been dug at the entrance to the cattle kraal, and each relative throws three handfuls of earth on it and then into the cattle kraal as at the green funeral, muttering "May I throw earth ?" "*Purzhu tukama?*" to which a Peiki[1] replies "Purzhul," "Throw earth." It is curious to note that whilst a "*Peiki*" performs this office for the lower clans, a "*Tarserzhál*" performs it for the high caste, "*Déválydl.*"

After this the pújári approaches with garlands of creepers, which he throws at the buffaloes. This is the signal for the *coup-de-grâce*. The poor terrified creatures, who have been half maddened by the treatment they have received from the young men who have spent the preceding hours in exciting them in every way, rush madly about and sometimes leap the kraal wall and make their escape to some distance before they can be caught and despatched. Their bodies are dragged back and placed in a line with the *pútkúli* and *Kéd* beside them, and men and women sit round it, mourning in couples as at the green funeral.

What follows next is weird and cruel, and the Tódas evidently fear that Government may prohibit it on the score of cruelty, for they "make a secret[2] of this part of their proceedings." A buffalo cow and calf are brought; the latter is held by three men, whilst the former receives a blow between the horns which stuns without killing her.[3] A gash is made under the fore leg of the poor animal, and the *Varzhál*[4] dipping some pieces of bark into the wound, gives some of the blood to the kinsmen, who smear it upon the *Kéd*, muttering "*Karma odi pona,*" "May the sin run away," and some other sentences containing the words *Karma*, sin, and *Ammunád*, heaven. The conclusion of this strangely significant rite I give in Mr. Breeks' own words :—

"A *Peiki* man then puts on the *putkúli* in which the *Kéd* has been wrapped and a silver necklace, and taking the bow[5] and arrows, the latter laid across the bow as if in readiness for shooting, dips the points of the arrows into the blood on the *Kéd*, saying '*Birzhutu-kama?*' 'Shall I give a bow?' After this they walk to another stone near the *Kédmanei* in procession, shouting 'Hoh, Hoh,' the Peiki with the bow in the middle and the Varzhal in front, carrying the

---

[1] This *pújári* does not appear to be a priest or at least one of higher orders, but simply an officiating layman. Colonel Marshall made particular inquiries on this point and learnt that neither Pálál or Kávalál had any religious duties to perform on such occasions.

[2] BREEKS.

[3] See MACPHERSON'S *Khond Hills*.—The buffalo has now taken the place of the human meria as the most fitting sacrifice to the Earth-Mother among the Khonds.

[4] An inferior priest.

Made by the Kótas expressly for each occasion.

CHAP. IX, PART I. — ETHNOLOGY.

leaf vessel[1] out of which he takes two pieces of bark at intervals, throwing one behind him. The calf is dragged to this stone and let loose, when they all run after it, throwing themselves down at intervals so as to touch the ground with their foreheads and shouting '*Ammuadga seruma Karma dharma tilima*,' which may be rendered 'May he enter heaven; may it be well with his good deeds and his sins.'"[2]

The Kéd is burnt within an *Azáram* or circle of stones sunk in the ground, with a miniature bow and three arrows, a *Kef-katti* or sickle, an axe, a palm-leaf umbrella, some jaggery, gram and other articles. The fire is lighted at four in the morning, and as it burns the Tódas mourn and wail, sitting as before in couples and sobbing their rhythmical farewell to the dead, whilst the Kótas rend the air with their discordant music. Mr. Breeks continues:—

"Just as dawn is breaking the music is stopped, the mourning ceases, and in dead silence all cluster round the Azaram for the impressive closing ceremony. Water is sprinkled on the embers, a large stone at the entrance of the circle is taken up and a pit dug under it, into which they scrape the ashes and the stone is replaced.

* * * * * *

Finally a dim figure enters the circle, and raising a chatty high over his head, dashes it to pieces on the stone covering the ashes, bends down, touches the stone with his forehead, and hastens away. All the others perform in turn the same prostration, and flitting silently down the hill, a procession of hurrying shadows fades into the mist, through which twinkles the distant fire of the *Kédmanei*. Imagination might easily transform them into the departing spirits of the propitiated dead."

Traditions.

With the exception of one or two vague stories, some of which may have been picked up from the Badagas at a comparatively late date, the Tódas have nothing to say of their past history. They generally look on at the despoiling of the cairns and cromlechs with perfect indifference, and appear to attach no importance to them; although, it is said, they do lay[3] claim to some. Travellers from time to time have narrated crude stories, supposed to have been gathered from the Tódas, relating to their origin, but they are very contradictory. Captain Ward[4] says they have some idea that they were originally self-born, and that they have also a notion that their ancestors, in primitive

[1] Containing the bark steeped with blood.

[2] This is done at a Tódi funeral. Peikis and Pekhans do not sacrifice a buffalo or lose a calf at the dry funeral, but sacrifice a male buffalo at the next new moon.—BREEKS.

[3] See METZ.

[4] *Biographical and Statistical Survey of the Nelagherry Mountains*, 1824.

CHAP. IX, PART I. — ETHNOLOGY.

times, were the palanquin-bearers to the giant Rávana, and were expelled from Lanka on his being slain by Ráma. A few legends, taken from the lips of the Tódas, are related by Mr. Breeks and Mr. Metz, but they are too long to repeat here.

Language.

The Tóda language is by no means peculiar to themselves as was once thought. It is a dialect of old Kanarese, and closely allied to other Dravidian languages of the plains. There is no trace of any written character having ever been used by the Tódas.

Dr. Pope remarks : " This language, of which but a very scanty fragment remains in use, has more sounds than any other Dravidian dialect, and some of these are peculiar to it, seeming to have been modified by the position and habits of the tribe. The Tudas chiefly converse in the open air, calling to each other from one breezy hill-top to another. Their speech sounds like old Kanarese spoken in the teeth of a gale of wind." In concluding his analysis of the grammar, he writes, " on the whole I venture to think (1) That the Tuda is a language which was once highly inflectional, but having lost most of its inflections, the people who have evidently degenerated in every way as the result of isolation, have not replaced them by significant particles or auxiliaries to the same extent as the other South Indian tribes; and the language has thus dwindled down to a mere skeleton. It now barely suffices for the purposes of a very barbarous people. (2) The language seems to have been originally old Kanarese and not a distinct dialect. The Tudas were probably immigrants from the Kanarese country, and had dwelt on the Nílagiris for about 800 years. Their language was old Kanarese. A few Tamil forms were introduced by the Poligars. Intercourse with the Badagas has probably modernized a few of the forms and introduced some words. Of Telugu influence I see no trace. It is true that the Tuda for *tree* is mân, and in Telugu mânu, while in Tamil and Kanarese it is mara; but the soft *r* is always avoided by the Tudas who turn *vâram* into *vôm*. Nor can I trace any resemblance in Tuda to Malayalam in any of the points where that dialect differs from its sisters." [1]

This view of the Kanarese affinities of the Tóda language appears now to be endorsed by Dr. Caldwell, though he formerly considered it more nearly connected with Tamil.[1]

[1] I learn from Dr. Oppert, Professor of Sanskrit, Madras, that in his opinion the Tóda dialect is probably more nearly allied to Telugu than any other Southern dialect.

PART II.

The Kótas.

Length of residence.—Derivation of name.—Language.—Physical characteristics.—Dress.—Census.—Divisions.—Mode of life.—Habits.—Habitations.—Religion.—Rites.—Birth.—Marriage.—Death.—Traditions.

CHAP. IX, PART II. ETHNOLOGY.

Residence on the plateau.

Our knowledge of the origin of this people, who may be described as a clan of Helot craftsmen, is most meagre; but judging from their language and traditions, there seems ground for regarding them as next to the Tódas in the length of their residence on the Hills. They have a settlement at the foot of the western slopes near Gúdalúr, and, like the Tódas, their oldest village or street is in the western highlands of the Tóda land or *nád*.

Derivation of name.

The name is differently spelt Kótu, Kóter, Kótar, Kóhatur and Kotturs. Its derivation is doubtful. The Tódas call them *Kuof* or cow-men, and, arguing from this word, some connect it with *Kó* (Sans.) cow, and *hatya*, *i.e.*, cow-killing. The first part of the derivation is probably correct. They are emphatically men of the *cow*, as opposed to the *buffalo*, the animal of the Tóda. The latter they are never allowed to keep; the former they keep, but do not, for superstitious reasons, milk. Mr. Breeks observes that he has been informed that in Mysore, some workers in metal are called Kotars and worship Káma, but I can find nothing in support of this assertion in the *Mysore Gazetteer*, though the lists of castes and out-castes given in it seem very complete.

Language.

There can be no question but that like the Tódas, this tribe belongs to the great Dravidian family. Dr. Caldwell speaks of their language as "an old and very rude dialect of Kanarese," but it is more like that of the Tódas than any other. The chief difference between the two lies in the deep guttural[1] pronunciation of the Tódas, the Kótas' pronunciation being more dental. Their respective dialects appear to be mutually understood.

Physical characteristics.

Dr. Shortt gives the average height of twenty-five men as 62·61 inches, the women being considerably shorter, they only average 57·98. The color of the Kótas is lighter than that of the other tribes and more inclined to copper. They are, on the whole, better looking and of a stronger physique than Kúrumbas or Irulas, having well-formed heads and better-shaped noses. Their cheek bones are high and prominent, and they have generally an

[1] Mr. Metz.

CHAP. IX, PART II. — ETHNOLOGY.

air of decision. The men wear their hair, which is black, straight and long, parted down the middle, either loose or tied in a knot behind. In the men the forehead is inclined to be prominent. In the women this defect is more marked, and they are generally less good-looking. Their noses are shorter and incline to a snub, and the chin is short and angular.

Dress, &c.

The dress of the men consists of the usual coarse unbleached cloth. The women have a similar one, which is worn over one shoulder and under the other arm, and forms a kind of petticoat reaching just below the knees. They are fond of rude ornaments, bracelets, armlets, and necklaces of seeds and wire. The dress of the dancers who attend festivals is peculiar. It is a loose ill-made *gown* of calico, with a skirt gathered very full round the waist and reaching to the ankles. This is ornamented with country red cloth sown on in patterns, a bright-colored girdle or scarf, and a handkerchief round the neck. Trousers of colored cotton stuff and a turban complete the costume. Their national dance requires six or eight performers, who stand in a row, their motions being uniform. The effect of these dresses when the dancers twirl together from one side to the other is most quaint and laughter-moving. Indeed the main characteristic of the dance is the way in which their draperies swing to and fro with the measure.

Census and Divisions.

They recognise no caste among themselves. The only divisions are of a very indefinite nature, and are called Keris or streets, but appear to have very little to do with locality, for Mr. Breeks mentions that "inhabitants belonging to all three *Keris*" are found in one Kótagiri.[1] They always seek their wives from another *Keri*. They are distributed as follows :—

—	Tódanád.	Méka-nád.	Péranga-nád.	Kúnda-nád.	Total.	Male.	Female.
Villages ...	2	1	2	1	6	...	...
Inhabitants...	420	243	331	118	1,112	534	578

There is another Kótagiri near Gúdalúr in Wainád, which is not included because it was not within the district prior to the annexation.

Mode of life.

The Kótas are the artizans of the Hills, and are necessary to all the other tribes as their blacksmiths, carpenters, tanners, rope-makers, umbrella-makers, potters, musicians, and workers in gold and silver. Consequently, their villages have sprung up in the

[1] *i.e.*, Kóta hill. This probably is a Badaga corruption of Kótakeri, or Kota street.

localities which enabled them to pursue their handicrafts and to find a ready sale for their wares. CHAP. IX, PART II.

Every Badaga village has a number of *Muttu* Kótas (said to be from *Muttava*, Kanarese, to touch) living in the nearest Kótagiri. Each Badaga also has a particular individual among the Muttu Kótas who works for him, and who is repaid in grain at harvest time. They work in the same way for the other tribes, who pay them in the produce they possess. Tódas pay them in dead buffaloes and ghee, the Kúrumbas in grain, and the Irulas in plantains and grain. They are also well paid for their music, and often receive ¼ rupee each for playing at a feast. On their part they pay the usual tribute in grain, gúdú, to the Tódas. ETHNOLOGY.

Habits.

It is said that the Tódas as well as the other tribes have a great contempt for the Kótas on account of their filthy custom of eating carrion. They are not allowed to enter a Badaga temple or to join in their annual feast to Hetté, to which the Tódas are invited. They once, the story goes, attempted to sell milk, but the Tódas scouted the idea of such unclean people taking to so sacred a pursuit, and they were obliged to give way. Strange to say, their disgusting food seems to agree with them, for they are stronger and of a finer physique than any of the tribes, except the Tódas, and Mr. Metz observes, "at no time do they thrive so well as when there is a murrain among the herds of the Tódas and Badagas." They justify themselves by saying that when the three most ancient Hill-tribes, the Tódas, Kúrumbas and Kótas were formed by Kámataráya out of three drops of perspiration which fell from his forehead, he commanded the Tódas to live on milk; the Kúrumbas he allowed to eat meat, such as the flesh of buffaloes, calves, &c.; the Kótas had liberty to eat carrion if they could get nothing better. They are also addicted to drinking and opium-eating.

Habitations.

Their villages are large and generally contain sixty houses or more. Their houses are of mud and thatch, not by any means so regularly arranged as those of the Badagas, and only saved from an utterly poor and squalid appearance by the patches of cultivation which surround them. Though the houses are entirely devoid of ornament, the pillars of the verandah are sometimes of stone sculptured by cutters from the low country. In each village one or two houses are set apart, to which the women retire during seasons of purification.

Religion.

The Kótas had, it is said, formerly but one deity[1] Kámataráya, but they also worship his wife;[2] each is represented by a silver plate. The god is also called Kambata and Kámata. If Kámata is correct, it is probably the same as

[1] Siva. [2] Kahasumna or Kalikai.

Káma, the god of love. It is noteworthy that a town of the Kúrumbas in Tondarmandalam was called Kámakottam, and that the goddess Parvati was worshipped in the temple there (Winslow). If however the correct word is Kambata, then the worship may be the same as the Badaga worship of the "Pillar god." And this view seems to derive support from the story of the new deity, Mágale, (*Máha* + *kal*, big stone) represented by an upright stone, of the establishment of which Mr. Breeks speaks. Their temples are mere pent-houses of thatch, open at both ends, and supported by square stone pillars sculptured after much the same fashion as the pillars of their verandahs, but on a larger scale. There is no image of any kind it is said. There are two or more of these temples in each village.

Of their two great annual festivals one is in honor of Kámataraya. It lasts for a fortnight and gives them an opportunity for decorating themselves in any dresses, ornaments, &c., that they can borrow and of performing their national dance to the music of their drums and horns accompanied by singing. Occasionally a Kóta becomes possessed by a god. He yells, dances, rolls about, and performs the most frantic gestures until at last he falls down in a kind of fit. This phase of the worship recalls the demonology of Southern India. The other feast is in honor of the dead who have died during the year, and answers in some respects to the Tóda green funeral.

Rites and Ceremonies. —Birth.

Immediately after the birth of a child, it is removed, with its mother, to a temporary hut, made of boughs, and called Vollu gúdu, from vollu, inside, gúdu, a nest. After thirty days they inhabit one or two permanent huts set apart for women when they are considered unclean. When they leave these huts to return home, after the third month has passed, it is the custom for the women to take seven steps backwards among seven kinds of thorns. The Kótas can give no explanation of this ceremony, it is simply *mámúl*. On the seventh day, after the return of the mother and child, a feast is given to all the relatives. The child is fed with gruel, "congee," and named.

—Marriage.

The Kótas marry only one wife, unless she has no children, in which case a second is permissible, and both women live in the same house.

It is usual for boys of fifteen or upwards to be betrothed to girls of six or eight. When the girl becomes of age, she is sent for to the house of her future father-in-law. A feast is given with music and dancing, and the ceremony is concluded by the bride-groom's mother tying the *táli* round the bride's neck. Among the Kótas the *táli* is a silver necklace of Kóta workmanship.

—Funerals.

The Kótas seem to have borrowed some of their funeral rites from the Badagas and some from the Tódas. The *Teru* or scaffolding hung with cloth and erected before the house of the deceased is similar to the one used by the Badagas. Under this the body is placed on a cot, face upwards, as is the custom among the Badagas and Kúrumbas. It is then removed to a Dué or burning ground and burnt with the implements of the deceased. The skull-bones are collected next day and burned. This answers to the green funeral; the dry funeral rites are performed later. Then one or more skulls are placed on cots and burned with a bow and arrows and various other implements. The ashes are not buried.

Language. Their language is a vulgar dialect of Kanarese and helps to strengthen the notion that the Kótas are a low-caste people of the plains.

Traditions. There is a tradition among them that they once lived on a mountain in Mysore called Kollemalé, after which they named the first village they built on the Nílagiris. The Tódas say that they were brought from the plains to work for them. It is certain that the Kótas were dwellers in the Hills long before the Badagas came there, otherwise one would be inclined to think that as artizans their services would hardly be required by the Tódas, who are purely a race of herdsmen, whilst the Badagas, as agriculturists, are daily in need of their handicraft for making and repairing their ploughs and hoes. This anomaly is more apparent than real. It is probable that close intercourse with the plains has always existed, so that the Kótas, though living with the Tódas, would have found a market for their manufactures in the low country, to which they would naturally have to resort for the purchase of metal, &c. Meanwhile, their position could secure them from the oppression to which workers in metal would be sure to be subjected in troublous times, especially at the hands of the high caste artizans.[1] This tribe may yet prove very useful in the development of the Hills. They are intelligent and hardworking, and their monogamous customs seem likely to ensure their rapid increase in numbers.

[1] Can the existence of these metal workers on the hills have any connection with the gold-digging referred to in the following chapter?

PART III.

KÚRUMBAS.

Origin.—Physical characteristics.—Dress.—Census.—Divisions.—Mode of life.—Dwellings.—Livelihood.—Religion.—Rites.—Birth.—Marriage.—Death.—Traditions.

CHAP. IX, PART III. — ETHNOLOGY. — Origin and history.

THE Kúrumbas occupy the slopes of the Hills and are undoubtedly allied to, or derived from, the same stock as the tribes scattered about the districts of Malabar, Mysore, and Coimbatore, of whom several are mentioned by Buchanan. In the low country they are called Kúrubas or Cúrubáru, and are divided into numerous families, such as the Áné or Elephant, Náya or Dog, Málé or Hill Kúrumbas. According to Buchanan, there are two great divisions, Handi and Kumbali Kúrumbas. He speaks of the Kád Kúrumbas, an exceedingly poor tribe living south of the Káveri. As described by him they are not unlike their brethren of the Hills; he says "they build miserable low huts, have few rags for a covering, and the hair of both sexes stands out like a mop and swarms with vermin. Their persons and features are weak and unseemly, and their complexion is very dark." The word Kúrumba means a shepherd.[1] It seems probable that all the tribes still extant are remnants of a once powerful people composed probably of numerous small tribes possessing considerable territory in Canara,[2] Western Mysore and in the great[3] Carnatic Plain and sprung from a race of nomadic shepherds, one of the great Dravidian group of tribes who inhabited the Peninsula of South India before the historic period. In the early centuries of the Christian era, some tribes acquired a certain amount of civilization and obtained by conquest possession of some more ancient kingdoms. Several dynasties of Kadamba Rájas[4] reigned at Bánawási, once an important city near Onur (Honúr) in Sunda. This city was an important seat of the Jaina sect. This is noteworthy, as the Kúrumbas of the south were in some way mixed[5] up with the Jains.

---

[1] The derivation is doubtful, but it appears to be allied to *Kúru* (Tamil) short. The word *Kúrumba* signifies a village in a desert tract and also wickedness. The latter is a derivative meaning due to the predatory habits of these people. The word *Kúrumba* also in old Kanarese, it is said, signifies a sheep (Kurumbadu, Tamil). But this animal is probably so called from being kept by a Kúrumban or dwarf.

[2] A part of Malabar is still called the district of Curumbara.—BUCHANAN.

[3] There is also a caste in Malayalam condemned to slavery called Catal or Curumbal, and in the plural Catulum or Curumbalum.—BUCHANAN.

[4] May not this word be a compound of Kátu or Kátam (both meaning forest) and Kúrumba, and perhaps be the same as Kád-Kúrumba?

[5] *Catalogue Rais.*, Vol. III, p. 399.

CHAP. IX, PART III.

ETHNOLOGY.

In one of the Mackenzie MSS. they are spoken of as "a wild people who cared not for their lives;" but we are also told that they were "shepherds, weavers, lime sellers, traders," and that the Kings of Chóla and Pandya made war upon them. The wildness of this people has probably been greatly exaggerated by the more timid races of the plain country of the south. A people who built fortresses, who traded by sea and land, who manufactured goods and cultivated gardens, could not have been wild and uncivilized, though they may have been fierce and vindictive as Arab traders now are. This fierceness was their safety. Finally, the kingdom of the Kúrumbas, known as Kúrumba bhúmi, with its twenty-four forts, which seems to have become very extensive, occupying the track of the Carnatic between the Pennar and Palar and extending inland as far as the Western Ghâts, was overthrown by Adondái, the illegitimate son of Kulattungí Chóla, and the conquered country went henceforth by the name of Tondamandalam. Their power probably survived longest in North Kárnáta and in the Southern Hills of that ancient country. It was probably from the dry uplands of Kárnáta, so well suited for the pasturage of sheep, that like the Mahrattas in modern times they originally pressed wedge-wise into the dry jungle tracts of the Carnatic plain, whilst the rich alluvial lands remained in the possession of the enervated but wealthy races of the coast. The records which bear upon the subject are very contradictory and confused and so mixed up with fable that it is almost impossible to extricate from the tangled mass any intelligible account of this strange people. Some historians put the date of their conquest at 700 A.D. Others recognize in them the Rájas of Vijayanagar and fix it as late as 1500 A.D. This latter theory is improbable, as the southern tribes seem to have lost all traces of civilization and to have no recollection whatever of their previous history. It should not, however, be lost sight of that Buchanan mentions Kúruba horsemen, known as Handi Rasalas, living about the upper Kistna.

These, however, are but fragmentary notices. But when the inscriptions at Conjevaram and elsewhere have been deciphered, some connected history of South India from the times of Asóka to the fall of Vijayanagar will perhaps be written. In such a history it may be found that the Kúrumbas have played an important part in South India. At present the attempt to piece together the scraps of information which are scattered here and there seems to promise little profit. The paleographist must precede the historian.

Physical characteristics.

The Kúrumbas are small in stature, very uncouth, and wild and squalid in appearance. An average of 25 measured by Dr. Shortt[1] gives the height of the men as 60–64 inches. He says :—

[1] See *Tribes on the Nílagiris.*—SHORTT.

CHAP. IX, PART III. — ETHNOLOGY.

" They have a shortish and spare form of body, with a peculiar wedge-shaped face and obtuse facial angle, cheeks hollow, with prominent malars or cheek-bones; slightly-pointed chin; eyes moderately large and frequently blood-shot. Color of irides dark brown, the nose has a deep indentation at the root about 1¾ inches in depth, which is general, and when contrasted with the profile or line with the ridge of the nose and os frontis, it gives them a very peculiar expression of feature.

*   *   *   *

" The hair is long and black and is grown matted and straggling, somewhat wavy, and is sometimes tied into a knot, with a piece of cord on the crown or back of the head, while the ends are allowed to be free and floating. They have scarcely any moustache or whiskers and a straggling scanty beard; occasionally one is met with full moustache, whiskers, and beard. They are, as a body, sickly-looking, pot-bellied, large mouthed, prognathous, with prominent outstanding teeth and lips; frequently saliva dribbles away from their mouths.

" The women have much the same physiognomy as the men, only somewhat softened in expression and slightly modified in feature with a small pug nose and surly aspect. An average of 12 gives 54·25 as their height. They are very shy and dislike seeing strangers or being questioned by them."

Dress.

The men seldom have any covering except the *" lingúti ;"* some of the women have only a waist cloth, and others wear a square[1] cloth which reaches from under the arms to the knee. Occasionally, when they can afford it, both men and women adopt the ordinary dress of natives. The women, too, are fond of ornaments, and wear necklaces and nose rings, earrings, and bracelets of glass and iron.

According to the last census they numbered 613.

Caste and Divisions.

The following table gives the different castes and divisions and the localities in which they live :—

—	Arakád.	Búdinattam.	Mékanád.	Malachippa.	Péranganád.	Sembanaré.	Sembanattam.	Tódanád.	Ariyúr.	Kúndas.	Vagapáni.	Velléru Kambé.	Total.
Eda Kúrumbas	...	29	...	...	...	...	...	...	...	...	...	...	29
Karmadiya Kúrumbas ...	...	...	...	...	7	...	...	...	..	...	...	...	7
Kúrumbas Proper	41	11	60	23	201	2	1	6	36	15	2	55	453
Kúrumba Okkibiga ...	...	4	...	...	...	...	...	...	...	...	...	...	4
Málé Kúrumbas	...	109	...	...	...	...	...	...	...	...	...	...	109
Pál Kúrumbas	...	11	...	...	...	...	...	...	...	...	...	...	11
	Male 330.							Female 283. Total...					613

[1] Called *túndu*, lit. a piece.

These families or *bígas*[1] do not intermarry, and it will be observed that their distinguishing names, Pál, &c., resemble those of the plains. Mr. Breeks mentions four tribal divisions, the names of which he learnt from a Kúrumba—1, Botta K. who live on the northern slopes and in Mysore district; 2, Kumbali K. who make blankets and live in the low country; 3, Mullu K. (locality uncertain); 4, Handi K. who live on the eastern slopes. Mr. Metz seems to regard the Nílagiri Kúrumbas as belonging to the Mullu tribe. In the Bhavání valley there are some Jain[2] Kúrumbas who live mainly on the sale of the honey which they collect.

Mode of life. Dwellings.

The villages of the Kúrumbas are called *mottas*, probably from *maram*, a tree. They consist generally of only four or five huts made of mud and wattle with thatched roofs. The front of a house is sometimes whitewashed and ornamented with rude drawings of men and animals in red earth or charcoal.

Livelihood.

" They store their grain in large oval baskets and for bottles they use gourds. They clear a patch round about the village and sow the ground with rági (*Eleusine coracana*), Tenne (*Panicum Italicum*), or Kiri (*Amaranthus tristis*). They dig up roots (called gású) for food and collect jungle produce, honey, resin, gallnuts, &c., which they barter with low-country traders, and they are clever in catching game in nets and dispose of the flesh in a surprisingly short time. They pay no *gudu* to the Todas."[3]

Kúrumbas occasionally take work on coffee plantations and some earn a livelihood by officiating as priests to the Badagas. They are also employed as musicians at wedding feasts and funerals of the other tribes, where they play on clarionets, drums, and tambourines, as well as on the *búguri*.

The Kúrumbas make baskets of rattan and milk vessels out of a joint of bamboo, as well as nets; these last are made of a thread called *oilhatti*. Their women do not labor in the fields, but confine themselves to the limited work of their households, fetching water, cooking, &c.

Religion.

The following extract embraces all that can be said of the religion of the Kúrumbas:—

Some Kurumbas whom I have met with profess, in answer to inquiries, to worship Siva, and occasionally women mark their forehead with the Siva spot. Others, living near Barliár, worship

---

[1] *Biga* means lit. a lock.

[2] *Jain* said to be from honey, but it may refer to the connection of these tribes with the Jainas.

The tribal divisions of the Kúrumbas are very numerous. In Mysore Mr. Rice enumerates no fewer than fifteen, who occupy mainly the hills along the south-western boundary of Mysore. In Hassan alone the Kád and Jain Kúrumbas number 1,819.

[3] BREEKS.

CHAP. IX, PART III. — ETHNOLOGY.

Kuribattraya (lord of many sheep) and the wife of Siva under the name of Musni. They worship also a rough round stone under the name of Hiriadéva, setting it up either in a cave or in a circle of stones like the so-called "Kurumba Kovil" of the Badagas, which the latter would seem to have borrowed from the Kurumbas; to this they make *puja*, and offer cooked rice at the sowing time. They also profess to sacrifice to Hiriadéva a goat, which they kill at their own houses, after sprinkling water, and eat, giving a portion of the flesh to the *pujari*. Others say they have no *pujari*; among such a scattered tribe customs probably vary in each *motta*. They do not consider the stone as a *lingam*, although they profess to be Saivites. They make no *puja* at home. They profess some small caste scruple, and will not eat with any tribe but the Badagas; but they will accept uncooked food from Todas, though not from Kotas.—BREEKS.

They are very much dreaded as sorcerers by all the tribes except the Tódas. As these have some pretension to being workers in the black art too and are probably in a measure behind the scenes they do not appear to have any fear of their witchcraft. It is a curious fact that neither Kóta, Irula, or Badaga will slay a Kúrumba until a Tóda has struck the first blow; but so soon as his sanctity has been violated by a blow they hasten to complete the murderous work which the sacred hand of a Tóda has begun. I am not aware of any attempt ever having been made on the life of a Tóda by either Kúrumbas or other hill men. They probably owe this immunity to their general benevolence. The Badagas, on the contrary, are in such fear of them that one of their tribe has been known to die of terror merely from meeting a Kúrumba in a lonely place; nevertheless they recognize their services on many occasions, for example, to turn the first sod at the ploughing, to reap the first sheaf at the harvest. They, like the Pareiyar of the low country, enjoy some privileges which seem to have come down to them from a time when they were the occupants of the land who had to be propitiated by immigrant tribes. The following extract from an article in the "Antiquary" by Mr. Walhouse, quoted by Dr. Caldwell, forcibly expresses this:—

"It is well known," he writes, "that the servile caste of Southern India once held far higher positions, and were indeed masters of the land on the arrival of the Brahminical races. Many curious vestiges of their ancient power still survive in the shape of certain privileges, which are jealously cherished, and, their origin being forgotten, are much misunderstood. These privileges are remarkable instances of survivals from an extinct order of society—shadows of a long-departed supremacy, bearing witness to a period when the present haughty high caste races were suppliants before the ancestors of degraded classes, whose touch is now regarded as pollution."

Rites and Ceremonies. —Birth and Marriage.

They have no ceremony to celebrate the birth of a child, and their marriages are contracted without any early betrothal or any especial rites. It sometimes happens that after a couple have cohabited for some time they agree to live together for life, and then their friends are invited to a feast on the occasion. Widows are allowed to marry again.

—Funerals.

They burn their dead and, as a rule, take no care to collect the ashes, but allow them be scattered to the winds. The body is placed *under* a car hung with cloth but no ornaments, coins, or implements are burnt with it. After dancing round the car to the sound of their weird music, the corpse is burnt and the car with it. Some few deposit a bone from the pyre in a *Sávumané* or death house—a small cromlech surrounded by upright stones and bearing some resemblance to the more ancient cromlechs found on the hills, but these are the Kúrumbas who live near Rangasámi's Peak and Burliar. These[1] Sávumanés they say were made by their forefathers. They no longer make them. When they can afford it, they administer a small gold coin called a Birian hanna[2] to a dying man. This custom also obtains among the Badagas.

Language.

Mr. Metz describes their language as a corruption of Kanarese with some Tamil words intermixed, and asserts that the Kanarese dialect spoken by them is purer than that of the Badagas. Dr. Caldwell however speaks of their language as "rude Tamil," regarding that of the Badagas as "an ancient but organized dialect of the Canarese." The Mysore Kúrumba tribes speak old Kanarese.

Tradition.

They are said to have no traditions of any kind. But if this is true of the Nílagiri Kúrumbas it does not appear to be quite the case with some of the tribes in Mysore. Their habitual distrust of strangers probably renders them uncommunicative.

---

[1] BREEKS—*Tribes*, &c.

[2] Birian-hanna or *Viria raya*, a gold coin struck in Mysore. Value ¼ rupee.

PART IV.

IRULAS.

Origin.—Language.—Physical characteristics.—Dress.—Census and Divisions.—Mode of life.—Dwellings.—Religion.—Rites and Ceremonies.—Traditions.

CHAP. IX, PART IV. — ETHNOLOGY. — Origin.

THE Irulas[1]—the men of darkness—belong to a still more primitive race than the Kúrumbas, namely, the Bédas or hunters of the forests of the peninsula, some of whom, like the Kúrumbas, have attained to civil life and power in Mysore and the tract of country known as ancient Kárnáta. The Bédas of Mysore, who belonged in part to Kárnáta, in part to Telingána, became soldiers by profession and agriculturists, and to them belong most of the Mysore Pálegárs. The opinion that the Nílagiri Irulas are allied to these Bédas receives confirmation from the fact that they, like the Mysore Bédas, are worshippers generally of Vishnu, a remarkable circumstance considering the almost universal Sivaism of the aboriginal tribes of South India. This fact is still more remarkable when it is considered that the wilder tribes of Kúrumbas[2] in Mysore differ but little from the Mysore Irulas in appearance and mode of life, whilst those of the Nílagiris not only personally resemble the Irulas, but inhabit villages which are known by the same name—*motta*—alike situated in the lower slopes, and are occasionally found living in the same hamlets. The tribes of the plateau, however, do not confound them, in fact they hardly recognize the Irulas as inhabitants of the mountain. The identity of the Irulas of Mysore, Kurnúl, and elsewhere receives further confirmation from the fact that both speak a corrupt dialect of Tamil.

Language.

Buchanan, who had but a brief acquaintance with the Nílagiri Irulas, regarded them as speaking a dialect of Kanarese, and on this ground came to the conclusion that they were not related to the Mysore Irulas, although he observes that their customs and mode of life correspond. Subsequent inquiry has shown their speech to be not Kanarese but Tamil, but this refers to the Irulas proper only. I am not aware whether the speech of the Bédas approaches Tamil or Kanarese; probably the latter. If this be so, their civilized condition in the midst of a Kanarese population might well account for the gradual abandonment of their native idiom.

Physical characteristics.

They are superior in physique to the Kúrumbas, and rather better looking. According to Dr. Shortt, an average of twenty-

[1] From the Tamil *irul*, dark, black.

[2] Jain.

five men gave their height as 61·78 inches. They are very dark, as the term Irula denotes, and their hair, which is straight and seldom very long, is worn by the women parted in front and tied in a knot behind. The men shave their heads and wear the *Kúdumi*.

Dress.

The men seldom wear anything but the *lingúti* when at home in their villages, but when they work on plantations they occasionally adopt the loose cotton cloth worn by the other tribes. The women wear a square cloth reaching from the waist to the knees, the upper part of the body being nude. They are fond of ornaments, and wear ear and nose rings, wire bracelets and armlets, and strings of beads round their necks.

Census and Divisions.

Dr. Shortt gives two classes of Irulas—the *Urali* and *Kurutali*. "The Urali"[1] he says, "mean rulers of the country, the Kurutali the serfs or common people." Mr. Breeks distinctly states that "they have no castes or divisions." By the Census of 1871 the distribution was as follows :—

Arakád.	Aranád.	Búdinattam.	Kodád.	Mékanád.	Malachippa.	Péranganád.	Sembanaré.	Sembanattam.	Segúr.	Tódanád.	Kún'apáni.	Siral Kambé.	Vagapáni.	Velléru Kambé.	Ootacamand.	Total.
160	105	250	30	5	52	6	45	72	24	334	139	99	50	98	1	1,470

Number of males and females are equal.

Mode of life.

Near Rangasámi's Peak, and scattered about the slopes and base of the hills to the south and south-east, there are several *mottas*.[2] These villages consist of seven or eight huts, generally built round a square. Patches of rági and tenné surround them, in the care of which men and women take an equal share. Near their villages they have large gardens of plantain and lime trees, and cultivate the neighbouring ground in the Cátucádu fashion, changing the field every year.[3]

They attend the market (or shandy) held at Mettapollium every Saturday, carrying down jungle produce, such as timber, bamboos and game, &c., to exchange for tobacco, salt, and cloths. A few mottas are scattered on the northern and western slopes of the Hills, but their inhabitants lead a harder life from the severity of the monsoon and their isolated position.

They seldom make any provision for the winter, but subsist on a crop of grain as long as it lasts, and trust for seed and what

---

[1] Strictly village-men.
[2] Derived from *maram*, a tree.
[3] BUCHANAN.

CHAP. IX, PART IV. — ETHNOLOGY.

more they may require to the Badagas, with whom they barter wood, honey, bees' wax, and other forest produce.

Their method of preparing their food is thus described in Captain Harkness' account of the Nílagiris:—

"Each morning they pluck as much as they think they may require for the use of that day, kindle a fire upon the nearest large stone or fragment of rock, and when it is well heated, brush away the embers and scatter the grain upon it, which, soon becoming parched and dry, is then readily reduced to meal. This part of the process over, or as soon as the rock has cooled, the parched grain, which in the meantime has been partially cleansed of the husk, is, with the assistance of a smaller stone, rubbed into meal, mixed up with water, and made into cakes. The stone is heated a second time, and the cakes are put on it to bake; or, where they have met with a stone which has a little concavity, they will, after heating it the second time, fill the hollow with water, and with this, when warmed, they mix up the meal and form a sort of porridge. In this way the whole of the family, their friends, and neighbours will live till all the grain has been consumed, and it seems to be considered among them as superlative meanness to reserve any, either for seed or future nourishment."

Of late years they have mixed more with civilized tribes, and some are to be found among the coolies on coffee plantations. They will only eat with the Badagas.

Dwellings.

Their houses are made of split bamboo interwoven like basket-work and plastered with mud inside, without any attempts at ornament.

Religion.

The Irulas have two temples, which have a general interest apparently for all the tribes, one on Rangasámi's Peak dedicated to Vishnu under the name of Rangasámi. They are only circles of rough stones, each enclosing an upright one, with iron tridents fixed in the ground. They are called dodda and chikka, the great and the little. The pújári or priest is an Irula, and he wears the Vishnu mark on his forehead. Although the Badagas are for the most part Sivaites, they come in large numbers to these temples once a year about sowing time, and make offerings of plantains, milk, &c., to the god. No animals are sacrificed. In a cave on the hill there is earth regarded as holy, which is much valued by worshippers.

There is also a temple at Kallampalla in the Sattiamangalam Taluq near Dévanaikenkóta, where an Irula priest officiates, but this one is dedicated to Siva. In this temple there is a stone called Mariamma or Mariatha, a form of Dúrga, the goddess of small-pox. To her they make offerings of goats and cocks. A sheep is sometimes sacrificed. Irulas make no *púja* in their homes, and seem to have very vague ideas even of the Hinduism they profess. Having paid the *pújári* two annas for each village once a year, their consciences are at rest.

Rites and Ceremonies.

There is no marriage or birth ceremony. When a boy comes of age he chooses a wife for himself, and there is no previous betrothal. The Irulas bury their dead, and their funeral customs are entirely different to those of the other tribes. Having dug a grave, they place the body in it in a sitting posture with a lamp beside it. After dancing round the corpse for some time, they fill up the grave with earth and place a small upright stone to mark the spot. Each village or *motta* has its burial-ground. I can hear of no other ceremony.

Traditions.

They have no traditions whatever, though they appear to have been made the subject of some fables. Their neighbours below the ghâts declare that they possess the power of taming tigers, and that Irula women, when they go into the woods, leave their children to the care of a tiger. Their familiarity with the habits of game has probably given rise to these fables.

PART V.

THE BADAGAS.

Origin.—Physical characteristics. Dress.— Castes.— Wódeas.—Kongas.—Adhikáris.—Kanakas.—Chittre—Bellis.—Háruvas.—Minor Castes.—Mode of Life.—Music and Song.—Character.—Dwellings.—Religion.—Temples.—Rites and Ceremonies.—Traditions.—Language.

CHAP. IX, PART V. — ETHNOLOGY. — Origin.

THE Badagas or *Northmen* are the descendants of Kanarese colonists from the Carnatic country known now as North Coimbatore and South Mysore, which at one time formed an important part of the ancient Kongu kingdom. It is commonly reported that the principal migrations took place about three hundred years ago on the breaking up of the Vijayanagar Empire; but there can be no question that Kanarese colonists must have occupied portions of the plateau long before this and whilst the Nílagiris appertained rather to ancient Kárnáta than to Dravida or the land of the Tamils; in fact the latter can hardly be said to have gained a footing on the Hills, except in the case of the Kanakas or accountant class, until after our occupation. These Kanarese colonists probably migrated to the Hills when driven from home by famine, political turmoil, or local oppression. The Lingayat Wódeas were probably among the more recent immigrants. Among several facts which indicate the long residence of most of the sections of the tribe on the plateau, we may mention, (1) that the Badaga population are almost to a man Sivaites, whilst only two-thirds belong to this sect in the neighbouring district of Mysore, which shows that they were but little affected by the conversion of the Mysore Rájas to the Vishnuvite faith in 1610 A.D; (2) the names of several of the divisions of castes are almost unknown in Mysore, it being otherwise with the more recent immigrants; (3) their language is a dialect of old Kanarese, whilst their kinsmen below the gháts speak the modern dialect; (4) the local distribution of the other tribes, and the absence among them of a tradition of the advent of the Badagas to the hills; (5) the respect with which they are treated by the Tódas, whose mode of addressing them is honorific, indicating the Kanarese ascendancy at the time of their immigration.

The earliest notice of the Badagas that I have found is in Buchanan. He writes on 24th October 1800,—

"Honey and wax are gathered by a caste called Budugar, who inhabit the hilly country between this (Dévanaikenkóta) and the province of Malabar, and which lies south from Nelleala, or the

Wynaad of Major Rennell. They live in small villages and huts like the Eriligaru, and not only use the Cotu-cadu cultivation already described, but have also ploughs. The quantity of honey and wax which they procure is considerable, and they pay nothing for it, there being no forest renter in this district."

The word *Badaga* is Kanarese and is the same as the Tamil *Vadugan*[1] or Northman. It is applied not only to the Badagas of the hills who approached them from Mysore and Canara, but is of far wider significance and older date. By this name were designated also the "Telugu followers of the Náyakkas[2] of Madura, who spread themselves over the Tamil country and even made irruptions into South Travancore." French Missionaries seem to have considered the words Telugu and Badaga as synonymous ; thus confusing the different northern emigrants under one appellation, as our ancestors called every Teuton a Dutchman and every stranger a Welchman.

Compared with the other hill tribes, the Badagas are an Aryanized people, though probably descended from the same Dravidian stock. In their religion and manners they bear the impress of comparatively recent contact with Hindus of the plains ; whilst the Tódas, Kótas and Irulas and even the Kúrumbas must have taken refuge in the fastnesses of the Nílagiris, either before or soon after the great Aryan invasion of the peninsula. The superstitious reverence for a race far beneath them in intelligence and civilization which has induced the Badagas to choose Kúrumbas and Irulas for their priests has a parallel in the relations of the high caste people and the Pareiyas of the plains and in the privileges claimed by the Bhills, an aboriginal people, at the coronation of Rájput princes.

Unlike the other tribes almost every class of the Badagas has some sort of history of its own, and some even point to villages below the hills from which they came and where their relatives still live.[3]

Physical characteristics.

In appearance the Badagas are very distinct from their neighbours. They are an active race, of moderate stature, with the usual Hindu features and prepossessing expression and light skins. An average of twenty-five measured by Dr. Shortt gives 66-70 as the height of the men, and 58-47 for that of the women. They are accustomed to labor from their earliest youth ; boys of from seven to ten years of age being employed to break stones upon the roads ; whilst the women take an equal share with the men in working in the fields. This may in part account for

---

[1] From *Vadugu*, north, and *avan*, he, pronominal suffix.

[2] See CALDWELL'S *Grammar*.

[3] See METZ' *Tribes of the Neilgherries*.

CHAP. IX, PART V. — ETHNOLOGY.

their extreme thinness ; one meets with very few who can be called stout.

Dress.

The men wear the *lingúti*, and both sexes a large unbleached cloth, which is stiffened to render it water-tight and warm to an extent which makes it very ungraceful. It is loosely wrapped round them ; so loosely that as a Badaga works in the fields, he is obliged to stop between every few strokes of his hoe to gather up his cloth and throw one end over his shoulder. They wear turbans of the same cloth with an end hanging behind. Their ornaments consist of brass, iron, or filagree silver earrings, necklaces, bracelets, and armlets ; they also wear nose-rings. The men frequently carry a silver box for opium or any little treasure they may happen to possess, such as a charm, a title-deed, or paper. The women are tattooed in rows of dots about the chest and four marks thus ○ □ ○ ▲ on the forehead.

Castes or divisions—Wódeas.

They recognize eighteen different castes or sects ; of the seven highest each one has a little history of its own. The first, called the Wódeas, a branch of the reigning family of Mysore, are proud and aristocratic. They refuse to carry burdens and disdain to work for Europeans, and in consequence are very poor. They possess only five villages. The Wódeas will not eat with the other castes, and consider themselves as Gurus (priests or rather bishops), for they only perform certain ceremonies. They wear the lingam.

The following extracts from Mr. Rice's Manual of Mysore and Coorg throw some light on the previous history of the Wódeas. " Odeyar, Wodeyar," or Wadeyar, he says, " is the plural and honorific form of Odeya, a Kannada word meaning lord, master. Wilks states that it indicated at the period of which we are writing (1399–1422) the governor of a small district, generally of 33 villages. Vadêr, a modification of the word, is the title of respect by which Jangama (Lingayat) priests are addressed."

The first Rája who took the title was called Vijaya Wódeyar ; he reigned in 1399–1422. In 1578–1617, however, his descendant Rája Wódeyar extended the possessions of his family over all the south of the present Mysore district and captured several places towards the north from Yagadeva Ráya. He expelled the Wódea rája from Oomatur, south-west of Mysore, who fled to the Nílagiris then probably under his authority. " His rule was remarkable for the rigor and severity which he exercised towards the subordinate Wodeyars and his indulgence towards the ryots. The Wodeyars were generally dispossessed and kept in confinement at the seat of government" (Wilks' Mysore). This Rája Wódeyar had also abandoned the religion of the Jungum, and had become a Vishnuvite. Here we seem to have the reason for the emigration of the Wódeas to the Hills, presuming that chiefs of the caste were not already in authority there, and their pride and pretensions to the priesthood are both explained.

—Kongas.

Second are the *Kongas*. The Rev. W. Stokes considers them to be identical with the Wódea, but Mr. Metz, whose acquaintance with them was even longer, calls them a distinct sect.

He says their ancestors came from Sargúr[1] by the Gajalhatti Pass on the Coimbatore side of the Hills, where they still live, and they take their name from *Kongu*, the name by which Coimbatore is known to the hill tribes. They generally wear the lingam, but a part of the tribe have lost their caste and the privilege of wearing it through the weakness of one of their number. A Konga fell in love with a low caste girl, and to please her tasted meat which is forbidden to all Lingayats. Against this, however, the Kongas can boast that one of the Badaga rájas of former days once married a girl of their caste.[2]

—Adhikáris.

The *Adhikáris* are divided into two sets, Lingadhikáris who wear the lingam, and Meatadhikáris, who have come from the village of Nellitoré.

—Kanakas.

The *Kanakas* or accountants are the only class who can read and write. They are also physicians and exorcists. They were probably introduced when the hills were under the sway of Tamil chiefs, this officer (accountant) being called Shanbhóg in Mysore.

—Chittre.

The *Chittre* class came to the Hills with the Wódeas, it is said, in the train of the Rája of Málékóta, a ruined fort near the head of the Segúr ghát.

—Belli.

The *Belli* or silver class are said to be the most cunning of the Badagas. There is an outcaste of this name in Mysore. The village of Jackatalla is inhabited by this class, whence the Badaga proverb, "If you are not very wide-awake, do not go to Jackatalla," *i.e.*, Wellington.

—Haruvas.

The *Háruvas* are a degenerate class of Brahmans; they may be connected with the Harihara, *i.e.*, the Vishnu-Siva sect, who combine the worship of these divinities. They still wear the Brahminical string and officiate as priests at the harvest festivals. Every second year they profess to perform the miracle of walking with bare feet over burning coals. The first settlers of this caste do not appear to have brought any women with them.

Minor castes.

These are the seven principal castes. The remaining eleven are as follows:—The *Hatara* or marriage caste, the *Aneas*, who

[1] Sargúr is not near the Gajalhatti Pass, but north-west of Gúndelpet.

[2] See METZ' *Tribes of the Neilgherries*. By Badaga Rájas some Wódea Rája is probably meant.

This is now prohibited.

CHAP. IX, PART V. — ETHNOLOGY. — live exclusively in the Tódanád, the *Mari*, the *Khasturi*, who live at Kaity and are also called *Gangalúru* and whom Mr. Metz regards as Vellálas, the *Dumas*, the *Gonajas*, and the *Manika* or gem caste. The origin of this name I have been unable to trace.

—Toreas —Kumbaras. There are two castes of Vellálas scattered in different districts, as well as the *Toreas* or lowest class, and the *Kumbararu* or potters. These last occupy two villages near Kalhatti, and are probably the same caste as the Kumbararu of Mysore. They do not intermarry with other Badagas, which seems to point to their being late arrivals. It was a Torea[1] chief who sought to marry the maiden who was rescued by Vijaya, the founder of the Mysore house.

Mode of life, &c. Their villages form a pleasing contrast to those of the other tribes, although they are by no means so picturesque as the mands of the Tódas. Their long rows of neatly thatched or tiled houses stand in the midst of smiling fields of korali and sámi, and are surrounded by well-stocked farm yards. They have an air of thriving industry which is very characteristic; for the Badagas are becoming a comparatively wealthy race, thanks to their industrious habits. As the men constantly leave their villages to work in the nearest coffee plantations, much of the labor in their own fields, as well as ordinary household work, is performed by the women. They are so industrious and their services of such value to their husbands that a Badaga sometimes pays Rupees 150 or Rupees 200 as dowry for his wife.

Music and song. They are a gentle, light-hearted race, as any one will testify who has heard their ringing laughter as they wind their way in Indian file along any of the numerous paths which intersect the shólas or climb the hills about Ootacamand. On the afternoon of the market day especially large parties of them may be seen returning to their villages laden with fairings, the foremost man in the row relating some incident in a stentorian voice for the benefit of the rest, who show their attention by an occasional grunt, as they jog along, and their appreciation of his wit by a chorus of laughter.

They are fond of music and song; their tunes are quaint and original and, when heard from a distance, have an uncultured sweetness about them in keeping with the soft coloring and wild beauty of the scenery of the land which is their home. They have many ballads of great length, which are sung to a monotonous kind of chant, and are an endless source of amusement, judging by the eagerness with which a Badaga audience listens to them. They are divided into stanzas of unequal length, and when a 'break' occurs, or the performer pauses to take breath, the

[1] An account of this caste will be found in BUCHANAN.

audience chimes in with a general grunt which has a most ludicrous effect. The metre of these ballads is generally four feet of unequal lengths, varying in almost every line, but ending frequently in a spondee. The following lines are the opening verses of one of these ballads translated from a German version of the Badaga by Mr. Metz, who has made a large collection of similar ballads; the metre of the original is preserved as nearly as possible.

BÁLA SÉVANA.

Ōnce ĭn thĕ vĭllăge ŏf Hānnĭămānnū,
Nēar tŏ thĕ fōrtrĕss ŏf Kōlĕgă Kāmbē,
Lived there a youth named Bála Sévana,
Also his brother, Béla-Māda.

Like were they to one another,
E'en as the spreading horns of a buffalo.
Nineteen men bad Béla-Máda,
Nineteen ploughed the land for Sévana.

Once in the field of the gravel slope they
Met by the corner of the sacred seal-stone;
First to the Circar made they obeisance,
Then they made a salaam to the temple,
Folding their hands to the moon above them.

Deep in the earth they scooped a hollow,
and Then they fetched an armful of hillus,[1]
Played with a golden ball and with a
Bat of silver the game of Hilláta.

Lo! the daughter of Yerugatta,
The twice fallen, Yérade-blúi,
Took unto her eighteen maidens.

There stood she upon the green slope,
'Neath the richly laden Khávilu;[2]
There did she unbind her tresses,
Thick were they as the churn-stick, mlattu.

Meanwhile skilful Bála Sévana
Caught the hillus of Béla-Máda;
Máda caught not those of Sévana.

Then said Yérugatta's daughter,
The twice fallen, Yérade-blúi,
"Has not Béla in Témalé,
In the grazing ground of Máda,
To the brim milked eighteen pailsful?

"Then his loins with pure white kerchief
Girt he not and made the butter,

---

[1] *Hillus.* Pieces of wood, the projectiles in the game.
[2] A shrub which bears edible berries.

Made it with coir and churn of Pángni,
Allamadda[1] was the framework?

"Therefore Béla-Máda's weary,
Tho' his hands have still their cunning:
Widows' sons are three times gifted.

"But had skilful Bála Sévana
To the brim milked eighteen pailsful,
"*He* forsooth had been too weary,
He had never caught the hillus;
Poorly fed is Bála Sévana,
Drinking washings of the milk-pail.

Art thou rich like Béla-Máda?"
Thus spake mocking Yĕrade-blúi.
Prone fell Béla 'mid the rushes.

Bála Sévana too, exhausted,
Fell among the Hubbé bushes.
See his face is dull and faded,
Which anon shone like a platter,—
Fatal word of Yérade-blúi,
Word of dark and evil omen.

So the some time loving brothers,—
Like were they to one another
E'en as the spreading horns of a buffalo,—
Part for aye from that same moment.

* * * * *

The ballad, which is very lengthy, goes on to relate the adventures of Bála Sévana, how he labored twelve years for his wife, became very rich, performed heroic deeds, and eventually was appointed the chief Monegar of the Hills, receiving the seal of office from the cutcherry at Satiamangalam.

Character.

The morality of the Badagas is neither better nor worse than might be expected from a naturally gentle and industrious but timid and ignorant people. Their regard for truth is of the slightest, and a clever piece of cheating is sure to excite their warmest admiration. In the funeral song which has been translated by Mr. Gover, one of the crimes enumerated for which atonement must be made, is that of "preferring a complaint to the Sircar," and one of their numerous proverbs embodies the same idea: "If you prefer a complaint to a magistrate, it is as if you had put poison into your adversary's food."

Either the terrors of the Sircar are not what they were, or this precept is much disregarded, for the Court-house at Ootacamund is constantly thronged with Badagas, and they are now very much given to litigation.

[1] Wood of a jungle tree.

CHAP. IX, PART V. — ETHNOLOGY. — Dwellings.

There is nothing very remarkable about their dwellings. They are ordinary cottages or huts built of stones or mud, with a substantial roof of thatch, which is gradually giving place to tiles as the people become more wealthy. There are lofts over each house, and the back eaves are sometimes closed in so as to form an additional room. There is generally a verandah with a pial in the front of the house, and a terrace for thrashing and winnowing grain; whitewash is a good deal used, and of late years their houses have been much improved. They are built in lines with occasionally an intervening street. They contain but little furniture : a rice-pounder, a few brass salvers, and a mortar made in the floor being all the necessary additions to a Badaga dwelling.

Religion.

The Badagas are Hindus of the Siva sect, but their form of the worship of Siva has lost much of its purity since their settlement in the Hills and intercourse with the more savage tribes about them. A small number belong to the sect called Lingayats, of whose origin in Mysore Mr. Rice gives the following account :[1]

"About 1160, little more than 40 years after the establishment of the Vaishnava faith in Mysore by Ramanuja Chari, arose the well known sect of Siva-worshippers called Lingayats, chiefly composed of the Kanada and Telugu-speaking races.

"Basava, the founder of the sect, whose name literally means bull, and was in fact regarded as the incarnation of Nándi, the bull of Siva. His political career has been sketched in connection with the history of the Kalachuryas. He was the son of an Aradhya Brahman, a native of Bagwadi in Belgaum. According to the legends, he refused to wear the Brahmanical thread because its investiture required the adoration of the sun, and repaired to Kalyana, the capital of Biggala, where he became, as elsewhere related, the prime minister, and where he founded the new sect.

"Its distinctive mark was the wearing on the person of a *jungama lingam* or portable linga. It is a small black stone, about the size of an acorn, and is enshrined in a silver box of peculiar shape, which is worn suspended from the neck or tied round the arm.

* * * * *

"Basava rejected the authority of the Vedas and the Brahmans, together with the observances of caste, pilgrimage and penance.

* * * * *

"The Lingayat faith soon spread through the north-west of Mysore, and, according to tradition, within 60 years of Basava's death, or 1168—1228, it was embraced from Ulovi near Goa to Sholapore, and from Ballehalli in Balehonnur to Sivaganga. It was the state religion of the Wodeyars of Mysore from 1399 to 1610."

---

[1] See RICE's *Manual of Mysore and Coorg.*

CHAP. IX, PART V. — ETHNOLOGY. — Temples.

The Lingayat priests from Gúndelpetta pay a pastoral visit to the Badagas of the hills every two or three years, for which they receive a present of a cow or an ox.

There are some hundreds of deities in the Hills, some of their shrines being merely ruins of cromlechs or houses, but the following are the principal shrines and idols :—The list is from Mr. Metz.

Kal-Kambaraya, or the stone pillar god.

Koriaraya, a rusty knife preserved in the village of Jackanéri, and supposed to have belonged to a man who committed suicide by leaping from St. Catherine's Fall.

Kariabettaraya, a silver figure representing a charitable Badaga of the Adhikári caste, now deceased.

Hiriadéva and *Hetté*, a Badaga and his wife. The latter committed suicide when her husband died, and both are worshipped. Other Badaga women emulating the example of Hetté have received the same honors, notably one called *Manikamma*.

Máhádeswara, an image of Siva copied from the one at Nanjanagúdi, called *Nanjanda*.

Ráma, or Rangasámi, is worshipped at only two places; at Rangasámi's Peak, where the officiating priest is an Irula, and at Húlikal Drúg, there the priest is a Badaga and wears the Vishnu mark.

Yérnasámi, a refractory chief from Coimbatore, who took refuge in the Nílagiris and was betrayed by the Badagas and cursed them for their treachery.

Jedeasámi, a god said to have appeared to a Lingayat. He is supposed to make the hair grow.

Ketaraya, a gold nose-ring, a god worshipped by the Toreas.

Bétasámi, a god of sport.

Gangamma, who presides at every stream. The Tódas also worship this deity.

Kakkaraya, the god of vomiting, who is frequently *propitiated* by an offering of a quarter rupee.

Virabhataraya, a granite image well carved and supposed to have been brought by the ancestors of the Badagas from Mysore.

The principal temples are the Hétte Kóvil in the Péranganád, two dedicated to the *Máhálingasámi* at Ténád in the Péranganád, and at Mélúr in the Mékanád, Jedeasámi's temple at Nidúnk..um in the Péranganád, Hiriasámi temples, one at Kuddanád in the Tódanád and the one at Mélúr.

There are also three others dedicated to gods not included in the above list, one to *Kariabettaraya* at Athiyarhatti in the Mékanád, one to *Ranganátha* at Kurrachawadi in the Mékanád, and

BADAGA TEMPLE

Near CHINNA KÚNÚR .C.M.C,Billikal 1876.

Rites and Ceremonies.

one to *Kattakal Mariammen,* probably the small-pox goddess, at Shólúr in the Tódanád.

As far as I can learn, no special ceremonies are usual on the birth of a child among the Badagas. In this they seem to resemble ordinary Hindus. Their marriages, too, are contracted without any especial rites. The looseness of the marriage tie among them may in part account for this. A time of probation is permitted *after marriage,* during which either husband or wife may change their minds. It is not unusual for a Badaga to form a *temporary alliance* with two or more young women, sending them back to their parents when he is tired of them, or even turning them out of doors before he settles down in earnest with a wife for life. A little feasting and the music of the Kótas is all the display that most of the castes indulge in. The Wódeas and Toreas alone employ a priest to perform some marriage ceremonies and make offerings to the gods. They also erect a rustic pandal, hung with garlands, under which the bride and the bridegroom take their seat, while the women sing songs and betel-nut is handed round. Feasting and dancing to the music of the Kótas concludes the marriage rites.

Their funerals are far more elaborate. Their forms begin before life is extinct and continue for several days. When a man or a woman is pronounced hopelessly ill, a small gold coin, worth quarter rupee and called a Birian hanna, is dipped in ghee and placed between his lips. If he can swallow it all the better; if not, it is tied to his arm, for it is intended to go with him on his long journey to pay his expenses until he has crossed the bridge of thread which leads to the next world. When the end has come, messengers are sent in all directions to summon the friends of the deceased, to call from the villages far and near the Kóta musicians, and to bring in wood and branches from the neighbouring shólas. A funeral car, a tower-like structure, is made close to the house of the deceased and hung with cloth. When it is ready the body is brought out on a cot and placed under it.

Strangely enough, the Kótas are employed as at a Tóda funeral in making bows and arrows which are laid on the bier, though a long time must have elapsed since the Badagas have possessed, much less used, any weapon of war or of the chase. The hoe and other tools of the deceased are also placed beside him, with his walking stick and flute. In the case of a woman, a rice-beater is substituted as being a more fitting emblem of her duties when alive, although she has generally a claim to the agricultural implements as well. On the following morning, when a large number of people have assembled, the death dance begins. It continues until sun-set, growing wilder and wilder as the day draws towards its close. The near relations of the dead do not join in it, but walk round the bier, carrying food in their hands and weeping whilst they enumerate the good qualities of their relative. After this the corpse is carried outside the village and then begins the strange ceremony which the Tódas seem to have copied, and which so vividly recalls the scape-goat of the Jews. Instead of a goat, a calf is chosen to bear the sins of the dead. A long litany is chanted and as each sin is mentioned, the people join in the refrain, shouting "It is a sin!"

"He killed the crawling snake."
Chorus—"It is a sin."

"The creeping lizard slew."
Chorus—"It is a sin."

When the last sentence with its response "Let all his sins be forgiven, and may it be well with him, yea all be well," has died away, earth is thrown on the body, and it is carried away to be burnt with the car on the banks of the nearest stream. The ashes are afterwards collected and thrown into the water. It is customary with the Badagas to give occasional feasts in honor of all the dead who have died during the eight or ten previous years.

Traditions.

Although some of the castes can point to the villages in Mysore from whence they came, and can tell some stories of the ill-usage which they received from Tippu's troops and the followers of neighbouring chiefs, they know but little about their ancestors in a more remote degree. According to Mr. Metz, scraps of their history are to be found interwoven in the lengthy ballads which they delight to recite, and it is much to be regretted that that laborious and patient observer of the habits of the hill people has not given to the public the large collection of their poetry which he has already translated into German.

Language.

Dr. Caldwell thinks that their language approaches most nearly to old Kanarese.

CHAPTER X.

ANTIQUITIES.

Varieties of Monuments, by whom described.—CAVES.—CAIRNS, position, contents, size, probable age.—BARROWS, size, contents, compared with European tumuli.—KISTVAENS, size, contents.—STONE CIRCLES.—AZARAMS.—CROMLECHS OR DOLMENS, groups, contents, origin.—RUINED VILLAGES.—FORTS.

CHAP. X. — ANTIQUITIES.

THE antiquities of the Nílagiris, although numerous, do not possess any great variety, neither do they differ materially from similar remains to be found in almost every hill range in Southern India.[1]

Varieties of monuments.

They consist of caves, cairns, barrows, kistvaens, cromlechs or dolmens, and stone circles, and also of sculptured stones, one inscription and some scratches on the rocks at Belliki, which are most probably written characters too, but which have not as yet been deciphered, and some ruins of forts and villages. These may be roughly classed, for the sake of convenience, under three heads, each representing approximately the relics of a different period, though it is by no means intended to lay down any strict rule, and it is possible that one class may overlap the other more than at first appears.

To the first and earliest[2] would seem to belong the only two caves as yet discovered possessing any remarkable features in the Hills.

To the second, the cairns, barrows, kistvaens, unsculptured cromlechs and stone circles, which seem to correspond with the tumuli and rude stone monuments that have been described in the Kistna, Salem, and other districts.

To the third, the sculptured cromlechs, or at least the sculptures found upon them, and the Tamil inscription at Mélúr, the ruins of villages,[3] and the ruined forts.

---

[1] No antiquities exist on the Pulní Hills in Madura. See MR. NELSON'S *Manual*, Part V, Chap. VIII.

[2] "It cannot be too strongly insisted upon, or too often repeated, that stone architecture in India commences with the age of Asoka (B.C. 250). Not only have we as yet discovered no remains whatever of stone buildings anterior to his reign, but all the earliest caves either in Behar or in the Western Ghâts show architecture in the first stage of transition from wood to stone."—FERGUSSON, *Tree and Serpent Worship*.

[3] As mentioned in a former chapter, some of these ruins may be very much more ancient than others.

CHAP. X.

ANTIQUITIES.

Of the earliest forms of religion no traces exist, and if the Dásyus and Takshas, the worshippers of trees and serpents,[1] ever inhabited these hills, they have left behind them no traces of their religion.

—by whom described.

The subject of the antiquities of this district was first systematically taken up about the year 1847, when Captain, afterwards Colonel, Congreve published a valuable paper in the Madras Journal of Literature and Science (Vol. 14, No. 32) pointing out the similarity of the Nílagiri tumuli to Druidical remains of the Celto-Scythians in different parts of Europe, and arguing from this the Celto-Scythian origin of the Tódas, whose work he believed them to be. Subsequent investigations and a broader and more scientific acquaintance with the subject has confirmed this view in so far as the Scythian or Turanian[2] origin of the cairn builders is concerned, but whether the Tódas of the present day are the descendants of the people who built the cairns still remains an open question. Various writers followed in Colonel Congreve's steps, and finally the late Mr. Breeks, Commissioner of the Nílagiris, by order of the Madras Government, drew up an elaborate report, after having opened a large number of the cairns and barrows and made a collection of their contents.[3]

Caves.

The following account of the caves of Belliki is from Colonel Congreve's paper :—

"Although possessing none of the features of interest belonging to the cave temples of the west of India, they are nevertheless worthy of observation.

"Formed by rocks projecting from the mountain side, the two caves are the work of nature, though the hand of man has increased their dimensions. The first * * * is about 30 paces broad, 12 deep, and 20 feet high at the entrance, the roof sloping downwards inside until it reaches the floor. Several smaller caverns branch from the outer caves, most of which are now filled up by loose stones and trunks of trees—the performance, I conjecture, of the Korumbas, who use this as a place of sacrifice and poojah. * * * The roof and façade of the caves present the remains of old paintings of armed men, men on horseback, animals, and demons so rudely executed as to render it as likely they are the work of the Korumbas as of a more accomplished people.

* * * * *

"To reach the second cave it is necessary to proceed in the first instance to Arrawaddy, two miles below Conagherry, and procure the

---

[1] No ancient serpent stones, though common in Mysore, have, as far as I know, been found in the Nílagiris.

[2] "No Semite and no Aryan ever built a tomb that could last a century or was worthy to remain so long."—FERGUSSON'S *History of Architecture*, Vol. I, page 51, 1865.

[3] This collection is still in the Commissioner's Office, Ootacamand, but is about to be distributed between the Calcutta and Madras Museums.

services of Korumbar guides, the route being intricate and embarrassed with grass and jungle. * * On reaching the cave I proceeded to measure, and found its depth 13 yards, its breadth 6, and the height of its entrance 40 feet, the roof sloping downwards until it meets the inner walls 5 feet high. The rock in which this cave is situated is perforated with several passages intersecting each other and connecting the interior of the cave with the flat surface above it. I explored the passage, but found nothing except an old iron ring. The sides of the large cave were marked with outline intaglio figures, and what perhaps were once inscriptions are now so defaced as almost to defy an attempt to copy them. I however contrived to transfer the more legible to paper.[1] On the left sides of the cave are the following intaglio cuttings in the rudest style.

"A human figure having the head of a bird with its waist encircled by the fold of a snake seemingly expanding and raising its seven heads behind the figure. In front of this human figure is a symbol having some resemblance to one of the Buddhist symbols mentioned by Colonel Sykes. The seven-hooded snake is frequently seen accompanying images and drawings of Buddha. To the proper left of the figure is, what I take to be, another Buddha or Jain symbol of a gridiron form with a handle above it. To the right of the large figure and snake is the rude effigy of a human being from whose head rises a long shaft surmounted by a chuckrum or lotus. There is a Buddhist symbol not unlike these. The same figure which seems to be balancing the chuckrum has a broom in its hand, which it will be recollected is one of the symbols of officers of Jain priests who use it to sweep insects out of their way for fear of treading upon them. In front of the figure of the Jain priest is a tree. Below this a figure kneeling, and apparently intended to be placed in a square niche. * * * At the bottom of the left hand side wall of the cave are some characters not unlike the old Páli. Near the floor, on the right side of the entrance, are some other characters.

"Returning from the cave I copied the rock inscriptions in the Belliki valley. There are three."

Colonel Congreve thought that one was old Kanarese, another old Malayalum, and the third the old Sanscrit of the third century before the Christian era; but it is difficult to understand the grounds on which he hazarded this assertion. Doctor Oppert, the Sanscrit Professor in the Madras University, who was kind enough to examine for me both Colonel Congreve's drawings and the photographs in Mr. Breeks' book, has given it as his opinion that the scratches are characters, but so rudely executed that he could not identify them with those of any particular language.

Cairns.

In using the words cairns, cromlech, &c., I shall, to avoid confusion, adopt the definition of them given by Mr. Breeks.

---

[1] Photographs of the intaglios and scratches will be found in BREEKS' *Tribes and Monuments of the Nílagiris.*

CHAP. X.
ANTIQUITIES.

By the term cairn, is understood a circular enclosure, formed either of single stones, a wall, or a heap of stones and earth.[1] These are very numerous. Mr. Breeks mentions having opened forty, and a considerable number had been opened previously[2] and their contents removed. Many are still unexplored. They are of different forms and exhibit more or less care in their construction—some being surrounded by a wall of uncemented stones so built as to give them the appearance of a draw well; others

DRAW WELL CAIRN.
CONGREVE.

are less carefully built, or only heaped up on the outside and lined with slabs, until they dwindle down to a mere circle of stones embedded in the earth.

CAIRN.

[1] Phin is the Tóda name. Badagas call them Hokkallu or navel-stones.
[2] Colonel Congreve opened forty-six.

Cairns are most numerous in the thickly populated portions of the hills and are met with but rarely in the Kúndas. CHAP. X. ANTIQUITIES.

They occupy almost invariably commanding positions on hills, and the principal stone slabs within the circles lie most frequently south-west by north-east. Sometimes rather more to the north and south, but never in a contrary direction. —position.

The following articles had been discovered. Generally some burnt bones, and in some cases pieces of skulls and jaw bones which are still whole. Pottery, varying from vessels made of very coarse clay, like the common chatty, to very fine pottery containing specks of mica and well glazed. The shapes of these vessels are very varied. Some of the lids are ornamented with figures of men and animals. There are pots having lids with birds, pigs, deer, dogs, elephants, horses, buffaloes, and trees, and —contents.

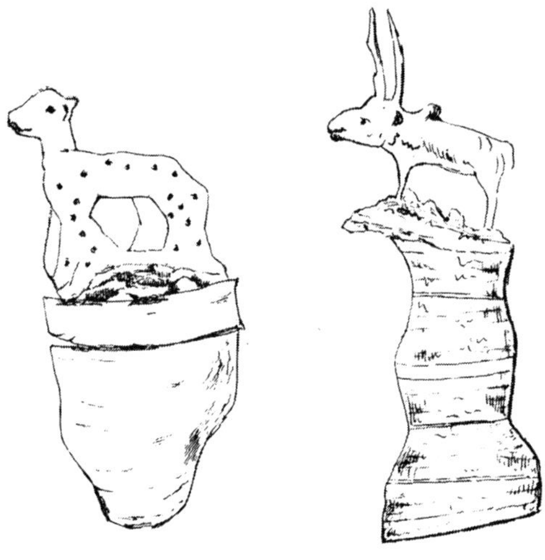

CINERARY URNS

one or two figures of men and women—some of the men on horse-back. One lid has a pillar or tower on it. Nearly all the implements found are of iron and present a curious similarity to those found in European tumuli. They include knives of various kinds, swords, razors, scythes, bells, and chains, also a few bronze vessels, some of them beautiful in shape and workmanship, and some gold ornaments—no silver.

CHAP. X. — ANTIQUITIES.

There are some long beads of agate, bored through longitudinally; also beads of cornelian and of gum.

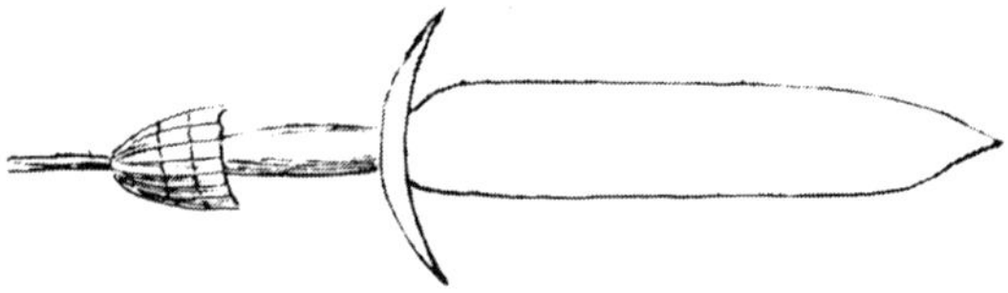

A SWORD

SPEAR HEAD FOUND IN CAIRNS

Walhouse

The absence of silver in the cairns may be an indication of their antiquity, gold having been much less common than silver as far back at least as the eleventh century. One Roman coin—an Aureus—has been found.

LIOS OF URNS CONGREVE

—size. The diameter usually varies from 20 to 28 feet, but there are some small cairns measuring only 9 or 10 feet. Most of the pots—cinerary urns—and implements are found within a few feet of the surface, either beneath stone slabs or resting on other slabs or a close pavement sunk a few feet down. The earth between the two layers of stones in which the pots are tightly packed is a black finely pulverized soil resembling decomposed animal matter.

CHAP. X.

ANTIQUITIES.

Large quantities of broken pots are frequently found embedded in it.

—probable age.

Of the age of the cairns it is difficult to form an opinion. That the most modern are from three to four centuries old is almost proved by the fact that the Badagas know nothing about them, whilst the enormous girth of some of the trees which have grown up within them, filling the interior of the circles with their roots, bears witness to an undisturbed possession of the locality for even a longer period. On the other hand the contents of the cairns do not point to any very remote antiquity. The weapons are mostly of iron, many of them such as are in use in the present day, and the few bronze vessels which have been found are always found with iron ones. This, as need hardly be explained, is significant, as it at once fixes the *era* to which these antiquities belong, though the actual *date* of the iron age in India may very likely differ materially from that of the iron age in Europe, the use of iron having been much earlier known in Asia.

Barrows.

The barrows[1] differ from the cairns chiefly in being surrounded by a ditch which is sometimes enclosed in one or more circles of loose single stones. The centre consists of a mound, which appears to have been like the cairns, almost invariably a place of interment for the ashes of the dead, if not the spot where cremation actually took place. They are very numerous, generally occurring near cairns or in similar elevated localities.

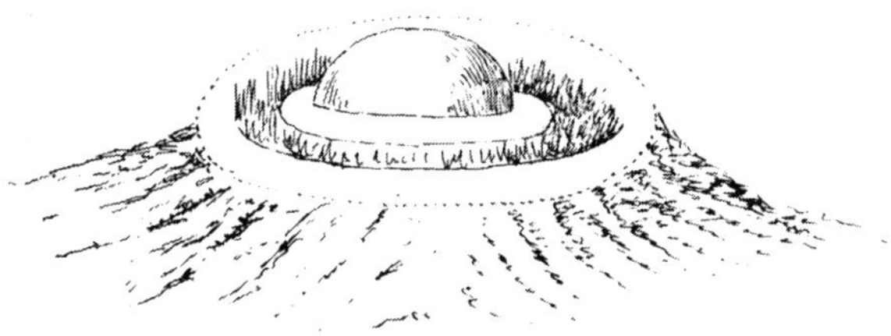

BARROW.

Congreve.

—size.

The diameter, measuring across the outer circle of stones or to the outer slope of the ditch when this forms the extreme edge of the barrow varies from 20 to above 60 feet.

—contents.

The contents are very similar to those of the cairns, leaving no doubt whatever of the sepulchral nature of these tumuli. The bones are most frequently found in small bronze vessels enclosed in an

[1] Badaga *Ponguli* or gold pit.

CHAP. X. — ANTIQUITIES. earthenware chatty or pot. The swords, daggers, spear-heads, and sickles are identical and do not belong to another era in art. The same may be said of the pottery, which is very plentiful. Mr. Breeks sums up thus :—

"The general features of the cairns and barrows vary very little. Above and beneath the slabs, which in a great majority of cases lie north-east and south-west exactly as if they had been placed by compass, and round the circle near the surface, lie the rough pots, large deep narrow vessels, pointed at the bottom so that they cannot stand upright, with rough figures of men and animals on the lid, and empty or containing only earth, as far as their almost invariably broken state allows one to judge. The number of these is surprising. Baskets full of heads and horns of buffaloes and other figures may be carried away from some cairns; but in most cases they lie so near the surface penetrated by the roots of trees and bushes that nothing can be recovered. Below at depths varying from one to four feet are the cinerary urns, superior in quality and make.

There does not seem to be any rule as to the arrangement of the interments. Sometimes the bones are at the bottom of the urn, sometimes in a bronze vase contained in it, sometimes under the inverted bronze. Often the bronze is not in or near the urn. Some of the urns do not contain bones but only implements and ornaments, and some only earth. Sometimes the number of interments corresponds with that of the slabs, but this does not occur often enough to prove design." [1]

BELL METAL VESSELS

—compared with European tumuli. In outward appearance the cairns and barrows of the Nílagiris differ very slightly from those in Europe; and their contents, as has been said before, exhibit even a more striking similarity. Each of the articles in the following list is found in the cairns of both countries.

[1] No very large urns, measuring as much as 4 feet in diameter, such as are found in Tinnevelly, have ever been found in the Nílagiris.

Taken out of the Nílagiri cairns by Mr. Breeks :—

Spearheads.
Knives.
Sickles.
Cornelian beads.
Pottery (varying in quality from very coarse to fine), small vessels containing a colorless fluid.
Miniature pots and weapons.
Lamps or censers.
Charcoal.
Burnt bones.
Ashes and decomposed animal matter.
Shreds of silk. (Woollen cloth is found in Europe.)
Gold ornaments.
Pavements on which the buried articles rest.
Bells.

Representations of the buffalo, horse, sheep, and deer are very common. Colonel Congreve writes: "When comparing the barrows of the Nílagiris with those in Dorsetshire I omitted to mention that in one of those ancient Celtic cemeteries was found a young bullock's head enclosed in a *patera* of earthenware."

The bright red glazing and the zigzag and harrow-headed mouldings of some of the urns are common to both.

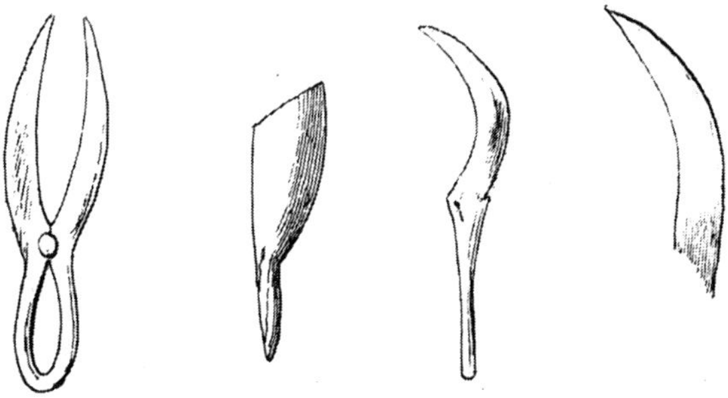

IRON IMPLEMENT CONGREVE.

Kistvaens.

Next in order—because they, too, have probably been used as tombs—are the Kistvaens. There is less danger of confusion as regards this term, for in every variety—and there are several—the *kist* or chest distinguishes them. The name, however, has sometimes been erroneously given to free-standing dolmens or cromlechs. The *kist* is almost invariably formed of large stone slabs so placed as to enclose a square space or vault, but the aperture varies from a round hole pierced in one side to a large space formed by the absence of one of the slabs. Those in the Nílagiris are of the first kind, the upper edge of the kist being level with the surface of the ground. They are surrounded by a circle of single stones. As far as is at present known, they

CHAP. X. ANTIQUITIES. exist in only one locality, on the slopes near Kótagiri—close to the site of the ruined fort of *Udiaráya.*

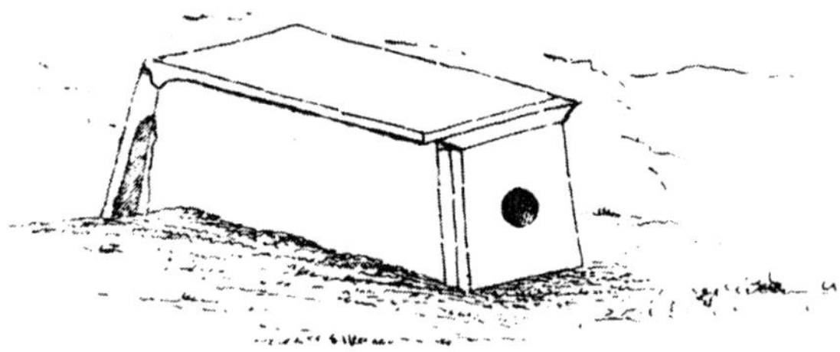

KISTVAEN-CONGREVE.

—size. Mr. Breeks found them all much alike. The size of the chest was about 3 feet 6 inches by 2 feet 6 inches, and the round aperture varied from 12 to 15 inches in diameter. They had all been opened, but the earth within the *kist* was mixed with —contents. charcoal, whilst that outside appeared to be the natural soil. A broken dagger and some fragments of pottery are all the "*finds*" recorded. These were not in the kist but beside it. One of the Kistvaens described by Mr. Boswell in the Kistna District exactly corresponds with these, the pottery being in "an adjacent chamber," not in the kist. In the plains Kistvaens are said to exist side by side with cromlechs, and to be undoubtedly tombs. In the Nílagiris, although they appear to have no connection with the cromlechs, there is every reason to suppose that they, too, were used as sepulchres.

Stone circles. It is almost impossible to distinguish these, in the few cases in which they exist apart from cairns, from modern Tóda Azárams. Mr. Breeks thinks that only one isolated ancient circle has been identified near the Paikaré Tiriéri-mand, but that there are circles in two places, which are perhaps neither kraals nor cairns. Of these he remarks :—

"They consist of two or three groups of circles of dry walling, to the right of the Segúr road, opposite Muttanád mand. One of these first dug out appears to be the kraal referred to in the story of Koten. It is built on sheet rock, in some places quite bare, in others covered only by a thin coating of turf and vegetable soil. Near this were several circles joined together, some large and some small. In one of the latter, about half a foot below the surface, were five small stones, about 12 × 6 × 6 inches laid in this form. Nothing was found within or below the stones."

The whole hill-side was covered with azárams, indicating that it was an ancient burial ground.

CHAP. X. — ANTIQUITIES. — Azárams.

A number of old Azárams had been opened. They contain exactly what an acquaintance with Tóda customs of the present day would lead one to expect. The only difference being that it seems formerly to have been the custom to bury bracelets and other valuables with the ashes, instead of withdrawing them when the burning has taken place as is now done.

These old Azárams supply one link in the chain which should connect the cairns with the modern ones, but many links are still missing, and it is impossible to assign the cairns and barrows to the Tódas on existing data, though they perhaps have a better claim to them than either of the other Hill tribes. Against this is to be set the fact that the Tódas do not generally claim them, and that they look on calmly at their spoliation, though they never seem to rifle them themselves.[1]

Cromlechs or Dolmens.

These terms are applied to monuments something like Kist-vaens, but above ground. They are formed of stone slabs enclosing a chamber, but open at one side, or in some cases only of two upright slabs with another resting tablewise upon them. They generally occur in groups in low-lying, secluded spots, and do not appear to have any connection with the cairns and barrows, although those with unsculptured stones may belong to the same period. The sculptured ones are probably more modern. In many respects they recall Buddhist reliquaries,[2] though the carvings resemble those of the Lingayats in Mysore, and the subjects are almost identical with some which are found in similar monuments in that kingdom. It is quite possible, however, that the carvings were executed long after the cromlechs were built.

The principal groups are as follow:—

– groups.

(1.) Shólúr. The cromlechs here have carvings on the side stones which, though rough in execution, deserve to be fully described if only for the sake of comparison with those described by Mr. Rice in his Manual of Coorg and Mysore. The slabs are divided into compartments by a raised line which forms a kind of frame to each picture, and is on a level with the figures in bas-relief. In the upper compartment of one stone, the central figure is a Basava, or sacred bull of Siva, kneeling before a kind of altar on which is a rude representation of a lingam. Behind the bull is a human figure, probably meant for the *pujári*. The rest of the stone is divided into compartments containing figures of men.

---

[1] The Tódas are moreover said to lay claim to some of the cairns. See Breeks.

[2] "The Buddhist reform altered the funeral tumulus into a relic shrine, modifying this, as it did most of the Turanian forms of utterance, from a literal to a somewhat more spiritual form of expression, but leaving the meaning the same."—FERGUSSON'S *History of Arch.*, p. 51.

CHAP. X.

ANTIQUITIES.

They are armed with spears and bows and arrows, and one figure is on horse-back. The women on the second stone are naked above the waist, and their hair is dressed in a knob on one side.

(2.) Mélúr. On one of the stones in this group at the back is the only inscription of any importance on the Hills. A description of it by Sir Walter Elliot will be found in Mr. Breeks' book. He regards the subject as a *virgal* (*vira-kal* or hero-stone) and a *Mastikkal* (*Maha Sati kal*, great Sati stone). It represents the death of a hero who was killed by a tiger, and whose wives performed sati. The inscription which is in modern Tamil has been deciphered by Dr. Pope as well as the broken condition of the stones would admit.

He says: "It reads thus:—'In the Vegudânya of the month Sittirai (April-May) in the Aswini Nak shetra the 42nd cycle of the Saka year 1518 (the character which I suppose to be 5 is ௫ which as a numeral is unknown) . . . . . for a gift . . . . for a tiger . . . . . this writing.' Dr. Pope seems to think, it is a grant; and he adds: "Saka 1518, *i.e.*, A.D. 1596, is late enough for the Badagas, but they do not seem to know anything of the cromlechs, and were or professed to be ignorant even of the second group which was hidden among some bushes."

The Badagas, however, do reverence some of the *bira kallu*, and offer fruit and flowers before them. This may only be because the "subjects have generally some reference to the worship of Siva. They oddly enough never claim these stones, but say sometimes that the *unsculptured* cromlechs were the work of their ancestors."

The other groups of cromlechs are as follow:—

(3.) Group at Mélúr. Only one of these sculptured, the subject being a double sati.

(4.) A single sculptured cromlech at Jakata Kambé. Here the Badagas perform an annual sacrifice.

(5.) A very fine group of cromlechs at Achenna. Some are built into the village kraal and used as pens for calves.

(6.) Group at H'laiúru between Kótagiri and Kódanád. The sculptures represent a hunting memorial.

(7.) Group at Kákúsi.

(8.) Group of sculptured cromlechs on Major Sweet's plantation near Kátéri.

(9.) One large cromlech sculptured and some small unsculptured ones at Mélkúnda.

Two groups have been entirely destroyed, one a "five-celled" dolmen in the direction of Húlikal Drúg, which has fortunately been described by Mr. Walhouse[1] and another near the Kúndas. CHAP X ANTIQUITIES

FIVE-CELLED DOLMEN

formerly existing near Nids Mand Nilagiris

Walhouse

As a rule, the cromlechs yield nothing but *déva kotta kallus*, but from those in Major Sweet's plantation some iron and brass armlets were taken by Mr. Breeks, as well as sickles, rings, two small iron hatchet-heads, and a common rough chatty or earthen-ware pot. No bones or charcoal have been found, and it is difficult to suppose that the cromlechs were ever intended to be used as sepulchres. contents

In a work of this description it would be out of place to put forward theories concerning the origin of these remains; indeed a very meagre account of what exists is all that can be attempted. It should, however, be borne in mind that the Tódas have been known to claim some of the cairns, though it is impossible to reconcile their utter apathy when these monuments are disturbed and desecrated with any genuine regard or veneration for them. According to Mr. Metz, the few Tódas who have "maintained that the cairns were the work of their ancestors" were men who had been examined by Europeans, and who had soon detected what information was desired, regulating their replies accordingly. On the other hand, their present mode of burning and burial in stone circles (azárams) as well as the conical shape of the Bóas (temples) seem to connect them with these remains, which are clearly the work of a Turanian people. —origin

As regards the third class of monuments, none of the present inhabitants of the Hills are capable of executing sculptures of even so elementary a degree of art as those on the cromlechs. The Sculptured cromlechs.

[1] *Indian Antiquary.*

Kótas alone possess the necessary tools, and they never use them for that purpose but employ sculptors from the lower country to decorate their houses. The present customs of the Kúrumbas and Irulas seem to point to the use of such structures as depositories of either smooth water-worn stones, to which they attach a superstitious reverence, or for stones which are placed in sacred spots in memory of the dead. No distinct traces of Buddhism are apparent in the meagre religion of either race, but if, as seems probable, they occupied the low country for centuries before they sought shelter in the Hills, they must, whether their status was as important as has been thought or not, have been more or less affected by that which was the paramount religion of the peninsula from B.C. 500 to A.D. 1000. Colonel Congreve thought that he saw in the monuments of the Nílagiris very clear traces of the Jain religion, but he was evidently led away by the word Pandya, which he took to refer to the Pandyan kings of the South, and whose dominion he thought was at one time established over the Hills. Be this as it may, it is now generally admitted that the word is used in a general sense, and has no especial reference either to the kings of Pandya or to the Pandava brothers, except in so far as the latter take the place of the giants and fairies of other countries, for "to them all over India ancient mysterious structures are ascribed."[1] However, it is possible that in the burial customs alone of the Kúrumbas and Irulas some traces remain of a religion which has all but died out among them. In Travancore a tribe still exists who make miniature cromlechs and place a stone in them in memory of each person who dies. This is held sacred and offerings made to it. That the wild and illiterate people of the Hills can tell nothing of the history of these monuments is not to be wondered at when the vague and unsatisfactory replies that are often elicited from comparatively learned Brahmins are remembered. It is no uncommon thing to be told by such that temples which cannot have been erected before our era are many thousands of years old, and such lapses of time as ten or twenty centuries are counted but as a span in their loose way of computing time. The Badaga name for the Kistvaens, *Máuryaru Mané* or Mauryars' houses, may give some clue to their origin. It looks at least as if they connected them with the dynasty of Magada, though it does not follow that they were erected by the subjects of that kingdom or even by their descendants, though both are possible. It is well

[1] See CALDWELL'S *Comparative Grammar of the Dravidian Languages*, p. 594, Appendix. "To call anything "a work of the Pandava" is equivalent to terming it "Cyclopian" in Greece, "a work of the Picts" in Scotland, or "a work of Nimrod" in Asiatic Turkey; and it means only that the structure to which the name is applied was erected in some remote age, by a people of whom nothing is now known."

known that Asóka caused topes and monuments to be erected far beyond the actual limits of his kingdom and there are also some grounds for connecting the present Kúrumbas of the Hills with the Kadamba Rájas whose suzerainty succeeded his in South India and who spread themselves over a large portion of the peninsula some centuries later. But the name may have been learned in Mysore, and merely applied by the Badagas to similar structures which they found when they came to the Hills.

Ruined villages.

Of these ruins there is very little to be said. They are met with not unfrequently on the plateau, but are not remarkable in any way. There is nothing to distinguish them from the ruins of modern huts, either as to size or as regards the quality of the masonry. Their age is mainly apparent by the overgrowth of shrubs and trees which frequently conceal them almost entirely. Those on the largest scale are at Fairlawns a few miles from Ootacamand, and Colonel Congreve was induced by the position of some of the walls and by the amount of ground they cover, to suggest that they might indicate the site of an ancient Capital. To me it seems more probable that this was once a village of gold diggers from the Wainád, for in this and other offshoots of Nanjanád valley [1] may be seen mounds of earth along the banks of the streams where the soil has been washed for gold. It is possible at one time that this part of the plateau yielded gold and as it lay within the Kongu or Coimbatore country, gold-seekers from the north and west would have to stand upon the defensive. This would account for the remains of a strong fort under shelter of which the village may have sprung up,[2] and may throw light on the remarkable fact of the existence on the Hills—which, for ages perhaps before the advent of the Badagas, were mere buffalo-walks—of an outcaste race of workers in gold and other metals, the Kótas.

Forts.

Besides the ruins at Fairlawns which have not been clearly identified, three forts originally existed, two of which are still in a fair state of preservation. The one best known is situated on summit of the Húlikal Drúg and commands the Coonoor ghát and the low country about Coimbatore. It is said to have been used by Tippu during his wars with the English as a stronghold for his prisoners, and among the stories of his cruelties is one which charges him with hurling some of them from the top when he found it expedient to get rid of them. But these stories are probably pure fictions.

---

[1] One of these is the valley behind Bishopsdown and Fernhill, the Tóda name of which is Púnthut, or gold-thut (?), *pat*, village. Mr. Brough-Smyth, the eminent Australian Mining Engineer, who recently examined the Fairlawns Valley, expressed a firm opinion that it contained ancient gold workings.

[2] See *Madras Journal of Literature and Science*, No. 32, 1847, p. 97. Article on "Antiquities of the Neilgherries" by Colonel Congreve.

CHAP. X. — ANTIQUITIES.

The second fort is in the Tódanád near the Segúr Pass and is called Málékóta or old fort.

The site of the third, called Udiaráya, is near Kótagiri, but although the position is known no ruins remain.

There is a tradition in the Hills that these three forts were once occupied by three Rájas who ruled over the whole of the Nílagiris, and that they were only strengthened by Haider Áli and used in his wars and subsequently in those of his son.

In the Kongu-désa Rájakal[1] mention is made of a *Nílagiri dúrga* which was taken by Hari-vari-déva, a king of the Chóla kingdom, but it is impossible to say if this really applies to one of the forts already mentioned.

As the architectural remains are closely connected with those of the neighbouring Districts of Coimbatore, I append a memorandum regarding them by Mr. William Fraser, District Engineer, Coimbatore, (1859). *Madras Journal of Literature and Science, May* 1860.

Memorandum on the interesting memorials of antiquity in the Coimbatore District.[2]

The memorials of antiquity in the Coimbatore District, although numerous, are not striking. The very ancient memorials consist of, so far as I have seen,

I. Cromlechs,
II. Sepulchral tumuli,
III. Pillar stones,
IV. Stone circles.

The memorials of more modern times are—

I. Temples,
II. Forts,
III. Palaces,
IV. Rock inscriptions,
V. Manuscripts.

2. As I am unacquainted with Indian antiquities, I have designated these remains by the names given to similar objects in other countries. These names are probably correct, for no one who is acquainted with Celtic antiquities can fail to be struck with the similarity between them and the ancient remains scattered over this district.

CROMLECHS.

3. Some of the cromlechs I have seen in this district are similar to those found in Ireland: three or more stones placed upright, and over them a large flat stone placed so as to form a small rude chamber.

---

[1] *Madras Lit. Journal*, No. 32, 1847.

[2] Mr. Fraser's remarks on stone circles are confined to those on the Nílagiris and contain nothing of importance. The remarks on the other memorials, rock inscriptions excepted, are also not note-worthy.—ED.

I do not allude to the numerous small buildings of this type, formed with dressed stones, and generally having one or two figures of Hindu deities carved upon them, but to those of a much ruder description, formed with unhewn stone, and without any carving or inscriptions.

4. In one respect these cromlechs differ from those in the British Islands.

The latter are ruder in construction: the upright stones are often without any particular form, as if they intended merely to support the top stone.

The number of supports too, varies greatly, sometimes only three, sometimes six; and thus the chamber is variable and rude in form.

The cromlechs in this district are, on the contrary, formed with carefully selected flat stones placed on edge, so as to form a chamber nearly square and nearly completely enclosed.

The covering stones have not so decided a slope as have those of the cromlechs of the British Isles.

5. Of unmistakable cromlechs, I *have seen* not more than six.

Four of these are in the valleys of the Bawáni and Moyár Rivers; and two in the valley of the Noyel River or the Bolamampatti Valley: one of the latter is close to the road from Coimbatore to Dambrapáleyam and about five or six miles from Coimbatore.

These two are remarkable for having, in a stone forming one side of the chamber, an oval shaped hole about 10 or 12 inches in diameter.

6. Major Hamilton when he visited the higher ranges of the Anamalais discovered a cromlech precisely similar to those in the Bolamampatti Valley.

It is on the east side of, and about 400 yards from, the Tora Kádavu River, about three or four miles south of Ponachi.

I did not see this cromlech, but having seen Major Hamilton's sketch and heard his description, I have no doubt but that it is a real cromlech.

SEPULCHRAL TUMULI.

7. These are found in every part of this district—in the cultivated plains—in the lands that have been irrigated for hundreds of years—around the base of the Anamalais—in the deep gorges at the foot of the Nílgiris—and in the now untrodden unhealthy jungles in the valleys of the Bawáni and Moyár, I have found these sepulchral tumuli, with their kistvaens, cinerary urns, and the other characteristics which distinguish the tumuli that are scattered over Northern and Western Europe.

8. These tumuli are not generally found isolated or singly here and there. In some places 10 or 12 acres are covered with them; and those burial places are so close to each other that it is impossible to resist the belief that the whole of the country must, at one time, have been thickly peopled: it is scarcely possible that these could be the results of the occasional visits of a nomadic race.

9. By far the finest specimens of these remains, that I have seen, are in the valley of the Moyár.

Generally, the tumuli are not much raised above the surface of the land; along the Moyár many of them are raised eight or nine feet and each tumulus is surrounded by a stone circle.

10. In some places there is one tumuli much larger than the rest, and surrounded by a larger circle of larger stones, flat, placed on edge, and standing about three feet above the ground.

11. In every instance there is a large flat stone upon the top of the tumulus; in a very few cases I have seen two within one circle; and I presume each covered a kistvaen, as was the case in all (perhaps 100) that I have seen open.

Some of the covering stones contained 150 to 200 cubic feet.

12. The kistvaens in these tumuli are precisely similar to those found in Europe: from four to five feet in length and two to three in width; thus evidently intended for the reception either of cinerary remains, or of bodies in a sitting posture: a mode of burial still observed by Lingadháris and others. The dimensions given above are those that generally prevail; but I have seen some much larger: there is a very large one in a rice field near Coimbatore close to the new road to the Railway Station: they are all, so far as I have seen, placed east and west.

13. I opened one of the tumuli in the valley of the Moyár, it contained the usual cinerary urns of baked clay, with portions of calcined and uncalcined human bones—I have been told that pieces of metal have been found in some but I never saw any.

14. Very many cinerary urns have been collected by the Railway Engineers, as their works laid open hundreds of tumuli. The Collector of this district, too, had and still has a considerable number.

They are of various shapes, and in size they vary from two or three feet to four or five inches in diameter: some are rudely ornamented, usually by wavy parallel lines; but none that I have seen are in this respect equal to those in European collections: I once thought I had discovered a black *glazed* one, but, on closer inspection, I found that the polished surface had been produced by friction.

15. Of the origin of these tumuli the same tradition is found in every part of the district. That they are the houses of a race of Pigmies called Pandúra, who, having angered the gods, were punished by fire rained upon them from heaven: that they sought protection in their houses and pulled these huge stones over them.

16. The people have no veneration for these remains, not even the Erulars and Kurambers, who inhabit the jungles around the hills and who are so like the descendants of aborigines. The only feeling they have about them is fear, that the spirits of the Pandúras might visit them if they interfered with their graves.

PILLAR STONES.

17. In a country where boundaries are still marked with pillar stones, it may naturally be expected that this class of memorial would

be numerous; such is the case in Coimbatore—pillar stones, marking boundaries, are found everywhere. CHAP. X. ANTIQUITIES.

Most of them are dressed stones: some are inscribed, and many have carvings of Hindu figures upon them.

18. Occasionally other pillar stones are met with, which seem to have been raised to commemorate some gallant deed in the destruction of tigers, as they are carved with representations of struggles between these animals and human beings. There are many of these throughout the district.

19. I found one half of an inscribed pillar stone a short time ago in an irrigation channel near the base of the Anamalais. So far as we could make out the inscription, from the one half that was present, it was to the effect that a large tract of jungle had been granted to some person by a rájá who reserved to himself certain privileges; this inscription is evidently very old. I have directed search to be made for the other half.

20. All these pillar stones are, however, comparatively modern, and have yet to exist for a few centuries before they become what is generally understood by the name. They are evidently of a date long posterior to that of the cromlechs and tumuli. I have, however, met with pillar stones which I consider coeval with those monuments of antiquity—rude, unhewn stones having an unmistakable family likeness to the Leagans of Ireland, the hoar stones of Scotland, and the hoar stones of England.

21. In a thick jungle in the valley of the Kódangíri, a tributary of the Bawáni, there are two or three of these stones at a place called Kutirai Kuttu[1] Palam, and there is a good specimen about nine or ten feet in height in the valley of the Bawáni near the village of Súndapatti.

22. In the valley of the Moyár near a place called Mángádu there are two.

Rock Inscriptions.

48. I have met with but one, near Anamalai: it is cut in a flat rock, which, up to the time of my seeing it, had been used by the villagers to beat out grain upon.

49. It is in old Tamil, and to the effect that a certain quantity of land had been granted for the support of the Anamalai Temple, and pronouncing anathemas against any one who should deprive the temple of those lands. The temple was demolished by Tippu, who I suppose by appropriating the lands earned the anathema in full.

By beating grain upon it a portion of the inscription has been destroyed.

I directed a low wall to be built around it.

---

[1] The "Kattu" here does not refer to *building* — but to *tying*. The Erulars who live near, say it is named from a tradition, handed down by their fathers, that a small band of predatory horsemen who were skulking in this valley tied their horses to these stones.

In an adjoining valley called Kalkattu Palam, there are about 20 sepulchral tumuli.

CHAPTER XI.

EARLY HISTORY.

Sketch of the history of peninsular India.—Early race movements.—Early religions of the peninsula.—Relation of early hill-tribes to race movements.—Divisions of South India.—Kongu or Chera.—Chólas.—Kadamba dynasty.—Hoysala Bellála.—Vijayanagar.—Mysore.—Fall of Seringapatam.—Malayálam.—Early Portuguese Missionaries.

CHAP. XI. — EARLY HISTORY. — Sketch of the history of peninsular India.—Early race movements.

ALTHOUGH the Nílagiris, prior to our occupation, have no history, that is, no written record of the changes in the varying peoples who have found a refuge on their heights from the turmoils of the open lands below, or of their doings, yet, from their peculiar geographical position, they possess an interest for the historian when considered in relation to the movements and development of the principal races of the south. The Nílagiri mountain-block stands forth, not only as a divider of winds and waters, but also as a divider of races and peoples, or, viewed in another way, as a pillar marking their point of contact, just as it marks the point of union of the great mountain systems of peninsular India.

Around its base, from the earliest ages, contending tribes and nations have struggled, the men of the north with the men of the south, and each and both of these with the people of the west, whilst in its wild recesses remnants of savage races have found a place of shelter and a home. To its south is the high road from the east to the west coast, the great Palghát Pass through which the Dravidians[1] pushed their way into Malabar; to its north the Gajalhatti Pass, through which the same people pressed upwards into the table-lands of Mysore; to its west Karkúr and other passes, through which the Malayálams penetrated into Wainád. But the tide of conquest was ever rising and falling, and downwards from Mysore or upwards from Malabar marched the avengers of these conquests.

Though small the area of the Nílagiris, yet it has probably at one and the same time been divided between the three great historic races of the south—the Tamulians, the Malayálams, and the Kanarese—and consequently its history combines in a measure that of Coimbatore, Malabar and Mysore, whose inhabitants

[1] They also entered, perhaps later, from the extreme south by Cape Comorin.

consist for the most part of these races; nor can the tale be satisfactorily told until the historical material of each of these provinces has been fully recorded and analysed. That of Mysore has hitherto engrossed the greater share of attention; that of Coimbatore and of Malabar has not as yet been pieced together.

In the two preceding chapters I have endeavored briefly to narrate the most important known facts regarding the tribes residing on the Nílagiris and the existing monuments thereon.

From these data three important conclusions may, perhaps, be derived : firstly, that these hills were once occupied by a race, the builders of the cairns and barrows, who spread themselves more completely over their surface than any of the existing tribes, but whether their occupation was prior to, or contemporaneous with, that of one or more of the extant tribes, or whether they were or were not Dravidians, is uncertain; secondly, that at least one race exists, the Tódas, who migrated thither without being subjected in any way to Brahmanical religious influences, but whether they are of the same stock as the rest of the Dravidian races of the peninsula cannot be said to be absolutely proven, though it is highly probable; and lastly, that the race which has exercised the longest and most powerful influence on the Nílagiris, and which first tilled the soil extensively, is the Kanarese.

At the dawn of Indian history we find the greater portion of India, south of the Vindya mountains and of the Nerbadda river, occupied by races who probably spoke dialects of one language —Dravidian— whilst to the east and west in Orissa and North Konkan the inhabitants already spoke dialects of the tongue of their Aryan conquerors. Among these Dravidian races there probably was at least one race differing in religion and possibly in language from the aborigines, known as the Nágas,[1] said to be a Scythian people who worshipped the serpent and took it for their national emblem. These Dravidian[2] races are now represented by the Tamils, the Telugus, the Malayálams, and the Tulu and Kodugu-speaking peoples, and by the more or less uncivilized races whose idioms are known as Tóda, Kóta, Gond, Khónd, Oráon, and Rájmahal, who occupy mainly the highlands of the Dekhan. These hill people are all regarded as Dravidians as opposed to Kólarians,—the generic appellation of tribes speaking dialects allied to the language of the Kóls,—in great measure by reason of the proved Dravidian nature of their speech and the absence of any

[1] The Yávanas appeared in the south much later. See the delightful account of these strangers in Dr. HUNTER's *Orissa*, Vol. I, Chapter V.

[2] See Dr. CALDWELL's *Grammar of Dravidian Languages* in Introduction.

CHAP. XI. — EARLY HISTORY.

traces of another language; and if unity of language were the only test of identity of race and origin, then the wilder races are very properly placed in the same family of men as their more civilized neighbours who use a cognate language; but whether the evidence drawn from the religion, manners, customs, and physical peculiarities of some of these tribes bears out fully this assumption is by some still regarded as an open question, though we find no certain traces of an older and essentially diverse people; for with wholly savage peoples it is conceivable that a race might disappear without leaving a trace of its language in the speech of its supplanters, or adopt that of its conquerors, losing every trace of its original tongue.

These wilder Dravidian races appear, as the curtain of history rises, to be occupying the highlands and mountains of the Dekhan, especially its western and southern borders and the upper tracts of the *Gódávari* and Kistna rivers. "At any rate it appears probable from the classical Geography," remarks Professor Wilson,[1] "as well as the imperfect character and general tenor of the traditions regarding this part of the peninsula, that a considerable tract of country between the *Gódávari* and *Kistna* rivers from the sea coast eastwards continued, to a comparatively modern date, in the possession of scattered and barbarous tribes, or an untenanted expanse of mountain and forest, such as it was when *Ráma*, with his wife and brother, resided in a cottage of leaves near the sources of the Gódávari." But although fierce and wild tribes occupied these forests and jungles, yet in the richer valleys of the great rivers and on the plains near the coast were people, dwelling in towns, far more advanced in civilization and the arts, who were engaged in commerce, the highway of which was the Arabian Sea or the Bay of Bengal; but there are no ruins to evidence to what degree of civilization they had attained. Meanwhile we find the Aryans pushing down along the east and west coast, their course along the sea-board being comparatively easy, and finally forcing their way from central Hindostan in a direct line southwards through the Dekhan. But the resistance of the tribes in possession appears to have been so determined that, although at last the power and civilization of the Aryans obtained a permanent footing in the more fertile and open portions of the Dekhan, and gradually extended to the most southern portions of the Peninsula and even to Ceylon, yet they were compelled to adopt the language of the people, and probably, in the first instance, much of their religion and many of their customs. The Aryan invaders

[1] *Descriptive Catalogue*, Vol. I, p. xcix.

were probably led by Kshatriya chiefs, though it may be their advent had been preceded by that of some holy rishi or sage, who sought seclusion in the forests of the south or escape from the religious dissensions of his native country. To these pale-faced immigrants the wild and black tribes of the country appeared monstrous and horrible. Hence with romantic exaggeration they have been handed down to us as giants (Asúras),[1] monkeys (Vanaras), and demons (Rakshasas). Indian legend and poetry are full of the conflicts, with varying fortune, between the incomers and the people of the soil, and again between these settlers and still later comers, who were often inspired by the reforming zeal of the Brahmans. For as the warlike Kshatriyas prevailed over the aborigines, so they in their turn yielded to the power of these religious enthusiasts; but gradually they brought the Kshatriya chiefs and the leaders of the aboriginal races under their power and, whilst leaving to such the headship of their people, succeeded in giving to prince and subject alike their civilization, such as it was, but along with it imposing the yoke of Brahmanical law and religion, whilst those who would not bow before the invader, whether Kshatriya or Brahman, became outcastes, or if they preserved their independence it was in isolation and retirement. A remarkable instance of such independence occurs in the case of the Coorgs, who, aided by the physical peculiarities of their country, not only repelled for long ages the invasion of armies, but also the subtle inroads of the Brahmans, who up to this day have never been able to found a colony in Coorg. Here and there chiefs of the wilder Dravidian races who had succumbed to the invaders, as for example the Kúrumbas, rose again to power, but this they obtained, or at least retained only in so far as they sought the aid of the church of the immigrant Aryan sacerdotalists and brought their people under its influence. At times probably the Brahmans made use of such converts to overthrow the hated Kshatriyas, and along with them their Buddhist or Jaina rivals.

Early religions of the peninsula.

What was the religion of the peninsula prior to the arrival of the Aryans from the north there is little to show, but it was probably rude and similar to those still prevailing among aboriginal tribes who have come but little into contact with these immigrants, viz., veneration for the Lingam, the emblem of life and power; reverence for household and village divinities; and also among some tribes respect for the serpent. This serpent worship was especially prevalent in Mysore; "there is scarcely a village

[1] This name still lingers in wild hill tribes, MALSIR's *Lords of the Hills*; in Malabar, BUCHANAN's *Journey*, Vol. II, p. 6.

CHAP. XI. EARLY HISTORY.

in that State in which there are not effigies of the serpent carved in stone, erected on a raised platform near the entrance for the adoration of the public."[1] The same is the case in Coimbatore; but the Nílagiris, as already stated, possess no such stones, though representations of the serpent are occasionally met with among those of other animals on the pottery in the cairns. The conclusion therefore seems to be, either that the Hills were not yet occupied when the Nágas possessed the neighbouring countries; for had this been the case it is probable that these enterprising serpent worshippers would have brought the dwellers thereon under their power, or that the people of a country where the serpent's bite is not death cared not to take measures to propitiate this reptile. The sustainer of life, the buffalo, never lacked reverencers.

The story of Ráma—the scene of some of whose exploits was in Mysore, and in whose history even the Tódas, as before mentioned, claim a place, asserting that they were the palanquin-bearers[2] of the giant Rávana and were expelled from Lanka,—would seem to indicate that the early religions of the peninsula, such as they were, were not formulated or organized. Ráma meets in his march no walled cities, no temples, no priests. His enemies are monkeys and serpents, demons and giants, birds and beasts of prey.[3] His aim is to rescue the holy ascetics, of whom Agastiya is the chief, from such enemies. As an evidence, however, that at this mythic period either the subjacent country was not thickly peopled, or that missionaries had not obtained a footing therein, the Nílagiris and also the neighbouring hills, so far as my information goes, possess no sacred hill bearing testimony, like the Agastiyamalé in Tinnevelly, to the devotion and piety of some saint. The spread of the Aryan cults seems to have been very gradual, but that of Brahmanism was especially slow in many parts of the peninsula; and although the Aryanised inhabitants of the richer and more accessible parts of the country along the Malabar and Coromandel coasts—the revolution in the former preceding that in the latter tract—were gradually Brahmanised about the beginning of the Christian era, the extension of this system to the Carnatic country was probably much later; in fact there is no certain proof that Brahmanism was ever established there until the overthrow of Buddhism in the tenth century and the missionary enterprise of Sankya Achárya.

---

[1] *Mysore Gazetteer*, Vol. I, p. 363.

[2] The tradition is remarkable as existing among a tribe of herdsmen, who would not be likely to invent it. It existed amongst the Tódas when Europeans first visited the Hills.

[3] WILSON's *Descriptive Catalogue*, Vol. I, Introduction.

Whether or not Buddhism, and simultaneously or subsequently Jainism,[1] had made much progress in the south peninsula prior to the introduction of Brahmanism is doubtful; but if the introduction of Brahmanism is placed about the Christian era, it probably succeeded these religions in some parts at least of the peninsula, and certainly in the Dekhan; for we know that Buddhism had been extending its domain rapidly in the fifth and fourth centuries B.C., and that in the eighteenth year of Asóka's reign (B.C. 245) Buddhist missionaries were sent to Máhishamandalam (perhaps Mysore) and to Wániwási or Bánawási, the capital of the Kadamba dynasty, on the river Varada, north of Mysore. The home of Buddhism and of Jainism in the south was probably Mysore and Kárnáta generally, but undoubtedly Buddhism[2] and still more certainly Jainism spread over the tracts further south. Buddhism probably lingered in Mysore until the tenth or eleventh century, whilst Jainism is not yet extinct.[3] The Jain faith was very prevalent in Mysore, increasing in power as Buddhism declined, becoming predominant in the early centuries of the Christian era. Its power fell with the conversion of Vishnu Varddhana, the Hoysala Bellála king, in the twelfth century.

"The rock inscription at Srávana Belgóla,[4] which describes the migration of a body of Jains from Ujjayani under the leadership of Badra Báhu in about the fourth century B.C., seems to record the period of their first introduction into Mysore. Of the history of their settlement in this country little is known, but the oldest authentic inscriptions[5] of the south show them to have long held an influential position in the early centuries of the Christian era, and all the earliest literature is Jain. Three Chera kings of Kongu in the first and second centuries had a Jain guru, and Jains were gurus to the same line of kings down to the fifth century. A Jain named Akalanka confuted the Buddhists at the court of Hemasitala in Kanchi in 788, and a century later, Amogha Varsha, king of Kanchi, had as his guru Jinasenachárya, reputed as the author of the chief Jain puranas. The state of Humcha, Shimoga District, founded in the seventh or eighth

---

[1] The Jains are distinguished from the Buddhists by the rejection of the doctrine of Nirvána and by the worship of saints, or Thirthankaras; but, like Buddhists, they are divided into monks and laymen. Some of these Jain monks went stark naked. The moral code of the Jains is expressed in five *maha-vratas* or great duties—refraining from injury to life, truth, honesty, chastity, and freedom from worldly desire. There are four *dharmas* or merits—liberality, gentleness, piety, and penance; and three sorts of restraints—government of the tongue, of the mind, and of the person.

[2] See CUNNINGHAM's *Ancient Geography, Southern India.* Huen Thsang did not visit the Mysore country or mention it, but proceeded north-west from Conjeveram to Konkanapura, probably Ánégundi on the Tungabadra, opposite to the site of Vijayanagar.

[3] There are still 13,000 Jains in the province.

[4] In Hassan, Mysore. Here is the gigantic image of Gomatesvara.

[5] Mercara Plates—*Indian Antiquities*, I, 363.

century was Jain and so continued till the eleventh. The Kalachurya kings of the twelfth century were Jains, and the Hoysala Bellála kings to Vishnu Varddhana belonged to the same faith. The conversion of this monarch to the Vaishnava faith in 1117, and the establishment of the Lingayet form of Siva faith at Kalyana about 1160, put an end to Jain predominance in Mysore as a state religion, though the Vijayanagar kings extended a partial favor to it, especially in Kanara and the west." *Mysore Gazetteer*, Vol. 1, page 371.

How near the Jain cult approached the Nílagiris is evidenced by the fact that one of the seats of Jainism was Máléyúr near Gúndelpet on the road from the Nílagiris to Mysore, and was the birthplace of Akalanka referred to above, who procured the expulsion of the Buddhists from South India. The absence of traces of Buddhists and Jains in the Nílagiris tends to show that these mountains were but sparsely populated during their supremacy, and further that though the Tóda customs have some strange resemblance to those of these religionists, yet they would appear to be anterior to the formulating of their creeds.

But before the fall of Jainism the old lingam or phallic worship of the ante-Aryan races, which had been developed in the north to an organized cult under the name of Sivaism, continuing the worship of Siva, the destroyer, and of Dúrga, the earth-mother, known also as Parvati or Bhavání,[1] had been revived. In the south this regenerated religion was preached by Sankya Achárya, the apostle of Sivaism and the founder of the Smárta sect. He was a native of Cranganúr in Malabar, and belonged to the tribe of Nambúri Brahmans. His era was about the eighth or ninth century A.D. His work was the abolition of Jainism and the reformation of the Brahmans. Professor Wilson[2] remarks :—

"It has been already observed that the prevalent division of the Hindu faith in the earliest period of its establishment appears to have been the worship of *Siva*, and the traditions of the different countries corroborate this view ; for the tutelary divinities of both the *Pandyan* and the *Chola* kingdoms were forms of that deity or his bride. In *Telingana* the first princes are reputed to have been *Vaishnava*, but this is the only division in which that faith predominated. In course of time however—probably by the seventh or eighth century—a variety of modifications existed, to reform which Sankara Achárya, it is related, was born. He did not attempt to abolish all the varieties of the Hindu faith, but whilst he recalled the attention of the Brahmans to the tenets of the Védas and the injunctions of the inspired legislators, and thence founded the division known in the south as the *Smartal* Brahmans, who disclaim, although they may practise, the exclusively preferential worship of any form of the Supreme Deity, he gave his sanction to the continuance of certain sects, over whom

[1] Compare TALBOYS WHEELER, Vol. III, p. 364.

[2] *Descriptive Catalogue*, Vol. I, p. 61.

he permitted sundry of his disciples to preside. These were the *Saivas*, *Vaishnavas*, *Sauras*, *Sáktas*, *Gánapatyas*, and *Kapalikas* or *Yogis*."

The Saiva form of Brahmanism dominated the south for about four centuries, when the great Vishnu revival was brought about by the preaching of Rámánuja Achárya, a native of Sripermatúr, near Madras, educated at Conjeveram, but who established the head-quarters of his sect at Srirangam, near Trichinopoly. As already stated, this apostle reduced the Jains to insignificance. In the Nílagiris the Sivaites now very greatly predominate among the Badagas and in the neighbouring tracts of Mysore. Taking Mysore as a whole, however, the sects are nearly equally divided, there being 2,564,846 Sivaites against 2,242,532 Vishnuites. At the period of the revival of the worship of Vishnu, the Preserver, arose the sect of Lingayats, the most revered sect on these hills,[1] and the sect peculiar to the Kanarese, just as the sect of Siva belonged to the west and that of Vishnu to the east coast. The Lingayat faith was a compromise between the teaching of the Sivaites and the Vishnuites, and seems indicative of the influence of the nations of the west[2] and east upon those of the central plateau, just as English Protestantism was the outcome of German, Lutheran, and French Calvinistic Propagandism. The compromise was known under the appellation Harihara, *Hari*, Vishnu, *Hara*, Siva, combined in one person. The founder of this sect was Bassava, a Brahman, native of Belgám. The name signifies bull, and he was regarded as the incarnation of Nándi, the bull of Siva. The mark of the sect was the Jangama Lingam. Bassava summed up the first principles of religion as the Gúrú, the Lingam, and the Jangam, *i.e.*, the teacher, the adorable emblem of divine power, and religious union. This faith prevailed extensively in Kárnáta, and was the state religion of the Wódeas of Mysore from the end of the fourteenth to the beginning of the seventeenth century, when Rája Wódeyar adopted the religion of Vishnu and persecuted the subordinate Wódeas or heads of districts, one of whom fled to the Nílagiris. This flight may account for the number of Wódea settlements on the Hills—which is remarkable considering the social pre-eminence of the class, it being that of the Mysore Rájas—and the number of Lingayat inhabitants. There are, however, still 419,900 Lingayats in Mysore, one-third of whom are in the Mysore Division contiguous to the Nílagiris.

---

[1] There are 1,467 Lingayats in the district.

[2] Only 1·5 per cent. of the inhabitants of Malabar are Vishnuites, 98·5 per cent. being Sivaites. In Coimbatore the proportions are—Vishnuites 22·8, Sivaites 76·9, Lingayats ·3.

CHAP. XI.

EARLY HISTORY.

All the religious movements thus far spoken of have in a measure their representatives among the ancient tribes on the plateau. This cannot be said of the great religious movement in Malabar, which dates from the conversion of Cheram Perumal, Rája of Kerala, to Mohammadanism in the ninth century, the resultant of which was the Mapillas, the offspring of Arab fathers and Malayálam mothers. The absence of this race from the Hills, though tolerably numerous in Wainád, shows that if the Nílagiris were conquered by Malayála, they were not incorporated with that country as the Wainád was, though also geographically a part of Kárnáta. The almost total absence of Lingayats[1] from the Wainád taluk and Malabar generally, though numerous in the Hills, points the same way.

The Christianity of the west coast—that of the Nazarens—appears never to have penetrated to the Hills, though some writers have attempted to connect the religion of the Tóda with it; and the similarity was such as even to impress the native mind, long before it was remarked by Europeans. I refer to the reports which reached the ears of the earliest Portuguese missionaries regarding the existence of Christians in the Hills, reports which induced them to make the expeditions referred to elsewhere.

Relation of early hill tribes to race movements.

Before sketching the history of the kingdoms adjacent to the Nílagiris, in whose destinies its history is involved, I would note the relation of the Tódas to the early race movements of the south. As already stated, in the Tódas we probably find a race of aborigines who came in contact with the Aryans, whilst the simple nature-worship of this people had still some of its power, and before it had been deeply influenced by Brahmanical sacerdotalism, though, perhaps, not before it had been subject to Buddhistic teaching. The tradition, almost the only one they possess, that they were the palanquin-bearers of the giant Rávana, and were expelled from Lanka on his being slain by Ráma, tends this way; but as regards their religion and religious customs, although they show few traces of Brahmanism, yet they differ in many ways from the ordinary cults of the wild tribes of the south. Moreover, the fact that the Tódas have no veneration for the serpent, but worship the sun, may show that they could not have been long under the power of the Nágas, but, on the contrary, were in close contact with a race of sun-worshippers—such worshippers were the Aryans. But that the Tódas did not come from the far north with these people seems probable, apart from linguistic and physical peculiarities, from the fact that they hold the buffalo in such affectionate regard,

[1] Only ·02 per cent. of the inhabitants of Malabar are Lingayats.

for it is improbable that this black, ungainly, wallowing animal could have become an object of affectionate regard to a people who knew and used the Brahmani ox, the horse, and the elephant. But this very peculiarity would connect them with the builders of the cairns and cromlechs, for whilst among the earthenware figures collected by Mr. Breeks there is only one figure resembling an ox, though it may also represent a bison, which has the distinguishing hump elongated, the makers of these figures seemed to have loved to linger over the forms of the buffalo, and though they also made figures of horses, elephants, and wild animals, their most successful representations are those of the buffalo. The sacred animal is never represented as bearing a burthen, but he often wears a bell. This love of the buffalo must have been common to a tolerably civilized race, for not only are bell-metal vessels of chaste design found along with such figures, with armed warriors, horse and foot, and also the representation of what may be a pillar of victory, but Dr. Shortt informs me that he has in his possession two artistic representations of the buffalo in bronze, which were dug up at Coimbatore.

CHAP. XI. EARLY HISTORY.

LID OF URN WITH PILLAR

It seems therefore not an unnatural inference that though aboriginal, this curious people was on very intimate relations with an Aryan race. The names of their deities, it will be remembered, are of Sanskrit origin, fairly direct, whilst their language has been but slightly influenced thereby. Can this be explained on any reasonable theory? It seems very doubtful; but we may perhaps find, in the history of the Dekhan, a clue which,

CHAP. XI. EARLY HISTORY.

if followed up, may throw light on the past of this people. Their traditions and their speech show them to be a Kanarese or Telugu people who approached the Nílagiris from the north, and this view is supported by the Brahman tradition, mentioned by Mr. Metz, that they came with Ráma from the north.[1] Also by the fact that they call the south-western portion of the district Pirgúr, which Mr. Metz interprets as the land of Feringis, *i.e.*, of strangers. The absence of any Tóda settlements on the southern slopes of the Hills also points the same way. They further call their grazing grounds (the uplands of Tódanad) Mélúr, but have no name, Mr. Metz states, for the western portions of the Kúndas, though they call the eastern portion Meurúr, or the land of rain. A people who lived from time immemorial on the uplands would not naturally call these uplands Mélúr; but a people coming from the lowlands would. It is also curious to observe that though the Tódas have settlements in Wainád near the Nílagiris, and even have a special reverence for a shrine there, where their hunting god Bétakan resides, yet they have not extended their settlements thither. It may be that incursions from Malabar drove them hillwards. Their presence in Wainád must, however, date back many centuries, for the absence of Lingayats in Wainád is an evidence that, for the last eight centuries at least, Kanarese dominion in that táluk, though the tract geographically is a part of Kárnáta, must have been very fitful. That they came from the north may then be admitted, but with what people were they connected there? Their religion may help us to find an answer. What is there unique in it? Veneration for the buffalo, adoration of the sun, moon, and fire—in a word, light—and the hermit character of their priests. These traits appertain to a race having a fire cult and to a land where the buffalo was held in special honor. Again, their marriage customs would connect them with a race of polyandrists. A race possessing several of these characteristics seems at one time, in the dim twilight of history, to have ruled in part of the Dekhan. There is mention[2] of a Máhishamati—city (?) of the buffalo—on the Nerbadda; again in the Máhábhárata, of a town of the same name situated apparently further south,—south probably of the Gódávari, on a tributary of the Kistna;—and again in Buddhist history (240 B.C.) of a Máhisha-mandalam, or buffalo country, probably

[1] This legend, though conflicting with the Tóda story, is noteworthy, as both legends would place them in close relation with great kings. It may indicate that they were a tribe adopted by the conquerors. I have noted elsewhere the presence of caste distinctions existing among them in a far more marked degree than in other aboriginal races.

[2] See LASSEN'S *Indian Alterthum*, Vol. I, pp. 567-69 and note. The common interpretation of Máhisha—buffalo—in this name is not universally admitted.

Mysore, in the south. Of Máhishamati on the Nerbadda, we are told that during the reign of a king of the solar line, the restorer of the kingdom of the Nágas,[1]—said by some to be a Scythian race—the Haihagas—also a race, seemingly, of Scythian origin—attacked the city and drove out the king. During his flight in the forest his son Sagara was born, who, on coming to man's estate, became a great conqueror, nearly destroyed the Haihagas and their allies, and imposed on the conquered the mode of shaving the head and wearing the hair known as *kudumi*. Of the Máhishamati of the Máhábhárata,[2] we read that in it one Níla ruled. Here was the worship of Agni (fire) maintained, and here prevailed a system of free love amongst the women. Mr. Rice thinks that this fact may indicate the dominion in the south of a Malabar chief. But against this view it may be urged that the religion of the Malayálams was essentially phallic. Níla was attacked by Sahadéva, one of Yudisthíra's generals, who, after conciliating the god Agni, conquered the city. Lastly we read, as already stated, in the Máháwanso that after the great Buddhist council in 241 B.C.—the third synod,—in the reign of Asóka, missionaries under the leadership of Máhádéva were despatched to Máhisha-mandalam to establish the religion of Buddha "and to bring them unto righteousness which passeth knowledge, and to deliver those bound in the fetters of sin."[3] There they made 80,000 converts.[4] I do not attempt to do more than draw attention to these facts, but it is strange to find that there existed in Southern India a race of polyandrists who were at the same time worshippers of the Vedic deity, the sun, and whose cities, situated in the land of rivers, were called after the buffalo, whose home is in the wide river basins of the Dekhan, where it attains its greatest vigor and size. And further that this race should not only have been in conflict with Scythian tribes, but have more or less mingled with them. Vedic, Scythian, and Dravidian cults seem here to have mixed. With such a race the Tódas must once have been in close contact. We find them using burial places and performing burial rites so similar that it makes it a question whether they were not the builders of the cairns, though we know that the Nílagiri cairns do not differ essentially from cairns found in other parts of the globe, which are generally admitted to have been built by Scythic tribes. They still adore the sun and light, though the sun has ceased to be a god; whilst

[1] For a notice of this race, see TALBOYS WHEELER, Vol. I, p. 147.

[2] The Máhábhárata, or great war, was probably about 1400 B.C., the Ramáyana about 1300 B.C.

[3] Dr. HUNTER's *Orissa*, Vol. I, p. 193.

[4] TURNOUR's *Máháwanso*.

CHAP. XI. — EARLY HISTORY.

the absence of snake-worship may indicate that they were connected with a race which did not adopt the religion of the Nágas. Moreover when we consider that there are the strongest grounds for believing that they were inhabiting the Hills when Buddhism and Jainism ceased to be the State beliefs of the powerful neighbouring Kárnáta kingdoms, the absence of marked traces of these religions may indicate that the Tódas left the plains before they became organized cults, for had they migrated thither during their ascendancy, surely some more distinctive traces of these creeds would survive amongst them.

Divisions of South India.

Of the great race divisions of South India, those which especially concern the Nílagiris are the Dravidian or Tamulian, the Malayálam, and the Kanarese. The Tamulian race, which seems to have ultimately divided itself into three great sections—Pandya, Chóla and Chera—occupied the whole champagne country of the peninsula south of the Eastern Ghát line and west of the Western Gháts; the Malayálam, the country west of the latter range and south of Mangalore; the Kanarese, the tract north of this town along the west coast as far as the Konkan, and the southern angle of the Dekhan table-land, more especially Mysore. These distributions are stated roughly, but a glance at the map will show that the Nílagiri range is the point of trijunction of the Tamulian divisions. We are only concerned with two, viz., Chóla and Chera. The Chólas had their principal seats in the lower Káveri, in the Trichinopoly and Tanjore Divisions; but as mentioned later, their dominions embraced the whole Carnatic plain north of this river. The Cheras occupied the country known as Kerala.[1] Dr. Caldwell remarks :—

"The Kerala of the ancients seems to have divided itself into two portions, one of which, the district lying along the sea coast, has always retained the Sanskritic name of Kerala, whilst it also called itself by the Tamil name of Chera; the other, an inland district including Coimbatore, Salem, and a portion of Mysore, seems to have dropped the name of Kerala altogether and called itself exclusively either Chera or Kongu. It is to the latter district that the papers of Professor Dawson[2] and Dr. Eggeling on the Chera dynasty refer. Though, however, the districts and dynasties differed, I have no doubt that the *names* Kerala and Chera were originally one and the same, and it is certain that they are always regarded as synonymous in native Tamil and Malayalam lists of synonyms. In the various lists of the boundaries of Chera given by Tamil writers, the Malabar coast from Calicut southward—that is, the whole of Southern Kerala—is invariably included. Probably Kera was the earliest form of the word Kerala, a Sanskritic derivative. The word *Kongu*, one of the names of

[1] Introduction, *Grammar Dravidian Languages*, p. 22.

[2] Vol. VIII, *R.A.S. Journal.*

the Chera country, means, like Kodagu (Coorg), crooked, curved, and is evidently a name derived from the configuration of the country."[1]

Allowing that the Malayálam people speak a dialect of Tamil, they are to all intents and purposes a separate Dravidian people, distinguished from the Tamils and the Kanarese by marked religious and social peculiarities. As regards Kárnáta, we are concerned with the Kadamba and Hoysala Bellála dynasties and those of Vijayanagar and of Mysore.

Kongu or Chera.

Kongu seems to have been the name of the country ruled by the Chera dynasty. Professor Wilson says :—

"The northern limit of Chera varied at different periods, being originally placed at *Palani* near *Dharapura*, whilst at a subsequent period the capital, *Dalavampur* or *Talcad*, above the Mysore Ghauts, indicates a considerable extension of the boundary in this quarter, and the *Chera* principality probably included the greater portion of *Karnata*. Its eastern limits were the possessions of *Chola* and *Pandya* and the western those of *Kerala*. In its early state, however, it comprehended the extreme south of the Malabar coast or *Travancore*, and consisted of that province, Wynad, the Nílagiri mountain district, the southern portion of Coimbatore and part of Tinnevelly. In this tract we have in Ptolemy the people called *Carei*, and not far from it *Carura Regia Cerebothri*, in which, making allowance for inaccuracies of sound and expression, we have the *Cheras* and *Carur*, still a city in this district, and *Cherapati*, the sovereign of *Chera*."[2]

An account of these kings will be found in the *Kongu-désa Rájakal*, already referred to, translated by W. Taylor. Their capital was at Skandapura, which is placed by Lassen near the Gajalhatti Pass. In the third century after Christ their capital was moved further north to Talkád on the Káveri, near Kollegal, just beyond the Coimbatore frontier, but their rule extended over all South-west Mysore, including, doubtless, the Nílagiris. They were a warlike race and delighted in the horse and elephant. It will be remembered that numerous figures of these animals caparisoned have been found in the Nílagiri cairns and cromlechs. Mr. Rice enumerates twenty-eight kings from about the beginning of the Christian era to 894 A.D. The early kings were apparently Jains. The seventh (A.D. 178 to 188), Sri Vikrama, joined the Siva faith. He was a great warrior, his conquests extending over Chóla, Pandya, Kerala, Malayála and Mysore. His successor, Kongani Varmma Dharma, was the founder of a new dynasty, and removed the capital to Talkád or Delavanapura. He lives in story as the divider, with one stroke of his sword, of

[1] See also Preface to the *Kongu-désa Rájakal*, Madras, p. xiv, 1, 1647, and Mr. NELSON's *Manual*, Part III, pp. 45-47.

[2] *Descriptive Catalogue*, Vol. I, Introduction, xcii.

CHAP. XI. EARLY HISTORY.

a Sila-stambha or pillar of victory, which may shadow forth a conflict with the Buddhists, who inscribed edicts on such erections. In the fifth century a monarch of this race married the sister of one of the Kadamba kings of Bánawási, an event which shows the importance of the dynasty at the time. At the close of this century the reigning monarch, Amrita or Druhva-niti, was "a great magician in the *mantras*; whenever he might go to war with his enemies, by the power of his *mantras* he would make a loud sound; the forces of his enemies remained mute and motionless, with their warlike arms upright in their hands, and without knowing how to make use of them."[1] Little wonder then that he is reported as conquering Kerala, Pandya, Chóla, Dravida, Andhra, and Kalinga, and many other countries. We find that in his reign South-west Mysore[2] was known as *Punnád*, ten thousand. The last ruler of this dynasty seems to have been Malladéva, at the close of the ninth century, when a Chóla king, Aditya Varmma, "being crowned in the Tanjavur-putnam, came to Kongu-désam, and conquered the Vardar (huntsmen or wild people) of the king of Kongu-désam and took the town of Talikad; and, giving many free endowments to many agraharas, he governed that country in addition to his own." The energy and perseverance of this kingly race was great. Driven from their ancestral dominions by the Chólas, they are said to have pushed their way to the north-east and ultimately to have founded the Gangavamsa dynasty in Orissa.[3] One of them, in the latter part of the thirteenth century, "raised the lovely pile that now overlooks the Bay of Bengal at Kanarak, the temple of the sun,[4] whose luscious ornamentation forms at once the glory and the disgrace of Orissa art."

On these hills we have the representatives of this Kongu people in the Kongas, a class of Badagas who wear the lingam and occupy villages near Rangasámi Peak, opposite the Gajalhatti Pass, the ancient home of their race. They are second only to the Wódeas in rank. To this day do the hill-people call North Coimbatore the Kongu country.[5] The name survives in the Kangiam Taluk of that district. The South Mysoreans still call Tamil Kangi.

Chólas.

This race may be described as that section of the Tamil people who ruled the river-basin of the Káveri below the gháts, though at one time their empire was probably counterminous with the Tamil language. In their progress towards the north

---

[1] *Kongu-désa Rájakal.*

[2] RICE. May not this be *pon-nád*, the district of gold?—a name which would be most appropriate to the Wainád and its neighbourhood.

[3] LASSEN, *Ind. Alt.*, IV. 14, and Dr. HUNTER's *Orissa*, Vol. I, pp. 277-290.

[4] Known to sailors as the black pagoda.

[5] Mr. METZ' *Neilgherry Hills*, p. 50; WILKS' *Mysore*, Vol. I, p. 4.

they encountered the Kúrumbas, who occupied the districts below the gháts westwards of the shore-line from Pulicat to Cuddalore. The subduer of these warlike clans was Adondái, the illegitimate son of Kulattungi Chóla. This conquest probably occurred in the eleventh century. The advance along the eastern coast may have been the result of their retirement from South Mysore, if we accept the latter half of the eleventh century as the period in which Adondái's conquest took place, for the dominion of the Chólas does not appear to have lasted in South Mysore for more than one hundred and fifty years after the taking of Talkád in A.D. 894. The Chóla conquests in Kúrumbanád seem to have been preceded by an alliance of the royal house with the eastern Chalukyas. The progress of the power of the Hoysala Bellála dynasty in South Mysore was probably the cause of the subversion of the Chóla dominion in that country. The Chóla monarch whose power appears to have been most extended was Hari-vari, who reigned at the beginning of the eleventh century. After conquering Madura, the writer of the *Kongu-désa Rájakal* relates that—

" Amarbhujangan, the general, set out with four kinds of forces towards the west of the mountain named *Saiya*, and thence proceeding to fight against the *Kerala-désa*, he heard that its king was performing the *Chatur-balaganam* and other ceremonies, in consequence of which he became greatly incensed and conquered (took) *Kotur*, *Indra-giri*, *Nilagiri-durga*, and other places; and as the entire strength of the king failed him, he embarked on boardship and fled into an island in the midst of the sea. Subsequently this general of the *Chola raja*, according to the permission of his master, collected and deposited all the plunder of riches acquired in this invasion in the *Saiva* temple on the top of the ghaut, and on the extreme west he fixed a conquest-pillar[1] with a flag, to denote his victory to that point; and he thus acquired great fame in the world."

Here a gap occurs in the manuscript. It proceeds to state :—

" Then the *Kongu-desa* and *Karnatica-desa* being subject to him, he, the *Maharaja Chola raya*, gave the name of Raja-raja-puram to the town of Keriur, in the Talicad district in the northern part of *Kongu-desa*, and gave it to the merchants (Vaisyar) of Dalavaira-puram."

Mr. Taylor remarks that the king referred to in the latter quotation is probably not Hari-vari but Kulattungi Chóla, the father of Adondái, the conqueror of the Kúrumbas. During the twelfth and thirteenth centuries the Chóla race appears to have been pushed back by the Hoysala Bellála kings and the vigorous Chalukyas and Kalachuryas. The Tamils, however, with the

[1] Jaya-stambha.

CHAP. XI. EARLY HISTORY.

pertinacity of their race, held to the best portions of the lowlands, whilst at the beginning of this period they gained a religious victory by the conversion of the Bellála king Varddhana from Jainism to the faith of Vishnu through the preaching of Rámanuja Achárya. It is possible that it was during these centuries that the earliest Kanarese colonists pushed forwards into the Nílagiris and on to the ranges to their south towards the Palghát Pass. Driven back by immigrants from the south-east, and then by new-comers from the north-east, the Kongu Kanarese would naturally retire to the highland part of their territory, and wait for better times, which came to pass during the empire of Vijayanagar.

Kadamba dynasty.

The Kadamba [1] dynasty, which was of great antiquity, ruled over North and South Canara and the western portions of ancient Kárnáta. Their capital, Bánawási, is mentioned by Ptolemy.[2] The date of the first king, Trinctra Kadamba, is fixed by Wilson as A.D. 168, and the kingdom appears to have lasted 1,168 years until the foundation of the Vijayanagar empire, but with probably greatly diminished power. Early in the fifth century a daughter of the house was married to Mádhara, king of Kongu, and, until the rise of the Bellála kings, they may be said to have divided the greater portion of Kárnáta between themselves and the Cheras. (*Des. Cat.*, p. cvii.)

"Up to the fifth century," says Mr. Rice, "they were independent, but being then subdued by the Chalukya king Kartti Varmma, they were reduced to the condition of feudatories. Their jurisdiction seems to have been thence limited to the province of Hanagal or Parangal until the tenth century, when they appear as lords of Banawasi as well as of Hanagal and other places. * * * Their capital was later established at Goa. The connection of the founders of Vijayanagar with the Kadambas has not been established, but the former were certainly descended from a Tuluva family of ancient origin and power, whose dominions extended towards the western sea,[3] and the Kadamba grants, which continue up to the time of the rise of Vijayanagar, then cease."

It is the unascertained connection of the rulers of Bánawási—with the Kúrumbas, perhaps prior to the rise of the Kadamba dynasty—which renders the history of this people interesting as regards the Nílagiris; but as notes [4] on the point will be found in Mr. Breeks' chapter on the Kúrumbas, it will not be discussed further here.

---

[1] Said to be so named from the *Kadamba* tree, a species of *nauclea*, one of the *Chinchoniaceæ*. See note 4, page 208, Chapter IX.

[2] *Descriptive Catalogue*, p. ci.

[3] WILSON, *McA. Coll.* I, civ.

[4] See CARR's *Seven Pagodas*; ELLIS' *Mirási Right*.

CHAP. XI. — EARLY HISTORY. — Hoysa'a Bellála.

The Hoysala Bellála dynasty possessed the suzerainty of Kárnáta proper from the beginning of the tenth to the middle of the fourteenth century, and at one period during the reigns of Vira Bellála and Vira Narasimha (1188-1249) the whole of Kárnáta as far as the Kistna was subject to their sway, "and the provinces of Malabar and Kanara on the west, the *Dravira* country on the south and east, and part of *Telingana* on the north-east, acknowledged them, if not as immediate masters, yet as exercising supreme authority over them through their officers, or through the native rajas as vassals and tributaries."[1] The early kings were Jains. Their capital was generally at Talkád, near Kollegal, on the Káveri, but it appears at one time to have been transferred to Tuluva, and again, at a later period, to Dwarasamudra near Bednore, south of the Kistna.[2]

The founder of the race, who was probably a petty feudatory of the Kongu or Chóla kings, was named Sola, and obtained the cognomen of Hoyi—strike (*Kanarese*)—from his good fortune and daring in killing, at the command of a rishi, a tiger which had infested the neighbourhood of the shrine of the goddess Vasantaka.[3] This race of kings was eminently warlike. The story in the *Kongu-désa Rájakal* shows them to have been constantly in conflict with the neighbouring princes, especially those of Malabar and Canara. Mr. Rice quotes from an inscription how the fourth king of the line, Vishnu Varddhana (1114-1145), is related to have overthrown the Tulu and Haihaga kings, became possessed of Talkád, subdued Kongu, overcame Nolambadi (Chitaldrúg), gained possession of Kovatúr (Coimbatore), sacked Toreyúr, and, passing Vellore, took up his residence at Conjeveram. The boundaries of the kingdom are given: "the lower ghaut of Nangala on the east; Kongu, Cheram and Anemal on the south; the Karkanar ghaut road of Konka on the west; and Sarimale on the north." These southern boundaries include the Nílagiris. This king's chief residence was at Belúr in Hassan, where he founded the celebrated temple. He became a convert to the Vishnu faith through the influence of his wife and the preaching of Rámánuja Achárya, whom "he received and trusted" when fleeing from the Chóla king, who sought to compel him to acknowledge the supremacy of Siva, and "with great devotion protected many *Vishnu* temples, and was a *Vishnu-bakti* (votary of Vishnu)."[4] His successors, however, were sometimes of the Saiva faith, but they appear generally to have shown toleration towards the Jains, whose religion had ceased to

[1] *Descriptive Catalogue*, Vol. I, p. cxi.
[2] *Kongu-désa Rájakal*.
[3] The other title, Bellála, is from *balam*, strength.
[4] *Kongu-désa Rájakal*.

CHAP. XI. — EARLY HISTORY.

be that of the State. This king was succeeded by his son Vira Narasimha (1145–1188), who seems to have been engaged chiefly in wars in the south, supporting the Chóla against the Pandya kings.[1] He was followed by Vira Bellála and Vira Narasimha, to whom reference has already been made. The latter monarch seems to have changed the State religion to that of Siva.[2] His successor was Bellála Rája, whose son, Someswara, followed him. During his reign the power of the Bellálas began to wane, and they seem to have received a crushing defeat in the Konkan. The Rájas of Kerala and Chóla rebelled, and finally, in the reign of Narasimha, Someswara's son (1268–1308), the dynasty succumbed to the attack of the Moslems under Kafur, the vizier of Ala-ud-Din of the house of Khilji (1295–1316). Their capital, Dora-samudra, was sacked, and the Bellála king is said to have been carried captive to Delhi.[3] This chief's conquests extended as far south as Madura. These Mahommadan chiefs held sway for forty-eight years, until the people were delivered from the hateful yoke by the prowess of a Kanarese or Mysore chief Kampana Wódea, who was probably in the service of the Rája of Vijayanagar.[4]

Vijayanagar.

But the Moslem conquest was not yet to bring the Hindus of the south under complete subjection. Dissensions at Delhi had enfeebled the administration in the distant provinces, and the fresh generation of Hindus in the Dekhan had forgotten the terrible punishment which followed the revolt in 1320. So in 1347 a fresh uprising took place, in which both Mussulmans and Hindus joined. The outcome was the establishment of an independent Mussulman kingdom, with its capital at Kalburga, by Hasan Gangu, the founder of the Bahmani dynasty, and the creation of two Hindu states, those of Telingána and Kárnáta. With the latter only are we concerned. Its capital was Vijayanagar, the city of victory (corrupted from *Vidyánagara*, the city of learning), on the south of the Tungabadra, opposite Ánégundi, the ancient seat of the mysterious Yávanas or Ionians. Here also was situated Kishkindha of the mythic age. The founders of this kingdom, which was destined to dominate the whole of the South Dekhan and the peninsula, were Bakka and Hakka, or Harihara, sons of Sangama, probably a petty Kárnáta chief of Kúrumba origin. Their minister was the sage Mádhava, a disciple of Sankya Achárya, who was probably "connected with the *Sringagiri*[5] establishment, the members of which, alarmed by the increasing numbers of the *Jangamas* and Jains, and the

[1] *Mysore Gazetteer*, Vol. I, p. 218.
[2] *Descriptive Catalogue*, Vol. 1, cxl.
[3] TALBOYS WHEELER, Vol. IV, 1st 1, p. 63.
[4] NELSON's *Manual*, Part III, pp. 81, 82.
[5] In the Kadur District, Mysore, the chief seat of the Siva priests.—*Gazetteer, Mysore*, Vol. I, p. 379.

CHAP. XI. — EARLY HISTORY.

approach of the Mahommadans, may have contributed their wealth to the aggrandisement of the sons of *Sangama*."[1] The date of the founding of the city usually given is 1336, but this is probably too early. The dynasty of Harihara possessed the throne until the year 1490, when it was superseded by that of Narasinga, whose descendants held the ráj until its final overthrow. The empire, which perhaps reached its zenith in the reign of Krishna Ráya (1508–1542), existed until the final decade of the sixteenth century; but its power was broken thirty years before by the defeat and death of the usurper Ram Rai at the battle of Talikóta in 1565. This victory marks the true beginning of the ascendancy of the Moslems in the peninsula. Hitherto their irruptions south of the Kistna were little better than predatory excursions. For more than two hundred years the able monarchs of Vijayanagar had withstood the Moslem immigrants ever pressing towards the south, and by their astute policy had combined the eternally conflicting princedoms of the peninsula into a confederation against the followers of the Prophet. In effecting this object they resorted to a system of military colonization,[2]—which they may have learned from the Mahommadans,—the establishment throughout the peninsula of bands of Telugu soldiers known as Náyaks, conferring on them lands, in return for which they preserved order in the subject or quasi-subject rájaships. Such settlements seem to be peculiar to this empire, for we find nothing similar to them in the policy of the earlier native conquerors of the south.

Mysore.

As the empire of Vijayanagar waned, and whilst the Mahommadan power was rising in importance, some of the native feudatories gradually advanced towards independence. The most important of these were the Náyaks of Madura and the Wódeas[3] of Mysore. In South Mysore, as elsewhere, several vassal chiefs had received small tracts of territory, and in return rendered military service. The principal were the Wódeas of Mysore, Kalala, Yelandúr and Ummatúr. The first and the last chiefly concern the Nílagiris. These chiefs were under the immediate authority of the viceroy of the Vijayanagar kings, whose seat was at Seringapatam.

The house of Mysore traces its origin to two Yadava cadets, Vijaya and Krishna, who came from Guzerat to push their fortunes in the south. On arriving at Hadinád, near Nanjangúdi, on the Mysore-Ootacamand road, they found the daughter of the Wódea of the place about to be forced into a marriage

---

[1] *Descriptive Catalogue*, Vol. I, p. cxii.

[2] WILKS' *Mysore*, Vol. I, Chapter I.

[3] See Chapter IX, Part V.

CHAP. XI. EARLY HISTORY.

with the Torea or low-caste chief of Karugahalli near Mysore. They espoused the maiden's cause and slew the bridegroom, and out of gratitude the lady became the willing bride of Vijaya, who changed his religion from that of Vishnu to the Jangama, and became the Wódea of Hadinád and Karugahalli. This event is placed at the beginning of the fifteenth century. Little is known of the history of his descendants until the reign of Chama Rája the Bold (1571–75), who reunited the dominion which his father Betad Cham Ráj had divided between his three sons.[1] This monarch, taking advantage of the weakness of Vijayanagar, was the first to refuse to pay tribute to its viceroy. He built or repaired the fort and tower hitherto called Puragiri,[2] but henceforth known and to be known to the world as Mysore (the buffalo-town). His son Rája Wódear (1578–1617) ousted the viceroy from Seringapatam (1610) and transferred thither the seat of government, and changed the religion of the State to that of Vishnu.[3] It was at this time that the Wódeas of Kalala (descended from the Vijayanagar family), which lies on the Ootacamand-Mysore road, identified their interests with those of the house of Mysore, and thenceforth the scions of this stock have filled the office of Dalavaye,[4] minister and general, of the Mysore kingdom. This alliance was perhaps in a measure due to the hatred of the Wódeas of Kalala for the Wódeas of Ummatúr. These chiefs, who undoubtedly for a long period exercised rule over the Nílagiris, and who in their adversity found a refuge here, and for a time, perhaps, preserved their partial independence in the Málékóta fort near Kalhatti,[5] possessed the fort of Ummatúr, lying three leagues to the east of Kalala near Yelandúr and the Billi-rangum hills. They were related to the Vijayanagar viceroy, Sri Ranga Ráyal, and their principality was an important fief of that empire. The house of Kalala had been nearly exterminated by the Ummatúr chief. The survivor, on coming to man's estate, allied himself to the Mysore king Rája Wódear, who thus aided, subdued Ummatúr and annexed it to the Mysore ráj (1613). Mr. Metz mentions that there are still living near Málékóta Bétar (huntsmen) whose ancestors were in the service of the Ummatúr Rája as tax-gatherers, and hence are still cordially hated by the Badagas. This fact is noteworthy, as it tends to show that the common view that the Badagas came

---

1 WILKS, Vol. I, Chapter II.

2 Said to be the same as Parikere, where the Kongu kings acquired the recognition of their dominion in the fifth century.—*Mysore Gazetteer*, Vol. I, p. 241.

3 WILKS, Vol. I, Chapter II.

4 Derived from *dala* (Kan.), army ; hence leader of an army.

5 See Mr. BREEKS' *Nilgherry Hills*, p. 45.

to the Hills on the break-up of the Vijayanagar empire is improbable, for they seem to have regarded the representatives of that empire with dislike, whilst they still call the Mysore chiefs (true Kanarese) their Kartas or lords. The name of the fort at Kótagiri—Udiaráya-kóta, *i.e.*, the Wódearáya's fort—seems also to indicate that it was the hold of a hostile ráya (title of the Vijayanagar kings) rather than of a friendly chief.[1]

Rája Wódear's conquests appear to have embraced the whole of the district of Mysore.[2] His rule, Colonel Wilks states, was "remarkable for the rigour and severity which he exercised towards the subordinate Wódeas and his indulgence towards the ryots." The Wódeas were generally dispossessed and kept in confinement on a scanty allowance at the seat of government; and it was the policy of Rája Wódear to reconcile the ryots to the change by exacting from them no larger sums than they had formerly paid. The comparatively impoverished condition of the Wódeas on the Hills, though they are still exceedingly proud, may have been the result of these stringent measures.

Rája Wódear's successor, Chama Rája (1617–1636), continued his predecessor's policy towards the Wódeas, and sought to extend his dominions below the ghâts towards Madura. Thus he came into conflict with the great Tirumala Náyak, who had recently come to the throne (1623). The invaders were defeated by the famous Rámapayya, who pursued them up the Gajalhatti Pass, and who is said to have taken Mysore.[3] Wilks is silent regarding this expedition. It should be remarked here that during the latter half of the sixteenth century Visvanatha and his successors, the founders of the Náyak dynasty, had gradually brought the Kanarese and Telugu chiefs of the country lying below the ghâts to the north and west of Madura under their hegemony, by inclusion in the feudal fraternity known as the Madura Palayakarans.[4] It was possibly during this period that the revenue system of Coimbatore was introduced on the hills, and along with it the Kanakan or writer class, for at no period subsequent

[1] Colonel Wilks assigns to the fifty years which succeeded the battle of Talikóta "the origin or improvement of most of the droogs or fortified places of the Karnatic proper and of Baramahal." Vol. I, Chapter III.

[2] In a map illustrating the history of Mysore, Mr. Rice does not include the Nílagiris in Mysore at Wódear Rája's death, but it is so included at Chikka Déva's death in 1704. He does not state when it was acquired, but in the absence of evidence to the contrary, we may reasonably infer it was virtually annexed when Ummatúr was conquered, for there can be little doubt that the Nílagiri plateau proper belonged to these rájas.

[3] NELSON's *Manual*, Part IV, p. 125.

[4] NELSON's *Manual*, Part III, p. 99.

CHAP. XI.

EARLY HISTORY.

thereto and prior to the English occupancy does the Tamil dominion seem to have extended over any part of the plateau.

The wars between the Rájas of Mysore and the Náyaks of Madura—the former generally aided by the Narasinga kings (the fading representatives of the Vijayanagar house), the latter by the Mussulmans—continued at intervals, and with varying success, during the reigns of the three following princes, Immadi Rája, R. Narasa Rája, and Dodda Déva Rája,[1] a period extending from 1637 to 1672, but they eventuated in the permanent annexation to Mysore of a large portion of Coimbatore, Karúr and Erode in 1667, and also Darapúr. Colonel Wilks' account necessarily loses sight of the Mysorean reverses whilst it magnifies their successes. The other, or Madura, side of the picture is given by Mr. Nelson.[2] Chikka Déva Rája (1672–1704) succeeded to the throne. His youth was passed at Yelandúr, where he became acquainted with the celebrated Jain pundit Visha Laksha. He was for a long time a prisoner at Hangala, a fort south of Gúndulpet. His father died here, and over his tomb he raised a pagoda to Aparamita Paravasa Déva (the god of perpetual exile). This spot is otherwise of historic interest, for near it is Tirkanambi, once the seat of a prince of the Kadamba line, and the temple, Tri-Kadamba, is said to mark the trijunction of the Kadamba, Kerala and Kongu territories.[3] The Kongus, it will be remembered, probably gained possession of all South Mysore in the seventh century, whilst the conquests gained by the Malayálams probably followed the decay of the Kadamba empire in the fifth century. Chikka Déva, whose early life was spent within view of these blue hills, was perhaps the most able monarch of the Mysore dynasty. He established a post, reformed the revenue system, and developed the administration generally. His energy raised the Jangamas against him, but they were ruthlessly reduced to submission. Early in his reign he came in contact with the Mahrattas. He managed, however, to divert their attention from his dominions whilst they ravaged the eastern portions of the Dekhan and the Carnatic. Meanwhile he strengthened his position and added to his prestige by an alliance with the Emperor Aurangazib. To him history must award the praise of having established a secure and prosperous state, "extending from Palni and Anemale in the south to Midagesi in the north, and from near Karnatic Ghur of Baramahal in the east to the borders of Coorg and Balam in the west."[4]

---

[1] This rája came to the throne in the year the great Tirumala Náyak died, 1659.

[2] *Madura Manual*, Part III, Chapter VI.

[3] *Mysore Gazetteer*, Vol. II, p. 279.

[4] *Mysore Gazetteer*, Vol. I, p. 247.

With Chikka Déva the house of Mysore seems to have lost the administrative energy which had raised it in little more than a century to be a considerable power in South India. Two princes occupied the throne between his death and 1731, but authority was gradually passing out of their hands into those of the Dalavaye, whilst the prestige of the house was greatly weakened by the successful invasion of Sadat Ulla Khan, Nawáb of Arcot, and his allies. These foes were, however, bought off by a crore of rupees. A similar procedure was followed to induce the Mahrattas to retire two years later. Two pageant princes followed, but the real rulers were the brothers Déva and Nanja Rája. These chiefs gradually got mixed up with the wars of the English and French in the Carnatic, into the details of which it is not necessary to enter here. But it was in these conflicts that an obscure Mussulman soldier, Haider, by military genius, courage, energy and cunning rose to eminence, and in the course of a few years succeeded not only in obtaining the chief place in the army and state by ousting Nanja Rája in 1759, whose brother Déva Rája had recently died, but after a seemingly desperate reverse usurped the government in 1761. This he retained till his death in 1782, when he was quietly succeeded by his son Tippu. Meanwhile Rájas continued nominally to occupy the throne, and were exhibited annually in regal state at the Dasara feast, but they were treated by Haider simply as state prisoners, and so continued until the death of Chama Rája Wódear in 1796, when Tippu deemed it unnecessary to appoint a successor. It is unnecessary here to narrate the events of Tippu's reign, which closed by his death at the storming of Seringapatam on the memorable 4th May 1799. It may, however, be remarked that during Haider and Tippu's operations in Coimbatore against the English, the importance of the Nílagiris as points of observation seems to have impressed itself on these strategists. Almost inaccessible except to hill people, they commanded a splendid view of North Coimbatore and the Gajalhatti Pass. From these outposts reports of an enemy's movements could be sent more readily and quickly to Seringapatam than from stations near Sattiamangalam. They seem, too, to have strengthened the three old forts for the purpose of preventing raids from the Wainád into Mysore and Coimbatore, for a raid of the kind is mentioned by Buchanan as happening immediately after the overthrow of Tippu. Whether it was for these or for revenue reasons, we find that the Nílagiris, or rather Dévanaikenkóta, which included the greater portion of the tract, was of sufficient importance to find a place and a name in the Proclamation of annexation issued at Seringapatam by General Harris, Colonel Arthur Wellesley, the Honorable Henry Wellesley, Colonel

CHAP. XI. — EARLY HISTORY.

Kirkpatrick and Colonel Barry Close on the 24th June 1799 as portion of the Sultan's territory ceded to the British.

Malayálam.

Thus far we have traced the history of the native states whose history was more or less connected with the Nílagiri mountains, but there is one race whose connection with the Nílagiris we have no means of ascertaining, though probably for several centuries past it has claimed a portion of the hills as its own— I allude to the Malayálam people. Their claim of suzerainty over any portion of the plateau (they never colonized any part of it) probably dates back to the age in which they forced back the indigenous races, and perhaps the Kanarese, from the Wainád plateau, which geographically is a portion of Kárnáta and not of Malabar. When this movement took place I am unable to say, but I have already noted that in the fifth century the boundary of Kerala (Malabar) extended to Tirkanambi east of Gúndulpet. It was probably prior to this extension of dominion that the Kanarese races took possession of the hills south of the Nílagiris. Buchanan writes:

"There is a tract of land occupying part of the mountains which separate *Malabar* from *Coimbatore*. The *Namburis* or *Nairs* had no authority over its inhabitants, who speak the language of *Karnata*. It is divided into two districts, *Attapadi* and Agrata Cadawa, each subject to a *Gauda* or hereditary chief. The pass leading to *Attapadi* goes by *Manaarghat*, which was subject to the Tamuri[1] as chief of a district called Nerunganada."

He thus accounts for the subject position of these Gaudas:

"Each raja took advantage of the hill chief, who could only have access to the commerce of the low country through his dominions and forced him to pay a tribute for permission to trade."

He goes on to say:

"From these hilly districts there are roads that lead to *Dan Nàyakan-cotay* and *Coimbatore;* and it would be of great importance to commerce to have these roads cleared, as also the passes which lead up from *Irnàda* in *Malabar* to the northern parts of Mysore."

Early Portuguese Missionaries.

It was, however, in consequence of the Malayálam suzerainty that Europeans first approached the hills at the opening of the seventeenth century. The following account of this expedition, which I extract from Mr. Breeks' work, apart from its great interest in other respects, is especially noteworthy as abolishing entirely, the ordinary, though unphilosophical, view that the Badagas came to the Nílagiris on the break-up of the Vijayanagar empire three hundred years ago; for here we find, at this very date, that

[1] So the natives call the Zamorin

the Badagas had not only reached the present western limit of their settlement on the Nílagiris, Mélkúnda, but that the plateau was divided into four districts, and that the Badagas were already in a relatively superior position to the Tódas; but at the same time it must be noted that the Tódas are said to be scattered pretty equally over the four districts, whilst two hundred years later they had been pushed back to the unculturable uplands of the plateau, and that their number had decreased to a half of what it was estimated to be by the Jesuit Ferreiri, but it must not be forgotten that those two hundred years comprised a period of endless turmoil and internecine strife. I now quote *in extenso* from Mr. Breeks' work Mr. Whitehouse's abstract of a manuscript in the British Museum.

"At the Synod of Udiamparur in the State of Cochin,[1] held under Archbishop Menezes in 1599, information having been received that there were certain villages of Christians in a country called Todamala, who anciently belonged to the Syrian Church of Malabar, but then had nothing of Christianity except the bare name, it was ordered that priests and preachers should be sent thither immediately to redeem them to the Catholic faith, baptise them, &c. Francisco Roy, the first Roman Catholic Bishop of the Syrian Christians, in 1602 sent a priest and deacon of the Christians of St. Thomas with a good guide to find out the place and collect information. They reached the Todamala; but, as the account brought back by them was not so sure and complete as was desirable, Bishop Roy requested the Vice-Principal of the Jesuits to depute a priest of his own order to make further inquiries. The Rev. Jacome Ferreiri was selected for this mission. He started from Calicut, the place of his residence, and was permitted to return safely, after undergoing great exposure and fatigue, with a good deal of information about the hill tribes, their manners and customs; but with no tidings of any Christian colony, which had either become extinct or removed elsewhere, if it had ever been there at all. At Calicut he wrote a formal report, dated April 1st, 1603, from which the following particulars are gleaned:—

He proceeded *viâ* Manarecate 13 leagues inland from Tanur. A native convert, a nephew of the Samuri Rajah, accompanied him and some others. Their route led them over steep and rugged mountains infested with elephants and tigers. At Manarecate they were told that the Todamala was 6 Canarese or 12 Malabar leagues distant, and that it would take them two days and a half to reach their destination. Here they provided themselves with extra clothing as a protection against the cold of the mountains, and also provision for their journey. The Nairs who accompanied them wisely left their weapons behind them, lest the hill people should take alarm. The evening of the

[1] Todamala is included in a list of Christian Churches given in Assemani Bible, Orient., but this only refers to the date of this same synod.

CHAP. XI. — EARLY HISTORY.

second day from Manarecate[1] found them at the foot of a steep hill up which their route lay. On the third day they reach a Badaga village called Meleuntao (? Melur or Melkundah), containing between one and two hundred inhabitants. The priest and deacon previously sent are said to have arrived thus far. Here they met also with the chief of the Todas, who agreed to call his people together so that they might have an opportunity of conversing with them. On the following day the Jesuit father tried to converse with the Badagas on the subject of Christianity. He also had an interview with the Toda priest called Pollem (Palal) outside the Badaga village, which he would not enter for fear of pollution. They saw some Toda women, and gave them looking glasses and hanks of thread, with which they were much pleased. The third day of their sojourn on the hills was spent in a visitation of some of the Toda settlements, which are very correctly described, as also their dress, diet, manners, and customs. They could not give much account of their own origin, and gave no information leading to the supposition that either they or their ancestors ever had anything to do with any form or profession of Christianity. They simply said that they had heard that their ancestors came from the east, that one party settled on these mountains, and another party descended into the plains. Their number was supposed to be about 1,000, scattered pretty equally over four mountain districts. Feeling the cold, and the Samorin's nephew beginning to be indisposed, they now began to arrange for their descent into the low country. Ere they left, they promised to return within a year and make a longer stay. Circumstances however prevented them from so doing. The friendly Badagas showed them a better road than that by which they made the journey there."

The route by which they returned may have been the Gúdalúr or Karkúr Gháts. Mr. Breeks quotes a notice (furnished by Dr. Gundert) of the Tódas by a Carmelite priest, gathered from reports of the tribe current on the west coast, who visited Malabar in 1657. It speaks of the mountains where they dwelt as "in the kingdom of the Zamorin." But how slight the hold was that the Zamorin had even on the ghát country below the Nílagiris is manifest from the fact that his nephew's retinue had to leave their weapons behind them before entering the country. The Badagas are simply spoken of as friendly. At this period the power of the Mysore house was rapidly rising.

---

[1] Mr. Whitehouse says, "I think the Manarecate must be the place called Manaur in Ward's Government Survey Map, about Lat. 11°, Long. 76° 30″, because it was 13 leagues inland from Tanor, and from thence 12 leagues to the Todamala. There is a Manaar at the foot of the Sundapatti Ghât, but this is too near. This idea receives support from Buchanan's Journey through Mysore and Canara, Vol. II, p. 434, where he speaks of a tract of land occupying part of the mountains between Malabar and Coimbatore, divided into two districts, Attapadi and Agrata Cadava, and says that the pass leading to Attapadi is called Manarghât."

Thus far I have endeavoured to raise an interest in the Nílagiris by connecting them not only with the great race movements and religious revolutions of Southern India, but also by collecting such fragmentary notices as link them, however loosely, with the story of the neighbouring countries. But for such scattered rays of light the darkness which envelopes their past would be impenetrable. I now pass on to their story from the time when they first became known to the English.

CHAPTER XII.

RECENT HISTORY.

Marquis of Wellesley's policy.—Dr. Buchanan's mission.—Colonel Colin Mackenzie's survey.—Mr. Keys' visit.—Mr. John Sullivan's exploration.—Attention of Governor-General drawn to the Hills.—M. Leschenault's remarks.—Infanticide.—Ootacamand.—Captain Ward's survey.—Mr. Sullivan opens out roads.—Ootacamand laid out.—Sir Thomas Munro's visit.—Mr. S. R. Lushington's scheme.—Ootacamand constituted a sanitarium. — Military Commandant appointed.—Official complications.—Convalescent Depôt established.—Mr. Sullivan's departure.—Portion of Nílagiris transferred to Malabar.—Mr. Sullivan protests.—Rapid extension of Ootacamand.—Bishop Daniel Wilson.—Court of Directors ask for report.—Committee of inquiry appointed.—Government Orders on report.—Mr. Lushington's departure.—Sir Frederick Adam succeeds.—Medical Report.—Abolition of Convalescent Depôt.—Administration defective.—Massacre of Kúrumbas.—Special legislation proposed, but negatived by Imperial Government.—Destruction of woods.—Draft Act.—Ootacamand constituted a Military bazaar.—Lord Elphinstone at Kaity.—Mr. Sullivan urges the re-annexation of that part of the plateau transferred to Malabar.—Government declines to make the transfer.—Commandant appointed Joint Magistrate and District Munsif.—Marquis of Tweeddale, Governor.—Retransfer of the second portion of the Hills to Coimbatore.—Coffee-planting begun.—Plans submitted for barracks at Wellington.—Coonoor Church built.—Small Cause Court Judge at Ootacamand.—Proposals to appoint Civil and Sessions Court rejected.—Assistant Judge transferred from Combaconum to Ootacamand.—Kúndas and Nídumalé annexed.—First Commissioner, Mr. Breeks.—Ouchterlony Valley added to the district.—Industries.—Prospects of District.

CHAP. XII. — RECENT HISTORY.

AFTER the fall of Seringapatam the Marquis of Wellesley "being justly of opinion that a more complete knowledge of these countries was indispensably necessary," resolved to have Mysore and the territories belonging to that state which had been recently annexed by the British carefully surveyed, and their physical, commercial, and agricultural conditions reported on. The survey operations were entrusted to that distinguished officer and oriental scholar Colonel Colin Mackenzie;[1] the other inquiries were confided to Dr. Francis Buchanan, in whose journal we possess invaluable notes on "the state of agriculture, arts and commerce; the religion, manners and customs; the history, natural and civil," of the provinces visited by him. Dr. Buchanan started from Seringapatam on the 19th May 1800, and, after traversing East and South Mysore, entered Coimba-

Marquis of Wellesley's policy.

[1] See *Cat. Rais.* Vol. 1. Preface, vii.

tore in October of that year, on the 24th day of which month he was at Dévanaikenkóta, a fort on the north side of the Bhavání, a little above its junction with Moyár, and the head-quarters of the taluk to which the Nílagiris proper belonged.

Dr. Buchanan's mission.

"It was built," he says, "by Dána, a Náyaka or Polygar dependent on Madura. * * * His descendants were deprived of it by Bal Raja, another dependent on the princes of Madura. From him, or at least a descendant of the same name, it was taken by the Raja of Mysore, and from its having been long dependent on that family, by far the greater part of its inhabitants speak the language of Karnata."

The disturbed state of the country as well as the relations of the hill-people are illustrated by the following occurrence :—

"About two months ago thirty or forty *Nairs* from *Wainad*, or from *Nelleala*, as it is here called, persuaded the chief of one of the hill villages subject to the Company to join them with sixty or seventy men. This united force came down to the low country and plundered three villages. A hundred *candashara*,[1] supported by a few *sepoys*, were sent out; and after an engagement, in which nobody was killed, took the chief and seven men prisoners. Of these three were *Nairs*. About ten years ago these banditti made some disturbance among the hill villages, but never before ventured down to the low country."

Then follows the first reference that I have met with to the Badagas :—

"Honey and wax," he writes, "are gathered by a caste called *Budugar*, who inhabit the hilly country between this and *Malabar*, and which lies south from *Nelleala* or the *Wainad* of Major Rennell. They live in small villages like the *Eriligaru*, and not only use the *cotu-cadu* cultivation already described, but have also ploughs. The quantity of honey and wax which they procure is considerable, and they pay nothing for it, there being no forest renter in the district."

On the following day, the 25th October, the unwearied doctor "took a long and fatiguing walk to the top of the western hills[2] in order to see a *cambay*, or village inhabited by *Eriligaru*."[3]

---

[1] I find reference to these incursions in a letter from the Board of Revenue to Lord Clive in June 1803, which is curious as containing the first reference to the Tódanad I have met with. It runs, "In consequence of the Hoblis of Devaroyapatam and Totanad having been threatened with invasion by the insurgents in Wainad, the former has been deserted by its inhabitants, and the Collector has found it necessary to detach peons for their protection." Mr. Garrow, the letter further states, on the outbreak of the rebellion in Malabar, engaged a band of 117 peons for the protection of this part of the Coimbatore District. In the following year (1804) the Government sanctioned the entertainment of 100 peons to protect the Hoblis of Dévaráyapatnam against invasions from the rebel Pyche Rája of Wainád.

[2] The spot was probably near Arakád, below Rangasámi's Peak, on the old track from Dévanaikenkóta to Kótagiri.

[3] Dr. Buchanan (Chapter IX) also refers to the Tódas, but he was evidently misinformed about them, not only placing them in the ranges south of the Nílagiris, but as cultivating with the plough and paying rent for their fields.

CHAP. XII.

RECENT HISTORY.

But he was more concerned with these wild people than with the grand hills on which they dwelt. Still the glorious panorama of hill and plain which was spread out before him could not pass unnoticed.

"Although the atmosphere was rather hazy, I had from the hills," he writes, "a noble view of the whole course of the *Bhavani* and of the country called *Chera*, as far as *Sandi-durga*, and other remote hills. Near the village I was refreshed by the cool water of a fine perennial spring, which in India is a great rarity."

Thus, whilst the first European who ascended these hills was a religious propagandist, upon whose eye their glorious scenery fell unheeded, the first Englishman was a scientist, whose first words were a tribute of praise to the hills, the river, and the refreshing spring, and the note he struck has been re-echoed by every fellow-countryman who has since climbed to this land of "springs of water" and of "sacred hills."

From Dévanaikenkóta Buchanan passed to Srimúgai, near Mettapollium, the residence in Tippu's time of an amildar, and thence to Coimbatore, where we part company with him.

Colonel Colin Mackenzie's survey.

We turn now to Colonel Mackenzie. His scheme of survey embraced "the statistics and history of the country as well as its geography." He had three assistants and a Naturalist, Dr. Heyne. Among the services to science which he performed may be mentioned the discovery of the Jaina religion, the accumulation of a mass of information regarding Lingayat and other sects, the Sassanams and other inscriptions, the monumental stones and trophies—*virakal* and *mastikal*,[1]—"the sepulchral tumuli, mounds, and barrows of the early tribes." This information was embodied in district survey memoirs. Although we know that Colonel Mackenzie did not ascend the Nílagiris, yet there can be little question that either one or more of his assistants did, for we find from his letter (11th January 1816) to the Madras Government, that in 1808 he had forwarded a notice of the Hills contained in his "6th Volume of Memoirs of the 18th and 26th October 1808" transmitted to the Court of Directors in 1809. I have endeavoured to obtain this notice from the Surveyor-General's Office, Calcutta, to whom these volumes were returned, but without success; the extract, however, is of interest.

"I have put up in the case for transmission to Europe a copy of a map of the Nilagiri mountains in the district of Danaikencotta, in the Coimbatoor province, on the original scale of survey of one mile to an inch. I have selected this as an original specimen of the work of the native assistant surveyors, and of the survey of a singular tract of

---

[1] See his letter quoted in Preface to Vol. 1 of the *Cat. Rais.*

mountainous country situated centrally in the limits between the countries of Malabar, Mysore and Coimbatoor, remarkable for their extraordinary height, and for being inhabited by two singular tribes of people described to be dissimilar to the natives of other provinces in habits, manners, language and complexion, some notices of whom are communicated in the memoirs of the Mysore Survey sent home in 1808, and in Colonel Wilks' History of Mysore.[1] This tract contains 495 miles of mountains and 250 of plain country, altogether 745 miles."

A copy of this map I have not seen, but Colonel Cloete, Revenue Survey, has courteously forwarded to me a copy of a map of the hills east of the Paikaré and Kúnda rivers, prepared from surveys from 1807–1814, that is, the Coimbatore portion of the Nílagiris, the tract west of these rivers not having been surveyed till 1821–23 by Captain Ward. Four years, however, subsequent to the despatch of the memoirs to the Honorable Court, we find that a European surveyor ascended the hills under instructions from Mr. Garrow,[2] Collector of the Coimbatore District. The name of this surveyor was William Keys.[3] His first letter is dated Ténád, 30th March 1812. On the 5th April he was at Péranganád, and on the 20th idem at Málékóta, or Kalhatti, returning to Dévanaikenkóta on the last day of the month. His report will be found in the appendix. I do not purpose to do more than quote from the letter forwarding the second portion, leaving the reader to judge for himself of the first known essay describing the Nílagiris. Mr. Keys writes in August:—

Mr. Keys' visit.

"It will be unnecessary for me to observe to you, Sir, that in the execution of this arduous duty, we have underwent considerable difficulties, and experienced great inconveniences from the inclemency of the climate, particularly of the Neelaghery mountains; but notwithstanding, I beg leave to suggest that I have made it my duty to be very particular in exploring those parts, and I flatter myself that the plan will be found an accurate and distinct delineation of them."

Mr. Keys found "no manufactures on the hills and much less of trade," though this is hardly consistent with the details of produce which he gives, and the fact that the Government at this time derived a revenue of about 15,000 rupees from this tract.

---

[1] I have not been able to trace the reference.—ED.

[2] It is noted that no reference is made to the Nílagiris, except the lowland portion about Dévaráyapatnam, in Mr. Hodgson's long and interesting report on the revenues of Coimbatore, 10th September 1807; but in the report of the Coimbatore Commission to Lord William Bentinck, 18th May 1804, reference is made to the rent of the hill villages. I would here note that the years 1803, 1804 and 1805 were marked by great deficiency in the rainfall.

[3] Another Surveyor, Macmahon, seems to have been on the hills about the same time.

CHAP. XII. RECENT HISTORY.

During the five years that followed I have not been able to trace any special notes on the Nílagiris, but with the year 1818 began the history of the European occupation and colonization of the plateau.

Mr. John Sullivan's exploration.

Early in 1818 two gentlemen[1] on a few weeks' leave visited the hills for 'shikar;' they ascended apparently by the old Dévanaikenkóta path by Ténád and Kíl-Kótagiri, south of Rangasámi's Peak, having slept a night *en route* near some Irula villages, still existing. They proceeded to Kótagiri, and on their return to Coimbatore, having "surprised their friends by the account they gave of it, particularly of the extreme coldness of the climate," a party was formed, who set out to repeat the tour on the 2nd January 1819. A long account of their tour will be found in the letter to the Editor of the *Government Gazette*, dated 30th January 1819, printed in the appendix. Of this party Mr. John Sullivan, Collector of Coimbatore, appears to have been one, and it is to the energy and enthusiasm of this friend of the native that we owe the final colonization of the hills. Mr. Sullivan, Mr. Thomas informs me, ascended by a narrow hill-path used by Irulas, and pitched his tent in the sheltered valley of Dimhatti near Kótagiri. He soon returned to Coimbatore, but again ascended the hills in May in company with the celebrated naturalist Leschenault de la Tour, who was completely restored to health by a residence here of a few months.

Mr. Sullivan, with characteristic energy and consideration for the people, in his first letter to the Board of Revenue, dated 6th March 1819, requests that a rough survey of the lands may be made, as "the inhabitants are extremely anxious to have their lands measured, under an idea that they are paying more than they ought to do." He incidentally remarks that surveyors had been sent to this tract "commonly known by the name of Neilgherry Hills" in 1800-1, but that "owing to the extreme inclemency of the climate" the surveyors were frightened, measured not an acre, and contented themselves with "making an estimate of the quantity and quality of the land, and fixing the old rates of *teerwa* upon it,"[2] which, he adds, were "extremely favorable to the ryots." Rupees 800 was the estimate for the work,

---

[1] Mr. E. B. Thomas, for many years Collector of Coimbatore, and whose personal acquaintance with the hills extends back to 1827, informs me that their names were Kindersley and Whish, Assistants to the Collector of Coimbatore; but I have not found the names mentioned in contemporary papers. In Jervis's book these names appear, but he states that they ascended in pursuit of a Poligar who had maltreated his ryots, and sought to escape the strong arm of the law in these hills. Another account is that they followed smugglers.—(BAIKIE.)

[2] He gives the revenue of the hills for twenty years ending 1819, which will be found in Chapter XIII.

which was sanctioned. He also asked for and obtained Rupees 300 to make the path to the Hills more accessible, observing that if this were not done, the revenue, which had been gradually diminishing, would in a short time waste to nothing, for the ryots pay as they please, their position rendering them "quite secure from any coercive measures." The formation of the road was entrusted to Mr. Macpherson in command of a party of pioneers, and to the same officer the survey of the lands. The road was reported as completed on 23rd May 1823. This was the old Srimúgai Pass, which preceded the Kótagiri Pass first cut by Mr. Thomas.[1]

The hills meanwhile were attracting attention, and we find that by June 1820 upwards of twenty gentlemen had visited the plateau, and one lady, name unknown, "without any inconvenience to herself and without giving particular trouble to the bearers"! A long and interesting letter was published in the *Madras Gazette*, 17th June 1820, containing extracts from the letters of M. Leschenault, Botanist to the King of France, on the region, its people and its vegetation; and contemporaneously a report written by Mr. Macpherson, printed in the appendix, was forwarded to Government, who appear to have passed on to the Governor-General these and other papers, for in the *Gazette of India* very shortly afterwards appears the following notice :—

Attention of the Governor-General drawn to the Hills.

"We trust that future reports of the salubrity of this spot will remove all the apprehensions that have been entertained, and that it will become a place of resort for those whose state of health may require that change of temperature which it unquestionably affords. Should a continued residence in these regions prove that the climate is favorable to the European constitution, it may perhaps be deemed expedient hereafter to form a military establishment for pensioners and invalids, with a regular hospital; and if it should become a military station, with Medical Officers attached to it, houses would soon become erected, and conveniences would be provided for those who might be compelled to seek the benefit of the climate; and, in all probability, many persons on the coast, who have withdrawn from active life, but who do not intend to return to their native country, would take up their future residence on the Nilgherry Mountains."

In his letter forwarding Lieutenant Macpherson's report, Mr. Sullivan urged on Government the desirability of employing on the new road the prisoners of Coimbatore and Salem, as labor could not be had on the hills or from Coimbatore, remarking that, as there was only one path and "the country on either side so rugged and steep that no prisoner would dare deviate from it, a sentinel therefore at the top and bottom of the pass would be

[1] JERVIS, p. 134.

CHAP. XII.

RECENT HISTORY.

sufficient to prevent the escape of any person working under the officer." His enthusiastic faith—a faith which succeeding years have proved to have been well founded—in the climate, which he tells us elsewhere did more to restore him to perfect health than a voyage to the Cape, finds expression in this letter.

"There is no Asiatic or African climate known to us (with the exception of that of the Nepaul mountains) so cool and equal throughout the year as the Neilgherries, and I have no doubt, when the road is made accessible and a medical man is stationed there, these mountains will become the general resort for invalids instead of the Cape and the Isle of France."

And further:

"My own mind is strongly impressed with the important results which may follow from the discovery of this country as affording an excellent asylum for invalids, both officers and soldiers. * * * It is *literally* true that out of the sun heat is not known on the mountains in any one month of the year. The soil is remarkably fertile, wheat and barley are already cultivated, and many of the European fruits grow wild and only require culture to attain perfection."

This latter prophecy has not been fulfilled, and even Mr. Sullivan had some fear that his readers would hold his fancy more lively than it ought to have been in the picture he had drawn, and so appeals to other gentlemen to bear him out.

Sir Thomas Munro, who had just succeeded to the Governorship of Madras, approved Mr. Sullivan's suggestions, anticipating "much advantage from the acquisition of an accurate statistical knowledge of that district," but, with his known economy, declined to sanction Rupees 26 for an English writer.

M. Leschenault's remarks.

Space will not permit of my giving M. Leschenault's account of the Hills, but as he was the first botanist who visited the mountains, I cannot refrain from quoting at length his monograph forwarded with a collection of Nílagiri plants to the Madras Literary Society.

"La collection des plantes que mon ami et moi avons recueillées sur les montagnes de Nilgerret, renferme plus de 200 espèces, parmi lesquelles un grand nombre de nouvelles. Nous avons pensé que la Société Littéraire de Madras recevroit avec intérêt quelques échantillons de ces plantes. Le temps que j'ai été obligé de donner à leur récolte, et à leur préparation, ne m'a permis que de les examiner rapidement. Je manquerois des livres, et des moyens de comparaison nécessaires pour fixer définitivement leur place, aussi je me suis contenté le plus souvent de reconnoître le genre j'ai donné avec reserve, quelques noms ne pouvent être que provisoires, car j'ignore si les plantes auxquelles je les ai données n'ont pas été nommées par MM. Roxburg, Rotteler, Buchanan, Blein, et Heyne, dont les recherches, sur d'autres montagnes de la peninsule, sont antérieures aux mienne, mais dont je ne connois point les herbiers.

" Le règne végétal sur le montagne de Nilgerret offre le plus grand intérêt, tant par le nombre des objets nouveaux, que par la différence qui existe entre les plantes de cette contrée et celles de la plaine—on y trouve un grand nombre de genres analogues avec ceux d'Europe, tels sont les Vaccinium, Rhododendron, Fragaria (strawberry), Rubus (raspberry), Anemoni, Balsamina, Geranium, Plantago, &c., &c. Ce rapport indique que les plantes utiles d'Europe s'acclimateraient parfaitement bien, et la vigoureuse végétation que l'on remarque partout, assure d'abondantes récoltes.

" Parmi les plantes les plus remarquables que nous avons recueillées, je citerai le Berberis Tinctoria, espèce nouvelle, dont le bois et l'écorce fournissent une belle couleur jaune, qui peut devenir importante pour les teintures, si l'on parvient à lui donner de la fixité. Elle n'est point employée par les indigènes.

" Le Leptospermum Scoparium arbuste, qui produit un fruit excellent que la culture rendrait encore meilleur; il seroit possible d'acclimater ce charmant arbuste dans plusieurs contrées d'Europe.

" Mr. ——— m'a adressé une excellente description d'une belle plante qui croît au sommet des plus hautes montagnes. Elle appartient à un genre nouveau. Je ne l'ai trouvée ni en fleurs, ni en fruits.

" Les bois offrent souvent des arbres d'une grandeur et d'une grosseur remarquables, bons pour le charpente et la menuiserie. Les bords des ruisseaux et des torrents sont parés de jolie plantes et d'arbustes élégants qui peuvent embellir nos jardins.

" Parmi les plantes céréales, le bled, l'orge, dont j'en ai vu que les grains, m'ont paru d'une qualité inférieure, et je crois nécessaire de renouveler les semences."

Infanticide.

In Mr. Sullivan's letter above referred to, he had brought to the notice of Government the strong reasons there were for believing that the Tódas practised female infanticide, and had suggested the institution by Mr. Macpherson of further inquiries. Sir T. Munro approved the proposals, but though the practice undoubtedly existed, and possibly still continues in remote mands, yet I have seen no report furnishing indubitable evidence on the point.

Ootacamand.

In March 1821 a letter appeared in the *Madras Gazette* giving an account of a visit to the Múkarté "belt." It is noteworthy for containing the first distinct mention of Ootacamand. The note runs:—February 22nd. "Marched Wotokymand. High wind evening and all night—to sensation extremely cold." To this letter is appended a thermometric table of the temperature at Jackanéri[1] for twelve months ending 28th July 1821.

In June 1822 appeared the first official Medical Report on the Hills, drawn up apparently by Assistant Surgeon Orton, of Her

[1] Two miles south-east of Kótagiri, elevation about 5,275 feet.

CHAP. XII.

RECENT HISTORY.

Majesty's 34th Regiment. The paper is a careful *résumé* of all the information then available on the suitability of the climate for Europeans, and discusses the several localities most suitable for a station. Of Ootacamand Mr. Orton says :—

"In the Torder village of Wuttacamund I was informed that no death had happened for three years."

He summed up as follows :—

"In the event of Government formingan establishment for invalids on the Neilgherries, it will require mature consideration to fix on the most proper situation for that purpose. The neighbourhood of Dimhutty would be most convenient for procuring supplies, &c., by the new road and on account of the Collector's establishment being placed there ; but the country about Codavomoody is much prettier, more cultivated, and populous. The Todiernaad, from its much greater height and coldness, would deserve the preference, were it not to be apprehended that its swamps and woods would be injurious. It does not, however, appear from experience that such is the case. The Toders are a more robust and healthy race than the other castes who occupy the less elevated tract. It is probable that a clean and dry tract may be found equally elevated with the Todiernaad. The country immediately west of Sooloor (Shólúr) seems to possess all these advantages, and it is close to Mysore and a pass leading down into it. It might be deemed eligible to erect a few small temporary buildings for the reception of sick officers—similar to some already raised by Mr. Sullivan for travellers—at several different parts of the table-land. The experiments of proving, on a sufficiently large scale, the effects of this singular climate on the European constitution would be a highly interesting one in a philosophical point of view, and, if successful, its results would be highly important and valuable."

Mr. Sullivan's energy, however, virtually solved the question as to the capital of the Nílagiris. In the year following his first visit he seems to have determined on selecting the grand valley of the western slopes of Doddabetta for his residence. The site chosen for his house was a spur projecting out into the eastern centre of the valley, commanding a grand view of the western range, whilst it was surrounded by grassy hills more or less covered, especially in the hollows, with magnificent shólas or woods. This valley seems to have been a favourite pasture-ground of the Tódas, containing two or three important mands, near one of which Mr. Sullivan fixed his house, and hence the settlement obtained its name—Ootacamand. It is strange that the terminations of the names of the four principal settlements of the hills represent its four principal tribes—Ootacamand, the Tódas ; Kótagiri, the Kótas ; Coonoor, the Badagas ; and Kólakambé, the Irulas. The Kúrumbamotté is not yet so distinguished. To return to Mr. Sullivan.—To this house he gave the name of Stonehouse, from the material, rough stone, of which it was built. This structure has since then passed through many hands. In 1860 the Lawrence Asylum was established there, and there continued till its removal to Lovedale in 1871, when it became the property of Government, and is now used for the Government Offices, to which is attached the new Council Chamber. The building appears to have been tolerably advanced to 1822, a European servant being in charge. In September 1822 Mr. Sullivan applied to Government for permission to enclose 500 ballas of waste land, having, with the consent of Government, procured a professional gardener and agriculturist with a view to making "experiments in horticulture and agriculture under his superintendence." "The experiments," he adds, "may eventually prove useful to the public, and the expense of making them will be my own." This gardener's name was Johnstone. Mr. Sullivan had also another assistant, an African named Jones, an excellent gardener and seedsman. Johnstone eventually took up the business of a market-gardener on his own account, made a good deal of money, and returned to England; whilst Jones carried on a similar business near the Málémand reservoir until his death. The land asked for and obtained by Mr. Sullivan was the valley to the south of Stonehouse, on parts of which the fruit trees planted by this true coloniser of the Nílagiris may still be seen, whilst others were planted by him, or by his aid, at the houses known as Lushington Hall, Shoreham, the Club, at Kaity and at Bellikal, and many other places. The presence of European grains and fruits on the hills, as already noticed, stimulated these pioneers to action.

Captain Ward's survey.

It was in this and the following year that Captain Ward, originally one of Colonel Colin Mackenzie's assistants, surveyed the Hills and completed the valuable memoir which will be found in the appendix, though it was not submitted to Government till July 1826. The following extract, written probably towards the end of 1822, is interesting as showing the progress made by the settlers on the Hills up to that date:—

"Since these regions have been visited by gentlemen," he writes, "several bungalows have been built in different pleasant situations, as at Dimhutty, and here is a very good kitchen garden, as also at Jackenery in a lower situation. A few temporary ones have been erected for the convenience of travellers at Kodavomoody, Nanjanaad, Keelur and Yellanhully, and another is now in some progress at Whotakary in the Mullanaad, with a spacious garden, laid out with taste on the shoulder of a low ridge, which promises in time to outstep those abovementioned. One great disadvantage attending building here is the want of materials. There is a variety of timber, but it appears to be of very indifferent kind, nor is it possible to burn firm bricks; the clay being of a bad quality, does not adhere together for any time."

CHAP. XII.

RECENT HISTORY.

Mr. Sullivan opens out roads.

In this year (1823) Mr. Sullivan obtained a grant from Government of 5,000 rupees to complete the road across the range to the Wainád by Gúdalúr, "thus completing the communication between the eastern and western coasts," rendering the Nílagiris "easily accessible to all persons approaching them from the sea." He also obtained permission to repair the communication with Mysore by the Gajalhatti Pass. In the following year he succeeded in obtaining a grant of Rupees 6,500 for opening out the Karkoot (Karkúr) Pass, which had been suffered to fall into decay after the capture of Seringapatam, and to repair the line connecting the pass with the Mysore frontier, which had originally been constructed by Tippu Sultan, making it practicable for wheel traffic. The opening of the road to the West Coast led to the importation of large supplies of grain, "thus affording timely relief to the market on the eastern side during this season of scarcity." In the following year (1824) Mr. Sullivan thus sums up the benefits the people had derived from his measures :—

"The whole produce of the hills was formerly carried down upon the backs of the natives for the person who rented it from the Government. The rent was a rigid monopoly,[1] and the demand upon the ryots undefined. Under this system the province and population were rapidly declining. Since the road was made the lands have been measured, assessed with money-rents, a regular ryotwári system introduced, and all the produce is now sold on the hills and carried down to the low country upon bullocks. Although these changes have been attended with a very considerable reduction of the public revenue, yet such is the demand and competition for the valuable products of the hills, and such the comparative facility of transferring them in all directions, that the loss will very soon be covered by increased cultivation."

Ootacamand laid out.

During the following two years little progress appears to have been made in inducing the Government to establish a sanitarium on the plateau, though Mr. Sullivan states he had long endeavoured to impress on the Government the great advantage which might be derived from the Nílagiris, being of opinion that "the judicious expenditure of thousands here would lead to the saving of lacs." But he had not been idle. It was about this time that the Ootacamand Lake was formed and many of the roads about the station cut. He built the house, and laid out the garden and grounds of Bishopsdown, then called Southdowns, having leased his houses at "Stonehouse" and gardens to Government for 460 rupees a month. Dr. Haines and Captain Macpherson also began to build, the one about the Club Hill, the other on the

[1] The renting system appears to have been introduced here, as in other parts of Coimbatore, in 1807.

western slopes of Elk Hill. But towards the close of the year 1826[1] Sir Thomas Munro—*clarum et venerabile nomen*—crossed the hills on his return from a tour through the southern districts. He seems to have well appreciated them, remarking that "no description hitherto given of them had done justice to the subject." He died at Bellary a few months later, and though he marked out no policy for the hills, he ordered Mr. Sullivan to report thereon. This report he submitted in September 1827. It contains a long account of the climate. It states that in Ootacamand there were then seventeen houses for Europeans, ten of which were private property unconnected with Government; that at Kótagiri there were five bungalows, these being occupied by private families.

CHAP. XII.

RECENT HISTORY.

Sir Thomas Munro's visit.

"Roads," he writes, "have been made in all directions about the settlement of Ootacamund, so that invalids may take either horse or palanquin exercise with almost as much facility as in the low country. A fine piece of water has also been constructed, on which boats are beginning to ply. A subscription has been set on foot for a public reading-room. Ootacamund, in short, is gradually approximating to a state of comfort and civilization."

Mr. S. R. Lushington's scheme.

But the times of indifference to the Nílagiris were at end when Mr. Stephen Rumbold Lushington succeeded to the Governorship of Madras three months after Sir T. Munro's death. Within thirty days of his assuming the government, we find a long series of questions addressed to the Ootacamand Station Committee,[2] composed of Mr. Sullivan, Dr. Haines and Captain Macpherson. From the answers to these queries, dated 27th November 1827, we learn that Government were in possession of four bungalows, accommodating ten bachelors and three families, upon which Government had spent 20,000 rupees, having received as rent above 3,000 rupees, and that forty or fifty Government officers had been accommodated in them; that there were four private bungalows available on rent at Ootacamand—one at Rallia, between Ootacamand and Kótagiri, and three at the latter place;—that Government had already advanced Rupees 32,000 to these gentlemen to build private residences, and that thirteen bungalows were being constructed by them; that "demand for accommodation" by intending visitors "was incessant;" that Mr. Sullivan had tendered his house, Stonehouse, with the garden to Government as a hospital for 100 soldiers, but that the project had fallen through, and that, consequently, he had made over the garden,

[1] It was in this year that two letters to the *Bengal Harkaru* by *Philanthropos* appeared, containing the first philosophic account of the Nílagiri tribes.

[2] Their powers were undefined, and I have not been able to trace the minute of their appointment.

CHAP. XII. — RECENT HISTORY.

measuring 10 acres, to a respectable European to cultivate, "on condition that the produce is to be appropriated to the supply of the public market." In reply to a proposal of Government to establish gardens, the Committee proposed no further outlay, but urged the propriety "of making Mr. Sullivan's garden the foundation for a botanical establishment," remarking that "a great many products largely used in medicine, and imported at a great expense from Europe, might be raised here in any quantities." We further learn from this report that, under orders from Government, advances had been made "at different times to people to establish bazaars here, and the market is now regularly and well supplied with every essential article. The prices of rice and some other grains, though cent. per cent. higher than those in the low country, are not above the usual bazaar rates at the Presidency; and when the passes into Malabar are fully opened, a very considerable reduction of them may be confidently expected." There were by this time about 500 people, with 23 shops, in the bazaar. The community were still dependent on the low country for bread. The Committee urged Government to establish a brewery for the manufacture of malt liquor for the European troops, as they believed the hill barley was capable of being converted into excellent malt. Hops, they thought, would grow if once introduced, but many efforts made by individuals to effect this had failed. They therefore urged that the Company should send out plants by the next year's ships. We find that an establishment of public palanquin-bearers was kept up. Villages, we are told, were beginning to spring up at the foot of the passes. They urged the employment of low-country bearers and coolies (ghaut condashars) for a curious reason, from which we may learn what a great change has come over the Nílagiri tribes.

"The hill people are so independent in circumstances and character," they write, "that no temptation of wages will induce them to engage themselves voluntarily as coolies, and they are only prevailed upon to work from a conviction that, refusing to do so, Government might make some just demands against them for increase of rent, which are now from motives of expediency withheld."

Ootacamand constituted a sanitarium.

The result of the deliberations[1] of Government was the establishment of Ootacamand as the sanitarium of Madras. After summing up the advantages of the hill climate, with the observation that the temperature was—what the late learned Doctor Baillie declared to be—"most favourable to the prolonged existence of man as an animal," they resolved, in order that invalids might "reap the benefit of this climate," that the Mysore

[1] *Extracts, Minutes Consultation*, 11th December 1827.

Pass (Segúr) should at once be made practicable for carts, and that ten companies of Pioneers should immediately be employed on the work; that travellers' bungalows should be built at Bellikal on the head, and at Segúr at the foot of the pass (also at Tippukádu and at Dondé in Mysore), and on completion of these bungalows, others were to be constructed on the Wainád and Coimbatore Passes. At Ootacamand the accommodation being "meagre and inadequate" compared with the pressing wants of the community, the following buildings were to be erected forthwith: a hospital to accommodate 40 or 50 invalid soldiers, costing 10,500 rupees; ten bungalows, each to accommodate four officers or two families, at 6,800 rupees each. These buildings were to be "durably and well" constructed, so as to bear a second story if necessary. The Commissary-General was ordered to supply chunam and the Gun Carriage Factory all the wood-work and furniture, and "the most vigorous exertions were to be used in carrying the resolution of Government into effect." The neighbouring Collectors and even the Resident at Mysore were warned to lend every assistance in building this new temple to Joy and Health in this land,—to many a land of dearth, drought, and dreariness.

Military Commandant appointed.

If in these energies Mr. Sullivan saw the approaching fulfilment of the dream which had for nearly ten years occupied his imagination, the pleasure was mixed with bitterness in the appointment of a Military Commandant, though he himself had advocated the appointment of a special officer. The duty of supervising the hills, which had "hitherto devolved upon a Committee of Public Officers or upon the Principal Collector, Coimbatore," was held sufficiently burdensome to constitute a separate charge. The Commandant was to control all public buildings, public works, and establishments, and "all military persons of inferior rank to his own who may proceed thither." All arrangements for purchase or sale of public property were to be made through him, and all applications for quarters to him. He was to report progress weekly. Major Kelso, of the 26th Native Infantry, was selected for the post, with a staff allowance of Rupees 400 per mensem.

Official complications.

But these activities induced conflicts. Mr. Sullivan being shortly afterwards ordered, in communication with this officer, to allot ground for a military bazaar, Major Kelso sought to mark out a large cantonment some ten or twelve square miles in extent for this purpose, and to construct the native bazaar at the spot now called Charing Cross, below Stonehouse; Mr. Sullivan to restrict it to a small space for a bazaar, which he wished to locate near the west end of the lake.

CHAP. XII. — RECENT HISTORY.

It is needless to detail the controversy that ensued, but it ultimately closed in a compromise, the part selected for the cantonment bazaars, public offices, hospital, &c., being the spur on which St. Stephen's Church, Bombay Castle, the jails and bazaars now stand.[1] The officer appointed to survey the station was Major Hansen, Deputy Quartermaster-General. His report[2] is interesting as drawing attention to the swamps of the station and suggesting their being drained, but he did not consider them necessarily unhealthy, for, although mostly impassable, springs were constantly oozing from the rising grounds in their vicinity, and thus they partook more "of the character of running streams than of stagnant water." He also earnestly urged on Government to limit and allot ground to private individuals who had already built or were building houses. He remarks, "At present the extent is very undefined, and the claims are, in many instances, so very unreasonable, that I think as little time as possible should be lost in defining the relative limits of each man's property." He urged that the Government bungalows for private individuals should be built on the slopes along the western lake, and that a suspension bridge should be thrown across this piece of water. He also discussed the passes to the hills, being strongly in favour of the Gúdalúr. It was also due to this officer that the central ridge already referred to was selected for the public buildings. His views were generally approved by Government, but they resolved to station only one company of sepoys, instead of two, at the place, and ordered the proposed native barrack accommodation to be reduced accordingly.

Convalescent Depôt.

The various military buildings as well as private residences were pushed on with great rapidity. On the 8th January 1830 "the Convalescent Depôt" at Ootacamand was notified as ready for occupation, and the first detachment of convalescents arrived in May following. During part of the year 1829 Mr. Lushington appears to have resided on the hills and to have taken a very active part in pushing on the works, visiting with this object the several gháts. He renewed, on behalf of Government, the lease of Mr. Sullivan's house "Stonehouse," and purchased from him for Government the Bishopsdown property as a residence for invalid officers for Rupees 35,000.

Mr. Sullivan's departure—Portion of Nílagiris transferred to Malabar.

But though Mr. Sullivan hailed Mr. Lushington's change of policy with enthusiasm, the views of these gentlemen differed

[1] The limits were soon extended, and two or three years later included the whole Ootacamand Valley.—See Map, 1st Edition of Dr. Baikie's work.

[2] The report is dated 23rd September 1828. In March of this year Surgeon Dalmahoy had submitted the report referred to in Chapter IV, Part I, but his remarks were mainly confined to Kótagiri.

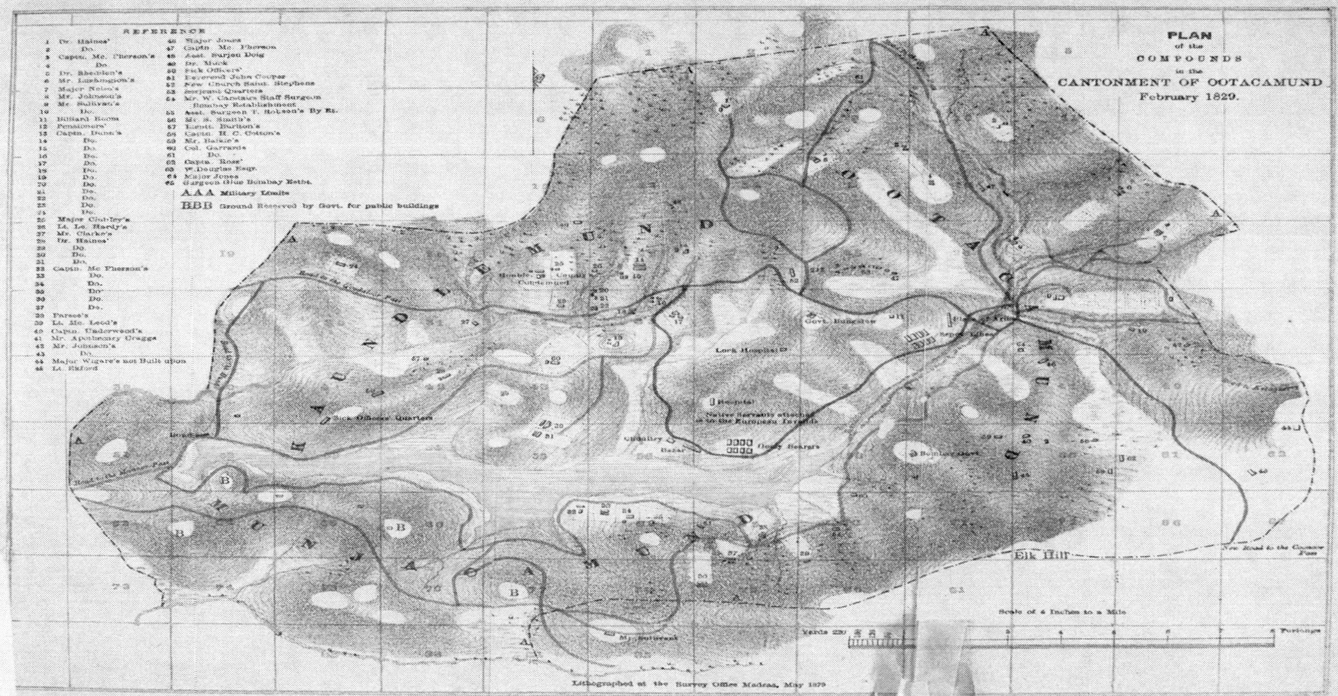
PLAN
of the
COMPOUNDS
in the
CANTONMENT OF OOTACAMUND
February 1829.
REFERENCE
AAA Military Limits
BBB Ground Reserved by Govt. for public buildings
Lock Hospital
Govt. Bungalow
Sick Officers' Quarters
Elk Hill
Scale of 4 Inches to a Mile

on many points, and the result of this disagreement was that advantage was taken of Mr. Sullivan's departure from the Hills at the close of 1829 (he was succeeded by Mr. J. Thomas) to transfer the greater portion of the Nílagiri Taluk, including the portion below the gháts at the northern base of the hills, to Malabar; Kótagiri and the adjoining portion of Péranganád alone remaining to Coimbatore. The transfer took place in January 1830. The ostensible reason was to check the smuggling of tobacco from Coimbatore across the range into Malabar, where there was a monopoly, the revenue in the latter district having been much affected by this illicit traffic.

"A free transit of tobacco," writes Mr. Lushington, "being permitted in every part of the Coimbatore District, a vast quantity of it is brought up during the fair season and concealed by the Malabar smugglers in different parts of the Neilgherry Hills adjoining the Kundahs, which are in the Malabar District. On a favourable opportunity the tobacco is conveyed to the low country by secret and almost inaccessible paths down the Kundah mountains, the smugglers keeping together in a large body on account of the numerous elephants and tigers with which the forest is infested, until they reach the open country of Malabar at the bottom, where they separate and disperse in different directions."

"The most obvious way of preventing this system of smuggling" was to transfer the Nílagiris to Malabar. The revenue of the portion transferred was said to be about Rupees 9,000 only. It was also thought desirable to place the two main passes under one authority. The Collector of Malabar at the time was Mr. Sheffield. Very shortly after this transfer it was found necessary to retransfer that portion of Péranganád which had been transferred to the Collector of Coimbatore, including, subsequently, the villages of Nellitoré, Odantoré, Velléru-Kambé and Anyúr-Kambé, in order that that officer might complete the Coonoor Ghát, which had now been begun. The Collectors of Malabar were allowed to please themselves regarding the retransfer of the Dévaráyapatnam tract, north of the Nílagiris.

Mr. Sullivan protests.

Mr. Sullivan, however, did not permit his beloved hills to be transferred from the district he had ruled so long without a severe struggle. He wrote a long and powerful minute on the subject, and, though his arguments were not to prevail at the time, twelve years later, during his term as a Councillor, they did prevail as stated hereafter. It was during this controversy that the contention in regard to the ancient dividing line of the Coimbatore and Malabar Districts came prominently forward, but it is not intended to sum up the arguments advanced on either side. The determination of the Governor in Council[1]

[1] *Extracts, Minutes Consultation*, 19th February 1830, No. 180.

CHAP. XII. — RECENT HISTORY.

on Mr. Sullivan's protest in regard to the boundary which had hitherto separated the Malabar and the Coimbatore Collectorates on the Nílagiris was as follows :—

"The Right Honorable the Governor in Council considers the evidence and information adduced by Captain Ward to be conclusive as to the fact that all the lands on the western bank of the Pykarra (or as he calls it, the Bukkarry) river belong to Malabar. Captain Ward could have no personal interest in the question; his duty was to survey the country; one of the chief objects of a survey is to mark distinctly the acknowledged boundaries of adjoining countries and to fix them in communication with the inhabitants when they are disputed. The boundary in this case was traced in 1822-23, and Captain Ward's accuracy in this respect was never, so far as the Government are aware, disputed[1] until the close of Mr. Sullivan's administration, when all other subjects of controversial disquisition had been exhausted."

This order is of interest in other ways, for it contains the first expression of the views of Government on the claims of the Tódas to be lords of the soil, and of the woods and of the wastes, a claim which was vigorously advocated by Mr. Sullivan, though they, *i.e.*, 450 of them, paid as grazing-tax Rupees 581 only. We learn that there was already a Tahsildar on the Hills with civil and criminal jurisdiction, but when appointed I have not been able to trace. It is noted that the average land revenue of the hills to 1813 was Rupees 14,762, but during the following fourteen years Rupees 6,499 only. In conclusion the Government ordered careful inquiries to be instituted into the alienation of lands, the prevention of which they considered of the greatest importance in view to the formation of a settlement on the Hills, and the minutes of Sir Thomas Munro on the rights of the Crown in the soil were commended to Mr. Sheffield for careful study.

Rapid extension of Ootacamand.

The transfer of the taluk to Malabar accomplished, the progress of the station was most rapid. Whilst in 1827 there were only seventeen houses in the station, within the following six years the number had risen to one hundred and two. A fine church, St. Stephen's, had been built at a cost of Rupees 24,000, provided in part by the Government, in part by the Church Mission Society, and in part by private subscriptions; and also a Roman Catholic chapel. A Grammar School[2] had been established by the Church Mission Society for the sons of Missionaries and of Europeans. Hospitals for Europeans and Natives, also

[1] This is hardly correct, as Mr. Sullivan called attention of the Survey Department to the error in his opinion on first receiving Captain Ward's map in July 1826.

[2] The building is now known as Sylk's Hotel. The prospectus will be found in Appendix V, 1st Ed., BAIKIE's *Nilgiri Hills*.

Jails, also a Club (the Club-house still used for this purpose was built by Sir William Rumbold, Bart., a partner of the famous house of Palmer and Co., Hyderabad), and lastly three large shops by Parsees from Bombay.[1] The Bombay authorities also had not been idle, and had established public quarters for their invalid officers at the house known as Bombay House, Elk Hill, and provided a Medical Officer for their care.[2] Meanwhile the selection and the opening out of the Coonoor Pass by Mr. Lushington led to the formation of a station at Coonoor, the first houses being those built by and for the Pioneers. An experimental farm had been begun at Kaity Valley under the Assistant Commissary-General Major Crewe. I would here mention that the establishment of a school, the building of the church, and the scheme for hill colonization by Europeans, were in great measure projected by Daniel Wilson, the eccentric but energetic Bishop of Calcutta, the only Indian Bishop at the time, and his zealous Assistant, Archdeacon Robinson of Madras. Bishop Wilson arrived in Calcutta in 1832, and shortly afterwards began his celebrated tour throughout his diocese which lasted five years, and during which he travelled 13,000 miles. Of him Lord Dalhousie remarked that he was the best man of business he had met in India. This zealous bishop also advocated a scheme for the Christian instruction of the native immigrants to the Hills. The consecration of St. Stephen's was a great day. Bishop Wilson took for his text the words "the wilderness and solitary place shall be glad for them and the desert shall rejoice and blossom as the rose." He referred to the natural wilderness as blooming around them, and "the valleys, till lately abandoned to solitude and desolation, teeming now with life, and in certain progress towards that time when they shall stand so thick with corn that they shall laugh and sing"—a prophecy which still remains to be fulfilled. He left the hills for the West Coast, journeying through Wainád. I cannot refrain from quoting his remarks on this district, though the conclusion will probably not meet with a response from the present settlers:—

CHAP. XII.

RECENT HISTORY.

Bishop Daniel Wilson.

"The cotton, coffee, and tobacco of this district, its mineral and other spontaneous productions, would, with even moderate care and pains, become an overflowing stream of wealth, and of that which statesmen love best—revenue. I never saw a country which, with a little management, might be rendered so *gloriously taxable*."

Court of Directors ask for report.

The station grew with marvellous quickness under Mr. Lushington's fostering care, but the expenditure he was incurring

[1] The principal, Nesserwanjee Jehangeer, is now represented by Framjee and Company.

[2] Several interesting sketches of Ootacamand and other places on the Hills will be found in HARKNESS, JERVIS, BAIKIE (1st Edition), and a series of large engravings by Captain McMurdy, all about 1834.

CHAP. XII. RECENT HISTORY.

was evidently viewed with doubtful favor by the Court of Directors, and about six months before he resigned office that eminently frugal and cautious body of rulers addressed a despatch to the Madras Government, asking for more definite information than had yet been given of the advantages which had attended the occupation of the Hills. They desired to know the number of houses, their cost; the names of owners and occupiers; past and present cost of establishments, and a list thereof; also to be furnished with a medical report; and ordered all correspondence on the subject of the Hills to be submitted to them. The Government, however, seem to have been forewarned; for in July, whilst the despatch was on its way, a Committee was appointed by Government to investigate the expenditure hitherto incurred, and that still necessary, on buildings, roads, and bridges, and the prospects of the Hills. The report of this Committee, which was composed of Major Strahan, Deputy Quartermaster-General, Major Hutchins, Adjutant-General, and Captain Eastment, who succeeded Major Kelso as Commandant of the Nílagiris, was submitted on the 10th August 1832, and contains much valuable information. The Committee enter at some length into the subject of the experimental farm established at Kaity Valley in April 1830, referred to in the chapter on agriculture; they recommend the employment of prisoners from Malabar on the Hills; they support Major Crewe's scheme[1] for encouraging colonization, having no hesitation in giving their opinion that cultivation might be carried to a very great extent, and remarking that "the flourishing appearance of the fields of grain around the small villages of the native Burghers prove the excellence of the soil, and the many flowing and unceasing streams of water from springs on the hills ensure constant irrigation during the driest parts of the season, and when the periodical rains may be scanty;" they recommend that great care should be taken in fixing the boundaries of lands granted to settlers and builders, and that the borders of the lake should be kept free from encroachment; they urge the desirability of forming an establishment for breeding cattle for the public service and supply of "salted provisions for the use of His Majesty's Navy," having observed "the herds of fine cattle belonging to the pastoral tribes." They then proceed to report on the public buildings, having "the advantage of the attendance of Lieutenant Pears,[2] of the corps of Engineers." The buildings detailed are St. Stephen's Church, the Convalescent Depôt, Southdowns, the Public Quarters, the Native Barracks, the Choultry, the Lock Hospital, and the Public Bazaar, portions of which they think

Committee of inquiry appointed.

[1] See Appendix VI, BAIKIE, 1st Edition.

[2] Now General Thomas Pears, R.E.

should be reserved as "a public granary." "These bazaars," they say, "were originally erected to encourage native merchants from the low country to settle at Ootacamand, and the arrangement appears to have succeeded perfectly, supplies of all kinds being in abundance;" but, as they are kept up at public expense, they suggest, after reserving the "granary," that the remainder should be granted to deserving occupants "on such conditions as may secure the several objects connected with them." The "Bake House" was to be treated likewise. They recommend the erection of permanent bridges in Ootacamand by the Pioneers and the completion of the bund. As regards the ghâts, they note that a road from Ootacamand to Coonoor was nearly completed; that the Coonoor Ghât was opened to an extent of five miles from the top, and only 2½ miles remained to be completed; they find the passage of the Bhavání at Mettapollium accomplished with difficulty in basket boats; so, whilst favoring the erection of a suspension bridge, they recommend the immediate construction of a "flying bridge" of boats. Two excellent travellers' bungalows had already been constructed, one at Coonoor and one at Mettapollium. On the road to the west by Gúdalúr they recommend that boats, "teengars," be provided for the Paikaré river, and suspension bridges for smaller streams. They find a "most excellent" travellers' bungalow at Neduwattam, but that at Paikaré fast going to decay. They advise the partial abandonment of the Kótagiri and Srimúgai Pass, as likely to be superseded by that of Coonoor, a road having been opened from that place to Kótagiri. They did not visit the Kúndas, but report the Sisapára ghât as already open, and recommend the construction of bungalows at the head and foot of the pass. At the Avalanché a large wooden bungalow, built at the Government Farm (Hoonsur?) in Mysore, had already been erected. The steepness of the gradients of some of the ghâts did not attract attention, for they remark that the Coonoor and Gúdalúr ghâts (the old with gradients of 1 in 8) will, on completion, "be easy for travellers and wheeled carriages of any description almost throughout the year." The times have changed; even one in nineteen does not suffice, but a railway is demanded for easy ascent. As regards the suitability of the hills as a sanitarium, they consider it "proved beyond a doubt," and submit a report from Dr. Baikie, Principal Civil Surgeon, in support of this opinion. They advise the establishment of a subordinate sanitarium at Dimhatti, where accommodation sufficient for ten officers already existed, originally intended for the use of a missionary establishment. They propose to provide also accommodation for fifty soldiers there. Their good opinion of the Nílagiri climate was unqualified, being "for the restoration of health unequalled in any part of India." "The Committee have never experienced and never heard of any place in

CHAP. XII.

RECENT HISTORY.

Europe where man's comfort and existence are so little endangered by the pressure or vicissitudes of climate." In conclusion they suggest that the Nílagiris should be committed to "the superintendence and undivided control of one active officer," who should be placed under the immediate orders of the Military Board; also that all the Medical Officers should be under "the immediate check and control of the Superintending Medical Officers."

Government Orders on report.

The recommendations of the Committee were mostly approved by Government. The employment of convicts was sanctioned; also one Overseer and two Sub-Overseers and fifty workmen for the Kaity Farm on 24, 12, and 8 rupees monthly respectively, the last "with a cloth jacket once in two years." These employés were to be chosen from the two companies of tent lascars employed by Government on the Farm "if they wished it;" a half-yearly statement of the produce of the land and expense of culture was to be submitted to Government. As regards grants of lands to settlers, they raised no objection if care be taken "that the new settlers have only land that has not been broken up, and that they make to the Todawars, when there is a mand in the vicinity, the same acknowledgments as the Burghers here also made to the Todawars. This will, of course, not preclude voluntary transfer and purchase of old lands from the Burghers in particular cases; but the general principle should be for the new settlers to occupy new unbroken land." Space was always to be left for public roads, an excellent provision, the neglect of which has cost the State dear in this district. The borders of the lake were to be reserved. The scheme for cattle-breeding was regarded favorably, but to be left to private enterprise. The bazaars were to be handed over to private persons, Government reserving the right to resume at any time on payment of the estimated value of the buildings. The works suggested in Ootacamand were to be carried out by Pioneer agency under Major Crewe, the special engineer establishment being dispensed with. The works recommended in the several passes were to be executed. The constitution of a sanitarium at Dimhatti was reserved for further consideration.

Major Crewe was appointed chief officer of the Hills as suggested, Captain Eastment going to Ganjam. The establishment on the Hills now consisted of eight officers costing 2,550 rupees monthly, of whom five were medical, the commanding officer drawing Rupees 400 staff allowance. In forwarding their report to the Court of Directors, Mr. Lushington expressed his confidence that the Home authorities would be gratified in observing at how small an expense his Government had been able "to open to the sick of all the Presidencies the use of the blessings which have been bestowed upon us in the Nilgiris in a temperate climate, a fertile soil, and a beauty of scenery not surpassed in any region of the globe," and desired that "similar statements of expense incurred at what are denominated the sanitaria of Bengal and Bombay" might be called for, as he had met with "no persons so deeply and so gratefully impressed with the superior benefits of the Nilgiris as those who visited the hills from Bengal and Bombay." CHAP. XII. RECENT HISTORY.

Mr. Lushington left the Hills, not to return, in August 1832, but on leaving, with thoughtful consideration for "subordinate ranks of the service," he placed the bungalow and gardens, which he had himself purchased at Dimhatti [1] from the Mission Society, on trust in the hands of the Collector of Coimbatore and of the Commanding Officer for the use of such free of all charge. The bungalows accommodated six families. Mr. Lushington's departure.

If it was a Civilian Collector, Mr. John Sullivan, who was the first to bring the Hills prominently to notice and to test their value in respect of climate and of soil, it was a Civilian Governor who first made them the permanent abode of Europeans, and placed their reputation as a seat for sanitaria and as a field of European enterprise almost beyond dispute. He seems to have created an enthusiasm in the hill country and its people which found expression in several works, such as Baikie's, Harkness' (Secretary to the Royal Asiatic Society), Jervis', and in other brochures; in fact the Nílagiri literary era belongs to his reign, though the works were not published until shortly after his retirement in the time of his successor Sir Frederick Adam. "It will be the glory of Mr. Lushington's Government," writes Captain Limond in June 1832, "without extravagant hyperbole, that he introduced Europe into Asia, for such are his improvements in the Nilgiris." Again: "The Coonoor and Koondah ghats (his own special works) will be to all succeeding times monuments of his beneficence and wisdom. * * * No power on earth can keep down the approved and tried celebrity of the Nilgiris. In the process of time they will become one of the noblest colonies in the known world. In future history Mr. Lushington will be recorded as their illustrious, enlightened, and early benefactor. * * * The Nilgiris were comparatively unknown before his day." And yet such is the absence of interest in the history of them displayed by Englishmen in this country, that probably not one in ten of the present residents have the vaguest notion of the debt they owe to this Civilian and his coadjutors. But the too bright hopes of these enthusiastic pioneers were destined soon to be overshadowed, though not quenched, by the rough lessons of experience.

---

[1] A note on the climate of Dimhatti will be found in the appendix to JERVIS.

CHAP. XII.

RECENT HISTORY.

Sir F. Adam succeeds. Medical report.

Mr. Lushington was succeeded by Sir Frederick Adam. The report on the extent and permanence of the benefits derived by Europeans from a resort to the Nílagiris, drawn up by the Medical Board (at that time composed of Messrs. Owen, Davies, and Hay), was submitted to Government, for transmission to the Honorable Court, on the 24th December, 1832. We find that to the end of October from date of establishment in January 1830 138 men of His Majesty and the Honorable Company's Services had been admitted, of whom 75 had been restored to good health, 11 much benefited, 14 discharged as incurable, 10 died, whilst 28 remained in the depôt. The majority of men sent to the Hills were young and not suffering from severe chronic complaints. In admitting that the public service had not derived extensive benefit from the Convalescent Depôt, the Board remark that it had hitherto labored under great disadvantages. "Placed in an elevated and unsheltered situation, without a surrounding wall, the building[1] was fully exposed to the south-west monsoon, while its vicinity to the bazaar afforded ready access to spirituous liquors." A more suitable building having been recently selected, they hoped that a more satisfactory trial might be made of the climate. They sum up the case as follows:—

"But, although the benefit hitherto derived from the Convalescent Depôt cannot, under these circumstances, be considered as indicating in a perfectly satisfactory manner the probable extent of the utility of a matured and well-regulated establishment of that nature, we think it proper on the present occasion to state that, from the information before us, we see no grounds for anticipating from such an establishment any results of much importance in a financial or political point of view, if indeed its maintenance should not be attended with positive loss. When the distance of the greater number of stations occupied by European troops from the Nilgiri Hills is considered, it will be obvious that a resort to them cannot be available for the cure of acute diseases, except in the cases of tedious and imperfect convalescence, which do not appear to have been numerous for some years past; and the medical reports received from the hills, while they generally represent the climate in a most favorable point of view, tend to show that it is not well adapted for the cure of chronic diseases attributable to a tropical climate, which chiefly lead to inefficiency, and consequently to discharge from the service or transfer to the invalid or pension establishments."

Taking the diseases which had led to invaliding in His Majesty's Army, they find that in very few cases would the climate be suitable for cure. So much for the soldiers.

As regards the officers of Government, civil and military, they note that, from the year 1826 to 1832, 238 sick Madras officers

[1] The present jail.

had been under the medical officers on the Hills, and during 1830, 1831, and 1832, 51 Bombay officers,[1] making a total of 289, of whom 136 had been cured, 54 improved, 25 sent to Europe, 12 died, 6 not improved, 16 transferred, and 40 remained. These figures show that the results in the case of officers were decidedly better than in that of the common soldiers.

Abolition of Convalescent Depôt.

The Convalescent Depôt, however, did not gain in popularity and on 4th July 1834, on the suggestion of Sir Frederick Adam, it was abolished, there being at the time only 16 patients in the depôt, the monthly cost of which was 413 rupees exclusive of the outlay on the hospital itself and repairs and commissariat charges. The cost for each soldier per annum was reckoned at Rupees 310. The benefits derived had fallen very short of those expected when it was established, and were in no way commensurate to the cost of the depôt. The medical establishment was reorganized, being reduced to two Assistant Surgeons at Ootacamand and an Apothecary at Kótagiri, the medical charges being thus reduced from 900 rupees to 570 rupees monthly. The lock hospital was abolished and converted into a common hospital. The books of the soldiers' lending libraries were distributed between Trichinopoly and Cannanore.

Administration defective.

Whilst the settlement was beginning to lose in reputation as a sanitarium, the general administration was found to have suffered greatly from the transfer of the greater portion of the plateau to Malabar. The result of this divided authority was that neither the Collector of Malabar nor Coimbatore took much interest in its affairs. Meanwhile the authority of the Commandant was confined to Ootacamand. The massacre in 1835 of no less than 58 Kúrumbas for witchcraft by the other hill tribes, the perpetrators of which crime were not detected, compelled the Government to action. Sir Frederick Adam had now the assistance of Mr. John Sullivan, who had succeeded to Council. In order to remedy the defects of the existing system and afford protection "to the lives and property of all classes of the inhabitants of the hills," the Government proposed to adopt a plan for placing the Nílagiris under an authority distinct from that of the Collectors of Malabar and Coimbatore, but resolved, in the meantime, to vest in the Officer Commanding police authority over all the Hills, and to appoint him Magistrate of the same, the revenue administration continuing as heretofore. The order of Government, 1st June 1832, constituting Ootacamand a general military bazaar was cancelled. The Foujdari Adálat were ordered to carry the magisterial arrangements into effect. This, however, the Court

Massacre of Kúrumbas.

[1] Under a medical officer of the Bombay Establishment.

CHAP. XII. RECENT HISTORY.

objected to do on the ground that it was opposed to Section 3, Regulation IX, 1816, and, on further reference by Government, declined to reconsider their opinion, but suggested the appointment of a Joint Magistrate. The Government then determined to legislate specially with the object of vesting in one officer, civil or military, the powers of a Collector, Magistrate, and Justice of the Peace, but limiting his civil jurisdiction to the powers of a Commanding Officer under Regulation VII of 1832. The Government observed that the annual net revenue of the Hills amounted to Rupees 9,427 only, and that it was necessary that the most economical system should be adopted for its realization. Moreover the hill tribes, it was noted, were most reluctant to attend the courts in the low country, it being beyond question that they frequently suffered oppression rather than complain to tribunals so distant from their homes. There was no resident European authority on the Hills, except the Commandant; and, as already stated, his jurisdiction was confined to Ootacamand. By this arrangement collision of authorities was to be avoided, the police and revenue administration improved, and the "concealed resources" of the hills developed. The Foujdari Adálat were to ascertain and report the proper limits of the separate charge to be created. After some further objections on the part of the Foujdari Adálat a draft Act was finally submitted to Government. This draft, amended by the omission of mention of Regulation VII of 1832, and the substitution in detail of the civil powers proposed to be conferred on the chief officer, was submitted to the Government of India in July 1836. Among the reasons urged in favor of special legislation were the necessity for controlling servants and of checking the destruction of woods. The Government remark that the felling of trees on the hills without authority would be attended with very injurious consequences to the low country, as the irrigation of the latter mainly depends upon the springs above, and that, if the wood is cut which shades them, the water would rapidly evaporate. This is the first indication of the care of Government for the woodlands. The Imperial Government, however,[1] would not hear of special legislation, being very averse, without the clearest necessity, to the enactment of special penal laws for particular portions of the country, whilst the Nílagiris possessed no such peculiarity in the circumstances of their position or population as to warrant their exemption from the ordinary criminal procedure. They, however, suggested that the Commandant should be invested with the powers of a Joint Magistrate, Deputy Collector, and Assistant Judge. The Sudr Adálat were directed to advise Government,

Special legislation proposed.

Destruction of woods.

[1] Lord Auckland had just succeeded Lord William Bentinck.

but they held that to carry out the Supreme Government's wishes it would still be necessary to legislate, as the Madras Government did not intend the Commandant to exercise so high civil power as indicated by the Supreme Government. They were urged to reconsider their views, but they adhered to their decision, and finally forwarded to Government a draft Act for adoption, which runs as follows :—

Draft Act.

"I. It is hereby enacted that it shall be competent to the Governor in Council of Fort St. George to vest in a separate officer, either civil or military, the powers of Collector and Magistrate under the Regulations of that Presidency, and of a Justice of the Peace upon the Nilagiri Hills, within such local limits as may be assigned by an order in Council, together with the special jurisdiction in civil suits described in the following section of this Act.

"II. The officer appointed under the provisions of this Act shall have exclusive authority to try and determine, in conformity with the rules prescribed for the proceedings of the Courts of Udalut generally, but as regards vakeels agreeably to the rules prescribed by clauses second and third, Section XIV, Regulation VI of 1816, or refer to arbitration under the rules prescribed by Regulation XXI of 1802 suits against any persons upon the Nilagiri Hills, those described in Article VII, Regulation V, 1827, not excepted, for personal property to an amount not exceeding four hundred rupees. The decisions of arbitrators shall be final, but an appeal within thirty days under the rules in force regarding appeals shall lie from all decrees of the said officer in suits exceeding twenty rupees, to the auxiliary court at Coimbatore, from whose decrees a special appeal shall be admissible by the Zillah Court of Salem under the provisions in force regarding special appeals."

Legislation finally negatived.

Lord Auckland, however, continued obdurate. His government would not admit the necessity of special legislation on the grounds urged by the Sudr, that the establishment of a special tribunal on the Nílagiris would, under existing regulations, "materially affect the rights, persons and property of the inhabitants," unless the court established differed from the ordinary tribunals, but they could not see why a court of ordinary jurisdiction should not be established there ; nor would they admit that the populations of the Nílagiris were worse off in the matter of civil courts than other parts of this Presidency, and therefore there was no reason for giving peculiar relief to persons who labored under no peculiar hardship. At the same time judicial reforms were promised to the people of the Nílagiris in common with the people of other districts.

Thus ended the first effort of the Madras Government to give a more complete form of administration to the Nílagiris. Thirty years and more were to pass before the district was to achieve independence and a constitution which in some

CHAP. XII. — RECENT HISTORY.

respects is inferior to that first proposed. Meanwhile the progress of the country was undoubtedly greatly retarded. It is possible that Lord Macaulay, who then guided the legislation of the Indian Empire, and who does not appear to have been very favorably impressed with the Nílagiris,[1] which he visited in 1834, may, on general principles, have thwarted the accomplishment of the wishes of the Madras Government.

Ootacamand constituted a Military Bazaar.

Sir Frederick Adam submitted, and orders were issued on 16th July 1837, abandoning the scheme and constituting Ootacamand a military bazaar. This Governor took considerable interest in the Hills and the people, and it was during his time that the Government first fixed the assessment to be paid for lands taken up by settlers, and virtually acknowledged the rights of the Tódas to the plateau—a policy that was approved by the Honorable Court of Directors in their despatch 10th April 1839, though qualified by the remark that they desired to "reconcile the interests of both parties," *i.e.*, Europeans and Natives. To this day do Government pay to the Tódas yearly compensation for the lands of the Ootacamand cantonment, excluding the mand reserves, amounting to Rupees 162-10-1—an undying witness to a policy, perhaps too generous, but comparing favorably with that which in 1862 deprived the Badagas of their immemorial right to obtain land under patta, compelling them equally with European settlers to purchase it under the Waste Land Rules.

Sir Frederick Adam resigned the Governorship of Madras 4th March 1837, and was succeeded by Lord Elphinstone, who held office till September 1842.

He, like his predecessor, took great interest in the Hills, and during his time, though the policy adopted in regard to the rights of the hill people was rigorously assailed, it remained unchanged as long as he held office. It was in his reign that the coffee industry first began on the eastern slopes, and other agricultural enterprises which have not been equally successful. He fixed his residence at Kaity, taking possession of the Government Farm buildings, and acquiring the land, which had been taken up for the farm in rather an irregular manner, in due form on a ninety-nine years' lease from the Badaga pattadars, paying them heavy compensation for their losses from the previous occupation, and a good price for the long lease. He expended considerable sums of money in building a large country house and laying out the grounds ornamentally, furnishing it in a style quite new to Indian experience. After he left the country the property

Lord Elphinstone at Kaity.

[1] He occupied Woodcock Hall when he joined Lord William Bentinck at Ootacamand.

was purchased by Mr. Casamajor of the Civil Service, formerly Resident at Mysore, for Rupees 15,000. This gentleman established a school here for Badaga children. On his death he left the greater portion of his property to the Basel Mission, who subsequently purchased the houses, which ever since have been the head-quarters of this Mission on the Nílagiris, and a convalescent depôt for their agents.

Mr. Sullivan urges the reannexation to Malabar.

In the year 1839 Mr. John Sullivan, on a petition from certain Badagas, revived the question of reannexing to Coimbatore that portion of the plateau which had been transferred to Malabar in 1830, and not retransferred in the following year. He urged that whilst this portion was, in regard to magisterial and police administration, under the Collector of Malabar, it was still under the court of Coimbatore, which was within the jurisdiction of the Southern Court of Circuit, whilst the Magistrate of Malabar was under the Western Court of Circuit; consequently, as Magistrate of the Nílagiris, he was not controlled at all, and the result was that the police were quite unchecked. Moreover, Ootacamand was under a military police, which was in reason whilst it was a military station, but not so now that it was practically a civil one. Further, the authority of the Tahsildar of Ootacamand was limited to the Malabar portion of the plateau, there being no similar functionary in the Coimbatore portion, which was consequently at a great disadvantage. He suggested the appointment of a Civil Assistant after the transfer of the tract to Coimbatore. The Government called on the Principal Collectors of Malabar and Coimbatore to report. The Collector of Coimbatore, Mr. Babington, whilst objecting to some of Mr. Sullivan's assertions and observing that the trade of the Hills was almost wholly with Malabar and Mysore, from which provinces the people drew their food supplies, thought reannexation on the whole desirable, though, in the interests of his own district, he urged that the tract should be constituted an independent district, or if this scheme, on financial grounds, could not be carried out, that it should be made a sub-collectorate. Mr. Underwood, Collector of Malabar, opposed the measure strongly on magisterial, financial, commercial and political grounds, holding that it was fraught with danger to his district and our rule there, and was likely to impede the progress of the Hills by separating them from the ports and commercial enterprise of the west coast. The Board of Revenue, however, were in favor of the change, remarking that there was no reason to expect that the revenue under the tobacco monopoly would decline, as urged by Mr. Underwood, if the transfer took place, for the increase in this revenue had been admittedly due to the manufacture of a superior article in Coimbatore and the vigilance of the preventive establishment of that district.

CHAP. XII. — RECENT HISTORY.

Government decline to make the transfer.

The Government however determined in July 1839 that sufficient grounds had not been adduced for the change, remarking that the objections urged by the Collectors of Malabar and Coimbatore thereto were equally strong and conclusive. This resolution was passed in Mr. Sullivan's absence, but he recorded a long minute of protest. In this paper he urged, as additional reasons, that the land tenure of the Hills differed from that of Malabar, and that the maintenance of a Military Commandant was unnecessarily expensive, and suggested the giving to the Tahsildar the powers of a District Munsif and of appointing a Civil Assistant. He also urged the expediency of employing the Coimbatore engineering staff instead of that of Malabar. Nothing was done. The matter came up again the following year in consequence of a dispute between two villages on the new Coonoor road, Bikhatti and Yellannallé, situated on the boundary line of Péranganád and Mékanád. In connection with this case Mr. Conolly, the ill-fated Collector of Malabar, recommended the appointment of a District Munsif on the hills. "Formerly," he writes, "all differences were settled by the Burghers among themselves. The influx of strangers, and the altered state of their society, has led them, as appears from the present instance, not to be always satisfied with this simple mode of administering justice."

The Commandant appointed Joint Magistrate and District Munsif.

The result, however, was a partial reform; the Commandant was appointed Joint Magistrate to the Magistrates of Malabar and Coimbatore, and also District Munsif. These changes appear to have been, in a measure, due to instructions from home. Colonel King, who had succeeded Colonel Crewe, resigned shortly afterwards (November 1840), and Colonel Jennings, his assistant, was appointed in his room by Lord Elphinstone, with the designation of Staff Officer of Ootacamand, on the same allowances, a designation which was again changed to Officer Commanding the Hills by the Marquis of Tweeddale in 1843. The Staff Officer was to be aided by two assistants, one of whom was in charge of the roads, the other of the post offices and other miscellaneous offices. All hill officers however were, under the imperative instructions of the Honorable Court (Despatch, 2nd March 1842), to hold office for two years only, and to be chosen from officers in the low country whose health required the change of climate. At this time also Lord Elphinstone had in contemplation the location of a European corps on the Hills, and one of the reasons for changing the designation of the resident officer was that he might have to be superseded by the officer commanding the corps. The Hills were still regarded less as a sphere for British enterprise than as a home for British troops.

Mr. Sullivan's arguments in favor of radical changes in the administration, which were opposed by the other Civilian Member of Council, Mr. Bird, were not to prevail in Lord Elphinstone's time, but just before his resignation the question of reannexation came up again, and by the irony of fate, on the motion of Mr. Charles May Lushington, Member of Council, a near relative of Mr. Stephen Rumbold Lushington, who was responsible for the transfer to Malabar. He ably represented the anomalous position of the Nílagiri administration, remarking that, although the Staff Officer had been appointed Joint Magistrate with jurisdiction over the whole tract, he was virtually subordinate to no Magistrate, and was permitted by an order in Council to try in one district offences committed in another. He writes:

"From the hill just above Ootacamund the sadr station of Coimbatore may be seen, but instead of allowing any of our revenue subjects aggrieved by the acts of the revenue officers at Ootacamund to proceed and lay their grievances before the Collector of a station they can see from their own doors, they are forced, by the present order of things, to go to a country inimical to their health and habits, and to travel through a dense feverish jungle upwards of 160 miles, being nearly four times the distance they would have to go for redress were Ootacamund placed under the authority of the Coimbatore Collectorate."

But Government is a slowly moving machine, and the only point gained was the referring of the subject with other matters appertaining to the Hills, for the decision of the Court of Directors, it being held that the powers of Joint Magistrate and District Munsif, recently conferred on the Staff Officer, met the most salient objections of Mr. Sullivan.

Marquis of Tweeddale, Governor. Retransfer of the second portion of the Hills to Coimbatore.

But the Marquis of Tweeddale, who assumed office on the 24th September 1842, resolved immediately to adopt Mr. Sullivan's proposal, and, on St. Valentine's day, 1843, ordered the retransfer to Coimbatore of the eastern portion of the Hills, or rather the portion of them which formerly belonged to it, leaving to Malabar the jurisdiction over the tract west of the Paikaré river, the position of the two districts previous to the year 1830.[1] The Collector of Malabar, however, was admonished to provide for the education of the Tódas within his range in accordance with the instructions of the Honorable Court of Directors, who, in their despatch, 14th December 1842, had expressed regret that the attempts of the Madras Government to introduce education and civilization among the Tódawars had hitherto been unsuccessful, but trusted "from the interest taken in the matter by the local officers" that no means, when available,

[1] The Nellambúr Rája was at the time mooting claims to the country west of this river.

CHAP. XII. RECENT HISTORY.

would be neglected to secure this important object. The Marquis of Tweeddale, like his predecessors, took a lively interest in the Hills, and was perhaps more friendly to European settlers than any of them, Mr. Lushington excepted. Early in his reign the policy of the Home Government underwent a marked change in regard to the grant of Government waste lands to Europeans, which finds expression in the celebrated despatch of the 21st June 1843. It was during his governorship, which lasted till 23rd July 1848, that coffee planting by Europeans was begun in the Wainád and on the western slopes of the Nídumalés. To him Ootacamand owes the Lake Road. But the principal act which will cause his name to be remembered was the determination to establish a military station on the Hills, not a mere convalescent depôt, but a cantonment, with a British regiment permanently located there. The abolition of the depôt at Ootacamand seems to have intensified the desire of the Government to have a home for soldiers in this salubrious climate at a lower elevation and on a more suitable scale. It will be remembered that Lord Elphinstone also favored a similar scheme. The subject of locating troops in the hills had for some time been occupying the attention of the Government of India and the Home Government, and already more than one such station had been established in the north of India. The immediate cause of its settlement was the determination of the Government to build barracks at Bangalore and Trichinopoly. The Marquis of Tweeddale desired to lay out the sum sanctioned for Trichinopoly, about £45,000, in building barracks on the Nílagiris, removing thither the European corps from Trichinopoly. Orders were issued to select two sites, one near Ootacamand and one near Coonoor, in the Jackatalla Valley; the latter site now known as Wellington, was pointed out to the Marquis by Captain Ouchterlony, then engaged on the survey of the Hills. The proposal to build near Ootacamand was abandoned for reasons with which I am not acquainted, but the Government resolved on building temporary barracks, similar to those used in Bengal, in the Jackatalla Valley, though the medical officer reporting on the site had brought to their notice that in one portion of the area, though not that on which buildings were to be placed, there existed ruins of a village which the Badagas asserted had been abandoned for its feverishness. Though the proposal to build barracks on the Nílagiris was approved by the Government of India in February 1847, yet, owing to political reasons regarding the disposition of European troops in India, the question was not settled in the time of the Marquis of Tweeddale. It must not be forgotten that at this time there were strategic objections to the Nílagiris as a station for troops, which hardly

Coffee planting begun.

CHAP. XII.

RECENT HISTORY.

apply now that a railway has been constructed to the foot of the ghâts. No carriage could then be obtained except from Mysore, Salem, and Coimbatore; and in view to meet this difficulty it was proposed to establish cattle depôts at Gúndulpet and Mettapollium. It was feared also that the troops would contract fever in marching from the Hills, especially on the Mysore side.

Sir Henry Pottinger. Plans submitted for barracks at Wellington.

Such was the state of affairs when Sir Henry Pottinger succeeded to office, which he retained until April 1854. He differed from his predecessor in regard to the character of the barracks, which he considered should be permanent, and consequently the plans for such a barrack, to accommodate 500 men, were called for, and the plans for temporary barracks remitted for further alterations. Meanwhile orders were given in the Revenue Department to acquire the site from the Badagas, and to collect timber on the Hills. This order was afterwards countermanded, and teak selected for the work. In November 1849 two sets of plans and estimates, the one for temporary barracks, amounting to Rupees 61,500, the other for permanent two-storied barracks, amounting to Rupees 4,20,000, were submitted to Government. If stone were to be used instead of brick, the extra cost was estimated at Rupees 30,000. Before sanction the Medical Board were called on for report on the sites and plans. Their reply was favorable as regards the site; they also approved a two-storied building. The scheme for a Convalescent Depôt was sanctioned by the Home authorities in 1850-51 and the work begun,[1] though the boundaries were not fixed and notified until 3rd May 1853. In 1852 Sir Richard Armstrong, the then Commander-in-Chief, recommended that the name should be changed from Jackatalla to Wellington, in honor of the illustrious duke, who from the first had evinced an interest in the establishment of a sanitarium on the Nílagiris, which he must have seen from afar in his youth, and had expressed his unqualified approbation of the measure. The proposal did not find favor with Sir Henry Pottinger, being unprecedented, and likely to be unintelligible to the natives. Eight years later, 3rd April 1860, Sir Charles Trevelyan thought otherwise, holding "that this interesting military establishment could not be connected with a more appropriate name" than Wellington, and ordered it to be so called henceforth. On the 30th November preceding this notification the post of Commandant on the Nílagiris was abolished, that of Joint Magistrate

[1] It was the building of the barracks, and consequent present and prospective demand for firewood, which led, in 1849, Captain Ouchterlony to suggest the establishment of Australian fire-wood reserves. In the first instance the trifling sum of Rupees 74 was sanctioned for raising nurseries.

CHAP. XII. — RECENT HISTORY.

continuing, and the Military police of Ootacamand transferred to the civil authorities. The office of Commandant, which is now represented by that office at Wellington, had existed thirty years.

Coonoor Church built.

Meanwhile the station of Coonoor had been rapidly growing in importance, partly from the extension of coffee plantations and partly from the preference shown by many for its mild climate, especially during the prevalence of the south-west monsoon. About the year 1850 the residents and others subscribed a sum of Rupees 6,000 for the erection of a church, Lieutenant-General Kennett granting the land for the site and burial ground. The designs were prepared by Captain Francis, the Executive Engineer at Jackatalla. The sum not being sufficient to complete the work—part of which, including the tower, having been constructed of brick and clay, was washed down during the monsoon rains of 1852—application was made to Government to complete the building at a cost of Rupees 6,500, and to take it over for the use of the Chaplain who had already been appointed for the charge of Jackatalla and Coonoor. This the Government ultimately consented to do. Fresh estimates were prepared, and the church with the tower finally completed at the beginning of 1854 at a total cost of Rupees 16,160, of which Rupees 8,982 were provided by private contributions.

Small Cause Court Judge appointed at Ootacamand.

The progress of the Nílagiris and the consequent increase of litigation induced the Government, Lord Harris being Governor, on the 1st November 1855 to establish a Principal Sudr Amín's Court at Ootacamand under Act VI, 1855, and Regulation VII, 1827, with Small Cause Court powers in suits of Rupees 500 and under. The Commandant was accordingly deprived of the powers of District Munsif, but continued to be Joint Magistrate. The salary of the new Judge, Mr. Burgess,[1] a Barrister and First Judge of the Madras Small Cause Court, was Rupees 800. Arrangements were made also for the Judge of Coimbatore holding criminal sessions at Ootacamand.

Proposal to appoint Civil and Sessions Court rejected.

It should here be stated that in the preceding year the Sudr Court, in view to improve the judicial administration of the Hills, proposed to establish a Civil and Sessions Court, as had been done at Tellicherry and Honúr, on a salary of Rupees 1,750. The Government rejected the scheme, partly because of the expense, and partly because the intermediate character of the salary would necessitate constant changes in the Judges. The Sudr Court then proposed an auxiliary Civil and Sessions Court, with an Uncovenanted Judge, who in criminal cases was to exercise the exceptional powers of the Agent to the Governor in Ganjam and

[1] Mr. Burgess was succeeded by Mr. James Ouchterlony, who opened out the coffee estates in the valley called after him.

Vizagapatam. An appeal was to lie to the Court of Coimbatore in suits exceeding Rupees 10,000 in value. The Government approved this plan, but it was opposed in the Viceregal Legislative Council by Mr. D. Elliott on the grounds (1) that it was impolitic to give an uncovenanted officer powers exceeding those of a covenanted Subordinate Judge; (2) that the litigation on the Hills did not demand a Judge with higher powers than a Principal Sudr Amín; (3) that the Criminal Sessions Court being light, could be provided for by the Judge of Coimbatore holding occasional sessions at Ootacamand. Mr. Elliott's views prevailed, and Act XXV, 1855, was passed.

Assistant Judge transferred from Combaconum to Ootacamand.

The Court continued until the 1st June 1858, when it was abolished, or rather transferred to Combaconum, and the Assistant Judge's Court at that town transferred to Ootacamand, Mr. E. W. Bird, C.S., being made Assistant Judge on a salary of Rupees 1,400. By notification on the 7th August 1858, the Kúndas, the Nídumalé tract west of the Paikaré river, and the Dévaráyapatnam tract north of the Nílagiris were included in the jurisdiction of the court. A proposal to include the Nambalakód amshom of South-East Wainád with the Ouchterlony Valley in the jurisdiction was negatived on the ground that a Malayálam-speaking people would be brought under the operation of a Tamil court.

Kúndas and Nídumalé annexed.

The opening out of the Government cinchona plantations west of the Paikaré river—narrated in a subsequent chapter—in 1860-61, the claims urged to one of the sites by the Nellambúr Rája, and the impending introduction of the Waste Land Rules, among other reasons, induced the Government in 1863 to annex to the Coimbatore collectorate the Kúndas and the tract west of the Paikaré already placed under the civil jurisdiction of the Ootacamand Court. About the same time the Madras Government, now presided over by Sir William Denison, who had succeeded to office in 1861, resolved on "the creation of a Civil and Sessions Judgeship on the Nílagiris on Rupees 2,000, in lieu of the Subordinate Judgeship, with the view of placing the administration of justice both in the lowlands of Coimbatore and on the Nílagiri Hills on a more efficient footing."

First Commissioner Mr. Breeks.

It had been found that the unnecessarily prolonged absence of the Judge of Coimbatore for the sessions on the Hills had greatly hindered business in the Coimbatore Court. This arrangement was sanctioned by the Imperial Government, but was not found to work satisfactorily, and was finally abolished by Act I, 1868, which provided for the separation of the district from Coimbatore, and fixes its present administrative and judicial constitution. The first Commissioner appointed under this Act

CHAP. XII. — RECENT HISTORY.

was Mr. James Wilkinson Breeks, who retained the office till his death on the 7th June 1872. He succeeded in securing the confidence of Government and the loving respect of all classes within his jurisdiction. The Memorial Schools which bear his name were built in great measure by public subscriptions as a testimony of this regard, whilst in St. Stephen's Churchyard is his tomb, erected by the members of his Service.

The Ouchterlony Valley added to the district.

During the commissionership of his successor, Mr. J. R. Cockerell, on the 15th July 1873, the tract known as the Ouchterlony Valley was added to the district, and on the 31st March 1877 three amshoms of the south-eastern division of Wainád.

Industries.

The transfer of the Indian Empire to the direct rule of the Crown, and the gradual extension of the provincial powers of the Madras Government, have resulted in the rapid progress of this district in common with the rest of the Presidency.

The great industries of coffee, tea, and cinchona cultivation have resulted from the liberation of private enterprise from former restrictions, the adoption of more considerate land rules, and, as regards cinchona, the fostering care of Government. The extension of the cultivation of cereals and other articles of food by natives and others has been equally rapid. Meanwhile public buildings and institutions have sprung into existence. Churches, libraries, and schools have been built, and newspapers established. Two important towns have been constituted Municipalities, and the district a Local Fund Circle. In a word, though much remains to bed one to place the prosperity of the Nílagiris on a sure footing, the progress of the past gives a good hope that this land has a bright future before it, and a place in the history of English enterprise and civilization in South India, which may, in the times to come, if our race is true to its traditions, be looked back upon with pride by future generations both of Englishmen and Natives.

Prospects of the district.

CHAPTER XIII.

REVENUE HISTORY.

INTRODUCTION.
PART I.—(a) THE CULTIVATING TRIBES; (b) THE GRAZIERS.
PART II.—EUROPEAN AND OTHER IMMIGRANTS.
PART III.—REVENUE SURVEYS.

INTRODUCTION.

Subject divided.—Revenue system of North Coimbatore prevails.—Major McLeod's settlement.

CHAP. XIII. — REVENUE HISTORY.

Subject divided.

THE history of the Land Revenue administration of the Nílagiris may be treated conveniently under three heads: firstly, that of the hill-tribes; secondly, that of the settlement of Europeans; thirdly, that of the revenue survey. The first head may be subdivided into that relating to (1) the cultivators, viz., the Badagas, the Kótas, the Irulas, and Kúrumbas; (2) the graziers, the Tódas. The land revenue economy of the Nílagiris, as far as the permanent cultivators—*i.e.*, the Badagas and the Kótas—are concerned, was and is practically that of the Coimbatore District, to which the tracts which had been partially brought under the plough at the time of the cession of the country to the British mostly belonged; whilst the position of the wandering or intermittent cultivators, the Irulas and the Kúrumbas, does not essentially differ from that of similar tribes or cultivators occupying the slopes of hill-ranges in Southern India; on the other hand the position of the grazing tribe, the Tódas, is perhaps unique.

Revenue system of North Coimbatore prevails.

At the date of the cession of the Dévanaikenkóta Taluk to the English, the Hills, which formed a portion of it, appear to have been under the same revenue system as the rest of North Coimbatore, although the village areas were still loosely defined and the use of land practically unrestricted. It may be mentioned in passing however that there was no renter[1] of the monopoly of the produce of the forests, such as honey, wax, and resin. This

[1] *Vide* Buchanan, Chap. IX.

CHAP. XIII.

REVENUE HISTORY.

exception is noteworthy, as it appears from a letter[1] from the Collector of Coimbatore to the Board of Revenue (3rd August 1843) that in other hill-tracts in that district the monopoly of the forest produce was farmed out.[2] The inference is that the Badagas were too powerful to submit to the exactions of a renter.

Major McLeod's settlement.

Immediately after the cession of the Coimbatore District the settlement of its revenue was entrusted to Major McLeod, the Principal Collector of Coimbatore and Malabar. The object of Major McLeod's settlement was to rectify the evils of Tippu's revenue system. It will be remembered that Haider Áli had abolished the ancient system of division of produce and had introduced a fixed money assessment on the cultivated lands of each village. The collection of the revenue was entrusted to amildars, whose charges were of considerable extent. Tippu increased the number of the amildars and decreased the area entrusted to each. He required the cultivators to pay for all cultivable lands, whether cultivated in the year or not. The result was that the ryots became terribly impoverished, and when the country came under our rule most of them were heavily in arrears. Major McLeod's first settlement was in December 1799. It was based upon the accounts rendered by the curnams. Being fully persuaded of the inaccuracy and falsity of many of these accounts, Major McLeod proposed to the Board of Revenue that the arable lands of each village should be measured by competent surveyors, trained in Salem. The project was approved. Operations began in North Coimbatore in March 1800 and were completed in March 1801. The area of each field was recorded, the cultivable area being distinguished from non-cultivable, whether waste, or grass, or occupied by water-courses, &c. The assessment of each field was noted, also the name of the holder or holders and the character and legality of the tenure, and such other particulars as were considered necessary for the completeness of a revenue register. After this information was complete the surveyors and others were employed to classify the lands according to their fertility after full consultation with the

[1] The following passage from Mr. Wroughton's letter is deserving of mention: "This (tax on forest produce) is one of a class of imposts which have the effect of marking the sovereignty and defining the boundary limits more effectually than could be arrived at under any other system, and with reference to the proximity of this district (Coimbatore) to the States of Travancore and Cochin, as also to Malabar, and its being bounded by dense and impenetrable jungles, it appears to me that the continuance of this tax is beneficial also in a political point of view, and that its interruption would be an inexpedient measure."

[2] *Vide* also letter from this Collector to the Board of Revenue, 15th March 1856.

heads of the villages. Subsequently the lands were assessed by the Collector according to a fixed scale, which provided twelve grades of assessment for dry and four for wet and garden lands. Topes of fruit trees were assessed separately. In fixing the grades the general character of the taluk or neighbourhood was taken into account. This survey and the subsequent settlement affected the land revenue considerably, but to relieve the people from any temporary inconvenience caused by the change it was provided that 'all diminution of the former rates were to be remitted to the inhabitants, but all augmentations above one-tenth of the actual assessment were to be divided among the two or three first years after the survey, instead of being demanded in the first.'[1] The result was that the revenue for Fasli 1211 showed a decrease on that of the preceding year of 7,224 star pagodas, though the ultimate increase was estimated at 30,426 star pagodas. The estimate was more than realized.

[1] See letter from Board of Revenue to Lord Clive, 18th November 1802.

PART I.

(a.) CULTIVATING TRIBES—The Badagas, Kótas, Irulas, Kúrumbas.

First settlement of the Nílagiris.—Mr. Sullivan proposes a survey.—Revenue.—Rates of assessment.—Changes proposed, 1862.—The shifting system.—"Ain" grass and "Grazing" puttas.—Revenue Board's proposals.—Decision of Government.—Revision of assessment.—Rates settled by Government—approved by Secretary of State.—Settlement introduced—extends to plateau only.—State of revenue accounts.—Settlement of Kúndas.—Lands for cultivation to be obtained under Waste Land Rules only.—Effects of the measure.—Kótas and other aboriginal cultivators.—Mode of assessing lands.

CHAP. XIII, PART I. — REVENUE HISTORY. — First settlement of Nílagiris.

I have above very briefly sketched the first recorded pymash, or settlement based on measurements, of the Coimbatore District, as its effects extended to the Nílagiri plateau, raising the revenue from Rupees 13,425 to Rupees 18,267. I say its effects, for Mr. Sullivan, in a letter to the Board of Revenue, 6th March 1819, states that although surveyors were sent in 1800-1 to the Nílagiris, they did not stay, but "sent accounts of their work, and it was taken for granted that they had completed it." On ascending the Hills he found that the survey was entirely nominal, and that not an acre of land had been measured. "The extreme inclemency of the climate indeed," he goes on to say, "frightened the surveyors and prevented them from doing more than making an estimate of the quantity and quality of the land, and of fixing the old rates of teerwa upon it." He accordingly proposed to survey the lands at a cost of Rupees 800, not with any intention of attempting a new classification or of interfering with the existing rates of assessment, which he regarded as extremely favorable to the ryots, but simply to ascertain accurately the extent of their occupations. With this letter he forwarded the following statement of the revenue derived from the Hills during the nineteen years ending 1818, which is interesting. He attributed the falling off in receipts to the want of a road. The survey was approved by Government, but I have not been able to trace any report of its completion :—

Mr. Sullivan proposes a survey.

Revenue of Nílagiris.

		RS.			RS.
Fasli 1209	...	13,425	Fasli 1219	...	15,067
" 1210	...	13,425	" 1220	...	15,067
" 1211	...	18,267	" 1221	...	12,055
" 1212	...	18,445	" 1222	...	10,052
" 1213	...	16,855	" 1223	...	9,639
" 1214	...	16,197	" 1224	...	9,533
" 1215	...	15,994	" 1225	...	14,350
" 1216	...	16,613	" 1226	...	8,393
" 1217	...	15,418	" 1227	...	8,925
" 1218	...	15,067			

CHAP. XIII, PART I. REVENUE HISTORY.

But whatever the results of the field measurements may have been, Mr. Sullivan did not attempt, during the period the Hills were under his control, to interfere with the settlement of Major McLeod as revised two or three years later by Mr. Garrow, who succeeded Major McLeod as Collector of Coimbatore. Writing in January 1835, Mr. Sullivan remarks that this assessment, which did not, on the average, exceed half a rupee a cawnie, and "which was in former times as much as the land could afford to pay, has become, under the improved circumstances of the people, little more than a quit-rent; but as the owners, in common with their neighbours in Malabar, have enjoyed the advantage of a light tax so long, the faith of Government is in fact pledged for its continuance."

Rates of assessment.

These rates[1] were as follows :—

Rate.		Per Bullah.			Per Acre.			Rate.		Per Bullah.			Per Acre.		
		RS.	A.	P.	RS.	A.	P.			RS.	A.	P.	RS.	A.	P.
1st	...	4	6	4	1	2	5	9th	...	1	12	2*	0	7	4
2nd	...	4	1	10	1	1	3	10th	...	1	7	6*	0	6	2
3rd	...	3	8	5*†	0	14	9	11th	...	1	2	10*	0	4	11
4th	...	3	3	8	0	13	6	12th	...	0	14	1†	0	3	8
5th	...	2	15	0*†	0	12	4	13th	...	0	9	5	0	2	5
6th	...	2	10	4*	0	11	1	14th	...	0	7	0	0	1	10
7th	...	2	5	7*†	0	9	10	15th	...	0	4	8	0	1	3
8th	...	2	0	11*†	0	8	7								

Changes proposed in 1862.

No change of any importance took place in the rates of assessment on lands held by hill cultivators without the Settlements for forty years after our advent, but in 1862 the question of the land system of the Nílagiris came under discussion, and this discussion resulted in important changes in the tenure of land by the hill-men and in the rates of assessment paid by them. The causes which induced these changes appertain mainly to the gradual extension of coffee and other plantations on the hills and slopes, and the consequent demand for land for such purposes; but there were certain evils in the land system of the Hills which aggravated the disadvantages of the position of the settler and

[1] Only the rates marked with an asterisk are mentioned in Mr. Conolly's letter to the Board of Revenue, 20th July 1833. Those which practically were in operation on the plateau are marked with a cross. Major Ouchterlony gives also two rates for potato cultivation, Rupees 7 and Rupees 5 per bullah for good and inferior land respectively. These, however, appear to have been special rates in the Settlements. The rates of assessment for lands taken up under the darkhast rules, where lands may still be so granted, differ according to the locality. In the Segúr tract it is Rupees 1-2-4 on dry and wet lands per cawnie of 1·32 acres, whilst garden lands are assessed at Rupees 2-5-7 per bullah of 3·82 acres. In South-East Wainád the rate is Rupees 1-4-0 per acre on cultivation, besides 8 annas jemnabhogam or landlord's fee. In the Wainád hill-tribes are permitted to cultivate hill slopes not being forest at the ordinary assessment without darkhast. The revenue so derived is debited to Seva jamma.

demanded a remedy. The evils lay in the Coimbatore shifting or "Bhurty" system, and in the unique custom of that district in regard to grass and fallow lands. Under the existing system of land tenure, under which holdings were both shifting and almost undefined, the hill cultivators were able easily to raise fictitious or seemingly fictitious claims to lands which strangers sought to acquire, and were thus enabled either to defeat the object of the applicant, or compel him to buy out the claimant in order to secure possession.

The shifting system.

The "Bhurty" or shifting system was a necessary consequence here, as elsewhere, of the poorness of soil and of the poverty of the cultivators. A poor soil is easily exhausted if called on to bear crops which abstract its food-producing qualities or essentials. To supply the loss a recuperative process is necessary. If left waste, nature herself slowly performs this process, but art renders such a rest or fallow unnecessary. Deep delving or ploughing, application of manure, and change of crop, will supply in a few months, and far more abundantly, the needs for which nature demands years. The hill cultivator was poor and ignorant, and so the State allowed him to possess a tract or tracts five or even ten times greater in extent than the portion for which he actually paid assessment, and which was shown in his annual putta. These several tracts might be miles apart, and sometimes even in different náds or villages. If 20 acres only were entered in the putta, the puttadar paid for, and was supposed to cultivate 20 acres only; but his claim might extend to over 200 acres in scattered fields, in which he selected the 20 acres, in one or many pieces, which he chose to cultivate each year, according to the condition of the soil or season, or other local or peculiar necessity. Nor had the separate lots which the putta was supposed to reserve to the ryot been ever properly defined or limited, or even identified. They were as often *in posse* as *in esse*, and the potentiality of possession really depended upon the will of the headmen and the connivance of the lower revenue officials. The position was rendered still more complicated by the ancient custom of joint or undivided family holdings, a system which is only now beginning to give way before the growing desire for individual and separate holdings consequent on the increasing prosperity and intelligence of the people. It may safely be said that, with the exception of the home-farm lands of each hamlet, the rest of the area, cultivable or uncultivable, forest or swamp, included within the bounds of the several náds or rural divisions was practically at the disposal of the village elders and subordinate revenue officials. The ill-defined and ill-understood rights of Government were virtually ignored, and Circar wood or waste on the agricultural portions of the plateau, that is, the tracts occupied by the Badagas, to all intents and purposes consisted only of deep forest or tracts which no man cared to claim for agricultural purposes, or which had never been cleared for cultivation.

Such was the shifting system—a system dear to the people, but inimical to agricultural progress. Its abolition was a necessity; but the way in which it was to have been carried into effect—had not a lenient system of demarcation or practically, though not technically, of revenue settlement prevailed—would undoubtedly have proved a violent and unexampled invasion of the rights and privileges of the hill cultivators.

"Ain" grass and "grazing" puttas.

The two other accidents of the Coimbatore agricultural system which were alleged to be abuses were that known as the "ain" grass and that of "grazing" puttas. As regards "ain" grass, it had been the usage of Coimbatore to permit the ryot to retain in his possession under this name a certain portion of his holding as fallow at one-fourth the original assessment. The extent thus held was not to exceed one-fifth of his regular holding. The grazing puttas were granted for inferior lands, known as "Paravapillu vari," to be retained as pasture at one-quarter the ordinary assessment until such land was required for cultivation by himself or another ryot. The evil complained of, in regard to the former, was that a ryot was practically at liberty to select any portion of his nominal holding as fallow, and thus defeat a selector in his desire to obtain land in his neighbourhood; as regards the latter, that it gave a preferential right to the occupier. The evils complained of in all these cases were, in the main, due to the absence of a definitive survey and settlement.

The Revenue Board's proposals.

When the alleged grievances were first discussed by the Board of Revenue, they recommended, as regards the "Bhurty" system, that it should practically cease, on the principle prevailing in the plains that when a ryot fails to pay his assessment, having no grounds for remission, his right to the land lapses; consequently, when a hill ryot "shifted" his cultivation, he was to be regarded as having relinquished his land, which accordingly was to be available for the first applicant to whom the Collector at his discretion might transfer it. So long as he cultivated or paid his assessment he might sell at his pleasure. In suggesting this radical measure they argued that—

"So long as unoccupied land is abundant there is no objection to the Burgher "shifting" his cultivation as much as he pleases, but he cannot naturally claim a right to all the land which in a series of years he has thus occasionally cultivated; still less can Government, in justice to the general community, admit such a right. Now that land required on the Hills by European settlers for agricultural purposes is invariably sold by auction, subject to an unvarying annual

CHAP. XIII, PART I. — REVENUE HISTORY.

assessment of Rupee 1 per acre, while the Burgher can at any time take up a portion at rates of assessment generally below that sum, there is clearly no reason why any further concession should be made to the latter."

As regards "grazing puttas" the Board strongly urged the inequity of restricting unnecessarily the privileges of the hill cultivators in regard to grazing rights. "The abuse of privilege" they observe, "is to be guarded against, but is not sufficient reason for withholding what general principles of good policy would concede, and that the original occupants of any particular locality have certain preferential rights of common over new-comers is recognised in every civilized system of polity. That such a right has been paid for by a villager should certainly strengthen his claim rather than weaken it. The paramount importance in an agricultural community of a sufficient extent of grazing land to maintain an ample stock is even more than ordinarily indisputable in a naturally poor country like Coimbatore, where the requisite extent must be greater to provide the same amount of nourishment for the cattle, and the necessity for an abundant supply of manure is more imperative, and the Board would strongly deprecate any innovations which might tend unduly to restrict the facilities for attaining these objects." But they were anxious to throw no unnecessary difficulties in the way of intending *bonâ fide* cultivators; and to prevent a ryot from paying temporary full assessment instead of one-quarter in order to defeat a settler from obtaining land, they proposed that whilst the land continued in the puttadar's possession no reduction from full assessment should be allowed, except in regard to the "ain grass" fifth, and that the putta should be required to be renewed annually. The "ain grass" privilege, it will be noted, was to be preserved intact.

Decision of Government.

The Government did not deal with the suggestions regarding "shifting" puttas, but as regards "grazing puttas" they questioned the validity of the Board's reasons, holding that, as the Badagas did not desire to take up the land with any intention of permanently improving it, their tenure should be regarded as annual, and as giving no preferential title; and, even as regards the immemorial "ain grass" privilege, the Government would not admit that so small a payment should secure more than the right of pasturage for a year. A preferential right would enable the Badagas virtually to exclude strangers, for whilst they held that in the plains, where boundaries are definitely fixed, there would be little risk of abuse, it was otherwise on the Hills.

Revision of assessments.

This order of Government did not touch the question of assessments, which, together with the general question of restricting the roving cultivation of the Badagas without ignoring their ancient rights, formed for some time previous to its issue the subject of correspondence between the Collector of Coimbatore, Mr. Thomas, and the Board. Mr. Thomas had, in the first instance, proposed that as a compromise a Badaga should be allowed an acre of fallow without payment for every acre of land for which he paid, or as an alternative that the assessment should be reduced 15 per cent. as compensation for the loss of the "shifting" system. The Board held that "the proper remedy was to make the assessment low enough to admit of the land being permanently held with profit to the owner," and directed the Collector to take the existing rates of assessment on the Hills into consideration, "bearing in mind that the poverty of the land-holder or his unthrifty culture was not the test by which the assessment was to be regulated." Mr. Thomas, however, held that in dealing with the assessment of the lands the intrinsic capabilities of the soil alone should be considered, and not accidents of "manure and capital." He pointed out that the proposed restriction of grazing privileges would limit the supply of manure, and that though the Badagas were better off than formerly, a large expenditure of capital on the land would probably not produce very favourable results, as though several practical European farmers had tried to get more out of the land than the Badagas, they had failed; and further that the Badagas were by no means unthrifty agriculturists. He therefore urged that a reduction of 15 per cent. in the assessment was the least that could be conceded. He subsequently submitted statements of holdings and assessments showing the effects of his proposals in detail, but for convenience of calculation substituted 12½ for 15 per cent. The Board admitted that considerable reduction was called for, but pointed out, very properly, that the "shifting" system had not necessarily resulted from the poverty of the soil, but was generally practised where unoccupied land was abundant. "The Burghers," they remark, "being wretchedly poor, and originally without a remunerative market, so long as they were able to change their occupancy at will, pursued the cropping system as the one by which they could draw their support from the soil with the least possible expenditure of labour and capital. They were put to no expense in supplying fertilizing materials of any kind to their outlying fields, for to use none is a necessary incident of this kind of cultivation, and by leaving the land fallow for long periods, the mere action of the atmosphere on the soil saved them some of the mechanical labour of ploughing. Under such a system, and poverty-stricken as they were, they had neither the inducement nor the means to obtain from the land the fullest return in the shortest period,

CHAP. XIII, PART I. — REVENUE HISTORY.

nor so long as they could betake themselves to fresh land at pleasure would they care what quantity of land was ultimately exhausted." They proceeded to argue that lands in the proximity of cattle kraals, where manure was easily available, were kept constantly under cultivation; and further urged that in assessing land it is right to assume that labour and capital will be expended on it sufficiently to maintain permanently its natural productiveness. One important fact, however, was forgotten, viz., that lands are allowed to lapse into jungle in order that ashes of the vegetation burnt when it is again cleared may add to its fertility and supply in part the manure necessary for the growth of crops. The kraal, especially as now constructed, without cover from sun and rain, supplies little more manure than is sufficient for the home-farm cultivation. The Board, however, were ready to deal even more liberally than Mr. Thomas with the Badagas, whose privileges and advantages under the "shifting" system they were proposing to abolish; and recommended a reduction of 25 per cent. in each of the existing fifteen rates of assessment, "on the understanding that claims to land for which payment is not made will cease to be recognised." The immediate consequent reduction of revenue was estimated at Rupees 1,900. The cultivable area, excluding inams, was returned as 29,912 acres, of which, according to the accounts of 1859-60, 18,857 were cultivated and 11,055 waste.

Rates settled by Government.

The Government generally concurred with the Board, but resolved to substitute for the manifold rates in force five rates as follow:—

		As.
For assessments	above 13 annas	10
Do.	below 13 annas, but above 9 annas.	8
Do.	below 9 annas but above 6 annas...	6
Do.	below 6 annas but above 4 annas...	4
For all assessments below 4 annas		2

The following was the cultivable area under each class:

	ACRES.
10 annas	3,943
8 "	4,611
6 "	13,221
4 "	5,517
2 "	2,620

Thus the average assessment would have been slightly over 6 annas per acre if the total cultivable area, 29,912 acres, were taken up. In 1876 the lands held under ordinary putta alone amounted to 57,925 acres, paying Rupees 20,560 or an average of Annas 5¾ per acre. This area will probably be very largely increased when the survey is complete. When the Government sanctioned the new rates, which were only to apply to the 29,912 acres of putta lands, and consequently not to interfere with the Waste Land Rules just passed, the concession was thought ample compensation for the loss of the "shifting" privilege; but the Badaga thought otherwise, for in fact the 29,912 acres was a fictitious number, and he continued to cultivate any lands lying within his village ayacut without scruple, and will continue to do so until the survey and settlement is complete and the subordinate revenue officials can be relied on to detect and report unauthorized cultivation.

CHAP. XIII, PART I. REVENUE HISTORY.

Approved by Secretary of State.

The determination of Government was reported to the Secretary of State for approval, and was sanctioned by Sir Charles Wood in a despatch dated 24th April 1863, who expressed a hope that the measures adopted would lead to the improvement of the condition of the Badagas; and that so far from the introduction of European capital being likely to injure the prospects of these people, he trusted that they would gain thereby in a better method of cultivation and many useful acquisitions of civilized life in addition to profitable employment of sorts.

Settlement introduced.

Mr. Grant, who had succeeded Mr. Thomas as Collector of Coimbatore, was entrusted with the carrying of the settlement into effect. This he did in Fasli 1272 (1862-63), and reported in May 1864 not only that the Badagas had been informed that the "shifting" system had ceased for ever, but he adds graphically: "It has ceased, and the people now regard it as a by-gone system; it is never alluded to." The Hindu is not wont thus readily to abandon his privileges and the institutions of his ancestors. He said "yes," but went on ploughing and planting as heretofore, until an accurate survey revealed the true position. In fact, each year has the area of cultivation and permanent occupation been extending with the growth in numbers of the hill-tribes, the increase of wealth among them, and the great extension of plantations. Meanwhile, possession or occupation has been the only test of ownership applied in the process of the demarcation that has been proceeding, and the only evidence available to support the truth of a claim was that of the claimants and of their kith and kin.

Settlement extends to the plateau only.

Mr. Grant pointed out that 29,912 acres shown in Mr. Thomas' statement included lands in ten villages or *arrondissements*, whilst virtually the Badagas only held lands in three *arrondissements* or parishes as he termed them—the Tódanád, the Mékanád and the Péranganád. He limited his settlement to these three villages. The aggregate extent of land held by the Badagas then, viz., in Fasli 1272, was 23,585 acres, paying Rupees 11,099 as revenue. The new rates produced a loss of Rupees 2,254 on this amount, but this loss was more than counterbalanced by the Badagas taking up 11,522 acres of waste yielding a revenue of Rupees 4,295, leaving the total assessment at Rupees 13,140 on 35,105 acres, against Rupees 8,114 on 17,333 acres in the preceding fasli. Thus it appeared that the Badagas had more than doubled their holdings. "The majority of the lands have been roughly demarcated, so that I think I may say," wrote Mr. Grant, "that the old practice of putting forward doubtful claims to lands applied for by Europeans and others has been put a stop to." There can be no question that the increase in the holdings was really nominal, or rather that it imperfectly represented cultivation which had hitherto been more or less concealed. The demarcation was practically useless. From the above assessment Rupees 1,961 were deducted for certain waste retained in puttas, caval lands, and "ain" grass lands, leaving the settlement figures at Rupees 11,179; but these items were in great measure temporary concessions.

The following remarks of Mr. Grant are noteworthy:—

State of the Revenue accounts.

"The revenue accounts, although they exhibit certain extents of land in each village as assessed and unassessed waste, do not define the boundaries of these lands. The result was, in carrying out the changes under report, it became impossible to say in cases in which unassessed waste lands had been cultivated, which portions belonged to the assessed and which to the unassessed lands; and as it was evident that many of the Burghers had both lands in their enjoyment, it was resolved, as the best way to meet the difficulty, to allow them to retain all the lands which had been cultivated under the "Bhurty" system, and which in reality formed portions of their existing holdings. The practical result has been that the lands taken up exceed the actual quantity of assessed waste exhibited in the accounts submitted to Government by 5,194 acres, and show a corresponding reduction in the available unassessed waste lands, of which many thousand acres still remain untouched. Although somewhat opposed to the letter of the Government order, the course followed seemed to be in accordance with its spirit; in fact it would have been difficult, if not impossible, to have carried it out differently, as, the lands not being demarcated and surveyed, there were no data as to which were the assessed and which the unassessed lands: almost all either were, or had been, under the plough at the time the settlement was made."

Settlement of the Kúndas.

Mr. Grant also introduced the new rates into the Kúndas, which had but recently (1860) been transferred to the Coimbatore District from Malabar. The revenue system hitherto existing in this tract seems not to have been thoroughly understood, as Mr. Grant speaks of the revenue being collected "on the number of fields locally termed 'Kottoocudoo' and 'Yercudoo' at so much on each description of field," but although these terms may have begun to represent the description of the field, that is, whether it was cultivated by the plough *er*, or the hoe *kottu*, instead of the possession of the right of using a plough or hoe, yet this change had not been sufficiently perfected to find a place in the revenue accounts; but the ryot still received a putta nominally for the right to use a plough or hoe, and not for so much land; for the former privilege he paid Rupee 1 to Rupees 1-8, and for the latter 4 to 8 annas; but the extent of land over which the right was to be exercised did not appear in the putta. Armed with this document he cultivated whatever land he liked and wherever situated. The result was that often fresh forest land was cleared whenever the land already under the plough or hoe began to show signs of exhaustion. The "Bhurty" system can hardly be said to have prevailed here, but an almost unrestricted and unlimited right to ear the ground and delve at choice. Mr. Grant reported that he had had the lands occupied by these Kúnda Badagas in 1862-63 (Fasli 1272) roughly surveyed by the taluk officials and classified according to the productiveness of the soil, and assessed at the five new rates. The total area was ascertained to be 1,220 acres, of which 118 acres appertained to the first class, assessed at 10 annas, 43 to the second, 606 to the third, and 299 and 154 acres to the fourth and fifth classes respectively. The total net assessment, after deducting Rupees 10 for *ain* grass, was Rupees 404, against Rupees 434, the settlement of the previous fasli. "The small decrease of Rupees 30," remarked Mr. Grant, "is nothing when the advantages of the new system are considered with reference not only to the Kúnda, but to the other villages on the Hills. The door to much fraud has been closed, and the sources of endless disputes and false claims to lands have been swept away; whilst the Burghers and Government have both immediately benefited, the former by the reduction of assessment and the latter by an increased revenue." These words read strangely after the lapse and experience of fifteen years; and it is to be regretted that the survey and settlement made by Mr. Grant had not been more complete. In the Kúndas, more especially, was the work so indifferently performed, that the particulars entered in the new puttas of area were utterly unreliable, whilst no boundaries were given, the only clue to the identification of the land being its name or designation. This usually helped to fix the rate only but not its area. Sources of dispute and false claims to lands, so far from being swept away, were rather more numerous and fruitful than heretofore.

Lands for cultivation by hill-tribes only to be obtained by auction under Waste Land Rules.

In making the settlement of the lands held by the cultivating tribes on the plateau,[1] Mr. Grant had proclaimed that henceforth

[1] It must not be forgotten that this settlement extended only to the plateau and higher slopes. The ancient settlement still exists in the tracts at the foot of the ghâts in the Moyar valley.

CHAP. XIII, PART I. — REVENUE HISTORY.

lands not appearing in the puttas of this settlement could not be obtained by the Badagas except by purchase in auction under the Waste Land Rules recently sanctioned. No exception appears to have been made even in the case of house sites. The Board of Revenue demurred to this restriction, pointing out at the same time that the final rule of the Waste Land Rules expressly reserves to Government the power to grant land on putta as heretofore; but the Government of the day were less liberally inclined, and resolved not to grant the Badagas any greater privileges in regard to waste lands, even though situated within the inmost circle of the hamlet farms, than were allowed to Europeans and other immigrants, remarking that the Badagas had been liberally dealt with, and as they acquiesced in the future adoption of the rules, there could be no objection to their being brought into operation. This arrangement, it was thought, would prevent disputes between Europeans and Badagas about lands. But this policy was in marked contrast with that of the Marquis of Tweeddale and of his successor Sir Henry Pottinger. In the rules issued by the latter in 1849, it was expressly declared that the native inhabitants of the Nílagiris should continue as heretofore to hold on putta the lands then in their enjoyment and any further lands which they might take up for their own cultivation; and this liberality was not confined to the hill-tribes, but any *native* settler from the low country was allowed to hold on similar tenure such lands as he might take *boná fide* for his own occupancy.[1] The views, however, of the Madras Government found acceptance with the Secretary of State, Sir Charles Wood, who, in a despatch dated 23rd November 1864, expressed his gratification at the result of Mr. Grant's settlement and acquiesced in the restrictions on the Badagas.

Effects of the measure.

This measure has been until recently virtually ignored, and consequently its restrictive effects have been but little felt; but there can be no question that had the revenue system of the succeeding twelve or fourteen years been strictly in accordance with rule, and had the rights of Government been secured by an accurate survey, its operation would have produced much discon-

[1] I cannot refrain from quoting the order of Sir Frederick Adam's Government, 31st October 1834, when granting compensation for the appropriation by Mr. Lushington's Government of Badaga ryots' lands for the experimental farm at Kaity. It runs:—"Supposing the rights of the Burghers to be merely a prescriptive right of occupancy, that right should not have been taken from them (so long as they fulfilled the condition of tenants by providing for the cultivation of the land and paying the Government revenue) without compensation in land or money. Restitution will now be made to them, but something more than restitution is necessary to do them full justice; they should be compensated for the loss of the profit they were accustomed to derive from the land after paying the revenue and all charges during the time they have been out of possession."

tent, which might have necessitated its abrogation. It has been urged that the rates fixed on ryots' lands are extremely low when compared with the rates paid under the Waste Land Rules, but this is only partially true, especially when it is considered that the greater part of Badaga cultivation is on grass and scrub land as opposed to forest. Moreover a Badaga, whilst cultivating yearly one acre, is compelled to pay assessment on, say, four acres, and in this way his assessment is virtually quadrupled.[1] Thus for land with 8 annas assessment he practically pays 2 rupees an acre, or the maximum rate on forest land held under the Waste Land Rules. The system adopted is akin to that of Tippu Sultan referred to earlier in the chapter, by which the ryots were compelled to pay for all arable lands, whether cultivated or not. The completion of the survey of putta lands, begun in 1870[2] at the request of the Commissioner, will soon put an end to the advantage which the hill cultivators have possessed under the settlement of 1863, and will test the question whether or not their lands as a whole are too heavily assessed.[3] A Badaga now clings to his land though he may derive little profit from it, because he fears it may be alienated for ever under the Waste Land Rules if it comes to the hammer for arrears of revenue. Meanwhile the well earned fruits of his labour on plantations and roads, and even at handicrafts, provide him with the means of paying the Government demand. In this respect his position compares most favourably with that of ryots in remote taluks in the plains. There can be little doubt that the whole land question of the district requires thorough and systematic treatment, and it will probably be found advisable, on completion of the survey, to have a fresh settlement of the country; and it would be well,

---

[1] The survey of the Mékanád increased the occupied area 80 per cent., but probably not more than one-third of this area is yearly cultivated. The fallow, however, has its value as grazing ground. To estimate rightly this increase, the home-farm lands, a fairly well fixed quantity, should be deducted.

[2] I would here remark that the resolution of Government when this survey was begun, to demarcate the lands found in the possession or occupancy of a ryot as his, although the area might be much greater than that entered in his putta, was a direct infraction of Mr. Grant's survey and settlement approved by the Secretary of State, which restricted the Badagas to the lands at that time ascertained to be in their possession, some 29,000 acres. It is well that the finality of the previous settlement was forgotten or ignored.

[3] Quite recently the following rules have been approved by Government for dealing with excess in demarcation:—

1. In cases of unauthorized occupation of primeval forest, title-deeds for the portion which has not been planted should be absolutely refused, except in special cases to be submitted for the orders of Government; retention of the area actually planted might be permitted, unless there is some strong ground for prohibiting further cultivation, on payment of the average auction price for similar land sold during the year, or during a series of three or five years, as may be thought most equitable with reference to the circumstances, such as enhancement of

CHAP. XIII, PART I. — REVENUE HISTORY.

in the interests both of Government and the villagers, if this settlement were accompanied by the introduction of a complete revenue, judicial, and police system among the hill peoples. The present village arrangements have outgrown the altered condition of things. Hamlets have grown into villages without being provided with a separate establishment of village officers, or, in a word, receiving the privileges of village autonomy.

Kótas and other aboriginal cultivators.

The land revenue arrangements of the Kótas differ in no respect from those of the Badagas, though they care less to extend their cultivation ; and of the practice existing in regard to the remaining tribes, the vagrant Irulas and the Kúrumbas, little has to be said except that the *shifting* system of cultivation, which hitherto prevailed amongst the Badagas, has prevailed amongst them in a still greater degree. A putta once granted for cultivating some undefined portion of land ostensibly for a season has been permanently held, and been made to represent, not the title to one piece of land of undefined extent, but an undefined number of pieces. These puttas have been, and it is believed still are, freely alienated, and form the title to valuable coffee and other plantations on the eastern slopes of the Hills. Efforts were made by Mr. Breeks to call in these puttas and to endorse them as non-transferable. In some cases this was done, but owing to a defective revenue administration the evil has continued. The completion of the survey and the improvement of the revenue administration will in time abolish the abuses. Hitherto the checks which an annual revenue settlement is supposed to afford to encroachments and other irregularities in regard to cultivated land have been in great measure inoperative.

Mode of assessing lands.

I would shortly note that the mode of assessing the lands of the hill cultivators is practically according to the intrinsic quality of

---

prices owing to unusual competition, &c. ; assessment on the area retained should be levied in arrears from the date on which it would have been payable had the land been procured in a regular manner and further encroachment prevented by imposition of prohibitive assessment.

2. In cases of unauthorized occupation by other than Badagas of grass or scrub, the reservation of which is not considered necessary, title-deeds should be offered on payment of the average auction price and assessment for the past years on the excess over the area covered by putta, subject to an allowance of 25 per cent. or 5 acres, whichever is more favorable to the occupant. This allowance will, the Board think, be a sufficient concession in cases of error of estimate on the part of *bonâ fide* purchasers, and will probably exclude all but the cases in which the discrepancy must have been palpable.

3. In the case of *bonâ fide* Badaga holdings, excess over the putta area within 100 per cent. should be charged with assessment for the future merely ; where the land demarcated is more than double the extent shown in the putta, the occupant should have the option of throwing up the excess over 100 per cent. or of retaining it on payment of the average auction price and back assessment.

4. In the case of specific grants the area demarcated should be strictly limited to the extent specified therein.

the soil, and the assessment, when once fixed in a putta on the report of the subordinate revenue official, who probably bases his opinion on the description of produce that may be raised thereon, is not, I believe, ordinarily disturbed. Formerly, however, it was the practice at the approach of harvest for the taluk officials with the curnums to make a tour through the different villages, "and form an estimate of the probable outturn of the crop on each field from its appearance, rating it as first class if it promises to be abundant, and as second class if otherwise. The highest rate levied is on lands cultivated for potatoes, which pay 7 rupees per vullam (bulla) for first-class ground, and 5 rupees for second-class. The next rate in the scale of assessment is applied to lands bearing wheat, which pay for first-class ground Rupees 3-8-5 and for second-class Rupees 2-5-7; barley, which pay for first-class Rupees 3-8-5 and for second-class Rupees 2-5-7 per vullam, and the same for poppy, vendium, mustard seed, garlic and onions. The lowest rate applies to raggee, samee, koralley, peas, shennugee and tenney, all of which pay Rupees 2-0-11 per vullam for first-class land, and for second-class Rupees 0-14-1 per vullam."
—OUCHTERLONY'S *Memoir*.

(b.) THE GRAZIERS—The Tódas.

Claim of Tódas to lordship over plateau—nature of claim—its extent—conditions operating against it.—Restrictions on purchases of land from Tódas.—Claims of the Tódas partially admitted.—Occupation of lands by Europeans attracts attention of Court of Directors.—Change in policy of Madras Government.—Grants made without mention of Tódas' claims.—Settlers continue to purchase from the Tódas.—Sir Frederick Adam's action.—Mr. Sullivan's views—endorsed by Government—approved by Court of Directors.—Difficulties in carrying policy into effect.—Matters still unsettled in 1839, and Court of Directors interfere.—Mr. Conolly's views.—Mr. C. M. Lushington strongly opposes policy of Government.—Marquis of Tweeddale refers questions to the Court of Directors.—After further report from the Collector of Malabar the Court's despatch, 1843, settles questions finally and orders payment of compensation for Ootacamand to Tódas.—Manual of Land Rules to be prepared—provisions of the manual relating to the Tódas—rescinded by the Waste Land Rules.—Present revenue system.

Tódas' claims to lordship over plateau.

Thus far I have treated of the cultivating tribes. I now turn to the graziers—the Tódas. The fact that they, relatively to the Badagas at least, the principal cultivating tribe, were the earliest occupants of the plateau, gave rise to pretensions on their part to lordship over the Hills, pretensions which received for many years the enthusiastic support of Mr. John Sullivan, of Mr. Hough, and of Captain Harkness, but which were as strenuously opposed by some distinguished members of the Civil Service, especially Mr. S. R. Lushington, Mr. C. M. Lushington, and Mr. Bird. Mr.

CHAP. XIII, PART I. — REVENUE HISTORY.

S. R. Lushington, whilst Governor, had practically ignored these claims, but his successor, Sir Frederick Adam, regarded them favourably, and made concessions which were opposed to the permanent rights in soil which throughout India belong to the State. Lord Elphinstone did not disturb the policy of his predecessor, although towards the end of his reign, in 1840, after Mr. Sullivan's retirement, the civilian members of the Government made a determined attack on the policy of the preceding five years; but on the accession to power of the Marquis of Tweeddale the papers were referred to the Honorable Court of Directors. In their reply of 21st June 1843 the question as to the rights of the Tódas in the land was finally set at rest.

—nature of claim.

The position claimed for the Tódas was similar to that known as the jenm tenure in Malabar, and was alleged to extend to the whole of the plateau. The "gudu," or basket of grain, which the Tódas received from the Badagas was regarded as rent paid by the tenants to the landlords for the lands occupied by them. The high position claimed for this tribe of barbarous herdsmen was in great measure due to the ignorance that existed in regard to the nature of this custom. But when it was ascertained that other tribes received from the timid Badagas *benevolences* of a similar nature, the argument grounded thereon lost much of its force. At first, too, it was believed that all Badaga ryots paid a contribution of the kind,[1] but later it was ascertained that the payment was not universal, but was mainly confined to Badaga villages neighbouring the Tóda grazing grounds of the uplands. The contribution, which is believed by Mr. Breeks[2] to amount to about two kuligas or four Madras measures of grain for an ordinary putta field, appears to be of a two-fold character. It is probably, to some extent, compensation for appropriation to cultivation of lands once grazed by Tóda buffaloes, but it also partakes of the nature of a free-will offering to secure the favour, or rather avert the displeasure, of the Tódas, who are supposed to possess necromantic powers. The fond advocates of Tóda rights also lost sight of the fact that they had from time immemorial paid to the Circar a tax on all female buffaloes in their possession, amounting to 2 cantarai fanams, or 9 annas 5 pies, per

---

[1] "The 'goodoo' is not collected into a common fund and then divided, but each 'mund' or 'moort' has the goodoo of a certain number of Burgher villages appropriated for its support, and if any difficulty should be made in payment, the aid of the monegar is called in for its collection."—MR. SULLIVAN.

[2] Major Ouchterlony states that the Tódas claim one-sixth of the produce, and that the Badagas admit that they paid at this rate before the advent of the English. He also states that the owner of a good house contributed 1 cundagam = 20 kuligas; the less opulent ½ or ¼ cundagam. Some interesting information on the custom will be found in his memoir.

animal, as well as an assessment of 1 cantarai fanam, or 4 annas 8 pies, per bullah on the grazing lands in the immediate neighbourhood of their mands, calculated at the rate of 10 bullahs (38 acres) for every hundred head of cattle herded at a mand. This latter tax produced Rupees 350 in 1828 and Rupees 400 in 1847.

—its extent.

When Mr. Sullivan first settled on the Hills, he appears to have regarded the Tódas' rights as extending to the whole of the plateau. "Referring to what has lately appeared in the public papers on the subject of colonizing the Hills," he writes on New Year's eve, 1829, "I would only beg leave to remind the Board that these hill people have rights. The Todawars can show as clear a proprietary right to the soil they now occupy as can be produced by the Mirassidars of Malabar, and to a certain share of the produce of all land now cultivated or that may hereafter be cultivated. The Todawars were originally in possession of the whole range, and it was only with their permission that the Burghers settled and cultivated upon mutual agreement, which is in force at this moment. The scanty number of the Toda population cannot be held to bar their claims. The Burghers again, holding from the Todawars on a fixed quit-rent, have a property in all the land they occupy. The cultivation and population in their nauds are rapidly increasing, and in a few years the Burghers, if left undisturbed, will occupy all the best descriptions and many of the inferior soils. In the Malnaud, or Todawar country, there is certainly room for a colony. That tract would support a very large population, but before any measures are taken for colonizing, the consent of the proprietors should be obtained, and a fair remuneration made to them for what they are to give up. They have been greatly injured by the formation of the cantonment of Ootacamand. The occupants of lands within this circle have paid for two cawnies for each house; for all the rest of the land from which the Todawars are debarred the use, they have received no remuneration at all. Having been the means of introducing Europeans and strangers to the Neilgherries, I am bound by every obligation of public duty and good feeling to assert the rights of the inhabitants whenever an attempt may be made to invade them." He had purchased from them, it will be observed, and not from Government, the lands occupied by him at Stonehouse, and later at Southdowns (Bishopsdown), and his example had been followed by several others, notably Sir William Rumbold, who thus acquired the site on which the Club and neighbouring houses now stand.

—conditions operating against it.

These transactions were not called in question by Government until the beginning of Sir Frederick Adam's reign, but were virtually admitted, for Government obtained by purchase properties so acquired without questioning the title. But the rapid growth

CHAP. XIII, PART I. — REVENUE HISTORY.

of the cantonment during Mr. S. R. Lushington's administration had brought the land question of the Ootacamand settlement into prominent notice early in that Governor's reign, and rendered it absolutely necessary that the position of Government in regard to such lands should be definitely settled. Each house-owner had endeavoured to secure as much as possible of the lands adjoining that on which his house stood, and to this day there are several instances in which owners of house properties have no documentary title to portions of their estates.

Restrictions on purchases of land from Tódas.

Early in 1828 the subject had engaged the attention of Government, and reports had been called for, but before full information was received as to the number and extent of these properties and the terms on which they were held, the Government, in November of this year, deemed it proper to limit the space to be allotted to each dwelling-house, exclusive of the site of the building and outhouses, to two cawnies, and directed that all ground held in excess of this area, which might have been enclosed or appropriated without permission from Government, should be resumed and incorporated with Circar land. Proprietors of houses already built, and persons desiring to build, were required, the former within three months, and the latter before beginning a building, to take out Government grants "in the usual form for the authorized extent of ground for each house, such grants being subject to the fees levied on the issue of similar instruments at the Presidency." The same order reserved all land between Stonehouse and the Willow Bund south of the lake for public buildings.

Tódas' claims partially admitted.

A few days after the issue of this order the Government dealt with the Tóda claims,[1] which had been strongly urged by Mr. Sullivan. The Board of Revenue had hesitated to admit the property rights of the Tódas, and held that such rights as they possessed did not stand in the way of Government allotting lands for building and other purposes; but the Government declined to enter into a discussion on the alleged property rights of the Tódas, but adopted the terms observed by Mr. Sullivan in purchasing their privileges from the Tódas as a sufficient guide for regulating the payment by other individuals "of compensation" for the usufruct of the land which the Tódas had hitherto enjoyed. The decision was that each occupant should pay to the Tódas as "compensation" 16 cantarai fanams for each bullah, being sixteen times the assessment paid by the Tódas for pasture land, and four times the lowest rate for cultivated lands in the plateau; and in addition to this the Government required the occupant to pay to the Circar, from the date of the grant, "quit-rent at the rate

[1] E. M. C., 14th November 1828.

usually assessed on lands for which Government grants are issued, and that from the same date rent *pro tanto* shall cease to be demanded from the Todawars." All applications for grants were to be accompanied by certificate that the prescribed compensation had been paid to the Tódas. The area allowed to each house, which had been originally recommended by Sir T. Munro, was maintained, subject to modification in special cases.

CHAP. XIII, PART I. — REVENUE HISTORY.

Occupation of lands by Europeans attracts attention of Court of Directors.

The occupation of lands for agricultural purposes on the Nílagiris had attracted the attention of the Honorable Court of Directors, and on the 2nd September 1829 the Court communicated to the Madras Government a copy of the Resolution of the Supreme Government, 7th May 1824, more particularly referred to later on in this chapter, and directed that the rules therein laid down should be "strictly observed in the case of every permission granted to a European to hold land on lease for purposes of cultivation." This Resolution provided that lands occupied by Native cultivators by hereditary right should not be transferred without their consent and that of "all parties possessing an interest in the soil or in the rents." Lands could only be obtained on lease for a period not exceeding twenty-one years.

Change in policy of Mr. Lushington's Government.

Meanwhile applications for grants of land, mainly in the Ootacamand settlement, began to flow in. Some of them were disposed of by the Government in April 1831. In sanctioning[1] these grants no mention is made of compensation to Tódas, nor were the grants limited to a period of twenty-one years, but were, "as at Madras, for an indefinite period." In fact the practice in the Presidency appears to have been adhered to in all respects. The quit-rent fixed was Rupees 5¼ per cawnie "to be assessed uniformly on all lands on the Nílagiris, whether within or without the cantonment."[2] The Government justified its departure from the instructions of the Court of Directors by alleging that those instructions referred exclusively to large tracts of land rented by indigo planters and others for agricultural purposes, and could not be held to apply "to the erection of dwelling-houses on small plots of ground at a place where, from local circumstances, the acquisition of very considerable landed property is almost impossible." The claims of the Tódas to any compensation, though so emphatically asserted in 1828, were now forgotten. East Indian settlers received grants of waste land according to the extent of their capital, beyond the limits of the cantonment, without any mention of paying assessment to Government.

Settlers continue to purchase from Tódas.

Meanwhile, however, settlers continued to purchase lands from the Tódas. These transactions are recounted in a letter from the

[1] 19th April 1831.

[2] E. M. C., 8th November 1831.

CHAP. XIII, PART I. — REVENUE HISTORY.

Collector of Malabar in 1833 as follows: "Land has, from time to time, been purchased from the Todawars by different persons for the purposes of building and cultivation, when a small compensation, generally from 10 to 50 rupees, always amply satisfied them; and these purchases were, until the recent orders of Government, generally effected through the Officer Commanding on the Hills, who, being on the spot, was able to see justice done to all parties." The Tódas, he remarks, had "learnt to assert and protect their own rights on all occasions, and never failed to make a good bargain in disposing of their lands;" and he adds that he had received no complaints of oppression being used towards them to induce or compel them to part with their lands. But there was a notable exception to this—Kandelmand—which the Tódas only alienated to Sir W. Rumbold, who required it to form part of the domain which he desired to attach to the house he was then building, after considerable compulsion on the part of the Peschar and the offer of Rupees 400, their unwillingness being due to the existence of a small temple in its centre, which they alleged contained "the effigies of their gods and the monuments of their ancestors."

Sir Frederick Adam's action.

So long as Mr. S. R. Lushington held the reins of Government the rights of the Tódas as well as the Badagas in the land were virtually ignored, but with the change of Governors came a violent reaction in the policy of the Government. Shortly after Sir Frederick Adam's accession to power the Government turned its attention to the land question, and caused a searching inquiry to be made into all land transactions with the Hill tribes. As regards the Badagas the Government had themselves been the chief transgressors in the matter of the Kaity Experimental Farm, where cultivated lands belonging to Badaga ryots had been appropriated by Government without payment of any compensation, the assessment only being remitted. As regards the Tódas the only important case was that of Sir W. Rumbold, above referred to; in both instances ample compensation was granted to the sufferers and the land restored.

The action of Sir Frederick Adam's Government was mainly in accord with the views of the Court of Directors, who, early in 1834, when calling for a report on the past and present condition of the Tódas, had expressed a strong desire that the rights of this people should be respected, and that they should not be deprived of any of their privileges without ample remuneration. The report called for by the Court opened up the whole question of the Tódas' rights in the soil. Mr. Sullivan was at this time Principal Collector of Coimbatore. He at once took up the cause of the Tódas, and, succeeding to Council in 1835, he was enabled to carry on the contest with advantage and final success, which was mainly due to a lengthened minute on the subject recorded on the 5th September 1835.

REVENUE HISTORY.

Mr. Sullivan's views.

His views border on the romantic. He admitted that the Tódas were not the first inhabitants of the Hills, grounding this assertion on the fact that they laid no claim to the cromlechs and tumuli, but as boldly asserted that, being in possession when the Badagas arrived, the latter were only "permitted to break up the soil of the Nilagiris upon an express compact with the Todawars that a portion of the produce of each cultivated plot should be rendered to them as the original occupants." "This compact," he continues, "is still religiously observed, and its origin is freely admitted by the Burghers themselves. The portion of the produce so rendered varies from a tenth to an eighth. It is called 'goodoo,' and bears an exact resemblance to that species of property in land in Arcot which is called 'Marah.'"

This position however he subsequently partially modifies, for, after remarking that the Badagas had spread over the Péranganád, Mékanád and the Tódanád, the Tódas having the exclusive occupation of the upland portion only of the last-named on the arrival of Europeans, he goes on to say, "The property of the land in the other divisions of the Hills vests in the Burghers, who hold it upon the prevailing tenure of Coimbatore, viz., the punctual payment of the Government assessment, but the Todawars have an inalienable claim to their 'goodoo.' The Malnaud, which extends from the boundary of the Todawarnaud to Nadoobett, is the property of the Todawars in the same sense as the lands of Malabar vest in Jemnikars, the Government in both cases retaining, of course, their full rights of revenue over the lands. The origin of the property is not to be traced in either instance: both have been in possession from a remote antiquity, and both have enjoyed their property under a light tax. No division has ever been made of the land amongst the Todawars. They enjoy the property in common, and when in 1822 I first became acquainted with their proprietary rights, the money which I then paid for the purchase of those rights over the lands I then occupied, and over other lands which I afterwards occupied, was divided amongst the Todawars resident on the Malnaud, but the few families who still remain in the other nauds were not considered entitled to a share. * * * No compensation has ever been made for the land included in the cantonment, which embraces a circle of several miles, and those of their favourite mands from which they have been entirely ousted; neither do they receive anything for the numerous herds which now graze upon their lands within the cantonment."

CHAP. XIII, PART I. — REVENUE HISTORY.

—endorsed by Government.

Mr. Sullivan's views were in the main approved by the Government, of which he had become a member, in October 1835. It was ordered that their rights should be "respected," and that they should not "on any account be disturbed in the possession of the lands heretofore held by them, which they may desire to retain for pasturage, so long as they pay the taxes at present payable [1] by them; that private persons shall not be permitted to appropriate any of those lands without the consent of the Todawars interested in them at terms mutually agreed upon, and no part of those lands shall be taken for public purposes without compensation to the Todawars who have previously occupied them." Subsequently the Board of Revenue recommended that "cattle belonging to persons holding lands for building and other purposes should not be allowed to graze indiscriminately on uncultivated lands within their mands or villages without the consent of the proprietors."

—approved by Court of Directors.

The determination of Government was fully endorsed by the Court of Directors in a despatch dated the 19th April 1837, the Court being anxious "to reconcile the interest of both parties." But prior to the receipt of this despatch orders had been issued to the Collector of Malabar to arrange with the Tódas for the settlement of compensation for lands occupied by Europeans at the rate before mentioned, and it was further directed that agreements should be entered into with the Tódas for the purchase of their common right and interest in their lands within or without the cantonment, and that the lands they desired to retain should be defined. Allowance was to be made in favour of Government for sums already paid by private individuals.

Difficulties in carrying policy into effect.

Difficulties however arose in carrying out this order. In the first place it could not be ascertained what had been paid to Tódas, and in the second place lands were frequently taken up and cultivated for a time and then abandoned. In regard to the latter point it was decided that it would be sufficient to make an allowance to the Tódas out of the assessment payable to Government, the amount so deducted to be specified in the jammabandi chittas and puttas; the former was ignored. In February 1847 the Board of Revenue reported that the area in the Ootacamand settlement to be reserved to the Tódas was under 100 cawnies or 133 acres, for which extent the Board stated at the rate sanctioned the compensation would be Rupees 162-10-1, but recommended that they should have compensation for the entire cantonment area, including the spots the Tódas desired to reserve. This proposal the Government sanctioned, and their order was

[1] About a fourth of the assessment receivable if the land were cultivated.

followed by the following curious notification by the Collector of Malabar:—

CHAP. XIII, PART I.

REVENUE HISTORY.

"Government having determined that compensation for the whole land included in the cantonment of Ootacamund shall be paid direct to the Todas from the public treasury, and that no demand shall be made on private occupants on this account, and further that the amount already paid by private individuals as compensation to the Todas for lands occupied by them shall be paid on their making over to Government the right and interest purchased by them from the Todas, in lieu of which a perfect and unquestionable title will be given them by Government to the lands in their occupation: Notice is hereby given that on proof by authenticated documents of any such payment having been made being furnished to the Sub Collector of Malabar at Ootacamund on or before the 1st April next, such sums shall be repaid to the parties on the terms above specified."

But many obstacles presented themselves to the completion of this arrangement, the chief of which was the refusal of the Tódas, instigated by the Tahsildar of Ootacamand, to accept the compensation offered. The Advocate-General also had pointed out to Government the legal difficulties involved in their policy.

Matters still unsettled in 1839; Court of Directors interfere.

Things remained unsettled, and when in April 1839 the Court of Directors expressed a hope that Government would soon be able to conclude an agreement with the Tódas, "either by payment of annual rent or otherwise," orders were thereupon issued to the Collector of Malabar to induce the Tódas to make over the lands on payment annually of Rupees 150 "as quit-rent for the same." In 1840 Mr. Conolly forwarded some important observations to Government, dealing with the Tódas' claims from a Malabar point of view. He pointed out that even in Malabar a man might cultivate waste, restoring it to the owner should a claim be established on receipt from the latter of full compensation; and further that a man is not allowed to leave his land waste unless he agree to pay to Government the tax they would receive if it were cultivated; and proceeded to remark that it was a serious question "whether the Tódas should have greater favour shown to them (allowing them to be proprietors of the soil) than is shown to the proprietors of Malabar; whether they should be allowed to keep the large portion of the Hills[1] which they claim as their peculiar property in a state which may fairly be called waste, to the prejudice of Government, who might derive a large emolument from its being brought under cultivation." And after observing that the Tódas only paid a land assessment on 190 bullahs (700 acres), and that the Government could hardly have intended in 1835 to have allowed them to occupy the rest of the uplands (in

Mr. Conolly's views.

---

[1] *i.e.*, the uplands—Mélnád—of the Tódas.—ED.

CHAP. XIII, PART I.

REVENUE HISTORY.

area fifty times greater than what they paid for) without payment of land tax, he proceeds :—

"All that the Todas have a right to expect by a fair construction of the resolutions of Government, is that these 190 bullahs, for which they *do* pay a tax, should be guaranteed to them so long as the amount, small as it is, is duly paid; and with regard to the remaining portion, I think the rule which prevails in Malabar * * * * * * might be fairly applied, although the cases are not in their nature exactly analogous. The Todas might be allowed the proprietary right to the whole of the soil, but it might be insisted that they should pay a tax for it, or, failing that, allow it to be occupied by those *who would* pay the assessed or assessable rates, receiving however, as in Malabar, 15 per cent. of the profits as the landlord's share. All land not tendered for might be left, as at present, in the Todas' possession with liberty to use it as their own till it was, piece by piece, taken up by those who would make a more profitable use of it. It would be very long ere, under this system, any such quantity would fall out of their hands (as far as the use of it goes) as to affect their interests as herdsmen; and by that time (if not before) it may be hoped they will have advanced in the scale of civilization and have seen the advantage of uniting husbandry to the mere tending of buffaloes. They may be compelled in time (and it is to be wished they should be) to change their mode of life by the operation of this system, but they can never be really injured by it; for, to say nothing of the moral consequences, every bullah of land that is lost to them in one way (saving the empty title to the proprietary right, on which they set much value) will be amply made up by the 15 per cent. which it is proposed should be given them from its produce."

In the following month Mr. Conolly submitted to Government an agreement concluded with the Tódas, by which they consented to make over to Government the lands in the Ootacamand settlement, deducting certain reservations on payment of a "quit-rent" of Rupees 150. In consideration of these reservations the Tódas consented to cede "such portions of land *without* the cantonment as have already been appropriated for building purposes."

Mr. C. M. Lushington strongly opposes policy of Government.

But Mr. Sullivan had now retired, and the proposal to pay "quit-rent" to the Tódas, and the decision of Government in 1835 to acknowledge these barbarians as "lords of the soil," met with the most determined opposition from Mr. C. M. Lushington, now senior Member of Council. In a very able minute, dated the 15th December 1840, he combated Mr. Sullivan's theories and the novel proceedings of the Board of Revenue, boldly asserting that "all opinions of any value were unanimously concurrent in maintaining that the ruling power in India not only possessed the right of making grants of waste land, but that its exercise from time immemorial was as frequent as undeniable." Passing in rapid review the opinions of eminent revenue officers from 1770 and the policy which was formulated in Regulation XXXI of 1802, he quoted Sir T. Munro's remark that "there is no reason to suppose that private landed property *ever* at any one time existed, except upon one footing. Over the greater part of India from Pulicat to Ganjam, in the Ceded Districts, the Baramahal and Coimbatore, it seems to have been always as now little known except as *inam* from the sovereign." After enlarging on this celebrated Governor's recorded opinions he proceeds to criticise the position taken by Mr. Sullivan and the evidence produced by Mr. Sullivan from Tóda and Badaga customs, upon which it is based. He demolished the analogy between Penn's purchase of Pennsylvania and the Government acquisition of Tóda lands, mentioning incidentally the notorious fact that Tippu had annually sent his Kichhana establishments to the Hills for pasturage whilst compelling the Tódas to pay tax for pasture. He enters fully into the import of the custom of paying "gudu," and, though ignorant of the meaning of the word, shows how it was admittedly paid to secure "the goodwill and protection" of the Tódas, its sanctions being moral. He shows that whilst demanding for the Tódas Malabar land-rights, Mr. Sullivan had from the first strenuously contended against the view that the Tódas or their country had ever anything to do with Malabar. He then goes on to point out that Mr. Sullivan, in issuing puttas on his first advent to the Hills, made no distinction between the puttas of Tódas and of Badagas, and finally closes his argument by stating the legal difficulties, urging that Government were in dilemma, for whilst by Regulation XXXI they denied that any length of tenure constituted a right without production of authentic documents, they had by orders of 1835 declared that the Tódas' rights in the soil were paramount; consequently no settler could obtain a valid title, for if he claimed by purchase from a Tóda, he was met by the objection that the law allowed no such rights in waste land; if by purchase from Government, by the objection that Government had declared they would not sell without the consent of the landlord Tóda. He then warns the Government against the policy adopted by urging that there were other claims involved in "this cession to the Toda." "These claims," he writes, "extend to a very large tract of the Neilgherries, and the person preferring them is the Nullumboor Zemindar, whose zemindari adjoins the Neilgherries. This is another reason against admitting the claims of the Todawars, except on legal proof, for, as justly observed by Sir Thomas Munro, 'We must not too hastily declare any right to be permanent, lest we give to one class what belongs to another.'" Mr. Lushington's views were fully endorsed by the other Civilian Member, Mr. John Bird, who, whilst agreeing that *compensation*, not *quit-rent* or "goodoo" should be paid, demanded that the claims of the Tódas to sovereign rights in the soil should be repudiated.

Marquis of Tweeddale refers the questions to the Court of Directors after further report from the Collector of Malabar.

Lord Elphinstone would not move, and it was not till the latter part of 1842 that his successor, the Marquis of Tweeddale, took up the matter. The Collector of Malabar was called on to explain the delay in making a final settlement with the Tódas. In December 1842 he reported that the Tódas had agreed to substitute the word "compensation" for "goodoo" in the agreement made with them in 1840, and that accordingly he had paid them Rupees 300, or two years' indemnity, leaving arrears to be settled later. In reporting the area "actually in the occupation of the Todas," he defines it as the land lying between Doddabetta and the Paikaré river and Segúr and the Mélúr cultivated lands. In February 1843 the Government submitted the question of the Tódas' rights for the decision of the Court of Directors. After pointing out that the chief difficulty in disposing of claims to land on the Nílagiris arose from the circumstance that the rights of the inhabitants in the soil had never been defined, and that the resolution of the Government in 1835 had been held virtually to apply to the Ootacamand settlement only, they proceed thus:—

"An attentive examination of the whole subject did not enable us to discover that the rights of the Todas in the land differed from those of the people of India generally in their relation to the existing Government. They seem always to have paid a land tax, and this was a light pasture tax only, because the Todas are a pastoral tribe in the lowest stage of civilization. Other classes of the hill population, we observed, of more settled habits, were not exempted from the payment of the usual agricultural tax. It is true we found that the latter were in the habit of offering certain gratuities or allowances of grain to the Todas under the name of "goodoo," the exact import of which is unknown, but similar payments are made to other rude tribes of the mountains without any acknowledgment of superiority claimed or service rendered."

The despatch goes on to state that Tódas had been maintained in possession of the lands occupied by them, but that the Government had been of opinion that these rights could not be suffered to bar the progress of improvement over the large tracts of land constituting the Nílagiris, nor to hinder the application of lands to more beneficial purposes, considering it sufficient that the Tódas should receive in such cases a compensation, or as Mr. Conolly had proposed with reference to the tenures of Malabar, a share of 15 per cent. on the net profits. On this point they desired to be furnished with the early orders of the Court, observing that the question in issue really was whether the Tódas were to have their absolute title acknowledged to the entire tract of the Hills at any time depastured by their herds, and to 15 per cent. "of all future produce resulting from the application of the capital and skill of others to the land," or whether their rights would be amply compensated by assigning to them "a liberal compensation (as in the case of Ootacamand), which shall indemnify them from all loss where their prescriptive right of pasturage is infringed, and the limit of their pasture-ground *bonâ fide* curtailed." They then suggest that instead of an annual payment, which might bear the semblance of a rent, a lump sum should be paid as compensation once for all. As regards the lands in more permanent occupation of the tribes, such as village sites and spots appropriated to religious rites, the Government suggested that the Tódas should be secured from all interference, and that their absolute right in them should be declared. They further requested orders on the amount of compensation for lands already occupied. In the same despatch, with reference to several applications by Europeans for lands on the Hills, they requested orders on the right of Europeans in the Company's service to hold lands, and under what restrictions; also as to the conditions to be attached to grants to Europeans not in the service and to Natives.

–the Court's despatch, 1843, settles questions finally.

The reply of the Court of Directors to this reference, conveyed in their despatch of the 21st June 1843, set the questions connected with the Tóda claims finally at rest. After summing up the case they proceed as follows:—

"From a consideration of the universally acknowledged rights of Government in respect to uncultivated lands, as well as of the peculiar circumstances of the case under discussion, we cannot admit the existence of any such proprietary rights in the soil on the part of the Todas as can in any way interfere with the right of Government to permit parties willing to pay the full assessment to bring it under the plough. It remains therefore to be determined whether they possess a right to be compensated for the abridgment of the grazing privileges which they have exercised over the lands on the Hills by their gradual cultivation and enclosure, and in the event of their being considered to possess such a right, on what principle the compensation shall be assigned to them.

"We have already observed that the only title which can be advanced on the part of the Todas is that of immemorial occupation, and the only advantage which they have derived from their occupancy (with the exception of the annual payments received from the Burghers) has been that of pasturing their herds. The injury which they will sustain from the settlement of strangers on the Hills will consequently arise from the diminution of their pasture grounds as the lands are gradually brought into cultivation. It must be admitted that this will be a positive disadvantage to them, and that the loss of a privilege

CHAP. XIII, PART I. — REVENUE HISTORY.

which they have enjoyed from time immemorial is a fair subject for compensation, although it is probable that many years will elapse before cultivation advances so far as to interfere to any serious extent with the means of feeding their herds; and in the mean time it is to be hoped that the Todas will be brought under the influence of more settled habits, and see the advantage of uniting the cultivation of the soil with their present occupation of tending buffaloes.

"There does not appear to us to be any such similarity between the circumstances of the Todas and those of the inhabitants of Malabar in respect to the occupation of the land as would entitle the former to the allowance of 15 per cent. on the profits of cultivating land by any other party than the actual proprietor, which is claimed by the landlords in Malabar. We should rather consider that they would be sufficiently compensated by a payment equivalent in amount to the "goodoo" which they now receive from the Burgher cultivators, especially as it would appear that they have not been in the habit of interposing any obstacle to the cultivation of the lands in their occupancy on these terms. In the event of land for which the pasturage tax is paid being brought under cultivation, an equivalent remission must of course be made from the amount of the tax.

"We are of opinion that the stipulated compensation should be added to the assessment which the land may be required to pay to Government in order that the Todas may receive it direct from the Collector's treasury. You consider that it would be desirable to afford the Todas compensation by the payment of a principal sum once for all as a full equivalent for all claims or interest which they may possess in the land. Our principal objection to such an arrangement is founded on the liability of the capital sum so raised being dissipated by the simple race for whose ultimate support it is intended to provide. Could the capital be invested so as to yield an annual income to be distributed in the same manner and in the same proportions as the compensation which we have sanctioned being made from the Collector's treasury, our objections would not only be obviated, but a fund would be provided for assisting any of the Todas to undertake agricultural operations, whenever they may be disposed to do so, with advantage to themselves.

"With respect to the lands which are in the more permanent occupation of the Todas, such as their mands or sites of villages and particular spots appropriated to religious rites, we agree with you that they should be secured from all interference, and their absolute right in them declared. We are further of opinion that you should abstain from making any grant of land in the immediate vicinity of their villages, as it is to be hoped that in course of time they may be induced so far to change their habits as to bring them themselves into cultivation.

"Before these instructions can be systematically acted on it will be necessary that you should be provided with a detailed survey and map of the Neilgherry Hills, distinguishing the lands in the occupation of the Government and private individuals, those brought under cultivation by the Burghers, those which are to be left in the permanent occupation of the Todas, and those entirely unoccupied, over a portion of which the Todas have been accustomed to pasture their herds. This work should be immediately commenced; but in the meantime we do not wish to restrict you from accepting any eligible proposals which may be made to you for bringing waste land into cultivation, care being taken that the rights of other parties are not infringed, and the general rules which we have laid down observed as far as practicable.

"In considering any claims which may be advanced by individuals to hold lands under titles derived by purchase from the Todas, you will bear in mind that they could not transfer any more extensive right than they themselves possessed, viz., the right of occupying the land for purposes of pasturage. Such land must be held liable for the full assessment whenever it shall be brought into cultivation by the actual occupants, or in the event of any other party proposing to reclaim it; in the latter case the occupant would be entitled to similar compensation as would have been assigned to the Todas had the land remained in their occupation."

—payment of compensation for Ootacamand ordered.

The Court in the same despatch ordered compensation to be paid to the Tódas for their exclusion from the lands of the Ootacamand cantonment from the 27th December 1837, the date on which it was resolved that the compensation should be made to them. The Court also forwarded a copy of the despatch of February 1842 to the Supreme Government regarding the acquisition of lands in Dehra Doon by Europeans, enunciating the policy of the Court of Directors regarding the acquisition of waste lands by Europeans, and the security which should be afforded for rights and privileges of the neighbouring native villagers.

Manual of Land Rules ordered to be prepared.

On receipt of these orders the Board of Revenue were called on to prepare a manual of rules for the approval of Government based thereon, and further to ascertain precisely the lands in the occupation of Europeans on the Nílagiris, and the circumstances under which such lands had been acquired.

—provisions of the Manual relating to the Tódas.

The manual of instructions, though submitted late in 1843, did not receive sanction until the end of 1849, on the completion of Major Ouchterlony's survey. The map prepared at the time exhibited, among other things, the lands in the occupation of the Tódas as well as the unoccupied tracts over portions of which these people had been wont to pasture their herds. These instructions, as far as concerned the Tódas, laid down that lands which had hitherto been "entirely unoccupied" or "used only as pasture grounds by the Tódas" should, on being taken up for agricultural purposes, be assessed "according to the rates paid on land of similar quality in the nearest agricultural village, unless where the land be within a specified distance of Ootacamund," (when special rates,

CHAP. XIII, PART I. — REVENUE HISTORY.

from which Badagas were exempt, prevailed). The rules also required the observance of the Court's orders regarding the non-proximity of land grants to mands and other Tóda sites, and as regards "goodoo" enacted that, "If it shall appear to the satisfaction of the Revenue authorities, upon inquiry made previous to the lease, or at any time during its currency, that the land leased is liable to the payment of goodoo or compensation fees to the Todas, the goodoo payable to these latter will be collected from the grantee in addition to the assessment, for the purpose of being paid to the Todas from the public treasury. The amount of goodoo in each case shall be determined by the Collector, subject to an appeal to the Board of Revenue." After reiterating the judgment of the Court of Directors as regards the pasture lands of the Tódas, that they could sell no "other right than that of pasturage," the rules declared, "if the land be required for cultivation, it must still be disposed of, under the rules in force, by public auction, for that purpose; the goodoo on the land, when such may clearly appear to be payable, being, in that case, paid to the party who has purchased the right of grazing from the Toda in the place of the Toda himself," which practically, though not overtly, deprived the Tóda of his ill-defined but admitted rights of pasture in the Nílagiri uplands.

—rescinded by the Waste Land Rules.

These rules remained in force, subject to certain modifications in 1858, until the 6th March 1863, when they were superseded by the present Waste Land Rules, which swept away for ever not only the fiction of the Tódas' grazing rights, but also the communal claims of a village to the lands within its ancient limits, by the decree that all lands were *waste* "in which no rights of *private* proprietorship or *exclusive* occupancy exist," and were liable to be disposed of by public auction. Were it not for the words in Rule XVII "a claim . . . . . of any other right incompatible with the sale of land under these rules," the conclusion might be drawn that little consideration for the rights and privileges of this ancient and simple race of herdsmen would be shown in future. In the period, scarce fifteen years, which has elapsed since then, we have done little to protect this race from the ultimate deprivation of the choicest spots they hold except by the measure of declaring the puttas for such grazing lands as they still hold non-transferable. But the intention of Government has been easily defeated by a system of sub-letting, which has converted the home-lands of several mands into potato fields and market gardens. Quite recently the Government have sanctioned the assessment at full rates of lands granted on favourable tenure if alienated by lease. This ruling will doubtless check the practice.

Present revenue system.

It remains simply to state that under the survey now proceeding about fifty acres of land, ordinarily to a considerable extent woodland, are demarcated as the site or reserve of each mand, the total number being about seventy. On this the Tódas pay an assessment of 2 annas per acre, *i.e.*, the lowest assessment under the present settlement. This is the only tax, which is about double the rate of the ancient "pillu-vari" or grass tax, now paid by them, the buffalo tax having been abolished with the Moturpha taxes in or about 1850. The ancient grazing tax was levied at the rate of one-tenth bullah or two-fifths of an acre to each buffalo.

PART II.

European and other Immigrants.

Absence of restrictions on acquisition of land by Europeans.—Policy of Lord Amherst's Government.—Rules promulgated.—Orders of Madras Government regarding acquisition of lands on the Hills.—Mr. Lushington encourages settlements of Anglo-Indians.—Rates on lands in the Mélnád prohibitive—Mr. Sullivan proposes changes—determination of Government—subsequent modifications.—Radical changes in the policy of Government in 1842.—Rules in the Dehra Doon despatch.—Manual of Land Rules to be prepared.—Right of settlers to use of water.—Résumé of the manual.—Modification in 1858.—Redemption of land-tax sanctioned.—Causes of variety of tenure on the Hills.—Discussion on land policy of Government of India after the Mutiny—Lord Stanley's despatches—Lord Canning's Resolution—action of the Madras Government—discussions in Parliament.—Waste Lands Bill.—Nílagiri Land Rules sanctioned.—Debate in the House of Commons.—Changes in the Rules and their causes.—Auction system called in question.—Appointment of a Committee of Inquiry and results.—Table of Sales of Waste Lands.—Absence of Tope Rules.—Firewood allotments.

CHAP. XIII, PART II. — REVENUE HISTORY. — Absence of restrictions on acquisition of land by Europeans.

It remains for us now simply to trace the history of the land in connection with immigrant settlers. When Europeans first took up their residence on the Hills no rules had been laid down, or the policy of the East India Company indicated, in regard to the acquisition of lands by Europeans, more especially by their own servants. As will be known to covenanted civilians, their covenant, whilst containing severe restrictions against trading, *i.e.*, privately competing with their employers in the trade of the country, is silent in regard to the acquisition or ownership of land. Consequently when Mr. Sullivan, who was the first purchaser of land on the Hills, acquired the Stonehouse, and subsequently other properties, there were no restrictions on transactions of this nature. Believing strongly in the Tódas' right to the uplands, he purchased direct from them, and his conduct in so doing was never questioned by the Government of the day; so far from so doing the Government about ten years later purchased his properties from him, accepting his titles as valid. Other original settlers followed the course adopted by Mr. Sullivan, and many of the oldest properties in Ootacamand were acquired in this way. For some time no assessment was demanded by Government. For several years such land alienations were confined to the cantonment of Ootacamand; but during the rapid development of this station under Mr. Lushington's Government, in consequence of the increasing number of applications for land and the disorder and indefiniteness that existed in relation of many of the properties already acquired from the Tódas, the Madras Government towards the close of 1829 received orders from the Court of Directors to adapt their policy to the rules and instructions laid down by the Supreme Government in their resolution of the 7th May 1824, and by the Court in the despatch of 8th July 1829, "conceiving it expedient that the rules observed in granting permission to Europeans to hold lands in India should be, as nearly as circumstances will permit, uniform at the several Presidencies." CHAP. XIII, PART II. REVENUE HISTORY.

Policy of Lord Amherst's Government.

The immediate cause of the issue of the resolution of the 7th May was the desire of Doctor Wallich, Mr. Gordon, and others to obtain lands for coffee cultivation in Bengal—a project which Lord Amherst's Government were anxious to encourage. This document is of great interest, which is my excuse for quoting from it at length.

"As far as a judgment can in such cases be formed until trial be made, there appears to be abundant reason to conclude that the cultivation of coffee may be successfully prosecuted in this country on an extensive scale, and that the article may indeed be produced at a cost considerably below that which the lowest prices hitherto known in the market would amply reimburse, while at the same time there is scarcely anything of which the consumption is likely to experience so large an augmentation in the event of any material reduction of price.

"The extension of the export trade of India is an object of the highest importance both to England and to India, and the introduction of a new branch of trade such as that in question may eventually become would be a great national benefit. The speculation appears therefore to be one which is in a high degree worthy of the support of Government. From the nature of the case it is indispensably necessary that those who undertake it should have an assured tenure in the lands appropriated to the cultivation for a considerable period of time, and although it is to be expected and desired that the Natives will before long enter on the speculation and be guided by the example set to them in the conduct of it, yet to its early and successful introduction on a large scale it appears to be essentially requisite to allow scope to European enterprise and intelligence."

After remarking that the land required would ordinarily admit of easy demarcation, Lord Amherst expressed a hope that little difficulty would be experienced "in providing for the satisfactory adjustment of all claims and the effectual protection of all rights attaching to land to be used in the cultivation of coffee, or other use necessarily included within the limits of the plantation. For this purpose, and especially for the protection of the ryots and the security of the real interests of the speculators," especial rules were considered necessary. The rules may be summed up as follows :—

—rules promulgated.

(1.) Arrangements for occupation of land by Europeans, between them and the owners and occupiers, were to be certified by the Collector.

CHAP. XIII, PART II. — REVENUE HISTORY.

(2.) This officer's award was to be binding, subject to appeal to the Board of Revenue touching rent, adjustment of boundaries, and the like.

(3.) The tenure was to be leasehold, not freehold; but the terms of the lease were undefined.

(4.) Only "Europeans of respectability, being persons of course duly licensed as to residence," might be authorized to take out lease.

(5.) Before establishing a coffee plantation the intending planter must apply to Government for permission to do so, naming the district and the quantity of land to be included in the plantation.

(6.) On receipt of the permission of Government the party had to forward to the Collector full information regarding the tract and its occupants.

(7.) This statement was to be duly published in the neighbourhood and at the Collector's office; objectors to appear within a month.

(8.) On objection being taken, the Collector to hold a regular inquiry, and, if he allow it, to report the matter for orders of the Board of Revenue.

(9.) If he do not allow it, he shall order an officer to proceed to the spot, and, after measurement, &c., of the land, shall see that the necessary deeds are exchanged between the parties.

(10.) The Board of Revenue to confirm these proceedings.

(11.) Persons licensed to bear all expenses.

(12.) Lands occupied under hereditary right of occupancy not to be transferred without consent of such occupiers. As regards zemindars and middle-men the right to object depended upon "the nature of the intermediate tenure, but in general it (was) the desire of Government that no lands should be taken by Europeans unless all parties possessing an interest in the soil or in the rents shall consent to the arrangement."

(13.) Collector's decision, subject to appeal to the Board of Revenue, to be final in disputes of every kind and description relating to the land, water-courses, wells, rents, &c.

(14.) Lands (except malgoozaree) liable to sale in satisfaction of a Collector's award; also, if a planter should "violently disturb the possessions of his neighbours or should otherwise be guilty of any act in breach of the peace," the enforcement of this penalty was reserved to the Governor-General.

In the despatch of 1829 the Court extended these rules, which related to coffee only, to the cultivation of indigo and other agricultural products, providing that the length of the leases must in all cases be regulated with reference to the nature of the cultivation, and must not be greater than would be necessary to afford the undertaker the prospect of a fair remuneration for the capital he may expend. In no case was a lease to exceed twenty-one years without the express sanction of the Court. In the case of a European every transfer of a lease was to be approved by Government, so that they might satisfy themselves "in regard to the respectability and good character of the individuals" who were to hold.

Orders of the Madras Government regarding acquisition of lands on the Hills.

Prior to the receipt of instructions from the Court of Directors the Madras Government had, in November 1828, at the request of the military authorities, issued orders limiting the space to be allotted to each dwelling-house, exclusive of the site of the building and outhouses, to 2 cawnies (about 2⅔ acres), the area suggested by Sir Thomas Munro; and had directed that all land in excess, enclosed or appropriated without permission of Government, should be incorporated with the Circar land; and further directed that all proprietors and intending purchasers should take out grants from Government for their lands, "such grants being subject to the fees levied on the issue of similar instruments at the Presidency." Existing proprietors were allowed three months for the purpose; intending purchasers until they began the erection of their houses. Under orders issued about a fortnight later, such occupants were required to pay the compensation of 16 cantarai fanams, already mentioned, to the Tódas, and to Government quit-rent at the rate usually assessed on lands for which Government grants were then issued. And as regards the enclosures already made which exceeded two cawnies, it was ruled that each case should be submitted for the orders of Government. It was subsequently settled in 1831 that these grants were all to be personal—no European hereafter, if purchasing the property described in the grant, being permitted to occupy it without a fresh certificate in his own name—and that it rested with Government when issuing title-deeds for such grants to insert any special conditions in the deed. In addition to this instrument the Collector was to issue to the party a certificate of permission to occupy the land. Later in the same year (1831) it was decided that applications should be made to the Principal Collectors of Malabar and Coimbatore, according as the land concerned was situate in the Malabar or Coimbatore portion of the Nílagiris, but the Officer Commanding at Ootacamand had a voice in the disposal of lands in the cantonment. The ordinary rate of quit-rent was 5¼ rupees or 1½ pagoda per cawnie, whether within or without the cantonment of Ootacamand. This high rate of Rupees 3-15 per acre was fixed in 1810 as the ordinary quit-rent on lands held under Government grants in the provinces; in no case was the quit-rent to be less than 1 pagoda (Rupees 3½) per cawnie (*vide* Note 1, page 269; also Note 4, page 270, Maskell's Board's Circular Orders, 1855). The Government further declared that the leases should, as at Madras, be for an indefinite period, holding that the Bengal rules could not apply "to the erection of dwelling-houses on small plots of ground at a place where, from local circumstances, the acquisi-

CHAP. XIII, PART II. — REVENUE HISTORY.

tion of any considerable landed property is almost impossible." These grants, under which many of the older properties in Ootacamand were acquired or secured, were issued by the Government Registrar; but the instructions regarding the area to be occupied seem from the first to have been practically a dead letter. There is hardly a property in Ootacamand which does not exceed the prescribed limit, nor does it appear that in any case the special orders of Government were obtained to secure possession of the larger area. Meanwhile, however, settlers continued to purchase lands from the Tódas, notably Sir William Rumbold in the case already referred to.

Mr. Lushington encourages settlement of Anglo-Indians.

At this time also Mr. Lushington was encouraging Anglo-Indian agricultural settlers to occupy waste land outside the cantonment in extent according to the amount of their capital. No assessment appears to have been fixed on such grants, and, in addition to this implied concession, I find from a letter from Mr. Lushington's Private Secretary to the Officer Commanding the Nílagiris, that they were to receive a moderate supply of potatoes as seed from the Government Farm, and also spare implements of husbandry, to be paid for by instalments, and "such other assistance as may tend to encourage their industry and enable them to overcome their first difficulties without expense to Government. Similar indulgences may be shown to the Native cultivators on the Hills, and the Government anticipates great benefit to them, to the community, and to the revenue from the extended cultivation of European grains and vegetables, especially potatoes, which judicious aid and encouragement are likely to produce." In a letter dated July 1833 the Collector of Malabar requests the Board's instructions regarding the assessment of such lands, and remarks, "but very few persons of this description (Anglo-Indian settlers) have as yet been induced to settle on the Neilgherries, and these are by no means in easy circumstances. Some of them have borrowed money from the Philanthropic Society to enable them to carry on the undertaking, and I have reason to believe they were led to expect they would be exempt from the tax, at least for some years." He then recommends that, considering the expense of labour and other disadvantages, lands cultivated by them might be given free of tax for two or three years, and that then they should not be assessed higher than the punja rates paid by Natives. No definite orders appear to have been issued upon this important matter, but it will be remembered that shortly afterwards Sir Frederick Adam was engaged in investigating the land history of the plateau, especially in regard to the Tódas and Badagas.

—rates on lands in the Mélnád prohibitive.

It however appears from a letter from Mr. Sullivan, dated January 1835, that the order of Government fixing the assessment on land in Ootacamand at $5\frac{1}{4}$ rupees per cawnie was held to apply to the whole of the Méluád, or the uplands of the Tódanád, and he urged that an adherence to this rate would inevitably drive stock and capital to the waste lands of the middle plateau of the Hills, where the average assessment did not exceed a half-rupee per cawnie. "This question is one of importance," he writes, "because from the great advantages which the Hills possess in soil, command of water, and certainty of seasons, they are capable of supporting a very large population, and of administering in seasons of scarcity to the wants of the country below. It is the interest therefore of Government, in the largest sense of the term, to encourage the investment of capital in their cultivation, and that will best be done by extending the assessment which was fixed thirty years ago upon the lands of the three great divisions to the Malnaad. * * * * The land within the cantonment (Ootacamand) and beyond it is occupied indiscriminately by Europeans, East Indians, and Natives, and it is obvious that there must be one assessment for all, or they to whom advantages are given will drive others out of the market." The force of this objection is borne out by the fact that six years later it was ascertained that no less than fifteen estates had been acquired by purchase from Badagas in the Coimbatore portion of the Hills near Kótagiri and Coonoor, aggregating some 800 acres, unsecured by a Government grant; whilst in the Malabar portion of the plateau it does not appear that a single estate was formed during that period.

CHAP. XIII, PART II. — REVENUE HISTORY.

—Mr. Sullivan's proposed changes.

Mr. Sullivan, however, shortly afterwards somewhat modified his views, and in his minute written in the month of August in the same year he suggested that lands situated at a certain distance from the cantonment of Ootacamand should be assessed according to the standard prevailing in the nearest Badaga village; but as regards the lands within the cantonment he observes, "considering that the land in Ootacamund is stated to be of the richest 'description, and capable, when worked, of producing as rich crops as are to be seen in any part of the world,' and, as already stated, a market is at hand for produce, an assessment for lands of the *first class* of double the amount which is now paid for the same class in the Burgher villages, or Rupees 7 per bullah, or Rupees 2-5-4 per cawnie, would be a very moderate charge; an increase of one-third might be made on lands of the second, of one-half upon the third, and of one-fourth upon the fourth class, beyond which it would not probably be necessary to go in the classification."

A year later we find the Board of Revenue approving generally of Mr. Sullivan's proposals, though raising no objections to the suggestions of the Collector of Malabar that the assessment on

CHAP. XIII, PART II. — REVENUE HISTORY.

enclosures should be fixed at the ordinary rates, Rupees 5¼ and 3½ per cawnie. In regard to Mr. Sullivan's proposal that lands occupied for agricultural purposes should be at the same rates as the lands held by Badagas, they remarked that they held the proportions just, "because were the assessment regulated so as to exceed the rates of assessment paid by the Burghers, the occupancy of new lands would be checked, or to avoid the higher assessment new-comers would hold of the Burghers, and thereby defeat the object of the comparatively high assessment. Besides it has been usual with Government to continue the rates of taxation which have been established. In the populous and rich district of Malabar the ancient light assessment has been preserved, and the private rights in the waste land have been continued to the proprietors. There seems no good reason, therefore, why the advantages of the established rates of assessment should not be secured to the scanty population of the Hills."

—determination of Government.

In their order of 25th July 1836 the Government accepted Mr. Sullivan's proposals as regards agricultural lands in Ootacamand and those at some distance therefrom, but maintained the ordinary rates, 5¼ and 3½ rupees, on lands enclosed for purposes of building. The territorial limit of the agricultural lands paying the enhanced rates was to be fixed by the Board with reference to their accessibility to the market. This limit was shortly afterwards fixed, on the Board's recommendation, roughly at three miles radius from the centre of the station—the present limits of the station, not municipal limits. Badagas already cultivating within this limit were to be exempt. The limiting line followed the extreme boundary of the Badaga villages situated nearest to a circle of three miles from the centre of the cantonment, and where there were no villages it ran through the points nearest the circle best suited to be used as landmarks.[1]

—subsequent modifications.

In December following, it having been brought to the notice of Government that the rates of assessment fixed for house enclosures pressed heavily on the house-proprietors of Ootacamand, they determined to maintain the highest rate, Rupees 5¼, for the cawnie of land which constituted the site of the house. The remainder was ordered to be assessed at the rate in force on fourth-class lands, viz., Rupees 1-2-4 per cawnie. At the beginning of the following year (1837) it was decided to raise the assessment on lands of the second class taken up for agricultural purposes within the cantonment by three-fourths instead of one-third the ordinary assessment, so that the gradation in the assessment might be more regular.

[1] The exact limits so fixed will be found in a memorandum by Mr. D. Elliott in the Board's Proceedings, 18th August 1836.

These orders still regulate the assessment on lands, whether for building or agricultural purposes, occupied within the cantonment of Ootacamand.

Radical changes in the policy of Government in 1842.

It is unnecessary to recount the position occupied by European settlers in relation to the Tódas during the five years ending 1842. The close of this year, however, marks an era in the history of European settlements in South India. The difficulties which existed in the issue by the Government Registrar of permission certificates[1] for lands acquired on the Hills was ascertained to be due to the fact that the rights of the ancient occupiers of the soil had never been defined, and that the existing land arrangements did not adequately provide for schemes of extensive improvement and the settlement of capitalists on the Hills. In issuing fresh rules and laying down new conditions, the Government appear to have calculated on the concurrence of occupiers; but, supported by the lawyers, they naturally demurred to accept conditions which more or less affected the validity of their titles and the value of their properties. The whole question was referred to the Court of Directors in despatches of 27th December 1842 and 15th February 1843. The Court's reply of the 21st June following has already been referred to at length in the matter of the Tódas' claims, but this document is of equal historical moment on account of the policy which it laid down for the disposal of waste lands. That policy is detailed in a despatch dated 23rd February 1842 regarding the grants of waste lands in Dehra Doon, and this Government were directed to act, as far as circumstances would admit, in accordance with the instructions contained in that despatch; but it was observed that before such instructions could be systematically acted upon, it would be necessary to survey and map the Hills, "distinguishing the lands in the occupation of Government and private individuals, those brought under cultivation by the Burghers, those which are to be left in the permanent occupation of the Tódas, and those entirely unoccupied, over a portion of which the Tódas have been accustomed to pasture their herds." This work was to be set in hand at once, but in the mean while the Government were permitted to accept eligible proposals for cultivation, care being taken that the rights of other parties were not infringed and the general rules laid down by the Court were observed as far as practicable. The Court also directed that the rates fixed for enclosures for dwelling-houses in Ootacamand should be charged for similar enclosures outside the limits of that cantonment.

---

[1] The rules regulating the issue of these certificates in the provinces were promulgated in April 1835, and will be found in Appendix No. 4, Maskell's edition of Circular Orders of Board of Revenue, 1855.

CHAP. XIII, PART II. — REVENUE HISTORY.

Land Rules in the Dehra Doon despatch.

The general rules laid down in the Dehra Doon despatch may be summed up as follows :—

(1.) Grantee to erect and keep in repair boundary marks.

(2.) Public thoroughfares or estates vest in the State and rights of way to be respected.

(3.) Grantee to pay 1 per cent. on his assessment for repair of public roads.

(4.) Right to minerals reserved to Government; right to remove lime and other stone from river-beds within grant to the public.

(5.) Right to distribute water reserved to the State.

(6.) Grantee to aid in the police arrangements of neighbourhood.

(7.) No grant to exceed 4,000 acres to one person; additional land might be granted at a certain sum per acre.

(8.) Grants to be made in section of 1,000 acres.

(9.) In grants of forest lands certain number of sections to be reserved for public timber requirements.

(10.) All grants to be on lease, subject at expiration of lease to ordinary assessment of the district.

(11.) Sale or transfer of lands not brought under cultivation null and void. Such uncultivated portions to be regarded as personal and hereditary only.

(12.) No grant to be made without previous survey and fixing of boundaries.

(13.) Public competition by tenders to be invited; highest to be accepted.

(14.) "Ancient common rights not to be abrogated until the land is actually brought into cultivation."

A Manual of Land Rules to be prepared.

The Board of Revenue were required by the Madras Government to submit a manual of instructions[1] embodying these principles, but, though submitted very shortly after the receipt of the order, the Government did not, as already stated, sanction it until the close of 1849, after the completion of Major Ouchterlony's survey.

Right of settlers to the use of water.

Whilst these subjects were engaging the attention of the Board, the question of the right of settlers on the Hills to apply the water of the streams of the mountains to the irrigation of their farms and gardens came before Government. The right so to utilize the streams had been disputed by Mr. Wroughton, the Collector of Coimbatore, especially in regard to the lands irrigated by the Bhaváni, on the ground that the water should descend unchecked into his district, "in virtue of mamool and prescriptive right, and the great extent of irrigated land under that river, and the high rate of assessment fixed upon it." The Board would not admit the claim on the ground of prescriptive right, although the plea

[1] The manual will be found as Appendix No. 5 of Maskell's edition of Board's Circular Orders, 1855.

that the Badagas and other hill tribes had never utilized streams as irrigants was not disputed, asserting that it would not be easy to establish "a principle which, conceding their title to the land (as Government had done), would deny their right to the water which rises in it or flows through it." They also argued that compared with the assessments charged on dry lands in Coimbatore, the Hill assessments were not low when all the countervailing circumstances were taken into consideration. "To exclude," the Board go on to say, "from the advantages of irrigation a tract of country so favoured by nature as the Neilgherry table-land, fitted for the culture of the mulberry tree, coffee, flax, and other valuable products both of the Torrid and the Temperate Zones, while it would be opposed to all true and enlightened policy, would, the Board submit, be productive of little or no benefit to the inhabitants of the low country. The quantity of water required for irrigation on the Hills is inconsiderable, and even of that quantity . . . . some portion percolates the earth and falls into the same stream at a lower level. On the other hand, the advantage to the ryots of the plains from an increased demand for their rice and other products on the Hills, consequent on the extension of agricultural speculations prosecuted there, is too obvious to need remark." But whilst holding these views as regards the rights of the ryots of the plains, they also held that a settler should not be permitted to turn the course of the stream, raise a dam, or cut a channel without first communicating with the local authorities, so as to prevent "one cultivator from engrossing water to the prejudice of another, and ensuring to all a fair and equal proportion of this necessary element of cultivation." The Government however did not dispose of the question raised for disposal of land applications submitted shortly afterwards, but determined to await the survey of the Hills, which was very shortly afterwards taken in hand. In a despatch, however, of the 17th June 1845, the Court of Directors entirely agreed in the views of the Board of Revenue regarding the disposal and control of the streams of the Hills.

Résumé of the manual.

In the manual, after reciting the settlement made in 1836 and 1837 as to assessment on lands in Ootacamand and lands taken up for cultivation, hitherto used as pasture by the Tódas, and declaring that the demand on Badaga arable lands had been determined, the Government laid down the following rules, which applied to Europeans or others taking up land for agricultural and building purposes:—

(1.) Native inhabitants of the Nílagiris to hold on putta lands occupied and any further lands they may take up for their own cultivation.

(2.) Native settlers to hold similarly "such lands as they may take up *boná fide* for their own occupancy."

CHAP. XIII, PART II. — REVENUE HISTORY. —

(3.) Collector empowered to allot for houses and gardens land not exceeding half cawnie, at ordinary rate of assessment, to "East Indians, Natives of the agricultural classes, Europeans of the lower orders, pensioners and others." The grant might contain any special conditions.

(4.) On receipt of application Collector to make full inquiry regarding claims thereto, character of land, if forest, whether it should be reserved.

(5.) Report to be sent to Board of Revenue with plan.

(6.) On their approval land to be put up to public auction, upset price ordinarily eight to ten years' assessment; ordinary assessment to be levied yearly.

(7.) Fee-simple not sold; lease for agricultural objects not to exceed 30 years, for building purposes 99 years, renewable every 33 years at option of lessee without fine or enhancement of assessment. Agricultural leases liable to re-assessment at termination of lease.

(8.) Applicant to satisfy Collector regarding his means.

(9.) Certain portion of grant to be brought in given period into cultivation, or lease liable to be declared null and void; portions not cultivated liable to forfeiture.

(10.) Uncultivated portions inalienable.

(11.) Lessee to erect and maintain boundary-marks.

(12.) Lessee to respect and grant rights of way, but in case of public roads, &c., &c., to be entitled to compensation, to be settled by arbitration.

(13.) Control over all streams, springs, reservoirs and channels of irrigation reserved "in the fullest manner" by Government. Diversion of streams requires sanction of revenue authorities.

(14.) Minerals reserved by Government.

(15.) Government may grant lands, without inviting competition, on special conditions.

These are the principal provisions relating to immigrants, minor articles and those relating to the Tódas having been omitted.

Modifications in 1858.

The instructions were amended in 1858 as follows:—

(1.) Upset price to be fixed by the Collector.

(2.) The rule regarding applicants' means to be omitted.

(3.) The penalties for non-cultivation to be omitted.

(4.) Alienation of uncultivated portions allowed, if first registered in Collector's Office.

Redemption of land-tax sanctioned.

In 1859 the redemption of the land-tax was authorised at twenty years' purchase, subsequently raised to twenty-five years.

Causes of variety of tenures on the Hills.

Such has been the history of the phases of the action of Government in relation to the occupation of lands prior to the introduction of the present Waste Land Rules; and tenures of land in the cantonment of Ootacamand in a special degree, and in the stations and outlying country tracts as far as immigrants are concerned, are as various as the phases of their action.

Not only is there marked differences in the tenures of the several properties, but many properties are occupied under several tenures; whilst much land, especially in the Native portions of the station, is held under a squatting tenure, which, until recently, was no recognised tenure at all, but simply an implied permission on the part of Government to the squatter to retain possession of the space originally occupied without permission. The ordinary rate for puttas for lands held by Native cultivators in Ootacamand is Rupees 1-13-6, and for squatter tenure in the station Rupees 10 per acre. The partial exclusion of the stations from the operation of the Waste Land Rules further complicated matters, and there can be little question that order will never be obtained until a complete settlement is effected on defined principles. Such a settlement is as much needed in the stations as it is in the district.

Discussion on the land policy of Government following the Mutiny. —Lord Stanley's despatches.

After the mutiny, for political reasons, the land systems of India were much discussed. This discussion was focussed by the Secretary of State's (Lord Stanley) despatch of 31st December 1858; it raised three questions—

(1) The redemption of the land-tax generally.

(2) The expediency of permitting "grantees of waste lands, under existing rules, to commute the annual payments stipulated under the rules by a single payment at the time of receiving possession of the grant."

(3) The expediency of disposing of waste lands in perpetuity, free of all prospective charge for land revenue.

Lord Stanley, in March 1859, desired information regarding the extent of land capable of cultivation, but uncultivated, at the disposal of Government in British India; and at the same time required the Government of India to state "the conditions which, having regard to the difference in revenue administration prevailing in the respective localities, they would recommend for disposing of such lands either for a term of years or in perpetuity, to persons desirous of bringing them into cultivation."

The Madras Government, whilst deprecating the redemption of the land-tax generally, resolved to deal with certain lands in accordance with the policy indicated by the Secretary of State. Their determination was (1) to put up to auction all lands required for building purposes at an upset price of twenty times the assessment of the land, (2) to allow lands occupied wholly or in part by buildings to be converted into freehold on payment of twenty times the annual assessment, (3) to give a fee-simple title in certain cases without payment (*e.g.*, lands included in village sites), (4) to make the orders applicable to the Nílagiris and the Wainád, the Shevaroys and the Pulnís.

—Lord Canning's Resolutions.

For nearly two years the Government of India had under discussion the questions raised by Lord Stanley. In October 1861

CHAP. XIII, PART II. — REVENUE HISTORY.

appeared Lord Canning's celebrated Resolution, enunciating the policy of the Government of India, first, regarding the sale of unassessed waste; secondly, regarding the redemption of the land revenue. The rules laid down were long known as the Fee-simple Rules, though this term does not appear in the Resolution, and although it contains no provision prohibiting the levy of an assessment where the full property was transferred to the purchaser. It defined the tenure of waste lands granted under its terms as "an heritable and transferable property, held in perpetuity, free from all claims, either of the Government or of third persons, prior to or inconsistent with the grant." The rules prescribed among other things that the land might be granted after thirty days' notice; that it should only be put up to auction in the event of there being more than one applicant, the upset price to be that of an ordinary grant; that the price of unassessed land (uncleared) should not exceed 2½ rupees per acre, of land unencumbered with jungle Rupees 5 per acre; that possession of unsurveyed lands might be given before survey. The Resolution fixed twenty years' assessment for the redemption of the land-tax.

—action of the Madras Government.

The Madras Government submitted draft rules as required, though the draft was opposed to their own views, remarking that the rules already in force in this Presidency provided for sales by auction, and consequently that there was no objection to the extension of the system proposed in the Resolution; but that lands in Madras so sold were subject to assessment. It was pointed out also that the upset price of Rupees 2½ and Rupees 5 was much too low for coffee and tea lands, and that the price of land was not the true obstacle to the introduction of European capital and skill; it was also urged that the price should bear a fair proportion to the profits derived from the land, and be sufficient to enable Government to perform its obligations. The propriety of selling lands, subject or not subject to a yearly assessment, at the option of the applicant was suggested, but the auction system was insisted on in all cases as fair to all concerned, and as removing all possibility of favouritism. It was further pointed out that the rules were quite unsuited to the Nílagiris, and the Government subsequently excepted these Hills from the operation of the rules of October 1861, the Government of India not objecting.

—discussions in Parliament.

Lord Canning's rules met with much adverse criticism in England, and were brought before the House of Commons by Mr. Smollett in May 1862 (Hansard, No. 166, p. 2136). In the July following Sir C. Wood addressed to the Government of India his celebrated despatch disallowing some of the most important provisions of the Resolution. He directed that waste lands should invariably be sold by public auction; that in all cases the boundaries should be marked out before sale; that each Provincial Government should fix the upset price suited to various descriptions of land in each district; that in no case should possession be given before survey; that the time allowed to third parties to object should be fixed by law; that the price of redemption should vary according to the market value at the time of four per cent. stocks.

Waste Lands Bill.

A fresh draft of rules was accordingly called for; meanwhile, however, the Waste Lands Bill engaged the attention of Government and finally became law, 10th March 1863, its operation extending to the Nílagiris.

The Nílagiri Land Rules sanctioned.

Shortly after this the Madras Government submitted the Unassessed Waste Land Rules and also special drafts for the Nílagiris, the Shevaroys, and the Wainád. These special drafts differed from the general code "in the reservation of assessment and the absence of a minimum upset price." The rules for the Nílagiris were finally approved by the Secretary of State in October 1863, on the ground that the lands on the Nílagiris were subject to an *annual general assessment* and did not fall within the scope of the rules for the sale of *unassessed waste.* This distinction is of the highest importance.[1] The rules for the sale of waste lands on the Nílagiris will be found in the appendix. It should be here observed that in practice they have been confined to the plateau and slopes, and that the lowlands to the north, between slopes and the Moyar, have heretofore been excluded from their operation, though I am not aware of any special sanction for this procedure.

Debate in the House of Commons.

The despatch upon which these rules were based raised much discussion in England, and came before the House of Commons, on the motion of Mr. Henry Seymour, for its cancelment in May 1863. A full report of the debate, in which several leading statesmen took part, will be found in Hansard, Vol. 170, p. 1610-1659. The main points raised were—the redemption of the land-tax; the declaring auction sales of waste lands compulsory throughout India; the necessity of a law of limitation connected with the occupation of land. It is unnecessary to detail the discussion, but it is noteworthy that Sir C. Wood, when objecting to the upset

---

[1] Mr. Breeks writing, in 1869, regarding objections to the Waste Land Rules, says:—"There is some ground no doubt for these objections, and individual cases of hardship could, I dare say, be adduced; but the lands on the Niligheries are not unassessed waste practically unlimited in area. * * * The lands are assessed lands, limited in area and dotted all over with villages of the hill tribes, who, by long use for grazing and cultivation purposes, have acquired a natural right to be consulted before large tracts are alienated."

CHAP. XIII, PART II. — REVENUE HISTORY.

prices fixed by Lord Canning, drew special attention to the Nílagiris, mentioning an instance of 45 acres of land having realized Rupees 1,310, which, with the assessment on the description sold, Rupees 2 per acre, with a twenty-five years' redemption right, gave a total value of Rupees 80 per acre, and urged that land which could fetch such a price could not reasonably be sold for 5 shillings per acre.

Changes in the rules and their causes.

Since the promulgation of the Waste Land Rules there have been a few relaxations favouring the planting industry. In 1869 the depressed condition of the planting interests, and the rather general disapproval of the auction system by that interest, led to the investigation of the matter. Much valuable information will be found in the Revenue Board's Proceedings, 18th March 1870, and the Government Proceedings, 22nd September 1876, Revenue Department. Under the original rules an assessment of Rupees 2 for forest and Rupee 1 for grass land per acre was charged from date of purchase, but in the order above quoted the assessment on forest land was postponed to beginning of the sixth year, that on grass land reduced to 8 annas per acre but levied from date of purchase. These orders had retrospective effect. In making this concession the Government remark that they "fully recognise the political and other incidental advantages to be derived from an influx of Europeans and European capital into India, and they would gladly give every reasonable encouragement to this movement. It is true that the grant of land by Government entirely free of tax would not make the cultivation of coffee, tea, or cinchona a profitable speculation under certain circumstances; but any modification of the existing rules which would render them more favourable to the planter could not fail, in some degree, to assist him ; and it is impossible to deny that at present the large majority of existing estates are in a languishing condition, and that their proprietors have been brought to the verge of ruin." The concession regarding forest land proceeded on the assumption that a coffee estate would be in full bearing by that time. The free period was extended to grass land taken up for tea and fuel plantations in August 1874, the concession being especially intended to encourage tea planting.

Auction system called in question.

When making these concessions the Government expressed an opinion that "the sale of land on the Hills by auction under the existing rules presents impediments to cultivation which it may be desirable to remove." "Many thousand acres of land" they observed, "are still available with scarcely an applicant, and this tends to show that precautions against land-jobbing may no longer be needed. His Excellency in Council is therefore willing to consider whether it may be possible to abrogate this system beyond certain limits, say, three to five miles round the hill stations, and in lieu thereof to charge a very moderate upset price, which might be fixed at different rates for different districts of the Hills for all comers, subject, of course, to the assessment and stipulations intended to secure the *bona fides* of the purchasers. Waste lands might be subjected to a special rate and valuation with reference to the standing timber." The questions were referred to the Board of Revenue for report, and the Commissioner was ordered to form a committee consisting of gentlemen "well acquainted with the condition of land on the Hills." The committee constituted under this order consisted of Mr. J. R. Cockerell, Major-General H. R. Morgan, Mr. W. G. McIvor, Captain Campbell Walker, Mr. W. Cotton Rhode, and Mr. E. J. C. Brace. Their report and draft of land rules, which contained many eminently radical alterations, will be found, with the Board of Revenue's review thereon, in G.O., 18th February 1876. This order was not final, but in pursuance of the policy already indicated the Government directed the Board to draw up another scheme of rules, abandoning the auction system, and "vesting in the Commissioner authority to dispose of individual applications, subject to an appeal to the Board of Revenue." The Commissioner was instructed to have forest reserves defined. The draft rules submitted by the Board will be found in G.O., 5th May 1876. The modification of rules has been postponed by Government, as it appeared that the sanction of the Secretary of State to any vital changes would be necessary. Meanwhile a commission was appointed to settle on forest reserves and the completion of the Nílagiri revenue survey ordered to be expedited. The result has been that the sale of forest lands under the rules has been practically stopped.

—appointment of a committee of inquiry and result.

The following table shows the lands sold under the rules since their introduction. It will be observed that the average price does not exceed 7 rupees an acre. The land however includes a considerable area of grass land. Good land may be obtained from Badagas for 10 rupees an acre, but *inter se* lands are often transferred for much less.

CHAP. XIII, PART II.

REVENUE HISTORY.

Statement of Lands sold under the Waste Land Rules.

Year.	Number of Lots.	Total Area ascertained by Survey.	Total Price realized.
		ACRES.	RS.
1863-64	21	2,450	12,934
1864-65	22	2,233	10,992
1865-66	90	2,788	4,610
1866-67	37	832	1,536
1867-68	27	305	3,700
1868-69	2	4	523
1869-70	9	58	745
1870-71	26	246	658
1871-72	21	93	2,076
1872-73	13	291	1,273
1873-74	13	538	16,856
1874-75	16	1,631	2,028
1875-76	15	607	11,906
1876-77	18	1,505	7,206
1877-78	27	1,008	8,051
1878-79	12	777	19,491
	369	15,373	104,590

Firewood allotments.

Before closing this section I would note that the Tope Rules do not apply to this district. The Board suggested their introduction in 1869, but the proposal was objected to by Mr. Breeks, as he feared the concession might lead to a few persons creating a monopoly. The Government, however, sanctioned the grant of blocks of land, not exceeding 50 acres, in the neighbourhood of the hill stations for *firewood* plantations, rent free for seven years, subject to confirmation at the end of that period, if fully planted up, at an assessment of Rupee 1 per acre and grant of title-deed; if not fully planted, to lapse to Government. The question of introducing the Tope Rules was revived in 1876 and is still unsettled.

PART III.

Revenue Survey.

First survey.—Major Ouchterlony's survey.—Surveyors appointed on introduction of Waste Land Rules.—Special Assistant Collector placed in charge.—Work transferred to Superintendent, Revenue Survey.—Settlement limits.—Rules for conduct of operations.—Survey operations after creation of Nílagiri Commission.—Work performed.

CHAP. XIII, PART III. — Revenue History.

The first revenue survey, as distinguished from topographical,[1] was carried out by the orders of Mr. Garrow, Collector in Coimbatore, in or about 1805. I have already quoted Mr. Sullivan to the effect that it was purely nominal. In 1820 Mr. Sullivan obtained permission to have a rough survey of the cultivated lands, but what the results of that survey were I have not been able to ascertain.

First survey.

The first systematic survey, however, of the Nílagiris was that ordered by the Court of Directors in 1843. It was completed in 1847. It combined, in a measure, revenue with topographical information. It did not extend to the Kúndas. The results are detailed in Major Ouchterlony's "Geographical and Statistical Memoir." It showed the area of the plateau of the Nílagiris proper to be 268,494 acres (no allowance being made for undulations in the surface); 23,772 acres had up to that date been brought under cultivation, of which between fifteen and sixteen thousand appear to have been kept ordinarily under the plough.

Major Ouchterlony's survey.

The Waste Land Rules necessitated a fresh and more detailed survey. This survey, however, succeeded the introduction of the rules, whilst Major Ouchterlony's preceded the promulgation of the "manual" of 1849. In May 1862, in reply to enquiries from the Collector of Coimbatore, the Government ordered (1) that one or two surveyors should be sent up to the Hills temporarily, but that the establishment sanctioned for Wainád would subsequently be available for some months in the year for work on the Hills; (2) that parties applying for land should specify boundaries; (3) that hill stations should embrace lands within three miles of the centre of Ootacamand and one-and-a-half mile of that of Coonoor and Kótagiri; (4) that the Collector should reserve lands required for public purposes. At the end of 1862 the establishment employed on the Hills consisted of two surveyors on Rupees 150 each. These surveyors worked under the supervision

Surveyors appointed on introduction of Waste Land Rules.

[1] Mr. Macmahon's notes in 1811-12 and Captain Ward's memoir of survey in 1820-24 will be found in the appendices.

CHAP. XIII, PART III. — REVENUE HISTORY.

of the District Engineer, Coimbatore. The rules as finally settled were promulgated in 1863. The articles especially relating to survey, are (1) that lots should not exceed 500 acres without, or 10 acres within, station limits; (2) that each lot should be compact, and as nearly as possible a parallelogram—road or water frontage not to exceed half the depth of the block; (3) no lot to be sold until surveyed and durable marks fixed.

Special Assistant Collector placed in charge.

In October 1863, partly with the view of expediting the disposal of applications for waste lands, the Special Assistant Collector was transferred from Malabar. Considerable sales of waste lands took place in 1863-64, and towards the close of 1864 the Government ordered three surveyors to work on the Nílagiris under the orders of the Superintendent of Revenue Survey, Colonel Priestly. It appeared that the rules had been disregarded; that the lots were not compact, and included streams which should have been excluded. The decision as to the shape, &c., of the land to be sold was, before survey, to be fixed by the revenue officers of the district. Whilst the Assistant Collector was in charge of the demarcation about 7,000 acres were marked out and subsequently surveyed prior to the transfer of the work to the Revenue Survey Department, but much of this had necessarily to be revised in accordance with the stricter requirements of this department. In some cases considerable discrepancies in area of estates were discovered. In 1865, on the representation of the Superintendent of Revenue Survey that the two surveyors were unaided by demarcators, draughtsmen, or computors, the Government sanctioned the employment of such assistants, but they were to be borne on the strength of the nearest survey party. Towards the close of the same year the Government ordered the Superintendent of Revenue Survey to arrange for the survey of the cinchona plantations, and in the following year directed that the Hill stations should be mapped on a large scale, as many surveyors being employed as might be necessary to complete the work in a year or eighteen months. Subsequently the employment of a detachment of No. 1 party on the Hills was sanctioned, and later in the year the party was strengthened by the transfer of the Wainád surveyors during the unhealthy season.

Work transferred to Superintendent, Revenue Survey.

Settlement limits.

In October of the following year the Government fixed the exact limits of the hill stations as follows:—

Ootacamand	...	3 miles radius from the Jail.		
Coonoor ...	...	2	do.	Gray's Hotel.
Kótagiri ...	...	2	do.	the Church.

Rules for conduct of operations.

At the same time the Government approved the following rule for preparation of survey plans. All reserves, whether of streams, roads, rights of way, wood, or any other right, to be clearly shown in the survey plans and exhibited in distinctive colour. The Collector to give survey officers the necessary information. The assessment on area reserved to be in all cases deducted.

Survey operations after creation of Nílagiri Commission.

Shortly after the constitution of the Nílagiri Commission Mr. Breeks reported that, owing to the delay in the survey and demarcation, it had been impossible to issue title-deeds, in many cases, of land sold under the rules, and consequently that no assessment had been levied on the lands sold. The demarcation was so defective that he recommended the transfer of the work wholly to the Survey Department, the boundaries being pointed out to the surveyors by the Commissioner or his Assistant in the presence of the demarcating clerk, who was to remain on the ground until the work was completed to aid in supply of labour and in other ways. This clerk was finally abolished by order of Government in 1873. These proposals were sanctioned; the responsibility of the surveyor extended little beyond seeing that the marks were fixed in the manner indicated by the Commissioner, on whom still devolved the adjustments of disputes and the settlement of the limits of blocks.

He at the same time recommended the location of a small but fully constituted party on the Hills, not only to be employed on survey of waste land blocks, but also in marking out the main lines of roads and also outlying estates, and in the preparation of a guide map. In the following year he urged the matter again, but it was not till 1870 that the sphere of the department's action was extended to all lands under occupation, including the putta lands occupied by the Hill tribes. Prior to this, with exception of occasional special surveys of estates, such as those in Kátéri Valley in 1869, the work undertaken was chiefly connected with waste land blocks and the survey of all properties in the Hill stations. About this time an Assistant Superintendent was placed in charge of the detachment in place of a Sub-Assistant, and he conducted its operations until the close of 1872 under the general superintendence of the Deputy Superintendent at Coimbatore. The old arrangement was then reverted to, but in 1876 the superior officer was again placed in immediate charge.

The following memorandum shows the position of the survey up to 31st March 1878:—

Work performed.

The total area of the Nílagiris, exclusive of the Ouchterlony Valley and the three amshoms annexed from Wainád, is 704·27 square miles. The area surveyed on 16-inch scale of coffee estates is 23·59 square miles; waste land blocks, 19·33 square miles; and puttas, building sites, Government forests, reserves, &c., 278·39 square miles. The number of holdings comprised in the district

CHAP. XIII, PART III. REVENUE HISTORY.

is 17,115, the average area in acres is 12·02, and the cost per square mile of demarcation and survey, including registry, is Rupees 1,606-14-10. This rate is based on cost of survey of settlements 24 inch, as well as other tracts 16 inches to a mile. The whole area (704·27 square miles) has been topographically surveyed on 2 and 4 inch scales at a cost per square mile of Rupees 37-8-8. The cost of revenue survey of the three settlements—Coonoor, Ootacamand and Kótagiri—which comprise an area of 53·70 square miles, is Rupees 3,137-6-11 per square mile, and of the remainder of revenue survey is Rupees 1,225-5-6 per square mile. The work remaining to be done on 16-inch scale is 0·10 square mile fields to be plotted, 21·97 square miles to be detailed, and 95·72 square miles to be finished; and these will be completed by the end of September 1879; and the work remaining to be done on 2 and 4 inch scales is 81·42 square miles to be plotted, 122·22 square miles to be detailed, and 249·50 to be finished, and these should be completed by the end of December 1879, excepting the Malabar boundary, which remains undecided.

CHAPTER XIV.

REVENUE ADMINISTRATION.

Revenue powers of the Commissioner and his Assistant.—Deputy Tahsildars.—Revenue Inspectors.—Maniyagar and Karnams.—Hukamnáma.—South-East Wainád.—Local Funds.—Pound Fund.

CHAP. XIV. — REVENUE ADMINISTRATION.

Revenue powers of the Commissioner and the Assistant Commissioner.

UNDER Act I of 1868 the Commissioner of the Nílagiris is invested with all the powers of a Collector devolving upon that official by any Act or Regulation, and is the head of the revenue administration. The Assistant Commissioner is invested also with similar revenue powers, but an appeal against his decisions lies to the Commissioner in his capacity of Collector. The district is not, as far as the Commissioner and his Assistant are concerned, split up into divisions, but their authority is conterminous, with the exception of the treasury,[1] which is practically in charge of the Assistant Commissioner. The revenue administration rests almost solely with the Commissioner and has the following establishment :—

	Per Mensem.
	RS.
Sheristadar and General Manager	200
Account Department (3 Clerks)	765
English Correspondence Department (3 Clerks)	165
1 Duffadar, 14 Peons, 1 Masalchy, 1 Sweeper and 1 Toty.	143
Vernacular Department (4 Clerks)	105
2 Deputy Tahsildars and their establishment ...	305
3 Revenue Inspectors	85
Temporary—	
1 Malayalam Clerk	50
2 License Tax Clerks	40

[1] The Madras Bank is practically the treasury. At the Commissioner's Office are kept the accounts of the district, all moneys being received directly by the Bank supported by a chellan or receipt from the Commissioner or his Assistant. In the same way disbursements are made directly by the Bank on the authorization of the Commissioner or the Assistant Commissioner.

CHAP. XIV. — REVENUE ADMINISTRATION. — Deputy Tahsildars.

The Commissioner is aided in the administration by two Deputy Tahsildars—one stationed at Coonoor, the other at Gúdalúr. The revenue jurisdiction of the former is conterminous with the magisterial jurisdiction of the Joint Magistrate of Wellington; that of the latter extends over South-East Wainád. The Deputy Tahsildar of Coonoor draws a salary of Rupees 65 monthly. His principal duties relate to inspection of waste land applications and reporting on petitions referred to him by the Commissioner. He is *ex-officio* stamp-vendor and Money Order Agent. He has no sub-treasury properly so called, as all collections are transmitted to head-quarters at the end of each month. The revenue establishment of the Deputy Tahsildar, Gúdalúr, consists of—

	RS.
2 Gumastahs, each at	20
1 Revenue Inspector at	30
Peons, &c.	35

His establishment as District Munsif costs 65 rupees monthly.

Revenue Inspectors.

There are two Revenue Inspectors on the Nílagiris. One works immediately under the Commissioner in the Tódanád and Kúndas, the other under the Sub-Magistrate of Coonoor. There is one Revenue Inspector in South-East Wainád.

Maniyagar and Karnams.

There are four head Maniyagar with colleagues, and six Karnams, one of each of the former officials being in charge of the great náds—the Mékanád, the Péranganád, Tódanád and Kúndanád. There are also Maniyagar or headmen for Ootacamand, Coonoor, Segúr, and for the villages below the gháts and on the slopes; and also inferior Maniyagar for the hamlets on the plateau. The Maniyagar, except in Ootacamand, are hereditary officials, the nearest male relation succeeding, provided he is considered by the Revenue authorities to be a fit and proper person to perform the duties of head of the village. These Maniyagar possess great power and influence in their respective náds, though only those of Ootacamand, Coonoor, and Kótagiri as yet hold regular court for the disposal of petty civil and criminal cases under the Regulations. They, with the exception of the Maniyagar of Ootacamand, belong to the Badaga race, and are practically the chiefs of the territory under their charge. They are wealthy and are generally much respected by the villagers within their divisions. The Karnams on the other hand are essentially Government nominees, this office not as yet having become hereditary, though the tendency is in this direction. There are six of these officials: two for Tódanád, one for each of the other three náds, and one for Segúr. Their pay and income appear in the following statement:—

Statement of Village Servants.

Division.	Number of Head and Sub-Maniyagar.	Inam. Extent.		Inam. Assessment.	Fees in Money.
		ACRES.	CENTS.	RS. A. P.	RS. A. P.
Tódanád.	3 Head Maniyagar and 2 Joint Maniyagar.	252	93	144 1 8	...
	1 Ooty Maniyagar ...	95	26	35 8 0	...
	11 Sub-Maniyagar ...	87	46	34 5 7	12 0 0
		435	65	213 15 3	...
	5 Thundals	92	42	51 15 3	...
	2 Karnams	123	24	68 7 9	...
		651	31	334 6 3	...
Mékanád.	3 Head Maniyagar ...	264	81	130 2 4	...
	6 Sub-Maniyagar ...	22	74	9 7 0	...
	1 Karnam	45	86	35 8 10	...
	2 Thundals	34	39	13 3 7	...
		367	80	188 5 9	...
Péranganád.	4 Head Maniyagar and 1 Joint Maniyagar.	249	89	136 11 3	...
	14 Sub-Maniyagar ...	62	57	25 7 5	...
	1 Karnam	87	89	53 7 7	...
	10 Thundals	61	14	27 0 6	...
		461	49	242 10 9	...
Kúnda ...	3 Head Maniyagar ..	...	...	...	84 0 0
	1 Sub-Maniyagar ...	...	...	...	8 0 0
	1 Karnam	...	...	...	40 0 0
	3 Thundals	...	...	...	18 0 0
		...	...	...	150 0 0
Segúr side.	1 Maniyagar	10	45	11 2 8	...
	1 Karnam	19	11	16 7 1	...
	2 Thundals	13	38	9 3 9	...
		42	94	36 13 6	...
Munnanád	1 Adicarry	...	...	...	63 0 0
	1 Menon or Karnam ...	...	..	...	72 0 0
	1 Peon	...	...	...	60 0 0
Cheramkód.	1 Adicarry	...	...	...	51 0 0
	1 Peon	...	...	...	60 0 0
Nambalakód.	1 Adicarry	...	...	...	63 0 0
	1 Menon or Karnam ...	...	...	...	72 0 0
	2 Peons	...	...	...	120 0 0
	Total ...	...	...	...	561 0 0

Hukamnáma.

In the chapter on the revenue history the position of the ryots on the plateau in regard to their lands has been explained. The result of their peculiar position in relation thereto is, that practically the ryotwari system with its privileges and incumbrances is in abeyance. Lands are seldom given on darkhast, and may not so

CHAP. XIV. REVENUE ADMINISTRATION.

be given except under the operation of the final rule of the Waste Land Rules. This remark, however, only applies to the plateau and slopes, the system prevailing in the Musnagúdi tract north of the Nílagiris being similar to that prevailing in North Coimbatore. Lands in this tract are still granted on darkhast, and the ryots' privileges and duties in regard to their holdings are those ordinarily prevailing, and need not here be detailed.

Method of collecting land-revenue in the plateau, in Musnagúdi and in South-East Wainád.

The Iyen land-revenue is collected throughout the district in six kists or instalments as follows:—

	AS.
November	2
December	2
January	4
February	4
March	2
April	2
Total ...	16

It is collected through the medium of the Head and Sub-Maniyagar. A register of plantation lands and houses and lands paying quit-rent is maintained at the Commissioner's Office.

South-East Wainád.

It does not fall within the scope of this manual to discuss the revenue system prevailing in South-East Wainád, which generally corresponds with that of the Malayalam Districts.

Local Funds.

The management of the funds raised under Act IV of 1871 devolves upon a Board, of which the Commissioner is *ex-officio* President constituted under that Act. The Assistant Commissioner acts as Honorary Secretary to the Board, a non-official being ordinarily Vice-President. All public communications, bungalows, and chattrams are vested in the Board. Its income is derived from land cess, levied at the rate of one anna in the rupee, tolls, and other petty sources. The house-tax is not levied. The roads are tolled at maximum rates, and there is at least one toll-bar on each of the important lines. Owing to the limited income of the Board, as shown elsewhere, its sphere of action is confined almost exclusively to supervision of the communications of the district, of vaccination, and of the bungalows and chattrams. It has as yet done little for the education of the people or for the sanitation of their villages, or for the health administration generally. The income of the Board is hardly sufficient for maintaining existing lines of communication in ordinary repair, and consequently it has to depend upon Government for grants-in-aid from Provincial Funds for all new works or exceptional repairs. The Board, however, performs a useful function in bringing the leading planters together to discuss matters appertaining to the welfare of the district within the scope of the Act, and also in giving the Commissioner a defined position with regard to the works, health, and education administration of the district. CHAP. XIV. — REVENUE ADMINISTRATION.

Cattle Pound Fund.

The administration of this fund is by law entrusted to the Assistant Commissioner in his capacity of District Magistrate. There are few cattle pounds in the district. A moiety of the surplus receipts, if any, is credited to Government for the Saidapet agricultural scheme, the other moiety to Local or Municipal funds.

CHAPTER XV.

HEADS OF REVENUE AND EXPENDITURE.

(a) IMPERIAL.—(b) PROVINCIAL.—(c) LOCAL.

(a) Imperial.

Land Revenue.—Excise on Spirits and Malt Liquors.—Stamps.—Forests.—Miscellaneous.

CHAP. XV. — Heads of Revenue and Expenditure. — Land Revenue.

The area of the Nílagiris proper, and the extent of land, and its distribution in each nád, will be found in Chapter II. In Fasli[1] 1285 there were 4,108 puttas; this would give the average ryot's holding under ordinary tenure at about 14 acres.

The following statement shows the extent and the land revenue assessment in that fasli. It includes lands held under all tenures:—

——	Extent.	Assessment.
	ACRES.	RS.
Dry	79,902	46,020
Wet[2]	...	90
Miscellaneous	...	9,267
Total ...	79,902	55,377

[1] This fasli is taken, as in the subsequent fasli the accounts of South-East Wainád are included. With South-East Wainád the number of puttas in Fasli 1287 was 5,350. The total holdings of the district as now constituted amount to 93,496, assessed at 65,610 rupees. Of this figure 13,550 acres appertain to South-East Wainád, assessed at 25,123 rupees. The area in South-East Wainád represents only that assessed and cultivated. The exact area of each holding is not ascertainable under the revenue system in force in Malabar. The areas may be classified as follows:—

		ACRES.
Iyen ...	Nílagiris	60,033
	South-East Wainád	4,428
Plantation.	Nílagiris	19,913
	South-East Wainád	9,122
		93,496

[2] There are no irrigation tanks in the district; the area entered as wet is watered by jungle streams. There are 2,258 acres classified as wet in South-East Wainád.

HEADS OF REVENUE AND EXPENDITURE.

The principal items under Miscellaneous are proceeds of waste land sales, Rupees 3,500, and quit-rent on house property, Rupees 5,061. Excluding this item the average ordinary land revenue for the ten faslis ending 1284 was Rupees 26,755; that of Fasli 1285 was Rupees 37,934. The increase is due to lands sold, and lands in excess of register areas discovered by the Revenue Survey. The figure Rupees 37,934 is made up as follows :—

	RS.
Lands held by hill-people	20,561
Lands held for plantations, &c.	17,373

The small revenue derived from plantations is due to the fact that a considerable extent of the land sold under the Waste Land Rules had not as yet passed out of the initial period of free tenure; the drawback on this account in this fasli was Rupees 8,014.

Excise on spirits and malt liquors.

The system of abkári in force in the district is the excise, superseding that of sale by auction under which the monopoly was worked until June 1875. In Fasli 1285, 32,000 Imperial gallons of spirits of various strengths were excised, yielding a revenue of 87,000 rupees. An excise [1] of 4 annas per Imperial gallon is levied on beer, yielding a revenue in Fasli 1285 of 18,994 rupees on 79,880 gallons excised. Licenses of the sale of liquor yielded 990 rupees.

Stamps.

The revenue derived from the sale of stamps was—

	RS.
Non-judicial stamps	7,696
Court fees	14,525

Forests.

Particulars of receipts under Forests will be found in Chapter XXVI.

Miscellaneous.

The most important items under Miscellaneous are the receipts from the Chinchona plantations and from the Government gardens.

Total revenue and charges.

Roughly the total revenue and charges of the Nílagiris proper debitable to Imperial, excluding chinchona, may be set at Rupees 1,60,000 and 2,00,000 respectively, viz. :—

	RS.
Land Revenue	30,000
Forests	46,000
Minor Departments	16,000
Law and Justice	42,500
Ecclesiastical	31,500
Medical	33,000
Miscellaneous	1,000
	2,00,000

[1] The excise has since this been reduced to 1 anna per gallon for below 6 per cent. alcoholic strength.

CHAP. XV.

HEADS OF REVENUE AND EXPENDITURE.

(b) PROVINCIAL.

Jails.—Registration.—Police.—Medical.—Printing.—Miscellaneous Charges.

Revenues.

The receipts from jails amount to about Rupees 1,200 annually, being the proceeds mainly of jail manufactures. The particulars of registration will be found in Chapter XVI. A sum, chiefly fines, is credited annually under Police. A sum of Rupees 900 is received under Medical, being grants of Rupees 500 and 400 respectively by the Ootacamand and Coonoor Municipalities towards the local Government dispensaries. A contribution of half per cent. on income is also paid by the Municipalities on account of the Madras Medical College. About Rupees 100 is realized annually from subscriptions to the District Gazette. Roughly the total revenues of the district under Provincial may be set at Rupees 4,000, including miscellaneous items.

Charges.

The charges may be estimated approximately at Rupees 66,000, viz. :—

	RS.
Jails	22,000
Registration	1,000
Police	27,000
Medical	6,000
Printing	3,000
Minor Establishments	1,500
Office rent	1,500
Miscellaneous	4,000
	66,000

(c) LOCAL.

Local Funds—Act IV of 1871—Pound Fund—Village Service Fund—Endowment Fund—Municipal Funds.

Local Funds.

The revenue of the Local Fund Board in the Nílagiris proper may be estimated at Rupees 35,000, of which approximately Rupees 30,000 are derived from tolls and Rupees 2,500 from land-cess at one anna in the rupee on assessment. The receipts from the Cattle Pounds amount to about 1,200 rupees annually against charges 1,000 rupees. The receipts of the Village Service Fund amount to Rupees 162 against charges of the same amount. The amount is received from Government. There is practically no Endowment Fund. Rupees 120 is, however, received from Government and paid for the maintenance of the Brahmins' Chuttrum in Ootacamand. For particulars of the Municipal Funds *see* Chapter XVII.

CHAPTER XVI.

CRIMINAL AND CIVIL JUSTICE AND REGISTRATION.

Constitution by Act I of 1868.—Sessions Judge and Magistrates—jurisdiction.—Benches of Magistrates—statement of operations.—Civil Courts—statement of operations.—Village Munsifs—appeals to the High Court.—Cost of Law and Justice.—Registration—operations.

CHAP. XVI. — CRIMINAL AND CIVIL JUSTICE, &c.

IN a previous chapter I have traced briefly the arrangements which existed on the plateau for the administration of justice generally, as well as of revenue, until the present constitution of the district was elaborated and then fixed by Act I of 1868 (Madras).

Constitution by Act I of 1868.

By this Act the chief criminal and civil powers are vested in the Commissioner of the district, whilst the chief magisterial power is entrusted to the Assistant Commissioner, the latter officer being aided in the magisterial administration by two Joint Magistrates, viz., the Joint Magistrate of Ootacamand and the Joint Magistrate of Wellington and Coonoor, the Sub-Magistrates stationed at Coonoor and in the South-East Wainád, and three benches of Honorary or *Special* Magistrates at Ootacamand, Kótagiri and Gúdalúr. A bench was created in Coonoor, but it ceased to exist at the end of 1876. The appointments of Joint and Sub-Magistrates are not specially referred to in Act I of 1868, but this Act provides that Government may invest any one residing on the Hills with any or all powers of a Magistrate.

Criminal Judge's and Magistrate's jurisdiction.

The Commissioner, in his capacity of Sessions Judge, holds a sessions ordinarily once a month at Ootacamand. The system of trial by jury has not yet been introduced, that of assessors still prevailing. The Assistant Commissioner, as Magistrate of the district, has no *special* territorial charge, but he directly supervises the work of the Sub-Magistrates of Coonoor and of the South-East Wainád, disposes of criminal appeals from these functionaries, and frequently presides at the sessions of the benches at Kótagiri and in South-East Wainád. The Joint Magistrate of Ootacamand exercises the full powers of a Magistrate, and is also President of the Ootacamand bench of Magis-

CHAP. XVI. — CRIMINAL AND CIVIL JUSTICE, &c.

trates. His territorial jurisdiction is as follows: Local limits included in the tracts known as Segúr, Kúndas, Tódanád (excepting the Ouchterlony Valley, the Ossington Estate, and the Government plantations at Neduwattam), and so much of Ootacamand as lies within the Tódanád.

The Joint Magistrate of Wellington, who possesses full magisterial powers, is also Magistrate of the Military Cantonment at that station. His territorial jurisdiction is as follows: the local limits included in the tracts known as Péranganád and Mékanád, excepting such portion of the latter as lies within the settlement of Ootacamand. He also presides occasionally at the sessions of the benches of Honorary Magistrates at Kótagiri.

The Sub-Magistrates of Coonoor and the South-East Wainád possess second-class powers only. The territorial jurisdiction of the Sub-Magistrate of Gúdalúr comprises the local limits included in the three amshoms (Cheramkód, Munnanád and Nambalakód) of South-East Wainád, the Ouchterlony Valley, the Government plantations at Neduwattam and the Ossington Estate.

The territorial jurisdiction of the Coonoor Sub-Magistrate is conterminous with that of the Joint Magistrate of Wellington.

Honorary Magistrate.

The bench of Magistrates at Ootacamand was constituted in 1875 under the orders of Government, dated 16th February 1875, No. 378, Judicial Department. The bench, however, at present rarely meets. The bench has first-class powers, with power to try summarily all offences mentioned in Section 222, Criminal Procedure Code. The benches of Magistrates in the South-East Wainád and Kótagiri were constituted under the orders of Government, dated 26th April 1878, No. 876. They consist of planters, and were especially constituted to aid the State in dealing more speedily and effectively with breaches of labor contracts and other offences which more or less impede or obstruct the progress of the planting industry. Their powers are as follows: First-class magisterial powers, provided that the Honorary Magistrate is a member of the bench and takes part in the proceedings, and power, under Section 224 of the Criminal Procedure Code, to try summarily all the offences mentioned in Section 222 of the said Code, when the bench is presided over by a Magistrate of the first class.

—statement of operations.

From the returns of 1878 it appears that the following work was performed by each of the Magisterial Courts above described:—

CHAP. XVI. — CRIMINAL AND CIVIL JUSTICE, &c.

Courts.	Trials.	Prelimi-nary Inquiries.	Appeals.
Suits instituted.			
Judicial Commissioner	11	...	8
Assistant do.	18	1	...
Joint Magistrate, Ootacamand	667	3	...
Cantonment Magistrate, Wellington ...	503	5	...
All Sub-Magistrates	[1] 218	...	...
Suits disposed of.			
Judicial Commissioner	11	...	7
Assistant do.	18	1	...
Joint Magistrate, Ootacamand	666	3	...
Cantonment Magistrate, Wellington ...	503	5	...
All Sub-Magistrates	[2] 218	...	...

Civil Courts.

In his civil capacity the Commissioner possesses the powers of a Civil Judge, and of a Subordinate Judge in civil suits, and, under Act XVIII of 1868, of a Small Cause Court Judge; the Assistant Commissioner, those of a District Munsif and of a Small Cause Court Judge under the Act above quoted. As District Munsif his jurisdiction is limited to suits not exceeding Rupees 2,500 in value. The Small Cause Court of the Nílagiris is constituted under the special Act referred to above, which empowers the Commissioner and Assistant Commissioner to exercise severally or jointly jurisdiction under Act XI of 1865. The Assistant Commissioner, as junior Judge, may refer any case, on application or otherwise, to a bench consisting of himself and the Commissioner as senior Judge; in case of difference of opinion, the opinion of the Commissioner prevails. The Cantonment Magistrate of Wellington, under Act I of 1866, possesses Small Cause Court powers, his jurisdiction extending to suits in value Rupees 400.

The Sub-Magistrate in the South-East Wainád also possesses civil jurisdiction to the following limits: Rupees 50 as Small Cause Court Judge, and Rupees 2,500 as Munsif.

—operations.

The following statement shows the work performed by each of these Courts in 1878:—

---

[1] Kótagiri Bench 67
Wainád do. 136
Salaried Sub-Magistrates 15
218

[2] Ootacamand Bench ... ... 1 Old case.
Kótagiri do. 65
Wainád do. 136
Salaried Sub-Magistrates 16
218

CHAP. XVI.
CRIMINAL AND CIVIL JUSTICE, &c.

Courts.	Ordinary Suits.	Small Cause.	Appeals.
Instituted.			
Judicial Commissioner	8	...	12
Assistant do.	51	211	...
Gúdalúr Munsif	30	16	...
Disposed of.			
Judicial Commissioner	6	...	11
Assistant do.	52	188	...
Gúdalúr Munsif	32	13	...

Maniyagar.

Three of the Maniyagar, viz., those having their head-quarters at Ootacamand, Coonoor, and Kótagiri, perform the functions of Village Munsifs under Regulation IV of 1816. According to the latest returns the number of cases disposed of by each was as follows:—

	No. of Cases disposed of.
Ootacamand	138
Coonoor	110
Kótagiri	45
	293

Only four appeals from the District Court were preferred to High Court in 1878 and one second appeal.

Cost of Law and Justice.

The cost of the administration of law and justice in the district (exclusive of South-East Wainád) is approximately 42,000 rupees, distributed as follows:—

	RS.	RS.
Half salaries of Commissioner and Assistant Commissioner	16,400	
Court Establishment	3,230	
Process Service Establishment ...	960	
Contingencies	300	
		20,890
Joint Magistrate, Ootacamand ...	10,558	
Contingencies	500	
		11,058
Joint Magistrate, Wellington ...	8,400	
Establishment	1,104	
Contingencies	500	
Process Service Establishment ...	250	
		10,254
		42,202

To this should be added about Rupees 500, a moiety of the charges of the Sub-Magistrate at Coonoor, the total charge for which is now debited to Land Revenue. Half the salary of the Commissioner and his Assistant is debited to Law and Justice under the orders of Government. The salary of the Joint Magistrate of Ootacamand is not consolidated, but depends upon the military rank of the officer. That above entered is the Staff Corps pay of a Lieutenant-Colonel, *plus* a special allowance of Rupees 70. The salary of the Joint Magistrate, Wellington, is consolidated and fixed at Rupees 700 a month.

CHAP. XVI — CRIMINAL AND CIVIL JUSTICE, &c.

Taking the population of the district, exclusive of South-East Wainád, at 60,000 souls, the cost of the civil and criminal administration is rather less than 12 annas per head. About one-fourth this cost is probably covered by the sale of judicial stamps.

Registration.

The Nílagiris was constituted a registration district in 1869. The Registrar was appointed in that year. His jurisdiction is limited by the jurisdiction of the Commissioner under Act I of 1868. There is a Sub-Registry Office at Gúdalúr. The Registrar's Office adjoins the Court House, Ootacamand. At the head office documents in Tamil and English, in original, will be admitted for registration; at the sub-office, Gúdalúr, in English, Tamil and Malayalam.

—statement of operations.

The following statement shows the operations of the department on the Nílagiris in 1876-77 and 1877-78:—

—	1876-77.	1877-78.
	RS.	RS.
Fees realized on registration ...	969	1,482
Receipts other than fees ...	158	464
Total ...	1,127	1,946
Expenditure	1,097	1,274
Aggregate value of property transferred by documents.	9,16,130	12,66,007
	NO.	NO.
Total number of documents ...	412	671

CHAPTER XVII.

MUNICIPALITIES AND STATIONS.

The four Settlements.—Description of *Ootacamand*—area and population—limits of the Municipality—elevation—Municipal Commission—receipts and expenditure—sanitation—market—public buildings—the gardens—hotels—rents—early sketch. —*Coonoor*—description—area—municipal limits—elevation—Municipal Commission—receipts and expenditure—public buildings—population—hotels and rents.—*Wellington*—description, &c.—*Kótagiri*—description.

CHAP. XVII. — MUNICIPALITIES AND STATIONS.

The four principal settlements or townships.

THERE are on the Hills four stations—Ootacamand, situated on the higher plateau or Mélnád; Coonoor, to the south-east, at the head of a great pass or gorge, the upper portion of which faces towards the town of Coimbatore; Wellington, at a short distance to the north of Coonoor, lying on the eastern slope of one of the two great valleys which bifurcate from near the head of the Coonoor pass; and Kótagiri, lying some ten miles to the north of Coonoor, on the ridge of the gháts. Ootacamand and Coonoor are Municipalities; Wellington is a Military Cantonment; Kótagiri is still a straggling settlement with no separate corporate existence.

OOTACAMAND.

Ootacamand, the chief town of the district, occupies the western slopes of the Doddabetta mountain range; the town proper lies within the basin formed by two spurs of this mountain, the highest point of the southern being Elk Hill, of the northern the Club Hill. These spur-ranges, like the western slopes of Doddabetta itself, are broken into somewhat deep and rocky, though open, valleys, which in early days were filled with beautiful forests. The ranges constituting the northern and southern shoulders of the town lose their rougher features towards the west and gradually pass into rolling downs, which stretch away for miles to the Kúndas and form a splendid riding country, with here and there a swamp or wood in the hollows from which spring innumerable streams. Owing to its peculiar natural features, Ootacamand is much exposed to the westerly winds, but is well protected upon the north and east. The bottom of the Ootacamand basin has been converted into a lake some two miles in length and one-third mile in width, by throwing a dam across the main stream at a narrow pass where it issues from the central valley. This lake is divided into two waters by means of a causeway and bridge known as the "Willow Bund," from the Indian willows which line its banks. It is situated towards the upper or eastern portion of the lake and is the means of communication between the north-west and south-west portions of the town. The western lake is sinuous in form with grassy headlands and reedy bays. Upon the hills which surround it, more or less concealed by woods of eucalyptus, acacia, cypress, and pine, stand some of the finest private residences in the town; whilst on a picturesque foreland of its southern bank stands the new Church of St. Thomas, a gothic edifice, and opposite to it, on the north bank, though at a greater distance from the lake, the Roman Catholic Church dedicated to the Blessed Virgin. Around the margin of the lake runs a wide carriage drive, from various points in which good views of the valley may be obtained.

The upper lake is an oval piece of water, which is at present much contaminated by the drainage of the Native town or bazaar which lies on its northern bank. The marsh at the head or eastern extremity of this lake has now been reclaimed and levelled, and is being formed into a park, known as the Hobart Park, for purposes of public recreation. The area, including the lands lying on the northern and southern margins of the lake as far as the Willow Bund, is about thirty acres. A portion of the ground (about seven acres) near the road to the south, at the foot of the western wood-covered slopes of Elk Hill, is appropriated to a gymkhána with a pavilion, a pretty octagonal structure of brick and teakwood with high-pitched roof and sharp gables. The grounds about it are laid out with shrubberies, trees and flowers. Opposite to the pavilion, at the eastern extremity of the Native bazaar, stands the Hobart School for Native girls, and to the east of it the public market. Beyond the latter is the agraharam, or Brahmins' village. On the slope of the hill behind the market are the Police lines and station, and above these ranges of buildings St. Bartholomew's Hospital, behind which, on the top of the ridge, are the jails for Europeans and Natives. At a short distance to the east, on the same spur, is the Public Library, and opposite to it the Post Office; a little further on are the Breeks' Memorial Schools and the public offices of the district. Nearer to the hill stands the Church of St. Stephen, the old station church, and opposite its gates the church and school of the Church of England Native Christians. The sides of the hill to the east and west of St. Stephen's are thickly studded with houses and cottages, including westward the Club House and the principal hotels, eastward the Assembly Rooms.

Looking to the east from St. Stephen's, but at a much lower elevation, on the western extremity of a minor spur of Doddabetta,

CHAP. XVII. — MUNICIPALITIES AND STATIONS.

stands "Stonehouse," which contains the Council Chamber and the offices of the Madras Secretariat. The hill commands a fine view of the Ootacamand valley and the distant Kúnda range. In the hollows and on the spurs of Doddabetta to the north and south of Stonehouse are many residences. The lands on these slopes are generally very fertile and well watered, and for this reason a considerable and greatly extending area is cultivated as garden land. In a steep ravine about half a mile to the north of Stonehouse are the Public Gardens and the Tóda mand from which Ootacamand takes its name. Above the Public Gardens, stretching across the Doddabetta saddle, is the Government Cinchona Plantation. On the northern shoulder of the ravine, adjoining the Public Gardens, lies Norwood, the hill residence of the Governor of Madras, backed by a fine wood of eucalyptus on the side of the Snowdon mountain.

From the foot of Stonehouse, towards the south, runs the highway to Coonoor, which disappears in the deep cutting (which separates Elk Hill from the Doddabetta range), bridged by the aqueduct of the south water-supply channel.

This is a simple description of the main valley, but the limits of the station lie far beyond it and include two other important valleys—to the south and parallel with it, Lovedale, with its picturesque little lake, above which stand the extensive storied buildings of the Lawrence Asylums with their lofty Italian tower—to the north, the valley of Málémand, which opens out towards the head of the Segúr Pass. Between the Ootacamand and the Málémand valleys is a hollow, across the outlet of which a dam has been thrown, forming the Málémand reservoir, from which, through a channel nearly three miles in length, the northern portion of Ootacamand is supplied with water.

One of the peculiar features of the town is the manner in which the population, Native and European, is scattered over the greater portion of the area lying within the municipal limits noted below. The houses occupied by Europeans generally have not less than five or six acres of land attached, and many possess domains from twenty to seventy acres in extent. In the chief Native bazaar on the border of the lake some two or three thousand persons are congregated, and perhaps half of this number in Kandel, a bazaar in a small valley to the west of the station; but a large number of Natives have their homes in scattered hamlets, chiefly in the eastern portions of the station. The inhabitants of these hamlets are chiefly Kanarese, with a fair sprinkling of Tamils. There is no Badaga village within municipal limits, and only three or four Tóda mands.

—area and population,

Area of station, lying within a circle with three miles' radius from the Jail Hill, is 19,297·74 acres, or about 30 square miles.

CHAP. XVII.

MUNICIPALITIES AND STATIONS.

The exact area of the Municipality I have not ascertained, but it is probably about ten or twelve square miles.

The Municipality contained, in 1871, 238 houses ordinarily occupied by Europeans and 1,064 houses inhabited by Natives.

The population of the bazaar may be estimated at 3,380 souls, taking the average number of inhabitants occupying each of the 676 houses at five persons. Population of Kandel, with 317 houses, in the same way is estimated at 1,585.

—limits of the Municipality.

The following are the limits of the Municipality: a line drawn from the north side of the Craigmore cutting to the top of the Craigmore Hill; from there to the top of Doddabetta, on to the top of Snowdon, and from thence to Málémand to the top of juncture of two roads leading from Ootacamand station. From this point at Málémand the boundary runs in a direct line to the top of Bétmand Hill; from thence to the top of a shóla planted with Australian trees, and then on to the second mile-stone on the Segúr road. From the Segúr road to a point on the Paikaré old road, from which the road to the Government brick-field diverges; then from the Paikaré old road through the brick-field valley to a point on the nullah below the new Paikaré road, at which a bridge formerly stood. From the point at which the bridge stood the boundary then runs to the road leading to the Governor's shóla to where three roads cross one another, and then on to a swamp close at hand, following the course of the water which crosses the Avalanché road, and falls into the stream below. From the stream the boundary then goes in a straight line to the top of the Cairn hill and down to the Lovedale stream, below the western boundary of what was Colonel Taylor's land. From this point to the boundary up the Lovedale stream until it gets close to Craigmore, when it strikes up to the cutting whence it first started.

—elevation.

The elevation of Ootacamand varies from about 7,150 feet above sea-level, at the ordinary water-level of the lake, to 8,642 feet at the summit of Doddabetta. (Latitude, 11° 24′ 5·40″; longitude, 76° 46′ 44·39″.)

The height of Elk Hill is 8,090 feet. St. Stephen's Church (tower) stands 7,429 feet above sea-level, and probably 7,350 feet represents the average height of private residences above the sea.

—Municipality.

The town of Ootacamand was first constituted a Municipality on the 3rd October 1866 under Act X of 1865 (now rescinded). Prior to this a Station Committee had existed and made some spasmodic efforts for the improvement of the town.

The Commissioner of the Nílagiris is *ex-officio* President of the Municipal Commission. The Commissioners have had conferred upon them by Government the power of nominating a Vice-

CHAP. XVII. — MUNICIPALITIES AND STATIONS.

President. The Assistant Commissioner, in the capacity of Honorary Secretary to the Commission, a title which has descended from the days of the old Station Committee, has hitherto performed the chief executive duties of the Commissioners. The number of Commissioners has generally been about eight or nine, of whom about half have been Natives. By recent order in Council the number of Commissioners is fixed at a maximum of ten, of whom one-half may be elected by the tax-payers under the rules promulgated by Government.

—receipts and expenditure.

The following table exhibits the receipts and expenditure of this Municipality during ten years :—

Ootacamand.

Years.	Receipts.[1]			Expenditure.			
	Taxes and Fees.	Miscellaneous.	Total.	Works.	Conservancy.	Other Objects.	Total.
	RS.	RS.	RS.	RS.	RS.	RS.	RS.
1868-69 ...	20,496	2,365	22,861	9,846	6,788	7,127	23,761
1869-70 ...	19,559	4,374	23,933	18,402	9,167	9,675	37,334
1870-71 ...	18,812	6,187	24,999	14,742	8,768	10,611	34,121
1871-72 ...	16,338	4,656	20,994	5,187	7,567	10,353	23,107
1872-73 ...	16,597	6,063	22,660	10,892	8,222	11,578	30,692
1873-74 ...	19,688	6,898	26,586	19,410	7,497	11,256	38,163
1874-75 ...	16,744	8,940	25,684	14,046	6,861	13,216	34,123
1875-76 ...	15,488	11,195	26,683	19,260	6,712	11,393	37,365
1876-77 ...	20,019	9,473	29,492	10,149	9,230	16,462	35,841
1877-78 ...	21,317	8,364	29,681	10,000	12,798	10,917	33,715
Total ...	1,85,058	68,515	2,53,573	1,31,934	83,610	1,12,678	3,28,222

At present all the taxes detailed in Act III of 1871 are in force with the exception of tolls, and are collected at maximum rates. In lieu of tolls the Government undertakes the repair of the principal thoroughfares of the station, which are excluded from the operation of the Municipal Act, at a cost of about 5,000 rupees annually. The tax on professions was abolished in 1874-75 by Lord Hobart's Government, but, owing to the financial necessities of the station, was reimposed in 1878-79. The Government, in consideration of the neglect of past years and the peculiar circumstances of the town as the chief sanitarium in South India, besides constructing the two large water reservoirs (at Málémand and Doddabetta), with supply-channels for the north and south portions of the station at a cost, direct and indirect, of probably

[1] The receipts are exclusive of grants from Government and loans, but the expenditure shows the outlay by the Municipality of moneys received by grant or loan from Government. Of the outlay on works probably 50 per cent. has been devoted to works connected with the sanitation of the town.

not less than Rupees 35,000, have expended considerable sums on the construction or reconstruction of roads within the station, and also on the improvement of the town bazaar and the reclamation of the upper lake, besides providing gratis for some years for these and other sanitary works the services of a large gang of convicts.

—Sanitation.

The sanitary condition of Ootacamand at the time of the establishment of the Municipal Commission was most deplorable. A detailed account of the state of affairs then existing will be found in the report of the Sanitary Commissioner (the late Mr. R. S. Ellis, C.B.) in 1868. Much had been done in the succeeding nine years to remedy some of the more crying evils, but in consequence of the outbreak of cholera in 1877 in the hill stations, when the district was suffering from drought and famine, the Government appointed a Committee, consisting of Surgeon-General Gordon, C.B. (British Army), Dr. Cornish, Sanitary Commissioner, and the Commissioner of the Nílagiris, to report upon the sanitation of the station. A history of the health of the town from 1855 and most of the important papers connected with the subject will be found in the Committee's report dated December 1877. It is not necessary to refer to the matter further here, beyond inserting a few remarks on the subject by Major Morant, R.E., District Engineer. "The site of Ootacamand," he writes, "has been well chosen, but from its commencement until now it has never been systematically treated, the town having been allowed to grow up uncontrolled. The gradients of many of the roads are inconveniently steep. The town would have been better served by fewer roads properly alligned. Houses have been allowed to be built without guidance; the locality of many is objectionable; the construction of most is poor and insanitary. Lands have also been recklessly sold to private individuals, who in many cases allowed them to remain unutilized and unenclosed. It is not now easy to obtain space for public wants. Thus difficulties exist in the way of much needed improvements. Ootacamand might have been a beautiful, convenient, and healthy town at no greater outlay than has already been incurred. The great desideratum is a copious supply of good drinking water, the present scheme in dry seasons not being adequate to requirements of the town. To this cause is due much of the sickness in dry years. More might be done by lease-holders in digging wells for themselves; a few have been successfully sunk, but near the bazaar and in low-lying parts densely occupied such wells would be exposed to contamination by soakage of sewage and filth through the adjoining strata. The drainage of the town may be regarded as a matter of secondary importance. The steepness of the ground upon which it is built and the wash of tropical floods effect a rude scavengering which is generally effective, and the

CHAP. XVII. — MUNICIPALITIES AND STATIONS.

passage of sewage into the lake, through which a current always flows, though objectionable, cannot be an insupportable evil. Outbreaks of disease are probably due to the necessity under which the Natives labor in seasons of drought of drinking impure water rather than to the imperfect drainage of their town." The system of sanitation in the populous portions of the station is to remove all excreta, without deodorization, and sweepings in carts drawn by bullocks, beyond the town. A system of dry-earth conservancy, including the manufacture of poudrette with ashes of sweepings and slaughter-house refuse and pulverized bone, was in vogue for two or three years, but has been, from various causes, discontinued, but may again be revived if a demand for the manure arises.

—market. There is a weekly market or *shandy* held every Tuesday, which yields to the Municipal Commission a revenue of about 3,000 rupees a year—the right to levy fees at certain approved rates being farmed out—for the sale of general produce, wares, poultry and vegetables, but there is at present no market for the sale of meat. Such an institution is much needed, as also a permanent market for the sale of vegetables, fruit, and poultry. The weekly market is supplied with staple food-grains and poultry from the low country, chiefly Coimbatore, and garden produce mostly from the neighbourhood of Ootacamand. The arrangements for the sale of meat are very defective. It is now ordinarily hawked about the town or exposed for sale in low ill-ventilated Native houses. The Commissioners have provided two slaughter-houses located below the jail, and obtain a considerable revenue from the slaughtering fees.

—principal buildings. The following are the principal public or *quasi*-public buildings in Ootacamand:—

St. Stephen's Church.
St. Thomas' Church.
The Tamil Mission Church.
The Church of the Blessed Virgin Mary (Roman Catholic).
The Goa Church.
Zion Chapel (Non-conformist).
Government House (Norwood).
The Council Chamber and Secretariat (Stonehouse).
The Courts and Offices of the Nílagiri Commission.
The Nílagiri Public Library.
The Breeks' Memorial Schools.
St. Bartholomew's Hospital.
The Jails.
The Police Station and Lines.
The Post Office.
The Telegraph Office.
The Madras Bank.
The Traveller's Home.
The Nazareth Convent and Schools.
The Subsidiary Jail (now used as a Municipal Workshop).
The Hobart Native Girls' School.
The Wesleyan Mission School.
The Pavilion.
The Ootacamand Club.
The Public Rooms (Misquith's).
Freemasons' Lodge.
The Market.

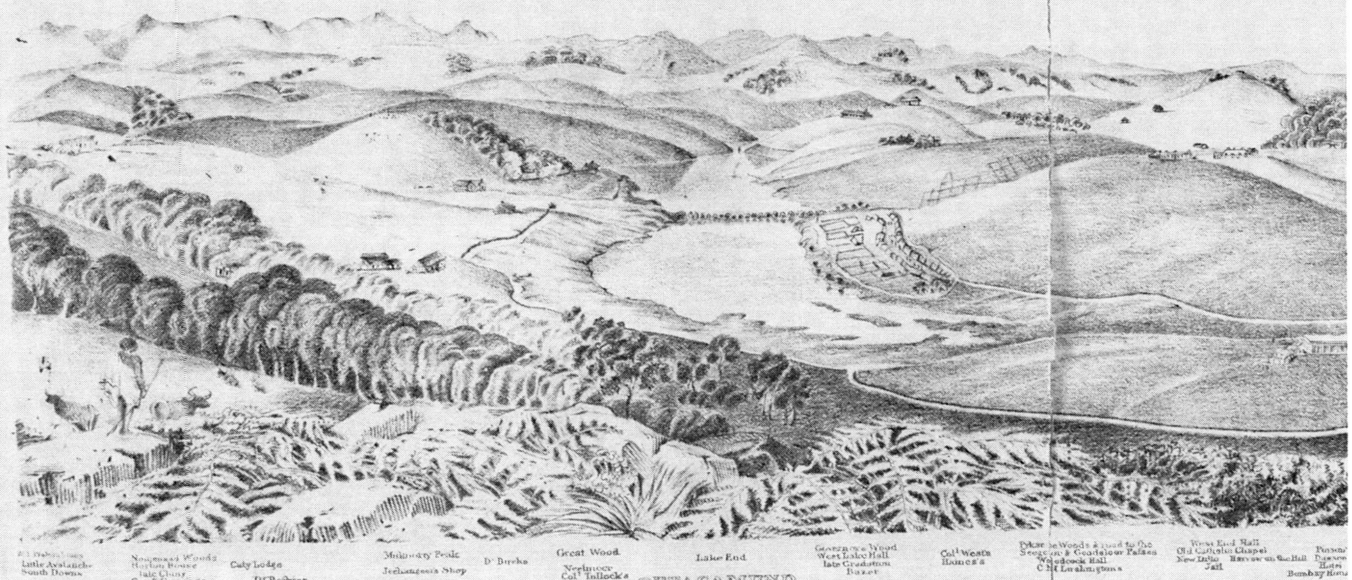

OTTACAMUND

WEST VIEW

1834

The architecture of several of these buildings is in good style, especially that of St. Thomas' Church, the Breeks' Memorial School, the Council Chamber, and the Pavilion.

CHAP. XVII. — MUNICIPALITIES AND STATIONS.

—societies.

Much has been done in Ootacamand by means of local committees formed for the attainment of a special, sometimes a purely temporary, object. To such agencies several of the buildings above enumerated owe their existence, more especially the hospital, the library, and the various churches and schools. Among those now existing may be mentioned the Library, the Hospital, and the Friend-in-Need Committees.

—the public gardens.

The Public Gardens are noticed elsewhere. They belong to Government and are under the management of a Superintendent who is directly responsible to the Commissioner.

—hotels.

There are several hotels in Ootacamand, though no single hotel has accommodation for more than a few families and single persons. The principal are Sylk's, Longwood, Bishopsdown, Shoreham, and Primrose House. The terms average about 6 rupees per diem, or Rupees 150 a-month for a single person.

—rents, &c.

The rent paid for houses is high during the season, ranging from about 75 rupees a-month for four-roomed bungalows to 300 rupees for the largest houses. This rental, however, ordinarily includes furniture, house rates, and the services of a house gardener. The value of house property is however low when compared with the rental. A house which would command a rental all the year round of Rupees 100 monthly would probably not realize 10,000 rupees if sold, unless the domain was large and the land good. This position is partly due to the absence of capital in the place, the changing character of the population, and also to the heavy cost of repair; many of the houses having, wholly or in part, been built of inferior materials, such as sun-dried brick and mud and poor timber covered with coarse stucco, chunam being very expensive. Some improvement however is taking place in building, especially by the use of sheet iron for roof linings.

—sketch of Ootacamand.

The sketch of Ootacamand as it was in 1834, taken from Captain McMurdy's Views, will be of interest to those who know the town as it now is. The change is chiefly due to the growth of Australian trees, which during the last few years have altered the face of the station. The planting of the public grounds and roads with ornamental exotics is much needed to relieve the present monotony in the tone and tint of the foliage. The absence of avenues on the public roads is a marked feature in the town.

COONOOR—description.

The picturesque little town of Coonoor lies at the head of the grand ravine and pass which bears its name; the ravine faces south-east, but a considerable portion of the town is situated on the western slopes of one of the valleys at the head of the pass, only a few of the houses being built on sites commanding a view down the ravine. The Native town spreads over the lower slopes of the spurs of two hills, which, divided by a central stream and bordered by two other streams on the east and west, terminate in a wedge-like promontory at a point where the united waters of these three streams break over the stony lip of the ghát and rush down the gorge under the name of the Coonoor river, until finally the stream discharges its volume into the Kátéri river. The three streams are crossed by three bridges—one, an old stone (laterite) structure, spans the river at the spot where it breaks over the gháts; the second, a black wooden suspension bridge, crosses the eastern affluent streams to the western spur, up which runs the road to Wellington; the third, of stone, spans the easternmost of these two affluents, which drain the Coonoor valley proper, and connects the eastern spur, up which passes the main road to Upper Coonoor, with the head of the ghát. On an eminence on the western spur stands the pretty Protestant Mission Chapel, and on the eastern the Roman Catholic Church; below the latter, on the extreme point of the interfluvial spur, is the market. The road to Upper Coonoor passes up the ridge and thence round the head of the valley, and along the wooded ridge which encloses it on the east and south. On this ridge stands the Coonoor Church, dedicated to All Saints, with a lofty square tower. The church is surrounded by a beautiful grave-yard planted with exotic trees and flowers. It commands one of the finest views in Coonoor. To the east of this ridge is a ravine separating it from the Tiger's Hill, round which winds Lord Hobart's road, which passes into the road to Lamb's Rock, Lady Canning's Seat, and the Dolphin's Nose some five miles eastward of Coonoor above the Kótagiri gorge. From the Dolphin's Nose there is a fine view of St. Catharine's Falls. The views along this road are very grand. Below it, stretching away to the east as far as the eye can see, are the great Coimbatore and Salem plains, the ancient Kongu realm; northwards the Bellirangan hills and the ranges which mark the line of the Balaghát country; whilst south and westwards is the great Coonoor pass, walled in on the south by the grand "Drúg" which is backed by the Lambton's Peak range, south of the Bhavání river and the distant Anémalé mountains.

At the head of the spur on which the church stands is the Coonoor Library, and above it Gray's Hotel. Behind the hill on which Gray's Hotel stands is another valley, one of the ravines on the western side of the Coonoor peak, along which runs the road to the Bleak House plantations, and onwards to Kótagiri. This valley, within the last five or six years, has been formed into a garden named Sim's Park—after Mr. J. D. Sim, a late Member of Council. It is an off-shoot of the deep ravine which divides Coonoor from Wellington, the upper portion of which has, by the energy of the Joint Magistrate, Lieutenant-Colonel Richards, been converted into a race-course, which, though small, is perhaps unrivalled by any in India for the picturesqueness and beauty of its position.

The drainage of this valley forms the middle stream of Coonoor, which meets the other streams at the old Coonoor bridge. This bridge is the central point of the Coonoor road system. Here the old and new ghât roads meet, and from it, along the right bank of the western stream as far as the Wellington bazaar, runs the main road to Ootacamand. Above this road to the left as the traveller ascends is the Sub-Magistrate's Court, the Police Station, Post Office, and a few private residences, and below it the Ashley Engineering Works.

The scenery of Coonoor differs very greatly from that of Ootacamand; its vegetation is semi-tropical, the contour of many of its hills rugged and severe, though softened by profuse vegetation; its coloring bright and warm. On the other hand the vegetation of Ootacamand is rather that of the Temperate Zones; its hill lines are unbroken and undulating, and its coloring ordinarily cold and grey. Its climate also differs as widely as its scenery. Warm, moist, and relaxing, breathing of the soft south, it seems calculated to induce a *dolce far niente* life; whilst that of Ootacamand, ordinarily cool, dry and invigorating, demands a life of energy and motion. Each, however, supplies a great need. To many the climate of the higher sanitarium is uncongenial and even, it may be, under certain conditions actually injurious. Such persons find in Coonoor a delightful and healthful retreat, and in any case a fitting preparation for the colder and rarer air of the upper plateau.

In an earlier chapter the rise of Coonoor has been referred to. Its prosperity has been in great part due to the excellent character of the land in its neighbourhood for planting purposes, but also in a measure to its proximity to the railway, as well as the attractions of its scenery and the lusciousness of its climate. Ootacamand had become an important station before a bungalow was built in Coonoor; in fact, its very existence is due to the demands of visitors from the southern districts for a nearer and easier road to Ootacamand than that by the Kótagiri Pass.

—area.

The Coonoor settlement, which includes the Wellington Cantonment, is limited by a line drawn roughly within a radius of two miles from Gray's Hotel. The area within these limits is 11·97 square miles, or 7,660 acres.

CHAP. XVII. — MUNICIPALITIES AND STATIONS.

—municipal limits.

The municipal limits are much less extensive and exclude the Wellington Cantonment. They were fixed by notification dated 27th July 1869 as follows :—

"On the east by a line drawn from the Sappers' burial-ground on the old ghát up to Nungappa Row's land adjoining Mr. Wait's plantation, and on the top of the hill on the north side of which Mr. Mann's tea plantation is situated, taking in the Bandy Sholah road and the houses named Woodhouselee, Mr. Hall's house, and Elk-hill House; then along to the top of the hill and down its slope to the nullah below Colonel Grant's house to a point in a line with the house; then along the nullah to the point at which it turns eastwards towards Coonoor. From this turn of the nullah the boundary runs in a direct line over the hill to the bridge on the Coonoor and Ootacamund road, in the east side of Wellington, and from the bridge including the Milk Village along its east side, and thence in a direct line to the Karteri stream; then eastward down the stream to the junction of the Karteri and Coonoor streams, then up to the latter stream, to the side of the new bridge, and from there in a direct line to the Sappers' burial-ground on the old ghát, whence it first started."

—elevation.

The height of All Saints' Church above the sea-level is 5,954 feet, that of the Coonoor bridge about 5,500 feet. Most of the houses occupied by Europeans are between 5,700 and 6,000 feet above sea-level. Coonoor Peak, however, is 6,893 feet above sea-level, or only 300 feet below the level of the Ootacamand lake.

—Municipal Commission.

Coonoor was constituted a Municipality by notification, under Act X of 1865, on the 19th October 1866. The Commission is administered almost wholly by European residents, but the Station Medical Officer ordinarily officiates as Vice-President. The Commission has done much to improve the station in sanitary as well as æsthetic matters, but the town still lacks an adequate water-supply and a systematic drainage. The steepness, however, of the ground, on which the greater portion of the Native town is built, supplies the want of drainage when scoured by the heavy rains, which wash down the debris of the town pretty thoroughly and thus mitigate the many existing sanitary defects. With the exception of the profession tax, the taxes laid down in Act III of 1871 are levied. The tolls however are in the hands of the Local Fund Board, and, as in Ootacamand, the Government maintain the main thoroughfares.

—receipts and expenditure.

The following statement shows the receipts and expenditure of the Commission during the ten years ending 1877-78 exclusive of loans, &c. :—

MUNICIPALITIES AND STATIONS.

Coonoor.

Years.	Receipts.			Expenditure.			
	Taxes.	Miscellaneous.	Total.	Works.	Conservancy.	Other Objects.	Total.
	RS.	RS.	RS.	RS.	RS.	RS.	RS.
1868-69 ...	5,336	1,336	6,672	3,532	2,322	3,745	9,599
1869-70 ...	6,054	1,888	7,942	3,919	2,573	2,002	8,494
1870-71 ...	4,265	2,148	6,413	1,120	2,424	4,253	7,797
1871-72 ...	5,304	2,031	7,335	1,291	2,369	4,200	7,660
1872-73 ...	4,984	4,220	9,204	2,241	2,898	3,849	8,988
1873-74 ...	4,337	3,264	7,601	1,026	2,871	4,248	8,145
1874-75 ...	3,409	7,030	10,439	2,287	2,929	4,238	9,454
1875-76 ...	4,441	8,973	13,414	3,058	4,900	5,283	13,241
1876-77 ...	4,901	7,586	12,487	8,288	5,430	6,003	19,721
1877-78 ...	4,414	7,534	11,948	2,748	5,084	4,740	12,572
Total ...	47,345	46,010	93,355	29,510	33,800	42,561	1,05,671

Coonoor possesses no public building of any size or importance besides All Saints' Church. The American Mission Chapel and the Roman Catholic Chapel dedicated to St. Anthony are comparatively small structures. The Public Library is a simple building; the Market (held on Sundays and Tuesdays) consists, as at Ootacamand, of plain tiled sheds. The Post Office was formerly the Travellers' Bungalow; the Sub-Magistrate's Office, the Police Station, the Hospital, the Native Chattram and the Coonoor Day School are all plain buildings. Sim's Park, artistically planted with beautiful trees and shrubs and laid out as a pleasure ground with summer houses, also with swings and poles, &c., bids fair to rival the Ootacamand Public Gardens. At present, however, it possesses no conservatories or green-houses. —public building, &c.

The population of Coonoor at the last census was 3,058, dwelling in 536 houses. The number of houses, however, has very considerably increased during the past seven or eight years. The number of inhabitants is now probably not less than 5,000. —population.

There are several hotels and lodging-houses in Coonoor, the chief being the Union (Gray's), Glenview, and Hillgrove House. The rates are generally the same as at Ootacamand. House property is much more valuable, and, as most of the land within the Municipality has passed into private hands, it is difficult to obtain building sites. Building materials being cheaper, the houses are probably in the main better constructed than at the principal station. Rents are much the same as at Ootacamand, though the population is less migratory than at that station, many planters residing there permanently. The future of Coonoor depends mainly on the success of agricultural enterprise on the eastern and southern slopes. —hotels, &c.

The account of Wellington in Chapter IV gives nearly all the information that is necessary in regard to this cantonment. WELLINGTON.

CHAP. XVII.

MUNICIPALITIES AND STATIONS.

It lies to the north-west of Coonoor, on the ridges lying between the western and middle streams which meet at the old Coonoor bridge. The Native bazaars however, with the Joint Magistrate's Court and the Police Station, lie on the right bank of the western stream, across which a fine suspension bridge has been thrown at a spot a short way above the bazaar. The hills and ravines in the cantonment were very bare of forest; the defect however has been remedied, especially in the neighbourhood of the barracks, by plantations of Australian eucalypti. Its climate is probably superior to that of Coonoor, the ghát mists ordinarily not extending in this direction. Its exact limits will be found in notification of 10th May 1865. It is a portion of the Coonoor settlement, and the Municipality is for the purposes of the Contagious Diseases Act under the surveillance of the Cantonment Magistrate.

The early history of the proposal to locate European troops on the plateau and the final decision to build barracks have already been related in Chapter XII.

KÓTAGIRI.

The only station remaining to be noticed is Kótagiri, lying some twelve miles to the north-east of Coonoor and at the head of a fine pass or ravine, in which are many coffee and tea estates. Kótagiri is especially interested in the tea industry, and hitherto may be said to have taken the lead on the Nílagiris in this enterprise. There are but sixteen large houses in the station, the principal being Kóta Hall, which stands on the ridge of the gháts, commanding a fine view of the eastern slopes and distant ranges. This house, built in 1830, was once occupied for several months by Lord Dalhousie, who preferred Kótagiri as a residence to the other stations. The little Native bazaar lies on the sides of the valley behind, at the foot of which is a neat, but small, church. The elevation of Kótagiri is at 6,500 feet above sea-level. Its climate, though less invigorating than that of Ootacamand, is colder and more bracing than that of Coonoor. The superior character of the climate is due partly to the greater elevation, but probably in a greater degree to the open character of the country. It is well protected from the violence of the south-west monsoon, but in the early months of the year the easterly winds are felt more here than at Coonoor. The area of the station, having a radius of two miles, is approximately 12 square miles, or 7,639 acres. The boundaries of this as of the other stations is marked by large stones and a deep trench. The population of Kótagiri at the last census was 641 only, and, unlike the other stations, it does not promise to increase rapidly, though that of the neighbourhood with the extension of plantations is doubtless growing steadily.

The only public buildings are the Church, the Dispensary, the Chattrum, and the Police station.

CHAPTER XVIII.

NOTES ON THE PUBLIC WORKS OF THE NÍLAGIRI DISTRICT.

(*By* Major J. L. L. Morant, R.E., *District Engineer.*)

Sums expended.—Establishment.—Roads.—Railway Scheme.—Military Buildings. —Lawrence Asylums.—Building materials.—Wages and cost of materials.—Nílagiris and Coimbatore compared.—Cost of the various edifices.

CH. XVIII. — Notes on Public Works.

Sums expended on public works.

This memorandum applies solely to the district prior to the annexation of a portion of South-East Wainád. The accompanying table (Appendix No. 16)[1] exhibits the sums which have been expended on public works on the Nílagiris during the seventeen years ending with 1876-77. From it we learn that (omitting cost of establishments) the annual expenditure on new works and repairs in this district during those seventeen years has averaged £20,265 and £3,993 respectively, distributed as follows:—

	New Works.	Repairs.
	£	£
Military Buildings	10,639	780
Civil Buildings	3,264	271
Communications	5,951	2,909
Miscellaneous Public Improvements...	411	33
Total ...	20,265	3,993

The cost of the establishment which has disbursed the above sums has averaged 13·2 per cent. of the entire expenditure.

Establishment.

In the year 1860-61 the Wellington barracks were completed. Excepting the officer employed on that work the Nílagiris had no resident Engineer until 1861-62; one from Coimbatore had paid it occasional visits. In the latter year a separate Engineer was appointed to the district. Thenceforth public works of all kinds were pushed on with vigour.

[1] In this and in all other tables the figures are given in English currency, the rupee being taken at two shillings.

CH. XVIII.

NOTES ON PUBLIC WORKS.

Roads.

In a lofty and isolated mountain district like the Nílagiris, which was formerly sparsely populated, difficult of approach, and but little known, to obtain access from the surrounding low-lying districts by means of roads to its elevated plateau was the first problem which Engineers had before them; and the subject of providing intercommunications to open up the plateau and make it everywhere more accessible has ever since engaged their attention. The passes rising up to the plateau which were first constructed were too steeply and unscientifically traced to allow of their being permanently retained. Large sums of money had subsequently to be expended in replacing them by proper roads fit for wheeled traffic. The existing passes, placed in the order of their construction, are—

1. The Kótagiri Pass on the south-east.
2. The Súndaputté Pass on the south.
3. The Sisapára Pass on the south-west.
4. The Segúr Pass on the north.
5. The Coonoor Pass on the south-east.
6. The Gúdalúr Pass on the west.

Of these the first and two last have been succeeded by new roads; the third is but little used; the second has been abandoned. In the year 1863-64 the more complete and correct roading of the district was actively begun, and has since been systematically carried out; but owing to limited funds these roads have been too much hurried on, quality having been sacrificed to quantity. The object seems to have been to make as many miles of road just passable for carts as possible, and not to expend too much money on their gradients, straightness, bridging or surface. The result is that the district possesses a large number of roads, most of which are indifferent in their original construction, and which will have to be improved as the district advances in prosperity. It would perhaps have been better if the roading of the district had been more concentrated, portions being taken up and properly completed before other parts were begun.

The only trunk road of the district is that which runs from the east in a westerly direction between the present railway terminus at Mettapollium and the south-east edge of the Wainád at Gúdalúr, through the only district towns of Coonoor and Ootacamand. Towards this arterial line flow feeders: most of these join it at Coonoor, which is situated on the top of the plateau at its south-east edge. One feeder taps the north-east portion of the district in the neighbourhood of Kótagiri and Kódanád, where there is a growing tea industry; a second high level line runs east along the edge of the plateau to Lady

CH. XVIII.

NOTES ON PUBLIC WORKS.

Canning's Seat, Lamb's Rock, and Dolphin's Nose, affording access to the town of Coonoor for numerous tea and coffee estates, the latter of which extend down the hill slopes towards Mettapollium; a third feeder opens access to the west and south of the district in the neighbourhood of Kátéri and Kólakambé, where lie most of the Nílagiri coffee estates.[1] From Kátéri branches a feeder which taps Dévashóla and Mélúr, where are large cinchona estates; and Kátéri is now connected with Ootacamand by a branch to Yellannallé. A line has been traced connecting the Kúndas with Dévashóla, and hence with Coonoor. A fourth feeder taps tea and coffee estates in the vicinity of the Húlikal Drúg. From Ootacamand runs a main feeder (once famous, now but little used except by the Forest Department), *viâ* the Segúr Ghát, almost due north towards Mysore. From Ootacamand also branches the line to Dévashóla and Mélúr, and from it a third but very incomplete line runs south-west towards Sisapára on the Kúndas. There are a few other connecting branches. It thus appears that very much has been effected to open out the district by roads. But much remains to be done before the Nílagiris can be said to be everywhere accessible. The lofty and in part promising western tract called the Kúndas,[2] with their western slopes, and the northern crests of the district plateau between Kódanád and Neduwattam may, without exaggeration, be said to be as regards communications in almost the same condition as when the Nílagiris were first discovered.

The following table of all the district roads, giving their cost, traffic, length, and annual maintenance will be of service :—

---

[1] Kótagiri has also been recently placed in direct connection with the Railway terminus at Mettapollium by a ghát road of 1 in 17 twenty miles long.

[2] North Kúndas or Nídumalé range.—ED.

CH. XVIII. — NOTES ON PUBLIC WORKS.

Roads in the Nílagiri District, giving their Original Cost, Annual Traffic, Length, and Sums spent on their Annual Repairs.

	No.	Description of Road.	Original Cost of Construction per Mile.	Annual Traffic in Tons.	Total Length in Miles.	Annual Repair Rate per Mile.	Total Annual Repair Allowance.
			£	TONS.	MILES.	£	£
Trunk Road.	1	Coonoor Ghát bridged, drained and metalled. Gradient 1 in 18½, 12 zigzags, 18 feet wide.	2,037	9,448	16	60½	968
Trunk Road.	2	Ootacamand to Coonoor bridged, drained and metalled. 15 feet wide	720	6,686	12	27½	330
Trunk Road.	3	Ootacamand to Neduwattam bridged and drained. One-fourth metalled, three-fourths of earth, 18 feet wide.	318	1,048	20	11	220
Trunk Road.	4	Gúdalúr Ghát bridged and drained. One-half metalled, one-half good soil, 7 zigzags, 14 feet wide.	814	1,048	12	11	132
S. Rds.	5	Ootacamand roads metalled with granite,[1] rolled and well looked after	...	...	9	33	297
S. Rds.	6	Ootacamand roads metalled with laterite, rolled and well looked after	...	...	7	22	154
S. Rds.	7	Kótagiri Station roads, very steep, much wash, unmetalled	...	...	2½	13¾	34
	8	Branch road from Coonoor to Kodanád through Kótagiri	280	400	17	11	187
	9	Roads chiefly unmetalled, of earth but well drained; worst parts here and there covered with broken stone.	320	400	104	11	1,144
	10	Roads chiefly good bridle-paths, 9 feet wide, are very little used by carts, and 12 feet wide, drained, &c., of earth.	200	...	52½	5½	289
	11	Bridle-paths, 4 or 5 feet wide, rough and steep, indifferently drained	...	...	13	2¾	36
		Total ...	...	...	265	...	3,791

Abstract.

	No. of Miles.
Roads metalled with granite or sienite	35½
Do. with decomposed granite or sienite	43½
Do. with laterite	58½
Earthen roads	79
Bridle-paths	48½
Total ...	265

[1] Gneissose rock.—ED.

CH. XVIII. NOTES ON PUBLIC WORKS. Railway scheme.

The Nílagiris are now occupied by Europeans chiefly for the purpose of growing shrubs yielding articles of export; they are resorted to for a portion of each year by the Madras Government and by European visitors mostly from Madras and Bangalore; and nearly all food-supplies, building materials, and other necessities of life are imported from the adjoining low-lying districts, mainly from the one on the eastern side. Hence the means by which all this traffic can best be served becomes the most important question relating to the Nílagiris. A glance at the map clearly shows that the inlet and outlet for all the district traffic is the railway terminus at Mettapollium. This is by far the nearest point of ingress and egress to the district, and it is the point towards which all the Nílagiri traffic now converges. Now Mettapollium is a station on the branch line which leaves at Pothanúr the main line of the Madras Railway; and this main line runs across the Indian peninsula from Madras on the east to Beypúr on the west coast, being connected with lines to Bombay and Allahabad. The extension of this branch along the arterial line of the district up the Coonoor Pass to Coonoor on the east, and thence through Ootacamand, its centre, to Neduwattam on the west, is that of which the Nílagiri District at present stands most in need. Statistics collected in 1874 show that the total charges on the annual traffic between Mettapollium and Coonoor amounted to £44,000; that this traffic had been increasing during the previous seven years at an average rate of 11 per cent. per annum; and that it had doubled itself within the previous ten years. Hence it is probable that a railway between Mettapollium and Coonoor, costing under half a million sterling, will return a paying dividend. There is only one system of mountain railways which will perfectly serve all the passenger and goods traffic, and which can be constructed between the above places for that sum. This is the rack-rail system of M. Riggenbach, a Swiss Engineer. He has offered to construct within four years a railway between Mettapollium and Coonoor. He undertakes himself to raise the necessary capital, which he estimates at £400,000. He requires Government to grant him, free of charge, all the land required for the line, and to guarantee him from the opening of the line and for the first ten years thereafter an interest of 4 per cent. per annum on only one-half of the outlay if the net receipts, after deducting all expenses, do not reach that figure. He proposes to construct the line between Mettapollium and Kalár (the foot of the Coonoor Pass) on the ordinary system, and that between Kalár and Coonoor on the rack-rail system, with a gradient of one in eight. His system has extended over the Continent, where eight lines and thirty-two locomotives are at work. The Government of Madras are disposed, it is understood, to favorably

CH. XVIII. — NOTES ON PUBLIC WORKS.

entertain his offer, and it is to be hoped that the line may shortly be begun. A branch railway on the metre gauge is about to be made between Bangalore and Mysore. Its extension from Mysore into the Wainád might be profitable, and would certainly develope that large coffee tract; but it could scarcely serve the Nílagiris.[1] Any point on it would be as far from Ootacamand as Mettapollium is, and Coonoor would be altogether out of its reach.

Though communications are obviously the most important of public works on the Nílagiris, nearly twice as much (excluding repairs) has been expended on military buildings. Of these there are but two, viz., the barracks for convalescent soldiers at Wellington and the asylum for soldiers' orphans at Ootacamand.

Military buildings.

The Wellington barracks were begun in 1848 and completed in 1860. In 1876 another block was added to them. Appendix No. 16-A gives particulars. They can accommodate 54 non-commissioned officers and 820 privates, and have cost in all £166,740. Each married soldier obtains 5,376 cubic and 384 square feet of living space, at a cost per head of £362. Each single soldier obtains 1,530 cubic and 77½ square feet at £166 per head. This cost covers that of every out-building, &c. Ample provision has been made for the comfort of the British soldier in the Wellington barracks, which are very substantial buildings, well built of the best materials. Indeed a larger number of soldiers might quite conveniently be accommodated by utilizing the wide back verandahs, which are enclosed. These barracks are amply provided with ablutionary water laid on in pipes by gravitation. The drinking-supply comes from a pure spring, and is piped to the point from which it is drawn. The barrack sites are all well drained. The latrines are worked on the dry-earth system, and the night-soil is daily removed from the buildings to a sufficient distance, where it is sold. The soldiers' food is admirably cooked in stoves. But the site on which these barracks are built has proved to be not altogether a healthy one.

Lawrence Asylums.

The Ootacamand Lawrence Asylums were begun in 1863, and all work upon them was stopped in 1871. They are incomplete. Appendix No. 16-B gives particulars. The Male Asylum has been completed at a cost of £57,500. Nearly £4,000 have been expended on the Female Asylum, the out-buildings of which have been temporarily converted into quarters: an additional outlay of some £34,000 for sergeants and masters will be needed to complete it according to the original design to accommodate 300 girls, with a chapel for both boys and girls. The girls are now lodged in what was intended to be the hospital for both branches: this was built for about £8,000. The buildings which have

[1] This view is not endorsed by me.—ED.

been completed can accommodate 1 Principal, 1 Matron, 3 Sergeants, 2 Mistresses, 400 boys and 144 girls, with workshops for the boys and quarters for native servants; but no separate hospital for either boys or girls having yet been provided, and the accommodation for the boys' staff (such as masters, &c.) being very limited, some of the dormitories are used as hospitals, tailors' shops, &c.; and sergeants and other Europeans are lodged in quarters intended, when designed and sanctioned, for native servants. The whole of the buildings, as they now stand, accommodate

CH. XVIII.

NOTES ON PUBLIC WORKS.

1 Principal,	2 Matrons,
1 Manager,	3 Mistresses,
5 Masters,	330 boys, and
6 Sergeants,	60 girls,
4 Farm servants (Europeans),	

besides numerous native servants. Each boy is supplied with 735 cubic and 25 square feet of sleeping space; he is also supplied with very large school and dining rooms, a covered play ground and every other convenience. This has cost, including everything, £164 per (boy) head. Each girl is supplied with 785 cubic and 38 square feet of sleeping space; other accommodation is in many respects limited; the building cost is £75 per (girl) head. The site selected for the asylums is very salubrious, being freely open to every breeze, and on ground which falls away from the buildings on all sides. The boys' asylum is a large, lofty, handsome, double-storied building, forming three sides of a quadrangle, and designed in the Italian Gothic style with a campanile 130 feet high. It is well built of the best materials. The boys' food is cooked in Duff's stoves. Water is supplied in open channels, and is pumped up some 50 feet to the building plateau. Its distribution might be improved. The latrines are on the dry-earth system, but are sanitarily too close to the main buildings. The girls' asylum (designed as the hospital) is a single-storied unpretentious but commodious and convenient building. Its sanitary arrangements are similar to those of the boys' branch.

Building materials.

All building materials are found on the Nílagiris except lime and timber. The stone is a gneiss of a very hard description, and is seldom chiselled. It is used as rough rubble in the retaining walls of roads, and answers well. Admirable clay for bricks is obtainable everywhere. The sand for mortar is very impure and dirty: no really good silicious sand can be procured except by breaking up the quartz pebbles which abound. Road metal is of three kinds—broken gneiss, which is very hard and makes a good surface; broken decomposed sienite, which bears moderate traffic; and broken laterite, or gravel, which binds well and carries

CH. XVIII. — NOTES ON PUBLIC WORKS.

light traffic on springs, but rapidly disintegrates in very wet weather. The Nílagiris have no limestone nor any indigenous timber. Lime is obtained from near Mettapollium. The stone from which it is burnt is semi-crystalline and honey-combed, with about 20 per cent. of silicates. The lime is good, but sets very slowly. It is burnt at Mettapollium and delivered on the hills unslaked. Morgan's cement is also sometimes used; it sets quickly, and is a very valuable article. Teakwood is obtained from the Government forests at Múdúmalé, north-west of Ootacamand. Of late years the supply has deteriorated, as those forests are being gradually worked out. At best the wood is full of holes and flaws, entailing great wastage, and the size of the logs is small. Such scantlings as are eventually obtained are very strong, but the timber is only half seasoned. On the Nílagiri plateau not a single indigenous tree is found which can be used as timber. As the slopes of the mountain are descended trees useful for building are met with, and the lower down the slopes the more numerous and vigorous are these trees. Efforts have been made to thin the plateau forests and to clear away the brushwood, leaving the larger trees to reassert their vigour, but without success; the trees are a prey to parasites. Australian trees have been introduced into the district with marked success, but many of them are also attacked by parasites of the mistletoe type. The blue-gum, *et hoc genus omne*, promise to best suit the soil and climate of the Nílagiris. But no real data regarding the value of the timber of these trees has as yet been afforded. They are cut down before maturity, and the wood is used before being in the least seasoned.

Wages and cost of materials.

Appendix No. 16-C gives the rates of wages and cost of materials at every triad during the last quarter of a century. Speaking roughly, during that period the rate of wages has doubled and the cost of materials has tripled. Improved communications have prevented imported articles like lime, teakwood, and Europe iron from increasing in the same ratio as local materials. Cooly labour being in great demand by owners of estates, it is difficult to procure, and is proportionately independent. About one-half of the coolies come from Mysore, the other half being the Badagas of the Nílagiris. The former are physically weaker, but do best as brick-makers and road repairers; the latter are stronger and more intelligent. All skilled labour is, as required by the Department Public Works, directly imported from the Coimbatore, Trichinopoly and Madura Districts. Private persons (in Ootacamand especially) find it almost impossible to obtain skilled labour in the bazaar, and generally apply to this department for it. Such skilled labour as is obtainable is not always the best. The cold wet climate induces to indulgence in ardent spirits, and wet days, when little or no work is done, have sometimes to be paid for in full. The climate is not appreciated by any class of imported Native, least of all by the skilled workmen. These latter, with few exceptions, leave the hills when the period for which they have been engaged terminates. Breaches of labour contract are also not infrequent. Very few women and boys are employed as labourers, proportionately far less than in most other parts of India.

Work by contract is seldom performed. It is nearly all done departmentally, by waged labourers who are tasked, their work of every kind being periodically measured and priced at certain rates. Suppliers of materials are not numerous, but lime, sand, firewood, road-metal, &c., are all furnished by contract. The procuring and managing of all labour and the obtaining of the means of transit for building materials, are the greatest difficulties against which an engineer has to contend on the Nílagiris.

Appendix 16-D compares rates of labour and materials in the Coimbatore and Nílagiri Districts, and gives the increased percentage of the latter over the former.

It will probably at the same time be useful to record the prices of food-grains in those two districts, as is done in following table :—

Statement showing Comparative Prices of Food-grains, &c., on the Nílagiris and at Coimbatore.

—	Rice, 1st sort.	Rice, 2nd sort.	Horse-gram.	Cholum.	Cumboo.	Salt.	Wheat.
	Number of lb. per Rupee.	Number of lb. per Rupee.	Number of lb. per Rupee.	Number of lb. per Rupee.	Number of lb. per Rupee.	Number of lb. per Rupee.	Number of lb. per Rupee.
Nílagiri Hills ...	17·42	19·75	30·10	34·59	38·22	19·05	21·62
At Coimbatore.	22·26	23·36	42·97	41·43	53·55	34·38	28·87
Per ton on Nílagiris, Rs.	125·5	114·7	80·6	64·4	63·2	114·4	103·6
Per Ton in Coimbatore, Rs.	100·6	95·8	52·1	54·0	41·6	65·1	77·5
Increase per ton, Nílagiris.	24·9	18·9	28·5	10·4	21·6	49·3	26·1

Cost of various edifices.

In conclusion I would draw attention to table (Appendix No. 16-E) showing the cost of the various edifices constructed throughout the Nílagiri District.

CHAPTER XIX.

PRISONS.

(*By* Lieut.-Colonel CLEMENTSON, M.S.C., *Superintendent of Prisons, Ootacamand, and Joint Magistrate, Nílagiris.*)

EUROPEAN PRISON—buildings—prisoners—discipline—industries — diet—dress—health—instruction—cost – establishment. — DISTRICT JAIL—situation—buildings—industries—diet—health.—SUBSIDIARY JAILS.

EUROPEAN PRISON AT OOTACAMAND.

CHAP. XIX. — PRISONS. — EUROPEAN PRISON. Description of the buildings.

THE European Prison was designed, as a Central Jail, for the accommodation of Europeans sentenced to penal servitude and long terms of imprisonment throughout India. It consists of a block of buildings containing two rows of small separate cells, thirty-six in number, arranged opposite each other in a lower and upper story with a corridor between. The capacity of the cells on the ground-floor is 977·65 cubic feet and of those in the upper 936·3 cubic feet, except the two at the west end, which are 1,656·32 cubic feet. These latter have flat roofs, but the roofs of all the others are dome-shaped. The ground-floor also contains a guard-room, office-room, and a hospital sufficiently large to accommodate four patients. The jail yard is divided into compartments with a workshed in three of them and two small store-rooms. In the fourth there is a kitchen.

Character and number of prisoners.

The jail was open for the reception of prisoners in 1862. The first convict admitted was a man sentenced by the Sessions Court of Mangalore in February of this year. In the March following twenty-nine convicts, chiefly civilian criminals, were received from Calcutta, and in June five military court-martial prisoners from different cantonments of the Presidency. In later years, as suitable jail accommodation became available in the other Presidencies, convicts ceased to be transferred from thence to this jail; and at present it is chiefly used for the confinement of military prisoners and civilians, Europeans and Eurasians, sentenced to long terms, or for shorter terms, if sentenced by the local Courts. The total number incarcerated up to November 1878 was 298, of whom 110 were sentenced by the Civil Criminal Courts and 188 by the Military Courts. The daily average in jail for the last five years ending 31st December 1877 was 25·73; 7·19 civilians and 18·54 military.

Female convicts are not admitted into this jail, nor are civil prisoners (debtors). For juveniles there is no separate accommodation. Of the latter only two have been admitted; they were not allowed to associate or work with the adults. CHAP. XIX. PRISONS.

All prisoners on arrival are considered on probation and liable to the discipline of the separate system for such period as the Superintendent may direct, but in no instance for less than three months, except in the case of prisoners who have less than six months of their imprisonment to undergo, or have already undergone three months of their sentence elsewhere, or solitary confinement as part of their sentence. On expiry of the probationary term, convicts work in association under the superintendence and control of European warders. They are required to rise at 6 in the morning on week days, and are employed in cleaning their cells and the corridor, &c., up to 7 o'clock, when they are allowed into the yards for washing and exercise. At 7-30 A.M. they return to their cells for breakfast and remain locked up until 8 o'clock. They then go to the worksheds and are kept steadily and industriously at labour of various descriptions until about 1 o'clock. They then retire to their cells for dinner and are locked up for an hour. At 2 P.M. work is resumed in the yards and continued till 5 o'clock. Half an hour is allowed for the afternoon exercise, and at 5-30 the prisoners are confined for the night after their evening meal is served to them. On Sundays convicts are allowed three hours exercise in the yards in the forenoon and two in the afternoon. For the rest of the day they are confined to their cells. —discipline.

None of the convicts are employed on extramural work. At present the intermural labour consists chiefly of weaving, coir mat making, rattaning, shoemaking, and beating out the fibre from the cocoanut husk, which latter has been recently substituted for stone-breaking. Other industries, as saddlery, carpentry, &c., for which a convict may be specially qualified, are occasionally introduced when there is a demand for such labour. All the jail work, such as sweeping out the yards, white and yellow washing the premises, cooking, tailoring, and the like, are done by the convicts themselves, except privy conservancy, which devolves on native convicts sent for that purpose from the neighbouring district jail. All prisoners are eligible for employment as cooks, for such period and at such times as the keeper may direct. The sale-proceeds on account of manufactures amounted in 1877 to Rupees 2,569-1-11, yielding a net profit to Government of Rupees 31-12-11 per head of effectives. —industries.

The ordinary diet of the convicts is as follows:— —diet.

Monday, Wednesday, and Friday.	Bread, 18 ounces. Potatoes, 1 pound. Soup (consisting of $4\frac{1}{2}$ ounces meat, 3 ounces potatoes, and 1 ounce dholl, 1 ounce onions). Suet Pudding (5 ounces flour and $\frac{3}{4}$ ounce suet).

CHAP. XIX. — PRISONS.

Monday, Wednesday, and Friday.	Gruel, 1 pint (2 ounces meal or rolong and 1 ounce sugar). Coffee, 1 pint. A little pepper and salt.
Saturday.	Curry-stuff is added to the soup to form mulligatanni, and 8 ounces of rice are substituted for potatoes. In other respects as above.
Tuesday and Thursday.	Cooked meat (bake), 7 ounces. Bread, Potatoes, Suet Pudding, Gruel, Coffee, Salt, &c. — As above.
Sunday ...	In all respects as above, excep bread 22 ounces.

Probationers are not allowed pudding. For the sick the doctor may prescribe special hospital diet.

For breaches of prison discipline convicts are liable to restrictions in diet. Bread and water or half rations may be awarded as a punishment, the former for a period not exceeding 3 days for any one offence, and the latter for a period not exceeding 7 days. The delinquent is subject to labour of the lightest description while on bread and water, and to that of medium severity while on half rations.

—dress. On admission each prisoner is supplied with a small kit, marked with his register number, consisting of 1 cap, 1 coat, 1 waistcoat, and 2 trousers of ordinary infantry blue grey cloth, 2 blue serge and 3 cotton check shirts, 2 flannel banians, 2 pairs of drawers, 3 pairs of socks, 2 handkerchiefs, 1 pair of boots and a pair of slippers, 1 comb and 4 towels. He is also allowed a coir mattress and 2 pillows, 4 sheets and 4 pillow slips, 2 blankets and a coverlet or cotton rug. During one month of his sentence and when undergoing punishment for breaches of prison discipline, a convict is deprived of his mattress and is required to sleep on a plank bed.

—health. Favoured by a salubrious climate, the health of the convicts has been remarkably good. Only two deaths have occurred since the opening of the jail, and in both cases heart disease was the immediate cause. The first was that of a convict who had undergone seven years of his sentence of imprisonment, and was at the time suffering also from pneumonia. The second was that of a military man who had had heart disease previous to admission, and succumbed to it in about a month after entrance. The more prevalent ailments are stomach affections and colds. There have been no epidemics. It has been found that convicts have generally gained weight during their imprisonment.

Divine service is performed once a week for Roman Catholics, and twice a week, Sundays and Wednesdays, for Protestants. There is a small library of useful and instructive books available for the use of the well-conducted prisoners. Each prisoner, if a Protestant, is supplied with a Bible and Book of Common Prayer; and, if a Roman Catholic, with a Douay Bible and Garden of the Soul. CHAP. XIX. PRISONS. —instruction.

The total cost of guarding and maintaining the prisoners in the European Jail for the year 1877 was as follows:— —cost.

	RS.	A.	P.
Establishment	7,206	15	8
Rations	4,059	11	3
Clothing	1,181	0	7
Contingencies	1,430	10	5
Hospital charges (including cost of medicines)	117	1	0
Total Rupees ...	13,995	6	11

or Rupees 559-2-0 per head of average strength.

The establishment consists of 1 Keeper, 5 Warders, 1 Messenger, 1 Medical Officer (also in charge of one of the two Ootacamand divisions), and 1 Assistant Apothecary, the Joint Magistrate of the station being *ex-officio* Superintendent. There is no Police guard over the prison, the warders having to act in the double capacity of guard and turnkey. —establishment.

DISTRICT JAIL, OOTACAMAND.

The building was originally the old Travellers' Bungalow, subsequently utilized as a Cutcherry for the Principal Sudder Amin, and was ultimately, in 1856, converted into a District Jail under the charge of the above officer, with a requisite establishment of subordinates. For many years the Joint Magistrate has been *ex-officio* Superintendent of the jail. DISTRICT JAIL.

The jail is well situated on a hill nearly in the centre of Ootacamand. The site is in every way good, except as regards its proximity to a bazaar, the sanitary condition of which is anything but satisfactory. —situation, &c.

The jail is not on the standard plan. It consists of a range of buildings facing the west, and contains ten wards and one under-trial ward, watchman's room, and at the northern end four solitary cells. There are four kitchens at the southern end, and at the north-western end latrines, &c., with earth stores. Opposite the main building is a range of stores and a workshop. The whole is surrounded by a wall about 7 feet high. The hospital is in a

CHAP. XIX. PRISONS.

separate yard, and contains four wards and accommodation for 26 patients. The wards, both jail and hospital, are generally well ventilated. There is also a separate building with a yard surrounding for civil debtors, European and Native.

—accommodation. The jail is wanting in separate accommodation for juveniles, and in a separate yard for females to work in during the day.

The jail is calculated to accommodate 72 convict males, 10 convict females, 3 under-trials, and 6 civil debtors; total 91.

—buildings. The area of ground occupied by the jail premises measures about 70 acres and is thus utilized up:—On the east and apart from the building is the vegetable garden, manured with poudrette, and producing excellent vegetables for the use of the prisoners. There is also on this side of the jail a temporary jail which is used for short-term prisoners. It is roofed in with corrugated iron, and partitioned into three wards capable of accommodating 88 inmates. The flooring is of earth tamped down, but the occupants sleep on raised boarded platforms.

The jailor's quarters are situated close to and west of the civil debtors' jail. The Police guard-room is just outside the main jail.

The hospital is a building 218 feet 6 inches long and 75 feet wide, having a verandah to the front and rear. The ends of the verandah at the back have been closed in and are used for a bath and store-room. Flanking it on the west, but detached, are the male and female latrines and dead-house. The accommodation provided by the hospital is ample, there being three wards for males and one for females. They are intended ordinarily to contain 24 male and 2 female inmates. There is also a surgery and a store-room. The wards of the hospital, as also those of the jail, are lighted nightly with kerosine lamps. The hospital staff is one Surgeon and one Apothecary. There is no quarantine ward.

The civil debtors' jail provides accommodation for 6 inmates, and is a comfortable building, but is rarely occupied.

Prisoners are received by drafts from the Coimbatore and other jails when the number in the jail falls very low. These drafts are needed to keep up the gang employed in public works to its full strength, about 100 prisoners.

Chinese are very rarely admitted into this jail.

—industries. The occupation of the convicts is chiefly extramural, at present on the works at Norwood and the Gardens; the work done is principally road-making, excavation, &c. These labouring convicts are supervised by an Overseer of the Public Works Department. They are guarded to and fro by the Police, and are in charge of prison warders assisted by convict maistries, who more directly see to the completion of their task. Within the jail and its precincts a number of the convicts are employed on the sanitary duties of the jail and in raggi-grinding, tailoring, cooking, and as dhobies; a little carpentry and smith's work is also done, and vegetable gardening. There are no manufactures. The jail garden supplies excellent vegetables sufficient for the prisoners' consumption; the surplus is sold and by this means a trifling sum is realized monthly and remitted to the treasury.

—diet, &c.

The cost of rations during 1877 for a daily average strength of 155·33 convicts was Rupees 11,625. The diet is ample and good, and in accordance with scale: 5 ounces of meat are supplied thrice weekly; no fish is used; also no tyre, as it is not obtainable in sufficient quantities; the vegetable ration is therefore increased to 7$\frac{3}{7}$ ounces in lieu of the tyre. There have been no scorbutic ailments, and the prisoners, as a rule, gain weight during their confinement. The water for drinking is obtained from the Málémand Lake; it is received into a reservoir, and pumped up into a covered masonry filter. It is sometimes very muddy even after filtration. The cost of clothing for 1877 was Rupees 737.

The nature of the clothing and bedding is thus:—1 cap, 2 cumbly jackets, 2 cotton breeches, 2 cumblies, 1 cumbly hood, and 1 coir mat for each male convict.

The following rules are enforced regarding ablution of the whole body for

(*a.*) MALES—Bathe twice a week within the jail. A large cistern is used as a bath. Cheakai is issued on each occasion, and oil every alternate week.

(*b.*) FEMALES—Bathe similarly, but in the compound of the debtors' jail.

—health.

The general health of the prisoners during 1877 as contrasted with former years was very unsatisfactory. Numbers were admitted in a state of starvation. Of 173 total admissions into hospital, 21 were for simple starvation, and of those admitted under the heads of general dropsy, debility, diarrhœa, and dysentery, the primary cause of disease in most instances was starvation, and twenty-four invalids were transferred to Coimbatore on medical grounds, being too emaciated to stand this cold climate. Almost all the deaths were due to privation. Ordinarily the ailments are such as are incidental to the nature of the climate, *e.g.*, dysentery, diarrhœa, and chest affections.

SUBSIDIARY JAILS.

SUBSIDIARY JAILS.

There is a lock-up for under-trial and short-term prisoners, *i.e.*, convicted persons whose sentence does not exceed one or two

CHAP. XIX. PRISONS.

weeks, at the Wellington Police Station, and another at the Sub-Magistrate's Court, Coonoor. The convicted prisoners are employed in out-door work in the proximity of the prisons. There are also lock-ups at Gúdalúr and Déväla.

CHAPTER XX.

POSTAL DEPARTMENT.

CHAP. XX. — POSTAL DEPARTMENT.

Number of Post Offices.—History of Ootacamand Post Office.—Old postal rates.—Hill Post Offices brought under inspection.—Present establishment.—Number of letters received and despatched.—Revenue.—Coonoor and Kótagiri.—Wellington.—South-East Wainád.—Old postal route of the Hills.—Tonga.—Rates for passengers.—Post hours at Ootacamand and other offices.

THERE are four Post Offices on the Nílagiris, viz., at Ootacamand, Coonoor, Kótagiri, and Wellington. *Number of Post Offices.*

Ootacamand is the first station at which a Post Office was opened. This was in the year 1826; the establishment then consisted of one writer and two delivery peons. In 1828 an additional writer and delivery peon were sanctioned, and in 1829 (as the Hills were becoming more generally known) the delivery staff was increased by two more peons. There appear to have been no fresh changes till the year 1837, when Colonel Thomas King was appointed Postmaster, drawing a subsidy of Rupees 100 per mensem, with two clerks, one on Rupees 35 and the other on Rupees 20, and four delivery peons. Mr. Hodges was the next Postmaster, and held office for a period of more than twelve years (from 1843 to 1855). During his time the establishment underwent several changes. *History of Ootacamand Post Office.*

The rates of postage prior to the year 1854 (when the postage labels were first introduced) were regulated according to distances and weight. The charge for a letter weighing a tola to Madras was in those days 8 annas, and it was five days in transit. A letter of the same weight now goes for 1 anna and is one day or twenty-four hours in transit. *Old postal rates.*

It was not till the year 1855 that the Post Offices on the Hills were included in the inspectoral circle of Coimbatore. Ootacamand is the head or disbursing Post Office, and all the others are subordinate to it. Mr. Hodges was the first inspector; Mr. Bower is the inspector at present. *Hill Post Offices brought under inspection.*

The present strength of the Ootacamand office is as follows:— *Present establishment.*

		Salary. RS.	A.	P.
1	Postmaster	100	0	0
1	Head Clerk	50	0	0
2	Clerks on Rs. 30 each	60	0	0
13	Peons	46	0	0
	Contingencies	18	12	0
	Total ...	274	12	0

CHAP. XX. — POSTAL DEPARTMENT.

Number of letters received and despatched. The number of covers received for delivery on an average at present in the season is 2,000 daily, and out of the season 700. The despatch is nearly the same as the receipt.

Revenue. The net revenue derived by this office yearly may be estimated at 68,000 rupees.

Coonoor and Kotagiri. The Coonoor and the Kótagiri Post Offices were the next opened; but the exact dates are not known.

Wellington. The Wellington (then called Jackatalla) Post Office was opened in the year 1855.

South-East Wainád. In the South-East Wainád, which now forms a portion of Nílagiris, there are five Post Offices:—Gúdalúr (opened in the year 1867), Guynd (1870), Déväla (1874), Cherambádi (1874), and Nellakóta (1877).

Old postal route of the Hills. Prior to the opening of the railway the mails were conveyed to Ootacamand *viâ* Mysore and Segúr Pass by dák runners. The road establishment then consisted of 26 runners and 2 mail overseers. The mails are now conveyed by rail up to Mettapollium, and till lately from thence by runners. The distance from Mettapollium to Ootacamand is 25 miles. There were 9 stages and 54 permanent runners; during the season the number of runners was more than doubled. The whole distance was run in 5 hours 10 minutes up-hill and 4 hours 30 minutes down-hill.

Tonga. The runners establishment between Ootacamand and Mettapollium was abolished on the 9th November 1878, from which date the mails (both letter and banghy) have been carried by tongas similar to those used in the Simla and other gháts in Northern India. The runners establishment on an average costs Rupees 650 per mensem, for which sum the agents of the Tonga Company have taken the contracts to convey the mails. The time allowed for the up journey is 5 hours 30 minutes and the down journey 4 hours 45 minutes, the distance between Ootacamand and Mettapollium being 34 miles.

Rates for passengers. A Tonga carries three passengers. The rates are as follows:—

Return Tickets by Pair Horse Tonga.

			RS.
Mettapollium to Ootacamand and back, or *vice versâ*, per seat.			30
Do. to Coonoor	do.	do.	18
Coonoor to Ootacamand	do.	do.	12

Up Journey.

	RS.
Mettapollium to Ootacamand, per seat	20
Do. to Coonoor	14
Coonoor to Ootacamand	8

Down Journey.

					RS.
Ootacamand to Mettapollium, 1 seat			...	...	16
Do.	to	do. 2 seats	...	...	24
Do.	to	do. 3 seats	...	...	32
Do.	to	Coonoor, per seat ...	...	...	6
Coonoor to Mettapollium, 1 seat		...	...	...	12
Do.	to	do. 2 seats ...	...	...	18
Do.	to	do. 3 seats ...	...	...	24

Post hours at Ootacamand and other offices.

The letter mail is now despatched from Ootacamand at 8-45 A.M. and the parcel mail at 5 P.M. The hours fixed for receiving registered letters is between 6 and 7-30 A.M. and from noon to 5 P.M. The letter-box is cleared for the last time at 8 A.M., but on overland days it is kept open till 8-15.

The following table shows the hours for despatch and delivery of letters at each of the stations on the Nílagiris:—

(1.) Ootacamand—

Despatch	8-30 A.M.
Delivery	4-30 P.M.

(2.) Coonoor—

Despatch	10 A.M.
Delivery	2 P.M.

(3.) Wellington—

Despatch	8-45 A.M.
Delivery	3 P.M.

(4.) Kótagiri—

Despatch	5 A.M.
Delivery	5 P.M.

CHAPTER XXI.

TELEGRAPH DEPARTMENT.

(Supplied by the Superintendent, Malabar Coast Division.)

Position.—The Indian system.—Strength of lines.—Number of Telegraph Offices.—Staff.—Cost of constructions.

CHAP. XXI. TELEGRAPHS.

THE Nílagiris are connected with the Indian telegraphic system *viâ* Mysore on one side and *viâ* Mettapollium on the other. On the latter route the Government line is joined to those belonging to the Madras Railway Company at Mettapollium.

The length of the line from Ootacamand to the Mysore frontier is about 23 miles, and to Mettapollium about 20 miles; total 43 miles.

There are two Telegraph Offices on the Nílagiris; one of the second class—working hours from 7 A.M. to 9 P.M.—at Ootacamand, and another of the third class—working hours from 10 A.M. to 5 P.M.—at Coonoor.

The staff attached to the former consists of one Telegraph Master and one Signaller, and the latter is worked by a Telegraph Master alone.

The above lines and offices are attached to what is designated the Mercara Sub-Division in the Malabar Coast Division of Government Telegraphs. The Superintendent is unable to furnish particulars regarding the cost of constructing the above lines. They formerly belonged to what was, prior to 1866, known as "the Madras Circle," the records of which were, it is believed, on the reorganization of the department in 1866 forwarded to the Director-General's Office, Calcutta; but whether they are still in existence or have been destroyed the Superintendent is unable to say.

CHAPTER XXII.

POLICE DEPARTMENT.

The village system.—Crime.—Reforms necessary.—New constabulary.—Present organization.—Stations on the Nílagiris—in Wainád section.—Proportion of Police to population, &c., &c.—Appendices.

CH. XXII.

POLICE.

The village system.

In respect of village police arrangements this district is peculiar; although there are headmen of rural divisions termed *gráma maniyagar*, and subordinate headmen, *úl maniyagar*, ruling in hamlets, many of which have grown into considerable villages, yet they have hitherto retained under them in many cases no regular village servants, as in the villages in the plains. Every able-bodied villager is required to obey the behests of his village chief, and to perform such customary duties as the exigencies of the village or district administration may demand. The result of this communal system is that intra-village crime is almost unknown, whether it concerns offences against person or property, and extra-village crime is even now almost wholly confined to crimes of intertribal violence, and seldom relates to property, except where land disputes are concerned.

Crime.

Violent offences are generally connected with superstitious feelings. The object of most of these assaults is the Kúrumba, and in such attacks all the other hill-tribes, and probably also some of the more recent Kanarese immigrants, are usually ready to take a part. The vaguest notion of their duties as village magistrate or police officer prevails among the headmen. So far from their understanding that it is their duty to repress such crime, they seem to regard it almost as a sacred duty not only to countenance and shield the wrong-doers, but even to aid in the perpetration. We may infer from this state of things that the Nílagiris, prior to our advent, had remained apart from the general police system of the neighbouring Kanarese and Tamil countries, for rough and rude though that system was, yet it had succeeded in training each village not only to do what was necessary to secure the lives and property of its members, but to take a share in protecting the lives and property of its neighbours, and in so doing to be ruled by a moral law of communal obligation which had grown, not out of the village life, but out of the wider life of a ráj or state.

CH. XXII. POLICE. Reforms necessary.

To the absence of anything approaching a village police, maintained by land endowments or the fees of the village, may also be attributed the fact that there are no hereditary thieves in the district, like the Dundassies in Ganjam, the Kavilgar of Trichinopoly, and the Talliaries of Cuddapah. There can however be no question that an effective police administration of the hills must have as an antecedent condition the organization of a domestic police, or at all events the education of the heads of villages to a due knowledge and appreciation of their responsibilities and duties as the dispensers of justice in petty cases and as the protectors of the lives and properties, not only of their fellow villagers, but also as guardians of the public peace generally.

New constabulary.

In establishing, therefore, a constabulary on the Nílagiris constituted on the European model, the Government met with no obstacles among the people arising out of the vested interests of the old watchmen, or the prejudice, conservatism, or fears of the people; but at the same time this new constabulary was deprived of the aid which it obtained elsewhere from the experience and knowledge of the ancient hereditary police, whether honest or dishonest. Prior to the introduction of the regular police system elaborated by Sir William (then Mr.) Robinson, it may be said that outside the limits of Ootacamand no police existed on the Hills. The peons of the Revenue officers—chiefly those of the Tahsildar—appear, under the system that prevailed from 1816 to 1859, to have done the little police work that was done, but how imperfectly this was performed has already been the subject of remark in Chapter XII. The failure of the police administration was one of the principal causes which produced changes in the higher executive agency of the district. Ootacamand possessed, from the year 1820 to 1855, a military police, and until the military control was finally and radically abolished in the civil stations this police remained under the orders of the military magistrate, under the style, at one time, of Officer Commanding, at another, of Commandant of the Nílagiris. The establishment of the military depôt at Wellington was the immediate cause of the abolition of this police.

Present organization.

The present police organization of the district is as follows. The Superintendent of Police, Coimbatore, exercises a general control over the Nílagiri district—an arrangement which has continued from the time when the Hills proper formed a taluk of that district. The officer immediately in charge is the Chief Inspector, on a salary of Rupees 350, who has under him 1 Inspector and 2 Sub-Inspectors. The Chief Inspector has taken the place of an Assistant Superintendent, an office which was abolished in 1875. The duties and responsibilities of the Chief Inspector have considerably increased by the annexation to the district of the South-East Wainád, not only from the fact that it adds to the population 38,000 souls, but also because it brings him into contact with a turbulent and dangerous class, the Malabar Moplas. The task, too, of detecting and repressing coffee thefts is also extremely difficult, though the recent passing of Act VIII of 1878—the law passed for the special object of repressing these offences—will doubtless afford the means of effectual repression. The head-quarters of the Chief Inspector are at Ootacamand; the subordinate Inspectors are stationed at Coonoor and Ootacamand.

Stations on the Nílagiris.

There are ten stations in the Nílagiris proper, viz., Ootacamand town, Ootacamand district, Paikaré, Neduwattam, Kalhatti, Masnikóvil, Kótagiri, Wellington, Coonoor district, Coonoor town.

The total strength, excluding Wainád, is 125 men. The details as to the force kept at each of these stations, the principal village within the beat, and the number of the beats will be found in Appendix No. 25.

—in Wainád section.

In Wainád the strength of the force is 34 men. There are four stations, as follows:—Gúdalúr, Cherambádi, Déväla, and Nádgáni.

Proportion of Police to population, &c., &c.

The proportion of the police to the population is 1 in 400 and to area 1 in 6¼ square miles on the Nílagiris proper, and 1 in 1,117 and 1 in 7 respectively in the Wainád; or taking the district as now constituted, 1 in 629 and 1 to 6⅕ square miles of territory. The cost per head of the population was in 1875-76 Rupees 0-9-3, and per square mile Rupees 37-4-6 in the Nílagiris proper, and Rupees 0-5-8 and Rupees 33-1-3 respectively in the South-East Wainád. The total cost for the district now is approximately Rupees 38,140 or Rupees 0-6-1 per head of population; and Rupees 38-9-8 per square mile. It must not be forgotten that a considerable portion of the area of the district is but sparsely populated.

Appendices.

In the appendices (Nos. 22 to 24) will be found some interesting information as to the crime statistics of the district prior to the annexation of South-East Wainád.

CHAPTER XXIII.

MEDICAL.

Establishments.—Cost.—Ootacamand—St. Bartholomew's Hospital.—Coonoor—Hospital.—Wellington.—Kótagiri.—South-East Wainád.

CH. XXIII. MEDICAL. Establishments. Cost.

The medical establishment of the district, exclusive of Wellington, which is under the supervision of the Deputy Surgeon-General of the Southern Division, consists of three Civil Surgeons, three Apothecaries, and four Hospital Assistants.

The cost of the establishments, exclusive of that at Wellington, may be estimated at Rupees 40,000 annually.

Ootacamand.—Two Commissioned Medical Officers, ordinarily of the rank of Surgeon-Major, are stationed here. The duration of the appointment is four years. One of these officers has charge of the northern half of the station, including St. Bartholomew's Hospital; the other of the southern half, along with the charge of the Native and European Jails. The officer in charge of the hospital has also care of the division of the district under the Joint Magistrate of Ootacamand. He supervises also the operation of the vaccinators, whether Municipal or Local Fund, and has generally a seat on the Municipal Commission. He also supervises generally the registration of vital statistics in the Municipality. He is aided by two Hospital Assistants, one of whom is restricted to the hospital; the other is available for the care of the Police and itinerant work generally. The Medical Officer in charge of the Jail is assisted by a medical subordinate of the grade of Apothecary.

St. Bartholomew's Hospital.

This institution has grown out of the old civil dispensary, and is strictly speaking the property of Government. By the Towns' Improvement Act it should have become vested in the Municipal Commission, who would thus have become responsible for its maintenance and management. The revenues of the Commission, however, were considered to be sufficiently burthened; consequently the institution was retained by Government, the Municipal Commission being required to contribute Rupees 500 annually towards its upkeep. This is still done. The management of the institution is entrusted to a committee, the Medical Officer in charge acting as Executive Officer and Secretary. There is a sub-committee of ladies upon whom devolves the care of all household matters, food-supplies, &c. The superior hospital establishment is maintained by Government with exception of the nurse. The general expenses of the institution are met by public charity, but the Government supplement all such receipts by a grant equal to fifty per cent. of the sum raised monthly. The institution originally cost about 21,500 rupees, and was opened for the reception of in-patients in 1867. It has, however, been very considerably added to since then by the erection of contagious and indigent wards, which are connected with the building by covered passages. The institution is highly appreciated by both Europeans and Natives. The accommodation is as follows :— CH. XXIII. MEDICAL.

Wards			
	for Europeans	Men	7
		Women	4
	for Natives ...	Men	12
		Women	5

besides two rooms for special cases, a contagious diseases ward, and a ward for pauper invalids.

The attendance in 1878 was as follows :—

—	In-patients.	Out-patients.
Europeans	46	950
Natives	1,012	7,890
Total ...	1,058	8,840

One of the Medical Officers of Ootacamand is Consulting Physician to the Lawrence Asylum, and receives a special allowance for the duty ; but an Apothecary is directly in charge.

There is one resident Commissioned Medical Officer at Coonoor, who, as at Ootacamand, is ordinarily of the grade of a Surgeon-Major. He is entitled to hold the office for four years. He is also in general charge of the Eastern Division of the plateau, including Kótagiri. His duties are similar to those of the Senior Medical Officer at Ootacamand. As the only Civil Officer of superior rank resident in Coonoor, he is generally entrusted with executive work of the Coonoor Municipality in the capacity of Vice-President. He is aided by a Hospital Assistant at Coonoor, whilst an Apothecary is directly in charge of the dispensary at Kótagiri. Coonoor.

There is a neat little hospital in Coonoor, a Government institution, which, as at Ootacamand, was not transferred to the Municipal Commission. There is, however, no managing committee. The Commission contribute Rupees 400 annually to the institution. The hospital contains two main wards affording accommodation for 8 men and 4 women.

CH. XXIII. MEDICAL.

The attendance in 1877 was as follows :—

In-patients	... ...	254
Out-patients	... ...	1,998
	Total ...	2,252[1]

Wellington. At Wellington there is ordinarily one Medical Officer; but the number depends on the number of convalescents there. He has also charge of the Observatory. Further particulars will be found in Chapter IV.

Kótagiri. As already stated, there is only a dispensary at Kótagiri. It is entirely supported by Government, though it has been transferred in a manner to the Local Fund Board, and has a sub-committee of that Board to supervise its working.

The attendance in 1877 was—

In-patients	... ...	22
Out-patients	... ...	3,033
	Total ...	3,045[2]

South-East Wainád. There is a hospital at Gúdalúr. It was originally a *quasi*-private institution, Government supplying an Apothecary, but the planters maintaining the institution by subscription. It is now vested in the Local Fund Board.

[1] Europeans and Eurasians 267.
[2] Europeans and Eurasians 123.

CHAPTER XXIV.

ECCLESIASTICAL.

Establishment—its cost.—Churches in Ootacamand, St. Stephen's, St. Thomas'.—Coonoor, All Saints'.—Kótagiri.—Wellington.—Roman Catholic Churches—Convent.—C. M. S. Tamil Mission.—The Basel Mission.

CH. XXIV. — ECCLESIASTICAL. — Establishment.

THERE are three Chaplains on the Hills, ordinarily of the grade of Senior Chaplains, stationed respectively at Ootacamand, Coonoor, and Wellington. The Chaplain of Ootacamand attends the European Jail, and has also spiritual charge of the western portions of the district, including the Ouchterlony Valley and Gúdalúr, whither he is expected to proceed for ministration once in every two or three months. The Chaplain of Coonoor has also spiritual charge of the eastern and southern portions of the district, including Kótagiri and Kátéri. The duties of the Chaplain of Wellington are exclusively confined to the military stationed at the depôt.

—cost.

The cost of the three Chaplains to Government, including establishment, &c., may be set at Rupees 30,000 annually. Hitherto nothing has been done to render the Church of England on the Nílagiris in any way self-supporting, though a considerable portion of the Europeans resident at Ootacamand and Coonoor are civilians, and consequently not strictly speaking entitled to the services of a Chaplain.

Churches in Ootacamand.

There are two churches belonging to Government in Ootacamand—St. Stephens' and St. Thomas'. The latter may be regarded as a sort of chapel-of-ease to the mother church, St. Stephen's. The lay trustees of St. Stephen's are also responsible for St. Thomas'. The Chaplain of Ootacamand has the right of attending meetings of the church committee at St. Thomas', even when a clergyman may be especially deputed to do duty there; but hitherto he has generally not interfered in the administration of this church.

St. Stephen's.

St. Stephen's Church was, as already stated in Chapter XII, built in 1830 partly by subscription, when Mr. S. R. Lushington was Governor of Madras. It was consecrated in 1831 by Dr. Daniel Wilson, the eccentric but admirable Metropolitan of India. The building is of no particular style; the square tower however is gothic, and forms a marked feature in the town. The church

CH. XXIV. — ECCLESIASTICAL.

has been recently much improved by the addition of a chancel, the gift of the widow of the late William Graham McIvor, the Superintendent of the Government Chinchona Plantations. The same lady has presented three handsome stained-glass windows to the church. There is a good organ. There are sittings for 300 persons. Pew-rents are charged for a large portion of the sittings at the rate of Rupees 2 a sitting. Within the church enclosure, but above the church, is the cemetery. It is neatly planted with trees and shrubs. This burial-ground has been used since 1830. Europeans who died in the station previously were interred in the old cemetery, adjoining the Woodlands domain at Stonehouse. The Government have ordered all burials at St. Stephen's to cease, and the Bishop has consecrated the enclosure of St. Thomas' as a cemetery. Only one burial has, however, hitherto taken place there. The cemetery has yet to be planted and laid out with paths.

St. Thomas'. The first proposal to build a second church in Ootacamand was made in 1860, when a public meeting was held and a committee formed to carry out the proposal. The death of Bishop Dealtry in 1861 for a time checked the carrying on of the scheme.

In 1865, however, when Archdeacon Dealtry became Chaplain of Ootacamand, the attempt to build a second church was revived, and Government having promised a grant of Rupees 30,000, a second appeal to the public was put forth in 1866 by a committee consisting of Bishop Gell, the original committee, and some fresh members. This appeal was so far successful that the site near the lake was purchased from Mr. A. Higginbotham, with a strip of ground on the lake side of the road, for Rupees 12,275, and the ground formally transferred to Government by Government Order of August 1st, 1866, No. 157.

The foundation-stone was laid by General Dowker on 1st May 1867, and, after many difficulties, the church was so far finished in 1870 as to be safe and usable, but the steeple is not yet built and the intended raised floor is not yet put in. The cost, Rupees 64,732-3-1 (site, *minus* cost of old buildings and contribution of Rupees 1,000 from Mr. Higginbotham, being Rupees 8,693-1-4), was met as follows :—

	RS.	A.	P.
Government grant	32,190	0	0
Contributions (including pew-rents of St. Stephen's from 1867 to 1872)...	32,542	3	1

The church, which is picturesquely situated, is gothic in style and cruciform in shape, with a chancel and sanctuary. It has a square tower. It was consecrated and dedicated to St. Thomas the Apostle on 20th October 1870 by the Right Reverend Bishop

Milman, D.D., Metropolitan of India, during the absence in England of the Diocesan. CH. XXIV. — ECCLESIASTICAL.

In the incumbency of Reverend J. M. Strachan, M.D., from April to October 1871 the following additions and improvements were subscribed for and carried out:—

	RS.
Seats, at a cost of	468
Hassocks, cushions, &c.	80
Lectern	270
Communion silver plate	376
Total ...	1,194

Subsequently, during the years 1875 to 1876, considerable sums were collected by the incumbents for the time being, especially the Reverend W. Barton, which were expended on church furniture and in enclosing and planting the churchyard.

The church now is seated to hold about 130 persons, and it will be further furnished as funds are available. A Church Improvement Fund was started in 1878, to which over Rupees 500 was subscribed in the incumbency of the Reverend A. C. Taylor, Chaplain of Vepery. Recently an organ has been presented to the church by Mrs. Allon of Bishopsdown.

All Saints' Church, Coonoor.

This church is gothic in style, and, though superior from an architectural point of view to St. Stephen's, is by no means equal to St. Thomas'. The history of its erection has been given in Chapter XII. It was consecrated on 18th March 1854. It has a fine tower, but no chancel. It contains sittings for about 200 persons. Pew-rents are collected. Efforts are being made to raise funds to build a chancel. The graveyard surrounding the church is the European cemetery of Coonoor. Coonoor was constituted a separate chaplaincy in 1865. The church is the property of Government, and is managed by a committee consisting of the Chaplain and two lay trustees.

Kótagiri Church.

The church at Kótagiri, though the property of Government, has not been consecrated. It was built by Major-General Gibson of Kóta Hall, and became the property of Government in 1864. It has accommodation for about fifty persons. Protestant Dissenters have the right of using the church for divine service when the Chaplain of Coonoor does not officiate. He ordinarily visits Kótagiri once in two months.

Wellington.

There is no church in Wellington, a large room in the barracks being fitted up for the purpose of divine worship.

Roman Catholic Churches.

There are three churches belonging to the Roman Catholic communion, one in Ootacamand, one in Coonoor, and one in Gúdalúr.

CH. XXIV. ECCLESIASTICAL.

I am indebted to the Reverend Father Triquet for the following information regarding the Roman Church's mission on the Hills :—

The Christians of this communion who accompanied Europeans to the Hills in the early days erected a chapel near the house now known as Kilburn. A priest named Paul, from near Somanúr, visited and administered to the congregation. He had another chapel built for the Pioneers, near Neduwattam, who were employed on the Gúdalúr Pass. Later these Pioneers were removed to Kandel, in Ootacamand, and they there built a chapel, which became the principal chapel on the Hills, the priest residing on the spot. In 1830, one Stephen Joachim, the butler of Sir William Rumbold, built another chapel above the old one on the Segúr road. The son of this Joachim now officiates there, though he has no canonical orders. In 1839 a priest named Beauclair resigned the old chapel, which is no longer the property of the Roman Catholic Church. This priest built a small chapel at Metucherri, near the site of the present church, in 1839-40, but the chapel (now used as a school-house) being found insufficient for the congregation, in 1859 the Reverend Father Pierron laid the foundation of the present church. It was consecrated on 15th August 1870. It cost upwards of 25,000 rupees, the Mission receiving a grant-in-aid from Government towards the building. The building has been recently much improved, and is now capable of holding a very large congregation. The Roman Catholic population is very numerous, being in the season nearly 3,000 souls. The resident priest receives a small allowance from Government of Rupees 30 monthly for the charge of the jail.

—Convent.

There is a convent of the Society of Marie Réparatrice in a building adjoining the church, established in January 1875. The convent bears the name of Nazareth, and the present community consists of twelve nuns. There are schools, an orphanage, a Magdalene refuge, an asylum for the destitute, and a dispensary attached to the convent. The head-quarters of this Society, whose branches are spread over the world, is at Rome.

Coonoor and Kótagiri.

The chapel here is dedicated to St. Anthony. It has accommodation for about 300 persons. There are about 800 Catholics in Coonoor and 200 in Kótagiri.

Church Missionary Society's Tamil Mission.

Other buildings in Ootacamand devoted to religious purposes are the Tamil Mission Chapel near St. Stephen's and Zion Chapel. The building and property of the former are vested in the Bishop and Archdeacon of the diocese. It was built about the year 1857. This mission is a branch of the Church Mission Society. It was formally superintended by a local committee. There is now a resident Native clergyman. Zion Chapel, which is open to all nonconformists, was built in 1857. It holds about 100 persons.

The building is vested in trustees. In Coonoor there is the American Mission Chapel, with accommodation for about 250 persons. The mission is superintended by the American Missionaries in North Arcot. There is a resident catechist.

The Basel Mission.

For the following notice of the Basel Mission I am indebted to the Reverend W. Stokes:—

The Nílagiri branch of the Basel German Evangelical Missionary Society's work in India has the following stations:—

First.—Kaity, with three Missionaries (Messrs. Stokes and Sayer since 1874, Rev. M. Mieg since 1878), a prayer-room, a congregation of 54 individuals not including the missionary staff, and sanitarium-quarters for the Society's Missionaries coming up from the plains. The Mission has likewise a sanitarium at Coonoor.

There is an orphanage and boarding school (with at present 16 boys and 25 girls) attached to the Mission for native children of both sexes, boys however only being retained to a certain age. The parents and guardians of the same are expected to contribute their mite towards the support of these children, who are in charge of a native matron under the supervision of a married Missionary. A native master conducts the school. The girls are also taught needle-work after school-hours, and have practice in household affairs. The boys are employed in different kinds of out-door work. The Mission having taken over a number of famine orphans from the Dévala Orphanage Committee, for whom there was not sufficient accommodation at Kaity, the Home Committee have directed the removal of the girls to Kótagiri, where a new building for them is in course of erection, towards which the Mission thankfully records having received from Government the liberal grant of Rupees 1,000.

Second.—Nirkambé, considered as an out-station of Kaity, lying three miles southward, with a congregation of 21 members, where there is a Mission chapel and a resident Badaga evangelist. The first Badaga convert, Abraham, baptized in 1858 (✝ 1870) was the father of this Christian village. The custom obtaining as to services is to hold them on alternate Sabbaths at each place, so that both congregations should be able to meet in worship one Sabbath at Kaity and the next at Nirkambé. There is a Mission school at this place for Christian and Heathen children. A school for Heathen children at Adikahatti (near Dévashóla) is about being transferred to Kátéri, as the people of the former village are growing indifferent about their school, whereas those of the latter are most eager to obtain instruction for their children.

Third.—Kótagiri, having a congregation of 108 souls. The Reverend A. Bührer, the pastor, assisted by a catechist who is a Badaga, has charge of the station. The native church at Kótagiri was built by Miss Cockburn and handed over to the Basel Mission. The same lady also supports a school which is attended by Christian and Heathen children and visited by the Missionary. Four Christian families live out on a plantation in Kódanád. They are regularly visited by the Missionary and the catechist. The station was established in 1867.

CH. XXIV. — ECCLESIASTICAL.

The head-quarters of the Basel German Evangelical Missionary Society's work is at Kaity, once the property and residence of Lord Elphinstone, Governor of Madras, where it commenced its operations in 1849. In that year the late G. J. Casamajor, Esq., of the Madras Civil Service, bequeathed the greater portion of his property to the Basel Society for the maintenance of a mission to the hill tribes on the Nílagiris. It should be remembered that three years previous to the bequest made by Mr. Casamajor, which constitutes the larger of the sinews of the present operations, the same work was being prosecuted with characteristic zeal by the good gentleman himself with the help of the German Missionaries. From 1846 some twenty Missionaries have lived and labored in this part of the mission-field. Some of these devoted servants have departed this life.

There are numbers of young men in the Kaity Valley and other villages who have not only received secular education, but have also a fair knowledge of the truths of Christianity.

Some Badaga youths have been sent to the training schools of the Society on the Western Coast to prepare themselves for work among their countrymen.

A few of the converts have been taught handicrafts, such as carpentry and weaving, and are able to earn their own livelihood.

Itinerating forms an important branch of the Hill Missionary's work. The Mission owns little cottages in the different districts, which the Missionaries make their head-quarters while working in the district. Where they have no cottages, tents are used.

The demeanour of the Badagas when preached to is in most cases respectful; they frequently testify to the truth and wisdom of the words spoken, but, alas! do not so frequently accept them. It must be stated, however, that although the converts on the Nílagiris are few considering the number of years the Mission has been at work, most of them have embraced the Christian religion from conviction and not from unworthy motives, as is very often the case in the plains where large numbers are gathered in.

The head-quarter station is embosomed in a pretty plantation of Australian and forest trees, which shelter it very much from the windy blasts so common to Kaity, situated as it is in the centre of an extensive valley.

There, too, in a clear space on the skirt of the plantation is a little acre containing the graves of members of missionary families and two Missionaries, while others lie buried in Ootacamand and Coonoor.

The pecuniary cost of the Kaity Mission during the year 1878 was Rupees 5,800, of which the sum of Rupees 3,000 was donated by the Casamajor Mission Fund, some Rupees 900 by public contributions, and the balance by the Parent Society in Basel. The Kótagiri station receives no help from the above Mission Fund, but is supported entirely by the Home Committee and local contributions.

CHAPTER XXV.

EDUCATIONAL.

History of education among the hill-tribes.—Badaga schools—Scheme of Union Schools.—Schools for Anglo-Indians.—The Breeks' Memorial School.—Convent Schools.—Tamil Mission School.—Hobart Girls' School.—Private Schools.—Educational needs.—Coonoor.—Lawrence Asylums—history—amalgamation with the Military Male Orphan Asylum—revenue—instruction—medical—domain.

CHAP. XXV. — EDUCATIONAL. — History of education among the hill-tribes.

As early as 1839 the Court of Directors desired the Government to take into consideration the provision of education for the Tódas. In December 1840 the Collector of Malabar explained the reasons which had prevented any steps being taken in this direction. Up to the close of 1842 he had been unable to bring forward any feasible plan for effecting this object. The Court of Directors thereon expressed their regret that the efforts of the Madras Government to introduce education and civilization among the Tódas had hitherto been unsuccessful, but they did not doubt that this Government would not neglect any available means, if they should offer, of effecting this object. The Collectors of Malabar and Coimbatore were again urged to do what they could. Nothing, however, was done until 1846, when the Basel Mission Society established an agency on the plateau and made attempts to instruct the Badagas and other hill tribes, though, owing mainly to the apathy of the people—their wild habits and indifference to learning—their labours were rewarded with but little success.

It was not until ten years later (1856) that the Badagas first appear to have shown any desire for instruction, especially in the Tamil language, being probably stimulated by the discovery that a knowledge of this tongue might be useful in their dealings with European planters who were then beginning to settle on the Hills, and also in their business in the courts and with native officials, who generally were unacquainted with Kanarese dialects. A report had also become current among them that only men able to speak Tamil would be selected for the post of maniyagar, the height of a Badaga's ambition. These facts we learn from the report of the Tahsildar of the time to the Collector of Coimbatore, Mr. E. B. Thomas. On the strong recommendation of this officer, Government, in August 1857, consented to the establishment of four schools under the supervision of Lieutenant-Colonel Pears, R.E., Inspector of Schools in North Tamil Division. The Govern-

CHAP. XXV. — EDUCATIONAL.

ment of India accorded their sanction to the scheme in November 1857. Their sanction was necessary, for, as in the case of the Khond Schools in the Ganjam Hills, these hill schools did not fall within the educational scheme then approved for the Presidency. A monthly grant of Rupees 40 was allowed for the salaries of four masters, and a sum of Rupees 400 was expended on the erection of four school-houses in the following localities:—

1. Túnéri, in the Tódanád, about 8 miles north-east of Ootacamand.
2. Adikahatti, in the Mékanád, south-west of Ootacamand, some 3 or 4 miles from Kátéri.
3. Káligiri, in the Péranganád, about 4 miles from Coonoor on the road to Kótagiri.
4. Dimhatti, near Kótagiri.

The teaching in these schools was free of charge to all. At first they were well attended, "probably because they were Government institutions and the Tahsildar interested." (Colonel Pears.)

In the course of a few months, however, three schools were made over to the German Missionaries at their request, Rupees 40 being disbursed to them as a grant-in-aid, on condition that they should expend an equal sum every month from their own resources upon the education of the hill tribes, one of their number being especially set apart to superintend them, the Missionaries for the time being the Revs. F. Metz, C. Mœricke, and F. Kittel. Their grounds for requesting the transfer were—(1), the district was too thinly populated to admit of two educational schemes; (2), for eleven years they had been maintaining schools in various parts of the district; (3), the Badagas had confidence in the Missionaries, and would raise no objection to their being entrusted with the sole management.

In April 1859 Colonel Pears reported that these Missionaries had more than fulfilled the conditions under which the schools were made over to them. The schools were then ten in number, six new ones having been added after the transfer.

The schools and attendance at this time were as follows:—

School		Attendance	Night schools	
Dimhatti	... ...	13		
Kótagiri	... ...	10		
Jackatalla	... ...	7		
Kereháda	... ...	8	Night schools ...	9
Nadahatti	... ...	6	Do. ...	8
Adikahatti	... ...	12		
Balakolla	... ...	10	Night schools ...	8
Túnéri	... ...	12		
Shólúr	... ...	13		
Kaity	... ...	7		
	Total ...	98 + 25 = 123.		

Colonel Pears remarks :—

"Among the difficulties which the missionaries have to contend with in carrying on the schools I may mention three; the first and greatest is the want of qualified masters: those first engaged were natives of the plains; for want of better they are still employed, but they are very bad, possessing but poor attainments, and generally not to be trusted. * * * Others of the masters are Badaga youths trained by the missionaries. These are better in every way, but there are but few such, and it will not be easy, at least for some time, to increase the number. * * * *

"The second difficulty that I refer to is the extreme poverty of the hill people, which, whatever may be their wish, makes it often impossible for them to dispense with the labour of their children at home or in the fields. * * * *

"The third difficulty is the opposition of the village headmen. This opposition, it is worth observing, does not arise from any religious feeling; on the contrary, it is a fact that those headmen who are most favourably inclined to the missionaries and their schools are those who pay most regard to the traditions and customs of their own religion, while those who oppose them are remarkable for nothing but gross immorality and brutish ignorance."

The expediency of transfer of the schools was noticed by the Secretary of State as questionable in that the hill people desirous of having their children taught had no longer the opportunity of obtaining for them secular instruction only, but on a further report from the Madras Government he withdrew his objection.

In reply to a suggestion from Government that opportunities of instruction provided for the Badagas should be extended to the other hill tribes, Colonel Pears, after giving a brief notice of the different tribes and dwelling on the marked differences between them, their wild, often brutish habits, and the dislike which the Badagas show for some of them, points out that it would be "quite impracticable to bring boys of any two tribes into one school." He adds—

"I would leave it to them (the missionaries) to decide (in communication with the Inspector) in what direction they could extend their operations, that is, whether to continue to confine them to one tribe, or to endeavour to embrace others."

It appears to have been found impracticable to interest any of the other tribes in education. Of the Tódas Colonel Pears says (1859)—

"The only attempt that I have ever heard of as having been made to instruct this tribe was made some years ago by a missionary who took three whole families into his house and maintained them in idleness in order to bring the children under instruction. It did not succeed, and I am informed that the children are now among the most disreputable of their tribe."

CHAP. XXV. EDUCATIONAL.

A school for Kótas was established by the missionaries, but it had to be closed through jealousy of the Badagas. The promise was good, as the Kótas are an intelligent race.

The Badaga schools did well for a time, the number increasing to eleven, and Government increased the grant to meet the increased expenditure. The teaching was quite elementary, being confined to reading in Kanarese and Tamil and to simple sums. In 1863 the number of the schools had fallen to five with a greatly reduced attendance. The grant was reduced to Rupees 40. Two causes are assigned by the Inspector for the falling off—(1), the frequent changes in the "*personnel*" of the missionaries; (2), the great demand for labour, which renders the work of even very young children valuable. In the following year the Government grant was withdrawn, as the total number of children in the day and night schools (4) had fallen to 44, of whom only 12 attended the inspectorial examination. Three schools—at Kaity, Nirkambé, and Kótagiri—have survived. An annual grant of Rupees 120 to each is provided from Local Funds, and, though not strictly in accordance with rule, has been approved by Government in consideration of the exceptional character of the schools and the difficulties the missionaries have to contend with.

—scheme of Union Schools.

On the introduction of the Local Funds Act, Mr. Breeks drew up a scheme of schools for the rural tracts, but the house-tax having been abolished, the scheme has not yet been introduced. The increasing prosperity of the Badagas is unquestionably inclining them to seek instruction for their children, and it is probable that a scheme of Union Schools if now introduced would meet with the approval of some of the leading villages. For some years past an Inspecting Schoolmaster has been employed by the Board, but his duties are practically confined to the Municipalities.

Above I have tried to trace the history of educational effort in regard to the hill tribes. I proceed to note briefly the educational position of the two chief towns.

Schools for Anglo-Indians.

A part of Mr. S. R. Lushington and Bishop Wilson's scheme for the utilization of this Hill Sanitarium was the establishment of a good school for the education of European and Eurasian children—a scheme somewhat similar to that with which Bishop Cotton's name is now associated. The Church Mission Society, a Society which aided in many ways the early development of the hill colony, undertook the scheme. A fine building, now known as Sylk's Hotel, was erected by the Society in 1831. The school was placed under the charge of the Rev. J. B. Morehead. It was chiefly intended for the sons of missionaries, but others were admissible. The institution was designated "The Church

CHAP. XXV. EDUCATIONAL.

Missionary Grammar School," and was "to be especially known and distinguished as a seminary for sound learning and religious education according to the doctrines and discipline of the United Church of England and Ireland." The property and management of the school was vested in the Madras Committee, Church Mission Society. "The new method of teaching, as detailed by Dr. Bell and practised in the Charter House and other European Grammar Schools (was) to be introduced as extensively as possible." There were foundationers and paying pupils, the charge of the latter being Rupees 70 monthly. A preparatory school was attached.[1] How long the institution existed I have been unable to trace.

Until communication with Europe became easy and cheap several private middle-class schools existed in Ootacamand. Among these may be mentioned the school at Snowdon House, established by the Rev. G. U. Pope, D.D. The school was begun between 1850 and 1860, and ultimately became a collegiate institution affiliated to the Madras University. It was closed in 1871, when Dr. Pope accepted the post of Warden of Bishop Cotton's School, Bangalore. There were as many as 70 or 80 boarders in the institution. The closing of this school was a great misfortune to the station, and no similar institution has as yet arisen in its place. It is deeply to be regretted that it was not converted into a public institution.

The Breeks' Memorial School.

In 1872, on the death of the late Mr. J. W. Breeks, Commissioner of the Hills, a committee was formed to raise subscriptions for a memorial to him. The great need of a school for the children of Europeans and Eurasians whose means did not admit of their sending their children to England or other parts of India to obtain a good education was considered, and it was determined that the memorial should take the form of a school, but as many natives were contributing to it, it was decided that children of natives of the respectable classes should also be admitted. Subscriptions were obtained amounting to over 4,000 rupees. A grant-in-aid was given by Government and also by the Municipality. The foundation-stone was laid on the 16th May 1873 by the Honorable J. D. Sim, C.S.I., in the presence of the late Lord Hobart, Governor of Madras. The building was completed in June 1874 at a cost of Rupees 9,487. The school was opened in that month, the services of a trained master of Highbury having been secured. The Government promised a grant of Rupees 150 monthly for three years. The progress of the school was so satisfactory in the first year of its existence that it was determined to extend the building. Subscriptions were solicited,

---

[1] The prospectus will be found in the first edition of Baikie's book, (1833).

CHAP. XXV. EDUCATIONAL.

and about Rupees 4,000 raised. This sum was supplemented by grants from Government and the Municipality. The balance required to complete the building was raised by debentures. The additional building, which has a lofty tower with a good clock,[1] was completed in 1878 at a cost of about Rupees 16,000. The main room has accommodation for about 50 boys, the additional room for 100. The buildings are well furnished. The early promise of the school has not so far been realized. Early in 1878 the grant of Rupees 150 was withdrawn by Government, and the school lost its head master. The first building has been utilized as a parish school for girls and little boys, the larger building being at present more than sufficient for the needs of the school, there being only about 30 lads in attendance. The standard is that of the entrance examination of the Madras University. Efforts have been recently made to develope the school, but without success. It is vested by order of Government in four trustees, the Commissioner, the Chaplain, the Senior Civil Surgeon, and the Vice-President of the Municipality, by deed of trust, and has a small endowment transferred to it in trust by the Church Committee, consisting of the house and premises known as "Bösinger's Shop." It yields a rent of Rupees 50 monthly.

Private Schools.

The late head master of the Breeks' Memorial School, Mr. H. Croley, on leaving that institution, established a private day and boarding school at Bombay House. The school educates to the Matriculation standard. There is a considerable number of boarders.

The Convent Schools.

The schools of the Nazareth Convent established in 1875 are doing good service in educating Europeans, Eurasians, and Natives.

The school for Europeans provides instruction in modern languages, music, drawing, and painting, and other necessary subjects. The pupils are divided into three sections—for the first section the rates are Rupees 50 and 20 for boarders and day scholars respectively; the second Rupees 30 and 5; and for the third Rupees 16 and 3.

The school for East Indians under the charge of two nuns affords a simpler scheme of education. There are two sections, the charges for which are Rupees 10 and 2 in the first, and Rupees 6 and 1 in the second section respectively for boarders and day pupils.

The *Native School* is under the charge of a nun assisted by native teachers; the children are admitted free.

---

[1] The clock was provided out of the fund raised for the reception of His Royal Highness the Prince of Wales, who had included Ootacamand in the scheme of his tour in India.

The total number attending these schools is about 120. The schools are under Government inspection.

The Catholic Mission has also a school for boys with native teachers; the school is still rather elementary. The school-house was once the Roman Catholic Church of the station.

Tamil Mission Schools.

The Church of England Tamil Mission has a school for boys held in the chapel near St. Stephen's Church. There are about 100 children in attendance. The school is under Government inspection, and receives salary grants from the Municipality. English is taught, but the standard of the school is low. The Mission has a small branch school at Kandel.

The Hobart Girls' School.

In the bazaar there is a neat school-house named the Hobart School, Lady Hobart having promoted a scheme of providing a school for native girls and contributed liberally towards its erection the sum of Rupees 500, the total cost being rather over 2,500 rupees. The school-yard is neatly fenced in and planted. A dwelling house within the enclosure for the schoolmistress has recently been erected. Funds were obtained by subscription. The property is vested in the Bishop and Archdeacon of the Diocese in trust. The trustees are required to maintain a school for native girls, the agency now employed being the Church Mission Society, who maintain and manage the school. It is under the "Results System." There are about 50 names on the books; there is accommodation for about 80 little children.

There is a small school-house and cottage in St. Stephen's, vested in the Church Committee. It was left in trust to the Committee for school purposes. An elementary school for girls has been maintained there.

Other Schools.

There are several small private schools in the town for the education of both Europeans and Natives.

Educational wants of the town.

The great educational need of Ootacamand is a good public middle-class school—higher and lower grades—for boys and girls, enabling boys to obtain entrance into the public service or the Madras University, and girls their livelihood, if necessary, as teachers or otherwise, supplemented by branches for the instruction of the children of the poor in letters and industries. At present the educational necessities of the most important European settlement in India are left to chance and spasmodic private effort.

Coonoor.

The principal school in this station for European and Eurasian children was established by Mr. T. Stanes and is maintained by subscription. It is located in a neat building, with a residence for the mistress attached. It is under Government inspection; there are about 40 children in attendance; there are four teachers. The children are offered for examination under the Results system.

CHAP. XXV. — EDUCATIONAL.

The Roman Catholics have two schools attached to the church—one for boys, the other for girls. The schools are under Government inspection, grants being sought under the Results system. There are about 100 children in attendance.

The American Mission also maintains an elementary school for natives, which is under Government inspection.

Lawrence Asylums. —history.

At the beginning of 1856 Sir H. Lawrence, K.C.B., made an offer of a donation of Rupees 5,000 and Rupees 1,000 annually if an institution similar to those established at Sunáwar and Mount Aboo were started at some hill-station in this Presidency, provided action was taken within three months. A meeting was held in Ootacamand on 13th February 1856, when it was resolved to accept the offer, and to make strenuous efforts to carry out the project. An address was issued and subscriptions invited. Some difficulty arose on the religious principles to be adopted for the institution. Finally a prospectus for an institution to be called "The Ootacamand Asylum for the Orphans and other children of European soldiers in India" was adopted. The proposed asylum was to be constituted on a strictly Protestant basis. The Committee chosen had for its President Bishop Dealtry. By the month of June 3,705 rupees in donations and 335 rupees in yearly subscriptions had been subscribed. The Committee sought the aid of Government, and noted that "should it ever be in contemplation to remove the Military Male and Female Asylums to these Hills, the two institutions might, if Government wished, be blended into one." The Government awaited the result of an appeal to the army. The Commander-in-Chief, though not objecting to an appeal, would not himself support it, "unless the children of soldiers of the Roman Catholic and all other Christian professions of Faith" were admitted to participate fully in the benefits of the proposed institution. In October of this year the Committee were told by Government that they had no power to transfer the Madras Asylums, and that their action would depend upon the support the scheme would receive from the army, and the adoption or otherwise of the present rules of the Sunáwar Asylum "in their full expression." The proposed deviation from the rules of the model institution resulted in an abandonment of the scheme for a time. The outbreak of the Mutiny also occupied public attention. Sir H. Lawrence in his will recommended the projected school at Ootacamand to the fostering care of the East India Company. In June 1858 the Honorable Court inquired what had been done. This inquiry resulted in the revival of the scheme. A meeting was held at Ootacamand in August 1858, when it was resolved to adopt the Mount Aboo rules for the proposed institution, and to invite subscriptions on this basis. Later a

Committee was formed, with Bishop Dealtry as Patron, and the Honorable Walter Elliot as President, Mr. E. W. Bird being Provisional Secretary. In a despatch, dated March 1859, the Secretary of State concurred in the view of the Government of India that "the best way to give effect to Sir Henry Lawrence's wishes, and to accomplish surely and satisfactorily his wise purposes, will be to take both the Mount Aboo and the Nílagiri School into the charge of Government as has been done in the Sunáwar School." When making this proposal the Governor-General had added—

"If this be thought too large a measure, I would advise that the Mount Aboo School be left under its present management, aided by a liberal subscription from Government, and that for the Nilgiri School a sum not less than the total of all donations received from the public be awarded for its establishment, and a subscription of Rupees 10,000 per annum for its maintenance, upon the understanding that the main rules in force at Sunáwar shall be observed."

The Madras Government referred the despatch to the Committee for report, and subsequently pointed out that "the Government could not recommend that the charge of the asylum should be assumed unless the Committee were prepared to consent to equal liberty in respect to religious instruction being allowed to all classes of Protestants and Roman Catholics." The Committee, however, considered themselves bound to abide by the fundamental rule laid down by Sir H. Lawrence regarding religious instruction, and declined to transfer the asylum to Government except "on the distinct understanding that the principles on which the institution was founded be adhered to in their integrity after it has been adopted by the State." By this time (June 1859) the asylum had been opened some months. The Stonehouse property valued at Rupees 22,600 having been purchased, 40 boys and 2 girls had been admitted; 30 were already in the institution. The Committee had admitted children of the military class in Ootacamand as day-scholars. They at this time had secured the following subscriptions :—

	RS.
Donations	37,727
Annual subscriptions	6,100
Monthly do.	396

Besides these sums they expected to receive 20,000 rupees from the "London Lawrence Memorial Fund," and other sums aggregating 6,500 rupees.

The scheme of the constitution was settled in detail. Subscribers had the right of nomination. An appeal at the same time was issued on behalf of the female branch.

CHAP. XXV. EDUCATIONAL.

Towards the close of the year the Government of India informed the Madras Government that unless the Committee agreed to adopt in principle or in entirety the rules of the Sunáwar Asylum relating to religious institutions the Government could not take over the institution. In January 1860 the managing body accepted these conditions, "as they knew it would be the desire of the late Sir Henry Lawrence," subject to a reference to the subscribers. Such reference however appears never to have been made. Meanwhile, the Committee of the Madras Military Male Orphan Asylum had under consideration the expediency of transferring their asylum to the Hills and amalgamating it with the Lawrence Asylum. The Committee of the latter asylum were favourably disposed to the project regarding the amalgamation "as a very desirable object," but they were unable to pledge themselves on the subject in consequence of their relation to Government. It was admitted that there were very serious obstacles in the way of the Government adopting the Madras Asylum. The question of uniting the asylums came before Government in November 1859; but Government, though appointing the Director of Public Instruction (Mr. A. J. Arbuthnot) as their representative on a Committee entrusted with the selection of a site in the event of the union taking place later, expressed no opinion on the desirability of combining the institutions. The two Committees, however, proceeded with their scheme, and after abandoning for the time the proposal to unite the Female as well as the Male Madras Asylum, determined to arrange for the maintenance and education of 400 boys. This number they expected to be able to provide for from the joint resources of the amalgamated asylums if the Government granted monthly Rupees 1,000, a sum equal to the income of the Lawrence Asylum (male branch). The Government were also requested to contribute towards the new building, for which the Committees of the two asylums expected to be able to provide about Rupees 1,25,000.

They proposed to appoint 8 Governors, 5 being ex-officio, viz., the Commander-in-Chief, the Bishop, the Director of Public Instruction, the Senior Civil and Senior Military Officers on duty on the Hills. These five were in the first instance to select three other members, and thenceforth the Board was to be self-electing.

It was urged that the arrangement would be far less costly to the State than the adoption of the Lawrence Asylum as a State institution. The scheme was before Government when the letter from the Government of India above alluded to was received. The Lawrence Asylum Committee having accepted the Government of India proposals, the Government resolved in February

1860 that the question of the union should remain in abeyance, whilst the Director of Public Instruction was called on to report on the necessary arrangements for the establishment and carrying on of the Lawrence Asylum on its transfer to Government. This officer reported against the Lawrence Asylum being constituted a State institution, remarking that the Madras Committee had determined that there was nothing in the Sunáwar rules precluding the amalgamation of the Lawrence Asylum with the Madras Military Male Orphan Asylum, and that they had solicited in addition to the grant of Rupees 23,905 already received from Government for these Madras asylums, a grant-in-aid equal to the amount the State was prepared to spend in maintaining a separate institution. He proposed, and the Government endorsed his proposal, that the amalgamation should be carried out under his direction, that the government of the asylum should be entrusted to the body above named, that a grant of Rupees 2,500 monthly should be made, Rupees 2,000 being for maintenance of 200 boys, and 500 rupees for general expenses (this sum being the estimated cost to the State of a State institution), together with a building grant-in-aid; that the female branch should be maintained by the State (estimated cost for 100 girls Rupees 1,500 monthly), pending any arrangement which might be made later with the Madras Female Military Orphan Asylum for their union. CHAP. XXV. EDUCATIONAL.

At this time (March 1860) the assets of the Ootacamand Asylum were stated to be—male branch Rupees 75,679, female Rupees 12,323. The monthly expenditure in the former was Rupees 926, in the latter Rupees 562.

Pending the orders of the Government of India, a monthly grant of Rupees 500 was made to the Ootacamand Committee.

The Government of India, though declining to sanction the scheme, the expenditure involved being too great, considered it a very good one, remarking—

> "The object of removing the Military Orphan Asylum to the Hills is one of great importance and incalculable benefit, and is well worth the proposed cost; while the amalgamation of the Male Orphan Asylum with the male branch of the Lawrence Asylum will enable the Government to maintain an efficient school at Ootacamund for 400 boys at a less expense than if it was called upon to defray the entire cost of a separate institution."

They, however, recommended the scheme for the approval of the Secretary of State in July 1860. At the same time the Public Works Department was called on by the Madras Government to prepare plans and estimates for a building sufficient to accommodate the united asylums.

CHAP. XXV. — EDUCATIONAL.

No intimation, however, of the views of the Home Government was received until the beginning of 1862. The delay which had occurred had been prejudicial to the progress of the institution. The knowledge that the Government had agreed to maintain it led to a large falling off in subscriptions, whilst the prospect of its immediate transfer to Government checked the energy of the Committee.

In reply, the Secretary of State, though commending the scheme for the male branch of the asylum, doubted whether it would be desirable to remove at once, and without a more careful examination of the question from a health point of view, the boys, who were mainly of mixed blood, from Madras to Ootacamand, believing the climate of Madras far more congenial for such than that of a very elevated table-land. The consideration of the question was accordingly to be postponed. "On the other hand," he remarked, "it is quite certain that children of pure European descent are far more likely to be reared and trained with vigourous bodies and energetic minds so as to become when grown up useful subjects or servants of the State at Ootacamund than at Madras, and for such it is my desire that a Lawrence Asylum should be established on the Neilgherries without loss of time." He approved the proposed grant of Rupees 2,500 for the maintenance of 200 boys, and required that a female branch should also be maintained. The despatch concluded in the following remarkable words :—

"I have to remark that while the State, from a regard to the last wishes of Sir Henry Lawrence, and from a desire to secure to a numerous class of Her Majesty's subjects, peculiarly calling for sympathy and assistance, the benefits which the Lawrence Asylums are calculated to afford, has undertaken the support of a given number of children in each of the three institutions above named, Her Majesty's Government would much regret that this measure should have the effect of checking the benevolence of the community in India, who contributed so liberally towards the original establishment of these asylums. It is desirable, therefore, that measures may be taken to make it publicly known that any contributions which may be made to the general objects of these asylums will be applied to extend their benefits still more widely. If sufficient funds for this purpose should, from time to time, be subscribed by the public, an additional number of children in each case might be taken in and provided for; and, as is the case in similar institutions in England, contributors to a certain amount might be invested with proportionate rights of nominating eligible pupils. When it is considered how largely the English army in India has been augmented within the last four years, I can have no doubt but that there will always be found many friendless orphans of our soldiers, to whom such an asylum would prove a boon of the highest value. To the living soldier these institutions will show that the Government take a real interest in the fate of his offspring, while to the State they will amply repay the public expenditure by affording the best means of bringing up a number of our race, who may, under God's blessing, prove a credit to the nation with whom they claim affinity."

The Director of Public Instruction, Mr. A. J. Arbuthnot, was directed to submit proposals for giving effect to the Secretary of State's instructions. His recommendations, which form the basis of the present institution, were—

(1.) That Lovedale should be the site of both asylums.

(2.) That a Committee of nine, four being Government nominees, should be constituted managers and trustees.

(3.) That the Government of India should be asked to contribute Rupees 4,000 monthly as a maximum grant-in-aid, leaving Rupees 1,000 monthly to be provided by public subscriptions.

(4.) That the Committee should submit a code of rules for the approval of Government.

(5.) That the Commander-in-Chief, Madras, and the Bishop of the Diocese should be visitors.

(6.) That the Director of Public Instruction should be the medium of correspondence with Government.

Accommodation was to be provided for 200 boys and 100 girls.

The Madras Government approved generally of his proposal, but, instead of fixing a grant, limited the number of children whom the Government should maintain and educate to 150 boys and 80 girls, leaving 50 boys and 20 girls to be provided for by public charity. The Government also agreed to pay the salaries of the Principal and the establishment. They directed that the rules should provide for the head of the institution being a clergyman of the Church of England, and that this appointment should be subject to the approval of the Governor in Council. (The appointment of a clergyman had not been part of the original scheme, but was suggested by the Military Male Orphan Asylum Committee, and was subsequently required by Government.)

Subscribers and donors of certain amounts had the right of nomination. These arrangements were reported to the Secretary of State in August 1862, and he was at the same time urged to reconsider his decision in regard to the amalgamation of the two asylums. In July 1863 the Home Government waived their objection to the amalgamation, and in April following the Lovedale site was finally selected, being preferred to sites proposed at Stonehouse, Governor's Shóla, and Málémand. The plans were to provide for the accommodation of 400 boys and the same number of girls with the necessary establishment. These plans were submitted early in the following year, the estimate being approximately eleven lakhs. The draft rules were about the

CHAP. XXV. — EDUCATIONAL.

same time adopted by Government. These rules are those under which the asylum is now administered. They will be found in the appendix. They were framed for the Lawrence Asylum proper, and have never been revised since the amalgamation with it of the Madras Asylum. This revision was especially necessary, as the Madras rules were more favourable to the Eurasian community than the Lawrence Asylum rules. The wisdom of the amalgamation scheme, which Sir Charles Trevelyan characterizes as "the greatest measure of Anglo-Indian colonization yet taken," is open to grave question. Neither the British nor the Eurasian soldier can be said to have benefited by it, and hitherto, as a colonization scheme, it has indisputably failed.

From this year (1863) the buildings were erected rapidly, but it was not until 1869 that they were sufficiently advanced to admit of the children, then numbering 120 boys and 63 girls, being removed to them from Stonehouse and Norwood. Difficulties arose regarding the excess in the expenditure by the Department Public Works, and the works for a short time were stopped; but in 1871 the main block of the male branch was completed, and in September of that year the amalgamation with the Madras Asylum was completed, and the children, 220 in number, transferred to Lovedale. The cost of the buildings and ground to Government has been approximately £75,000, but as yet only the foundations of the female branch have been laid and the church has not been begun. The girls are located in the hospital building. Further particulars regarding the buildings will be found in Chapter XVIII.

—amalgamation with Military Male Orphan Asylum.

It is unnecessary to detail the arrangements finally made for the amalgamation of the asylums. By it the Lawrence Asylum obtained the right to the interest and bonus at 4 per cent. on the funded property, amounting to 4,80,000 rupees, and the profits of the Asylum Press in Madras. The property is still vested in distinct trustees. The income so acquired may be roughly estimated at half a lakh of rupees.

—revenue.

The present income of the two branches is approximately as follows:—

Male Branch.

	RS.
Grant-in-aid	31,650
Interest	19,565
Bonus	19,260
Press profits	10,000
Orphan allowance and other funds ...	13,000
Industries	6,495
Total ...	1,00,000

Of this amount about three-fifths are expended on clothing and diet. CHAP. XXV. EDUCATIONAL.

Female Branch.

	RS.
Grant-in-aid	16,320
Orphan and other allowances	2,080
Miscellaneous	600
Total ...	19,000

There are ordinarily at the asylum about 325 boys and 60 girls; the average cost per annum of a boy is rather under 300 rupees, of a girl Rupees 260.

—instruction. The standard of instruction in either school is not very high, though girls are educated for the Teachers' tests. The Telegraph class in the male branch, the Instructor for which is provided by Government, has been very successful. There are other industrial classes, and a good band. The Head Master is aided by six Assistants in the school department. There are two Mistresses and a Matron in the female branch. The Government Inspector of Schools of the division annually reports upon the educational working of the institution.

—medical. There is a resident Apothecary, supervised by one of the Medical Officers of Ootacamand selected by the Committee. The health of the asylum has been noticed in Chapter IV.

—domain. A large farm is attached to the institution, but farming or gardening forms no portion of the industrial training. The area of the asylum reserve is about 1,200 acres, a considerable portion of which is natural woodland. Many acres have also been planted with *eucalyptus*, and a few acres with tea and chinchona.

CHAPTER XXVI.

FORESTS.

WOODS ON THE PLATEAU—early efforts to preserve shólas—first conservancy establishment—Dr. Cleghorn's suggestions—Conservancy Rules sanctioned in 1860—additional establishment—transfer of forests and plantations to the Commissioner under Jungle Conservancy—Special Forest Officer—retransfer to Forest Department—operations under Jungle Conservancy—Forest Commission—present system of firewood sales, &c. PLANTATIONS ON PLATEAU—early private enterprise—Government plantation at Jackatalla—planting at Ootacamand—other plantations—particulars—Ootacamand plantations—Wellington plantations—Conservator's remarks—yield of *eucalyptus*—financial statement—system of working. FORESTS AND PLANTATIONS BELOW THE GHÁTS—Múdúmalé forest—plantations—receipts and expenditure—Benné forest—plantation—Segór—forest—sandalwood plantation—receipts and expenditure—management—finances of the range—minor products—timber trees.

WOODS ON THE PLATEAU.

CH. XXVI. — FORESTS. — Early efforts to preserve shólas.

WITHIN a few years of the establishment of Ootacamand the tendency to destroy ruthlessly the woodlands of the settlement attracted attention, and efforts were made to check the mischief. The most important of these was the insertion in the title-deeds of lands granted by Government of a clause compelling the grantees to make good by planting saplings all vacancies caused by the felling of trees. Efforts were also made to prevent, as far as possible, the felling of trees held to be valuable timber. Few, if any, of the trees of the shólas of the plateau being of much value as timber, such restrictions were practically inoperative. Moreover, many of the shólas of the settlement were still unalienated. In the year 1837 the Government interfered directly to check the destruction of woodlands for private use, which, independently of their beauty, they regarded as highly useful in preserving by the shade they afford the springs from drying up. Accordingly orders were issued interdicting the practice of indiscriminately felling timber and forest trees within the military limits of Ootacamand, and directing that no trees in future should be cut down except by special sanction, which was never to be granted unless the trees selected were in situations in which they were not ornamental or of use in shading springs of water from the influence of the sun in the dry season.

CH. XXVI. — FORESTS. — —first conservancy establishment.

The mischief however continued, and apparently about the year 1852 the Government sanctioned an establishment of 1 Forester and 6 peons for conservancy purposes. We find that by 1857 Rupees 2,100 had been expended against receipts Rupees 1,368. Mr. E. B. Thomas was at this time Collector of the district. In a report regarding the Hill woodlands and plantations in 1858, Dr. Cleghorn[1] writes thus regarding this officer :—

"He has earnestly and unceasingly exercised a personal supervision of the woods around Ootacamund when he visited the Neilgherries, and has manifested a warm interest in the progress of this department as evinced by the establishment of his private garden at Burliar, which has been productive of much good in disseminating fruit and other trees. I do not hesitate to affirm with truth that but for his continued exertions the neighbourhood of Ootacamund would have been denuded of its remaining beautiful sholas long since."

This praise was fully acknowledged by Government.

—Dr. Cleghorn's suggestions.

Dr. Cleghorn's suggestions are summed up as follows : (1), improvement of establishment by appointment of an English Forester ; (2), portioning out the woods, limiting the period of cutting to one year in ten for each, preserving a certain number of the finest growing trees to the acre, planting (after cutting) quick-growing trees in and around each wood ; (3), the practice of removing dead wood, except at stated intervals, to be discontinued ; (4), encouraging use of peat instead of firewood ; (5), the formation of plantations at Wellington, the formation of avenues along the main lines of road, the planting of 10,000 trees for ornamental purposes in Ootacamand. The Government directed Dr. Cleghorn and Mr. Thomas to draw up rules for the conservancy of the Nílagiri woods, and sanctioned a grant from the proposed planting at Ootacamand. Nothing farther as regards the conservancy of woodlands seems to have been done at the time, and in the following year (1859), we find Dr. Cleghorn writing thus[2] :—

"In Ootacamund the ripe trees of the indigenous sholas are sold by auction, fetching a small return (Rupees 20 or 30 per shola). As the influx of settlers increases the original tree vegetation will disappear entirely, prohibitory rules will be futile, and then proprietors will plant according to their own requirements, and a few probably for profit."

Towards the close of this year Mr. Thomas again addressed Government on the urgent necessity of conserving the Nílagiri woodlands, especially in the neighbourhood of the stations. Persons were still permitted to cut *ad libitum* in Government

---

[1] First Conservator of Forests, appointed on creation of the department in 1856.

[2] Page 152, *Forests and Gardens of South India.*

CH. XXVI. FORESTS.

shólas without payment, and thus the most powerful incentive to private planting was lost.

—rules sanctioned in 1860.

After further report from the Conservator, the Government (Sir Charles Trevelyan being Governor) decided [1]—

" *First.*—The whole of the sholas or woods in the neighbourhood of the station to be absolutely reserved, not only for their beauty, but also from fear of injuring the water-springs; their limits to be marked; no private cutters to be allowed inside; old trees to be felled by servants of the department, and brought outside, and to be sold there by private auction; trees to be planted when required in vacant spaces.

" *Secondly.*—Suitable woods at a distance from the station to be selected and marked out in lots of moderate size, and a number of these lots, amply sufficient for a year's supply, to be put up to auction annually. The contractor to be permitted to clear the ground entirely within his lot or lots, with the exception of such trees as may be marked by the Conservancy Department previously to sale.

" *Thirdly.*—The cleared lots to be planted, as required, by the Conservancy Department.

" *Fourthly.*—No private felling of any kind, or for any person, to be allowed in woods or on land belonging to Government."

These rules which applied especially to Ootacamand were also to be adopted, so far as might be necessary, at Coonoor.

—additional establishment.

An additional Forester was sanctioned, and Government promised to increase the establishment if necessary to render the conservancy of the numerous and extensive woods effectual and to detect surreptitious cutting. About this time an Overseer was appointed for Coonoor, and not long afterwards Major Morgan, Deputy Conservator of Forests, was placed in charge of the Nílagiri shólas and plantations, including the forests northward of the Hills.

—transfer of forests and plantations to the Commissioner.

The conservancy however continued to be ineffectual, and on the creation of the Nílagiri Commission in 1868, the subject was reported on by the Commissioner. In October 1868 he wrote: " Day by day I feel more satisfied that, unless conservancy is taken in hand and organized on some efficient footing under the control of an experienced officer, the destruction of the surrounding sholas is but a question of time." Dr. Cleghorn had in 1867 proposed to place the general charge of the Nílagiri woods under the Special Assistant Collector—the resident revenue officer—prior to the creation of the Commission. The Board of Revenue supported the scheme of transfer and the appointment of a military officer having " some experience of forestry (and) * * of a standing, which would give his proceedings and opinion weight

[1] G.O., 20th March 1860.

with the European community on the Hills." The Government sanctioned the transfer of the plateau woods and plantations to the Commissioner under Jungle Conservancy Rules from 1st April 1869, but declined to sanction the entertainment of a special superior officer until they were satisfied that the services of such, as well as a stronger establishment, were needed. The grounds for transfer were—(1), in so small a district, no department should exist over which the Commissioner could not exercise full control; (2), the Forest Department had failed to check illicit felling and smuggling and had worked the Hill woods at a loss; (3) none of the Hill shólas contained valuable timber.

—Special Forest Officer.

The employment of a Special Officer was subsequently (September 1869) considered necessary, and Major Jago, attached to the Wellington Depôt, was placed in charge under the Commissioner, drawing a special horse allowance from the Conservancy Fund. The establishment was increased at an enhanced annual cost of Rupees 732, viz., Rupees 4,296 against Rupees 3,564. The Special Officer retained charge until 1874, when he was replaced by an officer of the Forest Department.

—retransfer to Forest Department.

At the close of 1874-75 the shólas and plantations were retransferred under sanction of Government of India to the Forest Department; the working expenses were to be kept within the income of the range, unless grounds were specially shown for an excess.

—operations under Jungle Conservancy.

The operations during the interval of this special arrangement were chiefly under plantations, and will be referred to below. The management, however, and the revenue derived from the natural woodlands somewhat improved; but the destruction of the forests continued, especially that of such as belonged to private proprietors in the neighbourhood of Ootacamand and Coonoor. Some forests had also been alienated under the Waste Land Rules in various parts of the Hills and slopes.

—Forest Commission.

The rapid decrease of the woods came prominently under the notice of the Government in 1877, and in January 1878 a Commission was appointed to report upon the woodlands to be reserved in the Péranganád, the Tódanád and the Kúndanád. At the same time the Government on the recommendation of the Commissioner, the Conservator of Forests, and the Board of Revenue, directed that all woodlands remaining in the Mékanád should be reserved, which were estimated not to exceed 1,000 acres. The Commission reported on the Péranganád and Tódanád in August 1878. They found still 11,700 acres of Government woodland in the latter, of which they proposed to reserve 10,800 acres; in the former they found but little remaining, except in the Coonoor Ghát, already reserved. They recommended that as in the Mékanád the remaining woodland in Péranganád should be strictly

CH. XXVI. FORESTS.

reserved. On this report the Government determined (November 1878) that "no application for forest or shola land be entertained on the Nilgiris until the whole district has been reported on, and the general question of land reservation, whether forest or grass land, considered, and future policy decided."

—present system of firewood, &c. sales.

The woodlands are now worked by the Forest Department on the seigniorage system—Rupees 1-4-0 is charged as seigniorage for a cart-load of 1,000 lb. if cut by the buyer in the shóla, 1 anna for a head bundle, and 3 annas for a bullock-load.

The seigniorage for charcoal[1] burners is 4 annas for a bag, or head-load of 50 to 70 lb. Firewood is also sold by the department at a depôt in Ootacamand at Rupees 2 per cart-load. The hill-tribes are also permitted to remove wood for agricultural implements, for funeral pyres, and some other special objects, free, on passes issued by the Forest Officer.

PLANTATIONS ON PLATEAU.

—early private enterprise.

I now proceed to notice the history of the plantations on the plateau. Much had been written on the subject of planting exotic trees on the Nílagiris prior to 1855, officially by Messrs. E. B. Thomas and McIvor, and Captain Campbell; otherwise by Mr. J. Sullivan (Agri-Horticultural Society's Proceedings) and Captain Allardyce, Dr. Wight, and Captain Ouchterlony (Madras Journal of Science), and plantations had been formed by private individuals near their houses, plants having been secured mainly from the arboretum in the Government Gardens.

—Government plantation at Jackatalla.

The construction of the Wellington barracks and the consequent large demand for firewood induced the Government[2] in 1856,

[1] The following extract, from a report of Mr. Gass, details the system of manufacture:—The process of making charcoal is as follows: A spot, close to a supply of water, is selected and the ground is slightly hollowed out. In and around this hollow are placed dry branches and on top the wood, cloven into thin strips, is loosely thrown. The branches are set fire to, and, as the wood on top burns away, fresh wood is added from a heap close by. When after four or five hours the fire has burned down, a mixture of ashes, earth, and water is thrown on the red embers to extinguish them thoroughly and the charcoal is finished.

One man and one woman are generally employed in the manufacture, and the trees chiefly used are *Cinnamomum Zeylanicum* and *Michelia Nílagirica*, the heartwood being best fitted for the purpose. But, with the exception of the Rhododendron, all kinds of timber may be employed. The bark, which is separated from the wood by the heat, makes the best charcoal, and that of *Cinnamomum Zeylanicum* is so far superior that the charcoal made from it sells at double price to the dhobies, who fill their hollow smoothing irons with it; and I was informed the natives, if permitted to strip off the bark without felling the tree, would willingly pay 12 annas seigniorage for a day-pass."

[2] Some interesting information on the scheme for plantations will be found in M. C. Rev., 8th June 1858; also in CLEGHORN'S *Forests and Gardens of South India*, page 171, *et seq*.

on the recommendation of Captain Campbell (then employed at Jackatalla (Wellington) as Assistant Executive Engineer) and Mr. E. B. Thomas, to sanction a grant of Rupees 10,000 for experimental plantations of exotic timber trees, chiefly Australian. The money was divided between Captain Campbell and Mr. Thomas. The site selected by Captain Campbell was 3½ miles from Wellington near Bleakhouse. The plot selected was 100 acres in extent, covered with coarse grass and bracken. It was purchased for Rupees 700. By the beginning of 1858, 8 acres had been planted chiefly with *Acacia robusta* (*melanoxylon*). Some *deodars* and pines were also planted. Captain Campbell also had made efforts to replant the felled portions of the Great Kóta Shóla with indigenous trees of sorts most esteemed by the Badagas. By the end of 1859 Captain Campbell had expended about Rupees 10,000 on these several operations. There were at this date already 90 acres planted, containing two lakhs of trees of various ages.

—planting at Ootacamand.

Meanwhile, Mr. Thomas at Ootacamand had planted out 8,000 Australian trees and resown certain denuded shólas with such seed. The presence of Australian *acacias* in the heart of some of the shólas near Ootacamand is due to this officer's practice of thus disseminating the seed of such trees.

The Government at this time ordered the planting of 10,000 trees in and about Ootacamand for ornamental purposes at a cost of Rupees 1,350, the operations to be under Mr. McIvor's direction. This sanction was made "under the conviction that the outlay (was) trifling in comparison with the advantages to be derived from the proposed plantation, even in an economical view, and that it is highly desirable that an example of successful planting should be placed before the residents on the Hills in each of the chief places of resort as an encouragement to others to engage in an enterprise which, while it will be generally beneficial, will also be individually remunerative."

Mr. McIvor had estimated that for an expenditure of 10,000 rupees in ten years Government would get a return in the same period of Rupees 50,000. The result of this planting is observable now, especially at the western extremity of the Lake.

—other plantations.

Subsequently some other plantations were formed on the Hills, notably the Governor's Shóla, about 3 miles to the west of Ootacamand; but in 1869, when the Nílagiri woods and plantations were handed over to the charge of the Conservator, the area of the plantations amounted to 191 acres only; when retransferred the area had risen to 919 acres. In 1876 the area was 960 acres, of which 339 acres were in the neighbourhood of Ootacamand, and 621 in that of Wellington and of Coonoor.

CH. XXVI.

FORESTS.

—particulars of plantations.

—Ootacamand plantations.

The following extract from the Conservator's inspection report in 1876 gives full particulars of each plantation:—

"*Aramby Plantation, distance from Ootacamund* $1\frac{3}{4}$ *miles.*—This is the oldest Government *eucalyptus* plantation at Ootacamund; it was planted in 1863, 1864, and 1865, and consists of about 38 acres, 30 of which was shola land and the rest grass; the plants were put down 6′ by 6′; it is almost entirely *Eucalyptus globulus*, but there are a few trees of other species which however have not succeeded so well.

"This plantation has not been treated systematically as a high timber plantation; the trees are not as straight as they should be, and they are of very unequal growth, many being 30 to 40 inches in circumference, whereas some are only 3 or 4 inches; about 504 are now standing to the acre and many are splendid specimens.

"*Governor's Shola Plantation, 5 miles from Ootacamund.*—This is about 80 acres. 70,000 Australian *acacias* were put down in 1863 and the two or three following years, and 45,000 *Eucalyptus globulus* in 1870, 1871, and 1872; the growth is very fair.

"*Snowdon Plantation,* 2 *miles from Ootacamund.*—About 7 acres planted with 9,000 *Acacia melanoxylon* and *dealbata;* planted by the Collector about the year 1860 before the Forest Department took charge.

"*Málémand Plantation,* $1\frac{1}{2}$ *miles from Ootacamund.*—About 9 acres planted with 7,000 *Acacia melanoxylon*, a few *Eucalyptus globulus;* planted by the Collector some fifteen or sixteen years ago.

"*The Sheffield Plantation,* $3\frac{1}{2}$ *miles from Ootacamund.*—Fifteen acres planted with *Acacia melanoxylon* and *dealbata* in trenches; planted by the Forest Department in 1862; the growth is not very good.

"*Madana Plantation,* 3 *miles from Ootacamund.*—Eight acres of *acacia* planted with 8,000 trees about twelve or fifteen years ago.

"*Brooklands Plantation,* $3\frac{1}{2}$ *miles from Ootacamund, lately purchased by the Forest Department.*—Ten acres planted about the year 1862 with 8,000 *Acacia melanoxylon* and *dealbata.*

"*Norwood Plantation,* $1\frac{1}{4}$ *miles from Ootacamund.*—Twenty-six acres planted in 1872 and 1873, 9′ by 9′, with 14,000 *Eucalyptus globulus;* stems more or less crooked from being planted too far apart, but growth good for a fuel plantation. It should give at least 100 tons to the acre and produce again from the stools. Reserved as an accessory to Government House.

"*Cally Plantation,* $3\frac{1}{2}$ *miles from Ootacamund.*—Fourteen acres planted 6′ by 6′ in 1870 with *Eucalyptus globulus;* when two years old in 1872 it was burnt clean down by a fire which crept in from the grass-land adjoining; it has however made splendid growth from the stool, and having been pruned down to one leader, no one without very close examination could detect that the trees were not the original seedlings.

"*Arnikal Plantation,* $5\frac{1}{4}$ *miles from Ootacamund.*—Eleven acres planted in 1873 with 6,000 *Eucalyptus globulus* at 9′ by 9′; growing well.

"*Andy Plantation, 4 miles from Ootacamund.*—Sixty acres planted in 1873 with *Eucalyptus globulus*; this plantation is in great part grass-land, and is too exposed to the monsoon for *eucalyptus* and has proved a failure. There are now only 5,000 *Eucalyptus globulus* established, and these are growing very poorly.

"*Baikie Plantation, 3 miles from Ootacamund.*—Thirty-three acres planted in 1874 with 39,000 *Eucalyptus globulus* at 6′ by 6′; growing well.

"*Chowghat Cally, 3½ miles from Ootacamund.*—Thirty acres planted in 1871 with 32,000 *Eucalyptus globulus* 6′ by 6′; the upper part of the plantation is much exposed to the monsoon, and there are many failures; the lower part has grown very well.

"*The Koolie Plantation, 1¾ miles from Ootacamund.*—About 58 acres.

"*Bleakhouse Plantation, about 2 miles from Wellington.*—About 235 acres. One hundred and fifty acres of this was planted nearly twenty years ago chiefly with *Acacia melanoxylon*; seventy-five acres are young, having been planted during the last few years, and are composed almost entirely of *Acacia dealbata* (the Wattle). —Wellington plantations.

"*The Newman Plantation, about 5 miles from Wellington.*—Thirty-five acres, of which 25 were shola and 10 grass-land; it was planted in 1870 and 1871 entirely with *Eucalyptus globulus* 6′ by 6′, and there are about 40,000 trees, and the growth is certainly splendid and beyond anything I have ever seen in any country.

"*Rallea Plantation, 4 or 5 miles from Wellington.*—Sixty acres planted in 1872, 9′ by 6′, with *Eucalyptus globulus* and *Acacia melanoxylon* alternately in broad strips.

"The growth of the *eucalyptus* is not straight.

"*The Old Forest Plantation, about 3 miles from Wellington.*—Two hundred acres planted in 1872-73, 9′ by 9′, with *Eucalyptus globulus*; this is the best soil and aspect of any of the plantations, and would have been a magnificent plantation if it had been planted 6′ by 6′; it was however planted 9′ by 9′, and the trees have consequently grown very crooked; the growth has been exceedingly rapid, the average height being 59¼ feet and the average girth 17½ inches, and, although there are only 537 trees to the acre, the weight per acre (exclusive of tops and branches, which average 70 lb. per tree) was computed at 39 tons per acre.

"*Blackbridge Plantation.*—Forty-eight acres in the immediate vicinity of Wellington, planted with *Eucalyptus globulus* two years ago; there have been many failures.

"*The Rock Plantation, 2 miles from Wellington.*—Eight acres planted in 1875 with *Eucalyptus globulus* 6′ by 6′.

"*Tippucachy, 2½ or 3 miles from Wellington.*—Thirty-five acres planted with *Eucalyptus globulus* 6′ by 6′.

"The firewood supply of the station of Ootacamund from Government sources for the year 1875-76 was 1,832 tons, and to be on the safe

CH. XXVI. — FORESTS. — Conservator's remarks.

side we may say we require to cut over annually from 25 to 30 acres of our plantations (*Acacia* [1] and *Eucalyptus*).

"I consider therefore that we have a sufficient area of plantations about Ootacamund for a permanent supply of fuel by felling in rotation, and I would not extend the plantations beyond planting up the remainder of the Koolie Plantation, the felled portion of the Buthery Shola and any other gaps; but if most of the *eucalyptus* is to be reserved for building timber as proposed by the Commissioner, though the supply from thinnings in the plantations (to be treated as high timber) will be very considerable, we may yet require some addition to our plantations and be compelled to fell the rest of the Buthery Shola and perhaps even other sholas; but after we begin working our older *acacia* plantations, time will soon show us if this is the case.

"If a railroad was ever made up to the plateau the conditions would be utterly different, and, immediately such is commenced, planting should be largely extended, wherever suitable sites are available, within five or six miles of the line. The railway scheme was abandoned, I believe, because it was supposed there was not sufficient traffic, but was it ever taken into consideration how enormously the traffic would increase, we should probably send annually thousands of tons of timber down for locomotive fuel, sleepers, building timber, &c. The *Eucalyptus globulus* is certainly much inferior to teak for the interior fitting of houses, &c., but it is known to be a valuable building timber, and it is largely used in Australia for beams, joists, and rafters, and in out-door work for piers, bridges, fence-rails, railway sleepers (duration about nine years), also for shafts and spokes of drays and a variety of other purposes.

Yield of plantations.

"The enormous yield per acre in the *eucalyptus* plantations on the plateau between 5,500 and 7,000 feet elevation is very astonishing. I calculate it about 1,450 cubic feet per acre per annum for the first five or six years, or in dry weight 25 tons per acre per annum (58 cubic feet to the ton); the *eucalyptus* grows splendidly from coppice, and five or six years would appear to be about the best period for rotation, so that a permanent supply of about 25 tons per annum per acre may be calculated on.

"I deputed Mr. Gass (trained Forest Assistant) to make very careful calculations in the "Newman" Plantations near Wellington, and the following was the result:—

---

[1] It has become very apparent that the planting of *Acacia melanoxylon* either for timber or firewood will never be as profitable as the planting of *eucalyptus;* its growth to begin with is very much slower, and it is everywhere attacked by the Loranth, which parasite in time kills the tree but very soon renders it sickly; this tree, besides, does not appear to grow at all well from coppice, unless when cut very young. The Wattle (*A. dealbata*) grows very readily from the stool, but it comes up such a dense mass of small twig-like stems that its treatment is very unmanageable, and without great expense in constant pruning and careful management it cannot be depended upon except for very small firewood, and it should only be planted where a constant supply of such is required, or as a shelter against the monsoon winds.—*Inspection Report,* 1878.

"It was found that 292 trees were standing on 10,890 square feet (the ¼ acre). The measurements taken were as follows: average height deduced from six trees = 69 feet, average girth deduced from ten trees = 19 inches. Three trees were felled respectively 28, 20 and 12 inches in girth; the first contained 13½, the second 7½, and the third 2 cubic feet (the upper part of the stem where less than 3 inches in diameter was not reckoned); this gives an average cubic content of 7⅔ to each tree, or multiplying by 292 and dividing by 58 = 38 tons to the ¼ acre = 152 tons per acre. The tops of the three felled trees together with the branches weighed 170, 100 and 80 lb. (average 116 lb. per tree); this however was not added in the calculation given above as the weight of the green wood gives a very erroneous result, the wood having been proved to lose about two-fifths of its weight in six months; the first tree felled, which was measured to be 13½ cubic feet, was weighed and found to be 880 lb., whereas its dry weight would only be about 500 lb. (or between 38 and 39 lb. per cubic foot).

"In the plains we only calculate for 2$\frac{5}{7}$ tons per acre per annum from babool and other plantations, so that the rate of growth of the *eucalyptus* up here may be said to be nine times as rapid as anything we can grow in the plains. Our fenced-in fuel reserves of indigenous trees in the plains are, as I have reported, only yielding 1 ton per acre per annum, but they may be worked up to a much greater yield, and cannot, of course, in their present state be compared with regular plantations.[1]

"Mr. Gass at my request also made careful measurements of some of the largest trees in the Aramby Plantation (now twelve or thirteen years old); fifteen trees were measured with the following results: average circumference 34 inches, height 85 feet, average cubical contents 23 cubic feet. The bole decreases to less than one foot in girth at about 14 or 15 feet from the top.

"Although there are many trees in this plantation averaging 23 cubic feet, there are many that are mere spindles (the result of too little and injudicious thinning), and if now cut over the yield would not be more than 150 tons to the acre, the same as that calculated for the "Newman" Plantation at Wellington, which is only half its age; it is true that thinnings have been removed from time to time, but allowing for this it is clear that the best period for *eucalyptus* as a coppice fuel plantation is about five to six years according to circumstances; the growth at Wellington is rather more rapid than at Ootacamund, as they get less frost during the winter months, and the plantations can be cut over at five or even four years of age, but at Ootacamund six to seven years will probably be found the best period of rotation."

—Financial statement of plantations, &c.

The statement given overleaf shows the receipts and expenditure on the Nílagiri forests and plantations from 1862-63 to 1877-78. Prior to this the Conservator believes the following sums were expended through the Department Public Works:—

[1] The indigenous shólas of the Nilgiris yield about 150 bandy-loads to the acre (say 65 tons). Their growth is exceedingly slow; reproduction probably not less than 150 years, so that the annual yield is considerably under half a ton per acre per annum.

CH. XXVI.

FORESTS.

	RS.	A.	P.
Expenditure from March 1856 to April 1858	5,460	10	10
Do. for the two years 1858-59 ...	5,259	8	6
Do. in 1860-61	1,656	0	0
Amount paid to D.P.W. for stores	692	7	3
Expenditure in 1861-62	333	6	0

Years.		Total Charges.	Receipts.
		RS.	RS.
Under Imperial Conservancy ...	1862-63 ...	1,639	83
	1863-64 ...	2,259	154
	1864-65 ...	1,583	780
	1865-66 ...	2,168	565
	1866-67 ...	1,821	514
	1867-68 ...	1,757	934
	1868-69 ...	1,518	108
Under Jungle Conservancy	1869-70 ...	6,411	3,294
	1870-71 ...	9,838	4,003
	1871-72 ...	9,703	3,554
	1872-73 ...	14,481	4,297
	1873-74 ...	17,111	3,168
	1874-75 ...	*16,730	*9,465
Under Imperial Conservancy ...	1875-76	*7,255	*13,200
	1876-77 ...	8,492	11,101
	1877-78 ...	10,026	7,259
	Total ...	1,12,792	62,479

—system of working.

The Conservator is now required to retain on the plantations trees likely to grow into good timber; to fell for fuel inferior trees only; to remove dead and dying trees from shólas; to plant up vacancies therein and generally carefully to conserve them; to get rid of Wattle (*Acacia dealbata*) as far as possible.

FORESTS BELOW THE GHÁTS.

It remains now to notice shortly the forests and plantations below the gháts, known as the Múdúmalé, the Benné, and the Segúr.

Múdúmalé forest.

The area of this tract of forest, which lies to the north-west of the Nílagiris on the Mysore frontier, extending from Tippukádu northwards beyond the Múdúmalé hill, until it joins the Wainád Teak hill, is approximately 300 square miles; of this extent 200 square miles have been leased by Government from the Tirumalpad of Nellambúr for 99 years at a rental of Rupees 3,500, dating from 1862. Prior to this date, in 1857, the Government had obtained the tract on lease for five years for the supply of teak for the Wellington barracks for Rupees 2,300 per annum. The lessor has the right to honey, wax, gall-nuts, lac, parthon (pitch), and cardamoms. This forest contains much teak, also other timber trees of value, such as blackwood (vengay). The number of teak

* Includes the receipts and charges of the shólas.

trees is estimated at 150,000, of vengay 40,000. It also contains large tracts of bamboo. The growth of the trees is very fine. Much timber has been removed from this forest not only for the requirements of the Nílagiris, but also for the Mysore market and for the Wainád. Large trees are said to be growing scarce, and consequently the felling has been restricted.

—teak plantation.

A plantation of young teak trees was formed here in 1868-69, in extent 20 acres. The growth is not promising. The spot is too much outside the influence of the south-west monsoon. Experience seems to show that the planting of teak in mountainous country does not promise so well as in rich valleys, *e.g.*, Nellambúr. The mountain teak yields, however, a superior timber to the product of richer and moister soils.

—receipts and expenditure.

The following table shows the receipts and expenditure on this forest. The forest was worked by the Public Works Department until 1860 :—

Year.	Receipts.			Expenditure, including Establishment and the rental of Rupees 3,500 per annum.		
	RS.	A.	P.	RS.	A.	P.
1861-62	37,936	5	1	34,346	14	7
1862-63	62,731	5	0	44,023	11	5
1863-64	15,287	6	5	37,292	7	4
1864-65	48,846	15	6	43,854	12	0
1865-66	67,570	11	6	64,891	2	10
1866-67	69,611	5	2	47,072	3	7
1867-68	64,914	9	7	54,162	14	9
1868-69	60,014	7	5	49,794	10	7
1869-70	47,978	7	4	47,380	4	6
1870-71	15,184	12	2	39,617	6	0
1871-72	21,528	0	0	44,521	7	8
1872-73	46,043	8	6	46,163	13	9
1873-74	41,823	0	0	39,429	0	0
1874-75	20,905	12	10	43,446	1	0
1875-76	53,928	1	8	36,797	5	0
1876-77	46,516	4	5	52,193	7	4
1877-78	40,276	10	10	41,901	10	8
Total ...	7,61,097	11	5	7,66,889	5	0
	(Minus)		−	99,395	2	7
	(Plus)		+	93,602	5	0
Balance against the Forests ...				5,792	13	7

—Benné forest.

This forest, properly speaking, is a portion of Wainád, lying north-west of Tippukádu, and comprises an area of 80 square miles. It is the property of Government. It is worked chiefly eastward to the Mysore road for the supply of timber to the Nílagiris. The description of forest is similar to that of Múdúmalé, but the growth finer.

CH. XXVI. — FORESTS. —plantation.

This plantation consists of teak. It is situated about nine miles to the north-west of Múdúmalé and is well within the influence of the south-west monsoon. It was begun in 1871-72 and has been gradually extended, now comprising about 80 acres. The soil and climate being more congenial than that of Múdúmalé the growth of teak is more rapid than in that plantation, as well as straighter. The expenditure on this plantation and that at Múdúmalé had amounted to Rupees 25,557 up to the end of 1877-78 exclusive of share of establishment. It is about double the rate per acre incurred in Nellambúr.

—Segúr forest.

This forest lies to the east of Segúr and the Mysore road, comprising the tract of country between the base of the Nílagiris and the Moyár river. Its area is about 40 square miles. The timber trees are generally of inferior growth and quality, the tract being almost beyond the influence of the south-west monsoon. It is very unhealthy. The forest is chiefly valuable for its sandalwood, from which a moderate revenue is derived. The forest is not worked for timber.

—sandalwood plantation.

This plantation, known as Sembra-geddi, is strictly speaking in South-East Wainád, a little to the E.N.E. of Gúdalúr, below the Paikaré Falls. It was begun in 1872-73, and has an area of 23 acres, containing about 23,000 saplings. The elevation is about 3,000 feet above sea-level. The artificial cultivation of sandalwood (*Santalum album*) is still in an experimental stage. The growth has been good, but the Conservator regards the soil as too rich for securing heartwood of the best quality. The plant prefers a poor soil and scrub jungle. Much care has been bestowed on the plantation. The expenditure to end of 1877-78 amounted to Rupees 8,841.

—receipts and expenditure.

The following statement shows the receipts and expenditure on the Segúr Forests since 1873-74 :—

Year.	Receipts.			Expenditure, including Establishment.		
	RS.	A.	P.	RS.	A.	P.
1873-74	2,194	0	0	2,800	0	0
1874-75	6,672	0	0	4,032	0	0
1875-76	7,815	0	0	4,756	0	0
1876-77	9,470	2	8	3,883	1	9
1877-78	7,275	2	0	6,338	12	0
Total ...	33,426	4	8	21,809	13	9
(Plus) +				12,222	6	11
(Minus) −				606	0	0
Balance in favour of the Forests ...				11,616	6	11

CH. XXVI. — FORESTS. — —management.

The Nílagiri range, which comprises the district as it stood prior to annexation, together with the tracts to the north-west just mentioned, is under the charge of a Deputy Conservator of Forests with the following subordinate establishment. The forests are all worked directly by the forest agency:—

	RS.
1 Sub-Assistant Conservator	150
1 First-class Ranger	100
1 Head Clerk	60

—finances of the range.

The following abstract shows the charges and receipts in 1877-78 for the range:—

Receipts.

	RS.
Timber	41,378
Firewood and charcoal	296
Bamboos	155
Sandalwood	6,021
Minor produce	123
Miscellaneous	49
Total ...	54,854

Expenditure.

	RS.	RS.
Conservancy works—		
Working	2,544	
Timber removed by purchasers ...	1,536	
Rent	3,800	
Cattle and tools	3,489	
Roads	902	
Planting	5,795	
Miscellaneous	490	
		40,490
Establishment—		
Salaries	16,500	
Travelling allowances	4,294	
Contingencies	224	
		18,168
Total ...		58,658

—minor products.

The Nílagiri forests proper have at no time been leased for minor products. The principal of these are—honey, resins, turmeric,

CH. XXVI. FORESTS.

ginger, soap-nuts, fibres, barks for tanning. The forest tribes, except at Múdúmalé, are permitted to collect such products without molestation.

—timber trees.

For the following lists of indigenous and imported trees, &c. I am indebted to General Morgan, formerly Deputy Conservator of this Range.

(1.)—*List of introduced Trees, Shrubs, &c., and their Uses.*

	Elevation. FT.	
Eucalyptus globulus (Tasmanian blue-gum).	6,000 to 7,000	Grows to 250 feet. Very useful for all purposes. First-class timber.
E. robusta	5,000 to 6,000	The mahogany of Australia. First-class timber. Swan River.
E. rostrata	5,000 to 6,000	The mahogany of Australia. First-class timber. Swan River.
E. calophylla	5,000 to 6,000	The mahogany of Australia. First-class timber. Swan River.
E. amygdalena ...	6,000 to 7,000	Grows 350 feet in height. Good timber.
E. species	...	Many kinds.
Acacia melanoxylon ...	5,000 to 7,000	The blackwood of Australia. Good for furniture.
„ molissima ...	5,000 to 7,000	Bark good for tanning. Good for firewood; burns green.
Araucaria Bidwellii (Buneya Buneya of Australia).	5,000 to 6,000	Good timber. Seed edible.
Casuarina muricata ...	6,000 to 7,000	Tough timber; good firewood.
Cryptomeria Japonica ..	6,000 to 7,000	Good cedarwood. Japan.
Cupressus Cashmeriana.	6,000 to 7,000	Good timber. Cashmere.
C. torulosa	6,000 to 7,000	Good timber. Cashmere.
Pinus maritima ...	6,000 to 7,000	Fair wood. England.
Cinchona succirubra or red bark.	4,000 to 6,000	Good for fever and dye. South America.
Cinchona condaminea or crown bark.	6,000 to 7,000	The best tree for producing quinine.
Coffea Arabica ...	2,000 to 5,000	Best in moist places and well manured soil.
„ Liberica	1,000 to 3,000	Stands drought; berries very large.
Thea Bohea	2,000 to 7,000	Well suited for moist places. Tea fine. China.
„ Assamica	2,000 to 6,000	Requires a warm, moist climate. Tea strong.
Jalap	5,000 to 7,000	A purge. South America.
Ipecacuanha	1,000 to 2,000	Good for dysentery. South America.
Digitalis (Fox-glove) ...	5,000 to 7,000	.....
Tobacco	5,000 to 6,000	Manilla, Havannah, &c. Good when well cured.
New Zealand Flax ...	5,000 to 7,000	The fibre of this when treated with oil is equal to Manilla hemp.
Annattoo	2,000 to 4,000	Grows well. Good to mix with chocolate. Coloring matter for cheese, butter, &c.
Cocoa	2,000 to 3,000	Grows well in a very hot, moist climate.
Nutmeg	1,500 to 3,000	Grows well.
All spice	1,500 to 3,000	Grows well.
Cardamoms	2,000 to 3,000	Grows well.

List of introduced Trees, Shrubs, &c., and their Uses—(Continued).

	Elevation. FT.	
Clove	2,000 to 3,000	Grows well.
Breadfruit	2,000 to 3,000	Grows well.
Pineapple	1,000 to 3,000	Grows well.
Orange	4,000 to 6,000	Various kinds. Malta, S. Michael, &c.
Limes	4,000 to 5,000	Various sorts.
Figs	4,000 to 5,000	Various sorts.
Apples	4,000 to 7,000	Various sorts.
Pears	4,000 to 7,000	Various sorts.
Strawberries	4,000 to 7,000	Various sorts.
Raspberries	4,000 to 7,000	Various sorts.
Dorian	1,000 to 2,000	Various sorts.
Mangosteen	1,000 to 2,000	Various sorts.
Peaches	4,000 to 6,000	Various sorts.
Plums	4,000 to 6,000	Various sorts.

(2.)—*List of Trees indigenous to the Nílagiris, their Uses, and at what Elevation found.*

	Elevation. FT.	
Michelia Nílagirica or Chumpek.	5,000 to 7,000	Useful wood for tea boxes and ordinary work.
Hydnocarpus alpina (Monkey fruit).	5,000 to 6,000 Coonoor.	Used for house-building; red wood, fair grain.
Gordonia obtusa ...	5,000 to 7,000	Fairly useful wood.
Ilex Wightiana and denticulata.	6,000 to 7,000	Very useful wood for tea boxes. Superior wood for rafters, planks, and grain like beech.
Euonymus crenulatus ...	5,000 to 6,000	Good for engraving.
Eugenia Jambolana or Jambur.	5,000 to 7,000	Good for charcoal, but having a twisted grain; of no use for planks.
Eugenia species ...	5,000 to 6,000 Paikaré.	Hard, dense red wood, good for rafters.
Cinnamomum Zeylanicum (Native name Dalchinee).	4,000 to 7,000 Wainád to Ootacamand.	Good for planks and rafters.
Mesua (Iron wood) ...	4,000 to 5,000 Slopes of the hills	Valuable timber.
Hopea parviflora ...	4,000 to 5,000	Second-class timber.
Calophyllum tomentosum or Poon spar.	3,000 to 4,000	Ship's spars, &c.
Tectona grandis (Teak).	1,000 to 4,000	First-class timber.
Dalbergia latifolia or Blackwood.	1,000 to 4,000	First-class timber, good for furniture.
Chikrassia tabularis (Red cedar).	2,000 to 4,000	Excellent timber.
Cedrela toona (White cedar).	3,000 to 5,000	Excellent timber.
Acrocarpus fraxinifolius.	3,000 to 4,000	Good timber; a gigantic tree.
Artocarpus hirsutus (Wild Jack. Ainee Native name).	2,000 to 3,000	Good timber.
Pterocarpus marsupium (Vengay Native name).	2,000 to 4,000	Good timber, fine grain.
Terminalia glabra (Kureemuradoo Native name).	2,000 to 3,000	Hard, heavy wood, valuable for being very straight and strong.
Lagerstrœmia (Ven Tek Native name).	1,000 to 6,000	Light but useful timber.

CH. XXVI.

FORESTS.

List of Trees indigenous to the Nílagiris, their Uses, and at what Elevation found—(Continued).

	Elevation. FT.	
Vatica laccifera (Sal Native name).	2,000 to 3,000	Hard, heavy, good timber.
Conocarpus (Velli Naga)	1,500 to 4,000	White wood, useful for planks; centre black, but always has heart shake.
Acacia speciosa (Native name Waghy).	1,000 to 5,000	Good timber.
Chloroxylon Swietenia (Satinwood).	2,000 to 4,000	Tough wood and handsome for furniture.
Santalinum album (Sandalwood.)	2,000 to 4,000	The most valuable wood of commerce; price has risen to 4 annas a pound for first-class wood.

CHAPTER XXVII.

AGRICULTURE.

(*By* Major-General MORGAN, *formerly Deputy Conservator of Forests, Nílagiris.*)

INTRODUCTION.

Mr. Sullivan's enterprise.—Mr. S. R. Lushington's farm at Kaity.—The Committee's report.—Major Ouchterlony's proposal.—Silk-worm culture.—Grant to Mr. John McIvor.—Private effort.—Lord Napier's Minute.—Major Ouchterlony's statement of produce.

CH. XXVII. — AGRICULTURE.

BY way of preface to the following interesting paper by Major-General Morgan, than whom no one has had a wider experience in experimental English farming on the plateau, I proceed to note briefly the history of agriculture in the district.

Mr. Sullivan's enterprise.

Mr. Sullivan may be well called the pioneer of improved agriculture and horticulture, especially on the higher plateau, and to his efforts in this way I have already referred in a preceding chapter. Soon after he had begun to build the house known as "Stonehouse," he obtained the consent of Government for procuring at his own charges the services of a professional gardener and agriculturist for the purpose of making experiments in agriculture and horticulture; and, on the arrival of this employé, the Government permitted Mr. Sullivan to enclose 500 bullas or nearly 1,900 acres, he having apparently purchased the land from the Tódas. His intention was only to cultivate suitable portions of this area. The tracts occupied by him appear to have been the hills and valleys extending from Stonehouse to the neighbourhood of Bishopsdown. On these properties which were portions of the original block passing into the hands of Government on Mr. Sullivan's leaving the Hills in or about 1830, they continued to maintain the gardens, though on a small scale, until the radical changes in the Hill administration under Sir Frederick Adam. I have not been able to find any account of Mr. Sullivan's agricultural enterprise, but from scattered notices it appears that to him is mainly due the introduction of European fruits and flowers. He also made attempts to introduce the culture of English cereals among the Badagas. Species of barley and wheat are still known as the *doré's* (gentleman) wheat or

CH. XXVII. AGRICULTURE.

barley, and crops of these species are said to be still grown, though the grain has degenerated greatly either from climate or hybridisation with the indigenous species. Vetches he also introduced, but the system of cattle-feeding prevailing among the Badagas does not necessitate the growth of fodder crops, and so the cultivation ceased. He appears also to have tried the culture of flax and hemp, for which the Hills are well suited. His experiments were chiefly confined to the plateau, but he also established a garden in the neighbourhood of Kalhatti.

Mr. S. R. Lushington's farm at Kaity.

On Mr. Sullivan's departure, the Governor, Mr. S. R. Lushington, brought the resources of Government to his aid in experimental English farming, and also offered the assistance of Government to Anglo-Indians who were willing to colonize the Hills. In April 1830 he established an experimental farm at Kaity, taking up Badaga lands for the purpose in a high-handed manner, which, after his departure, was the subject of a severe censure from the Court of Directors, who ordered the lands to be restored and ample compensation to be given to the landholders for loss of profits whilst their lands were improperly appropriated. Money however was not easily obtained, and accordingly the Government early in 1830 ordered two companies of tent lascars to proceed to the Hills for the purpose of relieving some of the people employed in protecting and improving the Government property at that station. They were placed under the orders of the Commissariat Officer, Major Crewe. About the same time orders were issued for the establishment of a store of implements of husbandry and horticulture at the Commissariat Depôt, such implements to be sold at prime cost to the public until they could be procured from other sources. The implements forwarded included light ploughs, wheel-barrows, rakes, &c. The articles were supplied from the Grazing Farm in Mysore. The history of the Kaity farm project I quote from the report of the Committee appointed to inquire into the progress of the Hills [1] on the eve of Mr. Lushington's departure. They write:—

Committee's report.

"The Committee have gone over the portions of the land which have been placed under Major Crewe's superintendence and control for the purposes of experiments in agriculture and horticulture in the Kaity valley. It is stated by Major Crewe that these experiments were commenced under his superintendence in the month of April 1830. The Committee found that fields to a considerable extent have been broken up in the English style of farming with ploughs of the English shape and by means of cattle trained for the purpose. Some of these fields have been planted with potatoes; others, on a smaller scale, have been laid out in wheat, oats, and barley, and more are now under

[1] E.M.C., Military Department, 5th October 1832.

preparation to secure seeds for second crops. Considering the short time these experiments have been in progress, the Committee beg to observe that the high appearance of the farm shows not only the capabilities of the soil, but that the exertions of the Superintendent in overcoming the many difficulties which he must have had to encounter in the commencement of operations of so novel a description have been great indeed. Several spots of ground at Kaity laid out as gardens are in a most flourishing condition, and the Committee have no reason to doubt but that the expectations which might have been entertained when these experiments were resolved on will be realized to the fullest extent. From a memorandum submitted by Major Crewe it appears that the farm at Kaity consists at present of about 150 acres, chiefly arable, with an extensive garden, the whole in its infancy, calling for enclosure, preparation of lands, roads, water-courses, &c., and that there are two large gardens at Ootacamund to be kept up."

Major Crewe had asked for a permanent establishment of 30 men for the farm, 8 for the garden at Bishopsdown, and 6 for that at Stonehouse. The Committee recommended the maintenance of a permanent establishment of 50 men and 3 overseers, to be selected from the tent lascars. They proceed :—

"Major Crewe has stated that good workmen cannot be procured on the Hills at a lower rate than 8 rupees per month (the pay and batta of the lascars at present employed being, however, within a fraction of Rupees 10). This appears high wages, but on the formation of all infant settlements and establishments a certain latitude must be granted, and the Committee have no doubt that, as the settlers on the Hills increase, the wages of work-people of all descriptions will fall to a lower scale. As a set-off against the expenses which have already been incurred and the expenditure proposed to be continued, Major Crewe states that last year, being the first, Rupees 2,000 were carried to the credit of Government, arising out of the produce and seeds, and that this season affords every expectation of realizing Rupees 5,000. Further, as Major Crewe justly observes, that, as the several grounds get into heart and the farm improved by culture and sheltered by enclosures and plantations, a considerable annual increase must result."

Major Crewe had written as follows on the public usefulness of the farm :—

"Sums already realized from the produce of the farm, as well as those to be derived this season will afford adequate means to justify the expense incurred in prosecuting this undertaking. Some stress also may be laid on its great public accommodation from the seeds and vegetables afforded to the local community and from the dissemination of the former of every description and of the best quality throughout India. Its utility is also showing itself by the encouragement and aid afforded to industrious but needy persons in the erection of cottages and the culture of potatoes and other saleable articles, whereby they will earn their livelihood."

After remarking that the Anglo-Indians—Rieley, Jones, and Joyce—with their families had already settled on the Hills and had

CH. XXVII. — AGRICULTURE.

been aided from the farm and that six more families were desirous of settling here, he proceeds :—

"There is every promise of extensive tracts of land now lying waste and capable of becoming most productive being brought under cultivation, to the increase of public revenue and to the useful employment of Indo-Britons and others for whom it has become difficult to find occupation."

On this the Committee remark that they "have no hesitation in giving their opinion, founded on the observations they have personally made in their several excursions, that cultivation might be carried on to a very great extent on the Hills. The flourishing appearance of the fields of grain around the small villages of the Native Badagas proves the excellence of the soil and the many flowing and unceasing streams of water from springs on the Hills ensure constant irrigation during the driest parts of the season and when the periodical rains may be scanty. The Committee therefore beg to recommend the adoption of Major Crewe's suggestions as to encouraging colonization to the greatest possible extent; materials for constructing the most comfortable dwellings for natives are to be had in abundance." The Government approved these suggestions, observing that there could be no possible objection, care being taken that the new settlers have only land that has not been broken up, and that they make to the Tódas when there is a mand in its vicinity, the same acknowledgments as the Badagas have made to the Tódas; but that this rule was not to preclude voluntary transfer and purchase of old lands from the Badagas in particular cases, but the general principle should be for the new settlers to occupy new unbroken lands. They at the same time sanctioned the Committee's proposals regarding the farm establishments.

But the scheme was destined soon to be abandoned under the orders of the Honorable Court and the lands to be restored to the Badagas. The Government however retained the buildings and the gardens immediately adjoining. Subsequently they were leased to the Marquis de St. Simon, the Governor of Pondicherry, who lived there for some time until 1839. In March 1840 Lord Elphinstone, the Governor, arrived on the Hills, and took up his abode at Kaity on account of the greater privacy of the place and of the mildness of its climate. He subsequently purchased the lands from the Badagas and the buildings from Government and continued to reside there occasionally. He built the large house and extended the plantation. On his departure the property was purchased by Mr. Casamajor of the Civil Service, by whom it was bequeathed to the German Mission.

This was the first and last effort by Government directly to establish a model farm on the Nílagiris.

Major Ouchterlony's proposal.

In 1847 Major Ouchterlony proposed the establishment of a Government farm, more especially for the growth of wheat and barley, recommending two sites for the purpose—one the elevated tract to the westward of the Paikaré river, commencing at the north-west angle of the plateau near Neduwattam, and extending southwards to Múkarté peak, the other the Kódanád promontory in which Mr. Hill has now formed his large tea estate. His proposed farms had special reference to the establishment of Government breweries on the Hills for supplying the troops with malt liquors. He also desired to promote immigration of farmers from Europe. His remarks are noteworthy as indicating the great change that has taken place in the price of labour, &c.

" Here cooly labor is very cheap, 2 annas, or $2\frac{3}{4}d.$, a day being the regular rate of pay for a working man who can perform any duty pertaining to spade husbandry, and undertake all the duties of a farm which in England fall to the lot of the common laborer, such as hedging and ditching, trenching, hoeing, reaping, stacking, thatching, &c., &c. A shilling a day, or $\frac{1}{2}$ a rupee, is the pay of a bricklayer or carpenter; men to look after 2 horses receive 14 shillings, or 7 rupees a month, cowherds 4 or 5 shillings, and all other labor in proportion. These advantages, coupled with those presented by a ready and ever-demanding market for such articles of produce as wheat, barley (oats if raised), clover, hay (of which article an immense quantity would be consumed in Ootacamund if it was procurable), turnips, potatoes (Ceylon offering a very favorable market for this vegetable), butter, eggs, and stock of all descriptions, both for butcher's meat and for salting for ship use, would surely, it is to be supposed, tempt many indigent farmers to this hilly region, whose necessities impel them to emigrate from the mother-country, but whose steps are stayed by the warnings uttered by the many hundreds of their unfortunate fellow-countrymen who have hurried heedlessly out to the Australian colonies, only to meet with disappointment and ruin."

Silk-worm culture.

I must refer to the Memoir for further information of the state of agriculture on the Hills at the time, but I would quote his notice of silk-worm culture, as the matter is now attracting attention.

" There remain yet a few articles of plantation produce to be noticed, the oldest of which, in the agricultural history of the Neilgherries, is silk. There are several plantations of mulberry trees in various parts of the Hills for the breeding of the silk-worm with establishments for preparing and winding the cocoons, the silk produced by which has, I understand, been pronounced in London to be of a quality very far superior to any produced in the plains, either in Bengal or other parts of India, and what has been sent to England appears to have realized very high prices. The quantity produced however has hitherto been very insignificant, and I confess, as far as I am able to judge, the scheme appears a complete failure. The mulberry trees do not shoot out fresh leaves with that redundant luxuriance which distinguishes all other descriptions of vegetation on these Hills; the weeding, watering, and pruning which they require involves much expense; the worms require the most delicate treatment both in regard to food and temperature, any mismanagement of which entails destruction on myriads, and the quantity of cocoons produced is not in a sufficiently large proportion to allow the superior quality of the silk reeled from them to secure a profit to the planter.

"Already one extensive plantation, and worm and silk-house, at Coonoor has been given up, and I should think it will not be found that this description of cultivation will be extended by future settlers."

Grant to Mr. John McIvor.

In 1850 the late Mr. W. G. McIvor obtained, with the sanction of the Court of Directors, on behalf of his brothers James and John a lease on very favorable terms for 10 years of 2,116 acres of land, part of which was selected at Ootacamand and part at Kátéri, with the object of establishing a "Scotch farm with improvements of grains, grasses, and cattle, &c." The project however was not carried into effect, the lands at Kátéri being utilized for the growth of coffee and potatoes. The land at Ootacamand was ultimately resumed, and that at Kátéri finally transferred to the late Mr. James McIvor by special agreement.

Private effort.

Although Government has not again interfered in agricultural enterprise, yet during the past twenty years, with the development of the settlement of Europeans on the plateau, more especially those connected with coffee-planting, many experiments have been made in a small way in the cultivation of exotic food-plants and to some extent in the introduction of sheep. The farm at Tudor Hall, on the northern slope of the Hills, which bounds Ootacamand on the north, was the most systematically conducted enterprise, and General Morgan's experience was mainly gained here; but within the last four or five years a farm has been established at the Lawrence Asylum, and the experience there obtained, which will be found briefly summarised in some of the recent annual reports, will prove of use to intending agriculturists. The establishment of a model farm in Madras and the appointment of a scientific agriculturist as its Superintendent gave rise to hopes that the Government might establish an experimental farm on the plateau. The scheme of provincial farms, which was contemplated in connection with the Madras project, did not embrace the Nílagiris, but the plains, which naturally had the first claim on the attention of Government. In September 1871, however, Lord Napier's Government determined to have the productive capabilities of the Hills reported upon by Mr. Robertson, the Superintendent of the Farms at Saidapet. Lord Napier writes in a minute dated 7th September 1871:—

Lord Napier's minute.

"The hill ranges of this Presidency do, however, also offer a legitimate subject of inquiry in this respect (improvement of husbandry), and the Neilgherries, as the seat of the Government sanitarium, of an increasing planting interest, of an independent English population, of large establishments for the support and education of English and East Indian youths, and of a Native population embodying a cultivating and pastoral tribe, would justify a special investigation."

He suggested that Mr. Robertson's attention should be drawn specially to the following subjects :—

(1.) The capabilities of the Hills for the purposes of breeding horses, horned cattle, and sheep.
(2.) The facilities which these Hills may afford for the institution of small farms on the European system, worked in part at least by European labor.
(3.) The improvement of the husbandry of the hill-people.

On the subject of European colonization His Lordship's remarks especially deserve attention. They are—

"Some discussion has occurred, from time to time, respecting the possibility of appropriating portions of the Neilgherry Hills for the purpose of establishing European agricultural settlers, for the purpose in fact of creating a self-supporting English rural population. On a first view of the plateau such an undertaking might seem promising to an inexperienced eye. The climate is fine for a large portion of the year, the temperature is congenial to the European constitution, the soil is rich, there are apparently large tracts of unappropriated ground, there is a market; these are conditions favorable to the production of cereal crops, garden crops, fruits, and valuable commodities for exportation, such as tea and coffee; there is a friendly and fostering authority. A close inspection and analysis, however, tend materially to qualify such favorable expectations. Much of the good land on the warm side of the Hills is subject to the rights of native cultivators; the cost of building is excessive; the price of labor is high; clothing is dear; medical attendance and education would be costly and difficult of access; the sale of grain crops, fruits, and vegetables would offer little money remuneration compared to the wants even of a humble European family; the returns of tea and coffee cultivation are slow and liable to great fluctuations. A poor man would find it difficult to establish and maintain himself; a richer man would prefer to go elsewhere. My own impressions are decidedly unfavorable to the Hills as a scene of agricultural settlement for Englishmen; but I think it would tend to the correction of erroneous impressions and to the formation of sound opinions that this question should be illustrated by the report of a person of unquestionable judgment and practical knowledge in such matters. The formation even of a limited working and self-supporting English community on these Hills, if it could be effected under favorable conditions, would not be without importance either in a commercial or political point of view, and the basis for such a community might be found, in part, in the Male and Female Military Orphan Asylums which are about to be permanently established on the Neilgherries. There is the land and

CH. XXVII. — AGRICULTURE.

there are the people; the question is whether they could be made to suit each other?"

Mr. Robertson submitted his report in 1875, and as it has been published, it is unnecessary to give the results of his investigation.

To the portion of the paper by General Morgan which relates to native agriculture I have added notes where from other information in my possession I think correction needed.

Major Ouchterlony's statement of produce.

The following statement of the agricultural products of the Nílagiris in 1847, extracted from Major Ouchterlony's paper, is of too great historic value to be omitted :—

Statement of the Agricultural Products of the Neilgherries in 1847—*Fasli* 1256.

Name of Production.	Quantity of Land cultivated.			Produce.		Ratio of Return of Crop from Seed.	Gross Amount produced.			Average Selling Price.		
		Equivalent.						Equivalent.			Equivalent.	
	In Vullums.	In Cawnies.	In Acres.	In Kolagums per Vullum.	Equivalent in Bushels per Acre.		In Kolagums.	In Bushels.	In Quarters.	Per Kolagum of 2 Seers.	Per Bushel.	Per Quarter.
										RS. A. P.	RS. A. P.	RS. A. P.
Wheat	70	202	267	400	11·12	40 to 1	28,000	2,978	372	0 2 8	1 6 0	12 8 0
Barley	1,419	4,901	5,433	400	11·12	20 ,, 1	567,600	60,383	7,548	0 1 1	0 10 2	5 1 4
Raggee	105	303	400	400	11·12	80 ,, 1	42,000	4,468	558	Not brought to market.		
Samee	364	1,052	1,391	300	8·4	60 ,, 1	109,200	11,617	1,452	......	......	......
Koralley	1,289	3,724	4,924	200	5·6	10 ,, 1	257,800	27,425	3,425	......	......	......
Tenney	102	294	385	300	8·4	30 ,, 1	30,600	3,255	407	......	......	......
Buttacudaley	83	240	317	200	5·5	40 ,, 1	16,600	1,766	221	0 2 8	1 9 0	12 8 0
Chanungee	55	159	210	300	8·4	30 ,, 1	16,500	1,755	220	0 2 8	1 9 0	12 8 0
Garlic	132	381	504	600	16·8	48 ,, 1	79,200	8,425	1,053	0 0 10	0 8 0	4 0 0
Onions	31	90	141	700	20·	56 ,, 1	21,700	2,308	288	0 1 1	0 10 2	5 1 4
Mustard Seed	122	352	491	300	8·4	150 ,, 1	36,600	3,893	487	0 0 10	0 8 0	4 0 0
Vendiem	67	194	256	200	5·6	100 ,, 1	13,400	1,425	178	0 1 0	0 9 5	4 11 4
Poppy Seed and Opium ...	93	269	353	100	2·8	100 ,, 1	9,300	990	124	0 4 0	2 5 7	......
				$2\frac{2}{3}$ lb. per vullum.			242 lbs. avoirdupois.			3 0 0	per seer = Rs. 5 per lb.	
Potatoes	49	141	186	600 mds. ,,		15 ,, 1	29,400 mds.=cwt. 6,562			0 6 0	per maund = Rupee 1 ,, 11 per lb.	
	3,981	11,510	15,220	Acres of land under cultivation.								

CH. XXVII.
AGRICULTURE.

MONOGRAPH ON AGRICULTURE.

(Major-General MORGAN's Paper.)

(a) SOILS.

Black soil.—Brown soil.—Yellow and red soils.

Soils. The soils on these hills may be roughly set down as four in number, viz., the black, brown, yellow, and red, sometimes running into each other.

—Black soil. These generally face the north, and very frequently overlie a rich retentive clay subsoil. Occasionally the soil is of a dense black and peaty nature. Such soil, until well worked and limed, is unproductive; but the true black soil of the Hills with a good subsoil is undoubtedly the most productive of all the soils. It may be called a rich loam.

—Brown soil. This is the soil next in value. It faces north-east or north-west, and is found even due east and west according to the shelter which the ground possesses. It is a fair soil for most crops, but rather stiffer than the black soil to work—a clay loam.

—Yellow soil. This soil may be called a stiff clay, poor until heavily manured. It requires under-draining even on steep hill-sides. It faces due south, south-west, south-east, and, having been exposed to the beat of the monsoon for ages, it has gathered no fertilizing matter, and is ruinous to cultivate except as grass-land.[1]

—Red soil. This soil is not so stiff as the yellow, but as far as productiveness is concerned is equally poor, and, facing ordinarily the same way, is exposed to the same disadvantages—the beat of the monsoon and a fierce southern sun. Except when sheltered, it is a hungry soil and ruinous to cultivate. It may be said of the soils on these Hills that there are two good soils and two bad soils, interspersed here and there with intermediate ones partaking more or less of the good or bad qualities of the one or the other. It may be laid down, as a rule, that all the soils require lime in large doses, the stiff soils to make them light, the peaty and black soils to sweeten them and render the vegetable matter in the ground suitable for the food of plants.

[1] I cannot concur with General Morgan in this view. When well worked and manured, these red and even the yellow soils become productive. *Eucalyptus*, *acacia* and other exotics grow tolerably well in them. They are very retentive of moisture which gives them an advantage in the hot and dry months. Mr. Robertson remarks: "When deeply ploughed, regularly worked, and adequately manured, they will yield well, especially when in the manure applied there is a fair proportion of lime. It is not that these soils are deficient in the elements of plant-food, lime excepted, but their physical condition is such that this food remains latent and useless until by deep cultivation the soils are brought fully under the influence of atmospheric agencies."—ED.

CH. XXVII. AGRICULTURE.

(b) NATIVE AGRICULTURE.

Crops—korali—raggi—barley—wheat—sámé—naomi—mustard—keré—poppy—onions—garlic—peas—potatoes.—Yield per acre.—Average price of staple food-grains.—Manuring.—Ploughing.—Sowing.—Weeding.—Area under each crop.—Cost of cultivation.—Implements.—Cattle.—Rotation of crops.—Terracing and fencing.—Reaping, thrashing, storing.—Price of cattle.—Land for pasturage.—Fodder.—Cows.—Modes of bringing produce to market.—Markets.—Results of agriculture.

The various crops cultivated by the indigenous tribes of the Hills, especially the Badagas, are as follow:— *Native agriculture. Crops.*

Korali is a millet, and is grown on every soil, from the richest to the poorest. On rich soils it may be seen nearly 2½ feet in height and bearing some 6 cwts. to the acre of grain, and from 1½ to 2 tons of excellent straw, much appreciated when fresh by horses, bullocks, and cows. This straw, whenever practicable, is all sold off the land and nothing in return put in—a ruinous process. This grain is the chief food of the Badagas.[1] *—korali.*

This grain is now grown to some extent. On good soils it produces heavily when manured, from 7 to 8 cwts. of grain the acre. It grows from 5,500 feet downwards. Its nutritive properties are very high, ranking with oats.[2] *—raggi.*

Barley is, with korali, the principal crop cultivated on the Hills. It grows best on the dark soils, but the return is wretched, the straw very inferior, deficient in silica; in fact, barley crops, only 2 feet in height, are frequently laid by heavy rain or wind, so deficient is the straw in silica. The straw is sold off the land. Barley of late years has risen in price enormously. Formerly 60 to 70 lb. could be purchased for the rupee, now 30 can hardly be procured. New seed[3] and a different style of cultivation is much needed. The soils and climate are well adapted for the growth of the best kinds of barley if properly manured; but the fatal system of non-manuring and fallows is the rule. A black barley shown at the Nílagiri Exhibition in 1869 was much approved of. It had been grown at Kótagiri, and the yield per acre was said to be great. The return expected *—barley.*

---

[1] From inquiries instituted I find that ordinarily the yield does not exceed 5 kandagams or 200 Madras large measures. This is also Major Ouchterlony's estimate. The yield of straw is about 10 to 15 bundles of 60 lb. or ⅓rd ton. About 60 lb. seed are sown to the acre. The yield is about tenfold. It is often sown with samé. The grain is very small, one-twentieth of a grain of wheat.—ED.

[2] This grain is chiefly grown in the lower Tódanád and Péranganád. It is a great favourite with the Hill-tribes and the Kanarese. The quantity raised by the Badagas is insufficient for their needs, and consequently much of that imported is consumed by them. The ordinary yield is eightfold.—ED.

[3] Grain of plants grown from seed introduced from Europe or Australia is found to deteriorate rapidly. In three generations it becomes thin and lean, with but little farinaceous substance and a hard kernel.—ED.

CH. XXVII. AGRICULTURE. by Badagas is but five to one, or, say, to two bushels of seed ten bushels crop, or about one-fourth of what the yield should be.[1]

—wheat. A fair amount of wheat is cultivated. It requires a stiffer soil than barley. The yield is small, the grain indifferent; in fact so inferior that the bakers procure their wheat from Coimbatore and even Bangalore in preference to using the wheat of the Hills. There is no good reason why this should be, as, like barley, the soil and climate is suitable for the growth of the best wheat, and it only requires good seed and intelligent husbandry to produce the best results.[2]

—samé. Samé[3] (*Panicum miliare*) is much esteemed by the Badagas and cultivated to some extent. The yield is small.

—naomi. Another small grain, naomi (*Panicum Italicum*), grows at a low elevation, but is not cultivated largely.

—mustard. This is grown in the Badaga villages to some extent. It is frequently found as a weed in the higher parts in the Hills amongst turnips, oats, &c.; and, though other weeds may be pulled up, this even in a garden is invariably retained by both Badagas and Kanarese.

—keré. Keré (*Amaranthus campestris*), Prince's feather, is often grown near the village in lines with raggi, and is much valued by the Badagas. This grain is small and white; it is produced only for house consumption.[4]

—poppy. A small field of poppy is always grown near every Badaga village. It grows best where the village is below 6,000 feet. The opium is collected in the cold months as the juice is then thicker.[5] The field generally receives some manure, though the yield is small owing to want of care in the cultivation. It sells for 8 annas an ounce. Opium is much eaten by Badagas.

—onion. The common small onion is grown regularly close to the village, and this crop of all others is heavily manured, but the yield is indifferent, one measure of onicns producing but two measures of crop.[6] The onions are very strong in flavour, quite unlike the onions of the low country, which are mild and delicate.

---

[1] Major Ouchterlony says the yield is twentyfold. The deterioration must have been great since his time, and probably General Morgan's estimate is too high now. See also Mr. Robertson's note on this grain in his report.—ED.

[2] See Mr. Robertson's report. The wheat chiefly cultivated is the *Triticum spelta*. Mr. Robertson considers the Hills promise well as a wheat-growing country.—ED.

[3] Mr. Robertson states that there are four kinds of samé.—ED.

[4] The leaves and stalks are also cooked when tender and much relished by the Hill-tribes.—ED.

[5] Before sunset a small incision is made in the pericarpium, whence the opium exudes, and is removed in the following morning. The seed is used for food.—ED.

[6] This yield seems too low; four or five fold is probably nearer the fact.—ED.

—garlic. This is also grown in the same manner as onions, and the yield is small; but the bulbs are far larger than low-country garlic.

—peas. These are grown as field peas, but the yield is small. The peas, too, are smaller than the English field pea.

—potatoes. Lately large crops of this tuber have been grown by Badagas, as the price has risen from Rupees 40 to at times Rupees 100 the ton, due in a measure to the prevalence of disease.[1] There is no doubt that the Badaga country is especially suitable for the growth of potatoes, which delight in a dry soil of a reddish brown colour and warm sun and moderate rainfall. With much rain they lose their starch and become watery. Kalhatti, Bellikal, Kaity, Coonoor and Kótagiri are well suited for the growth of the potato. The Kalhatti valley has for years produced the best potatoes on the Hills; the soil is a reddish brown loam, the climate moderately moist, and frosts only occur in January.

Yield per acre. The probable yield[2] of each crop per acre is—

	CWTS.
Wheat	3
Barley	3
Korali	3
Poppy	4 seers of opium and 40 lb. of seed.
Samé (*Panicum miliare*)	2
Naomi (*Panicum Italicum*)	2
Mustard	3
Keré	2
Onions	3
Garlic	3
Peas	2
Potatoes	40

Average price of staple food-grains. The following statement contains the prices of the staple grains during ten years ending June 1878, but, with the exception of wheat, raggi, and horse-gram, the grains named are imported.

[1] The manner in which the plant is cultivated, often in swampy ground, without cessation, so long as the land yields any return, may probably have been the cause. Efforts have been made by Government to remedy the evil by introduction of good seed of new varieties; but, until a more intelligent mode of culture is adopted and lime applied to the soil no permanent improvement can be expected.—ED.

[2] With the exception of korali and mustard, I believe the estimate is too low (*see* also Ouchterlony's statement).—ED.

CH. XXVII.

AGRICULTURE.

Prices of Grains per Garce of 3,200 Measures.

—	Rice.		Cholum.	Cumboo.	Wheat.	Horse-gram.	Raggi.
	1st Sort.	2nd Sort.					
	RS.	RS.	RS.	RS.	RS.	RS.	RS.
Fasli 1278 ...	620	563	295	276	520	320	303
„ 1279 ...	696	618	295	271	575	264	281
„ 1280 ...	558	494	277	203	558	226	218
„ 1281 ...	481	446	222	192	403	247	177
„ 1282 ...	530	477	237	205	412	263	198
„ 1283 ...	582	533	304	291	533	337	256
„ 1284 ...	582	512	298	291	457	337	256
„ 1285 ...	582	533	320	337	492	320	278
„ 1286 ...	753	674	457	400	674	522	441
„ 1287 ...	914	800	624	502	985	674	582
Total ...	6,298	5,650	3,329	2,968	5,609	3,510	2,990
Average ...	629¾	565	333	296¾	561	351	299
Madras full measures.	5·08	5·66	9·61	10·80	5·70	9·10	10·70

Manuring. Manure from the village cattle is carried to the adjoining hills in baskets. Cattle are never used for the carriage of manure. The quantity applied simply depends upon the fact whether or not murrain has visited the village herd. The amount of manure per acre does not exceed 2 tons. The manure is of poor quality, as Badaga cattle are never fed on manure-producing food. It is flung broadcast and ploughed in. When fallow land is broken up, the small bushes (*Dodonea*) are burnt and the ashes scattered over the land[1] and ploughed in.

Ploughing. From five to six ploughings are made.[2] The first ploughing is generally in April with the first showers. Sowing takes place towards the end of April, reaping in August. If a wet August comes, the crops suffer greatly.

Sowing. Grain crops are all sown broadcast by hand. Only headmen are entrusted with this important work. The Kanarese cultivators sow some crops in furrows, *e.g.*, onions, peas, &c.

---

[1] Probably half a ton per acre is the ordinary quantity used. The village debris of straw, &c., is mixed with it. It is not used until it is dry and powdery from decomposition and exposure to the sun. The manure is applied after the seed is sown. The thorough decomposition of the manure, though it is impoverished by the process, frees it from seeds of weeds and larvæ of insects.—ED.

[2] Four ploughings take place before sowing; one after it. The early ploughings first lengthwise, then across the field, then diagonally. The ploughs are of wood and the depth of the furrow not more than 6 inches. After each ploughing, stones, roots and weeds are carefully removed. The stones are piled up or used for terracing to prevent waste.—ED.

CH. XXVII.

AGRICULTURE.

Weeding.

The weeding is done by women and children and very clean the fields are kept. Some twenty women form line, using a small adze-shaped hoe for digging out weeds.[1]

Acres under each crop.

The number of acres under each crop in Fasli 1285 (1876) is reported to have been—

	ACRES.		ACRES.
Raggi ...	3,430	Mustard ...	355
Korali ...	15,728	Vendiem ...	144
Samé ...	4,662	Poppy ...	66
Wheat ...	3,199	Vegetables ...	189
Barley ...	3,761	Other crops ...	394
Other food-grains.	588		
Potatoes ...	754	Total ...	33,317
Horse-gram ...	67		

Cost of cultivation.

The cost[2] of ploughing, sowing, weeding, reaping and thrashing an ordinary grain crop is as follows:—

	RS.	A.	P.
Six ploughings at 8 As. each	3	0	0
Cost of seed, 67 lb., at 1 Re. per 30 lb. ...	2	4	0
Sowing	0	4	0
Rent of land	0	8	0
Weeding	2	0	0
Reaping	3	0	0
Thrashing	2	8	0
Total ...	13	8	0
Crop at 30 lb. per rupee = 336 lb. or 11 Rs. 3 As. 1 ton of straw at 10 rupees.	21	3	0

[1] Two weedings take place before harvest, at intervals of six weeks.—ED.

[2] With every respect to General Morgan's great experience I would estimate as follows for, say, a one-acre field of raggi:—

	RS.	A.	P.
5 ploughings at 8 annas	2	8	0
60 lb. of seeds	2	0	0
Dressing and sowing	1	0	0
2 weedings	6	0	0
20 headloads of manure	2	8	0
Reaping and thrashing	5	0	0
Assessment of land	0	8	0
Total ...	19	8	0
Proceeds—			
Grain, 4 cwts.	20	0	0
15 bundles straw	7	8	0
	27	8	0
Profit ...	8	0	0

Major Ouchterlony's estimate of charges is absurdly low.—ED.

CH. XXVII. — AGRICULTURE.

Implements. The implements used by the hill people in agriculture are—

The Plough	Weeding adze.
Harrow	Axe.
Bill-hook.	Momati.
Sickle.	

Cattle.

Number of ploughs in the district	... ...	3,496
Do. of ploughing cattle	... ...	10,156

One plough suffices to work about 10 acres.

Rotation of crops. There is some slight attempt near the villages to cultivate land by rotation of crops—such as onions after wheat or garlic, peas and potatoes after wheat or barley—but only on manured land.[1]

Terracing and fencing. Terracing on freshly-cleared land is also carried on where stones are abundant with manifest advantage. Fencing is confined to the fields immediately adjacent to the village.

Reaping, thrashing, storing. Women generally reap. A small reaping hook is used. Grain is thrashed out in the primitive fashion by the village bullocks muzzled. A post is set in the centre of the threshing-floor, which has been carefully plastered with cow-dung. The animals are fastened neck to neck some ten deep and driven round the circle. Of course the straw is rendered quite unfit for thatching, even if sufficient silica was in it for thatching straw. The grain is stored in huge conical baskets plastered inside and out with cow-dung. The small proboscis beetle is very destructive to many kinds of grain in store, such as wheat and barley. The oats and raggi are not attacked by it. It may be observed that raggi stored in pits in the ground of an oblong shape improves by keeping, and when seven years old is highly esteemed. The pits are called gows or cows; hence a man is called Timma Gowda or Timma of the pit-place. Hence to be a Gowda amongst Kanarese is to be a man of caste.

Prices of cattle. Badaga cattle may be valued at about 25 rupees a head for stout oxen.

Land for pasturage. It takes at least 4 acres of natural grass land to keep a bullock all through the year.[2]

Fodder. No artificial fodder is ever given, and trees are not even pollarded, as in the low country, during dry weather.[3]

Cows. The yield of milk of a cow is about half a quart in the morning and a quart in the evening. About ten quarts would yield a pound of butter. The price of a good milk cow is Rupees 30 to 35.

---

[1] The abrogation of the "shifting" system will probably necessitate the introduction of a rough rotation system.—ED.

[2] A hill buffalo probably requires 7 or 8 acres.

[3] A description of wild flax which grows in the shólas is much used as fodder in dry seasons. The cattle also eat the korali and other straw.—ED.

CH. XXVII. — AGRICULTURE.

Badagas bring grain in bags and baskets to the markets at Ootacamand, Coonoor, and Kótagiri. Their women also assist; bullocks are rarely used.

Modes of bringing produce to market.

Markets.

The weekly markets do not seem to have had much influence in developing among the Badagas a desire to improve the quality of the crops grown by them or to introduce new varieties of food plants into their farms, but they resort to them regularly to purchase the surplus grain they need.

Result of agriculture.

The Badaga agriculture does not maintain them: they have to go out to daily labour, and with the money so obtained to purchase grain to add to the village stock.

(c) English Farming.

Tracts and soils best suited.—Expenses.—Seasons for cultivating.—Field crops.—Degeneration of seed.—Draining, terracing, and ploughing.—Cultivation.—Manuring — lime — potash. — Horticulture. — Garden crops. — Fruit trees.—Market prices.— Live-stock — cattle — sheep — pigs — horses— poultry. —Diseases.—Treatment—murrain—foot-and-mouth disease.—General remarks.

Tracts of the hills and soils best suited.

As a general rule, it may be laid down that all the country west of Doddabetta is best suited for oat-hay and turnip crops; that east of Doddabetta for general grain crops, mangold wurtzel, and potatoes. For Guinea grass, Mauritius grass, and *Sorghum saccharatum* the northern aspect is the best.

Expenses.

The cost of breaking up grass land, manuring, sowing and reaping in the cultivation of cereals or wet crops may be calculated as follows per acre :—

First Year.

	RS.	A.	P.
Breaking up the land 9 inches deep ...	30	0	0
Cutting sods	10	0	0
Ten tons manure	30	0	0
Seed, 80 lb. (oats)	4	0	0
Sowing	0	4	0
Harrowing	1	0	0
Rent	1	0	0
Reaping	5	0	0
Stacking	2	0	0
Total ...	83	4	0

The return may be estimated at 2 tons of oat-hay at 40 rupees = 80 the first year. The second year the expense may be calculated as follows :—

	RS.	A.	P.
Three ploughings at 3 Rs.	9	0	0
Ten tons manure	30	0	0
Sowing 80 lb. oats	4	4	0

CH. XXVII.

AGRICULTURE.

	RS.	A.	P.
Harrowing	1	0	0
Cutting	5	0	0
Pitting	4	0	0
Rent	1	0	0
	54	4	0
Eight tons green fodder secured in pit at 5 Rs.	40	0	0
Second crop.—Ploughing twice at 3 Rs.	6	0	0
Ten tons manure at 3 Rs.	30	0	0
Transplanting turnips	5	0	0
Cost of plants	5	0	0
Pulling 20 tons	5	0	0
Weeding do.	5	0	0
	56	0	0
Return—20 tons of turnips at 5 Rs.	100	0	0
Thus Expenses for these two crops ...	110	4	0
Return	140	0	0

or a profit of 30 rupees the acre for green crops. Should a green and dry crop be taken, the expenses may be taken as follows, assuming that the land is in good heart and has been well cultivated for two years:—

	RS.	A.	P.
Ploughing three times at 3 Rs. ...	9	0	0
Manuring, 10 tons at 3 Rs. ...	30	0	0
Sowing 80 lb. oat-seed	4	4	0
Harrowing	1	0	0
Cutting	5	0	0
Pitting	4	0	0
Rent	1	0	0
	54	4	0
Eight tons green fodder in pit at 5 Rs. per ton	40	0	0
Ploughing three times at 3 Rs. ...	9	0	0
Five tons manure at 3 Rs.	15	0	0
Sowing seed 80 lb. oats	4	4	0
Cutting	5	0	0
Stacking	2	0	0
	35	0	0
Return—2 tons being at 40 Rs. ...	80	0	0

	RS.	A.	P.
Then expenses for two crops will amount to	85	0	0
The returns will be	120	0	0
or 35 rupees the acre.			

It must be understood that 30 rupees is the sum allowed for manure. Farm-yard manure may be alternated with poudrette with advantage, three tons of poudrette being equal to 10 tons of farm-yard manure, or they may be mixed together in the proportion of 1 ton poudrette (say) 10 rupees, to 7 tons of farm-yard manure (say) 20 rupees.

If potatoes are grown as a green crop, the rotation will be potatoes planted in February at a cost as follows :—

	RS.	A.	P.
One deep ploughing, Rs. 6 ... ... Two slight ploughings 3 Rs. each, Rs. 6	12	0	0
Ten tons manure	30	0	0
One ton seed	90	0	0
Planting	5	0	0
Ridging and weeding	10	0	0
Watching	14	0	0
Taking up	10	0	0
Rent	1	0	0
	172	0	0
Return, if no disease, six tons at Rs. 60 a ton	360	0	0
The second crop may be oats, and expenses will be the same as No. 5.	35	0	0
Return do. do.	80	0	0
Or expenses for two crops	207	0	0
Return	440	0	0
or Rupees 233 per acre.			

It must be borne in mind that the potato crop is one of more risk. At one time potatoes are down to 20 rupees a ton, then up to 100 rupees.[1] Again, disease may smite the crop and the return will hardly pay for the seed. Coolies and porcupines are also great enemies of the potato crop. The depredations they commit are most serious.

Seasons for cultivating crops.

The seasons vary exceedingly. A wet September means good turnips and damaged hay; late April rains mean a short potato crop; early frost is death to the second potato crop, and

[1] The variations in the prices obtained for potatoes depend mainly on the quality of the crop, and not so much on the fickleness of the markets. Good potatoes generally obtain a good price, but since disease has prevailed, sometimes the prevailing rates have been exorbitant.—ED.

CH. XXVII. — AGRICULTURE. — so on; but, as a general rule, west of Ootacamand the seasons of the various crops may be stated as follows:—Potatoes, first crop, plant in February, take up in August. Oats, first crop, sow in March showers, reap in August. As regards turnips, sow in June, transplant in August. Potatoes, second crop, plant in August, take up in December. Oats, second crop, for hay or grain sow in September, reap in February. Turnips, transplant from August to October, gather up to March.

East of Ootacamand crops are much later as there is but little frost. The south-west monsoon is slight and the north-east monsoon is prolonged into January, making the seasons later by two or three months.

Field crops. The climate west of Ootacamand is only suited for a limited number of root and fodder crops, amongst which may be noted turnips, swedes for bullocks, cows, and sheep, oats to be cut green and kept in an air-tight pit until they have fermented—a most valuable fodder for the dry weather—the great advantage being that this crop can be secured in the wettest seasons and simply requires to be buried in a pit, which may be, for convenience of filling, 4 feet wide, 4 feet deep, and 10 feet long. This pit, when the fodder is well pressed down, will hold about two tons. The earth must be heaped up over the fodder for at least 2 feet in height, sloping away from the centre to the sides. No air nor water must be allowed to enter; any cracks appearing must be closed up. The fodder will keep a year. The theory of this system is that fermentation develops the saccharine matter in the plant, and the exclusion of air prevents decay. This system is largely practised in France and is valuable on the Hills, where for six months all green crops flourish, but cannot be made into hay owing to excessive moisture. It also enables the farmer to take two crops off the ground with certainty. Korali also may be treated in the above manner. Oats, when sown in September, make excellent hay in January, the time for cutting being when the plant flowers. If it passes that stage all the saccharine matter leaves the stalk and is deposited in the grain; hence the hay loses much of its nutritious properties.

Lucerne grows better east of Ootacamand; vetches grow fairly and would do well if treated like green oats. Swamp grass makes excellent hay, but seeds before January, so it is difficult to secure it. Cocksfoot grass and sheep's fescue grow well and make good hay, but seed before January. In fact, as hay crops, they are very uncertain; a dry September alone enables the hay to be secured.

East of Ootacamand it may be laid down that the following grains all do well from 6,000 to 5,000 feet:—

Maize, all sorts.	Potatoes.
Barley.	Mangold wurtzel.[2]
Wheat.	Guinea grass.
Sorghum saccharatum.	Lucerne.
Buckwheat.[1]	Mauritius grass.

Degeneration of seed.

Fresh importations of seed require to be made constantly both from Australia and England.

Draining, terracing, ploughing.

The stiff yellow soils even on steep hill-sides would be much improved by draining, and all soils would benefit much by subsoil ploughing. In Australia lands subsoil ploughed suffer hardly at all from excessive drought; the soil remains free instead of being caked, and the roots of plants are enabled to penetrate much deeper, and of course to draw up much moisture. On the Hills it is much needed. Terracing on steep slopes where stones are available is undoubtedly a wise practice, but one that seldom can be followed owing to the lack of stones. Fences also are scarce and far between; in fact, they can be said hardly to exist. Ploughing to the depth of 9 inches is very necessary, and if the subsoil share is run in the furrows to the depth of another 6 inches, or 15 inches in all, the results would be very satisfactory. In breaking up grass-land the strain is very great; the dynamometer often showing 7 cwt. This is as much as four powerful bullocks can manage. Indeed, they must be first-class bullocks to do it; the ordinary bullock would consider half this strain as more than enough. Horses, being too fast, are of no use for this kind of work; but for earthing up potatoes or turnips a single powerful horse with one of Ransom's light single-horse ploughs will do more work and keep more ground clean in one day than 25 coolies could or would do.

Cultivation and manure.

Nothing is lost by heavy manuring and good cultivation. Ploughing 9 inches deep and 10 tons of good farm-yard manure to the acre may be considered fair cultivation and safe to produce average crops in average seasons; but even better than this may be accomplished if the subsoil plough is used and 2 tons of poudrette added to the 10 tons of farm-yard manure. It must be remembered that turnips and potatoes insist upon manure being applied direct in the furrows. Oats and other cereals do well enough if the manure is thrown broadcast over the field. At present the Hills are fain to content themselves with poudrette and farm-yard manure, the cost of carriage up the ghát effectually forbidding the use of any special manures, such as lime, saltpetre,

[1] This grows well at Ootacamand, but ripens its seed so irregularly that one-half the crop is in flower whilst the other half is shedding its seed.

[2] This will not grow in Ootacamand; the climate is too cold, and it requires much salt.

CH. XXVII. AGRICULTURE.

bones, guano, phospho-guano, &c., the cost per ton up the ghát to Ootacamand being not less than 30 rupees.

—lime. There is no denying that the Hills are prepared to absorb lime to any extent. Even in England on all but calcareous soils the amount of lime considered necessary is formidable ; 2 cwt. an acre annually for twenty years is not considered too large a dose on some soils. It is true that on the Hills, in the decomposing hornblende, we have some twelve per cent. of lime, but the question is, not the amount of lime in the hornblende, but the equal distribution of hornblende in the soil. The subsoils chiefly consist of felspar abounding in potash, a most valuable ingredient, but no lime ; at least Siberian felspar is credited with but three per cent., and many other felspars with not one per cent. It should be remembered that most of the soils on the Hills west of Ootacamand have never been broken up, and to enable the plant to assimilate the vegetable matters in the soil lime is necessary. On the stiff soils lime may be used with greater safety than on the light soils, because lime has a tendency to make a stiff soil lighter; hence the light soils only require sufficient lime to render the vegetable matter in them sweet, and therefore suitable for the food of plants. In fact lime may be said to be the beginning, the middle, and the end of agriculture; without it we cannot tell what the soils of the Hills are capable of. With a railway up the ghát lime would be delivered over the Hills at 20 rupees the ton ; even at this enormous rate the application of lime would be a success. Lime applied to fields in England rarely costs more than 6 rupees a ton. Lime has the property of releasing ammonia from manure ; hence it is not wise to combine the two. Lime should be slaked on the field, applied broadcast, and then ploughed in. Afterwards apply manure.

—potash. No doubt the subsoils contain much potash, as they chiefly consist of felspars, but it is a question if the felspar readily yields up its potash, or, in other words, if it does not require considerable exposure to the air to liberate or fit the potash in the felspar for the consumption of it by plant-life. When the felspathic subsoil is available, it would be advisable to spread some of it on the surface and plough it in. After a certain time had elapsed, the weathering it underwent would free the potash and render it fitting plant-food. In parts of Ireland granite rocks are burnt for potash; the burning sets free the potash for plant-food. Tobacco is well known to require an enormous amount of potash, and the Badaga country is well suited for its growth.

Horticulture. Under these heads we have to review products as widely apart as cinchona and strawberries, for arboriculture may be considered a branch of agriculture, and horticulture another branch. First, then, to deal with the cinchona tree. On these Hills this tree has found a home equally congenial with its native habitat. *Cinchona condaminea* may truly be said to flourish on these mountains of from 6,000 to 8,000 feet without a check, regardless of a burning sun by day or ten degrees of frost by night. The bark produced from this tree by skilful cultivators has in London realized prices surpassing that of all other barks produced in the world. Of coffee the same almost may be said of that grown here, with the addition that there are numerous coffee climates and numerous skilled coffee-growers in various parts of India and elsewhere. Of tea it may be said that the prices realized in the London market have been quite equal to those from other parts, such as Darjeeling, and it only requires more skilful and uniform manipulation, coupled with a larger outturn, to render the Nílagiri teas famous, the climate and the soil being fully equal to tea requirements. The Nílagiris may be said to export nothing but the above three products and a few potatoes, the export of garden produce without a railway being impracticable.

Garden crops.

Of garden crops, vegetable-marrows, beet-root, cauliflowers, and cabbages are produced in abundance and of fair flavour ; carrots indifferent, turnips indifferent, celery fair, not blanched enough for want of sand, which is very difficult of obtainment. Rhubarb is well grown in private gardens, so are marrow-fat peas. Natives grow fair knol-khols, radishes, salads, broad beans and French beans. These, if grown in Badaga land, are excellent ; but tomatoes, cucumbers, capsicum, and sweet herbs, which would grow well at Coonoor and Kalhatti, and for which there would be a large demand, are quite neglected.

Fruit trees.

In a mountainous region subject to perpetual changes of climate, with no settled seasons except those of wind and rain, fruit has an indifferent time of it, with now a burning sun, then misty, cloudy weather, then rain, next day a drying north-easter, fruit knows no regular season, hence, except on a southern exposure and a very sheltered spot, everything in the shape of fruit refuses to ripen. Very delicate management, such as wintering trees in September, pruning heavily, watering and manuring abundantly may produce a crop ; but west of Ootacamand the crop, except that of apples, is very problematical. Enormous crops of St. Michael and Malta oranges of a fine flavour have been obtained at Coonoor by skilled management—300 dozen of oranges from a single tree. Good pears have been produced on the slopes of Doddabetta, also strawberries ; but it requires generations, especially in such a climate as the Hills, to produce a first-class fruit-grower. It took three generations of Rivers', each man living to seventy and upwards, to produce the present Rivers, the greatest of

CH. XXVII. AGRICULTURE.

fruit-growers in England; hence in an equally difficult climate we may presume it will require the same amount of time and experience. The Hills produce a few fruits naturally, the hill guava, Brazil cherry, gualtheria, jamburs, wild strawberry, white and red raspberry and blackberry.

Market prices.

The vegetable market may be considered to be fairly well supplied; but the Natives, who are the principal market-gardeners, hardly aim at excellence, for which there are two reasons, first, that people's butlers, as they are called, do the marketing; this lets in the vicious system of "dustoorie," or what the Yankees call "stealings." The fellow yclept butler buys field peas and charges the price of marrow-fats to his mistress. The unfortunate grower of marrow-fats has the field pea price quoted, and is offered the same; the spirit of excelling is utterly cowed within him; there is no one to appreciate his efforts, and shortly he gives up marrow-fat growing and subsides into field peas. Thus it is with everything. Some few years ago an Agri-Horticulturist Society was established; shows were organized, prizes were given to Natives for the production of superior vegetables, good seeds were distributed, and for a time some impression was made; the market-gardener improved in his productions, and things looked promising; but unfortunately death stepped in—the able Commissioner, Mr. Breeks, who took the greatest interest in these matters, was carried off; members left, and once more the ever-present butler had it all his own way, and surprise is felt that such a climate and soil should be incapable of yielding vegetables equal to those grown in England.

Live-stock.

The live stock of these Hills may be considered to be of an inferior description, due to the following causes: first, the want of nourishment in the natural grasses; second, the excessive drought from January to April, occasioned by a hot sun during the day and frosts at night. During the three months of January, February, and March, the cattle, unless fed in sheds, are starved, and no breed in the world could thrive under such conditions. Indeed, even in England, a century ago, so impossible was it to carry the cattle through the winter, that a large percentage was annually slaughtered and salted for winter consumption. By the growth of turnips and improved cultivation this system has been altered; and it may be said of these Hills that until the system of agriculture is entirely changed and cattle stall fed through the dry months, an improved breed of cattle cannot be expected. The same may even with greater force be said of sheep, for they must be fed through the dry weather or die. Various breeds have been introduced with but little success, as stall-feeding has been neglected. With oat-hay, fermented green

—cattle.

fodder, turnips, and low country grain and oil-cake, no doubt the climate will support an improved breed of cattle with every certainty of success. Country sheep at the third cross with English cannot be distinguished from English sheep.

The best method of improving the breed of cattle would be to import, say, a Kerry bull and cross him with the best Nellore and Guntoor cattle; the produce, if stall-fed, would be good milking cows and draught bullocks. For the warm climate of Coonoor or Kótagiri Mr. Robertson recommends the Devon breed ; these, if fed on Guinea grass, *Sorghum saccharatum,* lucerne, and maize, would no doubt do well.

—sheep.

For sheep an imported Cotswold ram crossed with a large woolly sheep bred in Mysore would be most likely to succeed. A cross of Leicester and China has been introduced, and for flavour of meat and early maturity left nothing to be desired; but from want of fresh blood the sheep became delicate, and many lambs were lost from inflammation of the lungs brought on by continued exposure to cold in the monsoon. Shelter at night is necessary.

—pigs.

The Berkshire breed of pig crossed with the China has succeeded admirably, but Nílagiri bacon and hams have never been a success, the absence of winter weather preventing the due curing of the same.

—horses.

Horses could no doubt be produced on these Hills, as it may be laid down that where oats can be grown horses can be bred. The Arab horse, after a year on the plateau, becomes fully acclimatized ; the Australian horse fills out in an astonishing manner; and a cross of a thorough-bred Arab horse and Australian mare would produce a very serviceable horse, worth at four years old some seven hundred rupees. Mules, too, could be bred with great advantage, provided that the jackass sires were of the best kind from Spain. Australia could furnish the mares.

—poultry.

All poultry flourishes here. The young should be raised in the dry months from January to May.

Diseases.

Cattle diseases of two kinds are very prevalent. Murrain or *Doddah Róghu* sometimes decimates the native herds. Consequent upon the system common amongst Tódas and Badagas of allowing the Kótas to preside over the carcase of every animal that dies, the skin and meat being the Kótas' perquisite, the men carry these off and thus infect neighbouring herds. Foot-and-mouth disease is not uncommon.

Treatment —murrain.

Treatment should be—*food,* conjee-water of rice or raggi. *Medicine*—mouth to be washed with carbolic acid and water, and a decoction of 30 water to 1 carbolic acid administered

CH. XXVII. — AGRICULTURE.

internally. Chlorate of potash one tablespoonful to one quart of water—half a pint twice a day. Animal kept warm and separate.

—foot-and-mouth disease.

Make the animal stand in marshy ground. Diet, soup of rice or raggi. Wash out the mouth with carbolic acid and water.

General remarks.

The agriculture of the Nílagiris may be truly described as being in the progressive stage: nothing but tea, coffee, and cinchona bark can at present pay the cost of transit to the coast. Potatoes, it is true, are exported, but in very limited quantities. Until a railway from Mettapollium to Ootacamand is an accomplished fact agriculture must languish and the resources of the Hills remain undeveloped. It has been mentioned that the great want of the Hills is lime to develope the soil; the present rates of carriage being quite prohibitory, lime cannot be applied. The system of burying green fodder to ferment, if largely carried out on the Hills and in Wainád, where good grass is so abundant, would reduce the cost and risk of keeping all kinds of animals in the dry season. The cultivation of too large areas by the Badagas is a suicidal policy, and is the result of cheap land. Were the amount of labour and capital expended upon half the area, the results could not fail to be far more satisfactory than at present; but a Native is ever prone to have a greed for land, perhaps more so than Europeans, and it is very difficult to convince him that one acre well cultivated is far better and yields a better return than two indifferently farmed. In the Badaga valleys there are fair soils, an excellent climate, and a good market for many products which might be produced, but are not. In fact, if the Badagas would only exert their intelligence to grow good vegetables in addition to wheat, barley, raggi, and millet, they would soon improve their condition: they possess the intelligence, but not the assiduity. Much has been written about spade husbandry, and small European farmers have settled on various sites on the Hills, but hitherto no man has succeeded in realizing an ordinary living. It may be that the thrifty, hard-working, intelligent, small settler has never tried the Nílagiris, but only men deficient in those qualities so necessary for success in life. The retired soldier makes a bad settler in India; he has been accustomed to have so many things done for him that he has lost the art of doing anything for himself. The man who is not prepared to lead a frugal life and work hard need not hope to obtain a living from the soil, and it would only be by superior intelligence that he could with frugality and hard work succeed at all. Natives can afford to raise grain so cheaply in ordinary seasons that even high farming would hardly pay the European; nor, indeed, is it desirable that he should raise grain when he has so large a field open to his skill and capital in the cultivation of tea, cinchona, and coffee.

Much discussion has arisen regarding the sale of land by auction in opposition to selection, and various opinions have been given. This much may be said, that at a meeting some few years ago of various officials and non-officials the unanimous opinion was that auctions were detrimental to the agricultural interests of the Hills, and their abolishment was strongly recommended.

CHAPTER XXVIII.

COFFEE CULTIVATION.

Introduction.

Introduction of the coffee plant into South India.—Abbé Dubois.—Coffee on the Baba Booden Hills—in the Wainád—on the Nílagiris.—Major Ouchterlony's note.—The Ouchterlony Valley.—Area of coffee land under cultivation in the district.—Statistics of coffee exports.—Estimation of cost of cultivation and profits.—Books on coffee cultivation.

CH. XXVIII. — COFFEE CULTIVATION. — Introduction of coffee into South India. Abbé Dubois.

The coffee plant, belonging to the great order of Cinchonaceæ,[1] was introduced into South India towards the end of the eighteenth century, probably by Arab merchants trading to the West Coast. The first notice of the cultivation is contained in a letter from the Abbé Dubois to Colonel Miller, Resident of Mysore, dated 15th September 1805, replying to a request of the latter to obtain a man from the West Coast acquainted with the cultivation of the plant.[2] He writes :—

"I never understood that that plant grew in any part of the hills situated in the west of Mysore, although I have made many times enquiries on the subject with native botanists, who seem to have a tolerable knowledge of the plants of the country. However, as your information is by all means more extensive and more to be trusted than mine, I will not contradict it; but I may assure you that the produce of that plant (if it exist in the country) as an object of diet is entirely unknown to natives. That it would succeed if properly reared there can be no doubt. Any gentleman in this place (Seringapatam) who may cultivate for curiosity sake some plants of it will produce two crops in a year of good quality. * * * About ten years ago, when I was in the Baramahal, Colonel Read, Collector in that part of the country, undertook to make a large plantation at Tripatur by the means of an American he sent for from the coast, and to whom he gave a monthly pay of 25 pagodas. The plantation I saw many times had thriven well during the first year, and promised success, but the manager proving a man without conduct, Colonel Read was so soon disgusted of his services and dismissed him. At the same time, having found no one to replace him, and perceiving besides that the produce of that kind of cultivation would in no case equal the expenses necessary in that part of the country, the plantation was suffered to perish."

---

[1] Three plants of the order are said to be indigenous to the Nílagiris—*Coffea alpestris, grannuloides,* and *Wightiana* (*vide* Simmonds' *Tropical Agriculture*).

[2] Papers relating to the Coffee Districts, Madras, 1859.

CH. XXVIII. COFFEE CULTIVATION.

Coffee on the Baba Booden Hills.

Colonel Wilks mentions that a garden existed in the Baba Booden Hills,[1] attached to a mosque; the seeds are said to have been brought from Mocha. Prior to this, however, in 1801 Dr. Buchanan mentions having seen coffee trees in a very thriving condition near Tellicherry, but they had not as yet borne fruit.

—in the Wainád.

The seed appears to have been introduced into the Wainád from Anjarakandi by Major Brown in 1828. This was the beginning of the plantations in the neighbourhood of Manantoddi. Not long before this a few Europeans had begun to plant coffee in the Baba Booden Hills, and some years later on the Menzirabad mountain, the home of the celebrated Cannon's coffee. These plantations were practically the parents of coffee in Southern India.[2]

—on the Nílagiris.

Although coffee planting had been begun thus early in Wainád, it was not until the year 1839 that the cultivation became an enterprise, and about the same time the first gardens were formed on the Nílagiris. The cultivation of the plant on the Shevaroys had preceded its introduction into the Nílagiris, a plantation having been formed on the former hills about 1830. The extension however of the cultivation was rapid in the Wainád and more gradual on the Nílagiris, but in 1847 it had been fully established even in the latter tract, and by the year 1863-64 there were probably forty estates in various parts of the district.

Major Ouchterlony's remarks.

The following extract from Major Ouchterlony's Memoir in this year is deserving of record.

Coffee.

Numerous plantations of coffee trees are scattered about the Hills, principally situated on the slopes descending to the plains, where the elevation suitable for the growth of this shrub can be obtained. Until within the last two or three years, coffee plantations were only found on the eastern side of the Hills, but representations of the excellent quality of the berry, and of the advantages attending its cultivation

---

[1] "According to tradition the coffee-plant was introduced into Mysore by a Mahommadan pilgrim named Baba Booden, who came and took up his abode in the uninhabited hills in the Naggur Division, named after him, and where he established a college, which still exists, endowed by Government. It is said that he brought seven coffee berries from Mocha, which he planted near to his hermitage, about which there are now to be seen some very old coffee trees. The coffee plant has been known there from time immemorial; but the earliest official account of it is in 1822, when the revenue was under contract."—DRURY's *Useful Plants of India*. *See* also Colonel Onslow's remarks quoted in Shortt's Coffee-planting. In 1822 the revenue derived in Mysore from coffee was only 4,270 rupees annually; by 1837 it had risen to 7,472 rupees. The produce taxed in 1843 was 15,238 maunds of 28 lb.; in 1849 it had risen to 52,236 maunds; in 1861, 346,083 maunds.

[2] It will be remembered that Dr. Wallich and Mr. Gordon began coffee planting in Bengal in 1823 (*see* Chapter XIII), and that their enterprise led to the promulgation of the first code of rules for the sale of waste lands. In the preceding year the enterprise had been begun in Ceylon by Sir Edward Barnes and Mr. George Bird.

CH. XXVIII.

COFFEE CULTIVATION.

on the Neilgherries, having been made in Ceylon, the attention of the skilful planters of that island was attracted in this direction, and the result has been the opening of several plantations, where I ventured to predict, in a former memoir, that this description of cultivation would sooner or later be introduced, viz., on the western slopes of the Hills, where advantages are offered to the planter eminently superior to those, the possession of which has, of late years, so greatly enhanced the value and importance of the neighbouring islands.[1]

Cheap labour, 4 rupees a month.

The chief of all is the cheapness of labour, a cooly receiving even on distant plantations in the "Koondahs" 4 rupees a month, while in Ceylon 8, 9 and even 10 are given; while in the pay of artizans such as carpenters, sawyers, masons, &c., a still greater disparity exists in favor of this district.[2] Second to this is the abundance of labour which can always be commanded here, the neighbouring provinces of Malabar, Mysore and Coimbatore supplying coolies in sufficient numbers to meet all demands, and at all seasons of the year; while in Ceylon the utmost difficulty is experienced in most parts to obtain labourers when urgently required; and at all times the supply of coolies is extremely precarious. Planters here have also the advantage of a good public road passing through the heart of the forest land of the "Koondahs," and affording ready means for obtaining supplies, machinery, &c., or of sending away produce for shipment by a route, of which less than 30 miles are by land and 36 by water, to the port of Calicut.[3] One estate which was opened about two years ago near "Wallahkadoo," half-way down the Koondah ghaut, by the late Archdeacon of Ceylon and Mr. Hutson, also of that island, and which I had an opportunity of inspecting recently on my way up from the Western Coast, is in a very flourishing condition, and has every promise of turning out most successfully. In its neighbourhood are tracts of virgin forest land of immense extent, stretching away over the innumerable spurs and valleys into which the Koondahs are broken as they slope downwards towards the Ponany river, all eminently suitable for coffee planting, having the proper elevation, a good and rich soil, and enjoying a climate particularly favourable to the nourishment of this peculiar shrub. If the success which is looked for crowns the exertions and adventure of the first speculators, there can be little doubt that when the Koondah coffee appears regularly in the market as a production of this district, the attention of capitalists at home will be directed to it, and the western portion of this mountain tract become a source of great increase to the revenue of the country, while it will afford employment and subsistence to the many indigent people in the neighbouring provinces, who, at the

Western slopes of the Kúndas well suited for coffee cultivation.

---

[1] Works on Coffee Cultivation by Shortt, Hull, and Laborie, have been published by Higginbotham and Co., Madras.—ED.

[2] The market value of cooly and other labour has risen considerably since this memoir was published. A cooly now receives 6 annas per day, children 2 annas; farm servants, gardeners, &c. 8 rupees per mensem; carpenter 1¼ rupee, bricklayer 1 rupee, a day.—ED.

[3] The Sisapára Ghát is little used now.—ED.

present time, suffer such privations from the want of it, between the seasons of sowing and reaping the crops in the plains, and indeed for more than three-quarters of the year.

Plantations at Coonoor and Kótagiri too high.

The other, or what may be called the old plantations in the other parts of the Hills, but principally on the north-eastern slopes, are insignificant in point of size but remarkable for the peculiarly fine flavour of the coffee produced, which is considered to be owing to the high elevation at which most of them are situated. Some plantations near Coonoor and Kotergherry are 5,000 feet above the level of the sea, but it seems to me that the advantage derived from this superiority of flavour is more than counterbalanced by the general want of vigour and luxuriance of the coffee trees, which evidently do not thrive in this latitude so well at an elevation above 4,500 feet, as between that and 3,000 feet. It is not easy to estimate the amount of land at present under actual cultivation for coffee on the Neilgherries, as, in most cases, the coffee fields are so mixed up with the mulberry grounds, that it is difficult to arrive at the precise extent of each, but it may be pronounced not to exceed 280 acres on the eastern side, and 300 acres on the western. The general return of those on the eastern side, which are the only ones at present in bearing, is on an average about 6 to 7 cwt. per acre, which is a remunerative rate under the prevailing circumstances of cheap labour, but the trees require manure to keep them up to this rate of bearing, and more care in pruning and managing than is bestowed upon them.

Ouchterlony Valley.

The opening of the Ouchterlony Valley, the finest coffee tract in the district, was begun by the late Mr. James Ouchterlony about 1850. The difficulties encountered by this able and energetic pioneer in coffee planting are thus graphically described in a letter to Government in 1860:—

"I was equally a pioneer in the experiment of coffee planting on the Nilgiri slope near the Gudalur Pass, where I first commenced the cultivation. In a limited degree many of the features of a new colony were then presented: there was no resident population within any accessible distance; no articles of food to be had near the spot; we had no roads (properly so called), no police, and no law save at courts too distant to be reached. Labour and food had, in fact, to be imported from a remote district, the first being only obtained with difficulty, and then often scared away by the solitariness of the spot and an undefined dread of evil in the minds of the coolies. Doubts of success were even engendered in the minds of most of those who had embarked with me in the enterprise, and who necessarily withdrew from it. But at length a bright issue attended the efforts; and I will only say, let the changed aspect of the country around in respect of cultivation tell what the effect has been upon the general interests."

The area now under cultivation in this valley exceeds 4,000 acres.

Area now under cultivation in the district.

Coffee planting has now been tried on various portions of the slopes, and so far it seems to have succeeded best in the valleys and slopes to the east, to the south, and to the north-west

CH. XXVIII.

COFFEE CULTIVATION.

of the plateau, though there are some fine plantations lying towards the north-east; but generally speaking the northern slopes are too deficient in rainfall, and the western, *i.e.*, the Kúnda range, too much exposed to the violence of the south-west monsoon. The following statement shows the area under occupation and coffee cultivation according to the latest return in 1876-77. The subsequent returns include portion of the South-East Wainád.

Estates.	Elevation.	Area.		Taken up but not planted.	Total.	Approximate yield.
		Mature Plants.	Immature Plants.			
	FEET.	ACRES.	ACRES.	ACRES.	ACRES.	LB.
132 ...	3,000 to 6,000	11,184	2,434	6,825	20,443	3,560,480

Statistics of coffee exports.

The following are statistics of coffee exports from the Madras Presidency. In 1824-25 the quantity was 768,320 lb., value 1,79,764 rupees. For the five years ending 1830-31 it averaged 356,739 lb., value 59,912 rupees. The figures show no very significant variations until 1843-44, the average of the twelve preceding years being only 393,379 lb., value 75,277 rupees. In 1843-44 the exports rose to 811,000 lb., value 1,52,000 rupees ; in 1845-46 to 1,699,152 lb., value 2,69,750 rupees. The following year shows a slight decrease. Up to the close of this year the figures include re-exports, but in what proportion they stood to exports proper I am unaware. The exports proper in 1847-48 stood at 2,206,900 lb., value Rupees 3,38,000, but by the close of 1850-51 the figures had risen to 4,757,135 lb., value Rupees 4,79,000. By the close of 1855-56 they had reached 8,601,000 lb., value 8,92,000 rupees. The next five years saw a rise to 18,571,000 lb., value 32,41,000 rupees. These were nearly doubled by 1865-66, being 34,527,000 lb., value 78,13,000 rupees. They remained nearly stationary during the following five years, being 55,484,000 lb., value Rupees 82,84,000 in 1870-71, and showed only a slight rise in quantity in 1874-75, being 36,652,000 lb., but great in value, 1,36,13,000 rupees.

The figures for the following four years were :—

Years.	Quantity.	Value.
	LB.	RS.
1875-76	45,092,000	1,74,27,000
1876-77	36,166,000	1,43,32,000
1877-78	33,399,000	1,35,56,000
1878-79	38,476,000	1,56,01,000

Taking the area of coffee cultivation in the district at 12,000 acres roughly, of the quantity exported in 1876-77 probably not less than 4,500,000 lb. came from this district, excluding South-East Wainád, in value about 20 lakhs of rupees.

Estimate of cost of cultivation and profits. In the following paper by Mr. Steedman the principal points connected with the cultivation are carefully and clearly summarised. It contains, at my desire, no elaborated estimate of forming a plantation, as the cost differs in various parts of the district according to facilities of labour, nature of soil, and many other conditions. In Mr. Hull's work on coffee planting in South India and Ceylon a fairly approximate estimate will be found. It may be roughly stated that, exclusive of cost of land but inclusive of buildings, machines, roads, &c., it costs between 300 and 400 rupees an acre to bring a moderate sized estate of (say) 200 acres into full bearing. The cost of working may be set at 130 rupees per acre. The yield may be estimated at 4 cwts. per acre. This, at 50 rupees net per cwt., gives 200 rupees, an excess of 70 rupees over charges, or approximately 20 per cent. on capital expended, exclusive of shipping and brokerage charges, &c.[1]

Books on coffee cultivation. The works on the subject deserving especial mention are Mr. H. M. Elliot's "Coffee-planting in Mysore and Coorg," Dr. J. Shortt's "Hand-book to Coffee-planting in Southern India," Dr. Bidie's "The Borer," and Mr. H. P. Hull's "Coffee-planting in Southern India and Ceylon." A mass of general information on the subject will be found in P. L. Simmonds' treatise on "Tropical Agriculture."

MONOGRAPH ON THE CULTIVATION OF COFFEE.

(*By* A. H. STEEDMAN, Esq., *Balcarres Estate, Wainád.*)

Selection of land—elevation—opening out land—nurseries—shade—felling—burning—road tracing—lining—pitting—planting—weeding—draining—handling and pruning.—Manuring—composts—poudrette—fish-manure—bones—blood and slaughter-house refuse—guano—superphosphate of lime.—Irrigation.—Buildings—bungalow—cooly lines—pulper-house and store—barbacues and drying tables—cattle sheds.—Machinery—sprouting—pulper.—Crop—picking and curing.—Enemies of the coffee plant—bug—the borer—the coffee rat—leaf rot—leaf disease—its remedies.

Selection of land. In selecting a site for a coffee plantation a variety of considerations must be taken into account, and, foremost amongst

---

[1] Taking the area under coffee in bearing in the Presidency at 190,000 acres (Mysore 125,000, Madras districts 50,000, and Travancore 15,000), the exports, including Travancore, at 375,000 cwts., the internal consumption at 75,000 cwts., we have the average yield of coffee rather over 2½ cwts. per acre including native cultivation. These figures would seem to indicate that the margin of profit can

CH. XXVIII. — COFFEE CULTIVATION.

these, it behoves the planter to ascertain that the land which it is proposed to take up possesses a stream of water which runs all the year round, or, at any rate, will continue to flow until the crop season is over; for without a sufficient supply of water it is impossible to pulp the coffee. Unless, therefore, the land in question possesses a stream, or there are facilities for leading water from no great distance, the selector must make up his mind either to abandon it or to follow the native plan and dry his coffee in the cherry, which plan not only entails a serious diminution in the value of his coffee, but, in cases of plantations of any extent, is really impracticable owing to the enormous extent of drying ground that would be requisite. Then the land should be sheltered from the wind, situated, if possible, in the line of the showers which fall early in the year and go far to ensure good crops, and should not be exposed to the full fury of either the south-west or north-east monsoon, with the accompanying excessive damp and constant and injurious mists and fogs. Great care should be taken that frost never affects the land, as this is fatal to coffee, scorching and withering it as if fire had passed over it. Another deadly enemy to coffee is damp at the roots, so that swampy land or land that is nearly flat must be well drained before it will grow coffee.

—elevation. The range for coffee varies from about 3,000 to 4,500 or even to 6,000 feet on the eastern slopes above the sea level, and about the best possible site that could be selected is a well sheltered valley with a gentle declivity and a stream flowing through the centre. It should also be remembered that the greater the altitude the finer the quality of the berry, which is to a certain extent only neutralized by the smaller quantity yielded.

—opening out land. Having selected and obtained his land, the first thing for the planter to do is to run up temporary huts or cooly lines, unless he can rely upon a sufficiency of local labour, such as Badagas or Kúrumbas, to fell, pit, and plant his land. To save time and labour the planter should make arrangements to purchase plants from some of his neighbours, and these can usually be bought in sufficient numbers at from 8 to 12 rupees per thousand; but, if this is impracticable or the planter has a fancy for importing seed from a distance, he should lose no time in making a nursery.

—nurseries. A plot of ground as nearly level as possible and close to water should be selected, carefully dug all over to the depth of 2 or even 3 feet, all the stones picked out and beds made about

---

be but small, or about £2-10 per acre. If, however, the small yield of coffee cultivated in native gardens be taken into consideration, and the fact that abandoned or quasi-abandoned lands are often included in the areas returned, the net average profits probably do not fall short of £5 per acre, or £1,000 per annum for an estate of 200 acres.

4 feet in width and 10 or 12 in length with trenches between, down which the water may be led, so that there may be no difficulty in watering the plants. If cattle manure is easily procurable, it would be well to scatter a quantity broadcast over the beds and then dig it well in. The seed should be pushed in with the finger about an inch below the surface of the soil and carefully covered over, and when the seedlings spring up (which will vary very much in time according to locality,) and are about 2 inches above ground, they should be transplanted out at distances of about 6 or even 9 inches apart, so as to allow of their growing into healthy, sturdy plants. The nursery should be kept carefully watered and weeded, and a sufficient number of coolies should be told off specially to this duty. Some people erect a pandal or grass covering over their nurseries, but I think this is unnecessary if there is plenty of water. My own experience of planting seed is very unsatisfactory. A quantity obtained by me from one of the finest plantations on the Coonoor side was carefully planted in December 1874—a very large percentage of the plants threaten to turn out chicks—all were severely affected with leaf-disease (*Hemeleia vastatrix*), and a large quantity of the seed came to nothing. A friend in South Wainád, who obtained carefully selected seed from Ceylon, where they profess to have comparatively few chicks (so called from Chickmuglúr, from which place this miserable species has unfortunately been introduced), assured me that a very large percentage of this seed turned into chicks. Were I to plant seed again, I should be very much inclined to obtain either some of the renowned Cannon's Mysore, or else some from Travancore. My advice to a young planter would be, buy good plants, if you can, and, if this is impossible, plant seedlings in your nursery, taking care only to obtain those growing under or near fine healthy trees; and these seedlings, if well and carefully planted and tended in the nursery, ought to be ready for planting out in about eight months. A good, though rather expensive, plan is to plant the seedlings in small cane baskets, and then they can be planted out in the pits just as they stand, the basket soon decaying. This plan has the additional advantage that plants in baskets will stand a good deal of dry sunny weather without dying, and so can be planted out during the early showers in April and May, whilst as supplies amongst old coffee they are much more likely to succeed than any other.

CH. XXVIII. — COFFEE CULTIVATION.

—shade.

Before going any further, the planter should make up his mind whether he will make a clean sweep of the forest or leave some trees standing for the purposes of shade. The idea seems to be gaining ground that shade of one kind or another is the only real safeguard against attacks of leaf-disease, borer, and a

CH. XXVIII. — COFFEE CULTIVATION.

general decay and death of the coffee plant. In some parts of Mysore the coffee is regularly planted under the shade of the jungle, which is merely thinned out; and this plan saves, I have no doubt, a great deal of expense in weeding, &c.; but then the yield is very small indeed, not more, as a rule, than 2 cwts. per acre, as I am informed.

Whilst shade may be absolutely necessary in some exceptionally dry climates, I consider that it still remains to be seen if it will answer generally and prove the panacea that many predict; still, in the face of the continued serious attacks of leaf-disease, it is perhaps wise to try every prescription in the hope of ultimately overcoming this terrible plague. If the planter wishes to try the effect of shade, it would be well to leave trees standing at sufficient distances apart to allow of a moderate amount of light and sunshine reaching the coffee. The planting of the various kinds of wild fig, dwarf plantain and other trees for the purposes of shade, which is now largely done on many old plantations, is a tedious and costly operation, which the planter who has made up his mind on the question of shade and who is just starting, would do well to avoid by the simple expedient suggested above of leaving certain trees standing while felling the rest of the jungle or forest. Many however contend, and with some show of justice, that if shade trees—as jack and the various kinds of wild fig—are planted at the same time with the coffee, they will have grown sufficiently for purposes of shade by the time that shade is really required.

—felling. The best and simplest plan, if it can be managed, is to have the felling done by contract as is now generally done in Wainád, but, as far as I can learn, the old terms of felling at the rate of 10 rupees per acre with Kúrumbas or Punniahs are now past, and it will cost fully 15 rupees if not more. If the work is not done by contract and paid for after a rough and approximate survey is made, the planter should keep a close and constant watch over the coolies engaged, as felling is very hard and tiring work, and a cooly has not the very remotest idea of a really honest day's work unless well looked after and not allowed to shirk.

—burning. The forest having been felled, the usual plan is to allow the whole to stand for six or eight weeks until the branches and smaller saplings are dry and then to set fire, when a grand conflagration usually follows. The burn, as it is called, whilst clearing the way for the pitters and producing, as is natural, a quantity of ash, destroys the fine mould and soil which has been accumulating for years, and which is so very valuable for coffee.

But few planters, however, have the courage to incur the trouble and expense of lopping and piling the brushwood and branches in heaps and leaving the mass to decay (or even of burying, as has been done), which is rendered necessary if the aid of fire is not invoked. On one plantation in Wainád this plan was followed and the result, according to report, is a yield of more than a ton an acre, and this not once but repeatedly; but this is a long, tedious, and expensive operation, and is not likely to be the plan generally adopted.

—road tracing.

After the burn, and having selected a site for the store and pulper-house near a stream and as near the bottom of the estate as possible—since it is easier for the coolies to carry the picked coffee down than up hill,—it will be well to trace a cart or bandy road from the entrance of the plantation to the site of the proposed store. At the same time, in order to avoid making unnecessary pits or having to pull up plants subsequently, it is advisable to trace as many narrower paths as may be requisite, to enable the planter to go all over the plantation, for he may rely upon it that it is a great mistake to overtask himself or the coolies by rambling up and down hill more than is unavoidably necessary.

—lining.

And next comes the important task of lining, upon which depends in a great measure not only the symmetrical appearance of the plantation but the facility with which weeding, picking, manuring, and the various contract works are checked and examined. The best plan is to take two base lines running from north to south and east to west by the aid of a cross staff or road-tracer to ensure accuracy. Then having provided a number of pegs and a piece of stout hempen rope, with the distances marked off by means of pieces of cloth twisted into the strands as in a log line, and a pole to mark off the width between the lines, the planter should station two coolies one at each end of the line, and, commencing from the base line, should proceed to put down the pegs in parallel lines. The old rule used to be 6 feet by 6 feet apart, but my experience is that the proper distance is 6 feet by 5 feet, except in cases where the soil is unusually rich and the growth uncommonly luxuriant. Stumps and logs will more or less tend to throw the lines out a little, but if the planter insists upon the cooly making the pit exactly where the peg is placed, the lines will come out in the end with beautiful regularity. The marks on the hempen line will require occasionally to be set right in consequence of the unavoidable stretching of the rope. This need for correction is experienced even with the Surveyor's chain.

—pitting.

Armed with mamoties (some planters supply planting bars as well) and an axe to every three or four coolies to cut through

CH. XXVIII. — COFFEE CULTIVATION. —

roots, &c., the coolies should now be set to pitting. The usual contract is 25 pits, 2 feet cube, per man, or 10 rupees per thousand, and the planter should see that the pits are made full size, and that roots and stones are carefully taken out, as also that the pits are made exactly where the pegs were placed. These pits should be allowed to stand open till shortly before the rains set in, when they should be filled in with soil from the jungle (which would be a good, though an expensive, plan) or else with the surrounding earth, stones being carefully rejected and the peg replaced in the centre of the pit for a guide when planting.

—planting. Some planters maintain that it is not a good plan to plant during heavy rain or very early in the monsoon; but having planted in all weathers, I think that one cannot begin too soon after the rain has once fairly set in. At the same time the most favourable season (if you are so fortunately situated from having abundance of labour and work being well in hand as to be enabled to pick your days) is during dull showery weather. If the plants come from the planter's own nursery, a good though expensive plan is to take up each plant with a ball of earth attached and plant it thus in the pit, but with balls a cooly will not plant more than 60 or 70, and if the plants are brought from any distance this is out of the question. If planted without balls, the cooly should be provided with a sharp-pointed stick, with which he makes a hole in the loose earth of the pit, inserts the plant, gives it a slight pull upwards to provide against the tap-root being twisted, and then, with hand or foot, presses the earth firmly down all round the plant. A cooly should plant out 200 or 250 in this way, and should be carefully watched to see that he does not plant two in a pit, or even throw some away in order to get over his task the sooner.

—weeding. In about two months' time, or perhaps less, the newly-planted land will require weeding, and it will be a good thing if the planter makes two resolutions: the first, to keep constantly weeding so as never to allow the weeds to seed or get ahead of him, and secondly, never to allow a mamoty to be used in weeding. With constant care and attention hand-weeding can easily get rid of all the weeds, and these being few and far between, the weeding will be cheap and expeditious, as each cooly will easily be able to run over three or four long lines. In the evil olden days, when the rule was to take as much out of the soil as possible and high cultivation was unknown, the weeds were allowed to grow until they threatened to smother the coffee, and then gangs of coolies were sent with mamoties, and they dug and scratched away till, what with this constant scrape of the mamoty and the wash caused by the heavy monsoon rain, most of the old estates have lost all their surface-soil, and it is almost hopeless to expect to get the estates thoroughly clean. Indeed, some go so far as to say, cut down the weeds once or twice a year, and for the rest trust to manuring and pruning; but it seems to me a fatal mistake to disregard weed, though at the same time I would never allow a mamoty to be used for the purpose. Digging up and loosening the soil is a very good thing on very gentle slopes, but in my opinion, in the majority of cases, the less the soil is touched the better, as the great majority of coffee plantations are on very steep inclines, and the wash and loss of soil is very great.

A great variety of weeds are to be found on a coffee plantation—ferns, goat-weed or *ageratum*, Spanish needle, a thorn called the wild brinjal, the Sisapára creeper, the jungle sand-paper or fig (which, if allowed, grows into a tree), and a number of varieties of grasses, the Hurriali, the thatching grass, Dubber-ooloo, and a creeping grass of whose name I am ignorant, which last forms a regular mat on the surface of the soil, and is, in my opinion, the most pernicious of all. According to Dr. Bidie, the most hurtful weed is the goat-weed, which is said to take up all the ingredients which coffee requires.

—drainage.

As almost all coffee plantations are situated on steep slopes, the object of drainage is not so much to get rid of superfluous water as to prevent its carrying away soil in its rush. I am not a believer in an elaborate system of main and catch drains, which, as far as I have seen, are continually filling up, overflowing, and end in cutting dreadful chasms. If stones are abundant, as is often the case, the best plan, I think, is to revet or build round the lower surface of each tree; and if this is carefully done, the tree finally stands in a kind of natural flower-pot, and the lower surface instead of being sloped with the slope of the hill (thus exposing the roots) is flush with the upper surface. Renovation pits or trenches 3 or 4 feet long by 1 foot broad and 2 feet deep should be dug between each alternate group of four trees, and these pits not only serve to catch the soil which is washed down, but act as receptacles for weeds. Some planters make use of them as manure pits. As soon as these pits are filled up fresh pits between the alternate groups of four trees should be dug, and when the time comes round for the first pits to be opened the soil in them can be heaped up round the roots of the trees. Were it not for the constant and unceasing washing down of the soil that goes on, this heaping up of earth round the root of the trees would very likely cause rot, canker, and disease; but as it is, it only replaces what is being constantly washed away. A cooly can dig twenty-five to thirty of these renovation pits. Some planters, I believe, build terraces, but not having tried this plan

CH. XXVIII. — COFFEE CULTIVATION. —

myself or seen it done, I cannot say if it has answered. One planter in Ceylon proposed to take out a patent for prevention of wash by means of cylinders, made of wood, earthenware or iron, but the project fell through.

As coffee is very intolerant of constant damp at the roots, it is an absolute necessity to deeply drain the swamps, which, when thus treated, grow magnificent coffee and yield very heavy crops.

It may seem presumptuous, in the face of so many authorities who are strongly in favour of drains, to speak against them ; but my experience shows me that on the steep slopes which characterize most of the coffee plantations water does not stand but soon runs off; and whilst it is true that estates which are exposed to the full fury of the south-west monsoon do suffer from damp, I can only explain the seeming anomaly by saying that it appears to me that the excessive moisture is in the air, and that the best plan to counteract this is to keep the trees thoroughly well weeded and handled.

—handling and pruning.

When the plants are about two and a half or three years old (though this depends in some measure upon the climate, soil, and situation of the plantaticn), the trees will need topping to prevent their growing any taller. Coffee trees are usually topped at 3½ to 4 feet, but in windy or exposed situations they should be topped at 2 or 2½ feet in order to protect them as much as possible against being blown about. If alowed to grow at its own pleasure—and this is to be seen in native gardens—coffee will grow to a height of 15 to 20 feet with a number of stems and but few lateral branches. This is the plan followed in Arabia, where the berries are not picked as with us, but shaken off when fully ripe on to mats placed beneath the trees and then dried in the sun. Handling—an operation performed by hand and not with a knife—consists in pulling off the suckers or shoots which spring out from the stem, and which, if allowed to grow up, would grow into stems, and also in stripping off all the lateral branches (within a radius of 6 inches from the stem) sent out by the primaries, so as to allow of air and light reaching the centre of the tree. If cut off with a knife these suckers shoot out again with redoubled rapidity. Pruning, or the use of the knife, if systematically carried out from the opening of the plantation, is comparatively a simple operation, and consists in checking the tendency of the tree to run to wood and leaf instead of fruit, and the severity or leniency of pruning must, to a certain extent, depend upon climate. The coffee tree throws out pairs of lateral branches at right angles to each other and at distances of about 6 inches apart, which branches are called primaries and should never be cut off. These,

COFFEE CULTIVATION.

in their turn, send out alternate smaller branches called secondaries, and these, if allowed, throw out tertiaries. The tertiaries and every alternate secondary should be cut off, and occasionally from overbearing or weakness the ends of the primaries will die, when they should be cut back to the live wood. Some planters scarcely prune at all for two or three years, and then cut the trees to sticks; but the best plan is to prune steadily and regularly so as to ensure, as far as possible, a regular fair average crop instead of a bumper every now and then, with intermediate years of very small crops and rest for the trees. In old plantations where regular pruning has been neglected; drastic measures are often necessary, and in one notable instance, the planter gradually went through the whole of his plantation stumping or cutting down the trees to within a foot of the ground and then manured those stumps, and he has been nobly rewarded, for his plantation is now one of the finest in the district. The usual plan is to prune as soon as crop is finished and before the coolies leave for their country, and this plan has been strongly recommended; but if the planter has permanent labour always at command, pruning, in my opinion, should be deferred till showery weather, as the trees then bleed less, or, in other words, lose less sap than in hot sunny weather. The prunings should be carefully buried.

Manuring.

This is a subject on which there are perhaps more differences of opinion than on any other connected with planting. The best kind of manure, the best mode of applying it, as well as the quantity necessary, are still and are likely to remain vexed questions. Up to within the last few years high cultivation was quite the exception instead of the rule, and the results of this negligent treatment of the soil are startlingly put forth by Mr. Robertson, of the Model Farm in Madras, and in Mr. Schrottky's late work. Coffee-planters might, perhaps, have gone on for some time longer following the old plan despite the warning of bug and borer, but that fearful pest—the *Hemeleia vastatrix*—has startled them from their lethargy, and most are now awake to the fact that the choice only lies between high cultivation and ruin.

—cattle-manure.

This is generally allowed to be the best manure, and is said to contain almost if not all the ingredients required by coffee. The complaint made by some planters of its bulky nature and consequent expensiveness scarcely needs an answer, but the most telling argument against it is that grazing is limited; that only a certain number of cattle can be maintained on the grass-land usually attached to each plantation; and that until some such fodder as the prickly comfrey (*Symphytum asperrimum*) or the *Sorghum saccharatum*, which are *said* to flourish without manure and yield large quantities of food, are widely introduced, stall-

CH. XXVIII. — COFFEE CULTIVATION.

feeding to any large extent is out of the question. It is quite possible that ere long, under the pressure of reduced crops with increased expenditure, planters will follow the advice offered them by Dr. Bidie in his able and interesting Report on the Ravages of the Borer and Review of the existing Systems of Coffee Culture, and, abandoning the poorer portions of their estates, concentrate their efforts and expenditure on the finest fields of coffee. The abandoned fields might then be planted up with these much-praised fodder plants, and the herds of cattle might be largely augmented and stall-feeding become general. Cattle-manure should be well pulverized and mixed with jungle soil and a bushel applied to each tree, and even though the cattle may have been fed upon nothing but grass, the effect upon coffee is little short of marvellous. The usual plan is to apply manure after the crop season is over and before the coolies depart to their country, but if possible it should, in my opinion, be put out between the end of the monsoon and the picking season. In those very exceptional cases where the coffee grows on a very gentle slope there can be no better mode of application than to scatter the manure broadcast and then dig it well in, the mere forking or trenching of the ground where practicable being of great assistance to the trees; but I believe that this method is out of question on the generality of coffee estates. Whilst some bury the manure to the extent of two and even three bushels in the renovation pits and others dig shallow semi-circular pits above the trees, the plan I think most effectual is to remove the soil above the tree with a manuring fork, put in the manure, and replace the soil. The showers will soak through and carry the virtue of the manure to the lower roots. From all that I can read and learn, horticulturists ever strive to make fruit trees as much as possible surface-feeders, even to the extent of forcing them to do this by paving the subsoil with broken tiles, &c.

—composts. Some planters, however, do not own any grass-land, and are thus practically debarred from using cattle-manure; but it is always open to them to utilize the weeds, pulp, line refuse, ash, &c., which, with the aid of lime or chunam to hasten decomposition, make a valuable manure, and the planter cannot do better than study the Prize Essays on Manuring written by Mr. Arnold and Mr. G. White, both of Ceylon, which were published by the Planters' Association of that island.

—poudrette. Some planters in Wainád used to obtain poudrette prepared with ashes and dry earth from Ootacamand. Planters near Coonoor purchase the right of cleaning out the latrines, and use this manure in a liquid state more or less. It appears to me that the manure is more efficacious when used in a liquid state.

Large quantities of a kind of sprat are caught near Calicut and sent up in neat parcels in vast quantities to Wainád. Well mixed with pulp and jungle soil, I have found this manure very efficacious. I apply about a quarter of a bushel to each tree, and reckon that it takes a ton of fish to each acre; but I think the effect is not very lasting and that the manure should be applied yearly. Fish has long been used as manure for tea in Japan. CH. XXVIII. COFFEE CULTIVATION. —fish-manure.

Considering the vast herds of cattle slaughtered monthly in Australia and South America, and the large demand there would be for bone-manure if it were only well crushed and sold tolerably cheap, I am surprised that bone-crushing mills have not been started in those places and a large trade in bone-manure inaugurated. It is true that both crushed and steamed bones can be procured in India, but the price is very high, considering that, unless treated with sulphuric acid, this manure whilst lasting is slow in taking effect. Many planters hesitate to try so expensive a manure. I am informed that bone dust mixed with castor poonac makes a very fine manure, and I have found very good results from bone dust mixed with jungle soil. —bones.

This has been imported from Bombay by one of the firms at Calicut, but I am informed by a planter who tried it that it showed no results. —blood and slaughter-house refuse.

This is very expensive and very generally adulterated, and is usually considered too stimulating and evanescent in its effects. —guano.

Whether owing to adulteration or deterioration, this manure has by no means answered the expectations formed of it. —superphosphate of lime.

This mode of cultivation is but rarely employed, and my experience is that, except with a very large supply of water, and this favourably placed, it is impossible to do any good. Unfortunately just when irrigation is most required the streams are at their lowest, but perhaps something may be done towards saving and preserving the blossom in the absence of showers by the watering-engine of Messrs. Rhodes and Co., which has been used I learn with good effect by the agent of the Moyár Coffee Company. Irrigation.

These should be made as pucka and permanent as possible, as the constant renewal of temporary erections is not only twice or three times as expensive in the end, but takes up a vast amount of labour which might be much more beneficially employed in cultivation. Buildings.

Although, until the plantation is well under way—felled, pitted and planted—the planter may have to put up with a wattle-and-dab hut, he should not hesitate to erect a comfortable bungalow as soon as the labour can be spared, for, in order to keep his health, he must be comfortably housed. Some prefer wooden houses raised —bungalow.

CH. XXVIII. — COFFEE CULTIVATION. — from the ground on stone pillars, which may be obtained complete from Messrs. Massey and Co. of Calicut, or a substantial and tolerably cheap bungalow may be made of mud and stone walls faced with chunam and roofed with shingles, which, if made on the estate, cost Rupees 3-8-0 per thousand. Unfortunately these are apt to rot and be eaten by white-ants, and teak shingles are expensive, costing between 15 and 18 rupees per thousand. A very good kind of tile is manufactured at Calicut and Tellicherry, and if this were only glazed, it would make a perfect roof; as it is, those who have tried these tiles complain that they leak after the second or third monsoon. Most of the planters have been their own architects, and their bungalows, whilst as a rule not exactly ornamental, are useful and comfortable; but the great desideratum is a thoroughly water-proof roof: the best roof, though a very expensive one, is undoubtedly continuous iron covered by tiles. The site selected for the bungalow should be some hill above the coffee.

—cooly lines

Cooly lines should be built substantially of stone and mud or brick with shingle or tile roof, and provided with doors to each room or compartment. Planters usually reckon that a line 60 feet long by 12 or 15 feet broad and divided into 5 rooms will accommodate 40 or 50 coolies; but, as amongst the Kanarese there are a number of different castes, some of whom will not live in the same line with others, it is usually necessary to build two lines—one for the high and the other for the low caste coolies. The planter must always remember that without labour it is impossible to grow coffee, and that, whilst insisting upon obtaining a fair day's work for a fair day's wage (as things go in India), he should do everything in his power to make his coolies comfortable and healthy: pay them regularly and in person, and not through maistries; and then, unless the plantation is in an unhealthy district, he may rely upon it that his coolies will return to him year by year, as they are great creatures of habit, and as a rule unenterprizing and hard to turn out of the regular groove. The coolies are filthy in the extreme as regards their habits, and it is a matter of astonishment that fever and dysentery do not prove more often fatal. For sanitary purposes the planter should do his best to induce the coolies to make use of the renovation pits, and it may even in course of time become necessary for planters to erect regular latrines; but this entails keeping a number of scavengers or toties, as the lowest Pariah coolies would resolutely refuse to clean out these latrines. Chunam also might be frequently sprinkled about the lines.

—pulper-house and store.

The pulper-house should be erected rather above the store, unless the two are combined in one, the lower portion forming the pulper-house and the upper the store; but this combination building would scarcely answer except in the case of a small estate of 60 or 70 acres, or where there is always an abundant supply of bandies or bullocks to convey away the coffee as soon as it is ready. Some build their pulper-houses and stores entirely of wood, with wooden vats or cisterns, whilst others employ brick and chunam or Portland cement; but both are open to objection; the wooden cisterns shrink, rot, and are soon destroyed by white-ants so as to need renewing every second or third year, and the cement or chunam ones, though painted with tar, soon wash and wear away. A good and really permanent material both for pulper cisterns and barbacues has still to be found, but it has occurred to me that this material may perhaps be found in the liquid flint with which the floor of the Bombay Custom-house is paved; unless I have been misinformed, no planter has yet tried this. The following seems to me about the best kind of store to build if the combination pulper-house and store is not approved of. Stone and mud walls with large barred windows, to be closed if necessary with shutters; stone pillars about 3 feet high on which stout beams are placed, and on these rafters, over which are stretched rolls of double coir matting. This will ensure a thorough current of air, which will prevent the parchment coffee from getting heated and musty. In Ceylon, where they have rain almost throughout the crop season, Clerihew's apparatus for driving a heated current of air through the coffee by means of a fan is generally used, but, as far as I know, this has not been introduced into India, and unless the season here is unusually wet, as was the case in 1862, this is scarcely required.

—barbacues and drying tables.

For my part I prefer to use both, as I think that coffee dries sooner on the old drying tables covered with coir matting, so I leave my coffee on the drying tables to drain for a day or two, and then leave it to dry on the barbacues two or three days longer. The latter are usually made of brick covered with chunam and painted with a composition of tar and resin, but if ever so carefully made they soon crack and require to be re-done, and are expensive and not so lasting as they should be, considering their cost. My drying tables are made of sawn timber, which I take to pieces regularly every year after crop is over and store away in my store or pulper-house. Were the cement made by General Morgan not so expensive, this would, I think, be the best material for barbacues.

—cattle-sheds.

Cattle sheds should be dispersed about the plantation so as to save carriage as much as possible, and should be erected on sites suited either for carriage by bandies or despatch of the manure by wire ropes, which latter are coming into general favour. A good rough but strong and lasting cattle-shed may be made

CH. XXVIII. — COFFEE CULTIVATION.

of thick stone and mud-walls where stone is plentiful, otherwise of brick with a shingle or tile roof, and care should be taken also to thatch or cover the manure shed so as to prevent deterioration of the manure by exposure to the weather.

Machinery.

If sufficient water-power is available, the planter will find it a great saving of labour and even of expense in the end to put up a water-wheel, and in these days of great pressure on the labour-market and the very general complaint of an insufficient supply of coolies except in a few favoured districts, any saving of labour by means of machinery is a most decided gain.

—spouting.

For sending down cherry coffee from the elevated portions of the plantation to the pulper-house, spouting, though frequently used in Ceylon, is not much used in India as far as I am aware, but wire ropes for shooting down the cattle manure and jungle soil are coming into very general use. Chaff and litter-cutting machines, especially those made by Richmond and Chandler, are often used, and since manure is doubly efficacious if applied in a well-pulverized state, they are valuable if only to cut the daily supply of litter or bedding; but when stall-feeding becomes general, they will be still more valuable as cattle eat greedily well-cut-up fodder which they would otherwise refuse. When there is a water-wheel the chaff cutter can easily be attached to it and worked by it instead of by manual labour.

—pulper.

There are two kinds of pulper in general use—Gordon's breast and Walker's single and double disc, and in olden times the old Tellicherry chop-pulper, but this last has quite gone out of fashion and is now rarely seen. For my part I much prefer the Walker's double discs, which cost about Rupees 400 or Rupees 450, and of late years have been made entirely of metal.

Finally each estate should be provided with a pluviometer to register the rainfall.

Crop—picking and curing.

Crop season commences and ends in different seasons of the year in various districts, and even in the same district it varies very considerably owing to unusually wet or dry seasons. When crops are good, coolies, if they please, can earn very good wages, as the rate for picking never falls below 2 annas a bushel of cherry coffee, and active coolies can easily pick three and even four bushels a day, though many are so lazy as to be satisfied with earning the average 4 annas. Some planters merely supply their coolies with baskets, which often leads to a loss of coffee by spilling, and the passing of stones and other extraneous matter into the pulper. Towards evening the coolies come to the pulper-house carrying the coffee picked during the day, and on some estates they have two deliveries daily; the writer or superintendent, standing by the bushel measure (which is frequently a standing one with a door to open in front to let out the coffee), notes the quantity picked by each, and either gives tickets, or credits each cooly in the check roll with the quantity brought in. Some planters allow the cherry to stand till the next morning, but this plan is very apt to heat the coffee and make it "foxy," as it is called, that is, to cause red spots to appear in the beans, and I always have my cherry coffee pulped the same night. Strictly speaking, coffee should not be picked until it is fully ripe, that is to say, until each berry is of a rich purple verging on black, but in practice this is impossible even with the largest gangs, and sometimes when the coffee ripens simultaneously all over the plantation, a larger or smaller percentage drops before it can be picked, especially if there are showers or strong winds at the time. At the same time coolies are fearfully careless, and it is necessary to watch carefully that they do not strip the branches and bring in ripe and green berries and even leaves.

After it is pulped, the coffee will require to stand from 18 to 24 hours, according to the altitude of the plantation, to ferment, as until this process has been undergone it is found impossible to wash the coffee (now become parchment) clean, that is, to get rid of the mucilage which envelopes it when pulped. When thoroughly washed it is exposed to the sun on barbacues or drying tables until sufficiently dry, which operation takes from four to six days, and it is then transferred to the store to await the arrival of bandies or bullocks to convey it to the cleaning or shipping agents, as no planter cleans and packs his own coffee. As soon as the parchment coffee reaches the cleaning agent, it is exposed to the sun for another day or two, and it is then peeled by machinery, which operation gets rid of the parchment and silver skins.

The old plan was to have the coffee pounded in large wooden mortars in order to get rid of the parchment and silver skins, but of late years a double iron roller with fluted bottom, revolving very rapidly in an iron receptacle and driven by steam has been very generally introduced. This peeling machine is on the same principle as the chunam grinding and mixing mill so common in India, but made of iron instead of wood and driven by steam instead of horses or bullocks. After being peeled the coffee is poured into a winnowing machine, also driven by steam, which drives off the parchment skin (now reduced to a fine powder and used as fuel for the engine boilers) and delivers the clean coffee into bags. This coffee is then sized by means of a machine made of metal perforated with holes increasing in size as it reaches the end, and from these different holes the various sizes drop into boxes or bins. After being sized by machinery, the coffee is handed over to the garbling women who, with

CH. XXVIII. — COFFEE CULTIVATION.

morrums or native winnowers, separate all the pea-berry or round single beans and the black and broken berries, and each woman's work is then carefully examined by an inspector.

The coffee is finally packed in casks, cases, or bags, and marked with the name of the planter or plantation, and alphabetical letters A, B, C, PB and T to distinguish the different classes, 1st, 2nd, 3rd, Pea-berry, and Triage. Indian coffee is, as a rule, shipped to England generally by canal steamers, but a small quantity is yearly sent direct to France. There are now two coffee-cleaning establishments at Coimbatore, to which most of the coffee from Coonoor and Kótagiri is sent for preparation, and these crops thus have the great advantage of being cleaned and packed in a dry climate, and do not imbibe any moisture, as the coffee prepared on the coast is almost certain to do. For a long time Messrs. Stanes and Co. enjoyed the monopoly at Coimbatore, but lately Messrs. Binny and Co. have also started works there. From Coimbatore the coffee can be sent by rail either to Madras or Beypúr for shipment, at which latter place Messrs. Stanes and Co. have another coffee curing establishment. The coffee from the Segúr side is sent to the Bangalore Works of Messrs. Binny and Co. for preparation, whilst the crops from the Ouchterlony Valley are sent either to the works at Mamalé on the Nellambúr river, some little distance from Beypúr, or to one of the numerous coffee-cleaning houses in Calicut, viz., Messrs. Parry and Co., Pierce, Leslie and Co., Hinde and Co., Andrew and Co., or to Stanes and Co. at Beypúr.

Enemies of the coffee plant.

The coffee plant is a very hardy one, as spite of years of neglect and careless cultivation followed by repeated attacks from one foe after another, it still survives and yields, though in diminished quantities. Birds, monkeys, jackals, and squirrels, all have a decided liking for the berries when ripe, as the pulpy covering is sweet; but these can scarcely be called enemies of the tree, for, though they deprive the coffee planter of a larger or smaller share of his crop, they do no absolute harm to the tree as far as I have seen, and the birds are, in reality, friends, as they destroy millions of caterpillars and noxious insects.

—bug (*Lecanium caffeæ*).

This, the first pest that attacked the coffee tree, appeared in Ceylon in 1845 according to Dr. Bidie, and caused a great deal of alarm in 1847. The bug prevailed for a long time, appearing and disappearing in the most uncertain and perplexing manner, being especially well developed during the monsoon and giving the trees the appearance of being covered with soot. On one estate in Wainád a large portion of the plantation was infested with bug, looked as black as ink, and gave no crop at all for about five years; but this pest has apparently worn itself out and disappeared, except on a few spots here and there, at any rate temporarily. The only remedial measures found effectual are constant weeding, pruning and handling; in fact, allowing the sun and air to have free access to the trees. Dr. Bidie thus describes the bug in his Report on the Ravages of the Borer :—

"As the male and female, when mature, are very different in appearance, they will require to be described separately.

"*Male.*—Head sub-globular ; eyes black ; antennæ eleven-jointed, and with tufts of hair at the tips; thorax somewhat heart-shaped; wings two, horizontal, delicate, membranous and two-nerved; abdomen with two lateral and one long central appendage. Of pinkish brown color, but not often seen on the bushes.

"*Female.*—Apterous, capable of walking about until nearly full-grown, when, being impregnated, she becomes fixed to a young shoot or the margin of the under-surface of a leaf. She is then a conical-like scale of a brown color, which, to the naked eye, looks smooth, but under the microscope has a strong resemblance to the back of a tortoise. This scale contains several hundred eggs, which are smooth, oblong, and of a pale flesh color, and are hatched within it. When the young ones come out, there is but little difference in appearance between the sexes; but in a little while the males betake themselves to the underside of the leaves and the females to the young shoots.

"The male does not derive any nourishment from the tree, but the female has a proboscis with which she incises the bark and drinks the sap of the tree. The eggs being very minute, are easily transported from one place to another by adhering to clothing, birds, or animals, and this may account for the apparently mysterious way in which the pest often makes its appearance on an estate. During the first year of invasion it does not do much harm, but in the second year, owing to the increase in the number of scales, a good deal of the foliage is destroyed and a portion of the crop turns black and falls off. About this time, too, a saccharine substance called the honey-dew is secreted, apparently by the bugs, and shortly the plant acquires a dark, warty, and sordid appearance. A careful examination will now discover the presence of a fungus which gradually covers the branches and leaves. In the third year the plant will probably be completely devoid of leaves, and of course bear no crop. The fungus, which spreads over the plant in a dense, black, felt-like covering, was termed the *Triposporium Gardneri* by Berkeley and *Syncladium Nietneri* by Rabenhorst. The bug seems to appear first in sheltered damp hollows and ravines, but when once fairly established spreads over every part of an estate. It generally disappears in a few seasons, but leaves the trees in a weak and exhausted state, and is very apt to return. It seems to be prevalent in wet seasons. No effectual remedy has been discovered for it, and Dr. Gardner thought that the ravages of the insect were entirely beyond human control. Mr. Neitner says hand-rubbing will destroy an immense quantity of the bug, but is afraid the permanent good effect is

CH. XXVIII. — COFFEE CULTIVATION.

trifling. High culture, he also remarks, has the effect of throwing off the pest, and tar applied to the roots of the tree seems to be a valuable remedy. The bug has at times been very prevalent in Coorg and Wainad, but is not so well known in Mysore, and does not appear to be common or destructive on shaded estates."

—the borer (*Xylotocchus quadrupes*).

The attacks of this insect created so much alarm that Dr. Bidie, M.B., F.R.G.S., was in 1867 instructed by Government specially to report on the ravages caused by the borer in the different districts of Wainád. This report, which contains a mass of valuable and interesting information, was published in 1869 by Messrs. Gantz Brothers, and should be carefully read by every planter. Dr. Bidie ascribes the alarming increase of the borer which took place some years ago to drought, want of shade, bad culture, destruction of forest trees in which the insect used to live, and departure of some of its enemies; and whilst warning planters that high cultivation was essential, he suggested that shade should be tried, which recommendation has of late been very generally followed. The borer proved most destructive on bamboo lands and in very dry, hot climates, and in such situations, notably in Coorg, many plantations died out altogether; but of late years not so much has been heard of the borer, though there are rumours that it is appearing again in Coorg, and, as Dr. Bidie remarks, the insect, being indigenous to India, may appear again at any time owing to exceptional seasons, and consequently it is well to be prepared by having the plantations well shaded and well cultivated. The following is Dr. Bidie's description of the borer:—

"This is a very pretty insect, being slender and elegant in form and beautifully colored. The female is distinguished from the male by her superior size and by the ovipositer being often partially protruded. She is generally from six to seven-tenths of an inch in length and measures from eight to nine-tenths across the wings. The male is considerably smaller, head depressed and flattened in front, posterior portion lustrous black, anterior portion pale greyish green from numerous hairs of that color; labrum slightly exserted and rounded; mandibles horny, robust, sharp-pointed, and incurved; maxillary palpi somewhat slender and clavate, the last joint long and thick; labial palpi clavate, with the last joint thick and slightly truncated; eyes lunate, curved round the angles of the head, large and brilliant; antennæ of moderate length, eleven-jointed, filiform, first joint longest, thickest, and curved—third, fourth, fifth, and sixth joints slightly dentate; prothorax round or slightly oval, globular, covered with greyish green minute hairs and marked above with a black spot and on each side with a black dot; elytræ sometimes scarcely covering the abdomen, broad at their base and very slightly tapering, convex, rounded at their extremities, black, marked with white or yellow transverse, diagonal, and curved lines, the last of which form three figures like the inverted letter V; legs, the front pair shortest, the second pair longer, and the last pair about as long as the body; four posterior femora of a pink color, third joint of the tarsi bifid and the last armed with a sharp and double hook.

"*Pupa.*—The insect in this stage of its existence is generally found in a roomy cell prepared by the larva immediately under, or only separated by a thin layer of wood from, the bark of the tree. It is shorter and thicker than the larva, and exhibits the antennæ, limbs, clytra, &c., disposed in the manner usual in the family. Larva is at first not more than the tenth of an inch in length, and very slender; when full-grown it is from three-fourths to one inch in length, broadest at the head and gradually tapering towards the other extremity, of a pale yellow or whitish color and fleshy consistence. The body consists generally of eleven segments and is apodous, but three or four of the abdominal rings are each provided dorsally with a tubercle which aids the insect in moving forwards and in fixing its body while lengthening its tunnel. The head is hard and scaly, flattened above and armed with very powerful mandibles with which it reduces the wood to a fine powder. This forms the food of the voracious creature, and having passed through its body, is compacted behind it in the tunnel and so agglutinated by some mucilaginous fluid that it may be removed like a cast of plaster of Paris.

"*Ova.*—The eggs are placed deep in the little cracks which always abound in the bark, and fixed by some secretion that is voided at the time of deposition. The ovipositer is a telescopic split tube, and when not in use is drawn up into its sheath, which terminates the abdomen. It is capable of being protruded to a considerable length, which enables the female to place the eggs out of the reach of danger, and is armed at its extremity with two little round bodies bearing a few hairs, which are probably used to clear out and enlarge the crevice where the eggs are placed. It is difficult to ascertain the number which one female will lay, but the average is probably from 150 to 200. The eggs are placed in little clusters containing from five to eight each. They are very small, about the size of a pin point and of a white color. Under a low magnifying power they are found to consist of a pearly white membrane and are of a pyriform shape. They gradually enlarge in length as the embryo progresses, until at length the little larva can be seen through the membrane. They are mostly deposited in sunny places and hot sunshine favors, while cold damp weather retards or prevents, their hatching. Heavy showers destroy them, and they are eaten by several minute insects. They are not often deposited and do not hatch readily in shade.

"*General history of the insect.*—When the beetle emerges from its pupa covering, it finds itself in a dark chamber. At this time it has not attained its full size; the hard case of the body is not so strong as it afterwards becomes, and the colors of the clytra and other parts of the body are dull and imperfect. Accordingly it remains in the place of its birth from three to ten days, until every part of its frame has attained

CH. XXVIII. — COFFEE CULTIVATION.

its due development, when, moved by irresistible instinct, it sets to work, and with its powerful jaw cuts a tunnel through the barrier that separates its cell from the surface of the tree. One might suppose that in performing this operation the little creature would be just as likely to go in the wrong as the right direction, but this is prevented by the larva when about to be transferred to the pupa state always going to rest with its head towards the exterior of the tree. Very often the larva carries on its work of destruction in the root of the tree, and were it to undergo its transformations below ground, the beetle would never be able to escape. With marvellous instinct, however, the borer always returns to the stem to prepare the cell for the pupa and beetle, except in some rare instances in which the surface of a root has become exposed to the air by the washing away of the soil. The beetles may be met with at all seasons, but are most plentiful just after the monsoon and throughout the dry season. They live from twelve to twenty days, apparently feeding on vegetable matter, but are not often seen at large, although sometimes met with on the leaves or bark of the coffee tree. They delight in bright sunshine, and are very active in their movements and not easily caught. At the season when most abundant, they sometimes appear in considerable numbers in the windows of the planter's bungalow, and walking through a field of coffee, it is no unusual thing to find two or three adhering to one's clothes. Trees attacked by the borer always occur in patches, the mischief beginning in one and gradually extending to the others. The females in general select warm sunny places for depositing their eggs, avoiding exposed and shady situations. Indeed, shade seems to be obnoxious to them, and when the ova chance to be deposited in trees protected by it, they do not hatch. The female beetle is much more numerous than the male, and is active during her whole life in depositing ova. When engaged in this operation she moves about briskly on the bark of the coffee tree, looking for a convenient crack or chink in the bark, and having found this, the ovipositer is rapidly inserted and a few eggs deposited and fastened in their place, where they are so securely hidden that they can only be seen by carefully removing some of the outer portion of the bark. In from eight to fifteen days they are hatched, and the young grub, a very minute creature, begins to exercise its mandibles, and derives sustenance from the inner juicy layers of the bark. Its presence there causes the outer portion to rise in a well-defined ridge, as if a wire had been passed between it and the wood. This is an unfailing symptom of the enemy having taken possession of the plant, and enables the planter to detect an infested tree long before any other signs of the scourge have become manifest. As the larva increases in size and strength, it dips into the tender young wood, and at length drives its tunnel in all directions, having, apparently, rather a predilection for the hardest and most sapless portions of the stem. The tunnel pursues a very winding course, but rarely touches that of another individual, and never emerges on the surface of the stem. The empty part of the tunnel, in which the borer lives, is rather longer than itself, but it pushes forward, and fixes its body by the dorsal abdominal tubercles and the rings generally. The tunnel is lengthened by the action of the powerful gorge-like mandibles, and the wood-powder having passed through the intestine of the grub is, as already mentioned, excreted and firmly compacted behind it. The work of destruction is carried on by the larva for about or a little more than nine months, when, working its way towards the surface of the stem, it prepares a chamber immediately under or but a short distance from the bark, in which it goes to rest and becomes transformed into the pupa. In this state it continues for from thirty to fifty days, the time depending a good deal on the state of the weather. The entire existence of the insect from the deposition of the ova to the death of the beetle does not exceed twelve months, and in this it differs from other members of the *Cerambycidæ*, who are said to pass from two to three years in the larva state, although, it must be confessed, that we have but little accurate information concerning the obscurer points of their life-history. As regards the coffee borer there can be no doubt that the life of an individual in all its stages is comprised within twelve months, as instances have repeatedly come to my notice of the beetle existing in stems less than eighteen months old. The season at which the beetles appear differs slightly in different districts, but there is generally a numerous brood on the wing after the monsoon and again about the middle or end of the dry season The eggs are also of course deposited at these seasons, and the pupa are to be met with in greatest abundance in the month of September or about the beginning of October. A small percentage of the pupa are abortive or decay from water getting admission by old holes through which beetles have escaped, and it sometimes happens that the chamber in which the beetle appears is so far from the surface of the stem that it is never able to effect its escape."

—the coffee rat (*Golunda Ellioti*).

The ravages of this animal have been chiefly confined to Coorg and Ceylon, but during one year it threatened to prove a very serious foe to the planters in Wainád also. Driven, according to all accounts, by the absence of its usual food—either the nilloo or the bamboos,—the rat attacked the coffee trees in thousands, and gnawed away the primaries, giving the coffee trees the appearance of having been wantonly cut to pieces with pruning knives.

—leaf-rot.

This disease, which is unquestionably caused by excess of moisture, comes in and departs with the monsoon, and has been experienced to a greater or less extent since coffee was planted. It causes the leaves and a percentage of the berries also to turn black and drop off, and prevails most when the rain and mist are heaviest and most continuous. Planters, whose plantations are situated in unusually damp, misty climates, must be prepared to suffer from this pest, but it may be mitigated to a certain extent by keeping the plantation well weeded and pruned.

—leaf-disease (*Hemeleia vastatrix*).

We now come to the latest and most serious enemy of the long-suffering coffee plant, which made its appearance

CH. XXVIII. COFFEE CULTIVATION.

about six years ago and threatens to prove as lasting and damaging as the oidium in the vine, for which disease, according to all accounts, there has been found no cure, save digging up the vines and planting fresh ones. *Hemeleia vastatrix* seems to have spread simultaneously all over the coffee-growing countries of the world, and it attacks even the hardy Liberian variety which has been lately introduced into India and Ceylon. Startled by the general outcry of alarm, the Home Government, at the instigation of the Ceylon authorities, directed the Collectors of the various coffee-growing districts to circulate a series of questions drawn up by Mr. G. H. K. Thwaites, Director of the Royal Botanic Gardens of Peridinya and Hakgalla, amongst the planters, the replies to which were to be tabulated and sent to England for the consideration of some of the best horticultural authorities. As the outcome of the enquiry, a pamphlet has lately been largely distributed amongst the planters—Mr. Cooke's Report on Diseased Leaves. Mr. Cooke has come to the conclusions, 1st, that the ravages of the *Hemeleia vastatrix* are not to be compared to those of the leaf-rot; 2nd, that the planters should all simultaneously sponge the leaves of the affected trees with a solution of Condy's fluid. In my opinion and that of most planters with whom I have conversed on the subject, the leaf-disease has done more harm than all the other plagues combined, and it remains to be seen if the coffee will ever entirely throw it off or recover from its effects. As far as I can see, the disease is *now* at any rate in the sap of the tree,[1] and probably some application to the roots of sulphur, carbolic acid, petroleum or chunam may be found of use. The leaf-disease must by this time unfortunately be well known to all coffee planters, and its appearances are as follows :—The leaves present first of all a spotted appearance, and in due time are covered on the under surface with a golden rust, and finally shrink and drop off, leaving the tree quite bare; in many instances the fruit is also affected. A large percentage of the berries grow till they are nearly full sized and then drop off, and if examined are found to contain nothing. Some even grow to full size and ripen, but when pulped are found quite empty. Some planters thought this was a new disease and invented the term " shank ;"

[1] In a report to the Planters' Association, Ceylon, in 1879, Mr. Daniel Morris, Assistant Director, Royal Botanic Gardens, Kew, recommends, as the most efficacious remedy, flowers of sulphur mixed with unslaked coral lime, in the proportion of 1 of sulphur to 3 of lime; the mixture to be applied to the plant and to the soil. The disease is an external parasite—an organic fungoid growth—and not diffused in the juices of the coffee plant. In districts (Ceylon) affected by the south-west monsoon, it is generally present during December and the early months of the year as an external parasite in the form of long filamentous threads, which cover every part of the bark and leaves.—ED.

but in my opinion these empty berries are one effect of the leaf-disease, and as far as I am aware, were unknown till this disease appeared. The leaf-disease is most capricious in its attack, appearing and disappearing without any apparent cause, affecting both poor and healthy looking trees, on all kinds of soil and at all elevations ; but, as a rule, the "chicks" suffer most and earliest from its attacks, whilst it is beginning to be generally allowed that trees under shade are not so badly crippled as those in the open, so that, perhaps, as was found with the borer, shade combined with high cultivation may prove a remedy or at any rate a palliative.

None of these plagues seems to have affected the plantations on the Nílagiris as seriously as they have done those in the low country of Wainád, Mysore, Coorg, Travancore or even in Ceylon ; but I imagine that no coffee planter can say that his crops have not been more or less reduced by leaf-disease.[1]

[1] Replies to queries from Nílagiri planters on the leaf-disease will be found in G.Os., dated 30th November 1875, No. 1,715, Revenue Department ; 8th March 1876, No. 336, Revenue Department ; and 6th July 1876, No. 906, Revenue Department.

CHAPTER XXIX.

TEA.

INTRODUCTION.

Plant introduced, 1835.—Mr. Mann's efforts, 1854.—Dr. Cleghorn's reports.—Government policy.—Mr. Rae opens an estate near Ootacamand.—Government introduces tea-makers and forms a nursery at Doddabetta.—Agricultural Exhibition and its results as regards tea.—Area under tea.—Exports and imports.

CH. XXIX. — TEA. — Plant introduced.

THE history of tea cultivation in this district dates from the year 1835, when some boxes of plants were sent from Calcutta to the Nílagiris, and at the same time to Coorg, Mysore, and the Agri-Horticultural Society in Madras. The plants received on the Nílagiris were planted chiefly at the Experimental Farm at Kaity, and there cared for by Colonel Crewe and M. Perrottet, the French Botanist. They had been raised from seed brought direct from China by Mr. Gordon, the Secretary of a Committee specially appointed by Lord W. Bentinck (then Governor-General) to consider means for the introduction of the tea industry into India. The experiment appears on the whole to have been a failure, at least as regards the Madras Presidency, although a few plants seem to have survived in each locality to which they had been sent.[1] Attempts were made at different

[1] General Cullen, Resident, Travancore, writes to Government in October 1859 with reference to reports which he had received of the growth of tea at Coonoor as follows:—

"The tree thrives well in the Travancore territory, both at the level of the sea and altitudes of 1,800 and 3,200 feet. I first met with it in the coffee plantation of Mr. Huxham in the year 1841, on the route from Quilon to Courtallum, at a farm called Caldoorty, about 40 miles inland and 6 or 700 feet above the sea. There are some 10 or 15 trees from 20 to 25 and 30 feet high; they were, I believe, introduced during the government of Mr. Lushington, who I believe also introduced those formerly at Kaitee on the Neilgerries. I procured plants from Mr. Huxham and put them down in an experimental spice garden which I had established some twelve years ago at 1,800 feet on a hill in the south of Travancore near Oodagherry. They are now trees of 20 to 30 feet high, growing vigorously; and I have about 400 plants procured from their seed growing on another hill near the Tinnevelly frontier, at an elevation of 3,200 feet. There can be no doubt therefore of the facility of its introduction, although from the moderate altitudes and great atmospheric moisture of the localities hitherto selected, they may possibly be considered to grow more luxuriantly than is desirable; but which, if a defect at all, can probably be easily remedied by selecting ground more to the eastward, at greater altitudes, and with a less humid climate."

He proceeds to draw the attention of Government to the Travancore and Cochin "Cardamom Hills" as especially suited for tea culture.

times to manufacture tea from those on the Nílagiris, but without success. It was not until some years later that Mr. Mann of Coonoor succeeded in producing fair drinkable tea from the Nílagiri plants.

Mr. Mann's efforts.

Thus encouraged, Mr. Mann brought with him from China in February 1854 a good supply of seed of the best descriptions, collected by Mr. Fortune[1] from the finest plantations in the country, and applied at once to Government for land in the neighbourhood of Coonoor to form a nursery. After many delays, during which a large number of the seedlings died (the remainder was only saved by being sent to the Wainád), Mr. Mann succeeded in acquiring a piece of land near Coonoor, which is now known as the Coonoor Tea Estate.

Dr. Cleghorn's reports.

The seedlings were planted in grass land to save time, the forest land not being ready. As early as 1856 the tea produced from these plants was favourably reported on by the London brokers. Mr. Mann, however, appears to have been disheartened by the difficulty of procuring forest land to extend his estate, as is shown by the following extract from a letter to Dr. Cleghorn, then Conservator of Forests. Referring to a second importation he writes in April 1855: "I got another small supply of seed from China brought round in the same way" (*i.e.*, in earth in which the seeds germinated during the voyage) "which I put down in my nursery at Coonoor immediately they arrived, and scarcely lost a single plant. About 2,000 of these I planted out, though still very small, in the forest land in November of the same year, and the remainder, about 800, remained in the nursery until November 1856. I was convinced from the way these plants came on that the tea plant would grow well there, and applied through the Collector to the Government for a suitable piece of forest land for a tea plantation, which, if they had granted me, I would at once have returned to China and brought over a large quantity of seed; but I could get nothing but poor grass land, on which nothing would grow without being heavily manured, and to my repeated solicitations they at last sanctioned *two* cawnies of forest land, subject to all kinds of restrictions, so I gave the thing up and went on with the coffee, though I still think, if given fair play, the tea plant would not only grow well on the Neilgherries but pay well too."

Dr. Cleghorn in a visit made a few months later was struck by the thriving condition of the plants in Mr. Mann's nursery, and called his attention to the quantity of seed falling from the trees. In a letter dated August 1859, he writes:—

---

[1] Author of "Wanderings in China." This gentleman was sent by the Court of Directors to China to collect plants and seed with the view of introducing the culture into the North-West Provinces.

CH. XXIX. — TEA.

"I am happy to observe that you have acted on my letter of 25th ultimo, and that your new superintendent is collecting the seed carefully with a view to establishing a large nursery. * * * On a further consideration of the course which it seems desirable to adopt in reference to your tea plantations, I am inclined to recommend to Government that one or two Chinese manufacturers be brought down from the North-West Provinces at the public expense for the purpose of testing the actual qualities of the teas produced in these hills. * * * No doubt some satisfactory arrangement would readily be come to by which Government would obtain what they would consider an equivalent for their risk in the experimental manufacture.

"I cannot pledge Government to any special course, but personally I should think that if you would enable the Government to form a nursery from seed from your plantations, they would be satisfied, bearing in mind the great expense you have incurred in bringing your plantation to its present state."

Policy of the Government.

Dr. Cleghorn's representations to Government called forth the following characteristic minute from Sir C. Trevelyan:—

"I cannot understand why Dr. Cleghorn volunteered the assistance of Government in this matter. The experiment of growing and manufacturing tea had been commenced *as a mercantile undertaking*, which is the only wholesome and sound footing on which such enterprises can be conducted. * * * The manufacture of tea in India has been proved to be a profitable business, and ample experience has been acquired of it. All that private undertakers have to do, is to avail themselves of this advanced state of the art, with such modifications as the circumstances of South India may require, which they will be likely to do with much greater zeal and activity if they know that the Government will not do it for them. I see no necessity, therefore, for this industry in this part of India passing through the phase of a Government establishment. On the contrary, I believe that the vigorous and expansive period of the undertaking would be postponed by it for years to come, for when Government intrude into those operations which properly belong to private life, their hands are, as was truly described by Sir Robert Peel, torpid and wasteful. In Northern India the manufacture of tea did not begin to be remunerative until it was transferred from the Government to a private company; and what have all the expensive Government Farms done for the improvement of Indian cotton? The worst effect of this policy, however, is the morbid habit of dependence upon Government, which in some communities has amounted to a moral paralysis; and it ought to be our care to keep our Anglo-Indian settlements free from this taint."

Sir Charles' views were accepted by his Government (September 1859).

Mr. Rae's efforts.

Almost simultaneously with the formation of Mr. Mann's garden at Coonoor, Mr. Rae of Ootacamand had obtained a grant of land for tea near Kalhatti, constituting the estate now known as Dunsandle. He experienced similar difficulties to those of Mr. Mann in securing suitable land. Shortly after this a garden was begun at Kótagiri, and in 1863 the estate known as Belmont was formed on the Bishopsdown property in Ootacamand.

Tea manipulators introduced and a nursery formed at Doddabetta.

In Sir William Denison's reign some direct encouragement was afforded to the industry by introducing, in 1863, skilled manipulators from the North-West Provinces, distributing in 1864 a supply of tea seed procured from the same source gratuitously, and by forming (1864) a small tea nursery for raising good and fresh seed at Doddabetta within the Government Chinchona Plantations. The manipulators remained eighteen months; their services do not appear to have been much appreciated. The nursery at Doddabetta has been of little use to Government or the public, and is now leased to a private planter.

Agricultural Exhibition and its results as to tea.

The energy however of the Nílagiri planters has sufficed for the success of the enterprise without the fostering aid of Government. The introduction of the new Waste Land Rules in 1863 was, however, the measure which set this energy free. By the end of 1869 there were probably some two or three hundred acres of tea cultivation in the district. At the Agricultural Exhibition held at Ootacamand in October 1869 no less than eighteen exhibitors appeared. The exhibits were in some cases of very good quality. The teas were with two exceptions black. Reporting on this product, the Commissioner, Mr. Breeks, wrote: "I attach great importance to tea, viewed as an investment for English capital on these hills. Several private individuals have commenced its cultivation here, and it is most important to ascertain whether it can be carried on profitably. * * * * As far as soil and climate go the practicability of growing tea on the Neilgherries has been established. But the tea plant will grow almost anywhere; what we want to know is whether, under proper conditions of locality and management, tea planting in the Neilgherries will pay. Labour, means of transit, quantity of produce per acre, are all questions for the planter on the spot. * * * No two planters here manufacture alike; and colour, strength, and flavour are much affected by elevation."

He suggested to Government the forwarding of the specimens to England for brokers' opinions. The Government approved the suggestion. The brokers' report will be found in G.O., 16th September 1870. Many of the exhibits were pronounced good and some very good, the values ranging from 1*s*. 4*d*. to 6*s*. per pound. The Government, in agreeing to the above proposal, requested the Commissioner to report as to the steps to be taken to develope the enterprise. This report will be found in G.O., 5th October 1871, Revenue Department. The planting community suggested the following measures:—

I. Free tenure of land for a certain period.

CH. XXIX.

TEA.

II. The introduction by Government of experts to teach the best method of manufacture.

III. The purchase of Indian instead of China tea by the Commissariat.

IV. The importation and raising by Government of the best kinds of hybrid China and indigenous Assam seed.

The first concession was partially accorded by Government, the second refused, as also the third, the last was approved, but the approval was practically inoperative.

In treating of this enterprise, Mr. Breeks urged the importance of encouraging tea-planting to the utmost with the view of developing the resources of the Nílagiris and other hill plateaux, holding that as the plant flourished in climates congenial to the European constitution, it afforded " the best hope of inducing any number of them to people our hill plateaux." This forecast seems likely to be fulfilled as regards the Nílagiris, for in the eight years that have passed since he wrote the area taken up for this cultivation has risen to 4,200 acres, of which 2,550 are mature and 1,650 immature plants, the yield of which must approximate 400,000 lb., in value probably not less than Rupees 3,50,000. The land taken up for the cultivation exceeds 7,000 acres, being double the area so appropriated in 1876.

Exports and imports.

The following statement shows the quantity of tea exported from, and imported into, the Presidency from 1869-70 to 1878-79. The figures indicate a rapid increase in the local consumption of tea, as, although much of the tea manufactured in the Presidency is consumed in the country, the imports do not indicate a corresponding decline.

Imports and Exports of Tea into and from Madras Presidency (including foreign and coasting, but excluding British Ports within the Presidency).

Years.	Imports.		Exports.	
	Quantity.	Value.	Quantity.	Value.
	LB.	RS.	LB.	RS.
1869-70	183,176	1,84,552	6,245	9,238
1870-71	140,924	1,40,924	20,342	20,611
1871-72	256,433	2,56,433	37,922	50,001
1872-73	221,042	2,20,738	43,591	52,614
1873-74	149,641	1,49,681	80,907	89,496
1874-75	147,957	1,47,253	98,694	1,20,751
1875-76	220,636	2,14,197	122,981	1,47,926
1876-77	41,227 [1]	38,354	153,007	1,72,763
1877-78	167,643	1,40,050	183,620	1,93,294
1878-79	175,237	1,15,730	210,146	2,17,194

[1] Imports from Calcutta very small.

The following paper has been kindly prepared by Mr. Brace, one of the earliest tea planters in the district. Mr. Brace has also had considerable experience in tea cultivation in Northern India. I have omitted the introductory historical notice and remarks relating to climate and soil, regarding which information is given elsewhere.

CH. XXIX. — TEA.

MONOGRAPH ON THE CULTIVATION OF TEA ON THE NÍLAGIRIS.

(*By* E. J. C. BRACE, Esq., *of Kótagiri.*)

Suitability of climate and soils of the district for growth of tea.—Varieties of the plant—the China—the indigenous—the hybrid.—Selection of seed.—Selection of land—aspect and soil—lay of land—clearing—shelter—terracing—lining—pitting—planting.—Nurseries—propagation by cuttings—cultivation and pruning—yield.—Manuring—manures and their application.—Weeding.—Fodder crops.—Manufacture—difference between black and green teas.—Manufacture of black tea—withering—rolling—second rolling—rolling by machinery—colouring—drying appliances—drying off—storing—tasting teas.—Manufacture of green tea—sifting—packing.

Suitability of climate and soils for tea.

For all practical purposes the Nílagiris may, as regards their suitability for tea cultivation, be divided into two main divisions,[1] each having a different climate, which not only necessitates the cultivation of a different class of plant, but also a different course of treatment. A line drawn across the map of the Nilagiri District, from Kódanád on the north to Mélkúnda on the south, will as nearly as possible effect the desired demarcation. The eastern half will show the warm and sheltered side, which is not only protected from the violence of the south-west monsoon, but also less subject to the cold dry winds of the winter season. The

[1] Since the above lines were written the large tract of country known as South-East Wainád has been added to the Nilagiri District. I am of opinion that both the climate and soil are all that could be desired for successful cultivation of the tea plant, and am confident that with a good selection of plant, and equally high cultivation, gardens here will rival both in quantity and quality of their produce the best gardens of Assam and Cachar. Pure indigenous plants might be grown here with the greatest success. There are several classes of soils unsuited to coffee, but on which tea will thrive. The traveller passing through Wainád can hardly fail to notice, on almost every estate, a greater or less extent of exhausted or diseased coffee, the maintenance of which can hardly be compensated for by the crop. Yet these same poor fields might be made to yield excellent crops of tea. In some places the prevalence of bug, borer, or leaf disease renders coffee cultivation a very precarious investment, but as tea is never materially affected by these pests it may be grown with safety. The worst enemy of the tea plant is the red spider, but that has not hitherto, to my knowledge, been met with in Southern India.

Better grown tea plants than those now coming into bearing in the Ouchterlony Valley could not, I believe, be found in Assam or Cachar, and the teas produced there should, with careful manufacture, hold their own well in the London market.

CH. XXIX. TEA. western half will point out those parts of the district where plantations are not only as a rule situate at higher elevations, but where growth and yield are much curtailed by what amounts virtually to a double wintering, viz., during the high cold and damp winds of the south-west monsoon, and the clear sharp dry winds and nightly frost of the cold season. The severity of the climate checks the growth and yield of the plants to such an extent that bushes five years old will show less vigorous growth and constitution than plants of half that age grown at the same elevation on the eastern side of the hills. The black sour grass lands I look upon as wholly unfitted for tea cultivation; not but what they may be made capable of yielding some return after some years, but because the money so spent would have yielded a treble or quadruple return if invested on soil that had good drainage and was of a freer nature. The lands best suited to successful cultivation of the tea plant lie along the southern and eastern slopes of the hills. These have the advantage of getting a fair share of both monsoons, possess a warmer and more equable climate, and the atmosphere taken throughout the months of the year contains a greater percentage of humidity. In many parts these lands are very stony, but this is rather an advantage than a drawback, provided the stone present is in detached boulders, and not in the form of sheet rock at a short depth below the surface. Stones not only facilitate free drainage, a matter of no small importance to the health of the tea plant, but they retain moisture both beneath and around them; they absorb heat during the day and give it out at night, thus rendering the temperature in their immediate neighbourhood more equable; and also, by their constant decay under atmospheric influences, they provide a valuable supply of inorganic food for the roots of plants. That stony lands are less easy to cultivate in the first instance must be admitted, but their fertility makes ample amends for this defect.

Varieties of the tea plant. Before going further in my remarks on the climate and soils of these hills, it will be better to describe the several varieties of plant cultivated, as the suitability of the variety to the soil and elevation of the site selected has a great deal to do with the success of a garden.

—the China. First we have to deal with the pure China plant. This is a low-growing shrub with small, harsh, dark green leaves, growing at first with a single stem, but very soon throwing up additional suckers, and the more these are cut near the surface of the ground the more numerous do they become. The leaf hardens and the young wood ripens more rapidly than does that of either of the other varieties, and in consequence the plant bears seed earlier and to a very much greater extent. Amongst pure China plants a very great difference exists in the size and texture of the leaf of individual plants, even in cases in which the seed from which the plants were raised has been obtained direct from China. In its native country it has to endure great extremes both of heat and cold, and this natural hardiness is its sole merit. It is therefore the variety in some respects best calculated to succeed in the highlands of the western division.

—the indigenous.

The indigenous plant forms a marked contrast to the above. In the first place it is not a shrub, but a forest tree of moderate size, found in its wild state in the warm, moist valleys of Assam and Munnipoor. Unchecked, it will grow up with a single stem to a height of 25 to 30 feet. It has large light green leaves, of a very soft texture, broad in the centre, but very acuminate at the apex. This plant, as its natural habitat implies, is partial to tropical climates, and although it can, when two years old, with its roots well established, bear an extreme degree of heat with impunity, it suffers very much both in health and productiveness if subjected to frost or cold winds. At the higher elevations of these hills the growth of this variety is partially stunted. Its cultivation therefore, by itself, in gardens should not ordinarily be attempted at higher elevation than from 5 to 6,000 feet. On the eastern slopes of these hills, how low down tea of this variety may be grown is a point we have yet to ascertain, but on the western side, the whole of the Wainád, or at any rate all the lands suitable for coffee, are well suited for the cultivation of this and the hybrid variety. The plants seldom bear much seed unless allowed to grow unchecked.

—the hybrid.

I now come to the most generally useful variety of the tea plant in cultivation, viz., the hybrid plant. A first-class hybrid combines a great deal of the hardiness of the China plant with the vigorous growth, size, softness of leaf, and great productiveness of the indigenous plant. It seldom bears sufficient seed to hinder its yield of leaf, and the seed it does produce has too gréat a marketable value to make it advisable to strip it from the trees before it reaches maturity. There are, as is natural, plants of this kind of every type and quality, and although a garden may be planted with seed produced by bushes of the highest class, it may often be no easy matter to find among the plants so produced any half dozen exactly alike. Let it, however, approach the China plant ever so closely in appearance, it will be found to yield more than twice as much leaf as the latter, and, on the other hand, however closely it may resemble the indigenous, it will be found possessed of a more vigorous constitution and less liable than either of the other varieties to disease. It may be grown with advantage as high as 6 or 7,000 feet in sheltered localities;[1] and as low down as the indigenous plant is found to

[1] The plant flourishes in Ootacamand at elevations approaching 8,000 feet.—ED.

CH. XXIX.

TEA.

thrive; as a rule it grows naturally with a single stem, and in cases where it has a tendency to produce more, these may easily be removed without fear of their renewal. Individually I do not object to two or three stems, as these plants seldom throw out suckers unless the roots are injured close to the stem of the tree.

Both the indigenous and hybrid varieties need a better soil than that in which China plants may be grown, but I never advise tea planting on lands which do not possess to a considerable extent natural richness, and care must be taken that this standard of fertility is at any rate maintained if it cannot be improved.

Selection of seed.

The impression that the tea plant succeeds best in a cold climate is erroneous. Tea plants do not grow freely or mature their seed so well at a high elevation as they do lower down, and the plants raised from seed so grown must share to some extent the weakness of the parent plant. Thus seed procured from the Government garden in Doddabetta[1] would be held in small esteem by an experienced planter. European agriculturists lay great stress upon the selection for seed purposes of only the heaviest and best developed grains; and the same rule holds good in tea planting also.

It is but from a few gardens in Assam, and one or two only on the Nílagiris, and that in very limited quantities, that really first-class hybrid seed can be obtained. In Assam the gardens best known to me as supplying a good class of plant are the Bishnauth, Luckimpore, and Hool Maree Company's Estates. On very many gardens the mixed nature of the plant renders it undesirable that seed should be purchased from them. It seldom costs less than Rupees 80 to deliver a maund of seed on these hills, and its turning out good or bad is a mere lottery. I succeeded once in raising from two maunds of Bishnauth seed 45,500 plants; last year from the same quantity treated with great care I only obtained two seedlings. This uncertainty is a

---

[1] In paragraph 23 of his letter, G.O., 28th August 1874, Mr. Cockerell, speaking of the late Mr. W. G. McIvor, remarks:—

"He says that the seed grown on it is more adapted to the wants of planters than seed grown at Burliar could be, because seed from the latter spot would be planted out at a greater elevation, and would throw weakly seedlings owing to the greater cold, whereas seeds grown higher up do not suffer on being planted at a lower elevation.

"24. I take it that Mr. McIvor's opinion on this point must be considered decisive."

My experience is directly against Mr. Cockerell's theory regarding tea seed. I have never yet seen really well filled seeds of the indigenous and hybrid varieties grown at the higher elevations. The result is generally a shell of the usual size and a small undeveloped shrivelled nut inside. A well-developed seed grown at any elevation will, all other circumstances being the same, produce a stronger plant than a half-formed one. A visit to a well-cared-for nursery, situated about 5,500 feet elevation, filled with plants raised from seed imported direct from Assam, will serve best to upset the above theory.

very serious matter to a man who is opening out largely and dependent on Bengal for his supply of seed. An average of from 10,000 to 12,000 plants per maund of imported seed must be considered satisfactory.

From a maund of seed off my own hybrid plants grown at a mean elevation of 5,400 feet I can as a rule raise from 25,000 to 30,000 seedlings, and the plants so raised are in no way inferior to those imported direct from Assam. That the produce of plants grown on the hills at a moderate elevation is quite as good as that imported has been satisfactorily proved. Had the course I proposed been adopted at the time of its suggestion, I feel confident that great stimulus would have been given to tea planting on these hills.

Selection of land—aspect and soil.

Mr. Robertson, the Superintendent, Government Farm, Saidapet, as also did the late Mr. McIvor, lays great stress upon the subject of aspect. They maintain that the northern slopes of these hills are invariably better clothed with a natural growth of vegetation, and consequently better supplied with springs of water; also that in addition to these advantages the growth of vegetation on slopes facing the north was more rapid, and the heat during the dry months from the southerly declination of the sun's course less severely felt. It would be presumptuous on my part to pass over the opinion held by such scientific and experienced authorities, but I must confess that, after having cultivated the tea plant on all aspects, I have never been able to attribute the freer growth of any one plot of cultivation to aspect alone. Soil and shelter from wind were generally able to account for it. Nor am I of opinion that the richest soils, consequently those best adapted to the successful cultivation of the tea plant, are only to be met with on lands still covered with natural forest. There are large tracts of scrub grass and fern lands, more especially in the sheltered valleys of the eastern slopes, which, no doubt, previous to the immigration of the Badagas to these hills, were covered by natural forest; and many of these by the secondary growth give positive evidence of the fact. Doubtless the Badagas, on their establishing themselves on these hills, were possessed of sufficiently sound judgment to avail themselves of the right which lay in their power, viz., to select the most favourable sites for the erection of their villages and the cultivation of their crops; and a careful observer will note that they have almost invariably succeeded in doing so. One of the safest tests of the suitability of a plot of land for tea cultivation is a luxuriant growth of the common bracken fern (*Pteris aquilina*). It clearly indicates sufficient moisture, richness of soil, and good drainage. Such lands undoubtedly require constant weeding for the first three years, but amply repay the trouble and care taken with them.

CH. XXIX. TEA. —lay of land. With regard to the lay of the land, the less the slope the better; in fact flat lands, provided they possess good drainage and are not subject to frosts, are the most suitable. Steep lands, if stony, may be terraced, a practice which should be carried out more extensively than it now is on these hills. The soil is of as great importance to the planter as his capital. Whenever the surface soil with its strong proportion of organic matter has been lost, there remains little but the inorganic subsoil, which unless heavily manured cannot maintain the vigour of the plants.

—clearing. The first operation to be performed is the clearing of the natural growth on the land to be opened out. On heavy forest lands the general rule is to cut every thing, except a few of the trees whose timber is valuable: these are rung and left standing. The usual rate for clearing these lands by contract is Rupees 12 per cawny (1⅓ statute acres). On the more lightly wooded lands, many planters leave a few trees here and there for appearance sake; but this should be done with caution, as many of our jungle trees are infested throughout the greater part of the year by swarms of caterpillars, which descend at night and commit great havoc amongst the leaves of young plants. Moreover there are but few trees beneath whose shade, or within range of whose roots, tea plants will make a satisfactory growth. The trees where rung can subsequently, when seasoned, be felled and cut up for timber. They are not likely to injure the plants materially by their fall, as would be the case on a coffee or chinchona estate.

—shelter. It is very necessary on forest land to leave belts from 20 to 30 yards wide on all exposed ridges, or on the more open lands to plant belts of quick-growing trees (*eucalypti*, the larger varieties of chinchona, &c.) to check the violence of the monsoon gales. Shelter from strong wind is absolutely essential to good growth. Moreover the soil on ridges of the above description is seldom of very superior quality, and the planter must bear in mind that one acre of well sheltered tea is worth two that are exposed or planted in a hard gritty sub-soil. Both the sources and course of springs and streams must be left well protected by natural wood, or the water-supply will be much diminished, in some cases lost altogether. It is false economy in order to secure an extra acre or so of tea, to run the chance of losing one's water-supply or to lessen the power of attracting mists and clouds, and causing the moisture they contain to be precipitated.

A heavy burn is only desirable on strong clays. On the lighter lands it sets free, to a great extent, in the form of gases, the organic matters contained in the surface soil. Roots and stumps should, as far as practicable, be collected and either carried away or burnt in heaps. If left about on the ground they merely serve the purpose of breeding myriads of white-ants.

When the ground has been thoroughly cleared, the planter can easily determine the manner in which he will lay out his estate. The sites for the buildings and nurseries can now be selected, as also the course of the roads and drains.

—terracing.

In my opinion very steep slopes should not be cultivated unless means of terracing substantially are at hand, and even then drains at wide intervals may be necessary to break the force of a heavy fall of water. These drains should be laid out at a gradient of 1 in 30 to 1 in 40. The general cost of terracing comes as a rule to about the same as that of pitting, viz., Rupees 20 to 25 per acre. In the cases of light showers, the terraces absorb the rainfall instead of letting it run off the ground. It is always advisable to demarcate, at any rate, and if possible, to partially cut out the traces of the roads and drains before beginning to line the estate.

—lining.

The next business is to line the estate, *i.e.*, mark out by means of pegs or slips of bamboo, the exact spot at which a pit is to be dug for the reception of the plant. This is most easily accomplished by the aid of a Chesterman's land chain 100 feet long, in links of 1 foot each, and a staff indicating the distance between the rows for the men at each end of the chain. The whole appearance of the garden in after years depends upon the accuracy with which this work has been performed. The first step to be taken is to lay a horizontal base line as far as you can, and then from its centre set off a vertical line and work from that. The lines must be kept accurate, not following the curves of the hill. In spite of their somewhat set and square appearance they will be more pleasing to the eye than a succession of irregular curves. The cost of lining should not exceed Rupees 5 per acre.

—pitting.

The land has now to be pitted. A cylindrical pit of 18 inches in width and depth is the best size. These pits are usually made by contract at the rate of Rupees 12-8-0 per 1,000, or, if executed by the planter's own labour, at Rupees 10 per 1,000. When the land has to be terraced this work should be done after the lining and before the pitting. Some planters incline to horizontal trenches 18 inches wide and deep, but the cost is much greater, and while the roots have soft ground to work their way through on two sides, on the other two they are met by a hard compact surface.

In the earlier days of tea-planting, very wide distances were advocated, sometimes as much as 7 feet by 7 feet for indigenous plants. Experience has, however, taught us that shrubs planted

CH. XXIX. — TEA. — much closer, and confined to narrower limits, yield a very much larger return, and that too at a less cost.

At present it is the rule in Assam to put out hybrid plants at a distance of 4 feet by 4 feet, and very large returns are thus obtained at an early age. On the other hand, the very close system, 3 feet by 2 feet and 2½ feet by 2½ feet, frequently practised in Darjeeling and the North-West Provinces, is not to be recommended.

In my opinion for a fair class of hybrid plant 3 feet by 3 feet is the closest that the bushes should be planted at the high elevations on the western side of the Nílagiris; and 4 feet by 4 feet, or at the outside 4 feet by 3 feet at elevations of 6,000 feet and downwards on the eastern and southern slopes of the hills. Planting 4 feet by 4 feet will give on land perfectly free from stone, and excluding the space occupied by roads, drains, &c., 2,722 plants per acre, but making allowance for these, say a little over 2,000 plants clear per acre. Two small compact bushes 4 feet in diameter will yield a very much larger supply of leaf than would the bush of 8 feet diameter, and the amount of manure required per acre will remain the same.

A few planters incline to the hedge system of cultivation, say 3 feet apart in the row and 5 or 6 feet between the rows. The system is not one to be recommended: it is far better to let each plant have a regulated distance on all sides to which it can spread its roots in search of nourishment. Others incline to what is called the quincunx system, *i.e.*, commencing the second line from half way between the two first pegs and going back to the same line in the third row as shown. The system has little to recommend it.

When the pits have been exposed a short time to atmospheric influence, and the monsoon rains have set in, they may be refilled, care being taken that only the best soil is returned and that that is free from roots, weeds, stones, &c. The soil should be heaped up to some height in the centre, as the rains will soon compress it again, and a small pit in which water will lodge would be the result. The cost of this work will be about Rupees 2-8-0 per 1,000 pits.

—planting. The land is now ready to be planted. There are two ways of doing this, and both have their advocates, viz., planting the seed *in situ* and transplanting seedlings from nurseries. *In situ* planting is performed by sowing three or four tea seeds, germinated or fresh, in each pit, shading or not according to the state of the weather, and subsequently, when they are 2 or 3 inches high, leaving the strongest grower in the pit. Those removed serve to fill up vacancies that may exist, or may be planted in a nursery for use the following season. Some planters allow all to grow up together unchecked, but invariably one takes the lead and outstrips all the others in growth. A single plant in sole possession of the pit will always produce a finer and more vigorous bush than can several seedlings huddled up together. There is not the slightest doubt that on well-drained lands with a moderate incline and in favourable seasons the planting of germinated seeds *in situ* is a saving of both labour and money. The risk attached to so doing is that on these hills we can never rely thoroughly on the weather that may prevail at any particular season of the year, and close observation and record over a series of years have only led to very mystifying results. Tea seed that is imported from Assam ripens generally about the middle or end of October, and seldom reaches the Nílagiris earlier than the end of December or early in January. The first quarter of the year frequently passes without a drop of rain having fallen, and it naturally follows that planting *in situ* under such circumstances would be attended with great risk. If, however, the seed is sown in nurseries and carefully tended, the plants so raised may be planted out without any fear of undue loss in the first rains of the south-west monsoon, and even should that fail, as is sometimes the case, the planter is almost sure of suitable weather before October; but the earlier in the season the plants are put out the better, as they are then enabled to establish themselves well and make some growth previous to encountering the trials of a hot season. It is however as well to wait for the second or third shower to plant up pits that have been recently filled in. The loose soil has become more compact, and the heat generated by the first fall has had time to pass away.

Nílagiri seed, on the other hand, ripens between March and August, the crop lasting as a rule over three months, and the time of its commencement depending much on the quantity of rain that fell during the north-east monsoon and the dryness or otherwise of the first quarter of the year. If therefore the plants are well shaded up to the time of their attaining 2 inches or so in height, and no floods occur to wash the seedlings out of the ground, they have every chance of making a strong and vigorous growth, and the check occasioned by removal of a strong seedling is avoided. This is more especially the case when the seed has been germinated previous to its being sown in the pits. In the case of planting germinated seeds in the pits, two seeds to each pit will be found ample, and the nearer they are situate to the centre of the pit the better the subsequent appearance of the garden will be. *In situ* tea-planting on these hills, however, always involves more or less risk. A tea plant raised in a nursery, if planted with care and of a moderate size, is by far the most

CH. XXIX. — TEA. — likely ultimately to succeed, and this course will in the majority of cases be pursued by the planter who prefers certainty to chance.

There is a practice now coming much into favour of raising the germinated seed in small baskets of split bamboo: and thus transferring them to the pits they are meant to occupy. The outer covering of bamboo soon rots, and allows free passage to the lateral rootlets. In the case of filling up vacancies this system has much to commend it.

Nurseries. Concluding that the planter has in part at all events preferred the certainty to the chance, and made up his mind to raise at any rate a great portion of his plants in nurseries, we have now to consider the formation of the nurseries in which these seeds are to be sown. In all tea seed there is a proportion, seldom less than 8 per cent., of empty shells or unripe nuts, and these planted out in beds not only waste room, but give the beds an unsightly appearance when the plants have begun to show above ground.

The best site for a nursery is a piece of level ground, if such can be procured—failing that, a gentle slope on which terraced beds can be easily cut out. A very convenient size for nursery beds is in my opinion 30 feet long by 5 feet wide, with 2½ or 3 feet paths between the beds. The beds themselves should be well dug to a depth of 18 inches, and raised about 4 to 6 inches above the level of the paths. It is by no means a bad plan to lay the top soil of the paths on to the beds. The edges may be faced with stone, flat tiles, bamboo slips—on no account should solid manure be applied to nurseries; it attracts larvæ of all kinds, which do much damage by eating the tender roots of the seedling.

The surface should be made perfectly smooth and even. On this the seeds may be spread in a layer one seed thick, and covered over with an inch or an inch-and-a-half of good sandy loam. A good watering should be given in the first instance, and afterwards a lighter one from time to time as necessary. The seed of the tea plant, like most other seeds of a fleshy description, is very intolerant of an excessive supply of water, and this is more especially the case with seed that has travelled a long distance, say from Assam, and been allowed to dry partially on the journey. The greatest caution must be used therefore in giving these seeds just as much water as they can utilize and no more. At the end of five weeks the upper layer of soil may be removed, and those seeds that have commenced to throw out a radicle, or have burst their shell, may be taken out for sowing in the nurseries. The remainder should be covered over again and let alone for another fortnight.

For the purpose of sowing seeds with regularity and precision I generally employ a board about 2½ inches broad, and of a length equal to the width of the bed. Along each side of the board corresponding notches are cut 2½ inches apart, and these denote the spot on which each seed is to be placed. By always working with a few rows uncovered, the lines may be kept straight throughout the whole length of the bed. The seeds should be sown in shallow drills about 1½ inches deep. A board as described above makes the seedlings stand about 3½ to 2½ inches apart in the bed: and this is about as close as will admit of the young seedlings being taken up subsequently with a good ball of earth attached to their roots.

—propagation by cuttings.

If it is desired to produce seed that shall remain true to a certain type, that procured from plants raised from cuttings is most likely to attain the desired object; but for general purposes the planting out of cuttings cannot be too strongly condemned. But with regard to yield the experiment has been made over and over again in various districts during the past twenty years, and in no case with anything like the success that attends the planting out of seedlings. The reason is obvious. Let any one examine the roots of a four or five-year old plant raised from a cutting, and he will find that it shows no sign of possessing a tap-root. Such plants consequently suffer much in dry weather, and even in favourable seasons do not yield in anything like the same proportion as bushes that have been grown from seed. For these hills there is nothing like a small healthy seedling, taken up with a compact ball of earth adhering to its roots. Early or late in the season it stands the shift better, is sooner established, and when once started makes rapid growth. The utmost care is needed not to bend or otherwise injure the tap-root of the plant, and in transplanting the roots should be buried just up to the collar and no further. From 4 to 6 inches in height is a nice size at which to plant seedlings out. I have seen many planters fork up or pull like carrots both tea and coffee seedlings, and plant them out regardless of the tap-root being broken. No one could expect such a plant to thrive. Shading in favourable monsoon weather is in my opinion unnecessary and unadvisable, but in the case of planting of necessity, very early or very late, in broken weather, will do much to establish and keep the plants in health. I would strongly urge the importance of careful planting : vacancies are avoided, and a fine growth encouraged. It is best to leave the young plants alone for a month or six weeks after planting, when a good weeding may be given all over the estate. From this time however the land cannot be kept too scrupulously clean. A cooly should plant out 200 to 250 plants in a day. Sickly plants can generally be detected three months after planting, and these

CH. XXIX. TEA. should be replaced as early as possible by healthy individuals raised in bamboo baskets. English garden trowels are the best tools for transplanting purposes. The average cost of planting out may be said to be about Rupees 3 to 4 per acre.

—cultivation and pruning. The year after planting, so soon as the spring showers set in, the young plants will commence to shoot freely. Until they have attained a height of from 18 inches to 2 feet they are best left alone; but when the centre and main lateral shoots show an undue tendency to upward growth, they should be cut back. The more spindly the centre growth, the closer back it should be cut. This comparatively rough treatment of the centre will determine the flow of sap more strongly into the lower side branches, and cause the young plants to fill out into symmetrical bushes. Lateral growth might be equally well encouraged by stopping the lateral shoots, and the leaf so obtained might be made into tea. Much risk, however, attends this operation, as it is difficult to make the pickers understand clearly the difference between those shoots which should be picked and those that are best left alone. A light trimming with a knife to all straggling branches is a much safer course.

As far as possible the plants should be trained to a single stem for at least 6 inches above ground. A light surface trimming about the middle of the south-west monsoon, followed by a somewhat severer one at the end of the north-east rains, will probably be found sufficient during the second year. A couple of months or so after this second trimming a crowd of young succulent shoots will spring up all over the surface of each plant; and when these have attained a fair length, say from 6 to 8 inches, the upper leaves may be picked and manufactured. The greatest care however must be taken to allow the lateral branches to grow unchecked. From 2½ to 3 feet is about the best height at which to maintain the surface-level of the plants at pruning. This will allow them from 1 to 1½ feet of upward growth during the course of the picking season; and so long as they are maintained within these limits the women and children can reach with ease the shoots that have to be plucked. About July the plants will be old enough to undergo their first systematic pruning. The upward shoots from which crop has been taken will be shortened back to 1½ or 2 inches of young wood at their base, and those lateral shoots that show much growth will be shortened back to due limits. This course of treatment will be continued until the plants have fully covered their ground, by which time they will have nearly attained their full yielding power.

Judging from my own experience, the best time for pruning is from early June to middle of August, and it is generally about this season[1] that the seed crop of the preceding year has matured, and that of the coming season has formed its flower buds. Excepting at very low elevations hard pruning every year is not advisable. The growth at the higher elevations is not sufficiently strong to enable the plants to stand it. Severe pruning once in from 3 to 4 years is sufficient, and should in old estates be accompanied by forking and manuring wherever practicable.

—picking.

A few remarks are necessary on the subject of picking. It has been already stated that after the second trimming, plucking may be commenced from the centre shoots that have made a growth of from 6 to 8 inches: the lighter, within reasonable limits, that these shoots are picked the better. Young plants of this age have seldom many more leaves than are sufficient to keep the plant in health and support vigorous growth. It is only the supernumerary leaves produced in excess of the requirements by a course of artificial treatment that should be picked and made into tea. The planter's object is to produce an excessive and unnatural yield of leaf, and to do this and maintain the trees in health, skilful management is necessary.

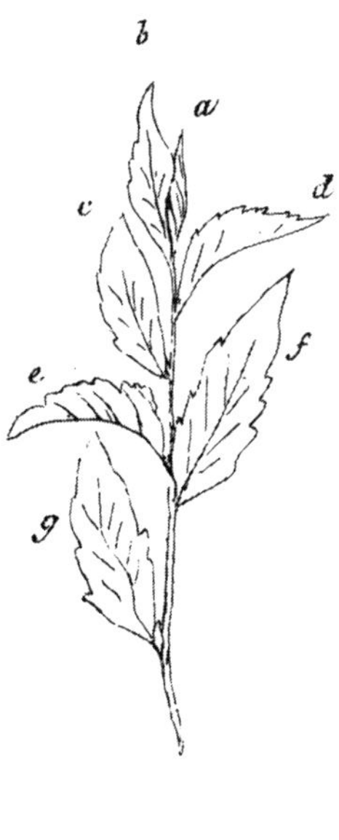

Each of the leaves on the above shoot are known to planters by technical names, as follows:—

---

[1] At high elevations February and March are the best months in which to prune.—ED.

CH. XXIX. — TEA. The convolute bud *a* is generally known as the flowery pekoe leaf, *b* and *c* as orange pekoe leaves, *e* and *f* as souchong, and *g* and *h*, were they sufficiently tender in our climate for the purpose of manufacture, would turn out the coarse leaf known as congou and bohea. But these leaves are not all picked separately, as their names would lead one to suppose; the sorting of the teas is accomplished by means of sieves subsequent to manufacture, and will be treated of in its proper place.

The leaves *a* and *b* should be picked together at the point marked in the diagram, the leaves *c*, *d*, *e*, *f* and *g* just above the bud at the axil of the leaf, care being taken to leave just sufficient of the leaf above the petiole to protect and support the latent bud. In cases where the planter picks all the leaves, the quality of his teas will be materially improved if the leaves are picked and manufactured separately, but there is little objection to the four leaves *a*, *b*, *c*, *d*, being picked and manufactured together. The shoots even of old bushes should be allowed to make fair growth for the first few pickings after pruning; afterwards, when leaves are more numerous, closer plucking may be resorted to.

The convolute bud at the apex of each shoot is what is ultimately known in the manufactured article as the pekoe tip, that white or orange downy leaf, a full proportion of which shows care in the plucking and manufacture and materially increases the value of the tea.

—yield. On the Nílagiris and other elevated hill ranges where tea is grown the yield cannot come up in quantity or strength to that of gardens situate in more tropical climates. The hill planter must therefore rely more on the quality than on the quantity of his outturn.

A good garden of hybrid plants at an elevation of 5,500 to 6,000 feet should, under proper treatment, yield when seven years old from 300 to 350 lb. per acre of manufactured tea, and there is every reason to believe that manured and highly-cultivated estates may be made to produce from 350 to 450 lb. per acre. On the western side of the hills, on the high elevations, I think that from 150 to 250 lb. should be looked upon as a satisfactory return.[1]

The following table will give an idea of what outturn may reasonably be expected under favourable circumstances :—

1st year	...	...	*Nil.*
2nd ,,	...	...	,,

[1] I think Mr. Brace has put these figures too low. From 200 to 300 lb. is in my opinion a moderate estimate.—ED.

3rd year	120	150
4th „	160	200
5th „	220	300
6th „	250	350
7th „	300	350

Low sheltered sites with good soil and sufficient rainfall will give far greater results than gardens that are less fortunately situated.

With regard to the manuring of tea estates, we know that where suitable manures can be purchased and applied at moderate rates, the yield of gardens has in several instances been more than doubled—in fact, that any advance towards high cultivation is found remunerative. No tract of land can go on steadily year after year yielding up its stores of organic and inorganic matter without becoming in time perfectly sterile, unless some restitution is made. The tea planter cannot avail himself of the rotation of crops, and the maintenance of fertility in his soil must be gathered from extraneous sources. Space will not allow of my dealing with this subject at length in this paper, but a few remarks on the chief constituents of the ash of the leaf of the plant, the manures most suited to supply its demand, and the best methods for their application may be treated of briefly. Manuring.

A sample of Nílagiri tea of my own manufacture, kindly analyzed by Professor R. Harvey, of the Madras Medical College, gave the following results:—

Leaves—	
Moisture	10·10
Ash	4·50
Ash—	
Potash	30·20
Phos. acid	16·89
Silica	·75

These are the chief constituents of the soil abstracted by the production of crops of tea, and unless these important elements are in proportion to their exhaustion returned to the soil, a decrease in yield, amounting in the end to absolute sterility, must result. So far as silica is concerned the soil contains, on all good tea lands, an almost permanent supply of this element; the other two, together with various other chemical substances that enter into the composition of the leaf, must be supplied as needed by regular manuring. The substances are found as a rule to a

CH. XXIX. TEA.

sufficient extent in the manures generally in use among planters. Lime, which is generally found present to a considerable extent in the ashes of most other plants, appears only to an inappreciable extent in the ash of the tea leaf, the ash of few of the best tea soils containing 1·50 per cent. of this substance in any form; but, considering the almost total deficiency of our soils as regards lime, it should not be altogether lost sight of in the manures applied. The plants will absorb sufficient for their requirements, rejecting any excess that the soil may contain.

I am indebted to the *Indian Tea Gazette* of June 20th, 1877, for the following extract:—

"In order to determine now what mineral plant-food a would-be good tea soil must contain, and in what proportion, we must base our remarks upon the tea-plant itself, and upon the inorganic substances in it as revealed by an analysis of its ashes.

"Mr. Schrottky gives the composition of the ashes of young leaves of the Assam hybrid tea-plant as follows:—

In 100 *Parts.*

Chloride of Sodium	2·247
Do. Soda	8·941
Do. Potash	36·514
Do Magnesia	10·089
Do. Lime	8·517
Oxide of Iron and Manganese	3·966
Phosphoric Acid	13·017
Silica	0·439
Total ...	99·944

and states that old leaves and stems will contain more lime and silica than here represented."

Present limits will not allow of my entering at any length on the chemistry of the tea-plant. I must content myself with making a few remarks on the object for which manures are applied, those best suited to the tea-planter's requirements, and the best method for their application.

The planter's object in applying manures must not merely be to return to the soil those substances of which previous crops have deprived it, but also, by the judicious application of those substances which form the chief constituents of the plant he intends to cultivate, to increase its capacity for producing crops.

The leading substances which enter into the composition of the tea plant, and in one or more of which the majority of our tea soils are presumably deficient, are phosphoric acid, potash, lime, and sulphuric acid. Silica is always present in abundance.

The manures chiefly in use and most easily procured are—

1. Poudrette.
2. Horse or Pig manure.
3. Cattle manure.
4. Oilcake.
5. Guano.
6. Fish.

Poudrette.

Night-soil has long been known to be one of the most powerful fertilizers. It contains a large proportion of nitrogen. The most valuable form is that manufactured on the principle in use by the Ootacamand Municipality, which process has, by the kind permission of the Honorary Secretary at that time, been published in my larger pamphlet on tea cultivation. To quote a few extracts from that:—

"The poudrette manufactured by the Municipality contains, in addition to poudrette proper, at least 10 per cent. of bone-ash and 10 to 15 per cent. of sheep and bullock's blood."

Many estates situate within a few miles of Ootacamand, Coonoor or Wellington, and possessed of good road communication, are thus enabled to procure a most valuable fertilizer at a moderate cost The only drawback to its application lies in the repugnance of all natives, and even of those of the lowest caste, to have anything to do with it. The bones it contains furnish a large supply of lime and phosphoric acid. Blood, though seldom used as a manure by itself, is a valuable addition to a compost on account of the large proportion of nitrogen it contains.

On large estates—and for that matter small ones too—a considerable supply of ordinary poudrette. may be obtained by establishing a good system of conservancy. The manure so obtained, when deodorised, may with advantage be mixed up with other manures, blood, burnt bones, lime, wood-ashes, charcoal, green weeds, &c. The surface of this and all other manures, while in the heap, should be well covered with a few inches of soil to prevent the escape of ammonia and other volatile gases. It is to be regretted that such a valuable product as this should be allowed, as is the case on most estates, to go to waste.

Horse and pig manure.

Horse and pig manure stand next in order to the above and are richest in nitrogen, and the urine of the pig furnishes a considerable proportion of phosphoric acid. In a fresh state they are somewhat too heating, and previous to application should either be well decomposed or applied in combination with some other substances as a compost. Horse manure is seldom procurable in any quantity, but such supplies as can be procured should be made use of.

In my opinion pigs should be kept to a much greater extent on estates than they are at present, not only on account of the

CH. XXIX. TEA. richness of their manures, as for the immense quantity that they make when well littered down, and the trifling cost of their keep. They will eat and thrive on almost every weed that grows on an estate.

Cattle manure. Cattle manure is the fertilizer most frequently used by the planter, and in many cases the only one procurable. It should be thoroughly decomposed before its application, and is always the better for being made into compost with other substances. Though less heating than horse or pig manure, its effects are more lasting, and it is the only medium with which the more powerful stimulant manures should in small proportion be applied to the soil. The effect of a bushel basket of cattle manure may be said to extend over four years. On all estates some cattle at all events may be maintained, and if these, or a portion of them, can be stall fed, a much larger outturn of manure will be obtained. Manure in a fresh and undecomposed state should not be applied to the roots of any plant, as it is very apt to promote, especially in wet weather, fungoid disease of the roots. A bushel basket of well rotted cattle manure in a fairly dry state will weigh on an average 25 lb., and one such basket to every tree once in four years may be considered sufficiently high cultivation. Allowing 2,000 plants on an average to the acre, this will give us a little over 22 tons to be applied per acre once in every four years. A garden of 100 acres, of which one-fourth is manured at a time, will require 550 tons of cattle manure per annum. In all cases where bone-dust, blood, wood-ashes, lime, &c. are added to the manure, the greater will be its value.

Sheep and goats' droppings are admirable manures, but they do not decompose rapidly.

Oilcake. In places where oilcake can be obtained cheap and in large quantities, a considerable increase of yield may be obtained by its application, and where the manures above named are not procurable in sufficient quantity I can recommend its use. Its effect, however, is very transitory, and frequent application will be needed if much good is to result. Far better feed cattle on it and use it in the second-hand form.

Guano. Guano is beyond doubt, when obtained in a pure state, the most powerful manure known. Its application, except in small quantities and then in conjunction with other less stimulating substances, is not unattended with danger. By itself its effect upon plants is much that of the free use of alcohol on the human system. An unnatural vitality is caused only to subside and bring on relapse directly the stimulant has ceased to act. For farm crops, where its effect is needed on a crop that only occupies the ground for a short time, its value is decidedly great; but for a permanent crop like tea or coffee its use, independent of combination with other substances, is not to be advised. A small quantity, say ¼ to ½ lb. per tree, mixed with half a basket of animal manure, may eke out a scanty supply of the latter, which latter will in its turn serve to check the reaction which would otherwise ensue when the stimulating properties of the guano had subsided.

Fish manure.

Fish is a very powerful and forcing manure, and should, in my opinion, only be used in combination with animal manures. It is very rich both in phosphoric acid and nitrogen. From 1 to 2 lb. fish to ½ to 1 basket of cattle manure should not only have a powerful, but also lasting, effect in increasing the yield of leaf in a garden.

Its direct action may be speedily noticed in the improved brilliance and vigour of the foliage of the plant to which it has been applied.

—application of manures.

Having fully discussed the respective merits of the manures generally in use, I now come to consider the best method of applying them. To illustrate this in the clearest form, I will avail myself of a short extract from Dr. Lindley's "Theory and Practice of Horticulture :"—

"As to the use of applying manure, it must be obvious that it can be of nc use unless it is in contact with the absorbing part of the roots; now these parts are young fibres and spongides as has been already stated, and, when plants have arrived at any size, the roots form the radii of a circle of which the circumference is the principal line of absorption. This being so, if a plant has arrived at the state of a bush or tree, it is useless to apply manure at the base of the stem, because that is precisely where the power of absorption is least, if it exists at all; and, as the circle formed by the roots is generally greater than that of the branches, the proper manner of applying manure is to introduce it into the ground at a distance from the stem about equal to the radius formed by the branches, and yet, although this is so evidently right, I have seen a gardener who ought to have known much better, sedulously administering liquid manure, by pouring it into the soil at the base of the stem, which is much the same thing as if an attempt were made to feed a man through the soles of his feet."

To further illustrate the object I have in view, I shall make another short extract from my lengthier paper on the cultivation of tea !—

"Now the part of the foregoing remarks of Dr. Lindley's to which I wish to draw most earnest attention is that relative to the distance from the stem at which manure should be applied. There are still, in Southern India at any rate, planters who believe that close to the stem is the proper place to bury manure, and many, evidently with a view to render it still more useless, lump it at a depth far below the range of feeding rootlets. Now the advice of Dr. Lindley that the manure

CH. XXIX. TEA.

should be laid at a distance from the stem about equal to the radius of the branches applies to a tree in the open. On a tea estate, where the bushes are grown as closely together as circumstances will permit, we have plants growing under unnatural circumstances, and as we find it necessary to curtail the lateral growth of the branches when they commence to touch one another, so must we deal with the roots also, more especially when supplying them artificially with food. In fact, we must endeavour that the feeding roots of each plant shall not, as a rule, spread much further than a circle formed from the stem with a radius of half the distance between the plants. It is my favourite plan therefore to fork a trench between each pair of plants.

Now as the feeding roots of the plant seldom extend downwards beyond 12 to 18 inches from the surface, and are by far the more numerous and active towards the top, it stands to reason that the nearer the manure is brought in contact with these, the greater its effect will be ; consequently from 9 inches to 1 foot is the best depth for these holes. When the soil has been removed to this depth (injuring the main roots as little as possible), the soil may be loosened with a fork a few inches deeper with advantage. The small fibrous roots torn or cut off will soon be reformed, and that in far greater numbers. I prefer, when practicable, lifting the soil all round the tree, nowhere nearer than from 15 to 18 inches from its stem, on flat or unterraced lands where serious wash is not to be apprehended. On terracing land pits must be dug between the trees. Many planters lay down their manure in trenches cut between the rows, but for my own part I prefer the practice above illustrated.

For loose soils and where the trees are planted at fairly wide distances apart, many planters like to lay their manure on the surface and then fork it in. As a rule much of the manure remains within reach of atmospheric influence and parts with its nourishment to the air instead of the plant.

The manure should not be thrown into the holes in a lump, but well mixed up with the soil, and the whole covered with a good 3 inches of earth to prevent the evaporation of its constituents during decomposition."

Weeding.

A few remarks are called for on this subject. I would most strongly urge that land that has been put under tea should be kept clean from the outset. All plants other than that which it is the planter's object to cultivate, abstract nourishment from the soil and do not, even when buried green, return all that they have absorbed. On light soils hand-weeding is to be preferred. On stiff soils a light scraping with the mamoty will not injure the trees, but will aid materially in keeping the soil open. Tea will not be found to thrive on lands which are overrun with grasses, *cyperaceæ*, or any other dense growth of weeds.

During the first year a weeding once in every six weeks will, in all probability, be found sufficient, and during the two following years once in every two months. By this time the seeds originally contained in the soil have been either extirpated by these frequent clearings or have in all probability lost their vitality, and but little trouble or expense will be hereafter incurred in keeping the land clean. Some weeds, such as the goat-weed (*Ageratum cordifolium*), exhaust the soil more than others, but as it is far better to allow none at all to grow, I shall not enter into further details regarding them. Grasses and ferns are, as a rule, the most troublesome to extirpate, but a good forking up of the roots will generally be found effectual.

Culture of green crops.

There are but few gardens which cannot spare a few acres for the culture of green crops for stall feeding cattle and other stock. The number of profitable plants from which the planter can take his choice is very considerable. Maize, Guinea, Mauritius, rye, and other grasses, cabbages, turnips, mangold-wurtzel, swedes, prickly comfrey, buckwheat, santung cabbage, lucerne, potatoes, *cum multis aliis*, offer a wide field for choice.

It was originally my intention to enter into some detail with regard to the various ills, insect and vegetable, to which the tea plant is heir. I have however arrived at the conclusion that it will be enough to point out the one unfailing panacea for all these evils, and that is, good systematic cultivation. Do not overpick your plants when young or overprune them ; do not let them become choked by weeds, or fail to feed them when they need it. There need be but little apprehension of disease if these principles are carried out : healthy plants are rarely attacked.

So far as the cultivation of the tea plant is concerned my task is now done. A few paragraphs on the manufacture and on one or two points of interest connected with tea planting in general will bring this paper to a close.

On manufacture.

In the third year the planter will begin to gather a small crop from his garden, and, although this cannot be expected to pay his working expenses, it will be found to go some considerable way towards doing so, and fully justify, at the end of the second year, the erection of a tea-house.

For an estate of 50 acres or less a building 50 feet long and 18 to 20 feet wide, the walls $1\frac{1}{2}$ feet thick and 9 feet high inside, of burnt brick, should give ample accommodation. The roof should be of corrugated or continuous iron. If a good pitch is given to the roof, a loft laid on the tie-beams will materially increase the accommodation.

The furnaces and trays for drying black tea should be laid along one end wall, their mouths facing outwards, and I most strongly recommend that all the black and fancy teas should be dried over iron plates and not by the direct action of charcoal, as so universally practised in our leading tea districts. Charcoal

CH. XXIX. — TEA. — has no direct influence on the quality of tea, whereas the saving from the use of wood is very considerable.

Though it may not be the planter's intention to manufacture green teas to any extent, it is a good plan to have two or three iron tea pans in every factory. They are of great service in warming broken teas previous to packing, and, if a demand for green teas should occur, can be turned to their legitimate use. One or two tables, say 12 feet long, 4 feet wide, and 3 feet high, will be needed for rolling the leaf gathered, and a few zinc-lined bins, capable of holding from 500 to 2,000 lb. of manufactured tea, will be found necessary.

I have no opportunity of providing plates to illustrate these necessary items of tea-house furniture, but as the majority of estates on these hills are more or less well supplied with them, an intending planter has only to visit one or two gardens in order to be fully acquainted with what is necessary.

For many of the details of this subject I shall have to quote a few extracts *verbatim* from my lengthier paper on Tea Cultivation in Southern India.

A slight notice has already been taken of the leaves ordinarily plucked for the purpose of manufacture. Whether four leaves as *a, b, c, d*, are all plucked and manufactured together, or *a, b, c*, and *d, e, f*, are plucked and prepared separately, matters little so far as the general description of the various processes to which the leaf is subjected are concerned.

First, to note the leading points of difference between black and green teas.

—difference between black and green teas.

1. The leaf of the former has a portion of its moisture evaporated by withering in the sun (or artificially) until quite soft or flaccid. The latter is rendered sufficiently soft for manipulation by a short but brisk panning.

2. With black teas, the juice is retained so far as practicable in the leaf, and subsequently evaporated by a slower process. In the manufacture of green teas it is expressed from the outset, and the leaf subsequently dried at a higher temperature.

3. Black tea is allowed, after the rolling has been completed, to stand and take colour, *i.e.*, incipient fermentation is allowed to take place, thereby converting a great portion of the tannin, the bitter principle contained in tea leaf, into gallic acid, and thus softening the astringency it would otherwise possess. If this process is carried too far, strength is lost, and what brokers term sourness results.

After these few introductory remarks I propose to deal with the treatment of the leaf from the time it is weighed in at the factory. If coarse leaves are picked, they should be manufactured separately from the finer leaves.

CH. XXIX.

TEA.

Manufacture of black tea.

The manner in which leaf should be plucked has already been explained. The next object is that the leaf plucked should be kept perfectly cool, not pressed down so hard in the picker's basket as to generate heat in the centre and thus cause fermentation to set in. As a safeguard against this, the leaf gathered is weighed in, as a rule, in most gardens twice during the day, first at from noon to 1 P.M., finally when work is left off. The leaf brought in is, so soon as it has been weighed, spread out thinly on racks covered with bamboo mats. A free circulation of air among the leaf is desirable, as this much hastens the evaporation of the moisture contained in it. The more moisture there is in the leaf and atmosphere, the thinner it should be spread out; when this has been done, the leaf is left on the racks until the following morning.

—withering.

The first operation now is to wither the leaf, *i.e.*, to extract by evaporation so much of the moisture it contains as to enable it to be rolled and take a good twist without breaking. To do this, the head tea maker, when the rays of the morning sun have become sufficiently powerful, spreads it out thinly in shallow flat baskets, or on bamboo mats, turning it over frequently. When thoroughly withered the hairy down on the pekoe tips will be seen to stand clearly out from the leaf when held to the light, and the stem may be bent back both ways without snapping. The feel of the leaf is in a great measure the best guide to go by, but practice only can teach the planters when the leaf is ready to roll. As in our climate the sun does not always attend on our wishes, we must at times manage to do without his aid, either by keeping the leaf until sufficient moisture is evaporated, or by making it into green tea. Some heat the leaf slightly in pans or on trays previous to rolling; but I cannot recommend the practice, as the leaf so treated either turns sour or colours badly afterwards—in the latter case the outturn shows very green. When sunshine fails, I advise the planter to spread his leaf out thinly in a warm corner of the tea-house, and wait patiently until the leaf is soft enough to roll, when he must do the best he can with it.

Over exposure to the sun is a mistake, as it blackens some of the leaf, and causes the fine pekoe tips to become discoloured and undistinguishable from the coarser leaf. Moreover it much weakens the infusion. On a moderately bright morning a quarter of an hour in the sun and an hour or so inside the factory will bring the leaf into fit condition for rolling.

Previous to the rolling process leaf should never be spread thickly or allowed to lie in mass, or heat will be generated in the centre and the tea turn sour.

CH. XXIX. — TEA. — —rolling.

Rolling is a process in which no small amount of dexterity is required to turn out first-rate work. Some planters roll the leaf straight out; others with a circular sweep of the hand, taking care always to work in the same direction. The latter motion may be best described as that of an eccentric set on a false axis. The latter method is the better in my opinion. Some roll their leaf very heavily, making a regular lather of the juice; this is bad, as in addition to weakening the tea by undue expression, the finer leaves get broken. The leaf should be lightly rolled, the juices being little more than brought to the surface, and only sufficiently expressed to cause the leaves to adhere when compressed by the hand into the form of a cone or ball. The fine twist and curl are communicated to the leaf not by hard pressure, but by frequently taking up and intermingling the mass as the rolling progresses, and picking out, for subsequent separate treatment, any hard coarse leaves that have been brought in. As to the amount that a man should take up at a time, sufficient to make when rolled a ball as large as a full-sized cricket-ball is enough; with a smaller quantity the leaf is apt to be broken, and with the larger the roll will not be even nor the twist good. The time taken to roll a handful will be from seven to fifteen minutes. It is better not to judge by time but from the appearance of the leaf. When ready the leaf should be taken up between the two hands and pressed into the form of a ball or cone. Ready for the reception of these a blanket is laid single-fold on a bin or at one end of the rolling table, the upper fold being rolled up until the exposed half has been fully covered with balls of leaf. Few men in Southern India will roll well more than 25 to 30 lb. of leaf a day.

—second rolling.

Some planters are in the habit of giving the leaf a slight panning and then a light second roll, in order to perfect the appearance of the tea: when the twist looks insufficient, or the get-up of the tea is of special importance, this is an excellent plan.

—rolling by machinery.

While on this subject I may as well venture a few remarks on the advantages of rolling tea by machinery. The only machine with which I am hitherto acquainted that can be said to do its work satisfactorily, and to save a vast expenditure of labour without in the least degree impairing the quality of the produce, is that patented by Messrs. W. and J. Jackson, late of Assam. The Calcutta Agents from whom these may be procured to order are Messrs. Williamson, Magor and Co.

The great drawback to the use of these machines, so far as the Nílagiris are concerned, is the excessive prime cost, somewhere about £110 sterling in Great Britain, and then only large estates of 100 acres or upwards, in full bearing, would be justified in incurring so heavy an outlay. In Bengal these machines are worked by steam-power, but on these hills there is hardly an estate to be found that has not a sufficient water-supply to work a 2 to 3-horsepower turbine or overshot water-wheel. CH. XXIX. TEA.

Where a number of small gardens lie within reasonable distances of one another, the owners might club together with advantage and set up one of these machines for their joint use, or some enterprising individual, who cultivated a somewhat larger acreage than his neighbours, might do well by manufacturing their tea for them at a moderate rate per pound.

Even with Jackson's machine a light hand rolling is afterwards necessary; but this takes so little either of time or labour, that the cost may be said to be merely nominal. I am convinced that this machine does as perfect work as machinery can ever attain to, and that its working is never likely to be materially improved on.

When the leaf is all rolled, the upper fold of the blanket should be folded closely down and the leaf left to take colour.

—colouring.

Many planters colour their tea loose and in heaps. It is not my practice to do so at first, but only towards the end of the process, or if I see that the cones are not colouring evenly throughout. Time is no test at all. I have coloured tea on these hills in 1½ hours, whereas on another occasion I have known it stand for eight hours and even then not take any colour. At an elevation of about 5,500 feet the thermometer will range as a rule between 70° to 86°, and the time required to colour the leaf properly will vary from 2½ down to 1½ hours.

The colour of the leaf when ready for drying should be a brownish olive. If the fine leaf is too brown there is risk of sourness, and the strength of the sample will be affected; if the larger leaves are too green there will be a raw acrid flavour in the liquor after infusion. So long as the leaves that still appear green are only a few coarse ones that have got in here and there, it does not much matter: these will come out in the sifting. Of the two evils, let your tea be under rather than over coloured. Constant attention and practice are the only things that can help you. A fairly trained staff, with whom a little trouble has been taken at the outset, may be trusted to work by themselves in a very short time. I have seen various means of forcing out the colour practised, but do not advise the adoption of any of them.

When this process has been completed, the cones should be broken up thoroughly, no small lumps being allowed to remain, and the whole spread out thinly until the trays are ready to receive it.

—drying appliances.

Now before going on any further with the manufacture, I will explain the various appliances in use for drying off

CH. XXIX. TEA.

teas. Previous to the introduction of the trays now in general use in Southern India, the tea used to be dried off in bamboo basket dhools over charcoal fires. The objections to these were very great: in the first place the sides were never air-tight and the greater portion of the heat was wasted. To obviate this, the sides were often plastered with cow-dung, and any stray spark catching this imparted a full but doubtfully desirable flavour to the tea. Secondly, the belt in the centre on which the bamboo sieve was almost always irregularly pitched did not fit accurately the sieve on which the tea rested. Thirdly, from the constant falling through, on to the fire, of fine leaf and dust, the chances of turning out "smoky burnt" tea were much enhanced. Lastly, an enormous number of these dhools, and a proportionate number of men to watch them, were necessary in order to dry off any quantity of leaf. A better form of dhool, *i.e.*, one made of cast-iron, was proposed by Mr. Haworth in his report on tea in Cachar, but even this did not provide a remedy for the last-named objection. In fact rather than use appliances of this nature I would prefer to dry off the teas in pans, but this is a tedious process, and the risk of sourness (perhaps the worst fault a tea can possess) is rendered much too probable.

The most satisfactory apparatus for drying off tea that I have hitherto met with, is the tray apparatus (the invention of an eminent Cachar planter, and also figured by Mr. Haworth in his report) now in almost universal use on the Nílagiris. I regret that I have no means of appending an illustration of it; but intending planters have but to visit the nearest tea estate to see it in full working. In Bengal these drawers are always laid on masonry over charcoal fires. The introduction of the hot-air principle by means of an iron plate let into the masonry of the furnace at a height of 18 inches was an improvement introduced by a Nílagiri planter, and, both as regards economy of fuel and excellence of quality of the article manufactured by its means, is worthy of universal adoption. The advantages of the iron plate system are—

1. That the heat can be better regulated.
2. That there is less risk of burning, or, as in the case of bad charcoal (the furnaces are fed from outside), of communicating a smoky flavour to the tea.
3. That as there is a false drawer with a zinc bottom to catch all the dust and broken tips when the teas are turned over in the course of drying, the risk of smoky burnt teas, caused by particles dropping on the fire or iron plate is obviated.
4. That the cost of preparing charcoal is done away with.

The iron plate should be 24 to 28 inches, and from $\frac{5}{16}$ to $\frac{3}{8}$ inches thick. Cast-iron plates procured from England are the best. The plates cast in this country are always uneven in thickness throughout, and, from the hardness of the metal, liable to crack right across. Wrought iron plates heat more readily, but from their expansion and contraction in proportion as they are influenced by heat or cold require to be more strongly fixed in the masonry. A good compound for plastering the inside face of the walls of the furnaces may be made as follows:—4 parts soorkee, 4 best stiff clay, 1 lime. Some planters use ordinary lime and sand, tempered with water infused with gall-nuts and to which jaggery and white of eggs have been added; but I have my doubts as to the efficacy of this mixture.

—drying off.

Above the plate, which should have an exposed surface of from 15 to 18 inches square, the masonry sides may widen out rapidly to the same dimensions at top as the trays that are about to be laid over them. The best size for the trays is 2 feet 6 inches square. The lowest tray is but half the depth of the upper ones, and the bottom is of block tin or zinc. Whenever any of the upper trays are drawn out, either to be filled or to have the tea they contain rearranged, this bottom tray is drawn out simultaneously with the other to catch all the dust and pekoe tips that fall through the wire gauze; otherwise these would fall upon the heated iron, and communicate a burnt flavour to the teas that were drying above. When the upper tray has been returned, the bottom tray is drawn out, and either laid on the top of the set or aside, as may be most convenient. A slab of wood covers the mouth to retain the heat.

The three upper trays are those which contain the leaf that is to be dried off. These are about 3 inches in depth, and the bottom of each covered with fine well-stretched galvanized iron wire gauze. The leaf to be dried should be spread over these drawers from 1 to 1½ inches thick, commencing with the bottom drawer. When the tea in the bottom drawer has begun to get dry, *i.e.*, when all fear of further fermentation has passed away, the drawer may change places with the empty one above it, and the latter be filled with fresh leaf. When almost dry, the same change may be effected with the uppermost drawer, the latter being placed lowest to receive fresh leaf. When the tea in the top drawer is thoroughly dried, it may be removed, and the same process continued until all the leaf in hand has been dried off.

The man who superintends the drying off must first ascertain, by placing his hand inside the mouth-place of the bottom drawer, that the furnaces have been heated to a proper degree. There

CH. XXIX. — TEA.

should be a good brisk heat at first, so much so that the hand can only just be held inside for a few moments without discomfort. If this is not carefully attended to, it is quite as easy to turn tea sour in the trays as by allowing it to ferment unduly during the colouring process. Thermometers are useless as a test, as the heat has invariably burnt the bulb of all that I have ever tried. Practice alone can decide when the heat is sufficient, and a few trials will give the requisite knowledge. When the whole process of drying off has been completed, the drawers may be filled up any how with the tea made, and laid one above the other on top of the wood-work to give the tea the benefit of the warmth given out by the cooling plates all through the night. The next morning the whole may be weighed, and, if not required for immediate sale, be thrown into a large bin to await the process of sifting.

Manufacture of green tea.

We now come to the manufacture of green teas. The chief drawbacks to the manufacture of these are that they require more labour, closer supervision, and are, as a class, wholly unsaleable in the local market. Their London value, too, fluctuates to such an extent as to render the manufacture of them a most precarious business. The advantage about them is that they can readily be turned out in dull cold weather, when the turning out of black teas of fine quality is a somewhat difficult task. The planter will do well to have a sufficient number of pans in his factory, so as to enable him to turn out teas of this description as occasion may require.

With regard to the setting up of these pans, some lay them in the masonry horizontally, others at a slight incline, say of 30°. I prefer the latter method. It lessens the risk of burning odd leaves here and there, renders it easier to empty the pans of leaf, facilitates the regulation of the temperature, and in the final process of bringing out the colour at a high temperature makes this process less trying to the workman's hands.

Leaf that is intended to be made into green tea is not withered in the sun; in fact manufacture may be commenced from the time of its being brought into the factory. Previous to commencing, the pans have, I conclude, been fired up to a moderate heat, but not sufficiently so to cause the leaf to crackle violently so soon as it touches the pan. One man will be required to warm the leaf for every eight to ten men employed in rolling. The quantity of leaf weighed out for each pan at a time should be from twenty to thirty pounds. This amount having been weighed out, the head tea-maker takes up enough leaf to make up a double handful for each man engaged in rolling, and pans it at a gentle heat until it is thoroughly warm, soft, and flaccid. The mass is then swept out of the pan into a basket and thrown out from this on to the rolling table. It is immediately taken up by the rollers, who set to work on it at once.

"In rolling green tea a considerably greater amount of pressure may be brought to bear upon the leaf than in the case of rolling for black teas, and the matter of the leaf being a little more broken does not signify so long as it is not literally cut to pieces and a fine close twist left on the leaf. This is only to be attained by frequently shaking up the leaf during rolling. When the leaf has been sufficiently rolled, each man should take up his handful and compress it into a firm ball, squeezing as much juice as he possibly can out of it. This done, the ball should be thoroughly broken up and the leaf spread out very thin on a table or mat. The latter point is of the greatest importance, as any slight heating of the leaf in this stage would cause fermentation to set in, and a dark colour would be communicated to the liquor after infusion.

"So soon as the first batch of leaf has been rolled once, a second is brought from the pan and similarly treated; and this is done until the whole twenty or thirty pounds has received the first roll. The whole is then again heated at a slightly increased temperature for about ten minutes and is then brought back to receive a second roll. The latter should take about five minutes, and the leaf should then be again compressed, and any superfluous juice squeezed out. The balls are now broken up again, and the whole returned to the pans for the final drying off. The temperature of the pans may now be materially increased, but not to an excessive degree, until nearly all the juice contained in the leaf has been evaporated and the latter has assumed a greyish black colour. The leaf will turn very dark in the drying process, but the colour will come out all right in the end. When the leaf seems nearly dry and assuming a greyish tint, the pan should be made as hot as the workmen's hands can bear it. Two men should now be set to each pan, and the leaf whirled round and round as quickly as possible, not a single particle being allowed to remain stationary at the bottom of the pan for a second, or burning will result. It is on this final process that the "colour" depends, and until the men have become expert at it, and their hands hardened, it is very difficult to get them, without close supervision, to keep the pans at the proper temperature. The men should relieve each other every half minute or so until the bloom has come out, which may be ascertained by taking up a handful and holding it to the light. As the tea cools the bloom will be more strongly developed.

"The colour to aim at is a bright pearly French grey; and if the planter has never seen a really first-class green tea turned out, he should procure a sample from a broker, and try to work up to it. It is of still more importance to keep green tea dry than black; it will absorb moisture freely, and the bloom will be lost, probably beyond hope of recovery, by another firing.

"The time taken in turning out a batch of green tea will occupy from two to three hours; an even steady heat up to the time of

CH. XXIX. — TEA.

commencing to bring out the colour is the point to aim at. If you hear your half-dried leaf hissing and crackling, heave it out into a cooler pan at once.

"The tasting of green teas is conducted in the same manner as that of black, but widely different results are looked for. The liquor should be a pale primrose straw-colour, and the flavour full strong and very pungent. The outturn of the leaf should be a bright pea-green. If the liquor be at all dark, we may rest assured that some leaves have been allowed to take colour either in the rolling or drying processes; and the colour of the outturn will tell the tale by showing a few discoloured leaves here and there. When the dried sample shows much yellow leaf we may be sure these latter have been burnt."

—tasting teas.

It is as well to taste every day's make. For the following general directions I was indebted some years back to Messrs. Morcen and Co. of Calcutta.

"Infuse the leaf, allowing it to draw for five minutes. If the tea is fine in quality, the leaf after infusion will be of a light salmony colour, or in other words the colour of a bright new penny-piece, and the liquor will be of a bright rich ruby colour. If under-fermented, some greenish leaf will be observed after infusion, and the liquor will be of a pale colour and have a sharp, pungent greenish taste. If over-fermented, the infusion will come out of a dusky olive green colour, and the liquor, although dark, will have a dull look and a soft insipid taste, and if much over-fermented, sourness will ensue."

"It often happens that the planter can get cup and bowls, but not the accompanying scales and weights. Under these circumstances any other scale will suit his purpose, and the weight of ¼ tola or of a 4-anna bit will tell him the exact amount of leaf to be infused. He must be careful to measure accurately the time allowed for infusion, viz., five minutes. Fresh spring water should be used: water that has been previously boiled and allowed subsequently to cool will not develope satisfactorily the qualities of the tea. The finer the leaf from which the sample is taken the stronger and richer the liquor will be. Dull dark leaves in the outturn after infusion may be owing to two causes, over-fermentation or burning in the trays; generally, in the latter case, the burnt flavour will be detected in the liquor. If the cement which lines the well beneath the trays has cracked and allows smoke to come through, the flavour of the tea will be affected, and the same thing may occur from particles of dust falling into the plate."

—sifting and storing.

It is advisable to keep the tea in bulk in the bins until there is enough accumulated to make up a moderate break for the London market. All damaged teas should be kept separate. Evenness in quality in each day's make is a great desideratum. Sifting is a dusty task, and one likes to have it going on in the tea-house as seldom as possible. With a large outturn and limited accommodation, it is true that sifted tea occupies much less space in the bins, but where ample space for all operations is provided, I prefer the former course. To repeat what I have said elsewhere,—

"One of the reasons for storing the tea in bulk is, that in no two consecutive days can one depend upon the tea manufactured being of the same quality and value; and if the daily teas turned out were sifted and packed separately, the quality of the teas packed in the several boxes might be found to differ materially. Sifting therefore just previous to despatch, and mixing in one heap all the tea according to its class, obviates this difficulty."

"Up to the present time our teas, both black and green, have been stored in the bins in the same state as they were at the end of the drying process. We now come to the business of assorting them for the London market. This is done, as a rule, by means of brass wire sieves of standard mesh, or, in large concerns, by machinery. I have seen planters in Southern India use bàmboo sieves of native make, but these are always irregular in mesh, and stand but a small amount of work. The best sieves are those procured from P. Jonas, Esq., 155, Fanwork Street, London, E.C. A full set will consist of Nos. 4, 6, 8, 10, 12, 14. The number of the sieve represents the number of spaces to the square inch. No. 4, the largest size, will only be required in case the planter manufactures the coarser leaves. No. 6 is the most useful all round. The tea that passes through this will, if well made, turn out a good pekoe, worth from 2*s*. to 3*s*. per lb., or at the worst a pekoe souchong worth from 1*s*. 10*d*. to 2*s*. 3*d*. per lb. If he sells his tea in this country, I advise the planter to use this sieve only. If no coarse leaf has been picked, and the rolling has been done properly, the tea that passes through this sieve may be classed as good pekoe, while that which remains will be a fair souchong. The dust, broken flat leaf, and tips will be subsequently winnowed out with a common bamboo rice fan, and be added to that which fell through from the trays in the process of drying.

"If, however, the planter means to sell his produce in London, he will find it advisable to assort it to a greater extent. He should begin with the finer sieves, and go on to the coarser. Thus:

Sieves 12–10 will turn out fine orange pekoes.
Sieve 8 do. pekoe.
Sieve 6 do. pekoe or pekoe souchong.
That which is left forms No. 6, souchong or congou.

"If he passed the dust, &c. through a No. 14, he may send this home as broken orange pekoe, but it is better perhaps not to do this, but to send the dust, tips, and broken flat leaf as broken pekoe. When there is much broken or flat leaf a decline of 2*d*. to 4*d*. per lb. in the value must be expected.

"The whole of the tea for despatch should be sifted out at once, and each quality kept separate until the whole is done, when packing

CH. XXIX. — TEA.

may commence. This ensures evenness of quality throughout the boxes which constitute the boreah.

"The sifting of green teas is conducted in exactly the same manner, but the teas are differently named. Sieve No. 12 will turn out Young Hyson, the flat and broken leaf winnowed out of this Hyson Skin, No. 10 will give Hyson No. 1, No. 8 Hyson No. 2, No. 6 Imperial Gunpowder, that which remains Gunpowder."

Messrs. W. and J. Jackson have patented a very powerful and satisfactory sifting machine, but its working capacities are too great for our small gardens. There is, however, procurable from Messrs. J. Savage and Sons, Eastcheap, London, a very excellent mixing and sifting machine, the price of which is £14. This will sift readily 1,000 lb. per day of 10 hours.

—packing. Boxes of excellent make and even weight are procurable at moderate rates from the Cochin Steam Mills Co., Cochin. These being worked by machinery are packed flat for travelling and put together (the sides being numbered) as required for use. The boxes I am in the habit of using are No. 1, 100 lb. full chests.

Inside measurement.			
Length 21 inches Depth 18 „ Width 17 „	will contain on an average	broken pekoe .. orange pekoe .. pekoe souchong .. souchong or congou..	110–125 lb. 110 „ 100 „ 90 „
No. 2, Half Chests.			
Length 14½ inches Depth 15½ „ Width 14½ „	will contain on an average	broken pekoe .. orange pekoe ..	50 lb. 45 „
No. 3, 20 lb. Boxes.			
Length 12 inches Depth 12 „ Width 12 „	will contain on an average	broken or orange pekoe pekoe	25 lb. 20 „

It is not advisable to pack the coarser tea for home shipment in boxes containing less than a Bengal maund of 82 lb.

The boxes must be put together securely, care being taken to drive in each nail perfectly straight. If any points project inside the lead will be torn. For 20 lb. boxes 1 inch French wire nails, and for the half and full chests 1½ inch similar nails should be used.

Previous to packing the boxes must be leaded. Tea lead is sold in sheets of regular size by the cut. Both Betts' and Compton's lead are of excellent quality. The best size of sheet is 37–22, and these sheets weigh, as a rule, about 1½ lb.

When the boxes are all ready and the teas have been sifted, they must, whether green or black, be fired again so as to be packed hot. Tea that has been fired will stand great pressure without the leaf breaking. When the required quantity has been packed in each box and well pressed down, the top should be carefully soldered. The top of the box is then nailed down, and the ends bound with ¾ inch iron hooping. CH. XXIX. TEA.

All that now remains is to brand the boxes. There should be a distinct mark of the estate on the top of each box, and on the front side below this the number of the box, the quality of the tea, and the tare and trett weight clearly marked. Nothing now remains but to despatch the teas for shipment.

CHAPTER XXX.

CHINCHONA CULTURE.

Botanical Order—species—native countries—distribution—discovery of medicinal qualities—by whom described.—Threatened failure of American supplies of bark.—Suggestions for introduction of chinchona into the East Indies—attempts to introduce made by the French and Dutch—the Indian Government recommends the sending of a collector to South America—the Court of Directors select Mr. Markham for the duty—his search—Mr. Spruce's search for *Red barks*—Mr. Pritchett's search for Grey barks—Mr. Cross procures *Crown bark* Seeds—Pitayo barks.—Selection of sites on the Nílagiris and formation of plantations—area of plantations—financial results.—Policy of Government in regard to the plantation scheme.—The manufacture of alkaloids in the country.—Mr. Broughton appointed quinologist—his researches—Amorphous quinine.—Alkaloid manufactory.—Analysis of barks.—Chief species and varieties of chinchona in India.—Cultivation.—Manure.—Harvesting the bark.—Drying the bark.—Packing.—Publications on chinchona.

CH. XXX.

CHINCHONA CULTURE.

Order.

THE genus Chinchona, the number of species of which has been reduced by Messrs. Hooker and Bentham to thirty-six, belongs to the order of *Chinchonaceæ*, one of the five natural orders appertaining to the chinchonal alliance—an alliance which, it is of interest to note, is not far removed from the Myrtles, to which order belongs the Eucalyptus or gum of Australia—being distinguished therefrom by the small embryo and large quantity of albumen. The order has two sub-divisions: (1) Coffeæ, (2) Chinchonaceæ. Of it Dr. Lindley remarks:—

"Cinchonads[1] are almost exclusively found in the hotter parts of the world, especially within the tropics, where they are said to constitute about one-twenty-ninth of the whole number of flowering plants. This order is not only one of the largest of which we have knowledge, but also contains a very considerable number of most important species largely employed for the use of man in the countries they inhabit. Many are accordingly the most valuable of remedial agents, acting as tonics, febrifuges, emetics, or purgatives; others, on the contrary, having their secretions in a state of great concentration, prove to be formidable poisons: nevertheless a few produce eatable fruit, and one is distinguished above all others for its agreeable stimulating seeds.[2] Dyeing qualities are also observed in a small number."

[1] Vegetable Kingdom, *Cinchonals.*
[2] Coffee.

Cephælis Ipecacuanha, the ipecacuanha of commerce, a native of the damp forests of Brazil, belongs to this order; also the *Gardenias*, so well known to the visitors to Hindu temples in the Peninsula.

CH. XXX. — CHINCHONA CULTURE.

The following table,[1] taken from the Pharmacographia of Messrs. Flückiger and Hanbury, exhibits the principal species their countries produce :—

—species.

Conspectus of the principal Species of Chinchona.

Species (excluding sub-species and varieties) according to Weddell.	Where figured.	Native Country.	Where Cultivated.	Product.
I.—Stirps Cinchonæ officinalis.				
1. Cinchona officinalis, Hook ...	Bot. Mag. 5364	Ecuador (Loxa)	India, Ceylon, Java.	Loxa or Crown Bark, Pale Bark.
2. ,, macrocalyx, Pav. ...	Howard N. Q...	Peru ...	...	Ashy Crown Bark. The sub-species *C. Palton* affords an important sort called *Palton Bark*, much used in the manufacture of quinine.
3. ,, lucumæfolia, Pav. ...	Do. ...	Ecuador, Peru	...	Carthagena Bark, confounded with Palton Bark, but is not so good.
4. ,, lanceolata, R. et P. (?)	Do. ...	Peru ...	...	
5. ,, lancifolia, Mutis ...	Karst. tab. 11, 12.	New Granada.	India ...	Columbian Bark. Imported in immense quantities for manufacture of quinine. The soft Columbian Bark is produced by Howard's var. *oblonga*.
6. ,, amygdalifolia, Wedd.	Wedd. tab. 6 ...	Peru, Bolivia...	...	A poor bark, not now imported.
II.—Stirps Cinchonæ rugosæ.				
7. Cinchona Pitayensis, Wedd. ...	Karst. tab. 22, *C. Trianæ*.	New Granada (*Popayan*).	India ...	Pitayo bark. Very valuable; used by makers of quinine; it is the chief source of quinidine.
8. ,, rugosa, Pav. ...	Howard N. Q.	Peru ...	...	Bark unknown, probably valueless.
9. ,, Mutisii, Lamb. ...	Do. ...	Ecuador ...	...	Bark not in commerce, contains only aricine.
10. ,, hirsuta, R. et P. ...	Wedd. tab. 21	Peru ...	...	
11. ,, Carabayensis, Wedd.	Do. 19	Peru, Bolivia.	...	Bark not collected.
12. ,, Pahudiana, How. ...	Howard N. Q.	Peru ...	India, Java	A poor bark, yet of handsome appearance; propagation of tree discontinued.
13. ,, asperifolia, Wedd. ...	Wedd. tab. 20	Bolivia ...	...	Bark not collected.
14. ,, umbellulifera, Pav...	Howard N. Q...	Peru ...	...	Bark not known as a distinct sort.
15. ,, glandulifera, R. et P.	Do. ...	Do. ...	...	Do. do.
16. ,, Humboldtiana, Lamb.	Do. ...	Do. ...	...	False Loxa bark; Jaen bark. A very bad bark.
III.—Stirps Cinchonæ micranthæ.				
17. Cinchona Australis, Wedd. ...	Wedd. tab. 8 ...	South Bolivia.	...	An inferior bark, mixed with *Calisaya*.
18. ,, scrobiculata, H. et B.	Do. ...	Peru ...	...	Bark formerly known as *Red Cusco Bark* or *Santa Ana Bark*.
19. ,, Peruviana, How. ...	Howard N. Q...	Do. ...	India	Grey Bark, Huanuco or Lima Bark. Chiefly consumed on the Continent.
20. ,, nitida, R. et P. ...	Do. ...	Do. ...	Do.	
21. ,, micrantha, R. et P...	Do. ...	Do. ...	Do.	

[1] Quoted in Dr. KING's *Manual of Chinchona Cultivation*.

Conspectus of the principal Species of Chinchona—(Continued).

Species (excluding sub-species and varieties) according to Weddell.	Where figured.	Native Country.	Where Cultivated.	Product.
IV.—Stirps Cinchonæ Calisayæ.				
22. Cinchona calisaya, Wedd. ...	Wedd. tab. 9 ...	Peru, Bolivia.	India, Ceylon, Java, Jamaica, Mexico.	Calisaya Bark, Bolivian Bark, Yellow Bark. The tree exists under many varieties; bark also very variable.
23. " elliptica, Wedd. ...	...	Peru (Carabaya).	...	Carabaya Bark. Bark scarcely now imported. *C. euneura*, Miq. (flower and fruit unknown), may perhaps be this species.
V.—Stirps Cinchonæ ovatæ.				
24. Cinchona purpurea, R. et P. ...	Howard N. Q...	Peru (Huamalies).	...	Huamalies Bark. Not now imported.
25. " rufinervis, Wedd. ...	Do. ...	Peru, Bolivia...	...	Bark a kind of light *Calisaya*.
26. " succirubra, Pav. ...	Do. ...	Ecuador ...	India, Ceylon, Java, Jamaica.	Red Bark. Largely cultivated in British India.
27. " ovata, R. et P. ...	Do. ...	Peru, Bolivia ..	India (?) Java (?)	Inferior Brown and Grey Barks.
28. " cordifolia, Mutis ...	Karst. tab. 8...	New Granada, Peru.	...	Columbian Bark (in part). Tree exists under many varieties; bark of some used in manufacture of quinine.
29. " Tucujensis, Karst. ...	Do. 9...	Venezu ela..	...	Maracaibo Bark.
30. " pubescens, Vahl. ...	Wedd. tab. 16	Ecuador, Peru, Bolivia.	...	Arica Bark, Cusco Bark, from var. *Pelletieriana*, Some of the varieties contain aricine. *C. caloptera*, Miq., is probably a variety of this species.
31. " pupurascens, Wedd....	Do. 18	Bolivia ...	...	Bark unknown in commerce.

—native countries.

"The trees producing the medicinal barks are all natives of tropical South America, where they are found in the dense forests of the mountainous regions of the western part of that continent at a height of from 2,500 to 9,000 feet above the level of the sea, and in an equable but comparatively cool climate. The cinchona-producing region forms a crescentic zone which follows the contour of the coast-line, but nowhere actually touches it, beginning at 10° N. and extending to 20° S. latitude. This crescentic belt is nowhere much above 100 miles in width, but its length (following its curve) is more than 2,000. During its course it passes through the territories of Venezuela, New Granada, Ecuador, Peru, and Bolivia."

—distribution.

It will be observed in the foregoing table that the trees yielding barks of commercial or medicinal value known as Red, Crown, Carthagena, Grey, and Yellow, are confined to distinct and comparatively limited areas, both as regards elevation above the sea and geographic position. Mr. Markham distributes them thus :

Crown barks, the Loxa region.
Red barks, the western slopes of Chimborazo.
Carthagena barks, the North Granada region.
Grey barks, the Huanuco region, North Peru.
Calisaya barks, Bolivia and South Peru.

—discovery of medicinal properties.

It is an unsettled point whether or not the therapeutic properties of this bark were known to the Indians before the arrival of the Spaniards, though the balance of evidence is in favour of this assumption. The name is Indian,[1] "quina-quina," "bark of bark." To the Countess of Chinchon, the wife of a Viceroy of Peru, and her Jesuit friends is the world indebted for the introduction of this inestimable febrifuge into Europe in 1640. It was long known as "Countess' powder" and "Jesuit's bark," and later as "Cardinal's bark;" hence arose the prejudices of Protestants against its use.

—by whom described.

A century elapsed before the genus of the quina tree was established by Linnæus (1742), who paid a just tribute to the Countess' memory by naming it after her. Nor has her service to humanity been forgotten by his followers, who have extended the name to the whole family of allied plants. He knew but two species. One of these, the *C. officinalis*, however, had been previously (1838) described by Dr. La Condamine, one of the members of the French expedition to South America, despatched in 1735 to measure an arc of a degree near Quito; the other members were Godin, Bouguer, and the celebrated botanist Joseph de Jussieu. Jussieu spent thirty-four years in prosecuting his investigations in South America, but he failed in his attempts to forward young chinchona plants to Europe. Seeds of *C. calisaya* were sent to the Jardin des Plantes by Dr. Weddell in 1846. They were procured from Bolivia. The plants which sprung of these seeds were the first grown in Europe.[2]

Dr. King remarks :—

"The species found in the region between 10° N. and the equator (the barks of New Granada) were described by Mutis in the last century and more recently by Karsten in his *Flora Colombiæ*. Mutis' notes remained in manuscript until 1867, when Mr. Clement Markham succeeded in unearthing and printing them, and both his notes and drawings have still more recently been published at Paris by M. Triana in his *Nouvelles Etudes sur les Quinquinas*. The cinchonas of the region between the line and 14° S. (the barks of Ecuador and Northern Peru) were first examined by Ruiz and Pavon, and a magnificent work founded on Pavon's specimens was published by Mr. J. E. Howard in 1862; while those indigenous in the region from the fourteenth parallel of South latitude to the extremity of the zone in 20° S. were described by M. Weddell in his splendid monograph published at Paris in 1849."

Threatened failure of American supplies of bark.

Fears had long existed that the bark supply from South America would fail owing to the wanton destruction of the

[1] MARKHAM'S *Travels*.

[2] The first plant grown in Java was one of these. It died shortly after arrival, but a numerous progeny has arisen from a cutting made from it.

CH. XXX. — CHINCHONA CULTURE.

chinchona forests by the bark-collectors,[1] and thus the importance of introducing the plant into other countries suited for its growth was generally acknowledged, especially by the two nations—the English and Dutch—who, by reason of their Eastern possessions, were the chief consumers. As early as 1835 Dr. Forbes Royle, then Superintendent of the Gardens at Seharunpore, suggested its introduction on the Khasia and Nílagiri Hills, and later (1839) in his "Illustrations of Himalayan Botany."[2] The subject attracted the notice of Lord William Bentinck. Dr. Royle wrote in 1852:

Suggestions to introduce chinchona into the East Indies.

"The probability of the entire success of the cinchona tree in India seems to admit of hardly any doubt, if ordinary care is adopted in the selection of suitable localities. I myself recommended this measure many years ago when treating of the family of plants to which cinchonas belong. I inferred from a comparison of soil and climate with the geographical distribution of cinchonaceæ plants that quinine yielding cinchonas might be cultivated on the slopes of the Nilagiris and of the Southern Himalayas, in the same way that I inferred the Chinese tea plants might be cultivated in the Northern Himalayas."

The French Academy had been urged by Jussieu and others to induce the French Government to make similar experiments, as the project was so uncertain that it was improbable that private capitalists would undertake it. Dr. Weddell had well written (Hist., p. 13):—

"The only remedy is cultivation, and it is absolutely necessary to have recourse to it. If any tree deserves acclimatization in a French colony, that tree is incontestably cinchona, and posterity will wish a blessing on the man who has carried the idea into execution."

—attempts made by the French and Dutch.

In consequence an attempt was made in Algeria by the French Government in 1850, but it failed.[3]

The Dutch Government, however, was the first to take the matter in hand. As early as 1829[4] scientific men had pressed on the Dutch Government the advisability of introducing into Java the

---

[1] "If no means be adopted," wrote Dr. Weddell in his History in 1849, "to arrest this destroying agency, posterity will have to regret, if not the total disappearance, at least the gradually occurring scarcity of the various kinds of quina."

[2] The desirability of introducing chinchonas into the East Indies was urged in a memorial addressed to the East India Company between 1838 and 1842 by Sir Robert Christison and backed by Dr. Forbes Royle, but no active step was taken till 1852, when again, on the motion of Dr. Royle, some efforts were made to obtain plants through Consular Agents.

In the original memorial presented by Sir Robert Christison he pointed out that "the transplantation, if successful, would become remunerative," because the trees might be cut down younger than was the case in America, and the bark might be collected like cinnamon bark.—*Encycl. Britan.*, Vol. V.

[3] "*Cultivation of the Chinchonas in Java*," by K. W. VANGORKOM, page 7.

[4] K. W. VANGORKOM'S *Cultivation of the Chinchonas.*

CHINCHONA CULTURE.

cultivation of chinchona, and one Textor was directed to proceed to South America to collect plants and seeds, but he died and the expedition was abandoned. Dr. Weddell's visit to the chinchona region (1845-48) was productive of a revival of interest in the matter. In the year 1852, in accordance with the grand and benevolent plan of the Dutch Minister of State, Pahud, the botanist M. Hasskarl was deputed to collect plants and seeds of valuable varieties and convey them to Java. The plants collected by him were landed in Java in 1854. These were more or less worthless varieties of *C. calisaya*. A plant of the true *calisaya* had, however, as mentioned above, been already introduced into Java. Seeds of other varieties, especially of the *C. lancifolia*, also arrived about the same time and germinated. This was the beginning of the Java plantations. At first the Dutch expended much money and time on the cultivation of inferior kinds on a faulty method, but in 1864 they changed their system. They have now a large number of very valuable species [1] and a far larger number of trees than exist on the Government Plantations of Southern India.

—the Indian Government recommends the sending of a gardening collector to South America.

In the year 1852 (the year of the Dutch expedition) Lord Dalhousie requested the early consideration of the Honorable Court of Directors to a proposal of the Government of Bengal to send a "gardening collector" to South America to collect plants and seeds. Dr. Royle, then employed at the India House, submitted a report on the subject to the Court, supporting the recommendation. But the Board of Control considered that the necessary supplies of seeds and plants should be forwarded through the Consular Agent. Some plants and seeds were collected, but they did not survive the voyage to Europe. In 1853 [2] a few plants of *C. calisaya* were sent to Calcutta from Kew; five survived the voyage, but two died during removal to Darjeeling, and the remainder was killed there by frost in the first winter. Early in 1856 Dr. Royle again urged the matter on the Indian Government, but without success. Lord Canning penned a minute, 20th October 1856, strongly supporting the recommendations of the Medical Board and Agricultural Society to employ a scientific collector in South America. "In six years," he observed, "the Government of India has expended nearly £54,000 [3] in quinine and cinchona bark, and, therefore, I believe that success will be well worth the cost." He concurred in the Board's views that there was every probability of

[1] Some bark of the *C. calisaya*, var. *Ledgeriana*, is reported to have yielded 10 to 13½ per cent. of crystalline sulphate of quinine.—Dr. KING.

[2] Blue Book, Vol. I.

[3] In 1876-77 India imported 4,648 lb. of quinine alone, value 3,34,437 rupees, against 3,925 lb., value 1,91,619 rupees, in 1875-76.

CH. XXX. — CHINCHONA CULTURE.

the successful cultivation of chinchona in the Eastern Himalayas, *e.g.*, in the mountainous regions of Assam and tracts eastward of Silhet; also on the sides of the Nílagiris, and probably also in parts of Malabar. Dr. Royle supported these proposals in a long memorandum (March 1857), which appears to be the last report this eminent botanist wrote on the subject. He had, however, the gratification of obtaining the sanction of the Directors to the despatch of a collector to South America,[1] but his death in 1858 prevented his carrying this into effect. Mr. Clement Markham, a clerk in the India Office well acquainted with the Cordilleras (where chinchona abounded) and the dialects spoken in those tracts, in April 1859 offered to superintend the collection of plants and seeds. His services were accepted.

—Court of Directors select Mr. Markham for the duty.

—Mr. Markham's search.

Mr. Markham's scheme was to collect simultaneously the seeds and plants in the three chief chinchona regions. For Ecuador, the home of the "Red bark," he selected Mr. Spruce, a botanist, aided by Mr. Cross, a gardener; for the Peruvian Province of Huanuco, with its "Grey barks," Mr. Pritchett; whilst he reserved for himself and his assistant, Mr. Weir, a gardener, the forests of Bolivia and South Peru, in which the Yellow barks or *calisaya* are found. The expedition arrived in Peru in January 1860. Mr. Markham proceeded inland in March and returned to the coast on the 1st June, bringing with him 497 plants of the *C. calisaya* and 32 of the inferior species, *micrantha* and *ovata*; and, in accordance with his instructions, started for England with his collection, it having been decided that the plants should be forwarded by the overland route to India. He reached the Nílagiris *viâ* Bombay and Calicut on the 12th October 1860. The plants suffered much during the latter part of the journey, the roots being much decayed. Mr. McIvor was, however, able to secure 207 cuttings, besides potting 125 of the original plants.

—Mr. Spruce's search for "Red barks."

Meanwhile Mr. Spruce, whose special task was the collection of "Red barks" (*Cascarilla roya*), began his exploration in 1859 with the view of settling on the tracts in which he could conduct his collecting operations. He selected a place named Limon for his head-quarters, and started on his expedition on the 11th June 1860, accompanied by Dr. Taylor of Riobambo. He was joined by Mr. Cross at Limon in July. They commenced operations, Mr. Cross remaining at Limon establishing a nursery of *Red bark* cuttings, whilst Mr. Spruce searched for seed. By the end of December they returned to the coast with a freight of 637 well-established plants and 100,000 healthy seeds. These were despatched from Guayaquil to England in charge of Mr. Cross on the 2nd of January 1861. He reached the Nílagiris on the 3rd April 1861 with 463 *C. succirubra* plants,

[1] Blue Book, Vol. I, page 20.

bringing with him also 6 *C. calisaya* plants.[1] The survival of these *calisaya* plants was fortunate, as only one of the cuttings of the plants of this kind brought by Mr. Markham was alive. The seeds were despatched by post. An interesting account of this journey will be found in Mr. Spruce's Report, No. 43, Blue Book, Vol. I, which is of special value, as he was an excellent naturalist.

—Mr. Pritchett's search for "Grey barks."

Mr. Pritchett, to whom the search for "Grey barks" had been committed, arrived at Huanuco on the 28th May, a town in the midst of the region where these trees abound. He returned to the coast with plants in Wardian cases and a collection of seeds towards the end of August. The plants and seeds were *C. micrantha*, *C. nitida*, and *C. Peruviana*. The plants in Wardian cases arrived in England in good order, but they perished before the cases reached Ootacamand. The seeds, however, germinated freely contrary to expectation.

—Mr. Cross procures "Crown bark" seeds.

Mr. Spruce had been unable to proceed to the Crown bark (*C. condaminea*)[2] region. This duty was entrusted to Mr. Cross on his return from England. He started from Guayaquil for the Loxa forests in the autumn of 1861, procured and despatched in December 1861 to India 100,000 *C. condaminea* seeds, also a small quantity of *crispa* seed, both varieties of *C. officinalis* of Linnæus. The packets arrived at Ootacamand in good order on the 4th March 1862.

—Pitayo barks.

The valuable species known as the Pitayo or Carthagena barks (*C. lancifolia* and *C. Pitayensis*) were not introduced into India until much later. A collection of seed had been made by Mr. Cross in 1863, but it lost its vitality. In 1868 this collector proceeded to the district of Popayan in New Granada, and there obtained a supply of seed which arrived on the Nilagiris towards the end of the year. They germinated freely. In the autumn of the following year Mr. Cross forwarded some plants of these species to India.

Selection of sites on the Nilagiris.

Previous to Mr. Markham's arrival in October 1860 Mr. McIvor had selected the wooded ravine above the Government gardens on the Doddabetta range, with an elevation of between 7,600 and 7,900 feet above sea level. Mr. Markham considered the site very suitable for varieties of chinchonas growing at high elevations in South America, such as *C. calisaya* (shrubby variety), *C. nitida*, *C. condaminea*, and *C. lancifolia*; but for the species requiring a warmer and moister climate, such as *C. succirubra*, *C. calisaya*, *C. micrantha*, and *C. Peruviana*, he, in communication with other officers of Government, selected a

---

[1] Blue Book, Vol. I, page 159.

[2] *C. Chahmarguera* (Pavon). For proper botanical names of these species see page 254, Vol. I, Blue Book.

CH. XXX. — CHINCHONA CULTURE.

forest glen at Neduwattam above Gúdalúr, on the north-western slope of the Nílagiris, having an elevation of about 6,000 feet. Towards the end of 1862 the Government approved Mr. McIvor's selection of the wooded slopes on either side of the Paikaré waterfall, having an elevation about the same as Neduwattam. These plantations are known as the Wood and Hooker estates. The former was so named in honour of the then Secretary of State, the latter in that of the celebrated botanist. Towards the end of the following year the Government sanctioned the opening of a plantation near Mélkúnda, about nine miles south of the Avalanché Bungalow, having an elevation of between 6,000 and 7,000 feet.

—area of plantations.

When these plantations were begun their ultimate extent does not appear to have been discussed. In the third year of operations, when the success of the experiment was partly assured, the Secretary of State sanctioned an extension aggregating 150 acres yearly for ten years, but in 1866 the same authority fixed 1,200 acres as the maximum limit of the cultivation. This limit was erroneously supposed to have been reached in 1869, at which time the cultivated area did not probably exceed about 800 acres. Small extensions have been carried out since that date. The area of the plantations, as ascertained by the recent survey (base measurement), is as follows:—

Doddabetta	... ...	320·47
Neduwattam	... ...	301·63
Paikaré { Wood	... ...	72·18
Paikaré { Hooker	... ...	154·19
		848·47

This area was planted up very gradually. Taking whole numbers, the area planted in each year stands thus, omitting Mélkúnda, where the area planted approximated 30 acres. This estate was abandoned in 1871 by order of Government. No great reliance is, however, to be placed in the figures.

—	Doddabetta.	Neduwattam.	Wood.	Hooker.	Total.
	ACRES.	ACRES.	ACRES.	ACRES.	ACRES.
1862	...	31	...	...	31
1863	9	5	3	...	17
1864	11	58	11	...	80
1865	41	44	24	...	109
1866	61	31	...	26	118
1867	23	...	29	40	92
1868	33	12	6	58	109
1869	119	104	...	19	242
1870	9	32	...	...	41
1871	8	...	...	...	8
1872	8	...	...	...	8
1873	2	...	...	11	11

CH. XXX.

CHINCHONA CULTURE.

For many years the number of plants on the estates was much exaggerated. The recent numeration and classification by Major J. Campbell Walker has set this vexed question at rest. The correct figures compare thus with those previously accepted by Government on the estimate of the late Superintendent :—

—	Estimated.	Actuals.
	NO.	NO.
Doddabetta	345,980	226,936
Neduwattam	474,740	208,780
Wood ... ... } Hooker ... ... }	304,484	45,758
Mélkúnda	65,254	87,557
Total ...	1,690,458	569,031

As regards the description of trees the estimated and actual figures stand thus :—

—	Estimated.	Actuals.
	NO.	NO.
Red Bark	579,938	260,837
Crown do.	531,282	305,432
Yellow do.	34,250	552
Grey do.	28,759	1,874
Other species	16,229	336
Total ...	1,190,458	[1]569,031

—financial results.

In the following statement, extracted from Major Campbell Walker's report, the financial history of the plantations is given. Interest on the annual balance of charges has been calculated at 4·50 per cent. The expenditure and receipts on account of the manufacture of alkaloids have been excluded. No allowance is made for cost of land or assessment thereon. The statement shows the position at the end of 1875-76. This year was chosen by Major Walker as it closes the initial stage in the history of the plantations, the termination of which is almost contemporaneous with Mr. McIvor's death. The area has not been extended since then.

[1] The figures do not include a few hundred trees which were remaining at Mélkúnda at the time, chiefly Red barks.

Account of Receipts and Expenditure on account of the Cinchona Plantations from the commencement up to the close of 1875-76, *taken from the Accountant-General's Books, Returns of Sale from India Office, and other sources.*

Years.	Receipts.				Charges.					
	Value of Bark supplied to the Quinologist.	Value of Bark sent to England.	Value of Bark supplied to other Governments and Cash Receipts.	Total.	Establishment including Superintendent's Salary.	Buildings and Plant.	Other Charges	Value of Convict Labour.	Interest on Balance of Charges.	Total.
	RS.	RS.	RS.	RS.	RS.	RS.	RS.	RS.	RS.	RS.
1860-61...	...	...	...	...	...	...	4,821	...	...	4,821
1861-62...	...	...	...	...	...	...	22,915	...	217	23,132
1862-63...	...	...	...	...	...	...	48,390	...	1,258	49,648
1863-64...	...	...	...	...	12,727	...	53,174	...	3,492	69,392
1864-65...	...	...	...	...	24,445	...	59,667	...	6,615	90,726
1865-66...	...	...	...	...	25,450	3,700	58,887	...	10,697	98,735
1866-67...	...	...	2,450	2,450	23,804	3,025	52,632	48,666	15,140	1,43,268
1867-68...	...	287	...	288	26,087	2,600	43,296	48,667	19,687	1,40,337
1868-69...	...	...	1,680	1,680	25,672	2,030	30,636	48,667	27,779	1,34,784
1869-70...	1,512	...	...	1,512	25,783	1,650	19,163	...	33,769	80,365
1870-71...	4,365	...	324	4,689	23,730	300	6,143	...	37,318	67,491
1871-72...	9,543	3,479	...	13,022	17,157	850	13,160	...	40,144	71,311
1872-73...	16,807	4,388	227	21,422	12,724	550	16,441	...	42,767	72,481
1873-74...	21,136	36,417	300	57,854	12,574	558	15,092	...	45,064	73,288
1874-75...	8,576	...	273	8,849	16,406	1,700	17,417	...	45,759	81,282
1875-76...	...	60,405	2,000	62,405	17,234	1,550	27,423	...	49,018	95,225
	61,939	1,04,976	7,254	1,74,171	2,63,793	18,513	4,89,257	1,46,000	3,78,724	12,96,287
1876-77...	...	4,33,746	3,058	4,36,804	12,467	...	58,408	...	50,495	1,21,371
	61,939	5,38,723	10,313	6,10,975	2,76,260	18,513	5,47,665	1,46,000	4,29,220	14,17,659

Net Results.

	RS.
Total charges up to 1875-76	12,96,287
Total receipts do.	1,74,171
Net charges	11,22,116
Add charges of 1876-77	1,21,372
	12,43,488
Deduct receipts of 1876-77	4,36,805
Net charges up to 1876-77	8,06,683

The receipts and expenditure for the two succeeding years, independent of the value of bark sent to England,[1] which probably did not fall short of £50,000 were as follows:—

—	Receipts.	Expenditure.		
	Sale of Plants.	Establishment.	Working Charges, &c.	Total.
	RS.	RS.	RS.	RS.
1877-78	17,543	8,199	69,349	77,548
1878-79	10,052	9,794	69,986	79,780

Policy of Government in regard to the Chinchona Plantations.

When establishing these experimental plantations the Secretary of State clearly indicated the object which Her Majesty's Government had in view in so doing.

[1] The value of the bark sent to England in 1877-78 was £33,231, but the price realized for the succeeding year's crop I have not been able to ascertain.

"The two first objects of the experiment (he writes) are the provision of an abundant and certain supply of bark for the use of hospitals and troops, and the spread of cultivation through the hill districts in order to bring the remedy within the reach of the frequenters of jungles and of the native population generally. Your Government has very justly deemed that the experiment cannot be regarded as a mere money-speculation, nor are the commercial advantages that may be derived from it to be considered as other than a secondary consideration, though, of course, a return of the outlay and the spread of chinchona cultivation by private enterprise[1] are very desirable in themselves."

In 1871 the propriety of selling the plantations, or of dispensing with two of the four, was considered by the Government with a view of leaving the development of chinchona to private enterprise, seeing that the successful cultivation of the tree had been proved; but it was ultimately decided that it was inexpedient for the Government to leave the undertaking to private industry, as in many respects it was still in an experimental stage;—"for (remark the Madras Government in a despatch to the Secretary of State) the barks of the already discovered species of cinchona yield a varying ratio of alkaloids at different stages of their growth, and it is possible that the species now least valued may, when more matured, be found rich in alkaloids, and *vice versâ*. The questions raised by the frequent discovery of fresh varieties of cinchona, or of an unprecedentedly large proportion of alkaloids in some of the known varieties, will be most expeditiously solved under Government supervision, which allows the freest scope for experiment." These views were accepted by the Secretary of State,[2] who inclined to the opinion that a portion of the plantations with the manufactories should remain permanently under the superintendence of Government; but he added:—

"It should be clearly understood that the intention of Government in sending their surplus bark to England for sale in the open market is not to enter into permanent competition with private growers, whose success would be viewed by Government with great satisfaction, but rather to act as the pioneer, and to establish the reputation of Indian-grown barks for their advantage. At the same time the Government will do rightly in continuing the sale of bark until the outlay attendant upon the introduction and cultivation of the plants is repaid."

These remarks have all special reference to the local manufacture of quinine alkaloids as well as to the trade transactions of Government. The question of the continuance of the plantations under the State has been much discussed in the recent inquiry, and the Secretary of State has decided that the plant-

[1] Blue Book, Vol. 1, page 255.
[2] Despatch, April 1871.

CH. XXX. — CHINCHONA CULTURE.

ations should be retained under the superintendence of a specialist.

The manufacture of alkaloids in the country.

So soon as it was ascertained by the analysis of barks sent to England for analysis, that they bid fair to yield quinine and other kinds of alkaloids, and that the yield of these alkaloids varied with, or was more or less dependent upon, artificial conditions of culture, the Madras Government suggested, on the advice of Mr. Markham, who visited the plantations in 1865, that an experienced chemist, having a thorough knowledge of chinchona and its product, should be appointed to investigate on the spot various points connected with the cultivation of the tree and the extraction and use of its alkaloids. The Secretary of State approved the proposal, as without such aid the various questions at issue—including that of undertaking the manufacture of quinine and other chinchona alkaloids locally—could not be satisfactorily settled.

Mr. Broughton appointed quinologist.

Mr. John Broughton, an Assistant at the Royal Institution, Albemarle Street, was selected, and reached India in November 1866. His salary was fixed at £1,000 yearly.

In the instructions[1] to Mr. Broughton the Secretary of State remarks:—

"The oldest trees on the Neilgherries have now been planted out for nearly four years, and the analyses of their barks, which have been made by Mr. Howard, prove that there is a very marked increase of the yield of febrifuge alkaloids under cultivation. The time has now come, therefore, when it is necessary to investigate the causes which regulate the yield of alkaloids from cultivated cinchona barks, and to ascertain the preparation of the febrifuge which will combine cheapness with efficacy in the greatest degree."

* * * * *

"The analysis of bark from plants growing in different situations, by a competent scientific chemist on the spot, will be a principal means of discovering the conditions, as regards elevation, climate, soil and exposure, best calculated to produce the largest possible yield of alkaloids, those conditions of course varying with the different species. There are several difficult questions connected with the formation of the alkaloids in bark, and particularly with the changes in the alkaloids themselves, caused probably by cultivation, which should be carefully and diligently investigated. It will also be an important duty of the chemist attached to the Cinchona Plantations to ascertain the difference, as regards yield and efficacy, between green and dried barks; and to make accurate analyses of the leaves, and hereafter possibly of the flowers, of the different species. The best method of drying the bark must be decided by scientific experiments; and,

[1] Blue Book, 1870.

finally, it will be expected from the chemist that he should, through his investigations, enable Her Majesty's Government to arrive at a decision with respect to the best and cheapest method of preparing the febrifuge for use among the labouring classes of the Natives of India. He will also be required to consider the questions connected with the manufacture of the cinchona febrifuge for the use of hospitals and troops in India."

—Mr. Broughton's researches.

It would be out of place here to detail the history of Mr. Broughton's valuable researches, which will be found in his reports, most of which have been published in the Blue Books on chinchona cultivation. The most important facts either discovered or proved by him were, (1) that the alkaloids were at a maximum in October and May, (2) that barks covered by moss yielded a greater amount of alkaloid and in a state which admits of their crystallization as sulphates easily, (3) that the alkaloids are chiefly deposited in the cellular tissue, (4) that the direct rays of the sun are inimical to the development of alkaloids in the bark, (5) that the alkaloids in the bark are injuriously affected in the process of drying in sunshine, or in heat above 100°, or in steam-heat, (6) that the leaves, blossoms, and wood of chinchona contained either very little alkaloid or none at all, (7) that Nílagiri chinchonas contained more chinchonidine than quinine, and that the proportion of the former to the latter increased after about the eighth year.

—Amorphous quinine.

During the first four years of his service Mr. Broughton conducted many experiments with a view of ascertaining a cheap febrifuge suitable for use in the hospitals of the country, but it was not until 1870 that he finally adopted a combination of alkaloids known as *Amorphous Quinine.* It consisted of the "total alkaloids of cinchona bark in the form of a non-crystalline powder, mixed to some extent with resin and red colouring matters so abundant in the red bark." A full description of the process of manufacture is given in Mr. Broughton's report to the Madras Government, 1st December 1873. The drug was acknowledged as an efficient febrifuge by the Madras Medical Department.[1] The manufacture continued for three years, when doubts having arisen as to its economy and expediency, a Special Commission was appointed in June 1874 by the Madras Government, consisting of Dr. Cornish and Mr. Cockerell, to report as to its value as a medicine and the cost of manufacture. The Commission found that after calculating the price of the bark at its market

[1] Mr. Broughton in a private communication gives the following directions for a cheap febrifuge decoction, the bark used being not less than three years old. A pound of freshly dried bark, cut up finely, boiled for half an hour and then squeezed; boiled again for the same period in fresh water, and again a third time in the same manner. Mix the decoctions and evaporate to small bulk.

CH. XXX. — CHINCHONA CULTURE.

value, the product cost more than ordinary quinine; whilst as prepared and issued, it was of uncertain composition, sometimes rich in quinine, at others chinchonidine and chinchonine predominating. The Government accordingly resolved to abandon the manufacture. Mr. Broughton thereupon, January 1875, resigned his appointment and left the country. The manufacture has not since been resumed, nor has a scientific chemist been appointed to observe the history of the trees. Rather less than 1,000 lb. of *Amorphous Quinine* was produced during the continuance of the manufactory.

Alkaloid manufactory.

The financial results connected with this experiment may be roughly estimated as follows :—

Receipts.	RS.	*Expenditure.*		RS.
Value of 922 lb. amorphous quinine manufactured[1] ...	30,737	Salary of Quinologist... ...		79,027
Excess expenditure balance...	1,71,703	Establishment and laboratory.		18,125
		Cost of manufacture, including buildings—		
		(a) Ootacamand ...	11,735	
		(b) Neduwattam ...	21,458	
				33,193
		Bark supplied (at market rates)		72,095
Total ...	2,02,440	Total ...		2,02,440

Analysis of barks.

During Mr. Broughton's service systematic analyses of the barks of the several kinds of chinchona grown on the Hills were conducted with special reference to mode of culture, site, elevation, age of trees, and the seasons of gathering the bark. Numerous analyses of specimens sent to England, by Messrs. Howard and DeVriz, exist, but the results are so varying and conflicting as to be of little use except to the specialist. A complete comparative history of the analysis of each variety under known variations of age, culture, &c., remains to be perfected.

The highest yield of alkaloids discovered by Mr. Broughton was on Doddabetta in 1868 in the variety of species of *C. condaminea* known as *angustifolia*, amounting to no less than 11·50 per cent. of total alkaloids, of which 10·13 per cent. were crystallised sulphate of quinine. A higher percentage still of alkaloids, namely, 12·30, is reported to have been obtained by Mr. McIvor from a hybrid known as *C. pubescens*; but although Mr. Howard stated

[1] This calculation is based on the supposition that each pound contained in five parts, 1 of crystallizable quinine, 2 of chinchonidine, 1 of chinchonine and 1 of uncrystallizable residue. * * * If the amorphous quinine is taken to have displaced an equal weight of quinine at 130*s*. a pound, its actual value to Government will have been Rupees 59,930. (See note on the Chinchona Plantations.)

that this variety excelled the *angustifolia*—especially, it would seem, in the size and vigour of the tree—yet I am not aware that its merits have been as systematically tested as those of *C. angustifolia*.

The following table, taken from Mr. Broughton's report of 1873, gives analyses of Nílagiri barks, which may be taken as a fair example of their yield of alkaloids :—

—	Mossed Red Bark, Neduwattam.	Renewed Red Bark, Neduwattam.	Grey Bark.	Red Bark, Neduwattam.	Red Bark, Paikaré.	Branch Red Bark.	Crown Bark, Neduwattam.	Crown Bark, Paikaré.	Mossed Crown Bark, Doddabetta.	Crown Bark, Doddabetta.	Branch Crown Bark.
Total Alkaloids ...	6·20	5·82	2·75	4·45	5·11	3·58	4·32	3·42	6·60	3·61	0·91
Quinine and Quinidine ...	1·14	3·25	...	1·31	0·97	1·33	3·08	2·32	3·89	2·07	...
Cinchonidine and Cinchonine.	5·06	2·57	2·75	3·14	4·14	2·25	1·24	1·10	2·71	1·54	...
Pure Sulphate of Quinine obtained crystallized.	0·74	2·62	...	0·74	0·62	0·81	3·11	2·39	3·86	2·04	...
Pure Sulphate of Cinchonidine obtained crystallized.	3·47	0·88	1·00	1·61	2·22	1·14	0·85	0·67	1·00	0·99	...

Chief species and varieties of chinchona in India.

Dr. Bidie, in his "*Cinchona Culture*," 1879, gives the following list of chinchonas in India:—

Crown and Pale Barks.

Chinchona officinalis (*and varieties*).	C. uritusinga.
C. condaminea.	C. angustifolia.
	C. lancifolia.[1]

Yellow Barks.

C. calisaya (*and varieties*).	C. Javanica.
C. Ledgeriana.	

Red Barks.

C. succirubra (*two varieties*).

Grey Barks.

C. Peruviana.	C. micrantha.
C. nitida.	

Other Barks.

C. Pitayensis.[2]	C. Pahudiana.

Hybrids.

C. pubescens.	C. lanosa.

The instructions given in the preceding chapter on tea, as to the selection of land and the forming and laying out of a tea estate,

[1] Columbian or Carthagena bark.

[2] Pitayo bark.

CH. XXX. — CHINCHONA CULTURE. — Cultivation.

may be followed generally in the formation of a chinchona estate. Further detailed information will be found in Mr. McIvor and Dr. King's Manuals. The experience of past years seems to favour close planting,[1] especially in the case of *condamineas* planted in exposed situations, also the propagation of plants by seed and not by cuttings or layering. Seed from plantations where natural facilities for hybridization exist is to be preferred, as the growth of hybrids is generally stronger, whilst the tendency in them seems to be towards a greater secretion of alkaloids. Hybrids of *condaminea* and *succirubra*, whilst partaking in great measure the vigour and strength of the *succirubra*, yield bark whose richness in quinine alkaloids approximates to that of the bark of the best varieties of *condaminea*. The natural tendency of the Nílagiri chinchonas to produce strong and rich hybrids is the most promising feature of the cultivation.

Manure.

The results of the experiments in the application of manures to the chinchona tree will be found in Mr. Broughton's report, April 1872. The effect on the growth of the tree was not marked, nor in the case of the Red barks was the secretion of alkaloids improved; but the Crown barks, to which guano, ammonia sulphate, and farmyard manure had been generally applied, showed a great increase in the alkaloids. In fact the result of applying the last-named manure was the doubling of the quantity of alkaloids. As regards the growth of Crown barks, subsequent experience goes to show that it is greatly favoured by the application of farmyard manure in the first few years after planting out.

Harvesting of bark.

There are four modes of gathering the bark: (1) by coppicing, (2) by stripping the bark in longitudinal sections, (3) by uprooting, (4) by scraping or shaving the bark. Of these methods, until recently, the second only had been followed in the Government plantations, and consequently nearly all the experience gained so far is of this method, which may be regarded as the discovery of Mr. McIvor. It therefore remains yet to be shown what mode of treatment is on the whole best suited to the several descriptions of chinchona with a view to obtaining the most valuable yield of bark from a given area of cultivation in a given series of years: in a word, what method is economically and scientifically the best.

There are two modes of coppicing: (1) cutting the tree down and allowing the shoots to spring from the bare stump, (2) felling the tree but leaving a root or stem shoot, or several such, to replace it. These methods—certainly the latter—are known to succeed as

[1] *C. succirubra* should be planted 4 feet × 4 feet and *C. condaminea* 3 feet × 3 feet ordinarily, and thinned out from about the fourth year if necessary.

regards the growth of the shoots, but the value of the bark of such growth, compared with that of an original plant, has yet to be satisfactorily ascertained.

The stripping is ordinarily known as the *mossing* process, though the application of moss, or other vegetable substance suited to exclude the light and protect the wound, is not absolutely essential to the renewal of the bark. The process is thus described by Mr. McIvor (*vide* report of the Commissioner of the Nílagiris, August 1875):—

Description of the process of Mossing.—" A labourer proceeds to an eight-year-old tree, and, reaching up as far as he can, makes a horizontal incision of the required width. From either end of this incision he runs a vertical incision to the ground, and then, carefully raising with his knife the bark at the horizontal incision until he can seize it with his fingers, he strips off the bark to the ground and cuts it off. The strip of bark then presents the appearance of a ribbon more or less long. Supposing the tree to be of 28 inches in circumference, the labourer will take nine of the above ribbons, each $1\frac{1}{2}$ inches wide. He will thus leave, after the tree has been stripped, other nine ribbons still adhering to the tree, each somewhat broader than the stripped ribbon and at intervals apart, occupied by the spaces to which the stripped ribbons had adhered. As soon as he has removed his strips, the labourer will proceed to moss the trunk all round, tying on the moss with some fibre. The decorticated intervals will thus be excluded from light and air, and this point is one of the capital points in the system. The mere exclusion of light and air from a stem partially bared of bark acts in two ways: it enables a healing process to be rapidly set up in the same way as a plaster does in the case of a wound in an animal organism: and it has this further curious effect, it increases the secretion of quinine in the bark renewed under its protection. This increase of quinine is admitted by Mr. Broughton in all his reports. At the end of six or twelve months the bands of bark left untouched at the first stripping are removed, and the intervals they occupied on the trunk are mossed. At the end of twenty-two months, on an average, the spaces occupied by the ribbons originally taken are found to be covered with renewed bark much thicker than the natural bark of the same age, and this renewed bark can be removed and a fresh process of renewal again be fostered by moss. In another six or twelve months the renewed bark of the natural ribbons left at the first stripping can be taken, and so on; harvests are obtainable from the trunk, alternately from the spaces left at the first stripping and the spaces left by the second stripping. Experience hitherto does not show any limit to the taking of these harvests from a tree. Of course it is understood that at every stripping the ribbons taken are longer than at the preceding stripping, because the tree each year increased in height and bulk, and, therefore, the top of every ribbon consists of natural bark and the lower part of renewed bark."

CH. XXX.

CHINCHONA CULTURE.

The following remarks of Dr. Bidie are noteworthy:—

"When moss is not available, grass is sometimes used to exclude the light, and it is probable that an envelope of soft thick cloth, tarred on one side to protect it from white-ants, might answer well. Indeed renewal on the barked surfaces will take place without any covering whatever, although there can be no doubt that protection expedites the process. On removing a strip of bark there is found between it and the wood a layer of mucilaginous-like consistence, the cambium. This consists of formative material, from which both bark and wood are developed, and the greatest care is therefore requisite not to injure it in any way, and to expose it as little as possible to air and sunshine. It should therefore be quickly and cautiously covered with the moss or other material. Mr. McIvor states that the average time required for the renewal of bark is about twenty-two months, but experience shows that a considerably longer period is requisite. It has also to be pointed out, that by the repetition of the stripping and mossing system the vigour of the tree is impaired, and the thickness of the renewed bark somewhat reduced. Some of the older Crown Bark trees on the Nilagiris have been barked and mossed four times, and some of the older Red Barks six times. Both kinds have shown a wonderful tolerance of the operation, but there are now obvious signs of its having reduced the vigour of the older plants. Thus most of the trees which have been frequently barked carry less luxuriant foliage, and show a greater tendency to produce an excessive crop of flower and seed than trees which have not been mossed. They also renew their bark very slowly, requiring nearly three years for the process, and even then the renewed bark is very thin. There can be no doubt, however, that up to a certain age the mossing system is a good and economical one. In the case of both Red and Crown Barks therefore I would recommend to the planter a combination of the mossing and coppicing systems. Cropping according to this method, he should begin by barking and mossing four times in successive years, as the bark becomes fit for the market. This would secure one crop of natural bark, one of mossed bark, and two of renewed bark. On the completion of the fourth stripping, moss should again be applied and kept on till complete renewal takes place. At this stage I would propose to coppice, which would bring in a third and large crop of renewed bark from the mossed, as well as a considerable amount of natural bark from the unmossed parts of the tree. In the case of the Red Bark trees too there can be no doubt that it will be found possible to repeat the mossing process on some of the bigger shoots which spring up after coppicing. It has already been mentioned that the mossing process increases not only the absolute quantity of alkaloids in renewed bark, but also the proportion of quinine. The source from which the increase in total alkaloids is derived is not very clear, but from Mr. Broughton's experiments in 1873 there is strong reason to believe that the gain in the renewed bark is obtained by a transfer to it of some of the alkaloids from the original bark on the upper unmossed parts of the tree.

Of such transfer we have other examples, as in the case of Loranthaceous parasites growing on *Nux vomica* trees, the alkaloid constituents of the host, viz., strychnia and brucia, being transferred to the parasite.[1] If this transfer in the case of the cinchonas be confirmed by future observations, it will follow that the main advantage of the mossing process will be the production of a superior product by the concentration of the alkaloid constituents of the tree generally in the strips of renewed bark. One good point of the mossing system, or of combined mossing and coppicing, is, that a crop can be got from the trees at an earlier age than would be desirable if coppicing alone or uprooting were adopted, as under either of the latter systems it would be uneconomical to collect the bark before it reached the stage of maximum yield. The process of mossing can only be conducted during the monsoon, when the trees are full of sap, as if done in the dry season the bark will not lift, and is renewed with difficulty. The collection of the bark at that time is, however, attended with some disadvantages, as that is the period of the year at which the cinchona contains the smallest amount of alkaloids."

CH. XXX. — CHINCHONA CULTURE.

So far the moss-renewing process, which is that generally practised in the district, may, on the whole, be pronounced a decided success; but it is of the first importance to remember that the essence of the system is the *renewal* of the bark, under moss, for the application of moss to the stem may be adopted with advantage in all the other systems of treating the bark. The system of up-rooting, that is, digging up the tree and removing the bark from the roots—generally rich in alkaloids—as well as the stem, though practised in Sikkim, has not been introduced. The system of scraping or shaving off the outer layers of the bark, leaving the inner layer or *liber* to protect the *cambium*—which has been recently introduced by the Dutch in Java—is being experimentally tried on some estates, but its suitability for the conditions of climate prevailing on the Nílagiris has yet to be ascertained. The alleged advantages of the system are (1) that it involves the removal of only the valuable portions of the bark, (2) that all such is removed, whilst under Mr. McIvor's process only sections are removed, (3) that the bark renews in a shorter period, (4) that the health of the tree is not affected, (5) that the protection of moss is not essential for renewal.

Drying the bark.

It is necessary that the bark should be dried in partial shade, as the action of sunlight and exposure to the heat of a fire dissipates the alkaloids. Sheds with shelves of bamboo laths, so as to admit of a free current of air, should be erected in convenient localities. When the bark is tolerably dry, it should be placed in a room artificially heated so as to evaporate the remaining moisture in it. The room may be heated by flues or charcoal

[1] See page 375, O'SHAUGHNESSY's *Bengal Dispensatory*, 1842.

CH. XXX.

CHINCHONA CULTURE.

fires, but the temperature should not be permitted to rise above 100° F. Green bark of tolerably mature age loses about two-thirds of its weight in the process of drying.

Packing.

The best mode of packing the bark for shipment to Europe is in bags made of gunny cloth, consisting of two layers, with an intermediate coating of tar, which ensures the purpose of uniting the layers and effectually excluding moisture.

The following list of books on chinchona is taken from Dr. King's Manual :—

List of books on chinchona.

List of the chief Modern Works relating to Cinchona (from Flückiger and Hanbury's Pharmacographia, page 328).

Berg (Otto), *Chinarinden der pharmakognostischen Sammlung zu Berlin.* Berlin, 1865, 4to, 48 pages and 10 plates shewing the microscopic structure of barks.

Bergen (Heinrich von), *Monographie der China.* Hamburg, 1826, 4to, 343 pages and 7 coloured plates representing the following barks :—China rubra, Huanuco, Calisaya, flava, Huamalies, Loxa, Jaen. An exhaustive work for its period in every direction.

Blue-books—*East India (Cinchona Plant)*, folio.—

A.—Copy of correspondence relating to the introduction of the Cinchona plant into India, and to proceedings connected with its cultivation, from March 1852 *to March* 1863. Ordered by the House of Commons to be printed, 20th March 1863. 272 pages. Contains correspondence of Royle, Markham, Spruce, Pritchett, Cross, McIvor, Anderson and others, illustrated by 5 maps.

B.—Copy of further correspondence relating to the introduction of the Cinchona plant into India, and to proceedings connected with its cultivation, from April 1863 *to April* 1866. Ordered by the House of Commons to be printed, 18th June 1866. 379 pages. Contains monthly reports of the plantations on the Nilgiri Hills; annual reports for 1863-64 and 1864-65, with details of method of propagation and cultivation, barking, mossing, attacks of insects, illustrated by woodcuts and 4 plates; report of Cross's journey to Pitayo, with map; Cinchona cultivation in Wynaad, Coorg, the Pulney Hills and Travancore, with map; in British Sikkim, the Kangra Valley (Punjab), the Bombay Presidency, and Ceylon.

C.—Copy of all correspondence between the Secretary of State for India and the Governor-General, and the Governors of Madras and Bombay, relating to the cultivation of Cinchona plants, from April 1866 *to April* 1870. Ordered by the House of Commons to be printed, 9th August 1870. Contains reports on the Nilgiri and other plantations, with map; appointment of Mr. Broughton as analytical chemist, his reports and analyses; reports on the relative efficacy of the several Cinchona alkaloids; on Cinchona cultivation at Darjeeling and in British Burma.

Delondre (Augustin Pierre) et Bouchardat (Apollinaire), *Quinologie*. Paris, 1854, 4to, 48 pages and 23 good coloured plates exhibiting all the barks then met with in commerce.

Gorkom (K. W. van), *Die Chinacultur auf Java*. Leipzig, 1869, 61 pages. An account of the management of the Dutch plantations.

Howard (John Eliot), *Illustrations of the Nueva Quinologia of Pavon*. London, 1862, folio, 163 pages and 30 beautiful coloured plates. Figures of Cinchona, mostly taken from Pavon's specimens in the Herbarium of Madrid, and three plates representing the structure of several barks.

Howard (John Eliot), *Quinology of the East Indian Plantations*. London, 1869, fol. x, and 43 pages with 3 coloured plates, exhibiting structural peculiarities of the barks of cultivated Cinchona.

Karsten (Hermann), *Die medicinischen chinarinden Neu-Granada's*. Berlin, 1858, 8vo, 71 pages and 2 plates shewing microscopic structure of a few barks. An English translation prepared under the supervision of Mr. Markham, has been printed by the India Office under the title of *Notes on the Medicinal Cinchona Barks of New Granada* by H. Karsten, 1861. The plates have not been reproduced.

Karsten (Hermann), *Floræ Columbiæ terrarumque adjacentium specimina selecta*. Berolini, 1858, folio. Beautiful coloured figures of various plants, including Cinchona, under which name are several species usually referred to other genera. Only the first three parts have been published.

Markham (Clements Robert). *The Cinchona species of New Granada, containing the botanical descriptions of the species examined by Drs. Mutis and Karsten; with some account of those botanists and of the results of their labours*. London, 1867, 8vo, 139 pages and 5 plates. The plates are not coloured, yet are good reduced copies of those contained in Karsten's *Floræ Columbiæ*; they represent the following:—*Cinchona corymbosa, C. Trianæ, C. lancifolia, C. cordifolia, C. Tucujensis.*

Miquel (Friedrich Anton Wilhelm), *De Cinchonæ speciebus quibusdam, adjectis iis quæ in Java coluntur. Commentatio ex Annalibus Musei Botanici Lugduno-Batavi excscripta*. Amstelodami, 1869, 4to, 20 pages.

Phœbus (Philipp), *Die Delondre-Bouchardat'schen China-Rinden*. Giessen, 1864, 8vo, 75 pages and a table. The author gives a description, without figures, of the microscopic structure of the type-specimens figured in Delondre and Bouchardat's *Quinologie*.

Planchon (Gustave), *Des Quinquinas*. Paris et Montpellier, 1864, 8vo, 150 pages. A description of the Cinchonas and their barks. An English translation has been issued under the superintendence of Mr. Markham by the India Office, under

CH. XXX.

CHINCHONA CULTURE.

the title of *Peruvian Barks*, by Gustave Planchon, London, printed by Eyre and Spottiswoode, 1866.

Soubeiran (J. Leon) et Delondre (Augustin), *De l'introduction et de l'acclimatation des Cinchonas dans les Indes néerlandaises et dans les Indes britanniques.* Paris, 1868, 8vo, 165 pages.

Triana (José), *Nouvelles études sur les Quinquinas.* Paris, 1870, folio, 80 pages and 33 plates. An interesting account of the labours of Mutis, illustrated by uncoloured copies of some of the drawings prepared by him in illustration of his unpublished *Quinologia de Bogotá*, especially of the several varieties of *Cinchona lancifolia*; also an enumeration and short descriptions of all the species of *Cinchona*, and of New Granadian plants (cheifly *Cascarilla*) formerly placed in that genus.

Vogl (August), *Chinarinden des Wiener Grosshandels und der Wiener Sammlungen.* Wien, 1867, 8vo, 134 pages, no figures. A very exhaustive description of the microscopic structure of the barks occurring in the Vienna market, or preserved in the museums of that city.

Weddell (Hugh Algernon), *Histoire naturelle des Quinquinas, ou monographie du genre Cinchona, suivie d'une description du genre Cascarilla et de quelques autres plantes de la même tribu.* Paris, 1849, folio, 108 pages, 33 plates and map. Excellent uncoloured figures of Cinchona and some allied genera, and beautiful coloured drawings of the officinal barks. Plate I exhibits the anatomical structure of the plant; Plate II that of the bark.

Weddell (Hugh Algernon), *Notes sur les Quinquinas, extrait des Annales des Sciences naturelles*, 56me serie, tomes XI et XII. Paris, 1870, 8vo, 75 pages. A systematic arrangement of the genus *Cinchona*, and description of its (33) species, accompanied by useful remarks on their barks. An English translation has been printed by the India Office with the title, *Notes on the Quinquinas by H. A. Weddell*, London, 1871, 8vo, 64 pages. A German edition by Dr. F. A. Flückiger has also appeared under the title *Uebersicht der Cinchonen von H. A. Weddell*, Schaffhausen and Berlin, 1871, 8vo, 43 pages, with additions and indices.

I would add the following to the above list :—

Blue Book (Chinchona Cultivation), East India. Ordered to be printed, 21st March 1876.

Report on the Government Chinchona Plantations, Nílagiris. By Captain Campbell Walker, 1878.

Report of the Committee on the Manufacture of Alkaloids, &c., 1878.

Lecture on Chinchona Culture, by Surgeon-Major Bidie, M.B., 1879, Madras.

Report by Robert Cross of his Mission to South America in 1877-78. London.

CHAPTER XXXI.

HORTICULTURE.[1]

Origin of the Ootacamand Gardens.—Mr. McIvor appointed Superintendent.—Site.—Defective management.—Dr. Wight's report.—Receipts and expenditure to 1852.—Gardens placed under Government.—Mr. Markham's description of the Gardens.—Medicinal plants.—Mr. Jamieson appointed.—Gardens placed under the Commissioner.—Agri-Horticultural Society.—Recent improvements.—Superintendent's reports.—Receipts and expenditure of each garden.

CH. XXXI. — HORTICULTURE. — Origin of the Ootacamand Gardens.

IN April 1847 it was first proposed to establish a Public Garden in Ootacamand, the chief promoters of the scheme being Mr. Bell, Bombay Civil Service, and Major A. Grant. A Committee was appointed, and a prospectus issued and widely circulated soliciting subscriptions and pointing out the advantages which the climate of the Hills offered for the formation of a nursery garden which would indirectly benefit all parts of India. At the same time application was made to Government for aid. The Marquis of Tweeddale, then Governor of Madras, approved of the undertaking, and in June of the same year a working Committee was appointed, and Rupees 100 granted by Government towards the expenses of the garden. On the suggestion of the Marquis of Tweeddale the Government proposed that the Court of Directors should be asked to send out "a scientific and practical gardener qualified to undertake the management of the gardens, and to sanction a grant of an annual contribution sufficient to meet his salary."

Mr. McIvor appointed Superintendent.

In June 1847 the sanction of the Court of Directors was communicated, and in January of the following year Mr. William Graham McIvor was engaged for five years on a salary of £150 a year with a leave allowance of £75. It was stipulated that he should not trade, and that he should conform to all the rules relating to the Uncovenanted Service. Mr. McIvor arrived in Madras early in the spring, and was ordered to proceed at once to Ootacamand and report himself to the Committee and the Commandant.

The portion of the gardens first brought under cultivation was the upper and steeper part, a piece of Government shóla running

[1] I had hoped to have given a paper on the history of horticulture on the Hills by a specialist, but have been disappointed in my expectation.

CH. XXXI. — HORTICULTURE. down a shallow ravine between two spurs of the Doddabetta range. The lower and more level portion of the ground which now forms the approach to Government House was not added until the year 1851, when its purchase from Mrs. Kyan was sanctioned by the Court of Directors at a price not exceeding Rupees 50 a cawny.

Site. The site is well chosen both as regards aspect and soil, and much of the present beauty of the gardens is due to the happy manner in which advantage has been taken of the picturesque lay of the land and of the trees and rocks with which it abounds. Bits of fine old shóla still nestle undisturbed in nooks and corners of the grounds, though they are now connected by gravel paths and grassy slopes intersected by beds of flowers. To Mr. McIvor the greatest credit is due for the taste and judgment displayed in the laying out of the grounds.

Defective management. For the first four years of its existence, however, the progress of the gardens appears to have been unsatisfactory, and in May 1852 Mr. McIvor was called upon to report on its state and prospects. The result of this report was the formation of a working Committee of three members. The Committee also determined to devote a sum of Rupees 100 a month to higher horticulture, the gardens having been utilized up to this time mainly for the cultivation of vegetables for the benefit of subscribers.

Dr. Wight's report. Little improvement appears to have been made in spite of these changes, chiefly owing to the want of unanimity between Mr. McIvor and the Committee. Dr. Wight's report a few months later, in which he supported Mr. McIvor, led to the abolition of the original Committee. The gardens were placed entirely in Mr. McIvor's charge, with an *ex-officio* Committee having the Collector of Coimbatore and the Commandant among its members.

Receipts and expenditure. The receipts and expenditure up to this time were as follows. Expenditure from October 1847 to June 1852, Rupees 15,122 exclusive of Mr. McIvor's salary. Receipts for the same period Rupees 14,600, that is, Government allowance Rupees 4,800, private subscriptions Rupees 9,800.

Garden placed under Government. In 1854 the *ex-officio* members of Committee again saw fit to form a Committee of Management, to whom Mr. McIvor was instructed to submit his accounts, and it was not until November 1855 that Lord Dalhousie recommended that the gardens should be taken over by Government. A Committee, however, appears to have existed under one form or another, although tacitly abolished, until September 1857, when the gardens were placed under the control of the Conservator of Forests, Dr. Cleghorn, the Commandant being still required to check the accounts.

CH. XXXI.

HORTICULTURE.

Their history from this date has been one of steady if not of rapid progress. Nor can it be doubted that they have given an impetus to horticulture in general, and have been the means of introducing and propagating a large number of useful as well as ornamental plants and shrubs which have been sent to many different parts of India. In 1856 the Government of India sanctioned a monthly sum of Rupees 50 and free carriage for plants and seeds to and from Calcutta.

As the gardens progressed the cultivation of vegetables was abandoned, as the available space was required for the growing of flowers and ornamental trees and shrubs, but not before they had been of much service in teaching the native gardeners how to supply the local market and in inducing them to cultivate better varieties from seed imported and distributed to them free of charge. The old conservatory was constructed and a fern-house built about this time. The following extract from Markham's "Travels in Peru and India" gives his impression of the gardens in 1860 :—

Mr. Markham's descriptions.

"The English settler on the Neilgherries will find English fruits, flowers, vegetables and grasses, the introduction of which is mainly due to the exertions of Mr. William G. McIvor, the Superintendent of the Government Gardens at Ootacamund, and now also Superintendent of Cinchona Plantations in Southern India. This gentleman has been in charge of the gardens at Ootacamund since 1848, and unites zeal, intelligence, and skill to the talent and experience of an excellent practical gardener. Under his auspices the steep slopes of one of the spurs which run off from the Peak of Dodabetta and overlook the cantonment of Ootacamund have been converted into a tastefully laid out garden, in a succession of terraces. Hampered at first by the interference of a useless committee, and with no assistance beyond that of an East Indian foreman and labourers from the Mysore plains, he has succeeded in changing the wild mountain side into a very beautiful public garden. Every point of view is taken advantage of with admirable taste, and numerous trees and flowering shrubs have been introduced from England, Australia, and other countries, while the native flora of the hills is fully represented. There are English roses and geraniums, ponds bordered by white arums, shady walks overarched by trellis-work, tasteful vases filled with showy flowers, thickets of rhododendrons, hedges of heliotrope and fuchsias, fine clumps of tall spreading trees,—and from the upper terraces, between the leafy branches, there are glorious views of the Ootacamund valley and of the finely broken range of the distant Koondah hills."

Of the branch garden at Kalhatti on the Segúr ghát, which had been added for the cultivation of plants requiring a warmer climate and less elevation, Mr. Markham writes as follows :—

"A magnificent waterfall descends into a rocky basin close beside it, and the garden contains oranges of many kinds, shaddochs, lemons,

CH. XXXI. — HORTICULTURE. — limes, citrons, nutmegs, loquats and plantains. On this spot the delicious Chirimoyas, the seeds of which we brought from Peru, will hereafter ripen and enable the people of India to taste the 'masterpiece of nature.'

* * * * *

" These gardens are self-supporting."

Medicinal plants. Up to the year 1856 the only medicinal plant which had been largely cultivated was the *digitalis*, but on a suggestion of the Medical Department that more attention should be given to this branch, it was suggested that a special garden should be made for this purpose at Mélkúnda. Whether this project was ever carried out or not is uncertain, but it was probably found that the gardens at Ootacamand, Burliar, and another nursery or branch garden established shortly afterwards at Kalhatti on the Segúr ghát offered sufficient varieties of soil and climate for experiments in the growth of medicinal plants.

Mr. Jamieson's appointment. Government experiments in the rearing of chinchona plants from seeds and cuttings, which had their beginning in 1860, soon occupied a large proportion of Mr. McIvor's time, and it was found necessary to give him a European assistant. The present Superintendent, Mr. Jamieson, from the gardens at Kew, was accordingly engaged as Deputy Superintendent of the Chinchona Plantations, but his work was mainly confined to the gardens. He began his duties at Ootacamand in 1868, continuing as assistant to Mr. McIvor until 1871, when he was promoted to the appointment of Superintendent on Mr. McIvor becoming Superintendent of the Government Chinchona Plantations.

Gardens placed under Commissioner. Soon after the Commission was formed the gardens were placed under the Commissioner, and this arrangement has continued. An Agri-Horticultural Society[1] was formed mainly

Agri-Horticultural Society. through Mr. Breeks' influence, which did good service in encouraging the native growers by distributing seeds and offering prizes for vegetables, which were awarded by a Committee appointed to inspect the vegetables brought for sale to the local market. During Mr. Breeks' life agri-horticultural shows were held from time to time in the gardens, but since his death only one has taken place. Though its affairs were never finally wound up, the Society seems to have virtually died out, and it is much to be regretted that it is not revived, for although the show of flowers and vegetables was never so good as might reasonably

[1] In June 1869 the Government sanctioned the transfer of the gardens to the Agri-Horticultural Society, the Commissioner being President of the Committee of Management. Mr. McIvor, who was relieved of the superintendence of the gardens, being an *ex-officio* member of the Committee, whilst Mr. Jamieson, as Superintendent, was to work under the orders of the Committee. The transfer was not carried into effect, as Mr. Jamieson declined to act as Superintendent under the orders of the Committee.

have been expected, the effect of these exhibitions could not have been other than beneficial as an incentive to both native growers and amateur gardeners.

Recent improvements.

Among the most noteworthy improvements since Mr. Jamieson has taken charge are some which come more especially within the province of landscape gardening. Portions of the lower part of the grounds have been cleared of the *Acacia dealbata* and *A. melanoxylon* and laid out in grass studded with *auracarias* and other handsome trees, including some rare varieties of the *eucalyptus*, and many additional flower beds have been introduced. Handsome gates flanked by lodges, one of which is used for a herbarium and the other as an office, have been placed at the entrance of the gardens. The approach to Government House is now through these gates, and the carriage drive which has been cut along the lower slope and first terrace having made it necessary to lay out these portions of the grounds afresh, a good deal has been done to improve their general appearance. A spacious conservatory has been recently erected above the terrace near the band stand.

Sim's Park.

As regards natural beauty, however, the Ootacamand gardens must yield the palm to the more recently formed garden at Coonoor, called after the late Member of Council, Sim's Park. During the last few years of his stay in India Mr. Sim devoted much time and attention to the formation and laying out of these gardens. The site is a particularly suitable one, and the climate of Coonoor being milder, is more adapted for the cultivation of flowers, and especially of roses. The ground embraces some stretches of natural shóla which are finer than any in the gardens at Ootacamand. The tree ferns are especially beautiful, and many foreign varieties have been placed in the shady hollows which are the natural habitat of this graceful family of plants. A miniature lake has been formed by damming up the stream which flows at the foot of the gardens, and a number of paths cut through the wilder portions of the enclosure.

Superintendent's reports.

The Superintendent's reports for the last few years are of special interest, showing the number of useful plants which have been introduced and propagated, among others the Santung cabbage, prickly comfrey (*Symphytum asperrimum*), and the mahogany tree. The list of medicinal plants now includes the ipecacuanha, jalap, rhubarb, peppermint, lavender, digitalis, taraxicum. A medicinal garden was formed in 1878 at the head of the Botanical Gardens, Ootacamand, five acres in extent, on the suggestion of the Surgeon-General, Indian Medical Department. A special grant is given for this purpose. In 1878-79 no less than three acres were cultivated with jalap. A quantity of

CH. XXXI. — HORTICULTURE.

dried jalap, as well as of *Berberis cortex* and dried digitalis, was supplied to the Medical Department. The fruit trees at Burliar have been let for the last few years, thus rendering this garden self-supporting. It now contains fine specimens of the mangosteen, leechee, clove, nutmeg, Liberian coffee, and other valuable tropical fruit-bearing trees and shrubs.

Receipts and expenditure.

The receipts and expenditure for the year 1878-79 at the several gardens, including the grounds of the Secretariat at Stonehouse and at Government House, Norwood, which are also under the Superintendent, were as follows :—

Garden.	Receipts.		Expenditure.	
		RS.		RS.
Ootacamand Botanical Garden.	By sale of plants ...	2,838	Establishment ...	5,327
	By Government grants.	10,720	Minor Establishment and Contingencies..	5,514
	Sundries	40		
	Total ...	13,598	Total ...	10,841
Stonehouse Park ... (Secretariat.)	Government grant ...	1,100	Establishment ...	874
			Sundries	229
				1,103
Upper Norwood ... (Government House.)	Government grant ...	1,050	Establishment ...	1,028
			Sundries	26
			Total ...	1,054
Medicinal Garden ...	Government grant ...	498	Establishment ...	498
		RS.		RS.
Sim's Park	Government grant ...	2,379	Establishment ...	1,840
			Sundries	540
			Total ...	2,380
Kalhatti ...	Government grant ...	180	Establishment ...	180
	Rent, &c.	75		
	Total ...	255		
Burliar	Government grant ...	335	Establishment ...	276
	Rent, &c.	273	Sundries	59
	Total ...	608	Total ...	335
	Grand Total ...	19,488	Grand Total ...	16,391

CHAPTER XXXII.

WEIGHTS AND MEASURES.

Land measure.—Capacity measures.—Measure used for house sites.—Long measure.—Weights.—Precious metals and coins.

CH. XXXII. WEIGHTS AND MEASURES.

Land measure.

28 Adis, or country ft.	=	1 Kól ...	=	24 English ft.
1 Square Kól ...	=	1 Gúli ...	=	576 square ft.
100 Gúlis	=	1 Cawnie	=	57,600 square ft.
			=	1·322314 acres.
1 Balla	=	3·82 acres	=	166464 square ft.

In the Revenue accounts cawnies are subdivided into annas and 12 pies or part of an anna.

$\frac{1}{12}$ of an Anna ...	=	300 square feet.
12 Pies ...	=	1 Anna or 3,600 square feet.
16 Annas ...	=	1 Cawnie or 57,600 square feet.

A cawnie is to the English acre as 160 is to 121.

To convert cawnies into acres, the usual course is to multiply the cawnie by 160 and divide by 121.

Since the Revenue Survey was introduced, acres and decimals are generally used in all measurements.

Measure used for house sites.

In measuring house sites, the measure known as mané or ground (= 60 × 40 feet = 2,400 square feet) is used.

It is noted that the space (about 12 feet) between the beams (thúlam) which support the roof ordinarily is called an ankanam. A fair sized Tamil house would consist of about 4 ankanams of 12 feet each. The term is used by the Badagas also, but with them each section would ordinarily not exceed 9 or 10 feet in breadth.

Measures of capacity.

2 Alloks	=	1 Ullok = ¼ measure (½ Madras measure).
8 Alloks	=	1 Paddi or Measure.
8 Measures	=	1 Merkal.
5 Merkals	=	1 Para.
400 Merkals	=	1 Garisa.
50 Jodis (Mysore measures) or 100 Madras half-measures	=	1 Palla.

CH. XXXII.

WEIGHTS AND MEASURES.

A Madras half-measure filled to overflowing is used in all transactions. Its cubic contents equal 50·17 inches. In the weekly markets held at the several stations and other parts of the district this measure is used in selling articles such as chillies, pepper, turmeric, and other condiments, which are generally purchased by weight in other places. Ghee is also sold by measure. The aborigines of Nílagiris have a measure called kolagam, nearly equivalent in size and contents to the Madras half-measure.

25 Imperial bottles = 1 Kodam or pot. This sort of measurement is used in selling oil.

Long measure.

9 Angulams or Inches ... = 1 Jan or span.
12 do. ... = 1 Adi or foot.
18 do. ... = 1 Múra or cubit.
2 Cubits or 3 English feet = 1 Gaj or yard.

Weights.

1 Palam ... ... = 3 Rupees in weight.
8 Palams ... ... = 1 Seer = 24 Rs. weight.
5 Seers ... ... = 1 Viss = 120 Rs. weight.
1 Viss ... ... = $3\frac{1}{8}$ Rathal.
$1\frac{1}{4}$ Viss or 50 Palams ... = 1 Túk = 150 Rs. weight.
8 Viss .. .. = 1 Maund = 960 Rs. weight.
20 Maunds ... ... = 1 Baram or candy
= 19,200 Rs. weight.

Precious metals and coins, gold and silver.

32 Koondamani weight ... = 1 Star Pagoda or 1 Varaha weight.
10 Varaha weight ... ... = 1 Palam ($1\frac{1}{4}$ oz. Avoirdupois).
8 Palams ... . = 1 Seer.
1 Rupee weight ... ... = $3\frac{13}{40}$ Varaha weight.

Money.

12 Pies ... ... = 1 Anna.
16 Annas ... ... = 1 Rupee.

4 Kas (pies) ... ... = 1 Thúddú.
3 Thúddús ... ... = 1 Anna.
4 Annas ... ... = 1 Belli.
4 Bellis ... ... = 1 Rupee.
$3\frac{1}{2}$ Rupees ... ... = 1 Varaha.

Dodda-hana ... ... = 4 Annas.
Chicka-hana ... ... = 2 Annas.

APPENDIX.

APPENDIX.

No. 1.—*Statement showing the Number of Villages and Hamlets in the District of Nílagiris as they stood in Fasli*[1] 1285.

Taluqs.	Area in Square Miles.	Government.				Zamindári.				Inám.				Total.					
		Inhabited.		Uninhabited.		Inhabited.		Uninhabited.		Inhabited.		Uninhabited.		Inhabited.		Uninhabited.		Total.	
		Number of Villages.	Number of Hamlets.	Number of Villages.	Number of Hamlets.	Number of Villages.	Number of Hamlets.	Number of Villages.	Number of Hamlets.	Number of Villages.	Number of Hamlets.	Number of Villag es.	Number of Hamlets.	Number of Villages.	Number of Hamlets.	Number of Villages.	Number of Hamlets.	Number of Villages.	Number of Hamlets.
1	2	3	4	5	6	7	8	9	10	11	12	13	14	15	16	17	18	19	20
Nílagiris ... Tódanád* ...	‡786	1	§169	...	...	...	...	...	...	...	...	...	...	17	401	...	...	17	401
Mékanád ...		1	§ 77	...	...														
Péranganád ...		1	89	...	...														
Kambés† ...		10	17	...	...														
Búdinatam ...		1	7	...	...														
Sembanattam ...		1	4	...	...														
Segúr ...		1	3	...	...														
Kúndas ...		1	35	...	...														
Total ...	...	17	401	...	...	...	...	...	...	...	...	...	...	17	401	...	...	17	401

(1) The revenue year ending 30th June 1876.
* Includes the Ouchterlony Valley, measuring 37·12 square miles.
† The names of these Kambés are given in Chapter III.
‡ The entire area of the district is officially given as 749 square miles. The Ouchterlony Valley is 37 square miles. By recent survey the Mékanád Division is 59,247·86 square acres or 92·57 square miles.
§ One in Tódanád, three in Mékanád, are newly formed hamlets, *i.e.*, since Fasli 1283. The Coffee industry created them.

No. 2.—*Statement of Population arranged with reference to Caste, according to the Census of* 1871.

Nationality.	Caste.	Population.		
		Males.	Females.	Total.
Hindus ...	Brahmins	107	89	196
	Kshatriyas	31	19	50
	Chetties	362	110	472
	Vellálar (Agriculturalists)	2,851	1,779	4,630
	Idaiyar (Shepherds)	421	350	771
	Kammalán (Artizans)	270	220	490
	Kanakkan	65	49	114
	Kaikkalar (Weavers)	148	84	232
	Vanniau (Laborers and Cultivators) ...	708	526	1,234
	Kusavan (Potters)	20	3	23
	Satani (Mixed)	1,077	882	1,959
	Sembadavan (Hunters)	36	24	60
	Shánán (Toddy-drawers)	16	...	16
	Ambattam (Barbers)	51	57	108
	Vannán (Washermen)	107	87	194
	Others	12,965	11,914	24,609
	Pareiyas	5,705	4,523	10,228
	Total ...	24,670	20,716	* 45,386
Mahomedans..	Lubbéys	218	55	273
	Arabs	3	1	4
	Sheiks	461	392	853
	Syuds	92	64	156
	Pattans	104	74	178
	Moghuls	5	3	8
	Other Mahomedans	266	198	464
	Total ...	1,149	787	1,936
Europeans ...	......	818	521	1,339
Eurasians ...	......	523	273	796
Others ...	......	32	12	44
	Grand Total ...	27,192	22,309	49,501

N.B.—Of the Hindu population 2,935 are Native Christians.

No. 2-*A*.—*Statement showing the Male Population arranged with reference to Occupation according to the Census of* 1871.

Major Headings.	Minor Headings.	Number of Males employed.
Professional	Government Service	78
	Military	571
	Learned Professions	56
	Minor do.	481
Domestic	Personal Service	964
Commercial	Traders	814
	Conveyors	608
Agricultural	Cultivators	6,963
Industrial	Dress	548
	Food	480
	Metal	143
	Construction	311
	Books	15
	Household Goods	39
	Combustibles	2
Indefinite and non-Productive.	Laborers	3,930
	Property	71
	Unproductive	41
	Others	207
	Total ...	16,322

No. 2-*B*.—*Statement showing the Number of Houses, Population, and Cattle in each Taluq.*

Number of Houses	Terraced	69
	Tiled	1,845
	Thatched	11,864
	Unspecified	144
	Total ...	13,922
Population ...	Males	27,192
	Females	22,309
	Total ...	49,501
Agricultural Stock	Tilling Cattle	6,212
	Cows	6,341
	She-Buffaloes	6,196
	Sheep	3,464
	Ploughs	2,897
	Horses	Unknown.
	Ponies	Do.

No. 3.—*Statement of Rent Roll for Fasli* 1281.

	Puttas.	Single Puttas.		Joint Puttas.		Total Puttas.	
		Number.	Assessment.	Number.	Assessment.	Number.	Assessment.
			RS.		RS.		RS.
Iyen.	Tódanád	806	2,955	264	2,756	1,070	5,711
	Mékanád	291	1,343	299	2,588	590	3,931
	Búdinatam	86	1,135	4	36	90	1,171
	Sembanatham	21	176	...	...	21	176
	Segúr	14	116	1	23	15	139
	Péranganád and Kambés.	432	2,109	266	3,127	698	5,236
	Kúndas	115	401	26	109	141	510
	Total ...	1,765	8,235	860	8,639	2,625	16,874
Plantation.	Tódanád	87	2,162	2	37	89	2,199
	Mékanád	30	1,431	11	676	41	2,107
	Ségúr	9	801	...	...	9	801
	Péranganád	148	2,126	9	520	157	2,646
	Kúndas	2	4	...	...	2	4
	Múlachapoi	1	285	...	...	1	285
	Velléru Kambé	1	3	...	...	1	3
	Total ...	278	6,812	22	1,233	300	8,045
	Grand Total ...	2,043	15,047	882	9,872	2,925	24,919

No. 4.—*Statement showing the Rainfall for a Series of Ten Years in the District.*

Faslis.	Official Years.	July.	August.	September.	October.	November.	December.	January.	February.	March.	April.	May.	June.	Total.
		Inches.	Inches.	Inches.	Inches.	Inches.	Inches.	Inches.	Inches.	Inches.	Inches.	Inches.	Inches.	Inches.
1276 ...	1866-67.	1·90	2·00	1·05	14·00	1·00	3·80	0·40	...	1·10	3·60	3·00	3·40	35·25
1277 ...	1867-68.	10·40	0·90	3·70	7·30	0·30	0·00	4·50	0·00	0·10	1·20	3·80	10·46	42·66
1278 ...	1868-69.	7·35	7·89	9·87	18·38	2·80	0·10	0·00	0·00	2·04	4·01	6·20	6·49	65·13
1279 ...	1869-70.	4·36	4·50	1·63	3·97	7·46½	8·04	2·90¼	0·61	3·40¼	2·19½	2·32	5·74	47·14
1280 ...	1870-71.	4·10	4·68	2·20	7·25	11·05½	2·53	10·18	2·97	1·49½	6·73	3·53	4·31	61·03
1281 ...	1871-72.	3·39	3·77	6·11	14·99	9·77	1·04	0·12½	0·59	0·72½	4·78	3·50	4·81	53·68
1282 ...	1872-73.	4·51	4·20	9·81	3·73	14·22	3·12	0·0	8·26	0·00	3·48	10·55	2·65	64·35
1283 ...	1873-74.	3·90	4·10	5·72	11·37	4·27	1·63	0·37½	1·41	1·47½	2·98	9·43	6·04	52·70
1284 ...	1874-75.	4·12	3·16	4·54	10·21	5·44	2·71	0·54	0·30	1·50	2·15	5·70	6·47	46·84
1285 ...	1875-76.	3·00	1·49	3·92	10·88	7·89	4·28	...	0·00	2·62	3·83	5·78	1·58	45·27
Average ...		4·70	3·67	4·85	10·21	6·42	2·72	1·90	1·41	1·45	3·50	5·38	5·19	51·40

No. 5.—*Statement showing Rainfall in certain places in the District of Nílagiris from Fasli Year* 1870-71 *to* 1876-77.

No.	Fasli Year.	1870-71.	1871-72.	1872-73.	1873-74.	1874-75.	Average for the five years.	1875-76.	1876-77.
	Ootacamand.								
		IN.	IN.	IN.	IN.	IN.	IN.	IN.	IN.
1	July	5·06	3·33	4·89	4·46	5·51	4·65	4·42	6·81
2	August	6·33	5·02	4·20	6·05	2·95	4·91	1·98	3·99
3	September	2·04	4·23	10·08	6·42	2·78	5·11	4·24	1·50
4	October	10·10	10·45	3·99	7·32	10·24	8·42	8·33	1·66
5	November	1·69	13·92	6·93	2·35	2·10	5·40	2·30	·26
6	December	1·11	·06	1·90	0·44	·85	·87	2·55	·11
7	January	1·95	...	...	...	·05	1·00	...	...
8	February	·60	...	2·79	0·86	...	1·42	...	·36
9	March	1·55	·05	...	1·45	·80	·96	2·82	2·56
10	April	5·73	1·93	5·96	2·20	1·46	3·76	1·72	2·88
11	May	4·71	5·00	7·35	11·18	5·45	6·74	4·57	7·15
12	June	5·68	6·45	2·27	7·36	10·87	6·53	1·72	8·48
	Total ...	46·55	50·44	50·36	50·09	43·06	48·10	34·65	35·76
	Coonoor.								
1	July	3·14	3·29	4·70	2·30	2·85	3·26	1·55	3·95
2	August	3·03	3·95	6·70	1·00	2·75	3·49	2·10	3·35
3	September	2·36	5·85	9·10	5·80	5·35	5·69	3·50	5·05
4	October	4·40	22·04	3·55	8·40	10·50	9·78	9·65	14·05
5	November	20·42	15·55	24·35	9·10	13·00	16·48	21·80	8·95
6	December	3·95	3·58	7·10	4·45	3·10	4·44	8·65	1·90
7	January	18·41	·15	...	0·40	2·05	5·25	...	...
8	February	5·35	·90	16·90	3·30	·30	5·35	...	1·65
9	March	1·44	·70	...	0·15	1·70	1·00	3·60	5·80
10	April	7·68	8·97	2·60	4·25	3·50	5·40	2·90	4·65
11	May	3·25	2·58	12·25	8·14	3·80	6·00	4·35	2·70
12	June	3·21	3·95	2·20	3·80	3·00	3·23	3·75	2·60
	Total ...	76·64	71·51	89·45	51·09	51·90	68·12	61·85	54·65
	Wellington.								
1	July	1·83	1·95	3·95	3·02	2·84	2·72	1·97	3·15
2	August	2·95	3·26	3·79	4·37	2·97	3·47	1·51	3·10
3	September	2·07	6·90	8·62	4·37	7·56	5·90	5·02	3·02
4	October	5·33	13·90	2·92	7·71	10·48	8·07	7·17	5·81
5	November	12·36	11·72	12·00	3·20	6·46	9·15	9·54	...
6	December	3·23	1·44	2·97	1·84	3·72	2·64	7·02	1·47
7	January	13·45	·10	...	·35	·65	3·64	...	·15
8	February	2·13	·95	8·35	2·72	...	3·54	..	·27
9	Ma ch	2·54	...	...	·14	1·66	1·44	2·66	7·36
10	April	9·05	4·91	2·36	2·80	2·30	4·28	3·65	3·09
11	May	1·31	1·59	12·80	7·04	4·31	5·41	5·94	2·47
12	June	3·25	2·89	1·57	4·26	4·13	3·22	2·42	3·39
	Total ...	59·50	49·61	59·33	41·82	47·07	51·47	46·90	33·28

No. 5.—*Statement showing Rainfall in certain places in the District of Nílagiris from Fasli Year* 1870-71 *to* 1876-77—(Continued).

No.	Fasli Year.	1870-71.	1871-72.	1872-73.	1873-74.	1874-75.	Average for the five years.	1875-76.	1876-77.
	Mélkúnda.								
		IN.	IN.	IN.	IN.	IN.	IN.	IN.	IN.
1	July	...	3·03	8·50	5·90	5·50	5·74	2·80	6·70
2	August	...	2·01	3·55	2·85	1·75	2·54	·80	4·80
3	September	...	6·45	6·90	5·59	4·35	5·82	3·30	...
4	October	Not furnished	13·90	3·80	12·45	9·00	9·79	11·50	11·55
5	November		1·36	23·10	7·80	8·95	10·30	9·05	...
6	December		2·20	5·25	2·45	4·8	3·90	3·70	5·20
7	January		...	...	...	1·0	1·00	...	...
8	February		·50	8·20	1·50	·5	2·67	...	·50
9	March		·80	...	...	1·25	2·02	3·30	4·15
10	April	...	6·60	3·10	2·43	2·00	3·53	1·02	...
11	May	2·07	1·60	12·20	6·00	6·50	5·67	2·70	...
12	June	3·75	3·10	2·30	9·00	5·10	4·65	·95	8·15
	Total ...	5·82	41·55	76·90	55·97	50·70	56·28	39·12	41·05
	Kaity.								
1	July	...	3·35	5·35	4·05	3·18	4·23	3·55	3·78
2	August	...	3·85	5·00	4·85	3·45	4·29	·95	4·53
3	September	...	6·75	12·50	5·30	6·40	7·74	5·75	2·71
4	October	...	13·75	4·10	0·65	13·20	7·92	6·14	3·55
5	November	...	9·65	7·90	3·50	3·65	6·17	5·16	1·85
6	December	...	·65	2·95	...	1·65	1·75	2·15	1·22
7	January	...	...	...	...	·38	·38	...	...
8	February	...	·15	5·40	2·15	...	2·57	...	...
9	March	...	...	...	4·20	2·15	3·17	3·50	8·49
10	April	...	3·80	2·80	2·23	2·72	2·89	3·43	2·96
11	May	3·70	3·05	9·75	13·47	5·96	7·19	5·76	4·75
12	June	4·95	4·40	2·50	6·10	6·89	4·97	3·19	4·81
	Total ...	8·65	49·40	58·25	46·50	49·63	50·95	39·58	38·65
	Kódanád.								
1	July	...	3·98	6·84	2·15	3·89	4·21	2·41	2·51
2	August	...	4·56	3·16	5·32	4·82	4·46	1·65	4·93
3	September	...	7·25	12·19	5·71	4·59	7·43	3·39	6·32
4	October	...	17·60	3·60	16·81	17·89	13·97	16·03	3·38
5	November	...	11·54	14·32	5·20	6·85	9·48	8·02	2·99
6	December	...	1·30	5·70	1·31	4·46	3·19	1·60	·47
7	January	...	...	...	·10	1·34	·72	...	...
8	February	...	·45	7·95	·65	...	3·02	...	·65
9	March	...	...	...	·09	1·86	·97	1·12	5·11
10	April	...	2·49	1·90	4·21	3·96	3·14	2·60	...
11	May	3·92	4·80	11·06	7·56	3·85	6·24	10·50	5·27
12	June	3·98	6·25	3·94	8·02	5·23	5·48	·55	3·88
	Total ...	7·90	60·22	70·66	57·13	58·74	61·69	47·87	35·51

No. 5.—*Statement showing Rainfall in certain places in the District of Nílagiris from Fasli Year* 1870-71 *to* 1876-77—(Continued).

No.	Fasli Year.	1870-71.	1871-72.	1872-73.	1873-74.	1874-75.	Average for the five years.	1875-76.	1876-77.
	Neduwattam.								
		IN.	IN.	IN.	IN.	IN.	IN.	IN.	IN.
1	July	29·86	29·51	31·71	35·17	40·04	33·26	37·35	43·30
2	August	25·24	15·44	19·34	18·30	24·20	20·50	8·41	22·45
3	September	22·39	16·56	13·02	15·60	13·15	16·15	5·75	9·45
4	October	19·44	5·79	5·31	12·01	14·22	11·35	4·24	3·90
5	November	2·67	8·14	3·71	·79	1·47	3·35	...	·40
6	December	·39	...	2·19	·21	·26	·76	...	...
7	January	·35	...	...	...	·50	·42	...	...
8	February	·65	...	·72	...	...	·68	...	...
9	March	·74	·08	·40	·45	·83	·50	3·33	1·90
10	April	...	1·67	4·93	2·11	3·57	3·07	2·33	2·38
11	May	...	3·39	5·92	15·89	4·42	7·40	1·58	3·12
12	June	...	20·12	17·97	43·72	13·51	23·83	11·33	41·80
	Total ...	101·73	100·70	105·22	144·25	116·17	113·61	74·32	128·70

No. 6.—*Statement showing the Prices of Grain for a Series of Ten Years in the District of Nílagiris per Garce of 3,200 Madras Measures.*

Faslis.	Official Years.	Rice, 1st Sort.	Rice, 2nd Sort.	Paddy, 1st Sort.	Paddy, 2nd Sort.	Chólum	Cumboo.	Rágg y.	Varagu.	Horse-gram.	Ulundu.	Wheat.	Salt.
		RS.	RS.	RS.	RS.	RS.	RS.	RS.	RS.	RS.	RS.	RS.	RS.
1276 ...	1866-67 ...	1,010	838	Not sold in the District.	Not sold in the District.	552	474	471	Not sold in the District.	585	937	1,075	569
1277 ...	1867-68 ...	687	608			384	292	354		345	800	756	471
1278 ...	1868-69 ...	620	563			295	276	303		320	800	520	426
1279 ...	1869-70 ..	696	618			295	271	281		264	576	575	489
1280 ...	1870-71 ...	558	494			277	203	218		226	588	558	493
1281 ...	1871-72 ...	481	446			222	192	177		247	576	403	518
1282 ...	1872-73 ...	530	477			237	205	198		263	443	412	526
1283 ...	1873-74 ...	582	533			304	291	256		337	652	533	533
1284 ...	1874-75 ...	582	512			298	291	256		337	724	457	582
1285 ...	1875-76 ...	533	533			320	337	278		320	689	492	533

No. 7.—*Statement showing the Particulars of Cultivation, &c., for a Series of Ten Years.*

Faslis.	Cultivable Extent.	Area occupied. Dry. Extent.	Dry. Assessment.	Wet. Extent.	Wet. Assessment.	Charge for Water.	Total Assessment.	Deduct Remissions.	Remainder.	Add Miscellaneous Items.	Total Ryotwari Demand.	Revenue from permanently settled Estates	Jodi on Shrotriem Villages.	Total Land Revenue Demand.	Arrears previous Years.	Total Demand of the Year.	Gross Collections.	Balance at the end of Fasli.
1	2	3	4	5	6	7	8	9	10	11	12	13	14	15	16	17	18	19
	ACRES.	ACRES.	RS.	ACS.	RS.	RS	RS.	RS.	RS.	RS.	RS.	RS.	RS.	RS.	RS.	RS.	RS.	RS.
1276 ...	129,691	55,945	25,400	165	360	...	25,760	1,109	24,651	4,256	28,907	..	...	28,907	11,053	39,960	23,778	16,182
1277 ...	129,691	57,279	27,624	165	360	...	27,984	875	27,109	7,280	34,389	...	...	34,389	16,182	50,571	36,406	14,165
1278 ...	129,691	58,947	30,427	40	90	...	30,517	† 13,959	16,558	11,865	28,423	...	...	28,423	14,165	42,588 Remission	36,571 2,896	3,121
1279 ...	129,691	59,428	30,530	40	90	...	30,620	1,032	29,588	12,866	42,454	...	...	42,454	3,121	45,575 Remission	41,844 1,877	1,854
1280 ...	129,691	59,636	30,859	40	90	...	30,949	1,103	29,846	10,437	40,283	...	...	40,283	1,854	42,137 Remission	38,207 310	3,620
1281 ...	129,691	60,510	31,668	40	90	...	31,751	‡ 7,008	24,750	11,730	36,480	...	...	36,480	3,620	40,100 Remission	35,173 431	4,491
1282 ...	129,691	62,816	33,215	40	90	...	33,305	‡ 11,193	22,112	9,416	31,528	...	...	31,528	4,491	36,019	32,343	3,676
1283 ...	* 133,326	67,010	41,092	40	90	...	41,182	‡ 17,391	23,791	18,454	42,245	...	...	42,245	3,676	45,921 Remission	42,254 2,440	1,227
1284 ...	133,635	67,602	41,846	40	90	...	41,936	‡ 9,442	32,494	13,555	46,049	...	...	46,049	1,227	47,276 Remission	45,648 701	927
1285 ...	133,686	79,902	46,020	40	90	...	46,110	‡ 8,176	37,934	9,267	47,201	...	...	47,201	927	48,128 Remission	38,916 187	9,026
Total ...	1,308,484	6,29,075	3,38,681	650	1,440	...	3,40,121	71,288	2,68,833	1,09,126	3,77,959	...	...	3,77,959	60,316	4,38,275	3,79,987	58,288

* The difference in cultivable extent is accounted for by the *paying* coffee acreage in the Ouchterlony Valley.

† This large item is merely an account item and does not mean an actual remission. It resulted thus: Government, finding the difficulty of enforcing the collection of the demand of each year within that year, resolved to avoid the difficulty by making the demand of each year accrue after the 30th June; thus the land revenue due 30th June 1876 became the demand for the revenue year 1876-77.

‡ These large remissions were the result of two Government Orders in 1871 and 1874, which permitted free tenure for 5 years of all land taken up for coffee and tea cultivation.

No. 7-*A.—Statement showing the Area under the principal Crops cultivated in Fasli* 1285.

	ACRES.
Raggy	3,430
Wheat	3,199
Ganjee	3,761
Koralie	15,728
Samay	4,662
Other food grains	588
Potatoes	754
Castor-oil seeds	10
Opium	66
Mustard	355
Vendiem	144
Horse-gram	67
Tea	2,392
Coffee	12,593
Cinchona	1,311
Vegetables	169
Other crops	384
Total ...	49,613

No. 8.—*Statement showing the Collections under the several Heads of Revenue in the District of Nilagiris for a Series of Ten Years.*

Faslis.	Official Years.	Land Revenue.	Forest Revenue.	Abkári.	Income Tax.	Stamps.	Total.
		RS.	RS.	RS.	RS.	RS.	RS.
1276 ...	1866-67...	23,778	54,035	93,237	...	16,585	1,87,635
1277 ...	1867-68...	36,484	36,294	53,285	4,595	14,649	1,45,257
1278 ...	1868-69...	36,571	29,234	33,909	8,809	13,179	1,21,702
1279 ...	1869-70...	41,844	10,252	85,522	14,437	9,918	1,61,973
1280 ...	1870-71...	38,207	6,379	86,005	17,081	7,715	1,55,387
1281 ...	1871-72...	35,178	6,660	78,461	6,227	8,631	1,35,157
1282 ...	1872-73...	32,343	33,075	86,659	5,673	13,081	1,70,831
1283 ...	1873-74...	42,254	25,953	70,547	6	13,860	1,52,620
1284 ...	1874-75...	45,648	18,427	75,847	...	17,213	1,57,135
1285 ...	1875-76...	38,916	36,815	1,00,217	...	20,272	1,96,220

No. 9.—*Statement showing the Number and Value of Suits disposed of in the Civil and Revenue Courts for a Series of Ten Years.*

Years.	Number of Suits disposed of in different Courts.													
	Ordinary Suits.								Small Causes.					
	Village Munsifs'.	Revenue Courts.	District Munsifs', Civil Judge as District Munsif, and Assistant Judicial Commissioner as District Munsif.	Civil Judges and Judicial Commissioner as Principal Sadar Amins.	Judges of Small Cause Courts as Principal Sadar Amins.	Civil Judges' and Judicial Commissioners'.	Total Number of Suits.	Total Value in Rupees.	District Munsifs', Assistant Agent's and Assistant Commissioner's.	Principal Sadar Amin.	Judges of Small Cause Courts (Wellington).	Civil Judges' and Assistant Judicial Commissioner's.	Total Number of Small Causes.	Total Value in Rupees.
1	2	3	4	5	6	7	8	9	10	11	12	13	14	15
								RS. A. P.						RS. A. P.
1866 ...	601	...	103	32	...	2	738	8,389 3 11	...	...	...	398	398	2,655 11 10
1867 ...	677	...	50	13	...	3	743	4,112 3 2	...	...	...	385	385	1,404 9 4
1868 ...	356	...	41	9	...	2	408	3,549 0 0	199	...	...	...	199	1,853 3 9
1869 ...	759	...	48	6	...	1	814	30,000 0 0	193	...	24	...	217	20,000 0 0
1870 ...	316	...	42	...	...	7	365	2,858 10 0	136	...	20	...	156	14,285 6 5
1871 ...	307	...	49	...	...	5	361	15,710 3 6	148	...	60	...	208	10,596 15 5
1872 ...	423	...	51	...	..	3	477	21,559 14 7	129	...	102	...	231	14,152 14 10
1873 ...	683	...	54	...	...	6	743	37,565 0 0	196	...	103	...	299	19,990 0 0
1874 ...	645	...	62	...	...	2	709	34,025 0 0	197	...	69	...	266	17,312 0 0
1875 ...	827	...	92	...	...	10	929	1,82,876 0 0	164	...	92	...	256	19,019 0 0
Total ...	5,594	...	592	60	...	41	6,287	3,40,645 3 2	1,362	...	470	783	2,615	1,21,269 13 7

No. 10.—*Statement showing the Receipts and Expenditure of Local*

Receipts.	1871-72.	1872-73.	1873-74.	1874-75.	1875-76.
	RS.	RS.	RS.	RS.	RS.
1. Balance { a. Road Fund	-3,627	-3,834	-10,304	-3,877	-3,060
b. Endowment Fund...	-258	177	-194	309	404
2. Provincial Grant for General Fund	...	1,103	701	5,704	2,747
Do. for Road Fund	44,790	51,380	52,350	48,530	46,286
3. Do. for Schools	...	...	...	...	...
4. Do. for General Purposes... ...	...	...	4,390	680	...
Special Sanctions	...	...	10,580	...	...
5. Surplus Pound Fund	...	...	...	...	2,244
6. Avenue	...	...	...	...	...
7. Fishery Rents	...	...	...	...	...
8. Miscellaneous	98	...	...	...	...
9. Road Cess under Act III of 1866	...	...	...	...	...
10. Land Cess under Act IV of 1871	807	...	2,262	2,121	2,089
11. Tolls' Act IV of 1871	10,907	14,692	12,785	13,729	14,867
12. House Tax	...	...	...	...	...
13. Fees in Schools and Training Institutions ...	...	...	...	...	...
14. Contributions	...	175	125	430	100
15. Educational Receipts	...	...	...	...	...
Choultries, &c.	964	410	1,100	360	360
16. Sale of Elementary Books	...	...	...	...	...
17. Fees from Travellers' Bungalows	...	...	...	...	...
18. Balance of Bungalow Fund	...	...	...	...	...
19. Fines and Penalties	...	...	...	...	...
20. Sale of other Property	...	...	...	...	...
21. Public Works Receipts	...	...	...	...	...
22. Do. Refund of Expenditure ...	...	...	...	...	...
23. Miscellaneous	92	5,910	3,023	3,433	1,312
24. Miscellaneous Debt Account	...	...	...	...	...
Suspense Account	...	...	...	...	14
Grand Total ...	53,773	70,013	76,818	71,417	67,363

Funds under Act IV of 1871, *for the Five Years ending* 1875-76.

Expenditure.	1871-72.	1872-73.	1873-74.	1874-75.	1875-76.
New Works.	RS.	RS.	RS.	RS.	RS.
1. Communications { By P. W. D.	10,230	5,773	14,871	17,152	15,873
By other Agency	...	...	...	...	...
2. Educational ... By P. W. D.	...	...	...	...	...
3. Sanitary and { By P. W. D.	...	...	...	...	...
Miscellaneous. { By other Agency	...	...	...	...	...
Incomplete Works	2,341	9,906	...	...	200
Repairs.					
4. Communications { By P. W. D.	34,808	37,084	37,762	31,760	38,566
By other Agency	...	..	...	...	...
5. Educational ... { By P. W. D.	...	...	...	...	...
By other Agency	...	...	...	...	...
6. Sanitary and { By P. W. D.	200	...	2,691	2,043	200
Miscellaneous. { By other Agency	...	...	...	...	...
7. Public Works Department supervision ...	7,570	17,100	16,399	12,616	13,637
8. Petty Establishment	256	2,345	...	...	...
9. Tolls and Ferries	...	...	...	59	...
10. Tools and Plant	6	506	...	460	450
Contributions to Coonoor Municipality ...	...	...	...	2,065	1,815
Total Grant I ...	55,411	72,714	71,723	66,155	70,741
11. Payment for Inspection	...	...	125	467	482
12. Local Fund Schools	...	...	...	...	...
13. Purchase of Books, &c.	...	..	..	...	...
14. Salary Grants	...	...	...	...	60
15. Results Grants	158	..	...	220	...
Miscellaneous	...	275	250	175	...
Total Grant II ...	158	275	375	862	542
16. Hospitals and Dispensaries	...	...	...	...	...
17. Vaccine Establishment	...	414	558	552	595
18. Sanitary Establishment and cleansing of Tanks and Wells.	...	...	...	...	...
Choultries Establishments	422	444	330	328	718
19. Travellers' Bungalow Establishment	...	173	275	286	486
Miscellaneous	...	882	72	...	...
Total Grant III ...	422	1,913	1,235	1,166	1,799
20. Establishments at the Presidency and in the Collector's and Local Fund Board's Offices and Contingencies.	336	1,532	867	881	1,046
21. Write-backs of incorrect Credits of District Road Fund and Balances.	...	...	...	...	...
Total Grant IV ...	336	1,532	867	881	1,046
Advances Recoverable	...	...	484	...	...
22. Miscellaneous Debt Account	...	...	...	2,263	14
Total Expenditure ...	56,327	76,434	74,684	71,327	74,142
23. Balance ... { Road Fund	-3,834	-7,548	-3,879	-3,060	-8,971
Endowment Fund ...	177	216	309	403	138
General Fund	1,103	911	5,704	2,747	2,054
Grand Total ...	53,773	70,013	76,818	71,417	67,363

No. 11.—*Statement showing Receipts and Expenditure for Special Local Funds for the Five Years ending* 1875-76.

—	1871-72. Balance at the beginning of the Year.	1871-72. Receipts during the Year.	1871-72. Total.	1871-72. Expenditure during the Year.	1871-72. Balance at the end of the Year.	1872-73. Receipts during the Year, including Balance.	1872-73. Expenditure during the Year.	1872-73. Balance at the end of the Year.
1	2	3	4	5	6	7	8	9
	RS. A. P.	RS. A. P.	RS. A. P.	RS. A. P.	RS. A. P.	RS. A. P.	RS. A. P.	RS. A. P.
Jungle Conservancy Fund.	6,675 11 4	14,741 14 9	21,417 10 1	10,066 6 0	11,351 4 1	22,789 2 7	14,791 14 7	7,997 4 0
Cattle Pound Fund ...	177 14 11	860 12 6	1,038 11 5	572 13 9	465 13 8	1,264 13 2	551 12 0	713 1 2
Public Bungalow Fund ...	940 5 9	4,587 8 0	5,527 13 9	5,391 15 6	135 14 3	......	......	......
Endowment Fund ...	......	......	......	......	......	......	......	......
Village Service	75 0 0	148 0 0	223 0 0	162 0 0	61 0 0	237 0 0	237 0 0	......
Total ...	7,869 0 0	20,338 3 3	28,207 3 3	16,193 3 3	12,014 0 0	24,290 15 9	15,580 10 7	8,710 5 2

—	1873-74. Receipts during the Year, including Balance.	1873-74. Expenditure during the Year.	1873-74. Balance at the end of the Year.	1874-75. Receipts during the Year, including Balance.	1874-75. Expenditure during the Year.	1874-75. Balance at the end of the Year.	1875-76. Receipts during the Year, including Balance.	1875-76. Expenditure during the Year.	1875-76. Balance at the end of the Year.
	10	11	12	13	14	15	16	17	18
	RS. A. P.	RS. A. P.	RS. A. P.	RS. A. P.	RS. A. P.	RS. A. P.	RS. A. P.	RS. A. P.	RS. A. P.
Jungle Conservancy Fund.	21,015 9 4	17,443 13 10	3,571 11 6	13,044 13 9	13,250 8 4	− 205 10 7	− 165 7 7	98 0 0	−263 7 7
Cattle Pound Fund ...	1,608 7 8	1,408 13 7	199 10 1	1,093 0 10	957 5 4	135 11 6	1,014 10 9	591 0 0	423 10 9
Public Bungalow Fund ...	......	......	......	......	......	......	......	......	......
Endowment Fund ...	......	......	......	......	......	......	......	−120 0 0	−120 0 0
Village Service	162 0 0	162 0 0	......	87 0 0	87 0 0	......	262 0 0	262 0 0	......
Total ...	22,786 1 0	19,014 11 5	3,771 5 7	14,224 14 7	14,294 13 8	− 69 15 1	1,111 3 2	831 0 0	40 3 2

No. 12.—*Statement showing the Progress of Education for a Series of Ten Years.*

Description of Schools.		1866-67.			1867-68.		
		Number of Schools.	Number of Pupils. Boys.	Number of Pupils. Girls.	Number of Schools.	Number of Pupils. Boys.	Number of Pupils. Girls.
A.—Government Schools.							
1 Maintained from Imperial or Provincial Funds.	Higher ...	...	...	...	...	...	...
	Middle ...	...	...	...	...	...	...
	Lower ...	...	...	...	...	...	...
2. Maintained from Local or Municipal Funds.	Higher ...	...	...	...	...	...	...
	Middle ...	...	...	...	...	...	...
	Lower ...	...	...	...	...	...	...
Total ...		...	...	...	...	...	...
* Lawrence Asylum ...	Middle ...	1	123	51	1	124	70
B.—Schools Aided.							
1. By Salary Grants ...	Higher ...	...	...	...	...	...	...
	Middle ...	2	71	...	2	56	...
	Lower ...	...	...	...	...	...	...
2. By Results Grants ...	Higher ..	...	...	...	...	...	...
	Middle ...	...	...	...	...	...	...
	Lower ...	...	...	...	...	...	...
3. Combined Salary and Results Grants.	Higher ...	...	...	...	...	...	...
	Middle ...	...	...	...	...	...	...
	Lower ...	..	...	...	...	..	...
* (Omitting Lawrence Asylum) Total ...		2	71	...	2	56	...
C. Schools under Inspection for Results Grants but not aided.	Higher ...	...	...	...	...	...	...
	Middle ...	...	...	...	...	...	...
	Lower ...	...	...	...	...	...	...
Total ...		...	...	...	...	...	...
Number of successful candidates for the Uncovenanted Civil Service Examination educated in this district.		...	...	...	...	2	...
Number of successful candidates for Special Tests.		...	...	...	...	...	...
Number of successful candidates for Matriculation and F. A.		...	Mat. 6 F.A. 0	...	...	Mat. 8 F.A. 1	...

No. 12.—*Statement showing the Progress of Education for a Series of Ten Years*—(Continued).

Description of Schools.		1868-69.			1869-70.		
		Number of Schools.	Number of Pupils.		Number of Schools.	Number of Pupils.	
			Boys.	Girls.		Boys.	Girls.
A.—*Government Schools.*							
1 Maintained from Imperial or Provincial Funds.	Higher ...	...	...	...	...	...	...
	Middle ...	...	...	...	...	...	...
	Lower ...	...	...	...	...	...	...
2 Maintained from Local or Municipal Funds.	Higher ...	...	...	...	...	...	..
	Middle ...	...	...	...	...	...	...
	Lower ...	...	...	...	...	...	...
Total ...		...	...	...	...	...	...
* Lawrence Asylum ...	Middle ...	1	121	59	1	126	62
B.—*Schools Aided.*							
1. By Salary Grants... ...	Higher ...	...	...	...	...	...	...
	Middle ...	2	61	...	2	98	...
	Lower ...	...	...	...	...	...	...
2. By Results Grants ...	Higher ...	...	...	...	...	...	...
	Middle ...	...	...	...	...	...	...
	Lower ...	...	...	...	...	...	...
3. Combined Salary and Results Grants.	Higher ...	...	...	...	...	...	...
	Middle ...	...	...	...	...	...	...
	Lower ...	..	...	...	...	...	...
* (Omitting Lawrence Asylum) Total ...		2	61	...	2	98	...
C. *Schools under Inspection for Results Grants but not aided.*	Higher ...	...	...	...	...	...	...
	Middle ...	...	...	...	...	...	...
	Lower ...	...	...	...	...	...	...
Total ...		..	...	...	...	...	...
Number of successful candidates for the Uncovenanted Civil Service Examination educated in this district.		...	5	...	...	4	*4
Number of successful candidates for Special Tests.		...	...	...	...	...	...
Number of successful candidates for Matriculation and F. A.		..	Mat. 4 F.A. 2	...	...	Mat. 5 F.A. 0	...

* Teachers' Certificate Examination.

No. 12.—*Statement showing the Progress of Education for a Series of Ten Years*—(Continued).

Description of Schools.	1870-71.			1871-72.		
	Number of Schools.	Number of Pupils.		Number of Schools.	Number of Pupils.	
		Boys.	Girls.		Boys.	Girls.
A.—Government Schools.						
1 Maintained from Imperial or Provincial Funds. — Higher ...	...	...	...	...	...	...
Middle ...	...	...	...	...	...	...
Lower ...	...	...	...	...	...	...
2 Maintained from Local or Municipal Funds. — Higher ...	...	...	...	...	...	...
Middle ...	...	...	...	...	...	...
Lower ...	...	...	...	...	...	...
Total ...	...	...	...	...	...	...
* Lawrence Asylum ... Middle ...	1	140	72	1	344	68
B.—Schools Aided						
1. By Salary Grants ... — Higher ...	...	...	...	...	...	...
Middle ...	2	94	...	1	*	*
Lower ...	...	...	...	...	...	...
2. By Results Grants ... — Higher ...	...	...	...	...	...	...
Middle ...	...	...	...	2	153	...
Lower ...	...	...	...	2	36	29
3. Combined Salary and Results Grants. — Higher ...	...	...	...	...	...	...
Middle ...	...	...	...	...	...	...
Lower ...	...	...	...	...	...	...
* (Omitting Lawrence Asylum) Total ...	2	94	...	5	189	29
C. Schools under Inspection for Results Grants but not aided. — Higher ...	...	...	...	...	...	...
Middle ...	...	...	...	...	...	...
Lower ...	...	...	...	...	...	...
Total ...	...	...	...	...	...	...
Number of successful candidates for the Uncovenanted Civil Service Examination educated in this district.	...	2	†3	...	2	...
Number of successful candidates for Special Tests.	...	...	...	...	...	...
Number of successful candidates for Matriculation and F. A.	...	Mat. 1 F.A. 0	...	...	Mat. 1 F.A. 0	...

* Closed after 9 months. † Teachers' Certificate Examination.

No. 12.—*Statement showing the Progress of Education for a Series of Ten Years*—(Continued).

Description of Schools.		1872-73. Number of Schools.	1872-73. Number of Pupils. Boys.	1872-73. Number of Pupils. Girls.	1873-74. Number of Schools.	1873-74. Number of Pupils. Boys.	1873-74. Number of Pupils. Girls.
A.—*Government Schools.*							
1. Maintained from Imperial or Provincial Funds.	Higher ...	...	...	...	...	...	...
	Middle ...	...	...	...	...	...	...
	Lower ...	...	...	...	...	...	...
2. Maintained from Local or Municipal Funds.	Higher ...	...	...	...	...	...	...
	Middle ...	...	...	...	...	...	...
	Lower ...	...	...	...	1	97	...
Total ...		...	...	...	1	97	...
* Lawrence Asylum ...	Middle ...	1	329	65	1	324	64
B.—*Schools Aided.*							
1. By Salary Grants ...	Higher ...	...	...	...	...	...	...
	Middle ...	...	...	...	...	...	...
	Lower ...	...	...	...	...	...	...
2. By Results Grants ...	Higher ...	...	...	...	...	...	...
	Middle ...	...	...	...	...	...	...
	Lower ...	3	161	30	...	...	...
3. Combined Salary and Results Grants.	Higher ...	..	...	...	...	...	...
	Middle ...	...	...	...	...	...	...
	Lower ...	...	...	...	...	...	...
*(Omitting Lawrence Asylum) Total ...		3	161	30	...	...	...
C. Schools under Inspection for Results Grants but not aided.	Higher ...	...	...	...	...	...	...
	Middle ...	...	...	...	...	...	...
	Lower ...	..	...	...	...	...	...
Total ...		...	...	...	...	...	...
Number of successful candidates for the Uncovenanted Civil Service Examination educated in this district.		...	...	...	...	...	...
Number of successful candidates for Special Tests.		...	...	...	...	...	3*
Number of successful candidates for Matriculation and F. A.		...	Mat. 0 F.A. 0	...	...	Mat. 0 F.A. 0	...

* Teachers' Certificate Examination.

No. 12.—*Statement showing the Progress of Education for a Series of Ten Years*—(Continued).

Description of Schools.		1874-75. Number of Schools.	1874-75. Number of Pupils. Boys.	1874-75. Number of Pupils. Girls.	1875-76. Number of Schools.	1875-76. Number of Pupils. Boys.	1875-76. Number of Pupils. Girls.
A.—*Government Schools.*							
1. Maintained from Imperial or Provincial Funds.	Higher ...	...	...	...	...	...	...
	Middle ...	...	...	...	...	...	...
	Lower ...	...	...	...	...	...	...
2. Maintained from Local or Municipal Funds.	Higher ...	...	...	...	...	...	...
	Middle ...	...	...	...	...	...	...
	Lower ...	1	104	...	1	102	...
Total ...		1	104	...	1	102	...
* Lawrence Asylum ...	Middle ...	1	332	58	1	Not known.	
B.—*Schools Aided.*							
1. By Salary Grants... ...	Higher ...	...	...	...	...	...	...
	Middle ...	1	76	...	1	70	...
	Lower ...	2	34	10	2	38	7
2. By Results Grants ...	Higher ...	...	...	...	...	...	...
	Middle ...	...	...	...	3	152	34
	Lower ...	3	253	6	...	...	...
3. Combined Salary and Results Grants.	Higher ...	...	...	...	...	...	...
	Middle ...	...	...	...	...	...	...
	Lower ...	...	...	...	...	...	...
* (Omitting Lawrence Asylum) Total ...		6	363	16	6	260	41
C. Schools under Inspection for Results Grants but not aided.	Higher ...	...	...	...	...	...	...
	Middle ...	...	...	...	...	...	...
	Lower ...	2	189	...	7	276	38
Total ...		2	189	...	7	276	38
Number of successful candidates for the Uncovenanted Civil Service Examination educated in this district.		...	...	...	...	...	...
Number of successful candidates for Special Tests.		...	...	4	...	...	...
Number of successful candidates for Matriculation and F. A.		...	Mat. 0 F.A. 0	...	... ...	Mat. 1 F.A. 0	...

No. 13.—*Deaths registered in the Rural Circle and Towns of the District of Nilagiris during each Month from the Year* 1870 *to* 1877.

1	2	3			4				
Years.	Rural Circles and Towns.	Population for which Returns were received.			Total Deaths registered during the Year.				
		Males.	Females.	Total.	January.	February.	March.	April.	May.
1870...	Rural Circle ...	11,989	10,190	22,179	23	17	30	41	52
	Ootacamand ...	6,745	5,204	11,949	8	10	9	7	8
	Coonoor ...	2,124	1,890	4,014	2	1	4	8	1
	Total ...	20,858	17,284	38,142	33	28	43	56	61
1871...	Rural Circle ...	11,989	10,190	22,179	30	30	25	29	30
	Ootacamand ...	6,745	5,204	11,949	9	7	12	23	31
	Coonoor ...	2,124	1,890	4,014	10	14	10	11	4
	Total ...	20,858	17,284	38,142	49	51	47	63	65
1872...	Rural Circle ...	19,926	15,911	35,837	26	43	33	75	73
	Municipal Towns...	7,112	5,974	13,086	29	28	50	36	52
	Total ...	27,038	21,885	48,923	55	71	83	111	125
1873...	Rural Circle ...	20,269	16,192	36,461	30	20	24	38	43
	Municipal Towns...	6,923	6,117	13,040	23	32	30	39	47
	Total ...	27,192	22,309	49,501	53	52	54	77	90
1874...	Rural Circle ...	19,378	15,867	35,245	37	26	39	59	74
	Ootacamand ...	4,890	4,323	9,213	13	11	18	32	42
	Coonoor ...	1,583	1,325	2,908	2	5	7	4	6
	Total ...	25,851	21,515	47,366	52	42	64	95	122
1875...	Rural Circle ...	19,378	15,867	35,245	45	51	35	49	54
	Ootacamand ...	4,890	4,323	9,213	17	15	20	15	32
	Coonoor ...	1,583	1,325	2,908	8	6	5	6	8
	Total ..	25,851	21,515	47,366	70	72	60	70	94
1876...	Rural Circle ...	19,378	15,867	35,245	34	35	48	59	118
	Ootacamand ...	4,890	4,323	9,213	7	20	14	24	35
	Coonoor ...	1,583	1,325	2,908	6	6	7	9	31
	Total ...	25,851	21,515	47,366	47	61	69	92	184
1877...	Rural Circle ...	19,378	15,867	35,245	54	83	71	272	329
	Ootacamand ...	4,890	4,323	9,213	23	36	94	99	74
	Coonoor ...	1,583	1,325	2,908	9	13	13	29	61
	Total ...	25,851	21,515	47,366	86	132	178	400	464

No. 13.—*Deaths registered in the Rural Circle and Towns of the District of Nílagiris during each Month from the Year* 1870 *to* 1877—(Continued).

Years.	Rural Circles and Towns.	4—(*Continued*). Total Deaths registered during the Year—(*Continued*). June.	July.	August.	September.	October.	November.	December.	Total.
1870...	Rural Circle ...	47	41	31	30	30	29	27	398
	Ootacamand ...	7	12	10	7	13	7	8	106
	Coonoor ...	11	12	3	4	6	6	11	69
	Total ...	65	65	44	41	49	42	46	573
1871...	Rural Circle ...	46	44	51	68	47	45	25	470
	Ootacamand ...	27	28	23	21	15	16	20	232
	Coonoor ...	4	9	7	7	11	3	2	92
	Total ...	77	81	81	96	73	64	47	794
1872...	Rural Circle ...	134	73	37	40	38	36	43	651
	Municipal Towns.	68	43	33	26	25	17	36	443
	Total ...	202	116	70	66	63	53	79	1,094
1873...	Rural Circle ...	69	56	50	48	40	41	32	491
	Municipal Towns.	39	37	23	30	21	30	38	389
	Total ...	108	93	73	78	61	71	70	880
1874...	Rural Circle ...	71	55	39	25	40	51	37	553
	Ootacamand ...	24	35	29	21	24	20	20	289
	Coonoor ...	4	7	8	7	11	5	9	75
	Total ...	99	97	76	53	75	76	66	917
1875...	Rural Circle ...	45	52	50	49	56	46	44	576
	Ootacamand ...	31	15	22	24	15	21	20	247
	Coonoor ...	9	13	10	9	12	11	6	103
	Total ...	85	80	82	82	83	78	70	926
1876...	Rural Circle ...	154	125	56	57	52	66	43	847
	Ootacamand ...	41	35	32	15	22	26	23	294
	Coonoor ...	23	12	10	9	9	12	12	146
	Total ...	218	172	98	81	83	104	78	1,287
1877...	Rural Circle ...	269	215	192	199	242	181	159	2,266
	Ootacamand ...	76	70	42	51	61	46	42	714
	Coonoor ...	33	53	52	59	55	43	29	449
	Total ...	378	338	286	309	358	270	230	3,429

No. 13.—*Deaths registered in the Rural Circle and Towns of the District of Nilagiris during each Month from the Year* 1870 *to* 1877—(Continued).

Years.	Rural Circles and Towns.	5												
						Injuries.						Total Deaths from all causes.		
		Cholera.	Small-pox.	Fevers.	Bowel-complaints.	Suicide.	Wounds.	Accidents.	Snake-bite	Killed by Wild Beasts.	All other Causes.	Males.	Females.	Total.
1870	Rural Circle ...	...	5	280	..	...	...	2	...	...	111	...	...	398
	Ootacamand ...	...	...	73	...	...		2	...	...	31	...	...	106
	Coonoor ...	...	...	44	...	1	...	...	...	...	24	...	...	69
	Total ...	...	5	397	...	1	...	4	...	...	166	...	...	573
1871	Rural Circle ...	3	1	343	52	1	.	3	...	...	67	267	203	470
	Ootacamand ...	2	1	137	42	1	...	1	...	...	48	137	95	232
	Coonoor ...	..	...	51	8	...	..	2	...	...	31	48	44	92
	Total ...	5	2	531	102	2	...	6	..	...	146	452	342	794
1872	Rural Circle ...	1	2	465	98	1	..	3	...	...	81	364	287	651
	Municipal Towns.	...	6	112	44	1	..	2	...	...	248	218	225	443
	Total ...	1	8	607	142	2	...	5	...	...	329	582	512	1,094
1873	Rural Circle ...	...	19	320	44	...	2	7	...	...	99	285	206	491
	Municipal Towns.	...	14	86	60	1	2	5	...	...	221	178	211	389
	Total ...	...	33	406	104	1	4	12	...	...	320	463	417	880
1874	Rural Circle ...	...	6	426	41	1	1	3	...	...	75	327	226	553
	Ootacamand ...	...	6	86	51	...	...	3	...	...	143	165	124	289
	Coonoor ...	...	2	25	18	...	1	...	...	...	29	46	29	75
	Total ...	...	14	537	110	1	2	6	...	...	247	538	379	917
1875	Rural Circle ...	9	6	394	35	1	...	13	...	...	118	336	240	576
	Ootacamand ...	1	...	63	43	...	...	4	...	...	136	148	99	247
	Coonoor ...	2	...	37	28	...	1	...	...	...	35	60	43	103
	Total ...	12	6	494	106	1	1	17	...	...	289	544	382	926
1876	Rural Circle ...	23	...	655	39	2	1	3	...	1	123	465	382	847
	Ootacamand ...	...	8	128	43	...	...	1	...	...	114	148	146	294
	Coonoor ...	2	...	69	36	...	...	...	...	...	39	92	54	146
	Total ...	25	8	852	118	2	1	4	...	1	276	705	582	1,287
1877	Rural Circle ...	333	174	1,289	281	1	2	13	...	...	173	1,368	898	2,266
	Ootacamand ...	93	124	161	75	1	1	4	...	...	255	373	341	714
	Coonoor ...	50	29	77	220	...	..	...	...	...	73	264	185	449
	Total ...	476	327	1,527	576	2	3	17	...	...	501	2,005	1,424	3,429

No. 13.—*Deaths registered in the Rural Circle and Towns of the District of Nílagiris during each Month from the Year* 1870 *to* 1877—(Continued).

Years.	Rural Circles and Towns.	6							
		Ratio of Deaths per 1,000 of Population.							
		Cholera.	Small-pox.	Fevers.	Bowel Complaints.	Injuries.	From all Causes. Males.	Females.	Total.
1870...	Rural Circle ...	...	·22	12·62	...	·09	...	...	17·94
	Ootacamand ...	...	...	6·10	...	·16	...	...	8·87
	Coonoor	...	...	10·95	...	·24	...	...	17·18
	Total ...	...	·13	10·40	...	·13	...	...	15·02
1871...	Rural Circle ...	·13	·04	15·46	2·34	·18	22·27	19·92	21·19
	Ootacamand ...	·16	·08	11·46	3·51	·16	20·31	18·25	19·41
	Coonoor	...	...	12·70	1·99	·49	22·60	23·28	22·91
	Total ...	·13	·05	13·92	2·67	·20	21·66	19·78	20·81
1872...	Rural Circle ...	·02	·05	12·97	2·73	·11	18·26	18·03	18·02
	Municipal Towns ...	...	·46	10·85	3·44	·23	30·6	37·7	33·85
	Total ...	·02	·16	12·40	2·90	·14	21·52	23·39	22·36
1873...	Rural Circle ...	...	·5	8·7	1·2	·2	14·	12·7	13·4
	Municipal Towns ...	...	1·07	6·6	4·6	·6	25·7	34·5	29·9
	Total ...	...	·6	8·2	2·9	·3	17·0	18·6	17·7
1874...	Rural Circle ...	...	·1	12·08	1·1	·1	16·8	14·2	15·6
	Ootacamand ...	...	·6	9·3	5·5	·3	33·8	28·7	31·3
	Coonoor	...	·6	8·5	6·1	·3	29·05	21·8	25·7
	Total ...	...	·2	11·3	2·3	·1	20·8	17·6	19·3
1875...	Rural Circle ...	·2	·1	11·1	·9	·3	17·3	15·7	16·3
	Ootacamand ...	·1	...	6·8	4·6	·4	30·2	22·9	26·8
	Coonoor	·6	...	12·7	9·6	·3	37·9	32·4	35·4
	Total ...	·2	·1	10·4	2·2	·4	21·0	17·7	19·5
1876...	Rural Circle ...	0·6	...	18·5	1·1	0·1	23·9	24·07	24·03
	Ootacamand ...	...	0·8	13·8	4·6	0·1	30·2	33·7	31·9
	Coonoor	0·6	...	23·7	12·3	...	58·1	40·7	50·2
	Total ...	0·5	0·1	17·9	2·4	0·1	27·4	27·05	27·1
1877...	Rural Circle ...	9·4	4·9	36·5	7·9	0·4	70·6	56·6	64·2
	Ootacamand ...	10·09	13·4	17·4	8·1	0·6	76·2	78·8	77·4
	Coonoor	17·1	9·9	26·4	75·6	...	166·7	139·6	154·4
	Total ...	10·04	6·9	32·2	12·1	0·4	77·5	66·1	72·3

No. 13.—*Deaths registered in the Rural Circles and Towns of the District of Nilagiris during each Month from the Year* 1870 *to* 1877—(Continued).

Years.	Rural Circles and Towns.	7 Number of Births registered. Males.	Females.	Total.	8 Ratio of Births per 1,000 of Population. Males.	Females.	Total.	9 Excess of Births over Deaths per 1,000 of Population.	10 Excess of Deaths over Births per 1,000 of Population.
1870...	Rural Circle ...	344	293	637	28·69	28·75	28·72	·78	...
	Ootacamand ...	20	22	42	2·96	4·22	3·51	...	5·36
	Coonoor	17	12	29	8·00	6·34	7·22	...	9·96
	Total ...	381	327	708	18·26	18·91	18·56	3·54	...
1871...	Rural Circle ...	273	189	462	22·77	18·54	20·83	...	·36
	Ootacamand ..	118	102	220	17·49	19·60	18·41	...	·10
	Coonoor	39	35	74	18·31	18·51	18·43	...	4·48
	Total ...	430	326	756	20·61	18·86	19·82	...	·99
1872...	Rural Circle ...	219	156	375	10·99	9·8	10·46	...	7·78
	Municipal Towns.	280	285	565	39·37	47·7	43·17	10·32	...
	Total ...	499	441	940	18·45	20·15	19·21	...	3·15
1873...	Rural Circle ...	281	238	519	13·8	14·6	14·2	·8	...
	Municipal Towns.	284	238	522	41·02	38·8	40·03	10·23	...
	Total ...	565	476	1,041	20·7	21·3	21·02	3·32	...
1874...	Rural Circle ...	228	246	474	11·7	15·5	13·4	...	2·2
	Ootacamand ...	194	194	388	39·6	44·8	42·1	10·8	...
	Coonoor	45	40	85	28·4	30·1	29·2	3·5	...
	Total ...	467	480	947	18·06	22·3	19·9	·6	...
1875...	Rural Circle ...	395	290	685	20·3	18·2	19·4	3·1	...
	Ootacamand ...	170	139	309	34·7	32·1	33·5	6·7	...
	Coonoor	42	41	83	26·7	30·1	28·5	...	6·9
	Total ...	607	470	1,077	23·4	21·7	22·7	3·2	...
1876...	Rural Circle ...	338	281	619	17·4	17·7	17·5	...	6·5
	Ootacamand ...	170	165	335	34·7	38·1	36·3	4·4	...
	Coonoor	51	35	86	32·2	26·4	29·5	...	20·7
	Total ...	559	481	1,040	21·6	22·3	21·9	...	5·2
1877 ..	Rural Circle ...	466	348	814	24·0	21·9	23·1	...	...
	Ootacamand ...	187	172	359	38·2	40·7	38·9	...	...
	Coonoor	43	40	83	27·2	30·2	28·5	...	...
	Total ...	696	560	1,256	26·9	26·0	26·5	...	45·8

No. 14.—*Deaths registered among Europeans and Eurasians from different causes in the District of Nīlagiris.*

1	2	3			4	5	6	7	8	9			10			11					
Years.	Sect.	Population for which Returns were received.			Cholera.	Small-pox.	Fevers.	Bowel-complaints.	All other causes.	Total Deaths from all causes.			Total Births.			Ratio of Deaths per 1000 of Population. From all Causes.			Ratio of Deaths per 1000 of Population. Total Births.		
		Males.	Females.	Total.						Males.	Females.	Total.	Males.	Females.	Total.	Males.	Females.	Total.	Males.	Females.	Total.
1874 ...	Europeans ...	818	521	1,339	...	...	3	8	30	25	17	42	26	32	58	30·5	32·6	31·3	31·7	61·4	43·3
	Eurasians ...	523	273	796	...	...	2	2	3	2	5	7	5	8	13	3·8	18·3	8·7	9·5	29·3	16·3
1875 ...	Europeans ...	818	521	1,339	...	...	2	6	44	28	24	52	34	31	65	34·2	46·6	38·6	41·5	59·5	48·5
	Eurasians ...	523	273	796	...	...	2	3	7	4	8	12	16	8	24	7·6	29·3	15·1	30·5	29·3	30·1
1876 ...	Europeans ...	818	521	1,339	7	...	3	11	29	31	19	50	24	30	54	37·9	36·4	37·3	29·3	57·5	40·3
	Eurasians ...	523	273	796	...	1	4	2	9	9	7	16	4	4	8	17·2	25·6	20·1	7·6	14·6	10·0
1877 ...	Europeans ...	818	521	1,339	5	1	6	4	54	42	28	70	39	39	78	51·3	53·7	52·3	47·6	74·8	58·2
	Eurasians ...	523	273	796	1	1	2	5	8	9	8	17	14	12	26	17·2	29·3	21·3	26·7	43·9	32·6

No. 15-*A.*—*Wellington—Statement of Rainfall at the Observatory,* 1873—1876.

Months.	1873. Rain. Number of Days it fell.	1873. Rain. Amount collected.	1874. Rain. Number of Days it fell.	1874. Rain. Amount collected.	1875. Rain. Number of Days it fell.	1875. Rain. Amount collected.	1876 Rain. Number of Days it fell.	1876 Rain. Amount collected.
January	...	...	1	0·35	4	0·65	...	...
February	10	8·45	5	2·72	...	...	...	...
March	...	...	1	0·14	5	1·65	6	2·16
April	9	2·32	4	0·63	6	2·30	8	3·65
May	12	12·80	17	7·04	15	4·31	14	5·94
June	7	1·46	13	4·26	14	4·12	11	2·42
July	10	3·20	7	1·07	8	1·13	13	3·15
August	12	4·30	11	2·97	6	1·51	4	2·94
September	7	3·20	15	7·56	10	5·02	6	3·03
October	16	7·21	21	10·51	11	7·17	6	5·82
November	6	3·20	10	6·46	11	9·97	6	1·79
December	4	1·84	7	3·72	4	7·02	4	1·47
Total ...	93	47·98	112	47·43	94	44·85	78	32·37
Mean ...	7·75	3·99	9·03	3·95	7·83	3·74	6·5	2·69

No. 15-*B.*—*Wellington*—*Statement of Readings of Barometer at the Observatory*, 1873—1876.

Months.	1873. Reading of Barometer No. 626 N and Z.				1874. Reading of Barometer No. 626 N and Z.				1875. Reading of Barometer No. 626 N and Z.				1876. Reading of Barometer No. 626 N and Z.			
	Mean for Month.	Highest in Month.	Lowest in Month.	Range.	Mean for Month.	Highest in Month.	Lowest in Month.	Range.	Mean for Month.	Highest in Month.	Lowest in Month.	Range.	Mean for Month.	Highest in Month.	Low-est in Month	Range.
January ...	24·219	24·327	24·11	·117	24·276	24·343	24·183	0·160	24·316	24·369	24·263	·106	24·310	24·383	24·238	·195
February ...	24·186	24·322	24·050	·272	24·257	24·347	24·144	0·203	24·320	24·390	24·250	·140	24·312	24·392	24·234	·158
March	24·230	24·350	24·1110	·240	24·316	24·398	24·248	·140	24·346	24·438	24·254	·184	24·324	24·414	24·239	·181
April	24·208	24·245	24·170	·075	25·333	24·426	24·240	·226	24·279	24·356	24·200	·158	24·287	24·380	24·194	·186
May	24·203	24·255	24·150	·105	24·140	24·328	24·052	·276	24·276	24·360	24·192	·168	24·268	24·398	24·135	·260
June	24·192	24·241	24·112	·199	24·142	24·294	24·094	·204	24·205	24·390	24·110	·190	24·247	24·326	24·168	·158
July	24·179	24·241	24·117	·124	24·208	24·280	24·130	·150	24·225	24·290	24·180	·130	24·233	24·306	24·160	·146
August	24·178	24·285	24·070	·215	24·232	24·325	24·138	·188	24·221	24·314	24·128	·186	24·241	24·300	24·182	·118
September ...	24·214	24·327	24·100	·227	24·303	24·298	24·108	·190	24·256	24·334	24·156	·196	24·212	24·354	24·170	·184
October ...	24·185	24·285	24·085	·200	24·245	24·352	24·139	·213	24·370	24·376	24·160	·216	24·282	24·362	24·202	·160
November ...	24·188	24·325	24·058	·275	24·315	24·390	24·240	·150	24·323	24·109	24·240	·169	24·305	24·379	24·232	·147
December ...	24·252	24·320	24·183	·137	24·313	24·376	24·250	·126	24·309	24·372	24·234	·138	24·315	24·374	24·236	·118
Mean ...	24·203	24·294	24·111	·182	24·248	24·347	24·164	·186	24·289	24·368	24·198	·158	24·278	24·364	24·200	·167

No. 15-*C.—Wellington—Statement of Ozone readings at the Observatory,* 1873—1876.

Months.	1873. Ozone.		1874. Ozone.		1875. Ozone.		1876. Ozone.	
	Mean at 10 A.M.	Mean at 4 P.M.	Mean at 10 A.M.	Mean at 4 P.M.	Mean at 10 A.M.	Mean at 4 P.M.	Mean at 10 A.M.	Mean at 4 P.M.
January	75	65	67	60	70	60	75	65
February	75	65	68	60	75	60	70	60
March	70	60	70	65	70	60	78	63
April	75	63	75	60	75	65	70	60
May	70	62	65	55	70	60	65	57
June	65	58	70	60	65	60	70	60
July	70	62	65	60	70	65	68	58
August	76	65	65	55	75	65	70	60
September	72	63	65	55	70	60	75	65
October	70	62	65	60	70	60	68	60
November	65	60	70	60	75	65	71	60
December	70	60	75	60	70	60	68	58
Mean ...	71	62	68	59	71	70	70	60

No. 15-*D.*—*Wellington—Statement of readings of Thermometer at the Observatory,* 1873—1876.

Months.	1873. Temperature of Air.							1874. Temperature of Air.						
	Highest in Month.	Lowest in Month.	Range in Month.	Mean of all Highest.	Mean of all Lowest.	Mean Daily Range.	Approximate Mean for Month.	Highest in Month.	Lowest in Month.	Range in Month.	Mean of all Highest.	Mean of all Lowest.	Mean Daily Range.	Approximate Mean for Month.
January	70·5	41·9	21·4	67·2	53·9	13·3	61·1	70·0	36·8	33·2	67·4	44·2	23·2	55·8
February	68·5	48·5	20·0	65·0	54·7	10·3	60·3	72·7	45·4	27·3	68·7	50·6	18·1	59·6
March	72·7	51·1	21·6	68·3	56·3	12·0	62·6	78·0	54·0	24·0	77·3	50·5	16·8	63·9
April	73·0	54·2	18·8	69·7	58·9	10·8	61·4	82·0	54·5	27·5	78·4	52·4	26·0	65·4
May	75·5	50·5	25·0	71·1	59·7	11·4	63·7	76·1	56·0	20·1	75·3	51·4	23·9	63·3
June	73·5	50·5	23·0	70·2	59·9	10·3	64·5	75·8	57·4	18·4	74·3	53·2	21·1	63·7
July	71·5	53·3	18·2	67·1	58·0	9·1	62·6	74·8	57·4	17·4	74·2	54·1	20·1	64·1
August	72·9	56·4	16·5	69·6	57·3	12·3	63·5	74·1	57·4	16·7	73·5	58·0	15·5	65·7
September	70·3	55·0	18·3	66·7	56·0	10·9	61·7	76·9	57·2	19·7	73·9	57·8	16·1	65·8
October	69·5	52·1	17·4	66·2	55·8	10·4	62·3	72·2	54·5	17·7	68·9	57·2	11·7	63·0
November	68·0	50·5	17·5	64·6	54·2	10·4	59·7	71·0	48·7	22·3	69·8	51·7	18·1	60·7
December	69·0	49·2	19·8	63·4	53·0	10·4	57·6	71·1	47·2	24·0	70·4	48·2	22·2	59·3
Mean ...	71·2	51·7	19·7	67·4	56·4	10·9	61·7	74·5	52·2	22·4	74·3	52·4	19·4	62·5

No. 15-*D.*—*Wellington—Statement of readings of Thermometer at the Observatory*, 1873—1876—(Continued).

Months.	1875. Temperature of Air.							1876. Temperature of Air.						
	Highest in Month.	Lowest in Month.	Range in Month.	Mean of all Highest.	Mean of all Lowest.	Mean Daily Range.	Approximate Mean for Month.	Highest in Month.	Lowest in Month.	Range in Month.	Mean of all Highest.	Mean of all Lowest.	Mean Daily Range.	Approximate Mean for Month.
January	69·8	45·3	24·5	68·8	46·9	21·9	57·8	76·5	43·0	33·5	72·8	46·2	26·6	59·5
February	79·1	38·5	40·6	76·7	40·1	36·6	58·4	79·6	48·2	31·6	76·8	49·2	27·6	63·5
March	81·3	47·2	34·1	80·4	47·5	32·9	63·9	79·8	56·5	23·3	78·0	59·4	20·6	67·7
April	82·7	53·0	29·7	82·3	53·0	29·3	67·6	81·3	59·6	21·3	79·6	59·2	20·4	69·4
May	84·9	53·0	31·9	84·5	53·9	31·6	69·2	80·6	57·1	23·5	80·4	59·1	21·3	69·7
June	76·1	54·5	21·6	75·9	54·7	21·2	65·3	78·0	58·0	20·0	74·7	58·7	16·0	66·2
July	77·3	55·7	21·6	77·0	55·8	21·2	66·4	77·3	57·0	20·3	74·9	57·9	17·0	66·4
August	76·4	52·3	24·1	76·3	52·3	24·0	64·3	77·1	57·2	19·9	73·8	57·6	16·2	65·7
September	79·1	49·0	30·1	78·2	49·4	28·8	63·8	76·5	56·0	20·5	73·4	56·3	17·1	64·8
October	73·5	52·8	20·7	73·3	52·8	20·5	63·0	72·4	53·9	18·5	66·4	54·9	11·5	60·6
November	71·3	41·7	29·6	71·2	42·9	28·3	57·5	71·6	47·1	20·5	66·1	54·3	11·8	60·2
December	72·8	38·0	34·8	72·0	39·1	32·9	55·6	70·9	46·8	24·1	65·2	53·7	11·5	59·4
Mean ...	77·0	51·7	25·6	76·4	49·0	27·4	62·7	76·6	53·3	22·2	73·5	55·5	18·6	64·4

No. 16.—*Expenditure on Public Works in the Nílagiri District during the* 17 *Years from* 1860-61 *to* 1876-77, *a rupee being taken at two shillings.*

Years.	New Works.						Repairs.					
	Military.	Civil Buildings.	Communications.	Miscellaneous Public Improvements.	Establishment.	Total.	Military.	Civil Buildings.	Communications.	Miscellaneous Public Improvements.	Total.	Grand Total.
	£	£	£	£	£	£	£	£	£	£	£	£
1860-61	11,701	...	1,000	...	773	13,474	734	144	1,265	...	2,143	15,617
1861-62	1,691	...	335	...	367	2,393	2,302	385	1,000	...	3,687	6,080
1862-63	1,868	2,662	...	...	355	4,885	244	120	1,556	...	1,920	6,804
1863-64	1,362	5,776	855	109	1,998	10,100	789	226	2,455	...	3,470	13,570
1864-65	9,249	1,051	4,378	...	3,281	17,959	697	266	1,384	75	2,422	20,381
1865-66	9,793	4,506	3,793	434	5,026	23,552	888	114	2,475	28	3,505	27,057
1866-67	16,770	4,315	9,991	92	5,713	36,881	96	123	1,279	26	1,524	38,405
1867-68	13,884	6,552	10,213	50	6,827	37,526	598	333	3,738	40	4,709	42,235
1868-69	70,733	11,707	39,913	1,456	6,081	129,890	710	329	4,091	46	5,176	135,066
1869-70	16,723	1,093	7,703	990	5,758	32,267	700	257	3,163	40	4,160	36,426
1870-71	2,319	133	1,482	764	2,559	7,257	699	295	3,228	25	4,247	11,504
1871-72	3,026	1,174	1,358	1,086	2,708	9,352	893	374	3,791	95	5,153	14,505
1872-73	2,553	1,399	1,596	985	2,636	9,169	763	517	3,724	25	5,029	14,198
1873-74	1,551	553	6,553	741	2,655	12,053	780	305	4,046	41	5,172	17,225
1874-75	605	592	6,750	121	2,515	10,583	976	315	4,135	125	5,551	16,133
1875-76	8,008	3,000	2,601	60	2,618	16,287	683	138	4,179	...	5,000	21,287
1876-77	9,027	10,982	2,646	102	2,585	25,342	711	365	3,945	...	5,021	30,362
Total ...	180,863	55,495	101,167	6,990	54,455	398,970	13,263	4,606	49,454	566	67,889	466,859

No. 16-*A.—Detailed particulars of the*

Description of Barrack or Work.	Single or Double Storied.	Accommodation provided in each Building.			Space per Soldier unit exclusive of Verandahs.	
		No. of Men.	No. of Rooms.	Size of Rooms in Feet.	Cubic Space, Cubic Feet.	Square Space, Square Feet.
		In each block.			In each Block.	
No. 1 Barrack Block with detached Wash-houses and Latrines.	Double.	140 Privates and 8 Non-Commissioned Officers.	4	129 × 21	For Privates.	
„ 2 do. do. do. ...	„		4	354 × 12	1,530	77½
„ 3 do. do. do. ...	„		8	24 × 9½	For Non-Commissioned Officers.	
„ 4* do. do. do. ...	„		2	21 × 8		
„ 5 do. do. do. ...	„		4	21 × 12	4,503	228
			4	12 × 9½		
			4	9½ × 7		
		In each Block of Quarters.				
No. 1 Married Quarters with detached Wash-houses and Latrines.	„	Families 30.	2	286 × 10	For each Family.	
„ 2 do. do. do. ...	„		2	286 × 8	5,376	384
„ 3 do. do. do. ...	„		30	16 × 14		
„ 4 do. do. do. ...	„		30	16 × 10		
Staff Block	„	10 Sergeants ...	2	315 × 12	Married Non-Commissioned Officers.	
		Commandants.	4	54 × 21	16,677	981
		Rooms, Sergts.	4	54 × 12		
		Mess and ...	7	28 × 21		
		ReadingRooms.	7	28 × 12		
		Qr.-mr.'sStores.	6	21 × 18		
		Guard-Rooms	4	21 × 11		
		with Cells ...	6	17½ × 12		
		Offices and ...	4	12 × 12		
		Workshops...	5	12 × 5		
		Entrance covered way.	1	66 × 16		
Hospital with detached Wash-houses and Latrines, Dresser's Quarters, &c., in 3 blocks.	Single		2	220 × 12	2,050	102
		Four Wards for Soldiers.	2	80 × 21		
			2	65 × 21		
			1	160 × 10		
			1	142 × 10		
		Hospital Sergeant's Quarters.	1	21 × 16		
			1	21 × 10		
			1	28 × 10		
		Surgery and Medl. Stores.	3	21 × 14		
			1	45 × 10		
		Special Ward...	1	21 × 10		
		Women'sWard.	2	26 × 21		
			1	56 × 10		
School and Library Block with detached Cook-houses, &c.	Double.	School Room ...	1	77 × 33	For Librarian and Schoolmaster.	
		Library ...	1	32 × 46	11,700	780
		Class Rooms ...	2	32 × 20	For Schoolmistress.	
		Three sets of Quarters for Librarian, Schoolmaster, and Schoolmistress.	3	20 × 16	16,380	780
			3	20 × 10		
			3	16 × 10		
			3	10 × 10		
		Verandahs ...	2	198 × 10		
Racquet and Ball Court and Skittle Alley.	Single.	...	...	...	...	...
Canteen, Coffee Room and Ration Shed ...	Double.	...	...	...	...	...
Plunge-bath and Armourer's Forge ...	Single.	...	...	...	...	...
Cricket Shed, Powder Magazine and Privies for Native Camp Followers.	„	..	...	...	...	...
Commissariat Godowns and Staff Sergeants' Quarters.	„	...	...	...	...	...
Slaughter-houses	„	...	...	...	...	..
Burial-ground	...	...	...	...	...	...
Drainage of Barrack and Hospital Squares.	...	...	...	..	...	...
Water-service both potable and ablutionary, including Reservoirs, Channels, and Pipes.	...	...	...	...	..	...
Roads of approach and Cantonment Roads.	..	...	...	...	...	...
Excavating for site of Barracks ...	...	...	...	...	...	...
Total ...						

* Single story first roofed in and burnt down.

Wellington Barracks in the Nílagiri District.

Cost of each Main Building.	Cost of Auxiliary and Subsidiary Buildings.	Cost of Accommodation of each Married Soldier.		Cost of Accommodation of each single Soldier.		Total Accommodation and Cost.		
		Barrack alone.	Barrack with Auxiliary and Subsidiary Buildings and Works.	Barrack alone.	Barrack with Auxiliary and Subsidiary Buildings and Works.	Sergeants.	Privates.	Pounds.
£	£	£	£	£	£			
13,196	...	...	...	89	147	...	...	...
17,590	...	...	...	119	177	...	...	...
13,292	...	...	...	90 (Average £108.)	148 (Average £166.)	...	...	...
20,503	...	...	...	138	196	...	...	...
15,203	...	...	...	103	161	...	...	...
9,128	...	304	362	...	...	...	...	...
9,128	...	304	362	...	...	...	...	...
9,128	...	304	362	...	...	...	...	...
9,128	...	304	362	...	...	...	...	...
...	12,927	...	...	...	...	...	...	...
...	10,529	...	...	...	...	54	820	166,739
...	5,825	...	...	...	...	...	...	...
...	1,966	...	...	...	...	...	...	..
...	3,299	...	...	...	...	...	...	...
...	1,000	...	...	...	...	...	...	...
...	435	...	...	...	...	...	...	...
...	2,626	...	...	...	...	...	...	...
...	1,535	...	...	...	...	...	...	...
...	246	...	...	...	...	...	...	...
...	2,337	...	...	...	...	...	...	...
...	4,538	...	...	...	...	...	...	...
...	1,650	...	...	...	...	...	...	...
...	1,530	...	...	...	...	...	...	...
116,296	50,443	...	...	...	...	...	...	...

Upper story added and block completed in 1876.

No. 16-B.—Detailed particulars of the Ootacamand

Description of Building.	Single or Double Storied.	Accommodation provided in each Building.		Space per Boy, Girl, or other unit, exclusive of Passages.		Cost of the Main Building.
		Number of Boys, Girls, and other occupants.	Number of Rooms.	Cubic Space in Feet.	Square Space in Feet.	
Boys' School.						
Dormitories for boys ...	Double ...	Dormitories for 400 boys, about 30 boys in each Dormitory.	14	735	25	...
Store Rooms, Dining Hall and School Rooms, &c.	„ ...	400 boys ...	11	298 321	40 12	... ...
Principal's Quarters ...	Treble ...	One Principal and Secretary.	14	34,729	2,762	...
Sergeants' Quarters ...	Double ...	Quarters for 3 Sergeants.	21	11,428	776	...
Covered Play-ground, Staircases, Towers and Porch.	„ ...	400 boys, 1 Principal, and 3 Sergeants.	22	173	17	From I to VI £49,256.
Corridors and covered passage to Lavatories and Latrines.	Double and Single.	400 boys ...	11 1	... ...	... ...	... ...
Kitchens for boys, Principal, and Sergeants.	Single ...	400 boys, 1 Principal, and 3 Sergeants.	8	...	...	...
Lavatories and Latrines...	„ ...	400 boys ...	16	44 74	5 7	...
Play-sheds and Workshops for the boys.	...	...	...	...	...	...
		Total Number of Rooms in Boys' School.	118	...	...	...
Girls' School.						
Dormitories	Single ...	144 girls ...	12	785	38	...
Matrons and Mistresses' Quarters.	„	1 Matron or Lady Superintendent.	5	16,272	900	From X to XI £5,773.
		2 Mistresses ...	8	16,840	927	...
Kitchen	„ ...	For 1 Matron, 2 Mistresses, and 144 girls.	2	48	5	...
Lavatories and Latrines...	„ ...	For 1 Matron, 2 Mistresses, and 144 girls, or 147 units in all.	13	98	9	...
		Total Number of Rooms in Girls' School.	40	...	...	...

Lawrence Asylums, Nílagiri District.

Cost of Auxiliary and Subsidiary Buildings.	Cost of Accommodation of each Boy.		Cost of Accommodation of each Girl.		Total Accommodation and Cost of Boys and Girls, &c.	Remarks.
	Building alone.	Main Building with Auxiliary & Subsidiary Buildings.	Building alone.	Main Building with Auxiliary & Subsidiary Buildings.		
...	...	...	...	...		Out of these 14 Dormitories one is now used as a Tailors' Shop, and two as a Hospital.
...	...	...	...	...		
...	...	...	...	...		
...	...	...	...	...		
...	...	...	...	...		Of these 3 quarters one is now occupied by a Matron, one by the Sergeant-Major, and the third by the Head Master.
...	£123	£144	...	...		
...	...	...	...	...		
...	...	...	...	...		
...	...	...	...	...		
From VII to IX £8,298.	...	...	...	...	1 Principal, 3 Sergeants, 400 boys, 1 Matron, and 144 girls, £80,283.	
...	...	...	...	...		
...	...	...	...	...		
...	...	...	...	...		Of these 6 Dormitories one is now used as a Hospital, one as a Dining Hall, and one as a School Room.
...	...	...	£40	£56		
...	...	...	...	...		
...	...	...	...	...		
From XIII to XIV £2,313.	...	...	...	...		
...	...	...	...	...		

No. 16-*B.—Detailed particulars of the Ootacamand*

Description of Building.	Single or Double Storied.	Accommodation provided in each Building.		Space per Boy, Girl, or other unit, exclusive of Passages.		Cost of the Main Building.
		Number of Boys, Girls, and other occupants.	Number of Rooms.	Cubic Space in Feet.	Square Space in Feet.	
Buildings, &c., common to both Asylums.						
Servants' houses ...	...	...	...	...	...	...
Water-service to both Asylums.	...	...	...	...	...	...
Excavating Sites ...	...	...	...	...	...	...
Roads and approaches ...	...	...	...	...	...	...
Drainage of Plateaus of both Asylums.	...	...	...	...	...	...
Compensation for land and other sundries.	...	...	...	...	...	...
Latrines, Wash-houses, and Cook-rooms of proposed new Female Asylum.	...	...	...	...	...	...

Lawrence Asylums, Nílagiri District—(Continued).

Cost of Auxiliary and Subsidiary Buildings.	Cost of Accommodation of each Boy.		Cost of Accommodation of each Girl.		Total Accommodation and Cost of Boys and Girls, &c.	Remarks.
	Building alone.	Main Building with Auxiliary & Subsidiary Buildings.	Building alone.	Main Building with Auxiliary & Subsidiary Buildings.		
£						
4,054	...	...	...	...	...	
1,639	...	Inclusive of everything £164.	...	Inclusive of everything £75.	...	
2,126	...	...	...	...	...	
1,285	...	...	...	...	...	
511	...	...	...	...	...	
1,088	...	...	...	...	...	
3,940	...	...	...	...	...	

No. 16-C.—*Rates of Wages and Cost of Materials in the Nilagiri District during the past Quarter of a Century arranged in Triads, a Rupee being taken at two Shillings.*

Wages.		Rates per Diem. 1852.	1855.	1858.	1861.	1864.	1867.	1870.	1873.	1876.
Skilled Labor.		s. d.	s. d.	s. d.	s. d.	s. d.	s. d.	s. d.	s. d.	s. d.
Maistry ...	*Per diem.*	1 ¼	1 ¼	1 6	2 0	2 4⅓	2 4⅓	2 4½	2 8¼	2 10
Stone-cutter.	„	...	1 0	1 1⅓	1 4⅓	1 6	1 7⅓	2 0	2 6	2 6
Bricklayer ...	„	0 9¼	1 ⅛	1 1½	1 3⅓	1 5	1 5	1 5⅓	1 6	1 6
Blacksmith ...	„	0 10⅓	1 ¾	1 2½	1 4½	1 7½	1 9	1 9	1 10½	2 0
Carpenter ...	„	0 10⅓	1 ¾	1 1½	1 4	1 7½	1 9	1 9	1 10⅓	1 10½
Painter ...	„	...	...	1 0	1 3	1 7½	2 0	1 6	1 6	1 6
Common Coolies.										
Gangman ...	*Per diem.*	0 4¾	0 5	0 6	0 6¾	0 9	0 9	0 10½	1 3	1 3
Cooly man ...	„	0 3¾	0 3¾	0 4½	0 5⅓	0 6	0 9	0 7¼	0 7½	0 7½
Do. woman	„	0 3	0 3	0 3	0 3¾	0 4	0 4¼	0 4½	0 4½	0 4½
Do. boy ...	„	0 2	0 2	0 2	0 2½	0 2¾	0 3	0 3	0 3	0 3

Materials.	Rate per	1852.	1855.	1858.	1861.	1864.	1867.	1870.	1873.	1876.
		s.	s.	s.	s.	s.	s.	s.	s.	s.
Wall bricks ...	1,000	8	8	14	17	24	24	24	24	24
Paving do. ...	1,000	16	16	24	36	50	50	50	50	50
Pillar do. ...	1,000	17	17	30	40	48	48	50	50	50
Flat tiles ...	1,000	4	4	8	8	12	12	12	12	12
Pan do. ...	1,000	5	9	12	12	16	16	16	16	16
Rough rubble stones.	C. yard.	...	4½	4⅓	6	3	3	3	3	3
Flooring stones dressed.	100 sq. ft.	...	...	110	120	130	130	130	130	130
Limestone (unburnt).	C. yard.	29	29	29	54	50	48	48	48	48
Lime burnt and slaked.	„	12	18	24	24	36	36	29	26	24
Firewood ...	1,000 lb.	...	1¼	...	...	...	...	...	...	7¼
Sand for mortar.	C. yard.	1¼	1½	3	4⅓	6	6	6	6	6
Teakwood in the log.	C. foot.	2	2¼	2⅔	3	4	4	4	4	4
Europe bar iron.	Ton.	...	...	560	560	560	560	560	560	560

No. 16-*D.*—*Comparative Statement of the Rates for Labor, Carriage, and Work in Coimbatore and the Nílagiri Hills in the Year* 1877.

Details.	Per	Amount Coimbatore District. RS. A. P.	Amount Nílagiri Hills. RS. A. P.	Difference per cent.	Remarks.
RATES FOR LABOR.					
Skilled Workmen.					
Maistry	Month ...	15 0 0	45 0 0 and 35 0 0	200	Much private work being done on the hills by owners of houses and of estates, maistries of all kinds are very difficult to be obtained.
Stone-cutters, 1st class	Day	0 12 0	1 4 0	66·6	The stone on the Nílagiris is much harder than that in Coimbatore.
Do. 2nd "	"	0 10 0	1 0 0	60	
Bricklayers, 1st "	"	0 9 0	0 12 0	33·3	
Do. 2nd "	"	0 8 0	0 10 6	31·25	
Carpenters, 1st "	"	0 12 0	1 0 0	33·4	
Do. 2nd "	"	0 10 0	0 12 0	20	
Smiths, 1st "	"	0 10 0	1 0 0	60	It is at all times very difficult to obtain black-smiths and painters; very few of either class are ever needed.
Do. 2nd "	"	0 8 0	0 14 0	75	
Painters, 1st "	"	0 8 0	0 12 0	50	
Do. 2nd "	"	0 6 0	0 10 0	66·4	
Laborers.					
Head cooly or gangman	Day	0 4 6	0 10 0	122·2	Unless these head coolies or gangmen are paid highly, they refuse to procure coolies. Coolies are also always very difficult to be got, there being such a large demand for them by private parties and on estates. I and all the other officials on the Nílagiris find it very difficult to procure sufficient labor; and planters and others employ less labor than they otherwise would if it was more plentiful.
Cooly man	"	0 4 0	0 5 0	25	
Do. do.	"	0 2 0	0 4 0	100	
Do. woman	"	...	0 3 0	...	
Do. boy	"	0 1 6	0 3 0	100	
Do. do.	"	...	0 2 3	...	

No. 16-*D.—Comparative Statement of the Rates for Labor, Carriage, and Work in Coimbatore and the Nílagiri Hills, &c.*—(Continued).

Details.	Per	Amount Coimbatore District.	Amount Nílagiri Hills.	Difference per cent.	Remarks.
RATES FOR LABOR—(*Continued*).					
Carriage.		RS. A. P.	RS. A. P.		
Bullock cart to carry 1,000 lb.	Day	1 0 0	1 10 8	66·6	Owing to steep grades on roads and to the hilly country, a cart on the Nílagiris carries only about 750 lb. of load. The climate is also against bullocks. Numbers die annually.
WORK.					
Stone.					
Rough-stone quarried and stacked ...	C. yards ...	0 12 0	1 0 0	33·3	
Stone, hammer dressed, roughly squared.	100 C. feet ...	19 8 0	150 0 0	223·07	The stone on these hills is particularly hard, very much harder than that at Mettapollium. I have procured some cut-stone from Mettapollium, and found it cost less delivered here than the dressed stone does on the hills.
Stone, squared and dressed to size ...	" ...	31 0 0	200 0 0	545·16	
Flooring stones 12" × 12"	100 S. feet ...	50 0 0	65 0 0	30	
Stone slabs, rough, split	100 C. feet ...	25 0 0	100 0 0	290	
Line, Sand, &c.					
Limestone, broken	C. yards ...	0 6 0	26 0 0	6833·3	The excess here is due to carriage. There is no limestone of any kind on the hill plateau.
Do. burnt and delivered	" ...	4 5 0	15 0 0	246·3	
Sand, clean, sharp, on river bank ...	" ...	0 11 6	3 0 0	·317·3	
Firewood, cut and stacked	" ...	3 0 0	3 8 0	16·6	

No. 16-*D.*—*Comparative Statement of Rates for Labor, Carriage, and Work in the Coimbatore and the Nílagiri Hills, &c.*—(Continued).

Details.	Per	Amount Coimbatore District. RS. A. P.	Amount Nílagiri Hills. RS. A. P.	Difference per cent.	Remarks.
WORK—(*Continued*).					
Timber.					
Teakwood in log	C. feet ...	1 8 0	2 0 0	33·3	The Múdumalé teak used on these hills is much less sound than the Anémalé teak used at Coimbatore; consequently there is more wastage.
Do. sawn into scantlings	„ ...	2 4 0	3 8 0	55·5	
Do. wrought and fitted	„ ...	2 12 0	5 0 0	82	
Junglewood in the rough	„ ...	0 12 0	1 0 0	33·3	
Bamboo, large	Each	0 2 0	1 0 0	700	There are no bamboos of any size on these hills; all have to be imported from Mettapollium.
Do. 1st class	100	2 0 0	75 0 0	3650	
Do. 2nd „	„	1 8 0	50 0 0	3233	
Bundles of thatch, 5′ girth	Each	0 4 0	0 4 0	...	
Iron.					
Native iron wrought and put up	lb.	0 1 6	0 4 0	166·6	No Native iron is used on these hills; Europe iron of 1st and 2nd class only is used.
Europe iron	„	...	0 5 0	...	
Corrugated iron sheek, 7′ × 2½′	Each	3 12 0	4 0 0	6·6	

No. 16-*E.—Nature and Cost of Construction*

Locality.	Name of Building.	Single or Double Storied.	Description and Height: Foundation. Quality of Work.	Foundation. Depth.	Plinth. Quality of Work.	Plinth. Height
				Feet.		Feet.
Ootacamand.	Lawrence Asylum Male Branch.	Double and Treble with Campanile.	Brick and mortar on broken brick concrete.	6	Brick and mortar pointed with cut stone quoins.	2½
	Lawrence Asylum Girls' School (designed as Hospital).	Single ...	Brick and mortar.	3	Brick and mortar plastered with mortar.	2
	Commissioners' Office.	Do. ...	Do. ...	4	Do. ...	1½
	St. Stephen's Church.	Do. ...	Do. ...	4	Do. ...	2½
	St. Thomas' Church...	Do. ...	Do. ...	3½	Do. ...	2
	Nílagiri Public Library.	Do. ...	Do. ...	2½	Do. ...	2
	Stables and Coach-houses of Norwood Government House.	Do. ...	Broken blue stone in mortar well rammed, and brick in mortar.	1½	Do. ...	½
	Stonehouse, Council Chamber of the Madras Government.	Do. ...	Brick in mortar.	4	Brick in mortar and tuck pointed with mortar.	3½
	Breeks' School extension.	Do. ...	Do. ...	2½	Do. ...	1
	Breeks' Memorial School.	Do. ...	Do. ...	3	Do. ...	1
	St. Bartholomew's Hospital.	Do. ...	Do. ...	3½	Brick in mortar and plastered with mortar.	1½

of various Edifices in the Nílagiri District.

of Walls, &c.							
Walls to top of Wall-plate.		Roof.	Floor.	Cost.	Area.	Rate per Superficial Foot.	Year in which constructed.
Quality of Work.	Height.						
	Feet.			£	Sq. ft.	Shillings.	
Brick and mortar pointed with mortar.	13′ lower story, 11′ upper story.	Pent roof tiled over continuous iron; all timber teakwood.	Planked on dwarf walls with sub-ventilation; upper floors tongued and grooved. Teakwood.	57,500	48,300	24	1868
Brick and clay plastered with mortar.	15	Pent roof tiled over flat tiles; timber teakwood.	Planked on dwarf walls with sub-ventilation.	8,000	13,760	12	1867
Brick and mortar plastered with mortar.	16	Pent roof tiled over continuous iron; timber teak.	Do. ...	5,640	7,326	15½	1865
Do. ...	16	Flat terraced.	Concrete plastered.	5,000	4,900	20½	1830
Do. ...	18½	Corrugated iron over felt and planking steep pent Gothic trusses.	Brick in mortar on edge incomplete.	6,440	4,944	26	1868
Brick and mortar pointed with mortar.	18	Pent tiled over planking.	Planked on dwarf walls with sub-ventilation.	3,800	2,936	26	1867
Brick in clay plastered with mortar.	9½	Pent roof of corrugated iron to coach-houses and tiles to stables; all timber teakwood.	Brick concrete and mortar well rammed.	1,700	5,366	7	1876
Brick in mortar and tuck pointed with mortar.	13½	Pent roof, teak shingles; all timber teakwood, ceiling to roof planked.	Planked on dwarf walls with sub-ventilation.	3,000	3,167	19	1875
Do. ...	13	Pent roof, teak shingles; all timber teakwood.	Do. ...	1,700	2,892	12	1875
Do. ...	11	Pent roof of corrugated iron over felt and planking.	Do. ...	900	1,250	14	1873
Do. ...	14½	Pent roof tiled over continuous iron; all timber teakwood.	Do. ...	2,230	5,768	8	1866

No. 16-*E*.—*Nature and Cost of Construction*

Locality.	Name of Building.	Single or Double Storied.	Description and Height			
			Foundation.		Plinth.	
			Quality of Work.	Depth.	Quality of Work.	Height
				Feet.		Feet.
Ootacamand—(*Continued*).	European Jail ...	Double ...	Brick in mortar.	4	Brick in mortar and plastered with mortar.	2
	Native Jail	Single ...	Do. ...	2½	Do. ...	1¼
	Pair of Seed-houses with railings and gate.	Do. ...	Do. ...	2	Brick in mortar and pointed (tuck) with mortar.	1½
	Pavilion	Do. ...	Do. ...	3½	Brick in mortar and tuck pointed with mortar.	1
Wellington.	Barracks, Batchelors' quarters.	Double ...	Do. ...	5	Brick in mortar and plastered with mortar.	1½
	Barracks, Married quarters.	Do. ...	Do. ...	5	Do. ...	2
	Barracks' Hospital ...	Single ...	Do. ...	3½	Do. ...	1½
Coonoor.	All Saints' Church ...	Do. ...	Do. ...	4½	Do. ...	1
	Market	Do. ...	Do. ...	2	Brick in clay and plastered with mortar.	¾
	Dispensary	Do. ...	Do. ...	2½	Brick in mortar and plastered with mortar.	1

of various Edifices in the Nílagiri District—(Continued).

of Walls, &c.							
Walls to top of Wall-plate.		Roof.	Floor.	Cost.	Area.	Rate per Superficial Foot.	Year in which constructed.
Quality of Work.	Height.						
	Feet.			£	Sq. ft.	Shillings.	
Brick in mortar and plastered with mortar.	22	Flat terraced with brick on edge, brick jelly, three courses flat tiles, and two coats of plaster.	Planked on dwarf walls with sub-ventilation; upper floors tongued and grooved; teak-wood.	4,400	10,900	8	1863
Do ...	14	Pent roof tiled over teakwood scantlings.	Planked on dwarf walls with sub-ventilation.	5,060	15,318	6½	1851 and 1867
Brick in mortar and tuck pointed with mortar.	9	Pent roof, corrugated iron on rafters with louvred ventilators.	Do. ...	500	823	12	1874
Do. ...	15	Pent roof, teak shingles; all timber teakwood with glass sky-light turret.	Do. ...	600	1,964	6	1875
Do. ...	35	Pent roof tiled over flat tiles; all timber teakwood.	Planked on dwarf walls with sub-ventilation; upper floors tongued and grooved; teakwood.	280,000	41,148	14	1853 to 1860
Do. ...	31	Do. ...	Do. ...	19,000	27,382	13½	1856 to 1862
Brick in mortar and plastered with mortar.	16	Do. ...	Planked on dwarf walls with sub-ventilation.	11,000	24,224	10	1853
Do. ...	19	Pent roof corrugated iron over felt and planking.	Brick concrete in mortar and plastered with mortar.	3,600	4,293	16½	1850
Brick in clay and plastered with mortar.	9½	Pent roof tiled over teakwood scantlings.	Brick concrete and gravel well rammed.	500	2,940	3½	1865
Do. ...	13	Do. ...	Planked on dwarf walls with sub-ventilation.	760	2,618	5½	1850

No. 17.—A Topographical Description of the Neelaghery Mountains.

From a letter by WILLIAM KEYS, *Assistant Revenue Surveyor, to* W. GARROWS, *Collector of Coimbatore,* 1812.

This tract of the country, forming the elevated division of the Danaikencota Taluk, is situated on the extensive range of the Neelaghery or Blue Mountains, which stretches westward, and is separated by an adjoining high and lofty ridge called the Coonda and Neddimullay hills, terminating the eastern limits of the Wynaud country.

Extent and boundary.

1. It extends in length from east to west 30 miles, and in breadth 16½ miles, containing a superficies of 495 square miles, and is bounded on the north by the lands of Davaroypatnum and the Mysore Province; west by the Wynaud country in Malabar; and south and east by the lowlands of Sattimungalum and Danaikencota.

Divisions and Sub-divisions.

2. Porunganaud, Maicanaud (Mékanád), and Kothanaud are three divisions or mootahs on the hills, containing in the whole 41 principal and 119 subordinate villages. These villages are chiefly small, consisting of hardly more than five to ten houses, built quite low and confined, and generally placed in one or two rows, presenting the appearance of a few straggling huts rather than a village.

Climate and population.

3. The climate is extremely cold and unhealthful, from continual covering of mist and clouds. The population, male and female, in the three nauds amounts to 2,516 individuals, of which number 1,647 are Buddagurs, 292 Lingbund or Shevaacharas, 268 Thorayers, 179 Thothavurs, and 130 Cothurs.

The Buddagurs, so called from their having settled on the mountains from the northward,* speak the Cannady language, and are the principal inhabitants as well as cultivators of the land. The Lingbund and Thorayers likewise speak the same language and cultivate the land. The Thothavurs, said to be the first that peopled this mountainous tract, have a distinct dialect, which is unknown even to their neighbour sects. They cultivate no land, but only attend their flocks of buffaloes, with which they live about the most retired parts of the mountains by some spring or stream of water, on a part of the country in the Thothanaud Division, appropriated as pasture-lands, being from its sterile quality unsusceptible of cultivation. This space is distinguished by the appellation of Keelaurum and Mallanaud, signifying a barren mountainous tract, and consists of 70 square miles. Although the Thothavurs cultivate no land, they however have a small interest in the produce, allowed them by the Buddagurs and others, being considered as the aboriginal inhabitants. Their chief subsistence is the milk of their cattle. Lastly the Cothurs, or the lowest class of

* From Woomatoor in the Mysore Province.

inhabitants, who have also a peculiar idiom of their own, but converse mostly in the Cannady language, not only cultivate the land, but serve as artificers in the capacity of the gold, silver, and brass smiths, carpenter, blacksmith, potter and wicker worker, also dresser of hides and skins. Independently of these there are the Irelurs, whose number is not very large and who blend the Malabar with the Cannady language. They inhabit and cultivate the deep valleys on the sides of the mountains (dependant to the low-lands), and, unlike the inhabitants on the height of the hills, are induced to undergo the arduous labor of preparing their fields with a small instrument resembling the hand hoe, on account of the steep and stony nature of the soil, which however is extremely fertile. These are likewise expert in bringing down the large honey-combs or bee-hives that are abundant about the rocks and precipices, as also in felling large trees and conveying the timber down to the plains.

The whole of the inhabitants are very unclean in their persons and dress, as they have no barbers or washers among them, and more so, as they imagine it an abomination to the deity Neelagharry Rungasawmy, presiding over these mountains, either to have their clothes washed, or their faces shaved by a barber, but the latter they effect among themselves; nor do they wear anything for the protection of their feet, probably on the same account. In short they have altogether an uncommonly rude appearance, more especially the Thothavurs, who hold it as a sacred and inviolable custom never to keep their heads covered, whether under the scorching heat of the sun or heavy showers of rain or frost; and custom even forbids them to shave at all, wherefore they suffer the hair of their heads to grow, only cutting it from time to time, so as not to remain too long.

Nature of the surface.

4. The surface of the country is very unequal and wavy, and abounds with springs.

Forts and other buildings.

5. There are only two small forts, one called Oolicul Guggenchoky doorga, upon a high hill on the south, and the other Mullayacota, upon a gentle eminence on the north; they are built in the simple manner that fortifications are generally seen about this country, consisting of a common mud wall faced with rock stones and surrounded by a ditch, and it is evident that they had been constructed in order to check the restless disposition of the neighboring countries in former times. There are no other buildings deserving notice.

Rivers and other water communications.

6. The Bariggy-olay or the Moyar river in the north takes its source from the stupendous heights of the Neddimullay hills, and has several other streams running down into it from the Mullanaud pasture-lands. The Chicka-olay or Mannar river takes its rise from the Mulnaud hills about Cowah and runs down southward, discharging itself into the Bhavany river. Besides these, the mountains give rise to numerous other nullahs, both large and small, but of these may be particularly noticed the great nullah running down on the north of Mullayacota, which below the mountains is called the Sheegoor river, joining the Moyaur on the east of Davaroyputnum,

and another springing from the high ridges between Thothanaud and Porunganaud, discharging itself into the Moyaur river about five miles on the west of Gajelhutty, before which a small canal is branched off it for the irrigation of paddy lands of a small extent about the village Moyaur. The nullah rushing down the hills on the north of Nellithoray (having the appellation of Culaur or rocky river) from Maicanaud is considerable, and waters an extent of three square miles of paddy lands belonging to Nellithoray.

Roads and passes.

7. There are three passes leading up to the mountains from the low-lands. The first is from Danaikencota, which begins to get upon the hills from about two miles on the west of it, and continues its track over a pretty steep eminence till as far as half a mile on this side of Urracadoo, the first village on the mountains, and distant by the route seven miles. It is extremely difficult and impracticable to laden bullocks from the steep ascent and ruggedness of the path. From Urracadoo by Thaynaud and Neduncolum to Poranganaud is sixteen miles, the road not less difficult from the many acclivities and declivities to be passed over.

The second pass leads up from Davaroyputnum, the length of which from the foot to Mullayacota fort is nearly five miles, over a much gentler slope, but it is not in any way less difficult, and there are few parts so dangerous, where the least stumbling or slip of the foot will be attended with the most tragical consequences. It is entirely impracticable to horses and laden bullocks, although it is asserted that in the times of Tippoo Sultan a few horses and one or two pieces of cannon were carried over to the fort. From Mullayacota to Thothanaud is three and a half miles, and from the latter place to Porunganaud, over Cookul, it is eleven miles, the road pretty tolerable.

The third pass leads up from Aulhutty on the south, and it is very steep and rugged till the summit of the hill is gained at Serulcombay, a small village, whence the difficulty of the road becomes moderate to Porunganaud, which from Aulhutty is thirteen miles. From Porunganaud westward to Maicanaud is eighteen miles, and from Maicanaud to Mullayacota in Thothanaud, over the pasture-lands, is ten miles, road tolerable. In short the several roads leading through the mountains may with propriety be all called passes.

Jungle.

8. The sides of the mountains and the several deep valleys opening about them are covered with large trees of the black and teak wood, as well as many other kinds, and which supply a large quantity of timber; there is also a good share of bamboo trees on the sides, which grow up only to the summit of the hills, whence the jungle decreases to a low wood, and in several places only to brushwood. Although the surface of the mountains bear such a paltry covering, there is, however, a striking diversity of landscape from the immense and large shady thickets or clusters of overgrown trees, which lie interspersed generally by some spring of water. The deep valleys on the sides abound with plantain groves, the fruit of which is inferior in quality to that of the low countries and extremely unwhole-

some. There is a growth of rattans and canes on the hills, but not of good kind.

9. There are no manufactures on the hills and much less of trade. Manufactures and trade.

10. The soil of the cultivated lands is very fertile, and may be accounted as being prevalently loam, in some places rather light and inclining to gravel. A few spots of ground contiguous to the villages are manured on account of growing poppy plants and wheat. Soil and produce.

The principal produce of the mountains is opium, poppy seeds, wheat, mustard and garlic, and beside these there are the following articles of produce, viz., ventheum (seeds used for culinary purposes), black peas (a kind of pulse called Mysore dhall), gaunji (a grain resembling wheat), vussomboo or country gentian, ghee, honey, and bees' wax. The only kinds of dry grain that they grow on the mountains are two sorts of shaume, which article is used as the food of all classes of the inhabitants. With respect to cattle there are immense flocks of buffaloes, very large, and bordering much upon the wild kind; these are chiefly kept by the Thothavurs as observed above, but the Buddagurs and others also have a few of their own about the villages. It is the milk of these animals that they get in abundance, there being but very few cows (in comparison to the above), which are kept by the most opulent, and although they are the breed of the highlands, yet they suffer severely from the cold, frost, and dews, if kept in the nights exposed as the buffaloes. The bullocks are used in ploughing the fields, much after the manner in the low countries. There are no sheep or goats bred on the hills, and very little of poultry.

GANAPATHI AGRAHARA, WILLIAM KEYS,
24*th June* 1812. *Assistant Revenue Surveyor.*

N.B.—The highland tract of country about Davaroyaputnum on the north and below the mountains, containing a superficial extent of 140 square miles, has an unequal wavy aspect, is covered with thick wood, and contains not more than eight villages, all which are small, and have each about it a little space of ground cultivated. The road leading to the Wynaud country runs through this part. It is plain that it had been more largely cultivated some years back, and had likewise some paddy lands; but the depredations of wild elephants of late and the diminution of hands have almost laid it desolate. There is a thick forest of teakwood trees on the west of Davaroyaputnum, which extends to a considerable distance even in the Wynaud country; and on the east of Davaroyaputnum the jungle is interspersed with sandalwood trees. The soil here is fruitful, and the climate is mostly dry and distinguished for unhealthiness.

The country on the south of the mountains is diversified with hills, mostly high and disposed in ridges, and has likewise a wild aspect. The air about the plain country is warm and healthy than otherwise, but about the hilly parts of Gopenaury and Annacutty is observed to be inhospitable.

(Signed) WILLIAM KEYS.

No. 18.—Copy of a letter dated 30th January 1819, to the Editor of the Government Gazette, published in the "Madras Courier" of the 23rd February 1819.

TO THE EDITOR OF THE GOVERNMENT GAZETTE.

SIR,—You sometimes give your readers notices of the thermometer as it stands at Madras. They may perhaps be amused by a few observations of the same kind from a part of the country not more than 350 miles distant from the Presidency.

The low country of Coimbatore is separated from Malabar and Wynaad by a mountainous region 30 miles in length and 16 in breadth, and which contains about 500 square miles. It is divided into three naads or countries, the Paungnaad, the Todiernaad, and the Maiknaad. The name given to the whole by the lowlanders is "Nilgerries" or the blue mountains; this name, however, properly belongs but to one part of the range, and is by the highlanders, peculiarly applied to a high peak, the "Rungasawmy Coil" or Nilgerry. Two gentlemen having visited this region early in last year, and having surprised their friends by the accounts they gave of it, particularly of the extreme coldness of the climate, a party was formed, who set out to repeat the tour on the 2nd of January.

They left Denaigencottah (which is about ten miles from the foot of the Guzzlehutty Pass, and two miles from the bottom of the Nilgerry Mountains) at 6 A.M. on the morning of the 2nd, and after two days' painful march, reached Dernaad, the first village in the Paungnaad, on the evening of the 3rd—distance about 16 miles.

Thermometer on the 2nd at 6 A.M., 57; at 8, 71; at 11, 62; at 2 P.M. 68. On the 3rd, thermometer at 6 A.M., 52; at 8, 62; at 5 P.M., 50. 4th halted at Dernaad. Thermometer at 6 A.M., 44; at 8, 60; at 3 P.M., 64; at 6, 54; at 8, 48. 5th.—Marched from Dernaad to Tondernaad, principal village of Paungnaad, 9 miles. Thermometer at 6 A.M., 40; at 7, 50; at 11, 60; at 2 P.M., 62; at 6, 50; at 7, 48. 6th.—Halted at Toddiernaad. Thermometer at 5 A.M. near the tent 40; hoar frost in the valley below; the thermometer, when placed on the ground, sunk to 31; at 8 A.M. it was 48 outside the tent; at 9, 55 inside and 64 in the sun; at 2 P.M., 70 in the sun, 58 in the shade. 7th.—Marched to Kodaramoody, a village in the Toddiernaad, distance 8 miles. Thermometer at 6 A.M., 36. Hard frost this morning; the water in the chatties completely frozen three-fourths of an inch round the vessels, and the thickness of a dollar in the centre; at 9 A.M. thermometer 51 in the shade, and 60 in the sun; at 11 in the shade 58; at 12, 70 in the sun; at 2 P.M., 72 in the sun; at 7, 39; at 8, 38; at 9, 34. 8th.—Thermometer at 6 A.M. near the tent 34. A very hard frost this morning; the water in the chatties frozen, and the ice kept sufficiently well to enable us to make our wine (already cool enough) colder at dinner. Thermometer at 7 A.M., 36 in the shade, 46 in the sun; at 8, 50 in the sun; at 11, 72 in the sun; at 2 P.M., 34 in the sun; at 6 P.M., 48; at 8, 34. 9th.—Marched to

Mailkottay, another village in the Toddiernaad, distance 7 miles. Thermometer at 6 A.M., 33. A frost again, and the water also frozen; the ice not so thick as on the preceding morning, although the glass stood near the tent 3 degrees lower. 10th and 11th mornings mild and cloudy; the thermometer was not seen to sink below 44. 12th. —To Nella Courli, a village in the Maiknaad, distance 3 miles. Thermometer at 6 A.M., 40; at 8 P.M., 30. 13th.—No account of the thermometer taken, but the water in the chatties frozen during the night.

On coming to the low country on the 16th, the thermometer for the greater part of the day stood at from 80 to 84.

The thermometer from which the above register was taken hung upon the tent ropes, close to which large fires were burning all the night. It did not give, therefore, the real temperature of the air, for when the mercury was above the freezing point, we had hard frost and ice a hundred yards from the tent. In Hindostan, when the thermometer sinks to the freezing point, the extremes of heat and cold are often felt in the same day; but we have no example, I believe, in this part of the globe, of a temperature so cool and so even for a continuance as that which is shown from the register of the thermometer given in the preceding part of this paper.

We could not ascertain the exact height of our situation in this mountainous region, but we considered ourselves to be at least three times as high as the highest part of Mysore; and if this calculation is correct, the elevation would be from 9 to 10,000 feet above the level of the sea. In looking over Mysore on one side and the low country of Coimbatore on the other, it was hard to distinguish the country above from the country below the ghauts; we were so much higher than both. The party were on their legs most part of the day, and generally walked ten or twelve miles up and down steep hills from 10 o'clock in the morning until sunset, without experiencing the least inconvenience from heat, often indeed seeking the sunshine as a relief from cold. With the exception of two slight ague fits there was no sickness amongst our followers, notwithstanding the intense cold of the nights and mornings, and the little protection they had against it.

In every part of the high country we found raspberries, both red and white, and strawberries growing in the greatest luxuriance; we found also a fruit in shape resembling a medlar, but of much smaller size, and in taste not to be distinguished from the gooseberry: its interior arrangement is also the same. White roses, marrigolds, balsams were seen in abundance and in full flower; we found specimens also of cinnamon and black pepper, and a tree yielding a beautiful yellow dye. If the color should stand, as it promises to do, the discovery of this tree would be an important one. The country is inhabited by three classes of people, whose language, manners, and customs are entirely distinct, viz., Todevies, Koties and Bergies. The two first are considered the aborigines of the hills, and the Todevies to be a superior caste to the Koties. The Todevies are exclusively herdsmen; they have no fixed habitation, but wander with their herds of buffaloes from pasture to pasture. Their huts are of a semi-circular form, strongly built with bamboos and mud, having a hole near the ground sufficiently large for their own ingress and for the egress of the smoke from their fires. Only one marriage is permitted amongst the males of a family, and if it should consist of ten or more persons, they have a wife in common. The lady is exempt from household cares and duties, she is served by the men, whose duty it is to prepare and cook the victuals, and it is her privilege also to be carried on the shoulders of her husbands when she makes visits or journeys. She selects whom she pleases of the family as her companion at bed and board, and this freedom of choice produces no interruption of domestic harmony. It is necessary that all the men of a family should agree in the choice of a wife, and if there should be a dissentient voice amongst brethren when a lady is submitted for their approbation, she is forthwith sent back to her relations.

Many of the men whom we saw measured above six feet; they are robust and athletic, with a marked expression of countenance, Roman noses, and handsome features. The women, though much above the size of their sex below, have anything but a prepossessing appearance: their features are coarse and their mouths unusually wide, but, on the whole, they have much more of the European than the Asiatic cast of countenance. Their dress consists of a single cloth, which completely envelopes their persons, and effectually conceals any grace of figure that they may possess. Both men and women are fair—fairer, perhaps, than the fairest class of Mahomedans. The fairness of their complexions, and their singular expression of countenance, may have given rise to a report which has long been prevalent of the existence of a white race of inhabitants in this region. Men, women, and children go bare headed and bare-footed in all weathers. It is against the custom of their caste to wear either turban or sandal; they permit their hair and beards to grow without restraint. Both sexes, and indeed all the inhabitants of these hills, wear their cloths without washing until they drop into pieces from filth and rags.

The Koties in appearance have no resemblance whatever to the Todevies, and except that both classes go without covering head or foot, their manners and customs are as dissimilar. Their persons are more diminutive, their complexions darker, and their features much less expressive. They are cultivators and artizans as well as musicians and dancers. The discord or harmony of their pipe has a strong resemblance to the sounds produced from the Scotch bag-pipe, and the dance appeared to an amateur of the party to be either the original or a copy of the famed "quadrille."

The Bergies are the principal cultivators and landholders. They emigrated from the neighborhood of Mysore about 300 years ago, and obtained possession of their lands from the Todevies, to whom they continue to pay a few handfuls of grain from each field as an acknowledgment of the grant. The language of the Bergies is a dialect of the Canarese; that of the Todevies and Koties is supposed to be a dialect of the Tamil : but it is a singular fact that the Todevies cannot speak the language of the Koties, or the Koties that of the Todevies, and that the language of both these classes is equally unintelligible to the Bergies.

The soil of this region is remarkably fertile and yields two crops in the year, of wheat, barley, peas, opium, garlic, mustard, and various species of millets. We found the pea and poppies in full blossom notwithstanding the severity of the weather. The frost indeed appears to have no ill effect whatever on the vegetation. The valleys afford inexhaustible supplies of excellent water. It was impossible to move a quarter of a mile in any direction without crossing streams. Some of them are highly impregnated with iron, and one was found of a warmth much above the temperature of the outward air. These streams run throughout the year, and empty themselves into the Bovani river on the one side, and into the Moyar on the other, of the low country. There are no sheep here, though the climate, soil and pasture are admirably adapted for them, and there can be no doubt but that Merino sheep would thrive here as well as in the walks of their native country. Black cattle are numerous, and the breed has more substance and bone than the cattle below. The Todevies possess large herds of buffaloes of immense size, and live principally upon their produce. The domestic fowls are twice as large as those below, and excellent for the table. The sportsmen of the party remarked the game to be as large as game in Europe, particularly the hares, whose color is usually red. Wolves were the only beasts of prey we saw, though the inhabitants spoke confidently of tigers being in the hills.

I have not troubled your readers or yourself with any description of the scenery of this singular and interesting country, although it was impossible to move in any direction without being struck with its extraordinary grandeur and magnificence. Every thing that a combination of mountains, valleys, wood and water can afford is to be seen here. Your readers will perhaps be surprised to learn that frosty regions are to be found at no very great distance from the Presidency, and within 11 degrees of the equator.

I am, Sir,
Your obedient servant,

30th January 1819. A SUBSCRIBER.

No. 19.—*From Lieutenant EVANS MACPHERSON, Superintendent, Neelgherry Road, to JOHN SULLIVAN, Esq., dated Neelgherry,* 12*th June* 1820.

I have the honor to acknowledge the receipt of your letter, of the 1st instant, calling upon me to state my opinion of the climate of this lofty region, its effects upon myself, and the people under my orders, the diseases of the natives, and whether they are more or less liable to fever than the inhabitants of the low district, the capabilities and resources of the country, whether it is adapted for the growth of European productions, and generally to remark on any other topic worthy of being brought to the notice of the public or of Government.

Limited as is the information a person in my humble situation in this country has an opportunity of obtaining on some of those heads I am sensible I can do the subject but little justice, yet as a plain statement of facts may do much good by bringing to the notice of Government and the European community the temperature and salubrity which this extraordinary and interesting country enjoys above every other to which we can have convenient access, I undertake the task with pleasure but with much diffidence.

I. Temperature of the Climate.—With respect to the climate of the Neelgherry in as far as my experience has hitherto extended, I think I may venture to pronounce it one of the pleasantest in the world as it regards temperature. My residence in these mountains has been since the 14th of March (now about three months), and probably the hottest season of the year. A reference to the monthly registers of the thermometer, with which I have furnished you, will prove that this is incomparably the most temperate Asiatic climate with which we are yet acquainted, and far superior to that of the Cape or the Mauritius. Here at no season of the year is it too hot in the shade, and to sleep under a light blanket in the warmest months is always agreeable. To invalids and people suffering from the debility produced by a long residence in a hot climate this, I should think, must prove of the first importance. Neither hot winds nor sultry nights are here known. During the continuance of the milder months (for we have no hot ones) the mornings and evenings are so cool that a visitor from the low lands is very willing to seek the warmth of the sun, and one may almost every day take exercise in the open air suffering no other inconvenience than perhaps being a little sun-burnt. I am informed by gentlemen who have visited the hills in December, January, and February that the thermometer is frequently below the freezing point, and that ice is found on the chatties in the mornings. It is at that season very cold and chilly, and it will be absolutely necessary to furnish with warm clothing such natives as may accompany their masters to the hills, for otherwise they will be liable to attacks of ague and bowel-complaints from the excessive coldness of the night air.

The effects of the climate on myself and on the constitutions of the people under my orders.

2. So long back as 1815 I suffered an attack of the Ganjam epidemic which appears to be an intermittent in its most malignant form, since which period when in feverish situations, or after exposure to inclement weather, I have been subjected to occasional attacks of fever. At Madras, in December last, while residing in a house nearly surrounded by water (in Chintadrepetta), I had two attacks of ague;

in the February following at Coimbatore I was nearly brought to the brink of the grave by the same disorder. In March I ascended the Neelgherry, weak and debilitated; in a few days my appetite was restored, and I soon recovered health and strength, since which period I have not had a single day's sickness.

My followers and servants, without exception, had all the fever of the low country, and some of them ascended the hill suffering under its effects; in a few days they also completely recovered (bark was administered to them), and except in two instances there have been no relapses. The coolies employed under my orders joined me on the 22nd April, the very day, it will be seen by the register of the thermometer, on which the rains commence that usually fall here about that season, and though they were exposed to severe winds and rain for several nights without cover there were but seven or eight of them complaining of bowel-complaint or slight agues, and as the weather cleared up all of them recovered, and on this day amongst my followers of all descriptions but three are taking medicine.

Of the diseases of the natives, and whether they or the inhabitants below are most subject to fever.

I have been particular in my inquiries relative to the diseases of the natives, and whether or not epidemics or infectious maladies are ever prevalent amongst them; the result has been most satisfactory; their appearance indeed bespeaks them not a sickly race; no epidemic was ever known amongst them but the small-pox, of which they stand in much fear, and which occasionally makes dreadful ravages amongst them and causes a great waste of population. The scourge of the low lands, the cholera morbus, has never extended to these hills. More instances of fever have occurred in the hills within the last two years than was ever known before, but I believe for one case of fever here more than thirty occur below.

The resources of the country.

The hills produce a variety of grains. Pulses and other articles which are subjects of exportation, such as wheat, barley, peas, natchey, and a variety of small grains, onions, garlic, ghee, honey, bees'-wax, dammer, sandal-wood, hides, and rattans, some pepper and excellent opium are amongst their productions; the inhabitants reserve grains, &c., just enough for seed and for their own subsistence, so that nothing can be obtained here for money excepting milk and ghee.

Nature of the soil and whether adapted for the growth of European productions.

The soil is uncommonly good—generally a fine, rich dark vegetable mould mixed with red earth. It is perhaps not too bold an assertion to say that almost all European productions would grow here when we consider its advantages of climate, soil, and the great facility of obtaining water for the purposes of irrigation from innumerable and inexhaustible springs and rivulets gushing on all sides from the hills.

The face of the country, as far as I have seen, is uneven hills and bottoms, for they are too confined to be called valleys, but the hills to their very summits are generally covered with a fine soil, and their ascent is not so abrupt or steep, but they might easily be subjected to the labors of the plough. Unlike the other hilly regions of India, there is very little jungle (and to this and to its elevation must be attributed I think its temperature of climate and salubrity of air), and all that is required to bring the country under a more complete system of cultivation is the protection of the ryot against the tyranny and oppression of the heads of villages, more extended population, and a free market.

Division of the country into Nauds or Districts.

The region denominated the Neelgherry is divided into three nauds or districts, the Todur Naud, Mekenaud, and Purganaud. These are inhabited by a race of people differing in language, appearance, and doubtless in origin, and divided into twelve castes, the principal and most marked being the Todewars, Kothewars, and Burghers.

Todewars.

These appear to be the aborigines of the hills; they are acknowledged lords of the soil by the other castes by the universal practice prevailing amongst them of presenting to the Todewars a certain portion of each crop yearly. The Todewars themselves never engage in the labors of agriculture; they have large herds of buffaloes with which they range from pasture to pasture, and subsist entirely on their produce and on the tribute of grain presented to them by their vassals.

Their appearance.

The Todewar is fair and handsome, with a fine expressive countenance, an intelligent eye, and an aquiline nose; his appearance is manly, being tall, strong-built, and well set up; his limbs muscular and finely proportioned. It is not uncommon in a circle of twenty Todewars to find perhaps two or three above six feet high. Their hair generally curls, and some of the women have natural ringlets which many a fine lady might envy; but this is their only charm, possessing no other grace nor beauty. Men and women go bareheaded and barefooted. A single cloth which envelops their persons is the dress common to both sexes.

Singular customs amongst the Todewars.

A singular custom prevails amongst this caste, the brothers of a family having but one wife in common. They serve her on all occasions, and carry her on their shoulders when she journeys or chooses to visit. She selects whom she pleases as her companion at bed and board; in short her sway is universal in the family, and her orders not to be disputed. Neither the men nor women ever wash their clothes which they wear until it drops off from age and filth.

Female infanticide.

Amongst this people it is to be feared the practice of female infanticide prevails. I have had information on this head which leaves me little room to doubt the fact; they themselves disavow it if questioned, and account for the comparative paucity of the female sex by declaring that amongst them more men than women are born; it is my intention, at a future period, to prosecute further inquiry into this subject with a view of submitting some plan if possible for its prevention.

Kothewars.

This is esteemed a low caste—the paria of the hills, and none of the other castes will eat with them or even enter their houses. They are the artizans, being carpenters, braziers, silver and iron smiths, chucklers, and chatty-makers; they are also the musicians and dancers, in which amusement the women never engage; their dress is the same as the Todewars—a coarse loose cloth which they also never purify by washing; they go bareheaded and barefooted in all weathers; they speak a language different from, and not understood by, the Todewars; they are small men, but stout and muscular; the hair of very many of them is bushy and usually tied behind in a knot.

Burghers.

This caste are the cultivators of the soil; they have a tradition amongst them that they emigrated from Mysore many years ago; they wear a turband and shave the beard; sandals are not in use in the hills; like the former caste they do not employ a washerman on any occasion.

Their marriage ceremony.

The marriages of this caste remind one of what is called bundling in Wales. The bride and bridegroom being together for the night, in the morning the bride is questioned by her relatives whether she is pleased with her husband elect; if she answers in the affirmative it is a marriage; if not the bridegroom is immediately discharged, and the lady does not suffer in reputation if she thus discards half a dozen suitors.

Intoxicating liquors or drugs.

Liquors of an intoxicating quality are never distilled on the hills nor drunk by any of the castes; opium is chewed, but I believe seldom or never to excess.

Crimes.

As drunkenness is unknown here, so likewise is its usual attendant crime, robbery or murder being unheard of, and I believe petty pilfering even seldom if at all practised.

Their worship.

All the castes worship one God—the creator of heaven and earth; they sometimes make images, but they say these are not gods, but serve to remind one of him. Idols are not common, and I have never seen one. They pay a yearly visit to Rungasamy coil, which is, I believe, the only pagoda in the country. They make offerings of the fruits of the soil, but do not sacrifice.

Days of rest.

They have two holy-days or days of rest in the week (Saturday and Monday), on which they will on no account work their cattle; though they will do nothing for themselves on these days, they count it no sin to do service for me.

Eat animal food.

This caste eat animal food; but individuals born on a Friday are prohibited this indulgence; their diet must consist exclusively of milk and vegetables.

Mode of cultivation. And manuring the fields.

Cultivation is carried on with much pains and wonderful neatness. They plough the field five times and weed it carefully before they deposit the seed; the weeding is performed by the women and children with a crooked iron instrument. They make an enclosure or pound of loose stones near the field to be cultivated in which the cattle are confined at nights for a certain period, and they thus preserve and ripen the manure until it is fit for use.

Grains when sown.

Of the grains most of them may be said to be put in the ground soon after the first rains, that is, about the end of May and beginning of June, and reaped towards the end of August and beginning of September. It is singular that they make no use of their forage; they leave it to rot on the ground.

Opium when sown and reaped.

The opium is usually sown in October and gathered in January.

Wild fruits and flowers.

In the jungles are found a variety of wild fruits and a profusion of beautiful flowers; of the former there are wild figs, strawberries, raspberries, red and white; a fruit resembling the gooseberry both in taste and internal structure, a berry which the European visitors to the hill have called the barberry and the natives juckul (the root of the bush on which this berry grows yields a most beautiful yellow dye), and many others. Of the latter the white rose, sometimes showing itself 30 or 40 feet high (being a creeper), honey-suckles, marigolds, and a hundred others for which I have no name, adorn the jungles.

I am sensible the above account is very imperfect, and but little calculated to give a proper description of the hills or the manners and customs of its inhabitants. My opportunities of acquiring information have been necessarily confined, and the difficulty and expense of moving much about where tents, baggage, everything must as yet be carried by men has been no inconsiderable obstacle in the way of my being better acquainted with these subjects. On this account as well as because I am but little in the habit of writing on any subject I must solicit a partial perusal of the foregoing remarks.

No. 20.—*Geographical and Statistical Memoir of a Survey of the Neelgherry Mountains in the Province of Coimbatore made in* 1821 *under the Superintendence of Captain B. S. Ward, Deputy Surveyor-General.*

Description of the Neelgherry Mountains.

Its situation, nature, and extent.

This mass of mountains, situated between the parallels of 11° and 12° of North Latitude, and 76° and 77° of East Longitude, is bounded on the north by the table-land of Davaroypatam, a narrow tract divided from the table-land of Mysore by the windings of the Moyar river at the bottom of a deep narrow-wooded valley; to the south and east by the open country of Coimbatore; to the south-west a branch of the Bhowany, called the Maunar, divides it from the unpopulated mountains of Khoondahs dependent on Malabar; on the west by the chain of ghats, defined by the Murkurty peak; to the north-west by the windings of the Bukkary river, one of the sources of the Moyar from the table-land of Wynaad, its greatest length being from east to west 36 miles, and a medium breadth of 15 miles, in figure an irregular oblong, and contains on the whole a superficial area of 469¼ square miles, of which only 14 square miles may be said to be under cultivation. The surface is in no part even, being composed of ridges of different elevations, running parallel to each other and forming deep valleys between; about the centre it is divided by a loftier chain running in a north-east and south-west direction; from it lesser ridges branch off in all directions; on this are several conspicuous eminences as Dodabetta Devoybetta, their elevation above the sea being about 8,700 feet on the west of this range, and very elevated are a series of plain green undulating hills denominated Mullanaud affording extensive rich pastures, no part of it being cultivated; the broad valleys formed by these green ridges are somewhat extensive, their bottoms in general marshy, and the nullahs or mountain streams working their way through them in a variety of serpentine courses become however confined on approaching the fall or exterior of the mountain, which to the north presents a bold face of stupendous precipices, rising in most places almost perpendicularly from the table-land of Davaroypatam; to the east and south thay are seen to slope down in irregular woody ridges from an elevation of about 5,000 feet in some parts presenting bold rocky precipices. Most of the narrow streams have their sources in the main chain, flow down on all sides in devious windings, and where arrested by rocks fall in small cataracts, eventually discharging themselves into the Moyar on the north, the Bhowany on the south; the streams of these rivers unite near the village of Pungar, three miles from its eastern base. The surface is formed of innumerable ridges, perfectly open, covered with a short stunted grass, yet not entirely devoid of wood, being fringed with groves of forest trees; these are seen at the head of ravines not unfrequent along the streams in the valleys and a few on the summit of the ridges to the eastward; towards the west in Mullanaud they are very extensive, covering the whole side of the hills to one or two square miles. In the eastern portion of Parunganaud many of the lower slopes are overrun with a low jungle, principally by a plant which bears a delicious fruit in great abundance, much esteemed by the natives, and called the *Thowtahun*, in taste and flavor not inferior to a gooseberry. The southern hills in Maikanaud are overrun with a long grass intermixed with fern and other wild shrubs, and the exterior slopes and deep valleys on all sides with a variety of forest trees. Around the southern base the bamboo grows in great profusion, and, on the table-land of Davaroypatam, along the foot of the mountain the teak, blackwood, and sandal appear to thrive.

Divisions and villages.

It is divided into three Nauds, viz., Parunganaud, Maikanaud, and the Thodawanaud, and contains 160 hamlets or villages independent of the temporary habitations of the Todawars in Mullanaud with a population of above 4,000 souls. Parunganaud lying on the east is by far the most populous. Next to it is Maikanaud occupying the south-west portion and Thodawanaud including Mullanaud to the west, though the largest division is far inferior to the others including the Thodawar population. The hill hamlets are in general small, composed of from two to twenty houses, arranged in one or two lines, sometimes forming a street; they are built of mud and covered with thatch, low and excessively filthy, the entrance or doorway generally facing the east and situated on the slopes of the lower ridges. These are extensively cultivated and well attended to; some of the neighbouring ridges yearly undergo it partially; the most extensive tracts are cultivated by the Badagas. Each division has its Cotter village; this being a very low class, they are under the necessity of herding together, which gives their villages, from having a larger number of cottages, a respectable appearance, and, though they are the artizans, cultivate extensive tracts in the vicinage of their habitations; the Mullu Curumbers confine themselves to the exterior slopes and prepare their fields with the hand-hoe. The Todawars, a migratory race, only tend large herds of buffaloes, chiefly confining themselves to the Mullanaud pastures on the west. It is a singular circumstance that no regular temples or places of worship are to be seen here, but they have a house in some of the more extensive villages set apart for performing their ceremonies called Davurmannay, and sometimes a small detached hut in a grove for this purpose; the Todawars on occasions convert their dairy into a house of worship; there are three deities worshipped by the Badagas besides Rungasawmy, which, however, is considered to be the principal deity and held in great veneration by all the mountaineers, the Todawars even not excepted. He is worshipped on the peak called after him on the eastern side of the mountain which appears conspicuous from the plain country on the south-east. The only emblems of the deity seen on it are a few rude stones and iron tridents fixed in the ground and surrounded by a low, rude, circular wall of loose stone with a couple of large iron pans on it; these are on the festival of Shevaratry replenished with ghee or oil, and at night illuminated. The hill people during this festival come from their villages on the west and make offerings of fruit, ghee, &c.; this peak is also celebrated for a cavern on the north declivity, which contains some holy earth, in request by Brahmins and other castes; much of it is carried away to different parts by pilgrims who come here during the annual festival.* The hill hamlets or villages are often seen in clusters of three or four within half a mile of each other and sometimes nearer; in some cases they are alone in remote situations on the sides of the valleys; the scenery in all situations beautiful though somewhat naked from a scarcity of trees near them. The clear purling streams meandering in every direction at the bottom of the valleys afford a constant supply of water, of which however no advantage is taken, irrigation being in a great measure neglected in all parts. Since these regions have been visited by gentlemen, several bungalows have been built in different pleasant situations as at Dimhutty, and here is a very good kitchen garden, as also at Jackanairy in a lower situation. A few temporary ones have been erected for the convenience of travellers at Kodavanudy, Nunjanaud, Keelur, and Yellanully, and another is now in some progress at Whotakay in the Mullanaud, with a spacious garden laid out with taste on the shoulder of a low ridge, which promises in time to outstrip those above mentioned. One great disadvantage attending building here is the want of materials; there is a variety of timber, but it appears to be of a very indifferent kind, nor is it possible to burn firm bricks; the clay being of a bad quality does not adhere together for any time.

Soil and productions. The soil of the hills varies materially; to the east it is of a light red mixed with gravel; that peculiar to Mullanaud is a deep brown sometimes inclining to black; in the morasses and woods it is perfectly so,

* A further account of their customs and manners will be seen in another place.

perhaps owing to an accumulation of much putrid vegetation; in many parts about the tracts of cattle and the different paths are to be discerned red and yellow ochreous earth; yet is the soil not very stony; the laterite and granite is found a little below the surface in some situations. The soils on the whole are very rich, but a very small portion of the extensive slopes calculated for the plough is cultivated. European vegetables have been tried and thrive exceedingly well, as also apples, strawberry, &c., but it is a singular circumstance that the plantain and other fruit trees, even the common vegetables of the open country, have not been found to succeed. The chief productions are corally, gunja, a species of barley, shamay, buttacudla, field pease, poppy, the seeds of greens, and wheat; also garlic, onions, mustard, vendiem or fenugrick; the marshes yield spontaneously vussumbu, or the sweet-scented flag-root, in certain situations; honey and bees'-wax is collected from the exterior rocky precipices and from the hollows of trees. It may be necessary here to remark that the poppy capsules, from which the opium is extracted, are not punctured till the plants are full fourteen months old; this operation being performed by the women and children with a small iron nail, wounding the capsule on the sides towards evening, when during the night a milk or resin exudes and coagulates, which is collected on the following day a few hours after sunrise; this operation continues to be repeated every fourth day till the plant shows indications of fading. A few of the plants bear two capsules, but one of them in this case is only punctured from a supposition if extracted from both that the opium would then be of a weaker quality.

Implements and mode of husbandry.

The agricultural instruments in use here are precisely the same rude machines seen in the low country; the plough, &c., are all constructed by the Cotters. The agricultural season commences with April; after a few heavy showers of rain, the lands undergo the operation of ploughing three or four times; the seed is then sown of the following grains:—corally, gunja, shamay, wheat, mustard; garlic and onions also are planted; in August they reap gunja, wheat and mustard; garlic and onions are gathered at the same time. In January following they reap corally and Greens seed; during September the fields are again ploughed and manured, when poppy, peas, fenugrick seed is sown, and more garlic planted; in December they gather the poppy capsules and reap peas and fenugrick seed. From the above remarks it will appear that cultivation is continually going on for nine months in the year, during which interval some of the grains yield two crops; from January to March the ryots are employed in the repairs of their cottages and gathering fuel, which is laid up in large stocks in the vicinity, where it is cut and brought to the villages in small quantities when required.

Cattle and other animals.

The domestic animals seen on the hills are herds of black cattle and buffaloes. The cows produce rich milk in small quantities, and the bullocks are the only animals yoked to the plough; they are, however, of an inferior kind and generally thin. The buffaloes are superior in size and make to any in India, and are excessively savage; they roam at leisure in very large herds on the pastures in Mullanaud; are chiefly the property of the Todawars; they yield very large quantities of rich milk, which is manufactured into butter and ghee, and forms one of the principal articles for export. The wild animals are the elk, spotted deer, and hog; bears and tigers not a few; the latter have been known to attack men, and the buffaloes grazing on the pastures to the west frequently fall a prey to this ferocious animal. Hares abound in all parts, as also pea and wild fowl, and black quail, doves, and a variety of other birds, together with vultures, kites, and ravens, but the common crow is never seen to frequent these regions.

Climate. The climate of these mountains is perhaps the finest known between the tropics; during December, January, and February it is extremely cold; water is often frozen during night, and the ice is sometimes seen to remain on its surface after sunrise, but during the other nine months it is delightful the whole day; in the morning it is often below 50°, never above 60°, nor in the hottest day in this interval does it rise above 75° in the shade; notwithstanding the gelidity, the inhabitants appear on the whole to be extremely healthy; fevers are sometimes prevalent, but of a slight nature, arising perhaps more from exposure to the keen night air and rain; they are, however, in other respects free from most epidemic diseases, the small-pox excepted, which is much dreaded here. It is singular in so extensive a population that a deformed object is rarely seen; yet from the promiscuous intercourse of the sexes there is strong reason to believe they are not altogether free from venereal complaints. A very favorable idea of the salubrity of the climate may be drawn from the many instances of European gentlemen recovering their health after a short residence on them, a circumstance which of itself proves beyond a doubt its extreme healthiness; it is, however, injurious to health to be exposed the whole day to the keen air and sun, it having a tendency to make the face and lips very sore; the pain arising from it does in some individuals create fever. The south-west or Malabar monsoon has its influence here; it commences early in June ushered in with violent winds and sleet, with sometimes a heavy fall of rain; this continues with short intervals of fair weather to September, when the north-east monsoon shows indications of setting in; the wind blowing from that quarter is followed with heavy showers of rain, with thunder and lightning, during November and December; from the middle of the latter month to May the weather is generally fair and serene; in April some heavy showers are experienced, with thunder and lightning accompanied with hail, and the wind then blows from various quarters, mostly from south-east; during the prevalence of both monsoons the mountain is for many days together enveloped in dense fogs, which disperse after a heavy shower, when the atmosphere clears up and the weather continues fair for some days.

Nothing of note under this head is to be seen here, with the exception of the sight of two forts, which, though of modern date, have fallen to decay; Mullacottah, at the head of a valley, commands an extensive view of the Mysore country; it is situated three miles south-east of Sholoor, built of stone and mud, in form a square, and surrounded by a deep dry ditch, its interior overrun with jungle. Hollycul, on a conspicuous detached ridge to the south, is built on an inaccessible bold bluff rock, with many inequalities, occupies a large surface, its shape an irregular rectangle, the access to it leads over the saddle of the ridge through extensive lofty forest, then up a perpendicular rock admitting the passage of only one individual at a time; it commands an extensive view of the low country to the south and east, and also a large portion of the surface of the mountain on the north; these places were once garrisoned by a few of Tippu's troops with a design to keep the mountaineers in check and also to assist the Sultan's servants in collecting the yearly revenue. It is worthy of notice that there are circular towers on the top of most of the higher and flat eminences called Hokuls; a few of them are perfect at the present day, being in diameter about 20 feet and 5 feet high, built of loose stones, the interior strewed about with broken images of idols, &c.; from this circumstance it would appear that they were once places of worship; but no account of their origin can be obtained from the present inhabitants further than that these edifices were built by the Boopalans, predecessors of the present race of the Toduwars. *Fortifications and other ancient buildings.*

A coarse cloth wore by both sexes may be considered the only article imported, excepting bars of iron for implements, tobacco and other requisites being purchased by the inhabitants at the weekly markets held at a few large villages in the low country; the exports consist of wheat, poppy seed, opium, honey, wax, garlic, onions, mustard, fenugricks, vasambu, ghee, and little of the superior kinds of dry grain, all which find a ready sale below. *Imports and exports.*

Iron ore is found on many of the ridges impregnated with stones, a small hill to the south-west of Trichaguddy is remarkable for it; much of it is also to be seen mixed with sand of the different streams washed down the slopes of the hills; none of it is, however, smelted here, it being imported in bars from the low country. *Mines and minerals.*

There are no less than five roads or paths through different passes communicative with the villages on the surface of this mountain; of these the most easy of access is the one lately made by a party of pioneers; it is the most frequented by travellers and admits of palanquins; horses and laden cattle go up it with much ease. The road to the pass strikes off from the left bank of the Bhavani river at Sirmogay, proceeds thence waving north-west three miles over level ground and low jungle to the base of the ridge; here commences the ascent steep, zigzag and rugged for a mile northerly, to the shoulder of the ridge, along which it winds westerly with many inequalities, principally ascending till it gains a gap between two high woody tops near Conjapany; from thence descends rather steep on the southern slope of the ridge to a level surface, gradual descent to a nullah, and ascends from it to a temporary bungalow at Serulú, a delightful *Roads, passes and defiles.*

situation, amidst lofty wood, about 4,000 feet above the plain; the road now winding north-west descends gently for half a mile, then in forest over a level surface, west one mile; crosses a couple of small streams flowing to the east, and here leaves the forest; the ascent again commences winding round on the eastern brow of hills, in a general north-west direction in a deep valley, along a branch of the Kaunday river, close on the right, pouring down in cascades, and after crossing several small streams gains the cultivated slopes, passing the villages of Jackatalla and Jackanery on the left, to the bungalow Urravani on the right, from thence the ascent steep, and winding round, the east brow of a wooded hill, it arrives at a plain level surface, Mail Kotagherry village on the left, then gently winding almost on the summit of another ridge, deep valley on the left, descends gradually to the bungalow at Dimhutty, a distance of 16 miles 4 furlongs.

	M.	F.	Y.
From the left of the bank of the Bhavani			
to the base of the ridge is	3	2	160
to Coonjapany, ascent steep	3	1	0
to Arravani Bungalow, descent	1	2	20
to do. do. and descent	5	6	40
to Mail Kotagiri village, ascent	1	3	40
to Dimhatty Bungalow, gentle descent ...	1	4	180
Measure distant miles ...	16	4	0

The road leading from Danáikenkotai on the west will scarcely admit of laden cattle, being very rugged and rocky, the road from the above place waving over dry grain fields, and some low jungle for one and a half miles to the base of the ridge, which it commences to ascend and proceeds winding westerly on the summit, has a gentle descent to Urracode in a small valley, cultivated with plantain, jack, and other fruit trees, thence it descends to a large stream ascending very steep winds over the southern brow of the Rungasawmy Hill, thence down a valley crossing another steep ridge, ascends a slope winding gently. Daynaád on the left, descends a small rugged pass to a temporary bungalow on the right, again ascends gently to the summit of a ridge, winding round the west brow of a hill, descends northerly into an open valley between low hills for about a mile and a half, descends westerly another small pass to Nedancolum, a fine village on the right, from thence over low plain ridges crossing two large streams in swamp, ascends another ridge and descends by a zigzag rugged pass to a large stream north-west of Cuppanatharay, then up the low brow of a low hill, gently ascends through low jungle, and crossing another small stream rises up to Dimhatty being on the whole a distance of 20 miles 7 furlongs.

	M.	F.	Y.
From Danaikenkotai to the foot of the pass is	1	5	100
„ to Urracode generally ascending ...	5	3	0
„ to Daynaád Bungalow do. ...	10	6	100
Nedancolum, first part ascent, then descent ...	16	0	100
Dimhatty, ascending gently, steep descent, ascend-	20	7	0

This communication with Dimhatty though circuitous is for a considerable way carried over very easy ground, with the exception of the first portion of it to Daynaád. The pass on the whole is of an easy ascent, and may be made practicable at a small labor and expense for laden cattle. The pass leading up from Authutty, on the left bank of the Bhavani, is short and therefore difficult and steep, joins the new road near the Serulu Bungalow, the ascent up the ridge being only 2 miles. It may be made practicable for laden cattle, and is constantly traversed by the hill people in preference to the new road, the communication being shorter with the villages on the plain. The pass from Keelur down to Soondaputty, a deserted hamlet on the left bank of the Bhavani among hills, is in a great measure steep; from the bungalow at the above place, the path runs south-west half mile, having the hamlet of Munjacumba on the left; it winds easterly on the saddle of an open ridge, ascends gently almost to the summit of Soondabetta, in high grass and date bushes, and the western slope, southerly to a small pool on the right, then south-easterly to the exterior or fall of the mountain, descends gradually winding to a wood and hut, thence descent steep, passing over a flat rock south-westerly to a nullah, keeps along it for a short distance and crossing it passes over gentle ascent, descends and crosses the Manar River, and ascending from it takes a south-westerly course, descends then south-east, passing over a rather level surface to Soondaputty, and is on the whole a tolerable path, the pass excepted being tedious in the descent.

	M.	F.	Y.
From Keelur to the summit of the pass	3	7	160
„ to nullah at the foot of the pass ...	6	4	200
„ to the Manar River	8	1	40
„ to Soondaputty banian tree... ...	10	0	0

The road and pass on the north, leading down to the table-land of Devaroyapatam at present frequented, leads from the village of Kulhutty, descends and crosses a ravine near Tudukaly, thence on a flat cultivated surface intersected by three inconsiderable streams, ascends a low ridge, and descending gradually to a large nullah crosses it, and two smaller ones to a buffalo crib, on a flat table, on the margin of which it runs east-north-east to a nullah in wood, quitting it, descends abruptly by several zigzag winding north-east and north, latter part very rugged to Courmullay, a deserted village at the foot of the mountains, the whole length of the pass being two-and-a-half miles, the path and crossing the Mullayacotta River and some ruins to Shégoor northerly runs, north-north-west over some uncultivated paddy lands and through a jungle of sandal and bamboos, recrossing the above river, here called Cottoár, from thence again north-west by north over high ground covered with low and open wood, again crosses the above river to Shembanuttum Fort. This pass is the most difficult, yet does admit of laden cattle, is on the whole from Kulhutty to Shembanuttum, a distance of nine-and-a-quarter miles. The original road skirting the eastern side of the Mullayacotta Valley has been impracticable for years from parts of the ridges having fallen and barred the both in many places.

The communication on the surface to the westward from Dimhatty runs on a ridge south-west to Todanad, thence through the opening of a high ridge west-north-west between hills on easy slopes, and crossing a nullah half a mile north of Kulhutty, ascends a ridge, descends it to the Kookal stream, ascends a long slope in low jungle to a conspicuous tree, Cuggoochy, a small hamlet on the left, leaving it, ascends a small winding pass, then on a level slope, at the summit of the Kookal Valley. Trichaguddy on the left, descends and crosses a stream and marsh, rises gently from it, and descends rather steep to a bungalow near a winding stream, crosses to the village of Kodavamudy on a gentle slope; the road to the west descends, and crossing another winding stream rises gently to the village of Toonairy on the right, then descends on a brow and crossing another hill stream winds gently up to Hunnikúray on the right, thence ascending on a slope has a short descent to a winding stream; on crossing it, proceeds on a ridge, Kondahutty, two furlongs on the left, winds round a hill, steep valley on the right, and crossing a few small streams gains the village of Kondahutty. From thence over a level surface descends rather steep, and crossing a large stream ascends to Kulhutty on the right. Here branch off two paths, one described above leads easily down to the valley, crosses another rivulet, Mailcottah Fort, on an eminence on the left, descends steep and circuitous to the Mantar, a large winding rivulet, ascent on passing it very steep, for a quarter of a mile, then over waving ground to the village of Shoolúr; from this place paths lead off to the south and west, traversing the pasture lands of Mullanaád in all directions.

		M.	F.	Y.
From Dimhatty	to Tandanaád	0	6	50
„	to Kuggoochy	5	0	60
„	to Trichagandy	6	3	120
„	to Kadavanludy Bungalow ...	8	2	60
„	to Toonairy	9	4	60
„	to Hunnúvurroy	10	7	180
„	to Kadhutty	14	1	140
„	to Kulhutty	14	7	100
„	to the Mantár	16	5	100
„	to Sholur	17	6	100
From Kadvamoody	to Toomanhutty	3	1	0

The path from Dimhatty to Ootacamund leaves the former one two furlongs south-east of Taudanaád, proceeds south, crosses a small stream, keeps waving on a plain surface westerly, Orasholah village three furlongs on the right, continues to wind on gentle slopes south-west, crossing three inconsiderable streams gently descending and ascending high hill on the right, descends a small pass and crosses a large stream two furlongs west of Togalhutty, and ascends another ridge southerly, descends on the western slope of it, and crosses another irrigious stream at a junction a furlong north of the village of Yellithoray, situated on a cultivated eminence; the path then runs on a level to the south-west in a narrow valley, low steep ridge, covered with jungle on the left, ascends gently leaving a swamp on the right and a remarkable hill with a single tree beyond it; it then descends into a narrow vale crossing a large stream to the top of a ridge, on the slope of which it descends rather steep, crossing another large irrigious stream below a confluence, and rises southerly to the village Munjatulla; then on the north brow of a ridge, waving, descends into an open valley, and crossing a few smaller streams on a waving surface, ascends a high ridge rather steep, Yellanully village on the right, two furlongs from it, descent steep to another stream, and rising again waves round the southern brow of a hill, gently glides down westerly into a valley, Kaytee on the right, and crossing several hill streams at short distances, gains a ridge and ascends north-north-west to its summit, descends and crossing another stream, winds round the eastern brow of a hill to a gap, then waving gently down on the western brow of high hills to a small stream and marsh ascends the flat ridge of Whotakaymund, Mr. Sullivan's Bungalow on the left. It is in general a good path, but very circuitous.

		M.	F.	Y.
From Dimhatty	to Taudanaád	0	6	0
„	to Togulhutty	4	1	120
„	to Yellithoray	5	2	0
„	to Munjatulla	8	4	120
„	to Yellanully	11	0	120
„	to Kaytee	12	3	20
„	to Whotakaymund	15	4	20

The direct road now making by a party of pioneers to Whotakaymund runs south of the village of Orasholah, passing a ridge winds on a waving surface between Padhal and Culhutty; ascends a ridge and descends it rather steep on the west slope of a large rivulet, crossing which it ascends an easy slope, runs south of Ballycumba, descends from it to another stream, ascends an easy slope, and winds north of the village of Tatarvane, Puggala, and joins the summit of another ridge, on which is situated that of Cumbutty; it then descends on the northern slope of a hill, leaving Cumbagay on the right, and descends to a stream; from it ascends another gentle slope, on which it keeps waving for a considerable way. Tumanhutty on the right, two furlongs, ascending winds round the eastern brow of the Koonatachapu hill, village on the left, descends and crosses a few streams and uneven ground, and ascends to the summit of Dodabetta ridge, and ultimately winding in its descent, on a slope of the same to Whotaykamund.

		M.	F.	Y.
From Dimhatty	to Orasholah	1	2	0
„	to Culhutty	3	0	0
„	to Billacumba	4	1	0
„	to Puggala	5	2	0
„	to Cumbaghy	6	3	0
„	to Toomanhutty	7	1	0
„	to Coonatchapa	8	5	0
„	to Whotaykamund	0	3	0

To enter into a full description of all the paths would perhaps be superfluous, the surface of the hill being traversed by them in every direction. A few of those measured is, however, here inserted.

	M.	F.	Y.
From Mullacottah to Nunjanaád	8	6	20
„ Nunjanaád to Whotakaymund	6	4	0
„ Nunjanaád to Ootalmund	6	2	0
„ Nunjanaád to Keelúr	8	1	100
„ Keelúr to Kaytee	8	4	0
„ Whotakaymund to Baricooly...	7	2	0
„ Baricooly to Keelúr	4	3	0
„ Nunjanaád to Baricooly	3	6	100

(Signed) B. S. WARD, Lieutenant,
Assistant, Surveyor-General's Dept.

MISCELLANEOUS.

It may be necessary in this place to give some account of the different castes of people inhabiting this vast mountain; these principally consist of four castes—Budagers, Todawers, Cotters, and Mullucurumbers; the latter are the officiating priests to the former, who are the principal cultivators, occupying villages and lands in all the three naáds or divisions with the exception of the western portion or Mullanaád, dependent on the Todawanaád, a tract of low green hills in ridges affording pasture to large herds of buffaloes; about it are interspersed the králls or munds of the Todawars in remote places to the west, forming their summer, those again to the east, almost on the skirts of the Budager villages, their winter habitations. Each division has its Cotter village, distinct from the Budagers; they are in general extensive, having from forty to fifty houses arranged in lines. They are the artizans, and also cultivate large tracts of land around their habitations. The women of both these classes perform the principal labors of the field in common with the men, who, however, leave the more arduous service of watching, weeding, and cleaning them to the women after the plough has done its duty. In their physiognomy, habits, and language they materially differ from one another. The prevailing language among all is the Canarese, much corrupted with peculiar phrases and idioms of their own invention. They are perfectly illiterate. An attempt to establish a school among them at Daynaád not long ago has failed; on what account is not known.

Agriculture in primitive times was carried on on a very limited scale by the Mullucurumbers only in exterior valleys and slopes; to the Budagers must be attributed the merit of diffusing husbandry all over the face of the mountains; to these aërial regions they are said to have emigrated about four centuries ago from Woomatúr and other places in the south of Mysore, and consequently have derived the appellation of Vada or Budagers, having come from the north, the compound word Buda-ger signifying literally people of the north. It appears they were originally invited by a chieftain or rajah of

Woomatúr, who had about that period taken refuge on these mountains, who, on their arrival, finding the land fertile, settled on them and in course of time were followed by others, and now form the largest proportion of the population of the hills. This class of people are again sub-divided into the following sects :—Harruvars, Buddagur, Shevacharas, Odykary, and Torayen ; these do not intermarry, however agreeing in most other particulars. The Harruvars are of the superior class, and wear the sacerdotal thread similar to the Brahmans of the low country.

OF THE BUDAGERS.

An individual wishing to form a connection of this nature proceeds to pay court to one of the other sex for a month and upwards ; during this interval he is assiduous in making her small presents, and by attention he seldom fails of gaining his object. He then settles with her parents the stipulated sum to be paid, which varies from six to ten Puns (15 to 20 rupees). Matters being thus adjusted, he takes his partner home, and the ceremony concludes with a repast. The parents of the young woman make over with her a cow and bullock, a metal dish, and an ornament for the neck called a talley. It often happens that the present stipulated is not promptly liquidated, but payment deferred to a definitive period on ample security ; in default of non-payment the relatives of the woman endeavour to separate her from her husband. If she will not be prevailed on, it is then determined according to the circumstances of the husband—a part of whose cattle and other property is disposed of to meet the demand. Polygamy is not uncommon among them ; an individual may have two or more wives if his circumstances will admit of his maintaining them, and they generally speaking prove of infinite service to him in the labors of the field, the largest portion of that duty devolving on the women. The standard of union here appears very fickle and capricious ; divorces or separation are not uncommon arising from disgust or disaffection, and when such is the case are seldom reconciled; this disposition to incontinency is more predominant with the fair sex. In case of a separation of this nature, all the children remain with the father ; and the woman is moreover obliged to give up all presents, &c., she may have received, the dowry being left to be adjusted on her second espousal. In case the woman is in a state of pregnancy when she takes this measure, the child when weaned is also consigned to its father, who pays her six rupees, twenty cantirai fanams for her trouble; her next husband pays the amount of the dowry stipulated on the former marriage, and is moreover responsible for all debts she may have incurred during it, which, if not liquidated by her second husband, she is separated from him by coercion and married to a third person fixed upon by the community. While in a state of separation if she should have a clandestine intercourse with another individual and prove with child, the gallant is then compelled to take her on paying the stipulated dowry.

Marriages.

Funerals. Their funeral rites are performed in the following manner :—The corpse is laid on a cot opposite to the house under a canopy four feet high ; from the centre rises a pole of ten feet with cross yards decorated with pendants of white cloth ; beneath it is exposed in wicker baskets boiled victuals, grain, &c., as offerings to the defunct. The relations and neighbours for a considerable time keep singing and dancing round the canopy. The ceremony concludes by knotting in a corner of the shroud the roll of a palm leaf worn by the wife of the deceased on her ears, and the contrary if a woman dies, a piece of light wood worn by the husband; the corpse is then removed to the pile accompanied by music, and consigned to it with the oblation. The male children of the deceased shave their heads and face. The sect of Shevacaras bury their dead.

Worship. Besides Rungasawmy, the dieties worshipped in the interior are Hereadeo, and the goddess Hethadeo, also a subordinate deity called Kunkolú Karodia, or the eye-giving power; the latter is their tutular goddess ; the Harruvars and Shevacaras have their Mahalinga.

Dress, &c. The coarse clothing of the mountaineers, stiffened with starch, intended as a defence against the gelidity of the climate, gives to men and more especially to the women a most uncouth appearance; the men wrap round them a large sheet with colored borders, and a handkerchief about the head ; those individuals who can afford it have rings of gold to their ears, and of silver on their fingers. The dress of the women consists of a coarse cloth, four or five cubits in length, hemmed in at the upper and lower extremities by triple lines of cotton twist, and drawn up in a fringe, giving it the shape of a petticoat, fastened with ligatures below the arm and midriff ; yet in spite of thick starch and bandages exposes a great part of the legs ; their jewelry consists of heavy brass bangles, worn above the elbow of the right arm, and those that can afford it a silver bracelet graces the left wrist, rings of gold and brass to their ears, fingers and toes, with a pendant jewel affixed to the membrane of the left nostril. Very few, if any, of the women in years can be termed beauties ; the fine features of some of the young girls occasionally seen are eclipsed by their awkward dress and propensity to dirty apparel. A few of the males in circumstances are robust and well made, but the generality are meagre and of a phlegmatic temperament, occasioned by the poor diet they subsist on and the pernicious use of raw opium ; in their disposition, with but a few exceptions, it may with propriety be said they are cunning, suspicious, and incommunicative in their dealings with strangers, display a covetous desire for lucre, which stimulates them to duplicity and falsehood ; among themselves are tolerably social ; jealousy is perhaps a negative passion, as fornication appears to be the prerogative of both sexes.

Diet. They subsist generally on koralay and shamay (two species of millet), gunja or barley, and the flour of the keeray or Garden greens seed. Condiments are not in general use, but garlic gives a zest to all their meals ; they are not averse to animal food (beef excepted), but very little, if any, enters their fare, excepting at a marriage, or some grand day of feasting. Milk, tyre, and rancid ghee may be considered among their luxuries.

In all the duties of husbandry women partake more of the labors Labor. than the men—the holding the plough is perhaps one exception, being the sole duty of the men; performing all the duties of the field, beside their internal household affairs, to which in a great measure we may attribute their strong, harsh, masculine features and deportment. The dairy, it must be remarked, is, however, the exclusive duty of the men, the milk kept in an inner apartment, and there churned; the females are scrupulously prohibited from entering it. Tthe poorer class make good porters.

TODUWARS.

The remarkable dissimilarity of these people in their persons and features from the other mountaineers is very striking; they are evidently a distinct race, and are in fact the aborigines of these aerial regions; their origin it is impossible to trace. When interrogated on this point we could only learn that they have some idea that they were originally self borne, and they have also a notion that their ancestors in primitive times were the palanquin-bearers to the giant Rawan, and were expelled from Lunka on his being slain by Rama. This migratory tribe confine themselves and herds of buffaloes to the Mullanaád, Taranaád and Kulánum Hills, which afford excellent pastures; this tract, consisting of the western portion denominated Todanaád, is marked by several of their kralls or munds, with a circular roof of thatch and door scarce high enough to admit a dog, into which they crawl on all fours; their site in general retired, near a tuft of forest trees in delightful situations, with extensive circles fenced with wood and stone for their buffaloes; those towards the west are occupied during summer. On the approach of the Malabar monsoons they retire with their cattle to the east, on the skirts of the Badager villages; a few families, however, continually reside in Perunganaád and Maiknaád, and tend with their own the cattle of the Badagers. Their chief occupation is the care of their buffaloes and the dairy, for which purpose a house of large dimensions at each mund is reserved apart, is by them considered sacred, women not being permitted to enter; in it they also perform such ceremonies in use on the anniversary of their deceased relatives, having no temples or other places of worship. Each clan being in possession of from one to two hundred buffaloes, pays a tax annually for each cow half a rupee; this they are well enabled to do from the sale of raggy and poultry. Leading a pastoral life and abstracted from all agricultural pursuits, they are indebted to the Badagers for grain given them gratis at the annual harvest—a custom from time immemorial in consideration of their being the hereditary claimants of the soil. On the celebration of any marriage among the more wealthy Badagers they receive from quarter to half a rupee as a present; they also subsist in a great measure on a variety of bulbous fruits procured by digging, large quantities being obtained on all the hills in the Todawanaád. The Todawars are in general well made and robust, in stature tall—some of them exceed six feet in height, and approach nearer to the European in feature, with Roman noses; they evince a friendly propensity to strangers, and appear to display more candour than their eastern neighbours, but it must, however, be remarked from personal observation they are not now behind the Burghers in criminal deceit and falsehood. The women are reputed beauties; some of the younger ones are possessed of handsome lineaments and exceedingly fair, with some vivacity, but like all other native women are old and wrinkled before they attain their thirtieth year; the men are very much attached to them, and carry their affection for the sex to a most voluptuous degree. Their colloquial language is the Canarese as spoken by the Badagers, but they have a most difficult and intricate one of their own, perfectly distinct from all the languages in India, and only known to themselves (they are illiterate). The same neglect of cleanliness in their apparel is observed here. Both men and women wear a large white sheet with colored borders; the only difference observed is the manner of wrapping it about the person; with the female the habit is the perfect dishabille; the right hand, which is exposed, serves to keep the wrapper from disrobing or being blown away. The men wear a scanty piece of cloth round their middle in addition to the sheet thrown round the shoulder and hanging to the knees, wearing their hair thick and full six inches in length, with bushy beards, having recourse only to shears when either become troublesome to the wearer, and never by any chance are known to shave or cover the head. The women have flowing tresses waving down to the shoulders, and often curled up with short sticks; on the whole pay much attention to their hair, anointing it with rancid ghee in lieu of jewels, which all are unable to afford, with the exception of a couple of brass bangles on the right arm, and silver or brass rings on the fingers; they puncture with an indelible black dye their necks, hands, and legs in imitation of jewellery. A singular custom among them is wearing a brass chain or girdle next to the skin round the waist, an appendage that no grown up woman or girl should be without. They have no formal rites of marriage, concluding alliances by reciprocal choice, the present on the part of the man to the connections of the bride being from six to eight buffaloes. When arrived at the house of her husband, she is obliged, in case he has brothers, to acknowledge them as husbands, and to render them the services and submission due from a wife. Independent of her husbands, she is by their laws allowed to choose an individual from a separate family as a gallant, styled coombhal, who is as eligible to her embraces as any of the former; in short the coombhal has a discretionary power over her, for in case the young woman should be at the house of one of her husbands, and the coombhal comes in, the husband immediately retires, and leaves her to his alliance; the legal husbands contribute towards her maintenance, and the coombhal provides her with a cloth yearly, with tobacco and other small presents.

Notwithstanding this inconsistency, the Toduwars live very peaceably together; the partition of the boys begotten in this manner chiefly depends on the seniority of the brothers, the eldest claiming the first born, and so on consecutively; the girls, left to the care of the mother, are generally betrothed when very young. In a connection of this nature, when one woman is common to a plurality of husbands, it is natural to suppose that the males must far exceed those of the females; an investigation into the cause of this disparity in the sexes has led to a supposition that they have been in the habit of destroying the females hitherto, at least those born on ominous days of the week, by some unnatural means, leaving them, as has been conjectured, at the door of the pen to be trampled by the buffaloes rushing out furiously when liberated; and if what is above stated be a matter of fact, we have still to ascertain the cause from whence originates this unnatural deed. The duties of the women often lead them out to tend the cattle when grazing; they also attend to all domestic affairs, the dairy excepted, and when at leisure amuse themselves with needle-work, darning the hems of cloth with red and blue thread; in this performance they display some taste, and are by the Badagers, for whom they work, recompensed with grain or small money according to exigencies. In their migrations, the infirm and old women are removed on the shoulders of the men; this circumstance gave rise to a credulous report that they invariably transported their women in this manner. It has been an ancient practice among them that one of the males should devote himself to a life of pious solitude, such is denoted a Terriara, and sometimes Pollen, who is reverenced as a priest; this anchorite resides perfectly secluded in the recess of some deep forest in a state of nudity, a small hut being there prepared for him, seldom communicating with the laity. Such of those who have any temporal or spiritual business, accost him and hold a conference, taking care to keep at a respectable distance. The Terriara is generally the most wealthy of the tribe, having large flocks of buffaloes presented to him by the laity, the produce of which is chiefly distributed among the herdsmen, the anchorite reserving but a small part to himself; he however occasionally makes an eleemosynary excursion to the neighbourhood of the munds. The dairy or milk-house (having no pagoda or idol of worship) is consecrated annually in memory of departed relatives. On this occasion they burn a lamp fed with butter, and make offerings of milk, ghee, fruit, invoking the names of the departed souls with supplication; during the performance of these ceremonies the Terriara is invited to officiate as high priest. The office of a Terriara is by no means permanent; he may resign of himself, by signifying his intentions to the community at large, who appoints some other individual to his room. From what is above stated a conclusion may be drawn that they are not very zealous idolaters, yet are superstitious enough to have their lucky and unlucky days; this has a powerful influence in all their concerns; thus Thursday, Saturday, and Sunday are reckoned good days, and *vice versâ* with the remainder of the week. A person dies on any of the ominous days, the funeral rites are deferred to the succeeding good day; the ceremony on this occasion consists in assembling the relations of the deceased, when they utter their condolence in loud lamentations; after this follows a sacrifice of two or more buffaloes, which are killed with heavy clubs and their skull and horns chopped off; the corpse is then placed on the pile for cremation. On the anniversary following the relations convene at the same spot, each bringing a buffalo; to these are added others belonging to the stock of the deceased, and picketted near the place where the body was consumed; the ceremony being performed, eight or ten able men with heavy clubs enter on a promiscuous slaughter, when they proceed to part the horns from the head of the animals; it has been a perfect mystery hitherto what was done with the flesh of these animals; from some inquiries in another quarter it has been ascertained that the Toduwars eat of it, and are in the habit always, when they can afford it, to partake of the flesh of this animal, the hides serving them as beds, when clean and dressed; yet they pretend all animal flesh to be unclean.

MÚLLÚCOORMBERS.

The aggregate amount of this caste is very small, inhabiting the recesses of the valleys or slopes of the mountains, towards the plain country. They are a primeval race, almost contemporary with the Toduwars, and have an equal right to the inheritance of the soil; have from very remote times followed the occupations of husbandry, cultivating the steep acclivities, in the execution of which they only use the hand hoe, a species of culture called cottúkád, and assessed very moderately. The produce of their fields, however, is very precarious and seldom affords them a sufficiency for consumption, for which they are in a great measure indebted to the Buddagers, to whom they officiate as priests. The Badager will never undertake any agricultural affair without some ceremonies performed by the Múllúcoormber* to Kalibuntyan; this ceremony ended, he holds the plough and turns up the glebe in each field, when the duty of the husbandmen commences; he then receives from each ryot from four to ten colagays of grain, according to the circumstances of each individual, and retires. At harvest time his services are again required to apply the sickle to the ripe grain; when the reapers proceed for this duty, he is permitted to take as many of the sheaves as he can well bear away on his shoulders. Their marriages, funeral ceremonies, are similar to those of the Badagers, differing very little in their habits and manners from them; living in seclusion they are seldom seen abroad, visiting the villages from mere necessity.

KOTHURS.

This caste of people are the most industrious race on the Neilgherries, following all the most useful occupations as carpenters, black-

* Who is fed for his spiritual duty. At the commencement of the ploughing season a sacrifice of fowls and sheep are offered by the Múllúcoormbers.

smiths, potters, &c., and officiate as musicians at feasts, funerals, and marriages; in short they are the only artizans on the hills, and are moreover good husbandmen; paying more attention to agriculture, their fields appear to thrive better around their hamlets than those seen in the vicinity of the Badager villages; they are, however, of a very inferior caste, and by their neighbours considered in the same light as the chuckler in the low country; they have cattle, but from superstitious motives never milk the cow, are not permitted to have buffaloes, but such unserviceable old animals which the Badagers dispense with for a trifle; these are allowed to die, when they partake of them, in short of the flesh of all kinds of dead animals, not being allowed by their laws to kill any; the hides being dressed are disposed of to advantage; their exterior and filthy propensities render them so peculiarly disgusting to their neighbours that a Badager will not drink of the stream that flows in the vicinity of their villages, polluted, as it is supposed to be, with the flesh of the dead animals and their raw hides, these being generally dressed on the side of a stream. In all the three Divisions or Naáds are Kothur villages, denominated Kothagerrys; these hamlets, though few, have generally a large population, and always in pleasant situations, with a grove of large trees, present an agreeable prospect from a distance. They are a more ancient people than the Badagers, their dress similar to that of the Toduwars, both sexes wearing their cloths in the same manner as the latter race. The men go bareheaded, wear the hair long, tied in a knot behind; they are in general of the middle stature, ill-made, short and bad featured; some of the women, however, are fair, and withal well-made and handsome.

Marriages.

The ceremony, if such it may be called, takes place on the mutual consent of both parties, being allowed a previous cohabitation; the parents of the young woman receive from the husband a compensation of 3 to 5 rupees; the man is at liberty to take a second wife, provided the first has no male issue after three successive female births. A woman from any disagreement is allowed to separate herself from her husband; in this case she leaves all her children, and moreover returns the present on marriage, but to their credit it may be said, though mean and contemptible, that female infidelity is not common; their ornaments are of small value. Copper bracelets adorn their wrists, and brass bangles above the left elbow; the neck decorated with black beads of stone or glass. The Kothurs burn their dead, and worship the manes in some dark grove on the following anniversary. Their idol is Cumbatodeo; for the worship of this deity small thatched edifices are erected, and offerings made on certain occasions.

IRRELURS.

Irrelurs, Múdúmars, and Cússúwars.

These are a distinct race of people from the other highlanders of the mountains, classed among the lowest of the Soodra caste, are very little superior to the Pariahs, diminutive and ill-made, are grossly ignorant, and in their apparel scanty and excessively filthy; their cottages are situated on the exterior slope and valleys, the sides of which they cultivate with a variety of dry grain, also plantain, jack and other fruits, which are seen in groves in the bosom of low valleys; they have scarcely any communication with the people of the hills, but often come down to the plains to dispose or barter plantains and other hill productions at the market villages. Those occupying the ridges on the east towards Denkankotai are invariably called Irrelurs; to the south on the ridges forming the Bhavani Valley are called Múdúmars; and on the northern slopes towards Davaroypatam, they go by the appellation of Cússúwars; these also cultivate large tracts on the plain surface of the table-land, and yet are all one race, differing in no one instance; their customs, manners, and occupation being alike. In their marriages perhaps they are singular. This contract does not take place between the parties cohabiting till the second or third child is born, when the man agrees to pay a stipulated sum by instalments as a dowry to the friends of the woman, who give with her as a portion a buffalo; the contract now becomes binding. In case of her demise the man must make over the whole of the balance before he forms another connection; but if she should survive her husband who has a brother, she must immediately become his wife, and also to the next till all are extinct, so that a fruitful woman, according to their customs, is always provided for. In their cemeteries and burials they widely differ from the other castes, appearing to venerate the manes of their dead above every other consideration. The cemeteries are scattered in pleasant but lonesome situations, being a neat house quite open to the east. About the middle and against the inner walls of all of them are seen a heap of circular black stones; these are placed on one of the community being interred, and consequently are accumulating from day to day. The males are buried on one side, females on the other. The ceremonies and feasting on these occasions last a month, and during this interval the earth lies very loose on the corpse; it is then softened with water and beaten down after the last rites are performed. If one of the community should happen to die at a distance even, his corpse is sent for and the usual rites are performed, though it be in a putrid state. The deities worshipped by them is Rungasawmy and the goddess Másula or Buttrácály. Offerings of sheep, &c., are made to her on certain days of ceremony.

(Signed) B. S. WARD, Leutenant,
Assistant, Surveyor-General's Department.

Register of the Thermometer at Whotakay on the Neilgherry Mountains for April 1822, *kept by J. Sullivan, Esq.*

Date.	6 A.M.	9 A.M.	NOON.	3 P.M.	6 P.M.	Remarks.
8	48	64	66	61	60	Morning fine, afternoon rain; at 2 P.M. thermometer at 55.
9	50	63	64	61	58	Rain.
10	48	64	62	55	...	Do.
11	48	62	66	65	60	Afternoon rain; evening fine.
12	52	62	66	68	59	Fine throughout.
13	48	65	68	67	61	Fair.
14	52	64	68	67	60	Do.
15	50	66	63	64	59	Fine.
16	50	62	62	58	59	Rain in the afternoon.
17	51	63	68	66	59	Morning fine, heavy clouds in the afternoon, high wind at night.
18	...	58	67	...	59	Rain at night.
19	...	64	66	64	60	Fine throughout.
20	50	65	66	64	60	Slight rain in the evening.
21	...	64	68	67	59	A shower in the evening.
22	50	63	66	65	60	A slight shower in the afternoon, high wind at night with thunder.
23	51	62	64	62	59	Fine throughout.
24	51	...	68	66	60	Do.
25	50	63	66	62	59	A slight shower in the afternoon, heavy clouds and thunder.
26	53	63	66	65	60	High wind, thunder and rain during the night.
27	...	60	62	63	59	Fine.
28	...	63	64	63	59	Do.
29	54	63	69	64	60	Do.
30	...	64	68	66	62	Do.
Average	50	63	64	63	60	General mean 60.

Minimum 48, maximum 69, range 21.

Register of the Thermometer at Whotakay on the Neilgherry Mountains for May 1822, kept by J. Sullivan, Esq.

Date.	6 A.M.	9 A.M.	Noon.	3 P.M.	6 P.M.	Remarks.
1	55	65	69	68	63	Fine.
2	...	66	70	68	63	Do.
3	...	66	68	66	63	Do.
4	55	67	69	67	63	Do.
5	54	65	65	66	63	Do.
6	55	65	68	67	62	Do.
7	52	64	67	67	63	Do.
8	54	65	65	67	63	Do.
9	...	64	66	67	63	Do.
10	54	64	67	...	60	Hard shower in the evening.
11	...	64	64	65	60	Shower in the afternoon.
12	...	64	65	64	60	Fine.
13	...	67	68	64	62	Rain during the night.
14	...	64	68	66	63	Do.
15	54	65	71	68	62	Fine.
16	54	67	70	68	62	Do.
17	60	66	70	...	62	Do.
18	58	67	69	68	62	Do.
19	58	62	71	68	62	Do.
20	55	70	71	69	...	Do.
21	54	66	72	70	...	Do.
22	52	64	68	72	64	Do.
23	54	64	68	60	64	Hard shower in the evening.
24	54	62	64	64	61	Showers in the afternoon.
25	56	64	62	62	58	Hard shower during the day.
26	54	58	64	65	59	Fine.
27	52	64	64	64	59	Hard shower in the afternoon.
28	54	58	64	62	58	Showers in the afternoon.
29	52	59	64	63	58	Fine.
30	54	60	62	64	58	Shower in the afternoon.
31	54	60	63	62	58	Fine.
Average	54	65	66½	65	61	General mean 62.

Maximum 72, minimum 52, range 20.

Register of Thermometer at Whotakay on the Neilgherry Mountains for June 1822, *kept by J. Sullivan, Esq.*

Date.	6 A.M.	9 A.M.	NOON.	3 P.M.	6 P.M.	Remarks.
1	54	60	62	64	57	
2	53	57	58	59	55	The south-west monsoon set in with drizzling rain and high wind.
3	54	59	59	60	55	Do. do.
4	54	58	56	56	54	Do. do.
5	54	58	59	58	56	Drizzling rain for a short time.
6	55	57	60	58	57	Do. do.
7	55	56	62	63	58	Very fine.
8	55	60	64	63	59	Do.
9	55	60	63	66	60	Do.
10	56	60	65	64	59	Do.
11	55	60	62	64	58	Do.
12	54	60	64	60	56	Shower in the evening.
13	54	58	64	62	58	Slight showers at intervals.
14	55	58	61	62	58	Very fine.
15	55	...	...	64	58	Do.
16	53	58	64	62	58	Do.
17	53	62	...	64	59	Do.
18	54	59	63	60	57	Rain at intervals during the day.
Average	54	58	61	61	58	Mean 58.
19	52	57	55	54	52	Rain and high wind.
20	51	54	60	55	53	Showers at intervals.
21	53	62	65	58	58	Drizzling rain at intervals.
22	53	56	62	60	54	Fine.
23	53	60	64	55	52	Occasional showers.
24	51	61	70	71	58	Fine.
25	50	68	60	58	...	Showers during the day.
26	48	64	71	64	58	Do.
27	50	60	68	60	56	Do.
28	52	59	68	70	54	Showers in the evening.
29	52	59	74	57	64	Fine.
30	51	56	65	66	54	Do.
Average	51	60	65	60	55	Mean 59.

Register of Thermometer at Whotakay on the Neilgherry Mountains for July 1822, kept by J. Sullivan, Esq.

Date.	6 A.M. in the Hut.	6 A.M. in the Air.	9 A.M. in the Hut.	9 A.M. in the Sun.	Noon in the Hut.	Noon in the Sun.	3 P.M. in the Hut.	3 P.M. in the Sun.	6 P.M. in the Hut.	6 P.M. in the Air.	Remarks.
1	57	54	67	60	62	62	60	61	57	53	Fine.
2	55	53	58	55	61	58	59	58	56	54	Occasional slight showers.
3	55	53	55	54	57	56	57	56	55	54	Do. do.
4	55	53	56	53	58	58	57	61	56	54	Do. with high wind.
5	56	53	54	52	56	56	57	56	56	54	Do.
6	54	51	56	58	58	58	58	60	56	54	Fine.
7	55	52	57	56	57	57	59	59	57	54	Slight showers at intervals.
8	56	52	57	54	58	57	58	60	55	52	Hard showers & high wind.
9	55	52	57	55	58	58	58	56	57	54	Do. do.
10	55	52	58	55	58	62	59	58	55	52	Slight showers at intervals.
11	55	52	59	60	59	64	60	64	...	56	Fine.
12	57	54	58	58	58	58	59	62	58	57	Slight showers at intervals.
13	57	54	64	61	64	72	62	58	58	56	Hard shower in the afternoon.
14	58	54	61	66	62	60	60	61	58	56	Slight do. do.
15	57	54	55	53	58	55	57	54	57	53	Rain for the greater part of the day.
16	55	51	57	54	58	59	57	54	55	52	Drizzling rain and wind.
17	55	51	57	54	58	59	57	54	54	51	Do. at intervals.
18	55	53	59	56	58	58	58	59	55	55	Hard shower in the evening.
19	56	54	59	55	57	55	57	56	56	54	Drizzling rain.
20	...	...	57	56	57	61	60	60	57	54	Occasional slight showers.
21	55	52	56	59	62	68	64	64	58	54	Very fine.
22	57	54	60	74	65	68	63	70	60	57	Very fine in the morning; slight shower evening.
23	56	52	58	62	64	69	64	70	60	58	Very fine in the morning.
24	57	54	59	57	...	...	62	65	58	56	Fine; slight shower in the evening.
25	58	54	60	64	61	65	62	62	58	56	Rain in the evening.
26	56	50	58	60	62	70	62	62	60	55	Hard shower in the evening.
27	55	53	60	60	59	59	...	...	...	56	Do. in the evening.
28	57	52	60	62	61	59	61	61	60	58	Hard rain.
29	56	52	58	66	63	66	62	64	60	60	Fine.
30	56	51	61	64	58	56	60	60	60	56	Hard shower in the morning.
31	53	48	61	68	64	65	61	64	59	56	Fine.
Average	56	52	58	59	60	60	69	60	57	54	General average 57.

Maximum in the shade ... 65 | Maximum in the sun ... 72
Minimum do. ... 53 | Minimum in the open air 48

Elevation and Depressions of some of the most conspicuous Points on the Neilgherry Mountains with their Heights above the level of the Sea determined from Hallagamally, a Station whose height was ascertained by Colonel Lambton to be 1,407·6 Feet (see 2nd Vol. of his Memoir).

Stations at	Stations observed.	Apparent Elevation and Depression.	Continued Arcs.	Refraction.	Elevations above the Sea.	
					Stations.	Height.
Shavanumputty	Kallagamalli	0 14 10 D.	25 35 9	4 05 4⅙	Shavanumputty Hill ...	1654·9
Kallagamalli	Shavanumputty	0 3 15 D.				
Shavanumputty	Rungasawmy Peak ...	1 43 20 E.	21 59 2	3 39 6⅛	Rungasawmy Peak ...	5937·6
Rungasawmy Peak	Shavanumputty	1 58 00 D.				
Thavanumpatty	Villachy Curdú	0 4 30 E.	6 39 6	1 34 8⅙	Villachy Curdú	1728·1
Villachy Curdú	Shavanumputty	0 8 00 D.				
Do.	Rungasawmy Peak ...	2 30 10 E.	15 26 2	3 03 1⅕	Rungasawmy Peak ...	5936·5
Rungasawmy Peak	Villachy Curdú	2 39 30 D.				
Villachy Curdú	Dodabetta	3 22 30 E.	18 54 7	2 57 $3\frac{1}{18}$	Dodabetta	8716·9
Dodabetta	Villachy Curdú	3 35 30 D.				
Rungasawmy Peak	Dodabetta	1 38 30 E.	15 10 8	2 35 4	Do.	8719·2
Dodabetta	Rungasawmy Peak ...	1 48 30 D.				
Do.	Múrkúrty Peak	0 18 00 D.	13 0 3	2 15 0	Múrkúrty Peak	8402·7
Do.	Koonda Peak	0 21 00 D.	12 18 7	2 00 0	Koonda Peak	8353·0
Do.	Kudiakadbet	0 14 30 D.	11 44 0	1 4 0	Kudiakad	8502·1
Do.	Davarbetta	2 48 00 D.	7 26 5	7 0 0	Davarbetta	6595·2
Rungasawmy Peak	Do.	0 25 30 E.	13 27 5	2 0 0	Do.	6656·7
Villachy Curdú	Do.	3 50 00 E.	20 19 0	7 30 0	Do.	6460·2
Rungasawmy Peak ...	Koondamoga	1 24 30 E.	11 46 0	0 38 0⅐	Koondamoga	7816·9
Koondamoga	Rungasawmy Peak ...	1 35 00 D.				
Rungasawmy Peak	Koonda Hill	0 58 30 E.	6 38 0	0 38 0¼	Koonda Hill	6555·8
Koonda Hill	Rungasawmy Peak ...	1 4 00 D.				

Elevations and Depressions of some of the most conspicuous Points on the Neilgherry Mountains with their Heights above the level of the Sea determined from Hallagamally, a Station whose height was ascertained by Colonel Lambton to be 1407·6 *Feet* (see 2nd *Vol. of his Memoir*)—(Continued).

Stations at	Stations observed.	Apparent Elevation and Depression.	Continued Arcs.	Refraction.	Elevations above the Sea. Stations.	Height.
Koonda Hill	Kodanaád	0 26 00 E.	5 14 0	0 37 0$\frac{1}{3}$	Kodanád	6815·7
Kodanád	Koonda Hill	0 20 00 D.				
Dodabetta	Kokulbetta	2 38 0 D.	5 16 0	0 38 0	Kokulbetta	7267·5
Do.	Tantaurbetta	1 24 30 D.	2 17 0	...	Davursolay	8380
Do.	Bevoybetta	1 34 00 D.	1 07 0	...	Bevoybetta	8488·2
Oorbetta	Koonda Hill	1 15 00 D.	2 45 0	...	Oorbetta	69150
Do.	Dimhutty Bungalow ...	12 12 00 D.	0 39 0	...	Dimhutty Bungalow ...	65068
Shavanumputty	Kooreddy Peak	4 28 57 E.	7 02 0	0 45 0	Kooreddy Peak	5128·7
Villachy Curdú	Do.	4 6 30 E.	7 40 0	0 45 0	Do.	5113·1
Shavanumputty	Coimbatore Palace ...	0 16 00 D.	6 54 0	7 42 0$\frac{1}{4}$	Coimbatore Palace ...	14839
Coimbatore Palace	Shavanumputty	0 12 30 E.				
Shavanumputty	Iyasawmy Peak	1 31 10 E.	13 21 8	2 30 9$\frac{1}{5}$	Iyasawmy Peak	3901·4
Iyasawmy Peak	Shavanumputty	1 39 30 D.				
Rungasawmy Peak	Danaikencottah	9 9 30 D.	4 59 2	1 14 6$\frac{1}{3}$	Danaikencottah ...	1066·0
Danaikencottah	Rungasawmy Peak ...	9 6 00 E.				
Perriakunjee	Allattoor Hill	2 42 15 D.	19 44 3	3 00 0	Allattoor Hill Fort	5404·0
			Allattoor Hill height determined by Colonel Lambton		...	1228·4
					Perriakunjee	6627·4
Perriakunjee	Dodabetta	0 30 30 E.	28 35 3	2 32 0	Dodabetta	8752·9
Dodabetta	Perriakunjee	0 54 00 D.				

DARAPOORAM,
18th March 1873.

(Signed) B. S. WARD, Lieut. and Bt. Captain,
Assistant, Surveyor-General's Department.

The following bearings and distances may be requisite if the calculations are to be revised; they will properly appear in the series of triangles which will accompany the Coimbatore Survey.

Kallagannully to Shavanumputty	... 79 N, 10 W.	155,763	feet.
Shavanumputty to Villachy Curdú	... 12 N, 13 W.	40,289	„
Allattoor Hill to Perriakunjee	... 22 N, 44 E.	119,517	„
Perriakunjee to Dodabetta	... 9 N, 26 E.	173,954	„
Villachy Curdú to Dodabetta	... 50 N, 47 W.	114,814	„
Shavanumputty to Rungasawmy Peak.	3 N, 14 W.	132,991	„

(Signed) B. S. WARD.

No. 21-*A.*—*Statement showing the Strength and Cost of the Police Force of the Nílagiri District excluding South-East Wainád Division for the year* 1878.

Rank.	Strength on the 31st Dec. 1878.		Pay.	Horse Allowance.	Pay and Horse Allowance.	Cost of Clothing.	Total Cost.	Contingencies.	Cost per Head of Population.	Cost per Square Mile.
	Sanctioned.	Actual	RS. A. P.	RS. A. P.	RS. A. P.	RS. A. P.	RS. A. P.	RS. A. P.	RS. A. P.	RS. A. P.
Chief Inspector	1	1	4,200 0 0	300 0 0	4,500 0 0	...	4,500 0 0	824 3 6	0 9 3	37 4 6
Inspectors	1	...	900 0 0	300 0 0	1,200 0 0	...	1,200 0 0			
Sub-Inspectors	1	1	624 0 0	...	624 0 0	...	624 0 0			
Chief Constables	1	1	480 0 0	...	480 0 0	24 1 0	504 1 0			
Head Constables	19	16	4,608 0 0	...	4,608 0 0	310 12 2	4,918 12 2			
Constables	119	106	14,552 0 0	...	14,552 0 0	1,959 14 4	16,511 14 4			
Total ...	142	125	25,364 0 0	600 0 0	25,964 0 0	2,294 11 6	28,258 11 6	824 3 6	...	...

No. 21.*B.*—*Statement showing the Strength and Cost of the Police Force of the South-East Wainád Division in Nílagiri District for the year* 1878.

Rank.	Strength on the 31st Dec. 1878.		Pay.	Horse Allowance.	Pay and Horse Allowance.	Cost of Clothing.	Total Cost.	Contingencies.	Cost per Head of Population.	Cost per Square Mile.
	Sanctioned.	Actual								
			RS. A. P.	RS. A. P.	RS. A. P.	RS. A. P.	RS. A. P.	RS. A. P.	RS. A. P.	RS. A. P.
Inspectors	1	1	1,200 0 0	120 0 0	1,320 0 0	...	1,320 0 0			
Sub-Inspectors	...	...	...	...	...	...	...			
Chief Constables ...	...	...	...	...	...	...	...	97 5 6	74 5 8	33 1 3
Head Constables ...	4	3	1,248 0 0	...	1,248 0 0	110 11 10	1,358 11 10			
Constables	34	30	5,364 0 0	...	5,364 0 0	919 12 8	6,283 12 8			
Total ...	39	34	7,812 0 0	120 0 0	7,932 0 0	1,030 8 6	8,962 8 6	97 5 6	...	...

No. 22.—*Statement of Grave Crimes occurred in the Years* 1870-71 *and* 1875-76 *in the District of Nilagiris.*

Crimes.	1870-71.						1875-76.					
	Cases		Persons		Property		Cases		Persons		Property	
	Reported.	Detected.	Arrested.	Convicted.	Lost.	Recovered.	Reported.	Detected.	Arrested.	Convicted.	Lost.	Recovered.
Murder	...	...	...	...	...	...	2	2	21	10	...	...
Culpable homicide	...	...	...	...	...	...	1	1	1	1	...	...
Dacoity	2	1	7	5	41	10	...	...	...	...	...	...
Highway robbery	...	...	...	...	...	...	1	...	2	...	8	8
Robbery	2	2	2	2	23	13	5	2	17	3	160	100
House-breaking	18	5	17	6	1,333	35	22	9	20	11	328	43

No. 23.—*Comparative Statement showing the Result of Police Operations in regard to each Great Class of Crime usually dealt with by the Police in the Nílagiri District during the Year* 1875-76.

Number of Heading.	Class of Crime.	Cognizable Cases reported.		Persons arrested without Warrant.					
				Number of Persons arrested.		Released without Trial.		Acquitted including released on Appeal or at Sessions.	
		From 1st April 1875.	From 1st January to 31st March 1876.	From 1st April 1875.	From 1st January to 31st March 1876.	From 1st April 1875.	From 1st January to 31st March 1876.	From 1st April 1875.	From 1st January to 31st March 1876.
1	Offences relating to the Army and Navy.	...	...	...	...	...	...	...	...
2	Offences against public justice.	...	...	...	...	...	...	...	...
3	Offences relating to coin and stamps.	1	1	1	1	...	...	...	...
4	Murder for sake of robbery.	...	...	...	...	...	...	...	...
5	Murder from other motives.	2	...	21	...	...	...	11	...
6	Culpable homicide ...	1	...	1	...	...	...	...	...
7	Suicide	...	...	...	...	...	...	...	...
8	Other serious offences against the person not connected with attacks on property.	4	2	11	2	3	2	1	...
9	Public and local nuisances.	7	1	10	9	...	...	...	...
10	Offences against property accompanied with personal violence or preparation for hurt.	6	...	20	...	20	...	...	...
11	Theft by house-breaking.	21	2	18	3	7	2	1	...
12	Theft	178	36	271	51	69	8	33	4
13	Receiving stolen property.	9	2	16	2	5	...	3	...
14	Mischief of a serious character.	3	...	2	...	2	...	...	...
15	Belonging to a gang of dacoits, robbers, and thieves.	...	...	...	...	...	...	...	...
16	Vagrancy and bad character.	...	...	...	...	...	...	...	...
17	Breaches of special laws cognizable by Police.	903	220	956	251	154	71	61	30
18	Minor offences not cognizable by Police but prosecuted by information before Magistrate.	...	...	...	...	...	...	...	...

No. 23.—*Comparative Statement showing the Result of Police Operations in regard to each Great Class of Crime usually dealt with by the Police in the Nilagiri District during the Year* 1875-76—(Continued).

Number of Heading.	Class of Crime.	Persons arrested without Warrant—(*Continued*).						Cases prosecuted by information before Magistrate.	
		Ordered to find Security.		Finally convicted.		Average Number of Days occupied in each Case.		Number of Informations lodged.	
		From 1st April 1875.	From 1st January to 31st March 1876.	From 1st April 1875.	From 1st January to 31st March 1876.	From 1st April 1875.	From 1st January to 31st March 1876.	From 1st April 1875.	From 1st January to 31st March 1876.
1	Offences relating to the Army and Navy.	...	...	...	...	...	...	...	...
2	Offences against public justice.	...	...	...	...	...	...	1	1
3	Offences relating to coin and stamps.	...	...	1	1	...	...	...	...
4	Murder for sake of robbery.	...	...	...	...	...	...	...	...
5	Murder from other motives.	...	...	10	...	...	...	...	...
6	Culpable homicide ...	...	...	1	...	...	...	...	...
7	Suicide	...	...	...	...	...	...	...	...
8	Other serious offences against the person not connected with attacks on property.	..	...	7	...	...	...	...	...
9	Public and local nuisances.	...	...	10	9	...	...	3	...
10	Offences against property accompanied with personal violence or preparation for hurt.	...	...	...	...	...	...	...	...
11	Theft by house-breaking.	...	...	10	1	...	...	...	...
12	Theft	...	...	169	39	...	...	...	...
13	Receiving stolen property.	...	...	8	2	...	...	...	...
14	Mischief of a serious character.	...	...	...	...	...	...	...	...
15	Belonging to a gang of dacoits, robbers, and thieves.	...	...	...	...	...	...	...	...
16	Vagrancy and bad character.	...	...	...	...	...	...	...	...
17	Breaches of special laws cognizable by Police.	...	...	741	150	...	...	...	...
18	Minor offences not cognizable by Police but prosecuted by information before Magistrate.	...	...	...	...	...	...	...	...

No. 23.—*Comparative Statement showing the Result of Police Operations in regard to each Great Class of Crime usually dealt with by the Police in the Nílagiri District during the Year* 1875-76—(Continued).

Number of Heading.	Class of Crime.	Cases prosecuted by information before Magistrate—(*Continued*).							
		Number of Persons arrested.		Number acquitted.		Number ordered to find Security.		Number convicted.	
		From 1st April 1875.	From 1st January to 31st March 1876.	From 1st April 1875.	From 1st January to 31st March 1876.	From 1st April 1875.	From 1st January to 31st March 1876.	From 1st April 1875.	From 1st January to 31st March 1876.
1	Offences relating to the Army and Navy.	...	...	...	...	...	...	...	...
2	Offences against public justice.	1	1	...	1	...	...	1	...
3	Offences relating to coin and stamps.	...	...	...	...	...	...	...	...
4	Murder for sake of robbery.	...	...	...	...	...	...	...	...
5	Murder from other motives.	...	...	...	...	...	...	...	...
6	Culpable homicide ...	...	...	...	...	...	...	...	...
7	Suicide	...	...	...	...	...	...	...	...
8	Other serious offences against the person not connected with attacks on property.	...	...	...	...	...	...	...	...
9	Public and local nuisances.	5	..	...	...	...	...	5	...
10	Offences against property accompanied with personal violence or preparation for hurt.	...	...	...	...	...	...	...	...
11	Theft by house-breaking.	...	...	...	...	...	...	...	...
12	Theft	...	...	...	...	...	...	...	...
13	Receiving stolen property.	...	...	...	...	...	...	...	...
14	Mischief of a serious character.	...	...	...	...	...	...	...	...
15	Belonging to a gang of dacoits, robbers, and thieves.	...	...	...	...	...	...	...	...
16	Vagrancy and bad character.	...	...	...	...	...	...	...	...
17	Breaches of special laws cognizable by Police.	...	...	...	...	...	...	...	...
18	Minor offences not cognizable by Police but prosecuted by information before Magistrate.	...	...	...	...	...	...	...	...

No. 24.—*Comparative Statement showing the Result of Police Operations in regard to each Great Class of Crime usually dealt with by the Police in the Nilagiri District during the Year* 1870-71.

Number of Heading.	Class of Crime.	Cognizable Cases reported.		Persons arrested without Warrant. Number of Persons arrested.		Persons arrested without Warrant. Released without trial.		Persons arrested without Warrant. Acquitted including released on Appeal or at Sessions.	
		From 1st April 1870.	From 1st January to 31st March 1871.	From 1st April 1870.	From 1st January to 31st March 1871.	From 1st April 1870.	From 1st January to 31st March 1871.	From 1st April 1870.	From 1st January to 31st March 1871.
1	Offences relating to Army and Navy.	...	...	...	...	...	...	...	...
2	Offences against public justice.	4	...	4	...	...	...	...	...
3	Offences relating to coin and stamps.	1	...	1	...	...	...	...	...
4	Murder for sake of robbery.	...	...	...	...	...	...	...	...
5	Murder from other motives.	...	...	...	...	...	...	...	...
6	Culpable homicide ...	...	...	...	...	...	...	...	...
7	Suicide	1	...	...	...	...	...	...	
8	Other serious offences against the person not connected with attacks on property.	9	1	22	1	...	...	6	1
9	Public and local nuisances.	7	...	9	...	...	...	...	...
10	Offences against property accompanied with personal violence.	...	...	...	...	...	...	...	...
11	Theft by house-breaking.	15	3	16	1	...	...	11	...
12	Theft	123	29	182	52	...	...	11	30
13	Receiving stolen property.	11	2	11	3	...	...	4	2
14	Mischief of a serious character.	...	1	...	...	...	...	...	...
15	Belonging to a gang of dacoits, robbers, and thieves.	...	...	...	...	...	...	...	...
16	Vagrancy and bad characters.	...	...	..	...	...	...	...	...
17	Breaches of special laws cognizable by Police.	354	15	480	20	...	...	18	2
18	Minor offences not cognizable by Police but prosecuted by information before Magistrate.	67	...	69	...	...	...	40	...

No. 24.—*Comparative Statement showing the Result of Police Operations in regard to each Great Class of Crime usually dealt with by the Police in the Nílagiri District during the Year* 1870-71.—(Continued).

Number of Heading.	Class of Crime.	Persons arrested without Warrant—(*Continued*). Ordered to find Security. From 1st April 1870.	Ordered to find Security. From 1st January to 31st March 1871.	Finally convicted. From 1st April 1870.	Finally convicted. From 1st January to 31st March 1871.	Average Number of Days occupied in each Case. From 1st April 1870.	Average Number of Days occupied in each Case. From 1st January to 31st March 1871.	Cases prosecuted by information before Magistrate. Number of Informations lodged. From 1st April 1870.	Number of Informations lodged. From 1st January to 31st March 1871.
1	Offences relating to Army and Navy.	...	...	...	...	...	...	...	...
2	Offences against public justice.	...	...	4	...	...	...	...	...
3	Offences relating to coin and stamps.	...	...	1	...	...	...	...	...
4	Murder. for sake of robbery.	...	...	...	...	...	...	...	...
5	Murder. from other motives.	...	...	...	...	...	...	...	...
6	Culpable homicide ...	...	...	...	...	...	...	...	...
7	Suicide	...	...	...	...	...	...	...	...
8	Other serious offences against the person not connected with attacks on property.	...	...	16	...	...	...	...	...
9	Public and local nuisances.	...	...	9	...	...	...	...	...
10	Offences against property accompanied with personal violence.	...	...	...	...	...	...	...	...
11	Theft by house-breaking.	...	...	5	...	...	...	...	...
12	Theft	...	...	171	...	...	...	..	...
13	Receiving stolen property.	...	...	7	...	...	...	...	...
14	Mischief of a serious character.	...	...	...	...	...	...	...	...
15	Belonging to a gang of dacoits, robbers and thieves.	...	...	...	...	...	...	...	...
16	Vagrancy and bad characters.	...	...	...	...	...	...	...	...
17	Breaches of special laws cognizable by Police.	...	...	462	...	...	...	...	...
18	Minor offences not cognizable by Police but prosecuted by information before Magistrate.	...	...	29	...	...	...	...	...

No. 24.—*Comparative Statement showing the Result of Police Operations in regard to each Great Class of Crime usually dealt with by the Police in the Nilagiri District during the Year* 1870-71—(Continued).

Number of Heading.	Class of Crime.	Cases prosecuted by information before Magistrate—(*Continued*).							
		Number of Persons arrested.		Number acquitted.		Number ordered to find Security.		Number convicted.	
		From 1st April 1870.	From 1st January to 31st March 1871.	From 1st April 1870.	From 1st January to 31st March 1871.	From 1st April 1870.	From 1st January to 31st March 1871.	From 1st April 1870.	From 1st January to 31st March 1871.
1	Offences relating to Army and Navy.	...	...	...	...	...	...	...	...
2	Offences against public justice.	...	...	...	...	...	...	...	...
3	Offences relating to coin and stamps.	...	...	...	...	...	...	...	...
4	Murder for sake of robbery.	...	...	...	...	...	...	...	...
5	Murder from other motives.	...	...	...	...	...	...	...	...
6	Culpable homicide ...	...	...	...	...	...	...	...	...
7	Suicide	...	...	...	...	...	...	...	...
8	Other serious offences against the person not connected with attacks on property.	...	...	...	...	...	...	...	...
9	Public and local nuisances.	...	...	...	...	...	...	...	...
10	Offences against property accompanied with personal violence.	...	...	...	...	...	...	...	...
11	Theft by house-breaking.	...	...	...	...	...	...	...	...
12	Theft	...	...	...	...	...	...	...	...
13	Receiving stolen property.	...	...	...	...	...	...	...	...
14	Mischief of a serious character.	...	...	...	...	...	...	...	...
15	Belonging to a gang of dacoits, robbers, and thieves.	...	...	...	...	...	...	...	...
16	Vagrancy and bad character.	...	...	...	...	...	...	...	...
17	Breaches of special laws cognizable by Police.	...	...	...	...	...	...	...	...
18	Minor offences not cognizable by Police but prosecuted by information before Magistrate.	...	...	...	...	...	...	...	...

No. 25.—*Detail List showing Strength, &c., of the Police Force of the Nílagiri District*, 1878.

Number.	Names of Stations.	Force kept at each Station.					Total.	Names of principal Villages in each Police Station charge.	Beats.
		Inspectors.	Sub-Inspectors.	Chief Constables.	Head Constables.	Constables.			
1	Ootacamand Town...	...	1	...	3	29	33	1. Kandal	3 beats at night 5 at during day.
2	Ootacamand Taluq...	*1	...	...	2	13	16	1. Adjanakal. 2. Munnahatti. 3. Oosahatti, 4. Hulada.	3 beats.
3	Paikare	...	...	...	1	3	4	1. Kuriamand. 2. Kurdamand.	3 do.
4	Neduvattam ...	...	...	...	1	5	6	All estates in Ouchterlony Valley ; no villages.	3 do.
5	Kalhatti	...	...	...	1	3	4	1. Yalkoni. 2. Thataneri. 3. Hoolhatti.	3 do.
6	Masnikovil	...	...	...	1	8	9	1. Mavanalla. 2. Hossur. 3. Chokanalli. 4. Bustipur.	5 do.
7	Kotagiri	...	...	...	1	6	7	1. Thokalatti. 2. Danad. 3. Kunjapani. 4. Kodanad.	5 do.
8	Wellington	1	...	1	3	20	25	1. Jakatalla. 2. Yellanulla. 3. Thokalutti.	6 do.
9	Coonoor	...	...	...	1	5	6	1. Burliar	2 do.
10	Coonoor Town ...	...	...	...	1	3	4	1. Coonoor Town ...	3 do.
11	Distilling Guard at Ootacamand.	...	...	...	1	3	4		
	Total ...	2	1	1	16	100	120		

* Chief Inspector.

No. 26.—*Detail List showing Strength, &c., of the Police Force of the South-East Wainad Division in Nílagiri District*, 1878.

Number.	Names of Stations.	Force kept at each Station.					Total.	Names of principal Villages in each Police Station charge.	Beats.
		Inspectors.	Sub-Inspectors.	Chief Constables.	Head Constables.	Constables.			
1	Gúdalúr	1	...	...	2	18	21	......	4 beats.
2	Cherambádi ...	...	...	...	1	6	7	......	3 do.
3	Déválla	...	...	..	1	6	7	......	3 do.
4	Nádgáni	...	...	...	...	4	4	......	3 do.
	Total ...	1	...	...	4	34	39		

No. 27.—*Rules for the sale of Waste Lands on the Neilgherry Hills, passed by the Hon'ble the Governor in Council on the 6th March* 1863, *and numbered* 478*A*.

I. Waste lands in which no rights of private proprietorship or exclusive occupancy exist, and which may not be reserved as hereinafter* provided, may, until further notice, be sold under the following rules:—

* Rule XVIII.

II. Applications for land under these rules shall be addressed to the Collector of the Coimbatore District, and shall comprise the following particulars:—

(*a*.) The estimated area of the land applied for.

(*b*.) The situation of the land and its boundaries, as accurately as can be stated.

III. No lot shall exceed 500 acres, unless otherwise specially ordered by Government. Within towns and villages the maximum extent of a lot shall be ten acres. But any person may apply for several contiguous lots, each not exceeding the above limits.

IV. Every lot shall be compact, and as nearly as possible a parallelogram. When the land touches any road, or river, the length of the road or water frontage shall not exceed one-half of the depth of the lot, and in all other cases the blocks will be so laid out that, as far as practicable, their length shall not exceed half their depth.

V. No lot shall be sold until it has been surveyed, and durable boundary marks have been erected.

VI. If, on receipt of an application under Rule II, the Collector has reason to believe that the land applied for is saleable under these rules, he shall call upon the applicant to deposit with him the estimated cost of surveying the land and of marking it out with durable boundary marks, unless the land is already surveyed and demarcated. The Collector will refund to the depositor any portion of his deposit which may not be actually expended in the survey and demarcation, and the depositor shall pay any deficiency.

VII. If the applicant fails to deposit the sum required under Rule VI within six weeks from the date of demand, his application shall be null and void.

VIII. On receipt of the deposit required under Rule VI, the Collector shall, as soon as possible, cause the land applied for to be surveyed and marked out, and shall exclude from the lot all excess which may be found on survey beyond the limits prescribed in Rule III, and shall advertise the lot for sale on a given day, to be fixed so as to admit of the notice required in Rule IX being given.

IX. The advertisement shall be in English and Tamil, and shall specify the locality, extent, and boundaries of the lot, the aggregate annual assessment, and the place, time, and conditions of sale. It shall be posted for three clear months on the land itself, as well as in the neighbouring villages, in the offices of the Collector and the Tahsildar of the taluk, and the nearest police office. A notification of the intended sale shall also be inserted in the District Gazette. The Collector shall at his discretion fix the time and place of sale, and may alter both if necessary, provided that not less than fourteen days' notice be publicly given of every such alteration, and that no land be sold until it has been advertised, as aforesaid, for three full months.

X. The Collector shall send written notice of the place and time of sale, as also of any alteration, under the provisions of Rule IX, to the applicant; but no sale shall be disturbed in consequence of the non-receipt of such notice, or delayed in consequence of the non-appearance of the applicant.

XI. On receipt of applications for lands under these rules, the Collector will hold a preliminary inquiry, and if he sees reason to believe that claims will be put forward for the lands applied for, he will duly warn the applicant that the survey will be undertaken only at his request and at his risk. Should the applicant prefer that the survey should be proceeded with on these terms, the same will be done, and if after the survey it should prove that the lands are not saleable under these rules, the applicant must pay the expense of surveying them, as well as of surveying any excess beyond the limits prescribed in Rule III. If no such warning be given, and the land should eventually prove not to be saleable, then the survey will be at the expense of Government. An applicant withdrawing his application prior to the sale of the land will be entitled to the refund of so much only of his deposit under Rule VI as may not be expended.

XII. On the withdrawal of an application, it shall be discretional with the Collector to proceed with the sale of the land or not, as he considers best for the public interests.

XIII. The upset price shall in all cases be merely the cost of the survey and of the erection of durable boundary marks. If the original applicant be the purchaser, he shall receive credit for his deposit or payment; otherwise the amount shall be repaid to him at once from the sale proceeds.

XIV. If, before the time of sale, no claim of private proprietorship, or of exclusive occupancy, or of any other right incompatible with the sale of the land under these rules, be preferred to the land, the lot shall, as advertised, be put up to auction, and sold to the highest bidder above the upset price, subject to an annual assessment, payable on or before the 30th June of each and every year, of one rupee for each acre of land contained in the lot.

XV. The successful bidder shall, immediately on the sale being declared, pay down 10 per cent. of the price. The residue of the purchase-money may, at the option of the purchaser, be paid in full within thirty days, or in three yearly instalments of equal amount, bearing interest from the day of sale at the rate of 6 per cent. per annum. In the former case, on payment of the residue of the purchase-money, a deed, in the Form X annexed to these rules, shall be furnished to the purchaser and possession given. In the latter case the land will remain hypothecated to Government as security for the punctual discharge of the unpaid principal and interest as they fall due, and on default of any such payment the Government may re-enter and repossess themselves of the land, or, at their option, the land may be resold at the expense and risk of the defaulter. When the purchaser elects to pay the purchase-money by instalments, he shall not receive possession until he has duly executed the deed marked Y annexed to these rules. When the conditions of Deed Y have been duly fulfilled, a deed in the Form X will be issued in lieu of it.

XVI. The sale shall be conducted under and subject to the following conditions of sale :—

(1.)—" That the highest bidder above the upset price shall be the purchaser of the premises; and if any dispute arise between two or more bidders at the same price, the premises shall be immediately put up again at the last preceding undisputed bidding and resold.

(2.)—" That immediately after the lot is knocked down, the purchaser thereof shall pay to the Collector a deposit of Rupees 10 per centum in part of his purchase-money, and intimate to the Collector whether he elects to pay the residue within thirty days, or by three yearly instalments, as provided by the rules passed by the Hon'ble the Governor in Council, under date the 6th day of March 1863, No. 478A, and shall at the same time sign an acknowledgment in one of the Forms U or V* (as the case may require) annexed to the said rules.

(3.)—That if the purchaser shall elect to pay the residue of his purchase-money within thirty days, he shall within thirty days from the day of sale pay to the said Collector the residue of his purchase-money, and shall thereupon receive a conveyance of the premises in the form marked X annexed to the said rules.

(4.)—" That if the purchaser shall elect to pay the residue of his purchase-money by three yearly instalments, he shall within ten days from the day of sale execute a deed in the form marked Y annexed to the said rules.

(5.)—" That all persons desirous of becoming purchasers are to satisfy themselves as to the identity and correct description of the property, and the measurement and boundaries of the premises, previous to the sale; as by having the premises knocked down to him, the purchaser thereof shall be held to have waived all objections to any mistakes that may afterwards appear to have been made in the description of the premises, as well as to any other error whatever in the particulars of the property.

(6.)—" That if the purchaser elects to pay within thirty days, and if, from any cause whatever, the purchase shall not be completed by the thirtieth day from the day of sale, or if the purchaser shall elect to pay by instalments, and shall neglect for ten days from the day of

* These forms have been omitted in this Appendix.

sale to execute a deed in the form marked Y annexed to the said rules, then the purchaser shall pay to the Collector interest at the rate of Rupees 12 per cent. per annum on the remainder of his purchase-money from the day of sale until the purchase shall be completed in the one case, or until a deed in the form Y be executed in the other cases without prejudice, nevertheless, to the right of resale reserved by the seventh condition.

(7.)—"That if the purchaser shall neglect or refuse to comply with the above conditions, or any of them, his deposit money shall be forfeited and retained by Government, and the Government shall be at liberty to resell the premises either by public auction or private contract without the necessity of previously tendering a conveyance to the purchaser ; and the deficiency, if any, arising from such resale, together with all expenses attending it, shall be made good by the purchaser at the present sale, who shall so neglect or refuse, as and for liquidated damages."

XVII. If, before the time of sale, a claim of private proprietorship, or of exclusive occupancy, or of any other right incompatible with the sale of the land under these rules, shall be preferred to the land or any part of it, the Collector shall postpone the sale of the land until such claim shall be disposed of in due course of law.

XVIII. Reserves of grazing and forest land, of land for the growth of firewood, for building sites, parks, recreation grounds, and the like, and of land required for other special purposes, are not to be sold under these rules without the express sanction of the Government. A register of such reserves will be maintained in the Collector's office, and will be open to inspection by intending applicants at such times and under such rules as the Collector may prescribe by notification in the District Gazette.

XIX. The annual assessment on lands sold under these rules may at any time be redeemed by the owner by payment of a sum equal to twenty-five times the said annual assessment, and the lands so redeemed shall thereafter be for ever free from all demand on the part of the State on account of land-revenue. On payment of the redemption money the owner of the land shall be furnished with a deed in the form Z annexed to these rules.

XX. Arrears of annual assessment shall be recoverable in the same manner as arrears of ryotwary land-revenue are or may be recoverable by law for the time being in force in the Madras Presidency.

XXI. Lands sold or redeemed under these rules shall, nevertheless, continue subject to all general taxes and local rates payable by law or custom.

XXII. The existing and customary rights of Government, of other proprietors and of the public, in existing roads and paths, and in streams running through or bounding lands sold under these rules, are reserved, and in no way affected by the sale of such lands under these rules.

XXIII. Nothing contained in these rules shall be held to debar the Government from granting waste land on putta, cowle, or otherwise at their discretion as heretofore.

X.

No.

THIS INDENTURE made the (a) day of one thousand eight hundred and sixty (a) BETWEEN the Right Hon'ble the Secretary of State for India in Council of the one part and (A.B.) of in the district of (b) of the other part: WHEREAS under the rules for the sale of waste land passed by the Hon'ble the Governor of Fort St. George in Council on the sixth day of March one thousand eight hundred and sixty-three and numbered 478A the Collector of Coimbatore did on the (a) day of one thousand eight hundred and sixty (a) offer for sale by public auction the land described in the schedule here-under written subject to annual assessment in perpetuity on the said land of Rupees (a) AND WHEREAS at such sale the said (A.B.) offered the sum of Rupees (a) for such land subject to such assessment and being the highest bidder was declared to be the purchaser thereof according to the terms and conditions in such rules contained: AND WHEREAS previously to the execution of these presents the said (A.B.) has paid into the treasury of the said Collector to the credit of Her Majesty's Government of India the full sum of Rupees (a) NOW THIS INDENTURE WITNESSETH that in consideration of the said sum of Rupees (a) so paid by the said (A.B.) (the receipt whereof is hereby acknowledged), the said Secretary of State in Council doth sell alien and convey unto the said (A.B.) THE piece or parcel of land containing British statute acres (a) situated on the Shervaroy Hills in the collectorate of Salem bounded as mentioned in the schedule hereunder written and delineated in the map or plan hereunto annexed together with all erections and buildings (if any) thereon erected and built AND all products both above and below the surface ways paths passages waters water-courses wells fences ditches easements profits rights members and appurtenances whatsoever to the said land and premises and every or any part thereof belonging or appertaining EXCEPT and always reserved out of these presents all existing and customary rights of Government and of proprietors of lands adjoining or lying near to the land and premises hereby conveyed in all existing roads and paths and in streams of water running through or bounding the land and premises hereby conveyed to HOLD the said land and premises hereby conveyed with the appurtenances to the said (A.B.) his heirs personal representatives and assigns for ever SUBJECT nevertheless to the payment by the said (A.B.) his heirs personal representatives and assigns to the said Secretary of State in Council his successors or assigns yearly and every year for ever hereafter of the clear sum of Rupees (a) on or before the thirtieth day of June in each year AND LIKEWISE subject to the payment by the said (A.B.) his heirs personal representatives and assigns of all general taxes and local rates now existing or which at any time hereafter may be imposed by law as also to the covenants and conditions hereinafter contained and the said (A.B.) for himself his heirs personal representatives and assigns doth hereby covenant with the Secretary of State in Council his successors and assigns in manner following (that is to say) that he the said (A.B.) his heirs personal representatives and assigns will yearly and every year for ever hereafter pay on or before the thirtieth day of June in each year the said sum of Rupees (*a*) AND LIKEWISE will at his and their own costs and charges forthwith erect and at all times hereafter maintain and keep in good repair permanent boundary marks round the land and premises hereby conveyed AND FURTHER that in case he the said (A.B.) his heirs personal representatives or assigns shall make default in payment of the said annual assessment of Rupees (*a*) or any part thereof as and when the same shall become payable under the covenant hereinbefore contained THEN and in such case and so often as the same shall happen the said assessment of Rupees (*a*) and all arrears thereof shall and may be treated as arrears of ryotwary land-revenue and may be recovered in the same manner as ryotwary land-revenue is now or at any time hereafter may be recoverable PROVIDED always and it is hereby declared and agreed by and between the parties hereto that the said (A.B.) his heirs personal representatives and assigns shall at any time be at liberty to redeem such annual assessment by payment to the said Secretary of State in Council his successors or assigns of the sum of Rupees (*c*) of lawful money of British India and that immediately after such payment the land and premises hereby conveyed shall be for ever free from all demand for land-revenue. IN WITNESS whereof the Hon'ble the Governor of Fort St. George in Council on behalf of the said Secretary of State in Council hath hereunto affixed the seal of the said Governor in Council and the said (A.B.) hath set his hand and seal the day and year first above written.

Y.

THIS INDENTURE made the (*a*) day of one thousand eight hundred and sixty (*a*) BETWEEN the Right Hon'ble the Secretary of State for India in Council of the one part and (A.B.) of in the district of (*b*) of the other part: WHEREAS under the Rules for the sale of Waste Land passed by the Hon'ble the Governor of Fort St. George in Council on the sixth day of March one thousand eight hundred and sixty-three and numbered 478A the Collector of Coimbatore did on the (*a*) day of one thousand eight hundred and sixty (*a*) offer for sale by public auction the piece or parcel of land containing British statute acres (*a*) situated in the village of in the taluk of in the

Collectorate of Coimbatore bounded as mentioned in the schedule hereunder written and delineated in the map or plan hereunto annexed SUBJECT to the payment by the said (A.B.) his heirs personal representatives and assigns to the said Secretary of State in Council his successors or assigns yearly and every year for ever hereafter of the clear sum of Rupees (*f*) on or before the thirtieth day of June in each year : AND WHEREAS at such sale the said (A.B.) offered the sum of Rupees (*l*) for such land subject to such assessment and being the highest bidder was declared to be the purchaser thereof according to the terms and conditions in such rules contained : AND WHEREAS at the time of such sale the said (A.B.) paid into the hands of the said Collector the sum of Rupees (*a*) being the amount of deposit at the rate of Rupees 10 per cent. on the said purchase-money as required by the said rules and under the provision contained in those rules has elected to pay the balance of such purchase-money amounting to the sum of Rupees (*c*) in three yearly instalments of Rupees (*d*) each with interest on such balance or on such part thereof as shall from time to time remain unliquidated at the rate of Rupees 6 per cent. per annum.

NOW THIS INDENTURE WITNESSETH that in consideration of the said sum of Rupees (*e*) so paid to the said Collector as hereinbefore mentioned (the receipt whereof is hereby acknowledged) and of the covenants on the part of the said (A.B.) hereinafter contained the said Secretary of State in Council for himself his successors and assigns doth hereby covenant with the said (A.B.) his heirs personal representatives and assigns that on payment by the said (A.B.) his heirs personal representatives or assigns of the said sum of Rupees (*c*) with interest thereon as herein mentioned he the said Secretary of State in Council his successors or assigns will convey unto the said (A.B.) his heirs personal representatives and assigns for ever the said land and premises together with all erections and buildings (if any) thereon erected and built AND all products both above and below the surface ways paths passages waters water-courses wells fences ditches easements profits rights members and appurtenances whatsoever to the said land and premises and every or any part thereof belonging or appertaining EXCEPTING nevertheless all existing and customary rights of Government and of proprietors of lands adjoining or lying near to the said land and premises purchased as aforesaid in all existing roads and paths and streams of water running through or bounding the purchased land and premises TO BE HELD by the said (A.B.) his heirs personal representatives and assigns subject to the payment of the said yearly sum of Rupees (*f*) on the thirtieth day of June in each year as hereinbefore mentioned AND LIKEWISE subject to all general taxes and local rates now existing or which at any time hereafter may be imposed by law AND to the observance of the several conditions in the said rules contained AND the said (A.B.) for himself his heirs personal representatives and assigns doth hereby covenant with the said Secretary of State in Council his successors and assigns in manner following (that is to say) that he the said (A.B.) his heirs personal representatives and assigns will yearly and every year for ever hereafter pay on or before the thirtieth day of June in each year the said sum of Rupees (*f*) AND LIKEWISE will at his and their own costs and charges forthwith erect and at all times hereafter maintain and keep in good repair permanent boundary marks round the land and premises so purchased AND FURTHER that he the said (A.B.) his heirs personal representatives and assigns will on the (*g*) day of (*g*) which will be in the year one thousand eight hundred and sixty (*g*) pay or cause to be paid to the said Secretary of State in Council his successors or assigns the sum of Rupees (*d*) of lawful money of British India and on the (*h*) day of (*h*) which will be in the year one thousand eight hundred and sixty (*h*) a like sum of Rupees (*d*) and on the (*i*) day of (*i*) which will be in the year one thousand eight hundred and sixty (*i*) a like sum of Rupees (*d*) of like lawful money AND also will pay to the said Secretary of State in Council his successors or assigns interest at the rate of Rupees 6 per cent. per annum on the said balance of the said purchase-money or sum of Rupees (*c*) or on such part thereof as shall from time to time remain unpaid by two equal half-yearly payments on the (*j*) day of (*j*) and the (*k*) day of (*k*) in each year together with a proportionate part of like interest until the said balance shall be fully paid or satisfied or until the said Secretary of State in Council shall obtain possession of the said land and premises under the provisions hereinafter contained: AND it is hereby declared and agreed by and between the parties hereto that until default shall be made by the said (A.B.) his heirs personal representatives or assigns in payment of the said annual assessment or sum of Rupees (*f*) as and when the same shall become payable under the covenant hereinbefore contained or in payment of the said instalments or any of them or any part thereof respectively or of the said interest or any part thereof it shall be lawful for the said (A.B.) his heirs personal representatives and assigns peaceably and quietly to occupy possess and enjoy the said land and premises so purchased and receive and take the rents issues and profits thereof to and for his and their own use and benefit: AND the said (A.B.) for himself his heirs personal representatives and assigns doth hereby further covenant with the said Secretary of State in Council his successors and assigns in manner following (that is to say) that in case he the said (A.B.) his heirs personal representatives and assigns shall make default in payment of the said instalments or any or either of them or any part thereof respectively or in payment of the interest hereinbefore covenanted to be paid or any part thereof as and when such instalments and interest shall respectively become due THEN and in such case and within one month after demand of possession shall have been made on him or them by or on behalf of the said Secretary of State in Council his successors or assigns he the said (A.B.) his heirs personal representatives and assigns will deliver to any person authorized by an order passed by the Governor of Fort St. George for the time being in Council to receive the same the quiet and peaceable possession of the said land and premises together with all erections and buildings which now are or which at any time between the date of these presents and such delivery of possession may be erected and built or standing on the said land and all improvements made to the said land in the meantime: AND MOREOVER that in the event of such default being made by the said (A.B.) his heirs personal representatives and assigns or in case of the breach or non-performance of any of the covenants and arrangements herein contained on the part of the said (A.B.) his heirs personal representatives and assigns it shall be lawful for the said Secretary of State in Council his successors or assigns at any tine hereafter to resell the said premises either by public auction or private contract and if on such resale the said premises should be sold for a sum less than the said sum of Rupees (*l*) he the said (A.B.) his heirs personal representatives and assigns will pay to the said Secretary of State in Council his successors or assigns the difference between the sum for which such premises shall be re-sold and the said sum of Rupees (*l*) or it shall be lawful for the said Secretary of State in Council his successors or assigns at any time after such default or breach into and upon the said land and premises or any part thereof in the name of the whole to re-enter and the same to have again repossess and enjoy as in his and their former estate any thing hereinbefore contained to the contrary notwithstanding: AND FURTHER that in case he the said (A.B.) his heirs personal representatives and assigns shall make default in payment of the said annual assessment of Rupees (*f*) or any part thereof as and when the same shall become payable under the covenant hereinbefore contained THEN and in such case and so often as the same shall happen the said assessment of Rupees (*f*) and all arrears thereof shall and may be treated as arrears of ryotwary land-revenue and may be recovered in the same manner as ryotwary land-revenue is now or at any time hereafter may be recoverable: PROVIDED always and it is hereby declared and agreed by and between the parties hereto that the said (A.B.) his heirs personal representatives and assigns shall at any time be at liberty to redeem such annual assessment by payment to the said Secretary of State in Council his successors or assigns of the sum of Rupees (*m*) of lawful money of British India and that immediately after such payment the land and premises hereby conveyed shall be for ever free from all demand for land-revenue. IN WITNESS whereof the Hon'ble the Governor of Fort St. George in Council on behalf of the said Secretary of State in Council hath hereunto affixed the seal of the said Governor in Council and the said (A.B.) hath set his hand and seal the day and year first above written.

Z.

No.

THIS INDENTURE made the (a) day of one thousand eight hundred and sixty (a) BETWEEN the Right Hon'ble the Secretary of State for India in Council of the one part and (A.B.) of in the district of (b) of the other part: WHEREAS by an indenture dated the (a) day of one thousand eight hundred and sixty (a) and made between the said Secretary of State of the one part and the said (A.B.) of the other part the said Secretary of State for the considerations therein mentioned did sell alien and convey unto the said (A.B.) his heirs personal representatives and assigns for ever the piece or parcel of land containing British statute acres (a) situated in the village of in the taluk of in the collectorate of Coimbatore bounded as mentioned in the schedule thereunder written and delineated in the map or plan thereunto annexed with the appurtenances subject to the payment by the said (A.B.) his heirs personal representatives and assigns of the annual assessment or sum of Rupees (a) and to the payment of all general taxes and local rates then existing or which at any time thereafter might be imposed by law AS ALSO to the several exceptions covenants and conditions therein contained and in and by such reciting indenture it was declared and agreed that the said (A.B.) his heirs personal representatives and assigns should be at liberty to redeem such annual assessment by payment to the said Secretary of State in Council his successors or assigns of the sum of Rupees (a) and that immediately thereafter the said land and premises should be for ever free from all demand for land-revenue: AND WHEREAS the said (A.B.) under the said provision hath paid into the treasury of the Collector of to the credit of Her Majesty's Government of India the said sum of Rupees (a) and hath requested that the said land may be declared to be for ever hereafter absolutely freed and discharged from the payment of the said sum of Rupees (a) and of all land-revenue payable thereon and that the said land may be likewise declared to be and continue as freehold. NOW THIS INDENTURE WITNESSETH that in pursuance of the said provision and in consideration of the said sum of Rupees (a) so paid by the said (A.B.) as hereinbefore mentioned (the receipt whereof is hereby acknowledged) the said Secretary of State in Council doth remise release and for ever quit claim unto the said (A.B.) his heirs personal representatives and assigns the said annual assessment or sum of Rupees (a) AND FURTHER doth declare that the said land and premises may for ever be held as freehold fully and absolutely enfranchised exonerated acquitted and discharged by these presents from all demand on the part of Her Majesty for or on account of quit-rent assessment land-tax or other land-revenue: PROVIDED always and it is hereby declared and agreed by and between the parties hereto that in all other respects the said land and premises shall be subject to the several exceptions reservations covenants and conditions in the hereinbefore in part recited indenture contained. IN WITNESS whereof the Hon'ble the Governor of Fort St. George in Council on behalf of the said Secretary of State in Council hath hereunto affixed the seal of the said Governor in Council and the said (A.B.) hath set his hand and seal the day and year first above written.

No. 28.—Rules of the Ootacamand Lawrence Asylum.

1. The object of this Institution is to provide for the children of Soldiers of the British Army, who are serving, or have served, within the limits of the Presidency of Madras, a refuge both from the debilitating effects of a tropical climate and from the serious drawbacks to the well-being of children incidental to a barrack life; to afford them an education suitable to their condition in life, plain, practical, and essentially Christian; and, as far as practicable, to train them to useful occupations.

2. The Asylum received its designation, the "Ootacamund Lawrence Asylum," in honor of the memory of the late Sir Henry Lawrence, K.C.B. In January 1860 it was transferred to the Government of Madras; and, by an order of the Governor in Council, dated 2nd June 1862, it received its present constitution.

3. The Asylum consists of two separate branches, the male and the female, united under the general supervision and control of one head, designated the Principal, who is responsible to a governing body named the Committee of Management.

4. The Asylum is designed to provide accommodation for 300 children, viz., 200 boys and 100 girls, to which numbers it is at present limited.

5. The Institution depends for its support partly on a grant from Government and partly on voluntary contributions. The Government grant is calculated to provide for the salaries of the Principal and his staff and for the maintenance of 150 boys and 80 girls; all beyond those numbers will be maintained by the public.

6. No child will be admitted under five or above twelve years of age, except in special cases to be decided by the Committee.

7. Children entitled to the benefits of the Institution are classified as follows:—

CLASS I.—Children of pure European parentage who have lost both parents.

CLASS II.—Children of European fathers and East Indian or Native Christian mothers who have lost both parents, and children of pure European parentage who have lost only one.

CLASS III.—Children of European fathers and East Indian or Native Christian mothers who have lost one parent, and children of pure European parentage who have both parents living.

CLASS IV.—All other children of soldiers of the British Army not provided for in the preceding classes.

The order of precedence in the admission of candidates will be regulated in accordance with this classification.

8. Four years' annual subscription of Rupees 50, or a donation of Rupees 300, shall confer the title to nominate one child for each such subscription or donation ; and, in like proportion, for higher amounts; and these nominees will take precedence in admission of the other candidates in the several classes to which they belong.

9. The children of Soldiers of the ranks of Private and Corporal, who are only drawing the pay of those ranks, will be admitted free of charge. Children having living fathers above the rank of Corporal will be charged according to the following scale, except under extraordinary circumstances, when the power of exemption from, or reduction of, payment shall be exercised by the Committee:—

——	1st Child.	2nd Child.	3rd Child.
	RS. A. P.	RS. A. P.	RS. A. P.
Serjeant	3 0 0	2 0 0	*Nil.*
Serjeant-Majors	4 0 0	2 8 0	1 0 0
Soldiers retired or on Staff employ, if drawing Rupees 60, but less than Rupees 80, per mensem	5 0 0	3 0 0	2 0 0
Do. do. Rs. 80 do. Rs. 120.	9 0 0	6 0 0	4 0 0
Do. do. „ 120 do. „ 150.	12 0 0	9 0 0	6 0 0

MEMORANDUM.—In addition to the Government allowance (if any) of Rupees 2-8-0 per mensem.

10. In all cases where private Soldiers, Non-Commissioned Officers, hold appointments by which their income is increased, they shall pay the rate of that rank, the allowances of which most nearly approximate to their actual income from all sources.

11. From pensioned Soldiers whose incomes do not exceed the pay of a Private or Corporal no payment shall be demanded. Other Pensioners will be required to pay according to the foregoing rule.

12. Applications for the admission of children must be made through the Officers Commanding Regiments or the heads of depart-

ments to which the parents or guardians are attached; in the case of Pensioners, through their Paymasters or employers; and of nominations, through the Donor or Subscriber nominating. Such applications must be addressed to the Secretary, who will furnish printed forms of application and a descriptive roll to be filled up by the applicant. The baptismal certificate of the candidate will also be required with the last pay certificate, if in receipt of the Government allowance. The parents or guardians of candidates whose cases do not answer to any of the foregoing descriptions may apply direct to the Secretary.

13. The Secretary, in announcing the election of a candidate, will fix a reasonable time, to be determined by the Committee, for joining the Institution. If the summons be not attended to, the election will be considered void and another candidate chosen, excepting for reasons which shall satisfy the Committee.

14. Applications for the removal of children shall be made through the channels prescribed in Rule 12, giving one month's notice.

15. Illegitimate children, children laboring under any form of disease which is likely to incapacitate them for the ordinary duties of life, the children of fathers not Soldiers of the British Army who are serving or have served in India, and children of Soldiers who have been dismissed the service by sentence of Court Martial are ineligible.

16. The Government of the Asylum is invested in a Committee of Management, consisting of nine Members, resident for the time being on the Nilgiri Hills, four of whom are appointed by the Government and five elected.

17. The Lord Bishop of Madras and His Excellency the Commander-in-Chief are connected with the Institution in the capacity of Patrons, and are at liberty at all times to visit the Asylum, and to refer to the Committee, or to the Government, any point which they may consider demanding attention.

18. The five elective Members shall be chosen by the votes of Donors to the Institution to the amount of Rupees 300, and subscribers to the amount of Rupees 50 per annum, resident for the time being within the limits of the Presidency of Madras. Members of Committee, as such, shall be entitled to vote at each election.

19. A provisional Member shall also be elected, according to the conditions of the preceding rule, to take the place of any vacating elective Member.

20. The death or resignation of a Member, or his ceasing to reside on the Nilgiri Hills, or his failing to attend four successive monthly Meetings of the Committee without assigning satisfactory reasons shall create a vacancy.

21. A vacancy, as soon as it occurs, shall be reported by the Secretary to the Committee at their next ensuing regular Meeting; and if it be that of a Government Member, notice thereof shall forthwith

be given to the Government. If the vacancy be that of an elective Member, the provisional Member shall at once succeed thereto, and the election of a new provisional Member be proceeded with under Rule 19.

22. One month's notice of an election shall be given, and, with the voting papers to be furnished to the electors, the Committee shall submit the names of any gentlemen resident on the Nilgiris, whom they may see occasion to recommend, the majority of votes determining the election. In the event of an equality of votes in favor of any two or more candidates, the decision between them shall rest with the Committee. The notice of the election of new Members to the Committee shall also be published in the *Fort St. George Gazette*.

The Committee are empowered to frame such bye-laws as they may consider necessary for the despatch of business. They shall hold a Meeting regularly once a month on a day to be fixed by them. Four Members shall form a quorum.

24. Any three Members shall have the power of convening an Extraordinary Meeting of the Committee, giving the Secretary one week's notice of the same.

25. The Committee shall at each monthly Meeting appoint two of their Members to visit the Institution officially and to report their impressions at the next ensuing Meeting. Every department of the Institution shall be accessible to these visitors.

26. The Committee shall be at liberty to appoint, from time to time, two lady visitors, who shall be requested to visit the female branch once a month, or oftener if thought desirable, and to enter any remarks they may have to make in a book to be kept for the purpose, which, after each visit, is to be forwarded to the Secretary.

27. That Rupees 1,000 a year be paid to the Medical Officer in charge of the Asylum, and that he be required to pay a daily visit to each Institution and to make a weekly inspection of every thing affecting the health of the inmates, making a special report on such occasion; and with such arrangements the services of a simple Dresser will be sufficient for the duties to be performed with reference to those who may be sick.

28. The Principal of the Asylum shall invariably be a Clergyman of the Church of England, his appointment being subject to the approval of the Governor of Madras in Council. The appointments to all other offices in the Institutions shall be at the disposal of the Committee.

29. The Principal is in superior charge of the Institution in both its branches. He will be responsible for the general direction of the education and discipline and for the regulation of the interior economy of every department. As Principal he will hold periodical examinations of the classes both in their religious and secular studies; as Chaplain he has pastoral charge of the Institution; as Secretary he is the executive officer of the Committee. He will also take charge of the accounts. In communication with the Committee, or such

Sub-Committee as they may appoint, he will make all the necessary disbursements. In the event of his intending to resign his appointment, it is necessary that he should give six months' notice to that effect. The Committee will also give the same notice on their desiring to dispense with his services.

30. The Head Master will, under the direction of the Principal, superintend the tuition in the male branch, his special charge being the upper division of the school, and the training of pupil teachers under the provisions of Rule 45.

31. The Head Mistress will, under the direction and supervision of the Principal, have entire charge of the female branch. She will be responsible for the moral and intellectual training of the girls, who will be subject to her control both in and out of school. Her authority will be that of a parent as well as that of a teacher.

32. The domestic arrangements of the female branch will, for the present, be conducted by a Matron, who will be subordinate to the Head Mistress. She will also be required to instruct the girls in all duties of the housewifery, needle-work included, and to be present at their meals.

33. The education given in the schools shall be generally such as will fit the children to discharge their duties in that station of life in which the providence of God has placed them.

34. In the religious lesson given in open school all the leading truths of Christianity shall be inculcated without unnecessary allusion to controverted points of faith and practice.

35. The Catechisms of the various Protestant bodies may be taught in private to the children of each body.

36. The authorized version of the Bible shall be read in school.

37. At the hours in which religious instruction is given in the schools, Priests of the Church of Rome and accredited Ministers of Evangelical Protestant bodies may attend and give instruction to the children of their respective communions, a place being set apart for that purpose, on giving previous notice of their wish so to do to the Secretary.

38. Priests of the Church of Rome and accredited Ministers of Protestant bodies shall have free access to the sick of their respective communions in the Infirmary at all times.

39. Divine Service, in accordance with the rites of the Church of England, shall be celebrated twice on each Sunday in the Chapel of the Institution, all the inmates of the establishment being required to attend, subject however to the provisions of Rule 40.

40. On the application of a Priest of the Church of Rome, or accredited Minister of any Evangelical Protestant community, requesting permission to celebrate Divine Service on a Sunday with the members of his communion, a place shall be set apart for the purpose, and such members shall have permission to attend. Such application, however, must be made on the previous Saturday.

41. The form of prayers sanctioned for use in the Asylum shall be read every morning and evening throughout the year by the Principal, or such officer as he may appoint for the purpose.

42. The Institution is subject to Government inspection, and will be inspected and examined by the Government Inspector of Schools at such times as the Director of Public Instruction, in communication with the Committee, may direct.

43. There shall be an annual examination of the schools in the month of May or June, conducted by the Government Inspector of Schools, aided by such persons as may be appointed by the Committee, with the approval of the Director of Public Instruction, after which there shall be a public distribution of prizes.

44. The Committee shall have the power of selecting, from time to time, a limited number of the most promising children to be trained as pupil teachers (both boys and girls), with a view to their qualifying themselves for employment in the Educational Department of Government.

They shall be selected at about the age of 14 or 15, and continue under training for a period of (about) four years, entering into an engagement with the Committee for the time being to that effect. They shall receive 4 rupees per mensem for the first year, after which, providing their progress and conduct be satisfactory, their monthly salaries shall be increased to 5 rupees in the second, 7 rupees in the third, and 10 rupees in the fourth years of their apprenticeship. During the whole period of their engagement the half of each month's salary shall be deposited in the Government Savings' Bank, in the name of the Principal, in trust for each pupil teacher specified by name ; and should any of them be guilty of breach of engagement, the deposit shall be forfeited to the Institution.

45. Capitation money at the rate of 5 rupees per mensem shall be allowed for each of the pupil teachers to the Master or Mistress entrusted with their training.

46. According to the means at the disposal of the Committee, and to the opportunities that may be offered, they will adopt measures for qualifying the boys for employment in different trades and pursuits and for the creation of industrial branches of various descriptions.

47. The Principal will report to the Committee when any boy has attained the age of 16 and any girl that of 18 years. It will then be the duty of the Committee to take such measures as may seem suited for his or her settlement in life. Where any such boy or girl has parents, guardians, or other near relatives able to render assistance, they will be required to remove the child on the Committee's calling for the same. This rule, however, shall be no bar to the Committee accepting any suitable engagement for a girl who shall have attained the age of 16 years.

48. The Committee of Management shall, by the 1st June each year, submit to Government a report upon the condition and progress

of the Asylums during the preceding official year ; and, as appendices to the same, shall be furnished—

(1) A statement of accounts ;
(2) A list of the establishment, with salaries attached.
(3) A statement showing the studies pursued by the several classes in both Asylums ;
(4) A time-table for the teachers, *i.e.*, showing the disposal of their time ; and
(5) A time-table for the pupils.

The papers numbered 2, 3, 4, and 5 shall correspond to the 30th April immediately preceding the submission of the report. The Committee shall forward their Annual Report to the Director of Public Instruction for submission to Government. The Report of the Inspector of Schools can be added as an appendix to the same at the discretion of the Director of Public Instruction.

INDEX TO NAMES OF PLACES, PERSONS, &c.

**** Names in the Appendix have not been indexed.*

INDEX TO NAMES OF PLACES, RIVERS, &c.

Achenna, 240.
Adikahatti, 421, 424.
Agastiyamale, 252.
Agrata Cadawa, 272, 274.
Allahabad, 395.
Andhra, 262.
Anégundi, 253, 266.
Anémalés, 3, 67, 84, 152, 175, 245, 247, 265, 270, 386.
Anjarakandi, 483.
Anyúr kambe, 291.
Arakádholla stream, 15.
Arakád, 30, 210, 215, 277.
Aranád, 30, 215.
Aratapára hill, 11.
Arcot, 271, 333, 421.
Ariyúr, 30, 210.
Arrawaddy, 230.
Arriakód, 19.
Arvenkád valley, 7, 8.
Arvenkád, 23.
Assam, 137, 515, 517, 518, 519, 522, 523, 524, 530, 538, 554.
Attapadi, 272, 274.
Avalanché valley, 4, 7.
Avalanché, 19, 20, 21, 22, 23, 89, 90, 103, 295, 381, 556.

Baba Booden Hills, 483.
Bagwadi, 225.
Balaghát, 386.
Balakolla, 424.
Balam, 270.
Ballehalli, 225.
Bánawási, 208, 253, 262, 264.
Bangalore, 16, 306, 395, 396, 427, 466, 502.
Banghi Tappal, 21.
Baramahal, 269, 270, 337, 482.
Battery (Sultan's), 12.
Bear-hill, 5.
Bednore, 265.
Behar, 229.
Belgám, 225, 255.
Belúr, 265.
Bellary, 174, 287.
Bellikal, 18, 21, 165, 285, 289, 467.
,, lake, 165.
Belliki, 229, 230, 231.
Bellirangan Hills, 386.
Bengal, 40, 287, 297, 306, 345, 459, 483, 519, 539, 540, 553.
Benné Teak Forest, 12, 449.
Bétmand Hill, 381.
Beypúr river, 5, 6, 19.
Beypúr, 395, 502.
Bhavání river, 5, 6, 16, 17, 18, 19, 66, 85, 89, 245, 247, 277, 278, 295, 352, 386.
Bhavání valley, 5, 18, 89, 211.
Biggala, 225.
Biguli river, 14.
Bikhatti, 304.
Billi-rangum Hills, 268.
Bolamampatti valley, 245.
Bombay, 39, 40, 42, 293, 297, 299, 395, 497, 499, 554, 568, 571.
Búdinattam, 30, 210, 215.
Bukapatti, 196.
Burliár, 20, 23, 24, 132, 211, 213, 439, 518, 574, 576.

Cachar, 515, 540.
Cairn Hill, 381.
Calcutta, 39, 42, 230, 293, 400, 410, 510, 514, 553.
Calicut, 16, 18, 21, 260, 273, 484, 497, 498, 502, 554.
Canara, 208, 219, 254, 264, 265, 274.
Cannanore, 21, 299.
Cape Comorin, 137, 248.
Carnatic, 3, 90, 180, 184, 208, 209, 218, 252, 260, 263, 269, 270, 271.
Carura Regia Cerebothri, 261.
Ceded Districts, 37, 337.
Ceylon, 151, 153, 154, 155, 158, 250, 483, 484, 487, 489, 494, 496, 499, 500, 502, 507, 508, 509, 568.
Chera country, 253, 260, 261, 265, 278.
Cherambádi, 408, 413.
Cheramkód, 1, 11, 12, 367, 374.
Chickmuglúr, 489.
Chinna Bhavání (river), 5.
Chinna Coonoor (hill), 5.
Chinna Doddabetta, 5.
Chitaldrúg, 265.
Chóla Kingdom, 209, 244, 254, 260, 261, 262, 263, 266.
Choladi river, 12.
Club Hill, 378.
Cochin, 273, 312, 511.
Coimbatore, 6, 11, 16, 19, 67, 85, 87, 154, 184, 186, 189, 208, 218, 221, 226, 243, 244, 245, 246, 247, 248, 249, 252, 255, 257, 260, 261, 262, 265, 269, 270, 271, 272, 274, 276, 277, 278, 279, 280, 281, 289, 291, 292, 297, 299, 303, 304, 305, 307, 308, 309, 311, 312, 314, 315, 316, 317, 322, 333, 337, 347, 353, 361, 362, 363, 368, 378, 384, 386, 391, 398, 399, 404, 405, 407, 412, 423, 466, 484, 502, 572.
Coimbatore gap, 3.
Combaconum, 309.
Conagherry, 230.
Conjeveram, 209, 253, 255, 265.

Coonoor, 5, 8, 12, 13, 16, 17, 19, 20, 21, 23, 24, 28, 30, 37, 39, 40, 43, 45, 48, 50, 53, 62, 63, 64, 65, 66, 67, 68, 76, 77, 78, 93, 103, 131, 132, 159, 172, 174, 182, 183, 284, 295, 304, 306, 308, 349, 361, 362, 364, 366, 372, 373, 374, 376, 377, 378, 380, 385, 386, 387, 388, 389, 390, 392, 393, 394, 395, 396, 406, 407, 408, 409, 410, 413, 415, 417, 419, 420, 421, 422, 424, 429, 440, 441, 443, 453, 460, 467, 471, 477, 479, 485, 489, 496, 502, 510, 511, 512, 531, 575.
Coonoor Pass or Ghát, 16, 17, 19, 20, 23, 65, 85, 103, 172, 174, 179, 243, 291, 293, 295, 297, 378, 386, 392, 394, 395, 441.
Coonoor Peak, 5, 386, 388.
Coonoor river, 6, 7, 17, 386, 388.
Coorg, 37, 101, 159, 220, 225, 239, 261, 487, 504, 507, 509, 510, 568.
Courtallum, 516.
Craigmore, 23, 381.
,, Hill, 381.
Cranganúr, 254.
Cuddalore, 263.
Cuddapah, 412.

Dalavairapuram, 263.
Dambrapáliyam, 246.
Dan Nayakancotay, 272.
Darapúr, 270.
Darjeeling, 40, 477, 522, 553, 569.
Dehra Doon, 341, 351, 352.
Dekhan, 1, 88, 180, 184, 249, 250, 253, 257, 258, 259, 260, 266, 270.
Delavanapura, 261.
Delhi, 266.
Dérbetta Hill (Bear-hill), 4.
Dévála, 95, 96, 406, 408, 413, 421.
Dévanaikenkóta, 6, 17, 25, 216, 218, 271, 277, 278, 279, 280, 311.
Devar-betta, 4.
Dévaráyapatnam, 277, 279, 291, 309.
Dévashóla, 5, 7, 19, 21, 393, 421.
Dévashólabetta, 4, 92.
Dharapura, 261.
Dhobies' village, 86.
Dimhatti, 16, 17, 67, 280, 284, 285, 295, 296, 297, 424.
Dimhatti Hill, 5.
Doddabetta, 3, 4, 5, 6, 7, 8, 9, 10, 13, 14, 15, 19, 38, 41, 42, 47, 49, 56, 62, 63, 64, 65, 67, 77, 86, 87, 89, 92, 95, 238, 284, 378, 379, 380, 381, 382, 471, 477, 513, 518, 555, 556, 557, 562, 563, 572, 573.
Dodholla stream, 11.
Dolphin's Nose, 20, 66, 386, 393.
Dondé, 289.
Dora-samudra, 266.
Dravida, 218, 262, 265.
Drúg range, 20.
Drúg, 20, 66, 386.
Dwarasamudra, 265.

Eastern Gháts, 1, 2, 41, 85, 88, 89, 183, 260.
Elk Fall, 89.
Elk Hill, 95, 287, 293, 378, 379, 380, 381.
Ellanhalli, 21, 23, 24.
Ellémalé, 2.
E'rkád river, 16.
Erode, 270.

Fort St. George, 301.

Gajalhatti Pass, 2, 8, 171, 174, 176, 221, 248, 261, 262, 269, 271, 286.
Ganapathi, 12.
Gangavamsa Dynasty, 262.
Ganjam, 296, 308, 337, 412, 424.
Goa, 225, 264.
Gódáveri, 90, 250, 258.
Gúdalúr, 12, 18, 19, 20, 21, 95, 96, 203, 204, 286, 295, 366, 373, 374, 376, 377, 392, 406, 408, 413, 416, 417, 419, 450, 556.
Gúdalúr Ghát or Pass, 16, 18, 274, 290, 295, 392, 394, 420, 485.
Gúlúr Hill, 12.
Gúndulpet, 12, 221, 226, 254, 270, 272, 307.
Guntoor, 479.
Guynd, 408.
Guzerat, 267.

Hadinád, 267, 268.
Hakgala, 508.
Hanagal, 264.
Hangala (fort), 270.
Hassan, 211, 253, 265.
Hásanúr Pass, 183.
Himagála range, 2, 89, 93.
Himalayas, 103, 131, 155, 552, 554.
H'laiúru, 240.
Honúr, 208, 308.
Hoonsoor, 295.
Hope river, 166.
Hoysala Bellála, 253.
Húlikal, 21, 66, 182.
Húlikal Drúg, 5, 17, 93, 226, 241, 243, 393.
Humcha, 253.
Hyderabad, 293.

Ibex Hill, 5.
Indragiri, 263.
Irnada, 272.

Jabbalpur, 154.
Jackanéri, 195, 226, 283, 285.
Jackatalla, 65, 86, 92, 221, 307, 308, 408, 424, 443.
Jackatalla valley, 17, 75, 306.
Jackata Kambé, 240.
Jail Hill, 380.

Kadamba, 208, 243, 253, 261, 264, 270.
Kadur, 266.
Kalinga, 262.
Kalkuttu Palam, 247.
Kalyana, 225, 254.
Kaity, 2, 43, 151, 222, 285, 296, 302, 324, 421, 422, 424, 426, 456, 457, 458, 467, 510.
Kaity valley, 7, 8, 86, 87, 92, 293, 294, 422.
Kakkanholla stream, 11.
Kákúsi, 240.
Kalala, 267, 268.
Kalár, 17, 20, 65, 66, 395.
Kalár river, 17.

Kalburga, 266.
Káléri (hills), 4.
Kalhatti, 15, 18, 21, 22, 24, 132, 172, 173, 222, 268, 279, 413, 456, 467, 477, 512, 573, 574, 576.
Kalhatti Fall, 6, 18, 573.
,, Ghát, 103, 179.
Káligiri, 424.
Kalkúdiúr Hills, 4.
Kallampalla, 216.
Kámakottam, 206.
Kanarak, 262.
Kanchi, 253.
Kandel, 380, 381, 420, 429.
Kandelmand, 332.
Kangiam, 262.
Kangra valley, 568.
Karkanar Ghát, 265.
Kancunthuré river, 65.
Karkúr, 11, 21, 248.
,, Ghát, 274, 286.
Kárnáta, 209, 214, 218, 253, 255, 256, 258, 260, 261, 264, 265, 266, 272, 277.
Karrashóla, 86.
Karugahalli, 268.
Karúr, 261, 270.
Kátéri, 19, 20, 21, 64, 103, 240, 393, 417, 421, 424, 460.
Kátéri Hill, 5.
,, Fall, 6.
,, river, 6, 7, 13, 17, 66, 386, 388.
,, valley, 20, 363.
Káveri, 205, 260, 261, 262, 265.
Keel Kunda, 89.
Keelur, 285.
Kerala country, 256, 260, 261, 262, 263, 266, 270, 272.
Kereháda, 424.
Keriur, 263.
Khasia Hill, 552.
Kil-Kótagiri, 17, 280.
Kilnád, 15, 285.
Kishkindha, 266.
Kistna, 185, 209, 229, 238, 250, 258, 265, 267.
Kodagu, 261.
Kódanád, 20, 43, 182, 240, 392, 393, 394, 421, 459, 515.
Kódanád Hill, 5, 459.
Kódangiri valley, 247.
Kodavamoody, 284, 285.
Kokád, 30, 215.
Kólakambé, 20, 21, 284, 393.
,, (hills), 5, 6.
,, waterfall, 6.
Kollegal, 261, 265.
Kollemalé, 267.
Kónabetta, Peak 5.
Konka, 265.
Konkan, 249, 260, 266.
Konkanapura, 253.
Kongu country, 218, 221, 243, 253, 260, 261, 262, 263, 264, 265, 270, 386.
Kótagiri, 5, 6, 8, 12, 13, 16, 17, 19, 20, 23, 24, 36, 37, 38, 39, 40, 48, 62, 63, 64, 66, 67, 75, 76, 78, 85, 86, 89, 92, 103, 152, 173, 204, 238, 240, 244, 277, 280, 284, 285, 287, 290, 291, 295, 299, 349, 361, 362, 364, 366, 373, 374, 375, 376, 378, 386, 390, 392, 393, 394, 407, 408, 409, 413, 415, 416, 417, 419, 420, 421, 422, 424, 426, 465, 467, 471, 479, 485, 502, 513, 515.
Kótagiri Pass or Ghát, 3, 16, 17, 18, 281, 295, 387, 392.
Kotur, 263.
Kovatúr, 265.
Krúrmand, 21, 22.
Kuddanád, 226.
Kúdikádu, Hills 4.
Kúkalbetta, 5.
Kúndamúgi, 5.
Kúnda Ghát or Pass, 16, 19, 297, 484.
Kúndanád, 13, 14, 31, 204, 366, 441.
Kúnda river, 3, 5, 6, 7, 14, 22, 279.
,, valley, 7.
Kúndas, 1, 2, 3, 4, 5, 6, 8, 11, 12, 18, 19, 30, 43, 48, 49, 52, 67, 84, 85, 86, 89, 90, 91, 93, 94, 95, 172, 174, 182, 187, 196, 210, 233, 241, 258, 291, 295, 309, 322, 323, 361, 366, 367, 374, 378, 380, 393, 484, 486, 513.
Kúniapáni, 30, 215.
Kúrumbanád, 263.
Kurrachawadi, 226.
Kurnúl, 214.
Kúrumba bhumi, 209.
Kúrumbamotté, 284.
Kussowlie, 40, 77.
Kuttakádu Hills, 4.
Kutirai Kuttupalem, 247.

Lady Canning's Seat, 66, 386, 393.
Lamb's Rock, 20, 66, 386, 393.
Lambton's Peak range, 386.
Lanka, 202, 252, 256.
Lovedale, 7, 14, 28, 60, 61, 96, 380, 381, 435, 436.

Madras, 13, 18, 39, 40, 42, 64, 84, 137, 150, 152, 230, 255, 288, 302, 347, 356, 395, 417, 434, 435, 436, 460, 482, 484, 486, 487, 495, 502, 510, 514, 568, 571, 577, 578.
Madura, 175, 219, 229, 263, 266, 267, 269, 398.
Mahableshwur, 40, 42.
Máhishamandalam, 253, 258, 259.
Máhishamati, 258, 259.
Malabar, 1, 2, 3, 11, 16, 95, 151, 184, 208, 218, 248, 249, 251, 252, 254, 255, 256, 258, 259, 260, 261, 265, 272, 273, 274, 277, 279, 288, 290, 291, 292, 294, 299, 303, 304, 305, 312, 315, 322, 328, 329, 333, 335, 336, 337, 338, 340, 347, 348, 349, 350, 863, 364, 370, 410, 413, 423, 484, 554.
Malayála, 256, 261.
Malachippa, 30, 210, 215.
Málékóta, 221, 244, 268, 279.
Málémand Hill, 15, 92, 285, 380, 381, 382, 435, 444.
Málémand Lake, 465.
Máléyur, 254.
Mamalé, 502.
Manaar, 274.
Manantoddi, 483.
Manárghát, 18, 272, 273, 274.
Mángádu, 247.
Mangalore, 260, 400.
Marapannaddi, 96.
Marégathé stream, 11.

Masnikóvil, 413.
Matheran, 40.
McIvor's Bund, 21, 22.
Meezerabad, 483.
Mékanád, 12, 13, 14, 16, 25, 26, 30, 31, 182, 187, 204, 210, 215, 226, 321, 325, 333, 366, 367, 374, 424, 441.
Meleuntao, 274.
Mélkúnda, 3, 5, 11, 19, 20, 21, 43, 240, 273, 274, 515, 556, 557, 574.
Mélnád, 3, 15, 285, 329, 333, 335, 348, 349, 378.
Mélúr, 19, 21, 86, 93, 226, 229, 240, 258, 274, 338, 393.
Mélúr Pass, 16, 18.
Mercara, 253, 410.
Mettapollium, 16, 17, 18, 20, 64, 65, 67, 85, 215, 278, 295, 307, 392, 393, 395, 396, 398, 408, 409, 410, 480.
Metucherri, 420.
Meurúr, 258.
Midagesi, 270.
Molemava, 2.
Mount Aboo, 40, 430, 431.
Moyár river, 2, 5, 11, 13, 18, 95, 245, 246, 277, 357, 450.
Moyár valley, 5, 245, 246, 247, 323.
Múdukkádu stream, 13.
Múdúmalé, 12, 173, 174, 398, 448, 449, 450, 452.
Múkarté, 2, 4, 5, 6, 21, 87, 91, 93, 196, 283.
Múkarté Peak, 2, 4, 22, 85, 193, 459.
Múlachapoi Kambé, 13.
Munnanád, 1, 11, 367, 374.
Munnipoor, 517.
Mupeinád, 12.
Muree, 40, 77.
Musnagúdi, 368.
Muttinád-betta, 5, 195, 238.
Mysore, 2, 6, 11, 16, 18, 21, 67, 88, 90, 96, 137, 154, 184, 193, 203, 207, 208, 211, 213, 214, 218, 219, 220, 221, 222, 225, 226, 228, 230, 239, 243, 248, 249, 251, 252, 253, 254, 255, 259, 260, 261, 262, 263, 266, 267, 268, 269, 270, 271, 272, 274, 276, 277, 279, 284, 286, 288, 289, 295, 303, 307, 393, 396, 398, 408, 410, 448, 449, 450, 456, 479, 482, 483, 484, 487, 489, 490, 504, 509, 510, 573.
Mysore ditch (gorge), 6.
" stream, 11.
" gháts, 261.

Nadahatti, 424.
Nádgáni, 5, 95, 96, 413.
Nadoobett, 333.
Naggur, 483.
Nambalakód, 1, 11, 193, 309, 367, 374.
Nangala, 265.
Nanjanád, 23, 285.
Nanjanád valley, 7, 14, 243.
Nanjanagúdi, 226, 267.
Neduwattam, 11, 18, 21, 22, 23, 24, 43, 89, 91, 95, 96, 103, 165, 174, 295, 374, 393, 394, 395, 413, 420, 459, 556, 557, 562, 563.
Nellakóta, 408.
Nellambúr, 2, 19, 97, 305, 309, 337, 448, 449, 450.
Nellambúr river, 5, 6, 15, 502.
Nelleala, 218, 277.
Nellitoré, 221, 291.
Nellore, 479.
Nepaul, 282.
Nerbadda river, 249, 258, 259.
Nerunganada, 272.
Nídunkúlam, 17, 226.
Nídumalé range, 2, 3, 7, 306, 309, 393.
Nílagiri Peak, 2, 4, 11, 12.
Nílagiris proper, 1, 3.
Nirkambé, 421, 426.
Nolambadi, 265.
Northern Circars, 155.
North Konkan, 249.
North-west Provinces, 77, 185, 511, 512, 513, 522.
Noyel river, 245.

Odantoré, 291.
Oodagherry, 510.
Oomatur, 220.
Ootacamand, 5, 6, 7, 8, 12, 15, 16, 18, 19, 20, 21, 22, 23, 24, 28, 30, 34, 38, 39, 40, 41, 43, 44, 45, 46, 47, 48, 49, 50, 52, 53, 56, 60, 61, 62, 63, 66, 67, 68, 78, 85, 86, 87, 88, 90, 91, 92, 93, 103, 130, 131, 132, 142, 147 150, 159, 165, 171, 172, 173, 174, 176, 183, 189, 195, 199, 215, 222, 224, 230, 267, 268, 283, 284, 286, 287, 288, 289, 290, 292, 293, 295, 299, 300, 302, 303, 305, 306, 308, 309, 329, 330, 331, 334, 335, 336, 338, 339, 341, 344, 347, 348, 349, 350, 351, 353, 354, 355, 361, 362, 364, 366, 372, 373, 374, 375, 376, 377, 378, 380, 381, 382, 383, 384, 385, 387, 388, 389, 390, 392, 393, 394, 395, 396, 398, 400, 403, 407, 408, 409, 410, 412, 413, 414, 415, 417, 418, 419, 420, 422, 424, 428, 429, 430, 431, 433, 434, 437, 438, 439, 440, 441, 442, 443, 444, 445, 446, 447, 453, 457, 460, 471, 474, 475, 476, 477, 480, 496, 513, 517, 531, 555, 562, 571, 573, 574, 575, 576.
Ootacamand Lake, 6, 48, 165, 378, 381, 388.
Orange Valley, 7, 8, 13, 67, 95.
Orissa, 249, 262.
Ossington Estate, 374.
Ouchterlony Valley, 11, 12, 13, 15, 27, 137, 166, 172, 173, 174, 176, 309, 310, 363, 374, 417, 485, 502.

Paikaré, 20, 21, 22, 23, 24, 87, 88, 91, 93, 103, 176, 238, 295, 381, 413, 453, 556, 563.
Paikaré Falls, 6, 20, 21, 450, 556.
" Hill, 4.
" River, 4, 5, 7, 20, 22, 85, 89, 91, 93, 165, 279, 292, 295, 305, 309, 338, 459.
" Valley, 7, 89.
Palar river, 209.
Palghát, 3, 89.
Palghát Pass, 248, 264.
Pándi river, 6, 11.
Pandya Kingdom, 209, 242, 254, 260, 261, 262.
Paranga, 264.
Parikere, 268.
Pennar river, 209.
Pérambúr, 13.

Pérangalúr, 13.
Péranganád, 12, 13, 14, 25, 26, 30, 31, 64, 182, 187, 204, 210, 215, 226, 279, 291, 321, 333, 366, 367, 374, 424, 441, 465.
Peridinya, 508.
Pérmand, 21, 22.
Pichulbetta, 4.
Pillúr, 21.
Pirgúr, 258.
Ponachi, 245.
Ponany river, 484.
Pondicherry, 458.
Poonamallee, 79, 81, 82.
Poorendhur, 40.
Pothanúr, 16, 395.
Púdúkóta, 13.
Pulicat, 263, 337.
Pulnis, 40, 84, 155, 229, 261, 270, 355, 568.
Punjab, 568.
Punnád, 262.
Puragiri, 268.
Púrthé, 21, 22.
,, stream, 22.

Quilon, 510.

Raja-raja-puram, 263.
Rallia, 151, 287, 445.
Ramandroog, 40.
Rangasámi's Peak, 1, 5, 6, 11, 17, 213, 215, 216, 226, 262, 277, 280.
Richardson's Line, 11.

Sáhyádri Hills, 1.
Sáidapet, 460, 519.
Saint Catherine's Fall, 6, 89, 226, 386.
Saiya, 263.
Salem, 184, 229, 260, 281, 301, 307, 312, 386.
Sandi-durga, 278.
Sargúr, 221.
Sarimale, 265.
Sattiamangalam, 216, 224, 271.
Segúr, 15, 18, 21, 24, 30, 31, 92, 195, 215, 238, 289, 315, 338, 366, 367, 374, 381, 420, 450, 502.
Segúr Pass or Ghát, 5, 6, 13, 16, 18, 19, 24, 86, 221, 244, 289, 380, 392, 393, 408, 573, 574.
Segúr Peak, 5.
Seharunpore, 552.
Sembanaré, 30, 210, 215.
Sembanattam, 30, 210, 215.
Seringapatam, 267, 268, 271, 276, 286, 482.
Seven-Cairn Hill, 92.
Shevaroys, 40, 84, 355, 357, 483.
Shimoga, 253.
Shólakal, 19, 21.
Sholapur, 225.
Shólúr, 15, 172, 173, 196, 227, 239, 284, 424.
Sikkim, 567, 568.
Silent Valley, 18.
Silhet, 554.
Simla, 40.
Siral Kambé, 30, 215.
Sisapára, 19, 21, 86, 88, 94, 103, 174, 393.
Sisapára Ghát or Pass, 16, 19, 103, 111, 171, 172, 179, 295, 392, 484.
,, Peak, 5.
,, Rock, 19.
Sivaganga, 225.
Skandapura, 261.
Snowdon, 4, 85, 86, 88, 380, 381, 444.
Somanúr, 420.
South Canara, 101.
Srávana Belgóla, 253.
Sringagiri, 266.
Srimúgai, 16, 278, 281, 295.
Sripermatúr, 255.
Srirangam, 255.
Sultan's Battery, 12.
Sunáwar, 430, 431, 432, 433.
Sunda, 208.
Súndabetta Hill, 19.
Súndaputté, 18, 19, 247, 392.
,, Pass, 18, 274.
Sur-Bhaváni river, 5.

Talikóta, 267, 269.
Talkád, 261, 262, 263, 265.
Tallapoya Pass, 19.
Tanjore, 260, 262.
Tanur, 273, 274.
Telingána, 214, 254, 265, 266.
Tellicherry, 308, 483, 498, 500.
Témalé, 20, 21.
Ténád, 17, 226, 279, 280.
Terai, 155.
Tiger's Hill, 386.
Tinnevelly, 236, 252, 261, 510.
Tippukádu, 11, 18, 21, 289, 448, 449.
Tirkanambi, 270, 272.
Todamala, 273, 274.
Tódamand, 66.
Tódanád, 12, 13, 14, 15, 25, 26, 30, 31, 182, 187, 204, 210, 215, 222, 226, 227, 244, 258, 277, 284, 321, 333, 366, 367, 374, 424, 441, 465.
Torakádavu river, 245.
Toreyúr, 265.
Travancore, 101, 219, 242, 261, 312, 487, 489, 509, 510, 568.
Trichinopoly, 174, 255, 260, 290, 306, 398, 412.
Tripatur, 482.
Tukalhallibetta, 93.
Tuluva, 265.
Túnéri, 424.
Tungabadra, 253, 266.

Udiamparur, 273.
Udiaráya, 238, 244, 269 (Kóta).
Ujjayani, 253.
Ulovi, 225.
Ummatúr, 267, 268, 269.
Úrbetta (hill), 5.

Vagapáni, 30, 210, 215.
Varada river, 253.
Velingiri, 4.
Velléru Kambé, 13, 30, 210, 215, 291.
Vellore, 265.
Vijayanagar, 209, 218, 253, 254, 261, 264, 266, 267, 268, 269, 270, 272.

Vindya Mountains, 1, 249.
Vizagapatam, 309.

Walaghát, 171, 172, 173, 175, 176.
Wallahkadoo, 484.
Wainád, 1, 2, 11, 16, 18, 27, 95, 96, 97, 175, 184, 204, 219, 243, 248, 256, 258, 261, 262, 271, 272, 277, 286, 289, 293, 306, 309, 310, 315, 355, 357, 361, 362, 363, 366, 368, 370, 373, 374, 375, 376, 377, 391, 392, 396, 408, 413, 416, 448, 449, 450, 453, 480, 483, 486, 487, 489, 490, 491, 496, 497, 502, 504, 507, 509, 511, 515, 517, 568.
Washermen's village, 86.
Wellington, 13, 16, 19, 20, 28, 31, 34, 37, 38, 39, 40, 43, 45, 64, 65, 66, 67, 68, 69, 70, 71, 72, 73, 74, 75, 76, 77, 78, 79, 80, 81, 82, 86, 221, 306, 307, 308, 366, 373, 374, 375, 376, 377, 378, 386, 387, 388, 389, 391, 396, 406, 407, 408, 409, 412, 413, 414, 416, 417, 419, 439, 441, 442, 443, 445, 446, 447, 448, 531.
Western Gháts, 1, 2, 11, 41, 88, 89, 90, 151, 155, 209, 229, 260.
Whatakai mand, 6.
Wúndúr, 19.

Yelandúr, 267, 268, 270.
Yellamalé Spur, 11.
Yellannallé, 285, 304, 393.

INDEX TO NAMES OF PERSONS, TRIBES, &c.

Abbé Dubois, 482.
Abraham (Badaga convert), 421.
Adam, Sir F., 297, 298, 299, 302, 324, 328, 329, 332, 348, 455.
Adhikáris, 32, 221.
Aditya Varmma, 262.
Adondái, 209, 263.
Agastiya, 252.
Agni, 259.
Akalanka, 253, 254.
Ala-ud-Din, 266.
Allardyce, Capt., 442.
Allon, Mrs., 419.
Anderson, Mr., 568.
Aneas, 221.
Ané Kúrumbas, 208.
Amarbhujangan, 263.
Amherst, Lord, 345.
Amoga Varsha, 253.
Amrita, 262.
Aparamita Paravasa Déva, 270.
Arbuthnot, Sir A. J., 432, 435.
Armstrong, Sir R., 307.
Arnold, Mr., 496.
Arnott, 130.
Asóka, 209, 229, 243, 253, 259.
Asúras, 251.
Athiyarhatti, 226.
Auckland, Lord, 301.
Aurangazib, 270.

Baba Booden, 483.
Babington, Mr., 303.
Badagas, 2, 7, 9, 13, 25, 26, 27, 29, 30, 31, 32, 34, 180, 182, 184, 185, 186, 187, 188, 192, 193, 195, 197, 199, 201, 202, 205, 206, 207, 211, 212, 213, 216, 218, 219, 220, 221, 222, 223, 224, 225, 226, 227, 228, 232, 235, 240, 242, 246, 255, 262, 268, 272, 273, 274, 277, 284, 294, 296, 302, 303, 304, 306, 307, 311, 312, 316, 318, 319, 320, 321, 322, 323, 324, 325, 326, 328, 329, 332, 333, 337, 339, 341, 342, 348, 349, 350, 351, 353, 359, 366, 380, 398, 421, 422, 423, 424, 425, 426, 443, 455, 456, 458, 465, 466, 467, 468, 470, 471, 476, 477, 479, 480, 488, 519, 577.
Badakáru, 32.
Badra Báhu, 253.
Baikie, Dr., 37, 42, 43, 50, 182, 280, 290, 292, 293, 295, 297, 427.
Baillie, Dr., 288.
Bakka, 266.
Bal Raja, 277.
Barnes, Sir E., 483.
Barton, Rev. W., 419.
Bassava, 225, 255.
Beauclair (Priest), 420.
Bédas, 26, 180, 214.
Beddome, Lieut.-Col. R. H., 98, 130, 133, 171, 177.
Bell, Dr., 427, 571.
Bellálas. *See* Hoysala Bellálas.
Bellála Rája, 266.
Bellis, 221.
Bentham, 548.
Bentinck, Lord William, 279, 302, 510, 552.
Benza, Dr. *See* de Benza.
Beresford, Col., 97.
Berg Otto, 568.
Bergen Heinrich von, 568.
Berkely, 503.
Betad Cham Ráj, 268.
Bétakan, 193, 258.
Bétasámi, 226.
Bhaváni, 20.
Bhaváni, 20, 254.
Bhills, 219.
Bidie, Dr., 133, 150, 487, 493, 496, 502, 503, 504, 563, 566, 570.
Birch, Dr., 37.
Bird, Mr. G., 483.
Bird, Mr. J. (Councillor), 305, 327, 337.
Bird, Mr. E. W., 309, 431.
Blandford, Mr., 2, 7, 83, 84, 85, 86, 87, 88, 91, 92, 93, 94, 95.
Blein, 282.
Boswell, Mr., 238.
Botta Kúrumbas, 211.
Bougner, M., 551.
Bouchardat, M., 569.
Bower, Mr., 407.
Brace, Mr. E. J. C., 359, 515, 528.
Breeks, Mr. J. W., 8, 182, 187, 191, 192, 193, 194, 195, 197, 198, 200, 201, 202, 203, 204, 206, 211, 213, 215, 230, 231, 232, 236, 237, 238, 239, 240, 241, 257, 264, 268, 272, 273, 274, 308, 326, 328, 357, 360, 363, 426, 427, 478, 513, 514, 574.
Brough Smyth, Mr., 243.
Broughton, Mr. J., 43, 144, 560, 561, 562, 563, 564, 565, 566, 569.
Brown, Major, 483.
Browning, Mr. T., 18.
Buchanan, Dr., 208, 209, 214, 215, 218, 222, 251, 271, 272, 274, 276, 277, 278, 282, 311, 483.
Bührer, Rev. A., 421.
Burgess, Mr., 308.
Burrell, Dr., 83.

Caldwell, Dr., 1, 4, 182, 184, 185, 202, 203, 212, 213, 219, 228, 242, 249, 260.
Campbell, Capt., 442, 443.

Canning, Lord, 355, 356, 358, 553.
Cannon, 483, 489.
Carei, 261.
Carr, 264.
Casamajor, Mr., 303; 422, 458.
Chalukyas, 263, 264.
Chama Rája, 268, 269.
Chama Rája Wódear, 271.
Cheram Perumal, 256.
Cherapati, 261.
Cheras, 253, 260, 261, 264.
Chikka Déva, 269, 271.
Chinchon, Countess of, 551.
Chittre, 221.
Chólas, 260, 261, 262, 263, 265, 266.
Christison, Sir R., 552.
Cleghorn, Dr., 439, 440, 442, 511, 512, 572.
Clementson, Lieut.-Col., 400.
Clive, Lord, 277, 313.
Cloeté, Lieut.-Col., 12, 279.
Close, Col. Barry, 272.
Cockburn, Miss, 421.
Cockerell, Mr. J. R., 310, 359, 518, 561.
Congreve, Col., 83, 230, 231, 232, 237, 242, 243.
Conolly, Mr., 304, 315, 335, 336, 338.
Cooke, Mr., 508.
Corbett, Surg.-Major W. H., 45, 64.
Cornish, Dr., 27, 34, 383, 561.
Cotton, Bishop, 426, 427.
Crewe, Col., 293, 294, 296, 304, 456, 457, 458, 510.
Croley, Mr. H., 428.
Cross, Mr., 554, 555, 568, 570.
Cullen, Genl., 510.
Cunningham, Mr., 253.
Cúrubáru, 208.
Cussuvers, 26.

Dalavaye, 268, 271.
Dalhousie, Lord, 293, 390, 553, 572.
Dalmahoy, Surg., 36, 37, 290.
Dána, 277.
Davies (Profr.), 298.
Dawson, Mr., 260.
Day, Dr., 165, 166.
Dealtry, Archdeacon, 418.
Dealtry, Bishop, 418, 430, 431.
deBenza, Dr. P. M., 83, 86, 88.
DeCandolle, 130.
deJussieu, M. Joseph, 551, 552.
Delondre, A. T. M., 569, 570.
Denison, Sir W., 309, 513.
Déva Rája, 271.
Dévalyáls, 187, 200.
DeVriz, M., 562.
Dodda Déva Rája, 270.
Dowker, Genl., 418.
Druhvaniti, 262.
Drury, 483.
Dumas, 222.
Dundassies, 412.
Dúrga, 20, 254.

Eastment, Capt., 294, 296.
Eda Kúrumbas, 210.
Eggeling, Dr., 260.
Elliot, Mr. H. M., 487.
Elliot, Hon. W., 431.
Elliot, Sir W., 153, 240.
Elliott, Mr. D., 309, 350.
Ellis, Mr. R. S., 383.
Ellis, 264.
Elphinstone, Lord, 8, 302, 304, 305, 306, 328, 338, 422, 458.

Farewell, Col., 18.
Fergusson, 184, 229, 230, 239.
Ferreiri, Rev. Jacome, 273.
Flückiger, Dr., 549, 568, 570.
Fortune, Mr., 511.
Framjee and Co., 293.
Francis, Capt., 308.
Fraser, Mr., 4, 244.
Freeth, Capt., 6.

Gangaluru, 222.
Gangamma, 226.
Gardner, Dr., 503.
Garrow, Mr., 277, 279, 315, 361.
Gass, Mr., 442, 446, 447.
Gell, Bishop, 418.
Geoghegan, Mr., 84.
Gibson, Maj.-Genl., 419.
Godin, M., 551.
Gomatesvara, 253.
Gonajas, 222.
Gordon, Surg.-Genl., 383.
Gordon, Mr., 345, 483, 510.
Gover, Mr., 224.
Grant, Mr., 321, 322, 323, 324, 325.
Grant. Major A., 571.
Gundert, Dr., 274.

Haider Ali, 244, 271, 312.
Haihagas, 259, 265.
Haines, Dr., 286, 287.
Hakka, 266.
Hamilton, Major, 245.
Hanbury, 549, 568.
Handi Kúrumbas, 208, 211.
Handi Rasalas, 209.
Hansard, 356, 357.
Hansen, Major, 290.
Harihara, 266, 267.
Hari-vari-deva, 244, 263.
Harkness, Capt., 182, 216, 293, 297, 327.
Harris, General, 271.
Harris, Lord, 308.
Háruvas, 32, 221.
Harvey, Mr., R. 529.
Hasan Gangu, 266.
Hasskarl, M., 553.
Hatara, 221.
"Hawkeye," 150.
Haworth, Mr., 540.
Hay, 298.
Hemasitala, 253.
Hetté, 205, 226.
Heyne, Dr., 278, 282.
Higginbotham, Mr. A., 418.
Hill, Mr., 459.
Hiriadéva, 193, 212, 226.
Hiriasámi, 226.
Hobart, Lady, 429.
Hobart, Lord, 427.
Hoblis, 277.
Hodges, Mr., 407.
Hodgson, Mr., 159, 279.
Hooker, Dr., 130, 548, 556.

Hough, Mr., 327.
Howard, Mr. J. E., 551, 560, 562, 569.
Hoysala, Bellálas, 254, 261, 263, 264, 265, 266.
Huen Thsang, 253.
Hull, Mr. H. T., 484, 487.
Hunter, Dr., 249, 259, 262.
Hutchins, Major, 294.
Hutson, Mr., 484.
Huxam, Mr., 510.

Ideiyas, 180.
Immadi Rája, 270.
Ionians, 266.
Irulas, 13, 27, 29, 180, 181, 182, 203, 205, 212, 214, 215, 216, 217, 219, 226, 242, 246, 277, 280, 284, 311, 326.

Jago, Major, 441.
Jain Kúrumbas, 211.
Jamieson, Mr., 574, 575.
Jangamas, 270.
Jedeasámi, 226.
Jennings, Col., 304.
Jerdon, Dr., 150, 151, 152, 156, 158, 159, 174.
Jervis, 182, 280, 293, 297.
Jinasenachárya, 253.
Joachim Stephen, 420.
Johnstone, Mr., 285.
Jones, Mr., 285, 457.
Joyce, 457.
Jussieu. *See* de Jussieu.

Kadamba kings, 208, 243, 253, 261, 262, 264, 270.
Kád Kórumbas, 208, 211.
Kafur, 266.
Kahasumna, 205.
Kakkaraya, 226.
Kalachuryas, 225, 254, 263.
Kalikai, 205.
Kal-kambaraya, 225.
Kallas, 181.
Kámata, 205.
Kámataráya, 205, 206.
Kambata, 205.
Kampana Wódea, 266.
Kanakas, 32, 221, 269.
Kariabettaraya, 226.
Karmadiya Kúrumbas, 210.
Karsten, Dr., 551, 569.
Kartti Varmma, 264.
Kattakal Mariammem 227.
Kávaláls, 194, 195, 200.
Kelso, Major, 289, 294.
Kennans, 187.
Kennett, Lieut.-General, 308.
Kerala, 261.
Ketaraya, 226.
Keys, Mr. W., 25, 279.
Khasturís, 222.
Khilji, 266.
Khonds, 200.
Kindersley, Mr., 280.
King, Colonel, 304, 407.
King, Mr., 84, 95, 97.
King, Dr., 547, 551, 553, 564, 568.
Kirkpatrick, Colonel, 272.
Kittel, Rev. F., 424.
Knox, Mr., 165.
Kokvális, 195.
Kóls, 249.
Kongani Varmma Dharma, 261.
Kongas, 32, 221, 262.
Kongus, 264, 265, 270.
Konka, 265.
Koriaraya, 226.
Kótas, 25, 26, 27, 29, 180, 182, 184, 187, 199, 200, 201, 203, 204, 205, 206, 207, 212, 219, 227, 242, 243, 284, 311, 326, 426, 479.
Krishna, 267.
Krishna Ráya, 267.
Kulattungi Chóla, 209, 263.
Kumbali Kúrumbas, 208, 211.
Kumbararus, 222.
Kunth, 130.
Kuribattraya, 212.
Kúrpúlis, 195.
Kúrubas, 208, 209.
Kúrumbas, 27, 29, 180, 181, 182, 184, 186, 203, 205, 206, 207, 208, 209, 210, 211, 212, 213, 214, 219, 230, 231, 242, 243, 246, 251, 263, 264, 266, 299, 311, 326, 411, 488, 490.
Kúrumbaokkibiga, 210.
Kurutalis, 215.
Kuttans, 187.
Kycolens, 26.

Laborie, 484.
La Condamine, Dr., 551.
Lassen, 258, 262.
Law, Col., 17.
Lawrence, Sir H., 430, 431, 432, 434.
Le Hardy, Lieut., 17, 19.
Leschenault de la Tour, M., 280, 281, 282.
Limond, Capt., 297.
Lindley, Dr., 130, 533, 548.
Lingadhikáris, 32, 221, 246.
Lingavunts, 25, 26.
Lingayat Wódeas, 218.
Lushington, Mr. C. M., 305, 327, 336, 337.
Lushington, Mr. S. R., 287, 290, 291, 293, 296, 297, 298, 305, 306, 324, 327, 328, 330, 331, 332, 344, 348, 417, 426, 456, 510.

Macaulay, Lord, 18, 302.
Mackenzie, Col. C., 209, 276, 278, 285.
Macmahon, M., 25, 279, 361.
Macpherson, Capt., 281, 283, 286, 287.
Macpherson, 200.
Mádhara, 264.
Mádhava, 266.
Mágale, 206.
Máhádeswara, 226.
Máhádéva, 259.
Máhálingasámi, 226.
Makay, Dr., 37.
Maladéva, 262.
Málékóta Rája, 221.
Málé Kúrumbas, 208, 210.
Manikamma, 226.
Manikas, 222.
Mann, Mr., 511, 512, 513.
Maravas, 181.
Mariamma, 216.
Mariatha, 216.
Maris, 222.
Markham, Mr. C. R., 550, 551, 554, 555, 560, 568, 569, 570, 573.

Marshall, Col., 182, 183, 191, 192, 193, 194, 195, 196, 197, 198, 200.
Martin, Sir J. R., 62.
Maskell, Mr., 351, 352.
McIvor, Mr. J., 460.
McIvor, Mr. W. G., 6, 22, 165, 167, 359, 418, 442, 443, 460, 518, 519, 554, 555, 556, 557, 562, 564, 565, 566, 567, 568, 571, 572, 573, 574.
McLeod, Major, 312, 315.
McMurdy, Capt., 293, 385.
Meat-adhikáris, 32, 221.
Menezes, Archbishop, 273.
Metz, Rev. F., 1, 32, 182, 183, 185, 186, 187, 191, 193, 194, 201, 202, 203, 205, 211, 213, 219, 221, 222, 223, 226, 228, 241, 258, 262, 268, 424.
Mieq, Rev. Mr., 421.
Miller, Col., 482.
Milman, Bishop, 419.
Miquel, F. A. W., 569.
Mitten, 130.
Mœricke, Rev. C., 424.
Morant, Major J. L. L., 16, 383, 391.
Morehead, Rev. J. B., 426.
Morgan, Major-Genl., 359, 440, 452, 455, 460, 462, 464, 466, 469, 499.
Morris, Mr. D., 508.
Müller, 130.
Mullu Kúrumbas, 26, 211.
Munro, 100.
Munro, Sir Thomas, 282, 283, 287, 292, 331, 337, 347.
Musoni, 212.
Mutis, Dr., 551, 569, 570.
Muttu Kótas, 205.

Nágas, 249, 252, 256, 259, 260.
Nanja Rája, 271.
Nanjanda, 226.
Nanjappa Rou, 23.
Napier and Ettrick, Lady, 165.
Napier, Lord, 460.
Narasa Rája, R., 270.
Narasimha, 266.
Narasinga, 267, 270.
Narrainsámi, 24.
Náyaks, 219, 267.
Náyaks, 180, 269, 270, 277.
Náya Kúrumbas, 208.
Neitner, Mr., 503.
Nelson, Mr., 229, 261, 266, 269, 270.
Nesserwanjee Jehangeer, 293.
Nila, 259.

Oldham, Professor, 50, 84.
,, Mr., 510.
Onslow, Col., 483.
Oppert, Dr., 202, 231.
Orton, Assistant Surgeon, 283, 284.
O'Shaughnessy, Dr., 567.
Ouchterlony, Col. J., 12, 13, 27, 30, 37, 42, 83, 91, 182, 187, 306, 307, 315, 327, 328, 341, 352, 361, 442, 459, 462, 465, 466, 467, 469, 483.
Ouchterlony, Mr. J., 23, 308, 485.
Owen, 298.

Pachman, Mr., 37.
Pahud, 553.
Páláls, 194, 195, 200, 274.
Pálegárs, 214.
Pálkápals, 195.
Pál Kúrumbas, 210.
Pandúras, 246.
Pandyas, 260, 261, 266.
Parvati, 254.
Paul, Priest, 420.
Pavon, M., 551.
Pears, Genl. Thos. (R.E.), 294, 423, 424, 425.
Peel, Sir Robt., 512.
Pehkans, 187, 201.
Peikis, 187, 194, 200, 201.
Perrottet, M., 510.
"Philanthropos," 35, 287.
Phœbus, 569.
Pierron, Rev. Fr., 420.
Pillar God, 206.
Planchoni, G., 569, 570.
Pogson, Mr., 38.
Poligars, 202.
Pope, Dr. G.U., 182, 183, 185, 189, 192, 198, 202, 240, 421.
Pottinger, Sir H., 307, 324.
Priestly, Col., 362.
Prince of Wales, 428.
Pritchett, Mr., 554, 555, 568.
Ptolemy, 261, 264.
Pújáris, 200, 212, 216.
Puleiyas, 184.
Punniahs, 490.
Pyche Rája, 277.

Rabenhorst, 503.
Rae, Mr., 512.
Rája Wodeyar, 220, 225, 268, 269.
Rájputs, 219.
Rakshasas, 251.
Ráma, 202, 226, 250, 252, 256, 258.
Rámánuja Achárya, 225, 255, 264, 265
Ramapayya, 269.
Ram Rai, 267.
Ranganátha, 226.
Rangasámi, 5, 13, 216, 226.
Rávana, 202, 252, 256.
Read, Col., 482.
Rennell, Major, 219, 277.
Rhode, Mr. W. Cotton, 359.
Rice, Mr., 192, 193, 211, 220, 225, 239, 259, 261, 262, 264, 265, 269.
Richards, Lt.-Col., 387.
Rieley, 457.
Riggenbach, M., 395.
Rivers, Mr., 477.
Robertson, Mr., 460, 461, 462, 464, 466, 479, 495, 519.
Robinson, Archdeacon, 293.
Robinson, Sir W., 412.
Ross, Dr., 42, 50.
Rotteler, M., 282.
Roxburg, M., 282.
Roy, R. C. Bishop Francisco, 273.
Royle, Dr. Forbes, 552, 553, 554, 568.
Ruiz, M., 551.
Rumbold, Sir W., 293, 329, 332, 348, 420.

Sadatulla Khan, 271.
Sagara, 259.
Sahadéva, 259.
Sangama, 266, 267.

Sankya Achárya, 252, 254, 266.
Saxton, Col., 4.
Sayer, Rev. Mr., 421.
Schratthy, Mr., 560.
Schrottky, Mr., 495.
Seymour, Mr. H., 357.
Sheffield, Mr., 291, 292.
Sheva-acharas, 25.
Shortt, Dr., 182, 185, 188, 203, 209, 214, 215, 219, 257, 483, 484, 487.
Sim, Hon. J. D., 427, 575.
Simmonds, Mr. P. L., 487.
Smarta sect, 254.
Smollett, Mr., 356.
Sola, 265.
Someswara, 266.
Souberan, J. L., 570.
Spruce, Mr., 554, 555, 568.
Sri Ranga Ráyal, 268.
Sri Vikrama, 261.
St. Simon, Marquis de, 458.
Stanes, Mr. T., 429.
Stanley, Lord, 355.
Steedman, Mr. A. H., 487.
Stendel, 130.
Stokes, Mr., 2.
Stokes, Rev. W., 221, 421.
Strachan, Rev. J. M., 419.
Straham, Major, 294.
Subaon, 24.
Sullivan, Mr. J., 280, 281, 282, 283, 284, 285, 286, 287, 288, 289, 290, 291, 292, 297, 299, 303, 304, 305, 314, 315, 327, 328, 329, 330, 332, 333, 334, 336, 337, 344, 349, 350, 361, 442, 455, 456.
Sykes, Col. F. R. S., 38, 42, 231.

Tallaries, 412.
Tarserzháls, 187, 200.
Taylor, Mr. P. G., 38.
Taylor, Dr., 554.
Taylor, Mr. W., 261, 263.
Taylor, Rev. A. C., 419.
Tennent, 155.
Textor, 553.
Thomas, Mr., 22, 165, 280, 281, 291, 319, 320, 321, 423, 439, 442, 443.
Thwaites, Mr. G. H. K., 508.
Tippu Sultan, 228, 243, 247, 271, 278, 286, 312, 325, 337.
Tirumala Náyak, 269, 270.
Tirumalpad, 448.
Tódas, 7, 10, 25, 26, 27, 29, 180, 182, 183, 184, 185, 186, 187, 188, 189, 190, 191, 192, 193, 194, 196, 197, 199, 200, 201, 202, 203, 205, 206, 207, 211, 212, 218, 219, 222, 226, 227, 228, 230, 232, 239, 241, 243, 249, 252, 254, 256, 258, 259, 260, 273, 274, 277, 283, 284, 292, 296, 302, 305, 311, 327, 328, 329, 330, 331, 332, 333, 334, 335, 336, 337, 338, 339, 340, 341, 342, 343, 344, 347, 348, 349, 351, 353, 354, 380, 423, 425, 455, 468, 479.
Tódis, 187, 201.
Tondarmandalam, 206, 209.
Toreas, 25, 26, 32, 222, 226, 227, 268.
Trevelyan, Sir C., 307, 436, 440, 512.
Triana (Jos.), M., 551, 570.
Trinctra Kadamba, 264.
Triquet, Rev. Fr., 420.
Turnour, 259.
Tweeddale, Marquis of, 38, 65, 304, 305, 306, 324, 328, 338, 571.

Underwood, Mr., 303.
Urali, 215.

Vanaras, 251.
vanGorkom, K. W., 552, 569.
Varddhana, 264.
Varzháls, 195, 200.
Vasantaka, 265.
Vijaya Wódeyar, 220, 222, 267, 268.
Vijayanagar Kings, 209, 254, 264, 268, 270, 272.
Vira Bellála, 265, 266.
Virabhataraya, 226.
Vira Narasimha, 265, 266.
Visha Laksha, 270.
Vishnu Varddhana, 253, 254, 264, 265.
Visvanatha, 269.
Vogl, A., 570.

Walhouse, Mr., 212, 241.
Walker, Capt. J. Campbell, 359, 557, 570.
Wallich, Dr., 345, 483.
Wapshare, Mr., 165.
Ward, Capt. (B.S.), 25, 30, 201, 279, 285, 292, 361.
Weddell, Dr. H. A., 551, 552, 553, 570.
Weir, Mr., 554.
Wellesley, Marquis of, 271, 276.
Wellesley, Hon. H., 271.
Wentworth, Mr., 36.
Wheeler, Mr. T., 254, 259, 266.
Whish, Mr., 280.
White, Mr. G., 496.
Whitehouse, Mr., 273, 274.
Whitton, Surg.-Major, 45, 46.
Wight, Dr., 130, 150, 442, 572.
Wilks, Col., 220, 262, 267, 268, 269, 270, 279, 483.
Wilson, Mr. (Professor), 11, 250, 252, 261, 264.
Wilson, Bishop D., 293, 417, 426.
Winslow, 206.
Wódeas, 32, 218, 220, 221, 225, 227, 255, 262, 267, 268, 269.
Wódeyar Rája, 220, 225, 268, 269.
Wood, Sir Charles, 321, 324, 356, 357, 556.
Wroughton, Mr., 312, 352.

Yadava, 267.
Yagadeva Ráya, 220.
Yávanas, 249, 266.
Yérnasámi, 226.
Yudisthára, 259.